THE NAVY LIST
BICENTENNIAL OF TR[illegible]

The title Navy List first came into use with the public[illegible] being made of the remarkable Steel's Original and Correc[illegible] [illegible]enue Cutters, with their Commanders and Stations, publish[illegible] [illegible]ouse, Little Tower Hill.

The October 1805 edition runs to 55 pages only plus a[illegible] additions, mainly for charts. The ability to include so much detailed information was ac[illegible] by the simple expedient of using a tiny typeface. The entry for HMS VICTORY lists only one other officer in addition to Nelson, Hardy and Rear Admiral George Murray (Nelson's Chief of Staff who left the ship for family reasons and so missed Trafalgar) and that is the Purser - W Burke. The Ship's station is described as 'To the Mediterranean'. The November edition shows Nelson and Murray ruled though in ink, and shows the station as 'off Cadiz'. There are 124 ships of the line. The list also notes that Nelson, as a Vice Admiral would have received £2-10-0d a day in pay plus 20 shillings table money.

This Navy List for 2005 contains much of the same information, but presents it in a more readable form, and thus turns out to be some 325 pages long, listing officers of all specialisations in the Royal Navy including officers of the Royal Marines, RNR, RMR, RFA, SCC and CCF. It is an important source of reference for today and will remain so for as long as historians and others remain interested in the Naval Service and the men and women who are a part of it.

Admiral Sir Alan WEST GCB DSC ADC
First Sea Lord

2005

THE

NAVY LIST

2005

Corrected to 1st April 2005

LONDON; The Stationery Office

ISBN 0 11 773029 7

Printed in the United Kingdom by The Stationery Office
N181270 08/05 C16 313720 19585

The Navy List is compiled and published by order of the Defence Council for the convenience of the Naval Service, but as errors may occasionally occur the Council must expressly reserve the right to determine the status of any Officer according to the actual circumstances of the case, independently of any entry in the Navy List

By Command of the Defence Council,

SIR KEVIN TEBBIT

Published by TSO (The Stationery Office) and available from:

Online
www.tso.co.uk/bookshop

Mail, Telephone, Fax & E-mail
TSO
PO Box 29, Norwich, NR3 1GN
Telephone orders/General enquiries: 0870 600 5522
Fax orders: 0870 600 5533
E-mail: book.orders@tso.co.uk
Textphone 0870 240 3701

TSO Shops
123 Kingsway, London, WC2B 6PQ
020 7242 6393 Fax 020 7242 6394
68-69 Bull Street, Birmingham B4 6AD
0121 236 9696 Fax 0121 236 9699
9-21 Princess Street, Manchester M60 8AS
0161 834 7201 Fax 0161 833 0634
16 Arthur Street, Belfast BT1 4GD
028 9023 8451 Fax 028 9023 5401
18-19 High Street, Cardiff CF10 1PT
029 2039 5548 Fax 029 2038 4347
71 Lothian Road, Edinburgh EH3 9AZ
0870 606 5566 Fax 0870 606 5588

TSO Accredited Agents
(see Yellow Pages)

and through good booksellers

PREFACE

The Navy List is on sale to the public and is published annually in July or as soon as possible thereafter. The Navy List of Retired Officers, also on sale to the public, is published separately and biennially.

This edition of the Navy List has been produced largely from the information held in the Naval Manpower Management Information System and is corrected to include those promotions, appointments etc. promulgated on or before 1 April 2005 as becoming effective on or before 30 June 2005. Only Flag rank entries in Section one will be corrected after this date.

Serving officers who notice errors or omissions in Sections 2 and 3 of the List should complete the form found on the final page of the Navy List and forward it to their Career Manager. Other errors or omissions should be brought to the attention of the Editor of the Navy List. Any other reader who notices errors or omissions is invited to write to:

Mr Andrew Hiscutt
The Editor of the Navy List
DNCM
Room 208
Jago Road
HM Naval Base
PORTSMOUTH
Hants, PO1 3LU

quoting the page(s) in question. Every effort will be made to include corrections and omissions received by the Editor before 28 March 2006. Regrettably, letters cannot be acknowledged.

Officers who succeed to peerages, baronetcies or courtesy titles should notify their Career Manager so that their computer records can be updated and the changes reflected in the Navy List. The degrees shown after Active Service Officers' names are not necessarily a complete list of those held, but are generally confined to degrees of an honorary nature conferred specially upon an Officer, and those that are so related to the professional duties of an Officer as to give some indication of his professional qualifications.

The master Allowance List for the free distribution of the Navy List is controlled by the Editor. DSDC(L) at Llangennech is responsible for the issue of this publication strictly according to the Allowance List. Units are asked to ensure that the Editor and DSDC(L) are informed of any reduction in requirement. Requests for additional copies and amendment to the master Allowance List should be addressed to DSDC(L) at Llangennech (using RN Form 53001(Demand for Naval Books)). Firmly attached to this demand should be a letter addressed to the Editor with a clear supporting case.

CONTENTS

Section 9

Section 10

Index

Her Majesty The Queen

LORD HIGH ADMIRAL OF THE UNITED KINGDOM 1964

MEMBERS OF THE ROYAL FAMILY

HIS ROYAL HIGHNESS THE PRINCE PHILIP, DUKE OF EDINBURGH, KG, KT, OM, GBE, AC, QSO

Admiral of the Fleet .... 15 Jan 53
Captain General Royal Marines .... 1 Jun 53
Admiral of the Fleet Royal Australian Navy .... 1 Apr 54
Admiral of the Fleet Royal New Zealand Navy .... 15 Jan 53
Admiral of the Royal Canadian Sea Cadets .... 15 Jan 53

HIS ROYAL HIGHNESS THE PRINCE OF WALES, KG, KT, OM, GCB, AK, QSO, ADC

Vice Admiral .... 14 Nov 02

HIS ROYAL HIGHNESS THE DUKE OF YORK, KCVO, ADC

Admiral of the Sea Cadet Corps .... 11 May 92
Honorary Captain Royal Navy .... 27 Jun 05

HER ROYAL HIGHNESS THE PRINCESS ROYAL, KG, GCVO, QSO

Rear Admiral Royal Navy .... 1 Nov 93

HIS ROYAL HIGHNESS PRINCE MICHAEL OF KENT, GCVO

Honorary Rear Admiral Royal Naval Reserve .... 1 Jun 04

HER ROYAL HIGHNESS PRINCESS ALEXANDRA THE HON LADY OGILVY, KG GCVO

Patron, Queen Alexandra's Royal Naval Nursing Service .... 12 Nov 55

VICE ADMIRAL OF THE UNITED KINGDOM

Admiral Sir Kenneth Eaton, GBE, KCB

PERSONAL AIDES-DE-CAMP TO THE QUEEN

Vice Admiral His Royal Highness The Prince of Wales, KG, KT, OM, GCB, AK, QSO, ADC
Honorary Captain His Royal Highness The Duke of York, KCVO, ADC

FIRST AND PRINCIPAL NAVAL AIDE-DE-CAMP TO THE QUEEN

Admiral Sir Alan West, GCB, DSC, ADC ....30 Nov 00

FLAG AIDE-DE-CAMP TO THE QUEEN

Vice Admiral Sir James Burnell-Nugent, KCB, CBE, ADC ....28 Jan 03

NAVAL AND MARINE AIDES-DE-CAMP TO THE QUEEN

Commodore C.A. Snow, CBE	Appointed	20 Apr 04	Seniority	14 May 02
Commodore G.J. Thwaites	Appointed	24 Mar 05	Seniority	1 Apr 03
Commodore C.J. Stait, OBE	Appointed	15 Mar 05	Seniority	22 Jun 04
Brigadier G.S. Robison	Appointed	23 Apr 04	Seniority	15 Sep 03
Captain A.M. Picton (Commodore)	Appointed	18 Oct 03	Seniority	30 Jun 96
Captain W.M. Covington, CBE (Commodore)	Appointed	11 May 04	Seniority	31 Dec 96
Captain M.J. Potter (Commodore)	Appointed	27 Sep 02	Seniority	30 Jun 97
Captain M.K. Bowker (Commodore)	Appointed	21 Jan 03	Seniority	30 Jun 97
Captain A.J. Rix (Commodore)	Appointed	03 Sep 03	Seniority	30 Jun 97

EXTRA NAVAL AND MARINE EQUERRIES TO THE QUEEN

Vice Admiral Sir James Weatherall, KCVO, KBE
Vice Admiral T Blackburn, CB LVO
Lieutenant General Sir John Richards, KCB, KCVO
Rear Admiral Sir Paul Greening, GCVO
Rear Admiral Sir John Garnier, KCVO, CBE
Rear Admiral Sir Robert Woodard, KCVO
Commodore A.J.C.Morrow, CVO Royal Navy

NAVAL AND MARINE RESERVE AIDES-DE-CAMP TO THE QUEEN

Commodore N.J E Reynolds, RD, ADC RNR	Appointed	01 Feb 04	Seniority	30 Sep 99
Colonel B.L. Hough, RD, ADC RMR	Appointed	20 Jun 03	Seniority	01 Jun 97
Captain S.P. Thorne, RD, RNR	Appointed	01 Mar 05	Seniority	30 Sep 03

HONORARY CHAPLAINS TO THE QUEEN

The Venerable B.K. Hammett, QHC, MA
The Reverend Monsignor B.R.Madders, MBE, QHC, VG
The Reverend D Barlow, QHC, MA
The Reverend S M Rae, MBE, QHC, BD

HONORARY PHYSICIANS TO THE QUEEN

Surgeon Commodore N.E.Baldock, QHP, MB, ChB, FRCP, FFOM, MRCS, DipAvMed
Surgeon Commodore P.F.R. Tolley, OBE, QHP, MB, BCh
Surgeon Commodore T.R. Douglas-Riley, QHP, MB, BS, MRCS, LRCP, MRCGP, DA, jsdc
Surgeon Captain O.M. Howard, QHP, MB, BS, FRCP,

HONORARY SURGEONS TO THE QUEEN

Surgeon Vice Admiral I.L.Jenkins, CVO, QHS, MB, BCH, FRCS
Surgeon Rear Admiral M.A.Farquharson-Roberts, CBE, QHS, MB, BS, MA, LRCP, FRCS, rcds

---

HONORARY DENTAL SURGEON TO THE QUEEN

Surgeon Commodore (D) G.L. Morrison, QHDS, BDS, FDS, MBA, DRDRCS

NAVAL RESERVE HONORARY PHYSICIAN TO THE QUEEN

Surgeon Captain J.A. McM Turner, RD, QHP, FRCP

HONORARY NURSE TO THE QUEEN

Captain L. Gibbon, ARRC, QHN, QARNNS

HONORARY OFFICERS IN HER MAJESTY'S FLEET

ADMIRAL

His Majesty King Karl XVI Gustav of Sweden, KG .... 25 Jun 75

His Majesty Sultan Haji Hassanal Bolkiah Mu'izzaddin Waddaulah Sultan and Yang Di-pertuan of Brunei Darussalam, GCB, GCMG .... 4 Aug 01

HONORARY OFFICERS IN HER MAJESTY'S ROYAL MARINES

COLONEL

His Majesty King Harald V of Norway, KG, GCVO .... 18 Mar 81

THE DEFENCE COUNCIL

Chairman
THE RIGHT HONOURABLE DR JOHN REID MP
(Secretary of State for Defence)

THE RIGHT HONOURABLE ADAM INGRAM JP MP
(Minister of State for the Armed Forces)

LORD DRAYSON
(Parlimentary Under Secretary of State and Minister for Defence Procurement)

MR DON TOUHIG MP
(Under-Secretary of State for Defence and Minister for Veterans)

GENERAL SIR MICHAEL WALKER, GCB, CMG, CBE, ADC Gen
(Chief of Defence Staff)

SIR KEVIN TEBBIT, KCB CMG
(Permanent Under-Secretary of State)

ADMIRAL SIR ALAN WEST, GCB, DSC, ADC
(First Sea Lord and Chief of the Naval Staff)

GENERAL SIR MIKE JACKSON, GCB, CBE, DSO, ADC, Gen
(Chief of the General Staff)

AIR CHIEF MARSHAL SIR JOCK STIRRUP, KCB, AFC, ADC, FRAeS, FCMI
(Chief of the Air Staff)

GENERAL SIR TIMOTHY GRANVILLE-CHAPMAN, KCB, CBE, ADC, Gen
(Vice Chief of the Defence Staff)

SIR PETER SPENCER, KCB
(Chief of Defence Procurement)

PROFESSOR ROY ANDERSON
(Chief Scientific Adviser)

MR IAN ANDREWS, CBE, TD
(Second Permanent Under-Secretary of State)

GENERAL SIR KEVIN O'DONOGHUE, KCB, CBE
(Chief of Defence Logistics)

THE ADMIRALTY BOARD

Chairman
THE RIGHT HONOURABLE DR JOHN REID MP
(Secretary of State for Defence)
(Chairman of the Defence Council and Chairman of the Admiralty Board of the Defence Council)

THE RIGHT HONORABLE ADAM INGRAM JP MP
(Minister of State for the Armed Forces)

LORD DRAYSON
(Parlimentary Under Secretary of State and Minister for Defence Procurement)

MR DON TOUHIG MP
(Under-Secretary of State for Defence and Minister for Veterans)

ADMIRAL SIR ALAN WEST, GCB, DSC, ADC
(First Sea Lord and Chief of the Naval Staff)

ADMIRAL SIR JONATHON BAND, KCB
(Commander in Chief Fleet)

VICE ADMIRAL SIR JAMES BURNELL-NUGENT, KCB, CBE, ADC
(Second Sea Lord and Commander in Chief Naval Home Command)

REAR ADMIRAL RICHARD F CHEADLE, CB
(Controller of the Navy)

REAR ADMIRAL ALAN M MASSEY, CBE
(Assistant Chief of Naval Staff)

REAR ADMIRAL R PAUL BOISSIER
(Naval Member for Logistics)

MR IAN ANDREWS, CBE, TD
(Second Permanent Under-Secretary of State and Secretary of the Admiralty Board)

OFFICERS ON THE ACTIVE LIST OF THE ROYAL NAVY, THE ROYAL MARINES, THE QUEEN ALEXANDRA'S ROYAL NAVAL NURSING SERVICE; AND RETIRED AND EMERGENCY OFFICERS SERVING AND LIST OF RFA OFFICERS' NAMES

Name	Rank	Branch	Spec	Seniority	Where Serving
A					
Abbey, Michael Keith, MSc, CEng, MIMarEST	CDR(FTC)	E	MESM	31.12.00	DRAKE SFM
Abbey, Michael Peter, MBE, pcea	LT CDR(FTC(A)	X	P	01.10.88	FLEET AV VL
Abbot, Richard Leslie, BSc, PGDip	LT(IC)	X		01.09.03	RNAS CULDROSE
Abbott, David	CAPT RM(CC)	-	SO(LE)	01.04.03	846 SQN
Abbott, David Anthony, BTech	LT CDR(FTC)	E	WE	01.10.04	CAPT MCTA
Abbott, Grant Paul, MA	CAPT RM(CC)	-		01.09.02	FPGRM
Abbott, Sir Peter (Charles) GBE, KCB, MA, rcds, pce	ADM	-	C	03.10.95	
Abbott, Simon Saint Clair	LT CDR(FTC)	X	PWO(U)	01.06.92	FOST FAS SHORE
Abbotts, Michael Charles, BEng, MRAeS	LT(CC)	E	AE	01.04.02	750 SQN SEAHAWK
Abel, James Andrew, MEng	SLT(IC)	E	WESM	01.11.02	RALEIGH
Abel, Lucy, BSc	LT(IC)	X		01.09.02	NOTTINGHAM
Abel, Nigel Philip	LT(CC)	X	P	16.08.96	848 SQN HERON
Abernethy, James Richard Gordon, PGDIPAN, pce, psc(j)	CDR(FTC)	X	PWO(N)	30.06.04	FLEET HQ PORTS 2
Abernethy, Lee John Francis, pce	CDR(FTC)	X	PWO(C)	30.06.05	HQ SACT
Abey, John Ashton	LT(IC)	MS		01.07.04	DRAKE COB
Ablett, Eleanor Louise, BA	LT CDR(FTC)	S		01.10.02	INVINCIBLE
Ablett, Simon David, BEng, MIEE	LT(FTC)	E	WE	01.01.98	FLEET HQ PORTS
Abraham, Paul, pce(sm)	CDR(FTC)	X	SM	31.12.96	FWO DEVPT SEA
Ackland, Heber Kemble, MA(OXON), psc(j)	LT CDR(FTC)	S		01.11.99	MOD (LONDON)
Acland, David Daniel, pce, pcea (Act Cdr)	LT CDR(FTC)	X	P	01.10.93	JCA IPT USA
Adair, Allan Alexander Shafto, rcds, pce, psc(a)	CDRE(FTC)	X	PWO	04.11.03	RN GIBRALTAR
Adam, Ian Kennedy, pce	LT CDR(FTC)	X	PWO(A)	01.01.97	GRAFTON
Adam, Murray William, BSc	SLT(IC)	X		01.11.03	DARTMOUTH BRNC
Adams, Alistair John, BSc, pce	CDR(FTC)	X	PWO(C)	31.12.98	MOD (LONDON)
Adams, Andrew Mark, BEng, MA, CEng, MIMarEST, psc(j)	CDR(FTC)	E	MESM	30.06.02	DLO BRISTOL
Adams, Edwin Smyth, BEng	LT(CC)	X	P	16.09.99	848 SQN HERON
Adams, Geoffrey Hugh, BEng, MSc, CEng, MIMarEST	LT CDR(FTC)	E	ME	01.04.01	CUMBERLAND
Adams, George, MIMarEST	LT(FTC)	E	ME	01.05.97	SULTAN
Adams, Peter, BSc, PGCE	CDR(FTC)	E	TM	30.06.03	FLEET HQ PORTS
Adams, Peter, n	LT(FTC)	X	PWO(N)	01.05.97	YORK
Adams, Richard Anthony Skelton, BSc	CDR(FTC)	E	MESM	30.06.92	MOD (BATH)
Adams, Richard Joseph, BEng, CEng, MIMarEST	LT CDR(FTC)	E	MESM	01.03.03	VANGUARD(PORT)
Adams, William John	LT(IC)	X		01.05.02	NEPTUNE DLO
Adamson, Hazel Josie, BEng	SLT(IC)	E	ME U/T	01.01.04	DARTMOUTH BRNC
Adamson, Stephen Edward	LT(IC)	X		01.05.02	MWS COLLINGWOOD
Adcock, Graham Edward	CAPT RM(FTC)	-		01.01.01	CHFHQ
Ademokun, Gloria	LT(SC(MD)	Q		01.02.03	DARTMOUTH BRNC
Ahlgren, Edward Graham, SM(n), SM	LT CDR(FTC)	X	SM	01.10.00	TRENCHANT
Ahuja, Vijay	SURG SLT(SCC)	-		22.01.05	DARTMOUTH BRNC
Aiken, Stephen Ronald, OBE, BSc, MA, pce, pce(sm), psc(j)	CDR(FTC)	X	SM	30.06.03	SOVEREIGN
Ainscow, Anthony James	LT(IC)	E	ME	01.05.02	SULTAN
Ainsley, Andrew Malcolm James	LT(FTC)	X		01.08.00	EXCHANGE NORWAY
Ainsley, Roger Stewart, MA, jsdc, pce, hcsc	RADM	-	AWO(A)	27.04.04	FOST SEA
(FLAG OFFICER SEA TRAINING APR 04)					

Name	Rank	Branch	Spec	Seniority	Where Serving
Ainsworth, Alan J	LT(IC)	E	WE	01.07.04	CARDIFF
Air, Christopher	2LT(IC)	-		01.08.01	CTCRM LYMPSTONE
Airey, Simon Edward, MA, jsdc (Act Capt)	CDR(FTC)	S		31.12.94	DA KIEV
Aitchison, Kenneth James, MB, CHB, MRCGP, DObstRCOG	SURG CDR(SCC)	-	GMPP	04.02.96	MWS COLLINGWOOD
Aitken, Andrew John, BA, SM(n), SM	LT CDR(FTC)	X	SM	01.09.02	FWO FASLANE
Aitken, Kenneth Matthew, MAPM	CDR(FTC)	S	(S)	30.06.03	AFPAA(CENTURION)
Aitken, Lee-Anne, BSc	LT(IC)	X		01.01.05	WALNEY
Aitken, Steven Robert, MSc	LT(CC)	X	P	01.01.01	815 FLT 221
Ajala, Ahmed, BEng, MSc gw	LT CDR(FTC)	E	WE	01.10.04	MOD (LONDON)
Akers, Samuel John	SLT(IC)	X	P	01.01.03	RAF LINTN/OUSE
Alabaster, Martin Brian, MA, MSc, rcds, psc	CDRE(FTC)	E	WE	30.04.02	FLEET HQ PORTS 2
Alberts, Paul William	LT(FTC)	E	WE	01.04.01	SCU SHORE
Albon, Mark, BSc, Cert Ed, PGDip	LT CDR(FTC)	X	HM	12.08.98	NAVSEC
Albon, Ross, OBE, BSc, MBA (Barrister)	CAPT(FTC)	S	BAR	30.06.02	DLO/DG DEF SC
Alcindor, David John, BSc, SM(n)	LT(CC)	X	SM	01.04.97	VIGILANT(STBD)
Alcock, Christopher, OBE, pce, pcea, psc	CDR(FTC)	X	O	30.06.98	FLEET HQ PORTS
Alder, Mark Christian, BEng, MSc, CEng	LT(IC)	E	MESM	01.05.04	SULTAN
Alderson, Richard James, BA	MAJ(FTC)	-		01.10.04	45 CDO RM
Alderton, Paul Alexander, BSc	LT(IC)	E	WE	01.01.03	MWS COLLINGWOOD
Alderwick, Jason Royston Claude, BA	LT(IC)	X	H2	01.12.99	FLEET HQ NWD
Alderwick, Matthew	LT(IC)	E	MESM	01.05.04	DARTMOUTH BRNC
Aldous, Benjamin Walker, LLB	LT(FTC)	X		01.11.99	MONMOUTH
Aldous, Robert James	LT(IC)	X		01.10.04	PEMBROKE
Aldwinckle, Terence William	LT CDR(FCC)	Q	IC	01.10.01	RH HASLAR
Alexander, Amy Louisa, BA	LT(FTC)	E	WE	01.09.99	DLO BRISTOL
Alexander, Giles David, BSc	CAPT RM(FTC)	-		01.05.99	RMR LONDON
Alexander, Oliver Douglas Dudley	LT(FTC)	X	MCD	01.11.97	SDG PLYMOUTH
Alexander, Phillip Michael Duncan, MEng	LT(FTC)	E	MESM	01.01.01	SCEPTRE
Alexander, Robert Stuart, MA, pce, pcea, psc	CDR(FTC)	X	P	30.06.99	MOD (LONDON)
Alexander, William Augustus Dudley, BSc	SLT(IC)	X		01.01.03	MONTROSE
Alison, Lynn Alexander	LT CDR(FTC)	E	WE	01.10.94	FLEET HQ PORTS
Allan, Chris Ruthven, BSc, n	LT(FTC)	X		01.12.97	CYPRUS PBS
Allan, Fraser Stuart	CAPT RM(CC)	-		01.09.03	CTCRM
Allan, Owen James	LT(IC)	E	WE	01.01.05	DARTMOUTH BRNC
Allan, Victoria Elizabeth, BA	SLT(IC)	X		01.09.03	DARTMOUTH BRNC
Allcock, Edward Charles, BM	SURG LT(SCC)	-		07.08.02	RH HASLAR
Allen, Alexander Paul, BEng	SLT(IC)	E	ME U/T	01.01.04	DARTMOUTH BRNC
Allen, Anthony David, PGDIPAN, pce	LT CDR(FTC)	X	PWO(N)	01.02.98	EXCHANGE AUSTLIA
Allen, David Peter	LT(FTC)	E	WE	15.06.90	CAPT MCTA
Allen, Douglas James Keith, BEng	LT CDR(CC)	X	P	01.10.03	846 SQN
Allen, Leslie Bernard, FInstLM	LT CDR(CC)	X	MW	01.10.04	RALEIGH
Allen, Patrick Lyons, pce, pcea	LT CDR(FTC)	X	O	01.06.99	MIDDLETON
Allen, Paul Miles, MBA, MSc	LT CDR(FTC)	X	O	01.10.04	LOAN JTEG BSC DN
Allen, Richard, pce(sm), SM(n), SM	LT CDR(FTC)	X	SM	20.07.99	QUORN
Allen, Richard Mark, pce(sm)	CDR(FTC)	X	SM	30.06.99	FLEET HQ NWD
Allen, Russell William	LT(IC)	X	EW	01.07.04	RNU RAF DIGBY
Allen, Stephen Michael, pce, pcea	CDR(FTC)	X	O	30.06.04	PORTLAND
Allfree, Joseph, BSc, n	LT CDR(FTC)	X	PWO(A)	01.01.03	EXETER
Allibon, Mark Christopher, pce, psc(j), MA	CDR(FTC)	X	PWO(A)	30.06.00	FLEET HQ PORTS 2
Allinson, Michael David, BSc	SLT(IC)	X	O U/T	01.09.03	DARTMOUTH BRNC
Allison, Aubrey Stuart Crawford, MSc, MB, BS, MRCS, LRCP, MFOM, MRCGP, psc	SURG CAPT(FCC)	-	(CO/M)	30.06.91	MOD (LONDON)
Allison, Glenn	LT(FTC)	X	P	16.11.94	DHFS
Allison, Kenneth Richard, MBE, sq	MAJ(FTC)	-		24.07.95	COM MCC NWD
Allkins, Helen Louise, BSc	CDR(FCC)	Q	ACC/EM	30.06.03	RCDM
Allsford, Karen Marie, BA (Act Lt Cdr)	LT(CC)	S		01.12.97	NP IRAQ
Allsop, Alistair Roos Lonsdale, MB, BSc, BCH, MRCGP, Dip OM, Dip FFP, DipIMC RCSED	SURG LTCDR(FCC)			05.08.03	
Allwood, Christopher, BSc, PGCE, adp	CAPT(FTC)	E	IS	30.06.04	AFPAA JPA
Almond, David Edwin Magor, BA, psc	LT CDR(FTC)	S		01.07.89	MOD (LONDON)
Almond, Nicholas Andrew Barrie, BEng	LT(IC)	E	AE	01.09.04	702 SQN HERON
Alsop, Sweyn Hamish	LT(CC)	X	P	01.12.98	750 SQN SEAHAWK
Alston, Richard, BA	CAPT RM(CC)	-		01.09.02	CTCRM

Name	Rank	Branch	Spec	Seniority	Where Serving
Ambrose, Rachael Elizabeth Frakes, MB, BS	SURG LT(MC(MD)	-		07.08.02	RFANSU (ARGUS)
Ameye, Christopher Robin, pce, psc(j)o	CDR(FTC)	X	MCD	31.12.97	SUPT OF DIVING
Amorosi, Riccardo Guy Filippo Luigi, BA, MEng	SLT(IC)	E	WE	01.09.01	MWS COLLINGWOOD
Amos, John Louis	MID(IC)	X		01.09.03	BROCKLESBY
Amos, Julian Harvey James	MAJ(FTC)	-		01.09.98	JHQ/CIS LISBON
Amphlett, Nigel Gavin, BSc, MA, pce, pcea, psc(j)	CDR(FTC)	X	O	30.06.03	FLEET HQ PORTS
Ancona, Simon James, MA, pce, pcea, psc	CAPT(FTC)	X	O	30.06.03	MWS COLLINGWOOD
Anderson, Andrew	LT(CC)	X	ATC	01.05.03	OCEAN
Anderson, Bruce William Drysdale	2LT(IC)	-		01.09.00	45 CDO RM
Anderson, Christopher John, BSc, IEng, MIIE	LT(IC)	E	WE	13.04.01	DLO BRISTOL
Anderson, Fraser Boyd, BSc, gdas	LT CDR(FTC)	X	O	01.10.93	MERLIN IPT
Anderson, Garry Stephen, SM(n), SM	LT(FTC)	X	SM	01.10.98	SOVEREIGN
Anderson, Hugh Alastair, LLB (Barrister)	CDR(FTC)	S	BAR	30.06.02	FLEET HQ PORTS
Anderson, Jon Harvey	2LT(IC)	-		01.08.01	CTCRM LYMPSTONE
Anderson, Kevin	LT(IC)	E	TM	01.06.03	NTE(TTD)
Anderson, Kevin Peter, BSc	LT(IC)	E	TM	01.01.04	DARTMOUTH BRNC
Anderson, Lindsy Claire	LT(FTC)	E	WE	01.09.03	YORK
Anderson, Lynne Ann, BA	LT(IC)	S		01.12.02	YORK
Anderson, Mark, BSc, pce, pce(sm)	CDRE(FTC)	X	SM	30.03.04	MOD (LONDON)
Anderson, Mark Edgar John, BSc, n	LT(FTC)	X		01.12.97	MERSEY
Anderson, Neil	LT(IC)	E	WE	09.04.04	CHATHAM
Anderson, Robert Gordon, MSc, psc	CDR(FTC)	E	WE	31.12.95	MOD (LONDON)
Anderson, Stephen Ronald	LT(CC)	X	O	01.08.00	815 FLT 202
Anderson, Stuart Christopher, pcea	LT CDR(CC)	X	P	01.10.99	GANNET SAR FLT
Anderson-Cooke, Darren Christopher James, BSc	LT(IC)	E		01.05.02	MWS COLLINGWOOD
Anderson-Hanney, Philip	LT(IC)	X		01.10.04	MERSEY
Andersson, James Laverock	SURG SLT(SCC)	-		08.04.03	DARTMOUTH BRNC
Andrew, Peter, BEng	LT(CC)	E	MESM	01.11.99	TALENT
Andrew, William George, psc, pce	CDR(FTC)	X	PWO(A)	30.06.93	STG BRISTOL
Andrews, Christopher, BSc	LT(IC)	E	IS	01.05.00	ALBION
Andrews, Dominic Michel	LT(IC)	E	WE	01.05.03	2SL/CNH
Andrews, Iain Stuart, DipEd	LT(IC)	X		01.09.01	MWS DEF DIV SCHL
Andrews, Ian	LT CDR(FTC)	E	MESM	01.10.95	ASM IPT
Andrews, Justin Pierre	LT(IC)	E	WE	01.05.02	EXETER
Andrews, Paul Nicholas, DipEcon, pce	LT CDR(FTC)	X	PWO(A)	01.06.94	FLEET HQ PORTS 2
Angliss, Roger John	SLT(IC)	X		01.01.04	750 SQN SEAHAWK
Angus, Donald	SURG SLT(SCC)	-		28.09.04	DARTMOUTH BRNC
Aniyi, Christopher Bamidele Jost, BEng, MA, MSc, CEng, MIMarEST, psc(j)	LT CDR(FTC)	E	ME	01.10.00	FOST SEA
Ankah, Gregory Kofi Esiaw, BEng, MSc	LT CDR(FTC)	E	ME	01.12.04	DLO BRISTOL
Annett, Ian Gordon, BEng, MSc, CEng, FRGS, MIEE, psc(j), gw	CDR(FTC)	E	WE	30.06.02	ILLUSTRIOUS
Ansell, Christopher Neil, BA, SM(n), SM	LT(FTC)	X	SM	01.01.99	VENGEANCE(STBD)
Anstey, Robert James, pce(sm), pce, SM(n), SM	CDR(FTC)	X	SM	30.06.05	VIGILANT(PORT)
Antrobus, Stuart Ronald, BEM	LT(IC)	X	AV	05.08.01	FLEET PHOT PORTS
Aplin, Adrian Trevor, MBE, MA, MCIT, MILT, psc(j), ESLog	CDR(FTC)	S		30.06.02	RNAS YEOVILTON
Appelquist, Paul, BSc, MAPM, CEng, MIEE	LT CDR(FTC)	E	WESM	01.10.99	FOST SM SEA
Apps, Julian Crawford	CAPT RM(IC)	-		01.09.04	CDO LOG REGT RM
Arbuthnott, Edward Alexander Hugh, MEng	SLT(IC)	X	P U/T	01.02.03	DARTMOUTH BRNC
Archdale, Peter Mervyn	LT CDR(FTC)	X	PWO(U)	16.03.85	NEPTUNE
Archer, Graham William, BEng	CDR(FTC)	E	AE	30.06.02	IA BRISTOL
Archer, Timothy William Kendray	CAPT RM(CC)	-		01.09.03	AGRIPPA MAR CC
Archibald, Brian Robert, BSc, pce, psc(j)	CAPT(FTC)	X	PWO(A)	30.06.04	DLO BRISTOL
Arden, Victoria Grace	LT CDR(FTC)	X	P	15.03.05	MOD (LONDON)
Arding, Nicholas Miles Bennett, OBE, BSc, MA, psc	LT COL(FTC)	-		30.06.98	CTCRM
Arend, Faye Marie, BA	LT(FTC)	S		01.01.99	INVINCIBLE
Argent-Hall, Dominic, BSc, CEng, MIEE, psc	CDR(FTC)	E	WE	30.06.00	MOD (LONDON)
Argles, Edward	2LT(IC)	-		01.08.04	CTCRM LYMPSTONE
Arkle, Nicholas James, BA	LT(CC)	X	P	01.09.98	RAF WITTERING
Armand-Smith, Penelope Harriet, MSc(Econ)	LT(IC)	X		01.01.05	MWS COLLINGWOOD
Armour, Graeme Alexander, psc(j)	MAJ(FTC)	-		01.05.99	PJHQ
Armstrong, Christopher	2LT(IC)	-		01.08.01	CTCRM LYMPSTONE
Armstrong, Colin David	LT(CC)	X		01.09.00	COTTESMORE
Armstrong, David Morgan, BA	LT(IC)	X		01.01.04	EXETER

Name	Rank	Branch	Spec	Seniority	Where Serving
Armstrong, Euan McAlpine, MB, ChB, MRCS	SURG LTCDR(FCC)	-		05.02.02	NELSON (PAY)
Armstrong, Nicholas Peter Bruce, MSc, pcea, gdas	LT CDR(FTC)	X	O	01.10.96	829 FLT 01
Armstrong, Roger Ian, psc(m)	LT COL(FTC)	-		31.12.92	COS 2SL/CNH
Armstrong, Rory James, BSc	LT(IC)	X		01.01.03	NP BOSNIA
Armstrong, Russell Freddie	2LT(IC)	-		01.09.00	FPGRM
Armstrong, Scott Thomas	LT CDR(FTC)	X	P	01.10.04	EXCHANGE RAF UK
Armstrong, Stuart McAlpine, BSc, SM(n), SM	LT(FTC)	X	SM	01.09.00	RALEIGH
Arnell, Stephen John	LT CDR(FTC)	E	WE	01.10.98	AFPAA(CENTURION)
Arnold, Andrew Stewart	LT CDR(FTC)	S	(W)	01.10.02	FLEET HQ PORTS
Arnold, Bruce William Henry, MSc, CEng, MIMechE	CDR(FTC)	E	MESM	31.12.92	DLO BRISTOL
Arthur, Calum Hugh Charles, MB, ChB	SURG LT(SCC)	-		01.08.01	MDHU DERRIFORD
Arthur, Iain Davidson, OBE, pce(sm) (Act Capt)	CDR(FTC)	X	SM	30.06.94	ACDS(POL) USA
Asbridge, Jonathan Ian, MA, MHCIMA, MILT, psc(j)	LT CDR(FTC)	S	SM	16.11.97	MOD (LONDON)
Ash, Timothy Claudius Vincent, psc(j), MA	LT CDR(FTC)	X	MW	01.10.99	COS 2SL/CNH
Ashby, Keith John, BEng, MIEE	LT(CC)	E	WE	01.09.97	SAT IPT
Ashcroft, Adam Charles, MA, Hf, pce, pcea, psc(j)	CDR(FTC)	X	P	31.12.00	MOD (LONDON)
Ashcroft, Kieran Thomas, BEng	SLT(IC)	X	P U/T	01.06.03	RAF CRANWELL EFS
Ashley, Paul David	LT(CC)	S		01.05.00	HQ SACT
Ashlin, James Matthew, BSc	LT(CC)	X	P	16.09.98	INVINCIBLE
Ashman, Rodney Guy, ACMA	LT CDR(FTC)	S	CMA	28.02.00	PJHQ
Ashmore, Sir Edward (Beckwith), GCB, DSC, IRs, jssc, psc	ADM OF FLEET	-		09.02.77	
Ashton, James, BEng	LT(FTC)	E	MESM	01.09.02	VIGILANT(PORT)
Ashton, Richard Eric, MA, MD, MB, BCh, FRCP	SURG CAPT(FCC)	-	(CK)	31.12.85	RH HASLAR
Ashton, Roy David	LT CDR(FTC)	E	WE	01.10.96	DFTE PORTSMOUTH
Ashton Jones, Geraint, MSc, PGCE	LT CDR(FTC)	E	IS	01.10.96	FLEET HQ PORTS
Ashworth, Helen Joanne, BEng	LT CDR(FTC)	E	ME	01.10.04	DARTMOUTH BRNC
Askham, Mathew Thomas, BA	SLT(IC)	X	P U/T	01.06.03	RAF CRANWELL EFS
Aspden, Andrew Mark, MA, pce, pcea, psc(j)	CDR(FTC)	X	O	30.06.03	FLEET HQ PORTS
Asquith, Simon Phillip, SM(n), SM	LT CDR(FTC)	X	SM	01.06.03	TURBULENT
Astle, Dawn Sandra	LT(FTC)	X	PWO(A)	01.12.98	OCEAN
Aston, Mark William, BDS, MSc, MGDS RCS	SGCDR(D)(FCC)	-		30.06.97	EXCH ARMY SC(G)
Athayde Banazol, Claire Victoria Norsworthy, ACIS	LT CDR(FTC)	S		04.04.99	MARLBOROUGH
Atherton, Bruce William	MAJ(CC)	-	P	01.10.04	EXCHANGE USA
Atherton, Martin John, MA, psc(j)	CAPT(FTC)	S		30.06.03	NEPTUNE DLO
Atkins, Ian, BEng, MA, MSc, CEng, MIMarEST, psc(j), Eur Ing	LT CDR(FTC)	E	ME	01.07.00	MOD (BATH)
Atkins, Paul Ronald	LT(IC)	E	MESM	01.05.03	2SL/CNH
Atkinson, Anthony	LT(IC)	E	TM	01.06.03	CTCRM
Atkinson, Charlotte Penelope, BSc	LT CDR(FTC)	X	HM2	01.10.04	BRECON
Atkinson, Garth Carson, BSc	LT CDR(FTC)	X	PWO(U)	01.02.04	ST ALBANS
Atkinson, Lee Vickerman	LT(IC)	X		01.05.02	MWS COLLINGWOOD
Atkinson, Mark, pce	LT CDR(FTC)	X	MCD	01.02.96	PJHQ
Atkinson, Neil Craig, BPh	CAPT RM(FTC)	-		01.05.00	NP IRAQ
Atkinson, Richard Jonathan	LT CDR(FTC)	X	AAWO	01.07.04	INVINCIBLE
Atkinson, Simon Reay, BSc, MPhil, CEng, FIEE, Eur Ing	CDR(FTC)	E	WE	30.06.00	MOD (LONDON)
Attwater, Richard Phillip	LT(IC)	X		01.01.05	MWS COLLINGWOOD
Attwood, Keith Alistair, BEng	LT(IC)	X	P	01.09.04	RNAS YEOVILTON
Atwal, Kamaldip Singh, BSc	LT(IC)	E	TM U/T	01.01.02	SULTAN
Atwill, John William Owen, LLB (Act Lt Cdr) (Barrister)	LT(CC)	S	BAR	22.10.98	NEPTUNE 2SL/CNH
Atyeo, Kelly Emma	MID(IC)	X		01.06.03	DARTMOUTH BRNC
Auld, Douglas Martin, BEng	LT(FTC)	E	MESM	01.01.98	NEPTUNE BNSL
Austen, Richard Mark (Act Lt Cdr)	LT(FTC)	S	(W)	08.04.94	MAS BRUSSELS
Austen, Tiffany Victoria	SLT(IC)	S		01.04.02	801 SQN
Austin, John Damian, BTech	LT CDR(FTC)	X		01.10.92	PJHQ
Austin, Peter Nigel, BSc, BA(OU), IEng, MIIE	LT(FTC)	E	WESM	09.01.01	FOST FAS SHORE
Austin, Simon Alexander	SLT(UCE)(IC)	X		01.09.03	DARTMOUTH BRNC
Austin, Stephen Timothy, MSc	LT(FTC)	E	ME	01.05.00	ENTERPRISE
Avery, Malcolm Byrne, BSc, pce, pce(sm), psc	CDRE(FTC)	X	SM	24.06.02	MOD (LONDON)
Avison, Matthew James, pcea	LT CDR(FTC)	X	O	01.10.99	INVINCIBLE
Axcell, Matthew Frederick, BSc	CAPT RM(CC)	-		01.09.03	RNAS YEOVILTON
Axon, David Brian, pce, psc(j), MA	CDR(FTC)	X	AAWO	30.06.03	MOD (LONDON)
Axon, Gail Margaret, BA (Barrister)	LT CDR(FTC)	S	BAR	01.10.00	MOD (LONDON)
Ayers, Dominic Edwin Bodkin, BA, MB, BS, MRCS	SURG LTCDR(FCC)	-		03.08.00	NELSON (PAY)
Ayers, Oliver Richard Beedom, BA	SLT(IC)	X		01.11.03	DARTMOUTH BRNC

Name	Rank	Branch	Spec	Seniority	Where Serving
Ayers, Richard Peter Beedom, BSc, CEng, MIEE, psc	CDR(FTC)	E	WE	31.12.92	NC3 AGENCY
Aylott, Peter Richard Frank Dobson, MA, PGDIPAN, pce, n	LT CDR(FTC)	X	PWO(N)	29.01.00	CATTISTOCK
Ayres, Christopher Paul, BSc, pce, psc, psc(j)	CDR(FTC)	X	PWO(U)	30.06.96	MOD (LONDON)
Ayrton, Robert Edward	LT(IC)	X		01.12.02	CARDIFF

B

Name	Rank	Branch	Spec	Seniority	Where Serving
Backhouse, Anthony Wynter, BSc, psc, odc(Aus)	CDR(FTC)	S	SM	31.12.90	SHAPE BELGIUM
Backus, Robert Ian Kirkwood, BEng	LT CDR(FTC)	X	PWO(U)	01.10.03	ARGYLL
Baddeley, Robert	LT(IC)	E	TM	01.11.03	RALEIGH
Baden, James Martin, MB, BS, BDS, BMS, FDS RCPSGlas	SURG LTCDR(MCC)	-		17.03.99	MDHU DERRIFORD
Badrock, Bruce, n	LT CDR(FTC)	X	H CH	05.07.98	MWS COLLINGWOOD
Baggaley, Jason Antony Lloyd, BSc, CEng, MIEE	LT CDR(FTC)	E	WE	01.10.01	LANCASTER
Bagnall, Sally Anne Elizabeth, BSc	LT CDR(MCC)	Q		01.10.04	RCDM
Bagshaw, James Richard William, BA	LT(CC)	X	MW	01.09.98	PENZANCE
Baileff, Roger Ian, pce, ACMA (Act Cdr)	LT CDR(FTC)	X	CMA	01.12.89	AFPAA JPA
Bailes, Kenneth Peter, BA	LT(CC)	X	FC	01.09.00	MIDDLETON
Bailey, Daniel Standfast	MAJ(FTC)	-		01.09.02	FPGRM
Bailey, Ian John, BEng, AMIEE	LT(FTC)	E	WE	01.09.03	JSCSC
Bailey, Jeremy James, BEng, MSc, CEng, MIMarEST	LT CDR(FTC)	E	ME	01.10.02	MARLBOROUGH
Bailey, Michael	LT(IC)	X	EW	01.07.04	JARIC
Bailey, Sian, BSc, PGCE	LT(CC)	E	TM	01.08.99	DARTMOUTH BRNC
Bailey, Simon Glenn	LT(IC)	X		01.10.04	NORTHUMBERLAND
Bailey, Timothy David	LT(IC)	E	WE	01.01.03	DLO BRISTOL
Baillie, Robbie William, BSc, PGCE	LT(IC)	E	TM	01.05.00	NP BOSNIA
Bainbridge, John	LT(IC)	X	MCD	30.06.98	MWS DEF DIV SCHL
Bainbridge, Paul	SLT(IC)	S		01.02.04	DARTMOUTH BRNC
Bainbridge, Stuart Darryl	LT(CC)	X	P	01.03.95	824 SQN
Baines, Andrew Richard, BSc	LT(FTC)	X	P	01.07.97	848 SQN HERON
Baines, David Michael Llewellyn, BSc	LT CDR(FTC)	E	IS	01.10.01	ILLUSTRIOUS
Baines, Gary Anthony	CAPT RM(FTC)	-	SO(LE)	01.01.01	RMR LONDON
Bains, Baldeep Singh, MB, ChB	SURG LT(SCC)	-		01.08.01	RCDM
Baird, Elaine	LT CDR(SCC)	Q		11.03.01	UKSU AFSOUTH
Baird, George Mitchell	LT(IC)	X	P	01.09.03	DHFS
Baker, Adrian Bruce, MB, CHB, MSc, MFOM, DipAvMed, MRAeS	SURG CDR(FCC)	-	(CO/M)	30.06.94	RNAS CULDROSE
Baker, Adrian Paul, BEng, pcea	LT CDR(FTC)	X	O	01.11.99	FLEET HQ PORTS
Baker, Alasdair	CAPT RM(IC)	-	C	01.07.01	UKLFCSG RM
Baker, Helen Mary Hartley, BEd	LT(IC)	S		01.05.04	LAIPT
Baker, James Edward Gunn, BA, MPhil	LT(IC)	X		01.09.02	KENT
Baker, James Kieron, MSc	SLT(IC)	X	P U/T	01.05.03	RAF CRANWELL EFS
Baker, Michael Benson, BA	CAPT RM(CC)	-	P	01.09.98	847 SQN
Baker, Michael John, BEng, CEng, MIEE	LT CDR(FTC)	E	WE	01.06.98	DGMC SEA
Baker, Nicholas James	LT(FTC)	S	(W)	20.09.99	AGRIPPA MAR CC
Bakewell, Robert Andrew	SLT(IC)	X		01.01.04	DARTMOUTH BRNC
Bakewell, Timothy David, psc(j)	MAJ(FTC)	-		01.09.00	MOD (LONDON)
Balcombe, Jeremy Stephen, BEng, MSc gw	LT(CC)	E	AE	01.09.94	DLO YEO
Baldie, Steven Anthony Hamilton, BEng	LT(CC)	X	P	01.05.99	848 SQN HERON
Baldock, Nicolas Edwin, QHP, MB, ChB, FRCP, FFOM, MRCS, DipAvMed (Commodore)	SURG CAPT(FCC)	-	(CO/M)	31.12.92	FLEET AV SULTAN
Baldwin, Christopher Martin, BA, pce, MSc	LT CDR(FTC)	X	MCD	01.03.95	MANCHESTER
Baldwin, Simon Frederic, BSc, psc	CDRE(FTC)	E	AE	01.07.04	MERLIN IPT
Balfour, Ross Donald	LT(IC)	X		01.07.04	NP IRAQ
Balhetchet, Adrian Stephen, BEng, CEng, MRAeS, Eur Ing	LT CDR(FTC)	E	AE	01.03.00	JHCHQ
Ball, Andrew David, n, SM(n)	LT(FTC)	X		01.01.99	MWS COLLINGWOOD
Ball, Matthew Peter, BEng	LT(CC)	E	MESM	01.12.99	DLO BRISTOL
Ball, Michael Peter, BSc, MIEE, CEng	CDR(FTC)	E	WESM	30.06.04	HQ DCSA
Ball, Stephen James	LT CDR(FTC)	E	ME	01.10.02	DRAKE SFM
Ball, William John Edgar	LT(IC)	E	ME	01.05.03	FLEET HQ PORTS 2
Ballantyne, Craig, SM(n)	LT(IC)	X	SM	07.05.00	RALEIGH
Ballard, Adam Paul Vince	LT(CC)	X		01.09.04	LEEDS CASTLE
Ballard, Mark Lewis, BEng, MIEE, CEng	LT CDR(FTC)	E	WESM	01.12.00	VIGILANT(PORT)
Balletta, Rene James, n	LT CDR(FTC)	X	PWO(C)	01.11.04	EXCHANGE CANADA
Balm, Stephen Victor, psc(a)	LT COL(FTC)	-	LC	30.06.92	RMB STONEHOUSE

Name	Rank	Branch	Spec	Seniority	Where Serving
Balmer, Guy Austin	MAJ(FTC)	-		24.04.02	DARTMOUTH BRNC
Balston, David Charles William, BA, pce, pce(sm), psc	CDR(FTC)	X	SM	30.06.97	MOD (LONDON)
Bamforth, Christian John Milton, BEng, CEng, MIEE	LT(FTC)	E	WESM	01.12.97	MOD (LONDON)
Bance, Nicholas David, BSc	LT CDR(FTC)	X	P	01.10.04	750 SQN HERON
Band, James Wright, BEng, MA, psc(j)	CDR(FTC)	E	AE	30.06.04	DLO YEO
Band, Jonathon, KCB, BA, jsdc, pce, hcsc (COMMANDER-IN-CHIEF FLEET, CINCEASTLANT AUG 02)	ADM	-	PWO	02.08.02	FLEET HQ NWD
Bane, Nicholas St John, BEng	LT(CC)	X	P	01.07.00	846 SQN
Banfield, Steven David, BA	LT(IC)	X		01.09.04	CUMBERLAND
Banham, Alexander William Debower, BEng, CEng, MRAeS	LT(CC)	E	AE	01.12.97	HARRIER IPT
Bankier, Stewart	LT CDR(FTC)	X		19.02.96	FOSNNI
Banks, Morven Janet, BSc	LT(IC)	X		01.01.04	TYNE
Banning, Geoffrey Daniel	MID(IC)	X	P U/T	01.11.03	DARTMOUTH BRNC
Bannister, Andrew Neil, BSc	LT CDR(FTC)	E	WE	01.10.01	CAPT MCTA
Bannister, Jonathan	LT(CC)	X		01.02.03	MONTROSE
Barber, Alexander Stewart Leslie, BSc	LT(IC)	X		01.01.05	MWS COLLINGWOOD
Barber, Christopher James Harrison, BA	LT(CC)	X	O	01.02.95	RNAS CULDROSE
Barber, Mark, BSc	LT(IC)	X	P	01.09.03	771 SQN
Barclay, Michelle Teresa, LCIPD	LT(IC)	S		01.05.04	RALEIGH
Barden, Paul Edward	CAPT RM(IC)	-	SO(LE)	01.07.04	CTCRM
Barfoot, Peter Michael, BSc	LT(IC)	X	FC	01.09.03	NOTTINGHAM
Barham, Edward James, BA	SLT(IC)	X	O U/T	01.09.03	DARTMOUTH BRNC
Bark, James Spencer, pce(sm), SM	LT CDR(FTC)	X	SM	01.09.96	MWC PORTSDOWN
Barker, Charles Philip Geoffrey, MB, BS, MS, FRCS, FICS, DipTh, GB	SURG CAPT(FCC)	-	(CGS)	30.06.01	RCDM
Barker, David Charles Kingston, pce, pcea	CDR(FTC)	X	O	30.06.01	BDS WASHINGTON
Barker, John Wilson, MBE, pcea	LT CDR(FTC)	X	O	01.10.99	702 SQN HERON
Barker, Nicholas James, MA, pce, pcea, psc	LT CDR(FTC)	X	P	01.05.90	LAIPT
Barker, Paul David, BEng	LT(FTC)	E	AE	01.04.00	820 SQN
Barker, Peter Roy, BSc	SLT(IC)	S		01.01.04	DARTMOUTH BRNC
Barker, Piers Thomas, BSc, pce(sm), SM	CDR(FTC)	X	SM	30.06.05	VIGILANT(PORT)
Barker, Richard Demetrious John, OBE, MA, pce, pce(sm), psc(j)	CDR(FTC)	X	SM	30.06.97	COM MCC NWD
Barker, Ruth (Act Surg Lt)	SURG SLT(SCC)	-		22.07.04	DARTMOUTH BRNC
Barker, Timothy John	LT(CC)	X	O	16.10.99	771 SQN B FLT
Barker, Victoria Susan ,BM, BS, BMS	SURG LT(MC(MD)	-		07.08.02	ENDURANCE
Barlow, David, MA	CHAPLAIN	CE		04.04.78	AFCC
Barlow, Martin John	LT(FTC)	X	O	01.03.97	849 SQN HQ
Barnard, Edward Benjamin Graham ,BM, BS, BMS	SURG LT(SCC)	-		04.08.04	RNAS YEOVILTON
Barnard, Toby James, BEng	LT(IC)	E	TM	01.08.01	RMB STONEHOUSE
Barnbrook, Jeremy Charles, pcea	LT CDR(FTC)	X	P	16.12.96	771 SQN
Barnes, James Richard	LT CDR(FTC)	X	AAWO	01.08.99	CATTISTOCK
Barnes, Nicholas John	LT(IC)	S		01.05.03	DARTMOUTH BRNC
Barnes, Patrick Alan Lambeth, BSc	LT(CC)	X	P	01.04.94	EXCHANGE RAF UK
Barnes, Rex Warwick, MA, psc	LT COL(FTC)	-	LC	31.12.00	CTCRM
Barnes-Yallowley, Jonathan James Hugh, pce, pcea	LT CDR(FTC)	X	P	16.07.92	CV(F) IPT
Barnett, Alan Clive, BA, MSc	LT CDR(FTC)	E	AE	01.02.02	849 SQN HQ
Barnwell, Alan	CAPT RM(CC)	-	SO(LE)	21.07.01	COMATG SEA
Barnwell, Keith Leigh, GCIS	LT CDR(FTC)	S		23.04.91	AMC
Barr, David Jonathan	SLT(IC)	X	SM	01.09.02	TALENT
Barr, Derek Desmond	LT(IC)	E	AE	01.04.02	SULTAN
Barr, Simon Peter, BSc	LT(CC)	X	P	01.09.99	EXCHANGE ARMY UK
Barraclough, Carole Denise	LT CDR(FTC)	X	REG	01.10.04	SULTAN
Barrand, Stuart Martin, pce	CDR(FTC)	X	AAWO	30.06.02	NAVSEC
Barratt, Stephen Mitchell	LT CDR(FTC)	S	(W)	01.10.02	CUMBERLAND
Barrett, Benjamin Thomas, BA	LT(IC)	X		01.08.04	MWS COLLINGWOOD
Barrett, David Leonard, IEng, MIIE	LT CDR(FTC)	E	AE	01.10.01	LOAN JTEG BSC DN
Barrett, Scott	LT(IC)	X	SM	01.01.04	VENGEANCE(PORT)
Barrett, Stephen James	LT CDR(FTC)	E	WE	01.10.99	MOD (LONDON)
Barrick, Paul Vincent	LT CDR(FTC)	X	EW	01.10.98	MWS COLLINGWOOD
Barrie, Stuart, BEng	LT(IC)	E	SM	01.09.04	VICTORIOUS(PORT)
Barritt, Olivier David, BA	LT(CC)	X	H2	01.04.00	SCOTT
Barron, Jeremy Mark	LT(IC)	E	WESM	01.05.01	FWO DEVPT SEA
Barron, Patrick Joseph, BSc	LT CDR(FTC)	X	C	01.10.00	STRS IPT

Name	Rank	Branch	Spec	Seniority	Where Serving
Barron, Philip Robert	LT(CC)	X	O	01.01.04	815 FLT 215
Barron-Robinson, David Paul	LT(FTC)	E	WESM	01.04.01	FLEET HQ PORTS 2
Barrow, Charles Michael	LT(CC)	X	FC	01.01.02	ILLUSTRIOUS
Barrow, Jamie	2LT(IC)	-		01.08.01	CTCRM LYMPSTONE
Barrows, David Malcolm, BEng, MSc, MIEE	LT CDR(FTC)	E	WE	01.10.03	MWS COLLINGWOOD
Barrows, Susan Mary, BEng	LT CDR(FTC)	E	WE	01.10.03	MOD (LONDON)
Barry, John Peter	LT CDR(FTC)	X	PWO(U)	01.10.02	LANCASTER
Barter, Emma Charlotte, BEng	SLT(IC)	E	ME U/T	01.01.04	DARTMOUTH BRNC
Bartholomew, David John, BSc	LT(IC)	E	TM	01.05.00	NTE(TTD)
Bartholomew, Ian Munro, ARICS, psc	CDR(FTC)	X	H CH	31.12.92	2SL/CNH FOTR
Bartlett, David Stephen George, BSc	CDR(FTC)	E	AE	30.06.04	LOAN DARA
Bartlett, Ian David, BEng, MSc	LT CDR(FTC)	E	MESM	01.01.98	NP BRISTOL
Bartlett, Mark John, BEng, CEng, MIEE	LT(FTC)	E	WE	01.05.98	RMC OF SCIENCE
Bartley, David James, BSc	CAPT RM(IC)	-		01.09.02	FPGRM
Barton, Keith Jeffrey Atkinson, BEng, MSc	LT(CC)	E	AE	01.03.99	INVINCIBLE
Barton, Mark Alfred, BEng, CEng, MIMechE, MRINA	LT CDR(FTC)	E	ME	01.07.00	FLEET HQ PORTS 2
Barton, Peter Glenn, MSc	CDR(FTC)	E	WE	30.06.99	HQ DCSA
Barton, Sarah Jane, MB, BS	SURG LTCDR(MCC)	-		04.08.04	NELSON (PAY)
Bartram, Gregory James	LT(IC)	E	WE	01.05.02	NOTTINGHAM
Bartram, Richard James	LT(CC)	X	P	01.11.00	JSCSC
Bass, Emma Margaret, BEng	LT(CC)	E	WE	01.09.01	DLO BRISTOL
Bass, Paul William	LT(IC)	E	WESM	01.01.03	TORPEDO IPT
Bassett, Dean Anthony, BA, AMNI, n, MNI	LT CDR(FTC)	X	PWO(A)	01.10.02	CUMBERLAND
Bassett, Neil Edward	LT CDR(FTC)	E	WE	01.10.99	JSSU CYPRUS
Basson, Andrew Paul, MSc, FCIPD, MDA, psc	CDR(FTC)	E	TM	30.06.00	MOD (BATH)
Bastiaens, Paul Alexander	LT(IC)	E	AE	01.05.02	SULTAN
Bate, David Ian George	LT CDR(FTC)	X	MCD	01.10.95	MWS EXCELLENT
Bate, Rohan Christopher, BSc	SLT(IC)	X		01.06.03	DARTMOUTH BRNC
Bateman, Richard Michael, MB, CHB, FFARCSI	SURG LTCDR(MCC)	-		02.08.00	NELSON (PAY)
Bateman, Stephen John Francis	CDR(FTC)	X	AAWO	30.06.93	RNLO GULF
Bates, Andrew James, BSc	LT(CC)	X	P	16.04.98	820 SQN
Bates, Nicholas Stuart, BSc	LT(IC)	X	O	01.04.00	814 SQN
Bath, Edward George	LT CDR(FTC)	X	AAWO	27.12.95	MWS COLLINGWOOD
Bath, Michael Anthony William, BSc, psc(j)	CDR(FTC)	S	SM	30.06.00	MOD (LONDON)
Batham, Donald, MB, BS, DObstRCOG, Dip FFP, MRCGP (Act Surg Cdr)	SURG LTCDR(SC(MD)	-	GMPP	01.09.95	JSU NORTHWOOD
Batho, William Guy Pakenham, BSc	SLT(IC)	X		01.07.02	ILLUSTRIOUS
Bathurst, Sir (David) Benjamin, GCB, DL, rcds	ADM OF FLEET	-	P	10.07.95	
Batley, Jonathan Taylor ,BMus	SLT(IC)	X	P U/T	01.06.03	RNAS YEOVILTON
Battrick, Richard Robert	LT CDR(FTC)	X	AAWO	01.04.04	GLOUCESTER
Baudains, Terence John, BSc, pce	LT CDR(FTC)	X	CMA	01.04.89	2SL/CNH FOTR
Baugh, Adrian Joseph Edward, MA	SLT(IC)	E	WESM	01.02.03	MWS COLLINGWOOD
Baum, Stuart Richard, BSc, pce, pce(sm)	CDR(FTC)	X	SM	30.06.97	NAVSEC
Baverstock, Andrew Peter	LT(IC)	X	AV	01.10.02	RAF COTTESMORE
Baxendale, Robert Fred, BSc, MA, psc(j)	MAJ(FTC)	-		01.09.99	CDO LOG REGT RM
Baxter, Arran Charles	LT(IC)	E	MESM	01.05.02	TIRELESS
Baxter, Frederick Joseph	LT(FTC)	E	AE	01.04.01	SULTAN
Baxter, Iain Menzies, BEng, CEng, MRAeS	LT CDR(FTC)	E	AE	01.01.00	SULTAN
Baxter, John Charles, SM	LT(FTC)	X	SM	27.09.95	FLEET CIS PORTS
Bayliss, Richard	LT(IC)	X	EW	01.07.04	PJHQ
Beacham, Philip Robert, BA	LT CDR(FTC)	X	P	01.07.03	FOST SEA
Beadle, John Thomas	CHAPLAIN	SF		30.03.95	DARTMOUTH BRNC
Beadling, David John	LT(CC)	E	MESM	01.09.01	OCLC MANCH
Beadnell, Robert Mark, MSc	LT CDR(FTC)	E	TM	01.01.04	SULTAN
Beadon, Colin John Alexander, MBE, psc(a)	LT COL(FTC)	-		30.06.94	RMR BRISTOL
Beadsmoore, Emma Jane, MB, CHB, MRCGP	SURG LTCDR(MCC)	-	GMPP	06.08.02	RALEIGH
Beadsmoore, Jonathan Edgar, pce, n	LT CDR(FTC)	X	AAWO	01.02.98	WALNEY
Beale, Michael Dean	LT(FTC)	X	MCD	23.07.98	MWS DEF DIV SCHL
Beales, Nicola Susan	LT(IC)	S		01.01.03	NELSON
Beanland, Peter Louis, BSc	LT(CC)	X		01.06.00	OCLC MANCH
Beard, David John, MB, BCH	SURG LT(SCC)	-		01.08.01	MDHU DERRIFORD
Beard, Graham Thomas Charles, BA, psc	CDR(FTC)	S		31.12.98	COM MCC NWD
Beard, Hugh Dominic, pce, pce(sm), psc(j), SM(n), SM, MA	CDR(FTC)	X	SM	30.06.05	TRENCHANT

Name	Rank	Branch	Spec	Seniority	Where Serving
Beard, Richard Geoffrey	LT(FTC)	X	C	10.12.98	BOWMAN IPT
Beard, Stephen Anthony	LT(IC)	X		01.01.04	CAMPBELTOWN
Beardall, Michael John Doodson, pce, psc(j), MA	CDR(FTC)	X	AAWO	30.06.03	CARDIFF
Bearne, Jeremy Peter, pce, psc	CDR(FTC)	X	PWO(U)	31.12.90	2SL/CNH FOTR
Beats, Kevan Ashley, pce	LT CDR(FTC)	X	PWO(U)	16.02.90	FLEET HQ NWD
Beattie, Paul Spencer, pce, n	LT CDR(FTC)	X	AAWO	01.10.01	FLEET HQ PORTS 2
Beaumont, Ian Hirst, pce, pcea	CAPT(FTC)	X	O	30.06.04	NELSON
Beaumont, Steven John, BSc	LT CDR(FTC)	X	C	01.10.00	FLEET CIS PORTS
Beautyman, Andrew John, BEng	LT CDR(FTC)	E	MESM	01.10.03	VIGILANT(STBD)
Beaver, Robert Mark Steven, BSc, AMIMechE	LT(FTC)	E	ME	01.05.98	MOD (LONDON)
Beavis, John Alexander, BSc	LT(CC)	X	MCD	01.04.99	CATTISTOCK
Beazley, Phillip, sq	MAJ(FTC)	-	SO(LE)	01.10.99	RALEIGH
Beck, Simon Kingsley, pce	LT CDR(FTC)	X	PWO(A)	01.04.99	MOD (LONDON)
Becker, Robert Keith, BA	LT(IC)	X		01.05.03	MANCHESTER
Beckett, Keith Andrew, BSc, MDA, rcds	CAPT(FTC)	E	MESM	30.06.04	FLEET HQ PORTS 2
Bedding, Darren, BA	LT(CC)	X	P	01.06.00	801 SQN
Bedding, Simon William Edward, BEng, CEng, MIEE	LT CDR(FTC)	E	WE	01.04.00	MOD (LONDON)
Bedelle, Stephen James	LT CDR(FTC)	E	WE	01.10.03	EXCHANGE CANADA
Beech, Christopher Martin, pce	LT CDR(FTC)	X	PWO(C)	01.07.98	MHRF(F)
Beech, Daymion John, BSc	LT(CC)	X	P	16.03.98	801 SQN
Beedle, James Daniel Stephen	SLT(IC)	X		01.01.03	MWS COLLINGWOOD
Beegan, Clive Francis, SM	LT(IC)	X	SM	01.01.02	RALEIGH
Belcher, Darren	LT(IC)	E	WE	01.07.04	MANCHESTER
Bell, Adrian Scott, pce, psc, hcsc	CAPT(FTC)	X	PWO(U)	30.06.02	CAMPBELTOWN
Bell, Catriona Mary, BSc	LT(CC)	X		01.02.99	FOST MPV SEA
Bell, Charlotte	SURG SLT(SCC)	-		01.07.02	DARTMOUTH BRNC
Bell, David John, BEng	LT(IC)	X	P	01.05.04	INVINCIBLE
Bell, Fiona Jean	SLT(IC)	E	ME	01.09.01	SOMERSET
Bell, Jeffrey Mark, BEng, CEng, MRAeS, MDA	LT CDR(FTC)	E	AE	01.05.04	SABR IPT
Bell, Lewis George	SLT(IC)	X		01.02.03	OCEAN
Bell, Lucy Jane	LT(IC)	S		01.08.02	847 SQN
Bell, Mark	LT CDR(FTC)	S	SM	01.10.00	MWS COLLINGWOOD
Bell, Nicholas Andrew Graham, BEng	LT(IC)	X	P	01.05.04	RNAS YEOVILTON
Bell, Reginald Paul William	LT CDR(FTC)	X	AAWO	01.10.90	2SL/CNH
Bell, Robert Douglas, pce	LT CDR(FTC)	X	PWO(U)	01.03.97	DLO BRISTOL
Bell, Scott William, MinstAM	LT(FTC)	S	SM	01.04.01	TORBAY
Bell-Davies, Richard William, BSc, pce, psc (Act Capt)	CDR(FTC)	X	PWO(U)	30.06.93	AGRIPPA JFC HQ
Bellfield, Robert James Astley, pce, psc(j)	CDR(FTC)	X	PWO(U)	30.06.04	GRAFTON
Benarr, Christopher Michael	LT(FTC)	X		01.02.03	WESTMINSTER
Benbow, James Alexander Kennedy	LT(IC)	X		01.05.04	BROCKLESBY
Bence, David Elliott, pce	LT CDR(FTC)	X	MCD	01.02.98	MOD (LONDON)
Benfell, Niall Andrew	LT(FTC)	S	(S)	02.05.00	RALEIGH
Benn, Stephen William, BEng, MAPM, MSc, CEng, MRAeS	LT CDR(FTC)	E	AE	01.10.02	824 SQN
Bennet, George Charters	CAPT RM(CC)	-		01.09.03	EXCHANGE ARMY UK
Bennett, Alan Reginald Courtenay, DSC, FRAeS, jsdc, pce, pcea, psc, hcsc	CDRE(FTC)	X	P	15.07.03	RNAS YEOVILTON
Bennett, Anthony John	LT CDR(FTC)	S	(W)	01.10.97	NAVSEC
Bennett, Brian Cecil Harold, BSc	LT(IC)	E	TM U/T	01.09.01	DARTMOUTH BRNC
Bennett, Christopher David, BSc	LT(IC)	X	P	01.03.00	847 SQN
Bennett, Douglas Prasad, BEng	LT(IC)	E	IS	01.05.97	AFPAA JPA
Bennett, Gavin Charles	LT(IC)	MS		01.05.03	MSA
Bennett, Graham Lingley Nepean, pce	LT CDR(FTC)	X	PWO(U)	01.07.93	FOST NWD (JMOTS)
Bennett, Mark Anthony, BEng	LT(IC)	E	WESM	01.01.04	VANGUARD(PORT)
Bennett, Neil Malcolm, BA, psc, psc(j)o	LT COL(FTC)	-	C	30.06.04	LN BPST SAFRICA
Bennett, Paul Martin, BA, pce	CAPT(FTC)	X	PWO(A)	30.06.04	FLEET HQ PORTS 2
Bennett, Stuart Albin Frances James, MB, BS	SURG LT(MC(MD)	-		01.08.01	42 CDO RM
Bennett, William Dean, SM	LT CDR(FTC)	X	C	01.10.00	AGRIPPA MAR CC
Bennett, William Ellis, MEng	LT(CC)	E	ME	01.01.00	SULTAN
Bennetts, Neil (Act Lt Cdr)	LT(FTC)	X	C	03.04.97	NP BOSNIA
Benstead, Neil William John, BEng, MSc	LT CDR(FTC)	E	ME	01.10.04	DLO BRISTOL
Bent, Philip Michael, BEng	SLT(IC)	E	WE U/T	01.02.03	2SL/CNH
Bentham-Green, Nicholas Richard Heriot, psc	MAJ(FTC)	-	LC	01.09.92	ATTURM
Bentley, Grant Stockford	SLT(IC)	X		01.05.03	RNAS YEOVILTON
Benton, Angus Michael, BSc	LT CDR(FTC)	X	MCD	01.09.96	MWC PORTSDOWN

Name	Rank	Branch	Spec	Seniority	Where Serving
Benton, Peter John, MB, BCh, FFOM, CHB	SURG CDR(FCC)	-	(CO/M)	31.12.93	DRAKE CBS
Benzie, Nichol James Emslie, BSc	LT(CC)	X	P	01.10.98	EXCHANGE RAF UK
Beresford-Green, Paul Maxwell	LT CDR(FTC)	S		16.12.00	COS 2SL/CNH
Bergman, Bridget Frances	LT(IC)	X	P	01.01.03	846 SQN
Bernard, Alain Raymond, BA	LT(CC)	X	HM2	01.04.97	ROEBUCK
Bernau, Jeremy Charles, pce, pce(sm), SM	LT CDR(FTC)	X	SM	01.11.91	FOST NWD (JMOTS)
Berry, James Thomas, BSc	LT(IC)	X	P	01.09.03	846 SQN
Berry, Paul	LT CDR(FTC)	E	ME	01.10.00	DFTE PORTSMOUTH
Berry, Steven Mark	LT(IC)	E	WE	01.01.02	CTS
Berry, Timothy James, BSc, n	LT(CC)	X		01.09.98	PUNCHER
Bessant, Matthew, BSc	LT(IC)	X		01.01.05	MWS COLLINGWOOD
Bessell, David Alexander, BA, SM(n), SM	LT CDR(FTC)	X	SM	01.06.01	VENGEANCE(STBD)
Best, Robert Michael, BSc	LT(IC)	E	MESM	01.09.02	SUPERB
Best, Russell Richard, OBE, BA, pce, psc	CAPT(FTC)	X	PWO(U)	30.06.01	CUMBERLAND
Bestwick, Michael Charles, MA, psc(j)	MAJ(FTC)	-		01.05.01	40 CDO RM
Betchley, James William, MSc	LT(IC)	X		01.05.05	MWS COLLINGWOOD
Betteridge, Jeremy Trevor, MCMI, pce, pcea, psc	CDR(FTC)	X	P	30.06.96	DNR RCHQ SOUTH
Bettles, John	LT(IC)	X		01.12.03	MIDDLETON
Betton, Andrew, MA, pce, pcea, psc(j)	CDR(FTC)	X	O	30.06.03	WESTMINSTER
Betts, Andrew Thomas James	SLT(UCE)(IC)	E	AE U/T	01.09.03	DARTMOUTH BRNC
Betts, Peter Richard	SLT(IC)	E	WESMUT	01.09.03	CHATHAM
Bevan, Jeffrey Richard	LT(CC)	X	P	16.12.99	RAF SHAWBURY
Bevan, Noel Stuart, MB, BS, FRCGP, LRCP, MRCS	SURG CAPT(FCC)	-	GMPP	31.12.99	DPMD
Bevan, Simon, BSc, MBA, jsdc, psc(j)	CAPT(FTC)	X	METOC	30.06.03	MOD (LONDON)
Beveridge, Simon Alexander Ronald, BA, CertTh	CHAPLAIN	CE		28.04.93	BULWARK
Beverley, Andrew Peter, BSc	LT(IC)	E	IS U/T	01.02.03	ILLUSTRIOUS
Beverstock, Mark Alistair, BSc, CEng, MIEE, rcds	CAPT(FTC)	E	WESM	30.06.03	MOD (LONDON)
Bevis, Timothy John, psc(j)	COL(FTC)	-		30.06.04	MOD (LONDON)
Bewick, David John, pce, psc(j), MA	CDR(FTC)	X	PWO(U)	30.06.02	MOD (LONDON)
Bewley, Nicholas John	LT(FTC)	X	FC	01.08.99	EXCHANGE RAF UK
Bhattacharya, Debdash, BSc	LT CDR(FTC)	X	P	01.10.03	771 SQN
Bibbey, Mark William, BA, psc(m)	COL(FTC)	-		31.12.00	SA ISLAMABAD
Bickley, Gary Neil	LT(IC)	X		01.01.03	NP IRAQ
Biggs, David Michael, pcea, BSc	LT CDR(FTC)	X	O	01.10.96	FLEET HQ PORTS
Biggs, Peter	LT(IC)	X		01.05.02	RALEIGH
Biggs, William Patrick Lowther, BEng, MA, MSc, CEng, MIEE, psc(j)	CDR(FTC)	E	WE	30.06.04	IA BRISTOL
Bignell, Stephen, BEng	LT CDR(FTC)	E	WE	01.04.00	FLEET HQ NWD
Billings, Andrew	SLT(IC)	X	REG	01.02.04	DARTMOUTH BRNC
Billington, Nigel Stephen, BA, MinstAM, MILT, psc	LT CDR(FTC)	S	SM	01.02.88	DLO/DG DEF SC
Billington, Sam, BEng, AMIMechE	LT(FTC)	E	MESM	01.03.01	DRAKE SFM
Billington, Tony John	LT CDR(FTC)	X	EW	01.10.00	FLEET HQ PORTS 2
Bilson, John Michael Frederick, pce	LT CDR(FTC)	X	AAWO	01.01.93	EXCHANGE USA
Bing, Neil Adrian, BSc	LT(FTC)	X	P	16.12.93	LOAN OTHER SVCE
Bingham, Alexander Anthony John, MEng	LT(IC)	E	ME	01.05.03	MARLBOROUGH
Bingham, David Spencer	LT CDR(FTC)	X	AAWO	01.03.99	ILLUSTRIOUS
Binns, James Barnaby, BEng	SLT(IC)	E	MESMUT	01.09.03	SOUTHAMPTON
Binns, John Richard	LT(CC)	E	WE	01.01.02	HQ DCSA
Binns, Jon Frank, BA	LT(CC)	X		01.05.01	RFANSU
Binns, Jonathan Brian, MSc, CEng, MIMarEST	CDR(FTC)	E	MESM	30.06.87	2SL/CNH FOTR
Birbeck, Keith	LT CDR(FTC)	E	WESM	01.10.98	TIRELESS
Birch, Peter Laurence, BEng	LT(IC)	X	P	01.01.03	702 SQN HERON
Birchall, James Charles, BSc	LT(CC)	X	P	01.04.98	847 SQN
Birchall, Stephen John, BSc, CEng, MIMarEST	CDR(FTC)	E	MESM	30.06.02	MOD (BATH)
Bird, Andrew William	LT(IC)	X	P U/T	01.09.04	RNAS YEOVILTON
Bird, David Edward, pcea	LT CDR(FTC)	X	P	01.10.93	DHFS
Bird, Gary Michael, BA	CAPT RM(CC)	-		01.09.99	29 CDO REGT RA
Bird, Jonathan Michael, BEng, pcea, gdas, MSc	LT CDR(FTC)	X	O	01.10.03	LOAN JTEG BSC DN
Bird, Matthew Graham James, BEng, CEng, MRAeS	LT CDR(FTC)	E	AE	01.11.02	EXCHANGE USA
Bird, Michael Philip, BA	SLT(IC)	X		01.01.03	BLYTH
Bird, Richard Alexander James, PGDIP, pce, n	LT CDR(FTC)	X	H CH	01.07.98	MOD (LONDON)
Bird, Timothy Michael, BA	SLT(IC)	S		01.06.03	INVINCIBLE
Bird, Toby Samuel Varnam, MA	LT(IC)	E	TM	01.09.98	EXCHANGE RAF UK
Birkby, Christina, BSc	LT(IC)	X		01.12.04	MWS COLLINGWOOD

Name	Rank	Branch	Spec	Seniority	Where Serving
Birkin, Kay, BSc	LT(IC)	MS		01.01.04	DMSTC
Birleson, Paul Denzil, BSc	LT(FTC)	X	H2	01.09.99	RFANSU
Birley, Jonathan Hugh, pce	LT CDR(FTC)	X	PWO(U)	01.05.95	EXCHANGE USA
Birrell, Gavin Craig, BSc, MA	LT(FTC)	X		01.07.97	MWS COLLINGWOOD
Birrell, Stuart Martin, MA, psc(j)	LT COL(FTC)	-		30.06.03	HQ 3 CDO BDE RM
Birse, Gregor James, BA, MSc, PGDip	LT CDR(FTC)	X	METOC	01.10.02	FOST SM SEA
Birt, David Jonathan, MB, BS, FRCA	SURG CDR(FCC)	-	(CA)	30.06.01	MDHU DERRIFORD
Bishop, George Charles	LT(FTC)	X	AV	27.07.95	RNAS YEOVILTON
Bishop, Paul Richard, BSc, MIMechE, AMRAeS	CAPT(FTC)	E	AE	30.06.03	HARRIER IPT
Bissett, Ian Michael	LT CDR(FTC)	E	AE	01.10.00	EXCHANGE AUSTLIA
Bissett, Phillip Keith, BSc	LT CDR(FTC)	E	AE	01.10.00	RMC OF SCIENCE
Bissett, Roger William	LT(FTC)	E	AE	17.10.91	HARRIER IPT
Bisson, Ian Jean Paul, MSc, CEng, MIEE, psc, gw	CDR(FTC)	E	WE	30.06.99	NAVSEC
Black, Edward John, MA(CANTAB)	LT(IC)	X	MW	01.01.02	ATHERSTONE
Black, Joanna Mary, BSc	LT(IC)	X		15.05.03	BANGOR
Black, Kenneth James, BSc	SLT(IC)	X	O U/T	01.01.04	DARTMOUTH BRNC
Black, Sarah Beth, MA	LT(CC)	S		01.10.99	NELSON
Blackburn, Andrew Roland James, BEng, MSc gw	LT(FTC)	E	AE	01.12.98	LOAN DSTL
Blackburn, Craig Jonathan	LT(IC)	X		01.09.04	MONMOUTH
Blackburn, Emma Catherine, BEng, MSc	LT(CC)	E	AE	01.07.99	AD AIM
Blackburn, Lee Richard, BEng	LT(FTC)	E	ME	01.09.00	SULTAN
Blackburn, Stephen Anthony, BSc, CEng, MIMarEST	LT CDR(FTC)	E	ME	01.03.98	MOD (BATH)
Blackburn, Stuart James, SM(n), SM	LT CDR(FTC)	X	SM	01.05.02	FOST DSTF
Blackett, William Philip Harry	SLT(UCE)(IC)	X		01.09.03	DARTMOUTH BRNC
Blackler, Steven, BSc	LT(IC)	E	IS	01.01.01	MWS COLLINGWOOD
Blacklock, James Francis	LT(FTC)	X	MW	26.04.99	FOST MPV SEA
Blackman, Nicholas Trevor, BSc, MA, CEng, MIEE, psc(j)	CDR(FTC)	E	AE	30.06.03	MOD (LONDON)
Blackmore, Andrew Michael	SLT(IC)	E	WESMUT	01.09.03	CHATHAM
Blackmore, James, BSc	LT(FTC)	X	P	16.01.98	LOAN DSTL
Blackmore, Mark Stuart, pce, pcea, psc(j)	CDR(FTC)	X	O	30.06.02	MWS COLLINGWOOD
Blackwell, Richard Edward	LT CDR(FTC)	S	SM	01.12.96	NAVSEC
Bladen, Christopher Samuel	LT(IC)	X	P	01.05.04	RNAS YEOVILTON
Blair, Duncan Guy Sanderman, MB, BCh, MRCGP, Dip FFP	SURG CDR(FCC)	-	GMPP	30.06.03	HQ DMETA
Blair, Graeme John Livingston, BEng, CEng, MIMechE	LT CDR(FTC)	E	MESM	01.05.04	NP DNREAY
Blair, Lee David	LT(IC)	X		01.05.04	SOVEREIGN
Blake, Gary Edmund, BSc	CDR(FTC)	E	WESM	30.06.00	DLO BRISTOL
Blake, Matthew George	SLT(IC)	X		01.05.02	PENZANCE
Blake, Sherwyn, BSc	LT(IC)	E	MESM	01.09.04	SULTAN
Blakeley, Anne Louise	LT(SCC)	Q	CC	17.11.98	RN GIBRALTAR
Blakey, Adrian Lawrence	LT CDR(FTC)	X	MCD	01.03.92	KING ALFRED
Blanchford, Daniel, BEng	MAJ(FTC)	-		01.09.02	45 CDO RM
Bland, Christopher David, MEng, AMIEE	LT(CC)	E	WESM	01.05.01	DLO BRISTOL
Bland, Steven Aaron, MB, CHB, BSc, RCSEd	SURG LTCDR(MCC)	-		07.08.01	NELSON (PAY)
Blatcher, David John	SLT(UCE)(IC)	E	MESMUT	01.09.04	DARTMOUTH BRNC
Blatchford, Timothy	SLT(IC)	E	AE U/T	01.01.04	DARTMOUTH BRNC
Bleakley, Charles	SURG SLT(SCC)	-		02.07.03	DARTMOUTH BRNC
Bleasdale, Daniel Robert, BSc	LT(IC)	E	TM	01.04.01	FWO DEVPT SEA
Blethyn, Hugh Phillip, MSc	LT(IC)	E	IS	01.01.00	CINCFLEET FIMU
Blick, Sarah Louise	LT(IC)	S		01.01.02	NELSON
Bligh, Sarah Louise	LT(IC)	X	FC	01.05.04	GLOUCESTER
Block, Andrew William George, MA, MIEE	LT CDR(FTC)	X	AAWO	01.07.02	INVINCIBLE
Blocke, Andrew David	LT CDR(FTC)	MS	(AD)	01.10.04	RN GIBRALTAR
Blois, Simon Dudley, BSc, MIEE	LT(FTC)	E	WE	01.04.01	JSCSC
Blount, Derek Raymond, BSc, CEng, MIMechE	LT CDR(FTC)	E	MESM	01.04.94	NEPTUNE DSA
Blount, Keith Edward, pce, pcea, psc(j)	CDR(FTC)	X	P	31.12.00	JSCSC
Blow, Philip Thomas, BSc	LT(FTC)	E	MESM	01.09.95	FLEET HQ PORTS 2
Blowers, Michael David, pce, pcea, psc(a)	CDR(FTC)	X	O	31.12.00	COS 2SL/CNH
Blunden, Jeremy Jonathan Frank, LVO, BSc, pce	CAPT(FTC)	X	PWO(N)	30.06.05	MOD (LONDON)
Blunt, Carla Lisa	SLT(IC)	X		01.02.05	DARTMOUTH BRNC
Blythe, James	LT(CC)	X		01.12.01	CARDIFF
Blythe, Paul Christopher, pce, pce(sm), SM	LT CDR(FTC)	X	SM	01.10.99	FLEET HQ NWD
Blythe, Tom Stuart, psc(j)	MAJ(FTC)	-	LC	01.09.00	EXCHANGE ARMY UK
Boakes, Philip John	LT(IC)	E	ME	01.05.02	SULTAN

Name	Rank	Branch	Spec	Seniority	Where Serving
Boardman, Sarah Jane, MA	LT(CC)	S		01.01.02	JSCSC
Boddington, Jeremy Denis Leonard, BSc, MRAeS, MDA, pcea, tp	LT CDR(FTC)	X	P	16.12.95	700M MERLIN OEU
Boddy, Katherine Louise, MB, CHB	SURG LT(SC(MD)	-		06.08.03	MWS COLLINGWOOD
Bodman, Simon Alexander, BEng	LT(CC)	X		01.04.00	CUMBERLAND
Boeckx, Thomas Julius Francis, MSc	LT(FTC)	X		01.01.00	SUTHERLAND
Boissier, Robin Paul, MA, MSc, pce, pce(sm), psc (DCE WSA SEP 04)	RADM	-	SM	26.08.02	DLO BRISTOL
Bolam, Andrew Guy, BSc, CEng, MIMarEST	LT CDR(FTC)	E	ME	01.06.94	ARK ROYAL
Bollen. Johanna Michelle	LT CDR(FTC)	S		01.10.03	RICHMOND
Bolton, Jonathan Praed, BEng, CEng, MIMarEST	LT CDR(FTC)	E	ME	01.09.99	CV(F) IPT
Bolton, Matthew Thomas William, BEng, MSc, CEng, MIMarEST, MIMechE	LT CDR(FTC)	E	ME	06.02.00	MOD (BATH)
Bolton, Stephen Jack	LT CDR(FTC)	X	P	01.10.04	702 SQN HERON
Bond, Jason Eric, BA	LT(IC)	X	H2	01.05.02	NP IRAQ
Bond, Nigel David	CDR(FTC)	S		31.12.00	JHCHQ
Bond, Robert Douglas Acton	LT(IC)	X	P	01.09.04	846 SQN
Bond, Robert James	SLT(IC)	X		01.04.03	BRECON
Bone, Christopher John, AMRAeS	LT CDR(FTC)	E	AE	01.05.92	FS MASU
Bone, Darren Nigel, pce, psc(j)	CDR(FTC)	X	PWO(A)	31.12.99	2SL/CNH
Bone, Matthew Peter George	MID(NE)(IC)	X	P U/T	01.09.04	DARTMOUTH BRNC
Bone, Richard Charles, BSc, psc(j)	LT CDR(FTC)	E	TMSM	01.05.98	MOD (LONDON)
Bonnar, John Andrew, BEng, MIEE	LT CDR(FTC)	E	WE	01.06.01	ARGYLL
Bonnar, Susan Mary	LT(CC)	X	ATC	01.11.96	RNAS YEOVILTON
Bonner, Timothy John, MB, ChB	SURG LT(MC(MD)	-		09.08.01	MDHU DERRIFORD
Bonney, James Edward, BSc	CAPT RM(CC)	-	LC	01.09.01	OCEAN
Booker, Glenn Raymond	LT CDR(FTC)	X	ATC	01.10.89	FLEET AV VL
Boon, Gareth John	LT(FTC)	X	METOC	19.09.00	RFANSU
Boon, Simon Edward, BSc	LT(IC)	S		01.09.03	SCEPTRE
Boot, Stephen	LT(IC)	S		01.07.03	CHFHQ
Booth, Diccon Philip Paul, BSc, PhD	LT(IC)	E	TM	01.09.01	INVINCIBLE
Booth, Rachael	SURG SLT(SCC)	-		01.07.02	DARTMOUTH BRNC
Booth, Thomas Oliver, BSc	SLT(IC)	X		01.09.03	DARTMOUTH BRNC
Booth, William Norman, Cert Ed, IEng, MIEE, AMIMarEST	LT(FTC)	E	ME	02.09.99	DLO BRISTOL
Boraston, Peter John, BSc, CEng, MIEE	LT CDR(FTC)	E	WE	01.04.90	IA BRISTOL
Borbone, Nicholas	LT CDR(FTC)	X	AAWO	01.02.03	FLEET HQ PORTS 2
Borland, Stuart Andrew, BSc, MA, CEng, MIEE, psc(j)	CDR(FTC)	E	WE	30.06.01	MOD (LONDON)
Borley, Kim John, MA, CEng, MIEE, rcds, jsdc (FLAG OFFICER TRAINING & RECRUITING/DG SEP 04)	RADM	-	WESM	07.09.04	2SL/CNH FOTR
Borrett, John Edward, BSc	SLT(IC)	X		01.07.02	ATHERSTONE
Boschi, Paul Hamilton, BA	CAPT RM(CC)	-		01.09.99	EXCHANGE ARMY UK
Bosley, Benjamin Daniel, n	LT CDR(FTC)	X		01.10.03	LOAN SAUDI ARAB
Bosshardt, Robert George, pce, jsdc, MCIPD, MSc	CDR(FTC)	X	AAWO	31.12.93	2SL/CNH FOTR
Boston, Justin, BA	LT CDR(FTC)	E	TM	01.01.05	FLEET HQ PORTS
Bosustow, Antony Michael, BEng, CEng, MIEE	LT CDR(FTC)	E	WE	01.06.98	MWS COLLINGWOOD
Boswell, Daniel John, BEd	LT(CC)	X	MW	01.03.99	JSCSC
Botterill, Hugh Walter Scott	LT(IC)	X		01.05.03	CARDIFF
Botting, Neil Andrew, BSc	LT(IC)	X	SM	01.09.02	VANGUARD(PORT)
Bottomley, Steven (Act Lt Cdr)	LT(FTC)	E	AE	06.09.96	AH IPT
Botwood, Tudor, MBE, BD	CHAPLAIN	SF		09.09.02	ARK ROYAL
Boud, Colin Stanley, BEng, AMIMechE	LT(IC)	E	MESM	01.01.04	SULTAN
Boughton, Jonathan Anthony Lee, BEng	LT(IC)	E	WE	01.02.03	INVINCIBLE
Boughton, Timothy Frederick	LT(FTC)	X	P	01.07.97	DARTMOUTH BRNC
Bougourd, Mark Anthony, BEng, MRAeS	LT CDR(FTC)	E	AE	01.10.99	MERLIN IPT
Boulind, Matthew Angus, LLB	LT(IC)	X	O	01.01.02	815 FLT 219
Boullin, John Paul, BEng	LT(CC)	X		01.09.01	NOTTINGHAM
Boulton, Graham Russell, BSc	LT(IC)	X		01.01.05	MWS COLLINGWOOD
Boulton, Neil Andrew, BSc	LT CDR(CC)	E	TM	20.11.98	NELSON
Bourn, Sebastian	SURG SLT(SCC)	-		01.07.03	DARTMOUTH BRNC
Bourne, Christopher Michael, pce, psc(j)	CDR(FTC)	X	O	30.06.04	BDS WASHINGTON
Bourne, Donald Sidney	LT CDR(FTC)	E	AE	01.10.98	DLO YEO
Bourne, Philip John, MA, psc(j)	MAJ(FTC)	-	SO(LE)	01.10.02	FLEET HQ PORTS 2
Bourne, Stephen William	CAPT RM(IC)	-		01.04.04	1 ASSAULT GP RM
Bouyac, David Roger Louis	LT(CC)	X	P	01.11.00	FLEET AV VALLEY

Name	Rank	Branch	Spec	Seniority	Where Serving
Bowbrick, Richard Charles, MA, pce, psc(j)	CDR(FTC)	X	AAWO	30.06.05	MWC SOUTHWICK
Bowden, Matthew Thomas Edward, BEng	LT CDR(FTC)	X	PWO(C)	01.02.03	FLEET CIS PORTS
Bowen, Christopher Nicholas, BSc, PGCE	LT(IC)	X	MCD	01.10.99	FDU3
Bowen, Michael, ARRC, BA, MSc	CAPT(FCC)	Q	RNT	27.03.01	HQ DMETA
Bowen, Nigel Timothy, pce, pcea	CDR(FTC)	X	O	30.06.05	JSCSC
Bowen, Richard James	SLT(IC)	E	WE	01.09.01	MANCHESTER
Bower, Andrew John, BSc, SM(n), SM	LT CDR(FTC)	X	SM	01.08.01	SUPERB
Bower, John William	LT CDR(FTC)	S	(S)	01.10.02	OCEAN
Bower, Nigel Scott, pce(sm)	CDR(FTC)	X	SM	30.06.05	JSCSC
Bowers, John Paul, pcea	LT CDR(FTC)	X	O	01.10.01	702 SQN HERON
Bowers, Keith James, MEng	LT(IC)	E	WE	01.09.04	CORNWALL
Bowers, Mark	LT(IC)	E	IS	01.08.03	DCCIS FAREHAM
Bowes, Nigel	2LT(IC)	-		01.08.01	CTCRM LYMPSTONE
Bowhay, Simon, BSc	LT CDR(FTC)	E	WESM	01.05.99	DLO BRISTOL
Bowie, Alan Niven, MB, BCh, MRCGP	SURG CDR(FCC)	-	GMPP	30.06.05	RN GIBRALTAR
Bowie, Richard	LT(IC)	E	WESM	01.05.02	MWC PORTSDOWN
Bowker, Geoffrey Neil	LT CDR(FTC)	X	ATC	01.10.93	MOD (LONDON)
Bowker, Iain Cameron, BEng	LT CDR(FTC)	E	MESM	13.02.01	NBC PORTSMOUTH
Bowker, Jane Mary, MA	LT(IC)	X		01.05.03	RNAS YEOVILTON
Bowker, Michael Andrew, ADC, MSc, MIMechE, MIMarEST, rcds, jsdc (Commodore)	CAPT(FTC)	E	MESM	30.06.97	NP BRISTOL
Bowman, Robert James, BEng	LT CDR(FTC)	E	AE	01.04.03	SULTAN
Bowman, Simon Kenneth James	SLT(IC)	X	ATCU/T	01.06.02	RAF COTTESMORE
Bowness, Paul (Act Lt Cdr)	LT(FTC)	E	AE	15.10.93	FLEET HQ PORTS
Bowra, Mark Andrew	MAJ(FTC)	-		01.10.03	MOD (LONDON)
Bowser, Nicholas John (Act Lt Cdr)	LT(FTC)	E	AE	02.05.00	MERLIN IPT
Bowyer, Richard John	CAPT RM(CC)	-	MLDR	01.05.00	BDLS AUSTRALIA
Boxall, Pauline, BEng, MSc	LT CDR(FTC)	E	ME	01.04.05	STG BRISTOL
Boxall-Hunt, Brian Paul, OBE, AMNI, pce	CDR(FTC)	X	PWO(A)	30.06.91	DRAKE NBC/DBUS
Boyce, the Lord, GCB, OBE, rcds, psc	ADM			25.05.95	
Boyd, Elaine Marie, BSc	SLT(IC)	S		01.05.02	RALEIGH
Boyd, James Alexander, jsdc, pce(sm)	CAPT(FTC)	X	SM	30.06.96	FWO FASLANE SEA
Boyd, Nicholas, MA, MSc, CEng, MIMechE, psc(j)	CDR(FTC)	E	ME	30.06.05	NP IRAQ
Boyes, Gareth Angus, BA, MEng	LT(FTC)	E	ME	01.07.97	ARK ROYAL
Boyes, Martyn Richard, BEng, MSc	LT CDR(FTC)	E	MESM	01.02.03	TORBAY
Boyes, Richard Austen	LT(FTC)	X	P	01.03.89	829 SQN HQ
Boyle, Jonathan Bartley, BEng, MSc, CEng	LT CDR(FTC)	E	MESM	01.10.02	SCEPTRE
Boynton, Stephen Justin, BSc, MBA, pcea	LT CDR(FTC)	X	O	01.12.99	FOST SEA
Brace, Anna Frances, BA	LT(IC)	X	ATC	01.01.04	RNAS CULDROSE
Bracher, Hugh	LT CDR(FTC)	E	WESM	01.10.96	DRAKE SFM
Bradburn, Stephen Joseph, pcea	LT CDR(FTC(A)	X	P	01.10.93	FLEET AV VL
Bradbury, Simon	CHAPLAIN	RC		18.09.96	RALEIGH
Bradford, Giles Job, MEng	LT(CC)	X	P	01.06.02	845 SQN
Bradford, Malcolm Howard	CAPT RM(IC)	-		01.09.04	40 CDO RM
Bradford, Michelle Joy, BA	LT(IC)	S		01.09.04	DRAKE NBC/DBUS
Bradford, Terrance Horace Colin	LT CDR(FTC)	MS	(AD)	01.10.02	2SL/CNH
Brading, Roland David	CAPT RM(CC)	-		01.03.04	RNAS YEOVILTON
Bradley, Harriet Eleanor, MB, CHB	SURG LT(SC(MD)	-		01.08.03	DARTMOUTH BRNC
Bradley, Martin James, BSc	SLT(IC)	X	O U/T	01.01.04	DARTMOUTH BRNC
Bradley, Matthew Thomas, n	LT CDR(FTC)	X	PWO(U)	01.05.02	MWS COLLINGWOOD
Bradley, Patrick Martin, BEng, CEng, MIEE	LT CDR(FTC)	E	WE	01.06.00	CV(F) IPT
Bradley, Rupert Litherland, LLB	LT(CC)	X	P	01.11.96	849 SQN HQ
Bradley, Trevor Adrian, BEng	LT(CC)	E	WE	01.05.02	NP IRAQ
Brads, Wayne, BSc, ACMA	LT CDR(FTC)	E	CMA	14.01.94	2SL/CNH
Bradshaw, Kevin Thomas, BSc, MDA	LT CDR(FTC)	E	WE	01.10.02	DLO BRISTOL
Brady, Matthew Vincent, BA	SLT(IC)	X	P U/T	01.02.03	DARTMOUTH BRNC
Brady, Sean, BSc	MAJ(FTC)	-		01.10.04	FLEET HQ PORTS 2
Brady, Sean Edward, pce	LT CDR(FTC)	X	PWO(U)	01.09.96	CAPT IST STAFF
Brady, Thomas William	LT(FTC)	S	(W)	01.04.01	MOD (BATH)
Braham, Stephen Wyn, MSc, CEng, FIMarEST, psc	CDR(FTC)	E	ME	30.06.97	MOD (LONDON)
Brailey, Ian Stewart Fordyce	LT(FTC)	X	AV	04.04.96	ADAS BRISTOL
Brain, William James Whitelaw, FHCIMA	CAPT RM(CC)	-		01.09.00	CDO LOG REGT RM
Braithwaite, Geoffrey Charles	LT(IC)	E	ME	01.04.04	SUTHERLAND

Name	Rank	Branch	Spec	Seniority	Where Serving
Braithwaite, Jeremy Sean, n	LT CDR(FTC)	X	H2	01.01.03	FLEET HQ NWD
Bramley, Stephen, pce, pcea, psc	CAPT(FTC)	X	P	30.06.03	NAVSEC
Bramwell, John Gerald	LT(CC)	X	O	01.04.93	EXCHANGE RAF UK
Brand, Simon Martin, BSc, MA, pce, pcea, psc(j)	CDR(FTC)	X	P	30.06.97	D STRAT PLANS
Brann, Robert William	LT(IC)	X		01.05.04	MWS COLLINGWOOD
Brannighan, Ian Derek, MEng	LT(IC)	X	P	01.09.04	RNAS YEOVILTON
Bratby, Simon Paul	LT(FTC)	X	P	16.11.94	ILLUSTRIOUS
Bratt, James Richard	MID(IC)	X		01.11.03	PENZANCE
Bravery, Martin Anthony Edward, pce, pcea	LT CDR(FTC)	X	P	01.05.99	FOST SEA
Bray, Andrew John	SLT(IC)	S		01.09.04	MWC PORTSDOWN
Bray, Katherine Elizabeth, MB, BSc, BS, Dip SM	SURG LT(SCC)	-		01.08.01	MDHU DERRIFORD
Brayson, Mark	LT(FTC)	X	P	16.10.94	815 FLT 246
Brazenall, Benjamin Crawford, BEng	LT(IC)	X	P	01.01.04	DHFS
Brazier, Lars Frank, MA	LT(IC)	X	P	01.01.99	GANNET SAR FLT
Breach, Charles Edward Marshall	CAPT RM(IC)	-	MLDR	01.04.04	FPGRM
Brearley, Rosalind Lydia, BSc	LT(IC)	X		01.05.00	EXCHANGE USA
Breckenridge, Iain Galloway, pce, pce(sm), psc(j)	CDR(FTC)	X	SM	30.06.04	TIRELESS
Bree, Stephen Edward Peter, MB, BCh, FRCA	SURG CDR(FCC)	-	(CA)	30.06.00	MDHU DERRIFORD
Breen, Deborah Ann, BA	LT(CC)	X		01.05.99	MWS COLLINGWOOD
Breen, John Edward, MEng, CEng, MRAeS	LT(CC)	E	AE	01.09.01	RMC OF SCIENCE
Brember, Peter Bruce	LT(FTC)	X	AV	25.07.96	INVINCIBLE
Brenchley, Nigel Gerard	LT CDR(FTC)	S		17.02.00	RNAS YEOVILTON
Brennan, Paul Anthony, BSc, PGDip, IEng, MIIE	LT(FTC)	E	MESM	02.09.99	TURBULENT
Brettell, Jeremy Donald	LT(IC)	X		01.05.05	MWS COLLINGWOOD
Bretten, Nicholas John	SLT(IC)	X		01.07.03	SEVERN
Brewer, Christopher Edward, BSc, SM(n), SM	LT(FTC)	X	SM	01.01.00	TALENT
Brewin, David John, BSc	LT(CC)	X	P	01.03.99	EXCHANGE RAF UK
Brian, Neil, pcea	LT CDR(FTC)	X	O	01.10.02	824 SQN
Briant-Evans, Tom Arthur Hugh, BA	LT(IC)	X		01.12.04	HURWORTH
Bridger, David William, BSc, PGDip, HND	CDR(FTC)	E	TM	30.06.96	CMT SHRIVENHAM
Bridger, Richard John, MA, pcea, psc(j)	CDR(FTC)	X	O	30.06.04	COS 2SL/CNH
Brierley, Simon Paul John, BEng	LT(IC)	E	AE	01.09.02	IV (AC) SQN (RN)
Briers, Matthew Peter, pce, pcea, psc(j)	CDR(FTC)	X	P	30.06.03	MOD (LONDON)
Briggs, Cathryn Sarah	LT CDR(MCC)	Q	OTSPEC	01.10.04	RCDM
Briggs, Charmody Elizabeth, BSc	LT(IC)	X	FC	01.12.01	EXCHANGE RAF UK
Briggs, Mark David, BEng	LT(CC)	E	WE	01.06.97	DRAKE SFM
Briggs-Mould, Timothy Paul	LT CDR(FTC)	E	WE	16.03.99	MONMOUTH
Brighouse, Neil George	MAJ(FTC)	-	P	24.04.02	845 SQN
Brimacombe, Louise Marie, BSc	LT(CC)	S		01.02.00	FLEET HQ PORTS
Brims, Fraser John Hall, MB, ChB, MRCP	SURG LTCDR(MCC)	-		05.08.03	NELSON (PAY)
Brindley, Mark William	LT(IC)	E	WE	01.01.03	MWS COLLINGWOOD
Brinsden, Mark Dudley, MB, BS, FRCSTr&Orth, MRCS	SURG LTCDR(FCC)	-		01.08.99	NELSON (PAY)
Brint, Ian	LT(CC)	S	SM	29.04.01	AGRIPPA MAR CC
Briscoe, James William Austen, BEng, MAPM	LT(IC)	E	WE	01.05.03	IRON DUKE
Bristow, Paul Christopher, BA	LT(IC)	E	TM	01.09.98	FLEET HQ PORTS 2
Bristowe, Paul Andrew, BSc, FRGS, pce, pcea	LT CDR(FTC)	X	P	01.03.01	UKMARBATSTAFF
Britchfield, Alison Esther Phyllis, MA, BD	CHAPLAIN	SF		01.10.92	2SL/CNH FOTR
Britton, Nicholas John, MBE, BSc	LT CDR(FTC)	X		01.04.90	CSIS IPT
Broadbent, Peter Stephen, BSc, MEng, CEng, MIEE	LT CDR(FTC)	E	WE	01.03.02	LOAN DSTL
Broadbent, Sarah Elizabeth	LT(CC)	S		01.03.01	NELSON
Broadhurst, Michael Robert, BA	LT CDR(FTC)	X	AAWO	01.12.00	FOST SEA
Broadley, Kevin James, BSc, MA, MPhil, pce, pcea, psc	CDR(FTC)	X	P	30.06.00	UKMILREP BRUSS
Broadwith, Joanna Louise, BA	SLT(IC)	X		01.02.04	DARTMOUTH BRNC
Brock, Mathew Jonathan	LT(CC)	X		01.01.02	MWS COLLINGWOOD
Brock, Raymond Frederick	LT CDR(FTC)	S		01.03.02	FLEET HQ PORTS
Brocklebank, Guy Philip, BSc, FRSA, MIMgt, pce (Act Capt)	CDR(FTC)	X	PWO(C)	31.12.92	FLEET CIS PORTS
Brocklehurst, Kelly Paul, BA	CAPT RM(CC)	-		01.09.02	FLEET AV SUPPORT
Brockwell, Paul Edward Norman, MBE, BSc, CEng, MIMarEST	CDR(FTC)	E	MESM	30.06.94	DLO BRISTOL
Brodie, Duncan John, BEng	LT(IC)	E	AE	01.01.02	FLEET HQ PORTS
Brodie, Ross William James, pce, n	LT CDR(FTC)	X	PWO(U)	01.12.02	OCEAN
Brodie, Stephen David	LT(SCC)	Q		08.03.01	RH HASLAR
Brodier, Mark Ian	LT(FTC)	E	AE	04.09.98	SULTAN
Brodribb, Timothy John, MB, BS	SURG LTCDR(SCC)	-		04.08.04	NELSON (PAY)

Name	Rank	Branch	Spec	Seniority	Where Serving
Brogden, Thomas	SURG SLT(SCC)	-		01.07.02	DARTMOUTH BRNC
Brokenshire, Sarah Isobel, BA	SLT(IC)	S		01.01.04	DARTMOUTH BRNC
Bromage, Kenneth Charles	CHAPLAIN	CE		02.08.92	RN GIBRALTAR
Bromige, Timothy Robert James, pce	LT CDR(FTC)	X	AAWO	19.05.92	SACT USA (SEA)
Bromwell, Mark Steven, MEng, AMIEE	LT(IC)	E	WE	01.09.02	MOD (LONDON)
Brook, Roger Leslie	LT(FTC)	X	O	11.08.98	771 SQN
Brooking, Richard Robert	LT(IC)	E	WESM	01.05.02	NEPTUNE DLO
Brooks, Gary Lee, pce, PGDip	LT CDR(FTC)	X	H CH	01.04.99	SCOTT
Brooks, Graeme Christian Gibbon	LT CDR(FTC)	X	MCD	01.04.05	MONTROSE
Brooks, Kirsten Mary Louise, BA	LT(IC)	E	TM	06.04.97	MWS COLLINGWOOD
Brooks, Nicholas Robert, BEng	LT(IC)	E	MESM	01.09.01	TORBAY
Brooks, Paul Neil	LT(IC)	E	WE	01.01.03	RMC OF SCIENCE
Brooksbank, Richard (Act Lt)	SLT(IC)	S		01.05.02	DLO/DG DEF SC
Brooksbank, Richard James, BSc, pce, pcea	CDR(FTC)	X	P	31.12.97	INVINCIBLE
Brosnan, Mark Anthony, pcea	LT(CC)	X	O	16.07.93	GANNET SAR FLT
Broster, Lee	LT(IC)	E	WE	01.07.04	GRAFTON
Brothers, Anthony Herbert George	LT(FTC)	E	WE	18.02.94	FLEET HQ PORTS 2
Brotherton, John Darren, QCBA	LT CDR(FTC)	X	P	16.04.02	RAF SHAWBURY
Brotherton, Michael, MBE, BD	CHAPLAIN	CE		04.09.84	OCEAN
Brotton, Peter James, BSc, n	LT(FTC)	X		01.04.98	MWS COLLINGWOOD
Brough, Geoffrey Alan	CDR(FTC)	E	WESM	31.12.94	2SL/CNH FOTR
Browett, Jon James, BSc	LT(IC)	X		01.09.04	MWS COLLINGWOOD
Brown, Aaron Richard Andrew	LT(CC)	X	O	01.03.00	750 SQN SEAHAWK
Brown, Alastair David, BEng	LT(IC)	E	ME	01.09.04	SULTAN
Brown, Andrew, MA(OXON), BM, BCH, Dip SM	SURG LTCDR(MCC)	-	GMPP	05.08.03	CDO LOG REGT RM
Brown, Andrew Martyn, BEng	LT CDR(FTC)	E	WE	01.12.04	T45 IPT
Brown, Andrew Paul	LT CDR(FTC)	X	ATC	01.02.04	RNAS YEOVILTON
Brown, Andrew Paul	SLT(IC)	X		01.09.02	ST ALBANS
Brown, Andrew Scott, MSc	LT(CC)	X		01.09.01	GRAFTON
Brown, Bernard Craig	LT(MC(MD)	Q		11.06.00	MDHU DERRIFORD
Brown, Christopher Dennis, pcea (Act Cdr)	LT CDR(FTC)	X	P	01.09.87	LOAN JTEG BSC DN
Brown, David Campbell, MSc, MB, CHB, LRCP, MRCS, MSRP, FFOM	SURG CAPT(FCC)	-	CPDATE	30.06.02	2SL/CNH
Brown, Emma Louise, BA	LT(IC)	S		01.01.05	ENDURANCE
Brown, Howard Spencer, MBE, pce, pcea, psc(j)	CDR(FTC)	X	P	31.12.99	ILLUSTRIOUS
Brown, James Alexander, BSc	LT(CC)	X	H2	01.05.00	MWS COLLINGWOOD
Brown, James Alexander, BEng, MSc	LT(IC)	E	WESM	01.01.03	SOVEREIGN
Brown, Leonard Anthony, BA	MAJ(FTC)	-	P	01.09.03	847 SQN
Brown, Lynda	LT(IC)	S		29.10.04	RALEIGH
Brown, Malcolm Keith, MBE, BSc, pce	CDR(FTC)	X	AAWO	20.09.94	NAVSEC
Brown, Michael Andrew, BSc	SLT(IC)	X		01.09.02	RNAS YEOVILTON
Brown, Neil Logan, LLB (Act Capt) (Barrister)	CDR(FTC)	S	BAR	31.12.98	MOD (LONDON)
Brown, Nigel Peter, BSc, MA, psc(m), psc(j)	LT COL(FTC)	-	C	30.06.98	CTCRM
Brown, Paul Alexander Everett, BA, pce, n	LT CDR(FTC)	X	AAWO	01.08.99	JSCSC
Brown, Paul Angus (Act Lt Cdr)	LT(FTC)	E	AE	07.09.95	AH IPT
Brown, Peter St John, BEng, CEng, MIMarEST	LT CDR(FTC)	E	MESM	01.06.95	TALENT
Brown, Rebecca Josephine	MID(UCE)(IC)	X		01.09.03	DARTMOUTH BRNC
Brown, Richard	CAPT RM(IC)	-	P	24.07.04	CTCRM
Brown, Robert Andrew Mark, OBE, pce	CAPT(FTC)	X	AAWO	30.06.02	NAVSEC
Brown, Sarah Suzanne	MID(IC)	X		01.09.03	DARTMOUTH BRNC
Brown, Scott James, BD	CHAPLAIN	SF		20.04.93	MWS COLLINGWOOD
Brown, Sharon Mary Jean	LT(IC)	S		01.07.04	COS 2SL/CNH
Brown, Simon David, n	LT CDR(FTC)	X	PWO(N)	01.11.02	EXCHANGE CANADA
Brown, Stephen	LT(IC)	S		01.07.03	FLEET HQ PORTS 2
Brown, Stephen Glynn	LT(CC)	X	P	04.08.00	848 SQN HERON
Brown, Stephen Harry, pce	LT CDR(FTC)	X	PWO(U)	15.01.01	MCM2 SEA
Brown, William Clarke, pce	CDR(FTC)	X	AAWO	30.06.03	MWC PORTSDOWN
Browning, Rowan Susannah, BSc, adp, PGDip	LT CDR(CC)	E	IS	01.01.02	EXCHANGE USA
Bruce, Steven Leonard, BA(OU), MA, psc	LT COL(FTC)	-		30.06.96	MOD (LONDON)
Bruce-Jones, Nicholas William, BSc, psc(j)	LT COL(FTC)	-		31.12.00	MOD (LONDON)
Bruford, Robert Michael Charles, pce	LT CDR(FTC)	X	AAWO	01.04.00	EXCHANGE USA
Brundle, Paul Robert, MBE	LT CDR(FTC)	X	ATC	01.10.95	MOD (LONDON)
Brunell, Paul Jonathan	LT CDR(FTC)	E	AE	01.10.04	SULTAN

Name	Rank	Branch	Spec	Seniority	Where Serving
Brunsden-Brown, Sebastian Edward, pcea	LT CDR(FTC)	X	P	01.10.01	700M MERLIN OEU
Brunton, Steven Buchanan, MSc, CEng, FIEE, MCGI, mdtc	CAPT(FTC)	E	WESM	30.06.01	HQ DCSA
Brutton, Joseph Henry, BEng	LT(CC)	E	MESM	01.08.97	FLEET HQ NWD
Bryan, Rory John Lockton, BA, pce	LT CDR(FTC)	X	PWO(U)	01.01.00	MWS COLLINGWOOD
Bryant, Daniel John Grenfell	LT CDR(FTC)	S	SM	01.10.02	FLEET HQ PORTS
Bryars, Paul Murray	CAPT RM(CC)	-	SO(LE)	01.04.03	UKLFCSG RM
Bryce, Graeme Edward, BDS	SG LT(D)(MC(MD)	-		29.06.00	40 CDO RM
Bryce, Neville Anthony, MBE	LT CDR(FTC)	E	MESM	01.10.03	VICTORIOUS(PORT)
Bryce-Johnston, Fiona Lorraine Stirling, MA	LT(MC(MD)	Q		16.07.01	JSCSC
Bryden, David Gaskell	SLT(IC)	X		01.09.04	MIDDLETON
Bryson, Susan Ainee, BA, n, PGCE	LT(FTC)	X	PWO(U)	01.03.94	GLOUCESTER
Bryson, Vincent Leonard, BA	LT(IC)	X		01.01.05	MWS COLLINGWOOD
Bubb, Jonathan David (Act Maj)	CAPT RM(FTC)	-	C	01.05.99	CTCRM
Buchan, John Alan, MA	LT(IC)	X		01.09.99	MCM3 SEA
Buchan, Lindsay Helen, BSc	SLT(IC)	S		01.06.03	BULWARK
Buchanan, David	LT(IC)	E	ME	01.05.03	DRAKE SFM
Buchanan, Robert Michael, BEng	LT(CC)	E	AE	01.05.01	FS MASU
Buchan-Steele, Mark Anthony, BSc, MA, psc(j)	CDR(FTC)	S	SM	31.12.00	NEPTUNE DLO
Buck, James Edward, PGDIPAN, pce, n	LT CDR(FTC)	X	PWO(N)	01.04.00	BULWARK
Buck, Sarah Rachael, BSc, PGCE	LT(IC)	E	TM	01.05.98	DCTS HALTON
Buckenham, Peter James, BEng, AMIMechE	LT(CC)	E	ME	01.10.99	LEEDS CASTLE
Buckeridge, Vincent	LT(FTC)	E	WESM	18.02.94	SPLENDID
Buckingham, Guy, SM(n), SM	LT CDR(FTC)	X	SM	01.12.01	EXCHANGE USA
Buckland, Richard John Francis, pce, pcea, psc(j)o	CDR(FTC)	X	O	31.12.99	MOD (LONDON)
Buckle, Iain Lawrence, BEng, MBA, CEng, MIMarEST	CDR(FTC)	E	WE	30.06.05	MOD (BATH)
Buckley, Bryn	LT(IC)	X	O U/T	01.05.05	RNAS CULDROSE
Buckley, Dominic David George, BA	LT(CC)	X	H1	01.02.94	NELSON
Buckley, Phillip James Anthony, jsdc, pce(sm), pce	CAPT(FTC)	X	SM	30.06.05	MOD (LONDON)
Bucknall, Robin James Woolcott	MAJ(FTC)	-		01.05.00	CTCRM
Buczkiewicz, Mathew James	CAPT RM(CC)	-		01.09.03	OCLC ROSYTH
Bugg, Kevin John	LT CDR(FTC)	E	AE	01.03.02	JCA IPT USA
Buggins, Brian, QGM	LT(IC)	X	AV	01.05.02	DISC SEA
Bukhory, Hamesh, BEng	LT(CC)	E	AE	01.01.02	LOAN DARA
Bulgin, Martin Ronald	LT(IC)	X	ATCU/T	01.01.05	RNAS CULDROSE
Bull, Andrew John, pcea, psc	CDR(FTC)	X	O	01.10.95	HQ1GP HQSTC
Bull, Charlotte Vivienne Rachel, BA, MinstAM	LT CDR(FTC)	S		01.10.04	SOUTHAMPTON
Bull, Christopher Martin Sefton, MA, CEng, MIEE, psc(j)	CDR(FTC)	E	WESM	30.06.04	NEPTUNE DLO
Bull, Geoffrey Charles, BEng, MSc, MIMarEST, CEng	LT CDR(FTC)	E	MESM	01.11.94	MOD (LONDON)
Bull, Louis Paul, BA, SM(n)	LT(CC)	X	SM	01.07.00	SUPERB
Bull, Michael Antony John, BSc, SM(n), SM	LT(CC)	X	SM	11.09.99	TRENCHANT
Bullock, James Richard	LT(CC)	X	P	01.08.02	846 SQN
Bullock, John Barry	LT(IC)	E	ME	01.07.03	SULTAN
Bullock, Michael Peter, MBE	CAPT(FTC)	S	SM	30.06.05	DLO/DG DEF SC
Bullock, Robert Arthur, BSc	LT(CC)	X		01.09.00	MONTROSE
Bulmer, Renny John	MAJ(FTC)	-	SO(LE)	01.10.00	UKLFCSG RM
Bulmer, William Elliot, MA	LT(IC)	S		01.01.03	RALEIGH
Bulter, Danielle Barbara, BEng	LT(IC)	E		01.09.01	FLEET HQ PORTS
Bunney, Graham, BSc	LT(CC)	X	P	01.02.94	849 SQN A FLT
Bunt, Kevin John	LT CDR(FTC)	S	(S)	01.10.00	RALEIGH
Burbidge, Kay	LT(CC)	X	O	01.09.98	814 SQN
Burcham, Jason Richard	CAPT RM(IC)	BS	SO(LE)	01.04.03	FLEET HQ PORTS 2
Burcham, Veryan	LT(IC)	MS		13.08.04	2SL/CNH
Burden, John Charles	LT CDR(FTC)	X	MCD	01.11.91	FOST MPV SEA
Burdett, Richard Wyndham, BSc, CEng, MIMechE, MDA	LT CDR(FTC)	E	MESM	01.06.92	NEPTUNE DLO
Burdett, Vincent Charles	LT(IC)	E	ME	01.05.02	CAPT MCTA
Burge, Roger George	LT CDR(FTC)	E	WESM	01.10.00	VENGEANCE(STBD)
Burgess, Andrew James, MB, BCH, BSc, FRCA, FFARCS, DA	SURG CDR(FCC)	-	(CA)	30.06.96	MDHU DERRIFORD
Burgess, Gary Thomas Myles, BEng, MSc	LT CDR(FTC)	E	MESM	01.02.00	NAVSEC
Burgess, Lawrence	2LT(IC)	-		01.08.01	CTCRM LYMPSTONE
Burgess, Mark John	CAPT RM(CC)	-	SO(LE)	01.04.03	CHFHQ
Burgess, Philip Gordon, BEng	LT(IC)	E	ME	01.09.04	CORNWALL
Burgess, Stanley, pcea	LT CDR(FTC(A)	X	P	01.10.90	RNAS CULDROSE
Burghall, Rebecca Clare, BSc	LT(CC)	X	H2	01.08.01	ROEBUCK

Name	Rank	Branch	Spec	Seniority	Where Serving
Burgoyne, William Lawrence, BA	SLT(IC)	X		01.05.03	ILLUSTRIOUS
Burke, Michael Christopher, BSc	LT CDR(FTC)	X	SM	01.09.95	DRAKE NBC/DBUS
Burke, Paul Dominic, OBE, BA, pce, pce(sm)	CDR(FTC)	X	SM	30.06.02	FOST SM SEA
Burkett, Janis Ann, MB, BCH, BAO, DObstRCOG, Dip FFP, MRCGP, JCPTGP	SURG CDR(SCC)	-	GMPP	01.07.00	INVINCIBLE
Burley, Matthew Richard, BEng, MSc	LT(FTC)	E	MESM	01.06.97	NP BRISTOL
Burlingham, Alexander Charles Rains, BSc, MA	LT(IC)	E	TM	01.08.03	CAMPBELTOWN
Burlingham, Brett Limmer, BSc, MA, CEng, MIMarEST, psc(j)	CDR(FTC)	E	ME	30.06.03	CTS
Burnell, Jeremy Richard Jenner, fsc	LT COL(FTC)	-		31.12.00	RMR SCOTLAND
Burnell-Nugent, James Michael, KCB, CBE, ADC, MA, jsdc, pce, pce(sm) (SECOND SEA LORD AND CINCNAVHOME JAN 03)	VADM	-	SM	28.01.03	2SL/CNH
Burnet, Ewan, BA	SLT(IC)	X		01.05.02	MWS COLLINGWOOD
Burnett, Paul Henry	LT(IC)	MS		01.05.03	2SL/CNH
Burningham, Michael Robert, BA, psc(j)	CDR(FTC)	S	SM	30.06.03	UKMARBATSTAFF
Burnip, John Matthew, BSc	LT CDR(FTC)	E	ME	01.08.93	EXCHANGE CANADA
Burns, Adrian Conleth	LT CDR(FTC)	S	SM	04.03.02	RALEIGH
Burns, Andrew John, BEng	LT(IC)	X	P	01.01.03	846 SQN
Burns, Andrew Paul, pce, BA	CDR(FTC)	X	PWO(A)	30.06.05	NP IRAQ
Burns, David Ian, BSc, ARCS, pce, psc(j), MA	CDR(FTC)	X	PWO(C)	30.06.04	SOMERSET
Burns, Euan Paterson, BEng	LT(FTC)	E	WE	01.08.98	RMC OF SCIENCE
Burns, James Edward, BEng	LT(FTC)	E	WE	01.02.99	HQ DCSA
Burns, Robin Douglas James, BSc, PGDip	LT CDR(FTC)	X	METOC	01.03.99	MWS COLLINGWOOD
Burr, Christopher	2LT(IC)	-		01.08.01	CTCRM LYMPSTONE
Burrell, Aleck Michael George	MAJ(FTC)	-	LC	01.04.04	1 ASSAULT GP RM
Burrell, David James, MEng	LT(IC)	X	SM	01.09.02	VENGEANCE(STBD)
Burrell, Philip Mark, BSc, MCIPD, psc	CAPT(FTC)	E	TM	30.06.02	UKNMR SHAPE
Burrows, John Campbell	LT(FTC)	E	MESM	15.10.93	TALENT
Burrows, Michael John	LT CDR(FTC)	X	P	01.10.94	LOAN JTEG BSC DN
Burrows, Thomas George	MID(IC)	X	P U/T	01.09.03	RNAS YEOVILTON
Burstow, Nicola Suzanne, BA, n	LT CDR(FTC)	X		01.11.03	DRAKE COB
Burstow, Richard Stanley, pce	LT CDR(FTC)	X	PWO(U)	01.05.99	FOST SEA
Burt, Douglas James	LT(IC)	E	MESM	01.10.02	FWO FASLANE
Burt, Paul Ronald, BA, ACIS	LT CDR(FTC)	S	(S)	01.10.93	AFPAA JPA
Burton, Alex, BSc	LT(FTC)	X	O U/T	01.11.00	RNAS CULDROSE
Burton, Alexander James, BSc, pce, psc(j)	CDR(FTC)	X	PWO(U)	30.06.01	MOD (LONDON)
Burton, David Stephen, MSc	CAPT(FTC)	E	IS	30.06.03	MOD (LONDON)
Burton, James Harry	SLT(IC)	X		01.01.03	DUMBARTON CASTLE
Burton, Paul Richard	LT(FTC)	E	ME	02.05.00	MOD (LONDON)
Burton, Tanya Jane, BDS	SGLTCDR(D)(SCC)	-		04.07.04	NEPTUNE DDA
Burvill, Justin Paul, BEng, MSc, CEng, MIMarE	LT CDR(FTC)	E	MESM	01.03.03	TIRELESS
Burwin, Harvey Lee, BEng	LT CDR(FTC)	E	WE	01.11.96	MOD (BATH)
Bush, Alexander John Taylor, pce	LT CDR(FTC)	X	PWO(U)	01.06.99	MWS COLLINGWOOD
Bush, David Jonathon, MEng	LT(IC)	E	SM	01.05.04	SPARTAN
Bushell, Gary Robert	LT CDR(FTC)	X		09.07.99	FLEET HQ PORTS
Bussey, Emma Louise, BA	LT(FTC)	X		01.09.99	TEMERAIRE
Buston, David Christopher	CAPT RM(IC)	-		01.04.04	MOD (LONDON)
Butcher, David	CAPT RM(CC)	-	C	01.04.03	40 CDO RM
Butcher, Mark William	MID(IC)	X		01.09.03	ENTERPRISE
Butler, Ian Anthony, MAPM	LT CDR(FTC)	E	AE	01.10.04	INVINCIBLE
Butler, Jonathon Edward, MEng	LT(IC)	E	WESM	01.09.03	TRAFALGAR
Butler, Lee Peter, IEng, AMRAeS	LT CDR(FTC)	E	AE	01.10.03	OCLC MANCH
Butler, Nicholas Abraham Marsh, MBA, pce, pcea	CAPT(FTC)	X	P	31.12.97	SA PARIS
Butler, Philip Michael, BSc	LT(IC)	X	P	01.01.01	RNAS YEOVILTON
Butler, Robin Andrew, BSc	LT(IC)	E	TM	01.01.02	MWS COLLINGWOOD
Butler, Simon, BA	CAPT RM(IC)	-		01.09.02	DNR DISP TEAM
Butterfield, Neil Philip, MB, BS, DA, DipAvMed	SURG CAPT(FCC)	-	GMPP	31.12.92	NELSON
Butterworth, Charlotte Louise ,BMus	LT(FTC)	S		01.02.98	COS 2SL/CNH
Butterworth, Leslie	LT(FS)(CAS)	FS		16.01.99	DRAKE COB(CNH)
Butterworth, Paul Gerard, LLB, MInsD	LT CDR(FTC)	X		01.03.05	MWS COLLINGWOOD
Buxton, David Adrian, BEng, MIEE	LT(IC)	E	WESM	01.09.01	TRIUMPH
Buxton, Peter John, BA, BM, BCh, FRCR	SURG CDR(FCC)	-	CPDATE	31.12.95	RH HASLAR
Bye, Marc David, BEng, CEng, MIMarEST	LT CDR(FTC)	E	ME	01.05.00	CTS
Byers, Hannah Rebecca	SLT(UCE)(IC)	E	AE	01.09.02	DARTMOUTH BRNC

Name	Rank	Branch	Spec	Seniority	Where Serving
Byne, Nicholas	LT(IC)	X	ATC	01.05.04	EXCHANGE RAF UK
Byrd, Liam Bernard	LT(IC)	S		17.12.04	NBC PORTSMOUTH
Byrne, Adrian Charles, IEng, MIPlantE	LT CDR(FTC)	E	ME	01.10.03	RALEIGH
Byrne, Terence Michael	LT CDR(FTC)	X	REG	01.10.02	NAVSEC
Byron, Douglas Charles	LT(IC)	S		01.09.03	FLEET CIS PORTS
Byron, James David	LT CDR(FTC)	X	MW	01.05.03	MONMOUTH
Bywater, Richard Lewis, BEng, MSc, CEng, MIEE, gw	LT CDR(FTC)	E	WE	01.03.99	JSCSC

C

Name	Rank	Branch	Spec	Seniority	Where Serving
Cackett, Thomas Edward Robert	SLT(IC)	X		01.05.03	727 NAS
Caddick, Andrew	LT(IC)	E	MESM	01.09.03	TRENCHANT
Caddick, Stephen	LT(IC)	E	WE	01.07.04	MONMOUTH
Cahill, Karen Ann, BA	LT CDR(FTC)	X	FC	01.08.03	MWS COLLINGWOOD
Cain, Christopher William	LT CDR(FTC)	E	WESM	01.10.04	DLO BRISTOL
Caldwell, Daniel James	CAPT RM(IC)	-		01.09.03	OPTAG
Calhaem, Richard Tahi, BEng	LT(CC)	X	P	15.03.98	STRIKFORNATO
Callaghan, Paul Fraser, MBE, BSc	LT CDR(FTC)	X	P	01.10.99	829 SQN HQ
Callis, Gregory James, BEng	LT(IC)	E	ME	01.09.02	MWS DEF DIV SCHL
Callister, David Roy, pcea	LT CDR(FTC)	X	O	01.10.95	FSAST IPT
Callon, Andrew McMillan	CHAPLAIN	CE		05.06.90	RNAS YEOVILTON
Calvin, Aaron James, MB, BCH, BAO	SURG LT(SCC)	-		04.02.03	CFLT MED(SEA)
Cambridge, Grant Andrew, BA	CAPT RM(IC)	-		01.09.99	RMR SCOTLAND
Cameron, Andrew John Brunt, rcds, pce	CAPT(FTC)	X	PWO(U)	30.06.98	FLEET HQ PORTS 2
Cameron, Fiona, BSc	LT(IC)	E	TM	24.04.98	FLEET HQ PORTS
Cameron, Mark John, BEng, MDA, CEng, MIEE	CDR(FTC)	E	WE	30.06.05	MWS COLLINGWOOD
Cameron, Peter Stuart, OBE, MA, psc(j)	LT COL(FTC)	-		30.06.02	UKLFCSG RM
Campbell, Alastair, BEng	LT(IC)	X	P	01.05.04	RNAS YEOVILTON
Campbell, Alistair Lamont, BEM	LT(IC)	X	AV	12.04.02	DISC
Campbell, David John, MB, BS	SURG CDR(FCC)	-	GMPP	30.06.02	SULTAN
Campbell, Iain Angus	LT(CC)	X	P	16.04.96	GANNET SAR FLT
Campbell, James Colin, Cert Ed, HNC	LT CDR(CC)	E	IS	01.09.01	AFPAA JPA
Campbell, James Kininmonth, MB, BS, LRCP, FRCS, FRCSEd	SURG CAPT(FCC)	-	(CGS)	30.06.02	RH HASLAR
Campbell, Keith Reid	CAPT RM(IC)	-	C	01.04.04	45 CDO RM
Campbell, Leslie Michael, BA	LT CDR(FTC)	X	MW	01.07.00	NEPTUNE DLO
Campbell, Malcolm Alexander, BEd, MSc	LT CDR(CC)	E	IS	01.01.00	CINCFLEET FTSU
Campbell, Mark Alan McMillian, BEng (Act Lt Cdr)	LT(FTC)	X	P	01.09.96	FOST SEA
Campbell, Peter Robert	LT(CC)	X	O	01.01.94	LOAN DESO
Campbell, Robin David Hastings, BEng, CEng, MIEE	LT CDR(FTC)	E	WESM	01.02.95	EXCHANGE FRANCE
Campbell, Timothy Ross, BSc	LT(IC)	X		01.06.00	MERSEY
Campbell-Baldwin, James William, BA	LT(IC)	X		01.05.03	LIVERPOOL
Camplisson, Owen Gerard	SLT(IC)	X		01.07.03	RNAS YEOVILTON
Canale, Andrew James, BA, n	LT(FTC)	X		01.07.97	JSCSC
Cannell, Graham Martin, BA	LT(CC)	X	P	01.05.00	RNAS YEOVILTON
Canning, Christopher Paul, BSc, pcea	LT CDR(FTC)	X	O	01.10.02	DARTMOUTH BRNC
Canning, William Andrew, OBE, psc(m)	LT COL(FTC)	-		30.06.93	SA OSLO
Cannon, Leslie Brian, MB, BS, BSc, FRCS	SURG CDR(FCC)	-	(CO/S)	30.06.04	RH HASLAR
Cantellow, Richard Barry	LT(IC)	X		01.01.03	RNAS YEOVILTON
Cantellow, Stuart John, BEng	LT(FTC)	E		01.06.01	JF HARROLE OFF
Cantrell, Simon Richard David	SLT(IC)	X		01.07.02	ILLUSTRIOUS
Cantrill, Richard John, BSc	MAJ(FTC)	-	MLDR	01.09.04	42 CDO RM
Canty, Nigel Robert, BSc	LT CDR(FTC)	E	MESM	01.09.91	FOST SM SEA
Canty, Thomas Alexander, BEng, AMIMechE	LT(FTC)	E	ME	01.02.02	WESTMINSTER
Capes, Stuart George, SM(n), SM	LT CDR(FTC)	X	SM	01.10.02	SCEPTRE
Capewell, David Andrew, OBE, psc(m), fsc, hcsc	BRIG(FTC)	-		18.10.04	PJHQ
Caple, Jonathan Neil	LT(FTC)	S		01.07.99	RALEIGH
Capps, James Alan, BSc	LT(IC)	X	P U/T	01.01.05	RNAS YEOVILTON
Carbery, Stephen James	LT(CC)	E	WE	01.01.02	DLO BRISTOL
Carcone, Paul Nicholas, BSc	LT(CC)	S		01.12.99	2SL/CNH FOTR
Carden, Peter David, pce, pcea, psc(j)	CDR(FTC)	X	O	30.06.99	IRON DUKE
Carey, Trevor James	LT(IC)	E	ME	01.05.02	SULTAN
Cargen, Malcolm Robert, BSc, psc	CDR(FTC)	E	AE	31.12.00	DLO YEO
Carlton, Paul David, MSc	SLT(IC)	E	MESMUT	01.05.03	2SL/CNH

Name	Rank	Branch	Spec	Seniority	Where Serving
Carman, Felix Spencer Dylan, BSc	LT(IC)	X		01.12.04	MWS COLLINGWOOD
Carne, Richard James Power, BSc, MBA, pcea	LT(FTC)	X	O	16.05.87	700M MERLIN OEU
Carnell, Gregory James, pcea	LT(CC)	X	O	01.09.91	815 SQN HQ
Carnell, Richard Paul, BA	LT(MC(MD)	Q		06.11.98	2SL/CNH FOTR
Carnew, Sean Frederick, BA	LT(IC)	X	O	01.09.03	820 SQN
Carnie, Manson John, BA	LT(FTC)	X	P	01.09.99	815 FLT 209
Carns, Alistair Steve	CAPT RM(IC)	-	MLDR	01.09.04	29 CDO REGT RA
Carpenter, Bryony Helen, BSc, PGCE	LT CDR(CC)	E	TM	01.10.04	INVINCIBLE
Carpenter, Gary John, BEng	SLT(IC)	E	WESM	01.09.02	FWO FASLANE SEA
Carpenter, George Edward, MEng	LT(FTC)	X		01.10.02	WESTMINSTER
Carr, David John	SLT(IC)	X		01.07.02	RNAS YEOVILTON
Carr, David Leslie, pcea	LT CDR(FTC(A)	X	O	01.10.89	702 SQN HERON
Carr, Julia	SLT(IC)	S		01.06.03	OCEAN
Carr, Peter, BSc	CAPT RM(IC)	-	SO(LE)	01.07.03	FLEET HQ PORTS 2
Carretta, Mark Vincent, BSc, pcea (Act Cdr)	LT CDR(FTC)	X	P	01.10.95	846 SQN
Carrick, Richard James, BEng, MBA, MSc, CEng, MIMechE	LT CDR(FTC)	E	MESM	01.05.97	FWO DEVONPORT
Carrigan, Jonathan Andrew	LT CDR(FTC)	S		01.10.04	SULTAN
Carrington, Victoria Louise, BA	LT(IC)	X		01.01.99	EXCHANGE FRANCE
Carrington-Wood, Clive Gordon, pce, MSc	LT CDR(FTC)	X	AAWO	01.10.91	MOD (LONDON)
Carroll, Benjamin John, MA, n, pce, psc(j)	LT CDR(FTC)	X	PWO(U)	01.02.98	SOUTHAMPTON
Carroll, Paul Christopher, BEng, MSc, CEng, MIMarEST	LT CDR(FTC)	E	ME	01.03.02	SOUTHAMPTON
Carroll, Philip John, BSc	LT CDR(FTC)	X	H1	01.01.98	EXCHANGE GERMANY
Carroll, Stephen Laurence, BEng, MSc	LT(CC)	E	AE	01.01.99	DLO WYTON
Carson, Neil Douglas Ernest, BSc, pce(sm), SM	LT CDR(FTC)	X	SM	01.01.97	UKMARBATSTAFF
Carter, Christopher Antony	LT(IC)	X		18.02.05	ROEBUCK
Carter, Ian Paul, pce	CDR(FTC)	X	AAWO	30.06.00	NAVSEC
Carter, Jonathon Mark, BSc, BEng, MIEE	LT CDR(FTC)	E	WESM	01.06.96	NEPTUNE SWS
Carter, Kendall, BSc, pce	CDR(FTC)	X	PWO(N)	30.06.95	NBC PORTSMOUTH
Carter, Kevin Stanley	LT CDR(FTC)	X		27.08.02	TEMERAIRE
Carter, Nigel Robin	LT(CC)	X	AV	29.04.01	SULTAN
Carter, Paul, BSc, BEng, MIEE	LT(FTC)	E	WESM	01.04.01	FLEET HQ PORTS
Carter, Robert Ian	LT CDR(FTC)	X	ATC	01.10.95	RNAS YEOVILTON
Carter, Simon Neil, GCIS, psc(j)	CDR(FTC)	S	SM	30.06.04	JSCSC
Carter, Simon Peter	LT CDR(FTC)	S	CA	01.10.04	LANCASTER
Carthew, Richard James, BA	LT(IC)	S	SM	01.05.01	DRAKE COB
Cartwright, Darren, MA, pce, pcea, psc(j)	CDR(FTC)	X	O	30.06.05	FWO PORTS SEA
Cartwright, James Andrew, BEng	LT(FTC)	E	MESM	01.08.98	SULTAN
Carty, Michael Gareth	LT RM(CC)	-		01.09.02	RNAS YEOVILTON
Carver, Anthony Graham, BSc, MIEE	LT CDR(FTC)	E	WESM	01.05.89	MWC PORTSDOWN
Carver, Charles Alistair, BA	SLT(IC)	S		01.05.03	LIVERPOOL
Carvosso-White, Anna-Louise, BEng	LT(IC)	E	ME	01.09.02	PORTLAND
Case, Alexander Charles, BSc, psc(j)	MAJ(FTC)	-		24.04.99	40 CDO RM
Case, Anthony	LT(FTC)	S	CA	26.04.99	RALEIGH
Case, Paul, MILog	LT CDR(FTC)	S	(S)	01.10.98	RNAS YEOVILTON
Casey, Adam Mark	SLT(IC)	X	P U/T	01.01.05	DARTMOUTH BRNC
Cassar, Adrian Peter Felix, MA, pce, psc(j)	CDR(FTC)	X	MCD	30.06.98	JSCSC
Cassidy, Mark James	CHAPLAIN	RC		24.09.00	INVINCIBLE
Cassidy, Stuart Martin, BEng	LT(IC)	X	P	01.09.03	845 SQN
Casson, Neil Philip, BSc, MBA, psc(j)	LT CDR(FTC)	E	TMSM	01.03.99	FLEET HQ PORTS
Casson, Paul Richard, BEng, MBA, psc(j)	CDR(FTC)	E	ME	30.06.01	INVINCIBLE
Casson, Roy Frederick	LT(CC)	E	ME	01.07.00	MONMOUTH
Castle, Alastair Stuart, BSc, pcea	LT CDR(FTC)	X	P	01.12.01	INVINCIBLE
Castle, Colin David (Act Lt Cdr)	LT(FTC)	X	AAWO	19.09.00	ILLUSTRIOUS
Castledine, Benjamin	SURG SLT(SCC)	-		28.12.04	DARTMOUTH BRNC
Catton, Innes C	CAPT RM(IC)	-		01.09.04	45 CDO RM
Cattroll, David	LT CDR(FTC)	E	MESM	01.10.04	SOVEREIGN
Cattroll, Iain Murdo, BSc, MIEE	LT CDR(FTC)	E	WE	01.03.94	MOD (LONDON)
Causton, John Fraser	LT(IC)	X		01.09.02	DUMBARTON CASTLE
Cave, Joanne ,BMus	SLT(IC)	X		01.09.03	DARTMOUTH BRNC
Cavill, Niki Richard Dalgliesh	CAPT RM(CC)	-		01.05.01	CTCRM
Cawthorne, Matthew William Southworth, MA, psc(m)	LT COL(FTC)	-	MLDR	30.06.00	JACIG
Cessford, Richard Ian, BEng	LT(CC)	E	WE	01.12.99	CMT SHRIVENHAM
Chacksfield, Edward Nicholas, BA	LT(IC)	X	HM2	01.11.98	DARTMOUTH BRNC

Name	Rank	Branch	Spec	Seniority	Where Serving
Chadfield, Laurence James, BA	LT CDR(FTC)	X	PWO(C)	01.10.04	PJHQ
Chadwick, Kara, BA	LT(CC)	S		01.01.02	COS 2SL/CNH
Chalmers, Donald Peter, MA, pce, psc(j)	CDR(FTC)	X	PWO(U)	31.12.99	COM MCC NWD
Chamberlain, Nicholas Richard Lawrence, BEng	LT CDR(FTC)	E	WE	01.11.01	HQ DCSA
Chambers, Christopher Paul, BSc	LT(CC)	X	P	01.12.99	815 FLT 206
Chambers, Ian Richard, BEng, CEng, MIEE, CDipAF	LT CDR(FTC)	E	WESM	01.05.00	DALRIADA
Chambers, Nigel Maurice Christopher, BSc, pce	CAPT(FTC)	X	PWO(U)	30.06.04	COS 2SL/CNH
Chambers, Paul David, BEng	LT(FTC)	E	WE	01.12.97	MWS COLLINGWOOD
Chambers, Richard, BSc	LT(CC)	X	H2	01.04.00	ALBION
Chambers, Thomas George	LT CDR(FTC)	X	MCD	01.10.88	SUPT OF DIVING
Chambers, William John, pce	CDR(FTC)	X	MCD	30.06.93	AGRIPPA JFC HQ
Chan, Andrea	A/SG LT(D)(SCC)	-		25.06.04	DRAKE COB(CNH)
Chandler, Nigel James, pce	LT CDR(FTC)	X	PWO(C)	01.03.97	SUTHERLAND
Chandler, Philip John, BEng	LT(IC)	X	O U/T	01.01.02	RNAS CULDROSE
Chandler, Stephen Arthur	LT CDR(FTC)	X	PWO(U)	01.01.87	FOST DPORT SHORE
Chang, Christopher Joseph	LT(IC)	S		01.05.03	LANCASTER
Chang, Hon Weng, BEng	LT(IC)	E	TM	01.08.02	RMB STONEHOUSE
Chapell, Andrew, BA, GCIS	CDR(FTC)	S	SM	30.06.05	MARS IPT
Chapman, Charles Leslie, BEng	LT CDR(FTC)	E	WESM	29.11.99	TRENCHANT
Chapman, Darren Andrew	LT CDR(FTC)	X	P	01.10.98	MWS COLLINGWOOD
Chapman, James Lawrence John, BSc	LT(IC)	X	HM	01.01.02	814 SQN
Chapman, John Robert	SLT(IC)	X		01.09.02	INVINCIBLE
Chapman, Martin Stuart	LT(CC)	S		01.09.01	SUTHERLAND
Chapman, Nicholas John, BA, MBA, pce(sm)	LT CDR(FTC)	X	SM	01.05.90	MDC GIBRALTAR
Chapman, Nolan Phillip, MBE	LT CDR(FTC)	S	(W)	01.10.92	AFPAA WTHY DOWN
Chapman, Peter, BEng, MSc, CEng, MIEE	LT CDR(FTC)	E	WE	01.09.01	DLO BRISTOL
Chapman, Simon, MA, psc(j)	MAJ(FTC)	-		01.09.98	CDO LOG REGT RM
Chapman, Simon John, BSc, pce	LT CDR(FTC)	X	AAWO	01.04.98	MWS COLLINGWOOD
Chappell, Matthew William, BEd	LT(IC)	E	TM U/T	01.07.03	SULTAN
Chapple, Colin Peter, BSc, PGCE	LT CDR(FTC)	X	METOC	01.05.90	MWC PORTSDOWN
Chapple, Sean	CAPT RM(IC)	-	SO(LE)	01.04.04	CTCRM
Charlesworth, Graham Keith, MSc, CEng, MIEE, MCGI	CDR(FTC)	E	WESM	30.06.01	COS 2SL/CNH
Charlier, Simon Boyce, pce, pcea, psc	CDRE(FTC)	X	P	16.11.04	FLEET HQ PORTS
Charlton, Christopher Robin Alistair MacGaw, BA	CDR(FTC)	S		31.12.97	MOD (LONDON)
Charlton, Kevin William, BSc (Act Lt Cdr)	LT(MC(MD)	Q		14.01.00	RCDM
Charnock, Simon James	SLT(IC)	S		01.06.03	INVINCIBLE
Chartres, David	LT CDR(FC)	X		01.10.93	FLEET HQ NWD
Chaston, Stephen Paul, SM	LT CDR(FTC)	X	SM	01.03.01	RALEIGH
Chatterjee, Shatadeep, BEng, PGDip	LT(IC)	E	ME	01.09.02	EXETER
Chatterley, Dawn Alice	SLT(IC)	S		01.01.04	DARTMOUTH BRNC
Chattin, Antony Paul, BEng, MSc, psc(j)	MAJ(FTC)	-	MLDR	01.05.00	MOD (LONDON)
Chatwin, Nicholas John, BSc, pce, pcea	CDR(FTC)	X	P	30.06.05	PJHQ
Chaudhary, Rahul	SLT(UCE)(IC)	E	WE	01.01.02	DARTMOUTH BRNC
Chawira, Denis Nyarono, BSc	LT(CC)	X	MCD	01.08.97	MWS COLLINGWOOD
Cheadle, Richard Frank, CB, MSc, CEng, FIMechE, FCMI, jsdc (XD4/COFN DEC 03)	RADM	-	MESM	03.09.02	DPA BRISTOL
Cheal, Andrew James, BA	LT(IC)	E	TM	01.04.02	NELSON
Cheater, Christopher John	SLT(UCE)(IC)	E	SM	01.09.02	DARTMOUTH BRNC
Cheema, Sukhdev Singh	LT(IC)	E	WESM	01.07.04	TALENT
Cheesman, Christopher John, BEng, MSc	CDR(FTC)	E	AE	30.06.02	JFCHQ BRUNSSUM
Cheesman, Daniel James Edward, BSc	MAJ(FTC)	-	C	01.09.04	PJHQ
Chelton, Simon Roger Lewis, BA, MIL, CDipAF, OCDS(JAP)	CAPT(FTC)	S	SM	30.06.03	SA TOKYO
Cheseldine, David	LT CDR(FTC)	E	AE	01.10.03	RNAS CULDROSE
Cheshire, Thomas Edward, BEng, MSc, CEng, MIMechE	LT CDR(FTC)	E	MESM	01.10.02	TORBAY
Cheshire, Thomas Smith, BSc	SLT(IC)	X		01.01.04	DARTMOUTH BRNC
Chesterman, Graham John, pce, pcea	LT CDR(FTC)	X	O	01.02.93	MOD (LONDON)
Chesters, David Martin Brandon	LT(FTC)	S		01.09.02	ILLUSTRIOUS
Chestnutt, James Muir, BEng	LT(FTC)	E	P	01.01.98	RNAS YEOVILTON
Cheyne, Roger Duncan, BEng	LT(FTC)	E	AE	01.04.01	771 SQN
Chichester, Mark Arlington Raleigh, BSc, pce, pce(sm)	LT CDR(FTC)	X	SM	01.10.90	ASM IPT
Chick, Nicholas Stevens	LT(CC)	X	P	16.11.95	820 SQN
Chick, Stephen John, BSc, pce, hcsc	CAPT(FTC)	X	PWO(A)	30.06.01	CHATHAM
Chicken, Simon Timothy, OBE, MA, psc	COL(FTC)	-	LC	31.12.00	BDS WASHINGTON

Name	Rank	Branch	Spec	Seniority	Where Serving
Chidley, Timothy James, BSc, MA, CEng, MIMarEST, psc(j)	CDR(FTC)	E	ME	31.12.98	UKMARBATSTAFF
Chilcott, Peter Leslie Herbert, MISM	LT CDR(FTC)	MS	SM	01.10.03	HQ DMETA
Childs, David Geoffrey, BSc, CEng	CDR(FTC)	E	AE	30.06.02	INVINCIBLE
Childs, John Richard	LT CDR(FTC)	X	AAWO	01.04.02	CARDIFF
Chilman, Peter	LT CDR(FTC)	S		01.03.93	DCL DEEPCUT
Chilton, Denise June	LT(FTC)	S	(S)	01.04.01	LAIPT
Chilton, Jerard, BEng, MIEE	LT(CC)	E	WE	01.07.98	CAPT MCTA
Chilvers, Leah	LT CDR(MC(MD)	Q	ACCEM*	01.10.04	RN GIBRALTAR
Chisholm, David Thomas, BEng	SLT(IC)	E	MESMUT	01.05.03	2SL/CNH
Chisholm, Philip James Hampden, BSc	SLT(IC)	X		01.07.02	LIVERPOOL
Chittenden, Timothy Clive, MA, MSc, CEng, FIMechE, MINucE, jsdc (CHIEF OF STAFF (SUPPORT) AUG 03)	RADM	-	MESM	04.08.03	FLEET HQ PORTS 2
Chittick, William Brian Oliver, BDS, MSc	SGLTCDR(D)(FC(MD)	-		10.07.02	JSCSC
Chivers, Paul Austin, OBE, MA, pce, pcea, psc(j)	CDR(FTC)	X	O	30.06.00	MOD (LONDON)
Choat, Jeffery Hugh, pcea	LT(FTC)	X	O	16.08.93	EXCHANGE AUSTLIA
Choules, Barrie, MEng	LT CDR(CC)	E	TMSM	01.09.02	MWS COLLINGWOOD
Chrishop, Timothy Ian, pce, pcea	CDR(FTC)	X	O	30.06.03	FLEET HQ NWD
Christian, Johanna, GradInstPS	LT(FTC)	S		01.07.99	2SL/CNH
Christie, Andrew Bell	LT(CC)	S	(S)	29.04.01	UKSU SHAPE
Christie, Campbell Stuart, BEd, psc, psc(j)	CAPT(FTC)	E	TM	30.06.01	JSCSC
Christie, Neil	2LT(IC)	-		01.08.01	CTCRM LYMPSTONE
Christmas, Stephen Peter	LT(FTC)	X	P	16.08.91	FLEET AV CU
Chudley, Ian Vernon	LT(IC)	X	P	01.05.03	771 SQN
Church, Alan David	CDR(FTC)	S		31.12.96	NAVSEC
Church, Simon James, BEng	SLT(IC)	E	MESMUT	01.09.03	YORK
Church, Stephen Cofield	LT(CC)	X	P	16.07.96	RAF CRANWELL EFS
Churcher, Jeremy Edward, pce, n	LT CDR(FTC)	X	H CH	01.08.99	ROEBUCK
Churchill, Timothy Charles, BA, pce	CDR(FTC)	X	PWO(N)	31.12.93	MOD (LONDON)
Churchward, Matthew James	MAJ(CC)	-	LC	01.10.04	40 CDO RM
Ciaravella, Timothy James, BEng	LT(IC)	E	ME	01.01.04	ILLUSTRIOUS
Clague, John Joseph, MEng, n	LT(FTC)	X	PWO(U)	15.01.97	NOTTINGHAM
Clapham, Grantley Thom, BEng	LT(IC)	E	IS	01.04.01	2SL/CNH FOTR
Clapson, Keith, osc	MAJ(FTC)	-		01.07.85	1 ASSLT GP RM
Clare, Jonathan Francis	MAJ(FTC)	-	SO(LE)	01.10.04	45 CDO RM
Clare, Katharine, BSc, PhD	LT(CC)	E	IS	29.07.96	MOD (LONDON)
Claridge, Alexander Melville	LT(SC(MD)	Q		12.04.03	RH HASLAR
Clark, Alan Sutherland, SM	LT CDR(FTC)	X	SM	01.10.03	FLEET HQ NWD
Clark, Alastair William Charles, MA, pce, pcea, psc(j)	CDR(FTC)	X	O	31.12.98	BDS WASHINGTON
Clark, Andrew Nelham, BSc, CEng, MIMechE	LT CDR(FTC)	E	MESM	01.09.91	RNAS YEOVILTON
Clark, Caroline Louise	LT(CC)	S		01.08.00	MOD (LONDON)
Clark, Donald Kennedy, BSc, CEng, MIMarEST	CDR(FTC)	E	MESM	30.06.98	NEPTUNE DLO
Clark, Gavin	SLT(SC(MD)	Q		01.11.03	DARTMOUTH BRNC
Clark, Ian David, MSc, CEng, MIMarEST	CDR(FTC)	E	MESM	30.06.03	DLO BRISTOL
Clark, Kenneth Ian MacDonald, pce(sm)	CDR(FTC)	X	SM	31.12.94	UKMARBATSTAFF
Clark, Kevin Charles, BEng, MSc, CEng, MIMarEST, MCGI	LT CDR(FTC)	E	ME	01.11.94	DLO BRISTOL
Clark, Matthew Thomas	CDR(FTC)	S	SM	30.06.05	JSCSC
Clark, Michael Howard, n	LT CDR(FTC)	X	AAWO	01.03.04	EXETER
Clark, Paul Anthony, BSc	LT(IC)	E	TM	01.01.04	RALEIGH
Clark, Paul Anthony	MAJ(FTC)	-	SO(LE)	01.10.04	JSCSC
Clark, Paul Michael Colin	LT CDR(FTC)	X	ATC	01.10.93	RNAS YEOVILTON
Clark, Philip John, BSc	SLT(IC)	X	O U/T	01.09.02	RNAS CULDROSE
Clark, Russell Anthony	LT(FTC)	X	O	01.08.99	815 FLT 209
Clark, Simon Mansfield	CDR(FTC)	S	CMA	30.06.05	2SL/CNH FOTR
Clark, Simon Richard, BEng, adp, PGDip, CEng, MIEE	LT CDR(FTC)	E	IS	01.05.97	CSIS IPT
Clark, Stephen, BSc	LT(CC)	E	TM	01.09.97	SULTAN
Clark, Stephen Michael, BA(OU)	LT(IC)	S		01.01.04	NAVSEC
Clarke, Adam Gregory, BSc	LT(CC)	S		01.11.99	EDINBURGH
Clarke, Andrew Patrick	LT CDR(FTC)	X	P	01.10.00	CHFHQ
Clarke, Bernard Ronald, MA, FRGS	CHAPLAIN	CE		30.06.81	ILLUSTRIOUS
Clarke, Charles Maxwell Lorne, OBE, pce (Act Capt)	CDR(FTC)	X	PWO(U)	30.06.95	NP BOSNIA
Clarke, Daniel, pcea	LT CDR(FTC)	X	O	01.10.03	815 SQN HQ
Clarke, Daniel, SM(n), SM	LT(FTC)	X	SM	01.01.99	RALEIGH
Clarke, David	2LT(IC)	-		01.08.01	CTCRM LYMPSTONE

Name	Rank	Branch	Spec	Seniority	Where Serving
Clarke, Ian Bruce, n	LT CDR(FTC)	X	PWO(A)	01.10.01	MOD (LONDON)
Clarke, James	LT CDR(FTC)	E	WE	01.10.98	FLEET CIS PORTS
Clarke, John Martin, MB, BS, MRCGP, DObstRCOG, Dip FFP	SURG CDR(FCC)	-	GMPP	30.06.02	UKSU JHQ LISBON
Clarke, Mark, LICG, MNI, MCMI, SM(n), SM, NDipM	LT(FTC)	X	SM	01.04.01	FLEET HQ NWD
Clarke, Matthew	LT(IC)	X		01.01.02	TYNE
Clarke, Matthew David, BSc	LT(CC)	E	TM	01.05.98	2SL/CNH FOTR
Clarke, Nicholas John, pce, pcea	CDR(FTC)	X	P	30.06.99	RNAS CULDROSE
Clarke, Peter Martin	CAPT RM(CC)	-	SO(LE)	01.01.02	815 SQN HQ
Clarke, Richard, MA, MBA, psc(j)	LT CDR(FTC)	E	TM	01.10.96	MWS COLLINGWOOD
Clarke, Richard William, BEng	LT CDR(FTC)	E	AE	01.03.02	DLO YEO
Clarke, Robert	LT(CC)	X	P	16.08.96	829 FLT 01
Clarkson, Andrew Mark	LT(MC(MD)	Q		04.05.01	RN GIBRALTAR
Clarkson, Antony Michael	LT(IC)	E	WE	01.01.03	MWS COLLINGWOOD
Claxton, Andrew Geoffrey Douglas, BSc	LT(IC)	X		01.04.04	NOTTINGHAM
Claxton, Martin Geoffrey	CDR(FTC)	E	MESM	30.06.03	NEPTUNE DSA
Clay, Jason Christopher, BSc, SM(n), SM	LT CDR(FTC)	X	SM	01.10.03	TRENCHANT
Clay, Toby Charles De Candole, BSc	LT(CC)	X	P	01.05.98	815 FLT 217
Clayton, Christopher Hugh Trevor, pce, psc, hcsc	RADM	-	P	30.08.04	IMS BRUSSELS
(ASSISTANT DIRECTOR INTELLIGENCE DIVISION AUG 04)					
Clear, Nichola Jane, BEng	LT(CC)	E	ME	01.11.99	NP IRAQ
Cleary, Christopher Mycroft	LT(CC)	S		01.01.02	COMATG SEA
Cleary, Stephen Peter, pce	CAPT(FTC)	X	AAWO	30.06.00	TEMERAIRE
Clee, James Stefan	LT(IC)	X		01.10.02	MWS HM TG (D)
Clegg, Martin Leslie, BSc, FRGS	LT CDR(FTC)	X	H CH	01.06.90	SHERWOOD
Clements, Elizabeth Joanne	LT(CC)	S		01.05.99	RNAS YEOVILTON
Clements, Stephen James	LT CDR(FTC)	X		01.10.03	DPA BRISTOL
Cleminson, Mark David, BEng	LT CDR(FTC)	E	MESM	01.02.05	SUPERB
Clews, Alan	2LT(IC)	-		01.08.01	CTCRM LYMPSTONE
Clifford, Timothy John, BEng, MSc, CEng, MRAeS	CDR(FTC)	E	AE	30.06.02	MERLIN IPT
Clink, Adam Duncan, BSc, pcea	LT CDR(FTC)	X	P	01.10.01	HQ1GP HQSTC
Clink, John Robert Hamilton, OBE, PGDIPAN, pce, FRIN	CAPT(FTC)	X	PWO(N)	30.06.05	NP IRAQ
Cloherty, Andrew	SLT(IC)	E	WESM	01.01.04	MWS COLLINGWOOD
Cloney, Justin William John, BA	LT(IC)	X	SM	01.09.03	TURBULENT
Clough, Christopher Ralph, MA, MSc, CEng, MIEE, psc(j), gw	CDR(FTC)	E	WE	31.12.00	PAAMS PARIS
Clucas, Malcolm Richard, pcea	LT CDR(FTC)	X	P	01.10.97	DHFS
Clucas, Paul Richard (Act Lt Cdr)	LT(FTC)	X		04.04.91	PRESIDENT
Cluett-Green, Stephen Mark, pce, pcea	CDR(FTC)	X	P	30.06.02	DLO BRISTOL
Coatalen-Hodgson, Ryan, BA	SLT(UCE)(IC)	X		01.09.02	DARTMOUTH BRNC
Coates, Adam James, BEng	LT(IC)	E	WE	01.01.03	INVINCIBLE
Coates, Philip James Barton, MB, BS	SURG LTCDR(FC(MD)	-		04.08.04	MDHU DERRIFORD
Coats, Daniel Simon, LLB (Act Maj)	CAPT RM(CC)	-		01.09.98	LN SIERRA LEONE
Cobb, Jill Elizabeth	LT CDR(FTC)	W	S	01.10.97	NELSON
Cobban, Michael James, BSc, SM(n), SM	LT(CC)	X	SM	01.09.99	FWO FASLANE
Cobbett, James Frank, pcea	LT CDR(FTC)	X	P	01.10.03	ILLUSTRIOUS
Cochrane, Christopher Duncan, MEng	SLT(IC)	E	SM	01.09.02	VANGUARD(PORT)
Cochrane, David Smith, BA	LT(IC)	X		01.08.04	GLOUCESTER
Cochrane, Malcolm David	CDR(FTC)	E	AE	30.06.03	MERLIN IPT
Cochrane, Michael Charles Nicholas, OBE, pce	CAPT(FTC)	X	PWO(N)	30.06.02	MOD (LONDON)
Cockram, Alice Louise, MB, BCH, BA	SURG LT(SC(MD)	-		04.02.04	CFLT MED(SEA)
Cocks, Anthony Edward John, MEng	SLT(IC)	X	O U/T	01.01.04	DARTMOUTH BRNC
Codd, Justin Sandell, BSc, SM(n), SM	LT(FTC)	X	SM	01.02.97	SUPERB
Coffey, Ralph Bruce Dobson, BA, MEng, LCIPD, AMIMechE	LT(IC)	E	SM	01.01.05	SPARTAN
Cogan, Robert Edward Charles, BSc	LT CDR(FTC)	S		01.10.04	WESTMINSTER
Cole, Alan Charles, BA (Barrister)	CDR(FTC)	S	BAR	30.06.05	MOD (LONDON)
Cole, Benjamin Barry, LLB	LT(IC)	S		01.09.01	OCEAN
Cole, Simon Philip	LT CDR(FTC)	E	WE	01.10.97	NAVSEC
Cole, Stephen Paul, BEng	SLT(IC)	E	AE	01.09.02	SULTAN
Coleman, Alexander Peter Grant	SLT(IC)	X		01.07.04	CUMBERLAND
Coleman, James Martyn Peter, BA	SLT(IC)	X	P U/T	01.11.02	RNAS YEOVILTON
Coleman, Timothy John Anthony	LT(IC)	X		01.05.04	CHATHAM
Coles, Adam John	LT(IC)	X		01.05.04	MWS HM TG (D)
Coles, Andrew Laurence, OBE, MA, pce, psc(j), pce(sm)	CDR(FTC)	X	SM	30.06.03	TURBULENT
Coles, Christopher John, BEng	LT CDR(FTC)	E	MESM	01.09.96	EXCHANGE AUSTLIA

Name	Rank	Branch	Spec	Seniority	Where Serving
Coles, Christopher Paul, BEng	LT(FTC)	E	AE	01.05.00	ADAS BRISTOL
Coles, Simon Phillip, BSc, PhD	LT(IC)	E	TM	01.09.98	DEF NBC CENTRE
Coles-Hendry, Frances Ann, BA	SLT(IC)	S		01.05.02	RALEIGH
Collacott, Jonathan Steven, BSc	LT(CC)	S	SM	01.03.99	COMATG SEA
Collen, Sara Jean, BEng	LT(CC)	E	ME	01.12.97	ALBION
Collett, Stuart Mark ,BM	SURG LTCDR(MCC)	-	GMPP	05.08.03	1 ASSAULT GP RM
Colley, Ian Paul	LT(IC)	E	WESM	01.09.04	TALENT
Colley, Robert	LT(CC)	X	REG	01.09.01	NAVSEC
Collie, James Alexander, BA	SLT(IC)	X		01.05.03	GLOUCESTER
Collier, Alan Paul, BSc	LT(IC)	X		01.01.05	RNAS YEOVILTON
Collier, Andrew Sheldon, BA, FRGS	LT CDR(FTC)	X		01.06.93	CALLIOPE
Collier, Michael John	LT(IC)	E	WE	01.07.04	MANCHESTER
Collighan, Giles Thomas, pce	LT CDR(FTC)	X	AAWO	01.04.99	NOTTINGHAM
Collin, Martin	MAJ(FTC)	-		01.04.04	HQ 3 CDO BDE RM
Collins, Andrew Charles	LT(CC)	X	O	01.11.00	RNAS YEOVILTON
Collins, Benjamin Leigh, BA	SLT(IC)	X		01.11.03	DARTMOUTH BRNC
Collins, Charles Anthony, BSc	SLT(IC)	X		01.11.03	DARTMOUTH BRNC
Collins, Dale Anthony	LT(IC)	E		01.05.02	RNAS CULDROSE
Collins, Darren, MSc, IEng, MIIE	LT(FTC)	E	WE	09.01.01	STG BRISTOL
Collins, David Andrew	LT(FTC)	E	MESM	02.05.00	DLO BRISTOL
Collins, David Anthony, MSc, PGCE	LT CDR(FTC)	X	METOC	01.10.95	MOD (LONDON)
Collins, David Ivan	LT(IC)	S		01.07.04	FOSNNI
Collins, David Rudolf, BSc, PhD	LT(IC)	E	TM	01.01.97	SULTAN
Collins, Gary Vincent, IEng, MIIE	LT(IC)	E	ME	01.07.04	INVINCIBLE
Collins, Graham John Simon, pce	LT CDR(FTC)	X	PWO(U)	07.04.96	NELSON
Collins, John (Act Maj)	CAPT RM(FTC)	-	SO(LE)	01.01.01	1 ASSAULT GP RM
Collins, Lorna Jane, BSc	LT(IC)	E	TM	01.09.00	DCCIS BLANDFORD
Collins, Mark Andrew, MSc, adp	LT(FTC)	E	WE	09.01.01	MOD (LONDON)
Collins, Mark Christopher	LT CDR(FTC)	X		01.10.03	SCOTIA
Collins, Paul Nicholas, pce, pcea, psc	CAPT(FTC)	X	P	30.06.02	UKMILREP BRUSS
Collins, Paul Reginald, BSc	LT CDR(FTC)	E	WESM	01.09.95	MOD (LONDON)
Collins, Sarah Jane, BSc, PGDip	LT CDR(FTC)	E	IS	01.10.03	MWS COLLINGWOOD
Collins, Simon Jonathan Peter, BA	LT(CC)	X	O	16.01.01	815 FLT 212
Collins, Stephen Anthony (Act Lt Cdr)	LT(FTC)	E	WESM	07.02.97	SUPERB
Collins, Stephen James	MID(IC)	X	P U/T	01.11.03	DARTMOUTH BRNC
Collins, Tamar Louise, BEng, MSc, PhD	LT(CC)	E	IS	01.01.96	OCEAN
Collinson, Neal Paul	CAPT RM(IC)	-	SO(LE)	01.07.04	45 CDO RM
Collis, Martin John, BEng	LT CDR(FTC)	E	ME	01.08.99	FLEET HQ PORTS 2
Coltman, Timothy Patrick, MB, BS	SURG LTCDR(MCC)	-		01.08.00	NELSON (PAY)
Colvin, Michael Andrew Thomas, BSc	LT(IC)	X		01.05.04	ST ALBANS
Compain, Craig Herbert	LT(CC)	X	P	21.03.97	FLEET AV VL
Concarr, David Terry	LT(CS)(CAS)	-		19.09.99	DNR NEE 1
Congreve, Steven Chistopher, BSc	MAJ(FTC)	-		01.05.00	HQBF CYPRUS
Conlin, John Anthony, MA	LT(CC)	X		01.01.99	IRON DUKE
Conneely, Steven Andrew, IEng, MIIE	LT(FTC)	E	WE	09.01.01	DLO BRISTOL
Connell, Martin John, pce (Act Cdr)	CDR(FTC)	X	O	01.01.00	MOD (LONDON)
Connolly, Christopher John, BSc, MA, pce, psc(j)	CDR(FTC)	X	PWO(A)	31.12.00	BULWARK
Connor, Daniel James ,BMS, BM, BS, FRCA	SURG CDR(MCC)	-	(CA)	30.06.04	LOAN FIELD HOSP
Conran, Nicholas William Douglas, BSc	LT(IC)	S	SM	01.01.03	VANGUARD(PORT)
Conroy, David Alexander, MA	CHAPLAIN	RC		24.09.00	MWS COLLINGWOOD
Considine, Keith John	LT(CC)	X	P	01.02.00	846 SQN
Conway, Julian John	LT CDR(FTC)	X	PWO(C)	01.11.93	MWC SOUTHWICK
Conway, Michael John	LT CDR(FTC)	X	EW	01.10.04	COM MCC NWD
Conway, Suzy Helen, BA	LT(FTC)	S		01.03.99	PJHQ
Cooch, Timothy James, BEng	LT(IC)	E	TM	01.07.02	SULTAN
Cook, Christopher Buchan, MSc, MBCS, CITP	LT CDR(FTC)	E	IS	01.10.00	NTE(TTD)
Cook, David John, MSc, MCGI, pcea, gdas	LT CDR(FTC(A)	X	O	01.10.97	FLEET HQ PORTS
Cook, Gordon Edward	LT CDR(FTC)	X	O	01.10.00	FLEET AV VL
Cook, Michael Colin, BEng	LT CDR(CC)	E	TM	01.07.02	NAVSEC
Cook, Myles Fitzpatrick, BA, psc(j)	MAJ(FTC)	-	C	01.05.00	JSCSC
Cook, Neville John Hunter	LT(IC)	S		01.05.02	ECHO
Cook, Paul Roger, pce	CDR(FTC)	X	AAWO	31.12.98	NAVSEC
Cook, Peter William John, sq	MAJ(FTC)	-		01.05.92	MOD (LONDON)

Name	Rank	Branch	Spec	Seniority	Where Serving
Cook, Timothy Arnold, BA, psc(j)o	MAJ(FTC)	-	C	01.09.97	1 ASSAULT GP RM
Cooke, David John, MBE, pce, pce(sm), hcsc (DEPUTY COMMANDER (GXX 004). JUL 04)	RADM	-	SM	20.07.04	STRIKFORNATO
Cooke, David Phillip, BSc	LT(IC)	X		01.05.05	RALEIGH
Cooke, Graham John	LT CDR(FTC)	X		01.10.99	NELSON
Cooke, Graham Spencer, BSc, pcea	LT CDR(FTC)	X	O	01.10.01	815 FLT 204
Cooke, Joanne Madeleine, MB, ChB	SURG LT(MCC)	-		02.08.00	MDHU DERRIFORD
Cooke, Jonathan Edward, pce, n	LT CDR(FTC)	X	PWO(U)	01.02.03	FLEET HQ PORTS 2
Cooke, Michael John	LT CDR(FTC)	E	AE	01.10.02	FS MASU
Cooke, Robert Neale	LT(CC)	E	AE	29.04.01	HARRIER IPT
Cooke, Stephen Neil, BEng	LT(IC)	X	P	01.01.02	815 FLT 211
Cooke-Priest, Nicholas Charles Richard, pcea	LT(FTC)	X	PWO(U)	01.05.95	MARLBOROUGH
Cooksley, Richard Edgar Charles	LT(IC)	X	C	08.04.01	MWS COLLINGWOOD
Cooling, Robert George, BA, jsdc, pce, hcsc	CDRE(FTC)	X	PWO(N)	28.08.02	ILLUSTRIOUS
Coomber, Jonathan Martin, BA	MAJ(FTC)	-	MLDR	01.09.01	HQ 3 CDO BDE RM
Coope, Philip James, BEng, MIEE	LT CDR(FTC)	E	WE	01.03.03	CORNWALL
Cooper, Adam, BA	LT(CC)	S		01.08.98	HQ1GP HQSTC
Cooper, Adam, BEng	LT(IC)	E	WE	01.03.03	ILLUSTRIOUS
Cooper, Edwin Sigurd, MEng	LT(IC)	X	O	01.05.04	FLEET HQ PORTS
Cooper, Janette Lindsey	LT(SC(MD)	Q		01.11.01	UKSU JHQ LISBON
Cooper, Kevin Philip, BSc	CDR(FTC)	E	WE	30.06.05	FWO DEVPT SEA
Cooper, Lorna Jane	LT(IC)	S		01.05.04	AFPAA WTHY DOWN
Cooper, Mark Andrew, pce, pce(sm)	CDR(FTC)	X	SM	31.12.00	FOST SM SEA
Cooper, Neil (Act Maj)	CAPT RM(FTC)	-	SO(LE)	01.01.00	FLEET CIS PORTS
Cooper, Peter Frank, MBE, MSc, CEng, MIMechE	LT CDR(FTC)	E	MESM	21.04.89	DRAKE CBS
Cooper, Robert Terence, MBE	MAJ(FTC)	-	SO(LE)	01.10.96	1 ASSAULT GP RM
Cooper-Simpson, Roger John, MA, psc(j)	MAJ(FTC)	-	C	01.05.00	COMAMPHIBFOR
Copeland, Stephen Nicholas, BEng, psc(j)	LT CDR(FTC)	E	AE	01.02.99	EXCHANGE RAF UK
Copinger-Symes, Rory Sandham, psc(j)	LT COL(FTC)	-		30.06.02	JSCSC
Coppin, Nigel James	LT(IC)	S		01.01.03	TIRELESS
Copsey, Nicholas Robert Benham	CAPT RM(IC)	-		01.09.03	CTCRM
Corbally, Margaret Louise	LT(IC)	X		01.01.05	MWS COLLINGWOOD
Corbett, Andrew Scott, pce, pce(sm), psc(j)	CDR(FTC)	X	SM	30.06.03	VENGEANCE(PORT)
Corbett, Gerard John	LT CDR(FTC)	X	ATC	01.10.96	HQ STC
Corbett, Thomas James	LT(FTC)	X	PWO(A)	01.04.94	SUTHERLAND
Corbett, William Roger, BSc, FRMS, psc(m)	CDR(FTC)	X	METOC	30.06.01	COS 2SL/CNH
Corbidge, Stephen John, MBE, sq	MAJ(FTC)	-	SO(LE)	01.10.97	HQ 3 CDO BDE RM
Corcoran, Robert Martin, BA	SLT(IC)	X		01.05.03	YORK
Corder, Ian Fergus, MA, jsdc, pce, pce(sm), hcsc	CDRE(FTC)	X	SM	09.11.04	DLO BRISTOL
Corderoy, John Roger, BEng, MA, MSc, psc(j)	CDR(FTC)	E	MESM	30.06.01	MOD (LONDON)
Corderoy, Richard Ian, MEng, AMIEE	LT(FTC)	E	WESM	01.01.00	FLEET HQ PORTS
Cordner, Michael Anthony, BSc, MB, CHB	SURG LT(MC(MD)	-		01.08.02	SETT GOSPORT
Corkett, Kerry Stephen	LT CDR(FTC)	X	REG	01.10.04	DRAKE COB(CNH)
Cormack, Andrew James Ross, MB, CHB, BSc	SURG LTCDR(FCC)	-	GMPP	05.08.03	NELSON (PAY)
Cornelio, Stuart Michael, BSc	SLT(IC)	X		01.09.02	ECHO
Corner, Gordon Charles, pce	CDR(FTC)	X	PWO(C)	30.06.03	MOD (LONDON)
Corner, Ian Lindsey Ferguson, fsc, osc	MAJ(FTC)	-	P	01.11.83	CTCRM
Corness, Andrew Stuart	CHAPLAIN	CE		06.09.04	FWO PORTS SEA
Cornford, Marc, BEng	LT(CC)	X	P	01.10.99	845 SQN
Cornick, Robin Michael	LT CDR(FTC)	X	MCD	01.10.97	MCME IPT
Cornish, Michael Christopher, pce	LT CDR(FTC)	X	AAWO	01.07.95	FOST SEA
Corps, Stephen David	LT CDR(FTC)	E	WE	11.11.98	KENT
Corrigan, Niall Richard, BSc, pce	CDR(FTC)	X	PWO(A)	30.06.96	SACT BELGIUM
Corrin, Colby St John, LLB, jsdc, psc	MAJ(FTC)	-	MLDR	01.09.92	PJHQ
Corry, Simon Myles, BSc, MA, MIEE, psc(j)	CDR(FTC)	E	WE	31.12.00	MOD (LONDON)
Cory, Nicholas John	LT(IC)	X	EW	01.05.04	JSSU CHELTENHAM
Coryton, Oliver Charles Wyndham Spencer	CAPT RM(CC)	-		01.09.03	CHFHQ
Costain, Kathryn Ann, BA	SLT(IC)	S		01.09.02	RALEIGH
Costello, Gerard Thomas, BSc, CEng, MIEE, MDA	CAPT(FTC)	E	WESM	30.06.03	NEPTUNE DSA
Cottee, Benjamin Richard John (Act Lt Cdr)	LT(FTC)	X	ATC	01.09.94	INVINCIBLE
Cotterill, Bruce Maxwell, BEng, MSc, MIEE	LT CDR(FTC)	E	WESM	01.03.00	TRAFALGAR
Cottis, Mathew Charles	LT CDR(FTC)	S	SM	01.10.01	RNAS CULDROSE
Cotton, Emma Louise	LT(FTC)	S	CMA	01.04.01	LIVERPOOL

Name	Rank	Branch	Spec	Seniority	Where Serving
Cottrell, Ralph	2LT(IC)	-		01.08.01	CTCRM LYMPSTONE
Coughlan, Scott, BA	LT(IC)	X		01.09.03	VENGEANCE(STBD)
Coughlin, Peter James Leonard, BSc	LT(IC)	X	O	01.09.04	SULTAN
Coulson, Jeremy Richard, BEng, PGCE	LT CDR(FTC)	E	IS	08.12.85	COS 2SL/CNH
Coulson, Peter, BEng, MA, MSc, CEng, MIEE, psc(j)	CDR(FTC)	E	WE	30.06.04	MOD (LONDON)
Coulthard, Adrian John, BSc, C PHYS, MinstP, CMath, MIMA	LT CDR(CC)	E	TM	11.05.03	DHFS
Coulthard, John Kinnear, MSc, CEng, MIMechE, jsdc	CAPT(FTC)	E	MESM	30.06.05	DRAKE CBS
Coulton, Ian Christopher, MA, MBA, psc(j)	CDR(FTC)	MS		30.06.01	DMSTC
Coulton, Jamie Robert Spencer	LT(CC)	X	P	16.06.98	815 FLT 209
Counter, Paul Richard, MB, BS, MRCS	SURG LTCDR(MCC)	-		01.08.99	NELSON (PAY)
Course, Andrew James, MBE, MA, MSc, CEng, MIEE, psc(j), gw	CDR(FTC)	E	WE	30.06.02	T45 IPT
Courtney, Timothy Paul	LT(IC)	E	MESM	01.05.03	MWS COLLINGWOOD
Coverdale, Paul, BSc, PGDip	LT(CC)	X	HM2	01.03.00	OCEAN
Covington, William MacArtney, CBE, ADC, pce, pcea, psc (Commodore)	CAPT(FTC)	X	P	31.12.96	HQ1GP HQSTC
Cowan, Aidan Roland	LT(FTC)	X	PWO(C)	19.09.00	MWS COLLINGWOOD
Cowan, Kenneth Gordon	CAPT RM(CC)	-		23.04.99	FPGRM
Cowdrey, Mervyn Charles	CDR(FTC)	S		30.06.93	2SL/CNH FOTR
Cowell, Richard James, BSc	LT(IC)	E	WE	01.09.03	NORTHUMBERLAND
Cowie, Andrew David, BSc	LT(IC)	E	WE	01.01.02	FLEET HQ NWD
Cowie, Kevin Michael	LT CDR(FTC)	X	C	01.10.99	CMSG IPT
Cowin, Timothy James, BSc	LT(CC)	X	P	01.11.98	848 SQN HERON
Cowley, Richard Merlin, BSc	LT CDR(FTC)	X	MCD	01.04.97	OCLC MANCH
Cowlishaw, Nicholas David	LT(IC)	X	ATC	01.07.04	FOST DPORT SHORE
Cowper, Ian Robert, BSc, CEng, MIMarEST	LT CDR(FTC)	E	ME	01.10.00	DLO BRISTOL
Cox, Andrew David ,BMus	LT(IC)	X		01.05.05	MWS COLLINGWOOD
Cox, David John, BEng, MSc, CEng, MIEE	LT CDR(FTC)	E	WE	01.10.01	NAVSEC
Cox, Mark Bamber	LT CDR(FTC)	S		01.10.04	CORNWALL
Cox, Matthew John, BSc	SLT(IC)	E	WE U/T	01.09.03	CHATHAM
Cox, Michael Shaun	LT(IC)	X		01.05.04	DUMBARTON CASTLE
Cox, Pieter William Studley, BSc, CEng, MIEE	CDR(FTC)	E	WESM	30.06.93	FLEET HQ PORTS
Cox, Rex John, n	LT CDR(FTC)	X	AAWO	01.03.01	SEVERN
Cox, Sean Adrian Joel (Act Lt Cdr)	LT(FTC)	X	P	16.08.93	847 SQN
Cox, Simon	2LT(IC)	-		01.08.01	CTCRM LYMPSTONE
Cox, Simon James	LT(IC)	X		01.05.05	MWS COLLINGWOOD
Coxon, Helen Elizabeth Mary	SLT(IC)	X		01.09.02	DARTMOUTH BRNC
Coyle, Gavin James, BSc, pce, n	LT CDR(FTC)	X	PWO(U)	01.08.01	ILLUSTRIOUS
Coyle, Ross Daniel	LT(IC)	E	WE	01.05.02	SOUTHAMPTON
Coyne, John Derek	LT(FTC)	X	AV	17.12.93	RNAS YEOVILTON
Crabb, Antony John, MSc	LT CDR(FTC)	X	PWO(U)	01.10.04	UKMARBATSTAFF
Crabbe, Robert James, BSc	LT(CC)	X		01.12.98	SEVERN
Crabtree, Ian Michael, BSc, pce	CDR(FTC)	X	AAWO	31.12.90	FLEET HQ PORTS
Crabtree, Peter Dixon, OBE, BA, ACIS (Barrister)	CAPT(FTC)	S	BAR	31.12.00	FLEET HQ PORTS
Cragg, Richard Darryl, BEng	LT CDR(FTC)	E	MESM	01.10.04	TRAFALGAR
Craggs, Stuart, BEng, CEng, MIMechE	LT CDR(FTC)	E	AE	01.10.03	700M MERLIN OEU
Crago, Philip Thomas, BSc, CEng, FIMarEST	CDR(FTC)	E	ME	30.06.02	FWO DEVPT SEA
Craib, Alfred George	LT CDR(FTC)	E	WE	01.10.02	NC3 AGENCY
Craig, John Antony, pce	LT CDR(FTC)	X	MCD	01.05.02	UKMARBATSTAFF
Craig, Kenneth Mitchell, BSc	MAJ(FTC)	-		01.05.01	FLEET HQ NWD
Craig, Michael Jon, BSc	LT(IC)	X	P	01.05.03	845 SQN
Cran, Barrie Charles, BEng, MA, CEng, MIMechE, psc(j)	CDR(FTC)	E	MESM	30.06.03	COS 2SL/CNH
Crane, Oliver Richard, BSc	LT(CC)	X	P	01.10.98	DHFS
Craner, Matthew John, MB, BCh, MRCP	SURG CDR(FCC)	-		30.06.04	NELSON (PAY)
Crascall, Stephen John	LT CDR(FTC)	X	AV	01.10.03	FLEET HQ PORTS
Craven, Dale	LT(IC)	E	WESM	01.01.03	DLO BRISTOL
Craven, John Arthur Graham, MIL, MCMI	LT CDR(FTC)	S		01.09.85	2SL/CNH FOTR
Craven, Martin William, BEng	LT(CC)	X	P	01.08.98	702 SQN HERON
Craven, Oliver Edward	SLT(IC)	X		01.09.02	MWS COLLINGWOOD
Crawford, Adam Timothy Stephen, BSc	MAJ(FTC)	-		01.05.04	HQ 3 CDO BDE RM
Crawford, Richard	SLT(IC)	S		01.02.04	DARTMOUTH BRNC
Crawford, Valerie Elizabeth, BA, LLB	LT(CC)	X		01.04.02	ENDURANCE
Crawley, David Anthony	LT(FTC)	E	ME	01.04.01	DRAKE SFM
Creates, Keith Ian, BA, pce	LT CDR(FTC)	X	PWO(U)	01.04.87	PJHQ
Cree, Andrew Martin, BEng, MA, MSc, psc(j)	CDR(FTC)	E	TM	30.06.04	FLEET HQ PORTS

Name	Rank	Branch	Spec	Seniority	Where Serving
Cree, Malcolm Charles, BA, pce, psc(j), fsc	CDR(FTC)	X	AAWO	30.06.98	FLEET HQ PORTS
Creech, Richard David, gdas, MCGI, MRIN, FInstLM, MAPM	LT CDR(FTC)	X	O	01.10.96	MERLIN IPT
Creek, Stephen Brian	LT(IC)	E	WESM	01.01.02	DRAKE SFM
Crew, Julian Maynard, BA	LT(CC)	X	P	01.01.00	815 FLT 201
Crichton, Gary	LT(IC)	X		29.10.04	LANCASTER
Criddle, Gary David James	LT(CC)	X	O	01.06.96	815 FLT 234
Crimmen, David John, pcea	LT CDR(CC)	X	P	01.10.02	771 SQN
Cripps, Michael James, MEng, MRAeS	LT(IC)	E	AE	01.09.02	849 SQN HQ
Cripps, Nicola Jane, BA	LT(IC)	E	TM U/T	01.01.04	DARTMOUTH BRNC
Crisp, Dominic John Delves	2LT(IC)	-		01.09.00	FPGRM
Crispin, Toby Alexander Baldwin, BSc, pcea, gdas	LT CDR(FTC)	X	O	01.04.94	LOAN JTEG BSC DN
Critchley, Ian Joseph	SLT(IC)	X	SM	01.09.04	MWS COLLINGWOOD
Crockatt, Stephen Richard James	LT CDR(FTC)	X	P	01.10.03	EXCHANGE USA
Crocker, Dominic Thomas Alcard, BSc	SLT(IC)	X		01.02.04	DARTMOUTH BRNC
Crockett, Simon Keith	LT(IC)	E	ME	01.05.04	ILLUSTRIOUS
Croft, David Francis, MA	LT(CC)	X	H2	01.01.99	ENTERPRISE
Crofts, Alan Francis	SLT(IC)	X	P U/T	01.01.05	RNAS YEOVILTON
Crofts, David Jeffrey, BEng, MSc, MIEE	LT CDR(FTC)	E	WE	01.02.99	HQ DCSA
Croke, Anthony, pce, pcea, psc, ocds(Can)	CAPT(FTC)	X	P	30.06.99	LOAN OMAN
Crombie, Stuart, BA	SLT(IC)	X	O U/T	01.09.02	RNAS CULDROSE
Cromie, John Martin, MSc	LT(CC)	X	FC	01.05.00	EXCHANGE FRANCE
Crompton, Andrew Paul James, BSc	LT(IC)	X	ATC	01.09.02	RNAS YEOVILTON
Crompton, Philip John	LT(CC)	X	P	01.11.00	815 FLT 229
Crook, AndreaSusan, BA, jsdc	CDR(FTC)	S		30.06.97	MOD (LONDON)
Cropley, Andrew, BSc, MA, MA(Ed), MCIPD, psc(j)	CDR(FTC)	E	TM	30.06.03	FLEET HQ PORTS
Cropper, Fraser Brunel Nicholas, BEng, MSc	LT CDR(FTC)	E	AE	24.06.01	815 SQN HQ
Cropper, Martin Andrew Keith, BA	LT CDR(FTC)	S	SM	16.05.90	DRAKE COB
Crosbie, Donald Ernest Frederick	LT CDR(FTC)	X	PWO(U)	01.02.00	PENZANCE
Crosby, David William Malcolm	LT(IC)	X	SM	01.05.04	VIGILANT(PORT)
Crosby, John Paul, psc	LT COL(FTC)	-		30.06.93	JWC/CIS STAVANGR
Crosland, Stephen Andrew	LT(IC)	E	WE	01.01.04	CINCFLEET FTSU
Cross, Alexander Leigh, BEng, CEng	LT(FTC)	E	WESM	01.07.98	NEPTUNE DLO
Cross, Andrew George (Act Maj)	CAPT RM(CC)	-	SO(LE)	03.04.00	FLEET HQ PORTS
Cross, Eric John	CAPT RM(CC)	-	P	01.01.02	847 SQN
Cross, Nicholas, BSc	LT(IC)	E	IS	01.07.02	DRAKE DIS
Crossey, Matthew Darren, BSc, PGCE	LT(IC)	E	TM	01.06.01	CARDIFF
Crossley, Charles Crispin, BSc, MDA, CEng, MIMechE, MIMarEST	CDR(FTC)	E	ME	31.12.99	FLEET HQ PORTS
Crouch, Matthew, BSc	LT(IC)	X		01.05.01	MWS COLLINGWOOD
Crouden, Stephen Frederick, psc(j)	MAJ(FTC)	-	SO(LE)	01.10.98	MOD (BATH)
Crowe, David Michael, n	LT(FTC)	X		01.08.99	TRUMPETER
Crowe, Philip David, BA	SLT(IC)	X		01.06.03	DARTMOUTH BRNC
Crowson, Elizabeth, MB, CHB, MRCGP, Dip FFP	SURG LTCDR(SC(MD)	-	GMPP	06.05.01	RALEIGH
Crowther, Kevin Wayne, BSc, pce	LT CDR(FTC)	X	AAWO	29.03.91	MWC PORTSDOWN
Croxton, Damien Philip, BSc	SLT(IC)	S		01.02.03	EXETER
Crozier, Stuart Ross McDonald, BA (Barrister)	CDR(FTC)	S	BAR	30.06.01	2SL/CNH
Crudgington, Paul, AFC, pcea	LT CDR(FTC)	X	P	01.09.87	824 SQN
Crundell, Richard John, BEng, MSc, gw	LT CDR(FTC)	E	WE	01.07.00	YORK
Cryar, Timothy Martin Craven, pce, n	CDR(FTC)	X	AAWO	30.06.05	MWS COLLINGWOOD
Cubbage, Jamie, BEng, MIEE	LT CDR(FTC)	E	WE	01.04.02	GRAFTON
Cull, Iain, PGDIPAN, n	LT CDR(FTC)	X	PWO(N)	01.05.02	ALBION
Cullen, Nicola Leonie, BSc	LT(CC)	E	TM	01.09.95	1 ASSLT GP RM
Cullis, Christopher John, sq	MAJ(FTC)	-	LC	25.04.96	EXCHANGE FRANCE
Cullum, William Eric	SLT(IC)	X		01.11.03	DARTMOUTH BRNC
Culshaw, Joanne, BA	LT(IC)	X		01.04.04	MWS COLLINGWOOD
Culwick, Peter Francis, BDS, MSc, MGDS RCS, MA	SGCDR(D)(FCC)	-		31.12.96	MOD (LONDON)
Cumberland, Noel Stanley	SLT(IC)	X	P U/T	01.09.03	DARTMOUTH BRNC
Cummin, Michael Antony, BSc, CEng, MIMarEST	CDR(FTC)	E	MESM	31.12.95	MOD (BATH)
Cumming, Frazer Smith, MEng	LT(IC)	X	O	01.09.03	849 SQN B FLT
Cumming, Robert Angus, BEng	LT(FTC)	E	MESM	01.04.97	DLO BRISTOL
Cummings, Alan Thomas, pce, pcea, ocds(USN)	LT CDR(FTC)	X	O	01.03.97	ILLUSTRIOUS
Cummings, David John, BEng, MSc	LT CDR(FTC)	E	WE	01.11.02	MONTROSE
Cunane, John Richard, MCIT, MILT	LT CDR(FTC)	S	SM	01.10.98	BDLS CANADA
Cundy, Robert Graham, MBE, psc(j)	LT COL(FTC)	-		30.06.04	PJHQ

Name	Rank	Branch	Spec	Seniority	Where Serving
Cunnane, Keith John, BEng, MSc, CEng, MIEE	LT CDR(FTC)	E	WESM	01.10.01	CMT SHRIVENHAM
Cunnell, Rachael Louise, BA	LT(IC)	S		01.01.03	FLEET HQ PORTS
Cunningham, David Andrew, pcea	CDR(FTC)	X	O	30.06.05	JSCSC
Cunningham, David Brand	LT(CC)	E	MESM	01.09.01	DRAKE SFM
Cunningham, John Gavin, BA, pce, pcea, PSC(ONDC)	CDR(FTC)	X	O	30.06.03	JFCHQ BRUNSSUM
Cunningham, John Stewart	MAJ(FTC)	-	SO(LE)	01.10.98	FLEET HQ PORTS
Cunningham, Justin Thomas, MA, psc(j)	MAJ(FTC)	-		01.05.99	42 CDO RM
Cunningham, Nigel John Whitworth	LT CDR(FTC(A)	X	O	01.10.03	RNAS YEOVILTON
Cunningham, Paul, FCIPD, CDipAF	CAPT(FTC)	S		30.06.05	DLO/DG DEF SC
Cunningham, Richard Alister, MBE, pce, pcea, psc	CDR(FTC)	X	P	30.06.00	RNAS CULDROSE
Cunningham, Stuart Iain	LT(IC)	X		01.01.05	BRECON
Cunningham, Thomas Anthony, pce, pcea, psc	CDRE(FTC)	X	O	22.02.05	MOD (LONDON)
Curd, Michael Christopher, BA	LT(IC)	X	O U/T	01.01.05	RNAS CULDROSE
Curd, Timothy Allan, pce, psc	CDR(FTC)	X	MCD	31.12.93	DEF EXP ORD SCHL
Curlewis, Andrew John, BEng, MSc	LT CDR(FTC)	E	ME	01.04.00	FOST SEA
Curnock, Timothy Charles Ross, BEng	SLT(IC)	E	WE U/T	01.01.04	DARTMOUTH BRNC
Curnow, Michael David, BSc, CEng, MIMechE, psc	CDR(FTC)	E	ME	31.12.98	FLEET HQ NWD
Currass, Timothy David, BEng, MSc	LT CDR(FTC)	E	WE	01.03.99	FWO PORTS SEA
Currie, David William, BSc, pce	LT CDR(FTC)	X	AAWO	01.04.90	MOD (LONDON)
Currie, Duncan Gordon	LT CDR(FTC)	X	P	16.12.01	771 SQN
Currie, Michael John, BSc	LT(CC)	X	O	16.08.99	824 SQN
Currie, Stuart McGregor, BEng, CEng, MIMarEST	LT CDR(FTC)	E	MESM	01.08.99	SOVEREIGN
Curry, Benedict Rodney, MBE, psc	LT COL(FTC)	-	C	30.06.02	MOD (LONDON)
Curry, Jamie Hunter, BA, n	LT(CC)	X		01.02.98	INVINCIBLE
Curry, Paul Thomas	CAPT RM(IC)	-	SO(LE)	24.07.04	NAVSEC
Curry, Robert Edward, BSc, n	LT CDR(FTC)	X	PWO(C)	01.11.01	BULWARK
Cursiter, John Douglas, BEng	LT(IC)	X	SM	12.03.05	MWS COLLINGWOOD
Curtis, David	LT CDR(FTC)	E	WESM	01.10.04	ASM IPT
Curtis, Peter John	CAPT RM(IC)	-	SO(LE)	24.07.04	CTCRM BAND
Curtis, Robert John	LT CDR(FTC)	X	AAWO	01.10.00	LOAN DSTL
Curtis, Suzannah Elizabeth Hayton ,BMus	LT(CC)	S		01.09.99	DRAKE COB
Curtiss, Charlotte Jane, BSc	LT(IC)	E	IS U/T	01.01.04	DARTMOUTH BRNC
Curwood, Jenny Elizabeth, BSc	LT(CC)	S		01.11.98	DLO BRISTOL
Cusack, Nicholas James, MSc, jsdc	LT COL(FTC)	-	C	30.06.99	FLEET CIS PORTS
Cuthbert, Glen, BSc	LT(IC)	X		01.05.04	CFPS SHORE
Cutlan, Sarah Louise, BEng	SLT(IC)	E	WE U/T	01.09.03	EXETER
Cutler, Andrew, BSc, SM(n), SM	LT(FTC)	X	SM	01.10.99	SPARTAN
Cutler, David Terry	LT(IC)	E	ME	01.05.04	DUMBARTON CASTLE
Cutler, Tristan Paul, BSc	LT(CC)	S		01.10.99	KENT
Cutt, John James Douglas, pce(sm), psc	CDR(FTC)	X	SM	30.06.94	PSYOPS TEAM

D

Name	Rank	Branch	Spec	Seniority	Where Serving
Da Gama, Joseph Anthony Jude, BSc, CEng, MIEE, MRAeS, psc	CDR(FTC)	E	AE	30.06.96	COS 2SL/CNH
Dabell, Guy Lester, BSc, MA, psc(j)	CDR(FTC)	E	MESM	30.06.02	MOD (LONDON)
Dacombe, Carl Andrew, BSc	LT(IC)	X		01.09.04	RNAS YEOVILTON
Daglish, Hugh Blyth, LVO, pce, psc, psc(j)	CAPT(FTC)	X	AAWO	31.12.96	HQ SACT
Dailey, Paul George Johnson, MA, MSc, CEng, MIEE, MCMI, psc(j), Eur Ing	CDR(FTC)	E	WESM	30.06.03	FWO FASLANE SEA
Dainton, Steven, MA, pce, psc(j), n	CDR(FTC)	X	PWO(C)	30.06.04	ST ALBANS
Dainty, Robin Christopher, SM(n), SM	LT(CC)	X	SM	29.04.01	TURBULENT
Dale, Alistair	LT CDR(FTC)	X	ATC	01.02.04	RNAS CULDROSE
Dale, Jamie Richard	SLT(IC)	X	ATCU/T	01.09.03	RNAS YEOVILTON
Dale, Nathan Andrew	LT(IC)	X	P	01.09.04	846 SQN
Dale, Nigel	LT(FTC)	X	SM	25.07.96	FLEET HQ NWD
Dale-Smith, Guy, BA, PGDIPAN, pce	LT CDR(FTC)	X	PWO(N)	01.12.97	INVINCIBLE
Dalgleish, Grant Alastair, BA	LT(IC)	X		01.05.04	GRAFTON
Dalglish, Kenneth Michael	LT(IC)	E	WE	01.09.04	CHATHAM
Dallas, Lewis Ian, BEng	SLT(IC)	E	SM	01.09.02	SOVEREIGN
Dalton, David John	LT CDR(FTC)	E	AE	01.10.92	MERLIN IPT
Dalton, Feargal John, BEng, CEng, MIEE	LT CDR(CC)	E	WESM	01.10.03	FOST FAS SHORE
Dalton, Mark, BD	CHAPLAIN	SF		12.01.03	FWO DEVPT SEA
Daly, Julie Margaret, BEd	LT CDR(CC)	E	TM	01.10.02	2SL/CNH FOTR

Name	Rank	Branch	Spec	Seniority	Where Serving
Daly, Michael Philip	LT(IC)	E	WE	01.01.04	COS 2SL/CNH
Daly, Paul	LT(CC)	X	PWO(U)	01.05.99	EXETER
Danbury, Ian Gerald, BSc, MIEE	CDR(FTC)	E	WE	30.06.98	RNAS CULDROSE
Dando, Benjamin John	MID(NE)(IC)	X	O U/T	01.09.04	DARTMOUTH BRNC
Dando, Jonathon Neil, n	LT CDR(FTC)	X	PWO(A)	01.08.00	FLEET HQ NWD
Dane, Richard Martin Henry, MBE, pcea	CDR(FTC)	X	P	30.06.05	824 SQN
Daniel, Benjamin James Edward, BA	LT(IC)	X	P	01.01.04	DHFS
Daniell, Christopher John, pcea	LT CDR(FTC)	X	O	01.10.95	750 SQN SEAHAWK
Daniels, Ian James Russell, BSc, pcea, gdas	LT CDR(FTC)	X	O	01.10.95	DASC
Daniels, Stephen Anthony, pcea, psc, tp	CDR(FTC)	X	P	30.06.00	CHFHQ
Daniels, Stuart Paul	LT(FTC)	X		01.04.01	SULTAN
Daniels, Timothy Nicholas, BA, psc(j)	LT COL(FTC)	-	C	30.06.03	FLEET HQ PORTS 2
Dannatt, Timothy Mark, MSc, CEng, MIMechE, jsdc	CAPT(FTC)	E	ME	30.06.03	STG BRISTOL
Daramola, Olufunmilayo, BSc, MB, CHB, MRCOG, MRCGP	SURG LT CDR(MC(MD)	-	GMPP	01.12.98	SULTAN
D'Arcy, Paul Andrew, pcea	LT CDR(FTC)	X	O	01.10.02	RNAS YEOVILTON
D'Arcy, Tara	LT(SC(MD)	Q		14.07.02	RH HASLAR
Darley, Matthew Edward, BSc	CAPT RM(CC)	-	P	01.09.01	UNOMIG
Darling, James Ian	LT CDR(FTC)	E	WE	01.10.98	CAPT MCTA
Darlington, Alan, BA	LT(IC)	X	P	01.09.04	RNAS YEOVILTON
Darlington, Mark Robinson, BSc, pce	CAPT(FTC)	X	AAWO	30.06.04	FLEET HQ PORTS
Darlow, Paul Raymond	LT CDR(FTC)	S	CA	01.10.02	MWC SOUTHWICK
Dart, Duncan James	LT(IC)	X	P	01.09.04	846 SQN
Darwent, Andrew, BSc, MDA, CEng, MIEE	CDR(FTC)	E	WE	30.06.99	MOD (LONDON)
Darwent, Sean Anthony, BSc	LT(CC)	X	O	01.03.93	GANNET SAR FLT
Dathan, Timothy James, BEng, MSc, psc(j)	LT CDR(FTC)	E	ME	01.03.95	DLO BRISTOL
Daukes, Nicholas Michael, BSc	MAJ(FTC)	-	C	01.09.01	CTCRM
Daveney, David Alan, BSc, SM(n)	LT(FTC)	X	SM	01.10.97	VENGEANCE(STBD)
Davenport, Nigel Jefferson, BDS	SGLTCDR(D)(MCC)	-		16.01.97	JSU NORTHWOOD
Davey, Christopher Stephen, BSc	LT(IC)	X	P	01.01.04	DHFS
Davey, Gary Stuart, BEng, MSc	CDR(FTC)	E	AE	30.06.05	CV(F) IPT
Davey, Kelly (Act Surg Lt)	SURG SLT(SCC)	-		22.07.04	DARTMOUTH BRNC
Davey, Paul John, BSc, CEng, FIMarEST	LT CDR(FTC)	E	ME	01.06.89	DRAKE SFM
Davey, Timothy James, BSc	LT(FTC)	X	MCD	01.10.97	DARTMOUTH BRNC
David, Simon Evan James, MA, psc(j)	CDR(FTC)	S		30.06.03	SULTAN
Davidson, Justin David	LT(IC)	E	ME	01.07.04	WESTMINSTER
Davidson, Neil Richard	LT CDR(FTC)	X	P	01.10.03	JHCHQ
Davidson, Serena Rachel, BSc	SLT(IC)	X	O U/T	01.09.02	RNAS CULDROSE
Davies, Andrew James Albert, gdas	LT(CC)	X	O	01.08.90	NELSON
Davies, Anthony Robin, MA, psc, pce	CAPT(FTC)	X	PWO(A)	30.06.04	SA THE HAGUE
Davies, Christopher John, BSc, MIExpE, ACMI, pce, isc	CDR(FTC)	X	MCD	30.06.02	MOD (LONDON)
Davies, Christopher Ronald, BEd	MAJ(CC)	-		01.10.04	FLEET HQ PORTS 2
Davies, Christopher Stanley, MA (Act Cdr)	LT CDR(FTC)	X	METOC	01.09.90	BF BIOT
Davies, Daniel Tudor, BPh	LT(IC)	X		01.01.05	MWS COLLINGWOOD
Davies, Darren James	LT(IC)	S		01.01.05	829 SQN HQ
Davies, Gary	LT(FC)	E	SM	15.06.90	CAPT MCTA
Davies, Geraint William Tudor	LT(CC)	X	FC	01.12.97	EXCHANGE RAF UK
Davies, Henry George Alexander	LT(CC)	X	P	01.07.96	829 FLT 03
Davies, Huan Charles Ayrton, BSc	MAJ(FTC)	-	MLDR	01.09.00	NELSON (PAY)
Davies, Ian Ellis, pce, n	LT CDR(FTC)	X	H CH	01.12.98	LOAN HYDROG
Davies, James Somerfield Ayrton, BEng	SLT(IC)	E	AE U/T	01.09.03	GLOUCESTER
Davies, Jason John	LT(CC)	X	P	12.12.97	EXCHANGE RAF UK
Davies, Jason Lee	LT(CC)	MS		01.09.01	MSA
Davies, John Huw, MA, MSc, psc(j)	CDR(FTC)	X	METOC	31.12.00	HQ SACT
Davies, John Robert, osc(us)	LT COL(FTC)	-		31.12.98	MWC SOUTHWICK
Davies, Lee, BEng	LT CDR(FTC)	E	AE	01.01.02	RNAS YEOVILTON
Davies, Luke Magnus Ayrton	2LT(IC)	-		01.09.00	45 CDO RM
Davies, Lyndon James	LT CDR(FTC)	E	ME	01.10.98	DRAKE CBS
Davies, Mark Bryan, MA, pce, pcea, psc(j)o (Act Cdr)	LT CDR(FTC)	X	O	24.01.97	702 SQN HERON
Davies, Nicholas Mark Samuel, BSc	LT(CC)	X	HM	01.09.98	INVINCIBLE
Davies, Nicholas Stuart, BA	SLT(IC)	X		01.01.04	DARTMOUTH BRNC
Davies, Paul Nicholas Michael, pce, psc(m)	CAPT(FTC)	X	AAWO	31.12.98	SULTAN AIB
Davies, Richard (Act Maj)	CAPT RM(IC)	-		01.09.00	CTCRM
Davies, Sarah Jane, MA	LT(IC)	X		01.09.04	SUTHERLAND

Name	Rank	Branch	Spec	Seniority	Where Serving
Davies, Stephen Philip	LT CDR(FTC)	E	WESM	01.10.01	ASM IPT
Davies, Timothy Gordon, BSc, MRAeS, odc(Fr)	CDR(FTC)	E	AE	31.12.98	NAVSEC
Davies, Trevor Martin, BEng, MSc, MIExpE	LT CDR(FTC)	E	WE	01.10.97	LOAN OMAN
Davis, Bernard James, OBE, LLB, LLM (Barrister)	CAPT(FTC)	S	BAR	01.04.04	2SL/CNH
Davis, Christopher John	LT COL(FTC)	BS		30.06.02	HQ BAND SERVICE
Davis, Edward Grant Martin, MBE, MA, psc(m)	COL(FTC)	-		30.06.04	MOD (LONDON)
Davis, Gary (Act Lt Cdr)	LT(IC)	X	EW	01.01.01	JSSU CHELTENHAM
Davis, Martin Philip, BSc, pce, pcea, psc	LT CDR(FTC)	X	O	01.07.88	SA MALAYSIA
Davis, Peter Henry, BA	LT(IC)	X		01.09.04	HURWORTH
Davis, Stephen Rickard, BEng	LT(FTC)	E	WESM	01.11.96	DLO BRISTOL
Davis-Marks, Michael Leigh, BSc, MA, pce, pce(sm), psc, MNI	CAPT(FTC)	X	SM	30.06.04	FLEET HQ PORTS 2
Davison, Andrew Paul, BSc, MA, PGCE, psc(j), CMarSci, FIMarEST	CDR(FTC)	X	METOC	30.06.04	JWC/CIS STAVANGR
Davison, Gregory James	LT CDR(FTC)	X	P	01.10.02	824 SQN
Davison, Jeffrey Edward, pce	LT CDR(FTC)	X	AAWO	06.04.97	MWS DEF DIV SCHL
Davison, Laura Marie	SLT(IC)	S		01.09.03	CAMPBELTOWN
Daw, Simon James, pcea	LT CDR(FTC)	X	O	01.10.97	750 SQN SEAHAWK
Dawe, Christopher John	SLT(IC)	X	SM	01.04.02	TIRELESS
Daws, Richard Patrick Anthony, MSc, CEng, MIEE	CDR(FTC)	E	WESM	30.06.99	MOD (BATH)
Dawson, Alan James, BTech	LT CDR(FTC)	E	WESM	01.10.03	DRAKE SFM
Dawson, Allan	CAPT RM(CC)	-	SO(LE)	01.04.03	1 ASSAULT GP RM
Dawson, Graham Alexander Edward, BSc, BEng	LT(IC)	E	TM	01.09.00	DISC
Dawson, Nigel Julian Frederick, MSc, FRGS	LT CDR(FTC)	E	TM	01.10.03	MOD (LONDON)
Dawson, Paul	LT(FTC)	E	MESM	01.04.01	NEPTUNE DLO
Dawson, Peter John	CDR(FTC)	X	ATC	30.06.04	FLEET HQ PORTS
Dawson, Phillip Mark David	LT(IC)	X	SM	01.01.02	FLEET HQ NWD
Dawson, Stephen Lee, MA, PGCE, MDA, psc	CDR(FTC)	E	TM	30.06.02	COS 2SL/CNH
Dawson, Stewart Neville, BEng, MSc, CEng, MIEE	LT CDR(FTC)	E	WE	01.10.98	MWS COLLINGWOOD
Dawson, William, pce	LT CDR(FTC)	X	AAWO	01.11.98	IRON DUKE
Day, Anthony	LT(IC)	X	REG	01.01.03	JSCSC
Day, Benjamin Thomas, BA	LT(IC)	X		01.04.02	MWS HM TG (D)
Day, Michael Kershaw, BSc	LT(FTC)	X	P	15.06.95	BULWARK
Day, Simon Nicholas, BEng, MSc, CEng, MIMarEST	LT CDR(FTC)	E	ME	01.10.03	YORK
De Jonghe, Paul Trevor, IEng, HNC, MIIE	LT CDR(FTC)	E	WE	01.10.94	LOAN OMAN
De La Mare, Richard Michael	LT CDR(FTC)	S		01.10.94	NELSON
De La Rue, Andrew Nicholas, BA	LT(CC)	S	SM	01.09.01	VENGEANCE(PORT)
De Reya, Anthony Luciano, BA, psc(j)o	MAJ(FTC)	-		01.09.01	40 CDO RM
De Sa, Philip John, pce, psc	CDR(FTC)	X	PWO(A)	31.12.91	JSU NORTHWOOD
Deacon, Phillip Reginald	LT(IC)	S	SM	22.07.04	RALEIGH
Deacon, Stephen, pce, pcea	LT CDR(FTC)	X	O	01.06.98	LANCASTER
Deakin, Johanna, BEng	LT CDR(FTC)	E	AE	01.10.03	DLO YEO
Deakin, Scott	SLT(IC)	E	WE	01.01.04	MWS COLLINGWOOD
Deal, Charlotte, BEng, MIEE, MAPM	LT(CC)	E	WE	01.06.99	MWS COLLINGWOOD
Deam, Paul Andrew Victor, SM(n), SM (Act Lt Cdr)	LT(FTC)	X	SM	23.07.98	AGRIPPA MAR CC
Dean, James Robert, BA	LT CDR(FTC)	S		01.10.02	GRAFTON
Dean, Joanna Patricia, LLB	SLT(IC)	X		01.02.03	CARDIFF
Dean, Michael Robin, MB, BCH, FFOM, MRCGP, DObstRCOG	SURG CAPT(FCC)	-	(CO/M)	30.06.93	INM ALVERSTOKE
Dean, Simon Ian Robert	CAPT RM(IC)	-		01.09.02	40 CDO RM
Dean, Timothy Charles, BDS	SGLTCDR(D)(MCC)	-		22.07.02	RMB STONEHOUSE
Dean, William Michael Henry, BSc, gdas (Act Cdr)	LT CDR(FTC)	X	P	01.10.95	JCA IPT USA
Deaney, Mark Nicholas, BSc, CEng, MRAeS	CDR(FTC)	E	AE	31.12.00	HUMS IPT
Dearden, Steven Roy, MSc, CEng, FIMechE	CAPT(FTC)	E	MESM	30.06.02	DLO BRISTOL
Deavin, Matthew James	LT(FTC)	X	P	01.07.95	LOAN OTHER SVCE
Dechow, William Ernest, OBE, BSc, jsdc	LT COL(FTC)	-		30.06.99	MOD (LONDON)
Dedman, Nigel John Keith, pce, pcea, fsc	CAPT(FTC)	X	O	30.06.01	SA MADRID
Deeks, Peter, BEng, CEng, MIMarEST	LT(CC)	E	MESM	01.07.96	NEPTUNE DSA
Deighton, Derek Simpson, pce	LT CDR(FTC)	X	PWO(A)	01.05.92	FOST DPORT SHORE
Dekker, Barrie James, MB, BS, FRCA	SURG LTCDR(MCC)	-		01.08.99	NELSON (PAY)
Delahay, Jonathon Edward, BSc	CAPT RM(IC)	-		01.09.02	42 CDO RM
Dell, Iain Martin, MSc	LT CDR(FTC)	MS	(AD)	01.10.02	MOD (LONDON)
Deller, Mark Gareth, pce, pcea, psc	CDR(FTC)	X	P	30.06.05	FLEET HQ PORTS
Dempsey, Sean Patrick, n	LT(FTC)	X	PWO(A)	01.02.98	LIVERPOOL
Denby, William	SURG SLT(SCC)	-		25.09.04	DARTMOUTH BRNC
Denham, Daniel John	LT(FTC)	X	P	01.06.98	RNAS YEOVILTON

Name	Rank	Branch	Spec	Seniority	Where Serving
Denham, Nigel John	CDR(FTC)	X	SM	31.12.00	FLEET CIS PORTS
Denholm, Iain Glenwright, pce	LT CDR(FTC)	X	AAWO	13.08.94	DLO BRISTOL
Denholm, James Lovell, MB, ChB	SURG LTCDR(MCC)	-	GMPP	07.08.01	1 ASSAULT GP RM
Denise, Alexander	2LT(IC)	-		01.08.01	CTCRM LYMPSTONE
Denison, Alan Rae Van Tiel, MSc, CEng, MIMechE	LT CDR(FTC)	E	ME	01.02.89	DLO/DG DEF SC
Dennard, Kieron John, BEng	LT(IC)	E	ME U/T	01.09.04	MONTROSE
Denney, James Robert, BA	LT(CC)	X		01.02.99	SEVERN
Denning, Oliver	2LT(IC)	-		31.08.04	RE ENTRY(ARMY)
Denning, Paul Richard, OBE, MA, psc(m)	COL(FTC)	-	P	30.06.03	FPGRM
Dennis, James Alexander, BSc (Act Maj)	CAPT RM(CC)	-	C	01.09.99	MWC PORTSDOWN
Dennis, Mark John, BSc, PGCE	LT(IC)	E	TM	01.01.97	MOD (LONDON)
Dennis, Matthew John, SM(n)	LT CDR(FTC)	X	SM	01.10.01	FLEET HQ PORTS 2
Dennis, Philip Edward, BSc	LT CDR(FTC)	X	PWO(A)	01.07.04	LANCASTER
Denovan, Paul Andrew, BSc, CEng, MIEE	CDR(FTC)	E	WESM	30.06.04	DLO BRISTOL
Densham, Martin Philip John, BA, BSc	LT(CC)	X	H2	01.10.98	EXCHANGE USA
Derby, Byron Dylan, BEng, MSc, MSc gw, CEng, MIEE, gw, NDipM	LT CDR(FTC)	E	WE	01.04.02	LOAN DSTL
Derby, Peter John, MAPM	LT CDR(FTC)	MS	(PD)	01.10.98	MOD (LONDON)
Dermody, Ryan Thomas	LT(CC)	X	FC	01.12.00	RNAS YEOVILTON
Derrick, Gareth Gwyn James, BSc, MPhil, Eur Ing, CEng, MIEE, psc(j)o	CDR(FTC)	E	WESM	30.06.97	JDCC
Derrick, Matthew John George, BEng	LT(CC)	E	TM	01.12.99	RNSR BOVINGTON
Despres, Julian Peter, ARRC	LT(MC(MD)	Q		19.11.02	NELSON (PAY)
Devenney, David	CHAPLAIN	SF		06.01.03	1 ASSAULT GP RM
Devereux, Michael Edwin, BA	MAJ(FTC)	-	P	01.09.03	JHCHQ
Deverson, Richard Timothy Mark, pcea	LT CDR(FTC)	X	P	01.10.01	702 SQN HERON
Devlin, Craig John, BSc	LT(IC)	E	IS U/T	01.01.04	DARTMOUTH BRNC
Dew, Anthony Michael, MB, BCh	SURG LT(MCC)	-		02.08.00	MDHU DERRIFORD
Dewar, Duncan Andrew, BSc, psc(j)	LT COL(FTC)	-		30.06.03	FLEET HQ PORTS 2
Dewar, Joanna Clare ,BM	SURG LTCDR(SCC)	-		30.04.02	NELSON (PAY)
Dewar, Michael James, BSc	LT(IC)	X		01.01.04	ENDURANCE
Dewsnap, Michael David	LT CDR(FTC)	E	WE	01.10.01	FLEET HQ PORTS 2
Dewynter, Alison Mary, MB, BS	SURG LT(SC(MD)	-		06.08.03	RALEIGH
Di Maio, Mark David, BSc	LT(IC)	S		01.01.03	INVINCIBLE
Dible, James Hunter, MA, pce, psc(j)	CDR(FTC)	X	P	30.06.04	FLEET HQ PORTS 2
Dick, Colin Michael, BEng	LT(CC)	E	SM	01.01.97	RALEIGH
Dick, Faye Elizabeth, BEng	LT(IC)	E	TM	01.05.98	NEPTUNE 2SL/CNH
Dickens, David James Rees, OBE, pce, psc	CAPT(FTC)	X	PWO(U)	30.06.02	COS 2SL/CNH
Dickens, David Stephen, BEng, MSc	LT CDR(FTC)	E	WE	01.10.04	MOD (LONDON)
Dicker, Nicholas Martin	LT(IC)	X	SM	01.08.04	TORBAY
Dickins, Benjamin Russell, BA	LT CDR(FTC)	X		01.10.04	MWS COLLINGWOOD
Dickinson, Pamela Hepple, BEng, MSc	LT(IC)	E	ME	01.07.00	SULTAN
Dickson, James Ian, BSc	LT CDR(FTC)	S	SM	01.08.02	CARDIFF
Dickson, James Peter Edward, MSc	LT CDR(FTC)	X	METOC	01.10.96	MWS HM TG (D)
Dickson, Kenneth George, BEng	SLT(IC)	E	WESM	01.09.02	FWO FASLANE SEA
Dickson, Stuart James, MB, CHB, MRCP, DTM&H	SURG LTCDR(MCC)	-		02.08.00	NELSON (PAY)
Dillon, Ben, BEng, MIEE	LT(IC)	E	WE	01.04.03	EDINBURGH
Dilloway, Philip John, BA, BSc	LT(MC(MD)	Q	RMN	07.12.96	RCDM
Dineen, John Michael George, MA	LT CDR(FTC)	X	AAWO	01.04.02	MWS COLLINGWOOD
Dingley, Paul Alexander	LT(FTC)	X	O	01.01.01	771 SQN
Dingwall, Nils	2LT(IC)	-		01.08.01	CTCRM LYMPSTONE
Dinham, Alan Colin, BSc, PhD	LT CDR(FTC)	E	TM	01.10.88	MOD (LONDON)
Dinsmore, Simon	2LT(IC)	-		01.08.01	CTCRM LYMPSTONE
Disney, Luke	2LT(IC)	-		01.08.04	CTCRM LYMPSTONE
Disney, Peter William, pcea	LT CDR(FTC)	X	O	01.10.94	829 SQN HQ
Diver, Paul Harry, HND	LT CDR(FTC)	E	TM	01.10.04	2SL/CNH FOTR
Dix, Caroline Patrica, MEng	SLT(IC)	E	AE U/T	01.09.03	SOUTHAMPTON
Dixon, Arthur Kenneth, BEng	LT(IC)	E	MESM	01.09.00	SUPERB
Dixon, Mark Edward, BEng	LT(IC)	E	MESM	01.01.04	SULTAN
Dixon, Richard Andrew	LT(CC)	X	P	01.01.01	702 SQN HERON
Dixon, Robert James	SLT(IC)	X		01.09.02	LIVERPOOL
Dixon, Simon James	LT(IC)	X	P U/T	01.01.05	RNAS YEOVILTON
Dixon, Simon Peter	LT(IC)	X		01.05.04	CAMPBELTOWN
Dobbin, Vincent William	LT CDR(FTC)	E	WESM	01.10.96	MOD (LONDON)
Dobbins, Stuart James, BA	LT(IC)	S		01.06.97	CNH(R)

Name	Rank	Branch	Spec	Seniority	Where Serving
Dobie, Fiona Elizabeth (Act Lt Cdr)	LT(FTC)	W	X	01.09.96	PJHQ
Dobson, Amy Clare	LT(CC)	X	O	01.04.03	750 SQN SEAHAWK
Dobson, Brian John	LT CDR(FTC)	S	SM	01.10.95	CHFHQ
Dobson, Richard Andrew, BSc	LT CDR(FTC)	X	H CH	01.04.91	LOAN HYDROG
Dobson, Serena Caroline Sandcroft, BA	SLT(IC)	X		01.05.03	SOUTHAMPTON
Docherty, Paul Thomas, BA, FCIPD, MNI, pce, psc	CDRE(FTC)	X	AAWO	16.07.04	NAVSEC
Dodd, Kevin Michael, pcea	LT CDR(FTC)	X	O	01.04.99	820 SQN
Dodd, Laura, BEng	LT(CC)	E	ME	01.04.01	OCEAN
Dodd, Nicholas Charles, MA, psc(j)	LT CDR(FTC)	S	SM	01.04.99	DRAKE COB
Dodd, Peter Michael	LT(IC)	X	EW	01.01.04	UKMARBATSTAFF
Dodd, Stuart Eric, SM(n), isc	LT(CC)	X	SM	01.10.00	VENGEANCE(PORT)
Dodds, Matthew Lewis, BSc	LT(FTC)	X		01.04.99	MWS COLLINGWOOD
Dodds, Ralph Scott, pce, pcea	LT CDR(FTC)	X	O	01.05.93	FLEET HQ PORTS
Doe, James Richard, BSc	LT(IC)	X	SM	01.10.02	VIGILANT(STBD)
Doherty, Kenneth, MBE	LT CDR(FTC(A)	X	P	01.10.93	ADAS BRISTOL
Doherty, Melanie, BChD, MFGDP(UK)	SGLTCDR(D)(SC(MD)	-		05.01.02	NELSON
Doig, Barry John, BSc	LT(CC)	X		01.12.97	JSCSC
Dominy, David John Douglas, n	LT CDR(FTC)	X	AAWO	01.03.00	SOMERSET
Dominy, Victoria Leigh, BSc	LT(IC)	E	TM	01.09.00	NTE(TTD)
Donaldson, Andrew Michael, IEng, MIIE	LT(FTC)	E	WE	09.01.01	DLO BRISTOL
Donaldson, Stuart Bruce, pce(sm)	LT CDR(FTC)	X	SM	01.09.91	VANGUARD(PORT)
Donegan, Claire Louise, LLB	LT(CC)	X	P	01.10.96	DARTMOUTH BRNC
Donnelly, James Stephen, BEng, CEng, MRAeS	LT CDR(FTC)	E	AE	22.11.98	RMC OF SCIENCE
Donnelly, Samantha, BSc, PGCE, HND (Act Lt Cdr)	LT(CC)	E	TM	17.09.96	DEF SCH OF LANG
Donovan, Patrick, BEng, MSc	LT CDR(FTC)	E	MESM	01.10.03	ASM IPT
Donovan, Paul Anthony, MBA, MCMI, FRSA	CHAPLAIN	RC		22.04.85	AFCC
Donovan, Robin John, BA	LT CDR(FTC)	S	SM	01.01.01	RNAS YEOVILTON
Donovan, Simon James, BA	LT(IC)	X	SM	01.08.02	SOVEREIGN
Donworth, Desmond Maurice Joseph, n	LT(FTC)	X	PWO(A)	01.12.96	WESTMINSTER
Doolan, Martin, MA, pce, psc(j)	CDR(FTC)	X	PWO(U)	30.06.01	MWS COLLINGWOOD
Dooley, Martin Edward	LT(IC)	E	WE	01.01.04	MWS COLLINGWOOD
Doran, Catherine Margaret Campbell, BA, MB, CHB, BAO, MRCS	SURG LTCDR(SCC)	-		07.08.03	NELSON (PAY)
Doran, Iain Arthur Gustav, BA	LT CDR(FTC)	X	PWO(U)	01.10.04	FOST SEA
Doran, Katie Elizabeth, BSc	LT(FTC)	X		01.11.00	ST ALBANS
Doran, Shane Edmund, BEng, CEng, MIMarEST	LT CDR(FTC)	E	ME	01.07.02	CORNWALL
Dorricott, Alan Joseph	CDR(FTC)	E	ME	30.06.02	DSFM PORTSMOUTH
Doubleday, Steven, pcea	LT(FTC)	X	P	16.10.98	848 SQN HERON
Douglas, Patrick John	LT CDR(FTC)	X	P	01.12.00	849 SQN B FLT
Douglas, Paul Gordon, SM(n), SM	LT CDR(FTC)	X	SM	03.12.00	MOD (LONDON)
Douglas-Riley, Timothy Roger, MB, BS, MRCS, LRCP, MRCGP, DA, jsdc (Commodore)	SURG CAPT(FCC)	-	GMPP	31.12.96	2SL/CNH
Douglass, Martin Colin Marc, BEng	LT CDR(FTC)	E	ME	01.03.99	NAVSEC
Doull, Donald James Murray, BEng, MSc, CEng, MIMarEST	LT CDR(FTC)	E	MESM	01.10.02	FOST SM SEA
Dow, Andrew James Royston (Act Capt Rm)	LT RM(IC)	-		01.09.02	CTCRM
Dow, Clive Stewart (Barrister)	LT CDR(FTC)	S	BAR	01.10.04	UKMARBATSTAFF
Dow, William Allister McGowan, MB, ChB	SURG LTCDR(MCC)	-		06.08.02	NELSON (PAY)
Dowd, Jonathan Wyn, BEng	MAJ(FTC)	-		01.09.01	NELSON
Dowdell, Robert Edmund John, BSc, pcea	LT CDR(FTC(A)	X	P	01.10.94	FLEET AV VL
Dowell, Paul Henry Neil, BSc, MA, psc(j), MIEE	CDR(FTC)	E	WE	30.06.05	MOD (BATH)
Dowlen, Henry	SURG SLT(SCC)	-		01.07.02	DARTMOUTH BRNC
Dowling, Andrew Jonathan, BA	LT(CC)	X	O	01.03.01	702 SQN HERON
Downes, Colin Henry, BSc	LT CDR(FTC)	X	PWO(A)	01.09.01	ILLUSTRIOUS
Downie, Alan John, IEng, FIIE	LT CDR(FTC)	E	WE	01.10.97	RMC OF SCIENCE
Downie, David Ross MacLennan, BEng	LT(IC)	E		01.09.04	801 SQN
Downing, Iain Michael	LT(CC)	X	P	16.09.94	RAF CRANWELL EFS
Dowrick, Michael Paul, BA(OU), MA	CAPT RM(IC)	BS	SO(LE)	01.04.03	HQ BAND SERVICE
Dowsett, Patrick Giles, pce, n	LT CDR(FTC)	X	PWO(C)	01.09.01	COMATG SEA
Doyle, Gary Lawrence, pce, pcea, psc(j)	CDR(FTC)	X	O	31.12.99	COMATG SEA
Doyle, Nicholas Patrick	LT CDR(FTC)	X		01.08.02	EXCHANGE AUSTLIA
Drake, Edwin Denis	CDR(FTC)	E	WESM	30.06.96	DLO DEF MUN GP
Dransfield, Joseph Asa James, BSc	LT(CC)	X	O	01.05.99	JSCSC
Draper, Stephen Perry, pce	LT CDR(FTC)	X	AAWO	26.02.96	MWS COLLINGWOOD
Dray, Jake Michael	LT(IC)	X		01.05.03	GLOUCESTER

Name	Rank	Branch	Spec	Seniority	Where Serving
Dreelan, Michael Joseph, MSc, pce	LT CDR(FTC)	X	PWO(U)	01.08.99	NAVSEC
Dresner, Rupert James	MAJ(FTC)	-	P	24.04.02	EXCHANGE USA
Drew, Christopher, BSc, MIEE	LT(IC)	E	IS	01.05.01	AFPAA(CENTURION)
Drewett, Brian John Howard, MSc	SLT(IC)	X		01.06.03	DARTMOUTH BRNC
Drewett, Colin Edward, BEM	LT(CS)(CAS)	-		19.09.98	DNR RCHQ SOUTH
Drewett, Robin Edward, MBE, pce, pcea (Act Capt)	CDR(FTC)	X	O	30.06.99	NAVSEC
Drinkwater, Ross	2LT(IC)	-		01.09.00	42 CDO RM
Driscoll, Mark Sinclair, BA, MIL	SLT(IC)	X		01.07.02	COTTESMORE
Driscoll, Robert, BSc, PGCE	LT(CC)	E	TM	22.07.97	MWS COLLINGWOOD
Drodge, Andrew Paul Frank, pcea	LT CDR(FTC)	X	O	01.10.02	FOST SEA
Drodge, Kevin Nigel, BSc	LT(CC)	X	P	01.10.98	849 SQN B FLT
Droog, Sarah (Act Surg Lt)	SURG SLT(SCC)	-		01.07.04	DARTMOUTH BRNC
Drummond, Henrietta, BSc	LT(IC)	E	TM	24.11.96	NELSON
Drummond, Karl Bruce, BDS	SGLTCDR(D)(MCC)	-		13.07.03	RALEIGH
Dry, Ian, BSc	LT(IC)	E	TM	31.01.99	SULTAN
Drylie, Andrew John, BSc	LT CDR(FTC)	X	SM	01.02.92	EXCHANGE USA
Drysdale, Steven Ronald, pce(sm), SM	LT CDR(FTC)	X	SM	01.02.97	RALEIGH
Drywood, Tobias, BEng, MSc, MIMarEST	LT CDR(FTC)	E	ME	01.04.01	FWO DEVPT SEA
D'Silva, Daniel Mark, BEng, CEng, MIEE	LT(FTC)	E	WE	01.02.98	CMT SHRIVENHAM
Duby, Alon, MB, BCH, FRCS(ED)A&E, FFAEM	SURG LTCDR(SC(MD)	-	(CA/E)	23.04.99	RCDM
Duce, Matthew	LT(IC)	X		01.05.01	MONTROSE
Duckitt, Jack Nathan	2LT(IC)	-		01.09.00	42 CDO RM
Dudley, Stephen Mark Terence, MA	LT CDR(FTC)	S		20.02.01	MWS EXCELLENT
Duff, Alistair John	MID(IC)	X		01.01.04	MANCHESTER
Duff, Andrew	CHAPLAIN	CE		04.10.04	FWO PORTS SEA
Duff, Andrew Patrick	LT CDR(FTC)	X	PWO(U)	01.09.00	INVINCIBLE
Duffy, Henry, pce, psc(j)	CDR(FTC)	X	PWO(C)	30.06.05	MWS COLLINGWOOD
Duffy, James Christopher	LT(IC)	X		01.12.04	LEEDS CASTLE
Duffy, Mari Louise	LT(IC)	X		01.04.03	LANCASTER
Dufosee, Sean William, MBE, pcea	LT CDR(FTC)	X	P	01.10.00	EXCHANGE ARMY UK
Duke, Adam John, BEng	LT(IC)	X	SM	01.09.04	MWS COLLINGWOOD
Duke, Ronald Michael	CDR(FCC)	Q	CPN	30.06.04	MOD (LONDON)
Dumbell, Phillip, BSc, MA, CEng, MIEE, psc	CDR(FTC)	E	WESM	30.06.02	NW IPT
Dumbleton, David William	LT(FTC)	E	WE	01.04.01	DRAKE SFM
Duncan, Colin John	LT(FTC)	X	P	01.09.93	815 FLT 219
Duncan, Giles Spencer, BSc	MAJ(FTC)	-		01.05.04	EXCHANGE NLANDS
Duncan, Ian Stewart, BSc	CDR(FTC)	E	MESM	30.06.05	CMT SHRIVENHAM
Duncan, Jeremy	LT CDR(FTC)	X	P	01.10.01	820 SQN
Duncan, John Ernest	SLT(IC)	X		01.06.03	DARTMOUTH BRNC
Duncan, Kathryn Claire Louise, BSc	LT(CC)	X		01.10.99	PORTLAND
Dunford, Liam James, BSc	LT(IC)	X		01.05.05	MWS COLLINGWOOD
Dunham, Mark William, BSc, psc(m)	COL(FTC)	-		30.06.02	COMAMPHIBFOR
Dunkley, Simon Charles	LT(FTC)	X	AV	26.04.99	RNAS YEOVILTON
Dunlop, Peter Francis, BSc, pce	LT CDR(FTC)	X	PWO(U)	01.04.91	FLEET HQ PORTS 2
Dunn, Anthony	LT(FTC)	X	AV	01.04.01	RNAS CULDROSE
Dunn, Gary Russell, BEng, MSc, CEng, Eur Ing	LT CDR(FTC)	E	WESM	01.05.98	RALEIGH
Dunn, Nicholas Geoffrey, BSc, pcea	LT CDR(FTC)	X	P	01.10.92	814 SQN
Dunn, Paul Edward, SM, SM(n)	LT CDR(FTC)	X	SM	01.07.01	FOST SM SEA
Dunn, Paul Ernest	LT CDR(FTC)	X		01.10.01	TEMERAIRE
Dunn, Robert Paul, pce(sm), psc(j)	CDR(FTC)	X	SM	30.06.04	PJHQ
Dunne, James, BA	LT(IC)	X	SM	01.12.04	MWS COLLINGWOOD
Dunne, Michael Gerard, BEM	LT CDR(FTC)	X	AV	01.10.02	FLEET AV SUPPORT
Dunningham, Stephen, IEng	LT CDR(FTC)	E	ME	01.10.02	SULTAN
Dunsby, Nicholas Byron	LT CDR(FTC)	E	MESM	01.10.01	TRIUMPH
Dunt, Peter Arthur, CB, rcds	VADM	-	(S)	30.04.02	MOD (LONDON)
(CHIEF EXECUTIVE DEFENCE ESTATE AGENCY APR 02)					
Dunthorne, Julie Agnes	LT CDR(FTC)	S		04.01.00	PJHQ
Durham, Paul Christopher Langton, BEng, MRAeS, n	LT CDR(FTC)	E		18.05.03	DLO YEO
Durkin, Jane, BA (Act Surg Lt)	SURG SLT(SCC)	-		15.07.04	DARTMOUTH BRNC
Durkin, Mark Thomas Gilchrist, BSc, pce, psc(j)	CDR(FTC)	X	MCD	31.12.00	MWS COLLINGWOOD
Durning, William Munro	CDR(FTC)	MS		30.06.04	RH HASLAR
Durston, David Howard, MBA, pce, pcea, psc, psc(j)	CAPT(FTC)	X	P	30.06.03	LOAN DSTL
Durup, Jason Michael Stanley (Act Maj)	CAPT RM(CC)	-	LC	01.09.00	1 ASSLT GP RM

Name	Rank	Branch	Spec	Seniority	Where Serving
Dustan, Andrew John	CDR(FTC)	E	AE	30.06.03	AH IPT
Duthie, Andrew	SLT(IC)	E	AE U/T	01.01.04	DARTMOUTH BRNC
Dutton, Andrew Colin	LT CDR(FTC)	S	SM	01.02.03	EXCHANGE USA
Dutton, David, MA, pce, psc(j)	CDR(FTC)	X	PWO(C)	31.12.00	MOD (LONDON)
Dutton, James Benjamin, CBE, BSc, rcds, psc(m)	MAJ GEN	-	C	04.05.04	COMAMPHIBFOR
(ONE STAR FORMATION COMMAND ESSENTIAL MAY 04)					
Dutton, Philip John	LT CDR(FTC)	E	WESM	01.10.99	DLO BRISTOL
Dyer, Graham Richard	LT CDR(FTC)	E	WE	01.10.04	DLO BRISTOL
Dyer, Jonathan David Thomas, BTech, MSc, MBCS	LT CDR(FTC)	E	IS	01.09.99	IMS BRUSSELS
Dyer, Michael David James, BEng, MSc, CEng, MIEE	CDR(FTC)	E	WESM	30.06.00	MOD (LONDON)
Dyer, Shani Danyell	SLT(IC)	X		01.09.03	MERSEY
Dyke, Christopher Leonard, MA, pce, psc(j)	CDR(FTC)	X	PWO(C)	30.06.03	MWC SOUTHWICK
Dyke, Kenneth Andrew, BEng	LT CDR(FTC)	E	MESM	01.10.00	VIGILANT(STBD)
Dymock, Anthony Knox, CB, BA, pce, psc	RADM	-	AWO(C)	19.01.00	BDS WASHINGTON
(HEAD OF BRITISH DEFENCE STAFF WASHINGTON SEP 02)					
Dymond, Justin Roy Melville, BEng	LT(IC)	E	WE	01.09.03	LIVERPOOL
Dyter, Ross Courtney, MEng	LT(FTC)	E	ME	01.02.03	ALBION

E

Name	Rank	Branch	Spec	Seniority	Where Serving
Eacock, Jason	LT(IC)	X		29.10.04	ST ALBANS
Eaglestone, Stephen	LT(IC)	E	MESM	01.02.01	SULTAN
Ealey, Nicholas James, BA	LT(IC)	X	SM	01.12.04	MERSEY
Earle-Payne, Gareth Ellis, BEng	LT(IC)	E	MESM	01.09.03	SCEPTRE
Eastaugh, Andrew Charles, MSc, adp (Act Cdr)	LT CDR(FTC)	E	IS	01.10.89	COS 2SL/CNH
Easterbrook, Christopher, BSc	LT(IC)	X		01.09.04	MONTROSE
Easterbrook, Kevin Ivor Edgar, BEng, CEng, MIEE	LT CDR(FTC)	E	WE	01.12.99	FOST SEA
Easton, Derek William	LT CDR(FTC)	X		01.10.02	DRAKE COB
Eastwood, Richard Noah, MEng	LT(CC)	X	P	15.02.98	JATEBRIZENORTON
Eaton, David Charles, BA	LT(CC)	X	ATC	01.01.02	RNAS CULDROSE
Eaton, Paul Graham, BSc	LT CDR(FTC)	X	METOC	01.06.94	OCEAN
Eatwell, Russell Andrew	LT CDR(FTC)	X	P	01.10.01	FLEET AV VL
Ebbens, Andrew John, sq (Act Lt Col)	MAJ(FTC)	-		01.09.87	UN AFRICA
Ebbern, Gareth John, BSc	SLT(IC)	X		01.09.03	DARTMOUTH BRNC
Eberle, Peter James Fuller, pce, psc (Commodore)	CAPT(FTC)	X	PWO(C)	30.06.97	MOD (LONDON)
Eddie, Alan George Watt, BTech	LT CDR(FTC)	E	WE	01.10.03	DLO BRISTOL
Eden, Christopher	2LT(IC)	-		01.08.01	CTCRM LYMPSTONE
Eden, Jeremy Rodney Hugh	SLT(IC)	MS		01.01.04	DPMD
Edey, Michael John, BSc, n	LT CDR(FTC)	X	PWO(U)	01.12.01	MWS COLLINGWOOD
Edgar, Iain	SURG SLT(SCC)	-		31.08.04	DARTMOUTH BRNC
Edge, Helen Ruth, BEng	LT(IC)	E	AE	01.07.02	847 SQN
Edge, John Howard, MA, MILT, MCIPD, psc(j)	CDR(FTC)	S	SM	30.06.04	NAVSEC
Edgell, John Nicholas, OBE, pce, pce(sm), psc	CAPT(FTC)	X	SM	30.06.03	MOD (LONDON)
Edinburgh, His Royal Highness The Prince Philip, Duke of	ADM OF FLEET			15.01.53	
KG, KT, OM,GBE, AC, QSO					
Edmonds, Rebecca Mary, BEng	LT CDR(FTC)	E	TM	01.11.99	MOD (LONDON)
Edmondson, James Andrew	LT(FTC)	X		01.04.01	CHATHAM
Edmondson, Mark	LT(IC)	X		01.07.04	TRAFALGAR
Edmondson, Simon, BA	CAPT RM(FTC)	-	P	01.05.99	NP IRAQ
Edney, Andrew Ralph, MBE, BEng, pce, pcea, psc	CDR(FTC)	X	P	31.12.96	NAVSEC
Edson, Mark Andrew, HNC	LT(FTC)	E	WE	22.02.96	FOST SEA
Edward, Amanda Michelle, MB, CHB	SURG LT(SCC)	-		07.08.02	RNAS CULDROSE
Edward, Gavin James, BEng, MSc gw, CEng, MIEE	LT CDR(FTC)	E	WE	01.07.03	JSCSC
Edwards, Andrew Donald Pryce, MBE, BSc	LT CDR(FTC)	E	MESM	01.02.88	DRAKE DIS
Edwards, Andrew George, BEng, CEng, MRAeS	LT CDR(FTC)	E	AE	01.09.03	RNAS CULDROSE
Edwards, Carlos Carew, MBE, BSc	LT CDR(FTC)	S		01.07.85	DARTMOUTH BRNC
Edwards, Charles John Albert, MB, BS, FRCA	SURG CDR(FCC)	-	(CA)	31.12.97	RH HASLAR
Edwards, David	LT(IC)	MS		01.01.02	DRAKE SFM
Edwards, James, BSc, PGCE	LT(IC)	E	TM	01.09.96	DISC
Edwards, James Eustice, BEng, CEng, MIEE	LT(FTC)	E	WE	01.06.97	SONAR 2087 IPT
Edwards, John David	MID(NE)(IC)	X	P U/T	01.09.04	DARTMOUTH BRNC
Edwards, Luke	MID(IC)	X		01.09.03	RNAS YEOVILTON
Edwards, Michael Ian, BSc	SLT(IC)	X		01.11.03	DARTMOUTH BRNC

Name	Rank	Branch	Spec	Seniority	Where Serving
Edwards, Richard	LT CDR(FTC)	X	EW	01.10.99	RNU ST MAWGAN
Edwards, Richard Peter, BSc	LT(IC)	E	TM	01.04.02	SULTAN
Edwards, Thomas Hugh Hamish, MPhil	LT(IC)	X		01.05.03	MONMOUTH
Edwins, Mark Richard	LT(FTC)	E	ME	02.05.00	ECHO
Edye, Robin Francis	CAPT RM(CC)	-		01.05.00	FLEET HQ NWD
Eedle, Richard John, BA, psc(j)o	LT CDR(FTC)	X	SM	01.03.91	MWS COLLINGWOOD
Egeland-Jensen, Finn Adam, PGDIPAN, pce	LT CDR(FTC)	X	PWO(N)	01.04.95	FLEET HQ PORTS 2
Egerton, Stephen Brian	LT(FTC)	X	C	10.12.98	SHAPE BELGIUM
Eglin, Caroline Anne, BA	CHAPLAIN	SF		10.09.90	RALEIGH
Elborn, Teresa Kathleen, MHCIMA	LT CDR(FTC)	W	S	01.12.04	FLEET HQ PORTS
Eldridge, Stephen, BSc	LT(IC)	E	TM	01.02.03	SULTAN
Eldridge, Timothy John	LT(FTC)	X	P	01.04.91	LOAN JTEG BSC DN
Elesmore, John Douglas	LT(IC)	X	C	29.10.04	FLEET CIS PORTS
Elford, David Graham, MA, MSc, CEng, MIEE, MRAeS, psc(j)	CDR(FTC)	E	AE	30.06.98	MOD (LONDON)
Eling, Richard James, BA	LT(IC)	X		01.09.02	FOST DPORT SHORE
Elkins, Stuart Spencer	LT(IC)	S		01.05.02	CALEDONIA DLO
Ellerton, Paul	LT(FTC)	X	P	16.10.94	RAF CRANWELL EFS
Ellicott, Matthew James, BSc	SLT(IC)	X		01.05.03	SOUTHAMPTON
Elliman, Simon Mark, pce, psc(j)o	LT CDR(FTC)	X	PWO(U)	01.10.94	FOST SEA
Ellingham, Richard Edwin	CHAPLAIN	SF		17.04.00	FWO PORTS SEA
Elliot-Smith, Teilo John, BA	LT(IC)	X	FC	01.09.02	MANCHESTER
Elliott, Jamie Alistair	LT(CC)	E	AE	01.07.00	RNAS CULDROSE
Elliott, Mark Ferguson	CAPT RM(CC)	-		01.09.03	42 CDO RM
Elliott, Michael Edward, MBE	SLT(IC)	X		01.02.04	DARTMOUTH BRNC
Elliott, Oliver Luke, BSc	SLT(IC)	X		01.11.02	NOTTINGHAM
Elliott, Stephen Peter	LT(IC)	E	WE	01.01.04	MWS COLLINGWOOD
Elliott, Timothy Douglas	LT(IC)	X		01.09.04	MERSEY
Ellis, Andrew Christopher, BA	LT(CC)	X	P	01.05.99	771 SQN B FLT
Ellis, Charles Richard, BEng, MIEE	LT(FTC)	E	WESM	01.03.00	DARTMOUTH BRNC
Ellis, David Francis, BSc, MAPM, CEng, MBCS (Act Lt Cdr)	LT(FTC)	E	IS	15.07.92	FLEET HQ PORTS
Ellis, David Robert, BEng	LT(IC)	E	AE	01.09.02	824 SQN
Ellis, James Paul, BEng, MSc	LT CDR(FTC)	E	ME	01.10.04	AFPAA JPA
Ellis, Michael Philip, OBE, psc(a)	LT COL(FTC)	-	P	31.12.98	MOD (LONDON)
Ellis, Nicholas Mark	LT CDR(FTC)	X		18.07.97	DARTMOUTH BRNC
Ellis, Richard William, BSc	CDR(FTC)	E	AE	30.06.99	EUMS
Ellis-Morgan, Roger Terrence, MBE	LT(IC)	X	EW	01.05.02	2SL/CNH RNCMC
Ellison, Peter John Patrick	SLT(IC)	X		01.01.03	ST ALBANS
Ellison, Toby George	LT CDR(FTC)	X	PWO(A)	01.10.03	WESTMINSTER
Ellwood, Peter George, SM	LT CDR(FTC)	X	SM	01.10.03	MOD (LONDON)
Elmer, Timothy Brendan, BDS	SGCDR(D)(FCC)	-	GDP UT	30.06.02	SULTAN
Elmore, Graeme Martin	CHAPLAIN	CE		30.09.86	NEPTUNE 2SL/CNH
Elsey, David John, BSc (Act Lt Cdr)	LT(CC)	E	TM	01.09.97	2SL/CNH FOTR
Elsom, Geoffrey Keith	LT CDR(FTC)	X	C	01.10.00	MOD (LONDON)
Elston, Adrian John	LT CDR(FTC)	X	REG	01.10.03	NELSON
Elvin, Andrew James, pce	LT CDR(FTC)	X	MCD	06.11.93	EXCHANGE USA
Elwell-Deighton, Dean Carl, pcea (Act Lt Cdr)	LT(FTC)	X	P	16.09.93	MOD (LONDON)
Emerson, Martin John	LT(IC)	X		01.01.05	DUMBARTON CASTLE
Emery, Christian Stanley	LT(IC)	E	WESMUT	01.05.03	2SL/CNH
Emmerson, Debra Marie, BSc	LT(MC(MD)	Q	ONC	22.06.00	RFANSU (ARGUS)
Emmerson, Graham John, pce	LT CDR(FTC)	X	AAWO	01.06.92	LOAN OMAN
Emms, Stuart Michael, IEng, MIIE	LT(FTC)	E	WE	09.01.01	PJHQ
Enever, Shaun Andrew	LT(CC)	X	O	01.09.96	702 SQN HERON
England, Lorraine, BSc	LT CDR(FC(MD)	Q	REGM	01.10.04	RALEIGH
England, Philip Morgan, MSc	LT(IC)	E	TM	01.04.00	DARTMOUTH BRNC
Ennis, John Lee	LT(IC)	X	ATC	01.07.04	RNAS YEOVILTON
Enticknap, Kenneth, QGM, BSc	CDR(FTC)	E	ME	30.06.98	FLEET HQ PORTS 2
Entwisle, William Nicholas, OBE, MVO, MA, pcea, psc(j)	CDR(FTC)	X	P	30.06.02	815 SQN HQ
Entwistle, Stephen Charles, pce, psc(j), MA, MNI	CDR(FTC)	X	AAWO	30.06.00	SACT BELGIUM
Epps, Matthew Paul, BSc, PGCE	LT(IC)	E	IS	17.07.99	BULWARK
Errington, Ridley James Bentley	SLT(UCE)(IC)	E	ME	01.09.02	DARTMOUTH BRNC
Erskine, Peter Anthony, BA, MSc, MIMechE, psc	CDR(FTC)	E	ME	30.06.96	DLO BRISTOL
Essenhigh, Angus Nigel Patrick, BA	LT CDR(FTC)	X		01.10.04	MWS COLLINGWOOD
Essenhigh, Nigel Richard, GCB, rcds, pce, psc, hcsc	ADM	-	PWO(N)	11.09.98	

Name	Rank	Branch	Spec	Seniority	Where Serving
Etchells, Stephen Barrie, BEng, CEng, MIEE	LT CDR(FTC)	E	WESM	03.07.00	FWO FASLANE
Ethell, David Ross, BEng	MAJ(FTC)	-	LC	01.10.03	RM WARMINSTER
Euden, Christopher Peter, BA, n	LT CDR(FTC)	X	PWO(A)	01.06.03	GLOUCESTER
Evans, Andrew	LT(IC)	S		01.07.04	DLO YEO
Evans, Andrew William	LT CDR(CC)	X	SM	01.10.95	MWC PORTSDOWN
Evans, Benjimin Gwynn, BSc	LT(IC)	X		01.01.04	RAMSEY
Evans, Charles Alexander, BA	LT CDR(FTC)	S	SM	01.10.03	KENT
Evans, Charlotte	SURG SLT(SCC)	-		01.07.03	DARTMOUTH BRNC
Evans, Christopher Anthony, BSc	LT(IC)	X		01.05.03	SPARTAN
Evans, Christopher Charles	LT(IC)	E	MESM	01.07.04	VIGILANT(PORT)
Evans, David Anthony	LT(FTC)	X	ATC	20.12.95	RNAS YEOVILTON
Evans, David John, BSc, CEng, MIEE, MRAeS, psc	CAPT(FTC)	E	AE	30.06.03	DLO YEO
Evans, David Mark Mortimer, psc(m)	LT COL(FTC)	-	C	30.06.01	COMATG SEA
Evans, Edward Michael, MinstAM, MCIT, MILT	LT CDR(FTC)	S	SM	16.08.97	RNAS CULDROSE
Evans, Gareth Charles, BA, MB, ChB	SURG LTCDR(MCC)	-		05.08.03	NELSON (PAY)
Evans, Geraint, BEng, MSc, MIEE	LT CDR(FTC)	E	WE	01.06.98	DOSG BRISTOL
Evans, Geraint, MB, CHB, FRCS, FFAEM (Act Surg Cdr)	SURG LTCDR(SC(MD)	-	(CA/E)	17.10.95	MDHU DERRIFORD
Evans, Giles, SM(n)	LT(FTC)	X	SM	01.05.94	TALENT
Evans, Graham Roy, BSc, pce	LT CDR(FTC)	X	PWO(U)	01.12.90	SHAPE BELGIUM
Evans, Helen (Act Surg Lt)	SURG SLT(SCC)	-		31.07.04	DARTMOUTH BRNC
Evans, John Walter, pce	LT CDR(FTC)	X	PWO(C)	06.05.86	MWS COLLINGWOOD
Evans, Jonathan	SURG SLT(SCC)	-		01.07.03	DARTMOUTH BRNC
Evans, Karl Nicholas Meredith, OBE, pce, pce(sm), psc(j), MA	CDR(FTC)	X	SM	31.12.98	FOST SM SEA
Evans, Kenneth	LT(IC)	X	AV	29.10.04	RFANSU (ARGUS)
Evans, Lee Stewart	LT(CC)	X	P	01.05.01	815 FLT 239
Evans, Marc David, MILDM, AMIAM	LT CDR(FTC)	S		16.05.98	COMAMPHIBFOR
Evans, Martin Joseph, BSc, pce	LT CDR(FTC)	X	PWO(U)	01.09.95	JSCSC
Evans, Martin Lonsdale	CHAPLAIN	CE		01.09.98	JSU NORTHWOOD
Evans, Martyn Alun, BA, sq	MAJ(FTC)	-		01.09.93	PJHQ
Evans, Michael Clive, BSc, MA, MNI, MCMI, pce, pcea, psc	CAPT(FTC)	X	P	30.06.04	DASC
Evans, Michael Edward, BEng	LT(FTC)	E	MESM	01.08.97	SULTAN
Evans, Michael Russell	MID(IC)	X		01.01.04	LEDBURY
Evans, Paul John	LT(IC)	E	WE	01.07.04	OCEAN
Evans, Peter Colin, MA, MSc	LT(CC)	E	IS	01.05.96	UKMARBATSTAFF
Evans, Peter John, BSc, MA, psc(j), mdtc	LT COL(FTC)	-	LC	30.06.05	FLEET HQ PORTS
Evans, Robert	SLT(IC)	E	AE	01.01.04	DARTMOUTH BRNC
Evans, Robert Paul	LT(IC)	E	WE	01.01.04	RALEIGH
Evans, Stephen, BSc, BTech	LT CDR(FTC)	E	WESM	01.10.01	MOD (LONDON)
Evans, Thomas Edward, MB, CHB	SURG LT(SCC)	-		07.08.02	INM ALVERSTOKE
Evans, Thomas William	SLT(IC)	S		01.09.03	DARTMOUTH BRNC
Evans, William Quennell Frankis, MNI, pce	CDR(FTC)	X	PWO(N)	30.06.02	MANCHESTER
Evans-Jones, Thomas Matthew	2LT(IC)	-		01.09.00	42 CDO RM
Eve, Laurie	CAPT RM(CC)	-		01.09.03	CTCRM
Evered, Jonathan Francis, BSc	SLT(IC)	X	P U/T	01.05.03	RAF CRANWELL EFS
Everitt, Claire Julia, BDS, LDS RCS(Eng)	SGLTCDR(D)(MCC)	-		11.03.97	RNAS YEOVILTON
Everitt, Tobyn William	LT(FTC)	X	P	19.08.96	LOAN OTHER SVCE
Everritt, Richard, MBE, BSc, psc(j)	LT COL(FTC)	-	SO(LE)	30.06.04	MOD (BATH)
Evershed, Marcus Charles, MB, BCh, MRCGP, Dip FFP	SURG CDR(FCC)	-	GMPP	30.06.02	DRAKE COB
Evison, Toby, MSc	LT(IC)	E	IS	27.07.93	MWS COLLINGWOOD
Ewen, Andrew Philip, BEng, MSc	LT CDR(FTC)	E	AE	01.07.00	PJHQ
Ewence, Martin William, OBE, MA, pce, psc(j)	CDR(FTC)	X	AAWO	30.06.98	FLEET HQ PORTS 2
Exworthy, Damian Andrew Giles, BSc, MA	LT CDR(FTC)	S		01.10.04	NOTTINGHAM

F

Name	Rank	Branch	Spec	Seniority	Where Serving
Fabik, Andre Nicholas, BA	LT(IC)	X		01.05.01	MWS HM TG (D)
Fairclough-Kay, Matthew, BA	LT(IC)	X		01.05.03	MARLBOROUGH
Falk, Benedict Hakan Geoffrey, MNI, pce, psc(j)	CDR(FTC)	X	PWO(A)	30.06.02	EXCHANGE USA
Fallowfield, Jonathan Paul, BTech (Act Lt Cdr)	LT(FTC)	E	WE	24.02.95	2SL/CNH
Fancy, Robert, OBE, pce, pce(sm)	CDR(FTC)	X	SM	31.12.00	PJHQ
Fanshawe, Edward Leo	LT(IC)	E	WESM	01.05.03	RALEIGH
Fanshawe, James Rupert, CBE, jsdc, pce, hcsc, I(2)Fr (Commodore)	CAPT(FTC)	X	PWO(U)	30.06.96	FWO DEVPT SEA
Farquhar, John William, FRGS, nadc, jsdc	CDR(FTC)	S		30.06.87	MAS BRUSSELS

Name	Rank	Branch	Spec	Seniority	Where Serving
Farquharson-Roberts, Michael Atholl, CBE, QHS, MB, BS, MA(Lond), LRCP, FRCS, rcds (MEDICAL DIRECTOR GENERAL(NAVAL) DEC 03)	SURG RADM	-	(CO/S)	09.12.03	2SL/CNH
Farr, Ian Raymond	LT(CC)	X	P	01.04.01	814 SQN
Farrage, Michael Edward, BSc, psc	CAPT(FTC)	E	TM	30.06.05	DCTS HALTON
Farrant, James Derek	LT(FTC)	S		01.02.03	NEPTUNE DLO
Farrant, Sam, BEng	SLT(IC)	E	WE	01.11.02	MWS COLLINGWOOD
Farrington, John Lewis, BEng, MSc, CEng, MIEE, psc, psc(j)o	LT CDR(FTC)	E	WESM	01.10.01	TALENT
Farrington, Richard, OBE, BA, jsdc, pce	CDR(FTC)	X	PWO(C)	30.06.96	CENTCOM USA
Farrington, Stephen Paul, QGM, MPhil, CEng, FRINA, FIMarEST, psc	CDR(FTC)	E	ME	30.06.96	RCDS
Farrow, Richard Dunstan, BA	SLT(IC)	X		01.09.03	DARTMOUTH BRNC
Farr-Voller, Emma Marie, BSc	LT(IC)	E	TM	01.05.01	RALEIGH
Faulconbridge, David, MSc, CEng, MIEE, MIMarEST, psc	CDR(FTC)	E	MESM	31.12.94	ASM IPT
Faulkner, Daniel William, BEng, CEng, MRAeS	LT CDR(FTC)	E	AE	29.11.97	829 SQN HQ
Faulkner, Jeffrey James, ARICS	CDR(FTC)	X	H CH	30.06.01	FWO DEVONPORT
Faulkner, Richard Ian, BSc	LT CDR(FTC)	E	ME	01.08.89	SULTAN
Faulkner, Stuart Glen, MRAeS	LT(FTC)	E	AE	01.09.03	FS MASU
Faulks, David John	CDR(FTC)	S		30.06.02	MWC SOUTHWICK
Fawcett, Fiona Patricia, MA, psc(j)	LT CDR(FTC)	E	TM	01.05.98	2SL/CNH FOTR
Fear, Richard Keith, BSc, MIEE, MDA	CDR(FTC)	E	WESM	30.06.99	CSIS IPT
Fearn, Samual Richard	LT RM(IC)	-		01.09.04	CDO LOG REGT RM
Fearnley, Andrew Thomas	LT CDR(FTC)	S	CMA	01.10.01	NP IRAQ
Fearon, David John, BEng	LT(IC)	E	WE	01.09.03	WESTMINSTER
Feasey, Ian David	LT(CC)	X		01.09.02	UKMARBATSTAFF
Feeney, Matthew Blake, BA	LT(FTC)	X		01.04.00	HQ BFSAI
Feeney, Michael Leonard, BEng, CEng, MIMarEST	LT CDR(FTC)	E	ME	01.05.97	DEF SCH OF LANG
Fellows, Christopher Richard, MEng	SLT(IC)	X	O U/T	01.01.04	DARTMOUTH BRNC
Fennell, Charles Benjamin, BSc	LT(CC)	X	MCD	01.07.99	JSCSC
Fenton, Gregory Morris	CAPT RM(IC)	-	SO(LE)	01.07.04	ALBION
Fenwick, Julie Cheryl, BDS	SGCDR(D)(MC(MD)	-		30.06.05	MWS COLLINGWOOD
Fenwick, Robin John, BSc	MAJ(CC)	-	P	01.10.04	LOAN OTHER SVCE
Ferguson, Gordon Henry, IEng	LT CDR(FTC)	E	MESM	01.10.98	FOST SM SEA
Ferguson, Ian	SLT(IC)	X	O U/T	01.09.03	DARTMOUTH BRNC
Ferguson, Julian Norman, OBE, BA, BSc, pce, pce(sm)	CDR(FTC)	X	SM	30.06.91	QHM CLYDE
Ferguson, Robert Grant (Act Cdr)	LT CDR(FTC)	X	C	12.12.90	HQ DCSA
Ferguson, Vikki Sara	LT CDR(FC(MD)	Q	CC	01.10.02	MDHU DERRIFORD
Fergusson, Andrew Christopher, BSc	MAJ(FTC)	-		01.05.99	UKLFCSG RM
Fergusson, Duncan Campbell McGregor, jsdc, pce, pcea, psc (Commodore)	CAPT(FTC)	X	P	30.06.97	COS 2SL/CNH
Fergusson, Houston James	CDR(FTC)	S	SM	30.06.00	NP IRAQ
Fergusson, Iain Buchan	LT(CC)	X	SM	01.05.02	VENGEANCE(STBD)
Fergusson, Nigel Andrew, MSc, CEng, MIEE	LT CDR(FTC)	E	WE	01.02.99	FLEET HQ PORTS 2
Ferns, Timothy David, LLB	LT CDR(FTC)	S		01.06.99	BULWARK
Ferran, Simon Harold Michael	LT(IC)	X		01.05.03	COTTESMORE
Ferrey, Robert Michael	CAPT RM(IC)	-		01.09.03	45 CDO RM
Ferris, Daniel Peter Sefton, BEng, MA, MSc, CEng, MIEE, psc(j), gw	CDR(FTC)	E	WE	30.06.04	HQ DCSA
Ferris, Nathan	MID(IC)	X		01.05.03	MWS COLLINGWOOD
Ffoulkes, Wayne	LT(IC)	E	TM	01.02.03	MWS COLLINGWOOD
Fiander, Peter John, BSc	LT CDR(FTC)	E	MESM	01.02.87	ASM IPT
Fickling, James William Angus, BEng	LT(IC)	E	WE	01.09.04	EDINBURGH
Fiddock, Matthew Lee, BEng	LT(IC)	E	ME(L)	01.09.03	INVINCIBLE
Fidler, John Quentin, BSc	CAPT RM(CC)	-	LC	01.09.02	BULWARK
Fidler, Marcel Malcolm Graham	LT(IC)	E	WE	01.07.04	PORTLAND
Field, Charles Richard Howard, BEng, CEng, MIMechE	LT CDR(FTC)	E	ME	01.01.04	GLOUCESTER
Field, John Dobson, pce	LT CDR(FTC)	X	AAWO	16.04.87	T45 IPT
Field, Stephen Nigel Crawford	LT CDR(FTC)	X	MCD	01.09.86	MWS DEF DIV SCHL
Fields, David Graham, pce, psc(j)	CDR(FTC)	X	PWO(A)	30.06.03	COMAMPHIBFOR
Fieldsend, Mark Andrew, BEng, fsc	CDR(FTC)	E	ME	30.06.03	AFPAA JPA
Fillmore, Raymond Jeffrey, SM(n)	LT(CC)	X	SM	01.12.00	RALEIGH
Filshie, Sarah Jane, BA	LT(CC)	X	ATC	01.01.02	RNAS CULDROSE
Filtness, David Mark, BSc, SM(n)	LT(FTC)	X	SM	01.10.00	SCEPTRE
Finch, Bruce Andrew, BA, MinstAM, MIL, MInsD, MCIPD, ADIPM	LT CDR(FTC)	S		01.08.01	LIVERPOOL
Finch, Iain Robert	LT(CC)	X		01.11.99	MCTC
Finch, Robert Leonard, BEng, MSc, CEng, MIMarEST, AMIMechE	LT CDR(FTC)	E	ME	01.05.97	FLEET HQ PORTS 2

Name	Rank	Branch	Spec	Seniority	Where Serving
Finch, Steven	LT(CC)	E	AE	29.04.01	DLO YEO
Finch, Timothy Stuart Aubrey, MILT, MCMI	LT CDR(FTC)	S	CA	01.10.97	FLEET HQ PORTS
Fincher, Kevin John, pce	LT CDR(FTC)	X	PWO(C)	01.10.95	T45 IPT
Finlayson, Alasdair Grant, MA, fsc (Act Capt)	CDR(FTC)	S		30.06.96	DLO/DG DEF SC
Finn, David William	LT CDR(FTC)	MS	(AD)	01.10.03	2SL/CNH
Finn, Graham John, pcea	LT CDR(FTC)	X	P	01.10.00	JSCSC
Finn, Ivan Richard, BEng	LT CDR(FTC)	E	AE	01.10.00	MOD (LONDON)
Finn, James Sutherland, BSc	LT(IC)	X	P	01.01.01	814 SQN
Finn, Stuart Andrew, BSc	LT(FTC)	X	O	01.09.00	RNAS CULDROSE
Finn, Tristan Alec	CAPT RM(IC)	-		01.09.04	45 CDO RM
Finnemore, Richard Andrew, AMBIM, pce	CDR(FTC)	X	PWO(U)	30.06.05	DLO BRISTOL
Finney, Michael Edwin, pce, pce(sm)	CAPT(FTC)	X	SM	30.06.03	MOD (LONDON)
Finnie, Harry Morrison (Act Lt Cdr)	LT(FTC)	E	ME	13.06.97	CUMBERLAND
Firth, John Simon, BSc	LT(IC)	X		01.05.00	DUMBARTON CASTLE
Firth, Nigel Richard, pce, pce(sm)	LT CDR(FTC)	X	SM	01.03.95	TALENT
Firth, Rachel Jane Gardner	LT CDR(FTC)	X	ATC	08.04.00	RNAS YEOVILTON
Firth, Stephen Kenneth, OBE, MSc, CEng, MIEE (Act Capt)	CDR(FTC)	E	MESM	31.12.90	DRAKE SFM
Fisher, Aaron George, BSc (Act Maj)	CAPT RM(FTC)	-	LC	01.09.98	FPGRM
Fisher, Clayton Richard Allan, psc(j)	CDR(FTC)	S		30.06.04	NAVSEC
Fisher, Morleymor Alfred Leslie, MBE, BSc, CEng, FIMarEST, MIMechE, MCMI	CDR(FTC)	E	MESM	30.06.94	DNR RCHQ NORTH
Fisher, Nicholas Douglas	LT(IC)	E	WE	01.09.04	ALBION
Fisher, Nicholas Gorden, MB, BS, MRCP	SURG CDR(MCC)	-		30.06.03	MDHU FRIMLEY
Fisher, Robert	LT(FTC)	E	WE	10.06.88	DLO BRISTOL
Fisher, Robert James	LT(CC)	X	P	01.06.96	RAF SHAWBURY
Fisher, Rupert Vincent	LT(CC)	X	ATC	01.01.04	RAF WEST DRAYTON
Fisher, Stephen John, BA	LT(CC)	X	P	01.03.99	845 SQN
Fitter, Ian Stuart Thain, BSc, pcea	CDR(FTC)	X	O	30.06.02	FLEET HQ PORTS
Fitzgerald, Colin	LT CDR(FTC)	E	AE	01.10.03	DLO YEO
Fitzgerald, Gary Samuel	LT(CC)	E	WE	01.01.02	CAPT MCTA
Fitzgibbon, John Paul, BSc	SLT(IC)	X		01.01.04	DARTMOUTH BRNC
Fitzpatrick, John Aloysius Joseph, BA	LT(FTC)	X	O	01.07.97	MWS COLLINGWOOD
Fitzpatrick, Neil James, BSc	LT(IC)	X		01.05.03	RNAS YEOVILTON
Fitzpatrick, Paul John	CAPT RM(IC)	-	SO(LE)	19.07.02	1 ASSAULT GP RM
Fitzpatrick, Paul Stanley	CAPT RM(FTC)	-	SO(LE)	01.01.01	1 ASSLT GP RM
Fitzsimmons, Mark Brown, pce	LT CDR(FTC)	X	PWO(A)	01.09.95	LIVERPOOL
Flaherty, Christopher Lynton, BSc	LT(IC)	X		01.05.02	MWS COLLINGWOOD
Flannagan, Donna Louise, LLB	LT(IC)	S		01.01.04	DLO BRISTOL
Flannigan, Aiden, BSc	SLT(IC)	E	MESMUT	01.09.03	CAMPBELTOWN
Flatman, Timothy David, BSc	LT(CC)	X	P	16.05.99	LOAN OTHER SVCE
Flatt, Leslie Declan	LT(FTC)	E	WE	02.09.99	DFTE PORTSMOUTH
Flatt, Liam Barrie, BSc	SLT(IC)	X		01.09.03	DARTMOUTH BRNC
Flegg, Kirsty Gayle, MA	LT(FTC)	S		01.09.00	CORNWALL
Flegg, Matthew James, BEng	LT(FTC)	E	AE	01.04.01	DLO YEO
Flegg, William John, BSc	SLT(IC)	X		01.11.03	DARTMOUTH BRNC
Fleisher, Simon Matthew, MEng, CEng, MIMechE	LT CDR(FTC)	E	ME	01.06.00	MWS EXCELLENT
Fleming, David Peter, BSc	LT(IC)	X	P	01.09.04	RNAS YEOVILTON
Fleming, Kevin Patrick, BSc, ARCS, pcea	LT CDR(FTC)	X	O	01.10.97	JSCSC
Fleming, Stephen Anthony	LT CDR(FTC)	X		30.09.94	FOSNNI
Fletcher, Andrew Stuart	SLT(UCE)(IC)	X		01.09.02	DARTMOUTH BRNC
Fletcher, Helene	LT(SCC)	Q		24.12.00	RH HASLAR
Fletcher, Ian James, BSc	LT(IC)	X	HM2	01.10.98	FLEET HQ NWD
Fletcher, Jonathan Henry Gibbin, BSc	SLT(IC)	X		01.11.03	DARTMOUTH BRNC
Fletcher, Nicholas Edgar, BA(OU), pce, psc, FCIPD	CAPT(FTC)	X	PWO(A)	30.06.05	MOD (LONDON)
Flinn, John A	CAPT RM(CC)	-	SO(LE)	01.04.03	40 CDO RM
Flint, Helen Anne, BSc, PGCE	LT CDR(FTC)	E	TM	01.05.02	RALEIGH
Flintham, Jason Edward (Act Lt Cdr)	LT(FTC)	X	P	16.03.96	HQ1GP HQSTC
Flinton, Alexandra Rachel	SLT(IC)	S		01.02.04	GRAFTON
Flitcroft, Michael	LT(IC)	E	WESM	01.07.04	RALEIGH
Float, Roger Andrew, MA, MSc, MCGI, AMIEE, psc(j)	CDR(FTC)	E	WE	30.06.02	MOD (LONDON)
Flower, Neil	CAPT RM(CC)	-	P	01.04.03	847 SQN
Floyd, Robert Edward, BSc	LT(IC)	E		14.03.05	SULTAN
Flynn, Andrew, BEng, MSc, CEng, MIMechE	LT CDR(FTC)	E	AE	01.05.04	JCA IPT UK

Name	Rank	Branch	Spec	Seniority	Where Serving
Flynn, Christopher	MID(NE)(IC)	X	O U/T	01.01.05	DARTMOUTH BRNC
Flynn, Mark Christopher, BSC(EH)	LT(IC)	MS		01.07.04	DRAKE CBS
Flynn, Michael Thomas, MCIPD	CDR(FTC)	S		30.06.03	DCL DEEPCUT
Flynn, Simon John	LT(FTC)	X	O	09.01.01	849 SQN B FLT
Foers, Paul Stephen, BEng	LT(IC)	E	WESM	01.09.04	VANGUARD(PORT)
Fogell, Andrew David	LT CDR(FTC)	S	SM	01.10.03	MONMOUTH
Fogg, Duncan Stuart, MA, MSc, CEng, MIEE, gw	LT CDR(FTC)	E	WE	01.04.93	FLEET CIS PORTS
Follington, Daniel Charles	LT CDR(FTC)	MS		01.10.04	MSA
Fomes, Christopher John Henry	CAPT RM(CC)	-		01.04.01	CTCRM
Fooks-Bale, Matthew Edward	LT(IC)	X	P	01.09.04	FLEET AV VALLEY
Foote, Andrew Steven, BEng	LT(CC)	E	ME	01.07.00	CARDIFF
Forbes, Duncan Graham, LLB	CAPT RM(CC)	-		01.09.01	CTCRM
Forbes, Matthew Peter, BSc	SLT(IC)	S		01.01.04	DARTMOUTH BRNC
Forbes, Paul Thomas	LT(CC)	X	P	16.07.96	849 SQN B FLT
Forbes, Reuben Glenn	LT(IC)	X	C	01.07.03	HQ DCSA
Ford, Anthony John, SM(n), SM	LT(FTC)	X	SM	04.04.96	FOSNNI
Ford, Barry Emerson	LT(IC)	E	MESM	01.10.02	TRIUMPH
Ford, Graham Ronald, MSc, CEng, PGDip, MIMarEST	LT CDR(FTC)	E	MESM	01.10.04	NP BRISTOL
Ford, James Anthony, pcea	LT CDR(FTC)	X	P	01.10.00	COS 2SL/CNH
Ford, Jonathan Douglas, BEng, CEng, MIEE	LT CDR(FTC)	E	WE	01.12.01	MWS COLLINGWOOD
Ford, Martin John, AFC, pcea	LT CDR(FTC)	X	O	05.08.98	771 SQN
Foreman, John Lewis Rutland, MA, pce, psc(j)	CDR(FTC)	X	PWO(C)	30.06.01	EXCHANGE USA
Foreman, Simon Michael, BEng, MSc gw, CEng, MIEE	LT CDR(FTC)	E	WE	01.04.05	MOD (LONDON)
Foreman, Susan Louise, BSc	LT CDR(FTC)	X		24.12.03	MWS COLLINGWOOD
Forer, Duncan Anthony, BSc, PGCE, M ED	CDR(FTC)	E	TM	30.06.05	2SL/CNH FOTR
Forester-Bennett, Rupert Michael William	LT CDR(FTC)	X	H CH	24.07.97	FLEET MINING TM
Forge, Stephen Mieczyseaw, BSc	LT(FTC)	S		01.05.00	NEPTUNE DLO
Forrest, Paul Matthew	2LT(IC)	-		01.08.01	CTCRM LYMPSTONE
Forsey, Christopher Roy, MSc, MIEE	CAPT(FTC)	E	WE	30.06.05	DLO BRISTOL
Forshaw, David Roy	LT(FTC)	E	ME	02.09.99	MOD (LONDON)
Forster, Raymond Adrian	LT CDR(FTC)	X	ATC	01.10.01	RNAS CULDROSE
Forster, Robin Makepeace, MA, psc(j)	LT COL(FTC)	-		30.06.05	NAVSEC
Forsyth, Andrew Richard, BSc (Act Capt)	CDR(FTC)	S		30.06.94	DLO/DG DEF SC
Fortescue, Paul Wyatt, BSc	CDR(FTC)	X	METOC	31.12.91	AGRIPPA MAR CC
Fortescue, Robert Christopher, MA, pce, pcea, psc(j) (Act Cdr)	LT CDR(FTC)	X	O	01.03.93	HQ BFSAI
Fortt, Paul David John	LT(IC)	E	TM	01.05.01	RALEIGH
Forward, David James	LT CDR(FTC)	E	AE	01.10.04	792 NAS(SEA)
Forward, Kirsty Louise, MEng	SLT(IC)	E	AE U/T	01.09.03	KENT
Foster, Alan James	LT(IC)	E	MESM	01.05.03	TORBAY
Foster, Benjamin	CAPT RM(CC)	-	MLDR	01.09.00	1 ASSAULT GP RM
Foster, Bruce Michael Trevor, BSc	LT CDR(FTC)	E	TM	07.12.98	FLEET HQ PORTS
Foster, Crawford Richard Muir, MSc, MB, CHB, MRCGP, MFOM, Dip FFP	SURG CDR(FCC)	-	(CO/M)	31.12.00	INM ALVERSTOKE
Foster, David Hugh, psc(j)o	LT CDR(FTC)	X	MCD	01.05.99	FOST SEA
Foster, Duncan Graeme Scott, BSc, PGDIPAN, pce, psc(j)	LT CDR(FTC)	X	PWO(N)	01.07.95	BDLS INDIA
Foster, Geoffrey Russell Nicholas, psc	CDR(FTC)	X	P	30.06.91	MOD (LONDON)
Foster, Graeme Russell, BSc, psc(m)	LT COL(FTC)	-	LC	31.12.97	ALBION
Foster, Graham James, BSc, AMIMechE	CDR(FTC)	E	MESM	30.06.05	NP BRISTOL
Foster, Mark Andrew, BSc, MA, CEng, MIMarE, MInsD, psc	CDR(FTC)	E	TM	30.06.97	MOD (LONDON)
Foster, Nicholas Paul, MSc	LT(FTC)	X	HM	01.02.97	MWS COLLINGWOOD
Foster, Nicholas Paul, BA	CAPT RM(FTC)	-		01.05.00	1 ASSAULT GP RM
Foster, Simon James Harry, BEng, MSc, CEng, MIMarEST, MIMechE	LT CDR(FTC)	E	MESM	01.04.99	FOST SM SEA
Foster, Toby George, BSc	LT CDR(FTC)	X	H1	01.04.03	ECHO
Foubister, Robert, IEng, FIIE	LT(FTC)	E	WESM	18.06.87	DLO BRISTOL
Foulger, Thomas Edward, BDS	SGLTCDR(D)(MCC)	-		11.06.04	FWO DEVONPORT
Foulis, Niall David Alexander, BSc	LT CDR(FTC)	X	HM	01.03.03	FLEET HQ NWD
Fowler, James	LT(IC)	MS		13.08.04	CDO LOG REGT RM
Fowler, Peter James Shakespeare, MSc	LT CDR(FTC)	E	MESM	01.04.90	NEPTUNE DSA
Fowler, Peter John, MSc, MB, BS, MRCS, LRCP, MRCGP, DRCOG	SURG LTCDR(SC(MD)	-	GMPP	03.08.96	JSU NORTHWOOD
Fowler, Remington, BEng	SLT(IC)	E	WESMUT	01.09.03	INVINCIBLE
Fox, David John	LT(IC)	X		01.01.04	TORBAY
Fox, Kevin Andrew, BSc, CEng, MIEE	CDR(FTC)	E	AE	30.06.94	SULTAN

Name	Rank	Branch	Spec	Seniority	Where Serving
Fox, Richard George, pcea	CDR(FTC)	X	P	30.06.05	JHCHQ
Fox, Trefor Morgan	LT(CC)	X	HM	01.07.96	SCOTT
France, Sean Charles, BSc	LT(MC(MD)	Q		25.08.99	RH HASLAR
Francis, Derek Edward	LT(FTC)	X	PWO(U)	10.01.00	JARIC
Francis, John	LT CDR(FTC)	X	AV	01.10.94	RNAS CULDROSE
Francis, Steven John, MA, psc(j)	LT COL(FTC)	-		30.06.03	PJHQ
Francis, Thomas Dewolfe Hamlin, BA	CAPT RM(IC)	-		01.09.01	1 ASSAULT GP RM
Frankham, Peter James, BEng, MDA, CEng, MIMarEST	CDR(FTC)	E	WE	31.12.00	DARTMOUTH BRNC
Franklin, Benjamin James, pcea, psc(j)	LT CDR(FTC)	X	O	01.10.98	RNAS CULDROSE
Franklin, Ross William, BSc	LT(IC)	X	P U/T	01.01.05	RNAS YEOVILTON
Franklyn-Miller, Andrew David, MB, BS	SURG LTCDR(MC(MD)	-		04.08.04	DARTMOUTH BRNC
Franks, Christopher Stephen, BSc, CEng, MIEE	LT CDR(FTC)	E	WESM	01.02.98	MOD (LONDON)
Franks, Donald Ian, adp	LT CDR(FTC)	E	IS	01.10.94	FLEET HQ PORTS
Franks, Jeremy Peter, BSc, CEng, MRAeS	LT CDR(FTC)	E	AE	01.12.85	CTS
Franks, Peter Dennis, MSc	LT CDR(FTC)	E	IS	01.10.93	AFPAA(CENTURION)
Fraser, Donald Kennedy, pce, MRIN	LT CDR(FTC)	X	PWO(U)	01.07.84	FLEET HQ NWD
Fraser, Eric, BSc, pce, psc	CAPT(FTC)	X	PWO(C)	30.06.02	FOST NWD (JMOTS)
Fraser, Graeme William, MA	MAJ(FTC)	-	LC	01.10.01	FPGRM
Fraser, Heather Lee, BEng	LT CDR(FTC)	E	WE	01.07.04	RMC OF SCIENCE
Fraser, Ian David, MSc	LT CDR(FTC)	E	AE	01.07.02	ADAS BRISTOL
Fraser, Ian Edward	LT(CC)	X	P	16.04.96	824 SQN
Fraser, James Michael, BA	LT(IC)	X	P	01.07.03	RNAS YEOVILTON
Fraser, Michael John Simon, MSc, PGDip	LT(CC)	X	H2	01.09.01	EXCHANGE N ZLAND
Fraser, Patrick	LT CDR(FTC)	E	AE	01.10.03	DLO WYTON
Fraser, Robert William, MVO, LLB, rcds (Barrister)	CDRE(FTC)	S	BAR	11.01.05	COS 2SL/CNH
Fraser, Timothy Peter, pce	CAPT(FTC)	X	PWO(N)	31.12.00	COS 2SL/CNH
Fraser, Wilson Cameron	LT CDR(FTC)	E	WESM	01.10.96	FOST FAS SHORE
Fraser-Smith, Sharron	LT(SC(MD)	Q		23.11.02	MDHU DERRIFORD
Frazer, Hamish Forbes	LT(CC)	X	FC	01.08.99	MWS COLLINGWOOD
Frean, James Peter, BA	LT(CC)	X	P	16.05.97	MOD (LONDON)
Fredrickson, Charlotte Ann	SLT(IC)	X	O U/T	01.09.03	DARTMOUTH BRNC
Free, Andrew Stuart, BSc, HNC, MIIE	LT(IC)	E	IS	01.05.00	DLO BRISTOL
Freegard, Ian Paul, MBE	LT CDR(FTC)	S	(W)	01.10.99	NELSON
Freeman, David Russel, pce, psc(j), MA	LT CDR(FTC)	X	O	01.06.96	RNAS YEOVILTON
Freeman, Edmund Malcolm Roger, BA	SLT(IC)	X		01.02.03	MANCHESTER
Freeman, Mark Edward	MAJ(FTC)	-		01.09.96	CTCRM
Freeman, Martin John, AMIMarEST	LT(FTC)	E	MESM	01.04.01	SULTAN
French, James Thomas	CDR(FTC)	E	ME	30.06.02	FLEET HQ PORTS 2
French, Jeremy Hugh, BEng	LT(IC)	X	P	01.01.02	RAF SHAWBURY
French, Kevin Lawrence, pce	LT CDR(FTC)	X	AAWO	09.07.93	CV(F) IPT
French, Paul, BSc	LT(IC)	E	AE	02.08.02	JCA IPT USA
French, Stephen Amos, OBE, BEng, MSc, CEng, MIMarEST, MCGI, psc(j)	CDR(FTC)	E	MESM	31.12.99	ALBION
Freshwater, Dennis Andrew, MB, BS, MRCP	SURG LTCDR(FCC)	-		09.08.98	NELSON (PAY)
Fries, Charles Anton, BA, MB, BCH, MRCS	SURG LT(SCC)	-		02.02.05	DARTMOUTH BRNC
Frisby, Paul	LT(IC)	X	C	01.05.04	STRS IPT
Frith, Adele Marie, LLB	SLT(IC)	X		01.02.03	OCEAN
Frost, Laurence John, BSc, IEng	LT(IC)	E	WE	01.07.04	RICHMOND
Frost, Mark Adrian, BSc	LT CDR(FTC)	E	TM	01.01.03	DCL DEEPCUT
Frost, Michael John	CAPT RM(IC)	-	SO(LE)	01.01.01	848 SQN HERON
Frost, Timothy Simon, BEng	SLT(IC)	X		01.05.02	RNAS YEOVILTON
Frost, Ursula Elizabeth	LT(IC)	S		01.11.04	MARS IPT
Fry, Jonathan Mark Stewart, MSc, CDipAF, CEng, FIMarEST, MCGI, psc	CDR(FTC)	E	ME	31.12.98	FLEET HQ PORTS 2
Fry, Rebecca	SURG SLT(SCC)	-		20.09.04	DARTMOUTH BRNC
Fry, Robert Allan, KCB, CBE, BSc, MA, psc(m)	LT GEN	-		07.07.03	MOD DCDS(C)
(DEP CHIEF OF DEFENCE STAFF(COMMITMENTS) JUL 03)					
Fry, Timothy Graham	LT(CC)	E	WESM	01.01.02	MWC PORTSDOWN
Fryer, Adrian Clifford, BSc, pce	LT CDR(FTC)	X	AAWO	01.02.02	FOST SEA
Fulford, John Philip Henry, BSc, psc(m)	CAPT(FTC)	E	WESM	30.06.04	DLO BRISTOL
Fulford, Robin Nicholas, IEng, MIIE	LT CDR(FTC)	E	WE	01.10.03	RICHMOND
Full, Richard John	LT(CC)	X	O	01.06.98	849 SQN A FLT
Fuller, Charles Edward	LT(FTC)	X	P	16.08.97	RAF SHAWBURY
Fuller, James Bruce, BSc	CAPT RM(CC)	-	LC	01.09.99	1 ASSAULT GP RM
Fuller, James Edward	LT(IC)	X	FC	01.03.02	ILLUSTRIOUS

Name	Rank	Branch	Spec	Seniority	Where Serving
Fuller, Richard	LT(IC)	S		01.07.03	HQ DCSA
Fuller, Simon Roland, MA, psc(j)	MAJ(FTC)	-		01.09.01	42 CDO RM
Fuller, Stephen Paul	LT(IC)	E		01.05.02	FLEET HQ PORTSEA
Fullman, Gemma, BSc	LT(IC)	X		01.09.02	NP AFGHANISTAN
Fulton, Craig Robert, pce, pce(sm)	CDR(FTC)	X	SM	31.12.00	MWC PORTSDOWN
Fulton, David Marc	LT(IC)	E	MESM	01.05.02	VENGEANCE(STBD)
Fulton, Robert Henry Gervase, KBE, BA, rcds, psc(m), hcsc	LT GEN	-	C	03.06.03	MOD (LONDON)
(DEP CHIEF OF DEFENCE STAFF (EQUIP CAPABILITY) JUN 03)					
Funnell, Nicholas Charles, BSc, pce, pcea, psc(m)	CDR(FTC)	X	O	30.06.96	FLEET HQ PORTS 2
Furlong, Keith, pce	CDR(FTC)	X	AAWO	30.06.05	FOST MPV SEA
Furmston, Gareth Hadyn, BSc	LT(IC)	X		01.12.04	COTTESMORE
Furness, Stuart Brian, MSc, MPhil, MIMA, pce, pcea	CDR(FTC)	X	O	30.06.96	RNLO USNAVCENT
Fyfe, Karen Sabrina	LT(CC)	X	H2	01.10.00	MWS HM TG (D)

G

Name	Rank	Branch	Spec	Seniority	Where Serving
Gabb, John Harry, MB, BS	SURG CAPT(FCC)	-	GMPP	31.12.00	DRAKE COB
Gadie, Philip Anthony, sq	MAJ(FTC)	-		01.05.97	MOD (LONDON)
Gadsden, Andrew Christopher, BA	LT(CC)	X		01.09.01	2SL/CNH
Gaffney, Benjamin	2LT(IC)	-		01.09.00	40 CDO RM
Gahan, Richard James, BEng	LT(IC)	E	WESM	01.09.04	VICTORIOUS(PORT)
Gair, Simon David Henley, BEng, MSc, MIEE, adp	LT CDR(FTC)	E	WE	01.02.03	MOD (LONDON)
Galbraith, Lee Andrew	CAPT RM(IC)	-		01.09.03	40 CDO RM
Gale, Crystal Violet	LT CDR(FTC)	S		24.12.00	SULTAN
Gale, Mark Andrew, MA, MSc	LT CDR(FTC)	E	MESM	01.02.00	FWO FASLANE
Gale, Simon Philip, pce, psc(j)	LT CDR(FTC)	X	PWO(U)	01.11.96	UKMARBATSTAFF
Gall, Michael Robert Carnegie, BDS, MSc, MGDS RCS	SGCDR(D)(FCC)	-		30.06.95	DDA PORTSMOUTH
Gallimore, John Martin	LT(FTC)	X	EW	01.04.01	FOST SEA
Gallimore, Richard Myles	LT(IC)	X	P	01.10.00	FLEET AV VALLEY
Galvin, David	LT CDR(FTC)	E	WE	01.10.96	FLEET CIS PORTS
Gamble, Neil	LT(FTC)	X	P	01.11.93	RAF SHAWBURY
Gamble, Phillip, BSc	LT(CC)	X	O	15.05.93	849 SQN A FLT
Gamble, Stephen Boston, BA, BEng	LT(CC)	X	P	01.06.97	702 SQN HERON
Game, Philip Gordon, BEng, MSc gw, CEng, MIEE	LT CDR(FTC)	E	WE	01.10.00	WESTMINSTER
Gannon, Dominic Richard	CAPT RM(IC)	-	SO(LE)	24.07.04	1 ASSAULT GP RM
Gardiner, Dermot Richard Charles, MB, BCH	SURG LT(SC(MD)	-		06.08.03	MDHU DERRIFORD
Gardiner, Peter Fredrick David	LT CDR(FTC)	X	ATC	01.10.00	RNAS YEOVILTON
Gardner, Callum Brian, MB, ChB	SURG LT(MCC)	-		02.08.00	MDHU DERRIFORD
Gardner, Christopher Reginald Summers, LLB, DipFM, psc	CDR(FTC)	S	SM	31.12.99	DPA BRISTOL
Gardner, Ewan Stephen Edward, BSc	SLT(IC)	X		01.02.04	DARTMOUTH BRNC
Gardner, John Edward, BA, pce	LT CDR(FTC)	X	PWO(A)	01.07.00	CHATHAM
Gardner, Louis Philip	LT(IC)	X		01.05.04	TURBULENT
Gardner, Michael Peter, BSc	LT(CC)	X		01.05.00	EXETER
Gardner, Suzanne Lorraine	LT(MCC)	Q		05.11.98	CTCRM
Gare, Christopher James, n	LT(CC)	X		01.07.00	MWS COLLINGWOOD
Garey, Emma Jayne	LT(IC)	X		01.01.05	COS 2SL/CNH
Garland, Andrew Neil	CAPT RM(FTC)	-	SO(LE)	01.01.00	RMR BRISTOL
Garland, Nicholas, BSc, ACMA	CDR(FTC)	S	CMA	30.06.02	UKMILREP BRUSS
Garner, Michael Edward	LT(IC)	X		01.09.02	MWS COLLINGWOOD
Garner, Robert John	MID(NE)(IC)	X		01.09.04	DARTMOUTH BRNC
Garner, Sean Martin, BA (Act Lt Cdr)	LT(FTC)	X	ATC	01.08.94	ILLUSTRIOUS
Garnham, Simon William, BA	CAPT RM(IC)	-		01.05.99	RMR MERSEYSIDE
Garratt, John Kenneth, BA, pce, n	LT CDR(FTC)	X	AAWO	01.05.99	JSCSC
Garratt, Mark David, pce, pcea	CDR(FTC)	X	P	30.06.97	JSCSC
Garreta, Carlos Eduardo, BSc	LT(CC)	X	FC	01.05.01	YORK
Garrett, Stephen Walter, OBE, pce, pce(sm), psc(j)	CAPT(FTC)	X	SM	30.06.05	MOD (LONDON)
Gascoigne, James, BA	LT(IC)	X		01.01.03	NORTHUMBERLAND
Gaskell, Harvey David, BEng	LT(CC)	X	P	16.10.98	EXCHANGE RAF UK
Gaskin, Daniel Edward	LT(IC)	X		01.09.03	CARDIFF
Gaskin, Simon Edward, MNI, MRIN, pce	LT CDR(FTC)	X		01.11.87	STG BRISTOL
Gass, Colin Joseph, BSc, psc, pce (Commodore)	CAPT(FTC)	X	AAWO	30.06.97	BDS WASHINGTON
Gasson, Nicholas Simon Charles, pce, ocds(USN), MA	CDR(FTC)	X	PWO(U)	30.06.95	MWC SOUTHWICK
Gater, James Clive, BSc	LT(IC)	X		01.01.03	MARLBOROUGH

Name	Rank	Branch	Spec	Seniority	Where Serving
Gates, Nigel Sinclair, BEng	LT(CC)	X	P	16.03.93	MWC PORTSDOWN
Gaunt, Amy Victoria, BA	LT(IC)	X	O	01.09.04	RNAS CULDROSE
Gaunt, Neville Raymond, pce, pcea, psc, psc(j)	CDR(FTC)	X	O	30.06.98	MOD (LONDON)
Gay, David Allin Thomas, MB, BS	SURG LTCDR(MCC)	-		05.08.03	NELSON (PAY)
Gayfer, Mark Ewan, MA, MSc, CEng, MIEE	LT CDR(FTC)	E	WESM	01.12.99	VIGILANT(PORT)
Gaytano, Ronald Troy McDonald, BEng, MSc	LT(IC)	E	AE	01.04.02	845 SQN
Gazard, Philip Neil, BEng, MBCS	LT CDR(FTC)	E	WE	01.10.99	SOMERSET
Gazzard, Julian Henry, PGDIPAN, pce	LT CDR(FTC)	X	PWO(N)	01.06.96	FOST SEA
Gearing, Richard Malcolm, BEng	SLT(IC)	E	AE U/T	01.09.02	SULTAN
Geary, Timothy William, BEng	CDR(FTC)	E	ME	30.06.05	CMT SHRIVENHAM
Geddis, Richard Duncan, BEng, CDipAF	LT CDR(FTC)	E	WESM	01.09.96	ASM IPT
Geldard, Michael Andrew, sq	MAJ(FTC)	-		01.05.01	DLO BRISTOL
Gelder, George Arthur, psc	LT COL(FTC)	-		31.12.93	LOAN DSTL
Gellender, Paul Scott	CAPT RM(IC)	-	SO(LE)	24.07.03	FLEET HQ PORTS
Geneux, Nicholas Steven, BSc	LT(IC)	E	TM	01.09.00	2SL/CNH FOTR
Gennard, Anthony, BA	LT CDR(FTC)	S		01.03.03	NORTHUMBERLAND
George, Alan Peter, pcea	CDR(FTC)	X	O	30.06.05	HQ STC
George, Christopher Alan, BSc	LT(IC)	X		01.11.03	SUPERB
George, David Mark, pce	LT CDR(FTC)	X	PWO(A)	13.03.01	MARLBOROUGH
George, Nicholas David	CAPT RM(IC)	-		01.09.04	42 CDO RM
George, Seth Duncan, BSc, PGCE	LT(IC)	E	TM	01.06.00	2SL/CNH FOTR
Geraghty, Felicity (Act Lt Cdr)	LT(MC(MD)	Q		01.09.00	MDHU DERRIFORD
Gerrell, Frederick John	LT CDR(FTC)	MS		01.10.00	NAVSEC
Gershater, Stefan Craig, BSc	LT(IC)	S		01.01.04	RNAS CULDROSE
Getgood, James Ashley, BA, psc(m)	LT COL(FTC)	-		30.06.95	MOD (LONDON)
Gething, Jonathan Blair, pce(sm)	CDR(FTC)	X	SM	30.06.02	JSU NORTHWOOD
Gibb, Alexander	CAPT RM(CC)	-	SO(LE)	01.04.03	1 ASSAULT GP RM
Gibb, Roger Walter, BSc, nadc	CDR(FTC)	E	WESM	31.12.91	HQ SACT
Gibbens, Carolyn (Act Surg Lt)	SURG SLT(SCC)	-		24.07.04	DARTMOUTH BRNC
Gibbins, Paul	CAPT RM(IC)	-	C	01.04.04	EXCHANGE ARMY UK
Gibbon, Lynne, ARRC, QHNS	CAPT(FCC)	Q	ONC	28.07.03	2SL/CNH
Gibbons, Nicholas Philip	LT CDR(FTC)	X	O	01.10.02	750 SQN SEAHAWK
Gibbs, Anthony Edward	LT(IC)	X	ATC	08.04.01	RNAS YEOVILTON
Gibbs, Anthony Maurice	LT(CC)	X	P	01.03.99	702 SQN HERON
Gibbs, David John Edward, BEng	LT(CC)	X	P	01.02.98	771 SQN
Gibbs, Mark Peter, BEng	LT(FTC)	E	ME	01.04.02	SULTAN
Gibbs, Neil David, BSc, psc(j)o	LT CDR(FTC)	E	ME	01.07.95	MCME IPT
Gibbs, Philip Norman Charles, MSc, FRSA	LT CDR(FTC)	X	PWO(U)	01.02.89	EXCHANGE USA
Gibson, Adrian	LT(IC)	E	WE	01.01.04	HQ DCSA
Gibson, Alastair David, MBE, MA	LT CDR(FTC)	S		16.11.97	PJHQ
Gibson, Alexander James, BSc	CAPT RM(FTC)	-	LC	01.05.99	COMATG SEA
Gibson, Andrew	CDR(FTC)	E	AE	30.06.04	DLO YEO
Gibson, Andrew Richard, MB, BS, MRCS	SURG LTCDR(FCC)	-		01.08.99	NELSON (PAY)
Gibson, David Thomas, BSc	LT CDR(FTC)	E	AE	01.06.91	NP IRAQ
Gibson, Ian Alexander, pce, psc(j)	CDR(FTC)	X	PWO(A)	31.12.92	DRAKE COB
Gibson, Mark James	MID(UCE)(IC)	X		01.09.03	DARTMOUTH BRNC
Gibson, Martin Jonathan Stuart, AMRAeS	LT(FTC)	E	AE	01.04.01	EXCHANGE CANADA
Gibson, Sarah Jane, BA, MSc	LT(IC)	E	IS	01.01.99	MOD (LONDON)
Gibson, Terence Anthony	LT(CC)	E	WE	01.01.02	JSCSC
Gibson, Timothy Andrew, MBE, pce (Act Cdr)	LT CDR(FTC)	X	PWO(N)	16.03.87	NBC PORTSMOUTH
Gilbert, Jamie Stuart Davidson	MID(NE)(IC)	X	P U/T	01.11.04	DARTMOUTH BRNC
Gilbert, Mark Ashley	SLT(IC)	X	O U/T	01.09.04	RNAS CULDROSE
Gilbert, Peter David, BEng, MA, MSc, CEng, FIMechE, FIMarEST, FInstLM, MCGI, ACGI	CDR(FTC)	E	ME	30.06.03	MOD (LONDON)
Gilbert, Ross Grant, LLB	LT(FTC)	S	BAR	01.06.98	2SL/CNH
Gilbertson, Cheryl Jane, BA	SLT(IC)	X	O U/T	01.09.03	DARTMOUTH BRNC
Gilding, Douglas Robert, BSc	MAJ(FTC)	-		01.09.98	CTCRM
Giles, Andrew Robert	CDR(FTC)	S	(S)	30.06.04	COM MCC NWD
Giles, David William, MBE, MSc, CEng, MIEE, psc(j)	CDR(FTC)	E	WE	30.06.04	STG BRISTOL
Giles, Gary John	CAPT RM(FTC)	-	SO(LE)	01.01.01	EXCH ARMY SC(G)
Giles, Kevin David Lindsay, BSc, pce	LT CDR(FTC)	X	MCD	01.05.92	MWC PORTSDOWN
Giles, Peter Anthony Illson, BSc	SLT(IC)	X		01.02.04	DARTMOUTH BRNC
Giles, Robert Keith, BEng	LT CDR(FTC)	X	MCD	01.03.01	MCM1 SEA

Name	Rank	Branch	Spec	Seniority	Where Serving
Giles, Simon	CAPT RM(IC)	-	SO(LE)	24.07.04	45 CDO RM
Gill, Alastair Brennan, BEng	SLT(IC)	X	O U/T	01.01.03	RNAS CULDROSE
Gill, Christopher David, SM(n), SM	LT(FTC)	X	SM	01.01.00	VANGUARD(PORT)
Gill, Mark Hansen, BEng, pcea	LT CDR(FTC)	X	PWO(A)	01.07.02	SOUTHAMPTON
Gill, Martin Robert, BEng, MSc, psc(j)	LT CDR(FTC)	E	MESM	01.04.95	DRAKE SFM
Gill, Paul Simon, MA	LT(IC)	E	TM	01.01.00	MWS COLLINGWOOD
Gill, Steven Clark	LT(FTC)	S	(S)	12.12.91	UKSU SHAPE
Gillan, Gordon Maxwell, BEng, MSc, gw	LT CDR(FTC)	E	WE	01.04.95	DLO BRISTOL
Gillanders, Fergus Graeme Roy, pce	CDR(FTC)	X	AAWO	31.12.94	MWS COLLINGWOOD
Gillard, Katharine Ellen, BSc	LT(IC)	X		01.05.04	PENZANCE
Gillard, Victoria Anne	LT(FTC)	X	HM	01.07.99	PJHQ
Gillett, David Alexander	LT(FTC)	X	O	01.11.98	815 FLT 203
Gillett, Nathan David	LT(IC)	X	AV	01.01.04	RNAS CULDROSE
Gillham, Paul Robert	LT CDR(FTC)	E	WE	02.03.95	CORNWALL
Gilliland, Samuel Saunderson	LT(FTC)	E	WE	13.06.91	MWS COLLINGWOOD
Gillingham, George	SLT(IC)	X	O	01.01.04	RNAS CULDROSE
Gilmartin, Kieran Peter ,BM	SURG LT(SC(MD)	-		06.08.03	RNAS YEOVILTON
Gilmore, Jeremy Edward	LT(IC)	X	P	01.09.03	846 SQN
Gilmore, Martin Paul	LT(CC)	X	P	01.06.96	815 SQN HQ
Gilmore, Steven John, BEng, CEng, MIEE	LT(CC)	E	WE	01.04.00	JSCSC
Gilmour, Craig James Murray, MNI, pce	CDR(FTC)	X	PWO(A)	30.06.02	UKMARBATSTAFF
Ginn, Robert Danny (Act Capt Rm)	LT RM(IC)	-		01.09.03	FPGRM
Ginn, Robert Nigel (Act Maj)	CAPT RM(FTC)	-	SO(LE)	01.01.95	1 ASSAULT GP RM
Gittoes, Mark Anthony Warren	MAJ(FTC)	-		01.09.90	MOD (LONDON)
Gladston, Stephen Anderson	LT(CC)	X	P	01.07.91	771 SQN
Gladwell, Trevor John, SM	LT CDR(FTC)	X	SM	01.12.93	JSCSC
Gladwin, Michael David, BSc	LT(CC)	X	ATC	01.01.01	OCEAN
Glancy, James Alexander	2LT(IC)	-		01.09.01	CTCRM LYMPSTONE
Glass, Jonathon Eric, BSc	LT CDR(FTC)	X		01.09.94	MWS COLLINGWOOD
Glendinning, Andreana Sarah	LT(SC(MD)	Q		12.01.01	MDHU DERRIFORD
Glendinning, Christopher James Alexander	LT(IC)	X		01.05.03	ALBION
Glennie, Andrew Michael Gordon, BSc, CEng, MIMarEST, psc(j)	CDR(FTC)	E	ME	31.12.00	OCEAN
Glennie, Brian William, MBA	LT CDR(FTC)	E	WE	01.10.99	ILLUSTRIOUS
Goble, Ian John	LT CDR(FTC)	E	WE	01.10.95	COS 2SL/CNH
Goddard, David Jonathan Sinclair, MBE, BSc, AFRIN, pce	LT CDR(FTC)	X	PWO(N)	01.10.87	MWS COLLINGWOOD
Goddard, David Simon, BA	LT(IC)	S		01.05.04	VIGILANT(STBD)
Goddard, Ian Aleksis, BSc	LT(IC)	X		16.11.01	YORK
Goddard, Ian Kenneth, OBE, pce, psc	CAPT(FTC)	X	PWO(U)	31.12.97	SULTAN AIB
Goddard, Paul	LT(IC)	E	WESM	01.05.02	VIGILANT(STBD)
Godfrey, Kim Richard, BSc, pce	LT CDR(FTC)	X	MCD	01.09.93	SDG PLYMOUTH
Godfrey, Simeon David William, SM(n), SM	LT(FTC)	X	SM	01.04.01	SCEPTRE
Godley, David John	LT(CC)	E	WE	01.01.02	MWS COLLINGWOOD
Godwin, Christopher Anthony, pcea	LT CDR(FTC)	X	P	01.02.99	814 SQN
Gokhale, Stephen George, MB, CHB, BSc	SURG LT(SCC)	-		04.08.04	CTCRM
Gold, John William	LT CDR(FTC)	X	EW	01.10.03	SCU SHORE
Golden, Charles Alexander	SLT(IC)	E	ME	01.09.01	SOUTHAMPTON
Golden, Dominic St Clair	LT CDR(FTC)	X	FC	01.06.99	MWS COLLINGWOOD
Goldman, Paul Henry Louis, BEng, MSc, CEng, MIEE	LT CDR(FTC)	E	WE	01.04.99	FLEET HQ PORTS 2
Goldsmith, Darran, pcea	LT CDR(FTC)	X	O	01.10.99	820 SQN
Goldsmith, David Thomas, BEng, MSc, CEng	LT CDR(FTC)	E	WE	01.01.02	NORTHUMBERLAND
Goldsmith, Simon Victor William, BSc, pce	LT CDR(FTC)	X	PWO(C)	01.05.95	FOST NWD (JMOTS)
Goldstone, Richard Samuel, BA, n	LT CDR(FTC)	X	PWO(A)	01.08.02	MONTROSE
Goldsworthy, Elaine Tania	LT CDR(FTC)	S		01.10.04	MONTROSE
Goldsworthy, Peter Jarvis, BEng (Barrister)	LT CDR(FTC)	S	BAR	01.09.01	COS 2SL/CNH
Goldthorpe, Michael, MCIPD	CDR(FTC)	S		30.06.05	NAVSEC
Gomm, Kevin, BSc, pce, pce(sm)	LT CDR(FTC)	X	SM	01.06.91	FOST DSTF
Gooch, Michael David, BEng	LT(IC)	E	MESM	01.09.02	TRENCHANT
Goodacre, Ian Royston, pce	LT CDR(FTC)	X	PWO(U)	01.05.98	CORNWALL
Goodall, David Charles, pce, pcea, psc	CAPT(FTC)	X	P	31.12.98	NATO MEWSG VL
Goodall, Joanne Claire, BA	LT(IC)	E	TM	01.05.00	FWO DEVPT SEA
Goodall, Michael Antony, BEng, MSc	LT(FTC)	E	ME	01.05.98	DLO BRISTOL
Goodall, Simon Richard James, CBE, BA, psc(m), MSc (DG T&E OCT 02)	RADM	-	TM	03.10.02	MOD (LONDON)

Name	Rank	Branch	Spec	Seniority	Where Serving
Goode, Alun Nicholas	LT CDR(FTC)	X	PWO(A)	01.09.99	PJHQ
Goodenough, Raegan Elizabeth	SLT(IC)	E	ME	01.09.02	BULWARK
Goodenough, Robert Henry, BEng	LT(FTC)	E	MESM	01.09.02	TURBULENT
Gooding, David Christopher	SLT(IC)	X		01.01.04	COTTESMORE
Goodings, George James	LT CDR(FTC)	E	MESM	01.10.96	NEPTUNE BNSL
Goodman, Andrew Theodore, BSc, pce, n	LT CDR(FTC)	X	PWO(U)	01.03.98	MONTROSE
Goodman, David Frederick, SM(n), SM	LT(FTC)	X	SM	09.05.01	VIGILANT(STBD)
Goodman, William	2LT(IC)	-		01.08.03	CTCRM LYMPSTONE
Goodridge, Terence James	MAJ(FTC)	-	SO(LE)	01.10.02	RM BICKLEIGH
Goodrum, Simon Edward (Act Lt Cdr)	LT(FTC)	MS		19.09.99	DMSTC
Goodsell, Christopher David, MNI, pce, pce(sm)	LT CDR(FTC)	X	SM	01.02.99	LEEDS CASTLE
Goodsell, David Lee	LT(IC)	E	WE	01.01.03	DLO BRISTOL
Goodship, Joanna Sophie, BEng, AMIMechE	LT(CC)	E	ME	01.07.99	SULTAN
Goodship, Mark Thomas, BEng	LT(FTC)	E	ME	01.01.98	MOD (BATH)
Goodwin, David Robert, pce	CDR(FTC)	X	PWO(U)	31.12.93	2SL/CNH FOTR
Goodwin, Thomas	CHAPLAIN	SF		05.05.02	NEPTUNE 2SL/CNH
Goosen, Richard Davidson	LT(IC)	X		01.05.04	LANCASTER
Gordon, Andrew Jon	SLT(IC)	E	ME	01.09.01	MONTROSE
Gordon, David, BSc, psc	CDR(FTC)	E	TM	30.06.01	NTE(TTD)
Gordon, David	LT(IC)	E	AE	01.05.04	RNAS YEOVILTON
Gordon, David Iain, BSc	LT(CC)	X	H2	01.05.01	NELSON
Gordon, Duncan Alexander, MB, CHB	SURG LT(SC(MD)	-		06.08.03	CFLT MED(SEA)
Gordon, John	LT(IC)	X	C	01.05.03	FLEET CIS PORTS
Gordon, Neil Leslie, BSc	LT CDR(CC)	E	ME	01.11.04	DNR PRES TEAMS
Gordon, Robert Stewart	CAPT RM(CC)	-	C	01.04.03	UKLFCSG RM
Gordon, Stuart Ross, MA, pce, pcea, psc	CDR(FTC)	X	P	30.06.02	RN GIBRALTAR
Gorman, Darren Ashley, BSc	LT(IC)	X	P	01.09.02	845 SQN
Gorman, Glenn Kieran	LT(IC)	X		15.01.04	ATHERSTONE
Goscomb, Paul Andrew, BA	LT(IC)	S		01.01.04	801 SQN
Gosden, Daniel Richard	LT(FTC)	E	ME	01.08.04	SULTAN
Gosden, Stephen Richard, MSc, CEng, FIMarEST, psc	CAPT(FTC)	E	ME	30.06.02	SA BERLIN
Gosling, Darren John, MHCIMA, AMIAM	LT(CC)	S		01.04.01	INVINCIBLE
Gosney, Christopher	CAPT RM(FTC)	-	SO(LE)	01.01.99	NP IRAQ
Goss, Jonathan Renton Charles	2LT(IC)	-		01.09.00	42 CDO RM
Gothard, Andrew Mark, BEng	LT(FTC)	E	ME	01.11.96	DUMBARTON CASTLE
Gotke, Christopher Torben, BEng	LT(FTC)	X	P	16.01.94	LOAN JTEG BSC DN
Gott, Stephen Bruce	LT(IC)	S		01.05.03	MWS COLLINGWOOD
Goudge, Simon David Philip, BA	LT CDR(FTC)	S		01.04.02	MOD (BATH)
Gough, Martyn John	CHAPLAIN	CE		01.09.98	RNAS CULDROSE
Gough, Steven Roy	LT CDR(FTC)	X		01.10.01	CAMBRIA
Gould, Amelia Alice, MEng, CEng, MIEE	LT(FTC)	E	WE	01.10.00	DLO BRISTOL
Gould, Ian	LT(IC)	E	AE	01.05.03	CTS
Gould, James Davin	LT(FTC)	X	PWO(N)	01.10.98	MWS COLLINGWOOD
Goulder, Jonathan David, BEng, n	LT(CC)	X		01.11.97	FOST MPV SEA
Goulding, Jonathan Paul, BA, ACMI, pce, n	LT CDR(FTC)	X	PWO(N)	01.03.03	FOST MPV SEA
Gourlay, James Stewart, BSc, psc (Act Capt)	CDR(FTC)	E	AE	30.06.96	AFPAA JPA
Govan, Richard Thomas, OBE, pce, psc	CDR(FTC)	X	PWO(U)	30.06.92	COS 2SL/CNH
Goward, Rachel Jane, BSc, PGCE	LT(IC)	E	TM	01.05.98	DCTS PORTS
Gower, John Howard James, OBE, BSc, MNI, pce, pce(sm)	CAPT(FTC)	X	SM(N)	31.12.99	BDS WASHINGTON
Grace, Nicholas John, pdm (Act Maj)	CAPT RM(FTC)	BS		01.01.01	HQ BAND SERVICE
Grace, Trevor Paul	LT CDR(FTC)	E	WE	01.10.98	DLO BRISTOL
Grafton, Martin Nicholas, BSc, CEng, MIMechE, MINucE	CDR(FTC)	E	MESM	31.12.96	NEPTUNE BNSL
Graham, Alastair Neil Spencer, MVO, BSc, AMIEE	LT CDR(FTC)	E	WESM	01.08.01	VENGEANCE(STBD)
Graham, David Edward, MBE, pce	LT CDR(FTC)	X	AAWO	01.10.91	FLEET HQ PORTS 2
Graham, David Winston Stuart, BEng, MA, CEng, MIMechE, psc(j)	CDR(FTC)	E	MESM	30.06.03	2SL/CNH
Graham, Gordon Russell, BSc, psc(m)	CDR(FTC)	E	WE	30.06.97	MOD (LONDON)
Graham, Ian Edmund, pce, psc(j), n	CDR(FTC)	X	PWO(A)	30.06.04	MARLBOROUGH
Graham, Mark Alexander, pcea	LT CDR(FTC)	X	O	01.10.01	LOAN OTHER SVCE
Graham, Penelope Jane, BA	LT CDR(FTC)	W	S	22.10.99	JSU NORTHWOOD
Grainge, Christopher Leonard, MB, BSc, BS, MRCP	SURG LTCDR(MC(MD)	-		04.08.04	NELSON (PAY)
Grange, Alan Benjamin	LT(IC)	X		27.06.03	RALEIGH
Grant, Alan Kenneth, OBE, MA, pcea, pce	CDR(FTC)	X	O	30.06.93	DRAKE NBC/DBUS
Grant, David James	LT CDR(FTC)	E	MESM	01.10.03	SCEPTRE

Name	Rank	Branch	Spec	Seniority	Where Serving
Grant, Ian William, MA, psc(m), psc(j)	LT COL(FTC)	-	LC	30.06.91	FLEET HQ PORTS 2
Grant, Richard	LT(IC)	E	ME	01.07.04	GRAFTON
Grant, Wayne Graham, BEng	LT(FTC)	E	AE	01.06.00	HARRIER IPT
Grantham, Guy James, BA	LT(IC)	E	IS U/T	01.11.00	SULTAN
Grantham, Stephen Mark, MSc, MA, CEng, MIMechE, MCGI, psc(j)	CDR(FTC)	E	MESM	30.06.01	MOD (LONDON)
Graves, Michael Edward Linsan, BSc	CDRE(FTC)	E	WESM	11.11.03	MOD (BATH)
Gray, Anthony James, MA, CEng, MRAeS, psc(j)	CDR(FTC)	E	AE	31.12.98	MERLIN IPT
Gray, Anthony John, MSc, CEng, MIMechE, psc(j)	CDR(FTC)	E	MESM	30.06.02	NP BRISTOL
Gray, David Kingston, BEng, MIEE	LT CDR(FTC)	E	WE	01.04.95	EXCHANGE CANADA
Gray, Emma Jane, BA	LT(CC)	S		01.09.01	NP IRAQ
Gray, James Alan, MA	MAJ(FTC)	-		01.05.03	JSCSC
Gray, James Michael, MEng	LT(IC)	E	AE U/T	01.09.03	815 SQN HQ
Gray, James Nelson Stephen	LT(CC)	X	O	01.04.95	702 SQN HERON
Gray, John Allan, BEng, pce	LT CDR(FTC)	X	AAWO	01.06.00	FOST SEA
Gray, John Arthur, BSc, SM(n)	LT(CC)	X	SM	01.03.98	VIGILANT(PORT)
Gray, Karl Daniel, BSc	CAPT RM(FTC)	-	C	01.05.00	40 CDO RM
Gray, Mark Nicholas, MBE, MA, osc(us)	LT COL(FTC)	-		30.06.02	PJHQ
Gray, Michael John Henry	LT(FTC)	X	AV	09.01.01	CHFHQ
Gray, Nathan John, BEng	LT(CC)	X	P	01.12.99	LOAN OTHER SVCE
Gray, Oliver William John	2LT(IC)	-		01.08.01	CTCRM LYMPSTONE
Gray, Paul Reginald	LT CDR(FTC)	X	P	01.10.02	814 SQN
Gray, Richard, MSc, PGDIPAN, adp	LT CDR(FTC)	E	IS	01.03.99	PJHQ
Gray, Richard Laurence	LT(IC)	X		01.09.03	CAMPBELTOWN
Gray, Robert Stanley, BSc (Barrister)	CDR(FTC)	S	BAR	31.12.99	NAVSEC
Gray, Samuel Dennis	LT(IC)	X		01.08.04	MWS COLLINGWOOD
Gray, Simon Anthony Neatham, BSc	CAPT RM(CC)	-	C	01.09.02	42 CDO RM
Gray, Timothy	CAPT RM(IC)	-	P	01.07.04	727 NAS
Gray, Yvonne Michelle, BEd	LT CDR(FTC)	X	PWO(U)	01.02.03	WESTMINSTER
Grayson, Stephen	LT(IC)	S	SM	01.07.04	TRENCHANT
Grears, Jonathan, MSc	LT CDR(FTC)	E	IS	01.09.99	RNEAWC
Greatwood, Ian Mark, BEng, MSc	LT CDR(FTC)	E	WESM	01.01.99	TORPEDO IPT
Greaves, Martin Richard	LT(IC)	X	SM	01.08.04	SCEPTRE
Greaves, Timoth Michal	SLT(IC)	X		01.09.03	RAF SHAWBURY
Greedus, David Arthur, MA, psc(j)	LT COL(FTC)	-	SO(LE)	30.06.05	FLEET HQ PORTS 2
Green, Adam James, MEng	LT(IC)	X		01.12.04	ARGYLL
Green, Adrian Richard, MSc, CEng, MIMechE, MCGI	CDR(FTC)	E	MESM	31.12.98	FLEET HQ PORTS 2
Green, Andrew John, MA, psc(j)	LT CDR(FTC)	E	TMSM	01.05.98	2SL/CNH FOTR
Green, Andrew Michael, BSc	LT CDR(FTC)	E	ME	01.07.01	SULTAN
Green, David Patrick Savage, BEng, MA, MSc, CEng, MIEE, psc(j)	CDR(FTC)	E	WESM	30.06.03	MOD (LONDON)
Green, David Paul, SM	LT CDR(FTC)	X	SM	13.08.93	NAVSEC
Green, Gareth Mark, BA, psc(j)	MAJ(FTC)	-		01.09.98	FLEET HQ PORTS 2
Green, Gary Edward, psc(j)	MAJ(FTC)	-	SO(LE)	01.10.01	MOD (LONDON)
Green, Ian Andrew	LT(FTC)	X	ATC	01.04.97	RNAS YEOVILTON
Green, Janette Lesley	LT CDR(FTC)	W	AV	01.10.03	DISC
Green, Jayne Hannah, BSc	LT(CC)	X	O	01.09.99	815 FLT 210
Green, John	CHAPLAIN	CE		04.06.91	MWS COLLINGWOOD
Green, John Anthony, BSc, CEng, MIEE, AMInstP, CDipAF, rcds, jsdc	CAPT(FTC)	E	WESM	31.12.97	FLEET CIS PORTS
Green, Jonathan, MBA	LT CDR(FTC)	X		01.06.98	MOD (LONDON)
Green, Jonathan	LT(CC)	X	P	16.11.02	849 SQN HQ
Green, Laura, BSc	LT(IC)	X	O	01.09.02	849 SQN B FLT
Green, Leslie David	LT(IC)	E	MESM	01.05.03	FOST SM SEA
Green, Michael Gerald Hamilton, MA, psc(j)	LT COL(FTC)	-	LC	30.06.04	539 ASSLT SQN RM
Green, Michael Ronald	MAJ(FTC)	-	SO(LE)	01.10.99	RMB STONEHOUSE
Green, Patrick George	LT(IC)	MS		01.10.02	2SL/CNH
Green, Peter James, pce(sm), SM	CDR(FTC)	X	SM	30.06.05	MWS COLLINGWOOD
Green, Roger Richard, BA	LT(IC)	E	TM	08.01.00	CTCRM
Green, Stephen Noel, BSc, MA, CEng, MIEE, psc(j)	CDR(FTC)	E	WE	31.12.98	OCEAN
Green, Timothy Cooper, BA, SM(n), SM	LT CDR(FTC)	X	PWO(U)	01.10.01	PORTLAND
Green, Timothy John, pce(sm), psc(a)	CDR(FTC)	X	SM	31.12.98	JDCC
Green, William	LT(IC)	E	WESM	01.07.04	RALEIGH
Greenaway, Nicholas Mark, pce	LT CDR(FTC)	X	AAWO	01.08.95	FLEET HQ PORTS 2
Greenberg, Neil ,BM, BSc, Dip OM, MRCPsych, MMedSci	SURG LTCDR(FCC)	-		01.09.99	2SL/CNH
Greene, Michael John, BEd, MSc, psc	CDR(FTC)	E	TM	31.12.99	LOAN OMAN

Name	Rank	Branch	Spec	Seniority	Where Serving
Greener, Carl, MEng, MSc, CEng, MIEE	LT CDR(FTC)	E	WE	01.09.99	ST ALBANS
Greenhill, Matthew Charles, BA	LT(IC)	X		01.05.04	MWS COLLINGWOOD
Greenland, Michael Richard, pce, pcea	LT CDR(FTC)	X	P	16.04.95	MOD (LONDON)
Greenlees, Iain Wallace, I, W, GREENLESS, OBE, BSc, pce	CAPT(FTC)	X	PWO(A)	30.06.05	NBC PORTSMOUTH
Greenway, Stephen Anthony, BEng, CEng, MIMarEST, MIMechE, CDipAFLT	CDR(FTC)	E	ME	01.02.00	CAPT MCTA
Greenwood, Antony Wyn, BSc	LT(CC)	X	HM	01.02.99	ECHO
Greenwood, Michael John, BA	LT CDR(FTC)	X	METOC	01.09.91	OCLC ROSYTH
Greenwood, Peter, pce	CDR(FTC)	X	MCD	30.06.01	BDS WASHINGTON
Greenwood, Peter Adam	LT(CC)	X	P	16.10.99	820 SQN
Greenwood, Stephen, BSc, CEng, MRAeS, MDA	CDR(FTC)	E	AE	31.12.97	FLEET HQ PORTS
Greenwood, Stephen James, BA	SLT(IC)	X		01.05.02	BRECON
Gregan, David Carl, psc	CDR(FTC)	X	H CH	30.06.92	NS OBERAMMERGAU
Gregory, Alastair Stuart, BEng, MSc, CEng, MIMarEST, MRINA	LT CDR(FTC)	E	ME	01.06.00	DLO BRISTOL
Gregory, Anthony Edward, MB, CHB	SURG LT(SC(MD)	-		01.09.02	RH HASLAR
Greig, Judith Anne, BEng	LT(IC)	E	TM	01.11.98	NELSON
Grenfell-Shaw, Mark Christopher, MA, MSc, CEng, MIEE	CDR(FTC)	E	WESM	30.06.05	DLO BRISTOL
Grennan, Eamonn Fergal, BEng, MSc (Act Lt Cdr)	LT(CC)	E	AE	01.05.98	COS 2SL/CNH
Grey, Christopher Sidney, BSc	LT(CC)	X	O	01.01.02	815 FLT 218
Grey, Edward John William, BA	LT(IC)	E	TM	03.04.99	1 ASSAULT GP RM
Grice, Matthew Gordon, BEng	LT(IC)	E	AE	01.09.03	847 SQN
Grierson, Andrew Douglas, MEng	LT(IC)	E	TM U/T	01.11.01	SULTAN
Grieve, Lynne Helen, BEng	LT CDR(FTC)	X		01.10.04	MWS COLLINGWOOD
Grieve, Steven Harry, BSc, MA, CEng, MRAeS, psc	CDR(FTC)	E	AE	30.06.01	CV(F) IPT
Griffen, David John, BSc	LT(IC)	X		01.04.00	MWS COLLINGWOOD
Griffin, Niall Robert, pcea	LT CDR(FTC)	X	P	01.10.01	846 SQN
Griffin, Peter John	LT(FTC)	X	ATC	19.09.00	RNAS CULDROSE
Griffin, Stephen	LT(IC)	X	AV	01.09.01	INVINCIBLE
Griffiths, Alan Richard	LT(FTC)	E	WE	09.06.89	MWS COLLINGWOOD
Griffiths, Andrew John, MSc, psc(j)	LT CDR(FTC)	E	TM	26.07.94	MWS COLLINGWOOD
Griffiths, Anthony	LT CDR(FTC)	X	MW	01.10.97	MOD (LONDON)
Griffiths, Christopher John James	LT(CC)	E	ME	29.04.01	1 ASSAULT GP RM
Griffiths, Colin Stuart Henry, BSc	LT(CC)	X	P	01.12.99	846 SQN
Griffiths, David Thomas, BSc, pce	LT CDR(FTC)	X	MCD	01.04.90	MOD (LONDON)
Griffiths, Francis Mark	SLT(UCE)(IC)	E	ME U/T	01.09.03	DARTMOUTH BRNC
Griffiths, Glyn	LT(IC)	E	WESM	01.01.03	RALEIGH
Griffiths, Michael Owen John	LT CDR(FTC)	X	PWO(U)	16.01.00	EXCHANGE NLANDS
Griffiths, Neil, BA	LT(CC)	X	MW	01.09.98	RAMSEY
Griffiths, Nicholas Alan (Act Maj)	CAPT RM(FTC)	-		01.05.00	42 CDO RM
Griffiths, Nigel Colin	LT(IC)	E	WE	01.01.03	DLO BRISTOL
Griffiths, Nigel Mills, QGM	LT(IC)	X	C	01.01.04	DCSA GIBRALTAR
Griffiths, Richard Hywel, SM(n), SM	LT CDR(FTC)	X	SM	01.06.04	VENGEANCE(PORT)
Grigg, Shelton Kent	LT(IC)	S	(W)	08.01.01	RALEIGH
Grimley, Daemon Marcus John, pce, pce(sm)	LT CDR(FTC)	X	SM	01.11.89	FOSNNI
Grimley, Timothy Paul, BSc	SLT(IC)	S		01.04.03	ALBION
Grimshaw, Ernest	CHAPLAIN	SF		02.05.00	RNAS CULDROSE
Grindel, David John Stuart, BEd, MSc, psc(j)	CDR(FTC)	E	TM	30.06.02	MWS COLLINGWOOD
Grindon, Matthew Guy, BEng	LT CDR(FTC)	X	P	01.10.00	848 SQN HERON
Grinnell, Jason, BSc, HND	LT(IC)	E	IS	01.10.01	AFPAA JPA
Gritt, Louisa Ann, BSc	LT CDR(FTC)	X	H1	17.12.01	FLEET HQ PORTS 2
Grixoni, Martin Reynold Roberto	MAJ(FTC)	-		01.09.90	1 ASSLT GP RM
Grocott, Peter Clark	LT CDR(FTC)	S	(W)	01.10.00	AFPAA(CENTURION)
Groom, Ian Stuart, MBE, BEng, CEng, FIMarEST, MIMarEST	LT CDR(FTC)	E	ME	01.03.99	JSCSC
Groom, Mark Richard, MB, ChB, DipAvMed, MRAeS, MFOM, MRCGP, AFOM, aws	SURG CDR(FCC)	-	(CO/M)	30.06.00	JSCSC
Grove, Jeremy John	LT(IC)	X	H2	01.07.04	ROEBUCK
Groves, Christopher Keith, pce(sm), SM(n)	CDR(FTC)	X	SM	30.06.04	TORBAY
Groves, Richard, BEng	LT(IC)	E	MESM	01.09.04	SULTAN
Gubbins, Victor Robert, MBE, BSc, CEng, MIMarEST, fsc	CDR(FTC)	E	ME	31.12.93	DRAKE CBS
Gubby, Adrian William, BEng	LT(FTC)	E	WE	01.05.02	CINCFLEET FIMU
Guild, Ian William	SLT(IC)	E	WE U/T	01.09.03	INVINCIBLE
Guild, Nigel Charles Forbes, CB, BA, PhD, FIEE, MIMA, jsdc (DIRECTOR GENERAL CAPABILITY (CS) DEC 03)	RADM	-	WE	06.01.00	MOD (LONDON)
Guilfoyle, Victoria Marion	LT(CC)	S		15.05.01	OCEAN

Name	Rank	Branch	Spec	Seniority	Where Serving
Guiver, Paul, BEM	LT(FTC)	X	MCD	03.04.97	EXCHANGE USA
Gullett, Humphrey Richard, MA	LT CDR(FTC)	S	SM	01.10.03	YORK
Gulley, Trevor James, MSc, CEng, MCGI	CDR(FTC)	E	ME	30.06.98	RALEIGH
Gulliver, Jeffrey William, BEng	LT(IC)	X		01.09.02	LOAN NEW ZEALAND
Gunn, William John Simpson, BSc, PGDip	LT CDR(FTC)	X	METOC	01.11.94	FOST SEA
Gunter, John Jeffrey	LT(IC)	X		01.07.04	MWS COLLINGWOOD
Gunther, Paul Thomas	LT CDR(FTC)	E	WESM	01.10.99	NAVSEC
Gurmin, Stephen John Albert, pce	CDR(FTC)	X	PWO(C)	30.06.03	MOD (LONDON)
Gurr, Andrew William George, pce	LT CDR(FTC)	X	AAWO	01.05.00	PJHQ
Gutteridge, Jeffery	LT CDR(FTC)	E	WE	01.10.02	COS 2SL/CNH
Guy, Charles Richard, BA, n	LT(FTC)	X	PWO(A)	01.03.98	SOMERSET
Guy, Frances Louisa	SLT(IC)	X		01.01.04	LEEDS CASTLE
Guy, Mark Andrew, MBE, BEng, MSc, MIEE	LT CDR(FTC)	E	WE	13.11.98	FWO DEVPT SEA
Guy, Terry John, MIExpE, psc	CDR(FTC)	E	WESM	30.06.93	MOD (BATH)
Guy, Thomas Justin, pce, psc(j), n	CDR(FTC)	X	PWO(U)	30.06.05	NORTHUMBERLAND
Guyer, Simon Thomas Glode, psc(m)	LT COL(FTC)	-	LC	30.06.95	LOAN ABU DHABI
Guyver, Paul Michael, MB, BS	SURG LT(MC(MD)	-		04.08.00	MDHU DERRIFORD
Gwatkin, Nicholas John	LT(CC)	X	MCD	29.04.01	HURWORTH
Gwilliam, Elizabeth Kate, BSc	LT(IC)	E		01.07.02	DRAKE COB(CNH)
Gwillim, Vivian George	MAJ(FTC)	-	ML2@	01.09.93	DEF NBC CENTRE

H

Name	Rank	Branch	Spec	Seniority	Where Serving
Hackland, Andrew Stuart	LT(IC)	X	ATCU/T	01.04.03	RNAS YEOVILTON
Hackman, James David, BA	LT(IC)	S		01.05.04	NEPTUNE DLO
Haddon, Richard William James, MB, BS, FRCA, MRAeS, MRCGP, MRCS, LRCP, AFOM, DipAvMed	SURG CDR(FCC)	-	GMPP	01.04.03	MDH
Haddow, Fraser, psc	COL(FTC)	-	MLDR	30.06.00	UKMILREP BRUSS
Haddow, Timothy Rowat, BEng	LT CDR(FTC)	E	PWO(C)	01.03.05	CV(F) IPT
Hadfield, David, MSc, CEng, MIMarEST	CDR(FTC)	E	MESM	30.06.99	SULTAN
Hadland, Giles Vincent	LT(CC)	X		01.10.00	NP IRAQ
Hadley, Clive	SLT(IC)	E	WESM	01.01.04	MWS COLLINGWOOD
Haggard, Amanda, BA	LT(FTC)	S		01.03.98	2SL/CNH FOTR
Hagger, Michael John, BSc	SLT(IC)	X		01.09.02	ENTERPRISE
Haggerty, Shaun Michael, BEng	LT(FTC)	E	AE	01.10.97	MERLIN IPT
Haggo, Jamie Robert, BSc	LT(CC)	X	P	16.04.98	RNAS YEOVILTON
Haigh, Alastair James, BSc	LT CDR(FTC)	X	P	01.10.03	815 FLT 203
Haigh, Julian Joseph, BA	LT(FTC)	S	SM	01.02.98	FLEET HQ PORTS
Hailstone, Jonathan Henry Steven, BA, MDA, pce, pcea, psc(m)	LT CDR(FTC)	X	O	16.05.94	FLEET HQ PORTS 2
Haines, Paul Roger	CDR(FTC)	E	WE	30.06.01	MOD (LONDON)
Haines, Russell James	LT(CC)	S		01.02.99	OCLC ROSYTH
Hains, Justin, BSc	LT CDR(FTC)	X	MCD	01.04.04	SDG PORTSMOUTH
Hairsine, William, BA	SLT(IC)	X		01.07.02	BANGOR
Hale, Alexandra	SURG SLT(SCC)	-		20.11.04	DARTMOUTH BRNC
Hale, Amanda, BSc	LT(IC)	X	O U/T	01.09.00	NEPTUNE 2SL/CNH
Hale, Bradley William, BEng, IEng, MIPlantE	LT(IC)	E	ME	01.09.03	CTCRM
Hale, John Nathan, BSc	MAJ(FTC)	-	LC	27.04.02	539 ASSLT SQN RM
Hale, Stuart Dennis	SLT(SC(MD)	Q		01.04.01	RH HASLAR
Haley, Christopher	LT(IC)	X	EW	13.08.04	FOSNNI
Haley, Colin William, MA, pce, psc(a)	CDR(FTC)	X	AAWO	30.06.99	MOD (LONDON)
Haley, Timothy John, MSc, CEng, FIMarEST	CDR(FTC)	E	ME	30.06.96	FOST SEA
Hall, Alexander Peter, BSc, MDA, pce, pcea, ARCS	LT CDR(FTC)	X	O	01.03.93	LOAN OTHER SVCE
Hall, Andrew Jeremy, BSc	LT CDR(FTC)	E	AE	01.08.98	MOD (BATH)
Hall, Barry James, BEng, MAPM, MSc, CEng, MIMechE	LT CDR(FTC)	E	MESM	01.11.98	FLEET HQ PORTS
Hall, Christopher John	LT(CC)	X		01.12.00	NP IRAQ
Hall, Christopher Langford, BEng, AMIMechE	LT(IC)	E	MESM	01.09.02	SPARTAN
Hall, Christopher Mark Ian	CAPT RM(CC)	-		01.04.01	FLEET AV SUPPORT
Hall, Darren	LT(FTC)	X	P	16.08.96	845 SQN
Hall, David James, BDS, MSc, MGDS RCSEd	SGCDR(D)(FCC)	-		31.12.99	DRAKE COB(CNH)
Hall, David William, BSc, gdas	LT CDR(FTC)	X	O	01.10.90	771 SQN
Hall, Derek Alexander	LT CDR(FTC)	S	(W)	01.10.00	MWS COLLINGWOOD
Hall, Edward Charles Malet	2LT(IC)	-		01.09.00	42 CDO RM
Hall, Elizabeth Clair, BSc, MBA, PGCE	CDR(FTC)	S		30.06.02	COS 2SL/CNH

Name	Rank	Branch	Spec	Seniority	Where Serving
Hall, Graham William Russell, BSc	LT(IC)	X	H2	01.01.03	FWO DEVPT SEA
Hall, James Edward, BSc	LT(IC)	X	O	01.05.03	849 SQN A FLT
Hall, Kilian John Darwin, BSc	LT(IC)	X	FC	01.05.01	RNAS YEOVILTON
Hall, Richard Mark, MA, psc	MAJ(FTC)	-		01.09.90	CTCRM
Hall, Robert Langford, BSc, pce, CEng, MIEE	CDR(FTC)	X	PWO(C)	30.06.03	PJHQ
Hall, Ryan S	SLT(IC)	X		01.07.04	ECHO
Hall, Sasha Louise	LT(IC)	X		01.05.02	FOSNNI
Hall, Simon Jeremy, OBE, MSc, psc	LT COL(FTC)	-	MLDR	31.12.99	MOD (LONDON)
Hall, Steven John, BA	SLT(IC)	X		01.07.02	PEMBROKE
Hallam, Stuart Peter, BA	CHAPLAIN	CE		05.05.02	CTCRM
Hallett, Daniel John, BA	LT(IC)	E	TM U/T	01.11.02	SUTHERLAND
Hallett, Simon John, BA	LT CDR(FTC)	S		01.03.01	COMAMPHIBFOR
Halliday, David Alistair, BA, jsdc, pce	CAPT(FTC)	X	AAWO	30.06.00	MOD (LONDON)
Halliwell, David Colin, BEng, MSc, psc(j)	CDR(FTC)	E	MESM	30.06.04	FLEET HQ NWD
Halls, Bernard Charles, MSc, CEng, MIExpE, MIIE (Act Lt Cdr)	LT(FTC)	E	WE	18.10.85	DOSG BRISTOL
Hally, Philip John, BSc	LT CDR(FTC)	S	CMA	01.11.00	MOD (LONDON)
Halpin, Andrew (Act Surg Lt)	SURG SLT(SCC)	-		12.07.04	DARTMOUTH BRNC
Halsey, Karen Elizabeth, BSc	LT(CC)	S		01.05.00	UKMARBATSTAFF
Halsted, Benjamin Erik, MA (Act Maj)	CAPT RM(IC)	-		01.09.01	CTCRM
Halton, Paul Vincent, pce, pce(sm)	CDR(FTC)	X	SM	30.06.04	SPARTAN
Hamblin, Paul Anthony	SLT(IC)	X		01.02.03	NOTTINGHAM
Hambly, Brian John, BEng, CEng, MIEE	LT(FTC)	E	WESM	01.09.95	MOD DIS SEA
Hamiduddin, Iqbal, BA	LT(IC)	X	SM	01.05.02	SPARTAN
Hamilton, Graham Douglas, MSc	LT(CC)	E	AE	29.04.01	MERLIN IPT
Hamilton, Gregory Robert	LT CDR(FTC)	X		01.10.94	PJHQ
Hamilton, Mark Ian, BEng	LT(FTC)	E	ME	01.12.99	FWO PORTS SEA
Hamilton, Matthew Sean, BDS	SG LT(D)(SCC)	-		26.06.01	42 CDO RM
Hamilton, Richard Alexander, MSc, CEng, MBCS	LT CDR(FTC)	E	IS	01.10.93	CINCFLEET FIMU
Hamilton, Stuart John David	2LT(IC)	-		01.09.99	45 CDO RM
Hamilton, Susanna Mary, BEng	LT CDR(FTC)	E	ME	01.10.03	NORTHUMBERLAND
Hammett, Barry Keith, QHC, MA	DGNCS CE	CE		11.07.77	2SL/CNH
(DIRECTOR GENERAL NAVAL CHAPLAINCY SERVICE. FEB 05)					
Hammock, Edward Richard Frederick, BEng	SLT(IC)	E		01.09.02	TRAFALGAR
Hammock, Simon George, BEng	LT(CC)	X	P	16.08.98	846 SQN
Hammon, Mark Alexander, BSc	LT(CC)	X		01.10.99	EXETER
Hammond, Christopher Robert, BA	SLT(IC)	S		01.01.04	DARTMOUTH BRNC
Hammond, David Evan, BSc	MAJ(FTC)	-		01.09.02	2SL/CNH
Hammond, Mark Christopher	MAJ(FTC)	-	P	01.05.00	LOAN OTHER SVCE
Hammond, Meirion Mark Vivian, BSc	LT(CC)	X	P	01.04.00	846 SQN
Hammond, Paul Adrian, BEng, MSc, FIEE, MIEE, gw	CDR(FTC)	E	AE	31.12.99	RNAS CULDROSE
Hammond, Paul John, n	LT CDR(FTC)	X	PWO(U)	01.05.04	MONTROSE
Hamp, Colin John, BSc, pce, pcea, psc	CAPT(FTC)	X	O	30.06.04	MOD (LONDON)
Hampshire, Tony	LT(CC)	X	MCD	01.10.00	QUORN
Hampson, Alexander Glendinning	LT(IC)	X		01.01.05	727 NAS
Hancock, Andrew Philip, pce, psc(j)	LT CDR(FTC)	X	PWO(U)	01.01.99	JHQSW MADRID
Hancock, James Henry, BA	LT(IC)	X		01.10.00	MOD (LONDON)
Hancock, Robert Thomas Alexander, BEng, MSc, MIEE	LT CDR(FTC)	E	WE	01.10.01	JES IPT
Hancock, Zena Marie Alexandra	LT(CC)	X		01.11.97	INVINCIBLE
Hancox, Jamie	SLT(IC)	X		01.09.03	MWS COLLINGWOOD
Hancox, Michael John, BEng, CEng, MIMarEST	LT CDR(FTC)	E	MESM	01.02.99	TURBULENT
Hand, Christopher John, MB, CHB, FRCS, FRCSTr&Orth	SURG CDR(FCC)	-	(CO/S)	30.06.03	RH HASLAR
Handley, Jonathan Mark, MA, jsdc, pce, psc(j)	CAPT(FTC)	X	PWO(U)	30.06.05	PJHQ
Handoll, Guy Nicholas George, MEng	LT(FTC)	E	MESM	01.09.02	TORBAY
Hands, Adrian Peter, pcea	LT CDR(FTC(A)	X	P	01.10.94	FLEET HQ PORTS
Hands, Anthony James, BDS	SGLTCDR(D)(MCC)	-		26.06.02	LOAN BRUNEI
Hands, Edward	2LT(IC)	-		01.08.01	CTCRM LYMPSTONE
Hankin, Robert Simon, MEng	SLT(IC)	E	WESM	01.11.02	RALEIGH
Hanks, Oliver Thomas	SLT(IC)	S		01.05.02	SUTHERLAND
Hannah, William Ferguson, MBE	MAJ(FTC)	-	SO(LE)	01.10.01	RMB STONEHOUSE
Hannam, Darrell Brett, BSc	LT(CC)	X	O	01.08.99	EXCHANGE RAF UK
Hannam, Samantha Jane, BA	LT(IC)	S		01.05.03	RNAS CULDROSE
Hannigan, Paul Francis, pcea	LT CDR(FTC)	X	P	01.10.01	845 SQN
Hanson, Mark Nicholas, BA	LT CDR(FTC)	S		01.10.02	FLEET HQ NWD

Name	Rank	Branch	Spec	Seniority	Where Serving
Hanson, Nicholas Anthony, BEng, CEng, MIEE, MIMarEST	LT CDR(FTC)	E	WE	01.06.98	EXCHANGE USA
Hanson, Steven Jon, BSc	LT(IC)	X		01.05.04	VENGEANCE(PORT)
Hanson, Sven Christopher, BSc	CAPT RM(CC)	-		01.05.01	1 ASSAULT GP RM
Harcombe, Andrew, BSc	LT(CC)	X	P	16.07.00	847 SQN
Harcourt, Robert James, BSc, PGCE, PGDip	LT CDR(FTC)	X	PWO(U)	01.01.00	MWS COLLINGWOOD
Hardacre, Paul Vincent, BSc, SM	LT CDR(FTC)	X	SM	01.06.94	FOST DSTF
Hardern, Simon Paul, MNI, pce, psc(j), MA	CDR(FTC)	X	PWO(U)	30.06.01	MOD (LONDON)
Hardie, Mark John, BA	CAPT RM(CC)	-		01.09.00	45 CDO RM
Hardiman, Nicholas Anthony, BEng, MSc	LT CDR(FTC)	E	MESM	01.05.03	TRENCHANT
Harding, Carl Sinclair, BEng, MBA	LT CDR(CC)	E	TM	01.09.04	MWS COLLINGWOOD
Harding, David Malcolm, BSc, MAPM, CEng	CDR(FTC)	E	AE	30.06.03	HARRIER IPT
Harding, David Victor, BEng	LT(IC)	E	WESM	01.09.02	VENGEANCE(STBD)
Harding, Ellen Louise	LT(IC)	S		12.11.02	NELSON
Harding, Emma (Act Surg Lt)	SURG SLT(SCC)	-		13.07.04	DARTMOUTH BRNC
Harding, Gary Alan, BEng, MIEE, psc	LT CDR(FTC)	E	WE	01.12.94	T45 IPT
Harding, Russell George, OBE, BSc, pce, pcea	CAPT(FTC)	X	O	30.06.03	MOD (LONDON)
Hardman, Mathew James, BSc	LT(FTC)	X		01.10.99	FLEET HQ PORTS
Hardwick, Mark John	LT(FTC)	S	SM	01.09.98	DPA BRISTOL
Hardy, Duncan Mark, psc(j)	MAJ(FTC)	-	C	24.04.02	FPGRM
Hardy, Gareth	SURG SLT(SCC)	-		01.07.03	DARTMOUTH BRNC
Hardy, Jonathon	SLT(IC)	X	ATCU/T	01.02.04	DARTMOUTH BRNC
Hardy, Lee Charles, pce	CDR(FTC)	X	AAWO	30.06.02	MOD (LONDON)
Hardy, Leslie Brian (Act Lt Cdr)	LT(FTC)	X	PWO(U)	16.12.94	FLEET HQ PORTS 2
Hardy, Robert John	LT(CC)	E	ME	29.04.01	SULTAN
Hardy-Hodgson, David Nicholas	LT(IC)	E	AE	01.07.04	800 NAS (GR7)
Hare, John Herbert, BA, PGDip	LT CDR(FTC)	X	METOC	01.09.97	RNAS YEOVILTON
Hare, Nigel James, pce	CDR(FTC)	X	PWO(N)	30.06.02	RNLO JTF4
Harford-Cross, Peter James, MA, SM(n), SM	LT(IC)	X	SM	01.02.00	FLEET HQ NWD
Hargreaves, Neale, MBE, MCGI, gdas	LT CDR(FTC)	X	O	01.10.97	849 SQN HQ
Harland, Nicholas Jonathan Godfrey, BSc, jsdc, pce, psc(j)	CDRE(FTC)	X	O	13.09.04	UKMILREP BRUSS
Harlow, Simon Richard	LT(FTC)	X	P	01.05.93	LOAN JTEG BSC DN
Harman, Michael John	CHAPLAIN	CE		20.09.79	RALEIGH
Harman, Stephen John, BSc	LT(CC)	S		01.12.01	SOVEREIGN
Harmer, Jason Neil Jonathon	LT CDR(FTC)	X	P	01.10.97	LOAN OMAN
Harper, Ian Lorimer	LT CDR(FTC)	X	AV	01.10.02	STG BRISTOL
Harper, James Andrew	LT CDR(FTC)	X	O	01.10.97	702 SQN HERON
Harper, Kevan James	SLT(IC)	X		01.05.03	LEDBURY
Harper, Philip Robert, BA, n	LT CDR(FTC)	X	PWO(U)	01.10.04	RICHMOND
Harradine, Paul Anthony, psc(j)	LT COL(FTC)	-	SO(LE)	30.06.02	CTCRM
Harrap, Nicholas Richard Edmund, OBE, MNI, jsdc, pce, pce(sm)	CAPT(FTC)	X	SM	30.06.04	FOST FAS SHORE
Harriman, Peter	LT(FTC)	X	C	26.04.99	FLEET CIS PORTS
Harrington, Jonathan Barratt Harley, BEng	LT CDR(FTC)	E	WE	01.10.03	MOD (LONDON)
Harrington, Lee, BEng	LT(FTC)	E	ME	01.03.98	JSSU CYPRUS
Harriott, Ceri Louise, BA	LT(IC)	S		01.05.04	ST ALBANS
Harris, Alastair Mark, BA	SLT(IC)	X		01.02.03	CARDIFF
Harris, Andrew Gordon, BEng, MAPM, MIEE	LT CDR(FTC)	E	WE	12.04.97	CV(F) IPT
Harris, Andrew Ian, MA, pce, pcea, psc(j)	CDR(FTC)	X	O	31.12.99	OCEAN
Harris, Carl Christian, BA	MAJ(FTC)	-		01.09.01	JSCSC
Harris, Hugh James Leonard	LT(IC)	X		01.05.05	MWS COLLINGWOOD
Harris, Keri John, BEng, pcea	CDR(FTC)	X	O	30.06.05	CAMPBELTOWN
Harris, Michael Trevor	LT CDR(FTC)	S	CA	01.10.99	EXCHANGE USA
Harris, Nicholas Henry Linton, MBE, pce, pce(sm), ocds(US) (NBC CLYDE MAY 03)	RADM	-	SM	13.05.03	FOSNNI
Harris, Philip Norman, OBE, MPhil, MNI, pce, psc	CDR(FTC)	X	O	31.12.85	NELSON
Harris, Richard Alun, BEng	LT(IC)	E	WE	01.09.04	IRON DUKE
Harris, Richard Paul, BA	LT CDR(FTC)	S		01.10.02	DARTMOUTH BRNC
Harris, Robert, BEng	SLT(IC)	X	O U/T	01.01.03	RNAS CULDROSE
Harris, Timothy Ronald, pce	CDRE(FTC)	X	PWO(U)	24.06.04	DARTMOUTH BRNC
Harris, Tristan	MAJ(FTC)	-		01.09.02	MOD (LONDON)
Harrison, Andrew David	LT(CC)	E	AE	29.04.01	ADAS BRISTOL
Harrison, Anthony	SLT(IC)	X		01.02.04	DARTMOUTH BRNC
Harrison, David, BEng	LT CDR(FTC)	E	WESM	05.01.97	DLO BRISTOL
Harrison, Ian	LT(IC)	X	O	01.10.02	RNAS YEOVILTON

Name	Rank	Branch	Spec	Seniority	Where Serving
Harrison, James Colin, MB, BS	SURG LT(MCC)	-		02.08.00	RH HASLAR
Harrison, John Andrew George	LT(IC)	X		01.05.02	PENZANCE
Harrison, Leigh Elliot, BSc	LT(IC)	X		01.04.03	RNAS YEOVILTON
Harrison, Mark Andrew, BEng, MIEE	LT(FTC)	E	WESM	01.11.97	RALEIGH
Harrison, Matthew Sean, BEng, MSc, CEng, MIEE, psc(j), gw	CDR(FTC)	E	WE	31.12.99	ILLUSTRIOUS
Harrison, Paul Dominic, gdas	LT CDR(FTC)	X	O	01.10.03	849 SQN A FLT
Harrison, Paul Geoffrey, CEng, MRAeS, BEng	CDR(FTC)	E	AE	30.06.04	JSCSC
Harrison, Richard Anthony, MSc, MDA, CDipAF, psc, gw	CDR(FTC)	E	WESM	31.12.89	SA BRAZIL
Harrison, Richard Simon, BA	LT CDR(CC)	X	P	01.10.04	MWC PORTSDOWN
Harrison, Stuart, BSc	LT(IC)	E	TM	10.05.04	SULTAN
Harrison, Thomas Iain, BEng, MPhil	LT(CC)	E	SM	01.01.96	NTE(TTD)
Harrop, Ian, BEng, MSc, CEng, MIMarEST	CDR(FTC)	E	MESM	30.06.05	JSCSC
Harry, Andrew David, BEng	LT CDR(FTC)	X		01.04.96	MOD (BATH)
Hart, Jonathan, MSc, CEng, MIEE, psc	CAPT(FTC)	E	WESM	31.12.99	DLO BRISTOL
Hart, Mark Alan, BSc, MA, pce, psc(j)	CDR(FTC)	X	AAWO	30.06.04	FLEET HQ NWD
Hart, Neil Lawrence Whynden	LT CDR(FTC)	S	SM	01.10.02	ARGYLL
Hart, Paul Andrew, BSc, FRGS, MInsD	LT CDR(FTC)	E	TM	01.10.98	DRAKE COB(CNH)
Hart, Stephen John Eric, BA	CAPT RM(FTC)	-		01.09.99	29 CDO REGT RA
Hart, Steven David	LT(FTC)	X		01.08.02	CYPRUS PBS
Hart, Steven James	LT(IC)	X	ATCU/T	01.05.04	RNAS YEOVILTON
Hart, Tobin Giles De Burgh	LT CDR(FTC)	X	P	01.10.00	LOAN JTEG BSC DN
Hartley, Andrew Paul, BEng, CEng, MIMarEST	LT CDR(FTC)	E	ME	02.03.00	CARDIFF
Hartley, Benjamin Paul Iles, BSc	LT(CC)	X	P	01.12.98	829 FLT 03
Hartley, James Henry Dean, BSc, PhD	LT(IC)	E	TM	01.05.98	RALEIGH
Hartley, John Laurence, BSc	LT CDR(FTC)	X	P	01.10.99	DHFS
Hartnell, Stephen Thomas, OBE, MA, rcds, psc	COL(FTC)	-		30.06.98	1 ASSLT GP RM
Harvey, Barrie, BEng	LT(FTC)	E	ME	01.06.97	DLO BRISTOL
Harvey, Colin Ashton, BSc	CDR(FTC)	E	MESM	30.06.00	NAVSEC
Harvey, Graham Anthony	LT(IC)	E	WE	01.01.03	AGRIPPA JFC HQ
Harvey, Keith, pce	CDR(FTC)	X	MCD	30.06.93	MWS COLLINGWOOD
Harvey, Paul Anthony, BSc (Act Cdr)	LT CDR(FTC)	X	ATC	01.10.91	DASC
Harvey, Paul Geoffrey	LT(IC)	E	WE	01.01.04	CAPT MCTA
Harvey, Paul John	LT(IC)	S	CA	08.01.01	AFPAA HQ
Harvey, Robert Matthew Malvern Jolyon, pce	CDR(FTC)	X	AAWO	30.06.03	YORK
Harwood, Christopher George, HNC, BTech	LT CDR(FTC)	E	WE	01.10.02	DRAKE SFM
Haseldine, Stephen George	LT CDR(FTC)	X	ATC	01.02.98	FLEET AV VL
Haskins, Benjamin Stuart, BA	LT(IC)	X		01.01.05	MWS COLLINGWOOD
Haslam, Philip James, pce	CDR(FTC)	X	PWO(A)	30.06.04	SUTHERLAND
Hassall, Harry, MEng, MSc, MA(Ed)	LT CDR(CC)	E	TM	01.10.95	EXCHANGE ARMY UK
Hassall, Ian, BEng	LT(FTC)	E	ME	01.12.97	FLEET ROSYTH
Hasted, Daniel	CAPT RM(FTC)	-	C	01.05.99	UKLFCSG RM
Hastings, Craig Steven	MID(IC)	S		01.06.03	DARTMOUTH BRNC
Hastings, Stephen Brian, BSc	LT(IC)	X		01.12.04	SEVERN
Hatch, Giles William Hellesdon, pce	CDR(FTC)	X	PWO(A)	31.12.98	RALEIGH
Hatchard, John Paul, FRGS	LT(FTC)	X	P	04.03.92	846 SQN
Hatchard, Peter John, BSc, MBA, jsdc, pce	CDR(FTC)	X	PWO(C)	30.06.94	NELSON
Hatcher, Rhett Slade, MA, pce, psc(j)	CDR(FTC)	X	P	30.06.04	PJHQ
Hatcher, Timothy Robert	LT CDR(FTC)	E	WESM	01.10.00	SOVEREIGN
Hattle, Prideaux McLeod	LT(IC)	X	PWO(U)	29.04.01	CAMPBELTOWN
Hatton-Brown, Oliver Robin, BEng	LT(IC)	E	ME U/T	01.09.04	ILLUSTRIOUS
Haughey, John Patrick, MCIEH	LT(FTC)	MS		01.04.01	MSA
Havron, Paul Richard	LT(FTC)	E	WE	01.04.01	DLO BRISTOL
Haw, Christopher Edward, MC, BSc	MAJ(FTC)	-	MLDR	01.10.04	FLEET HQ PORTS 2
Hawkes, Jonathan Derrick (Act Lt Cdr)	LT(FTC)	X		23.07.93	MOD (LONDON)
Hawkins, James Seymour, pcea	LT CDR(FTC)	X	O	16.08.98	FLEET HQ PORTS
Hawkins, Martin Adam Jeremy, pce, pcea, psc(j)	CDR(FTC)	X	O	30.06.03	849 SQN HQ
Hawkins, Richard Culworth, BA, jsdc, pcea	CAPT(FTC)	X	P	30.06.01	PJHQ
Hawkins, Robert Henry, pce	LT CDR(FTC)	X	MCD	01.10.91	FOST MPV SEA
Hawkins, Shane Robert, BEng, CEng, MIEE	LT(FTC)	E	WE	01.12.97	DLO BRISTOL
Hawkins, Stephen	LT(IC)	X	REG	01.07.04	DCPPA HALTON
Hawkins, Stuart	LT(CC)	E	WE	01.01.02	DLO BRISTOL
Haworth, Christopher	LT(CC)	X	O	01.09.91	815 FLT 214
Haworth, John, IEng, MIIE	CDR(FTC)	E	ME	30.06.99	SULTAN

Name	Rank	Branch	Spec	Seniority	Where Serving
Haworth, Jonathan Hywel Tristan, BEng, CEng, MIEE	LT CDR(FTC)	E	WE	01.10.04	MOD (LONDON)
Hawthorne, Michael John, MA, pce(sm), psc(j), pce	CAPT(FTC)	X	SM	30.06.05	HQ DCSA
Hay, James Donald, BSc	CAPT(FTC)	E	WE	30.06.05	HQ DCSA
Hay, Michael, BEng, MIEE	LT(FTC)	E	WE	01.03.98	DLO BRISTOL
Hay, Richard Harvey Iain, BSc	SLT(IC)	X		01.07.02	SCOTT
Hayashi, Luke Ronald, BSc	LT(CC)	X		01.11.99	DULVERTON
Haycock, Timothy Paul, BSc, pce, pcea, psc	CDR(FTC)	X	O	30.06.05	PJHQ
Hayde, Phillip John, BSc, MRAeS	LT CDR(FTC)	X	P	01.10.99	JCA IPT USA
Hayden, John Michael Leonard, BSc	LT(IC)	E	IS	01.05.01	AFPAA(CENTURION)
Hayden, Timothy William, BSc, pcea	LT(CC)	X	P	01.12.96	DHFS
Hayes, Brian John (Act Lt Cdr)	LT(FTC)	X		03.04.98	TEMERAIRE
Hayes, Claire Louise, BSc	LT(FTC)	S		01.09.97	RALEIGH
Hayes, James Victor Buchanan, BSc, psc(j)	CDR(FTC)	E	WESM	31.12.98	MOD (LONDON)
Hayes, Mark Andrew	LT(IC)	X		01.01.03	DEF SCH OF LANG
Hayes, Sean, BSc	LT(IC)	X		01.11.00	YORK
Hayes, Stuart John, pce	CDR(FTC)	X	MCD	30.06.00	FLEET CIS PORTS
Hayle, Elizabeth Anne, BA, MSc, isc	LT CDR(FTC)	W	X	01.10.98	MWC PORTSDOWN
Hayle, James Kenneth, psc(j)	CDR(FTC)	S	SM	30.06.05	DLO/DG DEF SC
Haynes, John Graham	SLT(IC)	X		01.01.03	MWS HM TG (D)
Haynes, John William	LT CDR(FTC)	X		01.10.98	2SL/CNH FOTR
Hayton, James Charles, BA, MB, ChB	SURG LT(MC(MD)	-		02.08.00	MDHU NORTH
Hayton, Stephen Robert Charles, pcea	LT(FTC)	X	O	05.09.95	820 SQN
Hayward, Clive Edward William, BA, SM	LT CDR(FTC)	X	SM	01.06.96	MOD (LONDON)
Hayward, Geoffrey	LT CDR(FTC)	X	O	01.10.03	MWS COLLINGWOOD
Haywood, Andrew James, BA	SLT(IC)	X	ATCU/T	01.11.02	DARTMOUTH BRNC
Haywood, Guy, pce, pcea	CDR(FTC)	X	P	30.06.02	PJHQ
Haywood, Peter James, BEng, pcea	LT CDR(FTC)	X	P	01.10.03	824 SQN
Haywood, Simon Anthony	CDR(FTC)	E	WESM	30.06.02	HQ SACT
Hazard, Lee	LT(IC)	MS		01.01.04	INM ALVERSTOKE
Hazelwood, Christopher David (Act Maj)	CAPT RM(FTC)	-	SO(LE)	01.01.00	FLEET HQ PORTS
Hazlehurst, Jody Alan, BEng	LT(IC)	X		01.05.05	RALEIGH
Head, Steven Andrew, BEng, MSc, CEng, MIEE	LT CDR(FTC)	E	WE	01.03.01	MARLBOROUGH
Headley, Mark James, BSc	LT(CC)	X		01.04.00	SOMERSET
Heal, Jeremy Phillip Carlton, psc	COL(FTC)	-		31.12.99	FLEET HQ PORTS 2
Heal, Tristan Stephen, MEng	LT(CC)	E	WESM	01.04.01	FLEET HQ NWD
Healey, Mark Jon	LT(CC)	E	AE	01.09.99	ADAS BRISTOL
Healy, Anthony John	CDR(FTC)	X	EW	31.12.99	JSSU CHELTENHAM
Heames, Richard Mark ,BM, FRCA	SURG LTCDR(MCC)	-		01.08.99	NELSON (PAY)
Heaney, Martin Joseph, BSc	LT(CC)	X	O	16.04.97	824 SQN
Heap, Graham George	LT(IC)	E	MESM	01.05.04	TURBULENT
Heap, Steven A	LT(IC)	E	MESM	01.07.04	TORBAY
Hearn, Samuel Peter, BA	LT(IC)	X	SM	01.09.00	SUPERB
Hearty, Stephen Patrick	LT(IC)	E	ME	11.04.03	CAMPBELTOWN
Heath, Eduardo Juan, BEng	SLT(IC)	E	WE U/T	01.01.04	DARTMOUTH BRNC
Heath, Stephen Philip Robert, MEng	LT(IC)	E	MESM	01.09.02	SCEPTRE
Heatly, Robert Johnston, MBE, osc(us)	LT COL(FTC)	-		31.12.95	HQ SACT
Heaton, Henry Gerald, BSc	LT(IC)	X	HM	01.05.02	ECHO
Heaver, David Gerard Verney, MA, psc(m)	COL(FTC)	-		30.06.96	SHAPE BELGIUM
Hecks, Ian James, BA	CAPT RM(IC)	-		01.09.02	42 CDO RM
Hedgecox, David Colin, BEng, MIEE	LT CDR(FTC)	E	WE	01.06.04	RMC OF SCIENCE
Hedges, Justin William, BSc	MAJ(FTC)	-		01.09.01	JSCSC
Hedworth, Anthony Joseph, BComm	LT(CC)	X	P	01.06.94	702 SQN HERON
Hefford, Christopher John, BSc	LT(FTC)	S		01.03.97	DLO/DG DEF SC
Heighway, Martin Richard, MSc, PGCE, MA(Ed)	LT(IC)	E	TM	01.01.96	DCTS HALTON
Heirs, Gavin George, MA	LT(CC)	X	P	01.08.98	771 SQN A FLT
Helby, Philip Faulder Hasler, MBE, BSc, MBA, AMIEE, CDipAF	LT CDR(FTC)	E	MESM	16.07.82	DRAKE CBS
Heley, David Nicholas, pce	CDR(FTC)	X	PWO(U)	30.06.00	NELSON
Heley, Jonathan Mark, BEng, MSc, CEng, MIMarEST	CDR(FTC)	E	MESM	31.12.00	MOD (LONDON)
Helliwell, Michael Andrew, BEng, CEng, MRAeS	CDR(FTC)	E	AE	30.06.05	RALEIGH
Hellyn, David Robert	LT CDR(FTC)	E	WE	01.10.97	T45 IPT
Hember, Marcus James Christopher, n	LT(FTC)	X		01.05.00	JSCSC
Hembrow, Terence	MAJ(FTC)	-	SO(LE)	01.10.97	RMB STONEHOUSE
Hembury, Lawrence	CAPT RM(CC)	-	C	01.04.03	42 CDO RM

Name	Rank	Branch	Spec	Seniority	Where Serving
Hemingway, Darren Graham, BSc	LT(IC)	E	TM	01.01.00	SULTAN
Hemingway, Ross, MB, CHB	SURG LT(SCC)	-		07.08.02	MCM1 SEA
Hempsell, Adrian Michael, n	LT CDR(FTC)	X	PWO(A)	01.06.02	FOST SEA
Hemsworth, Kenneth John, BEng, CEng, MIMarEST	LT CDR(FTC)	E	ME	01.01.98	FLEET HQ PORTS
Henaghen, Stephen John	LT(IC)	X	PWO(A)	13.07.01	BULWARK
Henderson, Andrew Graham, BSc	SLT(IC)	X	O U/T	01.01.04	DARTMOUTH BRNC
Henderson, Arthur	SURG SLT(SCC)	-		20.09.04	DARTMOUTH BRNC
Henderson, Peter Philip, HNC, NDipM	LT CDR(FTC)	E	WE	01.10.03	INVINCIBLE
Henderson, Robert John	LT CDR(FTC)	E	AE	01.10.04	MERLIN IPT
Henderson, Sam Charles, BA	LT(IC)	S		01.10.00	RALEIGH
Henderson, Stuart Philip, BEng, MSc, CEng, MIMarEST	LT CDR(FTC)	E	ME	01.03.99	CAPT MCTA
Henderson, Thomas Maxwell Philip, BSc, pce	LT CDR(FTC)	X	PWO(U)	01.04.91	CINCFLEET FIMU
Hendrickx, Christopher John, BEng	LT CDR(FTC)	E	WE	01.01.04	CINCFLEET FTSU
Hendy, Richard	LT CDR(FTC)	S		01.10.04	RAF COTTESMORE
Henley, Simon Michael, MBE, BSc, CEng, MRAeS, jsdc (Commodore)	CAPT(FTC)	E	AE	30.06.97	JCA IPT UK
Hennessey, Timothy Patrick David, BSc, pce, psc	CAPT(FTC)	X	O	30.06.03	CMT SHRIVENHAM
Henning, Daniel Clive Walker, MB, BCH, BAO	SURG LT(SC(MD)	-		19.09.03	CFLT MED(SEA)
Henry, Gavin Paul, BA	LT(IC)	X	P U/T	01.01.02	COS 2SL/CNH
Henry, Mark Frederick, MB, BCh, MRCS	SURG LTCDR(FCC)	-		06.08.02	MDHU DERRIFORD
Henry, Timothy Michael, pce, n	CDR(FTC)	X	PWO(U)	30.06.05	WESTMINSTER
Henson, Andrew John	LT(IC)	E	WESM	01.07.04	MWS COLLINGWOOD
Hepplewhite, Mark Barrie	LT(CC)	E	AE	01.09.99	RMC OF SCIENCE
Hepworth, Andrew William David, BEng, MSc	LT CDR(FTC)	E	IS	01.05.98	MOD (BATH)
Herbert, Lara (Act Surg Lt)	SURG SLT(SCC)	-		23.06.04	DARTMOUTH BRNC
Herman, Thomas Rolf, OBE, BSc, pce(sm)	CDR(FTC)	X	SM	30.06.92	FLEET HQ PORTS
Hermer, Jeremy Peter	MAJ(FTC)	-		01.09.01	CTCRM
Herridge, Daniel Jonathon	SLT(IC)	X		01.08.02	ST ALBANS
Herriman, John Andrew, BSc, MA, DipEd, FCIPD, MIMgt	LT CDR(CC)	X	MCD	01.04.03	FDG
Herring, Jonathan James Auriol, BSc, MA, psc	LT COL(FTC)	-		30.06.98	FLEET HQ PORTS 2
Herzberg, Mark	SLT(IC)	E	WE	01.01.04	MWS COLLINGWOOD
Hesketh, John James, BSc	LT(IC)	X	O U/T	01.11.01	RNAS CULDROSE
Hesketh, Michael (Act Sg Lt(D))	SG SLT(D)(SCC)	-		25.06.04	SULTAN
Hesling, Gary, pce, n, PGDip	LT CDR(FTC)	X	H1	28.02.02	ENDURANCE
Hester, James Francis William, BA	CAPT RM(CC)	-		01.09.01	40 CDO RM
Hetherington, Thomas Angus, BSc	LT(IC)	E	ME	01.12.03	NORTHUMBERLAND
Hett, David Anthony, BSc, FRCA, LRCP, MRCS, DA	SURG CDR(FCC)	-	(CA)	31.12.93	RH HASLAR
Heward, Mark George	LT(IC)	X		01.01.04	CATTISTOCK
Hewitson, Jonathan George Austin, BSc	LT(CC)	X		01.08.00	SHOREHAM
Hewitt, Antony, BEng	LT CDR(FTC)	E	MESM	01.06.95	MOD (LONDON)
Hewitt, David Leslie, pce	LT CDR(FTC)	X	AAWO	01.07.99	JSCSC
Hewitt, Lloyd Russell	LT CDR(FTC)	S		16.11.97	AFPAA JPA
Hewitt, Mark John, MIIE	LT(CC)	E	ME	29.04.01	MWS COLLINGWOOD
Hewitt, Nigel	SLT(IC)	E	AE U/T	01.01.04	DARTMOUTH BRNC
Hewitt, Richard Paul	LT(IC)	X		01.01.04	CHIDDINGFOLD
Hewlett, Philip James Edward, MEng	SLT(IC)	E	WESM	01.11.02	RALEIGH
Heycocks, Christian John, MA	CHAPLAIN	CE		24.09.00	DRAKE COB(CNH)
Heywood, Robert Hugh, BEng	SLT(IC)	E	MESMUT	01.09.03	INVINCIBLE
Hibberd, Nicholas James, pce, pce(sm), psc(j), MA	CDR(FTC)	X	SM	30.06.04	SUPERB
Hibbert, Martin Christopher	LT CDR(FTC)	X		01.10.96	MWS COLLINGWOOD
Hibbert, Peter Nigel, MNI, MInsD, jsdc, pce, pce(sm)	CDR(FTC)	X	SM	31.12.90	UKMILREP BRUSS
Hickey, Ruth	SG SLT(D)(SCC)	-		01.04.03	DARTMOUTH BRNC
Hicks, Nicholas John Ivatts, BSc, n, SM(n), SM	LT(CC)	X	SM	01.06.98	VANGUARD(PORT)
Hickson, Michael Stuart Harris, BEng, MRAeS	LT CDR(FTC)	E	(AE)	01.08.03	RNAS YEOVILTON
Higgins, Andrew John	LT(CC)	X	FC	01.08.95	RAF COTTESMORE
Higgins, Damian James, BSc	SLT(IC)	X		01.07.02	RNAS YEOVILTON
Higgins, Godfrey Nigel, BEng, CEng, MRAeS	CDR(FTC)	E	AE	30.06.04	ADAS BRISTOL
Higgins, Peter Martin, BEng	LT(IC)	X	P	16.12.01	815 FLT 214
Higginson, Nicholas John, BEng	LT(CC)	X		01.06.00	ILLUSTRIOUS
Higgs, Robert James	LT CDR(FTC)	X	C	01.10.00	2SL/CNH
Higgs, Thomas Arthur, BSc	LT CDR(FTC)	S		01.02.02	FLEET HQ NWD
Higham, Duncan John	CAPT RM(IC)	-		01.09.04	FLEET HQ PORTS 2
Higham, James Godfrey, BEng, MSc, MIEE, gw	LT CDR(FTC)	E	WE	01.01.00	JSCSC
Higham, Stephen William James Andrew, MA	LT CDR(FTC)	X		01.10.04	MWS COLLINGWOOD

Name	Rank	Branch	Spec	Seniority	Where Serving
Hignett, Geraldine	LT(IC)	E	TM	01.06.03	ILLUSTRIOUS
Higson, Beverly Lynn, BSc, PGDip, MIMA, CMath	LT CDR(CC)	E	IS	01.10.03	SHAPE BELGIUM
Higson, Glenn	SLT(IC)	X	AV	01.02.04	RE ENTRY(RM)
Hill, Adrain Jason, BSc	LT(CC)	X	O	01.10.96	RNAS CULDROSE
Hill, Christopher John, BSc	LT(IC)	X		01.04.04	RALEIGH
Hill, David, BEng, CEng, MRAeS, MIL, psc(j)o	LT CDR(FTC)	E	AE	01.03.99	DLO YEO
Hill, George Alexander	LT CDR(FTC)	E	WESM	01.10.98	NEPTUNE DLO
Hill, Giulian Francis, BEng, MSc, CEng, MCGI, MIMarEST, psc(j)	CDR(FTC)	E	ME	30.06.04	DLO BRISTOL
Hill, Graham Allen, MB, ChB, FRCS, FRCS(ORTH)	SURG CDR(FCC)	-	(CO/S)	31.12.00	RH HASLAR
Hill, John	CHAPLAIN	CE		17.01.94	RH HASLAR
Hill, Jonathan Paul, BSc (Act Maj)	CAPT RM(FTC)	-		01.05.99	UN AFRICA
Hill, Mark Robert, pce, pcea	LT CDR(FTC)	X	P	22.06.96	HQBF CYPRUS
Hill, Philip John, BEng, CEng, MIEE	CDR(FTC)	E	WESM	30.06.04	PJHQ
Hill, Richard Andrew	LT CDR(FTC)	X	MW	01.09.95	ALBION
Hill, Roy Keith John, MA, ACMA, psc(j)	CDR(FTC)	S	CMA	30.06.03	MOD (LONDON)
Hill, Thomas Edward, BEng	LT(IC)	X	O	01.05.03	849 SQN B FLT
Hilliard, Robert Godfrey, MA, DipTh	CHAPLAIN	CE		01.08.80	FLEET HQ PORTS
Hillier, Colin Andrew	SLT(IC)	X	O U/T	01.05.02	RNAS CULDROSE
Hillman, Christopher Mark, MB, BCH	SURG LT(SC(MD)	-		03.08.04	DARTMOUTH BRNC
Hills, Anthony Alexander, pce, pcea	LT CDR(FTC)	X	P	01.12.94	RAF CRANWELL EFS
Hills, Michael John	CHAPLAIN	CE		21.04.98	45 CDO RM
Hills, Richard Brian, MA, psc(j)	MAJ(FTC)	-		01.05.99	FLEET HQ PORTS
Hilson, Steven Millar, MBA, pcea	LT CDR(FTC)	X	O	01.10.04	MWS COLLINGWOOD
Hilton, James N	CAPT RM(CC)	-		01.09.03	CTCRM
Hilton, Simon Thomas, BEng	LT(CC)	X	O	01.04.99	815 FLT 239
Hinch, David Graham William	LT CDR(FTC)	X	P	01.10.00	RAF AWC
Hinch, Neil Eric	CDR(FTC)	X		30.06.03	2SL/CNH FOTR
Hinchcliffe, Alan, BSc	LT(CC)	X	P	01.03.94	GANNET SAR FLT
Hind, Kristian Nicholas	LT(IC)	X	AV	01.07.04	RFANSU
Hindmarch, Stephen Andrew, BA	LT(CC)	X	P	01.09.96	RAF CRANWELL EFS
Hine, Michael Joseph	LT(IC)	S		01.07.04	PJHQ
Hine, Nicholas William, pce, pce(sm), psc(j), SM(n), MA, BSc	CDR(FTC)	X	SM	30.06.00	JSCSC
Hipsey, Stephen Jon, MSc	LT CDR(CC)	X	METOC	01.10.89	MWS HM TG (D)
Hirons, Francis Durham, BSc, n	LT(CC)	X		01.02.99	BITER
Hirstwood, John Laurence	LT(IC)	X		01.09.01	LEEDS CASTLE
Hitchings, Deborah Louise, BA	LT(CC)	X	FC	01.01.94	RNAS YEOVILTON
Hitchings, Michael James, BEng	SLT(IC)	E	MESMUT	01.09.03	INVINCIBLE
Hitchins, Edward Graham David	CHAPLAIN	CE		06.01.03	CDO LOG REGT RM
Hoare, Peter Francis	CAPT RM(CC)	-	SO(LE)	21.07.01	RMR MERSEYSIDE
Hoare, Peter James Edward, pcea	LT CDR(FTC)	X	O	01.10.04	OCEAN
Hoather, Martin Stephen, MA(CANTAB), MEng, MSc, CEng, MIEE	LT(FTC)	E	WE	01.09.99	MOD (LONDON)
Hobbs, Alan Ronald	LT CDR(FTC)	X	PWO(A)	01.04.93	NEW IPT
Hobbs, Richard, IEng, FIIE	CDR(FTC)	E	WE	01.10.98	CAPT MCTA
Hobbs, Thomas Peter	LT(IC)	E	WE	01.09.04	KENT
Hobson, Ian Stuart, BTech	LT CDR(FTC)	E	WESM	01.10.00	FWO FASLANE
Hocking, Mark John Eldred, IEng, MIIE	LT(FTC)	E	WE	01.04.01	DLO BRISTOL
Hockley, Christopher John, MSc, CEng, MIMarEST, psc	CAPT(FTC)	E	ME	30.06.99	MOD (BATH)
Hodder, Philip James	LT(IC)	X	SM	01.09.03	TRENCHANT
Hodds, Sara	LT(SC(MD)	Q		01.11.02	NELSON (PAY)
Hodge, Christopher Michael, MSc, BEng, MIMarEST	LT CDR(FTC)	E	MESM	01.10.04	VENGEANCE(STBD)
Hodgkins, Jonathan Mark, pce, pcea, psc(j)	CDR(FTC)	X	O	30.06.02	MOD (LONDON)
Hodgkinson, Samuel Peter	LT(IC)	X	P	01.09.04	RNAS YEOVILTON
Hodgson, Jonathan Richard, MIIE	LT(FTC)	E	ME	02.05.00	MWS COLLINGWOOD
Hodgson, Richard Stephen, BSc	LT(IC)	X	SM	01.03.00	OCEAN
Hodgson, Timothy Charles, MBE, MA, CEng, MIMarEST, MIMechE, psc(j)	CDR(FTC)	E	MESM	31.12.99	CNNRP BRISTOL
Hodkinson, Christopher Brian, pce, MA, psc(j)	CDR(FTC)	X	PWO(A)	30.06.02	MOD (LONDON)
Hofman, Alison Jayne, BSc	LT CDR(MCC)	Q	IC	01.10.04	RCDM
Hogben, Andrew Lade, pce	LT CDR(FTC)	X	AAWO	01.03.99	UKMARBATSTAFF
Hogben, Michael John, BEng	LT(IC)	E	MESM	01.01.04	SULTAN
Hogg, Adam James	LT(IC)	X	P	01.05.03	RNAS YEOVILTON
Hogg, Christopher William, BSc	LT CDR(FTC)	X	PWO(A)	01.03.97	EXCHANGE NLANDS
Hogg, Graham David	2LT(IC)	-		01.09.99	FPGRM
Holberry, Anthony Paul, psc, psc(j)	CAPT(FTC)	E	WE	30.06.04	MOD (LONDON)

Name	Rank	Branch	Spec	Seniority	Where Serving
Holburt, Richard Michael, BSc	SLT(IC)	X		01.09.03	DARTMOUTH BRNC
Holden, John Lloyd, BA, SM	LT(IC)	X	SM	01.12.99	PJHQ
Holden, Neil	LT CDR(FTC)	X	MCD	01.04.01	STANAVFORMED
Holden, Paul Andrew	LT CDR(FTC)	E	AE	01.10.02	HARRIER IPT
Holden, Robert John	LT CDR(FTC)	X	O	01.10.99	849 SQN HQ
Holder, John Michael, BSc	LT(CC)	X	P	01.08.97	824 SQN
Holdsworth, Howard William, LLB, MSc	CAPT(FTC)	E	AE	30.06.04	DPA BRISTOL
Holdsworth, Rachel Ann, BEng	LT(IC)	E	WE	01.01.03	ST ALBANS
Holford, Stephen James, BEng	LT(FTC)	E	MESM	01.05.01	VIGILANT(STBD)
Holgate, James Alan	LT(CC)	E	WE	01.08.02	LANCASTER
Holihead, Philip Wedgwood, pce, psc(a) (Act Capt)	CDR(FTC)	X	AAWO	30.06.93	NELSON
Holland, Amanda Louise	LT CDR(MCC)	Q	IC	01.10.04	MDHU DERRIFORD
Holland, Charlotte Claire, BA	LT(IC)	S		01.05.02	ENTERPRISE
Holland, Christopher	LT(IC)	E	AE	01.05.03	RNAS YEOVILTON
Holland, Nicholas Roy, BSc	LT CDR(FTC)	S	(S)	01.10.99	AFPAA JPA
Holland, Simon Martin Walkington, BSc	LT CDR(CC)	E	TM	01.05.01	FOST FAS SHORE
Holland, Steven	SLT(IC)	E	AE U/T	01.01.04	DARTMOUTH BRNC
Holland, Toby	SURG SLT(SCC)	-		23.09.03	DARTMOUTH BRNC
Hollidge, John Howard, BSc, CEng, FIMarE, FIMarEST, MBIM, MCMI, psc	CAPT(FTC)	E	ME	30.06.98	SA ROME
Holliehead, Craig Lewis, BSc	LT(CC)	X	O	01.01.02	815 FLT 229
Hollins, Rupert Patrick, MA (Barrister)	CDR(FTC)	S	BAR	30.06.03	NAVSEC
Holloway, Benjamin Scott Vere	SLT(IC)	S		01.05.04	RALEIGH
Holloway, Jonathan Toby, MSc, CEng, MIMechE, jsdc	CAPT(FTC)	E	MESM	30.06.02	SA MOSCOW
Holloway, Nicholas, BEM (Act Maj)	CAPT RM(FTC)	-	SO(LE)	01.01.98	RM CONDOR
Holloway, Steven Andrew	LT CDR(FTC)	X	PWO(U)	01.10.03	FOST SEA
Hollyfield, Peter Richard, BSc	LT(IC)	E	IS	01.05.00	2SL/CNH
Holmes, Annabel Mary	LT(CC)	X	ATC	15.03.00	RNAS YEOVILTON
Holmes, Christopher John, psc(j)	MAJ(FTC)	-	C	01.05.98	UKLFCSG RM
Holmes, Graham, pce(sm)	LT CDR(FTC)	X	SM	01.12.87	MWC PORTSDOWN
Holmes, Helen Jane, LLB	LT(CC)	S		01.01.02	2SL/CNH
Holmes, Jamie John	SLT(UCE)(IC)	X		01.09.04	DARTMOUTH BRNC
Holmes, Jonathan David	LT CDR(FTC)	X	H1	04.02.99	BANGOR
Holmes, Mark Daniel	LT(IC)	X	ATCU/T	01.08.03	RNAS CULDROSE
Holmes, Matthew John, MA, psc(j)	LT COL(FTC)	-		30.06.03	COMAMPHIBFOR
Holmes, Patrick James Mitchell, BA, BSc	LT(IC)	X	P	01.05.02	824 SQN
Holmes, Paul Stewart, BDS	SGLTCDR(D)(SCC)	-		20.07.03	DRAKE COB(CNH)
Holmes, Rachel Mary, BA	LT(IC)	E	IS	01.09.00	ILLUSTRIOUS
Holmes, Robert, pce, psc(a)	CDR(FTC)	X	PWO(A)	31.12.95	TEMERAIRE
Holmes, Rupert Womack, BEng	LT CDR(FTC)	E	AE	01.04.95	FLEET HQ PORTS
Holmes, Sammy McLlroy, BA	LT(IC)	X		01.09.04	ALBION
Holmwood, Mark Alan Gresert, BEng	LT(CC)	E	ME	01.08.99	FOST MPV SEA
Holroyd, Jonathon Edward James, BSc	LT(CC)	X	O	16.02.98	824 SQN
Holt, John David, BSc, BA, MIIE	LT(IC)	E	IS	01.05.00	FOST FAS SHORE
Holt, Justin Sefton, MBE, MA, psc(j)	LT COL(FTC)	-	LC	30.06.05	JSCSC
Holt, Steven, PGDIPAN, pce, psc(j)	CDR(FTC)	X	PWO(N)	30.06.03	NOTTINGHAM
Holvey, Paul Jonathan	LT(FTC)	E	MESM	01.04.01	NP BOSNIA
Holyer, Raymond John, MSc	CAPT(FTC)	MS	(P)	06.07.04	RCDM
Honey, John Philip, BSc, CEng, MIMarE, MIMechE	LT CDR(FTC)	E	MESM	01.03.88	DRAKE SFM
Honnoraty, Mark Robert, pce(sm), SM(n)	CDR(FTC)	X	SM	30.06.05	MOD (LONDON)
Hood, Kevin Christopher, MA, psc(j)	CDR(FTC)	S		30.06.03	INVINCIBLE
Hood, Kevin Michael, BEng, MSc	LT CDR(FTC)	E	MESM	01.04.98	FLEET HQ PORTS 2
Hood, Matthew John	MAJ(FTC)	-		25.04.96	CTCRM
Hook, David Arnold, psc(m)	COL(FTC)	-	C	30.06.03	NP IRAQ
Hooper, Gary Peter, IEng, MIIE	LT CDR(FTC)	E	WE	01.10.01	FOST SEA
Hooper, Thomas	LT(IC)	S		01.01.05	FOST NWD (JMOTS)
Hooper, William Robert, MSc(Econ)	SLT(IC)	X	O U/T	01.01.03	RNAS CULDROSE
Hope, Karl, BSc, CEng, PGDip, MBCS, adp	LT CDR(FTC)	E	IS	01.09.96	AFPAA(CENTURION)
Hope, Mark Roger, BEng	LT CDR(FTC)	E	AE	01.07.04	DLO WYTON
Hoper, Paul Roger, MCGI, pcea, gdas, BSc	LT CDR(FTC)	X	O	01.10.96	FLEET HQ PORTS
Hopkins, Anthony Edward Tobin, BSc	LT(IC)	X	H2	01.04.02	RFANSU
Hopkins, Catherine	LT(CC)	X	ATC	01.05.01	EXCHANGE RAF UK
Hopkins, Nicola Sari, BSc	LT(IC)	X		01.01.05	MWS COLLINGWOOD
Hopkins, Rhys, MA	CAPT RM(IC)	-		01.09.01	FPGRM

Name	Rank	Branch	Spec	Seniority	Where Serving
Hopkins, Richard Michael Edward (Act Maj)	CAPT RM(CC)	-		01.09.00	CTCRM
Hopkins, Steven David	LT CDR(FTC)	X	P	01.10.03	750 SQN SEAHAWK
Hopley, David Alan, OBE, jsdc, psc	COL(FTC)	-		31.12.96	MOD (LONDON)
Hopper, Gary	LT(IC)	E	WESM	01.01.04	VENGEANCE(STBD)
Hopper, Ian Michael	LT CDR(FTC)	X	MW	09.04.02	MARLBOROUGH
Hopper, Simon Mallam, BA, pce, n	LT CDR(FTC)	X	PWO(A)	01.02.01	NAVSEC
Hopper, Stephen Owen, pce, psc(j), MA	CDR(FTC)	X	PWO(N)	31.12.99	JSCSC
Hopton, Matthew James, BA	SLT(IC)	X		01.07.02	WALNEY
Hopwood, Adrian	LT(IC)	X		17.12.04	LEDBURY
Hore, Robert Charles, psc	CDR(FTC)	E	ME	31.12.93	NAVSEC
Horlock, Andrew	SLT(IC)	MS		01.01.04	INM ALVERSTOKE
Horn, Neil Richard, BEng	SLT(IC)	X	P U/T	01.02.04	DARTMOUTH BRNC
Horn, Peter Barrick, MBE, pce	CDR(FTC)	X	PWO(A)	30.06.99	PJHQ
Hornby, Simon	SURG SLT(SCC)	-		01.07.02	DARTMOUTH BRNC
Horne, Archibald (Act Cdr)	LT CDR(FTC)	X	C	01.10.99	IMS BRUSSELS
Horne, Jason Richard, SM(n)	LT CDR(FTC)	X	PWO(U)	01.10.02	HURWORTH
Horne, Timothy George, MA, MSc, pce, psc, psc(j)	CDR(FTC)	X	PWO(A)	30.06.97	COS 2SL/CNH
Horne, Trevor Kingsley, MA, PGDip, FRICS, FCMI, pce, psc	CDR(FTC)	X	H CH	31.12.94	LOAN HYDROG
Horner, Patrick Andrew, MBA, pce	LT CDR(FTC)	X	AAWO	01.08.94	MOD (LONDON)
Horobin, Peter James, MSc	LT(IC)	X		01.12.04	RALEIGH
Horrell, Michael Ian, OBE, BSc, CEng, FIMarEST, rcds, psc	CAPT(FTC)	E	ME	30.06.97	DRAKE SFM
Horsburgh, Ben	SURG SLT(SCC)	-		07.02.05	DARTMOUTH BRNC
Horsley, Alan Malcolm Ronald, MA, pce, psc(j) (Act Cdr)	LT CDR(FTC)	X	PWO(N)	01.07.94	LOAN BMATT GHANA
Horsted, James Alexander, MEng	LT(FTC)	E	MESM	01.09.02	VENGEANCE(PORT)
Horswill, Mark Nicholas, NDipM	LT CDR(FTC)	S		01.08.97	DLO BRISTOL
Horton, James Robert, BEng	LT(IC)	X	P	01.11.00	815 FLT 202
Horwell, Brian Bernard	LT CDR(FTC)	E	WE	01.10.01	LOAN BRUNEI
Horwood, Neil Anthony	LT(CC)	S		01.01.02	MOD (LONDON)
Hosker, Timothy James, MA(CANTAB), MCIPD, psc	CAPT(FTC)	S		30.06.04	FLEET HQ NWD
Hosking, David Blaise, MBE, MA, pce, psc	CDR(FTC)	X	MCD	31.12.94	NELSON
Hough, Peter Jonathan, MEng	SLT(IC)	X	SM	01.09.02	TYNE
Hougham, Thomas Neil	SLT(IC)	X	P	01.09.02	DHFS
Houghton, Philip John, MA, pce, MDA	LT CDR(FTC)	X	PWO(U)	01.07.94	LOAN DSTL
Houlberg, Kenneth Mark Torben, pce, n	LT CDR(FTC)	X	PWO(A)	01.11.97	CHIDDINGFOLD
Houlberg, Kristian Anthony Niels ,BM, MRCP	SURG LTCDR(FCC)	-		01.08.99	NELSON (PAY)
Houlston, Ian James Edward, BEng	LT(IC)	X		01.01.05	RNAS YEOVILTON
Hounsom, Timothy Rogers, n	LT CDR(FTC)	X		01.04.05	MWS COLLINGWOOD
Hounsome, Jonathan Robert	LT(IC)	X	O	01.01.04	771 SQN A FLT
Hourigan, Mark Peter	LT CDR(FTC)	X	P	01.10.03	845 SQN
Houston, Darren John McCaw, n	LT CDR(FTC)	X	PWO(N)	01.10.01	FOST SEA
Houvenaghel, Ian Michael	MAJ(FTC)	-		01.10.04	FOST SEA
Howard, Charles William Wykeham	CHAPLAIN	CE		28.09.82	FWO PORTS SEA
Howard, Daniel Gordon, MA, MBA, MIL, psc(j)o (Act Cdr)	LT CDR(FTC)	X	ATC	01.10.99	SHAPE BELGIUM
Howard, James William	MID(IC)	X		01.02.04	DARTMOUTH BRNC
Howard, Keith Anthony, MSc, CEng, MIMarEST	LT CDR(FTC)	E	ME	01.07.90	DRAKE COB
Howard, Naomi Avice, BSc	LT(CC)	X	H1	01.09.98	ENTERPRISE
Howard, Neil, BEng, MRAeS, psc(j)o	LT CDR(FTC)	E	AE	31.10.94	JCA IPT UK
Howard, Nicholas Henry, BEng, CEng, MRAeS	LT CDR(FTC)	E	AE	01.06.00	CHFHQ(SHORE)
Howard, Oliver Melbourne, MB, BS, FRCP	SURG CAPT(FCC)	-	(CM)	31.12.94	HQ DMETA
Howard, Richard David, BEd	CAPT RM(CC)	-		01.05.00	RM WARMINSTER
Howarth, Dillon Wharton, MSc, pce, pcea, gdas	LT CDR(FTC(A)	X	O	01.06.90	LOAN JTEG BSC DN
Howarth, John	CAPT RM(FTC)	-	SO(LE)	01.01.00	RMR TYNE
Howarth, Stephen Joseph (Act Maj)	CAPT RM(FTC)	-		01.09.99	RM WARMINSTER
Howe, Craig Michael, BSc	LT(CC)	X	P	01.07.98	814 SQN
Howe, Johnathan Karl Alexander, MEng	SLT(IC)	E	AE	01.09.03	ILLUSTRIOUS
Howe, Julian Peter, BA	LT CDR(FTC)	X	PWO(A)	01.10.01	FOST SEA
Howe, Sarah Elizabeth, BDS	SGCDR(D)(FCC)	-		31.12.98	NEPTUNE DDA
Howe, Scotty (Act Maj)	CAPT RM(CC)	-		01.04.01	LN BMATT (CEE)
Howe, Thomas, BSc, SM(n)	LT(FTC)	X	SM	01.11.97	MWS COLLINGWOOD
Howell, Henry Roderick Gwynn, MSc, PGDip	LT CDR(CC)	X	METOC	01.10.00	LOAN DSTL

Name	Rank	Branch	Spec	Seniority	Where Serving
Howell, Michael Alfred, MB, BS, MA, MA(CANTAB), FRCS, FFAEM, psc(j)	SURG CDR(FCC)	-	(CA/E)	30.06.99	NAVSEC
Howell, Peter Charles Henry	LT(IC)	E	MESM	01.05.04	FWO FASLANE
Howell, Simon Brooke, pce, psc(j), MA	CDR(FTC)	X	PWO(A)	30.06.04	FLEET HQ PORTS 2
Howells, Martin John	LT CDR(FTC)	MS	SM	01.10.03	NELSON
Howells, Simon Murray	LT(FTC)	X	EW	19.09.00	EXCHANGE USA
Howes, Francis Hedley Roberton, OBE, BSc, MA, rcds, psc	COL(FTC)	-	MLDR	30.06.02	JSCSC
Howes, Nicholas James	CDR(FCC)	Q	ACC/EM	30.06.04	RH HASLAR
Howes, Richard Jonathan	SURG SLT(SCC)	-		27.08.02	DARTMOUTH BRNC
Howie, Emma Jane	LT(CC)	X	O	01.01.01	849 SQN A FLT
Howorth, Keith, BSc, MNI, pce, pcea	LT CDR(FTC)	X	O	01.12.92	FOST SEA
Hubschmid, Spencer Raymond, BSc	LT(CC)	E	WESM	01.11.99	VANGUARD(PORT)
Hucker, Oliver Charles	SLT(IC)	X		01.08.02	MWS COLLINGWOOD
Hudson, Andrew, SM(n)	LT(IC)	X	SM	01.10.02	VENGEANCE(PORT)
Hudson, Jeremy David, MA, psc(j)	LT COL(FTC)	-	MLDR	30.06.02	CDO LOG REGT RM
Hudson, Melanie, BA	LT(IC)	X	ATC	10.10.97	RNAS YEOVILTON
Hudson, Peter Derek, CBE, BSc, pce	CDRE(FTC)	X	PWO(N)	31.12.04	FLEET HQ PORTS
Hudson, Philip Trevor	LT CDR(FTC)	X	AV	01.10.96	DLO WYTON
Hudson, Rachel Elizabeth, BA	LT(IC)	X	P	01.05.04	RNAS YEOVILTON
Huggett, Clare Louise	SLT(IC)	E	WE	01.09.01	COS 2SL/CNH
Huggins, Kathryn Elizabeth, BSc	LT(SC(MD)	Q		01.11.02	LOAN FIELD HOSP
Hughes, Andrew Simon, MB, BCh, MRCGP	SURG CAPT(FCC)	-	GMPP	31.12.95	NEPTUNE DLO
Hughes, Benjamin Frederick Mostyn, BA	LT(IC)	S		01.01.03	DCL DEEPCUT
Hughes, Charlotte (Act Surg Lt)	SURG SLT(SCC)	-		24.07.04	DARTMOUTH BRNC
Hughes, Christopher Bryan, BSc	LT(CC)	X	O	01.06.99	849 SQN HQ
Hughes, David James, MB, ChB	SURG LTCDR(MCC)	-	SM	01.08.99	NELSON (PAY)
Hughes, Frank Charles	LT(IC)	E	WE	01.01.03	JARIC
Hughes, Gareth David, BEng	LT(CC)	E	ME	01.01.02	SCOTT
Hughes, Gareth Llewelyn, psc	CDR(FTC)	S		31.12.00	FLEET HQ PORTS
Hughes, Gary Edward	LT(IC)	X	AV	01.05.02	RFANSU
Hughes, Gary George Henry	LT CDR(FTC)	X	C	01.10.98	LOAN DSTL
Hughes, Geoffrey Alan, BA	LT(IC)	S		01.09.03	MONMOUTH
Hughes, John James, BEng	LT(CC)	X	P	01.08.99	846 SQN
Hughes, Jon-Paul Hudson, MA, psc(j)	MAJ(FTC)	-	C	01.09.97	FLEET CIS PORTS
Hughes, Mark Jonathan	MAJ(FTC)	-		01.09.01	COMAMPHIBFOR
Hughes, Nicholas Justin, pce, pce(sm)	CDR(FTC)	X	SM	31.12.96	FLEET HQ PORTS 2
Hughes, Paul Antony, MB, BS, FRCGP, DObstRCOG, Dip FFP, JCPTGP	SURG CDR(FCC)	-	GMPP	30.06.98	NELSON (PAY)
Hughes, Richard	SURG SLT(SCC)	-		01.07.03	DARTMOUTH BRNC
Hughes, Robert Ian, BSc, CEng, MIEE, jsdc	CAPT(FTC)	E	WESM	30.06.02	ASM IPT
Hughes, Scott Maurice, BSc	LT(CC)	X	P	16.07.97	849 SQN A FLT
Hughes, Stephen John, psc(m)	LT COL(FTC)	-		30.06.94	SULTAN AIB
Hughes, Thomas William, BEng	LT(IC)	E	MESM	01.01.04	SULTAN
Hughesdon, Mark Douglas, BEng, MSc, CEng, MIEE	LT CDR(FTC)	E	WE	01.02.98	HQ DCSA
Hugo, Ian David, pce, pce(sm), MNI	CDR(FTC)	X	SM	31.12.96	DRAKE COB
Hulme, Timothy Mark, BA, pce, pcea	LT CDR(FTC)	X	O	01.03.97	JSCSC
Hulse, Anthony William	CAPT RM(FTC)	-	C	01.04.01	45 CDO RM
Hulse, Rebecca Jane, LLB	SLT(IC)	S		01.05.02	RALEIGH
Hulse, Royston Matthew, BA	LT(IC)	X	FC	01.09.03	LIVERPOOL
Hulston, Lauren Marie, BSc	LT(IC)	X	O	01.09.01	820 SQN
Hume, Charles Bertram, BSc, CEng, MIMechE	CDR(FTC)	E	MESM	31.12.91	NP DNREAY
Hume, Kenneth John, BEng	LT(CC)	X	HM	01.03.99	ENDURANCE
Humphery, Duncan, BEng	LT(CC)	E	ME	01.06.98	INVINCIBLE
Humphrey, Ian Robert	LT(IC)	X		01.12.01	FLEET HQ PORTS 2
Humphrey, Ivor James	LT CDR(FTC)	E	WE	17.09.98	EXETER
Humphreys, John Illingworth, MNI, pce(sm)	CDR(FTC)	X	SM	30.06.94	IMS BRUSSELS
Humphries, Graham David	LT(IC)	X	P	01.05.01	845 SQN
Humphries, Jason Eric, n	LT(FTC)	X	PWO(U)	01.04.95	INVINCIBLE
Humphries, Mark, MSc	LT(IC)	X	P	01.07.00	LOAN OTHER SVCE
Humphrys, James Alan, BSc, MA, pce, psc	CAPT(FTC)	X	PWO(U)	30.06.04	JDCC
Hunkin, David John, pce	LT CDR(FTC)	X	MCD	01.12.99	HURWORTH
Hunnibell, John Richard	LT(IC)	X		01.05.04	SOMERSET
Hunt, Andrew James	LT(IC)	X	FC	01.05.04	SOUTHAMPTON

Name	Rank	Branch	Spec	Seniority	Where Serving
Hunt, Ben Paul, BSc	LT(IC)	X	P	01.09.03	DHFS
Hunt, Darren, MM	CAPT RM(CC)	-	P	01.01.01	CHFHQ
Hunt, Fraser Brain George, pcea	LT CDR(FTC)	X	P	01.10.03	829 FLT 02
Hunt, Jeremy Simon Paul, BSc, PGDip	LT CDR(FTC)	X	METOC	05.02.95	MWS HM TG (D)
Hunt, Patrick Edward Robin David, HNC	LT CDR(FTC)	E	WE	01.10.03	FLEET HQ PORTS 2
Hunt, Patrick Simon, BEng, MIEE	LT(FTC)	E	WE	01.01.99	UKCEC IPT
Hunt, Rachel Eleanor, MA	LT(IC)	X		01.01.03	FOST DPORT SHORE
Hunt, Robert James Campbell, LLB	LT(IC)	S		01.09.02	NELSON WF
Hunt, Stephen Christopher	LT CDR(FTC)	X	PWO(A)	01.10.03	CARDIFF
Hunter, Clare Roberta, MB, BS, DipAvMed	SURG LT(SCC)	-		07.08.02	FLEET AV HENLOW
Hunter, Kevin Patrick, BSc, CEng, FIMarEST, MIMechE	LT CDR(FTC)	E	ME	01.08.87	DRAKE CBS
Hunter, Neil Mitchell, BSc, pce, pcea, psc(j)o	CDR(FTC)	X	P	30.06.04	DPA BRISTOL
Huntingford, Damian Jon, BA	CAPT RM(CC)	-	MLDR	01.09.00	EXCHANGE ARMY UK
Huntington, Simon Peter, BSc, pce, psc(j), n	CDR(FTC)	X	PWO(U)	30.06.05	MOD (LONDON)
Huntley, Ian Philip, BA, psc(m), psc(j)	COL(FTC)	-		30.06.02	HQ 3 CDO BDE RM
Hunwicks, Sarah Elizabeth, BEng, CEng	LT(FTC)	E	AE	01.01.97	824 SQN
Hurley, Christopher, BSc	LT CDR(FTC)	X	PWO(A)	01.06.02	PJHQ
Hurley, Karl Antony	LT(MCC)	Q	ACC/EM	26.05.99	JSCSC
Hurman, Richard Nicholas	SLT(IC)	X		01.09.02	LIVERPOOL
Hurrell, Piers Richard, pce, n	CDR(FTC)	X	AAWO	30.06.05	JSCSC
Hurry, Andrew Patridge, pcea	LT CDR(FTC)	X	P	01.11.94	FLEET HQ PORTS 2
Hurst, Charles Nicholas Somerville	LT(IC)	X	SM	01.02.01	FLEET HQ NWD
Husband, James, MEng	LT(IC)	E	SM	01.01.05	TRENCHANT
Hussain, Amjad Mazhar, MSc, CEng, MIEE, jsdc	CDRE(FTC)	E	WE	09.07.02	NBC PORTSMOUTH
Hussain, Shayne, MBE, BSc, PhD, PGDip	LT CDR(FTC)	X	METOC	01.03.99	UKMARBATSTAFF
Hussey, Steven John, BSc, MA, psc(j)	MAJ(FTC)	-	P	01.09.99	847 SQN
Hutchings, James Stewart	LT CDR(FTC)	E	AE	01.10.00	FLEET AV VL
Hutchings, Justin Robert, MA, SM(n), SM	LT(CC)	X	SM	01.04.99	TORBAY
Hutchings, Richard Peter Hugh, MA, SM(n)	LT(FTC)	X	SM	01.12.97	GIBRALTAR PBS
Hutchings, Sam David ,BM, DipIMC RCSED, MRCS	SURG LTCDR(FCC)	-		06.08.02	NELSON (PAY)
Hutchins, Iain David MacKenzie, n	LT(FTC)	X	PWO(N)	01.09.98	MWS COLLINGWOOD
Hutchins, Richard Frank, BEng, MSc	LT CDR(FTC)	E	MESM	01.06.01	TRAFALGAR
Hutchins, Timothy Simon, BSc (Act Lt Cdr)	LT(FTC)	X	H2	16.06.96	JSCSC
Hutchinson, Alexander Paul	MID(NE)(IC)	X	P U/T	01.05.04	RAF CRANWELL EFS
Hutchinson, Christopher John, BSc, PGDip	LT CDR(FTC)	X	METOC	01.09.00	JHQ/CIS LISBON
Hutchinson, Michael Robert	LT(IC)	X	FC	01.01.05	GLOUCESTER
Hutchinson, Nicholas James, BA	LT(CC)	X		01.01.02	EXCHANGE ITALY
Hutchinson, Oliver James Procter	LT CDR(FTC)	X	AAWO	01.09.97	KENT
Hutchinson, Peter, IEng, AMIMarEST	LT(FTC)	E	ME	14.06.96	DSFM PORTSMOUTH
Hutchison, George Bruce, pcea, psc(j)	CDR(FTC)	X	O	30.06.03	HQ SACT
Hutchison, Paul Gordon, BEng, MSc, MIMarEST, CEng	LT CDR(FTC)	E	MESM	01.05.98	FLEET HQ PORTS 2
Hutton, Graham, pcea	LT CDR(FTC)	X	O	01.10.04	MWC SOUTHWICK
Hutton, James Kyle, psc(m) (Act Col)	LT COL(FTC)	-		30.06.97	STRIKFORNATO
Hutton, Katharine Denise, BEd, LCIPD	LT CDR(FTC)	E	TM	21.01.02	NTE(TTD)
Huxford, Stephen, BSc	LT(CC)	X		01.08.01	MWS COLLINGWOOD
Huynh, Cuong Chuong, BA	LT(CC)	S		01.03.02	MOD (LONDON)
Hyde, James William, MEng	LT(IC)	E	WE	01.09.02	CAMPBELTOWN
Hygate, Alison Margaret, BEng	LT CDR(FTC)	X		01.05.02	OCLC BIRM
Hyland, Roger Alan, BSc, PGDip, MIEE, MAPM	LT(FTC)	E	WE	22.02.96	CAPT MCTA
Hyldon, Christopher John, BSc, FRAeS, jsdc, sondc	CAPT(FTC)	E	AE	30.06.99	SA BUENOS AIRES
Hynde, Claire Louise, BSc	LT(CC)	S		01.07.00	NP IRAQ

I

Name	Rank	Branch	Spec	Seniority	Where Serving
Ibbotson, Richard Jeffery, DSC, MSc, CGIA, pce (NAVAL SECRETARY JUN 05)	RADM	-	PWO(U)	23.06.05	NAVSEC
Iliffe, David Ian, BD, MLITT	LT(IC)	X		16.11.98	BDS WASHINGTON
Imm, Nicholas David Harvey ,BM, DRCOG, MRCGP	SURG LTCDR(SC(MD)	-	GMPP	23.11.01	OCEAN
Imrie, Peter Blain, DSM	LT CDR(FTC)	X	AV	01.10.04	RFANSU (ARGUS)
Imrie, Samantha Jane, BA	LT(IC)	S		01.09.03	DLO/DG DEF SC
Ince, David Peter	LT CDR(FTC)	X	MCD	01.12.97	EXCHANGE USA
Ingamells, Stephen David, BSc	LT(IC)	X	P	01.01.04	DHFS
Inge, Daniel Jon (Act Lt Cdr)	LT(FTC)	X	ATC	01.05.95	RAF COTTESMORE

Name	Rank	Branch	Spec	Seniority	Where Serving
Ingham, Andrew Richard, BEng, n	LT(FTC)	X	PWO(A)	01.09.98	CHATHAM
Ingham, Nicholas Hampshire	LT(CC)	X		01.09.04	FWO FASLANE
Ingham, Phillip Clayton, pce, psc	CDR(FTC)	X	PWO(N)	30.06.92	LOAN KUWAIT
Inglis, David John, BSc	LT(IC)	X	P	01.01.02	RNAS YEOVILTON
Inglis, Graham Douglas, BSc	LT(IC)	X		01.05.04	IRON DUKE
Inglis, William Sinclair	SLT(IC)	X		01.01.04	MWS COLLINGWOOD
Ingram, Gareth John, BSc	LT CDR(FTC)	X	O	01.12.03	815 FLT 201
Ingram, Richard Gordon, pce, psc(a)	CDR(FTC)	X	AAWO	30.06.98	MOD (LONDON)
Innes, Ross	SLT(IC)	X	P U/T	01.09.03	DARTMOUTH BRNC
Inness, Matthew John, BEng	LT(IC)	E	MESM	01.01.03	SPARTAN
Insley, Andrew David, BSc	SLT(IC)	X		01.09.02	OCEAN
Instone, Malcolm John, BA, n	LT(CC)	X		01.11.98	DARTMOUTH BRNC
Ireland, Alasdair Robbie, MNI, pce, psc(j), MA	CDR(FTC)	X	AAWO	30.06.99	UKMARBATSTAFF
Ireland, John Mitchell	LT CDR(FTC)	E	MESM	01.10.02	DLO BRISTOL
Ireland, Philip Charles, DSC, pce	CDR(FTC)	X	MCD	30.06.04	STRIKFORNATO
Ireland, Roger Charles, MBE, MILT, ACIS	CDR(FTC)	S	SM	31.12.95	FLEET HQ PORTS
Irons, Paul Andrew	LT CDR(FTC)	X		01.07.97	NP IRAQ
Irons, Rupert Charles St John, BSc, n	LT CDR(FTC)	X	PWO(C)	01.10.03	CAMPBELTOWN
Irving, David Michael (Act Lt Cdr)	LT(FTC)	X	PWO(C)	10.01.00	ILLUSTRIOUS
Irving, Paul John, BA	SLT(IC)	X	P U/T	01.09.02	MWS COLLINGWOOD
Irving, Thomas Charles, BA	LT(IC)	S		01.05.03	CUMBERLAND
Irwin, Mark Andrew, BEng, MSc, CEng, MIMechE	LT CDR(FTC)	E	ME	09.01.97	DLO BRISTOL
Irwin, Stuart Gordon	LT(CC)	X	P	01.06.00	FLEET AV VALLEY
Isaac, Philip, ACIS	CDR(FTC)	S		31.12.99	FLEET HQ PORTS
Isaacs, Nathan James, BSc	LT(IC)	X		01.05.04	IRON DUKE
Isbister, Elspeth Joy, MB, CHB	SURG LT(SC(MD)	-		06.08.03	CFLT MED(SEA)
Isherwood, Carl Richard, BD	LT(IC)	X		01.05.04	WESTMINSTER
Issitt, Barry David	LT(IC)	X	P	01.01.02	RNAS YEOVILTON
Issitt, David James, BA, BSc, jsdc	CDR(FTC)	E	AE	30.06.90	FS MASU
Ives, David Jonathan, BSc	LT(CC)	X		01.06.00	FWO DEVPT SEA
Ivill, Stephen, QCBA	LT(IC)	X	O U/T	01.07.04	RNAS CULDROSE
Ivory, Thomas Joel, BEng	SLT(IC)	E	WE U/T	01.11.02	MWS COLLINGWOOD

J

Name	Rank	Branch	Spec	Seniority	Where Serving
Jackman, Andrew Warren, pce	CDR(FTC)	X	PWO(C)	30.06.98	MOD (LONDON)
Jackman, Richard William, BSc, MIEE, psc	CDRE(FTC)	E	WE	26.08.03	NC3 AGENCY
Jackson, Andrew Stephen, MSc	CDR(FTC)	E	MESM	30.06.05	JSCSC
Jackson, Anthony	LT(IC)	S		21.12.01	DRAKE COB
Jackson, David John, BEng, MSc	LT CDR(FTC)	E	AE	01.03.00	DLO YEO
Jackson, Howard Charles, BEng	LT(CC)	X	P	01.05.01	845 SQN
Jackson, Ian, SM	LT(CC)	X	H2	01.03.97	ENTERPRISE
Jackson, Ian Anthony, MSc, psc(j)o	LT CDR(FTC)	E	ME	01.04.96	FLEET HQ PORTS 2
Jackson, Mark Harding, MA, Cert Ed	CHAPLAIN	CE		19.04.83	CMT SHRIVENHAM
Jackson, Matthew John Andrew, MA	MAJ(FTC)	-		01.09.02	JSCSC
Jackson, Pamela, BSc	LT(CC)	X	ATCU/T	01.02.00	EXCHANGE RAF UK
Jackson, Paul Anthony	LT CDR(FTC)	S	(W)	01.10.01	FLEET HQ PORTS
Jackson, Peter Neil, BA, BEng, CEng, MIEE, LLB, LLM	LT CDR(FTC)	E	AE	01.02.99	ADAS BRISTOL
Jackson, Stephen Norman, BSc	LT(CC)	E	IS	01.01.00	COS 2SL/CNH
Jackson, Stevan Kenneth, FRGS, FInstLM	CAPT(FTC)	MS		31.08.04	MOD (LONDON)
Jackson, Stuart Harry, BSc, MBA, MRAeS (Act Cdr)	LT CDR(FTC)	E	AE	01.07.89	MOD (BATH)
Jackson-Smith, Stuart Paul	LT(CC)	X	ATC	01.09.01	EXCHANGE RAF UK
Jacob, Andrew William, BA	LT(CC)	X	H2	01.07.00	ECHO
Jacobs, Matthew Philip, BEng	LT(CC)	E	ME	01.02.98	DLO BRISTOL
Jacques, Karen Michelle, BA, n	LT CDR(FTC)	X		01.05.05	MWS COLLINGWOOD
Jacques, Marcus James	LT CDR(FTC)	X	AAWO	01.07.02	UKMARBATSTAFF
Jacques, Nicholas Adrian	LT CDR(FTC)	X	O	01.10.02	815 SQN HQ
Jagger, Paul Richard Albert, MSc, AMIEE	CAPT(FTC)	E	WESM	30.06.05	ASM IPT
Jaggers, Gary George, pcea	LT CDR(FTC(A)	X	O	01.10.01	FLEET AV CU
James, Adam Jon	LT CDR(FTC)	X	H CH	01.10.97	FLEET HQ PORTS 2
James, Alexander Williams, BSc	LT(FTC)	X	FC	01.04.99	EXPRESS
James, Andrew George, BEng, AMIMechE	LT(FTC)	E	MESM	01.09.02	TRAFALGAR
James, Christopher, BSc, CEng, MIMarEST, MIMechE	LT CDR(FTC)	E	MESM	01.06.91	ASM IPT

Name	Rank	Branch	Spec	Seniority	Where Serving
James, Christopher William, pce	LT CDR(FTC)	X	AAWO	27.10.93	SA MALAYSIA
James, David Russell, pce, pcea, psc	CAPT(FTC)	X	O	30.06.04	FLEET HQ PORTS
James, Gareth Clark Miguel	LT(IC)	S		01.05.03	NEPTUNE BNSL
James, Ian, BChD, MA, MFGDP(UK), psc(j)	SGCDR(D)(FCC)	-		30.06.05	DDA HALTON
James, Katherine Jeanette (Act Lt Cdr)	LT(FC(MD)	Q	CC	26.11.96	RCDM
James, Mark	LT(FTC)	E	WE	01.04.01	FOST SEA
James, Paul Melvyn, psc(j)	MAJ(FTC)	-		01.09.01	HQ ARRC
James, Richard Michael, BSc	LT(IC)	X	SM	01.11.01	VANGUARD(PORT)
James, Robert	LT(IC)	X	AV	01.07.04	RFANSU
Jameson, Andrew Charles, LLB, psc(j) (Barrister)	CDR(FTC)	S	BAR	31.12.98	SULTAN
Jameson, Andrew John, BA	LT(IC)	E	TM	01.09.98	2SL/CNH FOTR
Jameson, Roger Mark, BSc	LT(FTC)	X	P	16.07.92	815 FLT 212
Jamieson, Paul Andrew	SLT(IC)	X	SM	01.01.03	VENGEANCE(STBD)
Jamieson, Scott	SURG SLT(SCC)	-		13.09.04	DARTMOUTH BRNC
Jamison, James Scott	CAPT RM(IC)	-		01.09.04	45 CDO RM
Janaway, Paul, BSc, CEng, MIEE	CDR(FTC)	E	WE	30.06.05	HQ DCSA
Jane, Samuel Charles, BSc	SLT(IC)	X		01.07.02	TYNE
Janzen, Alexander, BA	MAJ(FTC)	-	C	01.10.04	42 CDO RM
Jaques, David Anthony (Act Lt Cdr)	LT(CC)	X		16.08.92	PJHQ
Jaques, Simon Christopher David, MB, BS, MSc	SURG LT(SC(MD)	-		06.08.03	CFLT MED(SEA)
Jardine, Darren Scott, MRIN, n, MSc	LT CDR(FTC)	X	AAWO	01.10.03	EXCHANGE CANADA
Jardine, Graham Andrew, pce, pcea, psc(j)	CDR(FTC)	X	O	30.06.98	FOST NWD (JMOTS)
Jardine, Iain, BEng	LT(IC)	X	P	01.05.04	RNAS YEOVILTON
Jarman, Paul Richard	LT(CC)	E	WESM	01.01.02	RALEIGH
Jarvis, David John, BSc, CEng, MIEE, psc	CAPT(FTC)	E	WESM	31.12.99	MOD (LONDON)
Jarvis, Ian Lawrence, BSc, psc	CAPT(FTC)	E	WE	30.06.97	MOD (LONDON)
Jarvis, Laurence Richard, BSc, psc(j)	CDR(FTC)	E	ME	30.06.02	T45 IPT
Jarvis, Lionel John, MB, BS, LRCP, FRCR, MIEE, MRCS, rcds	SURG CAPT(FCC)	-	CPDATE	31.12.99	2SL/CNH
Jayes, Neil John	LT(FTC)	X	REG	01.04.01	MWS COLLINGWOOD
Jaynes, Peter Robert William, BSc, CEng, FIMechE, psc	CAPT(FTC)	E	ME	30.06.99	NBC PORTSMOUTH
Jefferson, Peter Mark, pcea	LT CDR(FTC)	X	O	01.10.96	849 SQN B FLT
Jefferson, Toby Simon, BEng	LT CDR(FTC)	E	AE	01.10.04	JCA IPT UK
Jeffery, Samuel	SURG SLT(SCC)	-		01.07.03	DARTMOUTH BRNC
Jeffs, Samuel George	MID(NE)(IC)	X		01.11.04	DARTMOUTH BRNC
Jemmeson, Susannah Hazel, BA, MSc	LT(IC)	S		01.05.03	UKMARBATSTAFF
Jenkin, Alastair Michael Hugh, BSc, MA, CEng, MIEE, psc(m)	CDR(FTC)	E	WE	31.12.96	NBC PORTSMOUTH
Jenkin, James Richard Saint Lawrence	LT CDR(FTC)	X	SM	01.05.92	LOAN DSTL
Jenking-Rees, Damian, LLB	LT(CC)	S		01.10.97	PJHQ
Jenkins, Alastair Rodney, BSc	LT(CC)	X	P	16.06.98	RAF CRANWELL EFS
Jenkins, David Gareth, BSc, SM(n)	LT(CC)	X	SM	01.09.01	TRENCHANT
Jenkins, Gari Wyn, BEng, MSc, gw	CDR(FTC)	E	WE	30.06.03	HQ DCSA
Jenkins, Gwyn	MAJ(FTC)	-		01.09.01	JSCSC
Jenkins, Ian Lawrence, CVO, MB, BCH, FRCS (SURGEON GENERAL (SL 01) OCT 02)	SURG VADM	-	CPDATE	21.10.02	MOD (LONDON)
Jenkins, Robert Christopher, BSc	LT(IC)	E	TM	01.12.99	DEF SCH OF LANG
Jenkins, Thomas Richard	SLT(IC)	X		01.09.02	LANCASTER
Jenks, Anthony William Jervis, FIMarEST, CMarSci	LT CDR(FTC)	X	H CH	16.04.87	MWS HM TG (D)
Jenner, Andrew Christopher, BEng	LT(IC)	E	TM	16.09.97	SULTAN
Jennings, Christian Rubin, MBE	LT(IC)	S		01.01.04	AFPAA(CENTURION)
Jennings, William, BEng	LT CDR(FTC)	E	ME	01.03.03	IRON DUKE
Jepson, Nicholas Henry Martin	MAJ(FTC)	-	C	01.09.03	NAVSEC
Jermy, Stephen Charles, BSc, MPhil, pce	CDRE(FTC)	X	O	10.09.02	MOD (LONDON)
Jermyn, Nicholas Charles, BA	MAJ(FTC)	-	LC	01.09.00	45 CDO RM
Jerrold, William Harry, MEng	LT(IC)	E	ME U/T	01.09.03	GLOUCESTER
Jervis, Neil David, pce(sm)	CDR(FTC)	X	SM	30.06.99	SHAPE BELGIUM
Jess, Aran Ernest Kingston, BSc, MPhil	MAJ(FTC)	-	MLDR	01.10.04	45 CDO RM
Jess, Ian Michael, MA, MA, MSc, CEng, MIMarEST, psc	CAPT(FTC)	E	ME	31.12.00	DLO BRISTOL
Jessiman, Sarah Irene, BDS	SGLTCDR(D)(MCC)	-		20.06.02	FORT BLOCKHOUSE
Jessop, Paul Edward, MBE, BEng, MSc, CEng, MIMechE	CDR(FTC)	E	MESM	31.12.00	NP BRISTOL
Jewitt, Charles James Bagot, MSc, BA	CDR(FTC)	S		30.06.03	FLEET HQ NWD
Jewson, Benjamin David, BEng	LT(IC)	X	O	01.05.04	702 SQN HERON
Johansen, Stephen Paul	LT(IC)	E	ME	01.05.04	SULTAN
John, Gareth David, MBE, BSc, PGDip, CEng, MIEE	LT CDR(FTC)	E	WE	01.09.92	AGRIPPA JFC HQ

Name	Rank	Branch	Spec	Seniority	Where Serving
Johns, Adrian James, CBE, BSc, pce, pcea, psc, hcsc	RADM	-	P	27.05.03	MOD (LONDON)
(ASSISTANT CHIEF OF THE NAVAL STAFF MAY 03)					
Johns, Andrew William, SM(n), SM	LT(FTC)	X	SM	01.03.98	CHARGER
Johns, Leslie Ernest	LT(FTC)	X	REG	23.07.98	CALEDONIA DLO
Johns, Michael Glynn, BSc, pcea	LT CDR(FTC)	X	O	01.10.99	824 SQN
Johns, Sarah Alice Bedford, MSc, MCIPD	LT CDR(FTC)	E	TM	01.10.96	2SL/CNH FOTR
Johns, Tony, MSc, psc	CAPT(FTC)	E	MESM	31.12.00	RCDS
Johnson, Alex David, BSc	LT(CC)	X	P	01.01.99	815 SQN HQ
Johnson, Amanda Constance	LT(CC)	S		01.09.00	NAVSEC
Johnson, Andrew Martin	SLT(IC)	X		01.07.02	LANCASTER
Johnson, Andrew Stephen, pce	CDR(FTC)	X	AAWO	31.12.99	MOD (LONDON)
Johnson, Anthony Robert	LT(FTC)	X	O	16.02.95	702 SQN HERON
Johnson, Bryan, BSc, pce	LT CDR(FTC)	X	PWO(U)	01.05.88	MWS COLLINGWOOD
Johnson, Chad Colin Burnett, BEng	LT CDR(FTC)	E	AE	01.04.02	RNAS YEOVILTON
Johnson, Grenville Philip, MBE, jsdc, pce (Act Capt)	CDR(FTC)	X	MCD	31.12.91	SAUDI AFPS SAUDI
Johnson, James Charles, MBE, BEng, MBA, CEng, MIEE (Act Capt)	CDR(FTC)	E	WESM	31.12.99	DPA BRISTOL
Johnson, Kevin, MBE	LT(FTC)	S	(S)	09.01.01	DLO BRISTOL
Johnson, Lee Samuel, n	LT CDR(FTC)	X	PWO(A)	01.03.00	MWC PORTSDOWN
Johnson, Mark	CAPT RM(CC)	-	P	01.09.99	848 SQN HERON
Johnson, Mark Ralph Edward, BSc	LT(FTC)	X		01.07.98	EXPLOIT
Johnson, Mark William, BSc	LT(IC)	X		01.09.02	MWS HM TG (D)
Johnson, Michael David, ACMI	LT CDR(FTC)	S	(W)	01.10.03	AGRIPPA MAR CC
Johnson, Michael John	LT CDR(FTC)	E	WE	01.10.01	DLO BRISTOL
Johnson, Paul Raymond, BEng	LT(CC)	E	AE	01.02.99	DLO YEO
Johnson, Scott, SM(n), SM	LT(FTC)	X	SM	01.09.99	TRAFALGAR
Johnson, Sharon Valerie	LT(SC(MD)	Q		01.09.03	NELSON (PAY)
Johnson, Symon	LT(CC)	X	P	16.01.97	848 SQN HERON
Johnson, Thomas	MID(UCE)(IC)	E	WE U/T	01.09.03	DARTMOUTH BRNC
Johnson, Tim Paul	SLT(IC)	X		01.07.02	ILLUSTRIOUS
Johnson, Voirrey (Act Lt Cdr)	LT(FC(MD)	Q		25.01.96	MOD (LONDON)
Johnston, Andrew Iain, BA	LT(IC)	X	P	01.05.04	RNAS YEOVILTON
Johnston, Charles Gardner, MB, BCh, BAO, FFARCSI	SURG CAPT(FCC)	-	(CA)	31.12.00	INVINCIBLE
Johnston, David Raymond	LT(IC)	S		01.05.02	TRAFALGAR
Johnston, Gavin Stewart, MA	LT(CC)	X	P	01.12.98	RAF SHAWBURY
Johnston, Jeffrey Joseph, BA	LT(IC)	X		01.01.03	CHATHAM
Johnston, Karl George	CAPT RM(IC)	-		01.09.03	42 CDO RM
Johnston, Kirsten Iona, MSc	LT(IC)	E	TM	01.05.99	NAVSEC
Johnston, Richard Patrick, MB, BS, MRCP, MFOM, DipAvMed	SURG CDR(FCC)	-	(CO/M)	30.06.97	DRAKE CBS
Johnston, Timothy Alan, pce, pcea, psc(j)	CDR(FTC)	X	P	30.06.03	FWO PORTS SEA
Johnstone, Clive Charles Carruthers, BSc, pce	CAPT(FTC)	X	PWO(A)	30.06.03	FLEET HQ PORTS 2
Johnstone-Burt, Charles Anthony, OBE, MA, FCIPD, pce, pcea, hcsc	CDRE(FTC)	X	P	10.01.02	OCEAN
Joll, Simon Mark, BA, MInstAM, AMIAM	LT CDR(FTC)	S	SM	01.10.01	FLEET HQ PORTS
Jones, Adam Edward, BEng, pcea	LT CDR(FTC)	X	P	01.11.02	ALBION
Jones, Aled Lewis, MB, CHB, BSc	SURG LT(SCC)	-		06.08.03	FLEET AV SULTAN
Jones, Alun David, BA, pce, pcea	LT CDR(FTC)	X	P	01.11.97	CARDIFF
Jones, Anna Louise, BA	LT(IC)	S		01.11.04	RALEIGH
Jones, Christopher David	LT(CC)	E	WE	01.01.02	MWS COLLINGWOOD
Jones, Collin Raymond	LT(CS)(CAS)	-		08.01.99	DNR NWE 2
Jones, Craig Antony, n	LT CDR(FTC)	X	PWO(C)	01.11.99	FLEET HQ NWD
Jones, Darren Paul, MEng	SLT(IC)	E	AE U/T	01.09.03	INVINCIBLE
Jones, David Allen, MSc	LT CDR(FTC)	E	MESM	01.10.99	TIRELESS
Jones, David Bryan, BEng, MSc, AMIMechE	LT CDR(FTC)	E	MESM	01.07.99	FLEET HQ PORTS 2
Jones, David Kenneth	LT(IC)	S		01.05.03	RALEIGH
Jones, David Lloyd, BTech	LT CDR(FTC)	E	WE	01.10.02	CAMPBELTOWN
Jones, David Michael, BEng, MIEE	LT CDR(FTC)	E	WE	01.07.04	NP IRAQ
Jones, Emmanuel Nelson Lomotetteh	LT(IC)	X		01.01.03	WESTMINSTER
Jones, Gareth David, BSc, PGCE	LT CDR(FTC)	E	TM	01.09.03	NTE(TTD)
Jones, Glyn Robert, MA(CANTAB), MA, pce, psc(j)	CDR(FTC)	X	METOC	30.06.05	MOD (LONDON)
Jones, Gordon James Lyn, BSc	LT(IC)	X		01.09.03	RFANSU (ARGUS)
Jones. Hayley, BEng	SLT(IC)	E	WE U/T	01.01.04	DARTMOUTH BRNC
Jones, Huw Ashton, MSc	CDR(FTC)	E	MESM	31.12.00	ASM IPT
Jones, Ian Michael, BEng	LT(FTC)	E	AE	01.11.99	ILLUSTRIOUS
Jones, Lyndsey Helan, BEng	LT(IC)	E	TM	14.02.99	SULTAN AIB

Name	Rank	Branch	Spec	Seniority	Where Serving
Jones, Marc Robert	SLT(IC)	S		01.01.04	DARTMOUTH BRNC
Jones, Mark Douglas, BEng	LT(CC)	X	O	16.01.95	815 FLT 244
Jones, Mark Robert	LT(IC)	E	WE	01.07.04	CAMPBELTOWN
Jones, Mark Roger, BEng	LT(CC)	E	WE	01.06.00	FOST SEA
Jones, Martin Clifford, BSc, FIMarEST, pce, psc(j), n	CDR(FTC)	X	H CH	30.06.01	MOD (LONDON)
Jones, Martin David, BA	LT CDR(FTC)	X	PWO(A)	01.01.03	CAPT MCTA
Jones, Martyn Aubrey, BA, IEng, MIPlantE, MSE (Act Lt Cdr)	LT(FTC)	E	ME	13.06.97	SOUTHAMPTON
Jones, Matthew Russell, MBE, BA	MAJ(FTC)	-		01.09.98	45 CDO RM
Jones, Michael, pce	LT CDR(FTC)	X	AAWO	01.03.95	EXCHANGE CANADA
Jones, Nigel Patrick, SM(n), SM	LT CDR(FTC)	X	PWO(U)	01.02.99	SOMERSET
Jones, Paul, pce, psc(j), MA	CDR(FTC)	X	MCD	30.06.04	FLEET HQ PORTS 2
Jones, Paul Andrew, MSc	LT(FTC)	E	WE	09.01.01	MWS COLLINGWOOD
Jones, Paul David, SM(n), SM	LT CDR(FTC)	X	SM	01.10.04	TORBAY
Jones, Philip Andrew, MA, jsdc, pce	CDRE(FTC)	X	PWO(C)	13.12.04	FLEET CIS PORTS
Jones, Richard John, BA	LT(IC)	X		01.05.01	2SL/CNH
Jones, Richard William, MA, MSc, CEng, MIMarEST, psc(j)	CDR(FTC)	E	ME	30.06.02	MOD (LONDON)
Jones, Robert Peter Martyn, BA	CAPT RM(FTC)	-		01.09.03	CDO LOG REGT RM
Jones, Russell Keenan, IEng, MIEE	LT(FTC)	E	MESM	19.06.98	SOVEREIGN
Jones, Simon Sean	LT(FTC)	X	AV	01.04.01	ILLUSTRIOUS
Jones, Stephen	LT(IC)	E	ME	01.05.03	RNAS CULDROSE
Jones, Timothy Mark, BSc, DIPRP	LT(FTC)	MS		01.04.01	INM ALVERSTOKE
Jones, Toby, BA	SLT(IC)	X		01.02.04	DARTMOUTH BRNC
Jones, William Colston	SLT(IC)	X	P U/T	01.02.04	DARTMOUTH BRNC
Jones-Thompson, Michael John	LT(FTC)	X	AAWO	01.04.01	MANCHESTER
Jordan, Adrian Mark, BDS, MSc, LDS RCS(Eng)	SGCDR(D)(FCC)	-	GDP UT	31.12.98	RALEIGH
Jordan, Andrew Aidan, BA, pce, psc(j), n	CDR(FTC)	X	PWO(U)	30.06.05	IRON DUKE
Jordan, Anna Frances, LLB	LT(FTC)	X		01.09.99	RNP TEAM
Jordan, Craig, BEng, MSc	LT(CC)	E	IS	01.01.95	MWS COLLINGWOOD
Jordan, Emma Lesley, LLB	LT(IC)	X	HM	01.05.97	RNAS YEOVILTON
Jordan, Mark David, BSc, BEng	LT(IC)	E	WE	01.05.01	SUTHERLAND
Jordan, Nicholas Stuart	LT CDR(FTC)	E	WE	01.10.98	LOAN DSTL
Jose, Steven, BA	LT CDR(FTC)	E	AE	01.03.02	LOAN JTEG BSC DN
Jowett, Adrian	SURG SLT(SCC)	-		05.11.04	DARTMOUTH BRNC
Joyce, David Andrew, BEng, MSc, MPhil, CEng, MIEE	LT CDR(FTC)	E	WE	01.10.00	FLEET HQ PORTS
Joyce, David James, BEng	LT(IC)	E	ME	01.09.04	RICHMOND
Joyce, Philip, BSc, psc(j)	LT COL(FTC)	-		30.06.04	MOD (LONDON)
Joyce, Thomas Jeremy, pcea	LT CDR(FTC)	X	P	01.11.99	FLEET HQ PORTS
Joyner, Adam, pce, pcea	LT CDR(FTC)	X	P	01.05.89	RN GIBRALTAR
Juckes, Martin Anthony	LT CDR(FTC)	E	AE	16.08.95	NAVSEC
Julian, Timothy Mark	LT CDR(FTC)	X	P	01.10.04	849 SQN A FLT

K

Name	Rank	Branch	Spec	Seniority	Where Serving
Kadinopoulos, Benjamin Alexander, BA	LT(FTC)	E	WE	01.09.03	CORNWALL
Karsten, Thomas Michael, BA, jsdc, pce	CAPT(FTC)	X	PWO(U)	31.12.00	ENDURANCE
Kassapian, David Lee, BA, psc(j)	LT COL(FTC)	-		30.06.04	FLEET HQ NWD
Kay, Paul Stuart, SM(n), SM	LT(FTC)	X	SM	01.04.01	VANGUARD(PORT)
Kay, Victoria Joanne, MEng	SLT(IC)	E	WE U/T	01.11.02	2SL/CNH
Keam, Ian	LT(IC)	E	AE U/T	13.08.04	702 SQN HERON
Keane, Brendan Michael	LT(IC)	E	WE	01.05.03	2SL/CNH
Keane, Joseph Patrick	SLT(IC)	X	O U/T	01.05.03	750 SQN SEAHAWK
Kearney, Paul Leonard, BDS, psc(j)o	MAJ(FTC)	-		27.04.02	MOD (LONDON)
Keble, Kenneth Wayne Latimer, OBE, jsdc, pce, pcea	CAPT(FTC)	X	O	30.06.05	NP IRAQ
Keefe, Patrick Charles, BSc	CDR(FTC)	S		31.12.95	MOD (LONDON)
Keegan, Amanda Claire, BSc	SLT(IC)	X	P U/T	01.09.02	RNAS YEOVILTON
Keegan, William John, BSc, CEng, MIEE, psc	CDRE(FTC)	E	WE	26.04.05	NAVSEC
Keeley, Stephen Peter	LT CDR(FTC)	E	MESM	01.10.02	DRAKE SFM
Keen, Neil, BEng, MIEE	LT CDR(FTC)	E	WE	01.06.01	SOUTHAMPTON
Keenan, Benjamin F, BEng, MSc	LT(IC)	E	MESM	01.09.02	TIRELESS
Kehoe, Anthony Desmond, MB, ChB	SURG LTCDR(FCC)	-		01.12.00	LOAN FIELD HOSP
Keillor, Stuart James, SM(n)	LT(CC)	X	SM	01.09.04	SCEPTRE
Keith, Benjamin Charles, BSc	LT(CC)	X	P	01.05.00	815 FLT 226
Kelbie, Ewan, MA, pce, pcea, psc(j)	CDR(FTC)	X	P	30.06.02	MOD (LONDON)

Name	Rank	Branch	Spec	Seniority	Where Serving
Kellett, Andrew, BEng, CEng, MIMarEST	LT CDR(FTC)	E	ME	01.10.03	MONTROSE
Kelley, Alexandra Louise, BSc	SLT(IC)	X	O U/T	01.01.04	DARTMOUTH BRNC
Kelly, Anthony Paul	MAJ(FTC)	-	SO(LE)	01.10.01	45 CDO RM
Kelly, Frank Aidan	LT(SC(MD)	Q		01.02.02	RCDM
Kelly, Grant Jason, MA	LT(CC)	E	TM	01.09.96	ILLUSTRIOUS
Kelly, Howard Clifton, BEng	LT CDR(FTC)	E	MESM	01.04.02	SPARTAN
Kelly, John Anson, BEng	LT CDR(FTC)	E	ME	01.02.00	CAPT MCTA
Kelly, John Anthony ,BMus	CAPT RM(CC)	BS	SO(LE)	01.01.01	JSCSC
Kelly, Nigel James	CHAPLAIN	CE		26.05.92	RCDM
Kelly, Philip Michael, BEng, MSc	MAJ(FTC)	-	P	01.09.02	LOAN OTHER SVCE
Kelly, Richard, pce(sm)	LT CDR(FTC)	X	SM	03.04.91	ASM IPT
Kelly, Simon Peter, BA	LT(FTC)	X	MCD	01.07.99	EXCHANGE FRANCE
Kelly, Stephen	LT(IC)	X		01.01.03	MONMOUTH
Kelly, Thomas James, BA	CAPT RM(IC)	-	MLDR	01.09.00	45 CDO RM
Kelynack, Mark Trevellyan, pcea	LT(FTC)	X	O	16.04.95	MWS SOUTHWICK PK
Kemp, Alexander Charles	CAPT RM(FTC)	-	LC	01.04.02	539 ASSLT SQN RM
Kemp, Peter	SURG SLT(SCC)	-		20.09.04	DARTMOUTH BRNC
Kemp, Peter John (Act Lt Col)	MAJ(FTC)	-	MLDR	01.09.98	STRIKFORNATO
Kemp, Richard Lee, BA	LT(IC)	X		01.09.04	MERSEY
Kempsell, Ian, BSc, CEng, MIMarEST	LT CDR(FTC)	E	ME	26.06.96	DRAKE SFM
Kenchington, Robin Anthony Warwick	MID(NE)(IC)	X	P U/T	01.11.04	DARTMOUTH BRNC
Kendall, Philip Colin	MID(NE)(IC)	X	O U/T	01.09.04	DARTMOUTH BRNC
Kendall-Torry, Guyan Charles	SLT(UCE)(IC)	E	WE	01.09.03	DARTMOUTH BRNC
Kendrick, Alexander Michael, BEng	LT CDR(FTC)	E	WE	01.02.05	DLO BRISTOL
Kennan, Nicholas Paul, LLB	LT(IC)	S		01.06.02	DSDA
Kennaugh, Alastair John, BSc, PGCE, psc	CDR(FTC)	E	TM	31.12.88	SULTAN AIB
Kenneally, Sean Joseph	CAPT RM(FTC)	-	SO(LE)	01.01.00	1 ASSAULT GP RM
Kennedy, Ian Christopher	LT(SCC)	Q	RMN	26.05.02	DRAKE COB(CNH)
Kennedy, Ian James Andrew, BEng, MA, CEng, MIMarEST, psc(j)	CDR(FTC)	E	ME	30.06.03	MOD (LONDON)
Kennedy, Inga Jane, DipEd	CDR(MC(MD)	Q		30.06.05	MDHU DERRIFORD
Kennedy, Nigel Henry, MSc, MIMarEST, psc	LT CDR(FTC)	E	ME	01.05.92	EXCHANGE CANADA
Kennedy, Roger John, BEng	LT(CC)	X	O	01.07.99	849 SQN A FLT
Kenney, Ronald Paul	CDR(FTC)	MS		30.06.04	PJHQ
Kennington, Lee Alexander, BSc	LT(CC)	X	O	01.05.94	JSCSC
Kennon, Stanley, BA, BD	CHAPLAIN	SF		24.09.00	FWO DEVPT SEA
Kenny, Luke E	CAPT RM(IC)	-		01.09.04	42 CDO RM
Kenny, Stephen James, pce, MA	CAPT(FTC)	X	AAWO	30.06.05	BDS WASHINGTON
Kent, Isabel Maria, BEd	LT CDR(FTC)	W	X	20.02.99	2SL/CNH FOTR
Kent, Martin David, BSc, pce (Act Cdr)	LT CDR(FTC)	X	PWO(N)	01.05.89	2SL/CNH FOTR
Kent, Matthew John	LT(IC)	E	ME	01.05.01	ST ALBANS
Kenward, Peter David, BSc, MA, DipFM, CEng, MRAeS, psc	CAPT(FTC)	E	AE	30.06.05	DLO YEO
Kenworthy, Richard Alan, BA, sq	MAJ(FTC)	-		30.04.98	CTCRM
Keogh, Joanna Mary Elizabeth, MB, BS	SURG LTCDR(FC(MD)	-		04.08.04	RH HASLAR
Kerchey, Stephen John Victor, BSc, CEng, MIEE	CDR(FTC)	E	WE	31.12.00	MOD (LONDON)
Kerley, Benjamin John	LT(IC)	X	P	01.05.03	RNAS YEOVILTON
Kern, Alastair Seymour	MAJ(FTC)	-		01.09.00	STRIKFORNATO
Kerr, Adrian Nicholas, BEng, CEng, MIEE	LT CDR(FTC)	E	WESM	01.01.01	TORBAY
Kerr, Alan Thomas Frederick	LT CDR(FTC)	X	PWO(U)	01.10.01	MWS COLLINGWOOD
Kerr, Jack	LT CDR(FTC)	X		01.10.01	LOAN BMATT(EC)
Kerr, William Malcolm McTaggart	LT CDR(FTC)	X	MCD	09.03.90	LOAN OMAN
Kershaw, Christopher Robert, MA, MB, BCh, FRCP, MRCS, DCH	SURG CAPT(FCC)	-	(CC)	30.06.85	RH HASLAR
Kershaw, Richard James ,BM	SURG LT(MC(MD)	-		07.08.02	CFLT MED(SEA)
Kershaw, Simon Henry Christopher, BDS	SG LT(D)(SCC)	-		18.07.01	NELSON
Kershaw, Steven, MA, MSc, CEng, MIEE, psc(j)	CDR(FTC)	E	WESM	30.06.01	DLO BRISTOL
Kerslake, Richard William, pce	LT CDR(FTC)	X	P	01.02.99	FLEET HQ PORTS
Kestle, Mark Edward	LT(IC)	E	ME	01.05.02	DLO BRISTOL
Kestle, Ryan	2LT(IC)	-		01.08.01	CTCRM LYMPSTONE
Kettle, Richard Andrew, BA, psc(j)o	MAJ(FTC)	-		24.04.99	CDO LOG REGT RM
Kewley, Ian David, BA, n	LT(FTC)	X		01.08.98	MWS COLLINGWOOD
Key, Benjamin John, BSc, pce	CDR(FTC)	X	O	31.12.99	MOD (LONDON)
Khan, Mansoor Ali, MB, BS	SURG LT(MC(MD)	-		01.08.01	MDHU PETERBRGH
Kidd, James Christian, MSc, CDipAF, psc, gw	CDRE(FTC)	E	WE	19.04.04	DPA BRISTOL
Kidd, Robert	2LT(IC)	-		01.08.04	CTCRM LYMPSTONE

Name	Rank	Branch	Spec	Seniority	Where Serving
Kiernan, Colin Graham, BEng	LT(IC)	X	P	01.05.02	815 FLT 246
Kierstan, Simon Janusz James, BEng	LT(IC)	E	TM	01.01.01	CMT SHRIVENHAM
Kies, Lawrence Norman, BSc, PGCE	LT CDR(FTC)	E	TM	01.10.03	CTCRM
Kiff, Ian William	LT(IC)	E	WE	01.01.03	MWS COLLINGWOOD
Kilbane, Dominic Kevin John, BSc	LT(IC)	X		01.04.03	SUPERB
Kilby, Stewart Edward, MA, pce, pcea, psc(j)	CDR(FTC)	X	O	30.06.04	JSCSC
Kilmartin, Andrew, BSc	LT(IC)	E	ME	01.02.99	CMT SHRIVENHAM
Kilmartin, Steven (Act Maj)	CAPT RM(IC)	-		04.04.97	NAVSEC
Kimberley, Robert, BSc, n	LT CDR(FTC)	X	PWO(U)	01.07.98	FLEET HQ NWD
Kimmons, Michael, BA, rcds	RADM	-		15.03.05	COS 2SL/CNH
(CHIEF OF STAFF TO 2SL/CNH MAR 05)					
King, Anthony Michael, BSc, CEng, MDA, MRAeS, MInsD	CAPT(FTC)	E	AE	30.06.04	DCAE COSFORD
King, Charles Edward William, BA, MILT, MCIPD, jsdc	CAPT(FTC)	S		30.06.04	DCL DEEPCUT
King, David Alexander, BA	LT(IC)	X		01.09.04	DUMBARTON CASTLE
King, David Christopher Michael, BSc, MA, psc(j)	LT COL(FTC)	-		30.06.01	40 CDO RM
King, Edward Michael, MSc, CEng, MIEE, CDipAF, gw	CAPT(FTC)	E	WE	30.06.03	AGRIPPA JFC HQ
King, Gordon Charles	LT CDR(FTC)	E	MESM	01.10.03	SPARTAN
King, Iain Andrew, BSc	LT(IC)	X	P	01.09.02	771 SQN
King, Ian Jonathan, BEng	SLT(IC)	E	AE U/T	01.09.02	SULTAN
King, Jason Matthew	LT(IC)	E	MESM	01.07.04	VENGEANCE(STBD)
King, Michael Andrew	SLT(UCE)(IC)	E	WE	01.09.02	DARTMOUTH BRNC
King, Nicholas William, BEng, MSc	LT CDR(FTC)	E	MESM	01.05.97	FWO FASLANE
King, Nigel Alan, pcea, psc(m)	LT CDR(FTC)	X	P	01.12.84	HANDLING SQN
King, Paul Christopher, MSc	LT CDR(FTC)	E	ME	01.09.92	SULTAN
King, Richard John, BSc, MA, psc(j)	MAJ(FTC)	-		01.05.01	EXCHANGE ARMY UK
King, Richard William, BSc, MPhil, pce, pcea	CDR(FTC)	X	P	30.06.02	DARTMOUTH BRNC
King, Steven John	LT CDR(FTC)	X	P	01.10.04	771 SQN
King, William Robert Charles, BSc	LT(FTC)	X		01.10.00	SOUTHAMPTON
King, William Thomas Poole, BEng	LT(IC)	E	MESM	01.09.01	TRAFALGAR
Kingdom, Mark Andrew, BEng	LT(FTC)	E	AE	01.02.97	FS MASU
Kingdon, Simon Charles	LT(IC)	S		01.01.02	MOD (LONDON)
Kings, Simon John Nicholson, MBE, DipFM, FCMI, pce, pcea	CAPT(FTC)	X	O	30.06.05	MOD (LONDON)
Kingsbury, James Arthur Timothy, BSc (Act Cdr) (Barrister)	LT CDR(FTC)	S	BAR	01.02.91	NAVSEC
Kingsbury, Simon Hugh, BEng, MSc, CEng, MIEE	LT CDR(FTC)	E	WE	01.04.96	HQ DCSA
Kingsbury-Smith, Rosemary (Act Surg Lt)	SURG SLT(SCC)	-		15.07.03	DARTMOUTH BRNC
Kingston, Earl Anthony, BEng	LT(IC)	X	P	01.09.02	814 SQN
Kingwell, John Matthew Leonard, pce, psc(j), MA	CAPT(FTC)	X	PWO(U)	30.06.05	NP IRAQ
Kirby, Stephen Redvers, BSc, MA, pce, pcea, psc, ocds(USN)	CDRE(FTC)	X	O	06.12.02	FLEET HQ PORTS 2
Kirk, Adrian Christopher, BEng	LT CDR(FTC)	E	AE	01.05.05	AH IPT
Kirk, Trevor Leslie, BSc, PGDip, psc (Act Cdr)	LT CDR(FTC)	E	WE	01.06.87	EXCHANGE AUSTLIA
Kirkby, Stephen James, BSc	LT(IC)	X		01.09.03	CATTISTOCK
Kirkham, Simon Philip, pcea	LT CDR(FTC)	X	P	01.10.04	727 NAS
Kirkman, Thomas Mark	2LT(IC)	-		05.01.03	42 CDO RM
Kirkup, John Paul, BSc, MA, psc(j)	CDR(FTC)	E	TM	30.06.03	FLEET HQ PORTS
Kirkwood, Tristram Andrew Harry, BSc	LT CDR(FTC)	X	PWO(U)	01.11.02	GRAFTON
Kirman, Christopher Richard	MID(IC)	X	P U/T	01.01.04	DARTMOUTH BRNC
Kirwan, John Anthony	LT(CC)	S		07.04.02	AFPAA(CENTURION)
Kissane, Robert Edward Thomas, BEng, MSc	CDR(FTC)	E	WE	30.06.03	CV(F) IPT
Kitchen, Bethan, BEng	LT(CC)	E	AE	01.07.00	JF HARROLE OFF
Kitchen, Stephen Anthony, BEng	LT CDR(FTC)	E	AE	01.01.98	LOAN DARA
Kitt, Robert George	LT(FTC)	E	WE	01.09.99	DL IPT
Kitteridge, Daniel James, BA	LT(CC)	X	P	01.01.00	846 SQN
Klar, Phillip	LT(IC)	MS	SM	01.07.04	FLEET HQ PORTS 2
Klidjian, Michael Jeffrey, BSc	LT(CC)	X	FC	01.05.01	RNAS YEOVILTON
Knibbs, Mark, BA, pce, psc(j)	CDR(FTC)	X	PWO(U)	30.06.99	D STRAT PLANS
Knight, Alastair Cameron Fergus, BSc	LT(CC)	X	P	01.03.94	771 SQN
Knight, Alexander James	MID(IC)	X		01.11.03	DARTMOUTH BRNC
Knight, Andrew Robert, pcea	LT CDR(FTC)	X	P	01.10.01	824 SQN
Knight, Anthony William, MBE, BSc, pce	LT CDR(FTC)	X	PWO(C)	01.02.90	AGRIPPA JFC HQ
Knight, Damon Ashley, MBE, pce	CDR(FTC)	X	AAWO	30.06.01	JDCC
Knight, Daniel Simon, BSc, SM(n), SM	LT(FTC)	X	SM	01.09.99	COTTESMORE
Knight, David William, BSc, pce	LT CDR(FTC)	X	AAWO	01.12.00	MWS COLLINGWOOD
Knight, Diane Joy	LT CDR(FC(MD)	Q	IC	01.10.01	MDHU DERRIFORD

Name	Rank	Branch	Spec	Seniority	Where Serving
Knight, James	2LT(IC)	-		01.08.04	CTCRM LYMPSTONE
Knight, Jeremy Denis	LT CDR(FTC)	X	EW	01.10.04	FLEET CIS PORTS
Knight, Jonathan Michael	SLT(IC)	X		01.01.03	2SL/CNH
Knight, Keith John, MBE, BSc, BTech	LT CDR(FTC)	E	WESM	01.10.03	MTS IPT
Knight, Paul James, BSc, psc(j)	CDR(FTC)	E	AE	30.06.03	JHCHQ
Knight, Paul Richard, BSc, psc	CDR(FTC)	E	MESM	30.06.03	DRAKE CBS
Knight, Robert Harry	LT CDR(FTC)	E	MESM	01.10.03	VENGEANCE(STBD)
Knight, Stephen	SLT(IC)	S		01.01.03	RNAS YEOVILTON
Knill, Robin Lloyd	LT CDR(FTC)	S	(S)	01.10.97	MOD (BATH)
Knock, Gareth Paul	LT CDR(FTC)	S	SM	01.10.01	MOD (BATH)
Knott, Michael Bruce, AMNI, pce	LT CDR(FTC)	X	PWO(N)	01.02.01	ILLUSTRIOUS
Knott, Thomas Michael	SLT(IC)	X		01.02.04	CUMBERLAND
Knowles, Christopher James, BSc	LT(IC)	X	P	01.03.01	814 SQN
Knowles, David	LT(IC)	X		01.09.04	SUTHERLAND
Knowles, Gareth Robert	CAPT RM(IC)	-	SO(LE)	01.04.04	42 CDO RM
Knowles, John Michael, rcds, pce, pcea, psc	CAPT(FTC)	X	P	30.06.99	RNAS CULDROSE
Knox, Graeme Peter, LLB	LT(FTC)	S		01.10.99	2SL/CNH
Koheeallee, Mohummed Cassim Rashid Charif, BEng	LT(IC)	X	P	01.05.04	RNAS YEOVILTON
Kohler, Andrew Philip	LT CDR(FTC)	X	PWO(A)	01.04.02	MWS COLLINGWOOD
Kohn, Patricia Anne, n	LT(FTC)	X		01.07.00	TRACKER
Kongialis, James Allyn, BSc	CAPT(FTC)	E	WESM	30.06.97	DLO BRISTOL
Kopsahilis, Alexandros	MID(IC)	X		01.05.03	GLOUCESTER
Kroon, Zoe	LT(CC)	X	FC	01.10.00	CAPT IST STAFF
Krosnar-Clarke, Steven Matthew, MSc	LT CDR(FTC)	E	TM	01.10.98	JSCSC
Kurth, Rolf Peter Ernst, SBSTJ (Act Lt Cdr)	LT(CC)	X	PWO(C)	18.05.98	FOST NWD (JMOTS)
Kyd, Jeremy Paul, PGDIPAN, pce, n, BSc	CDR(FTC)	X	PWO(N)	30.06.04	MONMOUTH
Kyle, Ryan	2LT(IC)	-		01.09.00	45 CDO RM
Kyte, Andrew Jeffery, MA, psc(j)	CDR(FTC)	S		30.06.03	PJHQ

L

Name	Rank	Branch	Spec	Seniority	Where Serving
Lacey, Catherine Margaret, BEng	LT CDR(FTC)	E	WE	01.10.00	DPA BRISTOL
Lacey, Ian Nigel, MSc, PhD	LT CDR(FTC)	E	IS	16.06.91	CMT SHRIVENHAM
Lacey, Stephen Patrick, pcea	CDR(FTC)	X	O	30.06.02	RNAS YEOVILTON
Lade, Christopher John, BSc, pce	CDR(FTC)	X	MCD	30.06.98	MWS DEF DIV SCHL
Ladislaus, Cecil James, BEng	LT(IC)	X	SM	01.01.02	TURBULENT
Laidlaw, Jonathan Murray, BEng	LT(IC)	X	P U/T	01.01.05	RNAS YEOVILTON
Laidler, Paul James, MEng	LT(CC)	E	WE	01.12.01	CAPT IST STAFF
Lai-Hung, Jeremy Jean Paul	LT(IC)	S	SM	01.07.03	TURBULENT
Laing, Iain, BEng, CEng, MIEE, NDipM	LT CDR(FTC)	E	WE	01.09.01	NOTTINGHAM
Lake, Andrew, BA	SLT(IC)	X	P U/T	01.01.04	DARTMOUTH BRNC
Lamb, Andrew Gordon, n	LT CDR(FTC)	X	PWO(A)	01.10.02	KENT
Lamb, Robert John Favell	SLT(IC)	X		01.01.03	SOUTHAMPTON
Lamb, Scott Innes	CHAPLAIN	CE		06.01.03	FWO DEVPT SEA
Lambert, Allison	LT CDR(CC)	X	ATC	01.10.03	FLEET AV VL SEA
Lambert, Anthony Wayne, MB, BS, FRCS	SURG CDR(FCC)	-	(CGS)	30.06.99	MDHU DERRIFORD
Lambert, Brian, pce, BSc	CDR(FTC)	X	PR	31.12.96	NAVSEC
Lambert, Nicholas Richard, BSc, pce	CAPT(FTC)	X	AAWO	30.06.00	ENDURANCE
Lambert, Paul, BSc, MPhil, DipFM, rcds, pce, pce(sm), hcsc (COM(OPS) JUN 04)	RADM	-	SM	29.06.04	FLEET HQ NWD
Lambourn, Peter Neil, pce, pcea, psc	CDR(FTC)	X	O	31.12.96	EUMS
Lambourne, David John, BSc, pcea	LT CDR(FTC)	X	P	01.10.97	849 SQN A FLT
L'Amie, Christopher Andrew, BA	LT(IC)	X		01.01.03	NORTHUMBERLAND
Lamont, Neil, SM(n) (Act Lt Cdr)	LT(FTC)	X	SM	06.10.94	TIRELESS
Lamont, Samuel Neville James, MB, BSc, BCh, BAO, MRCP	SURG LT(MCC)	-		02.08.00	NELSON (PAY)
Lancashire, Antony Craig, MA (Act Maj)	CAPT RM(CC)	-	LC	01.09.97	ALBION
Lancaster, James Henry David, LLB	LT(IC)	X	SM	01.01.03	VANGUARD(PORT)
Lander, Martin Christopher, MA, MDA, pce, pcea, psc, psc(j)	CDR(FTC)	X	O	30.06.95	LOAN DSTL
Landrock, Graham John, pce	LT CDR(FTC)	X	MCD	01.09.93	SAUDI AFPS SAUDI
Lane, Elizabeth Helen	MID(IC)	X		01.08.03	DARTMOUTH BRNC
Lane, Matthew John	MID(NE)(IC)	X		01.11.04	DARTMOUTH BRNC
Lane, Nicholas, BSc	LT(IC)	S	SM	01.05.00	FLEET HQ NWD

Name	Rank	Branch	Spec	Seniority	Where Serving
Lane, Roger Guy Tyson, CBE, FCMI, rcds, jsdc, psc(m), fsc, hcsc (DEPUTY COMMANDER HRF(L) NOV 03)	MAJ GEN	-	WTO	06.11.03	AGRIPPA MAR CC
Lang, Alasdair John Mathieson, BA	LT(IC)	X	O U/T	01.01.05	RNAS CULDROSE
Lang, Andrew James Nicholas, BEng	LT CDR(FTC)	E	AE	01.02.02	RNAS YEOVILTON
Lang, Justine Suzanne, DCHS	LT(MCC)	Q		30.09.98	SULTAN
Langbridge, David Charles, MSc, CEng, MIMechE, MCGI, jsdc	CAPT(FTC)	E	MESM	30.06.01	DLO BRISTOL
Langford, Timothy Duncan, BSc	SLT(IC)	X	ATCU/T	01.02.03	RAF SHAWBURY
Langhorn, Nigel	CDR(FTC)	X	AAWO	30.06.96	NAVSEC
Langley, Eric Steven, pce	CDR(FTC)	X	AAWO	30.06.05	LOAN DSTL
Langmead, Ben	SLT(IC)	X	O U/T	01.05.03	RNAS CULDROSE
Langrill, Mark Philip, BEng, MSc, CEng	LT CDR(FTC)	E	AE	01.10.01	820 SQN
Langrill, Tracey Jane, MA	LT(IC)	E		01.02.95	MWS COLLINGWOOD
Langrish, Gary James	LT CDR(CC)	X	P	01.10.02	750 SQN HERON
Lanigan, Ben Ryan	LT(IC)	S		01.12.02	MWS DEF DIV SCHL
Lankester, Peter, BTech, pce, pcea, psc	CDR(FTC)	X	P	30.06.92	SA PRETORIA
Lankester, Timothy John, BSc, CEng, MIMechE, psc	CDR(FTC)	E	ME	30.06.92	DRAKE SFM
Lanni, Martin Nicholas, pcea	LT(CC)	X	P	01.09.95	GANNET SAR FLT
Lanning, Kerry Anne, BA	LT(CC)	S		01.01.00	RALEIGH
Lanning, Roderick MacGregor, BSc	LT(CC)	X	FC	01.03.00	INVINCIBLE
Large, Stephen Andrew, BEng, MSc	LT CDR(FTC)	E	ME	01.03.03	BULWARK
Larmour, David Rutherford, OBE, pce	CAPT(FTC)	X	O	30.06.98	DRAKE COB
Latchem, Andrew James, BEng	SLT(IC)	X	P U/T	01.01.04	DARTMOUTH BRNC
Latham, Mark Anthony	CAPT RM(IC)	-	C	01.04.04	CTCRM
Latham, Neil Degge, MSc, CEng, Hf, MIMechE, jsdc (COMMANDANT CMT FEB 05)	RADM	-	ME	28.02.05	CMT SHRIVENHAM
Latus, Simon Harry, BSc	LT(CC)	X		01.01.02	MWS COLLINGWOOD
Lauchlan, Robert Alexander, BSc	LT CDR(FTC)	E	WESM	01.08.00	VANGUARD(PORT)
Laughton, Peter, MBE	LT CDR(FTC)	X	MCD	01.04.04	LANCASTER
Laurence, Simon Timothy	LT(CC)	X	O	16.01.01	MWS SOUTHWICK PK
Laurence, Timothy James Hamilton, MVO, BSc, Hf, pce, psc(j) (ASST CHIEF OF DEF. STAFF(PROGRAMMES) JUL 04)	RADM	-	PWO(U)	05.07.04	MOD (LONDON)
Lauste, William Emile, BA	LT CDR(FTC)	E	TM	01.03.99	DGMC SEA
Laverty, Robert Edwin, BA, SM(n)	LT CDR(FTC)	X	SM	01.02.03	LANCASTER
Lavery, John Patrick, MVO	CDR(FTC)	S		30.06.99	NAVSEC
Law, James Samuel	LT(IC)	E	WE	01.05.03	2SL/CNH
Law, John	LT CDR(FTC)	X	MCD	27.03.95	NORTH DIVING GRP
Law, Richard, BEng, MIEE	LT(FTC)	E	WE	01.01.00	MOD (LONDON)
Law, Samuel James, MA	LT(IC)	S		01.09.03	FOST SEA
Lawler, Jon Andrew, MBE	CDR(FTC)	X	P	30.06.05	BDS WASHINGTON
Lawrance, Gregory Michael	LT(CC)	X	P	16.05.92	RNAS YEOVILTON
Lawrence, Linda Jane, BA	LT(CC)	X	HM	16.09.99	DARTMOUTH BRNC
Lawrence, Stephen Paul, n	LT CDR(FTC)	X	H CH	01.10.93	MWS HM TG (D)
Lawrence, Stuart Peter	LT CDR(FTC)	S		14.01.01	NAVSEC
Lawrenson, Timothy Alfred Horace, MEng	SLT(IC)	E	WE	01.07.02	MWS COLLINGWOOD
Laws, Philip Eric Arthur, LLB, FCMA	CDR(FTC)	S	CMA	30.06.02	2SL/CNH FOTR
Lawson, Alexandra Florence, BA	LT(IC)	S		01.01.03	GLOUCESTER
Lawson, Geoffrey John	LT CDR(FTC)	X		01.10.03	EXCHANGE USA
Lawson, Stephen Jonathan, pce, pce(sm)	LT CDR(FTC)	X	SM	01.09.91	RN GIBRALTAR
Lawton, Peter, MBE (Act Maj)	CAPT RM(FTC)	-	SO(LE)	01.01.99	HQ 3 CDO BDE RM
Laycock, Antony, BSc, pcea	LT(CC)	X	O	16.07.94	848 SQN HERON
Layland, Stephen, BSc, pce, psc(j), MA	CDR(FTC)	X	PWO(N)	30.06.02	MWS EXCELLENT
Layton, Christopher, BEng	LT(IC)	E	MESM	01.05.01	SOVEREIGN
Le Gassick, Peter James, BEng	LT CDR(CC)	E	TM	01.10.04	RMB STONEHOUSE
Lea, John, pce, pcea	LT CDR(FTC)	X	O	01.01.98	JSCSC
Lea, Sebastian Augustine Pollard, n	LT CDR(FTC)	X	PWO(C)	01.11.03	NP IRAQ
Leach, Sir Henry (Conyers), GCB, DL, jssc, psc	ADM OF FLEET	-		01.12.82	
Leach, Sarah Jane, BEng	LT CDR(FTC)	E	ME	01.10.03	CHATHAM
Leadbetter, Andrew John, BA	LT(CC)	X		01.11.97	PJHQ
Leaker, Daniel Thomas	LT(IC)	X	P	01.05.04	RNAS YEOVILTON
Leaman, Richard Derek, OBE, pce, hcsc (Commodore)	CAPT(FTC)	X	AAWO	31.12.96	JSCSC
Leaman, Thomas Peter	SLT(IC)	X		01.05.04	ILLUSTRIOUS
Leaney, Michael John, MBE, BSc	LT CDR(FTC)	X	MCD	01.03.90	SUPT OF DIVING
Leaning, David John	LT CDR(FTC)	E	MESM	01.10.01	TRIUMPH

Name	Rank	Branch	Spec	Seniority	Where Serving
Leaning, Mark Vincent, MA, pcea, psc	CDR(FTC)	X	P	30.06.03	COS 2SL/CNH
Leaphard, Daniel Paul	SLT(IC)	X		01.06.03	DARTMOUTH BRNC
Lear, Stuart Francis, BA	LT(CC)	S		01.09.00	2SL/CNH FOTR
Leason, Nicholas Charles	LT(CC)	X		01.05.01	NP IRAQ
Leather, Nicholas William Fishwick, MSc, MB, BS	SURG LT(SC(MD)	-		07.04.03	CFLT MED(SEA)
Leatherby, James Hawton	CDR(FTC)	S	SM	31.12.90	NEPTUNE DLO
Leaver, Andrew Michael	LT(FTC)	E	AE	02.09.99	RNAS CULDROSE
Leaver, Ashley	LT(IC)	E	WE	01.07.04	DLO BRISTOL
Leaver, Charmian Elizabeth Lucy, MA, MSc, PGDip	LT CDR(FTC)	X	HM2	01.07.03	INVINCIBLE
Leckey, Elizabeth Helen, BEng	LT(IC)	E	AE	01.05.05	SULTAN
Ledward, Karen Louise	LT(CC)	S		01.01.01	DRAKE SFM
Lee, Daniel John, MDA, pce, psc (Act Capt)	CDR(FTC)	X	AAWO	31.12.96	FLEET HQ PORTS 2
Lee, David Alexander, BSc	SLT(IC)	X		01.09.03	DARTMOUTH BRNC
Lee, Jonathan Coling	LT CDR(FTC)	X	MW	01.10.94	FLYING FOX
Lee, Nicholas Foden, BEng, MIMechE, pcea	LT CDR(FTC)	X	P	01.03.99	750 SQN SEAHAWK
Lee, Nigel David, pce	LT CDR(FTC)	X	AAWO	16.06.03	YORK
Lee, Oliver Andrew, MA	MAJ(FTC)	-		01.05.04	45 CDO RM
Lee, Peter Alan, BEng	LT CDR(FTC)	E	ME	01.08.99	FWO PORTSMOUTH
Lee, Philip Marsden, BSc	LT(CC)	X	P	16.07.94	801 SQN
Lee, Raymond Andrew	LT(IC)	E	WESM	01.01.04	RALEIGH
Lee, Robert	SURG SLT(SCC)	-		15.09.04	DARTMOUTH BRNC
Lee, Steven Edward, MEng, MIEE	LT(FTC)	E	WE	01.11.99	DLO BRISTOL
Lee, Steven Patrick, MA, psc(j)	MAJ(FTC)	-		27.04.02	42 CDO RM
Lee, Steven Yiu Lam, BEng, CEng, MIEE	LT(FTC)	E	WE	01.12.95	DLO BRISTOL
Lee, Warren, BEng	LT(FTC)	E	WE	01.06.97	HQ DCSA
Leech, Sarah Louise, BA	SLT(IC)	S		01.05.02	RALEIGH
Leeder, Timothy Rupert	LT(CC)	X		01.05.02	EDINBURGH
Lee-Gallon, Timothy James	2LT(IC)	-		01.09.00	42 CDO RM
Leeming, Robert John, BSc, CEng	CAPT(FTC)	E	ME	30.06.00	MOD (BATH)
Leeper, James Stephen, BSc	LT(CC)	X		01.01.02	GLOUCESTER
Lees, Adrian Christopher Slater, MEng	SLT(IC)	E	ME U/T	01.01.05	DARTMOUTH BRNC
Lees, Edward Charles, n	LT CDR(FTC)	X	PWO(C)	01.02.99	NELSON
Lees, Sarah Elizabeth	SLT(SC(MD)	Q		01.09.02	RH HASLAR
Lees, Simon Neville, BEd	LT CDR(FTC)	E	TM	01.10.02	MWS COLLINGWOOD
Leese, James Frederick	LT(IC)	E	AE(L)	01.05.02	MERLIN IPT
Leeson, Antony Richard	LT(CC)	X	FC	01.08.02	801 SQN
Leigh, Clara Jane	SLT(IC)	X		01.08.03	GLOUCESTER
Leigh, John, osc(us)	LT COL(FTC)	-	MLDR	31.12.96	LOAN KUWAIT
Leigh-Smith, Simon ,BM, BCH, DObstRCOG, Dip FFP, FFAEM, FRCS(ED)A&E, MRCGP	SURG CDR(MCC)	-	GMPP	30.06.04	NELSON (PAY)
Leightley, Simon Mark	LT(CC)	X		01.04.04	MWS COLLINGWOOD
Leighton, Matthew Richard, BA	LT(CC)	X	P	01.06.97	848 SQN HERON
Leitch, Iain Robertson, BSc, pce	LT CDR(FTC)	X	AAWO	01.10.96	RNAS YEOVILTON
Leivers, Andrew James	LT(CC)	E	ME	01.09.99	539 ASSLT SQN RM
Lemkes, Paul Douglas, pce	CAPT(FTC)	X	AAWO	30.06.05	FWO PORTS SEA
Lemon, Robert Gordon Arthur, BSc	LT CDR(FTC)	E	WESM	01.09.84	DLO BRISTOL
Leonard, Mark, BEng, MIEE	LT CDR(FTC)	E	WE	01.10.97	NELSON (PAY)
Leonard, Thomas Andrew	SLT(IC)	X		01.07.04	WESTMINSTER
Leong, Melvin	SURG SLT(SCC)	-		23.06.04	DARTMOUTH BRNC
Lerwill, Sean Simon Guy	CAPT RM(IC)	-		01.09.04	UKLFCSG RM
Leslie, Bruce Duncan	LT(IC)	X	O	01.05.03	849 SQN B FLT
Lester, Rodney Leslie	LT(FTC)	X		10.01.00	DISC
Lett, Jonathan David, n, BA	LT CDR(FTC)	X	PWO(U)	01.10.00	UKMARBATSTAFF
Lettington, Paul David William, BEng	LT(IC)	E	TM	01.01.04	CDO LOG REGT RM
Letts, Andrew John, BEng, CEng, MIEE	LT CDR(FTC)	E	WE	01.08.03	SAT IPT
Lew-Gor, Simione Tomasi Warren, MB, CHB, MRCS	SURG LTCDR(MCC)	-		05.09.00	NELSON (PAY)
Lewins, Grant	LT CDR(FTC)	S	(W)	01.10.04	NEPTUNE DLO
Lewis, Andrew James, BEng, CEng	LT CDR(FTC)	E	MESM	01.03.04	SULTAN
Lewis, Barry Morgan	CAPT RM(IC)	-		01.09.04	40 CDO RM
Lewis, Benjamin'Charles, BSc	LT(FTC)	X	P	16.05.97	LOAN OTHER SVCE
Lewis, Daniel, BEng	LT(IC)	E	AE	01.12.01	RNAS YEOVILTON
Lewis, David James	LT CDR(FTC)	X	O	01.10.98	MWC PORTSDOWN
Lewis, David John, BEng, MIEE	LT CDR(FTC)	E	WE	01.09.01	PJHQ

Name	Rank	Branch	Spec	Seniority	Where Serving
Lewis, Gary David	LT CDR(FTC)	S		01.09.89	DLO BRISTOL
Lewis, Guy David, BEng, CEng, MIMarEST	LT CDR(FTC)	E	ME	03.02.00	FWO PORTS SEA
Lewis, James A E	CAPT RM(IC)	-		01.09.04	42 CDO RM
Lewis, John Keene, BEng, MDA, AMIEE	CDR(FTC)	E	WESM	30.06.99	MWS COLLINGWOOD
Lewis, Jonathan Munro	LT(IC)	X	SM	25.02.05	VIGILANT(STBD)
Lewis, Kay Elisabeth	LT(CC)	X		01.07.00	MWS COLLINGWOOD
Lewis, Keith Alan	LT CDR(FTC)	X	PWO(C)	01.10.03	RN GIBRALTAR
Lewis, Mark David, MEng	LT(IC)	E	AE	01.09.02	829 SQN HQ
Lewis, Matthew J	2LT(IC)	-		01.09.00	40 CDO RM
Lewis, Paul Leonard	LT(IC)	X		08.01.01	FLEET HQ NWD
Lewis, Simon John, MSc, CEng, MBCS, CITP	LT CDR(CC)	E	IS	01.01.05	RMC OF SCIENCE
Lewis, Stephen Bernard, pce, psc	LT CDR(FTC)	X	PWO(U)	01.01.87	DRAKE COB
Lewis, Timothy John, pce, psc(j)	LT CDR(FTC)	X	PWO(U)	05.02.95	FLEET HQ NWD
Lewis, Wesley Darren, BSc	LT(IC)	X	ATCU/T	01.09.03	RNAS CULDROSE
Ley, Alastair Blevins, SM(n), SM	LT CDR(FTC)	X	SM	01.11.03	RALEIGH
Ley, Jonathan Ashley, pce, n	LT CDR(FTC)	X	PWO(A)	01.08.00	SEVERN
Leyden, Tristan Neil (Act Maj)	CAPT RM(FTC)	-		01.09.99	45 CDO RM
Leyshon, Robert John, BDS, MFGDP(UK)	SGLTCDR(D)(MCC)	-		09.01.99	LOAN BRUNEI
Lias, Carl David, BSc, MEng	LT CDR(FTC)	E	MESM	01.10.96	MOD (LONDON)
Liddell, Matthew Lewis	LT(FTC)	E	ME	02.05.00	ENDURANCE
Liddle, Richard David, BEng	LT(CC)	X	P	01.04.00	GANNET SAR FLT
Liddle, Stephen Johnstone, MA	MAJ(FTC)	-		01.09.01	JSCSC
Ligale, Eugene	LT(IC)	X		01.01.03	MWS COLLINGWOOD
Lightfoot, Charles David, BSc, pce, pce(sm), psc(j), MA	CDR(FTC)	X	SM	30.06.03	MOD (LONDON)
Lightfoot, Richard Alan	LT(CC)	X	O	16.02.01	GANNET SAR FLT
Lilley, David John, BSc, pce, pcea, psc(m), psc(j)	CDR(FTC)	X	O	31.12.96	UKMFTS IPT
Lilly, David Mark, BEng	LT(CC)	X	P	01.12.98	LYNX OEU
Lincoln, Keith James, BEng, MBA, CEng, MIEE	LT CDR(FTC)	E	WE	01.07.03	SUTHERLAND
Linderman, Ian Ronald, BSc, MBA	LT CDR(FTC)	E	TM	01.10.99	2SL/CNH FOTR
Lindeyer, Matthew James, BSc	LT(IC)	X	HM	01.05.02	ENTERPRISE
Lindley, Jeannine, BSc	LT(IC)	X		01.05.04	GRAFTON
Lindley, Nicholas Paul, BSc, MA, psc(m)	LT COL(FTC)	-		31.12.99	45 CDO RM
Lindsay, David Joseph, BEng	LT CDR(FTC)	X	P	01.10.03	LOAN OTHER SVCE
Lindsay, Irvine Graham, MA, pce, pce(sm), psc(j)	LT CDR(FTC)	X	SM	01.04.96	FOST FAS SHORE
Lindsay, Jonathan Mark, BSc	CAPT RM(CC)	-	MLDR	01.05.01	42 CDO RM
Lindsay, Michael Henry, MB, BSc, BS	SURG LT(SC(MD)	-		06.08.03	VIGILANT(STBD)
Lindsey, Richard, pce(sm), SM(n)	LT CDR(FTC)	X	SM	30.04.00	EXCHANGE USA
Lines, James Micheal, FCIPD, MDA	CDR(FTC)	S		30.06.02	ALBION
Ling, Christopher, MSc, MRAeS	LT CDR(FTC)	E	AE	01.03.04	FLEET HQ PORTS
Ling, John William Legrys, BEng, MSc, pcea, gdas	LT(FTC)	X	O	16.09.94	LOAN JTEG BSC DN
Lintern, Robert David, BA, MSc, PGDIP, MRIN, n	LT CDR(FTC)	X	HM	01.10.01	MIDDLETON
Lipczynski, Benjamin James, BEng	SLT(IC)	E	WESM	01.11.02	RALEIGH
Lippe, Peter William	LT(IC)	X	C	02.08.02	STRS IPT
Lippitt, Simon Thomas, BEng	LT(CC)	X	ATC	01.04.98	ILLUSTRIOUS
Lipscomb, Paul, BSc, CEng, MIMarEST	LT CDR(FTC)	E	MESM	01.11.95	RN GIBRALTAR
Lipson, Christopher Nicholas	LT(IC)	X		01.09.04	GRIMSBY
Lison, Andrew Christopher, BEng, MAPM, MSc, AMIEE, psc(j), MA	CDR(FTC)	E	AE	30.06.04	MOD (LONDON)
Lister, Mark, pce(sm)	CDR(FTC)	X	SM	30.06.04	VENGEANCE(STBD)
Lister, Matthew John Laurence, BEng	SLT(IC)	E	MESMUT	01.09.03	ILLUSTRIOUS
Lister, Simon, SM	LT(FTC)	X	SM	08.04.94	MOD DIS SEA
Lister, Simon Robert, OBE, MSc, AMIMechE	CDRE(FTC)	E	MESM	06.07.04	DRAKE NBC/DBUS
Lister, Stephen Richard	LT CDR(FTC)	S	SM	01.04.93	RN GIBRALTAR
Litchfield, Julian Felix, FCIPD	CDR(FTC)	S		30.06.98	BDS WASHINGTON
Litster, Alan, MBE, BSc, psc(j)o	MAJ(FTC)	-	LC	01.09.98	40 CDO RM
Little, Charles Stewart Anderson, BSc, pce, pce(sm)	LT CDR(FTC)	X	SM	01.02.90	NSRS IPT
Little, Craig Martin	LT(IC)	X	O	01.10.02	814 SQN
Little, George	2LT(IC)	-		01.08.01	CTCRM LYMPSTONE
Little, Graeme Terence, BEng, MSc, psc(j)	CDR(FTC)	E	ME	30.06.00	MOD (LONDON)
Little, Matthew Iain Graham, BSc	LT(IC)	X		01.05.01	NP IRAQ
Little, Rhoderick McKeand, BSc, CDipAF, CEng, MIEE, psc	CAPT(FTC)	E	WESM	31.12.98	LOAN DSTL
Liva, Anthony, BSc	CAPT RM(CC)	-		01.09.01	45 CDO RM
Livesey, John Edward, SM(n), SM	LT(FTC)	X	SM	01.10.97	SPARTAN
Livingston, Martin Philip James, BEng	LT(IC)	E	AE	01.05.02	SABR IPT

Name	Rank	Branch	Spec	Seniority	Where Serving
Livingstone, Alan James, MBE, ocds(No)	LT COL(FTC)	-		30.06.04	IMS BRUSSELS
Livsey, Andrew Everard John, BA	LT(FTC)	X		01.09.99	NP IRAQ
Llewellyn, Jonathan Gwyn	LT(FTC)	X	AV	20.09.99	RFANSU
Llewelyn, Kevin	LT CDR(FTC)	X	ATC	01.10.97	MOD (LONDON)
Lloyd, Bruce Jeremy, BSc	LT(CC)	X	P	01.04.00	815 FLT 234
Lloyd, Christopher John	CDR(FTC)	MS		30.06.03	NAVSEC
Lloyd, David Philip John, MBCS, MCIT, MILT	LT CDR(FTC)	S		01.09.91	FLEET HQ PORTS
Lloyd, Matthew Rome	LT(IC)	S		01.09.02	SPARTAN
Lloyd, Paul Robert, pce, psc(j), MA	CDR(FTC)	X	PWO(N)	31.12.97	RNP TEAM
Lloyd, Stephen John, MSc, CEng, MIMarEST, psc	CAPT(FTC)	E	MESM	30.06.00	RCDS
Loane, Michael MacAire (Act Lt Cdr)	LT(CC)	X	MCD	01.06.93	NP IRAQ
Lochrane, Alexandre Edmond Ross, pce, psc(j)(o)	CDR(FTC)	X	PWO(U)	30.06.04	MOD (LONDON)
Lock, Alan Matthew, BEng	LT(IC)	E	MESM	01.09.04	SULTAN
Lock, Andrew Glen David	MAJ(FTC)	-		01.04.04	NELSON (PAY)
Lock, William James, BSc	LT(IC)	X	O	01.05.02	814 SQN
Locke, Nicholas Michael, BEng	LT(IC)	E	MESM	01.09.04	SULTAN
Lockett, David John, n	LT CDR(FTC)	X	PWO(U)	01.04.04	EDINBURGH
Lockhart, John Brian	LT(IC)	E	AE	01.07.04	849 SQN B FLT
Lofthouse, Ian, MA	CAPT(FTC)	E	MESM	30.06.05	NEPTUNE DLO
Logan, John Gordon, BA, PGCE, MISM	LT(SC(MD)	Q	RNT	27.07.96	RH HASLAR
Logan, Joseph Majella	LT CDR(FTC)	X	FC	01.10.03	FOST SEA
Lombard, Didier, rcds, pce, pce(sm), odc(Fr), SM(n), sondc	CAPT(FTC)	X	SM	30.06.05	NAVSEC
London, Nicholas John	SLT(IC)	E	WESMUT	01.09.03	INVINCIBLE
Long, Adrian Montague, BEng, MSc, CEng, MIEE	LT CDR(FTC)	E	WE	01.04.00	JSCSC
Long, Anthony Donald, pce, pcea, psc(j)	CDR(FTC)	X	O	30.06.04	PJHQ
Long, Hugh Andrew	2LT(IC)	-		01.09.00	FPGRM
Long, Michael Selden	LT(FTC)	X	MW	01.04.96	PJHQ
Long, Richard Peter	CAPT RM(IC)	BS		01.04.04	BRNC BAND
Longman, Matthew Stephen, BEng	LT(IC)	E	ME	01.09.04	LANCASTER
Longmore, David ,BM	SURG LT(SCC)	-		04.08.04	DARTMOUTH BRNC
Longstaff, Thomas William	LT(FTC)	S	SM	19.09.00	DRAKE COB
Lord, Andrew Stephen, BA, PGCE, M ED, MCIPD	LT CDR(FTC)	E	TM	01.09.87	SULTAN
Lord, Martin	LT CDR(FTC)	E	WE	01.10.98	CAPT MCTA
Lord, Richard James	LT(FTC)	X	P	01.10.94	EXCHANGE DENMARK
Lorenz, Rudi	SLT(IC)	X	P U/T	01.06.03	RAF CRANWELL EFS
Loring, Andrew, BSc, MA, CEng, MIMechE, psc(j)	LT CDR(FTC)	E	ME	01.03.93	FLEET HQ PORTS
Louden, Carl Alexander	LT(FTC)	X	C	23.07.98	FOST SEA
Loughrey, Neil Charles	LT(CC)	E	AE	29.04.01	JHCHQ
Louis, David Richard Anthony	LT(FTC)	X		01.12.04	MWS COLLINGWOOD
Louw, Len	LT(IC)	E	WESM	01.01.02	VENGEANCE(STBD)
Lovatt, Graham John	LT CDR(FTC)	X	AAWO	01.04.03	COMATG SEA
Love, John James	LT(IC)	E	AE	01.05.03	2SL/CNH
Love, Julie Dawn	LT(FTC)	S	(W)	19.09.00	DLO YEO
Love, Lee-Ann, LLB	LT(IC)	X		01.09.01	MOD (LONDON)
Love, Richard J, BEng	LT(FTC)	E	AE	01.08.98	ILLUSTRIOUS
Love, Robert Thomas, OBE, BSc, CEng, FIMarEST, psc	CDRE(FTC)	E	ME	04.05.04	BDLS AUSTRALIA
Love, Tristram Simon Nicholas, BEng, MSc, CEng, MIEE	LT CDR(FTC)	E	WESM	01.10.00	TRENCHANT
Lovegrove, Raymond Anthony, MSc, CEng, MIEE, gw	CDR(FTC)	E	WE	30.06.04	MOD (BATH)
Lovell, Alistair, BDS	SG LT(D)(SC(MD)	-		25.06.03	DRAKE COB(CNH)
Lovell, James Edward Charles, BA	LT(IC)	X		01.01.03	KENT
Lovelock, Richard Benjamin, psc(m) (Act Col)	LT COL(FTC)	-		30.06.94	NP IRAQ
Lovering, Tristan Timothy Alan, BSc	LT CDR(CC)	E	TM	01.10.04	FLEET HQ PORTS
Lovett, Andrew Robert	LT(CC)	E	AE	01.06.00	SULTAN
Lovett, Michael John, BSc	CDR(FTC)	E	WE	30.06.96	SA CAIRO
Lovett, Stephen Andrew, SM	LT(FTC)	X	SM	26.04.99	COM MCC NWD
Low, Simeon Alexander Sava, BA	SLT(IC)	X		01.11.02	BULWARK
Lowe, Christopher	LT(FTC)	E	MESM	02.05.00	SULTAN
Lowe, Gavin James, BA	LT(IC)	X		01.05.04	PORTLAND
Lowe, Julian Charles, BEng, MSc, CEng, MIMarEST	LT CDR(FTC)	E	ME	01.08.99	FOST SEA
Lowe, Stuart Michael, BEng, MSc, MIEE	LT CDR(FTC)	E	WE	01.12.00	IRON DUKE
Lowe, Timothy Miles, jsdc, pce	CAPT(FTC)	X	PWO(N)	30.06.03	SHAPE BELGIUM
Lower, Iain Stuart, BSc, pce, n	LT CDR(FTC)	X	AAWO	01.10.99	SHOREHAM
Lowson, Roderick Mark, pce	LT CDR(FTC)	X	AAWO	01.04.97	GLOUCESTER

Name	Rank	Branch	Spec	Seniority	Where Serving
Lowther, James Marcus, BA, PGDIPAN, pce, n	LT CDR(FTC)	X	PWO(N)	01.07.98	TYNE
Lucas, Darren Philip, BEng	LT(IC)	E	WE	01.05.02	UKMARBATSTAFF
Lucas, Nicholas Hugh, BA	LT(IC)	X		01.05.04	TYNE
Lucas, Simon Ulrick	CAPT RM(FTC)	-	SO(LE)	01.01.01	CTCRM
Luckraft, Christopher John, BD, AKC	CHAPLAIN	CE		05.08.87	NELSON
Lucocq, Carolyn Marie, LLB	LT(CC)	S		01.05.01	2SL/CNH
Lucocq, Nicholas James, BSc, MRIN, n	LT CDR(FTC)	X	PWO(A)	01.10.04	INVINCIBLE
Ludlow, Julian Andrew, SM(n)	LT(CC)	X	SM	01.01.02	SPARTAN
Lugg, John Charles	MAJ(FTC)	-	SO(LE)	01.10.04	CDO LOG REGT RM
Luke, Christopher James	SLT(IC)	X		01.01.05	CUMBERLAND
Lumsden, Peter Imrie, BEng	LT CDR(FTC)	X	P	01.04.05	LOAN OTHER SVCE
Lunn, Adam Christopher, pce, pcea	LT CDR(FTC)	X	P	01.06.94	LOAN OMAN
Lunn, David Vaughan, MB, CHB, FFARCS, DA	SURG CDR(FCC)	-	(CA)	30.06.91	LOAN FIELD HOSP
Lunn, James Francis Clive, BSc, CEng, MIMarEST, MIMechE, psc	CDR(FTC)	E	MESM	31.12.93	MOD (LONDON)
Lunn, Mark Henry Bernard, MSc, CEng, MIMarEST	LT CDR(FTC)	E	MESM	01.07.00	SUPERB
Lunn, Thomas Ramsay	LT CDR(FTC)	X		01.01.03	BULWARK
Lupini, James Martin, BA	LT(IC)	X		01.10.02	ARGYLL
Luscombe, Michael David, pcea	LT CDR(FTC)	X	P	01.10.99	FLEET AV CU
Lusted, Roy Peter, BSc (Act Lt Cdr)	LT(FTC)	E	AE	13.10.89	RNAS YEOVILTON
Lustman, Arnold Marc, GCIS	CDR(FTC)	S	SM	30.06.02	ILLUSTRIOUS
Luxford, Charles Alexander, BA	LT(IC)	X		01.05.02	MWS COLLINGWOOD
Lynas, Jonathan Francis Alistair	LT(CC)	X	P	01.09.00	849 SQN B FLT
Lynch, Paul Patrick, MC, BA	MAJ(FTC)	-		01.10.04	45 CDO RM
Lynch, Rory Denis Fenton, BA	LT CDR(FTC)	X	P	16.04.02	771 SQN B FLT
Lynch, Stephen, pcea	LT CDR(FTC)	X	O	01.10.00	FLEET HQ PORTS
Lynn, Henry William	LT(FTC)	X		19.09.00	MWS COLLINGWOOD
Lynn, Ian Herbert, pce	LT CDR(FTC)	X	PWO(U)	30.06.03	MERSEY
Lynn, Sarah Louise, MSc	LT(IC)	X	O	01.02.03	814 SQN
Lynn, Steven Robert, BEng	LT CDR(FTC)	E	WE	01.04.98	UKCEC IPT
Lyons, Alan Gordon, BEng	LT(CC)	E	MESM	01.03.98	NP DNREAY
Lyons, Michael John, BEng, CEng, MIMechE, AMIMechE	LT CDR(FTC)	E	MESM	01.06.04	NP BRISTOL

M

Name	Rank	Branch	Spec	Seniority	Where Serving
MacAskill, Colin Hugh (Act Lt Cdr)	LT(FTC)	S	CA	11.12.92	NEPTUNE BNSL
Macaulay, Scott Charles	LT(IC)	X	SM	01.05.05	VENGEANCE(PORT)
MacColl, Andrew Alexander James	LT(FTC)	X	ATC	01.05.96	RNAS CULDROSE
MacCormick, James, BSc	LT(IC)	E	WESM	01.05.02	MOD (LONDON)
MacCorquodale, Mairi Ann, MA, MPhil	LT(IC)	E	IS	01.09.98	CENTCOM USA
MacCrimmon, Stuart Stanwix	2LT(IC)	-		01.09.00	FPGRM
MacDonald, Alasdair Iain, BSc, MDA, CEng, MIEE, MCMI	CDR(FTC)	E	WE	30.06.98	INVINCIBLE
MacDonald, Alastair James, BEng, MSc, CEng, MIEE	LT CDR(FTC)	E	WE	01.09.02	MOD (LONDON)
MacDonald, Douglas Hugh Lawson, BSc, MA, MNI, pce, ocds(US)	CDR(FTC)	X	MCD	30.06.91	NELSON
MacDonald, George Ewen, LLB	CAPT(FTC)	S		30.06.00	NAVSEC
MacDonald, Glen Dey, BA	LT CDR(FTC)	X		01.05.91	JHQ/CIS LISBON
MacDonald, Ian Robert, MBE, sq	MAJ(FTC)	-		08.02.93	EXCHANGE NLANDS
MacDonald, John Robert, BEng, MA, MSc, psc(j), gw	CDR(FTC)	E	WESM	30.06.04	FOST SM SEA
MacDonald, Katrina Louise	LT(IC)	X		01.09.03	2SL/CNH
MacDonald, Michael	CAPT RM(IC)	-		01.09.04	42 CDO RM
MacDonald, Stuart Brewey	LT(IC)	S		01.11.00	RNAS CULDROSE
MacDonald-Robinson, Nicholas Ulric Spencer, pce, n	LT CDR(FTC)	X	AAWO	01.04.98	EDINBURGH
MacDougall, Gavin Ross	LT CDR(FTC)	S		01.10.98	JSCSC
MacDougall, Stewart John	LT CDR(FTC)	E	WESM	01.10.03	CAPT MCTA
Mace, Stephen Barry, BEng, CEng, MIEE	CDR(FTC)	E	WE	30.06.04	JSCSC
Macey, Kevin, MSc	LT(IC)	MS		01.07.04	RCDM
MacFarlane, Gordon Thomas ,BMS, MB, CHB	SURG LT(SC(MD)	-		08.10.03	VENGEANCE(PORT)
MacFarlane, Iain Stuart David, BSc	LT(CC)	X	P	01.11.93	700M MERLIN OEU
MacGillivray, Ian, BEng, MA, psc(j)	LT CDR(FTC)	E	WE	01.04.98	FLEET HQ PORTS 2
MacIntyre, Ian Douglas	LT(CC)	E	WESM	01.01.02	DLO BRISTOL
MacKay, Andrew Colin, BA	LT CDR(FTC)	S		01.02.04	DISC
MacKay, Colin Ross, MSc, adp	CDR(FTC)	E	IS	30.06.02	CMT SHRIVENHAM
MacKay, Graeme Angus, pce, pcea, ocds(Can)	CDR(FTC)	X	O	31.12.97	MOD (LONDON)
MacKay, Peter, BEng	LT CDR(FTC)	E	WE	01.12.98	DARTMOUTH BRNC

Name	Rank	Branch	Spec	Seniority	Where Serving
MacKay-Brown, Alan, MB, CHB	SURG LT(SC(MD)	-		01.08.00	CTCRM
MacKenow, Helen Rebecca, LLB	LT(IC)	S		01.09.04	DLO/DG DEF SC
MacKenzie, Jessica-Rose Emily, BA	LT(IC)	S		01.07.99	JSU NORTHWOOD
MacKenzie-Green, William	2LT(IC)	-		01.08.01	CTCRM LYMPSTONE
MacKett, Duncan Geoffrey, pce	LT CDR(FTC)	X	PWO(A)	01.05.88	NELSON
Mackey, Martin Christopher, pce	LT CDR(FTC)	X	PWO(U)	01.06.99	RAMSEY
Mackie, David Francis Sarsfield, BEng, MSc, gw, MIEE, CEng	LT CDR(FTC)	E	WE	01.03.99	FLEET HQ PORTS
Mackie, Simon John, MB, BS, MRCS	SURG LTCDR(FCC)	-		12.08.01	NELSON (PAY)
MacKinnon, Donald James, BEng, MPhil	LT CDR(FTC)	X	PWO(U)	01.01.01	UKMARBATSTAFF
MacLaughlin, Richard Adrian, BA	LT(CC)	X	P	01.08.98	GANNET SAR FLT
MacLean, Graham Francis	LT(IC)	X		01.09.03	CUMBERLAND
MacLean, Juliet Anna, BA	LT(CC)	X		01.04.00	702 SQN HERON
MacLean, Malcolm Thomas	LT(FTC)	E	ME	02.09.99	DSFM PORTSMOUTH
MacLean, Richard Gregor (Act Capt Rm)	LT RM(IC)	-		01.09.02	MOD (LONDON)
MacLean, Shamus MacFarlane	LT(IC)	X	SM	01.09.04	PJHQ
Macleod, Alanna	SG SLT(D)(SCC)	-		01.04.03	DARTMOUTH BRNC
Macleod, James Norman, BEng, MA, MSc, CEng, MIEE, psc(j)	CDR(FTC)	E	WE	30.06.04	STG BRISTOL
Macleod, Mark Stuart, BEng	LT CDR(FTC)	E	AE	01.02.02	LOAN JTEG BSC DN
MacMillan, Steven James	LT(IC)	E	AE	01.07.04	846 SQN
MacNaughton, Francis George, MBE, BA, pce	LT CDR(FTC)	X	PWO(A)	01.05.87	STG BRISTOL
MacNeil, Stephen William, pcea	LT CDR(FTC)	X	P	01.10.04	824 SQN
MacPhail, Neil MacTaggart	LT(IC)	MS		01.05.03	DRAKE SFM
MacPherson, Craig Alexander Cameron, BSc	LT(IC)	X		01.01.03	SEVERN
MacPherson, William Gordon Clark	CAPT RM(CC)	-	MLDR	01.04.02	1 ASSAULT GP RM
MacQuarrie, Gary, BEng	LT(IC)	E	ME	01.05.02	MWS COLLINGWOOD
MacRae, Justin Russell	CAPT RM(IC)	-		01.09.03	OCLC BRISTOL
MacRae, Kirk, BSc	SLT(IC)	X		01.01.04	DARTMOUTH BRNC
Madders, Brian Richard, MBE, QHC	PR CHAPLAIN	RC		09.09.85	2SL/CNH
(DIRECTOR NAVAL CHAPLAINCY SERVICE (FAITH AUG 02)					
Maddick, Mark Jeremy, MA, psc(j)	LT COL(FTC)	-	LC	30.06.02	MWC SOUTHWICK
Maddison, Hugh Richard, BEng	LT(IC)	E	ME	01.01.03	ILLUSTRIOUS
Maddison, John David (Act Maj)	CAPT RM(FTC)	-	SO(LE)	01.01.98	UKLFCSG RM
Maddison, Paul	LT(IC)	E	WE	01.07.04	ILLUSTRIOUS
Maden, Steven	SLT(IC)	E	WESM	01.01.04	MWS COLLINGWOOD
Madgwick, Edward Charles Cowtan, BDS, MFDS,RCS	SGLTCDR(D)(MCC)	-		23.07.01	CTCRM
Madigan, Lee, BA	LT(IC)	X	H2	01.03.00	ECHO
Maese, Philip Andrew	MAJ(FTC)	-	SO(LE)	01.10.97	1 ASSAULT GP RM
Magan, Michael James Christopher, BEng, MA, MSc, CEng, MIEE, psc(j), gw	CDR(FTC)	E	WE	30.06.02	PAAMS PARIS
Magill, Alasdair Fraser	SLT(IC)	X		01.07.04	INVINCIBLE
Magowan, Robert Andrew, MBE, BSc, odc(US) (Act Col)	LT COL(FTC)	-		30.06.03	MOD (LONDON)
Magzoub, Mohayed Mohamed Mustafa	SLT(UCE)(IC)	E	ME	01.09.02	DARTMOUTH BRNC
Maher, Michael Patrick, pce	CDR(FTC)	X	AAWO	30.06.05	2SL/CNH FOTR
Mahoney, Andrew John	SLT(IC)	X		01.07.02	YORK
Mahony, Christopher David Copinger, psc(j)	LT CDR(FTC)	X	P	03.04.99	RNAS YEOVILTON
Mahony, David Grehan, pce, pcea	CDR(FTC)	X	O	30.06.03	FLEET HQ PORTS
Mailes, Ian Robert Arthur, pcea	LT CDR(FTC)	X	O	01.10.03	824 SQN
Main, Edward Stafford, BSc, CEng, MIMarEST	CDR(FTC)	E	ME	30.06.98	T45 IPT
Main, Matthew George	SLT(UCE)(IC)	E	WESM	01.09.04	DARTMOUTH BRNC
Mains, Graham	LT(CC)	X	O	18.03.99	814 SQN
Mair, Brian, pce	CDR(FTC)	X	MCD	30.06.02	MOD (LONDON)
Malcolm, Paul Stuart, BA	LT(IC)	X		01.09.02	ENTERPRISE
Malcolm, Stephen Robert, MA, FIMarEST, CMarSci, pce, psc(j)	CDR(FTC)	X	H CH	31.12.00	SCOTT
Maley, Catherine Elizabeth, LLB	LT(FTC)	X	O	16.01.98	MWS SOUTHWICK PK
Malin, Michael John	LT CDR(FTC)	X	H CH	01.04.88	FLYING FOX
Malkin, Sharon Louise, MA	LT CDR(FTC)	E	AE	01.10.02	FLEET HQ PORTS
Mallabone, James John Kenneth, BSc, PGCE	LT(CC)	E	TM	01.08.97	DCTS HALTON
Mallen, David John, BEng	LT CDR(FTC)	E	AE	01.10.03	RNAS CULDROSE
Malley, Mark Paul, BEng	LT CDR(FTC)	E	WESM	01.01.01	VICTORIOUS(PORT)
Mallinson, Ian Paul	LT(IC)	X		01.09.04	NORTHUMBERLAND
Mallinson, Laurence John, BSc	LT(IC)	S		01.05.03	ALBION
Mallinson, Robert, BEng, MA, pcea, psc(j)	CDR(FTC)	E	AE	30.06.05	DLO YEO
Mallows, James	2LT(IC)	-		01.08.04	CTCRM LYMPSTONE
Malone, Martin Thomas	LT(IC)	S		01.05.03	ROEBUCK

Name	Rank	Branch	Spec	Seniority	Where Serving
Malone, Mick	LT(IC)	X		29.07.01	ILLUSTRIOUS
Malone, Roger William, BSc	LT(IC)	X	H2	01.01.03	SCOTT
Malster, Dudley Andrew	LT(IC)	X		01.05.05	MERSEY
Maltby, Michael Robert James, BSc, CEng, MIMarEST	CDR(FTC)	E	ME	31.12.99	DLO BRISTOL
Maltby, Richard James	MAJ(FTC)	-		01.05.03	EXCHANGE USA
Mandley, Philip John, MSc	LT CDR(FTC)	E	TM	01.05.02	NTE(TTD)
Manfield, Michael David, pce(sm), SM	LT CDR(FTC)	X	SM	01.01.99	EXCHANGE AUSTLIA
Manger, Garth Stuart Cunningham, osc(us)	LT COL(FTC)	-	C	30.06.02	COMAMPHIBFOR
Mann, Andrew William	LT(CC)	E	WE	01.01.02	MWS COLLINGWOOD
Mann, Colin Andrew	LT(CC)	E	AE	01.10.02	771 SQN
Mann, David Michael, BEng	LT(CC)	X		01.06.99	MWS COLLINGWOOD
Mann, Gary Digby, BA, FCMA	LT CDR(CC)	E	TMSM	01.10.97	RALEIGH
Manning, Duncan, MA	MAJ(FTC)	-		01.09.02	1 ASSAULT GP RM
Manning, Gary Paul	LT(CC)	S		01.09.01	MOD (LONDON)
Mannion, Robert Victor, pce, SM	LT CDR(FTC)	X	SM	01.06.95	SETT GOSPORT
Mannion, Timothy Shaun	LT CDR(FTC)	X	P	01.09.86	RNAS YEOVILTON
Mansergh, Andrew Christopher, BA	CAPT RM(CC)	-	LC	01.09.01	COMAMPHIBFOR
Mansergh, Frances Antonia, BA, n	LT(FTC)	X		01.08.98	RNP TEAM
Mansergh, Michael Peter, BA, pce, hcsc	CAPT(FTC)	X	PWO(C)	31.12.00	MOD (LONDON)
Mansergh, Robert James, LLB, pce, pce(sm)	CAPT(FTC)	X	SM	30.06.00	RCDS
Mansfield, James Alexander, BA, n	LT(FTC)	X		01.10.97	MWS COLLINGWOOD
Manson, Colin Robert, BSc, PGDip, MIMarEST	LT CDR(FTC)	X	METOC	01.10.98	FLEET HQ NWD
Manson, Peter Duncan, BSc	MAJ(FTC)	-	P	01.09.99	OCEAN
Manson, Thomas Edward, BSc, MA, psc(j)	CDR(FTC)	E	AE	30.06.05	SABR IPT
Mant, James Nicholas, BSc, CEng, MIEE	LT CDR(FTC)	E	WE	01.10.89	FLEET HQ PORTS 2
Mantle, Mark, MB, BS	SURG LTCDR(MCC)	-		07.08.01	NELSON (PAY)
Mantri, Anand Harishankar, BEng	LT(IC)	E	TM	22.05.00	DARTMOUTH BRNC
Manwaring, Roy Geoffrey	LT CDR(FTC)	MS		01.10.04	INM ALVERSTOKE
Maples, Andrew Thomas, MB, ChB	SURG LT(MC(MD)	-		01.08.01	MDHU DERRIFORD
Marden, Tony, MEng	LT(IC)	E	WE	01.02.02	MWS COLLINGWOOD
Mardlin, Stephen Andrew, DipFM	LT CDR(FTC)	S		01.04.99	DLO/DG DEF SC
Mardon, Karl Fraser	LT CDR(FTC)	X	PWO(U)	02.09.92	PJHQ
Marino, David Jones, MBE, MA, MCMI, psc	LT COL(FTC)	-	SO(LE)	01.10.98	NAVSEC
Marjoram, Gareth Keri, BEng	LT(FTC)	E	WESM	01.05.96	FOST DSTF
Marjoribanks, Charlotte	LT(IC)	X		01.09.03	MARLBOROUGH
Mark, Robert Alan, MSc, MNI, MRIN, MInsD (SENIOR DIRECTING STAFF (NAVAL) JAN 05)	RADM	-	H CH	06.01.05	RCDS
Markey, Adrian Philip, BEng	LT CDR(FTC)	X	PWO(U)	01.08.01	EXCHANGE USA
Markwick, Kenneth William, BSc	LT(IC)	E	AE	01.05.03	JCA IPT UK
Marland, Eunice Elizabeth, BSc	LT(CC)	S	S	01.01.02	MOD (LONDON)
Marlborough, Marcus John, BEng	SLT(IC)	X	P U/T	01.01.04	DARTMOUTH BRNC
Marlor, Andrew, MEng	SLT(IC)	E	WESMUT	01.09.03	ILLUSTRIOUS
Marmont, Kerry Lewis, BSc, CEng, MIEE	CDR(FTC)	E	WESM	31.12.00	DLO BRISTOL
Marok, Jani, BSc, MA, psc(j)	LT COL(FTC)	-		30.06.02	MOD (LONDON)
Marquis, Adrian Colin, BEng	LT(CC)	X	P	01.12.93	EXCHANGE GERMANY
Marratt, Richard James, BSc, MA	LT CDR(FTC)	E	TM	01.09.02	RNSR BOVINGTON
Marriott, Mark Nicholas, BEng, MSc	CDR(FTC)	E	AE	30.06.04	FLEET HQ PORTS
Marriott, Matthew James	LT(FTC)	X	FC	01.09.02	LIVERPOOL
Marriott, Neil Kenneth	LT(FTC)	X	MCD	01.12.95	INVINCIBLE
Marrison, Graham	LT(IC)	E	MESM	02.08.02	FOST FAS SHORE
Marsh, Brian Henry, MBE, BSc, pcea	LT CDR(FTC)	X	O	01.10.99	UKMARBATSTAFF
Marsh, David Julian, BSc, MCMI	CAPT(FTC)	S		30.06.03	NAVSEC
Marsh, David Richard	LT(IC)	S		01.01.04	HQ 3 CDO BDE RM
Marsh, Michael Peter Alan	LT CDR(FTC)	X		01.10.02	PJHQ
Marsh, Stephen William	LT(IC)	S		01.01.04	SOMERSET
Marsh, Stuart David, BA	LT(IC)	X	H2	01.05.02	SCOTT
Marshall, Alistair John, BA	LT(CC)	X	SM	01.12.99	TRAFALGAR
Marshall, Andrew, MEng	SLT(IC)	X	P U/T	01.05.03	RAF CRANWELL EFS
Marshall, Colin George	LT(FTC)	X		01.12.04	PENZANCE
Marshall, Fleur Tiffany, MB, CHB, MRCGP, DObstRCOG, Dip FFP	SURG LTCDR(MCC)	-	GMPP	07.08.01	FOST SEA
Marshall, Gavin Peter, MEng	LT(CC)	E	ME	01.01.02	CV(F) IPT
Marshall, Jason	LT(IC)	X		01.01.04	IRON DUKE
Marshall, Leon	2LT(IC)	-		01.08.01	CTCRM LYMPSTONE

Name	Rank	Branch	Spec	Seniority	Where Serving
Marshall, Matthew, BEng	LT(CC)	X	P	01.05.98	FLEET AV VL
Marshall, Paul, BEng, MSc, psc(j)	LT CDR(FTC)	E	ME	01.09.00	MOD (LONDON)
Marshall, Richard Anthony, pce, psc(m)	CDR(FTC)	X	MCD	31.12.92	JHQ/CIS LISBON
Marshall, Richard George Carter, pce	LT CDR(FTC)	X	PWO(C)	01.05.95	DARTMOUTH BRNC
Marson, Gary Michael	LT CDR(FTC)	E	WE	14.10.96	DRAKE DIS
Marston, Peter Alan, MA, psc(j)	LT CDR(FTC)	S		16.04.96	PJHQ
Marston, Robert	2LT(IC)	-		01.08.01	CTCRM LYMPSTONE
Marten, Andrew David (Act Lt Cdr)	LT(FTC)	X	ATC	01.04.95	RAF SHAWBURY
Martin, Antony John	LT(FTC)	X	C	10.12.98	SAT IPT
Martin, Bruce Anthony, BSc, CEng, MIMechE	CDR(FTC)	E	MESM	30.06.05	MOD (LONDON)
Martin, Christopher Gavin, MEng	SLT(IC)	E	WE U/T	01.01.04	DARTMOUTH BRNC
Martin, David Charles Sarsfield	LT(CC)	X	PWO(U)	01.09.01	MWS COLLINGWOOD
Martin, David Leslie	SLT(IC)	X		01.09.03	YORK
Martin, Elizabeth Janet, BSc	LT CDR(FTC)	E	TM	01.04.91	PJHQ
Martin, Graham	LT(IC)	E	ME	01.07.04	SULTAN
Martin, James Nigel, BSc	SLT(IC)	X		01.01.03	HURWORTH
Martin, Lisa (Act Surg Lt)	SURG SLT(SCC)	-		16.07.04	DARTMOUTH BRNC
Martin, Michael Peter, CEng, PGDIPAN, AMRAeS	CDR(FTC)	E	AE	30.06.01	LAIPT
Martin, Michael Terence, BEng, MA, psc	CDR(FTC)	E	ME	30.06.01	ILLUSTRIOUS
Martin, Neil, MB, ChB, BSc	SURG LTCDR(SCC)	-		04.08.04	NELSON (PAY)
Martin, Neil Douglas, BSc, pcea, psc, gdas	LT CDR(FTC(A)	X	O	01.06.87	LOAN JTEG BSC DN
Martin, Nicholas Peter, MB, BS	SURG LTCDR(SCC)	-		26.08.04	RN GIBRALTAR
Martin, Nigel, DipFD	LT(FTC)	X	C	20.09.99	HQ DCSA
Martin, Paul John, BSc, psc(m)	LT COL(FTC)	-	C	31.12.93	BDS WASHINGTON
Martin, Rebecca Jane Whitehead, BA, MA(OXON)	LT(IC)	X		01.09.04	SEVERN
Martin, Rebecca Liane	LT(IC)	X	O	01.05.04	702 SQN HERON
Martin, Robert James, BEng	LT(CC)	E	AE	01.02.00	EXCHANGE ARMY UK
Martin, Roger Graham, pce	LT CDR(FTC)	X	AAWO	01.09.95	LOAN DSTL
Martin, Ronald Charles John Richard, BA	CHAPLAIN	SF		03.09.96	EXCHANGE USA
Martin, Simon Charles, LVO, pce, pce(sm), psc	CAPT(FTC)	X	SM	30.06.98	FWO DEVPT SEA
Martin, Simon James, BEng, MSc, CEng, MIEE	LT CDR(FTC)	E	WESM	01.02.00	TRIUMPH
Martin, Stuart William, MSc	LT(CC)	E	AE	01.08.99	FS MASU
Martin, Timothy Frederick Wilkins, LLB, MA, rcds (Barrister)	CAPT(FTC)	S	BAR	31.12.98	NAVSEC
Martindale, Holly	MID(IC)	X	ATCU/T	01.02.04	DARTMOUTH BRNC
Martyn, Alan Wallace, MSc, CEng, MRAeS	CDR(FTC)	E	AE	31.12.00	ILLUSTRIOUS
Martyn, Daniel, BA, MSc, SM(n)	LT(CC)	X	SM	01.05.01	SOVEREIGN
Martyn, Julie	LT(SC(MD)	Q		22.02.05	DARTMOUTH BRNC
Masilamani, Nithyanand Samuel, MB, BS, FRCS	SURG LTCDR(SCC)	-		14.01.98	RH HASLAR
Maskell, Bernard Malcolm, BEng	LT(IC)	E	WESM	01.05.04	CAPT MCTA
Maskell-Bott, John Malcolm, adp (Act Lt Cdr)	LT(FTC)	E	MESM	16.02.84	HQ BFSAI
Maskew, Tammy Anne, BA	SLT(IC)	X		01.09.03	DARTMOUTH BRNC
Mason, Andrew Clive, BSc	LT(CC)	X		01.07.98	EXPLORER
Mason, Andrew Harold, MSc	CDR(FTC)	E	AE	31.12.99	JCA IPT USA
Mason, Angus Edward, BSc	SLT(IC)	X	P U/T	01.01.04	DARTMOUTH BRNC
Mason, Darren Jon, BEng, SM(n)	LT(FTC)	X	SM	01.03.97	TORBAY
Mason, David, BSc	SLT(IC)	X		01.11.03	DARTMOUTH BRNC
Mason, Jeffrey Sinclair, MBE, psc	COL(FTC)	-	LC	30.06.01	PJHQ
Mason, Lindsay Colleen, MSc	LT CDR(FTC)	E	TM	01.10.02	DCTS PORTS
Mason, Mark John, BSc	LT(CC)	X	MCD	01.01.00	MWS COLLINGWOOD
Mason, Martin	LT CDR(FTC)	E	AE	01.10.99	ADAS BRISTOL
Mason, Nicholas Hugh, BSc, MinstP, MIIT, C PHYS	CDR(FTC)	E	TM	31.12.98	NELSON
Mason, Richard James, BSc	LT(IC)	X		01.05.04	SCEPTRE
Mason, Richard William, BSc, MA, CEng, MIEE, psc	CAPT(FTC)	E	WE	30.06.01	CAPT MCTA
Mason-Matthews	Angela	LT(IC) X		01.09.04	JARIC
Massey, Alan Michael, CBE, BA, PGCE, rcds, pce, psc (Commodore)	CAPT(FTC)	X	AAWO	30.06.96	PJHQ
Massey, Paul	LT CDR(FTC)	X	AV	01.10.04	RNAS YEOVILTON
Masson, Neil Graham, BSc	LT(IC)	X	SM	01.05.02	TORBAY
Masterman, Andrew Paul, BA, MLITT	LT(IC)	X		01.09.02	ALBION
Masters, James Christopher, pce	LT CDR(FTC)	X	AAWO	01.05.96	JSCSC
Masters, Richard Hilary, BTech, MA, MA(Ed), FCIPD, psc(j)	LT CDR(FTC)	E	TM	01.01.92	SHAPE BELGIUM
Mather, Graeme Philip	CDR(FTC)	E	ME	30.06.04	2SL/CNH FOTR
Mathews, Andrew David Hugh, MSc, CEng, MIMechE, rcds, psc	RADM	-	MESM	24.03.05	MOD (LONDON) (MAR 05)
Mathias, Philip Bentley, MBE, pce, pce(sm), psc	CAPT(FTC)	X	SM	31.12.99	RCDS

Name	Rank	Branch	Spec	Seniority	Where Serving
Mathias-Jones, Peter David, pce	LT CDR(FTC)	X	PWO(U)	01.09.90	MWS COLLINGWOOD
Mathieson, Kevin Richard, pcea (Act Cdr)	LT CDR(FTC)	X	P	01.10.95	FSAST IPT
Mathieson, Neil Braid, BEng, isc	LT(FTC)	E	AE	01.03.00	HARRIER IPT
Matthew, Mark Jonathan	LT(CC)	S	SM	01.09.99	NP BOSNIA
Matthews, David William, BEng, MSc	CDR(FTC)	E	WESM	30.06.05	JSCSC
Matthews, Gary Anthony, MB, BCH, MRCP, FRCA	SURG CDR(FCC)	-		30.06.04	NELSON (PAY)
Matthews, George, psc	LT COL(FTC)	-	SO(LE)	31.12.00	1 ASSAULT GP RM
Matthews, Jonathan James, MB, ChB	SURG LTCDR(MCC)	-		01.08.01	NELSON (PAY)
Matthews, Justin	LT(CC)	X	O	16.05.94	849 SQN HQ
Matthews, Paul Brian, BEng, PGDip	LT CDR(FTC)	E	TM	01.10.99	FWO PORTS SEA
Matthews, Paul John	SLT(IC)	X	O U/T	01.09.03	DARTMOUTH BRNC
Matthews, Paul Kinley	LT CDR(FTC)	S		01.10.03	FOST SEA
Matthews, Peter Ronald	LT(FTC)	E	AE	01.04.01	815 SQN HQ
Mattin, Paul Roger	MAJ(FTC)	-	MLDR	01.05.00	JWC/CIS STAVANGR
Mattock, Nicholas John	LT(IC)	X	P	01.01.05	RAF LINTN/OUSE
Maude, Christopher Philip, MRAeS, pcea (Act Cdr)	LT CDR(FTC)	X	P	01.10.92	LOAN JTEG BSC DN
Maude, Colin David, BEng	LT(CC)	E	AE U/T	01.03.03	HARRIER IPT
Maude, David Howard	LT CDR(FTC)	E	AE	01.10.99	DLO YEO
Maumy, Jonathan Marc	MID(NE)(IC)	X	P U/T	01.01.05	DARTMOUTH BRNC
Maunder, James Gilmore	LT(IC)	E	AE	01.05.04	771 SQN
Maw, Martyn John, BSc, CEng, MIEE	LT CDR(FTC)	E	WESM	01.12.90	TCM IPT
Mawdsley, Gareth Richard	LT(FTC)	S		01.09.01	DARTMOUTH BRNC
Mawer, Kieren Jon, BEng	LT(IC)	E	ME U/T	01.09.04	MANCHESTER
Mawer, Paul Rutherford	CAPT RM(IC)	-	SO(LE)	01.07.04	1 ASSLT GP RM
Mawson, John Robert, BA	CAPT RM(IC)	-	LC	01.05.99	1 ASSLT GP RM
Maxwell, Malcolm Scott, BSc	LT(IC)	E	TM	01.09.01	ILLUSTRIOUS
Maxwell, Rachel, BA, n	LT CDR(FTC)	X	PWO(U)	01.05.02	JSCSC
May, Colin	LT CDR(FTC)	X		01.07.04	MWS COLLINGWOOD
May, Damien John	CAPT RM(CC)	-	P	01.04.02	847 SQN
May, David Mark	LT(IC)	X	REG	01.10.02	MWS COLLINGWOOD
May, Dominic Peter, MBE, MDA, sq	LT COL(FTC)	-		30.06.05	NAVSEC
May, John William	LT(CC)	X	P	01.07.95	RNAS YEOVILTON
May, Nigel Peter, pce, pcea	LT CDR(FTC)	X	P	01.09.98	GRIMSBY
May, Oliver Buchanan, BA	SLT(IC)	X		01.06.03	DARTMOUTH BRNC
May, Peter James (Act Lt Cdr)	LT(FTC)	X	C	29.10.93	HQ DCSA
May, Steven Charles, BEng, MSc	LT CDR(FTC)	E	ME	01.07.03	EXETER
Mayberry, Peter James, MEng	LT(IC)	X	SM	01.09.04	MWS COLLINGWOOD
Maybery, James Edward, psc(j)	LT COL(FTC)	-		30.06.05	1 ASSAULT GP RM
May-Clingo, Martin Stephen (Act Lt Cdr)	LT(FTC)	X	AV	04.04.91	FLEET HQ PORTS
Mayell, Julie Ann, BA	LT CDR(FTC)	W	S	01.10.02	JSCSC
Maynard, Andrew Thomas Westenborg, MA, osc(us)	LT COL(FTC)	-		30.06.02	COMAMPHIBFOR
Maynard, Charles Ian, BA, n	LT CDR(FTC)	X	PWO(A)	01.02.03	ARGYLL
Maynard, Paul Andrew, BSc (Act Maj)	CAPT RM(CC)	-		01.09.01	BF BIOT
Mc Allister, Steven Edward, SM(n)	LT(CC)	X	SM	01.01.02	TORBAY
Mc Currach, Robert Henry	LT(CC)	X	FC	01.08.00	MWS COLLINGWOOD
Mc Laren, James Patrick	MAJ(FTC)	-		30.04.98	FLEET HQ PORTS 2
McAlpine, Paul Anthony, pce, psc(j)	CDR(FTC)	X	MCD	31.12.98	FOST SEA
McArdle, Martin James, BA	SLT(IC)	X	P U/T	01.02.04	DARTMOUTH BRNC
McArthur, Calum James Gibb ,BM, BCh, BAO, MRCGP, LRCP, DObstRCOG, Dip FFP	SURG CAPT(FCC)	-	GMPP	30.06.02	RCDS
McAteer, Dominic John	SLT(IC)	X		01.01.03	MWS COLLINGWOOD
McAuslin, Thomas McDonald, MMedSci	CDR(FTC)	MS	SM	30.06.04	MDHU DERRIFORD
McBain, Mandy Sheila	LT CDR(FTC)	W	S	01.12.04	NELSON
McBarnet, Thomas Francis, BSc, pce, psc(j)	CDR(FTC)	X	PWO(U)	31.12.97	FLEET HQ PORTS 2
McBeth, Gary, BEng	SLT(IC)	E	SM	01.09.02	VIGILANT(PORT)
McBratney, James Alexander Grant, SM(n), SM	LT CDR(FTC)	X	SM	01.11.04	SOVEREIGN
McCabe, Joseph, BA, MCIPD, psc (Act Col)	LT COL(FTC)	-		31.12.92	FLEET HQ PORTS
McCabe, Shane Edward Thomas, MB, BSc, BS, FRCA	SURG LTCDR(MCC)	-		01.08.00	LOAN FIELD HOSP
McCall, Gary, BA	LT(CC)	X	P	01.11.98	RAF SHAWBURY
McCall, Iain Robert, PGDIPAN, pce	LT CDR(FTC)	X	PWO(N)	01.07.96	EXETER
McCallum, Guy Peter, BSc	LT(IC)	X	P	01.09.03	DHFS
McCallum, Malcolm Donald, BA	LT(IC)	X		01.05.03	MWS HM TG (D)
McCallum, Neil Ritchie, BEng, MSc	LT(FTC)	E	ME	01.06.97	DLO BRISTOL

Name	Rank	Branch	Spec	Seniority	Where Serving
McCallum, Nicola	LT(IC)	X		01.05.05	2SL/CNH
McCamphill, Paul Joseph, BEng	LT(IC)	E	WE	01.01.02	DLO BRISTOL
McCann, Toby, BEng	LT(FTC)	E	AE	01.12.98	829 FLT 04
McCardle, John Alexander, BSc, jsdc	LT COL(FTC)	-	P	30.06.02	FLEET HQ PORTS 2
McCarrick, Michael James	2LT(IC)	-		01.09.00	CTCRM LYMPSTONE
McCartain, Michael Brendon William, OBE, BSc, pce, pcea, psc	CDR(FTC)	X	O	31.12.98	COS 2SL/CNH
McCarthy, Daniel John, BEng	LT(IC)	E	ME	01.09.02	IRON DUKE
McCarthy, Steven James, BEng, MSc, CEng, MIMarEST	LT CDR(FTC)	E	ME	01.10.02	OCEAN
McCaughey, Vincent Joseph, BComm, PGCE (Act Lt Cdr)	LT(FTC)	E	IS	01.03.93	2SL/CNH FOTR
McCavour, Bryan Darrell	SLT(IC)	X		01.09.02	OCEAN
McCleary, Simon Paul, BEng	LT(FTC)	E	WESM	01.03.98	MOD (LONDON)
McClement, Duncan Lewis, BEng, PGDip	LT(FTC)	E	MESM	01.01.99	NP BOSNIA
McClement, Timothy Pentreath, OBE, jsdc, pce, pce(sm), hcsc (DEPUTY COMMANDER IN CHIEF FLEET JUN 04)	VADM	-	SM	07.06.04	FLEET HQ PORTS 2
McCloskey, Ian Michael, BEng, CEng, MIMarEST	LT CDR(FTC)	E	ME	01.10.04	DLO BRISTOL
McClurg, Robert James, BEng	LT(FTC)	E	WE	01.03.02	MWS COLLINGWOOD
McCombe, John, MIMarEST	LT CDR(FTC)	E	ME	01.09.04	SUTHERLAND
McConochie, Andrew David, BSc	LT CDR(FTC)	S		16.04.96	DRAKE COB
McConville, Claire Wendy	LT(MC(MD)	Q		28.03.00	RN GIBRALTAR
McCormack, Gary	LT(FTC)	E	ME	01.09.03	LIVERPOOL
McCormack, Stuart	SLT(IC)	X	ATCU/T	01.01.04	RNAS YEOVILTON
McCormick, Peter Edward, MEng	LT(CC)	X	P	15.03.98	EXCHANGE CANADA
McCowan, David James (Act Lt Cdr)	LT(FTC)	X	P	16.06.95	846 SQN
McCowen, Polly Anne Charlotte, BA	LT(IC)	S		01.05.01	INVINCIBLE
McCoy, Mark, BEng	LT(FTC)	E	AE	01.11.98	DARTMOUTH BRNC
McCrea, Mark John, BEng	LT(IC)	E	ME U/T	01.05.05	WESTMINSTER
McCue, Duncan, MA, MSc, CEng, MIMarEST	LT CDR(FTC)	E	ME	01.10.98	JSCSC
McCulley, Steven Cameron	CAPT RM(CC)	-	LC	01.04.01	COMAMPHIBFOR
McCulloch, Alen John Ronald, MA, BD	CHAPLAIN	SF		12.06.04	FWO DEVPT SEA
McCullough, Karen Margaret	LT(SC(MD)	Q		01.11.04	MDHU DERRIFORD
McCutcheon, Graeme	LT(FTC)	X	P	01.02.95	815 FLT 215
McDermott, Owen David, BEng	LT CDR(FTC)	E	WE	01.10.99	DLO BRISTOL
McDermott, Paul Andrew	LT(FTC)	X	MCD	24.07.97	FDU2
McDermott-Evans, Rachel, BA	LT(IC)	X	O	01.01.05	RNAS CULDROSE
McDicken, Ian Neil, BDS	SGLTCDR(D)(SCC)	-		25.06.03	FORT BLOCKHOUSE
McDonald, Andrew, BEng	LT(CC)	E	AE	01.03.00	FLEET HQ PORTS
McDonald, Duncan James, BEng	LT(FTC)	E	ME	01.09.98	DARTMOUTH BRNC
McDonald, Morgan James	LT(IC)	X		01.01.05	MWS COLLINGWOOD
McDonald, Norman	LT(CC)	X	P	01.09.94	771 SQN
McDonnell, David Shaw, BEng, PGDIP	LT CDR(FTC)	X	METOC	01.03.99	FLEET HQ NWD
McDonnell, Peter William, pce, pce(sm)	CDR(FTC)	X	SM	30.06.98	RALEIGH
McDonough, Ambrose Gerrard, BSc, pce	LT CDR(FTC)	X	PWO(U)	01.07.96	DARTMOUTH BRNC
McDougall, William	LT(IC)	E	MESM	01.07.04	VIGILANT(STBD)
McElwaine, Richard Ian, BSc	CAPT(FTC)	E	AE	30.06.03	MOD (LONDON)
McEvoy, Lee Patrick	LT CDR(FTC)	X	EW	01.10.03	FLEET CIS PORTS
McEwan, Rory Daniel, BEng	LT(IC)	E	WESM	01.09.02	MWS COLLINGWOOD
McEwen, Craig James	SLT(IC)	X		01.09.03	DARTMOUTH BRNC
McFadden, Andrew	CHAPLAIN	RC		01.09.98	NELSON
McFarland, Noeleen	LT(MC(MD)	Q	REGM	14.01.99	RH HASLAR
McFarlane, Andrew Lennox, OBE, BSc, CEng, MIMechE, rcds	CDRE(FTC)	E	MESM	05.01.04	CNNRP BRISTOL
McGannity, Colin Stephen, BEng	LT(CC)	X	O	16.03.00	849 SQN HQ
McGarel, David Francis (Act Cdr)	LT CDR(FTC)	S	CA	01.10.96	AFPAA(CENTURION)
McGhee, Craig, BEng	MAJ(FTC)	-	P	01.09.02	847 SQN
McGhie, Ian Andrew, pce, pce(sm)	CDR(FTC)	X	SM	31.12.99	MOD (LONDON)
McGinley, Christopher Thomas, BSc, PGCE	LT(IC)	E	TM	01.05.97	45 CDO RM
McGivern, Ryan Patrick, BSc	LT(IC)	X	P	01.09.04	RNAS YEOVILTON
McGlone, Fergus Robert	MID(NE)(IC)	X		01.11.04	DARTMOUTH BRNC
McGlory, Stephen Joseph, BA	LT CDR(FTC)	X	PWO(A)	01.06.02	FLEET HQ NWD
McGowan, Angela Bridget, BA	LT(CC)	X	O	01.09.01	GANNET SAR FLT
McGrane, Richard John, pce	LT CDR(FTC)	X	C	01.10.03	UKMARBATSTAFF
McGrath, Wayne James (Act Lt Cdr)	LT(IC)	S	(S)	08.01.01	HQBF CYPRUS
McGreal, Benjamin, BEng	LT(IC)	X	P U/T	01.01.03	DRAKE COB
McGrenary, Andrew	LT CDR(FTC)	X		01.01.94	MOD (LONDON)

Name	Rank	Branch	Spec	Seniority	Where Serving
McGuire, James, SM(n), SM	LT CDR(FTC)	X	SM	24.08.04	SOVEREIGN
McGuire, Michael Joseph, pce, n	LT CDR(FTC)	X	PWO(A)	31.08.98	GIBRALTAR PBS
McGunigall, Roy	LT CDR(FTC)	MS	(AD)	01.10.04	NELSON (PAY)
McHale, Gareth John, BSc, pce, pcea	LT CDR(FTC)	X	O	01.12.91	MERLIN IPT
McHale, Kevan	CDR(FTC)	E	AE	30.06.05	JHCHQ
McHugh, Richard Henry, BEng	LT CDR(FTC)	E	ME	01.03.05	DLO BRISTOL
McInerney, Andrew Jonathon, BSc, MA, MDA, psc(j)	MAJ(FTC)	-		01.09.99	HQ 3 CDO BDE RM
McInnes, James Gerard Kenneth, BSc, MIEE	CDR(FTC)	E	WESM	30.06.05	FOST SM SEA
McIntosh, James Declan, BA, MB, BS, DRCOG, MRCGP	SURG LTCDR(MCC)	-	GMPP	26.08.02	BULWARK
McIntosh, Jane Rachel	SLT(IC)	X	ATCU/T	01.02.04	DARTMOUTH BRNC
McIntyre, Alastair William	LT CDR(FTC)	X		01.10.04	MOD (LONDON)
McIntyre, Caroline	SLT(IC)	S		01.06.03	ILLUSTRIOUS
McIntyre, Louise, MA	LT(CC)	X		01.01.00	SHOREHAM
McJarrow, Duncan James, BDS, MGDS RCS, LDS RCS(Eng)	SGCDR(D)(FCC)	-		30.06.00	RNAS YEOVILTON
McKay, Thomas Westley, LLB	LT(CC)	X		01.01.02	EDINBURGH
McKeating, Paul Michael	CAPT RM(IC)	-		01.09.03	FPGRM
McKee, Hamish McLeod, BA, BComm	LT(CC)	X	O	01.07.97	824 SQN
McKee, Robert William	LT(IC)	X	O	01.05.04	849 SQN A FLT
McKeen, Stephen Alexander, BSc	SLT(IC)	X	P U/T	01.07.02	RNAS YEOVILTON
McKeever, Shaun Alexander	LT(IC)	X	MCD	01.07.04	QUORN
McKendrick, Andrew Michael, OBE, pce, pce(sm), psc(j)	CDR(FTC)	X	SM	31.12.98	JSCSC
McKenna, Danelle Rosanne	LT(IC)	X		01.07.03	GRAFTON
McKenzie, David, BSc, CEng, MIMarEST	CDR(FTC)	E	ME	30.06.00	SHAPE BELGIUM
McKenzie, Hannah Kathryn	SLT(IC)	S		01.02.04	INVINCIBLE
McKenzie, Malcolm, MBE, pce, pcea	LT CDR(FTC)	X	O	03.03.98	HQ1GP HQSTC
McKernan, James	LT CDR(FTC)	X	C	01.10.01	MOD (LONDON)
McKie, Andrew, MBE, MA, pcea, psc	CDR(FTC)	X	P	31.12.00	DHFS
McKinlay, Jayne	SURG LT(SCC)	-		01.02.05	DARTMOUTH BRNC
McKnight, Derek James Stewart	LT CDR(FTC)	X	MCD	01.07.03	SOUTHAMPTON
McKnight, Nicholas William, MSc	LT CDR(FTC)	S		01.10.93	AFPAA JPA
McLachlan, Andrew Charles, BA	LT(IC)	E	TM	19.01.04	40 CDO RM
McLachlan, Jennifer Kim, MB, ChB, FRCA	SURG LTCDR(MCC)	-		17.08.00	NELSON (PAY)
McLachlan, Michael Paul, AMIMarE	LT CDR(FTC)	E	ME	01.10.02	LIVERPOOL
McLaren, Stuart Caldwell	CAPT RM(IC)	-		01.09.04	FPGRM
McLarnon, Christopher Patrick Charles, MSc	LT CDR(FTC)	E	IS	01.09.99	FLEET CIS PORTS
McLaughlin, Steven, MA, PGCE	LT(IC)	E	TM	01.12.98	FLEET HQ PORTSEA
McLaughlin, Vincent, BEng	LT(IC)	E	ME	01.09.04	BULWARK
McLean, Christopher Richard, MB, BS, MRCS, DP	SURG LTCDR(SCC)	-		07.08.01	MDHU FRIMLEY
McLean, Daniel James	SLT(IC)	S		01.09.04	NEPTUNE DLO
McLean, David, BSc, BD	CHAPLAIN	RC		18.09.96	DARTMOUTH BRNC
McLean, Rory Alistair Ian, CB, OBE, pce, hcsc	VADM	-	P	16.09.04	MOD (LONDON)
(DEPUTY CHIEF OF DEFENCE STAFF (HEALTH) SEP 04)					
McLellan, James Douglas, BEng, CEng, MIEE	LT(FTC)	E	WE	01.11.97	DRAKE SFM
McLelland, Peter Holmes	CAPT RM(IC)	-	P	01.04.02	849 SQN A FLT
McLennan, Andrew	LT(CC)	X	O	01.04.95	824 SQN
McLennan, Richard Glenn, BSc, fsc	CDR(FTC)	E	AE	30.06.98	AGRIPPA JFC HQ
McLeod, Katherine Yvonne Louise	LT(IC)	X		01.12.03	CAMPBELTOWN
McLocklan, Lee Michael	LT(CC)	S		01.04.00	MWS COLLINGWOOD
McLone, Simon Peter, BSc	SLT(IC)	X	P U/T	01.05.02	RNAS YEOVILTON
McMahon, Damien Patrick, BSc	LT(IC)	X		01.08.04	LEEDS CASTLE
McMahon, Daniel Steven, BSc	LT(IC)	X		01.01.04	EXETER
McMaster, Garry Thomas, BSc	LT(IC)	X		01.01.03	MARLBOROUGH
McMeekin, Nicola Sarah, BDS, BSc	SGLTCDR(D)(MCC)	-		15.07.95	DRAKE COB(CNH)
McMenamin, Diarmaid Martin, MB, BS	SURG LT(SCC)	-		06.08.03	CFLT MED(SEA)
McMichael, James Stewart, BSc	LT(CC)	X	O	01.01.98	815 FLT 228
McMichael-Phillips, Scott James, BSc, ARICS, pce	CDR(FTC)	X	H CH	31.12.99	MOD (LONDON)
McMillan, Nelson	LT(CC)	X		01.09.04	2SL/CNH
McMullan, Neil Leslie, BA, MSc	LT CDR(FTC)	E	TM	01.01.01	JSCSC
McNab, Gillian Jane, BDS	SG LT(D)(SCC)	-	GDP	19.06.02	DRAKE COB(CNH)
McNair, Euan Alan, AFC, pce, pcea, psc	CDR(FTC)	X	P	30.06.95	DASC
McNair, James	LT(FTC)	E	AE	02.05.00	FLEET HQ PORTSEA
McNally, Neville James	LT CDR(FTC)	S		01.11.98	DLO/DG DEF SC
McNally, Nicholas Anthony	LT(IC)	E	ME	01.07.04	SULTAN

Name	Rank	Branch	Spec	Seniority	Where Serving
McNamara, Ian Martin, BEng	LT CDR(FTC)	E	WESM	01.08.04	DLO BRISTOL
McNaughton, John Alistair, BSc, adp, SM	LT CDR(FTC)	E	IS	01.07.93	FLEET CIS PORTS
McNeill Love, Robin Michael Cox, MSc, MB, BS, MRCGP, MFOM, DA, DRCOG, DipAvMed, Dip FFP	SURG CDR(FCC)	-	GMPP	30.06.96	R
McPhail, Thomas Cameron, BSc	LT(IC)	X		01.05.04	BRECON
McPherson, Alan	LT(IC)	S		01.05.04	VENGEANCE(STBD)
McQuaker, Stuart Ross, MSc, PGDIPAN, pce, psc(j)	CDR(FTC)	X	PWO(N)	31.12.98	ILLUSTRIOUS
McQueen, Jason Bedwell, BSc, n	LT CDR(CC)	E	TM	01.10.03	FLEET HQ PORTS
McQueen, Patrick Graham, BSc	LT(IC)	X		01.09.04	SOUTHAMPTON
McQuire, Duncan Ewen Alexander, BEng, MSc, CEng, MIMechE	LT(IC)	E	ME	01.01.03	SUTHERLAND
McRae, Philip Compton, BEng, CEng, MIEE	LT CDR(FTC)	E	WESM	01.12.99	DPA BRISTOL
McSavage, Robert Ian, BSc	SLT(IC)	X	O U/T	01.05.02	RNAS CULDROSE
McTaggart, Douglas Alexander	LT(FTC)	E	WE	07.02.97	JES IPT
McTear, Karen, BSc	CDR(FTC)	E	TM	30.06.05	SA MOSCOW
McTear, Nigel James	LT CDR(FTC)	X	AV	01.10.02	NELSON
McTeer, Ian James, BA	LT(CC)	X	P	16.08.98	845 SQN
McWilliams, Adrian Robert	LT(CC)	X	O	01.05.98	815 FLT 211
McWilliams, Jacqueline Elizabeth, BA, MSc	LT CDR(FTC)	X	MW	01.09.03	FLEET HQ PORTS 2
Meacher, Paul Graham, BA	LT(IC)	X		01.04.03	SOUTHAMPTON
Meachin, Michael Charles	CHAPLAIN	SF		07.07.97	ALBION
Meakin, Brian Richard, BSc, MBA, pcea, psc(j)	CDR(FTC)	X	O	30.06.03	MOD (LONDON)
Mealing, David William, BEng	LT CDR(FTC)	E	AE	01.10.04	CTS
Mealing, Steven, BEng	LT(FTC)	E	ME	01.12.97	SULTAN
Mearns, Craig McDonald, MA, psc(j)	CDR(FTC)	S		30.06.05	RN GIBRALTAR
Mears, Richard John, BSc	CAPT RM(FTC)	-	C	01.05.00	HQ 3 CDO BDE RM
Meeds, Kevin, pce, pcea, psc(j)	LT CDR(FTC)	X	O	16.12.95	FLEET HQ PORTS
Meek, Camilla Simpson, BEng, CEng, MIMarEST	LT CDR(FTC)	E	ME	01.03.02	EDINBURGH
Mehlsen, Nigel Mark Nicholas	SLT(IC)	X		01.01.04	DARTMOUTH BRNC
Mehta, Kim Louise, BEng	LT(CC)	E	TM	01.09.95	DARTMOUTH BRNC
Meigh, Peter David, BSc	LT(IC)	X		01.09.04	RNAS YEOVILTON
Meikle, Robert	LT(CC)	X		01.04.01	MWS SOUTHWICK PK
Meikle, Stuart Andrew, BSc, IEng, MIIE	LT(FTC)	E	AE	01.04.01	SULTAN
Melbourne, Steven	CAPT RM(IC)	-	SO(LE)	02.04.04	COMAMPHIBFOR
Mellor, Adrian John, MB, BCh, FRCA	SURG CDR(FCC)	-	(CA)	30.06.03	MDHU NORTH
Mellor, Barry John, MA, FCMI, psc(j)	CDR(FTC)	S		30.06.04	HQ DCSA
Mellor, Daniel Peter, BEng	SLT(IC)	E	SM	01.09.02	VENGEANCE(PORT)
Mellor, Rex Geoffrey, MB, BS, BSc	SURG LT(SC(MD)	-		01.12.04	CFLT MED(SEA)
Melville, Arran, IEng, AMIMarEST	LT(IC)	E	ME	01.02.01	SULTAN
Melville-Brown, Martin Giles	LT CDR(FTC)	S	CA	01.10.01	FOST SEA
Mennecke-Jappy, Gavin William George, BA	LT(CC)	X		01.08.97	EXCHANGE GERMANY
Menzies, Angus, MInsD, AMNI	CDRE(FTC)	S	SM	04.02.03	NAVSEC
Menzies, Bruce, BSc	LT(IC)	X	P	01.09.01	815 FLT 218
Menzies, Gregor Malcolm, BSc	CAPT RM(IC)	-	MLDR	01.09.02	40 CDO RM
Mercer, Andrew Jude, MB, CHB	SURG LT(MC(MD)	-		01.08.01	MDHU DERRIFORD
Mercer, David Crispian	LT CDR(FTC)	X	P	01.10.03	FLEET HQ PORTS
Mercer, Simon Jude, MB, ChB	SURG LT(MCC)	-		02.08.00	MDHU DERRIFORD
Mercer, Stuart James ,BM, BCh, MRCS	SURG LTCDR(MCC)	-		03.08.00	NELSON (PAY)
Merchant, Ian Charles	CDR(FTC)	S		31.12.00	MOD (LONDON)
Merchant, Jeremy Mark, CGC	MAJ(FTC)	-	SO(LE)	01.10.04	1 ASSAULT GP RM
Meredith, Nicholas, BSc, pce(sm)	LT CDR(FTC)	X	SM	01.04.94	EXCHANGE FRANCE
Merewether, Henry Alworth Hamilton, MA, pce, pcea, psc(j)	CDR(FTC)	X	O	30.06.04	FOST DPORT SHORE
Merriman, Peter Orrill, BSc, CEng, MIMechE	CDR(FTC)	E	MESM	30.06.99	FWO FASLANE SEA
Merritt, Jonathan James, BEng, MSc, CEng, MCGI, MIMarEST	CDR(FTC)	E	ME	30.06.05	DLO BRISTOL
Mervik, Christopher Fields, OBE, rcds, pce, pcea, ocds(Can)	CAPT(FTC)	X	P	31.12.99	MOD (LONDON)
Messenger, Gordon Kenneth, DSO, OBE, BSc, psc	COL(FTC)	-	MLDR	30.06.02	PJHQ
Metcalf, Robin	LT CDR(FTC)	E	ME	01.10.01	CARDIFF
Metcalf, Stephen William, IEng, AMIMarEST	LT(FTC)	E	MESM	01.04.01	FOST SM SEA
Metcalfe, Anthony Paul Warren, pce	LT CDR(FTC)	X	PWO(U)	01.12.91	FLEET HQ PORTS
Metcalfe, Liam Michael	CAPT RM(CC)	-	LC	01.09.03	FPGRM
Metcalfe, Philip Geoffrey, BEng, MSc, MIEE	CDR(FTC)	E	WESM	30.06.03	MOD (LONDON)
Metcalfe, Richard John	LT(FTC)	E	WE	04.09.98	MCM3 SEA
Methven, Paul, BEng, MSc, CEng, MIMarEST	CDR(FTC)	E	MESM	30.06.04	DLO BRISTOL
Mettam, Samuel Richard, MA	LT(FTC)	S		01.09.02	846 SQN

Name	Rank	Branch	Spec	Seniority	Where Serving
Mewes, David Bruce	CAPT RM(CC)	-	SO(LE)	01.04.02	CTCRM
Meyer, Alexander James, BA	LT(CC)	X	FC	01.12.98	JSCSC
Miah, Jahangir Hussain, BSc	LT(IC)	E	IS	01.09.01	AFPAA(CENTURION)
Miall, Merlin Christopher, BSc	LT(IC)	X	SM	01.05.03	TIRELESS
Mickleburgh, Allan	LT CDR(FTC)	X	REG	01.10.97	JPS UK
Middleditch, Thomas Clifford	MID(UCE)(IC)	E	ME U/T	01.09.03	DARTMOUTH BRNC
Middleton, Christopher Sydney, BEd	MAJ(FTC)	-	LC	01.10.04	40 CDO RM
Middleton, Donna Marie, BA	LT(CC)	S		01.03.99	NELSON
Middleton, Judith Elizabeth, BSc	LT(MC(MD)	Q	IC*	26.04.01	RCDM
Middleton, Simon William Frederick, MB, BS	SURG LT(SC(MD)	-		11.09.03	CDO LOG REGT RM
Middleton, Toby Patrick Windsor, BSc, psc(m)	LT COL(FTC)	-	LC	31.12.00	COMATG SEA
Middleton, Wayne Trevor	LT(CC)	S		01.08.00	FLEET HQ PORTSEA
Midmore, Martin Jonathan	LT CDR(FTC)	E	AE	01.10.03	FLEET AV VL
Midwinter, Mark John, MD, MB, BS, BSc, FRCS	SURG CDR(FCC)	-	(CGS)	31.12.98	MDHU DERRIFORD
Mifflin, Michelle Jane	LT(CC)	X	X	01.01.05	MWS SOUTHWICK PK
Miklinski, Anthony Stanley, BSc, DipEd, psc	CDRE(FTC)	E	TM	02.03.04	MOD (LONDON)
Milburn, Philip Kenneth, pce	CDR(FTC)	X	AAWO	31.12.00	OCEAN
Milburn, Victoria	LT(FTC)	MS	(AD)	01.04.01	INM ALVERSTOKE
Miles, Graham John, BSc, BEng, MRAeS	LT CDR(FTC)	E	AE	07.08.00	RAF COTTESMORE
Miles, Philip John, BA	LT(CC)	S		01.08.98	CTS
Miles, Rebecca Lewis, BSc, PGDip	LT CDR(FTC)	X	HM	01.01.05	FLEET HQ NWD
Miles, Richard, MB, BS, FRCR, MRCP	SURG CDR(FCC)	-	(CX)	30.06.03	MDHU DERRIFORD
Miles, Sean (Act Surg Lt)	SURG SLT(SCC)	-		02.07.04	DARTMOUTH BRNC
Mileusnic, Christopher John, BA	SLT(IC)	X	P U/T	01.02.04	DARTMOUTH BRNC
Millar, Gordon Craig, BEng	LT CDR(FTC)	E	AE	15.05.98	MOD (LONDON)
Millar, Kevin Ian, MIIE	LT(FTC)	E	MESM	02.09.99	SUPERB
Millar, Stuart William Sinclair, MB, BS, MRCGP, Dip FFP	SURG CDR(FCC)	-	GMPP	30.06.02	JSCSC
Millard, Andrew Robert	LT CDR(FTC)	X		01.01.99	PJHQ
Millard, Jeremy Robert, BEng, AMIEE	LT(CC)	E	ME	01.02.98	1 ASSLT GP RM
Millen, Ian Stuart, psc(j), MA	CDR(FTC)	X	EW	30.06.05	MOD (LONDON)
Millen, Stuart Charles William	LT(FTC)	X	P	01.04.93	849 SQN HQ
Miller, Alexander David, BA	SLT(IC)	S		01.05.03	ALBION
Miller, Colin Robert, pcea	LT CDR(FTC)	X	O	01.10.99	FLEET HQ PORTS 2
Miller, David Edward	LT CDR(FTC)	MS	(AD)	01.10.03	DRAKE SFM
Miller, Gary	LT CDR(FTC)	X	AV	01.10.02	SULTAN
Miller, Ian, MEng	LT(FTC)	E	MESM	01.01.00	SULTAN
Miller, John Charles, IEng, MIMarEST	LT(FTC)	E	MESM	17.10.86	SULTAN
Miller, Kevin Roy, BEng	LT(IC)	E	WE	01.05.01	SOUTHAMPTON
Miller, Mandy Catherine, BEng, MSc gw	LT CDR(FTC)	E	WE	01.10.04	MOD (LONDON)
Miller, Paul David	LT CDR(FTC)	X	AAWO	01.02.01	YORK
Milles, Olivia Kate, BA	LT(IC)	X	P	16.06.00	846 SQN
Milligan, Robert James Charles, pcea	LT(FTC)	X	O	16.04.92	PJHQ
Mills, Andrew, BEng	LT CDR(FTC)	E	WESM	01.05.95	SETT GOSPORT
Mills, Gary Anthony	LT(FTC)	X		19.09.00	MWS COLLINGWOOD
Mills, Gordon William	LT CDR(FTC)	E	WE	01.10.98	CAPT MCTA
Mills, Ian, BEng, CEng, MIEE	LT CDR(FTC)	E	WE	01.10.01	GLOUCESTER
Mills, Sydney David Gareth	LT(CC)	X	P	01.01.95	FLEET AV VL
Mills, Thomas Clark, BSc, MA, psc(j)	LT CDR(FTC)	E	TM	01.10.93	SULTAN
Millward, Jeremy, MBE, pcea (Act Capt)	CDR(FTC)	X	P	31.12.99	HQ1GP HQSTC
Milne, Andre Paul, MA	LT(CC)	X	P	16.12.00	MWS COLLINGWOOD
Milne, Andrew Richard, BA (Act Lt Col)	MAJ(FTC)	-	MLDR	01.09.88	2SL/CNH FOTR
Milne, Jason	CAPT RM(IC)	-	SO(LE)	24.07.04	FLEET HQ PORTS 2
Milne, Peter Barkes, BEng (Act Lt Cdr)	LT(FTC)	X	P	16.09.91	FLEET AV VALLEY
Milne, William John Connington, BEng	LT(FTC)	E	MESM	01.03.00	VANGUARD(PORT)
Milner, Hugh Christopher, ocds(No)	MAJ(FTC)	-		01.09.89	RMC OF SCIENCE
Milner, Lisa Deni, BSc	SLT(IC)	X	O U/T	01.05.02	RAF SHAWBURY
Milner, Robert Adrian, MB, BS, MRCP	SURG LTCDR(MCC)	-		07.08.01	NELSON (PAY)
Milsom, Jonathan, BEng	LT CDR(FTC)	E	AE	01.10.99	DLO WYTON
Milton, Gary Peter, pcea	LT CDR(FTC)	X	O	01.10.04	820 SQN
Milton, George James Gordon, BSc, CEng, FIEE, MIEE, psc	CDR(FTC)	E	WESM	31.12.90	NEPTUNE SWS
Mimpriss, Graham Donald, PGDip, pce, n	LT CDR(FTC)	X	H CH	01.04.99	EXCHANGE USA
Minall, Mark Lee	LT(IC)	X	PWO(C)	01.05.02	ALBION
Minall, Paul Alan, BDS, FDS	SGLTCDR(D)(SCC)	-		24.07.96	FWO DEVONPORT

Name	Rank	Branch	Spec	Seniority	Where Serving
Mincher, David Joseph Francis, BEng	LT CDR(FTC)	E	MESM	01.07.02	VENGEANCE(STBD)
Minnikin, Stephen Barry, MSc	LT(IC)	X		01.01.05	MWS COLLINGWOOD
Minshall, Darren (Act Surg Lt)	SURG SLT(SCC)	-		16.07.04	DARTMOUTH BRNC
Minty, Darren, MEng	SLT(IC)	E	ME U/T	01.09.02	ILLUSTRIOUS
Mitchell, Christopher David	LT CDR(FTC)	X	MW	01.12.04	COM MCC NWD
Mitchell, Henry George Murray, pcea, psc(j)	CDR(FTC)	X	P	30.06.01	HQ1GP HQSTC
Mitchell, Jamie Dundas, SM(n)	LT(CC)	X	SM	01.09.01	TORBAY
Mitchell, Michael	LT CDR(FTC)	X	AV	01.10.04	MOD (BATH)
Mitchell, Patrick, IEng, MIIE	LT CDR(FTC)	E	WESM	01.10.04	CAPT MCTA
Mitchell, Paul Jeffrey	LT(IC)	X		01.05.03	RNAS YEOVILTON
Mitchell, Shouna Elizabeth, BSc	LT(IC)	S		01.01.05	DLO YEO
Mitchell, Stephen Derek, IEng, AMINucE	LT CDR(FTC)	E	MESM	01.10.01	SULTAN
Mittins, Simon	LT(IC)	X	ATCU/T	01.05.03	RAF COTTESMORE
Mockford, James Arthur	LT CDR(FTC)	E	AE	01.10.96	JCA IPT USA
Moffat, John William, BEng	CAPT RM(CC)	-		23.04.99	NAVSEC
Moffatt, Danny	CAPT RM(IC)	-	MLDR	01.09.03	29 CDO REGT RA
Moffatt, Neil Robert, BSc, CEng, MIMarEST	CDR(FTC)	E	MESM	30.06.02	DLO BRISTOL
Moffatt, Roger, pcea, tp	LT CDR(FTC(A)	X	P	01.10.95	LOAN JTEG BSC DN
Mole, Andrew James, MEng	LT(IC)	E	MESM	01.09.03	VANGUARD(PORT)
Molloy, Lynne, BSc	LT(CC)	X	ATC	01.09.02	INVINCIBLE
Molnar, Richard Mark	LT(FTC)	X	PWO(A)	01.04.01	NOTTINGHAM
Molyneaux, Dean George, BSc, CEng, MIEE, psc	CAPT(FTC)	E	WE	30.06.04	MOD (BATH)
Molyneux, Ian Thomas, BEng, CEng, MIEE	LT(FTC)	E	WESM	01.08.99	DLO BRISTOL
Monachello, Paolo Gino, BSc, SM(n), SM	LT(CC)	X	SM	01.01.99	MWC PORTSDOWN
Moncrieff, Ian, BA, pce	CDRE(FTC)	X	PWO(C)	10.11.03	HQ BFSAI
Money, Christopher John, BA	LT(CC)	X	H2	01.06.00	FWO DEVPT SEA
Monger, Paul David, MSc, PGDip	LT CDR(FTC)	X	METOC	01.10.94	RNAS CULDROSE
Monk, Kevin Neil	LT(IC)	X	O	01.10.02	815 FLT 246
Monk, Stephen, n	LT CDR(FTC)	X	PWO(N)	01.10.04	EXCHANGE USA
Monnox, Jill	LT(CC)	X		01.09.01	LIVERPOOL
Montagu, Timothy Benjamin Edward Paulet, BSc	SLT(IC)	X		01.01.04	DARTMOUTH BRNC
Montague, Andrew David, BSc	SLT(IC)	X		01.07.02	MIDDLETON
Montague, Richard James, BSc	LT(FTC)	X	SM	01.12.01	SCEPTRE
Montgomery, Charles Percival Ross, BEng, rcds, pce, psc	CDRE(FTC)	X	PWO(U)	25.11.03	COS 2SL/CNH
Montgomery, Harvie Ellams, BSc	LT(IC)	E	TM U/T	01.11.04	CTCRM
Montgomery, Michael Henry, BSc, SM	LT CDR(FTC)	X	SM	01.12.97	AST(N)
Moodie, Graeme Russell, jsdc, pce, pcea	CAPT(FTC)	X	O	31.12.96	MOD (LONDON)
Moody, Alistair Charles, BEng, MSc, CEng, MIMarEST	LT(FTC)	E	MESM	01.02.99	NP BRISTOL
Moody, David Christopher, BEng, CEng, MIEE	LT CDR(FTC)	E	WE	01.07.00	FLEET CIS PORTS
Moon, Ian Langland, BEng	LT(IC)	E	ME	01.05.01	YORK
Moore, Christian Benedict, psc(j)	MAJ(FTC)	-		01.09.96	1 ASSAULT GP RM
Moore, Christopher, BA, MSc	LT CDR(FTC)	X		05.12.99	FLEET HQ PORTS
Moore, Christopher Ian, pce	CDR(FTC)	X	AAWO	30.06.99	FWO PORTS SEA
Moore, Jonathan Peter	SLT(IC)	X	P U/T	01.06.03	RNAS YEOVILTON
Moore, Martin, BA	LT CDR(FTC)	X	PWO(U)	01.06.00	FOST SEA
Moore, Martin Nicholas, MBE	CDR(FTC)	E	WESM	31.12.00	MOD (LONDON)
Moore, Matthew James	LT(CC)	X	MCD	01.04.01	CHIDDINGFOLD
Moore, Michael Ronald, IEng, MIL	LT(FTC)	E	WE	29.10.82	VICTORY
Moore, Nicholas Gerald Arthur	LT(IC)	S		17.12.04	RNAS CULDROSE
Moore, Nicholas James, BSc	LT(IC)	X	P	01.04.00	LOAN OTHER SVCE
Moore, Paul Grenville, BDS	SGLTCDR(D)(FCC)	-		31.12.98	ILLUSTRIOUS
Moore, Piers Henry George, psc(j)	LT CDR(FTC)	X	SM	01.06.96	MOD (LONDON)
Moore, Richard	2LT(IC)	-		01.08.04	CTCRM LYMPSTONE
Moore, Sara, BSc	LT(IC)	E	TM U/T	01.02.03	ILLUSTRIOUS
Moore, Sean Barry, LLB (Barrister)	LT CDR(FTC)	S	BAR	01.04.02	MOD (LONDON)
Moore, Suzanne Kathryn, BEd, pce, n	LT CDR(FTC)	X	PWO(U)	01.11.01	FLEET HQ NWD
Moore, William Ian	CAPT RM(IC)	-		01.09.04	FPGRM
Moores, Colin Peter, BEng, CEng, MIMarEST	LT CDR(CC)	E	ME	01.10.02	COS 2SL/CNH
Moores, John	LT CDR(FTC)	S	(S)	01.10.03	SUTHERLAND
Moores, John Keith, BSc, pce, pce(sm)	CAPT(FTC)	X	SM	30.06.03	VANGUARD(PORT)
Moorey, Christopher George, pce, psc(j)	LT CDR(FTC)	X	PWO(A)	01.03.94	MWS COLLINGWOOD
Moorhouse, Edward James	MAJ(FTC)	-		24.04.02	FLEET HQ PORTS
Moorhouse, Stephen Mark Richard, BSc	LT CDR(FTC)	X	O	01.02.04	BULWARK

Name	Rank	Branch	Spec	Seniority	Where Serving
Moorhouse, Suzanne Marie, BA	LT CDR(FTC)	S		01.06.02	NELSON
Moran, Benjamin Michael	LT(IC)	X	SM	01.01.02	VIGILANT(STBD)
Moran, Craig Andrew	LT(FTC)	X	REG	10.01.00	AGRIPPA JFC HQ
Moran, John-Paul	SLT(IC)	E	MESMUT	01.09.03	MANCHESTER
Moran, Julian Toby	CAPT RM(CC)	-		28.04.99	RM WARMINSTER
Moran, Russell James	LT(CC)	X		01.06.99	FOST MPV SEA
Moreby, Martin Francis	LT(FTC)	X	AV	02.04.93	CHFHQ
Moreland, Michael John, BSc, CEng, MIMarEST, psc(m)	CDR(FTC)	E	MESM	30.06.00	FWO FASLANE
Morey, Kevin Norton	LT(FTC)	X		01.09.02	DULVERTON
Morey, Roland George	LT(IC)	E	ME	11.04.03	BULWARK
Morgan, Benjamin Penoyre, BSc	LT(IC)	X	P	01.01.02	814 SQN
Morgan, Christopher William	LT(IC)	X	SM	01.05.02	TIRELESS
Morgan, David	LT(IC)	X	EW	01.05.02	PJHQ
Morgan, David Henry, BSc	LT CDR(FTC)	X	PWO(U)	01.10.02	FOST SEA
Morgan, Edward	LT(CC)	X		12.02.99	845 SQN
Morgan, Fiona Caroline Frances, BA	SLT(IC)	X		01.07.02	WALNEY
Morgan, Forbes Scott, BEng, MSc, MIMarEST	LT CDR(FTC)	E	ME	01.11.97	PORTLAND
Morgan, Gareth Lee	LT(IC)	X	P	01.09.04	845 SQN
Morgan, Huw Lloyd, BSc	CAPT RM(CC)	-		01.09.01	1 ASSAULT GP RM
Morgan, Nicholas Vaughan, MB, BS, FRCSEd, Dip SM, jsdc	SURG CAPT(FCC)	-	GMPP	30.06.00	MOD (LONDON)
Morgan, Peter Thomas, DSC, pce, psc	CDR(FTC)	X	PWO(A)	30.06.97	FLEET HQ PORTS 2
Morgan, Rachel Sara	LT(MC(MD)	Q	REGM	06.09.99	NELSON (PAY)
Morgan, Stephen Alexander, HNC	LT CDR(FTC)	E	WE	01.10.97	LOAN DSTL
Morgan-Hosey, John Noel, BEng, CEng, MIMarEST	LT CDR(FTC)	E	MESM	01.10.01	NP BRISTOL
Morisetti, Neil, BSc, jsdc, pce, hcsc	CDRE(FTC)	X	PWO(A)	26.03.02	INVINCIBLE
Morley, Adrian, BA	MAJ(FTC)	-	LC	01.05.03	2SL/CNH FOTR
Morley, James David, MA, pce, psc(j)	CDR(FTC)	X	PWO(A)	30.06.04	LANCASTER
Morley, James Ian, MSc, CEng, MIMechE	LT(FTC)	E	ME	01.11.97	DLO BRISTOL
Morphet, Kathryn, BSc, MA	LT(IC)	E	TM	01.01.01	FOST FAS SHORE
Morrell, Andrew John	LT CDR(FTC)	X	SM	01.10.04	PJHQ
Morris, Alistair John, MB, BSc, BS	SURG LT(SC(MD)	-		03.08.04	NELSON (PAY)
Morris, Andrew Julian, BSc, MDA, CEng, MIEE, MInsD	CDR(FTC)	E	WESM	31.12.99	DLO BRISTOL
Morris, Anthony Martin	LT(FTC)	X	P	01.07.93	829 FLT 04
Morris, Daniel Rowland	LT(CC)	X		01.10.02	MWS COLLINGWOOD
Morris, Daniel William, BEng	LT(CC)	E	ME	01.01.02	SULTAN
Morris, David Simon, pce, pce(sm)	CAPT(FTC)	X	SM	30.06.02	NAVSEC
Morris, Harriet Sophie, BA	LT(IC)	S		01.09.02	SOUTHAMPTON
Morris, James Andrew John, BSc, MA, psc(j)	LT COL(FTC)	-		30.06.05	NAVSEC
Morris, James Edward Dallas	2LT(IC)	-		02.09.03	40 CDO RM
Morris, John Owen, BComm, MA	CHAPLAIN	CE		06.10.92	FWO DEVPT SEA
Morris, Kevin Ian	LT CDR(FTC)	S	CA	01.10.03	CHATHAM
Morris, Louisa Elizabeth, MB, BS	SURG LT(SC(MD)	-		06.08.03	CFLT MED(SEA)
Morris, Paul, BSc, MA(Ed), PGDip, PGCE	LT CDR(FTC)	E	TM	01.10.99	SHERWOOD
Morris, Paul Edward Mannering, sq	MAJ(FTC)	-	P	01.05.97	847 SQN
Morris, Paul John, BA	LT(IC)	X	FC	01.09.01	CAPT IST STAFF
Morris, Paul William	LT(IC)	X	AV	01.05.04	JSCSC
Morris, Peter John, BEng, CEng, MIEE, MDA	LT CDR(FTC)	E	WESM	10.06.92	DA SOFIA
Morris, Philip John	LT CDR(FTC)	X	C	01.10.97	2SL/CNH FOTR
Morris, Richard Charles, BSc	CAPT RM(CC)	-	LC	01.09.03	539 ASSLT SQN RM
Morris, Richard John, pce	LT CDR(FTC)	X	PWO(A)	01.04.97	FLEET HQ PORTS
Morris, Simon Timothy, BEng, CEng, MIEE	LT CDR(FTC)	E	WESM	01.10.97	FWO DEVONPORT
Morrison, Graham Lindsay, BDS, MBA, DRD, FDS RCSEdin, jsdc (Commodore)	SGCAPT(D)(FC(MD)	-		31.12.96	DDA HALTON
Morrison, Jurgen	LT(IC)	S		01.05.04	TALENT
Morrison, Paul	LT CDR(FTC)	X	O	01.10.02	824 SQN
Morrison, Robert William, IEng, MIMarEST	LT CDR(FTC)	E	ME	01.10.97	LOAN BMATT(EC)
Morrison, Shaun	LT(IC)	E	MESM	01.07.04	TALENT
Morritt, Dain Cameron, BEng, MA, MSc, psc	CDR(FTC)	E	WE	31.12.98	MOD (LONDON)
Morrow, Oliver James, BSc	SLT(IC)	X		01.01.04	DARTMOUTH BRNC
Morse, Andrew Charles, pcea	LT CDR(FTC)	X	O	01.01.92	UKMFTS IPT
Morse, James Anthony, BSc, pce	CAPT(FTC)	X	PWO(N)	30.06.03	JSCSC
Morse, Jeremy, BSc	LT(CC)	X	P	01.12.99	845 SQN
Morshead, Christopher, BEng, CEng, MRAeS	LT CDR(FTC)	E	AE	14.05.98	DLO YEO

Name	Rank	Branch	Spec	Seniority	Where Serving
Morson, Myles Geoffrey	SLT(IC)	X	O U/T	01.05.04	750 SQN SEAHAWK
Mortimer, Philip Robert	LT(IC)	E	WESM	01.01.04	TRENCHANT
Mortlock, Philip Alun, BEng, MIEE	LT(CC)	E	WESM	01.01.00	FLEET HQ NWD
Morton, Benjamin Alexander, BA	LT(IC)	X		01.08.04	PORTLAND
Morton, James Henry	2LT(IC)	-		01.09.00	40 CDO RM
Morton, Justin Clarke	CAPT RM(CC)	-	SO(LE)	01.04.02	JSCSC
Morton, Nigel Peter Bradshaw, BSc, MA, psc	CDR(FTC)	S		30.06.99	MOD (LONDON)
Morton-Haworth, Charlotte Elizabeth Jayne, BSc	SLT(IC)	S		01.09.03	DARTMOUTH BRNC
Moseley, Stephen Huw, BEng	LT(IC)	X	P	01.09.02	824 SQN
Moss, Patrick John, MIIE	LT CDR(FTC)	E	WESM	01.10.00	DLO BRISTOL
Moss, Peter, psc(m)	CDR(FTC)	X	O	30.06.04	LANG TRNG(UK)
Moss, Richard	LT(IC)	E	TM	01.01.02	MWS COLLINGWOOD
Moss, Richard Ashley, BSc, pce	LT CDR(FTC)	X	O	01.03.99	FWO PORTS SEA
Moss, Timothy Edward, MBE, CEng, IEng, FIIE, MIMarEST	LT CDR(FTC)	E	ME	01.10.97	FOST SEA
Moss-Ward, Edward George	SLT(IC)	X		01.09.03	SOMERSET
Mould, Philip	LT CDR(FTC)	X	P	01.10.02	LOAN OTHER SVCE
Moules, Matthew Alexander John, BSc, SM(n)	LT CDR(FTC)	X	SM	01.08.04	RALEIGH
Moulton, Simon John, BSc, pcea	LT(FTC)	X	O	01.01.92	GANNET SAR FLT
Mount, James Bruce	LT(CC)	X	P	01.06.00	771 SQN
Mountford, Penny Claire, BEng, MSc, CEng, MIMechE	LT(FTC)	E	ME	01.04.98	DLO BRISTOL
Mountjoy, Brian John, MIOSH	LT CDR(FTC)	E	WESM	01.10.01	MOD (BATH)
Mountjoy-Row, Robin Eric	LT(IC)	E	AE	01.05.04	LYNX OEU
Mountney, Gemma Ann, BSc	LT(IC)	X		01.04.02	RAMSEY
Mowat, Andrew Duncan John, MA	LT(IC)	S		01.01.03	NOTTINGHAM
Mowatt, Patrick, PGDip	LT CDR(FTC)	X	H1	01.05.04	EXCHANGE AUSTLIA
Moy, David Keith	LT(FTC)	E	ME	02.05.00	SUPT OF DIVING
Moys, Andrew John, MSc, FRMS	LT CDR(FTC)	X	METOC	01.10.97	EXCHANGE USA
Muddiman, Andrew Robert, BA	MAJ(FTC)	-		01.09.03	RM WARMINSTER
Mudford, Hugh Christopher, psc	LT COL(FTC)	-		30.06.99	OCEAN
Mudge, Adrian Michael, BSc	LT(FTC)	X	O	01.07.93	849 SQN B FLT
Mugridge, Anthony Robert, MB, ChB, FRCSEd	SURG CAPT(FCC)	-	(CGS)	30.06.98	MDHU DERRIFORD
Mugridge, David Robert, BA, MNI, pce, n	LT CDR(FTC)	X	PWO(C)	01.02.98	JSCSC
Muir, Andrew, MEng	SLT(IC)	E	ME U/T	01.02.03	UKMARBATSTAFF
Muir, Katie Marie, BA, PGDipL	SLT(IC)	X		01.11.03	DARTMOUTH BRNC
Muir, Keith, pce, pcea, psc(j)	CDR(FTC)	X	O	31.12.98	MWC SOUTHWICK
Muirhead, Barry George, BEng	LT(CC)	X	P	01.08.98	829 FLT 02
Mules, Anthony John, n	LT CDR(FTC)	X	H1	01.03.98	ENTERPRISE
Mullen, Jason John, BA	LT CDR(FTC)	X	MCD	01.10.04	CORNWALL
Mullin, Peter, BSc, MIMechE	LT CDR(FTC)	E	MESM	01.07.93	SULTAN
Mullins, Andrew Dominic, BEng, CEng, MIMarEST	LT CDR(FTC)	E	MESM	01.12.04	NP IRAQ
Mullins, Natalie Elizabeth, BEng	LT(IC)	E	AE U/T	01.09.04	824 SQN
Mullis, Geoffrey, MEng	SLT(IC)	E	WE U/T	01.01.04	DARTMOUTH BRNC
Mullowney, Paul, BEng	LT(CC)	X	O	01.02.99	750 SQN SEAHAWK
Mulroy, Paul	LT(IC)	E	MESM	18.02.05	FWO FASLANE
Mulvaney, Paul Andrew, BSc	LT CDR(FTC)	E	AE	01.06.00	801 SQN
Muncer, Richard A, BEng	CAPT RM(CC)	-		01.09.00	CDO LOG REGT RM
Munday, Ian Vernon, MBE, pce, pcea, psc	LT CDR(FTC)	X	O	01.04.85	824 SQN
Munday, Stephen William, BSc	LT(IC)	E	WE	01.01.04	GLOUCESTER
Mundin, Adrian John, BSc, CEng, MIMechE	LT CDR(FTC)	E	ME	01.04.92	MOD (LONDON)
Mundy, Alan Richard	LT(IC)	MS		01.05.02	HQ 3 CDO BDE RM
Munns, Andrew Robert, BEng, CEng, MIMarEST	CDR(FTC)	E	ME	30.06.03	JWC/CIS STAVANGR
Munns, Christopher Ronald, jsdc, pce, pce(sm), hcsc (Commodore)	CAPT(FTC)	X	SM	31.12.96	PJHQ
Munns, Edward Neil	SLT(UCE)(IC)	X		01.09.03	DARTMOUTH BRNC
Munro, Helen Louise, BSc	LT(IC)	E	TM	01.09.02	SULTAN
Munro, Kenneth, BEng, CEng, MIMarEST	LT CDR(FTC)	E	ME	01.04.95	DLO BRISTOL
Munro, Michael	LT(IC)	E	WE	01.07.04	CUMBERLAND
Munro, Niall Frank Hamilton, LLB	LT(IC)	X	FC	01.01.99	RNAS YEOVILTON
Munro-Lott, Peter Robert John, pcea, psc(j)(o), MA	LT CDR(FTC)	X	O	01.10.96	829 SQN HQ
Murchie, Alistair Duncan, BEng, MSc	LT CDR(FTC)	E	ME	01.10.03	SULTAN
Murchison, Ewen Alexander, BSc, MA, psc(j)	MAJ(FTC)	-		01.09.00	HQ 3 CDO BDE RM
Murdoch, Andrew Peter, BSc (Barrister)	LT CDR(FTC)	S	BAR	01.11.02	2SL/CNH FOTR
Murdoch, Andrew William, MSc, MIEE, CEng	CDR(FTC)	E	WESM	30.06.05	FLEET HQ PORTS 2
Murdoch, Gillian Agnes, BDS	SGLTCDR(D)(MCC)	-		20.07.03	JSCSC

Name	Rank	Branch	Spec	Seniority	Where Serving
Murdoch, Stephen John, MBA	CDR(FTC)	S		31.12.99	MOD (LONDON)
Murgatroyd, Andrew Clive, MBE, BSc, jsdc, pce	CDR(FTC)	X	AAWO	31.12.94	MOD (LONDON)
Murgatroyd, Kevin John, BEng	LT(CC)	X	O	01.04.00	824 SQN
Murphie, John Dermot Douglas, pce, psc(m)	CAPT(FTC)	X	MCD	30.06.04	2SL/CNH FOTR
Murphy, Andrew, IEng, MIIE	LT(FTC)	E	WE	09.01.01	RMC OF SCIENCE
Murphy, Anthony, MBA	CDR(FTC)	MS		30.06.02	NAVSEC
Murphy, Christian John, MEng	LT(IC)	E	AE U/T	01.09.04	814 SQN
Murphy, Diccon Andrew, BSc	LT(CC)	X	P	01.04.92	815 SQN HQ
Murphy, James, BSc	LT CDR(FTC)	S	SM	01.06.92	DRAKE COB
Murphy, Kian Stuart, BA	CAPT RM(CC)	-		01.05.98	40 CDO RM
Murphy, Nicholas, MBE, MNI, pce, psc(j)	LT CDR(FTC)	X	PWO(U)	01.09.90	PJHQ
Murphy, Paul Anthony, BA, ACMA	LT CDR(FTC)	S	CMA	01.03.00	MWS COLLINGWOOD
Murphy, Peter William, MSc, BEng	LT CDR(FTC)	E	MESM	01.09.95	NP DNREAY
Murphy, Richard James, BA	LT(IC)	X	MCD	01.09.99	GRIMSBY
Murphy, Stephen Mark, BEng	LT CDR(FTC)	E	ME	01.08.04	ARGYLL
Murphy, Steven Robert Anthony, BA, pce(sm)	LT CDR(FTC)	X	SM	01.09.98	FLEET HQ PORTS 2
Murphy, Vanessa Jane, BA	LT(CC)	S		01.07.99	RNSR BOVINGTON
Murray, Alexander Bruce, psc(j)	MAJ(FTC)	-		26.04.00	42 CDO RM
Murray, Alister	LT(CC)	MS		01.09.01	NP IRAQ
Murray, Andrew Sidney	LT CDR(FTC)	X	P	01.10.99	771 SQN
Murray, Grant McNiven, BEng	LT CDR(FTC)	E	WESM	01.06.98	FOST SM SEA
Murray, Greig Martin, BSc	LT(IC)	X		01.09.02	ARGYLL
Murray, Jamie Cameron	SLT(IC)	X	P U/T	01.05.04	RNAS YEOVILTON
Murray, Robert Henry, MBE, BSc, MIMechE	LT CDR(FTC)	E	MESM	01.01.82	DRAKE CBS
Murray, Simon David	CAPT RM(IC)	-		01.09.04	NP IRAQ
Murray, Stephen John, pcea, gdas	CDR(FTC)	X	O	30.06.03	LOAN JTEG BSC DN
Murray, William Justin, BSc	LT(IC)	X	P	01.05.04	RNAS YEOVILTON
Murrison, Richard Anthony, MA, GCIS, ACIS, psc(j)	CDR(FTC)	S		30.06.04	FOSNNI
Mustafa, Habeeb	SLT(IC)	X		01.05.02	MWS COLLINGWOOD
Musto, Edward Charles, BA, psc(m)	LT COL(FTC)	-		31.12.96	EXCHANGE USA
Mutch, Jonathan Rocliffe, BSc, pcea	LT(CC)	X	P	01.09.94	815 FLT 210
Muyambo, Nomalanga Nosizo, BSc	LT(IC)	E	TM	01.01.00	MWS COLLINGWOOD
Myatt, Marie-Claire	SLT(UCE)(IC)	E	WE U/T	01.09.04	DARTMOUTH BRNC

N

Name	Rank	Branch	Spec	Seniority	Where Serving
Naden, Andrew Charles Keith, BSc, CEng, MIMarEST, psc(j)	CDR(FTC)	E	ME	30.06.02	FLEET ROSYTH
Naden, James Ralph, MSc, BA, PGDip, Cert Ed	LT CDR(FTC)	E	IS	01.10.94	CMT SHRIVENHAM
Nail, Vaughan Anthony, MA, psc	CDR(FTC)	X	H CH	31.12.97	ENTERPRISE
Nairn, Alan Barclay, BSc	LT CDR(FTC)	S		01.02.99	JSCSC
Nairn, Robert, OBE, psc	CDR(FTC)	S		31.12.96	RALEIGH
Naismith, David Hamilton, BSc, pcea	LT CDR(FTC(A)	X	O	01.05.91	824 SQN
Nance, Adrian Ralph, OBE, BSc, pce (Commodore)	CAPT(FTC)	X	PWO(A)	30.06.97	JSCSC
Napier, Graham Andrew	LT CDR(FTC)	E	AE	01.07.01	JHCHQ
Nash, Philip David, BSc	LT CDR(FTC)	X	PWO(A)	01.10.02	GRAFTON
Nash, Robin David Cory, BSc	LT(CC)	X	H2	01.01.02	ROEBUCK
Nash, Rubin Piero, BSc	LT(IC)	X		01.01.02	EXETER
Nash, Russell Frank Roger	LT(IC)	E	WESM	01.01.04	TORBAY
Nathanson, Helen, BA	LT(CC)	S		01.02.97	RNAS CULDROSE
Naylor, Andrew James	LT(CC)	X	P	16.06.94	824 SQN
Neal, Simon Matthew, pcea	LT CDR(FTC)	X	O	01.10.03	814 SQN
Neale, Daniel Frederick	SLT(IC)	X		01.09.02	DULVERTON
Neary, Joseph, MSc, MB, BCH, FRCGP, DCH (Act Surg Cdr)	SURG LTCDR(SC(MD)	-	GMPP	01.10.96	2SL/CNH
Neave, Andrew Michael	LT CDR(FTC)	X	ATC	01.10.98	FLEET HQ PORTS
Neave, Christopher Bryan, OBE, BSc, pcea	CAPT(FTC)	E	AE(L)	30.06.01	NP IRAQ
Neave, James Robert	SLT(IC)	X		01.09.04	OCEAN
Necker, Carl Dominic, PGDIPAN	LT CDR(FTC)	X	PWO(N)	01.11.99	PORTLAND
Neil, David Alexander	SLT(IC)	X		01.05.02	EDINBURGH
Neild, Timothy, n	LT CDR(FTC)	X	PWO(C)	01.10.03	ILLUSTRIOUS
Nekrews, Alan Neil Laurence Michael	LT(IC)	X		01.01.04	CUMBERLAND
Nelson, Andrew	LT CDR(FTC)	E	WESM	01.10.95	MWC PORTSDOWN
Nelson, Christopher Stuart, BSc, n	LT CDR(FTC)	X	PWO(N)	01.03.01	FOST SEA
Nelson, David Lawrence	LT CDR(FTC)	X	P	01.10.92	702 SQN HERON

Name	Rank	Branch	Spec	Seniority	Where Serving
Nelson, Digby Theodore, BSc, psc	CAPT(FTC)	S		30.06.05	NAVSEC
Nelson, Dominic Edward, BSc	LT CDR(FTC)	X	PWO(A)	01.04.88	DRAKE COB
Nelson, Lisa Marie, BEng	LT CDR(FTC)	E	ME	01.01.03	ILLUSTRIOUS
Nelson, Matthew Rodney	LT(CC)	X	P	16.11.98	NELSON
Nelson, Paul Moffat, BA, PGCE	LT(FTC)	E	TM	01.01.97	SULTAN
Nelson, Victoria, BA	LT CDR(FTC)	S		01.10.03	CAMPBELTOWN
Nelstrop, Andrew Marcus, BA, MB, BCH	SURG LTCDR(MC(MD)	-		10.02.04	NELSON (PAY)
Neofytou, Andrew George Kleopas, BEng	LT(IC)	X		01.08.99	RNAS YEOVILTON
Netherwood, Lyndsey Dawn, BA, n	LT(FTC)	X		15.09.99	MWS COLLINGWOOD
Neve, Piers Charles, pce(sm)	LT CDR(FTC)	X	SM	11.02.94	EXCHANGE USA
New, Christopher Maxwell, BEng, MSc, CEng, MIMechE	LT CDR(FTC)	E	ME	01.04.97	DLO BRISTOL
New, Richard Ashley	LT(CC)	S		01.02.01	NEPTUNE DLO
Newall, Jeremy Andrew	LT CDR(FTC)	X	ATC	01.03.94	RNAS YEOVILTON
Newall, Paul John, MA	LT(IC)	E	TM	01.09.02	RALEIGH
Newby, Christopher	LT(IC)	X	O U/T	01.01.05	RNAS CULDROSE
Newby Stubbs, Rebecca Louise	LT(MCC)	Q	IC	15.08.99	DRAKE COB
Newell, Gary David	LT(CC)	E	ME	29.04.01	DFTE PORTSMOUTH
Newell, Jonathan Michael, MBE, MSc, CEng, FIMarEST, MIL, fsc	CAPT(FTC)	E	ME	30.06.05	NAVSEC
Newell, Phillip Russell, BEng	LT CDR(FTC)	X	H CH	01.06.01	ECHO
Newing, Stephen Geoffrey, psc	LT COL(FTC)	-	MOR	30.06.98	FLEET HQ PORTS 2
Newland, Mark Ian, BSc, pce, psc(j)	CDR(FTC)	X	PWO(U)	30.06.03	MWC SOUTHWICK
Newman, Christopher Richard Spencer	LT(IC)	X	H2	01.05.02	RNAS CULDROSE
Newman, David	LT(CC)	E	AE	01.01.99	EXCHANGE ARMY UK
Newman, Paul Henry, MBE, BSc	LT CDR(FTC)	X	METOC	01.05.89	FWO DEVPT SEA
Newth, Christopher, BSc	LT(CC)	E	IS	01.05.00	INVINCIBLE
Newton, David John, pce, psc	CDR(FTC)	X	P	31.12.98	MOD (LONDON)
Newton, Garry Arnold, pce(sm)	CDR(FTC)	X	SM	30.06.00	MOD (LONDON)
Newton, James Lloyd, DFC	LT CDR(CC)	X	P	01.10.04	FLEET AV VL
Newton, Michael Ronald, FIEIE, FIIE	LT CDR(FTC)	E	WE	22.09.87	CTS
Newton, Nicholas John Patrick, BSc, MB, BS	SURG LT(SC(MD)	-		06.08.03	VIGILANT(PORT)
Newton, Owen Robert Alan	SLT(IC)	X		01.02.05	DARTMOUTH BRNC
Newton, Robert William	CAPT RM(IC)	-		01.09.03	40 CDO RM
Neyland, David A, BEng	LT(IC)	X	P	01.09.04	RNAS YEOVILTON
Nguyo, David Ngibuini, MEng	LT(IC)	E	WE	01.09.02	DCCIS FAREHAM
Nicholas, Bryan John, BSc, pcea	LT CDR(FTC)	X	P	01.10.01	EXCHANGE USA
Nicholas, Jeremy Richard	CAPT RM(CC)	-	SO(LE)	01.04.03	1 ASSLT GP RM
Nicholas, Stephen Paul, BEng, CEng	LT(CC)	E	MESM	01.04.94	NEPTUNE BNSL
Nicholls, Barry Austin	MAJ(FTC)	-	SO(LE)	01.10.04	NAVSEC
Nicholls, Guy Anthony, IEng, MIEE	LT CDR(FTC)	E	WE	01.10.99	MWS COLLINGWOOD
Nicholls, Larry Roy	LT(IC)	E	WE	01.05.03	PORTLAND
Nichols, Elizabeth Anne, MB, BS, MRCGP, DObstRCOG	SURG CDR(FCC)	-	GMPP	31.03.01	RALEIGH
Nicholson, Brian Harold	LT(CC)	E	AE	29.04.01	MERLIN IPT
Nicholson, David Andrew Gore, BEng	LT(CC)	X		01.01.01	CFPS SHORE
Nicholson, David Peter, BSc	CAPT RM(FTC)	-	LC	01.09.99	45 CDO RM
Nicholson, Graeme, MB, CHB, MFOM, MRCGP	SURG CDR(FCC)	-	(CO/M)	31.12.00	INM ALVERSTOKE
Nicholson, Jonathan Craig, BSc	LT(FTC)	E	WE	02.09.99	SANS IPT
Nicholson, Kristin James, BA	LT CDR(FTC)	S		01.08.02	RMC OF SCIENCE
Nicholson, Simon Charles Lawrence, pce	CDR(FTC)	X	MCD	30.06.96	MWC SOUTHWICK
Nicklas, Colin James, BEng, MSc, CEng, MIEE	LT CDR(FTC)	E	WE	01.06.00	MOD (LONDON)
Nicklin, Gareth James Edward, BEng	LT(CC)	E	MESM	01.01.00	JSCSC
Nickolls, Kevin Paul, BEng	LT CDR(FTC)	E	AE	01.01.00	COS 2SL/CNH
Nicol, Allan MacKenzie	SLT(IC)	E	MESMUT	01.09.02	VENGEANCE(STBD)
Nicol, Peter James Stewart, MB, BS, LRCP, MRCS, JCPTGP	SURG CDR(FCC)	-	GMPP	30.06.94	ILLUSTRIOUS
Nicoll, Andrew John, BEng, MIEE	LT CDR(FTC)	E	WE	01.04.05	LOAN DSTL
Nicoll, Steve Kenneth (Act Maj)	CAPT RM(FTC)	-	SO(LE)	01.01.96	DGES LAND
Nielsen, Erik Michael	CAPT RM(IC)	-	SO(LE)	01.07.04	RMB STONEHOUSE
Nightingale, Samuel David, BSc	LT(IC)	X		01.01.05	MWS COLLINGWOOD
Nimmons, Paul, BEng, MSc	LT(FTC)	E	MESM	01.06.96	NP BRISTOL
Nisbet, James Henry Thomas, BSc, pce, psc(j), MA	CDR(FTC)	X	PWO(U)	30.06.03	KENT
Nixon, Alexander	2LT(IC)	-		01.08.03	CTCRM LYMPSTONE
Nixon, Paul William, MSc, CEng, MIMechE, MInstPS	CDR(FTC)	E	MESM	30.06.96	DRAKE SFM
Nixon, Sophie Elizabeth Kate	LT(IC)	X		01.09.03	MOD (LONDON)
Noakes, Kevin Massie, BEng, MSc, CEng, MIEE, gw	LT CDR(FTC)	E	WE	01.05.02	EDINBURGH

Name	Rank	Branch	Spec	Seniority	Where Serving
Noble, Kevan Leslie	CAPT RM(IC)	-	SO(LE)	01.04.03	CDO LOG REGT RM
Noble, Mark Jonathan Dean, psc	COL(FTC)	-	P	31.12.99	JHCHQ
Noble, Robert Vincent, BA	SLT(IC)	X		01.05.03	YORK
Noble, Tom Mark Dean	2LT(IC)	-		01.09.00	40 CDO RM
Noblett, Peter Gordon Arthur, MNI, pce, pce(sm)	LT CDR(FTC)	X	SM	01.10.01	PJHQ
Nokes, Oliver	SLT(IC)	X		01.09.03	RAMSEY
Nolan, Anthony Laurence	CDR(FTC)	X	C	30.06.01	COM MCC NWD
Nolan, Paul Ernest	CAPT RM(CC)	-	P	01.04.02	847 SQN
Nolan, Robert	LT(IC)	X	C	01.07.03	MWS COLLINGWOOD
Noon, David, MBE	LT CDR(FTC)	S	CA	01.10.03	COS 2SL/CNH
Noonan, Charles Daniel, BA	LT(CC)	X		01.05.01	MWS COLLINGWOOD
Norcott, William R	CAPT RM(IC)	-		01.09.04	DNR PRES TEAMS
Norford, Michael (Act Lt Cdr)	LT(FTC)	X		03.04.97	MOD (LONDON)
Norgan, David James, BA, pce, n	LT CDR(FTC)	X	PWO(C)	01.07.01	FOST SEA
Norgate, Andrew Thomas, BSc, PGDip, SM(n), SM	LT(FTC)	X	H2	01.11.98	BULWARK
Norgate, Perry Raymond Edward, BSc (Act Lt Cdr)	LT(FTC)	E	ME	19.06.98	ALBION
Norman, Jaimie McCoy, BA	CAPT RM(CC)	-		01.09.02	FLEET HQ PORTS 2
Norman, Phillip Douglas	LT CDR(FTC)	E	WE	01.10.99	DLO BRISTOL
Norman, Toby Benjamin	LT(IC)	X		01.04.03	SEVERN
Norris, Guy Patrick	LT(FTC)	X	O	16.07.93	750 SQN SEAHAWK
Norris, James Garnet, BA	LT CDR(FTC)	E	AE	01.11.00	JSCSC
Norris, Richard Edward, BDS, MA, LDS RCS(Eng), MGDS RCS, psc(j)	SGCAPT(D)(FCC)	-		30.06.96	DDA PLYMOUTH
Norris, William Desmond, BSc, PhD, MB, CHB	SURG LTCDR(FCC)	-	GMPP	20.05.02	NEPTUNE DLO
Norriss, Mark William	LT(IC)	X	P	01.01.05	DHFS
North, Adam Christopher, MEng	SLT(IC)	E	AE U/T	01.09.03	ILLUSTRIOUS
Northcote, Mark Richard	LT(CC)	X	MCD	01.12.00	EXCHANGE AUSTLIA
Northcott, Michael Kevin, BEng	LT(FTC)	E	WE	01.03.99	HQ DCSA
Northcott, Philip James, BEng	LT(FTC)	E	MESM	01.09.02	SOVEREIGN
Northeast, Paul	LT(FTC)	S	SM	01.04.01	RALEIGH
Northover, Adam Frederick, BSc, n	LT(FTC)	X	PWO(U)	01.08.97	YORK
Northwood, Gerard Rodney, pce	CDR(FTC)	X	AAWO	30.06.99	LIVERPOOL
Norton, Alexandra Louise Elizabeth, MEng	LT(IC)	E	ME	01.09.02	OCLC BIRM
Norton, Ian Andrew	LT(IC)	E	AE	01.07.04	DLO YEO
Norton, Thomas Charles Horatio, MA(OXON)	CAPT RM(FTC)	-	C	01.09.03	CHFHQ
Norwood, James Kenneth, BSc	LT(IC)	X		01.01.04	SHOREHAM
Norwood, Jeffrey Michael, BA, MB, BCH, DCH	SURG CDR(SCC)	-	DPHC	01.03.97	2SL/CNH
Notley, Edward John, LLB	LT(IC)	X	SM	01.01.03	TRAFALGAR
Notley, Louis Paul, BSc, MDA	CDR(FTC)	S	SM	30.06.04	FLEET HQ PORTS 2
Nottley, Simon Matthew	LT(FTC)	E	WESM	01.04.01	MOD DIS SEA
Nowosielski, Frank, MBE	LT CDR(FTC)	X	AV	01.10.93	VICTORY
Noyce, Nigel Roderick	LT CDR(FTC)	X		15.01.97	DISC
Noyce, Roger Grenville, MBE, MRINA	LT CDR(FTC)	X		01.10.04	FLEET CIS PORTS
Noyce, Vincent Robert Amos, pce	LT CDR(FTC)	X	PWO(A)	01.11.01	MWS COLLINGWOOD
Noyes, David James, MA, psc(j)	CDR(FTC)	S		30.06.01	FLEET HQ PORTS 2
Nugent, Helen Ann	SLT(IC)	X	O U/T	01.09.04	RNAS CULDROSE
Nunn, Christopher John, OBE, nadc, psc(a)	LT COL(FTC)	-	P	30.06.88	DA TBILISI
Nunn, Gerald Eric, BSc, CEng, PGCE, PGDip	LT CDR(CC)	E	TM	01.10.95	NTE(TTD)
Nunnen, Catherine Rebecca, MA	LT(CC)	X	O	01.05.01	815 FLT 226
Nurse, Michael Talbot, BSc, psc (Act Cdr)	LT CDR(FTC)	E	AE	01.06.88	IMS BRUSSELS
Nursey, Adrian Paul, IEng, MIIE	LT(FTC)	E	MESM	02.09.99	TIRELESS

O

Name	Rank	Branch	Spec	Seniority	Where Serving
Oakes, Ian James	LT(FTC)	X	P	16.06.94	RAF SHAWBURY
Oakes, Michael Carson	LT(IC)	X		01.05.02	1 ASSLT GP RM
Oakley, Andrew J, BSc	LT(IC)	E	TM	01.01.01	SULTAN
Oakley, Claire Marie	LT(CC)	X	HM	01.05.01	820 SQN
Oakley, Sarah Ellen, MA, n	LT CDR(FTC)	X		01.05.05	JSCSC
Oatley, Timothy Peter	LT(FTC)	X	O	16.07.94	EXCHANGE USA
O'Brien, Ian Patrick, BTech, IEng, MIIE, MIIT	LT(FTC)	E	WE	24.02.95	MCM1 SEA
O'Brien, Kieran John, BEng	LT CDR(FTC)	E	AE	01.02.00	JSCSC
O'Brien, Patrick Michael Christopher, BEng, MSc, CEng, MIEE	CDR(FTC)	E	IS	30.06.04	COS 2SL/CNH

Name	Rank	Branch	Spec	Seniority	Where Serving
O'Brien, Peter Charles, BSc, PGCE, adp (Act Cdr)	LT CDR(FTC)	E	IS	23.04.88	AFPAA JPA
O'Brien, Thomas Patrick	LT(IC)	E	WESM	01.01.04	VANGUARD(PORT)
O'Byrne, Patrick Barry Mary, pce(sm), SM(n)	LT CDR(FTC)	X	SM	01.11.00	FLEET HQ PORTS 2
O'Callaghan, Patrick Francis	LT(IC)	X		01.05.02	FOST MPV SEA
O'Connor, David McPherson	CAPT RM(IC)	-	C	01.07.04	UKLFCSG RM
O'Connor, David Paul	LT(IC)	E	WESM	01.01.03	OCLC BIRM
Oddy, David Mark, pcea	LT CDR(FTC)	X	P	01.10.00	COMATG SEA
O'Donnell, Ian Mark, MBE, MA, psc	LT COL(FTC)	-	P	30.06.03	CHFHQ
Officer, Robert Lennie	LT(CC)	X	MW	01.02.96	FOSNNI
Offord, Matthew Ronald	LT CDR(FTC)	X	MCD	01.04.02	QHM CLYDE
Offord, Stephen John Joseph, BA	SLT(IC)	E	AE U/T	01.05.03	2SL/CNH
O'Flaherty, Christopher Patrick John, pce	LT CDR(FTC)	X	PWO(U)	01.03.99	NORTHUMBERLAND
O'Flaherty, John Stephen, BEng, CEng, MIMarEST, psc(j)	LT CDR(FTC)	E	ME	03.10.97	SULTAN
O'Grady, Matthew James, fsc	CDR(FTC)	S	SM	30.06.01	RNAS CULDROSE
O'Hara, Gerard Connor	MAJ(FTC)	-		01.09.03	NELSON
O'Herlihy, Simon Ian, MA	MAJ(FTC)	-		01.09.02	COMAMPHIBFOR
O'Kane, Robert James, BSc	LT(CC)	X	O	16.05.00	RNAS CULDROSE
O'Keefe, Thomas Declan (Act Capt Rm)	LT RM(IC)	-		01.09.03	CDO LOG REGT RM
Okell, Peter	2LT(IC)	-		01.08.01	CTCRM LYMPSTONE
Okukenu, Dele, pcea	LT(CC)	X	P	01.01.96	848 SQN HERON
Oldfield, Christian Adam William, BEng	SLT(IC)	E	AE U/T	01.09.02	SULTAN
Oliphant, William, MA, psc(j)	CDR(FTC)	S		30.06.05	COMATG SEA
Olive, Peter Nicholas, pce, n	CDR(FTC)	X	PWO(A)	30.06.05	JSCSC
Oliver, Carlton James	LT(IC)	X	AV	01.05.04	SULTAN
Oliver, Graeme John, BSc	LT(CC)	S		01.12.99	ILLUSTRIOUS
Oliver, Graham, PGDip, BSc	LT CDR(FTC)	X	METOC	01.05.03	RNAS YEOVILTON
Oliver, Kevin Brian, BEng, MA, MSc, psc(j), mdtc	LT COL(FTC)	-	MLDR	30.06.04	CTCRM
Olivey, Timothy Douglas	LT(IC)	X	O	01.05.02	LYNX OEU
Ollerton, Justin Clive	LT(CC)	X	P	16.11.96	849 SQN B FLT
Ollis, Victoria	LT(CC)	S		01.05.01	FWO DEVONPORT
Olliver, Adrian John, MILT	LT CDR(FTC)	S	SM	01.10.96	NP IRAQ
O'Neill, Conor Mark	SLT(IC)	X		01.09.01	MWS COLLINGWOOD
O'Neill, Henry Larence	LT(IC)	X	P	01.01.03	845 SQN
O'Neill, James, BA	LT(CC)	X	H2	22.11.99	ENTERPRISE
O'Neill, Patrick John, MA, MSc	CDR(FTC)	E	WESM	30.06.97	FLEET HQ PORTS 2
O'Neill, Paul Joseph, BEng	LT CDR(FTC)	E	MESM	01.10.03	TRAFALGAR
O'Neill, Timothy James	LT(CC)	X		01.01.02	MWS COLLINGWOOD
Onions, Judith Mary, ARRC	CDR(FCC)	Q	IC	30.06.02	NAVSEC
Onyike, Chinyere Eme, NDipM, BEng, MSc, CEng, MIEE, MCMI	LT CDR(FTC)	E	WE	01.01.02	CUMBERLAND
O'Nyons, Yorick Ian, BA, SM(n)	LT CDR(FTC)	X	SM	01.07.02	FLEET HQ PORTS
Orchard, Adrian Paul, pcea	CDR(FTC)	X	P	30.06.05	JSCSC
Ordway, Christopher Norman Maurice Patrick	CAPT RM(FTC)	-		01.09.99	HQ 3 CDO BDE RM
O'Reilly, Christopher Andrew	LT(IC)	S		01.05.04	FLEET HQ PORTS
O'Reilly, Sean Anthony, pce, psc	CDR(FTC)	X	MCD	31.12.95	MOD (LONDON)
O'Reilly, Terence Michael, MRAeS, psc(j)	CDR(FTC)	E	AE	31.12.98	DLO YEO
O'Riordan, Michael Patrick, BSc, pce, pcea	LT CDR(FTC)	X	P	01.04.89	UN AFRICA
Orme, William Benjamin	LT(IC)	X	P	01.05.02	845 SQN
Ormshaw, Martin Andrew, BA	SLT(IC)	X	O U/T	01.09.02	RNAS CULDROSE
O'Rourke, Richard Michael	LT(IC)	S		01.05.02	MOD (LONDON)
Orr, Keith John, BEng	LT(CC)	E	MESM	01.11.99	NEPTUNE DLO
Orr, Simon David	CAPT RM(CC)	-	SO(LE)	03.04.02	CHFHQ
Orton, David Michael, BSc, DPhil	LT CDR(FTC)	E	TMSM	01.10.00	MWS COLLINGWOOD
Orton, Trevor	LT(IC)	X		01.10.04	MWS COLLINGWOOD
Osbaldestin, Richard Alan	LT(FTC)	X	MCD	01.10.98	EXCHANGE USA
Osborn, Colvin Graeme, BSc, SM	LT CDR(FTC)	X	SM	01.06.02	FLEET HQ NWD
Osborn, Richard Marcus	LT CDR(FTC)	X	AAWO	01.02.99	MWS COLLINGWOOD
Osborne, John Michael, BSc	LT(IC)	E	TM	01.10.99	SULTAN
O'Shaughnessy, David John, BEng, CEng, MIMarEST	LT(FTC)	E	ME	01.06.97	CAPT MCTA
O'Shaughnessy, Paul Charles, BEng, MIEE	LT(FTC)	E	WE	01.01.99	DLO BRISTOL
O'Shea, Eamon Patrick, BEng	LT CDR(FTC)	E	AE	01.07.98	845 SQN
O'Shea, Matthew Kent, MPhil, MB, CHB, BSc	SURG LT(SC(MD)	-		06.09.04	VANGUARD(PORT)
Osman, Mark Ronald, pcea, psc	LT CDR(FTC)	X	P	01.09.86	RNAS CULDROSE
Osmond, Justin Bruce, BEng, MA, MSc, psc(j)	CDR(FTC)	E	AE	30.06.05	DCAE COSFORD

Name	Rank	Branch	Spec	Seniority	Where Serving
O'Sullivan, Aidan Marian, pcea	CDR(FTC)	X	O	30.06.02	FLEET AV VL
O'Sullivan, Barrie Oliver	LT CDR(FTC)	X	P	01.10.00	MOD (LONDON)
O'Sullivan, Matthew Richard John	CAPT RM(CC)	-	P	01.09.04	847 SQN
O'Sullivan, Michael Louis James, BSc, PGDipL	LT CDR(FTC)	X	H1	01.08.01	ENTERPRISE
O'Sullivan, Paul Benedict, BEng	LT(IC)	E	MESM	01.06.03	TURBULENT
Oswald, Sir (John) Julian (Robertson), GCB, rcds, psc	ADM OF FLEET	-	G	02.03.93	
O'Toole, Mathew Charles, BEng	LT(FTC)	E	MESM	01.10.97	MOD (LONDON)
Ottaway, Thomas Arthur	LT(IC)	X	SM	01.05.03	SPARTAN
Ottewell, Paul Steven, BSc, SM(n)	LT CDR(FTC)	X	SM	01.01.05	TURBULENT
Oulds, Keith Antony, BEng	LT CDR(FTC)	X	MCD	01.09.00	ARK ROYAL
Oura, Adrian Nicholas, BA	CAPT RM(FTC)	-		01.09.00	UNOMIG
Ouvry, Janet Elisabeth Delahaize	LT(MCC)	Q		25.03.97	NELSON
Ovenden, Neil Stephen Paul, pce	LT CDR(FTC)	X	PWO(U)	01.02.95	EXCHANGE CANADA
Ovens, Jeremy John, BSc, MBA, pce, pcea, psc	CDR(FTC)	X	O	31.12.99	MOD (LONDON)
Owen, Douglas Philip Collinson	LT(IC)	X		01.09.02	CYPRUS PBS
Owen, Glyn	LT(CC)	X	O	16.02.97	815 FLT 221
Owen, Peter Clive, pcea	LT CDR(FTC)	X	P	01.10.91	824 SQN
Owen, Samuel Thomas Louis, SM(n)	LT(CC)	X	SM	01.11.00	MWS COLLINGWOOD
Owen, Vincent Frederick	LT(IC)	X		01.05.02	RNAS CULDROSE
Owens, Daniel Tudor, BEng, CEng, MIMechE	LT CDR(FTC)	E	ME	01.08.99	FLEET HQ PORTS 2
Owens, John Whittal, MA	LT(IC)	X		01.01.05	RALEIGH
Oxlade, Andrew Thomas, BSc	SURG SLT(SCC)	-		01.07.03	DARTMOUTH BRNC
Oxley, James David	SLT(IC)	X		01.02.05	DARTMOUTH BRNC

P

Name	Rank	Branch	Spec	Seniority	Where Serving
Packer, Robert Graham	LT(IC)	X		01.07.04	RNAS CULDROSE
Packham, Craig Nicholas Ronald	LT(CC)	X	P	01.03.96	LYNX OEU
Padbury, Sarah	SLT(IC)	S		01.02.04	DARTMOUTH BRNC
Padget, Joanna	LT(IC)	E	TM	01.05.00	1 ASSLT GP RM
Page, Carrie, BA	SLT(IC)	S		01.09.02	RALEIGH
Page, David Michael, BSc, MDA, CEng, MIEE	CDR(FTC)	E	WE	30.06.97	DLO BRISTOL
Page, Durward Charles Miller, BSc, MA, psc(j)	MAJ(FTC)	-		01.09.01	UKMARBATSTAFF
Page, Mark Robert	LT(CC)	X	O	01.05.00	CAPT IST STAFF
Page, Michael Christian, MA, MBA, psc	LT COL(FTC)	-	LC	30.06.99	MOD (LONDON)
Page, Trevor Andrew	LT(FTC)	E	ME	10.06.94	SULTAN
Paget, Simon James	LT(FTC)	X		02.05.00	RALEIGH
Pakes, Danyel Tobias, BEng, CEng	LT CDR(FTC)	E	WESM	01.01.04	ASM IPT
Palethorpe, Nicholas, BSc	LT(CC)	X		01.09.97	MWS COLLINGWOOD
Palin, Giles Roland, LLB, n	LT(FTC)	X		01.12.97	RAIDER
Pallett, Angela Julie, MA	LT(IC)	S		01.01.03	BULWARK
Palmer, Alan Charles, MB, ChB, MRCGP	SURG LTCDR(FCC)	-	GMPP	01.03.97	SETT GOSPORT
Palmer, Christopher Laurence, BSc, MIMgt, pce, pcea, psc	CAPT(FTC)	X	O	31.12.00	FLEET HQ PORTS
Palmer, Christopher Richard, MSc, IEng, AMINucE	LT(CC)	E	MESM	01.09.01	NP BRISTOL
Palmer, James Ernest, MSc, CEng, MIEE, MBCS, MInsD	CDR(FTC)	E	WE	31.12.96	FLEET CIS PORTS
Palmer, John, MA, CEng, MIEE	LT CDR(FTC)	E	WE	01.10.03	MWS COLLINGWOOD
Palmer, Martin David, BSc	LT(IC)	X	H2	01.01.03	RFANSU
Palmer, Michael Edward, BEng, MSc, CEng, MIEE	LT CDR(FTC)	E	WE	01.11.01	FLEET HQ PORTS 2
Palmer, Phillip Alan, BA, SM	LT CDR(FTC)	X	SM	01.07.89	MOD (LONDON)
Palmer, Rhoderick Adrian Nigel, BSc, ACGI, psc (Commodore)	CAPT(FTC)	E	AE	31.12.96	DPA BRISTOL
Pamphilon, Michael John, pcea, psc	LT CDR(FTC(A)	X	P	01.03.88	824 SQN
Pancott, Brian Michael, BSc, LRPS, FRGS, CITP, MBCS, MCGI, psc, mdtc	CDR(FTC)	E	WE	31.12.91	AFPAA JPA
Panic, Alexander, BSc (Act Lt Cdr)	LT(CC)	E	TMSM	15.04.95	FOST FAS SHORE
Panther, Andrew Mark, BEng, MSc, CEng, MIEE	LT CDR(FTC)	E	WE	01.07.00	FOST SEA
Pardoe, Elton Ramsey, MB, CHB, BSc	SURG LT(SC(MD)	-		06.08.00	FLEET AV SULTAN
Pariser, Andrew Maurice, BSc	SLT(IC)	X		01.05.03	INVINCIBLE
Park, Brian Campbell, BA	LT CDR(FTC)	S		01.10.03	GLOUCESTER
Park, Ian David, MA	LT(CC)	S		01.08.98	ILLUSTRIOUS
Park, Lindsay, BDS	SG LT(D)(SC(MD)	-		27.06.03	SULTAN
Parker, Anthony Richard	LT(IC)	S	(W)	29.10.04	RALEIGH
Parker, Daniel John	SLT(IC)	S		01.05.02	RALEIGH
Parker, Darren Stuart	LT(IC)	MS		01.07.04	NEPTUNE DLO
Parker, Henry Hardyman, MA, PhD, CEng, MIEE, psc	CAPT(FTC)	E	WESM	30.06.02	BDS WASHINGTON

Name	Rank	Branch	Spec	Seniority	Where Serving
Parker, Ian Robert, BSc	CDR(FTC)	E	MESM	31.12.93	DLO BRISTOL
Parker, Jeremy Vaugn Vernham, BSc, psc(m)	LT COL(FTC)	-		30.06.92	COS 2SL/CNH
Parker, Jonathan Donald, BEng, MIEE, NDipM	LT(IC)	E	WE	01.04.03	NOTTINGHAM
Parker, Mark Neal, BEng, MSc, CEng, FIMarEST, MAPM, MCGI	CDR(FTC)	E	ME	30.06.01	EXCHANGE USA
Parker, Matthew Charles, BA	CAPT RM(FTC)	-		01.09.02	CTCRM
Parker, Matthew James, BA	LT(IC)	X	H2	01.01.04	ROEBUCK
Parker, Sarah Anne Marie, BA	LT(IC)	X		01.09.00	NP IRAQ
Parker, Timothy Stephen, BSc, MIMarA, MBCS, CMath	LT(CC)	E	IS	01.11.95	PJHQ
Parkin, Brett	SLT(IC)	E	WESM	01.01.04	MWS COLLINGWOOD
Parkin, James Miles Benjamin, MA	LT(FTC)	X	FC	01.09.98	RANGER
Parkin, Malcolm Ian, BEng	LT CDR(FTC)	E	ME	01.07.99	EXCHANGE NLANDS
Parkin, Matthew James, BA	SLT(IC)	X		01.05.03	CAMPBELTOWN
Parkinson, Andrew Philip	LT(FTC)	X	AV	23.07.98	ILLUSTRIOUS
Parkinson, Henry Michael Larissa	LT(FTC)	E	AE	01.09.04	RNAS YEOVILTON
Parkinson, James Hugh George, MEng	LT(FTC)	X	SM	01.09.02	TRENCHANT
Parks, Edward Patrick, jsdc, psc (Act Lt Col)	MAJ(FTC)	-		01.09.90	MWC SOUTHWICK
Parmenter, Alan John	LT(FTC)	E	AE	01.04.01	FS MASU
Parnell, Adam David, BEng, pce	LT CDR(FTC)	X	AAWO	01.04.01	PJHQ
Parnell, Daniel Christian	SLT(IC)	E	ME U/T	01.01.04	SULTAN
Parr, Matthew John, BSc, pce, pce(sm)	CAPT(FTC)	X	SM	30.06.02	FLEET HQ NWD
Parr, Michael John Edward	LT(FTC)	X	HM	01.10.96	FLEET HQ NWD
Parrock, Neil Graham	LT(CC)	X	P	01.07.95	DHFS
Parrott, James Philip	LT CDR(FTC)	X	PWO(A)	01.07.04	EXETER
Parrott, Stuart Steven	SLT(IC)	X		01.01.03	MWS COLLINGWOOD
Parry, Alexander Keith Illiam, BSc, psc(j)	CDR(FTC)	S		30.06.05	MOD (BATH)
Parry, Christopher Adrian, MB, BS, BSc, MRCS	SURG LTCDR(FCC)	-		12.08.99	NELSON (PAY)
Parry, Christopher John, CBE, MA, rcds, pce, pcea, psc (DGJDC JAN 05)	RADM	-	O	25.01.05	JDCC
Parry, Gareth Richard	LT(IC)	X		01.10.03	MWS COLLINGWOOD
Parry, Jonathan Allan, BSc	MAJ(CC)	-	P	01.10.04	JHCHQ
Parry, Jonathan David Frank, MRAeS, pcea	LT CDR(FTC)	X	P	01.05.00	815 SQN HQ
Parry, Mark Roderick Raymond, BEng, MSc	LT CDR(FTC)	E	AE	01.05.04	NAVSEC
Parry, Nicholas Thomas, BSc, AMIEE, CGIA, psc, mdtc	CDR(FTC)	E	WESM	31.12.94	NEPTUNE DLO
Parry, Roger John	LT(FTC)	E	AE	16.10.92	GANNET SAR FLT
Parry, Stephen Joseph, BSc	SLT(IC)	X		01.01.03	FOST DPORT SHORE
Parry, Stuart David, LLB	LT(IC)	S		05.03.02	IRON DUKE
Parsons, Andrew David, BSc, n	LT CDR(FTC)	X	PWO(C)	01.01.00	PJHQ
Parsons, Brian Robert, BSc, MBA	CDR(FTC)	E	AE	31.12.00	DLO WYTON
Parsons, Christopher Graham, BSc, MDA, CEng, MIEE	CDR(FTC)	E	WE	31.12.00	FLEET HQ PORTS 2
Parsons, Patrick Hugh, osc(us)	LT COL(FTC)	-	MLDR	31.12.92	LN BMATT (CEE)
Parsons, Robert John, BSc	LT(IC)	X	MW	01.11.00	BANGOR
Parsons, Robert Martin James	LT(CC)	X		01.01.02	MWS HM TG (D)
Parton, Alan	LT(FTC)	X	MCD	19.09.00	MWS COLLINGWOOD
Partridge, Simon Christopher, BSc	LT(IC)	X	HM	01.12.00	FLEET HQ NWD
Parvin, Philip Stanley, BEng, MBA, MSc, CEng, FIMarEST, MIMechE, MCMI	LT CDR(FTC)	E	MESM	01.02.97	FWO DEVONPORT
Parvin, Richard Alan, MA	MAJ(FTC)	-		01.05.03	JSCSC
Pascoe, James Roderick Munro	CAPT RM(CC)	-		01.09.03	45 CDO RM
Paston, William Alexander	LT(IC)	X	FC	01.05.02	HQ STC
Patch, Stirling John	LT(IC)	E	ME	02.08.02	DFTE PORTSMOUTH
Pate, Christopher Michael	LT(CC)	X		01.01.04	MWS COLLINGWOOD
Patel, Devang Ramesh, MB, BSc, BS, DipIMC RCSED	SURG LT(SCC)	-		01.08.01	RH HASLAR
Paterson, James	SLT(IC)	X		01.01.03	BROCKLESBY
Paterson, Michael Paul, PGDIPAN, pce, n	CDR(FTC)	X	PWO(N)	30.06.05	JSCSC
Paterson, Thomas John	CAPT RM(CC)	-	MLDR	01.04.02	CTCRM (SEA)
Paton, Alan John Malcolm	LT(FTC)	E	ME	19.06.98	DLO BRISTOL
Paton, Christopher Mark, BEng	MAJ(FTC)	-		01.09.02	NELSON (PAY)
Paton, Martin Stirling	LT(IC)	E	MESM	01.05.04	TRIUMPH
Patrick, James, MSc, rcds, psc	CDRE(FTC)	E	TM	08.02.05	2SL/CNH FOTR
Patrick, John Andrew	SLT(IC)	X		01.01.03	ROEBUCK
Patten, Michelle Louise, BEng	SLT(IC)	E	WE U/T	01.09.03	BULWARK
Patterson, David, BEng	LT CDR(FTC)	E	WE	01.10.02	ALBION
Patterson, John David, BSc, n	LT CDR(FTC)	X	PWO(A)	01.08.04	CAMPBELTOWN

Name	Rank	Branch	Spec	Seniority	Where Serving
Patterson, Pascal Xavier, BSc	SLT(IC)	X	O U/T	01.01.04	DARTMOUTH BRNC
Patterson, Scott Douglas, BEng, CEng, MIEE (Act Lt Cdr)	LT(FTC)	E	WE	01.07.97	DLO DEF MUN GP
Patterson-Hollis, Christopher, BEng, MIEE	LT CDR(FTC)	E	WE	01.04.97	DLO BRISTOL
Pattinson, Ian Howard, MSc	CDR(FTC)	S		30.06.98	OCEAN
Patton, Richard	LT(IC)	MS		01.05.02	DPMD
Paul, Gillian Morag	SLT(IC)	X		01.06.03	DARTMOUTH BRNC
Paul, Russell William Fordyce, MA, psc	LT COL(FTC)	-	LC	30.06.01	BULWARK
Paulet, Michael Raoul	LT(CC)	X	P	01.02.01	849 SQN A FLT
Paulson, Richard Brian, BEng, MSc, MIEE	LT CDR(FTC)	E	WE	01.08.03	MWS COLLINGWOOD
Payne, Daniel	LT CDR(FTC)	E	ME	01.10.99	MWS EXCELLENT
Payne, John Durley, BSc, pce, n	LT CDR(FTC)	X	PWO(U)	01.06.98	JSCSC
Payne, Joseph Oliver, BEng	SLT(IC)	E	MESMUT	01.09.03	INVINCIBLE
Payne, Matthew John	LT CDR(FTC)	X	PWO(C)	01.10.03	MWS COLLINGWOOD
Payne, Michael Thomas	CAPT RM(IC)	-		01.09.03	42 CDO RM
Payne, Philip John, BA	LT CDR(FTC)	X	HM	01.07.02	FWO DEVONPORT
Payne, Richard Charles, pce, pcea	CDR(FTC)	X	P	30.06.01	ALBION
Payne, William Dudley	LT(IC)	X		01.05.03	LEDBURY
Peace, Richard William	LT CDR(FTC)	E	MESM	02.07.97	DLO BRISTOL
Peach, Graham Leslie, BSc, psc	CAPT(FTC)	E	WE	30.06.00	FLEET HQ PORTS 2
Peachey, Richard Matthew, BSc	LT(CC)	X	P	01.11.94	847 SQN
Peacock, Joel David	MID(IC)	X		01.09.03	SHOREHAM
Peacock, Laura Gillian Joan ,BMus	SLT(IC)	X		01.05.03	KENT
Peacock, Stephen, BSc, MDA, CEng, MIEE	CDR(FTC)	E	WESM	30.06.03	EXCHANGE AUSTLIA
Peacock, Timothy James, MA, pce, pcea (Act Cdr)	LT CDR(FTC)	X	P	01.01.98	COS 2SL/CNH
Peak, Martyn (Act Lt Cdr)	LT(FTC)	X		03.04.98	MWS COLLINGWOOD
Peake, Stephen Peter	LT(IC)	MS		01.07.04	JSCSC
Pearce, Elizabeth Anne, MA	LT(IC)	X		09.04.02	DARTMOUTH BRNC
Pearce, Jonathan	LT(IC)	E	WE	01.01.04	CAPT MCTA
Pearce, Robert James, BA	LT(CC)	X		01.01.02	ALBION
Pearce, Sarah Louise	SLT(IC)	X		01.09.02	WALNEY
Pearch, Sean Michael	LT(FTC)	X	ATC	26.04.99	CHFHQ
Pearey, Michael Scott, DSC, BSc, jsdc, pce, pcea	CDR(FTC)	X	O	31.12.96	MOD (LONDON)
Pearmain, Stephanie Rosina, BSc	LT(IC)	E	TM	14.05.00	DCTS PORTS
Pears, Ian James, MSc, adp	LT CDR(FTC)	E	IS	01.10.00	COS 2SL/CNH
Pearson, Alan James, BSc	SLT(IC)	X	O U/T	01.01.02	DARTMOUTH BRNC
Pearson, Charles Peter Bellamy, BEng, CEng, MIMarEST	LT CDR(FTC)	E	ME	01.10.00	FOST SEA
Pearson, Christopher Robert, MA, MBA, MB, BChir, FRCS, DLO	SURG CDR(FCC)	-	(CE)	30.06.02	RH HASLAR
Pearson, Ian Thomas, BA, MEng	LT(IC)	E	AE	01.09.04	RNAS YEOVILTON
Pearson, James Carden	LT(CC)	X	MCD	01.12.00	JSCSC
Pearson, Michael Forbes	LT CDR(FTC)	X	O	01.03.01	STANAVFORMED
Pearson, Neil, BEng, MSc, CEng, MIMarEST	LT CDR(FTC)	E	ME	01.08.97	FOST SEA
Pearson, Robert James, BA	SLT(IC)	X		01.01.04	DARTMOUTH BRNC
Pearson, Stephen John, MA, pce, psc(j)	CDR(FTC)	X	O	30.06.00	FOST SEA
Pearson, Susan, BEd	LT(CC)	S		01.05.01	NELSON WF
Peasley, Helen Susan	LT(IC)	E		01.04.02	ILLUSTRIOUS
Peattie, Ian William, BSc	LT(IC)	S		01.05.02	MARLBOROUGH
Peck, Ian John, BSc, CEng, MRAeS, MDA	CDR(FTC)	E	AE	31.12.97	DASC
Peck, Simon Russell, MEng	LT(FTC)	E	AE	01.09.02	SULTAN
Pedler, Mark David, BEng	LT(CC)	X	P	01.07.97	EXCHANGE USA
Pedre, Robert George, BSc, ARCS	LT CDR(FTC)	X		01.10.04	JSCSC
Pegg, Russell Montfort, pce, fsc	CAPT(FTC)	X	PWO(U)	30.06.05	AGRIPPA MAR CC
Pegrum, Terrence Allen, pcea	LT CDR(FTC)	X	P	01.10.99	JHCHQ
Peilow, Benjamin Francis, BA, MILT, psc	CDR(FTC)	S		31.12.92	FLEET HQ PORTS
Pelly, Gilbert Ralph	MAJ(FTC)	-		25.04.96	HQ 3 CDO BDE RM
Penalver, Warren Craig	LT(IC)	X	SM	01.01.04	VIGILANT(PORT)
Pendle, Martin Erle John, BSc, CEng, MIMarEST, jsdc	CDR(FTC)	E	ME	30.06.95	BULWARK
Pengelley, Tristan Anthony Hastings	CAPT RM(IC)	-		01.09.04	CTCRM
Pengelly, Steven Paul, MB, CHB	SURG LT(SCC)	-		06.08.03	CFLT MED(SEA)
Penketh, Mark Geoffrey	LT(FTC)	E	ME	02.09.99	FWO PORTS SEA
Penkman, William Alfred Vincent, BSc	MAJ(FTC)	-	P	01.09.04	JHCNI
Penn-Barwell, Jowan George, MB, CHB	SURG LT(SCC)	-		07.10.03	UKLFCSG RM
Pennefather, Douglas Cameron John	CAPT RM(IC)	-		01.09.04	45 CDO RM
Pennington, Charles Edmond, BSc	CAPT RM(IC)	-		01.09.01	EXCHANGE ARMY UK

Name	Rank	Branch	Spec	Seniority	Where Serving
Penny, Anthony David, MSc, CEng, MIEE	CAPT(FTC)	E	WE	31.12.00	T45 IPT
Penprase, Jason Michael	LT(CC)	X		01.10.94	RALEIGH
Pentreath, Jonathan Patrick, BSc, pce, pcea, psc(j)	CDR(FTC)	X	P	30.06.03	MOD (LONDON)
Peppe, Alasdair George	LT CDR(FTC)	X	PWO(U)	01.06.03	PJHQ
Pepper, Martin Richard, BSc, pce, pcea, psc	CDR(FTC)	X	O	31.12.92	JDCC
Percharde, Michael Robert, BSc, pce, psc(j)	CDR(FTC)	X	AAWO	31.12.98	FLEET HQ PORTS
Percival, Fiona	LT CDR(FTC)	S		01.10.03	IRON DUKE
Percival, Michael Christopher	LT CDR(FTC)	S		01.07.99	UKMARBATSTAFF
Percival, Victoria Helen, MEng	SLT(IC)	E	ME U/T	01.01.04	DARTMOUTH BRNC
Percy, Nicolas Andrew, BSc	LT(CC)	X	MCD	01.04.99	GRIMSBY
Perkins, Ben, BEng	LT(FTC)	E	P	01.07.01	DLO YEO
Perkins, Michael Jonathan, BA, MDA, pce	CDR(FTC)	X	AAWO	30.06.96	FLEET CIS PORTS
Perkins, Ross John, BEng, CEng, MIMarEST	LT CDR(FTC)	E	ME	01.01.04	NP IRAQ
Perks, Andrew Barry, MEng	SLT(IC)	X		01.11.02	BULWARK
Perks, James Le Seelleur, pce(sm), SM(n)	CDR(FTC)	X	SM	30.06.05	MWS COLLINGWOOD
Perrin, Mark Stephen, BA	CAPT RM(CC)	-		01.09.01	EXCHANGE ARMY UK
Perry, Andrew James	LT CDR(FTC)	S	SM	16.07.99	RALEIGH
Perry, Carl Steven Leslie, BSc	LT(IC)	X	TM	01.03.05	MWS COLLINGWOOD
Perry, Jonathan Neil, MB, ChB, FRCR	SURG CDR(FCC)	-	(CX)	31.12.96	MDHU PETERBRGH
Perry, Richard, BSc, BA(OU), MA, psc	LT CDR(FTC)	E	MESM	01.11.90	FLEET HQ NWD
Perry, Robert William, sq	MAJ(FTC)	-	SO(LE)	01.10.00	1 ASSLT GP RM
Perry, Russell John	LT(CC)	X	MW	01.11.93	FLEET HQ PORTS
Perryman, Ian Thomas Charles, BSc	LT(IC)	E	TM	01.01.00	JSCSC
Perryment, Claire Patricia	LT(CC)	X		01.08.01	CAMPBELTOWN
Peschardt, Charles William Hagbarth, BA, MCIPD	SLT(IC)	X	P U/T	01.07.02	RNAS YEOVILTON
Peskett, Daniel Mark, BEng, AMIMechE	LT(IC)	E	ME	01.03.03	CHATHAM
Petch, Alan Napier, BEng	LT(IC)	X	P	01.09.03	DHFS
Peters, Adam John Urlin, BSc (Act Cdr)	LT CDR(FTC)	X		01.08.87	MOD (LONDON)
Peters, Andrew Douglas	CAPT RM(CC)	-	SO(LE)	01.04.03	CTCRM
Peters, Matthew Keith, BEng	SLT(IC)	E	ME	01.05.02	ARGYLL
Peters, William Richard, BA, n	LT CDR(FTC)	X		01.03.04	SOUTHAMPTON
Peterson, Keith Andrew, BEng	LT(IC)	E	WESM	01.09.03	SCEPTRE
Petheram, Anthony John, pce	LT CDR(FTC)	X	PWO(C)	01.09.97	FOST SEA
Petheram, Michael John, MBE, MA, pce, psc(j)	CDR(FTC)	X	PWO(U)	30.06.02	NAVSEC
Petherick, Jason Stewart, pce, psc(j)	LT CDR(FTC)	X	AAWO	01.04.98	COMATG SEA
Pethybridge, Richard Alan, PGDIPAN, pce, n	LT CDR(FTC)	X	PWO(N)	01.05.97	ATHERSTONE
Petitt, Simon Richard, BEng, MBA, CEng, MIEE	CDR(FTC)	E	WE	30.06.03	MOD (LONDON)
Pett, Jeremy Graham, BSc, MinstP, C PHYS	CDR(FTC)	E	TM	30.06.99	MOD (LONDON)
Pettigrew, Thomas Robert, BEng, IEng, MIIE	LT(CC)	E	TM	01.09.97	FOST FAS SHORE
Pettitt, Gary William, pce	CDR(FTC)	X	PWO(U)	31.12.97	MOD (LONDON)
Petzer, Garth Stephen, MBE, DipTh	CHAPLAIN	CE		01.08.04	FWO PORTS SEA
Peyman, Tracy Anne	LT(CC)	S		01.09.00	MOD (BATH)
Pheasant, John Christian Stephen, BSc (Barrister)	LT CDR(FTC)	S	BAR	01.10.00	FOST DPORT SHORE
Phenna, Andrew, BEng	CDR(FTC)	E	WE	30.06.01	JFCHQ BRUNSSUM
Phesse, John Paul Lloyd, IEng, AMRAeS	LT CDR(FTC)	E	AE(L)	01.10.00	814 SQN
Philip, Alistair David, BSc, n (Act Lt Cdr)	LT(CC)	X	HM2	01.03.97	FLEET HQ PORTS 2
Philips, Thomas James, MEng	SLT(IC)	E	ME U/T	01.01.03	SULTAN
Philipson, Matthew James	SLT(IC)	E	WE U/T	01.09.03	OCEAN
Phillippo, Duncan George, MEng	LT(IC)	E	MESM	01.05.04	SULTAN
Phillips, Andrew Graham, BSc, CertTh	CHAPLAIN	CE		14.02.00	NEPTUNE 2SL/CNH
Phillips, Andrew Ralph, BA, IEng, MIIE	LT CDR(FTC)	E	AE	01.10.01	DCAE COSFORD
Phillips, David George, pce, pce(sm)	CDR(FTC)	X	SM	30.06.95	SHAPE BELGIUM
Phillips, David Guy	CAPT RM(CC)	-	SO(LE)	01.04.03	CTCRM
Phillips, Edward Henry Lloyd, BA	SLT(IC)	X		01.02.04	DARTMOUTH BRNC
Phillips, Ian Michael	LT CDR(FTC)	MS		01.10.01	NELSON (PAY)
Phillips, James Charles, MB, CHB	SURG LT(MC(MD)	-		01.08.02	JSCSC
Phillips, James Nicholas, BEng, MSc, CEng, MIEE	LT CDR(FTC)	E	WE	01.03.03	CSIS IPT
Phillips, Jason Peter, pcea	LT CDR(FTC)	X	O	01.10.00	814 SQN
Phillips, Laura Claire	LT(CC)	X		01.09.04	EXCHANGE SPAIN
Phillips, Mark Christopher, MBE	MAJ(FTC)	-	SO(LE)	01.10.04	1 ASSAULT GP RM
Phillips, Matthew Benjamin, BSc	LT(IC)	X	P	16.08.95	EXCHANGE RAF UK
Phillips, Matthew Rhys	LT(IC)	S		01.09.04	MWS COLLINGWOOD
Phillips, Richard Edward	LT(IC)	X	P	01.09.03	801 SQN

Name	Rank	Branch	Spec	Seniority	Where Serving
Phillips, Richard Mark, MSc	LT(CC)	X		01.01.00	TYNE
Phillips, Simon Miles, MB, BS, MRCGP, Dip OM	SURG LTCDR(SCC)	-	GMPP	03.09.02	NELSON (PAY)
Phillips, Stephen John, MA, psc	LT COL(FTC)	-		30.06.04	RMR TYNE
Philo, Julian Quentin, BEng, CEng	LT CDR(FTC)	E	ME	01.06.98	FLEET HQ PORTS
Philpot, David John, BEng, MIEE, CEng	LT CDR(FTC)	E	WESM	18.07.00	SCEPTRE
Philpott, Marcus Cornforth, MB, CHB, MRCGP, DRCOG, DCH, Dip FFP (Act Surg Ltcdr)	SURG LT(SC(MD)	-	GMPP	04.01.05	NP IRAQ
Philpott, Nigel Edward, psc(j)	CDR(FTC)	S		30.06.04	MOD (LONDON)
Phipps, Tracey Anne, BA	LT(FTC)	X	H1	01.02.94	ROEBUCK
Piaggesi, Gareth Fiorenzo	LT(IC)	E	AE	01.09.04	RAF WITTERING
Pickard, David Malcolm	CAPT RM(FTC)	-	SO(LE)	01.01.99	1 ASSLT GP RM
Pickard, Richard James ,BM, RCSEd	SURG LTCDR(SC(MD)	-		23.04.02	NELSON (PAY)
Pickard, Stephen Richard	LT(CC)	E	AE	01.09.00	FLEET HQ PORTS
Picken, Christopher Robert, MB, BCH, BAO	SURG LT(MC(MD)	-		07.08.02	VENGEANCE(STBD)
Pickering, Coralie Ann	LT(CC)	S		04.05.00	NELSON
Pickering, David Allan	LT(IC)	MS		01.05.04	MDHU DERRIFORD
Pickering, Ian Jeffery, BA, SM(n)	LT(FTC)	X	SM	01.07.96	VIGILANT(PORT)
Pickering-Wheeler, Christopher William, BSc, SM(n)	LT(FTC)	X	SM	01.01.98	SUPERB
Pickles, David Richard	LT(FTC)	X	ATC	01.01.01	DARTMOUTH BRNC
Pickles, Ian Seaton, pce, pce(sm)	CDR(FTC)	X	SM	30.06.97	BDS WASHINGTON
Pickles, Martin Richard, BSc	LT(IC)	X	P	01.05.01	815 FLT 200
Picksley, Michael Raymond	LT CDR(FTC)	E	WE	01.10.00	SANS IPT
Pickthall, David Nicholas, BSc, CEng, MIEE	CDR(FTC)	E	WE	31.12.97	EXCHANGE FRANCE
Pickup, Richard Allan, CBE, BSc, MA, psc(m), psc(j)o	COL(FTC)	-		30.06.03	FLEET HQ NWD
Picton, Annette Mary, ADC, psc (Commodore)	CAPT(FTC)	W	SEC	30.06.96	MOD (LONDON)
Pierce, Adrian Kevern Maxwell, PGDIPAN, n	LT CDR(FTC)	X	PWO(N)	01.02.00	BLYTH
Pierson, Matthew Fraser, odc(Fr)	LT COL(FTC)	-		30.06.04	FLEET HQ PORTS 2
Pike, Martin Stephen, BSc	LT CDR(FTC)	S		01.03.91	HQ RHINE/EURO SG
Pike, Robin Timothy	LT(IC)	E	WESM	01.01.04	ASM IPT
Pilkington, Alex Gregory Howarth, BSc	MAJ(IC)	-		01.10.04	CTCRM
Pilkington, Barry Mark, MEng	SLT(IC)	X	P U/T	01.02.04	DARTMOUTH BRNC
Pilkington, Will James	CAPT RM(IC)	-		01.09.04	FPGRM
Pillai, Sonia	SURG SLT(SCC)	-		20.09.04	DARTMOUTH BRNC
Pillar, Christopher David, pce	LT CDR(FTC)	X	PWO(U)	01.03.95	NELSON
Pilsworth, Dermod Scott, CGIA	LT CDR(FTC)	E	WE	01.06.85	T45 IPT
Pimm, Anthony Richard, BSc	LT(IC)	X		01.09.04	PORTLAND
Pimpalnerkar, Ashvin Lakshman, MSc, MB, BS, MChOrth, FRCS(ORTH)	SURG CDR(MCC)	-	(CO/S)	30.06.04	LOAN FIELD HOSP
Pinckney, Mathew Robert Nicholas	CAPT RM(IC)	-		01.09.04	FOST SEA
Pinder, Christopher David, BEng	LT CDR(CC)	E	TM	01.10.04	DCAE COSFORD
Pine, Paul Martin, BSc, PGCE	LT(IC)	E	TM	06.12.98	NTE(TTD)
Pinhey, Andrew David	LT(IC)	MS		01.01.02	NEPTUNE BNSL
Pink, Simon Edward, n	LT CDR(FTC)	X	PWO(N)	01.01.02	FOST SEA
Pinney, Richard Francis	2LT(IC)	-		02.09.00	FPGRM
Pinnington, Adam John	SLT(IC)	X		01.01.04	DARTMOUTH BRNC
Piper, Benjamin James	SLT(IC)	X		01.05.03	FDG
Piper, Neale Derek, ARRC, BSc	LT CDR(FC(MD)	Q	IC	01.10.03	HQ DMETA
Pipkin, Christopher, MB, BS, FRCPath	SURG CAPT(FCC)	-	CPDATE	30.06.94	2SL/CNH
Pipkin, Peter John, BEng, CEng, MIEE	LT(FTC)	E	WE	01.04.00	CAPT MCTA
Pipkin, Simon Christian, pcea	LT CDR(FTC)	X	P	01.10.95	UKMARBATSTAFF
Pirie, Ian Thomas	LT(IC)	X	C	01.07.04	MWS COLLINGWOOD
Pirrie, James Alexander	LT(FTC)	X	C	19.09.00	OCLC ROSYTH
Pitcher, James	LT CDR(FTC)	E	AE	01.10.93	ADAS BRISTOL
Pitcher, Paul, BA	LT CDR(FTC)	X	PWO(C)	01.10.02	UKMARBATSTAFF
Pitman, Lisa Jill, BEd	LT(IC)	S		01.01.03	SULTAN AIB
Pitt, Jonathan Mark, SM(n), SM	LT CDR(FTC)	X	SM	17.02.99	FWO DEVONPORT
Pitt, William Thomas	LT(IC)	X	EW	01.01.03	UKMARBATSTAFF
Pittard, David Campbell, BSc	LT(IC)	X		01.06.99	FOST DPORT SHORE
Pittock, Stephen James	LT(IC)	X	SM	01.01.05	VENGEANCE(PORT)
Plackett, Andrew John, BSc, MA	LT CDR(FTC)	E	TM	01.10.03	FLEET HQ PORTS
Plaice, Graham Conyers	LT CDR(FTC)	S	SM	01.10.00	AGRIPPA MAR CC
Plant, Ian Robert, BSc	LT CDR(FTC)	E	AE	01.07.90	LOAN JTEG BSC DN
Plant, Jeremy Neil Melrose, BSc, MDA	CDR(FTC)	E	AE	31.12.99	MOD (LONDON)

Name	Rank	Branch	Spec	Seniority	Where Serving
Plant, Martin Gary	LT CDR(FTC)	E	WE	13.06.91	STRS IPT
Platt, Jonathan Howard, BSc	LT(CC)	X	P	16.06.96	DHFS
Platt, Nicola	LT(FTC)	S	(W)	03.04.98	RH HASLAR
Pledger, David	LT CDR(FTC)	X	AV	01.10.02	RFANSU
Pledger, Pippa May, BSc, FRGS	LT(IC)	X		01.01.05	MWS COLLINGWOOD
Plenty, Andrew Justin	LT(IC)	X	ATC	01.09.03	RNAS CULDROSE
Plewes, Andrew Burns, BSc	MAJ(FTC)	-		27.04.02	COMAMPHIBFOR
Plunkett, Gareth Neil	SLT(IC)	X	P	01.09.03	RNAS YEOVILTON
Pocock, David	LT CDR(FTC)	S		16.10.00	EDINBURGH
Podger, Kevin Gordon Ray, BSc, psc	CDR(FTC)	E	MESM	30.06.95	COS 2SL/CNH
Podmore, Anthony, BSc	CDR(FTC)	E	TM	30.06.01	2SL/CNH FOTR
Pointon, Bryony Margaret, MB, CHB	SURG LT(SCC)	-		04.05.02	RH HASLAR
Polding, Martin, BA	LT(FTC)	X	P	01.11.93	EXCHANGE USA
Polhill, Joanne Victoria	MID(IC)	X		01.11.03	DARTMOUTH BRNC
Poll, Martin George, BA, DipTh	CHAPLAIN	CE		14.06.90	2SL/CNH
Pollard, Alexandra Eleanor, BA	LT(CC)	X	FC	01.08.98	BLAZER
Pollard, Andrew John	LT(FTC)	E	ME	01.04.01	SULTAN
Pollard, Jonathan Richard, BEng, MSc gw, MIEE, NDipM	LT(FTC)	E	WE	01.12.99	MWS COLLINGWOOD
Pollitt, Alexander William	SLT(IC)	X	P U/T	01.05.03	RAF CRANWELL EFS
Pollitt, David Nigel Anthony, pce, pce(sm), psc	LT CDR(FTC)	X	SM	01.04.89	FLEET HQ NWD
Pollock, Barnaby James, BSc	SLT(IC)	X		01.11.02	CATTISTOCK
Pollock, David John, BSc, pce, pce(sm)	CDR(FTC)	X	SM	30.06.99	FLEET HQ PORTS 2
Pollock, Malcolm Philip, MA, pce, pcea, psc(j)	CDR(FTC)	X	O	30.06.05	MWC PORTSDOWN
Pollock, Sir Michael (Patrick), GCB, LVO, DSC, psc	ADM OF FLEET	-		01.03.74	
Pomeroy, Mark Anthony	CDR(FTC)	E	ME	30.06.03	FWO PORTS SEA
Pomeroy, Philippa Mary, BEd, psc(j)	LT CDR(FTC)	S		01.02.00	MOD (LONDON)
Pond, David William, BEd, rcds	CDRE(FTC)	X	METOC	08.07.03	RALEIGH
Pond, Robert James	LT(IC)	E	MESM	01.05.03	JSCSC
Ponsford, Philip Kevin, BSc, MInsD	LT CDR(FTC)	X	PWO(U)	01.01.99	FOST SEA
Poole, Daniel Charles, BA	SLT(IC)	S		01.09.02	RALEIGH
Poole, Jason Lee, pce, psc(j)	CDR(FTC)	X	MCD	30.06.04	PJHQ
Poole, Timothy James, MRAeS, MCGI, pcea, gdas, MSc	LT(FTC)	X	O	16.01.92	700M MERLIN OEU
Pooley, Steven William, BSc	LT CDR(FTC)	E	WESM	01.07.96	DLO BRISTOL
Pope, Catherine Manuela, MA, MSc, psc	CDR(FTC)	X	METOC	24.06.98	HQ DCSA
Pope, Kevin David	LT(IC)	X	P U/T	01.01.05	HQ BFSAI
Porrett, Johnathan Anthony	LT CDR(FTC)	S	SM	14.11.95	NAVSEC
Porritt, Colin	LT(IC)	E		01.05.02	ADAS BRISTOL
Porteous, Russell	SLT(IC)	E	ME U/T	01.01.04	SULTAN
Porter, Derek Lowry, BA	LT(CC)	S	SM	01.06.97	RAF WITTERING
Porter, Matthew Edward, MBE, BSc, psc(j)	LT COL(FTC)	-		30.06.04	1 ASSAULT GP RM
Porter, Simon Paul, pce, psc(j)	CDR(FTC)	X	AAWO	31.12.99	INVINCIBLE
Porter, Suzanne, MB, ChB, BSc	SURG LTCDR(MCC)	-	GMPP	01.08.01	ALBION
Porter, Timothy Benedict, BA	LT CDR(FTC)	S		01.05.02	UKSU JHQ LISBON
Postgate, Michael Oliver	LT RM(IC)	-		01.09.02	40 CDO RM
Pothecary, Richard Edward, FCMI, MNI, pce	CDR(FTC)	X	AAWO	31.12.93	COS 2SL/CNH
Potter, David John	LT(FTC)	X	O	24.07.97	824 SQN
Potter, David Lloyd, MB, CHB	SURG LT(SC(MD)	-		04.08.04	CTCRM
Potter, Michael John, ADC, MA, MSc, CEng, MIMarEST, MINucE, MInstP, C PHYS, psc (Commodore)	CAPT(FTC)	E	TM	30.06.97	2SL/CNH FOTR
Potter, Stephen	MAJ(FTC)	-	SO(LE)	01.10.98	1 ASSAULT GP RM
Potts, Duncan Laurence, BSc, pce	CAPT(FTC)	X	PWO(U)	30.06.00	MOD (LONDON)
Potts, Gary, BEng, MSc, CEng, MIEE	LT CDR(FTC)	E	WESM	01.10.04	MOD (LONDON)
Potts, Kevin Maxwell	LT CDR(FTC)	X	P	01.02.92	815 SQN HQ
Potts, Ruth Ernestine, BSc	LT(CC)	S		01.08.00	FWO PORTSMOUTH
Powell, David Charles, MSc, CEng, MIMarEST	CDR(FTC)	E	ME	31.12.95	FLEET HQ PORTS 2
Powell, Gregory Mark John	SLT(IC)	X		01.01.04	ATHERSTONE
Powell, Rebecca Jane	LT(CC)	X		01.01.03	GRIMSBY
Powell, Richard Laurence, MA, pce, pcea, psc(j)	CDR(FTC)	X	P	31.12.00	MOD (LONDON)
Powell, Steven, MA, pce, pcea, psc(a)	CDR(FTC)	X	O	30.06.03	MOD (LONDON)
Powell, Steven Richard, pce	LT CDR(FTC)	X	PWO(C)	01.07.98	MWS COLLINGWOOD
Powell, William Glyn, pce, pcea	LT CDR(FTC)	X	O	16.12.98	JHQ/CIS LISBON
Power, Benjamin	SLT(IC)	X		01.09.03	MWS COLLINGWOOD
Powis, Jonathan, pce, pce(sm)	CDR(FTC)	X	SM	31.12.92	FLEET HQ NWD

Name	Rank	Branch	Spec	Seniority	Where Serving
Powles, Derek Anthony, MEng	LT CDR(FTC)	E	ME	01.02.04	RICHMOND
Powne, Simon Philip Watts	LT(IC)	E	ME	01.05.02	SULTAN
Precious, Angus P	CAPT RM(IC)	-		01.09.04	CDO LOG REGT RM
Preece, David Graeme, BA	LT CDR(FTC)	S	SM	01.08.01	FOST SM SEA
Preece, Simon Edward, BSc	LT(IC)	X		01.09.04	DULVERTON
Prendergast, Sally Ann, MSc, PGDip, FCIPD, MCIPD	LT CDR(CC)	E	TM	25.06.02	2SL/CNH FOTR
Prentice, David Charles (Act Cdr)	LT CDR(FTC)	X	PWO(C)	22.12.97	COS 2SL/CNH
Prescott, Shaun, BEng, MA, CEng, MIEE, psc(j)	CDR(FTC)	E	WE	30.06.01	FWO PORTS SEA
Pressdee, Simon John	LT(FTC)	X	MCD	01.07.98	MWS DEF DIV SCHL
Pressly, James Winchester, BSc, MA, psc(j)	LT COL(FTC)	-		30.06.05	FLEET HQ PORTS 2
Prest, Neal Andrew	LT CDR(FTC)	S	(W)	01.10.04	MANCHESTER
Prest, Stephen Frederick, MEng, MIEE	LT(CC)	E	WE	01.06.00	SUTHERLAND
Preston, Jacqueline Natalie, BSc	SLT(IC)	X	O U/T	01.01.04	DARTMOUTH BRNC
Preston, Mark Richard, BEng, CEng, MIMechE	LT CDR(FTC)	E	ME	01.10.99	FOST SEA
Preston, Ross Walker, BSc	MAJ(FTC)	-		01.09.02	CTCRM
Preston, Thomas Edward, MA	CAPT RM(CC)	-		01.09.02	40 CDO RM
Price, Andrew Michael, sq	MAJ(FTC)	-	C	01.05.97	42 CDO RM
Price, David Glyn	CAPT RM(FTC)	-	SO(LE)	01.01.01	EXCHANGE AUSTLIA
Price, David John, pce	LT CDR(FTC)	X	AAWO	01.04.93	MWC PORTSDOWN
Price, David William	CDR(FTC)	X	REG	30.06.05	NAVSEC
Price, Frederick Earle Francis, MBE, MA, MSc, MBA, PhD, CEng, Eur Ing, MIOA, MInsD, psc	CDR(FTC)	E	TM	30.06.95	MOD (LONDON)
Price, James Edward Owen, BSc	CAPT RM(CC)	-		01.09.02	29 CDO REGT RA
Price, John Philip, MA, MInsD, psc	CDR(FTC)	E	ME	30.06.96	MOD (LONDON)
Price, Joseph Charles, BSc	LT(CC)	X	MCD	05.03.01	LEDBURY
Price, Martin John, MA, psc	LT COL(FTC)	-	MLDR	31.12.98	CDO LOG REGT RM
Price, Raymond Terence	CAPT RM(CC)	-	SO(LE)	01.04.02	CTCRM
Price, Tania Lucille, BSc, MA(Ed), Cert Ed, MCIPD	LT CDR(FTC)	W	TM	01.10.92	JSCSC
Price, Terence Peter, MSc	LT CDR(FTC)	E	WE	01.10.97	FLEET HQ PORTS 2
Price, Timothy Andrew, pce, n	LT CDR(FTC)	X	AAWO	01.07.98	BROCKLESBY
Price, Tracie Evelyn, BSc	LT CDR(CC)	E	TM	01.10.02	NAVSEC
Price, Trevor William, BSc, MA, psc(j)	CDR(FTC)	X	METOC	30.06.05	FLEET HQ NWD
Price, Victoria Juliette, MB, ChB, BSc	SURG LTCDR(MCC)	-		04.08.04	MDHU FRIMLEY
Priddle, Alexandria C, BA	LT(IC)	E	TM	01.01.02	FLEET HQ PORTS
Priddle, Steven Michael R	CAPT RM(IC)	-	P	01.04.04	AACC MID WALLOP
Prideaux, Robert John	LT(IC)	E	MESM	01.07.04	SULTAN
Priest, James Edward, BEng	LT(CC)	X	P	15.02.98	848 SQN HERON
Priestley, Catherine, BSc	LT(IC)	E	TM	01.01.00	NP IRAQ
Prince, Mark Edward, BEng, CEng, MIMarE	LT CDR(FTC)	E	MESM	01.10.00	TRENCHANT
Pring, Stuart James, BA	LT(CC)	S		14.08.97	COM MCC NWD
Pringle, Anthony, pce, pcea	LT CDR(FTC)	X	P	01.07.90	MOD (LONDON)
Prinsep, Timothy John, BEng, CEng, MIEE	LT CDR(FTC)	E	WE	01.06.00	CARDIFF
Prior, Grant Michael, IEng, FIIE	CDR(FTC)	E	WE	30.06.05	MOD (BATH)
Prior, Iain Alexander	LT(FTC)	E	ME	01.04.01	MWS EXCELLENT
Prior, Kate Rebecca Edna Jane, MB, BS	SURG LTCDR(MCC)	-		06.08.02	NELSON (PAY)
Pritchard, Gavin Scrimgeour, pce	CDR(FTC)	X	PWO(U)	30.06.01	MWS COLLINGWOOD
Pritchard, Lloyd	2LT(IC)	-		01.08.00	CTCRM LYMPSTONE
Pritchard, Simon Andrew, MA, psc (Act Lt Col)	MAJ(FTC)	-		18.04.94	MWC SOUTHWICK
Procter, Jamie Edward, BEng, MSc, Cert Ed, PGDip	LT CDR(FTC)	E	TMSM	01.10.01	JSCSC
Proctor, Anna Rachael ,BM	SURG LT(MC(MD)	-		01.08.01	RH HASLAR
Proctor, Nicholas Stephen	LT(IC)	S	SM	01.05.03	UKSU JHQ NORTH
Proctor, William John Gibbon, BEng, CEng, MIEE, MSc	LT CDR(FTC)	E	WE	01.03.02	2SL/CNH FOTR
Prodger, Andrew Phillip	LT(IC)	E	WESM	01.01.03	DLO BRISTOL
Proffitt Burnham, Julia Marie, BSc	LT(CC)	E	TM	01.09.95	MWS COLLINGWOOD
Prole, Nicholas Mark	LT(CC)	X	P	16.09.97	848 SQN HERON
Prosser, Matthew James	LT(CC)	X		01.08.01	MWS COLLINGWOOD
Proud, Andrew Douglas, BEng	LT CDR(FTC)	E	AE	11.06.99	846 SQN
Proudman, Michael Paul	SLT(IC)	X		01.05.03	MWS COLLINGWOOD
Prowse, David George	LT(FTC)	E	ME	01.04.01	ENTERPRISE
Pruden, Ian, BSc	MAJ(CC)	-		01.10.04	FLEET HQ PORTS 2
Pryce, Helen Claire, BEng	LT(IC)	E	ME	01.09.04	SOMERSET
Pugh, Geoffrey Noel John, BEng	LT(IC)	X	ATCU/T	01.10.03	RNAS CULDROSE
Pugh, Jonathan, BEng	LT CDR(FTC)	E	WE	08.03.00	CAPT MCTA

Name	Rank	Branch	Spec	Seniority	Where Serving
Pullan, Keith James (Act Lt Cdr)	LT(CC)	X	H1	29.06.96	DGIA
Pulvertaft, Rupert James, odc(Fr)	LT COL(FTC)	-		30.06.03	EUMS
Punch, John Matthew, BSc	LT(CC)	X	P	01.01.01	845 SQN
Punton, Ian Matthew, BEng, CEng, MRAeS, psc(j) (Act Cdr)	LT CDR(FTC)	E	AE	01.09.99	20(R) SQN (RN)
Purdy, Richard John	LT(IC)	E	AE	01.09.04	DLO YEO
Purvis, David Mark, MEng	LT CDR(FTC)	E	AE	16.10.04	815 FLT 207
Purvis, Stephen Graham	SLT(IC)	X		01.05.02	BROCKLESBY
Puxley, Michael Edward, BEng, CEng	LT CDR(FTC)	E	WESM	01.09.04	MOD (LONDON)
Pye, Philip Martin	LT CDR(FTC)	S	CA	01.10.98	JHCHQ
Pyette, Marc Daniel Victor Crosby, BA, MSc	SLT(IC)	X		01.02.04	DARTMOUTH BRNC
Pyne, Robert Leslie, BA, DipTh	CHAPLAIN	CE		23.01.90	SULTAN

Q

Name	Rank	Branch	Spec	Seniority	Where Serving
Quade, Nicholas Alexander Clive, BEng	LT(FTC)	E	MESM	01.10.97	NP IRAQ
Quaite, David Geoffrey, BSc	LT(IC)	X		01.01.03	MWS HM TG (D)
Quantrill, Steven William, BSc (Act Lt Cdr)	LT(CC)	S		01.03.97	AFPAA HQ
Quaye, Duncan Thomas George, MSc, CEng, FIMarEST	CDR(FTC)	E	ME	30.06.98	DFTE PORTSMOUTH
Quekett, Ian Peter Scott, BEng, MSc, MIEE, psc(j)	LT CDR(FTC)	E	WE	01.08.99	MOD (LONDON)
Quemby, Sarah Elizabeth	LT(MC(MD)	Q		20.02.03	RN GIBRALTAR
Quick, Benjamin Paul, BSc	SLT(IC)	X		01.06.03	DARTMOUTH BRNC
Quick, Neville Hellins, BSc, CEng, MIEE	LT CDR(FTC)	E	WE	01.05.91	FLEET CIS PORTS
Quick, Stephen James, BA	LT(IC)	X		01.05.01	LEEDS CASTLE
Quine, Nicholas John, MA, MIEE, psc	LT CDR(FTC)	E	WE	01.12.88	RMC OF SCIENCE
Quinn, Antony David, BSc, PGDip	LT(IC)	E	TM	01.07.00	MWS COLLINGWOOD
Quinn, Mark Eugene, MSc	LT(IC)	E	IS	01.03.00	DCCIS BLANDFORD
Quinn, Michael Gerard, BA	LT(IC)	X	FC	01.01.02	INVINCIBLE
Quinn, Paul Anthony, BA, FCMI, FHCIMA, FCIPD, MHCIMA, MInstPS, CDipAF, jsdc	CAPT(FTC)	S	SM	30.06.00	FLEET HQ PORTS
Quinn, Shaun Andrew, pcea	LT CDR(FTC)	X	O	01.10.04	UN AFRICA
Quirk, Anthony Thomas, IEng	LT(FTC)	E	WE	02.09.99	DSFM PORTSMOUTH

R

Name	Rank	Branch	Spec	Seniority	Where Serving
Raby, Nigel John Francis, OBE, MSc, jsdc (STLB MERGER PROJECT TEAM LEADER SEP 04)	RADM	-	WE	02.09.04	FLEET HQ PORTS
Race, Nigel James, MA, pce, psc(j)	CDR(FTC)	X	PWO(C)	31.12.99	RN SINGAPORE
Rackham, Anthony David Henry, BSc	LT CDR(FTC)	X	PWO(A)	01.10.02	MWS COLLINGWOOD
Rackham, Katharine, BSc, n	LT CDR(FTC)	X		01.03.05	TEMERAIRE
Radakin, Antony David, LLB, pce, psc(j), MA	CDR(FTC)	X	PWO(U)	30.06.02	MOD (LONDON)
Radbourne, Neville Ian	LT CDR(FTC)	E	WE	01.10.02	HQ DCSA
Radford, Andrew James, BEng	LT(CC)	X	P	01.06.92	846 SQN
Rae, Alistair Lewis, BEng, CEng, MIEE	LT CDR(FTC)	E	WE	01.04.05	CSIS IPT
Rae, Anthony James William, BSc, pcea (Act Cdr)	LT CDR(FTC)	X	P	01.10.99	801 SQN
Rae, Derek Gordon, BSc, PGDip	LT CDR(FTC)	X	H1	01.03.04	MWS COLLINGWOOD
Rae, Scott MacKenzie, MBE, BD	CHAPLAIN	SF		02.02.81	2SL/CNH
Rae, Stephen Gordon, AGSM	LT CDR(FTC)	S		01.02.00	MOD (BATH)
Raeburn, Craig, BSc, SM(n)	LT(FTC)	X	SM	01.09.96	MANCHESTER
Raeburn, Mark, n	LT CDR(FTC)	X	PWO(N)	01.07.02	MWS COLLINGWOOD
Raffaelli, Philip Iain, MSc, MB, BCH, MRCGP, FFOM, rcds, jsdc (CHIEF EXECUTIVE MAY 04)	SURG RADM	-	CPDATE	04.05.04	HQ DMETA
Rainey, Owen (Act Surg Lt)	SURG SLT(SCC)	-		06.07.04	DARTMOUTH BRNC
Ralls, Damien William, BEng	LT(IC)	E	WESM	01.09.04	SUPERB
Ralston, William Archibald, BSc, PGCE	LT(IC)	E	TM U/T	01.01.02	SULTAN
Ramaswami, Ravi, MB, BS (Act Surg Cdr)	SURG LTCDR(SC(MD)	-	(CO/M)	27.07.96	INM ALVERSTOKE
Ramm, Steven Charles, pce, pce(sm), psc	CAPT(FTC)	X	SM	31.12.98	JSCSC
Ramsay, Alastair, BSc	LT(IC)	E	TM	01.07.02	RALEIGH
Ramsey, Jeremy Stephen, BSc	LT CDR(FTC)	S		16.04.89	AFPAA JPA
Ramsey, Ryan Trevor, pce(sm), SM(n)	LT CDR(FTC)	X	SM	01.11.00	FOST SM SEA
Ramshaw, George William Lilwall, BSc, MDA, CEng, FCMI, MIEE	CDR(FTC)	E	WE	30.06.99	FLEET HQ PORTS 2
Rance, Maxwell George William, MA, psc(j)	CDR(FTC)	S		31.12.99	DARTMOUTH BRNC
Rand, Marc James, BEng, MSc	LT CDR(FTC)	E	ME	01.05.01	NOTTINGHAM
Rand, Mark Andrew	LT(CC)	E	WESM	01.01.02	NEPTUNE BNSL

Name	Rank	Branch	Spec	Seniority	Where Serving
Rand, Mark Conrad	CAPT RM(IC)	-		24.07.04	1 ASSAULT GP RM
Randall, David Frederick, BA, MSc	CDR(FTC)	S		30.06.02	AFPAA JPA
Randall, Richard David, BSc, MDA, CEng, MIMechE	CDR(FTC)	E	MESM	30.06.03	MOD (LONDON)
Randle, Martin Philip, MB, CHB, FRCSEd, MRCOG, JCPTGP (Act Surg Cdr)	SURG LTCDR(SC(MD)	-	GMPP	01.09.95	MWS COLLINGWOOD
Randles, Steven, BA	LT(CC)	X		01.06.00	ARGYLL
Rankin, Graham Johnathon	LT(IC)	X	PWO(A)	01.09.01	PORTLAND
Rankin, Suzanne Jayne	LT CDR(FC(MD)	Q	ONC	01.10.03	NELSON (PAY)
Rankine, Ivor Matthew	LT(FTC)	E	MESM	19.06.98	VENGEANCE(PORT)
Ransom, Benjamin Robert James	LT(IC)	X		01.09.00	TYNE
Ranson, Christopher David, MSc, DipFM, CEng, MIEE	CDR(FTC)	E	WE	30.06.99	CAPT MCTA
Rant, Oliver James, BA, SM(n), SM	LT(IC)	X	SM	01.01.00	FLEET HQ NWD
Rapp, James Campsie, pce, pcea, psc (T200SL AUG 04)	RADM	-	O	20.11.01	COS 2SL/CNH
Rasor, Andrew Martin, pcea	LT CDR(FTC)	X	P	01.10.04	845 SQN
Ratcliffe, John Paul, BSc, PGDip (Act Capt)	CDR(FTC)	E	TM	30.06.92	DISC
Rawal, Krishna Mark, MB, BS, DObstRCOG	SURG CDR(MCC)	-	GMPP	30.06.05	HQ 3 CDO BDE RM
Rawles, Julian Roy (Act Lt Cdr)	LT(FTC)	X	ATC	01.04.99	CHFHQ
Rawlings, Damian Paul, BEng, MDA	LT CDR(FTC)	E	ME	01.08.95	FLEET HQ PORTS
Rawlings, Gary Andrew	LT(FTC)	E	ME	01.04.01	ECHO
Rawlins, Simon Terence	LT(CC)	X	P	01.04.02	LOAN OTHER SVCE
Rawlinson, Kathryn Elizabeth	SLT(IC)	X		01.05.03	BLYTH
Rawlinson, Stephen James, BEng, CEng, MIMarEST	LT CDR(FTC)	E	MESM	01.03.99	MANCHESTER
Rawson, Scott Michael, BEng	LT CDR(FTC)	E	MESM	01.04.03	DLO BRISTOL
Ray, Benjamin Timothy, BEng	SLT(IC)	E	WE U/T	01.01.04	DARTMOUTH BRNC
Ray, Louise Barbara, LLB	LT(IC)	X		01.08.04	MANCHESTER
Raybould, Adrian Glyn, MA, MSc, CEng, MIEE, psc(j)	CDR(FTC)	E	WESM	30.06.01	FLEET CIS PORTS
Rayner, Andrew, BEng, MSc, MIEE	LT CDR(FTC)	E	WE	01.12.00	PORTLAND
Rayner, Brett Nicholas, psc	CAPT(FTC)	S		30.06.99	HQ SACT
Raynes, Christopher, BSc	LT(CC)	X	P	16.09.98	848 SQN HERON
Raynor, Sean David	LT(FTC)	E	WE	04.09.98	COS 2SL/CNH
Rea, Maria Elizabeth	LT(SC(MD)	Q		01.10.03	RH HASLAR
Rea, Stephen Dennis	LT(CC)	X		01.07.00	YORK
Read, Alun John	LT CDR(FTC(A)	X	P	01.10.04	DHFS
Read, Clinton Derek (Act Maj)	CAPT RM(FTC)	-		01.05.00	CTCRM
Read, Jonathon Asher Jason Marcus, MB, BS	SURG LTCDR(MC(MD)	-	O U/T	04.08.04	MDHU DERRIFORD
Read, Paul Steven, BEng, MSc gw, CEng, MIEE	LT(FTC)	E	WE	01.03.97	LOAN DSTL
Read, Richard John, BA	MAJ(FTC)	-	LC	01.09.02	FLEET HQ PORTS 2
Readwin, Roger Roy, BA	LT CDR(FTC)	X	PWO(A)	01.04.04	MONMOUTH
Reah, Stephen, BEng	LT CDR(FTC)	E	ME	02.05.00	FLEET HQ PORTS 2
Rearden, Richard Joseph	MAJ(FTC)	-	SO(LE)	01.10.03	JSCSC
Reaves, Charles Edward, LLB	LT(IC)	S		01.01.03	RALEIGH
Redding, Andrew Mark	LT(IC)	MS		01.07.04	RH HASLAR
Redman, Charles Jeremy Rufus, n	LT CDR(FTC)	X		23.11.98	OCEAN
Redman, Christopher Douglas Jeremy, BDS, MSc, LDS RCS(Eng), MGDS RCS, MFDS,RCS	SGCDR(D)(FCC)	-		31.12.00	EXCHANGE USA
Redman, Rachel ,BMus	LT(IC)	E	TM	01.04.02	FWO DEVPT SEA
Redmayne, Mark Edward, BA	LT(CC)	X		01.06.99	GIBRALTAR PBS
Redmayne, Michael Julian, BSc	LT(IC)	X	H2	01.01.03	NP 1016 IN SURV
Redstone, Colin	CDR(FTC)	S	SM	31.12.98	PJHQ
Reece, Nigel David, BEng, MSc, CEng, MIMechE	LT CDR(FTC)	E	MESM	01.03.00	CNNRP BRISTOL
Reed, Andrew William, OBE, BSc, pce	CDR(FTC)	X	AAWO	31.12.00	EXETER
Reed, Darren Keith, BA, PGDipL	LT CDR(FTC)	S		01.12.04	2SL/CNH
Reed, Edward Christopher Dominic	2LT(IC)	-		01.09.00	45 CDO RM
Reed, Frank, OBE, BA, MSc, psc	CDRE(FTC)	MS	(P)	12.06.02	INM ALVERSTOKE
Reed, James Hamilton, pce, pcea, psc(j)o	LT CDR(FTC)	X	P	01.04.95	JDCC
Reed, Jeremy Jameson, BSc	MAJ(CC)	-		01.01.01	JACIG
Reed, Jonathan Charles	LT CDR(FTC)	E	AE	01.10.02	RNAS CULDROSE
Reed, Mark, BSc, PGDip	LT CDR(FTC)	X	METOC	01.10.98	ILLUSTRIOUS
Reed, Nicholas	LT CDR(FTC)	S	SM	01.10.04	RALEIGH
Reed, Peter Kirby	SLT(UCE)(IC)	E	ME	01.09.01	DARTMOUTH BRNC
Rees, Adam Martin, BA, MSc	LT(IC)	E	TM	01.09.98	FLEET HQ PORTSEA
Rees, Daniel Simon James, LLB	LT(IC)	X	SM	01.12.02	TURBULENT

Name	Rank	Branch	Spec	Seniority	Where Serving
Rees, John Blain Minto, BSc, jsdc	CAPT(FTC)	E	TM	31.12.99	2SL/CNH FOTR
Rees, John Patrick, MSc	LT CDR(FTC)	S		29.06.99	ADAS BRISTOL
Rees, Justin Harrington, BSc, MCIT, MILT, ACIS	CDR(FTC)	S		01.07.00	DLO/DG DEF SC
Rees, Karen Margaret Mary, LLB	LT(CC)	S		01.10.99	DARTMOUTH BRNC
Rees, Paul Stuart Chadwick, MB, BS, MRCP, DipIMC RCSED	SURG LTCDR(MCC)	-		06.08.02	NELSON (PAY)
Rees, Richard Matthews, BSc	LT(IC)	X		01.08.04	LEDBURY
Rees, Richard Thomas, BEng, n	LT CDR(FTC)	X	PWO(U)	01.12.03	NORTHUMBERLAND
Rees, Simon Geoffrey	SLT(IC)	X		01.12.02	SUPERB
Reese, David Michael, BSc	LT CDR(FTC)	X	O	01.09.02	LOAN OTHER SVCE
Reeves, Andrew Philip, SM(n)	LT(CC)	X	SM	01.01.03	RALEIGH
Reeves, Paul Keith	LT(CC)	E	MESM	01.08.00	TIRELESS
Reid, Benjamin William	2LT(IC)	-		01.09.00	40 CDO RM
Reid, Charles Ian, BSc, pce, pce(sm), psc(j)	CDR(FTC)	X	SM	31.12.99	MOD (LONDON)
Reid, Douglas Russell	LT(IC)	X	AV	01.07.04	RFANSU
Reid, James Lyle, BSc	LT(CC)	X		01.05.00	BULWARK
Reid, James Robert, BA	SLT(IC)	X		01.11.04	DARTMOUTH BRNC
Reid, Jason Charles James, BEng, CEng, MIEE	LT CDR(FTC)	E	WESM	01.04.01	SUPERB
Reid, Joseph Anthony William, MSc	SLT(IC)	X	O U/T	01.05.02	RNAS CULDROSE
Reid, Martyn, pce, pcea, psc	CDR(FTC)	X	O	30.06.94	SHAPE BELGIUM
Reid, Martyn Richard	LT(CC)	X		01.04.95	ILLUSTRIOUS
Reidy, Paul Alan, pce(sm), SM	LT CDR(FTC)	X	SM	01.11.98	MOD (LONDON)
Reilly, John	SURG SLT(SCC)	-		20.09.04	DARTMOUTH BRNC
Reilly, Paul, BA	LT(IC)	E	TM U/T	08.06.04	ALBION
Reindorp, David Peter, PGDIPAN, AFRIN, pce	CDR(FTC)	X	PWO(N)	30.06.02	JSCSC
Relf, Elizabeth Mary	LT(IC)	X	O U/T	01.05.05	RNAS CULDROSE
Relf, Kerry Marie, BA	LT(CC)	S		01.07.99	AGRIPPA MAR CC
Renaud, Gavin Andrew Richard	LT(CC)	X	O	16.10.01	771 SQN
Rendell, Derrick John, MSc (Act Lt Cdr)	LT(FTC)	E	MESM	14.06.96	SPLENDID
Rennie, James Gibson	LT(CS)RM(CAS)	-		18.09.98	DNR W CENTRAL
Rennie, Richard Anthony	SURG SLT(SCC)	-		01.07.03	DARTMOUTH BRNC
Renshaw, Paul	CAPT RM(IC)	-		01.09.04	40 CDO RM
Renwick, John	CDR(FTC)	S	SM	30.06.02	MOD (LONDON)
Reston, Samuel Craig, MB, ChB	SURG LTCDR(FCC)	-		07.08.01	NELSON (PAY)
Retter, Rachael Louise, BA	LT(IC)	X	H2	01.07.00	GLEANER
Revell, Aaron Daniel	MID(IC)	X		01.09.03	MONMOUTH
Rex, Colin Antony	LT(CC)	X	P	01.10.99	848 SQN HERON
Reynolds, Andrew Charles James, BEng	LT(IC)	E	ME	01.09.02	JSCSC
Reynolds, Andrew Graham, BEng, MSc, CEng, MIMechE, MCGI	CDR(FTC)	E	ME	30.06.04	BDS WASHINGTON
Reynolds, Ben K M	CAPT RM(IC)	-		01.09.04	CDO LOG REGT RM
Reynolds, Darren Paul	SLT(IC)	E	WE	01.01.04	MWS COLLINGWOOD
Reynolds, Huw Francis, BEng	LT(CC)	E	P	01.03.02	702 SQN HERON
Reynolds, James	LT(IC)	X		01.01.03	CUMBERLAND
Reynolds, Mark Edward, BEng	LT(FTC)	E	ME	01.09.03	NOTTINGHAM
Reynolds, Matthew Jowan	LT(CC)	X		01.05.01	MWS SOUTHWICK PK
Reynolds, Timothy Edward, MA	CDR(FTC)	X	METOC	30.06.98	RMC OF SCIENCE
Reynolds, Timothy Paul, BSc, MDA	LT CDR(FTC)	E	IS	30.04.95	CTCRM
Reynolds, Zoe Anne	LT(IC)	X		01.12.03	TYNE
Rhodes, Andrew Gregory, BEng, psc(j)o	CDR(FTC)	E	WE	30.06.02	BDS WASHINGTON
Rhodes, Andrew William	LT(FTC)	E	WE	01.04.01	NCSA SECTOR NWD
Rhodes, Martin James, MSc, gdas	LT CDR(FTC)	X	O	01.10.04	MOD (LONDON)
Rhodes, Paul Edwin, MCGI (Act Maj)	CAPT RM(CC)	-	SO(LE)	21.07.01	FLEET HQ PORTS 2
Rich, David Charles, pce(sm), pce	LT CDR(FTC)	X	SM	20.05.97	MWC PORTSDOWN
Rich, Jonathan George, MA, MIPD, MCIPD, pcea, psc(j)	CDR(FTC)	X	P	30.06.04	COS 2SL/CNH
Richards, Adam Vivian, BA	LT(IC)	X		01.03.99	OCLC BRISTOL
Richards, Alan David, jsdc, pce, pcea	CDRE(FTC)	X	P	24.06.02	MOD (LONDON)
Richards, Anthony Jeremy	LT(CC)	S	SM	01.10.00	JSCSC
Richards, Christopher Martin, pce, psc	CAPT(FTC)	X	AAWO	30.06.04	UKMARBATSTAFF
Richards, Fraser Charles, SM	LT CDR(FTC)	X	SM	01.10.03	MOD DIS SEA
Richards, Guy Benjamin	LT(IC)	S		01.01.04	COM MCC NWD
Richards, James Ian Hanson, BEng, CEng	LT CDR(FTC)	E	WESM	01.10.04	FOST FAS SHORE
Richards, Paul, BSc, MIIE	LT(CC)	E	ME	29.04.01	RALEIGH
Richards, Simon Timothy	LT(CC)	X	O	16.02.04	849 SQN B FLT
Richards, Stephen William, psc(j)	MAJ(FTC)	-	SO(LE)	01.10.99	COMAMPHIBFOR

Name	Rank	Branch	Spec	Seniority	Where Serving
Richards, Steven Charles Arthur	LT(CC)	E	WE	01.01.02	MWS EXCELLENT
Richardson, Adrian Paul	LT(CC)	E	WESM	01.01.01	VIGILANT(PORT)
Richardson, Benjamin	2LT(IC)	-		01.08.04	CTCRM LYMPSTONE
Richardson, David MacBeth	MID(NE)(IC)	X		01.09.04	YORK
Richardson, Gary	LT(IC)	X		18.02.05	MERSEY
Richardson, Gavin Andrew, BSc, pcea	LT CDR(FTC)	X	O	01.10.01	824 SQN
Richardson, Geoffrey Leslie, BSc	LT CDR(FTC)	X	P	01.10.02	848 SQN HERON
Richardson, George Nicholas, BA	LT CDR(FTC)	S		01.07.01	MOD (BATH)
Richardson, Ian Hayden	LT(CC)	X	MCD	01.03.00	FOST MPV SEA
Richardson, John Francis, BEng	LT(IC)	X		01.09.04	EDINBURGH
Richardson, Mark Anthony, BSc	LT CDR(FTC)	E	IS	01.09.97	AFPAA JPA
Richardson, Mark Francis	LT(IC)	X		13.08.04	MWS COLLINGWOOD
Richardson, Michael Colin (Act Maj)	CAPT RM(FTC)	-	SO(LE)	01.01.95	RMDIV LECONFIELD
Richardson, Michael Peter, FHCIMA	CDR(FTC)	S		30.06.97	FLEET HQ PORTS
Richardson, Peter	LT CDR(FTC)	X	P	01.10.02	848 SQN HERON
Richardson, Peter Stephen Mark, BEng, MIEE	LT CDR(FTC)	E	WE	01.08.99	FLEET HQ PORTS
Richardson, Philip Charles, BSc	LT(FTC)	X	P	01.03.98	815 FLT 228
Richardson, Sophie Charlotte, BA	LT(FTC)	S		01.09.03	702 SQN HERON
Riches, Anthony Ian, BA	LT(IC)	X		01.05.03	PEMBROKE
Riches, Ian Charles, pce(sm)	CDR(FTC)	X	SM	30.06.04	DLO BRISTOL
Richman, Paul George, BA	LT(CC)	X	P	16.11.97	848 SQN HERON
Richmond, Iain James Martin, BA, pce, pcea	CDR(FTC)	X	P	31.12.96	MOD (LONDON)
Richter, Alwyn Stafford Byron, BEng, CEng, MIEE	LT CDR(FTC)	E	WE	01.09.00	SCU SHORE
Rickard, Jack, BSc	LT(CC)	S	SM	12.11.97	CAPT IST STAFF
Rickard, Rory Frederick, MB, BCh, BAO, FRCSEd	SURG CDR(FCC)	-		30.06.04	NELSON (PAY)
Riddett, Adam Owen, BSc	LT(IC)	X		01.09.02	ST ALBANS
Rider, John Charles Raymon, BSc, n, SM(n)	LT(CC)	X	SM	01.01.02	TIRELESS
Ridge, Mervyn Henry	LT CDR(FTC)	E	WESM	01.10.04	DLO BRISTOL
Ridgwell, Daniel Robert, BEng	SLT(IC)	E	ME U/T	01.09.02	MANCHESTER
Ridley, George Edward	MID(IC)	X	P U/T	01.02.04	DARTMOUTH BRNC
Ridley, Jon	CAPT RM(IC)	-	SO(LE)	24.07.04	MWS RM SCH MUSIC
Rigby, Jeremy Conrad, MA, MILDM, psc(j)	CDR(FTC)	S		31.12.00	BULWARK
Riggall, Andrew Derek	LT CDR(FTC)	X	P	01.10.03	702 SQN HERON
Riggs, Matthew George Winston, BA	LT(IC)	S		01.01.04	ILLUSTRIOUS
Riley, Graeme Alexander	LT(FTC)	E	MESM	14.06.96	TALENT
Riley, Michael Jaeger, BSc, jsdc, pce	CDR(FTC)	X	AAWO	31.12.93	JSCSC
Riley, Ralph Aidan, BA	LT(IC)	X	O	01.01.04	824 SQN
Rimington, Anthony Kingsmill, BA	LT CDR(FTC)	X	P	01.10.03	MWS COLLINGWOOD
Rimmer, Heather Elizabeth, BA, psc(j)	LT CDR(FTC)	E	TM	22.07.96	FLEET HQ PORTS
Rimmer, Owen Francis, BA, SM(n)	LT(CC)	X	SM	01.01.02	TRAFALGAR
Rimmer, Robin	LT CDR(FTC)	E	WE	01.10.98	DFTE PORTSMOUTH
Riordan, Shaun Paul	SLT(UCE)(IC)	E	WE U/T	01.09.03	DARTMOUTH BRNC
Ripley, Benjamin Edward, n	LT CDR(FTC)	X	PWO(U)	01.11.02	MWS COLLINGWOOD
Ripley, Stephen	LT(IC)	E	WE	01.07.04	GLOUCESTER
Rippingale, Stuart Nicholas, MSc, PGCE	CDR(FTC)	E	IS	30.06.05	AFPAA(CENTURION)
Risdall, Jane Elizabeth, MA, MB, BS, FFARCSI	SURG CDR(FCC)	-	(CA)	31.12.98	MDHU PETERBRGH
Risley, James Grant, BEng	LT(CC)	E	MESM	01.02.00	SULTAN
Risley, Jonathan, BSc, MA, CEng, MBCS, CITP, CDipAF, adp	CDR(FTC)	E	IS	31.12.00	HQ SACT
Ritchie, Douglas Brian	LT(CC)	E	MESM	01.09.01	SULTAN
Ritchie, Iain David, BSc	LT(IC)	X	HM	01.08.02	RAF WITTERING
Ritchie, John Noble, SM	LT CDR(FTC)	X	SM	01.04.02	BDS WASHINGTON
Ritchie, William James, MSc, sq (Act Lt Col)	MAJ(FTC)	-	SO(LE)	01.10.97	FLEET CIS PORTS
Ritson, Jonathan	SURG SLT(SCC)	-		19.10.03	DARTMOUTH BRNC
Ritsperis, Athos, MAPM, MSc, DIC, PGCE, MIEE, MBCS, MIL, ACGI, ARCS	LT(CC)	E	IS	01.01.92	RNEAWC
Rix, Anthony John, ADC, pce, psc (Commodore)	CAPT(FTC)	X	PWO(U)	30.06.97	UKMARBATSTAFF
Robb, Michael Edward, BA	LT(CC)	S		01.08.97	COS 2SL/CNH
Robbins, Harry Vincent	CAPT RM(CC)	-	P	01.01.02	846 SQN
Robbins, Jeremy Matthew Francis, MBE, BSc, psc(m), hcsc	COL(FTC)	-	C	30.06.99	HQ 3 CDO BDE RM
Robbins, Margaret Joy, psc	CDR(FTC)	W	C	31.12.92	MWS EXCELLENT
Robert, Iain Andrew	LT(CC)	E	AE	29.04.01	MERLIN IPT
Roberts, Andrew Paul, BEng	LT(IC)	E	AE	01.05.02	SULTAN
Roberts, Benjamin, BA	LT(IC)	S		01.09.03	ARGYLL
Roberts, Daniel Llewellyn	SLT(UCE)(IC)	E	MESM	01.09.03	DARTMOUTH BRNC

Name	Rank	Branch	Spec	Seniority	Where Serving
Roberts, David Alan, pce	LT CDR(FTC)	X	PWO(A)	01.05.92	COM MCC NWD
Roberts, David Howard Wyn, BA, pce	LT CDR(FTC)	X	AAWO	01.04.91	JCTS IPT
Roberts, David Stephen, BSc	SLT(IC)	X		01.11.03	DARTMOUTH BRNC
Roberts, Dean, BEng	LT CDR(FTC)	E	WE	04.04.99	FOST SEA
Roberts, Ellis William	LT CDR(FTC)	E	AE	01.10.95	RNAS YEOVILTON
Roberts, Iain Gordon, BSc, BEng	LT CDR(FTC)	E	WESM	01.10.03	HQ DCSA
Roberts, Ian Thomas, OBE, pce(sm), psc(j), MA	CDR(FTC)	X	SM	30.06.02	VIGILANT(STBD)
Roberts, Kenneth Eric, BEng, MSc, CEng, MIEE, gw	LT CDR(FTC)	E	WE	01.01.99	MOD (LONDON)
Roberts, Martin Alan	LT(FTC)	X	O	01.11.94	750 SQN SEAHAWK
Roberts, Martyn, BEng	LT CDR(FTC)	X	O	01.10.02	RNAS YEOVILTON
Roberts, Michael John, LLB	LT(IC)	S		01.09.04	824 SQN
Roberts, Nicholas Steven, BEng, MSc, Hf, psc(j)	CDR(FTC)	E	WE	30.06.99	MOD (LONDON)
Roberts, Nigel David	LT(CC)	X	O	10.02.98	702 SQN HERON
Roberts, Nikke	LT(CC)	S		01.07.00	NELSON
Roberts, Peter Andrew	CAPT RM(IC)	-		01.04.04	1 ASSAULT GP RM
Roberts, Peter Stafford	LT CDR(FTC)	X	AAWO	01.10.01	COS 2SL/CNH
Roberts, Selvin Clive, BEng	LT CDR(FTC)	E	MESM	01.10.99	NEPTUNE DLO
Roberts, Stephen David, BEng, MSc, CEng, MIEE, psc(j)	CDR(FTC)	E	WE	30.06.03	LOAN DSTL
Roberts, Stephen Mark	SLT(IC)	X	ATCU/T	01.02.03	RAF SHAWBURY
Roberts, Suzi	LT(IC)	S		23.03.03	CHATHAM
Roberts, Timothy John, BEng, MSc	CDR(FTC)	E	MESM	30.06.03	DLO BRISTOL
Robertshaw, Ian Weston, BEng, CEng	LT CDR(FTC)	E	WESM	01.04.04	MWC PORTSDOWN
Robertson, Adam Joseph	SLT(IC)	E	WE	01.09.02	MWS COLLINGWOOD
Robertson, David Cameron, BSc, PGDIPAN, MRIN, pce, n	CDR(FTC)	X	H CH	30.06.05	JSCSC
Robertson, Douglas Malcolm, BSc	LT CDR(FTC)	X	ATC	01.10.93	CV(F) IPT
Robertson, Frederick William, MBE, pcea (Act Cdr)	LT CDR(FTC)	X	P	01.03.86	CHFHQ
Robertson, Ian Wallace, BEng	LT(IC)	E	WE	01.08.03	YORK
Robertson, Kevin Francis, pce	CDR(FTC)	X	PWO(C)	30.06.98	SCU SHORE
Robertson, Michael George, BSc, pce, psc(j)	CDR(FTC)	X	O	30.06.03	SULTAN AIB
Robertson, Neil Bannerman, psc(j)	MAJ(FTC)	-		01.05.00	45 CDO RM
Robertson, Paul Noel, LLB, pcea	LT CDR(FTC)	X	O	01.10.00	LOAN JTEG BSC DN
Robertson, Stuart Thomas, BA	LT(CC)	S	SM	01.03.99	HARRIER IPT
Robertson Gopffarth, Alexander Alistair John, BSc, SM(n)	LT CDR(FTC)	X	SM	01.02.05	FWO FASLANE
Robey, James Christopher	LT(CC)	X		01.10.00	MWS SOUTHWICK PK
Robey, Stephanie Jane	LT(IC)	X		01.08.01	MWS COLLINGWOOD
Robin, Christopher Charles Edward, pce, pcea, psc(j)	LT CDR(FTC)	X	P	01.09.94	FLEET HQ PORTS 2
Robin, Julie Isobel, MB, ChB	SURG LT(MCC)	-		02.08.00	NELSON (PAY)
Robinson, Andrew, BSc, jsdc	CDR(FTC)	X	METOC	30.06.97	COS 2SL/CNH
Robinson, Andrew (Act Lt Cdr)	LT(FTC)	MS		01.04.01	HQ DMETA
Robinson, Charles Edward Thayne, pce, psc(j), MA	CDR(FTC)	X	PWO(U)	30.06.99	MOD (LONDON)
Robinson, Christopher Paul, MBE, pce, pcea, psc (Act Capt)	CDR(FTC)	X	O	31.12.87	MOD (LONDON)
Robinson, David	LT(IC)	S		01.10.02	EXETER
Robinson, David Ian, MSc, MIEE, psc, gw	LT CDR(FTC)	E	WE	01.02.84	T45 IPT
Robinson, Guy Antony, MA, pce, psc(j)	CDR(FTC)	X	PWO(A)	30.06.02	MOD (LONDON)
Robinson, Lee David	LT(IC)	E	WESM	01.07.04	VIGILANT(PORT)
Robinson, Matthew Steven	LT(IC)	X	P	01.05.04	820 SQN
Robinson, Michael	SURG SLT(SCC)	-		16.09.04	DARTMOUTH BRNC
Robinson, Michael Peter, MA, MSc, CEng, MIMarEST, psc(j)	CDR(FTC)	E	MESM	30.06.02	DLO BRISTOL
Robinson, Paul Henry, pce, pce(sm)	CDRE(FTC)	X	SM	30.09.03	JSCSC
Robinson, Paul James, BA	SLT(IC)	S		01.09.02	RALEIGH
Robinson, Philip James Owen, BSc	CAPT RM(CC)	-		01.09.01	CTCRM
Robinson, Pollyanna, BEng	LT(CC)	E	AE	01.01.00	COS 2SL/CNH
Robinson, Richard John	LT(FTC)	X	ATC	01.04.01	FOST DPORT SHORE
Robinson, Steven Leslie, BEng	LT(FTC)	E	WE	01.01.01	HQ DCSA
Robinson, Timothy George (Act Surg Lt)	SURG SLT(SCC)	-		20.07.04	DARTMOUTH BRNC
Robison, Garry Stuart, ADC, MPhil, psc(m), psc(j), hcsc	BRIG(FTC)	-		15.09.03	CTCRM
Robley, William Forster	LT(FTC)	X	P	01.06.96	771 SQN A FLT
Robson, Christine Jane	LT CDR(FCC)	Q	IC/CC	01.10.00	HQ DMETA
Rochester, Andrew David, BSc	CAPT RM(CC)	-		01.09.02	40 CDO RM
Rochester, Richard William	MAJ(IC)	-	LC	01.10.04	BULWARK
Roddy, Michael Patrick, MBE, BSc, psc(j)o	MAJ(FTC)	-		27.04.02	PJHQ
Rodgers, Darren	LT(CC)	X	P	01.07.93	LOAN OTHER SVCE
Rodgers, Steven	CDR(FTC)	E	WE	30.06.04	FLEET HQ PORTS

Name	Rank	Branch	Spec	Seniority	Where Serving
Roe, Roma Jane	LT(IC)	E	AE	01.07.04	820 SQN
Roffey, Kevin David, BEng	LT(IC)	E	AE	01.09.04	846 SQN
Rogers, Alan	LT CDR(FTC)	X	AV	01.10.01	792 NAS(SEA)
Rogers, Andrew Gavin, BEng, MDA, CEng, MIEE (Act Cdr)	LT CDR(FTC)	E	WE	01.02.98	MTS IPT
Rogers, Christopher Mark, BEng, PGDip, CEng, MIEE	LT CDR(FTC)	E	WE	01.06.00	FLEET HQ PORTS 2
Rogers, Julia Ann	LT(CC)	X	P	01.08.99	JSCSC
Rogers, Julian Charles Everard, SM	LT CDR(FTC)	X	SM	01.03.03	FOST DSTF
Rogers, Malcolm Stuart, BSc, AMIEE	CDR(FTC)	E	TM	30.06.90	2SL/CNH FOTR
Rogers, Matthew Stideford, BA	SLT(IC)	X		01.01.03	PORTLAND
Rogers, Orlando	2LT(IC)	-		01.09.03	42 CDO RM
Rogers, Philip Scott, BSc (Act Lt Cdr)	LT(CC)	E	TM	01.01.95	NP IRAQ
Rogers, Simon James Peter, BA	LT(FTC)	X		01.07.98	JSCSC
Rogers, Simon Milward, BSc	CAPT RM(CC)	-		01.09.02	CTCRM
Rogers, Stella Monica, BEd	LT(IC)	S	TM	01.09.03	NELSON
Rogers, Timothy Hugh Goddard	LT CDR(FTC)	X		04.12.98	DARTMOUTH BRNC
Rogerson, Alison Elizabeth ,BMus	SLT(IC)	S		01.05.03	CUMBERLAND
Rollason, Caroline Anne	LT(CC)	S		01.11.00	DARTMOUTH BRNC
Rolls, Edward Christopher, BSc	SLT(IC)	X		01.01.03	RNAS YEOVILTON
Rolph, Andrew Peter Mark, pce	CDR(FTC)	X	PWO(C)	30.06.04	MWS COLLINGWOOD
Rom, Stephen Paul, IEng, MIIE	LT(FTC)	E	WE	02.09.99	JSCSC
Romney, Paul David, PGDIPAN, MRIN, pce	LT CDR(FTC)	X	PWO(U)	01.01.98	FOST SEA
Ronald, Euan Taylor, BSc	LT(IC)	X		01.05.03	RNAS YEOVILTON
Rook, David John	LT CDR(FTC)	E	WE	01.10.96	2SL/CNH FOTR
Rook, Graeme Inglis, BSc, CEng, MIEE	LT CDR(FTC)	E	WE	01.04.98	FLEET CIS PORTS
Rooke, Adam Edward, MEng	SLT(IC)	E	MESMUT	01.09.03	INVINCIBLE
Rooke, Kate Elizabeth, MEng	SLT(IC)	E	AE U/T	01.09.03	ILLUSTRIOUS
Rooke, Zoe Selina, BA	LT(IC)	E	TM	01.01.02	SULTAN
Rooney, Michael, BEng, MIEE	LT(CC)	E	WE	01.09.00	CAPT MCTA
Rooney, Thomas	SLT(IC)	E	WE	01.01.04	MWS COLLINGWOOD
Roper, Martin, pcea	LT CDR(FTC)	X	O	01.11.90	MARS IPT
Roscoe, David, MB, CHB	SURG LT(SCC)	-		04.08.04	RH HASLAR
Roscoe, Robert David, BEng	LT CDR(FTC)	E	WE	01.04.99	FWO DEVONPORT
Rose, Alan, BSc	LT(IC)	E	WESM	01.09.02	VIGILANT(STBD)
Rose, Andrew Donald, BA	LT(CC)	X	O	16.12.97	INVINCIBLE
Rose, Caroline Mary, BEng, MSc, CEng, MIMechE, AMIMarE	LT CDR(FTC)	E	ME	30.08.02	2SL/CNH FOTR
Rose, John Gordon, MBE, psc(m), hcsc	BRIG(FTC)	-		30.06.00	HQ 3 CDO BDE RM
Rose, Marcus Edward	SLT(IC)	E	WE U/T	01.09.03	NOTTINGHAM
Rose, Michael Frederick, BEng, MSc, CEng, MIMarEST	LT CDR(FTC)	E	ME	28.12.99	NAVSEC
Rose, Simon Paul, BEng	SLT(IC)	E	WE U/T	01.01.04	DARTMOUTH BRNC
Rose, Simone, BA	LT(IC)	S		01.05.03	SCOTT
Roskilly, Martyn, MSc	CAPT RM(CC)	-	P	01.05.01	847 SQN
Ross, Andrew Charles Paterson, BT, BSc, ocds(No), psc	LT COL(FTC)	-		30.06.05	JDCC
Ross, Angus Allan, BA, MSc	CAPT(FTC)	S		30.06.02	FLEET HQ PORTS
Ross, Gareth Donald Anthony	LT(IC)	X	AV	01.05.03	RNAS CULDROSE
Ross, Gawain (Act Maj)	CAPT RM(FTC)	-	SO(LE)	01.01.99	1 ASSAULT GP RM
Ross, Ian, BEng, CEng, MIMarE	LT CDR(FTC)	E	ME	01.08.00	SAUDI AFPS SAUDI
Ross, Jonathan Hubert, BSc, MA, ACGI, psc(j)	LT COL(FTC)	-		30.06.02	MOD (LONDON)
Ross, Paul William, BSc	LT(IC)	E	TM U/T	01.01.02	SULTAN
Ross, Robert Alasdair, MB, BS, FRCS, Dip FFP	SURG CDR(FCC)	-	GMPP	31.12.99	UKSU AFSOUTH
Roster, Shaun Patrick	LT(FTC)	X	O	16.11.94	702 SQN HERON
Rostron, David William, BEng	LT CDR(FTC)	E	MESM	01.01.04	SPLENDID
Rostron, John Harry	LT(IC)	E	WESM	01.01.03	OCLC MANCH
Roue, James Llewellyn, BA	LT(IC)	S		01.01.03	FLEET HQ PORTS
Roue, Kathryn Sian, MB, BCH, BSc	SURG LT(SCC)	-		03.08.04	MDHU DERRIFORD
Round, Matthew James, BA, BSc, PGCE	LT(IC)	X	O	01.05.02	849 SQN B FLT
Routledge, William David	LT(FTC)	X		10.12.98	DISC
Rowan, Mark Edward (Act Lt Cdr)	LT(FTC)	X	C	24.07.97	AGRIPPA MAR CC
Rowan, Nicholas Anthony, BEng	LT CDR(FTC)	E	MESM	01.10.01	VENGEANCE(PORT)
Rowberry, Adrian Graham, BSc	LT(IC)	X		01.01.02	PEMBROKE
Rowe, Andrew James	LT CDR(FTC)	E	WE	01.10.04	DLO BRISTOL
Rowe, Paula Elizabeth, MBA	LT CDR(FTC)	E	TM	01.10.97	PJHQ
Rowe, Phillip James	LT(IC)	X	H2	01.05.02	ECHO
Rowe, Richard Dudley, BD	CHAPLAIN	SF		24.09.00	NELSON

Name	Rank	Branch	Spec	Seniority	Where Serving
Rowell, Graham Edward, MSc	CAPT(FTC)	E	AE	30.06.04	DLO WYTON
Rowland, Paul Nicholas, BEng, CEng, MIMarEST	LT CDR(FTC)	E	MESM	01.01.00	VICTORIOUS(PORT)
Rowlands, Andrew Richard, BEng, MSc gw	LT CDR(FTC)	E	WE	01.06.04	DLO BRISTOL
Rowlands, Kevin, BSc, MA, pce	LT CDR(FTC)	X	PWO(A)	01.10.01	ALBION
Rowley, Thomas Patrick	SLT(IC)	X		01.02.04	DARTMOUTH BRNC
Rowse, Mark Lawrence, BEng, CEng, MIMarEST, psc(j)	CDR(FTC)	E	WE	30.06.03	FOST SEA
Rowson, Marcus Jonathan, BSc	LT(CC)	X	P	16.11.99	845 SQN
Roy, Alexander Campbell, OBE, osc(us)	LT COL(FTC)	-		31.12.90	FPGRM
Roy, Christopher Alan	LT(IC)	X	P	01.01.04	801 SQN
Royce, Roderick Henry, BEng	SLT(IC)	X	P U/T	01.02.03	DARTMOUTH BRNC
Roylance, Jaimie Fraser, MA	MAJ(FTC)	-	P	01.09.01	JSCSC
Royle, Nigel Alexander	LT(IC)	E	ME	01.05.03	CAPT MCTA
Royston, James Lawrence, MA	LT(IC)	X	SM	01.09.03	TORBAY
Royston, Stuart James, pce, n	LT CDR(FTC)	X	PWO(C)	01.05.98	ST ALBANS
Rucinski, Peter Gerard, BEng	LT(IC)	E	WE	01.01.04	EXETER
Rudd, Philip	CAPT RM(IC)	-	P	01.04.04	DHFS
Ruddock, Gordon William David, n	LT CDR(FTC)	X	PWO(A)	01.07.03	ST ALBANS
Ruddock, Jane, MA	LT(IC)	E		01.01.99	MWS COLLINGWOOD
Rudkin, Adam Llywelyn, MEng	SLT(IC)	E	AE U/T	01.09.02	SULTAN
Rugg, Christopher Phillip, BSc	LT(IC)	X	P	01.09.04	RNAS YEOVILTON
Runchman, Phillip Charles, MA, BM, BCH, FRCS	SURG CAPT(FCC)	-	(CGS)	30.06.85	INVINCIBLE
Rundle, Anthony Littlejohns, BEng, CEng, MIEE	LT CDR(FTC)	E	WE	01.10.00	MWS COLLINGWOOD
Rusbridger, Robert Charles, MSc, psc	CAPT(FTC)	E	ME	30.06.03	DLO BRISTOL
Rushworth, Andrew William Edward, BEng	SLT(IC)	E	ME U/T	01.09.02	CAMPBELTOWN
Rushworth, Benjamin John, BSc, ARCS, n	LT(FTC)	X	PWO(U)	01.05.98	CARDIFF
Russell, Bruce, BEng, MA, CEng, MIEE, psc(j)	LT CDR(FTC)	E	WESM	01.05.00	TURBULENT
Russell, Colin	LT(FTC)	E	AE	01.01.00	ILLUSTRIOUS
Russell, Gillian Spence, BEng	LT CDR(FTC)	S		01.08.03	2SL/CNH
Russell, Katherine Elizabeth Filshie, BSc	LT(IC)	X	FC	01.05.02	ILLUSTRIOUS
Russell, Mark James	LT(IC)	E	MESM	01.05.03	DRAKE CBS
Russell, Martin Simon, BA	LT(CC)	X	O	01.01.02	849 SQN HQ
Russell, Nigel Anthony David	LT CDR(FTC)	X	PWO(A)	01.10.04	MWS COLLINGWOOD
Russell, Paul, MNI	LT CDR(FTC)	X	AAWO	01.05.01	NAVSEC
Russell, Philip Robert, BTech, MSc, CEng, MRINA, MIMarEST	CDR(FTC)	E	ME	30.06.05	JSCSC
Russell, Simon Jonathon, MSc, MInstPS, MILT, MRAeS, psc, psc(j)	CDR(FTC)	E	AE	30.06.98	RNAS YEOVILTON
Russell, Thomas, pce, psc(j)	LT CDR(FTC)	X	MCD	01.07.93	MWS COLLINGWOOD
Russell, Timothy James, BSc	LT CDR(CC)	X	MW	01.07.02	MWS COLLINGWOOD
Ruston, Mark Robert, BEng, MSc, MIEE	LT(CC)	E	WE	01.01.99	2SL/CNH FOTR
Rutherford, Adam Todd	CAPT RM(IC)	-	MLDR	24.07.04	CTCRM
Rutherford, Kevin John, BSc	LT(CC)	X	P	01.10.93	846 SQN
Rutherford, Timothy James, BEng	LT CDR(FTC)	E	AE	30.12.00	848 SQN HERON
Ruthven, Stuart Christopher, MB, ChB	SURG LT(SCC)	-		01.08.01	DRAKE COB
Ryall, Tom Armstrong Scott, BA	CAPT RM(IC)	-		01.09.04	42 CDO RM
Ryan, Dennis Graham, BSc	CDR(FTC)	E	AE	30.06.02	AH IPT
Ryan, John Benedict	LT CDR(CC)	S		01.10.01	EAGLET
Ryan, John Peter	LT(FTC)	E	MESM	02.05.00	DLO BRISTOL
Ryan, Nicholas, BEng, CEng, MIMarEST	LT CDR(FTC)	E	ME	01.07.03	CAMPBELTOWN
Ryan, Patrick Douglas Blackwood	LT(FTC)	X	SM	01.09.02	TURBULENT
Ryan, Paul Justin, BEng	LT(IC)	X	P	01.09.02	824 SQN
Ryan, Richard Michael, BSc, pce, pcea	LT CDR(FTC)	X	O	01.04.97	NAVSEC
Ryan, Sean Joseph, BA, pce(sm), SM(n)	LT CDR(FTC)	X	SM	01.04.01	PEMBROKE
Ryan, Stephen James, BEng	SLT(IC)	E	MESMUT	01.09.03	MANCHESTER
Rycroft, Alan Edward, pce, pcea, psc(j)	CDR(FTC)	X	O	30.06.96	PJHQ
Ryder, Matthew Robert, BEng	SLT(IC)	E	WE U/T	01.02.03	2SL/CNH
Ryder, Tony	LT(IC)	X		13.07.04	SHOREHAM
Rye, John Walter, MA, psc	MAJ(FTC)	-	C	01.09.84	CTCRM
Rymer, Alan Robert, BSc, CEng, MIMarEST, psc	CDRE(FTC)	E	ME	11.12.03	DLO BRISTOL

S

Name	Rank	Branch	Spec	Seniority	Where Serving
Saddleton, Andrew David, psc(j)o	LT COL(FTC)	-	LC	30.06.05	MOD (LONDON)
Saleh, Jenny, BSc	LT(IC)	E	TM	01.01.02	MWS COLLINGWOOD
Salim, Muttahir, BSc	LT(IC)	E	TM	01.09.98	NP IRAQ

Name	Rank	Branch	Spec	Seniority	Where Serving
Salisbury, David Peter, OBE, pce, pcea, psc(j)	CDR(FTC)	X	P	30.06.03	AGRIPPA MAR CC
Salmon, Andrew, OBE, MA, psc	BRIG(FTC)	-		13.04.04	FLEET HQ PORTS 2
Salmon, Michael Alan, pcea	CDR(FTC)	X	O	30.06.04	RAF AWC
Salter, Jeffrey Alan, BEng, MSc, CEng, MIEE, MIMarEST, psc(j)o	CDR(FTC)	E	WE	30.06.03	MOD (LONDON)
Saltonstall, Hugh Francis Rous, LLB	LT(IC)	X	P	01.05.02	815 FLT 207
Saltonstall, Philip James Rous, BA	LT(CC)	X	P	01.07.99	702 SQN HERON
Salzano, Gerard Mark, MBE, psc	LT COL(FTC)	-		30.06.00	42 CDO RM
Sambrooks, Richard John, BEng	LT(CC)	X	P	01.08.99	RNAS YEOVILTON
Sampson, James Peter, BA	LT(IC)	E	IS U/T	01.06.03	OCEAN
Sampson, Philip Henry, psc(m)	LT COL(FTC)	-		30.06.97	CTCRM
Samuel, Christopher David Robert, BSc	CAPT RM(CC)	-	C	01.05.01	CDO LOG REGT RM
Samuels, Nicholas	LT(FTC)	X	SM	01.04.98	TIRELESS
Samways, Michael James	LT(IC)	X		01.07.03	MWS COLLINGWOOD
Samwell, Michael Guy, BEng	LT(IC)	E	WESM	01.09.04	TRIUMPH
Sanderson, Christopher Peter, MA	LT(FTC)	X	H2	01.10.99	JSCSC
Sanderson, Lee David, BEng, CEng, MIEE	LT CDR(FTC)	E	WE	01.10.04	DARTMOUTH BRNC
Sanderson, Robert Christopher, BDS, FDS RCPSGlas	SGCAPT(D)(FCC)	-	(COSM)	30.06.00	RH HASLAR
Sandle, Neil David, BEng, CEng, MIMarEST	LT CDR(FTC)	E	ME	01.08.03	ST ALBANS
Sandy, David	LT(IC)	X		17.12.04	MIDDLETON
Sangha, Randeep Singh, BEng	LT(CC)	E	AE	01.12.98	820 SQN
Sanguinetti, Hector Robert, MA, pce, psc(j)	CAPT(FTC)	X	PWO(C)	30.06.05	MOD (LONDON)
Sansford, Adrian James, BEng, MSc	LT CDR(FTC)	E	MESM	27.05.99	SULTAN
Santrian, Karl	LT(FTC)	X	AV	01.01.97	OCEAN
Santry, Paul Matthew	LT(FTC)	X	C	01.04.01	MWS COLLINGWOOD
Sargent, David Reginald	LT(IC)	S		01.01.02	MONTROSE
Sargent, David Stuart, MB, BS, BSc	SURG LT(SCC)	-		06.08.03	NP BOSNIA
Sargent, Lindsay, BSc	LT CDR(IC)	E	TM	01.10.04	NTE(TTD)
Sargent, Nicholas Matthew, BEng	LT(FTC)	E	AE	01.05.98	MERLIN IPT
Sargent, Philippa Mary, MA, n	LT CDR(FTC)	E	TM	01.10.04	JSCSC
Sarkar, Tirthankar	LT(IC)	X	SM	01.04.04	FOST FAS SHORE
Satterly, Robert James, BEng	LT(CC)	E	ME	01.01.01	DFTE PORTSMOUTH
Satterthwaite, Benjamin John, BA	LT(CC)	X	PWO(A)	01.02.95	NORTHUMBERLAND
Sauer, Alexis Charlotte, BSc	SLT(IC)	X		01.11.02	SOMERSET
Saunders, Christopher Edmund Maurice, MSc	LT(FTC)	X	PWO(C)	01.06.97	CHATHAM
Saunders, Jason Mervyn, BEng	LT(CC)	E	TM	01.09.94	NTE(TTD)
Saunders, John Nicholas	LT CDR(FTC)	X	PWO(N)	01.10.90	NBC PORTSMOUTH
Saunders, Timothy Mark, BSc, MA, psc(j)	CDR(FTC)	E	TMSM	30.06.04	JSCSC
Savage, Alexander Frederick, BSc	LT(IC)	S		01.01.05	PORTLAND
Savage, Daniel Liam, BEng	LT(IC)	E	ME	01.01.03	SULTAN
Savage, Mark Roger, pce	LT CDR(FTC)	X	MW	01.09.98	FLEET HQ PORTS 2
Savage, Shane, BSc	LT CDR(FTC)	X	ATC	01.10.94	RNAS CULDROSE
Saward, Justin Robert Ernest, BEng, MRAeS	LT(FTC)	E	AE	01.07.97	FLEET HQ PORTS
Sawford, Gavin Neil	LT(CC)	E	WE	01.01.02	DLO BRISTOL
Saxby, Christopher James, BEng, MSc, CEng, FIMarEST, MCGI, MIMarEST	CDR(FTC)	E	ME	30.06.03	DRAKE SFM
Saxby, Keith Alan (Act Cdr)	LT CDR(FTC)	X	AAWO	24.02.94	FLEET HQ PORTS 2
Say, Russell G	LT(IC)	E	WE	01.01.04	CARDIFF
Sayer, Jamie Michael, BA, BEng	LT(FTC)	E	AE	01.06.97	MERLIN IPT
Sayer, Russell Joe	2LT(IC)	-		01.08.01	CTCRM LYMPSTONE
Saynor, Roger Michael, MBE	LT CDR(FTC)	X		01.10.96	MWS EXC BRISTOL
Saywell-Hall, Stephen Eric	LT(FTC)	E	AE	02.09.99	SULTAN
Scales, Dean Robert	LT(IC)	X		18.02.05	CHIDDINGFOLD
Scandling, Rachel Jane	LT CDR(FTC)	S		01.10.02	2SL/CNH
Scanlon, Meredith Patricia, MSc	LT(IC)	X		01.04.04	OCEAN
Scanlon, Michael, BSc	CAPT RM(CC)	-		01.05.01	OCLC BIRM
Scarborough, David Colin	LT(IC)	MS		01.05.03	INM ALVERSTOKE
Scarlett, Christopher Joseph	LT(IC)	E	WESM	01.01.04	MOD (LONDON)
Scarth, William, BSc, jsdc, pce, psc(j)	CDR(FTC)	X	MCD	30.06.97	HQ SACT
Schillemore, Paul Colin (Act Lt Cdr)	LT(FTC)	E	WE	18.10.85	MWS COLLINGWOOD
Schleyer, Jonathan	CAPT RM(IC)	-		01.09.02	45 CDO RM
Schnadhorst, James Charles, pce	LT CDR(FTC)	X	PWO(U)	01.05.95	JACIG
Schofield, Julie Claire	LT(CC)	X		01.09.04	EXCHANGE GERMANY
Schofield, Susan Ruth, MB, BS, JCPTGP	SURG LTCDR(MCC)	-	GMPP	08.08.01	UKSU AFSOUTH
Scholes, Neil Andrew, MSc, CEng, MINucE, MIMarEST	LT(FTC)	E	MESM	02.09.99	DLO BRISTOL

Name	Rank	Branch	Spec	Seniority	Where Serving
Schwarz, Paul Michael Gunter	CDR(FTC)	X	ATC	30.06.02	AGRIPPA MAR CC
Scivier, John Stapleton, MCMI	LT CDR(FTC)	X	ATC	01.10.01	NAIC NORTHOLT
Scoles, Jonathon Charles, OBE, FCMI, pce, psc (Act Capt)	CDR(FTC)	X	PWO(U)	31.12.89	NAVSEC
Scopes, David, BEng, MRAeS	LT CDR(FTC)	E	AE	01.12.02	HARRIER IPT
Scorer, Andrew James, BA	LT(IC)	X		01.05.05	GRIMSBY
Scorer, Samuel James, nadc, jsdc, pce	CAPT(FTC)	X	PWO(U)	30.06.00	FWO DEVPT SEA
Scorer, Thomas	SURG SLT(SCC)	-		01.07.03	DARTMOUTH BRNC
Scott, Alexander James, BEng	LT(IC)	X		01.05.04	CHIDDINGFOLD
Scott, Christopher Ralph, OBE, MA, psc	COL(FTC)	-		30.06.05	PJHQ
Scott, James Baxter, BEng, CEng, MIMechE	LT CDR(FTC)	E	MESM	01.05.96	JSCSC
Scott, Jason Andrew, BA, pce	CDR(FTC)	X	MCD	30.06.03	MCM1 SEA
Scott, Julian Vivian	LT(IC)	X	EW	01.07.04	RALEIGH
Scott, Mark Robert, pcea	LT CDR(FTC)	X	P	01.10.04	MOD (LONDON)
Scott, Michael, BEng, CEng, MIEE	LT CDR(FTC)	E	WESM	01.05.99	NAVSEC
Scott, Michael, BEng	LT(IC)	X	P	16.08.97	771 SQN
Scott, Neil	LT(CC)	X		01.09.01	FLEET HQ NWD
Scott, Neil	LT(IC)	X		01.05.03	BLYTH
Scott, Nigel Leonard James, BEng, CEng, MIEE, ACGI, psc(j)	CDR(FTC)	E	WESM	30.06.02	MOD (LONDON)
Scott, Peter Darren	SLT(IC)	X	ATCU/T	01.02.04	DARTMOUTH BRNC
Scott, Peter James Douglas Sefton, OBE, BD	CHAPLAIN	CE		03.09.91	DARTMOUTH BRNC
Scott, Richard Antony, BEng, MSc	LT(FTC)	E	WE	01.08.94	T45 IPT
Scott, Robert John, pce, pcea	LT CDR(FTC)	X	O	02.03.98	FLEET HQ PORTS 2
Scott, Samantha Leigh	LT(CC)	X		01.08.00	ARCHER
Scott, Simon John, MA, psc(j)	LT COL(FTC)	-	LC	30.06.05	JDCC
Scott, Stephen Charles	MAJ(FTC)	-	SO(LE)	01.10.03	RM NORTON MANOR
Scott, Thomas	2LT(IC)	-		01.08.01	CTCRM LYMPSTONE
Scott, Timothy Edward, MB, BS, MRCP	SURG LTCDR(MC(MD)	-		04.08.04	MDHU PETERBRGH
Scott, Wendy Ann, BDS	SGLTCDR(D)(SCC)	-		13.01.02	RNAS CULDROSE
Scott-Dickins, Charles Angus, MSc	LT CDR(FTC)	X	METOC	01.10.94	GANNET SAR FLT
Scotter, Claire Marie, BSc	LT(IC)	E	IS	01.09.99	MWS COLLINGWOOD
Screaton, Richard Michael, BEng, CEng, MIEE	LT CDR(FTC)	E	ME	01.03.04	DLO BRISTOL
Screen, James	LT(IC)	E	WE	01.07.04	UKMARBATSTAFF
Scutt, Martin Jason, PhD, BM, BSc	SURG LT(SC(MD)	-		04.02.04	VENGEANCE(STBD)
Seaborn, Adam	LT(IC)	X	AV	01.05.02	SULTAN
Seagrave, Suzanna Jane, BEng	LT(FTC)	E	ME	01.11.00	NEPTUNE FD
Seal, Martin Richard	SLT(IC)	X		01.04.03	MONMOUTH
Seal, Michael Owen, BA	LT(IC)	X		01.09.04	RALEIGH
Sealey, Nicholas Peter, BSc, CEng, MIMarEST, psc	CAPT(FTC)	E	ME	30.06.02	DLO BRISTOL
Seaman, Alec	2LT(IC)	-		01.08.01	CTCRM LYMPSTONE
Seaman, Philip John	LT CDR(FTC)	E	WE	01.10.03	HQ DCSA
Sear, Jonathan Jasper, MA, psc(j)	MAJ(FTC)	-		01.09.98	EXCHANGE ARMY UK
Searight, Mark Frederick Chamney, psc(j)	MAJ(FTC)	-		01.05.97	CTCRM
Searle, Andrew James Arthur, BEng	LT(IC)	E	WE	01.09.04	LIVERPOOL
Searle, Christopher Richard	LT(IC)	S		01.07.04	SOUTHAMPTON
Searle, Emma Louise, BSc	LT(IC)	S		01.01.05	INVINCIBLE
Seatherton, Elliot Frazer Kingston, MBE, pce, psc(j)o	CDR(FTC)	X	PWO(N)	31.12.95	JDCC
Seddon, John Stephen Maurice	LT CDR(FTC)	S	SM	16.10.88	VIVID
Seddon, Jonathan David	SLT(IC)	X		01.04.03	EXETER
Sedgwick, Hugo George, BSc	LT(IC)	X	SM	01.01.04	VENGEANCE(STBD)
Segebarth, Robert Andrew	LT(FTC)	X	P	16.02.96	RAF LINTN/OUSE
Selden, John David Alan, BSc	LT(IC)	E	IS U/T	01.11.03	SULTAN
Sellar, Trevor Jefferson	CAPT RM(FTC)	-	SO(LE)	01.01.97	1 ASSAULT GP RM
Sellars, Scott John, BA, MinstAM	LT CDR(FTC)	S	CMA	01.10.04	FLEET HQ PORTS 2
Sellers, Graham Donald, BEng, MSc, CEng, MIEE	LT CDR(FTC)	E	WE	01.02.01	CHATHAM
Selway, Mark Anthony, BEng (Act Lt Cdr)	LT(FTC)	E	AE	01.07.97	AH IPT
Semple, Brian	LT(IC)	X	P	01.01.03	RNAS YEOVILTON
Sennett, Michael	LT(IC)	E	TM	01.05.02	MWS COLLINGWOOD
Sennitt, John William, MBE, MSc, PGDip, MIEE	LT CDR(FTC)	E	WE	01.08.92	DLO BRISTOL
Sephton, John Richard, BSc, FRMS, psc	CDR(FTC)	X	METOC	30.06.00	NAVSEC
Sergeant, Nicholas Robin, CDipAF	LT CDR(FTC)	E	WE	01.10.99	SULTAN
Seton, James, BA	LT(IC)	X		01.01.04	ARGYLL
Seward, Stafford Allan, MBE	LT CDR(FTC)	X		01.10.02	NP IRAQ
Sewed, Michael Antony, BSc, pcea, gdas	LT CDR(FTC)	X	O	01.10.94	LYNX OEU

Name	Rank	Branch	Spec	Seniority	Where Serving
Sewry, Michael Ronald, BSc, CEng, MIEE, psc(a)	CDR(FTC)	E	AE	31.12.95	MOD (LONDON)
Sexton, Michael John (Act Capt)	CDR(FTC)	E	WE	30.06.98	SHAPE BELGIUM
Seyd, Miranda, BSc	LT(IC)	X		01.05.03	MONTROSE
Seymour, Kevin William, pcea	LT CDR(FTC)	X	P	01.10.96	LOAN OTHER SVCE
Shackleton, Scott James Sinclair, PhD, BA, BD	CHAPLAIN	SF		20.04.93	DRAKE COB(CNH)
Shadbolt, Simon Edward, MBE, BSc, psc(m), psc(j)	BRIG(FTC)	-	C	01.10.04	MOD (LONDON)
Shah, Rajesh Radhakrishna, MChOrth, FRCS	SURG LTCDR(SCC)	-		12.01.00	NELSON (PAY)
Shakespeare, Benjamin, BSc	LT(IC)	X		01.01.05	SCOTT
Shakespeare, Christopher Allan, BEng	LT(IC)	E	AE	01.09.04	848 SQN HERON
Shallcroft, John Edward, pcea	LT CDR(FTC)	X	P	01.10.98	RAF CRANWELL EFS
Shanahan, Lloyd Anthony	LT(IC)	X	P	01.05.03	845 SQN
Shand, Christopher Michael, BSc	LT CDR(FTC)	E	WESM	01.11.82	DRAKE SFM
Shanks, Diana Zoe, BSc	LT(IC)	X		01.01.03	CFPS SHORE
Sharkey, Elton Richard, BEng, MSc	LT CDR(FTC)	E	MESM	01.06.03	TRENCHANT
Sharkey, Michael	CHAPLAIN	RC		01.10.90	42 CDO RM
Sharkey, Philip Joseph, BEng	LT(IC)	E	ME	01.09.03	INVINCIBLE
Sharland, Simon Patrick, BA, sq	MAJ(FTC)	-	LC	01.09.90	NAVSEC
Sharman, Max Christopher (Act Capt Rm)	LT RM(IC)	-		01.09.03	FPGRM
Sharp, Andrew Peter	LT(IC)	E	MESM	01.05.02	SETT GOSPORT
Sharp, Christopher	LT(IC)	E	WE	12.04.02	ARK ROYAL
Sharp, John Vivian	LT(CC)	X	P	01.07.03	846 SQN
Sharpe, Gary Anthony	CAPT RM(FTC)	-	SO(LE)	01.01.93	CTCRM
Sharpe, Grantley James, pce	LT CDR(FTC)	X	PWO(U)	01.02.88	AGRIPPA MAR CC
Sharpe, Marcus Roger	CAPT RM(IC)	-	SO(LE)	01.04.03	CTCRM
Sharpe, Thomas Grenville	LT CDR(FTC)	X	PWO(A)	01.10.02	MWS COLLINGWOOD
Sharples, Joseph Henry, BA	SLT(IC)	X	P U/T	01.11.02	RNAS YEOVILTON
Sharples, Mark James, BSc	SLT(IC)	X	O U/T	01.05.03	750 SQN SEAHAWK
Sharpley, John Guy, MA, MB, BCh, MRCPsych	SURG CDR(FCC)	-	(CN/P)	30.06.02	RH HASLAR
Sharrott, Christopher, BSc	LT(IC)	X	P	01.09.03	DHFS
Shaughnessy, Sophie Louise, BEng, MIEE	LT CDR(FTC)	E	ME	01.10.02	GRAFTON
Shaughnessy, Toby Edward	LT(FTC)	X	FC	01.10.97	ST ALBANS
Shaw, Alexander	SURG SLT(SCC)	-		06.09.04	DARTMOUTH BRNC
Shaw, Andrew Thomas	CAPT RM(CC)	-		01.09.03	FPGRM
Shaw, Callam Roderick, BEng	SLT(IC)	E	MESMUT	01.01.03	FWO FASLANE
Shaw, Ian Brian, BEng	LT CDR(FTC)	E	WESM	15.09.91	ACDS(POL) USA
Shaw, Kevin Norman Graham, MA, PhD, CEng, MIEE, MRAeS, MRIN, psc(j)	CDR(FTC)	E	WE	30.06.02	BDS WASHINGTON
Shaw, Mark Alexander, BEng	LT(IC)	X		01.05.04	NORTHUMBERLAND
Shaw, Michael Leslie, BEng, CEng, MRAeS	LT CDR(FTC)	E	AE	11.02.00	847 SQN
Shaw, Neil Andrew	LT(FTC)	E	WE	01.04.01	DFTE PORTSMOUTH
Shaw, Paul James, MBE	CDR(FTC)	S		30.06.04	FOST SEA
Shaw, Simon James, BA	SLT(IC)	S		01.09.02	RICHMOND
Shaw, Steven Matthew, MA, psc(j)	CDR(FTC)	S		30.06.01	UKMARBATSTAFF
Shaw, Stewart Andrew	SLT(IC)	X		01.07.02	RAF SHAWBURY
Shawcross, Paul Kenneth, BSc, pcea	CDR(FTC)	X	P	30.06.03	CMT SHRIVENHAM
Sheals, Emma Jane, BSc	LT(IC)	X		18.01.05	MWS COLLINGWOOD
Shearman, Alexander James, MB, BMS, CHB	SURG LT(SCC)	-		06.08.03	RFANSU (ARGUS)
Shearn, Matthew Arthur, BA	LT(IC)	X		01.04.00	MWS HM TG (D)
Shears, Gary Raymond, BSc	LT(IC)	X	ATCU/T	01.09.03	RNAS YEOVILTON
Sheehan, Mark Andrew, pce, pcea, psc	CDR(FTC)	X	O	30.06.01	RNAS YEOVILTON
Sheehan, Neil Marc	SLT(IC)	X		01.02.03	ALBION
Sheehan, Thomas John	LT(IC)	E	WESM	01.01.04	TIRELESS
Sheikh, Nabil, BSc, PGDipL, CDipAF (Act Lt Cdr)	LT(FTC)	S	BAR	01.11.97	PJHQ
Sheils, Damian Edmund Tyrie	LT(CC)	X	P	16.07.94	771 SQN
Sheldon, Mark Laurence	LT(FTC)	E	WE	07.02.97	MWS COLLINGWOOD
Shepherd, Alan, IEng, MIIE	LT CDR(FTC)	E	WE	01.10.92	SAUDI AFPS SAUDI
Shepherd, Anya Clare, BSc	LT(IC)	X	FC	01.12.02	HQ STC
Shepherd, Charles Scott, BSc, pce(sm)	LT CDR(FTC)	X	SM	01.01.97	JSCSC
Shepherd, Christopher Edward	SLT(IC)	E	WESM	01.09.02	FWO FASLANE SEA
Shepherd, Fiona Rosemary, MBE, MSc, LRPS	LT(CC)	S		01.09.99	NAVSEC
Shepherd, Martin Paul, pcea	LT CDR(FTC)	X	P	01.04.04	MWS SOUTHWICK PK
Shepherd, Oliver James	MID(NE)(IC)	X		01.09.04	DARTMOUTH BRNC
Shepherd, Paul Rodney, pcea	LT CDR(FTC)	X	O	01.10.92	RNAS CULDROSE

Name	Rank	Branch	Spec	Seniority	Where Serving
Shepherd, Roger Guy, BEng, MIEE	LT CDR(FTC)	E	WESM	01.05.96	FLEET HQ NWD
Sheppard, Heidi Clare	SLT(IC)	X		01.04.03	DUMBARTON CASTLE
Shergold, Paul James	CAPT RM(FTC)	-	SO(LE)	01.01.97	RM CHIVENOR
Sherriff, David Anthony, pce, pcea, psc(j)	CDR(FTC)	X	P	30.06.03	FLEET AV CRANWEL
Sherry, James Mark, BSc	LT(IC)	X		01.01.05	MWS COLLINGWOOD
Sherwin, Antony John, BA	LT(IC)	X	O U/T	01.01.05	RNAS CULDROSE
Sherwood, Gideon Andrew Francis	LT(IC)	X	FC	01.05.01	EXETER
Shield, Simon James, pce(sm), psc	CDR(FTC)	X	SM	31.12.98	ASM IPT
Shields, Kristofer Neil, BA	SLT(IC)	X	SM	01.01.03	OCEAN
Shipperley, Ian, BSc, CEng, MIMechE	CDR(FTC)	E	ME	30.06.98	DLO BRISTOL
Shirley, Andrew John, BEng, CEng, MIMechE	LT CDR(FTC)	E	MESM	01.08.01	MOD (BATH)
Shirley, Wayne Peter, MA, MBA, psc(j)	CDR(FTC)	E	WE	30.06.04	NEW IPT
Short, Gavin Conrad, BEng, MA, CEng, MIEE, psc(j)	CDR(FTC)	E	WESM	30.06.00	IMS BRUSSELS
Short, John Jeffrey, BEng, AMIMechE	CDR(FTC)	E	ME	30.06.05	JSCSC
Short, Katherine Jane, BDS	SG LT(D)(SCC)	-		04.07.02	NELSON
Shortall, James John, BSc	SLT(IC)	X		01.05.02	PENZANCE
Shortland, Karen, BA	LT(IC)	S		01.01.04	MOD (BATH)
Shrestha, Shekhar, BEng	LT(IC)	E	ME	01.01.04	ARGYLL
Shrimpton, Helen Diane, MB, BCh, MA(CANTAB), DObstRCOG, Dip FFP, MRCGP	SURG LTCDR(MCC)	-	GMPP	04.02.98	NELSON
Shrimpton, Matthew William, pcea	LT CDR(FTC)	X	P	01.10.03	EXCHANGE N ZLAND
Shrives, Michael Peter, MA, pce, pcea, psc, psc(j)	CDR(FTC)	X	P	30.06.95	MWC PORTSDOWN
Shropshall, Ian James	LT(IC)	X	SM	01.09.03	TRENCHANT
Shropshall, Kelly Ann	SLT(IC)	X		01.08.02	2SL/CNH FOTR
Shrubsole, Gareth Mark, BA	SLT(IC)	X		01.09.02	SEVERN
Shuttleworth, Stephen	LT CDR(FTC)	E	ME	01.10.04	LANCASTER
Shutts, David, BEng, CEng, MIMarEST, psc(j)	CDR(FTC)	E	ME	30.06.05	CAPT MCTA
Sibbit, Neil Thomas, pce, pcea, psc, psc(j)o	CDR(FTC)	X	O	30.06.96	LANG TRNG(UK)
Sibley, Andrew Keith	LT CDR(FTC)	E	ME	01.10.04	PORTLAND
Sidebotham, Simon Charles, BSc	LT(IC)	E	WE	01.01.03	HQ DCSA
Sidoli, Giovanni Eugenio, BDS, MSc, MGDS RCS	SGCAPT(D)(FCC)	-		31.12.95	DPMD
Sidoli, Luigi Tomasso Angelo, BSc	SLT(IC)	X		01.02.03	EXETER
Sienkiewicz, Maryla Krystyna, LLB	LT(CC)	X		01.09.01	MANCHESTER
Siggers, Benet Richard Charles, MB, CHB, DipIMC RCSED	SURG LTCDR(MCC)	-		02.08.00	NELSON (PAY)
Sillers, Barry, BSc, SM(n)	LT CDR(FTC)	X	SM	01.12.02	FOST FAS SHORE
Silver, Christina Kay	LT CDR(FTC)	W	C	01.10.93	JSSU CHELTENHAM
Sim, Donald Leslie Whyte, MA, FCMI, MNI, pce, pcea, ocds(USN)	CAPT(FTC)	X	O	30.06.02	NAVSEC
Simm, Craig William, BEng	LT(FTC)	E	AE	01.07.98	LOAN JTEG BSC DN
Simmonds, Daniel Douglas Harold	LT(CC)	X	SM	01.05.03	FLEET HQ NWD
Simmonds, Gary Fredrick	LT CDR(FTC)	E	AE	01.10.98	FLEET HQ PORTS
Simmonds, Peter Bruce, psc(a)	MAJ(FTC)	-		01.08.83	CTCRM
Simmonds, Richard Michael, OBE, jsdc, pce, psc(a)	CDR(FTC)	X	MCD	31.12.90	SA LISBON
Simmonite, Gavin Ian	LT(CC)	X	P	16.11.00	846 SQN
Simmons, Nigel Douglas, MSc, CEng, MIEE	CDR(FTC)	E	WESM	30.06.99	MOD (LONDON)
Simmons, Robert Leigh	CAPT RM(IC)	-		01.09.03	UKLFCSG RM
Simms, David Martin	LT(CC)	X	O	16.03.96	824 SQN
Simpson, Christopher John, BA	LT(IC)	X	P	01.01.04	RNAS YEOVILTON
Simpson, Colin Chisholm	LT CDR(FTC)	X	P	01.10.04	815 SQN HQ
Simpson, David	CHAPLAIN	CE		07.03.05	DARTMOUTH BRNC
Simpson, David Keith, pcea	LT(CC)	X	O	16.11.93	RNAS CULDROSE
Simpson, Emma Jane, BA	LT CDR(FTC)	W	X	01.10.01	AFPAA HQ
Simpson, Erin Leona	SLT(UCE)(IC)	E	WE	01.01.02	DARTMOUTH BRNC
Simpson, Mark	LT(IC)	E	ME	05.08.01	DLO BRISTOL
Simpson, Martin Joseph, PGDIPAN, pce	LT CDR(FTC)	X	PWO(N)	01.07.96	MWS COLLINGWOOD
Simpson, Paul Emmanuel	LT(MCC)	Q		27.10.00	RCDM
Simpson, Robin Frank	2LT(IC)	-		01.09.00	40 CDO RM
Simpson, Scott Forsyth	LT(CC)	X	O	01.02.01	815 SQN HQ
Simpson, Thomas Westgarth, BA	CAPT RM(IC)	-		01.09.04	42 CDO RM
Simpson, William James Stuart, BEng	LT(IC)	E	MESM	01.01.02	VANGUARD(PORT)
Sims, Alexander Richard	LT(CC)	X	O	15.06.00	702 SQN HERON
Sinclair, Andrew Bruce, odc(Aus)	LT CDR(FTC(A)	X	P	01.02.84	RNAS YEOVILTON
Singleton, Mark Donald	LT(FTC)	X	AV	10.12.98	ILLUSTRIOUS
Sinha, Raman	SLT(IC)	X	P U/T	01.06.04	RAF CRANWELL EFS

Name	Rank	Branch	Spec	Seniority	Where Serving
Sitton, John Barry, BEng, MSc	LT(FTC)	E	MESM	01.11.95	TORBAY
Skeer, Martyn Robert, MBE, pce, pcea	CDR(FTC)	X	P	30.06.02	CMT SHRIVENHAM
Skelley, Alasdair Neil Murdoch, MA, n	LT CDR(FTC)	X	PWO(U)	01.03.03	MONMOUTH
Skelton, John Steven, BEng, CEng, MIMarEST	LT CDR(FTC)	E	ME	01.10.04	CTS
Skidmore, Christopher Mark, BA, FCIS, FCMI, FCIPD, MILog	CDR(FTC)	S	SM	31.12.98	MOD (BATH)
Skinner, Amy Louise, BA	SLT(IC)	X		01.02.04	DARTMOUTH BRNC
Skinner, Jonathan Jeffery, BA	SLT(IC)	X		01.02.03	NOTTINGHAM
Skinsley, Terry John	LT(IC)	X		01.05.03	SEVERN
Skipper, James Alexander	LT(FTC)	X		01.11.02	PJHQ
Skittrall, Steven David, BEng	LT(FTC)	E	AE	15.10.97	849 SQN HQ
Skuse, Matthew, BSc, psc(j)o	MAJ(FTC)	-	MLDR	01.09.99	MOD (LONDON)
Skyrme, Laura	SURG SLT(SCC)	-		01.07.03	DARTMOUTH BRNC
Slack, Jeremy Mark	MAJ(FTC)	-	LC	01.05.97	EXCHANGE AUSTLIA
Slade, Christopher, pcea	LT CDR(FTC(A)	X	P	01.10.90	RNAS CULDROSE
Slater, Sir Jock (John Cunningham Kirkwood), GCB, LVO, rcds, pce	ADM	-	N	29.01.91	
Slattery, Damian John, BSc	LT(CC)	X	MCD	01.01.00	QUORN
Slawson, James Mark, BSc, CEng, MIMarEST, psc	CAPT(FTC)	E	ME	30.06.04	NBC PORTSMOUTH
Slayman, Emily	SLT(IC)	S		01.09.03	DARTMOUTH BRNC
Slight, Oliver William Lawrence	SLT(IC)	X		01.09.02	EDINBURGH
Slimmon, Kevan William, NDipM	LT CDR(FTC)	E	WESM	01.10.04	FWO FASLANE
Sloan, Ian Alexander, BEng	LT(FTC)	X	P	01.12.99	EXCHANGE RAF UK
Sloan, Mark Usherwood, BSc, pce, psc	CAPT(FTC)	X	PWO(U)	31.12.99	MWC SOUTHWICK
Sloan, Patrick Alexanxder	MID(NE)(IC)	X		01.02.05	DARTMOUTH BRNC
Slocombe, Christopher Alwyn, pcea, psc(j) (Act Cdr)	LT CDR(FTC)	X	P	01.10.96	845 SQN
Slocombe, Nicholas Richard	LT CDR(FTC)	X	ATC	01.10.02	FOST DPORT SHORE
Slowther, Stuart John, BEng	LT(CC)	E	WE	01.09.01	RMC OF SCIENCE
Small, Richard James, BSc, SM(n)	LT CDR(FTC)	X	SM	01.03.05	TRAFALGAR
Smallwood, Anthony John	CAPT RM(IC)	BS		19.07.02	RM BAND SCOTLAND
Smallwood, Justin Patrick, MA(CANTAB), MBA, sq	MAJ(FTC)	-		05.09.95	UKLFCSG RM
Smallwood, Richard Iain, pce(sm), SM(n)	LT CDR(FTC)	X	SM	12.10.01	FLEET HQ PORTS 2
Smart, Caroline Rose, BSc	LT(IC)	E	TM U/T	01.07.03	DARTMOUTH BRNC
Smart, Mark James	LT(FTC)	E	AE	02.05.00	EXCHANGE GERMANY
Smart, Steven Joe	LT(FTC)	E	ME	23.02.90	SULTAN
Smedley, Rachel Laura, BA	SLT(IC)	S		01.05.02	RALEIGH
Smerdon, Christopher David Edward, BA	LT CDR(FTC)	S	SM	01.07.94	RNAS CULDROSE
Smith, Adam Hewitt	SURG SLT(SCC)	-		01.07.03	DARTMOUTH BRNC
Smith, Adrian Charles, BSc	LT CDR(FTC)	E	AE	16.03.84	CV(F) IPT
Smith, Adrian Gerard, BA, MA(CANTAB)	LT CDR(FTC)	E	WE	01.02.99	FLEET HQ PORTS 2
Smith, Andrew, BA	LT(CC)	X		01.04.99	TRUMPETER
Smith, Andrew Paul	LT CDR(FTC)	X	PWO(A)	01.04.98	HQ BFSAI
Smith, Anthony, MEng	LT(CC)	E	TM	09.01.99	CAPT IST STAFF
Smith, Ashley Mark	MID(IC)	X	O U/T	01.09.03	RNAS CULDROSE
Smith, Austin Bernard Dudley	LT CDR(FTC)	X	P	01.10.02	846 SQN
Smith, Barbara Carol	CDR(FCC)	Q	SCM	30.06.05	HQ DMETA
Smith, Benjamin, BA	SLT(IC)	X		01.05.02	MWS COLLINGWOOD
Smith, Brian Joseph, n, BA	LT CDR(FTC)	X	PWO(A)	01.12.99	YORK
Smith, Brian Stephen, BDS, MGDS RCSEd	SGCDR(D)(FCC)	-		30.06.01	RN GIBRALTAR
Smith, Charles John	LT(IC)	X	C	01.05.03	COM MCC NWD
Smith, Christopher John Hilton, CEng, MIEE, BEng	LT CDR(FTC)	E	WE	01.10.04	JSCSC
Smith, Christopher Julian, MA, psc(j)	LT CDR(FTC)	S		16.03.96	COM MCC NWD
Smith, Clive Peter, pce	LT CDR(FTC)	X	PWO(U)	26.04.95	NAVSEC
Smith, Clive Sherrif, OBE, MSc, CEng, MIMarEST	CDR(FTC)	E	MESM	30.06.92	DLO BRISTOL
Smith, Craig Adam, BEng	SLT(IC)	E	WE U/T	01.02.03	2SL/CNH
Smith, David Jonathan	LT(IC)	X	SM	01.05.03	TIRELESS
Smith, David Leslie	LT CDR(FTC)	X	AAWO	01.10.04	MWS COLLINGWOOD
Smith, David Munro	MAJ(FTC)	-	SO(LE)	01.10.04	FPGRM
Smith, David Thomas	LT(CC)	X	O	16.06.91	824 SQN
Smith, Edward George Giles, BA	LT(IC)	X	H2	01.08.02	MWS COLLINGWOOD
Smith, Fiona	SURG SLT(SCC)	-		11.03.04	DARTMOUTH BRNC
Smith, Gordon Kenneth	CAPT RM(CC)	-	LC	01.10.00	539 ASSLT SQN RM
Smith, Graeme Douglas James, BSc	LT CDR(FTC)	X	PWO(C)	01.01.01	MWS COLLINGWOOD
Smith, Gregory Charles Stanley, pce, pcea	LT CDR(FTC)	X	O	01.01.98	HQ1GP HQSTC
Smith, Gregory Kenneth, BSc, CEng, MIEE, MBCS, adp	CDR(FTC)	E	IS	30.06.05	PJHQ

Name	Rank	Branch	Spec	Seniority	Where Serving
Smith, Jason Edward, MB, BS, MSc, Dip SM, FFAEM, MRCP (Act Surg Cdr)	SURG LTCDR(FCC)	-		01.08.98	MDHU DERRIFORD
Smith, Jason James, MB, BS	SURG LTCDR(MCC)	-		07.08.01	NELSON (PAY)
Smith, Jennifer Clare, BEng	SLT(IC)	X		01.01.04	DARTMOUTH BRNC
Smith, Kenneth Marshall	LT CDR(FTC)	X		16.11.88	FLEET HQ PORTS
Smith, Keven John, pcea	LT CDR(FTC)	X	P	01.10.95	JHCHQ
Smith, Kevin Alexander, BSc, CEng, MIMarEST	CDR(FTC)	E	MESM	30.06.03	FWO DEVPT SEA
Smith, Kevin Donlan, MEng	LT(CC)	E	IS	01.02.97	DCCIS BLANDFORD
Smith, Kristian Mark	LT(IC)	X	P	01.05.04	DHFS
Smith, Laurence Michael	MID(NE)(IC)	X	P U/T	01.09.04	DARTMOUTH BRNC
Smith, Lesley Ann, BA	LT(IC)	X		01.01.05	INVINCIBLE
Smith, Lynnette	LT(CC)	S		01.01.02	JSU NORTHWOOD
Smith, Malcolm, CDipAF	CAPT(FTC)	S	SM	30.06.05	PJHQ
Smith, Mark MacFarlane, BEng, MAPM, CEng, MRAeS	LT CDR(FTC)	E	AE	01.11.98	RNAS CULDROSE
Smith, Mark Peter	LT CDR(FTC)	MS		01.10.04	FLEET HQ PORTS 2
Smith, Mark Richard, BEng	LT CDR(FTC)	E	ME	14.07.95	LOAN OMAN
Smith, Martin Linn, MBE, BSc, psc	LT COL(FTC)	-		31.12.99	MOD (LONDON)
Smith, Martin Russell Kingsley, BA, PGDip, MDA	CDR(FTC)	X	METOC	30.06.03	JHQ/CIS LISBON
Smith, Matthew David, MA	LT(IC)	S		01.09.04	NEPTUNE DLO
Smith, Matthew Roy Thomas, BA	SLT(IC)	X		01.07.02	MONTROSE
Smith, Melvin Andrew, MSc, mdtc	CDR(FTC)	E	WE	31.12.95	AGRIPPA JFC HQ
Smith, Michael Daren	LT CDR(FTC)	X	O	01.10.02	FLEET HQ NWD
Smith, Michael John, BEng, MIEE	LT CDR(FTC)	E	WESM	01.05.04	NEW IPT
Smith, Neil	SLT(IC)	E	ME	01.02.04	DARTMOUTH BRNC
Smith, Nigel John, pce	LT CDR(FTC)	X	PWO(U)	01.10.01	FOST SEA
Smith, Nigel Paul, BA, pce, psc	CDR(FTC)	X	PWO(U)	31.12.89	DA MANAMA
Smith, Nigel Peter, BA, MSc, pce	LT CDR(FTC)	X	PWO(U)	01.07.91	SONAR 2087 IPT
Smith, Owen John	LT(CC)	E	ME	01.04.02	ILLUSTRIOUS
Smith, Paul	LT(FTC)	X	MCD	01.04.01	BLYTH
Smith, Paul Martin, MEng	SLT(IC)	E	WE U/T	01.01.04	DARTMOUTH BRNC
Smith, Richard David	LT CDR(FTC)	X	PWO(U)	01.07.03	CUMBERLAND
Smith, Richard William Robertson	LT CDR(FTC)	X	PWO(U)	01.05.93	DRAKE COB
Smith, Robert Charles Vernon, pcea	LT CDR(FTC)	X	O	01.10.00	815 SQN HQ
Smith, Robert Edward	LT(FTC)	X	O	10.12.98	ILLUSTRIOUS
Smith, Rudi Adam	LT(IC)	X		01.09.01	RNAS YEOVILTON
Smith, Simon Ronald Frederick (Act Lt Cdr)	LT(IC)	X	ATC	28.07.96	OCEAN
Smith, Stephen Clive	LT(IC)	X	SM	01.05.04	VIGILANT(STBD)
Smith, Stephen Frank	MAJ(FTC)	-	SO(LE)	01.10.02	CHFHQ
Smith, Steven Luigi, pce	CDR(FTC)	X	AAWO	30.06.05	UKCEC IPT
Smith, Steven Rhodes Clifford, MB, ChB, FRCS, FRCSTr&Orth	SURG CDR(FCC)	-	(CO/S)	30.06.03	MDHU DERRIFORD
Smithson, Peter Edward, MSc, CEng, MRAeS	CDR(FTC)	E	AE	30.06.97	RNAS YEOVILTON
Smye, Malcolm Alexander, BEng	LT(IC)	E	AE	01.01.02	HARRIER IPT
Smyth, Clive Robert	LT(IC)	MS		01.05.02	DMSTC
Sneddon, Russell Neil	LT CDR(FTC)	X	P	01.10.01	RAF SHAWBURY
Snee, Paul	LT(IC)	X		17.12.04	SUTHERLAND
Sneesby, Nicholas	LT(IC)	E	AE	01.07.04	815 SQN HQ
Snel, Karen Elizabeth	SLT(IC)	X		01.01.03	RNAS CULDROSE
Snell, Andrew James	LT(IC)	E	ME	01.05.02	DRAKE SFM
Snell, David Micheal	LT(CC)	E	WE	01.01.02	DLO BRISTOL
Snelling, Paul Douglas, BEng, MSc	LT CDR(FTC)	E	MESM	01.10.02	VIGILANT(PORT)
Snelson, David George, CB, FCMI, MNI, pce, psc, hcsc (POST CVS/LPH COMMAND JUN 04)	RADM	-	AWO(A)	05.11.02	FLEET HQ PORTS 2
Sneyd, Eric Patrick Bartholomew, MBE, BEng, MSc	LT CDR(FTC)	E	TM	20.06.93	2SL/CNH FOTR
Snook, Raymond Edward, pce, pcea, psc(j)	CDR(FTC)	X	O	30.06.98	LANG TRNG(UK)
Snow, Christopher Allen, CBE, ADC, BA, pce	CDRE(FTC)	X	SM	14.05.02	MOD (LONDON)
Snow, Maxwell Charles Peter, BSc, DipFM, pce, pcea, psc	CDR(FTC)	X	P	30.06.93	FLEET AV VL
Snow, Paul Frederick, BSc, CEng, MIMarEST	LT CDR(FTC)	E	ME	01.10.94	FLEET HQ PORTS 2
Snowball, Simon John, MA, psc	CDR(FTC)	X	PWO(N)	30.06.00	COS 2SL/CNH
Snowden, Michael Brian Samuel, MB, CHB, MRCGP, DObstRCOG, Dip FFP	SURG LTCDR(MCC)	-	GMPP	01.08.99	NEPTUNE DL
Soar, Gary, pcea	LT CDR(FTC)	X	O	01.10.02	700M MERLIN OEU
Soar, Trevor Alan, OBE, pce, pce(sm) (CM(PA) MAY 04)	RADM	-	SM	18.05.04	MOD (LONDON)

Name	Rank	Branch	Spec	Seniority	Where Serving
Sobers, Scott, BEng	LT(IC)	E	MESM	01.09.03	VIGILANT(PORT)
Solly, Matthew MacDonald, BSc, n	LT CDR(FTC)	E	TMSM	01.10.02	2SL/CNH FOTR
Somerville, Nigel John Powell, MBE, MA	MAJ(FTC)	-		01.05.04	MOD (LONDON)
Somerville, Stuart James	LT(FTC)	S	SM	01.04.01	JSCSC
Soul, Nicholas John, BEng	LT CDR(FTC)	X	P	01.10.04	CHFHQ
South, David John	LT CDR(FTC)	X	AAWO	15.06.97	FOST NWD (JMOTS)
Southall, Emma Louise, BDS	SG LT(D)(SCC)	-		24.09.00	RN GIBRALTAR
Southall, Timothy Edward, BA	SLT(IC)	X	O	01.09.02	FWO PORTS SEA
Southern, Mark John	CAPT RM(CC)	-		01.09.03	UKLFCSG RM
Southern, Paul Jonathan, BSc, IEng, AMIMarEST	LT CDR(FTC)	E	ME	27.02.99	MWS COLLINGWOOD
Southorn, M, pce	LT CDR(FTC)	X	PWO(U)	21.07.99	ARGYLL
Southwell, Neil Peter (Act Lt Cdr)	LT(FTC)	X	C	24.07.97	HQ DCSA
Southwood, Shaun Christopher	LT(IC)	E	MESM	01.05.03	VICTORIOUS(PORT)
Southworth, Christopher, MEng	SLT(IC)	X	O U/T	01.01.03	RNAS CULDROSE
Southworth, Mika-John, BSc	LT(IC)	X		01.09.02	NP IRAQ
Sowden, Lesley Margaret, MB, CHB, MRCGP, DObstRCOG, Dip FFP	SURG LTCDR(MCC)	-	GMPP	02.08.00	RNAS CULDROSE
Spacey, Craig David, BEng	SLT(IC)	E	MESMUT	01.09.03	ILLUSTRIOUS
Spalding, Richard Edmund Howden, BSc, CEng, FIEE, FCMI, jsdc (Act Capt)	CDR(FTC)	E	WE	30.06.97	STRS IPT
Spalton, Gary Marcus Sean, BSc, pce	CDR(FTC)	X	PWO(U)	31.12.92	SACT BELGIUM
Spanner, Paul	MAJ(FTC)	-		01.05.01	MOD (LONDON)
Spark, Stephen Michael	LT(IC)	X		01.05.03	VIGILANT(PORT)
Sparke, Philip Richard William, BA	LT CDR(FTC)	S		01.03.00	EXCHANGE FRANCE
Sparkes, Peter James, BSc, pce, n	CDR(FTC)	X	PWO(C)	30.06.04	MOD (LONDON)
Sparkes, Simon Nicholas, pcea	LT CDR(FTC)	X	P	01.10.02	2SL/CNH FOTR
Sparks, Simon	CAPT RM(IC)	-		01.09.04	40 CDO RM
Sparrow, Mark Jonathan, BSc	LT(CC)	X	P	16.04.99	LOAN OTHER SVCE
Spayne, Nicholas John, n	LT CDR(FTC)	X	PWO(U)	01.10.98	WILDFIRE
Spears, Andrew Graeme, SM(n)	LT(CC)	X	SM	01.11.00	DARTMOUTH BRNC
Speedie, Alan Carrick	2LT(IC)	-		01.09.00	45 CDO RM
Speller, Nicholas Simon Ford, pce(sm), MDA, MCMI, MNI	LT CDR(FTC)	X	SM	01.05.88	FLEET HQ PORTS 2
Spence, Andrei Barry, BSc (Barrister)	CDR(FTC)	S	BAR	30.06.00	NELSON
Spence, Nicholas Anthony, pce	CDR(FTC)	X	PWO(U)	30.06.97	EUMS
Spence, Robert Graeme, BA	LT(FTC)	X	P	16.12.93	845 SQN
Spencer, Ashley Carver, BA	LT(CC)	X		01.05.01	MWS COLLINGWOOD
Spencer, Elizabeth Anne, BEd, MA, psc(j)	CDR(FTC)	X	METOC	30.06.99	FLEET HQ PORTS 2
Spencer, Jeremy Charles	LT(FTC)	E	ME	02.09.99	FLEET HQ PORTS 2
Spencer, Richard Anthony Winchcombe, OBE, BA, psc(j)o	LT COL(FTC)	-	C	31.12.99	JSCSC
Spencer, Steven John	LT CDR(FCC)	Q	CC	01.10.00	NP IRAQ
Spicer, Clive Graham, BSc, CEng, MIMarEST	CDR(FTC)	E	ME	31.12.95	NELSON
Spicer, Mark Nicholas, BSc, psc	BRIG(FTC)	-		16.06.03	IMS BRUSSELS
Spike, Adam James, BSc	LT(IC)	X	P	01.05.02	846 SQN
Spillane, Paul William	LT(CC)	X	O	01.07.96	EXCHANGE USA
Spiller, Michael Francis, BSc, psc	CDR(FTC)	S		31.12.98	PJHQ
Spiller, Stephen Nicholas, BEng	LT(FTC)	E	WE	01.08.97	RMC OF SCIENCE
Spiller, Vanessa Jane, pce, psc(j)	CDR(FTC)	X	PWO(U)	30.06.05	FLEET HQ NWD
Spink, David Andrew	CAPT RM(CC)	-		01.09.02	RM WARMINSTER
Spinks, David William	LT(FTC)	X	PWO(A)	01.08.97	EXCHANGE FRANCE
Spinks, Robert John, BSc	LT(IC)	X	P	01.05.01	845 SQN
Spires, Trevor Allan, BSc, CDipAF, nadc (CHIEF EXECUTIVE OCT 03)	RADM	-	TM	21.10.03	AFPAA HQ
Spooner, Ross Sydney, BEng	LT CDR(FTC)	E	AE	01.04.04	RNAS CULDROSE
Spoors, Brendan Mark, BEng	LT(CC)	X	P	01.01.98	RAF SHAWBURY
Spring, Andrew Ralph James, pce, n	LT CDR(FTC)	X	PWO(U)	01.03.98	FOST DPORT SHORE
Springett, Simon Paul, LLB, CertTh	CHAPLAIN	CE		10.09.91	CTCRM
Spurdle, Andrew Peter	LT(FTC)	X	PWO(A)	20.09.99	INVINCIBLE
Squire, Paul Anthony, BSc, adp, CEng, CITP, CDipAF, MIEE, MAPM, MBCS	LT CDR(FTC)	E	WE	01.10.90	DCCIS FAREHAM
St Aubyn, John David Erskine, BSc	CDR(FTC)	E	WESM	30.06.01	NWR
Stace, Ivan Spencer, BEng, MA, MSc, CEng, MIEE, MCGI, psc(j), mdtc	CDR(FTC)	E	WESM	30.06.04	FWO DEVPT SEA
Stacey, Andrew Michael, BSc	LT CDR(FTC)	X	PWO(A)	01.06.02	DUMBARTON CASTLE
Stacey, Elizabeth Jane	SLT(IC)	X		01.07.02	CHATHAM

Name	Rank	Branch	Spec	Seniority	Where Serving
Stacey, Hugo Alister	LT CDR(FTC(A)	X	P	01.10.93	MERLIN IPT
Stack, Eleanor Frances	LT(CC)	X		01.09.01	LANCASTER
Stackhouse, Martyn Carl	SLT(IC)	X	P	01.01.04	RNAS YEOVILTON
Stafford, Benjamin Robert, MEng	LT(FTC)	E	MESM	01.02.00	DLO BRISTOL
Stafford, Derek Bryan	MAJ(FTC)	-	P	01.10.03	846 SQN
Stafford, Wayne	LT(FTC)	E	WESM	09.01.01	DLO BRISTOL
Stagg, Antony Robert, BEng, MSc	LT CDR(FTC)	E	AE	01.03.03	JCA IPT UK
Stait, Benjamin Geoffrey	LT(FTC)	X	MCD	01.04.99	FDU1
Stait, Carolyn Jane, OBE, ADC, FCIPD, psc	CDRE(FTC)	W	S	22.06.04	NEPTUNE DLO
Stait, Emma Jane	LT(CC)	S		01.04.99	DFTE PORTSMOUTH
Staley, Simon Peter Lee, pce, pcea	LT CDR(FTC)	X	O	01.02.99	NAVSEC
Stallion, Ian Michael, BA, pce, pce(sm)	CDR(FTC)	X	SM	31.12.94	MOD (LONDON)
Stamper, Jonathan Charles Henry, BSc	LT CDR(FTC)	E	IS	01.01.00	RMC OF SCIENCE
Stamper, Valerie Louise, BA	LT(IC)	X		01.09.04	FLEET HQ PORTS
Stancliffe, Andrew Eden	LT(IC)	E	AE	01.07.04	RAF COTTESMORE
Standen, Colin Anthony	CAPT RM(FTC)	-	SO(LE)	01.01.01	RMB STONEHOUSE
Standen, Gary David	LT(IC)	E		01.05.02	DLO YEO
Stanford, Jeremy Hugh, BA, jsdc, pce	CAPT(FTC)	X	P	30.06.01	BULWARK
Stangroom, Alastair, pce	CDR(FTC)	X	MCD	30.06.03	LOAN OMAN
Stanham, Christopher Mark	LT CDR(FTC)	E	AE	01.10.01	ADAS BRISTOL
Stanhope, Mark, KCB, OBE, MA, MNI, rcds, pce, pce(sm), psc, hcsc (DEPUTY SACT JUL 04)	ADM	-	SM	10.07.04	HQ SACT
Stanistreet, Georgina Clare, BEng	LT(IC)	E	ME U/T	01.05.04	IRON DUKE
Stanley, Andrew Brian	LT(IC)	E	MESM	01.10.02	FWO DEVONPORT
Stanley, Christopher Edward, pce, psc	CDR(FTC)	X	AAWO	30.06.94	MWC PORTSDOWN
Stanley, Nicholas Paul, MPhil, pce, psc	CAPT(FTC)	X	MCD	30.06.02	MOD (LONDON)
Stanley, Paul, BEd, jsdc, ODC(SWISS)	CDR(FTC)	E	TM	30.06.92	SULTAN
Stanley-Whyte, Berkeley John, BSc, MA, CEng, MIEE, psc(j)	CDR(FTC)	E	WESM	31.12.98	DLO BRISTOL
Stannard, Adam, MB, ChB, BSc	SURG LT(MCC)	-		02.08.00	MDHU NORTH
Stannard, Mark Philip	LT CDR(FTC)	X		01.08.97	LOAN SAUDI ARAB
Stant, Mark Simon, BEng	SLT(IC)	X	P U/T	01.11.02	RNAS YEOVILTON
Stanton, David Vernon, MBE, pcea, psc(j)	CDR(FTC)	X	O	30.06.03	RNAS CULDROSE
Stanton, Keith Victor	CAPT RM(CC)	-	SO(LE)	01.04.03	CTCRM
Stanton, Paul Charles Maund, BSc, ACMA	LT CDR(FTC)	S	CMA	16.02.97	NAVSEC
Stanton-Brown, Peter James, BSc, SM(n)	LT CDR(FTC)	X	SM	01.02.01	FOST DPORT SHORE
Stanway, Charles Adrian, BSc, SM(n)	LT(FTC)	X	SM	01.09.00	SUPERB
Stapley, Sarah Ann, MB, ChB, MD, FRCS, FRCSTr&Orth	SURG CDR(FCC)	-	(CO/S)	30.06.02	RH HASLAR
Starkey, David Samuel	SLT(IC)	X		01.02.03	EXETER
Starks, Michael Robert, BSc, MA, CEng, MRAeS, psc	CDR(FTC)	E	AE	30.06.97	FLEET HQ PORTS
Stead, Abigail, BSc	LT(IC)	X	P	01.01.04	RAF LINTN/OUSE
Stead, Andrew Michael, BSc	LT(IC)	E	TM	01.07.99	RALEIGH
Stead, John Arthur, BSc	LT(TC)	E	WESM	02.09.99	CLYDE MIXMAN1
Stead, Richard Alexander, MBA	LT CDR(FTC)	MS	(AD)	01.10.01	MOD (LONDON)
Steadman, Rebecca Angharad Jane, BSc	LT(FTC)	X	O	01.04.02	849 SQN A FLT
Steadman, Robert Paul, BA	LT CDR(FTC)	X	PWO(A)	01.05.04	MWS COLLINGWOOD
Stearns, Rupert Paul, MA, psc, psc(j)	COL(FTC)	-	LC	30.06.03	CDO LOG REGT RM
Steeds, Sean Michael, pce, pcea, psc(j)	CDR(FTC)	X	P	30.06.98	LANG TRNG(UK)
Steel, Christopher Michael Howard, BSc, CEng, MIEE, MCMI, jsdc	CAPT(FTC)	E	WESM	30.06.04	2SL/CNH FOTR
Steel, David George, BA, FCIPD, jsdc (Barrister)	CAPT(FTC)	S	BAR	31.12.00	MOD (LONDON)
Steel, David Goodwin	LT CDR(FTC)	MS	(CDO)	01.10.98	MDHU DERRIFORD
Steel, Peter St Clair, BSc, jsdc, pce	CAPT(FTC)	X	P	30.06.01	NELSON
Steele, Matthew Stuart, BSc	LT(IC)	X	HM	01.05.02	ILLUSTRIOUS
Steele, Trevor Graeme	LT(FTC)	X	O	11.12.92	MWS COLLINGWOOD
Steen, Kieron Malcolm, BSc	LT(CC)	X	P	01.01.98	801 SQN
Steer, Rebecca	SURG SLT(SCC)	-		01.07.03	DARTMOUTH BRNC
Steiger, Robert Carl	LT(IC)	E	IS U/T	01.11.03	FLEET HQ NWD
Stein, Graham Kenneth, BSc	LT(CC)	X	P	01.11.98	846 SQN
Stembridge, Daniel Patrick Trelawney	LT CDR(FTC)	X	P	01.10.03	EXCHANGE USA
Stemp, Justin Edward, BA	MAJ(FTC)	-		01.09.04	FLEET HQ PORTS
Stenhouse, Nicholas John, BSc, MA, CEng, MIEE, psc	CDR(FTC)	E	WE	31.12.93	CALEDONIA DLO
Stephen, Barry Mark, BA, n	LT CDR(FTC)	X	PWO(U)	01.03.02	IRON DUKE
Stephen, Thomas	2LT(IC)	-		01.08.01	CTCRM LYMPSTONE
Stephens, Christopher	SLT(IC)	E	WE	01.01.04	MWS COLLINGWOOD

Name	Rank	Branch	Spec	Seniority	Where Serving
Stephens, Patrick George	SLT(IC)	X		01.07.02	ALBION
Stephens, Richard James, MBE, MA, psc(j)	LT COL(FTC)	-		30.06.03	MOD (LONDON)
Stephens, Richard John, BSc, PGDip	LT CDR(CC)	X	METOC	01.09.02	EXCHANGE NLANDS
Stephens, Richard Philip	LT CDR(FTC)	X	EW	01.10.99	FLEET CIS PORTS
Stephens, Samuel Jolyon Roderick, MSc	SLT(IC)	X		01.01.03	MONMOUTH
Stephenson, Christopher John, BSc	LT(IC)	X		01.04.03	MWS COLLINGWOOD
Stephenson, David, BEng, MSc, CEng	LT CDR(FTC)	E	ME	22.11.95	CV(F) IPT
Stephenson, John Michael, BSc	SLT(IC)	X		01.05.03	DARTMOUTH BRNC
Stephenson, Keith James MacFarlane, BA	LT CDR(CC)	E	IS	01.10.02	RMC OF SCIENCE
Stephenson, Philip George, BSc, MILog	LT CDR(FTC)	S	(S)	01.10.03	ALBION
Stephenson, Richard	SLT(IC)	S		01.11.03	RALEIGH
Sterry, Jasen Edward Baxter	LT(CC)	X	REG	01.09.01	NEPTUNE 2SL/CNH
Stevens, Andrew John	LT(SC(MD)	Q		24.09.99	RH HASLAR
Stevens, Andrew Mark Robert	LT(FTC)	X	MCD	01.10.97	MCM3 SEA
Stevens, Anthony, BA	LT(IC)	E	TMSM	04.12.97	DARTMOUTH BRNC
Stevens, Christopher Kenneth	MID(NE)(IC)	X		01.09.04	DARTMOUTH BRNC
Stevens, Derek George	LT(IC)	E	TM	01.01.02	NTE(TTD)
Stevens, Joseph Iain, BEng	LT(IC)	E	AE U/T	01.09.03	848 SQN HERON
Stevens, Robert Patrick, CB, pce, pce(sm) (COS TO CDR ALLIED NAVAL FORCES S.EUROPE JAN 02)	RADM	-	SM(N)	04.08.98	AGRIPPA MAR CC
Stevenson, Adam Peter, BA	LT(IC)	X		01.09.04	MWS COLLINGWOOD
Stevenson, Geoffrey Stewart, BDS, MFGDP(UK)	SGLTCDR(D)(SCC)	-		14.01.99	RALEIGH
Stevenson, Julian Patrick, BEng	LT(FTC)	E	MESM	01.11.93	TRIUMPH
Stevenson, Laura, BDS	SG LT(D)(SC(MD)	-		27.06.03	DRAKE COB(CNH)
Stevenson, Paul Michael, BEng	LT(IC)	E	MESM	01.09.04	SULTAN
Stevenson, Robert MacKinnon, BDS, MSc, MGDS RCS (Act Sgcapt(D))	SGCDR(D)(FCC)	-		31.12.90	DDA PORTSMOUTH
Stevenson, Simon Richard	LT(IC)	X	P	01.01.02	820 SQN
Stewart, Andrew Carnegie, pce, MIL	CDR(FTC)	X	PWO(C)	30.06.00	MWS COLLINGWOOD
Stewart, Benjamin Christopher	LT(IC)	X		01.05.03	NP IRAQ
Stewart, Charles Hardie, BSc	LT(IC)	X		01.09.01	MWS COLLINGWOOD
Stewart, David James, OBE, MC, BSc, MA, psc	COL(FTC)	-	C	30.06.05	CTCRM
Stewart, James Neil, BSc, MA, psc(j)	CDR(FTC)	E	TMSM	30.06.03	FLEET HQ PORTS
Stewart, Kenneth Currie, BSc	LT CDR(FTC)	E	TM	01.09.98	NEPTUNE 2SL/CNH
Stewart, Marcus Patrick Michael	CHAPLAIN	CE		29.03.04	RNAS YEOVILTON
Stewart, Michael David, MB, ChB, MRCP	SURG CDR(FCC)	-	(CM)	30.06.01	RH HASLAR
Stewart, Nicholas John, MSc	LT(IC)	X		01.05.04	ATHERSTONE
Stewart, Robert Gordon, BSc, psc	CAPT(FTC)	X	H CH	30.06.04	MOD (LONDON)
Stewart, Rory William, BSc	LT CDR(FTC)	E	MESM	01.07.91	DRAKE SFM
Stickland, Charles Richard, BSc, MA, psc(j)	LT COL(FTC)	-	LC	30.06.04	MOD (LONDON)
Stidston, Ian James, BSc, MDA, MCIPD	CDR(FTC)	E	TM	31.12.00	NAVSEC
Stillwell-Cox, Andrew David Robert, MHCIMA, MCFA, MinstAM	LT CDR(FTC)	S	CA	01.10.00	RNAS CULDROSE
Stilwell, James Michael, BA, SM(n)	LT(CC)	X	SM	01.01.98	SCEPTRE
Stinton, Carol Ann	LT CDR(FCC)	Q	OTSPEC	01.10.99	PJHQ
Stirzaker, Mark, BSc, MA, CEng, MINucE, AMIMechE	CDR(FTC)	E	MESM	30.06.05	FLEET HQ PORTS 2
Stitson, Paul	CAPT RM(IC)	-		01.09.03	RMR BRISTOL
Stiven, Timothy David, MSc	LT CDR(FTC)	E	ME	01.03.04	DLO BRISTOL
Stobie, Paul Lionel	LT CDR(FTC)	E	AE	01.10.01	DLO WYTON
Stock, Christopher Mark	LT CDR(FTC)	X	O	01.10.04	MWC PORTSDOWN
Stockbridge, Antony Julian, MA	LT(FTC)	S	SM	01.03.97	2SL/CNH
Stockings, Timothy Mark, BSc, pce, pcea, psc(j)	CDR(FTC)	X	P	30.06.00	MOD (LONDON)
Stockton, Kevin Geoffrey	LT CDR(FTC)	X	PWO(U)	19.11.00	FOSNNI
Stoffell, David Peter, GCIPD	LT CDR(FTC)	S	SM	27.11.98	NAVSEC
Stokes, Alan William	LT CDR(FTC)	E	WESM	01.10.98	HQ DCSA
Stokes, Richard, BSc, MDA, DipFM, CEng, MIEE	CDR(FTC)	E	WESM	31.12.98	NAVSEC
Stone, Colin Robert Macleod, pce	LT CDR(FTC)	X	PWO(U)	01.05.85	FLEET HQ NWD
Stone, James William Gray, BSc	LT(IC)	X	O	01.05.02	849 SQN B FLT
Stone, Nicholas Joseph John, BA	LT(CC)	S	SM	01.07.00	FLEET HQ PORTS 2
Stone, Nicholas Stuart	MID(UCE)(IC)	X		01.09.03	DARTMOUTH BRNC
Stone, Paul Christopher Julian, BSc, pcea, tp	CDR(FTC)	X	P	30.06.04	MOD (LONDON)
Stone, Richard James	LT(FTC)	E	ME	19.06.98	ENDURANCE
Stoneman, Timothy John, BSc, MA, pce, psc	CDR(FTC)	X	AAWO	31.12.91	CAPT MCTA
Stonier, Paul Leslie (Act Maj)	CAPT RM(FTC)	-	SO(LE)	01.01.01	CTCRM

Name	Rank	Branch	Spec	Seniority	Where Serving
Stonor, Philip Francis Andrew, pce, pcea, odc(Fr)	CDR(FTC)	X	P	31.12.95	UKMILREP BRUSS
Storey, Andrew Eric	LT(IC)	X	SM	01.05.02	VIGILANT(STBD)
Storey, Anne-Louise	LT(IC)	MS		01.11.03	2SL/CNH
Storey, Ceri Leigh, BEng, MBA	LT CDR(FTC)	E	MESM	01.08.03	SCEPTRE
Storrs-Fox, Roderick Noble, BSc, MBA	CDR(FTC)	S		31.12.95	DLO BRISTOL
Storton, George Houston	SLT(IC)	X		01.07.03	SEVERN
Story, Ruth Siobhan, BA	SLT(IC)	X		01.01.03	BLYTH
Stott, John Antony, MIEE	LT CDR(FTC)	E	WESM	26.05.91	FLEET HQ PORTS 2
Stovin-Bradford, Matthew, psc(j)o	MAJ(FTC)	-	C	01.09.99	PJHQ
Stowell, Perry Ivan Mottram, pce, n	LT CDR(FTC)	X	PWO(U)	01.04.98	MONMOUTH
Stowell, Robin Barnaby Mottram, BEng, MSc, CEng	LT CDR(FTC)	E	ME	01.09.03	FLEET HQ PORTS
Strachan, Richard Parry, MB, CHB	SURG LT(SC(MD)	-		06.08.03	NEPTUNE DLO
Strange, Steven Paul, BEng, CEng, MIEE	LT(FTC)	E	WESM	01.09.97	RALEIGH
Stratford, Peter John	LT(CC)	X	ATC	01.04.95	RAF SHAWBURY
Strathern, Roderick James	LT CDR(FTC)	X	PWO(U)	01.10.98	FOST SEA
Strathie, Gavin Scott	LT(CC)	X	ATC	01.06.96	RNAS CULDROSE
Stratton, John Denniss, BSc, CEng, FRAeS, psc	CAPT(FTC)	E	AE	30.06.02	DLO YEO
Stratton, Matthew Paul, BEng, MSc	LT(FTC)	E	WE	01.05.99	MWS COLLINGWOOD
Stratton, Nicholas Charles, SM(n)	LT(CC)	X	SM	01.05.00	VENGEANCE(PORT)
Stratton, Stuart John	LT(IC)	E	MESM	01.05.01	VENGEANCE(PORT)
Straughan, Christopher John, MBE, pce	LT CDR(FTC)	X	PWO(U)	01.12.90	FWO DEVPT SEA
Straughan, Harry, MSc, psc	CDR(FTC)	E	IS	31.12.97	DCCIS BLANDFORD
Straughan, Scott Richard, BEng	LT(CC)	E	IS	01.05.97	IMS BRUSSELS
Straw, Andrew Nicholas	CDR(FTC)	S		30.06.03	FLEET HQ PORTS
Strawbridge, Chantal Marie, BA, BSc	LT(IC)	X		01.09.04	KENT
Street, Paul M	LT(IC)	E	WESM	01.07.04	RALEIGH
Street, Sarah Caroline	LT(IC)	S		01.05.04	RNAS YEOVILTON
Streeten, Christopher Mark, BSc, CEng, MIEE, nadc	CDR(FTC)	E	WESM	30.06.02	MOD (LONDON)
Streets, Christopher George, MB, BCh, BSc	SURG LTCDR(FCC)	-		01.08.98	NELSON (PAY)
Stretton, Darrell George	LT(FTC)	X	AV	03.04.97	FLEET HQ PORTS
Strickland, Timothy John, BEng	SLT(IC)	X	P U/T	01.02.04	DARTMOUTH BRNC
Stride, James Alan, BA	LT CDR(FTC)	X	HM2	01.10.03	MWS COLLINGWOOD
Stride, Jamieson Colin	LT CDR(FTC)	X	O	01.04.03	815 FLT 200
Stringer, Graeme Ellis	LT(FTC)	X	ATC	19.09.00	RNAS YEOVILTON
Stringer, Roger Andrew, pcea	LT CDR(FTC)	X	P	01.10.97	GANNET SAR FLT
Stroude, Paul Addison, BEng, n	LT CDR(FTC)	X		01.08.04	CORNWALL
Strudwick, Russell	LT CDR(FTC)	S	(W)	01.10.03	ST ALBANS
Strutt, Jason Fearnley, BEng, MSc	LT CDR(FTC)	E	WE	01.05.00	LIVERPOOL
Stuart, Euan Edward Andrew	LT CDR(FTC)	X	PWO(A)	01.10.04	EXCHANGE AUSTLIA
Stuart, Simon Alexander, BSc	LT(IC)	X	O	01.09.04	815 SQN HQ
Stubbings, Paul Richard	CDR(FTC)	E	MESM	31.12.99	FWO DEVONPORT
Stubbs, Benjamin Duncan, BEng	LT(IC)	X	P	01.09.03	FLEET AV VALLEY
Stubbs, Ian	LT(CC)	X	O	16.05.95	JSCSC
Stubbs, Ian	LT(IC)	E	TM U/T	01.02.03	MWS COLLINGWOOD
Stubbs, Martin Andrew	LT CDR(FTC)	E	WESM	01.10.03	JSSU CHELTENHAM
Sturdy, Clive Charles Markus	LT CDR(FTC)	X	PWO(U)	01.06.04	SUTHERLAND
Sturgeon, David Marcus	LT(IC)	S	SM	01.05.02	DRAKE COB
Sturgeon, Mark, BEng	LT(IC)	E	WESM	01.09.02	JSCSC
Sturman, Richard William, BSc	LT(CC)	X	P	01.08.00	846 SQN
Stuttard, Mark Christopher, pce	LT CDR(FTC)	X	PWO(A)	01.07.94	FLEET HQ PORTS 2
Stuttard, Stephen Eric	LT CDR(FTC)	X	AV	01.10.97	FLEET HQ PORTS
Style, Charles Rodney, CBE, MA, rcds, pce, hcsc (COMASWSTRIKFOR MAY 04)	RADM	-	PWO(U)	21.01.02	UKMARBATSTAFF
Suchet, Robert	CAPT RM(IC)	-		01.09.04	EXCHANGE ARMY UK
Suckling, Robin Leslie, pcea	LT CDR(FTC)	X	O	01.10.02	FOST NWD (JMOTS)
Suddes, Lesley Ann, BA, psc(j)	CDR(FTC)	X	METOC	30.06.03	MOD (LONDON)
Sugden, Michael Rodney, BSc, MBA	LT CDR(FTC)	E	ME	01.10.94	DLO BRISTOL
Sugden, Stephen Robert, HNC	LT CDR(FTC)	E	WE	01.10.99	DSFM PORTSMOUTH
Sullivan, Anne Gillian, BSc, MA, FRMS, psc(j)	CDR(FTC)	X	METOC	31.12.99	MOD (LONDON)
Sullivan, Colin, BA, psc	CDR(FTC)	X	METOC	31.12.96	COM MCC NWD
Sullivan, Mark, BSc, BEng, CEng, MIEE	LT CDR(FTC)	E	WE	01.07.01	MANCHESTER
Sullivan, Mark Nigel, BEng, MIMechE	LT(FTC)	E	ME	01.12.97	FOST SEA
Sullivan, Timothy Ernest, MSc, BA(OU), DEH, MIOSH	LT(IC)	MS		29.04.01	MOD (BATH)

Name	Rank	Branch	Spec	Seniority	Where Serving
Summerfield, David Edward, osc(us)	LT COL(FTC)	-		30.06.00	RMR LONDON
Summers, Alastair John	LT(CC)	X	P	01.12.00	849 SQN HQ
Sumner, Michael Dennis, MIIE	CDR(FTC)	E	WESM	30.06.03	MOD (LONDON)
Sunderland, John Dominic, MSc, CEng, MIEE	CDR(FTC)	E	WESM	31.12.97	MOD (LONDON)
Surgey, Ian, SM	LT CDR(FTC)	X	SM	26.10.97	FLEET HQ NWD
Sutcliff, Jonathan David, MEng	SLT(IC)	E	WE U/T	01.11.02	MWS COLLINGWOOD
Sutcliffe, Edward Diccon, BA (Act Lt Cdr)	LT(CC)	S	SM	01.05.98	JSCSC
Sutcliffe, John, pce, pcea	CDR(FTC)	X	O	30.06.04	EXCHANGE USA
Sutcliffe, Paul Matthew, BA	LT(IC)	X		01.01.05	INVINCIBLE
Sutcliffe, Roy William	LT CDR(FTC)	E	WESM	01.10.00	MOD CSSE USA
Suter, Francis Thomas	LT(CC)	X	O	01.01.02	815 FLT 208
Sutherland, Gayl, BSc, Dip ICN	LT(FC(MD)	Q		25.10.00	MDHU DERRIFORD
Sutherland, Iain Duncan	LT RM(CC)	-		01.09.03	CTCRM
Sutherland, Neil, MSc	MAJ(FTC)	-	C	24.04.02	JSCSC
Sutton, David, MBE	CAPT RM(CC)	-	P	01.04.01	847 SQN
Sutton, Gareth David, MSc, CEng, MIMarEST	LT CDR(FTC)	E	ME	01.06.93	CTS
Sutton, Gary Brian, pce	CAPT(FTC)	X	PWO(N)	30.06.05	DGMC SEA
Sutton, Richard Michael John	LT CDR(FTC)	X	P	01.10.02	846 SQN
Sutton, Stephen John	CAPT RM(CC)	-	P	29.04.97	845 SQN
Swain, Andrew Vincent, MBE, AFRIN, pce	CDR(FTC)	X	H CH	30.06.05	COMATG SEA
Swain, David Michael, BSc, FNI, pce, pcea	CAPT(FTC)	X	O	30.06.01	PJHQ
Swan, Wendy	LT(CC)	W		19.01.96	MWS COLLINGWOOD
Swann, Adam Peter Drummond, BA	SLT(IC)	X		01.03.03	MANCHESTER
Swann, John Ivan, BSc (Act Lt Cdr)	LT(FTC)	X	EW	28.07.89	RNU RAF DIGBY
Swannick, Derek John, BSc, psc(j)	CDR(FTC)	X	METOC	30.06.02	MWS HM TG (D)
Swarbrick, Richard James, BA, pce, pcea, psc(j)	CDR(FTC)	X	P	30.06.04	PJHQ
Sweeney, Craig, BSc	LT(CC)	X	P	16.02.99	845 SQN
Sweeney, Keith Patrick Michael, BEng	LT CDR(FTC)	E	ME	01.08.03	SOMERSET
Sweeney, Rachel Jane, BEng	LT(IC)	E	AE	01.01.01	849 SQN A FLT
Sweetman, David James	SLT(IC)	E	WE U/T	01.11.02	2SL/CNH
Sweny, Gordon	2LT(IC)	-		01.08.01	CTCRM LYMPSTONE
Swift, Robert David	LT(IC)	S		01.09.04	TRIUMPH
Swift, Robin David, pce	CDR(FTC)	X	PWO(U)	30.06.05	HQ SACT
Swindells, Mark, BEng	LT(CC)	X	P	16.07.99	815 FLT 212
Swire, Barry John, BA	LT(SC(MD)	Q		26.07.02	RH HASLAR
Sykes, Hannah Elizabeth, BA	SLT(IC)	X		01.01.04	DARTMOUTH BRNC
Sykes, Jeremy James William, MSc, MB, CHB, FRCP, FFOM (Commodore)	SURG CAPT(FCC)	-	(CO/M)	31.12.98	DPMD
Sykes, Karen Dawn	LT(IC)	MS		01.11.02	MDHU DERRIFORD
Sykes, Malcolm, BEng, MSc, psc	CDR(FTC)	E	MESM	30.06.02	DRAKE SFM
Sykes, Matthew John	LT(FTC)	X		01.09.02	NOTTINGHAM
Sykes, Robert Alan, BSc	LT CDR(FTC)	X	O	01.10.96	MOD (LONDON)
Symcox, Charles Michael	SLT(IC)	X	P U/T	01.01.05	815 FLT 209
Syrett, Matthew Edward, BSc, PGDip, PGDIPAN, n	LT CDR(FTC)	X	HM2	01.08.03	FOST SEA
Syson, Carl Frederick, MEng	LT(IC)	X	P	01.01.04	RAF CRANWELL EFS
Syvret, Mark Edward Vibert, BSc, psc(j)o	LT COL(FTC)	-		30.06.01	MOD (LONDON)

T

Name	Rank	Branch	Spec	Seniority	Where Serving
Tabeart, George William, pce	LT CDR(FTC)	X	H CH	01.11.97	ENDURANCE
Taberham, Hazel, BEng	SLT(IC)	E	AE U/T	01.09.03	ILLUSTRIOUS
Taborda, Matthew Anthony, BSc	SLT(IC)	X		01.09.02	NOTTINGHAM
Tacey, Richard Haydn	LT(CC)	X	PWO(A)	01.12.95	STRIKFORNATO
Tait, Martyn David, BEng	LT(CC)	E	TM	27.08.02	ASM IPT
Tait, Stacey Jane, BSc, MIEE	LT(CC)	E	WE	01.01.02	JSCSC
Talbot, Christopher Martin	LT CDR(FTC)	X	C	01.10.99	FOSNNI
Talbot, Richard John, BSc	LT(IC)	X		01.05.02	FDG
Talbot, Richard Paul, MA, pce, psc(j)	CDR(FTC)	X	PWO(A)	30.06.00	MOD (LONDON)
Talbot, Simon James	SLT(IC)	X	FC	01.05.02	CARDIFF
Talbot, Stephen Edward, BSc	SLT(IC)	X		01.05.02	MWS COLLINGWOOD
Talbott, Aidan Hugh	LT CDR(FTC)	S		01.12.99	COS 2SL/CNH
Tall, Iain	LT(IC)	E	WE	01.07.04	BULWARK
Tamayo, Brando Christian Craig, MB, ChB, DipIMC RCSED	SURG LTCDR(MCC)	-		01.08.99	NELSON (PAY)

Name	Rank	Branch	Spec	Seniority	Where Serving
Tamlyn, Stephen John, BSc	CAPT RM(CC)	-		01.05.01	UKLFCSG RM
Tanner, Michael John, psc(j)	MAJ(FTC)	-		01.09.02	COMAMPHIBFOR
Tanner, Richard Carlisle, SM(n), SM	LT CDR(FTC)	X	SM	01.03.03	VIGILANT(STBD)
Tanser, Susan Jane, MB, BS, FRCA	SURG CDR(FCC)	-	(CA)	30.06.03	RH HASLAR
Tantam, Robert John Geoffrey, MEng	LT(IC)	E	MESM	01.09.03	TORBAY
Tapp, Steven John	CAPT RM(FTC)	-	SO(LE)	01.01.01	EXCHANGE ARMY UK
Tappin, Simon John, BEng	LT(IC)	X		01.01.02	GLOUCESTER
Targett, Helen Anne	SLT(IC)	S		01.09.04	815 SQN HQ
Tarmey, Sarah Louise, BSc	LT(IC)	S		01.09.04	2SL/CNH
Tarnowski, Tomasz Adam, MSc, MIL	MAJ(IC)	-	LC	12.11.04	CTCRM
Tarr, Barry Stuart, BSc(Eng), MSc, CEng, MIMarEST	CDR(FTC)	E	MESM	30.06.02	NP BRISTOL
Tarr, Michael Douglas, OBE, BSc, pce, psc(a)	CAPT(FTC)	X	AAWO	30.06.02	MWS COLLINGWOOD
Tarr, Richard Nicholas Vaughan, BSc, CEng, MIMechE	CDR(FTC)	E	MESM	30.06.04	FOST SM SEA
Tarrant, Robert Kenneth, pce, pce(sm)	CAPT(FTC)	X	SM	30.06.04	MOD (LONDON)
Tasker, Adam Murray, BA	LT(IC)	X	O U/T	01.05.05	RNAS CULDROSE
Tasker, Greg, psc(m)	LT COL(FTC)	-		31.12.95	MOD (BATH)
Tate, Andrew John, BSc, MIEE, psc	CAPT(FTC)	E	WESM	30.06.02	NELSON
Tate, Nicholas Mark	LT(IC)	E	ME	01.05.02	MWS EXCELLENT
Tate, Simon John, OBE, BSc, MA, CEng, MRAeS, psc(j)	CDR(FTC)	E	AE	31.12.99	JFCHQ BRUNSSUM
Tatham, Stephen Alan, BSc, MPhil	LT CDR(FTC)	E	TM	01.09.99	MWS COLLINGWOOD
Tattersall, Richard Brian	LT CDR(FTC)	X	P	01.10.01	EXCHANGE USA
Tatton-Brown, Hugh Trelawny	SLT(IC)	E	WE	01.09.01	MWS COLLINGWOOD
Tawse, Lawrence Oliver John, BSc	LT(IC)	X	P U/T	01.01.05	RNAS YEOVILTON
Tayal, Manish, MB, CHB, BSc	SURG LT(SCC)	-		01.08.04	RH HASLAR
Taylor, Andrew	LT(IC)	X		18.02.05	SUTHERLAND
Taylor, Andrew Ian, BSc, SM(n), SM	LT(IC)	X	SM	01.12.99	MWS HM TG (D)
Taylor, Andrew Lyndon, BA, MSc	LT CDR(CC)	E	IS	01.05.03	AGRIPPA JFC HQ
Taylor, Anna, HND, PGDip	LT CDR(CC)	E	IS	01.10.00	DNR N IRELAND
Taylor, Anthony Richard, BA, MA(CANTAB), pce, n, SM(n)	LT CDR(FTC)	X	PWO(U)	01.11.98	WESTMINSTER
Taylor, Brian David	LT CDR(FTC)	X		01.07.96	FWO PORTS SEA
Taylor, Carl Richard	LT CDR(FTC)	S		01.08.02	EXCHANGE USA
Taylor, Christopher Simon, MSc	LT(CC)	E	TM	01.01.97	FWO FASLANE SEA
Taylor, Gordon David, BA	LT(IC)	X	SM	01.01.02	SCEPTRE
Taylor, Ian John, BEng	LT(CC)	E	TM	05.05.96	FOST DPORT SHORE
Taylor, Ian Kennedy, MSc	LT CDR(FTC)	S	(S)	01.10.01	ENDURANCE
Taylor, James Edward, BSc	LT(IC)	X	P	01.09.04	RNAS YEOVILTON
Taylor, James Edward Henry, BSc	LT(IC)	X		01.09.02	ILLUSTRIOUS
Taylor, James Tremayne, BSc	LT(IC)	X	O U/T	01.09.04	RNAS CULDROSE
Taylor, John Jeremy, MSc, CEng, FIMarEST	CAPT(FTC)	E	MESM	30.06.05	NP BRISTOL
Taylor, John William, MIPM	CDR(FTC)	X	ATC	30.06.01	2SL/CNH FOTR
Taylor, Jonathan Paul, SM(n), SM	LT CDR(FTC)	X	SM	01.10.03	MOD (LONDON)
Taylor, Keith Milbrun, BEng	LT(FTC)	E	WE	01.08.98	RMC OF SCIENCE
Taylor, Kenneth Alistair, BSc, pce, pcea, psc	CDR(FTC)	X	O	31.12.97	CV(F) IPT
Taylor, Kenneth John	LT CDR(FTC)	E	WESM	01.10.99	FLEET HQ PORTS 2
Taylor, Leslie, MBE, pcea	LT CDR(FTC(A)	X	P	01.10.94	849 SQN HQ
Taylor, Lisa Margaret	LT(MC(MD)	Q		05.07.99	JSU NORTHWOOD
Taylor, Marcus Anthony Beckett	MAJ(FTC)	-	LC	01.09.01	FLEET HQ PORTS 2
Taylor, Mark Andrew, pce, pcea	LT CDR(FTC)	X	P	01.02.99	NAVSEC
Taylor, Mark Richard	LT CDR(FTC)	X	C	01.10.00	HQ DCSA
Taylor, Martin Kenneth, OBE, osc	LT COL(FTC)	-	C	30.06.94	STRIKFORNATO
Taylor, Neil John	CAPT RM(CC)	-		01.09.02	JWW
Taylor, Neil Robert, BEng, AMIMechE	LT CDR(FTC)	E	ME	01.10.02	DRAKE SFM
Taylor, Neil Robert, BSc	SLT(IC)	X		01.02.04	DARTMOUTH BRNC
Taylor, Nicholas Frederick, MA, pce	LT CDR(FTC)	X	PWO(C)	16.02.87	HQ DCSA
Taylor, Nicholas Simon Charles, BA	SLT(IC)	X		01.11.02	CATTISTOCK
Taylor, Nigel Anthony, BSc, MIOSH (Act Lt Cdr)	LT(IC)	MS		06.03.96	2SL/CNH
Taylor, Peter George David, BSc, MA, psc(j)	LT COL(FTC)	-		30.06.03	HQ 3 CDO BDE RM
Taylor, Peter John, MB, BS, FRCS, DA, DTM&H	SURG CDR(MCC)	-	(CGS)	30.06.05	LOAN FIELD HOSP
Taylor, Robert, BEng, MSc, CEng, MIEE, gw	LT CDR(FTC)	E	WE	01.09.99	DLO BRISTOL
Taylor, Robert James	LT(FTC)	X	O	16.02.94	RNAS YEOVILTON
Taylor, Robert Paul, BSc	LT(IC)	X	P	01.05.02	824 SQN
Taylor, Robert Scott, BSc, MB, BS	SURG LT(MC(MD)	-	SM	07.08.02	VENGEANCE(PORT)
Taylor, Scott Andrew, BEng	SLT(IC)	X		01.06.03	DARTMOUTH BRNC

Name	Rank	Branch	Spec	Seniority	Where Serving
Taylor, Spencer Alan, MSc, CEng, MIEE	CDR(FTC)	E	IS	30.06.98	NAVSEC
Taylor, Stephen John, BA (Barrister)	CDR(FTC)	S	BAR	30.06.03	COS 2SL/CNH
Taylor, Stephen John, BEng, CEng, MIEE	LT CDR(FTC)	E	WE	01.10.01	PJHQ
Taylor, Stephen Mark	LT CDR(FTC)	S		01.11.93	RNAS CULDROSE
Taylor, Stephen Robert, BEng	SLT(IC)	E	MESMUT	01.09.03	CAMPBELTOWN
Taylor, Stuart David, BSc	MAJ(CC)	-		01.10.04	CTCRM
Taylor, Terence Peter	LT(CC)	X	ATC	01.10.00	RNAS YEOVILTON
Taylor, William John, OBE, osc	COL(FTC)	-		30.06.04	FLEET HQ PORTS 2
Tazewell, Matthew Robert, BEng	LT(CC)	X	O	16.10.98	702 SQN HERON
Teasdale, James Paul, BEng	SLT(IC)	E	WE	01.11.02	MWS COLLINGWOOD
Teasdale, Robert Mark, BA	LT CDR(FTC)	S		16.01.93	RNAS CULDROSE
Tebbet, Paul Nicholas, pce	LT CDR(FTC)	X	PWO(U)	01.09.97	FOST SEA
Teideman, Ian Charles, BEng, MIEE	LT CDR(FTC)	E	WE	01.03.00	FOST SEA
Telfer, Duncan Deans	SLT(IC)	X	P U/T	01.11.02	DARTMOUTH BRNC
Temple, David Christopher	LT(FTC)	E	WE	01.04.01	MWS COLLINGWOOD
Tennant, Michael Ian, MB, BS	SURG LTCDR(FC(MD)	-		14.09.00	NELSON (PAY)
Tennuci, Robert George, pce	LT CDR(FTC)	X	AAWO	01.12.99	COMAMPHIBFOR
Terry, John Michael, MSc, CEng, MIMarEST	CDR(FTC)	E	ME	31.12.96	COS 2SL/CNH
Terry, Judith Helen, BSc	LT(CC)	S		01.12.98	FOST NWD (JMOTS)
Terry, Michael Charles Gadesden, MB, BS, FRCS	SURG CDR(MCC)	-	(CGS)	30.06.03	RH HASLAR
Terry, Nigel Patrick	LT(CC)	X	P	01.09.96	771 SQN
Tetchner, David James, BEng	SLT(IC)	E	WE	01.11.02	MWS COLLINGWOOD
Tetley, Mark	LT CDR(FTC)	X	O	01.10.03	829 FLT 03
Tetlow, Hamish Stuart Guy, BA	LT CDR(FTC)	X	SM	01.07.96	MOD (LONDON)
Thain-Smith, Julie Christina	LT CDR(MC(MD)	Q		31.03.99	RCDM
Thatcher, Louise Frances Victoria, BA	LT(FTC)	X		01.02.00	DULVERTON
Thicknesse, Philip John, MA, pce, pcea, psc	CAPT(FTC)	X	P	30.06.04	MOD (LONDON)
Thistlethwaite, Mark Halford, BSc, MCIPD, psc	CAPT(FTC)	E	AE	30.06.05	FLEET HQ PORTS 2
Thoburn, Ross, OBE, pce	CDR(FTC)	X	O	30.06.92	NELSON
Thom, Mathew Frank, BA	LT(IC)	X	SM	01.01.02	VICTORIOUS(PORT)
Thomas, Adam Joseph, BEng	LT(IC)	E	AE U/T	01.03.03	820 SQN
Thomas, Andrew Giles	SLT(UCE)(IC)	E	ME	01.09.02	DARTMOUTH BRNC
Thomas, Ann Louise, BEng	LT CDR(FTC)	E	TM	01.10.02	MOD (LONDON)
Thomas, Daniel Huw	LT(CC)	X	P	01.07.99	SUTHERLAND
Thomas, David Jonathan	LT CDR(FTC)	S	(S)	01.10.04	RALEIGH
Thomas, David Lynford, BDS, MSc, LDS RCS(Eng), MGDS RCS, MGDS RCSEd	SGCAPT(D)(FCC)	-		01.04.03	NELSON
Thomas, David William, BEng	LT(CC)	X	P	01.10.98	824 SQN
Thomas, David William Wallace, BA	CHAPLAIN	CE		18.10.88	CHFHQ
Thomas, Duncan James	SLT(IC)	X	O U/T	01.05.02	RNAS CULDROSE
Thomas, Francis Stephen	CDR(FTC)	S	(SM)	30.06.99	DRAKE COB
Thomas, Geoffrey Charles, OBE, BSc, pce, pce(sm), hcsc	CAPT(FTC)	X	SM	30.06.02	D STRAT PLANS
Thomas, Jeffrey Evans	CDR(FTC)	X	EW	30.06.04	D TIO
Thomas, Jeffrey Graham	CAPT RM(CC)	-		01.09.03	CTCRM
Thomas, Jeremy Huw, BEng, MLITT	LT CDR(FTC)	E	WESM	01.02.98	NELSON
Thomas, Jeremy Hywel, psc(m), hcsc	BRIG(FTC)	-	WTO	17.09.01	MOD (LONDON)
Thomas, Joseph Maximilian, BSc	LT(IC)	X	P U/T	01.05.04	RNAS YEOVILTON
Thomas, Kevin Ian, BSc	LT CDR(FTC)	X	METOC	01.10.92	MOD (LONDON)
Thomas, Leslie, BSc	LT CDR(FTC)	X	C	01.10.99	FLEET CIS PORTS
Thomas, Lynn Marie, MB, BS, BSc, MRCP	SURG CDR(MCC)	-		30.06.04	NELSON (PAY)
Thomas, Mark, BSc, n	LT(CC)	X		01.09.98	JSCSC
Thomas, Mark Anthony	LT(IC)	E	WE	01.01.04	HQ DCSA
Thomas, Mark Peter	SLT(IC)	X	O U/T	01.05.03	750 SQN SEAHAWK
Thomas, Martyn George, IEng, AMIMarE	LT(FTC)	E	ME	17.02.89	SULTAN
Thomas, Owen Hopkin, BSc	LT(CC)	X		16.10.99	PJHQ
Thomas, Patrick William, sq (Act Lt Col)	MAJ(FTC)	-	SO(LE)	01.10.96	FLEET CIS PORTS
Thomas, Richard Anthony Aubrey, MBE, pce, psc(j)	CDR(FTC)	X	PWO(U)	30.06.02	MOD (LONDON)
Thomas, Richard David	MID(IC)	S		01.09.03	DARTMOUTH BRNC
Thomas, Richard Kevin, BSc, pce, PSC(ONDC)	CDR(FTC)	X	PWO(U)	30.06.02	MOD (LONDON)
Thomas, Robert Paul, pce, pcea, psc	CDR(FTC)	X	O	30.06.95	SA MUSCAT
Thomas, Simon Alan, MA, pce, pcea, psc(a)	CDR(FTC)	X	P	31.12.93	2SL/CNH FOTR
Thomas, Stephen Mark, BEng	LT CDR(FTC)	E	ME	01.01.01	ARGYLL
Thomas, Stephen Michael	LT(CC)	X	P	16.02.96	814 SQN

Name	Rank	Branch	Spec	Seniority	Where Serving
Thomas, William Gwynne, BSc, pce, pcea	CDR(FTC)	X	O	31.12.00	MOD (LONDON)
Thompson, Alastair James	LT(IC)	X	P	01.01.04	RAF CRANWELL EFS
Thompson, Andrew, BSc	CDR(FTC)	E	AE	30.06.02	HARRIER IPT
Thompson, Andrew Robert	LT(CC)	X	O	01.02.92	815 SQN HQ
Thompson, Bernard Dominic, BA, pce	CDR(FTC)	X	MCD	30.06.02	FDG
Thompson, David Anthony, BSc	LT(IC)	X	P	16.04.99	846 SQN
Thompson, David Huw	CAPT RM(FTC)	-		01.09.99	1 ASSAULT GP RM
Thompson, David John	LT(IC)	X		20.02.04	LIVERPOOL
Thompson, Elizabeth Ellen, BEng	LT(IC)	E	ME U/T	01.01.05	CUMBERLAND
Thompson, Fiona	LT(MC(MD)	Q		24.09.98	RH HASLAR
Thompson, George Christopher	SLT(IC)	X	P	01.09.03	DHFS
Thompson, Graham Michael, BEM	MAJ(FTC)	-	SO(LE)	01.10.04	DISC
Thompson, James	LT(IC)	X		01.05.04	FLEET AV SUPPORT
Thompson, James Peter Bibby, BSc	CAPT RM(IC)	-	MLDR	01.05.00	MWS COLLINGWOOD
Thompson, Mark George, PGDIPAN, SM(n)	LT CDR(FTC)	X	SM	01.03.03	FOST DSTF
Thompson, Michael James, BEng, CEng, MIMarEST	LT CDR(FTC)	E	ME	01.10.03	KENT
Thompson, Neil James, pcea (Act Cdr)	LT CDR(FTC)	X	P	01.10.94	NP IRAQ
Thompson, Paul Leslie, BSc	CAPT RM(CC)	-		01.09.01	RMR TYNE
Thompson, Richard Charles, BEng, MA, psc(j)	CDR(FTC)	E	AE	30.06.02	JCA IPT UK
Thompson, Robert Anthony, BSc, pcea	LT CDR(FTC)	X	O	01.10.98	RNAS CULDROSE
Thompson, Robert Joseph, BSc, jsdc	CAPT(FTC)	E	ME	30.06.03	MOD (LONDON)
Thompson, Sarah Kay, BSc	LT(SC(MD)	Q		01.11.03	RH HASLAR
Thompson, Sarah Leanne	LT(IC)	X		01.05.03	SOMERSET
Thompson, Stephen John, MSc, CEng, MCGI, MIMarEST, psc(j)	CDR(FTC)	E	ME	31.12.99	ARK ROYAL
Thompson, William Alistair, BEng	LT(CC)	X	P	01.02.00	815 FLT 244
Thomsen-Rayner, Lisa, BSc	LT(CC)	X	PWO(C)	01.02.97	OCEAN
Thomsett, Harry Fergus James, BA	MAJ(FTC)	-	C	01.09.01	JSCSC
Thomson, Allan Brown, MBA, fsc, osc	COL(FTC)	-	MLDR	30.06.01	NAVSEC
Thomson, Colin Douglas, BSc, PGDip	LT CDR(FTC)	X	H CH	01.02.01	MOD (LONDON)
Thomson, David Forbes	LT(FTC)	E	AE	01.04.01	JCA IPT USA
Thomson, Duncan, pce, psc(j)	CDR(FTC)	X	PWO(U)	30.06.05	NAVSEC
Thomson, Iain Rodger, BSc	LT CDR(FTC)	E	WESM	22.05.97	MWS COLLINGWOOD
Thomson, Ian Wallace, MIIE	LT(FTC)	E	WESM	01.04.01	SCU SHORE
Thomson, James Christopher, BSc	LT(CC)	X	FC	01.01.99	INVINCIBLE
Thomson, Jane Margaret, BSc	LT(IC)	E	TM	01.01.01	DCTS PORTS
Thomson, Leighton George	CAPT RM(IC)	-		01.09.04	FPGRM
Thomson, Michael Lee, BEng, MSc	LT(FTC)	E	ME	01.04.99	DLO BRISTOL
Thomson, Paul Allan, MEng	SLT(IC)	E	AE U/T	01.09.02	SULTAN
Thomson, Paul Damian, BSc	LT(CC)	E	IS	24.02.97	FLEET CIS PORTS
Thomson, Roger Geoffrey, MB, BS, MRCGP, DCH	SURG CDR(MC(MD)	-	GMPP	05.11.03	CTCRM
Thomson, Steven, BSc, BD	CHAPLAIN	SF		13.09.04	FWO PORTS SEA
Thomson, Stewart McLean, BSc	LT(IC)	X		01.08.04	MWS COLLINGWOOD
Thorburn, Andrew	CDR(FTC)	X	AV	30.06.04	COS 2SL/CNH
Thorley, Graham	LT(IC)	X	SM	01.01.04	VIGILANT(PORT)
Thorne, Dain Jason, BEng, FRAeS	LT CDR(FTC)	E	AE	01.03.05	FLEET HQ PORTS
Thornhill, Andrew Philip, pdm	MAJ(FTC)	BS		01.10.04	MWS RM SCH MUSIC
Thornhill, Stephen	LT(IC)	MS		01.07.04	CDO LOG REGT RM
Thornley, Jeremy George Carter, BD	LT(IC)	X		01.05.03	VENGEANCE(PORT)
Thornton, Daniel Moss (Act Capt Rm)	LT RM(IC)	-		01.09.02	BF BIOT
Thornton, John	2LT(IC)	-		01.08.03	CTCRM LYMPSTONE
Thornton, Michael Crawford, pce, pcea, psc	LT CDR(FTC)	X	P	08.02.84	LOAN DARA
Thornton, Philip John, pcea	LT CDR(FTC(A)	X	P	01.10.93	RNAS YEOVILTON
Thorp, Benjamin Thomas, BEng, MSc	LT CDR(FTC)	E	ME	01.07.04	SULTAN
Thorp, David Brian, BEng, MIEE	LT(FTC)	E	WE	01.03.98	RMC OF SCIENCE
Thorpe, Conrad Dermot Biltcliffe, OBE, MA, psc(j)	LT COL(FTC)	-		30.06.03	CTCRM
Thorpe, Elaine	LT(MC(MD)	Q		03.08.99	JSCSC
Thorpe, Robert Michael, MA	CAPT RM(CC)	-		01.09.03	CDO LOG REGT RM
Thrippleton, Mark Graham, BEng	LT CDR(FTC)	E	AE	15.08.00	702 SQN HERON
Thurstan, Richard William Farnall, MA, psc(j)	MAJ(FTC)	-	LC	01.05.97	40 CDO RM
Thurston, Mark Stewart, BEM	LT(IC)	X	C	29.10.04	HQ DCSA
Thwaites, Gerard James, ADC, BSc, CEng, MIMechE, psc	CDRE(FTC)	E	MESM	01.04.03	SULTAN
Thwaitesm, Lindsey William	LT(IC)	E	WESM	01.07.04	VENGEANCE(PORT)
Tibballs, Laura Rosalind, BSc	LT(IC)	S		01.01.04	NELSON

Name	Rank	Branch	Spec	Seniority	Where Serving
Tibbitt, Ian Peter Gordon, MA, CEng, MIEE, jsdc	CDRE(FTC)	E	AE	15.04.02	DLO YEO
Tickle, Martin John, BSc	SLT(IC)	X		01.05.03	INVINCIBLE
Tidball, Ian Crofton, BEng	LT CDR(FTC)	X	P	01.10.04	801 SQN
Tidman, Martin David	CAPT RM(IC)	-	SO(LE)	21.07.01	1 ASSAULT GP RM
Tiebosch, Nicola Kate, BSc	SLT(IC)	X		01.02.04	DARTMOUTH BRNC
Tighe, Simon, SM(n), SM	LT(CC)	X	SM	30.03.99	FLEET HQ NWD
Tilden, Philip James Edward, BA, ACMI, n	LT CDR(FTC)	X		01.03.05	MWS COLLINGWOOD
Tilley, Duncan Scott Jamieson, pce	CDR(FTC)	X	H CH	30.06.00	RNAS YEOVILTON
Tilsley, David, BSc	LT(IC)	E	IS	01.05.01	CINCFLEET FIMU
Timbrell, Ian Philip James, BEng	LT(FTC)	E	ME	01.02.00	SULTAN
Timms, Stephen John, OBE, MBA, MSc, CEng, MIMarEST, MIMechE, jsdc	CAPT(FTC)	E	MESM	31.12.98	2SL/CNH FOTR
Tindal, Nicolas Henry Charles, MA, pce, pcea, psc(j)	CDR(FTC)	X	P	30.06.02	EXCHANGE USA
Tindall-Jones, Lee Douglas, BSc, MA, CEng, MIEE, psc	CDR(FTC)	E	WESM	31.12.99	MOD (LONDON)
Tinsley, Glenn Nigel, GCIS	CDR(FTC)	S		31.12.96	EXCHANGE AUSTLIA
Tinsley, Phillip	CAPT RM(CC)	-	SO(LE)	21.07.01	CDO LOG REGT RM
Titcomb, Andrew Charles, BEng, MA, MSc, psc(j)	CDR(FTC)	E	WESM	30.06.04	LAIPT
Titcomb, Mark Richard, BSc, pce, pce(sm), psc(j), MA	CDR(FTC)	X	SM	30.06.03	SCEPTRE
Titcombe, Adam James, BA	LT(CC)	S		01.05.99	COM MCC NWD
Tite, Anthony Damian	LT CDR(FTC)	X	O	01.10.04	LOAN JTEG BSC DN
Titerickx, Andrew Terry	CAPT RM(IC)	-	SO(LE)	01.07.04	CDO LOG REGT RM
Titmuss, Julian Francis, BA	LT CDR(FTC)	S	CMA	01.12.02	MOD (LONDON)
Titterton, Phillip James, OBE, pce, pce(sm)	CDR(FTC)	X	SM	30.06.99	MOD (LONDON)
Todd, Daniel Bevan, BEng	LT(IC)	E	ME	01.03.99	JSSU CYPRUS
Todd, Geoffrey Alan	LT(IC)	MS		01.05.03	MOD (BATH)
Todd, James William, BSc	CAPT RM(CC)	-	P	01.05.00	847 SQN
Todd, Michael Anthony	MAJ(FTC)	-	SO(LE)	01.10.03	40 CDO RM
Todd, Oliver James, LLB	CAPT RM(CC)	-	MLDR	01.09.00	UKLFCSG RM
Toft, Michael David, BEng, CEng, MIEE	CDR(FTC)	E	WE	30.06.04	DLO BRISTOL
Tok, Chantelle Fen Lynne, BSc	LT(IC)	X	ATC	01.05.00	NELSON
Toland, Martin James, BSc	LT(IC)	X		01.12.04	MWS COLLINGWOOD
Tolley, Peter Frederick Richmond, OBE, MB, BCh (Commodore)	SURG CAPT(FCC)	-	GMPP	31.12.95	2SL/CNH
Tomkins, Alan Brian	LT(FTC)	E	WE	19.02.93	MWS COLLINGWOOD
Tomkins, Bradley	SURG SLT(SCC)	-		11.09.03	DARTMOUTH BRNC
Tomlin, Ian Stephen, BEng	LT(IC)	E	WESM	01.02.03	FLEET HQ PORTS 2
Tomlinson, Amy Ruth, BA	LT(IC)	S		01.05.04	MANCHESTER
Tomlinson, David Charles	LT(FTC)	X	AV	03.04.97	INVINCIBLE
Tong, Steven Richard	MID(IC)	X	O U/T	01.09.03	RNAS CULDROSE
Tonge, Malcolm	LT(IC)	E	ME	01.05.03	DFTE PORTSMOUTH
Toomey, Nicholas John, BSc, MA, psc(j) (Act Cdr)	LT CDR(FTC)	S	SM	01.11.96	PJHQ
Toon, John Richard	LT CDR(FTC)	E	AE	01.10.92	DLO YEO
Toon, Paul Graham	LT(FTC)	X	AV	26.04.99	RNAS CULDROSE
Toone, Stephen Anthony, BSc	LT(FTC)	E	WE	01.04.01	DLO BRISTOL
Toor, Jeevan Jyoti Singh, BSc, PGDip	LT CDR(FTC)	X	PWO(U)	01.09.98	LIVERPOOL
Toothill, John Samuel, SM(n)	LT CDR(FTC)	X	SM	01.04.97	AGRIPPA MAR CC
Topham, Neil Edwin, BEng	LT(IC)	E	TM U/T	01.02.01	SULTAN
Topping, Jay Anthony	SLT(IC)	X	P U/T	01.01.05	RALEIGH
Torbet, Linda, MEng	LT(IC)	E	AE U/T	01.01.04	845 SQN
Torney, Colin James	LT(FTC)	E	MESM	02.09.99	VIGILANT(PORT)
Tothill, Nicholas Michael, MSc	CDR(FTC)	S		30.06.00	DLO/DG DEF SC
Tothill, Rachel Charlotte, MA	LT CDR(FTC)	S		17.08.00	MOD (BATH)
Totten, Philip Mark	CAPT RM(CC)	-		01.09.00	UKLFCSG RM
Tottenham, Geoffry John	MID(UCE)(IC)	X		01.09.03	DARTMOUTH BRNC
Tottenham, Timothy William	CAPT RM(IC)	-		01.09.03	FLEET HQ PORTS
Tough, Iain Shand, MEng	LT(IC)	E	WESM	01.09.03	VENGEANCE(PORT)
Towell, Peter James	LT CDR(FTC)	E	ME	01.07.01	FLEET HQ NWD
Towler, Alison, BSc, PGDipL (Barrister)	LT CDR(FTC)	S	BAR	14.12.97	2SL/CNH
Towler, Perrin James Bryher, BSc, pce	LT CDR(FTC)	X	PWO(A)	01.06.94	FLEET HQ NWD
Towner, Stephen	SURG SLT(SCC)	-		13.09.04	DARTMOUTH BRNC
Townsend, David John, BEng, CEng, MIEE	LT(FTC)	E	WE	01.03.96	2SL/CNH FOTR
Townsend, Graham Peter	LT(FTC)	X	O	01.05.94	771 SQN
Townsend, John Stafford, MB, BS, BSc, Dip FFP	SURG CDR(SCC)	-	GMPP	31.01.01	RNAS YEOVILTON
Townshend, Jeremy John, BSc, MBA, FCIPD	CDR(FTC)	E	TMSM	30.06.04	2SL/CNH FOTR
Toy, Malcolm John, BEng, CEng, MRAeS	CAPT(FTC)	E	AE	30.06.05	CTS

Name	Rank	Branch	Spec	Seniority	Where Serving
Tracey, Alan David, BEng (Act Lt Cdr)	LT(FTC)	E	AE	01.05.97	FLEET HQ PORTS
Trafford, Michael	LT RM(IC)	-		01.09.03	45 CDO RM
Trasler, Mark Farnham, MSc	LT CDR(FTC)	MS	(LT)	01.10.00	2SL/CNH
Trathen, Neil Charles, BSc, pce	LT CDR(FTC)	X	PWO(N)	01.02.92	DRAKE COB
Treanor, Martin Andrew, MSc, psc	CDR(FTC)	E	AE	31.12.99	NAVSEC
Tredray, Thomas Patrick, BA	LT CDR(FTC)	X	AAWO	01.02.01	MWS COLLINGWOOD
Tregale, Jamie, BSc	LT(IC)	X		01.04.04	DULVERTON
Tregunna, Gary Andrew, SM	LT CDR(FTC)	X	SM	08.08.03	PJHQ
Treharne, Mark Adrian, BEng	LT(CC)	E	MESM	01.08.00	VENGEANCE(STBD)
Tremelling, Paul Nicholas, BEng	LT(FTC)	X	P	16.04.98	801 SQN
Trent, Thomas, BEng	LT(IC)	X		01.09.03	KENT
Tretton, Joseph Edward, BSc	LT(IC)	X		01.01.04	LEEDS CASTLE
Trevethan, Christopher John	SLT(IC)	X		01.02.04	DARTMOUTH BRNC
Trevithick, Andrew Richard, BSc, PGCE, MIMA, CMath	CDR(FTC)	X	METOC	31.12.93	COS 2SL/CNH
Trewhella, Graham Gilbey, BSc, MA, psc	LT CDR(FTC)	E	TM	01.05.91	FLEET HQ PORTS
Trewinnard, Robin Michael, BEng	LT(IC)	E	AE	01.04.02	20(R) SQN (RN)
Tribe, Jeremy David, BSc	LT(FTC)	X	P	16.10.87	DLO YEO
Trigwell, Simon	SLT(IC)	E	AE U/T	01.01.04	DARTMOUTH BRNC
Trinder, Stephen John	LT(FTC)	S	CA	30.01.96	NP IRAQ
Tritschler, Edwin Lionel, BEng, BTech, MA, CEng, MRAeS, psc(j)	CDR(FTC)	E	AE	30.06.04	2SL/CNH FOTR
Trosh, Nicholas, BEng	LT(IC)	E	WE	01.09.04	CAMPBELTOWN
Trotman, Stephen Peter, IEng, MIIE	LT(IC)	E	WESM	01.01.03	MWC PORTSDOWN
Trott, Edward Alan, BEng, MSc	LT CDR(FTC)	E	AE	01.12.02	FLEET HQ PORTS
Trotter, Steven, MSc, CEng, MIMarEST	LT CDR(FTC)	E	ME	01.12.87	RALEIGH
Trubshaw, Christopher, pcea	LT CDR(FTC)	X	P	01.10.04	DHFS
Truelove, Samantha	LT(IC)	S		01.01.02	820 SQN
Trueman, Brian David	LT(CC)	E	AE	01.05.00	JSCSC
Trump, Nigel William, psc(j)	CDR(FTC)	S		30.06.03	RALEIGH
Trundle, Nicholas Reginald Edward, MA, pce, pcea, psc(j)	CDR(FTC)	X	O	31.12.98	MOD (LONDON)
Tucker, Philip James	LT(IC)	X	P U/T	01.09.04	RNAS YEOVILTON
Tucker, Simon James William, BA	CAPT RM(IC)	-	LC	01.09.02	ALBION
Tuffin, Michael Graham	LT(IC)	X		01.01.05	MIDDLETON
Tuhey, James Jonathan George, BEng	SLT(IC)	E	WESM	01.09.02	FWO DEVPT SEA
Tulley, James Robert, BSc	CDR(FTC)	S		31.12.99	MWS COLLINGWOOD
Tulloch, Frederik Martin, BSc, CEng, MIEE	LT CDR(FTC)	E	WE	01.04.93	MOD (BATH)
Tulloch, Stuart William	MAJ(FTC)	-	SO(LE)	01.10.04	42 CDO RM
Tumilty, Kevin	LT(IC)	E	WE	01.01.04	DL IPT
Tupman, Keith Campbell	MAJ(FTC)	-	SO(LE)	01.10.99	CTCRM
Tuppen, Russell Mark, MNI, pce, pcea, psc, psc(j)o	CDR(FTC)	X	O	31.12.99	GLOUCESTER
Turberville, Christopher Thomas Leslie, BA	LT(IC)	S		01.01.04	ILLUSTRIOUS
Turle, Paul James, IEng, MIIE	LT CDR(FTC)	E	ME	01.10.03	WESTMINSTER
Turnbull, Graham David, pce, psc(j)	CDR(FTC)	X	H CH	30.06.02	COS 2SL/CNH
Turnbull, Nicholas Robin, BDS, MSc, FDS RCSEdin, MOrth	SGCDR(D)(FCC)	-	ORTHC	30.06.03	DDA PORTSMOUTH
Turnbull, Paul Sands, MB, BS, AFOM	SURG CDR(FCC)	-	(CO/M)	30.06.01	EXCHANGE USA
Turnbull, Simon Jonathan Lawson, MA, MNI, pce, psc(j)	CDR(FTC)	X	PWO(U)	30.06.02	FLEET HQ PORTS 2
Turner, Antony Richard, BA	CAPT RM(FTC)	-		01.09.00	1 ASSAULT GP RM
Turner, David James, LLB, PGDip	LT(FTC)	S	SM	01.04.00	FWO FASLANE
Turner, David Neil	LT(CC)	X	P	01.06.95	RNAS YEOVILTON
Turner, Derek Bayard, MBE, BSc, ARICS, pce	CDR(FTC)	X	H CH	30.06.02	MOD (LONDON)
Turner, Duncan Laurence	SLT(UCE)(IC)	E	WE	01.01.03	DARTMOUTH BRNC
Turner, Ian, OBE, BSc, psc	CAPT(FTC)	X	H CH	30.06.02	FWO DEVONPORT
Turner, Jennifer Claire Belinda, BDS, BSc	SG LT(D)(SCC)	-		24.09.00	CDO LOG REGT RM
Turner, Jonathan Stephen, BA	LT(CC)	X	O	01.01.01	815 FLT 217
Turner, Joseph Seymour Hume, MA (Barrister)	LT CDR(FTC)	S	BAR	01.04.99	FLEET HQ PORTS
Turner, Kerry Ann, BEng, PGDip	LT CDR(CC)	X	METOC	01.10.01	RNAS CULDROSE
Turner, Matthew, BEng	LT(IC)	E	ME	01.01.04	KENT
Turner, Matthew John, MB, BS	SURG LTCDR(SC(MD)	-	GMPP	01.08.04	CFLT MED(SEA)
Turner, Neil	LT(IC)	E	AE	01.05.03	SULTAN
Turner, Phaedra Louise, BSc	LT(CC)	E	TM	01.02.99	RNAS YEOVILTON
Turner, Robert Francis, BSc	LT CDR(FTC)	S	(W)	01.10.00	RALEIGH
Turner, Shaun Mark, jsdc, pce, pce(sm) (Act Capt)	CDR(FTC)	X	SM	30.06.90	MOD (BATH)
Turner, Simon Alexander, BSc	MAJ(FTC)	-		01.09.02	FLEET AV SUPPORT
Turner, Stephen Edward, pce	CDR(FTC)	X	PWO(U)	31.12.93	RH HASLAR

Name	Rank	Branch	Spec	Seniority	Where Serving
Turner, Vicki Mary	SLT(UCE)(IC)	E	ME	01.09.02	DARTMOUTH BRNC
Tutchings, Andrew	LT(FTC)	X		01.04.01	SHAPE BELGIUM
Tweed, Christopher James, BSc, MDA	LT CDR(FTC)	E	WE	01.02.89	COS 2SL/CNH
Twigg, Katherine Louise, MSc	LT(CC)	X	HM	01.04.99	MWS COLLINGWOOD
Twigg, Neil Robert, BEng	LT(IC)	X	P	16.03.01	LOAN OTHER SVCE
Twine, John Harold, MA, PGDip, psc(j)	LT CDR(FTC)	E	TM	01.01.99	SULTAN
Twiselton, Matthew James	LT(IC)	E	AE	01.05.03	2SL/CNH
Twist, David Charles	LT CDR(FTC)	S	(W)	01.10.99	CSSG (SEA)
Twist, Martin Thomas, BSc	MAJ(FTC)	-		01.09.01	LOAN JSOC SLOV
Twitchen, Richard Christopher, pce, psc, psc(m)	CDRE(FTC)	X	AAWO	14.10.03	FWO PORTS SEA
Tyack, Terence James, pcea	LT CDR(FTC)	X	P	01.10.98	JSCSC
Tyacke, Richard Simon, BSc	SLT(IC)	X		01.05.03	CHATHAM
Tyce, David John (Act Maj)	CAPT RM(FTC)	-	SO(LE)	01.01.96	BDMT
Tyler, Jeremy Charles	LT CDR(FTC)	X	PWO(A)	01.07.04	MANCHESTER
Tyler, Peter Leslie	LT CDR(FTC)	S		10.07.93	RH HASLAR
Tyrrell, Richard Kim	MAJ(FTC)	-	LC	01.09.86	NP IRAQ

U

Name	Rank	Branch	Spec	Seniority	Where Serving
Ubaka, Philip Benizi Nnamabia	CAPT RM(IC)	-	SO(LE)	24.07.04	CDO LOG REGT RM
Ubhi, Wayne Gurdial, BEng, MSc	LT CDR(FTC)	E	ME	01.06.04	MONMOUTH
Udensi, Ernest Andrew Anene Anderson, BEng, MSc, CEng, MIEE	LT CDR(FTC)	E	WE	01.09.93	MWS COLLINGWOOD
Underwood, Nicholas John, BSc, psc(a)	MAJ(FTC)	-		01.09.88	RM CHIVENOR
Underwood, Paul John	MAJ(FTC)	-	SO(LE)	01.10.02	40 CDO RM
Underwood, Richard Alexander Howard, BA	LT(FTC)	S		01.08.01	UKMILREP BRUSS
Unwin, Nicholas Richard Forbes, BA	LT(IC)	X		01.08.02	MANCHESTER
Uprichard, Andrew James, BA	CAPT RM(IC)	-		01.09.04	LN SIERRA LEONE
Upright, Stephen William, BSc, pce, pce(sm)	CAPT(FTC)	X	SM	30.06.03	FWO FASLANE SEA
Upton, Iain David, BSc, CEng, MIEE	CDR(FTC)	E	WE	30.06.03	NELSON
Urry, Simon Richard, MBE, BSc	MAJ(FTC)	-		01.10.04	NAVSEC
Urwin, Stuart James, BA	LT(CC)	X		01.06.00	LANCASTER
Usborne, Andre Christopher, BSc, FCMI, psc (Act Capt)	CDR(FTC)	E	WE	31.12.92	JSU NORTHWOOD
Usborne, Christopher Martin, BSc, CEng, MIEE	CAPT(FTC)	E	WE	30.06.04	COS 2SL/CNH
Usher, Andrew Thomas	CAPT RM(CC)	-	P	01.04.02	771 SQN
Usher, Brian	CAPT RM(CC)	-	SO(LE)	01.04.02	CTCRM
Ussher, Jeremy Howard David, BSc	LT(IC)	E	TM	01.05.00	JSCSC
Utley, Michael Keith, n	LT CDR(FTC)	X	PWO(A)	01.10.00	NAVSEC
Utting, Roy Charles	LT(IC)	E	WE	01.07.04	JSCSC

V

Name	Rank	Branch	Spec	Seniority	Where Serving
Vale, Andrew John, MB, CHB	SURG LT(SCC)	-		07.08.02	CFLT MED(SEA)
Vallance, Michael Stefan, BSc	LT(CC)	X	P	01.05.98	AACC MID WALLOP
Van Beek, Dirk, BSc, CEng, MIEE, psc	CAPT(FTC)	E	WE	30.06.03	HQ DCSA
Van Beek, Luke, BSc, MBA, psc, psc(m)	CDRE(FTC)	E	WE	07.10.03	MOD (LONDON)
Van Duin, Martin Ivar Alexander, BSc	LT(IC)	X	P	01.01.02	FLEET AV VALLEY
Van-Den-Bergh, William Lionel, MBE (Act Cdr)	LT CDR(FTC)	X	FC	01.10.96	LN SIERRA LEONE
Vanderpump, David John, BEng, psc(j)	CDR(FTC)	E	ME	30.06.00	CV(F) IPT
Vandome, Andrew Michael, BSc, MIEE, psc(j)	CDR(FTC)	E	WE	30.06.99	DLO BRISTOL
Varaitch, Supinder, BEng	SLT(IC)	E	WE U/T	01.01.04	DARTMOUTH BRNC
Vardy, Kevin John	LT(IC)	E	WE	01.01.04	CSIS IPT
Varley, Ian Guy, BEng, pcea	LT CDR(FTC)	X	P	01.01.01	824 SQN
Varley, Peter George Sidney, BSc	LT(IC)	X		01.06.00	PORTLAND
Vartan, Mark Richard, BSc	LT CDR(FTC)	X	H1	01.10.03	SCOTT
Varty, Jason Alan, BSc	LT(CC)	X	H2	01.10.98	ECHO
Vaughan, David Michael, OBE, BA, MNI, pce, pce(sm), FRIN	CDR(FTC)	X	SM	31.12.90	NELSON
Vaughan, Edward Alexander, BSc	LT(IC)	X	P U/T	01.09.04	RNAS YEOVILTON
Vaughan, James Richard, BEng	LT(IC)	E	MESM	01.06.03	VICTORIOUS(PORT)
Veal, Alan Edward, BEng	LT CDR(FTC)	E	WE	01.08.03	DLO BRISTOL
Veal, Dominic Joseph	LT(CC)	X		01.05.02	WESTMINSTER
Venables, Adrian Nicholas, MBCS, pce	LT CDR(FTC)	X	PWO(C)	01.12.97	MOD (LONDON)
Venables, Daniel Mark	CAPT RM(CC)	-		01.09.02	CTCRM
Venn, Nicholas Spencer Collacott, BSc	MAJ(CC)	-	P	30.09.01	847 SQN

Name	Rank	Branch	Spec	Seniority	Where Serving
Vereker, Richard John Prendergast, BEng	SLT(IC)	X		01.01.03	WESTMINSTER
Verney, Kirsty Hilary, BDS, BSc	SGLTCDR(D)(SCC)	-		09.07.02	DDA PORTSMOUTH
Verney, Peter Scott, pce, psc(j), MA	CDR(FTC)	X	PWO(A)	30.06.05	EDINBURGH
Verrecchia, Joseph Romano	SLT(UCE)(IC)	X		01.09.02	DARTMOUTH BRNC
Vessey, Lee Matthew (Act Lt)	SLT(IC)	X		01.01.03	MERSEY
Veti, Mark Alister, LLB	SLT(IC)	X		01.02.03	CUMBERLAND
Vickers, Carl Geoffrey	LT(FTC)	E	WESM	02.09.99	NEPTUNE SWS
Vickers, Charles H	CAPT RM(IC)	-		01.09.04	OCLC MANCH
Vickers, John, BEng, MSc	LT CDR(FTC)	E	AE	01.11.98	JF HARROLE OFF
Vickery, Ben Robert, BA	LT(CC)	X	MCD	01.05.01	LEDBURY
Vickery, Robert James, IEng, AMRAeS (Act Lt Cdr)	LT(FTC)	E	AE	02.09.99	JF HARROLE OFF
Vickery, Timothy Kenneth, BSc, MDA	LT CDR(FTC)	X	PWO(U)	01.11.95	T45 IPT
Vierow, Michael Keith	LT(IC)	X		01.05.05	NORTHUMBERLAND
Vincent, Adrian, BEng, MPhil, CEng, MIMechE	LT CDR(CC)	E	TM	01.10.03	NTE(TTD)
Vincent, Christopher, BSc	SLT(IC)	X		01.02.04	DARTMOUTH BRNC
Vincent, Daniel, BSc, PhD	LT CDR(CC)	E	TM	01.10.04	NTE(TTD)
Vincent, Peter Hedley, MEng	LT(FTC)	X		01.01.04	WALNEY
Vines, Nicholas Owen, BSC(EH), MCIEH	LT(IC)	MS		01.12.02	2SL/CNH
Viney, Peter Michael	LT(CC)	S	(W)	29.04.01	FLEET HQ PORTS
Visram, Adrian Haider, BA	LT(IC)	X		01.01.04	HURWORTH
Vitali, Robert Charles, pce, psc(j)	CDR(FTC)	X	AAWO	30.06.04	SOUTHAMPTON
Vivian, Philip	LT(IC)	S		01.07.04	2SL/CNH FOTR
Vogel, Lanning David	LT CDR(FTC)	S	SM	01.10.04	RALEIGH
Voigt, Matthew Adam	LT(IC)	X		01.12.03	GLOUCESTER
Voke, Christen Alexander, BSc	LT(IC)	X	SM	01.08.02	TRAFALGAR
Voke, Helen Louise, BA	LT(IC)	X		01.05.02	CHATHAM
Vollentine, Lucy	LT CDR(FTC)	S		01.10.04	ILLUSTRIOUS
Vorley, Simon William, BSc	LT(FTC)	X	P	15.06.96	702 SQN HERON
Vout, Debra Kim	LT(IC)	X	C	01.10.02	MWS COLLINGWOOD
Vowles, Iain Robert	SLT(UCE)(IC)	E	WESM	01.09.02	DARTMOUTH BRNC
Vowles, Mitchell John	LT(FTC)	X		24.07.97	RALEIGH
Voyce, John Edington, BEng, MSc, MIMarEST	LT CDR(FTC)	E	ME	01.09.02	INVINCIBLE

W

Name	Rank	Branch	Spec	Seniority	Where Serving
Waddington, Andrew Kennneth, BSc, pce, psc(j)	CDR(FTC)	X	H CH	30.06.03	ECHO
Waddington, John, BSc	CDR(FTC)	E	WESM	30.06.02	MOD CSSE USA
Wade, Andrew	LT(IC)	MS		01.09.01	INM ALVERSTOKE
Wade, Claire Victoria, BChD, MFDS,RCS	SG LT(D)(MC(MD)	-		29.06.00	JSU NORTHWOOD
Wade, Jonathan Mark Robertson, BA	LT(IC)	X	P	01.02.99	814 SQN
Wade, Nicholas Charles, BSc (Act Cdr)	LT CDR(FTC)	X	PWO(C)	01.01.90	RNEAWC
Wadge, Guy David Ernest, BSc	LT(IC)	E	TM	08.05.01	42 CDO RM
Wadsworth, Richard York, BEng	LT(CC)	E	ME	01.03.99	SULTAN
Wagstaff, Andrew	LT(IC)	S		01.05.02	CHFHQ
Wagstaff, Neil	LT CDR(FTC)	MS	(LT)	01.10.02	DMSTC
Wagstaff, Sally Elizabeth, Dip OHN	LT(SC(MD)	Q		01.01.03	RH HASLAR
Wain, Alexis William, MEng, MIEE	LT(IC)	E	WE	01.09.04	MONTROSE
Wainhouse, Michael James, pce	CDR(FTC)	X	PWO(A)	30.06.02	MOD (LONDON)
Waite, Matthew Temple, MA	CAPT RM(CC)	-		01.09.02	HQ 3 CDO BDE RM
Waite, Tobias Gerard, BSc	LT(CC)	X		01.05.01	IRON DUKE
Wake, Charlotte	SURG SLT(SCC)	-		19.01.05	DARTMOUTH BRNC
Wakeling, Jonathan Lee, MA	CDR(FTC)	E	TM	31.12.94	RALEIGH
Waldmeyer, Edward	CAPT RM(CC)	-		01.09.03	FPGRM
Wales, Benjamin David, BSc	LT CDR(FTC)	S	CMA	01.03.03	2SL/CNH
Walford, Lance Scott	SLT(IC)	X	P U/T	01.02.05	DARTMOUTH BRNC
Walker, Alasdair James, OBE, MB, ChB, FRCS	SURG CAPT(FCC)	-	(CGS)	30.06.91	MDHU DERRIFORD
Walker, Andrew John, BA, PGCE	MAJ(FTC)	-		01.05.01	40 CDO RM
Walker, Clive Leslie	CDR(FTC)	S		31.12.00	NAVSEC
Walker, Daniel Haydn, BSc	LT(IC)	X	O	01.01.04	849 SQN A FLT
Walker, Donald William Alexander, BA	LT CDR(FTC)	S		01.10.01	DLO/DG DEF SC
Walker, Ellis George	LT CDR(FTC)	X	REG	01.10.00	FORWARD
Walker, Gavin Stewart Logan	MAJ(FTC)	-		01.09.90	MOD (LONDON)
Walker, George (Act Lt Cdr)	LT(FTC)	E	WE	02.09.99	DLO BRISTOL

Name	Rank	Branch	Spec	Seniority	Where Serving
Walker, Ian Michael, BEng	LT(IC)	E	MESM	01.01.03	SOVEREIGN
Walker, James John, MEng, ACGI	LT(CC)	X		01.09.04	QUORN
Walker, Jamie, BEng	LT(IC)	E	ME	01.01.03	NORFOLK
Walker, Jamie Joseph	LT(IC)	X	EW	01.07.04	PJHQ
Walker, Louise Linda, MB, BS	SURG LTCDR(MCC)	-		04.09.99	NELSON (PAY)
Walker, Mark Christopher, pcea (Act Cdr)	LT CDR(FTC)	X	P	01.10.94	848 SQN HERON
Walker, Mark John ,BMus	SLT(IC)	X		01.02.03	CARDIFF
Walker, Mark Justin, BEng	LT CDR(FTC)	E	TM	01.10.02	DCTS HALTON
Walker, Martin, BEng, MA, MSc, CEng, MIEE, psc(j)	CDR(FTC)	E	WE	30.06.00	MOD (BATH)
Walker, Martin Denis James, BA	LT(IC)	S		01.01.04	899 SQN HERON
Walker, Matthew John Emrys, MSc	LT(IC)	E	TM	01.01.02	DCTS PORTS
Walker, Michael John	LT CDR(FTC)	X		01.10.03	2SL/CNH FOTR
Walker, Nicholas John, MSc, psc(j)	CDR(FTC)	E	MESM	30.06.00	MOD (LONDON)
Walker, Nicholas Lee, pce	LT CDR(FTC)	X	PWO(U)	01.02.93	MOD (LONDON)
Walker, Nicholas MacLaren, BSc	LT CDR(FTC)	X	P	01.01.00	ALBION
Walker, Nicholas Michael Cleveland	LT(CC)	X	P	01.08.02	GANNET SAR FLT
Walker, Nigel Albert	LT CDR(FTC)	S	CA	01.10.00	PJHQ
Walker, Peter Richard, MBA, MSc	LT CDR(FTC)	E	IS	01.05.96	2SL/CNH FOTR
Walker, Richard Eden, MA, psc	LT COL(FTC)	-	C	31.12.97	CTCRM
Walker, Richard Paul	LT(IC)	X	O U/T	01.07.04	RNAS CULDROSE
Walker, Robin Stuart	LT(FTC)	X	MCD	19.09.00	WALNEY
Walker, Stephen James, BEng	LT(FTC)	E	WESM	01.04.02	SUPERB
Walker, Stephen Paul, SM, SM(n)	LT CDR(FTC)	X	SM	09.03.02	FLEET HQ NWD
Wall, Irene Joanne, BSc	LT(CC)	S		01.02.00	DRAKE COB
Wall, Karl	LT(IC)	X	SM	01.07.04	TRENCHANT
Wall, Steven Nicholas, BSc	LT(CC)	X	FC	01.02.99	EXCHANGE RAF UK
Wallace, Allan, BSc, PGDIPAN, pce	CDR(FTC)	X	PWO(N)	30.06.01	MCM3 SEA
Wallace, Anthony Robert, BEng	LT(CC)	X		01.01.02	HURWORTH
Wallace, David James, BSc	LT CDR(FTC)	E	IS	01.10.98	HQ DCSA
Wallace, George William Alexander, AFC, BSc, pce, pcea, ocds(Can), osc, hcsc	CAPT(FTC)	X	P	30.06.04	CHFHQ
Wallace, Iain Stephen, BEng, PGDip	LT(IC)	E		01.07.00	DCCIS FAREHAM
Wallace, Michael Rupert Barry, BA, jsdc, pce, hcsc	CAPT(FTC)	X	PWO(U)	30.06.03	NP IRAQ
Wallace, Richard Stuart, BSc	LT(IC)	X		01.09.02	GRAFTON
Wallace, Richard Stuart	CAPT RM(CC)	-		01.04.01	45 CDO RM
Wallace, Ryan Patrick, BSc	LT(IC)	E	IS	01.03.01	MWS COLLINGWOOD
Wallace, Scott Peter, BSc	CAPT RM(CC)	-		01.09.01	FLEET AV SUPPORT
Wallace, Simon Jonathan	LT CDR(FTC)	X	AAWO	01.03.02	NOTTINGHAM
Wallace, Stewart Andrew, BSc	LT(FTC)	X	ATC	01.12.97	RAF COTTESMORE
Waller, Ramsay	2LT(IC)	-		01.08.01	CTCRM LYMPSTONE
Waller, Steven Adrian, pce(sm), SM	LT CDR(FTC)	X	SM	01.03.99	NAVSEC
Walliker, Michael John Delane, OBE, BA, pce, pce(sm)	CDR(FTC)	X	SM	31.12.99	MOD (LONDON)
Wallington-Smith, James	MID(NE)(IC)	X		01.09.04	CAMPBELTOWN
Wallis, Adrian John, pce, pcea	CDR(FTC)	X	O	30.06.02	FLEET CIS PORTS
Wallis, Jonathan Spencer	LT CDR(FTC)	X	P	01.10.02	JHCHQ
Walls, Kevin Finlay	MAJ(FTC)	-	MLDR	01.05.00	CTCRM (SEA)
Walmsley, Elizabeth Ann, ACIS	CDR(FTC)	S		30.06.05	JSCSC
Walpole, Peter Kenneth, BSc, pce	CDRE(FTC)	X	PWO(C)	07.07.03	SACT USA (SEA)
Walsh, Andrew Harwood, BEng	LT(CC)	E		01.12.98	DLO WYTON
Walsh, David	LT(IC)	S		01.02.01	JSCSC
Walsh, Dennis Gerard	LT CDR(FTC)	E	AE	01.10.01	OCEAN
Walsh, Kevin Michael, BSc, n	LT CDR(FTC)	X		01.11.04	MWS COLLINGWOOD
Walsh, Mark Anthony	CDR(FTC)	S	CA	30.06.05	FOST DPORT SHORE
Walter, Stephen	SLT(IC)	E	ME	01.01.04	SULTAN
Walton, Andrew Paul	LT CDR(FTC)	MS	(AD)	01.10.02	2SL/CNH
Walton, Colin Peter, BEng, CEng, MIEE	LT CDR(FTC)	E	WE	01.09.00	2SL/CNH FOTR
Walton, George James	LT(IC)	X		01.05.03	BULWARK
Walton, Jonathan Charles, MSc, MIEE, MCGI	LT CDR(FTC)	E	WE	01.12.90	NBC PORTSMOUTH
Walton, Simon Phillip	LT(FTC)	X	SM	01.10.97	SOVEREIGN
Walton, Stephen David	LT(FTC)	X	MW	01.10.98	CHIDDINGFOLD
Walton, Stephen Paul	LT CDR(FTC)	E	AE	01.10.01	CV(F) IPT
Wappner, Gary Dean, BA	LT(CC)	X	P	10.10.98	771 SQN
Warburton, Alison Mary, BSc	LT(SC(MD)	Q		26.02.03	RH HASLAR

Name	Rank	Branch	Spec	Seniority	Where Serving
Ward, Alexander James, MA	LT(IC)	S		01.09.02	WESTMINSTER
Ward, Andrew James	LT CDR(FTC)	X	MCD	01.06.03	EXCHANGE CANADA
Ward, Andrew James, BSc	CAPT RM(CC)	-	LC	01.09.00	1 ASSLT GP RM
Ward, Christopher James, MA	LT(SCC)	Q		01.05.04	RH HASLAR
Ward, Colin David	MAJ(FTC)	-	SO(LE)	01.10.03	JSCSC
Ward, David Steven, BA	LT CDR(FTC)	X		01.10.97	DRAKE SFM
Ward, Douglas John, BSc	LT(FTC)	S	SM	01.11.98	2SL/CNH
Ward, Jared Maurice	LT(IC)	S		01.07.04	RNAS CULDROSE
Ward, Kristian Nigel	LT(FTC)	X	P	13.02.98	LOAN OTHER SVCE
Ward, Michelle Therese, MA	LT(CC)	X		01.04.99	DARTMOUTH BRNC
Ward, Nicholas John	CDR(FTC)	X	PWO(A)	01.10.94	BDS WASHINGTON
Ward, Nigel Anthony, BSc, MBA, IEng, MIIE, MCMI	LT(FTC)	E	WE	02.09.99	MWS COLLINGWOOD
Ward, Rees Graham John, CB, MA, MSc, CEng, FIEE, rcds, jsdc, gw, hcsc (CE DCSA JAN 02)	RADM	-	WE	27.04.99	HQ DCSA
Ward, Simon	LT(FTC)	X	P	01.09.97	MWS SOUTHWICK PK
Ward, Simon Ira, pce	CDR(FTC)	X	AAWO	30.06.05	JSCSC
Ward, Stephen David, BEng	LT CDR(FTC)	E	ME	01.01.98	MOD (LONDON)
Warden, John Mitchell, MA, MBA, MSc, CEng, MinstP, C PHYS, psc(j)	CDR(FTC)	E	TMSM	30.06.02	2SL/CNH FOTR
Wardle, Mark	LT(FTC)	X	C	17.12.93	INVINCIBLE
Wardley, Thomas Edward	LT(SC(MD)	Q		01.03.05	MDHU DERRIFORD
Ware, Andrew Travis, BA	LT(IC)	X		01.05.02	HQ BFSAI
Ware, Peter James, BSc	LT(IC)	X		01.01.05	TIRELESS
Wareham, Michael Paul, BEng, MSc	CDR(FTC)	E	MESM	31.12.99	NP BRISTOL
Waring, John Robert, BSc, PhD	LT CDR(FTC)	E	TM	01.04.99	NELSON
Warn, Christopher John, SM	LT CDR(FTC)	X	SM	09.12.98	OCLC BRISTOL
Warr, Caroline Helen	LT(IC)	X		01.01.05	MWS COLLINGWOOD
Warr, Richard Frank	LT CDR(FTC)	E	WESM	01.10.02	SPARTAN
Warren, Anouchka Jane Lenham, BA	SLT(IC)	X		01.09.02	CHATHAM
Warren, Brian Howard, OBE, BSc, pce	CAPT(FTC)	X	PWO(U)	30.06.05	MOD (LONDON)
Warren, Julian	SURG SLT(SCC)	-		01.07.02	DARTMOUTH BRNC
Warren, Matthew James, BSc	LT(IC)	X		01.05.04	IRON DUKE
Warren, Richard Alan, BSc	LT(IC)	X	P	01.09.03	DHFS
Warrender, William Jonathan, pce, psc(j)	CDR(FTC)	X	PWO(A)	30.06.04	ARGYLL
Warrick, Mark, BEng	LT(IC)	E	WE	01.09.04	SOMERSET
Warrington, Paul Thomas, BEng	LT CDR(FTC)	E	MESM	01.01.99	COS 2SL/CNH
Warwick, Philip David, pce, psc(j), MA	CDR(FTC)	X	PWO(U)	30.06.01	FLEET HQ NWD
Washer, Nicholas Barry John, BSc, pce	LT CDR(FTC)	X	PWO(C)	01.01.00	JSCSC
Waskett, Daniel, BEng	SLT(IC)	X	O U/T	01.01.04	DARTMOUTH BRNC
Wass, Martin James, BSc	LT CDR(FTC)	X	PWO(A)	01.08.90	FLEET HQ NWD
Watchorn, James	SURG SLT(SCC)	-		15.05.04	DARTMOUTH BRNC
Waterfield, Simon Jon, AMNI	LT CDR(FTC)	X		01.06.02	MWS COLLINGWOOD
Waterhouse, Phillip, MHCIMA	LT CDR(FTC)	S		01.10.00	JSCSC
Waterman, John Henry, BSc, MA, CEng, MIMarE, psc	CDR(FTC)	E	ME	31.12.97	COS 2SL/CNH
Waters, Michael Rhodri, BSc	LT(IC)	X		01.01.05	MWS COLLINGWOOD
Waters, Nigel Roger, BSc	LT CDR(FTC)	S	SM	16.04.96	MOD (BATH)
Watkins, Andrew Patrick Leonard, BSc	MAJ(FTC)	-		01.05.03	BDS WASHINGTON
Watkins, Dean Thomas	CAPT RM(IC)	-	SO(LE)	01.04.04	42 CDO RM
Watkins, Kevin John, BEng, MSc	LT(FTC)	E	ME	01.01.98	DLO BRISTOL
Watkins, Timothy Crispin, BSc, pcea	LT CDR(FTC)	X	P	01.10.00	845 SQN
Watson, Andrew Herbert, BEng, pcea	LT(FTC)	X	O	01.06.95	MWS COLLINGWOOD
Watson, Anthony Peter	LT(FTC)	E	MESM	02.09.99	DLO BRISTOL
Watson, Bradley Lawrence, BSc	LT(CC)	X	O	01.05.01	849 SQN HQ
Watson, Brian Robert	CAPT RM(CC)	-	SO(LE)	01.01.02	815 SQN HQ
Watson, Charles Robert, HNC	LT CDR(FTC)	E	WE	01.10.04	DCSA DHFCS FMR
Watson, Graham Brian	CAPT RM(IC)	-	SO(LE)	24.07.04	40 CDO RM
Watson, Ian, n, BA	LT CDR(FTC)	X	PWO(A)	01.03.03	IRON DUKE
Watson, James Richard, MEng	SLT(IC)	E	ME U/T	01.09.02	SULTAN
Watson, Patrick Halfdan, nadc, pce, psc	CAPT(FTC)	X	PWO	30.06.96	DA BRUNEI
Watson, Peter Gerald Charles, BEng, CEng, MIMarEST	LT CDR(FTC)	E	MESM	25.10.96	FOST SM SEA
Watson, Philip Frank	MAJ(FTC)	BS		01.10.00	RM BAND PTSMTH
Watson, Richard Douglas	LT(IC)	X	MCD	01.10.02	ATHERSTONE
Watson, Richard Ian	MAJ(FTC)	-	SO(LE)	01.10.04	1 ASSAULT GP RM
Watson, Richard John, SM	LT CDR(FTC)	X	SM	01.08.89	FLEET HQ PORTS

Name	Rank	Branch	Spec	Seniority	Where Serving
Watson, Simon Christopher	SLT(IC)	E	WE	01.09.02	MWS COLLINGWOOD
Watson, Stuart Benedict Cooper	LT CDR(FTC)	S	SM	01.10.04	SUPERB
Watt, Anthony James Landon, pce	CDR(FTC)	X	PWO(U)	30.06.05	MWS COLLINGWOOD
Watts, Alun David	CDR(FTC)	S	SM	30.06.02	2SL/CNH FOTR
Watts, Andrew Peter, pcea	LT CDR(FTC)	X	O	01.10.93	RNU ST MAWGAN
Watts, Graham Michael, BSc, CEng, FIMarEST, psc	CAPT(FTC)	E	ME	30.06.05	MOD (LONDON)
Watts, Jason Neil, BSc	LT(CC)	X	P	01.02.96	DHFS
Watts, Raymond Frederick, BSc, psc	CAPT(FTC)	E	WE	31.12.00	DLO DEF MUN GP
Watts, Richard Dennis, OBE, psc(m)	COL(FTC)	-	C	30.06.05	SULTAN AIB
Watts, Robert, pce(sm)	LT CDR(FTC)	X	SM	01.07.01	TRAFALGAR
Watts, Zoe Abigail, BSc	LT(CC)	X		01.01.99	SMITER
Waugh, Peter John, MA, MB, BCh, MFOM, LRCP, LRCS, DipAvMed.	SURG CDR(FCC)	-	(CO/M)	30.06.90	NBC PORTSMOUTH
Waugh, Richard Peter, BEng	LT(IC)	X	P	01.01.04	RAF CRANWELL EFS
Way, Robert Andrew	LT(IC)	X		01.01.01	UKMARBATSTAFF
Weale, John Stuart, pce, pce(sm), BSc	CDR(FTC)	X	SM	30.06.99	MOD (LONDON)
Weale, Jonathan	SURG SLT(SCC)	-		29.05.03	DARTMOUTH BRNC
Weare, Jonathan Bran, BA, MSc	LT(FTC)	S		01.09.99	2SL/CNH
Weaver, Neil	LT CDR(FTC)	E	MESM	01.10.02	ASM IPT
Weaver, Simon, n	LT(FTC)	X	H1	01.10.99	GLEANER
Weaver, Thomas Henry, BA	LT(IC)	X		01.01.03	IRON DUKE
Webb, Amy Francesca	SLT(UCE)(IC)	X		01.09.04	DARTMOUTH BRNC
Webb, Andrew James, BSc, pce	CDR(FTC)	X	PWO(C)	30.06.03	MONTROSE
Webb, Christopher McDonald, pcea	LT CDR(FTC(A)	X	O	01.10.96	824 SQN
Webb, Daniel, BEng	LT(FTC)	E	ME	01.07.01	MOD (LONDON)
Webb, Eleanor Lucy, BA	LT(IC)	S		01.09.02	NAVSEC
Webb, John Paul	LT(IC)	X		01.10.02	MOD (LONDON)
Webb, Martin Robert, BSc	LT(IC)	X	H2	01.09.01	ENDURANCE
Webber, Christopher John, BEng, FRMS, MDA, MCIPD, MCMI	LT CDR(FTC)	X	HM	26.08.97	MOD (BATH)
Webber, Joanne Patricia, BA	LT(FTC)	X	O	01.09.94	820 SQN
Webber, Kerry Jane	LT(CC)	X		01.11.96	OCLC MANCH
Webber, Richard James, MB, BS, Dip FFP, JCPTGP	SURG LTCDR(FCC)	-	GMPP	01.02.01	NELSON (PAY)
Webster, Andrew John, BSc	LT(IC)	E	TM	01.01.04	DARTMOUTH BRNC
Webster, Andrew Philip, BA	LT(CC)	X	PWO(C)	01.11.94	CUMBERLAND
Webster, Mark	SLT(IC)	X		01.04.04	DUMBARTON CASTLE
Webster, Richard James, BSc	LT(CC)	X	FC	01.12.98	MWS COLLINGWOOD
Webster, Richard John, BA	LT(FTC)	S		01.12.97	OCLC MANCH
Webster, Timothy John Cook, psc(m)	LT COL(FTC)	-	C	30.06.00	MOD (LONDON)
Weedon, Grant Antony	LT(FTC)	E	ME	01.09.04	SOUTHAMPTON
Weeks, Deborah Clare, BEd	LT(IC)	S		01.03.99	RALEIGH
Weightman, Nicholas Ellison	LT CDR(FTC)	X	P	01.10.01	NAVSEC
Weil, Daniel Gerard	SLT(IC)	E	AE	01.09.01	SULTAN
Weir, James Robertson	CAPT RM(CC)	-	SO(LE)	01.04.02	539 ASSLT SQN RM
Weir, Scott Duncan, BEng	LT CDR(FTC)	E	WESM	01.10.99	VIGILANT(STBD)
Welborn, Colin George, FRGS, MDA, pce, psc(m)	CAPT(FTC)	X	MCD	30.06.03	FWO PORTS SEA
Welburn, Roy Stuart, BSc	CDR(FTC)	E	AE	31.12.00	MOD (LONDON)
Welch, Alan	LT(FTC)	MS	(AD)	20.09.99	2SL/CNH
Welch, Andrew, MBE	LT CDR(FTC)	X	O	13.10.95	DASC
Welch, James Fleming, MB, ChB, BMS	SURG LTCDR(MCC)	-		05.08.03	MDHU DERRIFORD
Welch, Katherine Alice	LT CDR(CC)	S		01.10.04	MWS COLLINGWOOD
Welford, Robert Clive, BEng	LT CDR(FTC)	X	PWO(C)	01.02.99	PJHQ
Wellesley, Richard Charles Robert, OBE, MDA, pce, pcea	CAPT(FTC)	X	O	30.06.03	MOD (LONDON)
Wellington, Stuart, HNC, BEng, MIEE	LT CDR(FTC)	E	WE	01.02.98	MOD (LONDON)
Wells, Barry Charles, BSc	LT CDR(FTC)	E	WESM	01.10.02	VENGEANCE(PORT)
Wells, Jamie Duncan, BSc	LT(CC)	X		01.09.01	KENT
Wells, John Paul, BDS	SG LT(D)(SCC)	-	GDP	04.07.02	MWS COLLINGWOOD
Wells, Jonathan	LT CDR(FTC)	X	P	01.08.97	824 SQN
Wells, Laura	SURG SLT(SCC)	-		08.04.03	DARTMOUTH BRNC
Wells, Martin Neville	LT(IC)	X	O	01.01.05	849 SQN HQ
Wells, Michael Peter, BSc, PGCE	LT CDR(FTC)	S		01.03.05	FLEET HQ PORTS 2
Welsh, Georgina Louise, BA	LT(IC)	X	H2	01.05.02	ENDURANCE
Welsh, John, BSc, CEng	LT(IC)	E	TM	15.10.95	MWS DEF DIV SCHL
Welsh, Michaela Penelope	SLT(IC)	X		01.02.04	EXETER
Welsh, Richard Michael Karl	LT(CC)	E	AE	01.02.01	814 SQN

Name	Rank	Branch	Spec	Seniority	Where Serving
Wernham, William Frederick, MSc	LT(IC)	MS		01.04.04	NEPTUNE DLO
Wesson, Matthew	LT(SC(MD)	Q		01.07.03	2SL/CNH
West, Alan William John, GCB, DSC, ADC, rcds, pce, psc, hcsc (CHIEF OF NAVAL STAFF AND FIRST SEA LORD SEP 02)	ADM	-	AWO(A)	30.11.00	MOD (LONDON)
West, Andrew William	LT CDR(FTC)	S	(W)	01.10.01	UKSU AFSOUTH
West, Anthony Bernard	LT CDR(FTC)	X	REG	01.10.01	MWS EXCELLENT
West, Darren Colin, BSc	LT(FTC)	X	MCD	01.12.95	MWS SOUTHWICK PK
West, David John	CAPT RM(IC)	-	P	19.07.02	845 SQN
West, Diana Michelle, BSc	SLT(IC)	X		01.02.05	DARTMOUTH BRNC
West, Gillian Ann	LT(IC)	X	ATC	01.05.03	FOST DPORT SHORE
West, Graham George, BEng, CEng, MIMarEST	LT CDR(FTC)	E	ME	06.06.99	MOD (LONDON)
West, Michael Wallace, pce	LT CDR(FTC)	X	AAWO	05.08.92	LOAN OMAN
West, Nicholas Kingsley, BA	LT(CC)	S		01.04.00	FLEET HQ PORTS 2
West, Rory Julian, BSc, pcea	LT CDR(FTC)	X	PWO(U)	01.06.02	PJHQ
West, Timothy Lewis	SLT(IC)	S		01.09.02	VICTORIOUS(PORT)
Westbrook, Jonathan Simon, MBE, pce(sm), pce	CAPT(FTC)	X	SM	30.06.02	MOD (LONDON)
Westbrook, Kevin, BEng	SLT(IC)	E	AE U/T	01.09.03	OCEAN
Westerman, Richard Warwick, MB, CHB	SURG LT(MC(MD)	-		13.08.02	40 CDO RM
Westlake, Karly-Jane, BSc	SLT(IC)	X		01.07.02	RAF SHAWBURY
Westlake, Simon Richard	CAPT RM(FTC)	-	SO(LE)	01.01.98	RMR SCOTLAND
Westley, Alexander James Rayner	SLT(UCE)(IC)	E	WESM	01.09.03	DARTMOUTH BRNC
Westley, David Richard	LT CDR(FTC)	X	P	01.10.01	EXCHANGE ARMY UK
Westoby, Guy Thomas Richard, BSc	LT(IC)	X		01.08.04	YORK
Weston, Graham Kenneth	SLT(IC)	X	SM	01.09.03	SOVEREIGN
Weston, Helen Louise, BSc	LT(IC)	X		01.09.03	COS 2SL/CNH
Weston, Karl Nicholas Neville, BEng	LT(CC)	X	O	01.08.99	815 FLT 212
Weston, Mark William, BDS, MSc, MFGDP(UK)	SGCAPT(D)(FCC)	-		30.06.02	DDA HALTON
Weston, Paul Andrew, pdm	MAJ(FTC)	BS		01.10.03	RM BAND PLYMOUTH
Weston, Robert	LT(IC)	X	P	01.01.03	RNAS YEOVILTON
Westwood, Andrew James, BEng	LT(IC)	X	P	01.09.02	845 SQN
Westwood, Mark Robin Timothy, BEng, MSc, CEng, MIMarEST, MIMechE, MCGI, psc(j), Eur Ing	LT CDR(FTC)	E	MESM	01.07.94	CNNRP BRISTOL
Westwood, Martin William, MA, pce, pcea, psc, psc(j)	CAPT(FTC)	X	P	30.06.02	MOD (LONDON)
Westwood, Thomas Philip	LT(IC)	X		01.01.04	BRECON
Whale, Victoria Alice	LT(CC)	S		01.10.01	DLO/DG DEF SC
Whalley, Richard James	LT CDR(FTC)	S	CMA	01.04.01	FLEET HQ PORTS 2
Whalley, Simon David, MILT, psc	CAPT(FTC)	S	SM	30.06.04	FLEET HQ PORTS
Wharrie, Craig George, BEng	LT(CC)	E	ME	01.12.00	OCLC MANCH
Wharrie, Ewan Killen Balnave, BSc	LT CDR(FTC)	E	TMSM	01.10.01	OCLC ROSYTH
Whatley, Mark	MID(IC)	S		01.07.03	RALEIGH
Wheal, Adrian Justin, BEng	LT CDR(FTC)	E	MESM	01.09.00	SULTAN
Wheatley, Ian James	CHAPLAIN	CE		08.04.97	EXCHANGE USA
Wheatley, Nicola Sian, BSc	LT(IC)	X	H2	01.01.03	FWO DEVPT SEA
Wheatley, Wendy Joy, BA, PGDip	LT CDR(FTC)	X	METOC	04.10.97	750 SQN SEAHAWK
Wheaton, Bowden James Stewart, pcea, gdas	LT CDR(FTC)	X	O	01.10.98	LOAN JTEG BSC DN
Wheeldon, Matthew Alexander John, BA	LT(IC)	X		01.01.05	ENDURANCE
Wheeler, Nicholas Jules, SM(n)	LT CDR(FTC)	X	SM	01.10.03	SPARTAN
Wheen, Charles Jefferies David	LT(IC)	X		01.01.04	BANGOR
Whetter, Richard Scott, BSc	LT(IC)	E	TM	14.05.00	NTE(TTD)
Whetton, Julia Barbara Dawn	LT CDR(FTC)	W	S	01.10.96	RNAS CULDROSE
Whild, Douglas James (Act Lt Cdr)	LT(FTC)	X		24.07.97	NBC PORTSMOUTH
Whitaker, Martin Jeffery, BEng	SLT(IC)	X	P U/T	01.01.04	DARTMOUTH BRNC
Whitaker, Michael John, BSc, CEng, MIMechE, MDA	CDR(FTC)	E	AE	30.06.97	MOD (LONDON)
Whitaker, Rachel Elizabeth	SLT(IC)	E	AE	01.09.02	SULTAN
White, Alastair	2LT(IC)	-		01.08.01	CTCRM LYMPSTONE
White, Alistair John McIntosh	LT(IC)	X	P	01.05.04	RNAS YEOVILTON
White, Andrew Raymond, BSc, CEng, MIEE	CDR(FTC)	E	WESM	31.12.94	MOD (LONDON)
White, Briony Anghard	LT(SC(MD)	Q		01.09.04	MDHU DERRIFORD
White, David John, BSc	LT(CC)	X	P	01.03.98	DHFS
White, Douglas	LT(IC)	E	WESM	01.01.04	VANGUARD(PORT)
White, Haydn John, psc(j)o	LT COL(FTC)	-	LC	30.06.05	FLEET HQ PORTS 2
White, Ian Frank, SM(n), SM	LT CDR(FTC)	X	SM	18.11.99	FOST DSTF
White, Jason Paul	LT(CC)	X	MCD	01.02.01	BROCKLESBY

Name	Rank	Branch	Spec	Seniority	Where Serving
White, Jonathan Andrew Paul, pce(sm), psc(j)	CDR(FTC)	X	SM	30.06.03	TRENCHANT
White, Jonathan Eric, BSc	LT CDR(FTC)	S		01.11.02	AGRIPPA JFC HQ
White, Jonathan W	LT RM(IC)	-		01.09.03	45 CDO RM
White, Katharine Jane, BSc	LT(IC)	X	ATC	01.01.04	RNAS YEOVILTON
White, Kevin Frederick, BEng	LT(FTC)	E	ME	01.07.97	CAPT MCTA
White, Mark William, OBE, BSc, MA, pce, psc	CDR(FTC)	X	PWO(U)	31.12.98	JSCSC
White, Paul Donald, BSc	LT(IC)	X	P	01.05.03	771 SQN
White, Philip Alan, MSc, CEng, FIMarEST	LT CDR(FTC)	E	MESM	16.02.92	NEPTUNE DLO
White, Robert Fredrick	CDR(FTC)	E	WE	30.06.05	COS 2SL/CNH
White, Robert Leonard	LT CDR(FTC)	E	AE	01.10.04	FLEET AV VL
White, Ross Elliott, BEng	LT(IC)	X	P	01.05.04	RNAS YEOVILTON
White, Simon Henry Wilmot, BA, pcea	LT(FTC)	X	P	16.06.93	820 SQN
White, Stephen, BSc	LT(IC)	E	IS	01.01.00	AFPAA(CENTURION)
White, Stephen James	LT(FTC)	X	C	09.01.01	DARTMOUTH BRNC
White, Stephen Noel, BA	CDR(FTC)	S		31.12.97	MOD (BATH)
White, Stephen Paul, IEng, MIIE (Act Lt Cdr)	LT(FTC)	E	WESM	10.06.88	FLEET HQ PORTS
White, Steven, BSc	LT(IC)	X		01.05.03	FDG
Whitehall, Sally, BSc	LT(IC)	X		01.02.00	MWS COLLINGWOOD
Whitehead, Peter James	LT(CC)	X	O	01.12.98	RNAS YEOVILTON
Whitehead, Robert John, BSc	LT(IC)	E	TM	01.01.02	SULTAN
Whitehead, Steven John, BEng, CEng, MRAeS	LT CDR(FTC)	E	AE	01.03.00	771 SQN
Whitehead, Tom, BSc	LT(IC)	X		01.08.04	MWS COLLINGWOOD
Whitehorn, Iain James, BSc, CEng, MIMarEST	CDR(FTC)	E	MESM	30.06.94	2SL/CNH FOTR
Whitehouse, Andrew Paul, MEng	SLT(IC)	X		01.09.02	RNAS YEOVILTON
Whitehouse, David Spencer, SM(n), SM	LT(CC)	X	SM	01.04.00	SPARTAN
Whitehouse, Dominic Patrick, MSc, MB, CHB, MRCP, AFOM, DCH, DTM&H	SURG CDR(FCC)	-	(CM)	01.04.03	NELSON (PAY)
Whitehouse, Marie Louise, BA	SLT(IC)	X		01.11.02	SOMERSET
Whitehouse, Niall Robert	LT CDR(FTC)	E	AE	01.12.04	RNAS YEOVILTON
Whitehouse, Simon Robert, BSc, MIIE	LT(FTC)	E	WE	01.04.01	MCM2 SEA
Whitfield, Joe Alexander	LT CDR(FTC)	X	P	01.10.03	845 SQN
Whitfield, Kenneth David, BEng	LT CDR(FTC)	E	AE	01.03.00	MERLIN IPT
Whitfield, Philip Mark, BSc	MAJ(FTC)	-		01.09.03	FLEET HQ PORTS 2
Whitfield, Robert Matthew Patrick, BSc	LT CDR(FTC)	X	P	01.05.03	RAF LINTN/OUSE
Whitlam, John, pce	LT CDR(FTC)	X	PWO(A)	01.10.00	MWC PORTSDOWN
Whitley, Ian Derek Brake, pce, n	LT CDR(FTC)	X	PWO(C)	01.06.99	MWS COLLINGWOOD
Whitlum, Andrew Colin, BEng, pcea	LT(CC)	X	P	16.08.96	RAF SHAWBURY
Whitlum, Sarah, BSc, n (Act Lt Cdr)	LT(CC)	X	PWO(U)	01.11.96	COMATG SEA
Whitmarsh, Adam Thomas	CAPT RM(CC)	-		01.09.03	CTCRM
Whitson-Fay, Craig David	LT(FTC)	X	O	15.02.01	MWS COLLINGWOOD
Whittaker, Mark Adrian ,BM, MRCPath	SURG CDR(FCC)	-	(CL)	30.06.05	RH HASLAR
Whittingham, Debra Jayne	LT CDR(FTC)	W	X	01.10.98	MOD (LONDON)
Whittington, Christopher Charles	MID(IC)	X	P U/T	01.11.03	DARTMOUTH BRNC
Whittington, Rowland	LT(IC)	E	WE	01.07.04	CORNWALL
Whittle, David James, BA	SLT(IC)	X		01.09.03	DARTMOUTH BRNC
Whittles, Gary William	LT(IC)	S		01.07.04	TALENT
Whitwell, Nicholas Shaun, n	LT(FTC)	X		01.07.99	MWS COLLINGWOOD
Whitworth, Robert Maitland	LT CDR(FTC)	X	PWO(U)	01.10.99	EXCHANGE AUSTLIA
Whybourn, Lesley Ann, MB, ChB, Dip FFP, DRCOG	SURG LTCDR(MCC)	-	GMPP	28.11.02	NELSON (PAY)
Whyntie, Adrian, BSc, CEng, FIEE, jsdc	CDRE(FTC)	E	WE	01.04.05	HQ DCSA
Whyte, Gordon	LT(IC)	E	WE	01.07.04	ARGYLL
Whyte, Iain Paul, MA, MSc, psc(j)	LT CDR(FTC)	E	TM	01.04.01	FLEET HQ PORTSEA
Wick, Harry Mark Stephen	LT(CC)	X		01.09.00	SUTHERLAND
Wickett, Richard James, BEng	LT(CC)	E	ME	01.03.02	2SL/CNH FOTR
Wickham, Robert James, BEng	LT(IC)	X		01.05.01	BRECON
Wicking, Geoffrey Steven, BEng	LT CDR(FTC)	E	AE	01.10.03	MERLIN IPT
Wielopolski, Mark Leszek Christopher Carpenter	LT(IC)	X	P	01.05.01	FLEET AV VALLEY
Wightwick, Katherine Helen Torr, BA, BD	LT(IC)	X		01.08.01	DNR PRES TEAMS
Wilcocks, David Nicholas	SLT(IC)	X		01.07.02	RAMSEY
Wilcocks, Philip Lawrence, DSC, BSc, AMRINA, pce, psc(a) (LSN 100 (SR R3(5/16)) APR 04)	RADM	-	AAWO	19.04.04	PJHQ
Wilcockson, Roy	LT(CS)RM(CAS)	-		07.05.99	DNR SWE 2
Wilcox, Christopher Raymond	SLT(IC)	X	O	01.09.03	849 SQN B FLT

Name	Rank	Branch	Spec	Seniority	Where Serving
Wilcox, Thomas Colin	CAPT RM(CC)	-	P	01.04.01	847 SQN
Wild, Gareth, MB, CHB, BMS	SURG LT(MC(MD)	-		01.08.01	MDHU DERRIFORD
Wild, Richard James	LT(IC)	S		01.01.02	VIGILANT(PORT)
Wildin, Andrew, BEng, MSc, CEng, MIEE	LT CDR(FTC)	E	WE	01.10.04	JSSU CHELTENHAM
Wiles, Stephen John, MSc, CEng, MRAeS	CDR(FTC)	E	AE	30.06.98	ADAS BRISTOL
Wilkins, David Paul, SM(n)	LT(CC)	X	SM	01.05.01	VIGILANT(STBD)
Wilkins, Richard Ronald, BEng	LT CDR(FTC)	E	MESM	01.10.03	VANGUARD(PORT)
Wilkins, Robert Lloyd, BEng	LT(IC)	E	MESM	01.05.03	TRAFALGAR
Wilkinson, David Henry, n	LT CDR(FTC)	X	PWO(U)	01.06.00	FLEET HQ NWD
Wilkinson, Georgina	LT(MCC)	Q	OTSPEC	06.10.97	MDHU DERRIFORD
Wilkinson, John Richard	LT(IC)	X	AV	01.01.04	CHFHQ
Wilkinson, Michael French	LT(CC)	X	P	01.02.96	LOAN OTHER SVCE
Wilkinson, Peter John, BA, FCIPD, pce, pce(sm) (NAVAL SECRETARY JUL 04)	RADM	-	SM	27.07.04	NAVSEC
Wilkinson, Peter McConnell	LT CDR(FTC)	X	P	01.10.96	771 SQN
Wilkinson, Richard Murray, BSc, PGCE, MDA, nadc, jsdc	CAPT(FTC)	E	TM	30.06.00	NATO DEF COL
Wilkinson, Robin Nicholas	LT CDR(FTC)	X	P	01.10.98	FLEET AV VL
Wilkinson, Sarah Louise, MEng	SLT(IC)	E	ME U/T	01.01.04	DARTMOUTH BRNC
Wilkinson, Timothy Lindow, BA	CHAPLAIN	SF		04.03.97	RMB STONEHOUSE
Will, Andrew Watt, MBE, BSc	LT CDR(FTC)	E	WE	01.06.84	FOST FAS SHORE
Williams, Amanda Charlotte	LT(IC)	X	REG	01.07.04	NELSON
Williams, Anthony Michael	LT(IC)	X		01.09.04	SUTHERLAND
Williams, Anthony Peter, DSC, MA, pce, psc(j)	CDR(FTC)	X	MCD	31.12.00	MCM2 SEA
Williams, Anthony Stephen	LT(FTC)	X	FC	01.09.98	TYNE
Williams, Benjamin Ross, BDS	SG LT(D)(SCC)	-		27.06.00	NEPTUNE DDA
Williams, Brett, MEng	LT(IC)	E	P U/T	01.09.03	RNAS YEOVILTON
Williams, Bruce Nicholas Bromley, OBE, BSc, pce, psc	CAPT(FTC)	X	PWO(U)	30.06.01	FOST SEA
Williams, Caroline Mary Alexandra, PhD, BA	CDR(FCC)	Q	IC	30.06.05	RCDM
Williams, Cassandra Lyn, BEng	LT(CC)	E	AE	01.04.02	RAF COTTESMORE
Williams, Colin Nicholas Owen, BSc	LT CDR(FTC)	X	PWO(A)	01.06.01	STRIKFORNATO
Williams, Daniel Leslie, BA	LT(CC)	X	P	01.01.00	LOAN OTHER SVCE
Williams, David	LT CDR(FTC)	S	SM	01.10.99	SAUDI AFPS SAUDI
Williams, David	LT(CC)	X	P	08.06.00	847 SQN
Williams, David Ian, pce	LT CDR(FTC)	X	AAWO	29.05.92	DL IPT
Williams, David Spencer, BEng, pce, psc(j)	CDR(FTC)	X	PWO(U)	30.06.05	DRAKE COB
Williams, Dean Ashley	CAPT RM(IC)	-	SO(LE)	01.07.04	BULWARK
Williams, Dylan, BDS	SG LT(D)(SC(MD)	-		25.06.03	45 CDO RM
Williams, Gerwyn, ACMI, MinstAM	LT(IC)	S		01.05.04	AFPAA(CENTURION)
Williams, James Laurence	SLT(IC)	X		01.02.04	DARTMOUTH BRNC
Williams, James Phillip	LT CDR(FTC)	X	AAWO	01.06.00	LIVERPOOL
Williams, Jonathan Roland ,BMus	SLT(IC)	X	O U/T	01.09.03	DARTMOUTH BRNC
Williams, Lee John	LT(IC)	E	WESM	01.07.04	TURBULENT
Williams, Linda Jean, BA	LT(CC)	X		01.05.98	MWS SOUTHWICK PK
Williams, Luke Anthony John, BA	LT(IC)	X		01.01.05	MWS COLLINGWOOD
Williams, Mark Adrian, pcea	LT CDR(FTC)	X	O	01.10.00	FLEET HQ NWD
Williams, Mark Henry, MA, pce, pce(sm), psc(j)	CDR(FTC)	X	SM	31.12.98	TRAFALGAR
Williams, Mark Stuart, BSc	LT CDR(FTC)	S		29.03.97	NBC PORTSMOUTH
Williams, Martyn Jon, OBE, MA, CEng, MIEE, psc(j)	CDR(FTC)	E	WESM	30.06.00	ASM IPT
Williams, Matthew Charles	CAPT RM(IC)	-		01.09.03	RM WARMINSTER
Williams, Nicola Marie	SLT(IC)	X		01.09.04	RNAS YEOVILTON
Williams, Nigel David Blackstone, BSc, jsdc, pce	CDR(FTC)	X	PWO(U)	31.12.91	AGRIPPA MAR CC
Williams, Nigel Lamplough, BSc, CEng, MIMarEST	CAPT(FTC)	E	ME	30.06.00	NAVSEC
Williams, Oliver Charles Llewelyn	SLT(UCE)(IC)	X		01.09.03	DARTMOUTH BRNC
Williams, Paul Allan, BEng	LT(CC)	E	ME	01.01.02	CAPT IST STAFF
Williams, Paul Glynn, BA	LT(IC)	X		01.05.01	NEPTUNE
Williams, Peter Mark, BEng, MBA	LT CDR(FTC)	E	TM	01.10.03	FLEET HQ PORTS 2
Williams, Peter Michael	CAPT RM(IC)	-		01.09.03	EXCHANGE ARMY UK
Williams, Richard	SURG SLT(SCC)	-		01.07.02	DARTMOUTH BRNC
Williams, Robert Evan, OBE, LLB (Barrister)	CDR(FTC)	S	BAR	30.06.93	COS 2SL/CNH
Williams, Robert John Stirling, n	LT(FTC)	X	PWO(C)	01.09.96	ILLUSTRIOUS
Williams, Roderick Charles, BSc	LT CDR(FTC)	E	ME	01.10.89	DSFM PORTSMOUTH
Williams, Simon Paul, BSc, pce	CAPT(FTC)	X	PWO(C)	30.06.03	MWS COLLINGWOOD
Williams, Simon Thomas, OBE, BSc, pce, pce(sm)	CDRE(FTC)	X	SM	03.05.05	UKMCC BAHRAIN

Name	Rank	Branch	Spec	Seniority	Where Serving
Williams, Stephen Wayne Leonard	LT CDR(FTC)	S		01.04.01	PORTLAND
Williams, Thomas George Edward, BA	LT(IC)	X		01.06.04	COTTESMORE
Williams, Timothy Nicholas Edward, BSc, pce, pcea, psc (Act Capt)	CDR(FTC)	X	P	31.12.89	SA SEOUL
Williamson, Alexander Karl, MSc	MAJ(FTC)	-	C	01.05.04	FLEET CIS PORTS
Williamson, Peter James	LT(IC)	X		01.10.02	MWS COLLINGWOOD
Williamson, Tobias Justin Lubbock, MVO, BEng, MA, pce, pcea, psc(j)	CDR(FTC)	X	O	31.12.00	NAVSEC
Willing, Nigel Phillip, BSc	LT(CC)	X	P	16.08.93	EXCHANGE FRANCE
Willis, Alistair James, MA, MBA, MILT, MCMI, psc(j)	CDR(FTC)	S		30.06.04	FLEET HQ PORTS
Willis, Andrew Stephen, n	LT(CC)	X		01.01.98	BULWARK
Willis, Martyn Stephen	LT CDR(FTC)	S	CA	02.05.95	RALEIGH
Willmore, Simon	SLT(UCE)(IC)	E	WE	01.01.03	DARTMOUTH BRNC
Wills, John Robert, BSc, CEng, MIMarEST	CAPT(FTC)	E	ME	31.12.97	SA ATHENS
Wills, Philip John, BSc	LT CDR(FTC)	X	O	01.01.01	FLEET HQ PORTS 2
Wills, Robert Hartingdon, BEng	LT(IC)	E	MESM	01.05.03	VIGILANT(STBD)
Willsmore, Stuart Andrew	SLT(IC)	X		01.07.02	SOUTHAMPTON
Wilman, David Mark, BA (Barrister)	LT CDR(FTC)	S	BAR	01.10.01	SOMERSET
Wilmott, Sarah Catherine, MB, ChB	SURG LT(MC(MD)	-		01.08.01	MDHU DERRIFORD
Wilshaw, Gary	LT(IC)	E	AE	01.05.03	OCLC BRISTOL
Wilshire, Nicholas	SLT(IC)	E	MESM	01.11.03	FWO FASLANE
Wilson, Adrian Clive	MAJ(FTC)	-	SO(LE)	01.10.03	42 CDO RM
Wilson, Alexander Charles, MA, psc, psc(j)o	LT COL(FTC)	-	LC	31.12.95	SHAPE BELGIUM
Wilson, Allan John, n	LT CDR(FTC)	X	PWO(U)	01.10.03	SOMERSET
Wilson, Charles Dominick, OBE, BSc, jsdc, pce	CDR(FTC)	X	MCD	30.06.95	SA COPENHAGEN
Wilson, Charles Kenneth, BA	SLT(IC)	S		01.09.03	DARTMOUTH BRNC
Wilson, Christopher Gordon Talbot, pce, pcea	LT CDR(FTC(A)	X	P	01.08.85	DLO YEO
Wilson, Christopher John, BEng, MBA, CEng, MIMarEST	LT CDR(FTC)	E	MESM	01.12.96	MOD (BATH)
Wilson, David Robert, pce, n	LT CDR(FTC)	X	AAWO	01.05.00	BANGOR
Wilson, David Timothy	LT CDR(FTC)	E	WE	01.10.98	DLO BRISTOL
Wilson, David William Howard, psc(j)	LT COL(FTC)	-		30.06.03	NELSON
Wilson, Gary Paul	LT(IC)	X	SM	01.01.03	DEF SCH OF LANG
Wilson, Geoffrey John	LT(FTC)	X	REG	19.09.00	NAVSEC
Wilson, Graham John, MBE	LT CDR(FTC)	X	MCD	01.10.01	MWS COLLINGWOOD
Wilson, James Andrew	LT(FTC)	E	ME	15.06.95	SCOTT
Wilson, John, BEng	LT(CC)	X	P	01.07.97	848 SQN HERON
Wilson, Julian Graham, BA	MAJ(FTC)	-		01.09.04	UKLFCSG RM
Wilson, Kevin Paul, BSc, MDA, CEng, MIEE	CAPT(FTC)	E	WESM	30.06.05	HQ DCSA
Wilson, Michael George, BEng	LT(IC)	E	MESM	01.01.03	SUPERB
Wilson, Neil Andrew, BA	LT(IC)	X	SM	01.05.03	VICTORIOUS(PORT)
Wilson, Robert, ARICS (Act Cdr)	LT CDR(FTC)	X	H CH	01.07.83	LOAN OMAN
Wilson, Robert	LT CDR(FTC)	X	PWO(A)	01.09.00	LEDBURY
Wilson, Simon Allistair	LT(IC)	X	P	01.01.04	RAF CRANWELL EFS
Wilson, Stephen Gordon, MNI, pce, psc	CAPT(FTC)	X	AAWO	30.06.03	DA BRIDGETOWN
Wilson, Stephen Richard, psc	LT COL(FTC)	-		30.06.94	FOST SEA
Wilson-Chalon, Louis Michael, BSc, pcea	LT CDR(FTC)	X	P	01.04.97	815 SQN HQ
Wiltcher, Ross Alexander, BA	LT CDR(FTC)	S		01.08.93	NP IRAQ
Wilton, Mark, BSc	LT(IC)	X		01.12.04	LEEDS CASTLE
Winand, Francis Michael John, BA, SM(n)	LT(CC)	X	SM	01.05.00	EXCHANGE NLANDS
Winbolt, Neil, BEng	LT(IC)	E	TM	01.04.00	FLEET HQ PORTSEA
Winborn, David John, BEng	LT(IC)	E	MESMUT	01.05.05	TURBULENT
Winch, Emma Jane, BDS	SGLTCDR(D)(MCC)	-		24.01.99	MWS EXCELLENT
Winch, Joseph Adrian	CAPT RM(IC)	-		01.09.04	CTCRM
Windebank, Stephen John, pcea	LT CDR(FTC)	X	P	01.10.02	750 SQN SEAHAWK
Windsar, Paul Andrew, BEng	LT CDR(FTC)	E	WESM	27.11.98	FOST SM SEA
Windsor, Mark, BSc, MA, MIMechE, psc	CAPT(FTC)	X	METOC	31.12.00	2SL/CNH FOTR
Wingfield, Melissa Helen, BDS	SGLTCDR(D)(MC(MD)	-		01.07.01	INVINCIBLE
Wingfield, Michael James, BEng (Act Lt Cdr)	LT(FTC)	X	O	16.07.94	MWC PORTSDOWN
Winkle, Sean James, BA	CDR(FTC)	E	TM	30.06.05	NAVSEC
Winn, John Paul	LT(CC)	X	HM2	01.10.00	SCOTT
Winskell, Thomas Robert	MID(NE)(IC)	X		01.11.04	DARTMOUTH BRNC
Winsor, James, BSc	LT(CC)	X	H2	01.03.00	ECHO
Winstanley, Keith, MBE, pce, hcsc	CAPT(FTC)	X	PWO(N)	31.12.99	ALBION
Winstone, Nigel	SLT(IC)	E	MESM	01.02.04	DARTMOUTH BRNC
Winter, Richard Jason, BEng, CEng, PGDip, MIEE, adp	LT CDR(FTC)	E	WE	01.08.01	BULWARK

Name	Rank	Branch	Spec	Seniority	Where Serving
Winter, Timothy McMahon, BEng, MA, CEng, MIMarEST, psc(j)	LT CDR(FTC)	E	ME	01.05.98	MOD (LONDON)
Winterbon, Andrew Richard	LT(IC)	X	FC	01.05.01	MANCHESTER
Winterton, Paul	LT(IC)	X	O	01.05.04	820 SQN
Wintle, Geoffrey Lawrence, MSc, MCIT, MILT	CDR(FTC)	S	SM	30.06.03	MOD (LONDON)
Wise, Graham John, BEng, MSc, CEng, MIEE, psc(j)	CDR(FTC)	E	WE	30.06.02	HQ DCSA
Wise, Simon David, BSc, MDA, CEng, FCMI, MIEE, CDipAF	CDR(FTC)	E	WE	31.12.96	DLO BRISTOL
Wiseman, George Richard	CAPT RM(FTC)	-	SO(LE)	01.01.00	HQ 3 CDO BDE RM
Wiseman, Ian Carl, n	LT CDR(FTC)	X	PWO(N)	01.02.03	ENDURANCE
Wiseman, Neil Christopher	LT(CC)	X	O	16.06.96	RNAS YEOVILTON
Withers, James Warren, BEng, CEng, MIEE	LT CDR(FTC)	E	WE	01.04.96	DLO BRISTOL
Witt, Alister Kevin	LT(IC)	MS		01.09.01	DMSTC
Witte, Richard Hugh, LLB, n	LT(FTC)	X		01.12.97	MWS COLLINGWOOD
Witton, James William, pce	LT CDR(FTC)	X	PWO(U)	01.06.93	LOAN DSTL
Witton, Oliver Edward Nicholas John Charles	MID(UCE)(IC)	X		01.09.03	DARTMOUTH BRNC
Witts, Christopher Ian	CAPT RM(IC)	-		01.09.03	42 CDO RM
Woad, Jonathan Patrick Rhys, BSc	LT(IC)	X		01.11.01	CHATHAM
Wolfe, David Edward, pce, pcea, fsc	CAPT(FTC)	X	O	30.06.02	RCDS
Wolsey, Mark Andrew Ronald, BA, psc(m)	LT COL(FTC)	-		30.06.99	MOD (LONDON)
Wood, Alexander MacDonald, BSc, MB, CHB	SURG LT(SCC)	-		01.08.02	45 CDO RM
Wood, Andrew Graeme, BEng	LT(CC)	E	AE	01.07.97	DLO YEO
Wood, Christopher	SLT(IC)	X		01.01.02	CYPRUS PBS
Wood, Christopher Richard	LT CDR(FTC)	X	P	01.01.05	829 FLT 01
Wood, Christopher Taylor, BEng	LT(IC)	E	TM	01.01.00	NTE(TTD)
Wood, Craig, n	LT CDR(FTC)	X	PWO(A)	01.08.01	FLEET HQ PORTS 2
Wood, Graham Richard, BA (Act Lt Cdr)	LT(CC)	S		01.02.98	NEPTUNE DLO
Wood, Gregory, MB, BS	SURG CDR(MCC)	-	GMPP	30.06.04	NELSON
Wood, Iain	SURG SLT(SCC)	-		01.07.02	DARTMOUTH BRNC
Wood, Iain Leslie, BA	LT(CC)	X		01.01.99	BROCKLESBY
Wood, Ian Derrick, IEng, AMIMarEST	LT CDR(FTC)	E	ME	01.10.96	DLO BRISTOL
Wood, Joanne Tamar, BA	LT(IC)	X		01.01.02	RAF SHAWBURY
Wood, John Lindsay, MSc, CEng, FIMarEST, MCGI, psc(j)	CDR(FTC)	E	ME	30.06.01	DPA BRISTOL
Wood, Jonathan Richard	LT(IC)	E	WE	01.09.04	CUMBERLAND
Wood, Joseph Albert (Act Lt Cdr)	LT(FTC)	X		03.04.98	INVINCIBLE
Wood, Matthew David James	LT(IC)	E	TM	01.03.05	MWS COLLINGWOOD
Wood, Michael Leslie, BSc, MPhil, n	LT CDR(FTC)	X	PWO(U)	01.12.04	CHATHAM
Wood, Michael William, BSc	LT(IC)	X		01.05.04	MWS COLLINGWOOD
Wood, Nicholas Robert	LT(FTC)	X	PWO(U)	01.04.01	EXCHANGE AUSTLIA
Wood, Richard Ralph Thellusson, BA	LT(IC)	X	P U/T	01.09.04	RNAS YEOVILTON
Wood, Robert (Barrister)	CDR(FTC)	S	BAR	30.06.04	JDCC
Wood, Simon Andrew Hall, BEng	LT(CC)	X	P	01.05.00	846 SQN
Wood, Uvedale George Singleton, pcea	LT CDR(FTC)	X	P	01.04.99	EXCHANGE USA
Woodard, Jolyon Robert Alban, BA, pcea	LT CDR(FTC)	X	P	01.10.03	CHFHQ
Woodard, Neil Antony, BSc, GCIPD	LT CDR(FTC)	S		01.10.04	EXETER
Woodbridge, Richard George, BEng	LT CDR(CC)	E	ME	01.08.04	SULTAN
Woodcock, Simon Jonathan, BSc, CEng, MIMechE, psc(j)	CAPT(FTC)	E	ME	30.06.05	SULTAN
Woodford, Geoffrey Ian, MBE, BEng	LT CDR(FTC)	E	WESM	01.09.96	DLO BRISTOL
Wooding, Graham Allen, BSc	LT(FTC)	E	WE	19.02.93	DCSA NWD REGION
Wooding, Steven	LT(IC)	E	AE	01.05.04	MOD (LONDON)
Woodley, Stephen Leonard, BEng	LT(IC)	E	MESM	01.09.02	VICTORIOUS(PORT)
Woodman, Daniel Peter, BEng	LT(IC)	E	ME	01.09.03	EDINBURGH
Woodrow, Kevin, SM	LT CDR(FTC)	X	SM	01.10.03	MWS COLLINGWOOD
Woodruff, Anthony Desmond	LT CDR(FTC)	X	PWO(U)	01.10.99	MWC PORTSDOWN
Woodruff, Dean Aaron, BEng, MSc	LT CDR(FTC)	E	ME	01.12.99	T45 IPT
Woods, Jeremy Billing, pce, psc(j)	CDR(FTC)	X	AAWO	30.06.04	FLEET HQ PORTS 2
Woods, Michael James Peter, BEng	LT(FTC)	E	WESM	01.05.01	FOST FAS SHORE
Woods, Roland Philip, AMIAM, pce	CDR(FTC)	X	PWO(A)	31.12.98	BDS WASHINGTON
Woods, Timothy Christopher, MA, psc(j)	LT CDR(FTC)	E	TMSM	01.02.01	DARTMOUTH BRNC
Woodward, Darroch John, BA, BSc	LT CDR(FTC)	X	MCD	01.07.95	FLEET HQ PORTS 2
Wookey, Mark	LT(CC)	X	O	01.02.96	EXCHANGE BRAZIL
Woolfe, Kevin David	LT(IC)	E		01.05.02	ADAS BRISTOL
Woolhead, Andrew Lyndon, BA, n	LT CDR(FTC)	X	PWO(N)	01.10.03	OCEAN
Woolhead, Craig Morton, BA	LT(CC)	X		01.05.00	MARLBOROUGH
Woollcombe-Gosson, David James, pce	LT CDR(FTC)	X	AAWO	01.06.97	CUMBERLAND

Name	Rank	Branch	Spec	Seniority	Where Serving
Wooller, Mark Adrian Hudson, BA	LT CDR(FTC)	S	SM	01.10.01	NEPTUNE DLO
Woolley, Martin James	LT CDR(FTC)	X	MCD	01.01.93	LOAN OMAN
Woollven, Andrew Howard, pce	LT CDR(FTC)	X	PWO(U)	01.08.97	BROCKLESBY
Woollven, Christopher David, BSc	LT(CC)	X	O	01.08.99	815 FLT 206
Woolsey, Kevin Edward Keith	LT(FTC)	X	ATC	16.05.95	RNAS CULDROSE
Woosey, David Alan, BA	LT(IC)	S		01.09.03	NBC PORTSMOUTH
Wordsworth, Jonathan David, BSc	SLT(IC)	X		01.07.02	ILLUSTRIOUS
Workman, Rayner John	LT(IC)	X		01.09.03	INVINCIBLE
Worley, Thomas Frank, BA	LT(IC)	X		01.01.03	KENT
Wormald, Robert Edward, MSc, CEng, FIMarEST, psc	CDR(FTC)	E	MESM	31.12.92	MOD (BATH)
Wort, Roland Stephen, BA, BSc	CHAPLAIN	SF		27.07.93	FWO PORTS SEA
Worth, Malcolm Charles	CAPT RM(IC)	-	SO(LE)	01.04.04	CTCRM
Worthington, Jonathan Michael Francis, MA, psc(j)	LT CDR(FTC)	E	TM	01.05.96	MWS COLLINGWOOD
Wotherspoon, Steven Robert, psc	LT COL(FTC)	-		30.06.94	NS OBERAMMERGAU
Wotton, Alan Christopher	LT(IC)	X	P	01.07.04	847 SQN
Wotton, Ryan John	SLT(IC)	X		01.01.05	RNAS YEOVILTON
Woznicki, Stanley James	LT CDR(FTC)	X	AAWO	16.06.88	MWS COLLINGWOOD
Wragg, Gareth Terence, SM(n)	LT(CC)	X	SM	01.01.01	VANGUARD(PORT)
Wragg, Helen Claire	LT(IC)	S		01.06.03	FOST DPORT SHORE
Wraith, Neil	MAJ(FTC)	-	LC	01.09.00	BULWARK
Wray, Arthur Douglas	LT CDR(FTC)	E	WESM	01.10.01	FLEET HQ PORTS 2
Wren, Stephen James	LT(IC)	X		01.07.04	MWS COLLINGWOOD
Wrenn, Michael Reader William, FIIE, MIOSH	LT CDR(FTC)	E	WE	01.10.02	MOD (LONDON)
Wrennall, Eric Paul	LT(CC)	E	ME	29.04.01	FOST SEA
Wrigglesworth, Stephen Mark	LT(IC)	X	C	01.07.03	MWS COLLINGWOOD
Wright, Bradley Lee, BEng, MSc, CEng, MIEE, gw	LT CDR(FTC)	E	WE	01.06.99	COS 2SL/CNH
Wright, Daniel James, LLB, SM	LT(CC)	X	SM	01.12.98	VENGEANCE(STBD)
Wright, David Anthony (Act Lt Cdr)	LT(FTC)	X	MCD	29.07.94	ILLUSTRIOUS
Wright, David Ian, BEng, CEng, MIEE	LT CDR(FTC)	E	WE	01.09.04	RMC OF SCIENCE
Wright, Douglas	LT(IC)	E	AE	01.05.03	RNAS CULDROSE
Wright, Gabriel Joseph Trevillian, MEng, DPhil	SLT(IC)	E	WE U/T	01.11.02	ILLUSTRIOUS
Wright, Geoffrey Neil, MBE, BSc (Act Capt)	CDR(FTC)	E	MESM	30.06.93	DRAKE SFM
Wright, Gillian, BSc	LT(FTC)	S		01.04.98	UKMCC BAHRAIN
Wright, Helen Jane	LT(IC)	S		13.08.04	JHCHQ
Wright, James Nicholas	SLT(IC)	S		01.05.03	NOTTINGHAM
Wright, Jeffrey Robert	LT(IC)	S	(W)	01.07.04	814 SQN
Wright, Jennifer Sarah, BA	LT(IC)	S		01.09.04	FLEET HQ PORTS 2
Wright, Jonathon Stuart	SLT(UCE)(IC)	X		01.09.04	DARTMOUTH BRNC
Wright, Martin Glenn, BEng	SLT(IC)	E	ME U/T	01.01.05	DARTMOUTH BRNC
Wright, Neil, MBE	LT(IC)	E	AE	13.08.04	1 (F) SQN (RN)
Wright, Nigel Seymour, BEng, MSc, CEng, MIMarEST	LT CDR(FTC)	E	ME	01.02.99	JSCSC
Wright, Stuart Hugh (Barrister)	CDR(FTC)	S	BAR	30.06.05	DCPPA HALTON
Wright, Timothy Mark, BA	LT(FTC)	S		01.04.98	RALEIGH
Wright-Jones, Alexandra Elizabeth Megan	LT(SC(MD)	Q		29.11.02	NELSON (PAY)
Wrightson, Hugh Mawson, BSc, MA, CEng, MIEE, psc(j)	CDR(FTC)	E	ME	31.12.97	COS 2SL/CNH
Wrigley, Alexander John, MB, BS, BSc	SURG LT(SCC)	-		03.08.04	DARTMOUTH BRNC
Wrigley, Peter James	LT CDR(FTC)	X		16.10.88	NBC PORTSMOUTH
Wroblewski, Jefferey Andre	LT CDR(FTC)	E	MESM	31.10.01	VICTORIOUS(PORT)
Wuidart-Gray, Spencer	LT CDR(IC)	X	PWO(U)	01.03.02	MWS COLLINGWOOD
Wunderle, Charles Albert	CDR(FTC)	S	(W)	30.06.00	DLO BRISTOL
Wyatt, Christopher	LT(FTC)	S	(S)	17.12.93	RNAS CULDROSE
Wyatt, David James, MCMI, pce, NDipM	LT CDR(FTC)	X	H CH	01.11.93	MWS HM TG (D)
Wyatt, Julian Michael, BSc, MDA, CEng, FIMarEST, MIMechE	CDR(FTC)	E	MESM	30.06.03	COS 2SL/CNH
Wyatt, Steven Patrick, BSc	CDR(FTC)	E	WESM	31.12.95	HQ DCSA
Wykes, Thomas Edward Vernon, BEng	LT(IC)	E	MESM	01.01.05	SULTAN
Wyld, Anthony Wallace	LT CDR(FTC)	E	WE	01.10.02	JES IPT
Wylie, David	LT(IC)	X		02.08.02	RNAS YEOVILTON
Wylie, David Victor	CHAPLAIN	CE		01.12.98	40 CDO RM
Wylie, Ian Charles Henfrey, BEng, MBA, AMIEE	LT CDR(FTC)	E	WESM	01.11.00	MOD (LONDON)
Wylie, Robert, MB, CHB, AFOM, MRCGP, Dip FFP	SURG CDR(FCC)	-	GMPP	01.04.03	RNAS YEOVILTON
Wyness, Caroline Jayne, BEng, n	LT(FTC)	X		01.10.98	EXAMPLE
Wyness, Roger Simon, pcea	LT(FTC)	X	P	01.07.96	JSCSC
Wynn, Simon Raymond, PGDip, M ED, MSc	LT CDR(FTC)	X	METOC	01.09.97	MOD (LONDON)

Name	Rank	Branch	Spec	Seniority	Where Serving
Wynn Jones, Iago, BA	LT(IC)	X	O	01.05.02	849 SQN A FLT
Wyper, James Robert, BSc, SM(n)	LT CDR(FTC)	X	SM	01.09.00	FOST DSTF
Wyper, John	SLT(IC)	E	ME	01.01.04	SULTAN

Y

Name	Rank	Branch	Spec	Seniority	Where Serving
Yardley, Andrew Philip	LT CDR(FTC)	X	METOC	01.10.99	RFANSU
Yarham, Nigel Peter	LT(IC)	X		01.01.04	MONTROSE
Yarker, Daniel Lawrence, MBA, pce, NDipM	LT CDR(FTC)	X	AAWO	01.10.97	MOD (LONDON)
Yarnall, Nicholas John, MB, BCH, MRCGP, AFOM, DObstRCOG (Act Surg Cdr)	SURG LTCDR(FCC)	-	GMPP	01.08.97	NEPTUNE
Yates, David Martin	CHAPLAIN	RC		01.09.98	SULTAN
Yates, Elizabeth Helen, MB, BS	SURG LT(SCC)	-		01.08.01	RH HASLAR
Yates, Lauren Olivia, BA	LT(IC)	S		01.09.03	FLEET HQ PORTS
Yates, Neal Peter, MBE, pce, pcea, psc	LT CDR(FTC(A)	X	O	01.06.89	DLO YEO
Yates, Simon Peter	SLT(UCE)(IC)	X		01.09.04	DARTMOUTH BRNC
Yates, Stuart Edward, BSc, n	LT(CC)	X		01.05.98	MWS COLLINGWOOD
Yelland, Christopher Brian	LT CDR(FTC)	X	O	01.10.01	702 SQN HERON
Yemm, Matthew Alvin	SLT(IC)	X		01.02.03	OCEAN
York, Gideon Rufus James, BEng	LT CDR(FTC)	E	MESM	01.05.04	DLO BRISTOL
Youldon, Louisa Jane, BSc	LT(IC)	X	HM	01.05.01	SCOTT
Young, Angus, PGDIPAN, pce, n	LT CDR(FTC)	X	PWO(N)	01.06.99	YORK
Young, Christopher John, BEd, HND	LT CDR(CC)	E	TM	18.06.04	NTE(TTD)
Young, David Andrew	LT(IC)	E	AE	01.07.04	FLEET HQ PORTS
Young, Gavin Lee, pce, psc(j), MA	CDR(FTC)	X	AAWO	30.06.04	MWC SOUTHWICK
Young, John Nicholas	LT(FTC)	X	AV	24.07.97	NELSON
Young, Keith Hunter	LT(FTC)	E	ME	23.02.90	DRAKE SFM
Young, Michael Stephen, MBE, MA, MSc, ADipC, FCIPD, psc(j)	LT CDR(FTC)	E	TM	01.09.96	COS 2SL/CNH
Young, Nigel Alan, BSc	LT(CC)	E	TM	01.01.96	INVINCIBLE
Young, Peter	LT(FTC)	E	ME	02.05.00	EXCHANGE N ZLAND
Young, Rachel, BA, n	LT(CC)	X		01.12.94	NAVSEC
Young, Stephen William	LT CDR(FTC)	S	SM	01.10.00	NAVSEC
Young, Stuart Sheldon, MSc, CEng, FIMarEST, MIMechE, jsdc	CDR(FTC)	E	ME	30.06.95	CMT SHRIVENHAM
Youngman, Paul	LT(IC)	E	TM	01.02.04	DARTMOUTH BRNC
Youp, Allan Thomas, BSc, PGCE	LT CDR(CC)	E	TM	01.10.04	FWO PORTS SEA
Yuill, Ian Alexander, BSc, CDipAF, adp	CDR(FTC)	E	IS	01.10.96	CINCFLEET FTSU
Yule, Michael James, BA, n	LT(CC)	X	PWO(C)	01.08.95	CORNWALL

Z

Name	Rank	Branch	Spec	Seniority	Where Serving
Zambellas, George Michael, DSC, BSc, pce, pcea, psc, hcsc	CDRE(FTC)	X	P	29.11.02	COMATG SEA
Ziolo, Jan Mathieson Christopher, BEng	LT(IC)	E	MESM	01.01.05	SULTAN
Zipfell, Adam James, BSc	LT(IC)	X	P	01.09.02	RAF SHAWBURY

RFA OFFICERS

COMMODORE

P. J. LANNIN

COMMODORE (ENGINEERS)

M.D. NORFOLK

Captains

C.J. Fell
S.F. Hodgson psc
C.R. Knapp
D.M. Pitt
A.T. Roach
P.A. Taylor, OBE
J.P. Thompson, OBE
B.J. Waters, OBE
L.M. Coupland, OBE
N.A. Jones
J. Stones
D.J.M. Worthington
W.M. Walworth OBE
R.L. Williams
F. Brady
I.N. Pilling
R.A. Bliss
S.H. Cant
R.G. Ferris
J.P. Huxley
M.T. Jarvis
I.E. Johnson
J. Murchie
R. Robinson-Brown
R.C. Thornton
P.M. Farmer
D.I. Gough
R. H. Allan
R. Bennett
P.T. Hanton
T.J. Iles
S.P. Jones
D.P. Kehoe
P.S. Whyte
A.S. Swatridge

Captain (Engineers)

T. Adam
G.R. Axworthy
D.E. Bass
P.J. Beer, MBE
D.W. Birkett
R.J. Brewer
P.C.M. Daniels
A. Edworthy
I.W. Finlayson
I.E. Hall
K. Holder
R. Kirk
R.W. Langton
S.J. Mathews
M. Mission
D.W.G. Phasey
R. Settle
K. Smeaton
C.S. Smith
R.J. Smith
N.C. Springer
A.D. Wills
E.M. Quigley
G. T. Turner
K.R.C. Moore
A.C. Bowditch
J.E. Collins
I.M. Doolan-Phillip
A.J. Grant
B.S. Layson
J.J. Oakey
D.S.Simpson
D. Preston
I. Dunbar
P.I. Henney
A.G. Sinclair
C.L. Forrest
D.J. Moore
C.M. Brown
M.P. Cole

SENIORITY LIST

ADMIRALS OF THE FLEET

(This rank is now held in abeyance in peacetime (1996))

Edinburgh, His Royal Highness The Prince Philip, Duke of, KG, KT, OM, GBE, AC, QSO....... 15 Jan 53

Pollock, Sir Michael (Patrick), GCB, LVO, DSC, psc........ 1 Mar 74

Ashmore, Sir Edward (Beckwith), GCB, DSC, IRs, jssc, psc ....9 Feb 77

Leach, Sir Henry (Conyers), GCB, DL, jssc, psc .... 1 Dec 82

Oswald, Sir (John) Julian (Robertson), GCB, rcds, psc........2 Mar 93

Bathurst, Sir (David) Benjamin, GCB, DL, rcds .... 10 Jul 95

ADMIRALS

FORMER CHIEF OF DEFENCE STAFF, FIRST SEA LORD OR VICE CHIEF OF DEFENCE STAFF WHO REMAIN ON THE ACTIVE LIST

Slater, Sir Jock (John Cunningham Kirkwood), GCB, LVO, DL, rcds, pce .... 20 Jan 91
Former First Sea Lord and Former Vice Chief of Defence Staff

Boyce, the Lord, GCB, OBE, rcds, psc .... 25 May 95
Former Chief of the Defence Staff and Former First Sea Lord

Abbott, Sir Peter (Charles) GBE, KCB, MA, rcds, pce........3 Oct 95
Former Vice Chief of Defence Staff

Essenhigh, Sir Nigel (Richard), GCB, rcds, pce, psc, hcsc .... 11 Sep 98
Former First Sea Lord

ADMIRALS

West, Sir Alan (William John), GCB, DSC, ADC, rcds, pce, psc, hcsc .... 30 Nov 00
(FIRST SEA LORD AND CHIEF OF NAVAL STAFF SEP 02)

Band, Sir Jonathon, KCB, BA, jsdc, pce, hcsc........02 Aug 02
(COMMANDER-IN-CHIEF FLEET, COMMANDER ALLIED NAVAL FORCES NORTH AUG 02)

Stanhope, Sir Mark, KCB, OBE, MA, MNI, rcds, pce, pce(sm), psc, hcsc .... 10 Jul 04
(DEPUTY SUPREME ALLIED COMMANDER TRANSFORMATION JUL 04)

VICE ADMIRALS

Dunt, Peter Arthur, CB, rcds .... 30 Apr 02
(CHIEF EXECUTIVE DEFENCE ESTATES//CHIEF NAVAL LOGISTICS OFFICER (AS HEAD OF SPECIALISATION) APR 02)

Burnell-Nugent, Sir James (Michael), KCB, CBE, ADC, MA, jsdc, pce, pce(sm)........ 28 Jan 03
(SECOND SEA LORD AND CINCNAVHOME JAN 03)

McClement, Timothy (Pentreath), OBE, jsdc, pce, pce(sm), hcsc........ 07 Jun 04
(DEPUTY COMMANDER IN CHIEF FLEET/CHIEF NAVAL WARFARE OFFICER (AS HEAD OF SPECIALISATION) JUN 04)

McLean, Rory (Alistair Ian), CB, OBE, pce, hcsc .... 16 Sep 04
(DEPUTY CHIEF OF DEFENCE STAFF (HEALTH) SEP 04)

REAR ADMIRALS

Stevens, Robert Patrick, CB, pce, pce(sm) .... 4 Aug 98
(CHIEF OF STAFF TO THE MARITIME COMMANDER ALLIED FORCES SOUTHERN EUROPE Jan 02)

Ward, Rees (Graham John), CB, MA, MSc, CEng, FIEE, rcds, jsdc, gw, hcsc .... 27 Apr 99
(CHIEF EXECUTIVE DEFENCE COMMUNICATIONS SERVICES AGENCY JAN 02)

Guild, Nigel (Charles Forbes), CB, BA, PhD, FIEE, MIMA, jsdc .... 06 Jan 00
(DIRECTOR GENERAL CAPABILITY (CARRIER STRIKE)/CHIEF NAVAL ENGINEERING OFFICER (AS HEAD OF SPECIALISATION) DEC 03)

Dymock, Anthony (Knox), CB, BA, pce, psc .... 19 Jan 00
(HEAD OF BRITISH DEFENCE STAFF WASHINGTON SEP 02)

Rapp, James (Campsie), pce, pcea, psc .... 20 Nov 01
(DIRECTOR GENERAL TRAFALGAR 200 AUG 04)

Style, Charles (Rodney), CBE, MA, rcds, pce, hcsc .... 21 Jan 02
(COMMANDER UNTED KINGDOM MARITIME FORCE MAY 04)

Boissier, Robin (Paul), MA, MSc, pce, pce(sm), psc .... 26 Aug 02
(DIRECTOR GENERAL LOGISTICS FLEET SEP 04)

Cheadle, Richard (Frank), CB, MSc, CEng, FIMechE, FCMI, jsdc .... 03 Sep 02
(DIRECTOR LAND & MARITIME/CONTROLLER OF THE NAVY DEC 03)

Goodall, Simon (Richard James), CBE, BA, psc(m), MSc .... 03 Oct 02
(DIRECTOR GENERAL TRAINING & EDUCATION OCT 02)

Snelson, David (George), CB, FCMI, MNI, pce, psc, hcsc .... 05 Nov 02
(CHIEF OF STAFF (WARFARE) TO COMMANDER-IN-CHIEF-FLEET, REAR ADMIRAL SURFACE SHIPS (AS HEAD OF FIGHTING ARM)JUN 04)

Harris, Nicholas (Henry Linton), MBE, pce, pce(sm), ocds(US) .... 13 May 03
(FLAG OFFICER SCOTLAND & NORTHERN IRELAND/CHIEF OF STAFF (MARITIME PORT SECURITY) TO COMMANDER-IN-CHIEF-FLEET MAY 03)

Johns, Adrian (James), CBE, BSc, pce, pcea, psc, hcsc.. 27 May 03
(FORMER ASSISTANT CHIEF OF THE NAVAL STAFF, REAR ADMIRAL FLEET AIR ARM MAY (AS HEAD OF FIGHTING ARM) 03)

Chittenden, Timothy (Clive), MA, MSc, CEng, FIMechE, MINucE, jsdc................................04 Aug 03
(CHIEF OF STAFF (SUPPORT) TO COMMANDER-IN-CHIEF-FLEET AUG 03)

Spires, Trevor (Allan), BSc, CDipAF, nadc..21 Oct 03
(CHIEF EXECUTIVE ARMED FORCES PERSONNEL ADMINISTATION AGENCY OCT 03)

Wilcocks, Philip (Lawrence), DSC, BSc, AMRINA, pce, psc(a)... 19 Apr 04
(DEPUTY CHIEF OF JOINT OPERATIONS (OPERATIONAL SUPPORT) APR 04)

Ainsley, Roger (Stewart), MA, jsdc, pce, hcsc... 27 Apr 04
(FLAG OFFICER SEA TRAINING APR 04)

Soar, Trevor (Alan), OBE, pce, pce(sm)... 18 May 04
(CAPABILITY MANAGER (PRECISION ATTACK) MAY 04)

Lambert, Paul, BSc, MPhil, DipFM, rcds, pce, pce(sm), hcsc..29 Jun 04
(COMMANDER (OPERATIONS) TO COMMANDER-IN-CHIEF-FLEET, REAR ADMIRAL SUBMARINES (AS HEAD OF FIGHTING ARM) JUN 04)

Laurence, Timothy (James Hamilton), MVO, BSc, Hf, pce, psc(j)..05 Jul 04
(ASSISTANT CHIEF OF DEFENCE STAFF(RESOURCES & PLANNING) JUL 04)

Cooke, David (John), MBE, pce, pce(sm), hcsc..20 Jul 04
(DEPUTY COMMANDER STRIKE FORCE SOUTH JUL 04)

Wilkinson, Peter (John), BA, FCIPD, pce, pce(sm)..27 Jul 04
(DEFENCE SERVICES SECRETARY JUL 05)

Clayton, Christopher (Hugh Trevor), pce, psc, hcsc..30 Aug 04
(ASSISTANT DIRECTOR INTELLIGENCE DIVISION NATO INTERNATIONAL MILITARY STAFF AUG 04)

Raby, Nigel (John Francis), OBE, MSc, jsdc... 02 Sep 04
(STLB MERGER PROJECT TEAM LEADER SEP 04)

Borley, Kim (John), MA, CEng, MIEE, rcds, jsdc.. 07 Sep 04
(FLAG OFFICER TRAINING & RECRUITING/CHIEF EXECUTIVE NAVAL RECRUITING & TRAINING AGENCY SEP 04)

Mark, Robert (Alan), MSc, MNI, MRIN, MInsD..06 Jan 05
(SENIOR NAVAL MEMBER OF THE DIRECTING STAFF OF THE ROYAL COLLEGE OF DEFENCE STUDIES JAN 05)

Parry, Christopher (John), CBE, MA, rcds, pce, pcea, psc...25 Jan 05
(DIRECTOR GENERAL JOINT DOCTRINE AND CONCEPTS JAN 05)

Latham, Neil (Degge), MSc, CEng, Hf, MIMechE, jsdc...28 Feb 05
(COMMANDANT OF THE COLLEGE OF MANAGEMENT & TECHNOLOGY FEB 05)

Kimmons, Michael, BA, rcds .... 15 Mar 05
(CHIEF OF STAFF TO SECOND SEA LORD/COMMANDER-IN-CHIEF NAVAL HOME COMMAND MAR 05)

Mathews, Andrew (David Hugh), MSc, CEng, MIMechE, rcds, psc .... 24 Mar 05
(DIRECTOR GENERAL (NUCLEAR) (MAR 05)

Ibbotson, Richard (Jeffery), DSC, MSc, CGIA, pce .... 23 Jun 05
(NAVAL SECRETARY JUN 05)

Massey, Alan (Michael), CBE, MA, PGCE, rcds, pce, psc .... 5 Jul 05
(ASSITANT CHIEF OF THE NAVAL STAFF JUL 05)

COMMODORES

2002

X Johnstone-Burt, C.A. ...... 10 Jan
X Morisetti, N. .... 26 Mar
E Tibbitt, I.P.G. .... 15 Apr
E Alabaster, M.B. .... 30 Apr
X Snow, C.A. .... 14 May
MS Reed, F. .... 12 Jun
X Avery, M.B. .... 24 Jun
X Richards, A.D. .... 24 Jun
E Hussain, A.M. .... 09 Jul
X Cooling, R.G. .... 28 Aug
X Jermy, S.C. .... 10 Sep
X Zambellas, G.M. .... 29 Nov
X Kirby, S.R. .... 06 Dec

2003

S Menzies, A. .... 04 Feb
E Thwaites, G.J. .... 01 Apr
X Walpole, P.K. .... 07 Jul
X Pond, D.W. .... 08 Jul
X Bennett, A.R.C. .... 15 Jul
E Jackman, R.W. .... 26 Aug
X Robinson, P.H. .... 30 Sep
E Van Beek, L. .... 07 Oct
X Twitchen, R.C. .... 14 Oct
X Adair, A.A.S. .... 04 Nov
X Moncrieff, I. .... 10 Nov
E Graves, M.E.L. .... 11 Nov
X Montgomery, C.P.R. .... 25 Nov
E Rymer, A.R. .... 11 Dec

2004

E McFarlane, A.L. .... 05 Jan
E Miklinski, A.S. .... 02 Mar
X Anderson, M. .... 30 Mar
E Kidd, J.C. .... 19 Apr
E Love, R.T. .... 04 May
W Stait, C.J. .... 22 Jun
X Harris, T.R. .... 24 Jun
E Baldwin, S.F. .... 01 Jul
E Lister, S.R. .... 06 Jul
X Docherty, P.T. .... 16 Jul
X Harland, N.J.G. .... 13 Sep
X Corder, I.F. .... 09 Nov
X Charlier, S.B. .... 16 Nov
X Jones, P.A. .... 13 Dec
X Hudson, P.D. .... 31 Dec

2005

S Fraser, R.W. .... 11 Jan
E Patrick, J. .... 08 Feb
X Cunningham, T.A. .... 22 Feb
E Whyntie, A. .... 01 Apr
E Keegan, W.J. .... 26 Apr
X Williams, S.T. .... 03 May

CAPTAINS

1996

X Watson, P.H. .... 30 Jun
X Fanshawe, J.R. .... 30 Jun
X Boyd, J.A. .... 30 Jun
X Massey, A.M. .... 30 Jun
W Picton, A.M. .... 30 Jun
X Daglish, H.B. .... 31 Dec
X Moodie, G.R. .... 31 Dec
X Covington, W.M. .... 31 Dec
X Munns, C.R. .... 31 Dec
E Palmer, R.A.N. .... 31 Dec
X Leaman, R.D. .... 31 Dec

1997

X Eberle, P.J.F. .... 30 Jun
E Jarvis, I.L. .... 30 Jun
X Fergusson, D.C.M. .... 30 Jun
E Kongialis, J.A. .... 30 Jun
E Potter, M.J. .... 30 Jun
X Nance, A.R. .... 30 Jun
X Gass, C.J. .... 30 Jun
E Horrell, M.I. .... 30 Jun
E Bowker, M.A. .... 30 Jun
E Henley, S.M. .... 30 Jun
X Rix, A.J. .... 30 Jun
X Goddard, I.K. .... 31 Dec
E Wills, J.R. .... 31 Dec
E Green, J.A. .... 31 Dec
X Butler, N.A.M. .... 31 Dec

1998

X Martin, S.C. .... 30 Jun
E Hollidge, J.H. .... 30 Jun
X Larmour, D.R. .... 30 Jun
X Cameron, A.J.B. .... 30 Jun
X Goodall, D.C. .... 31 Dec
E Little, R.M. .... 31 Dec
E Timms, S.J. .... 31 Dec
X Ramm, S.C. .... 31 Dec
X Davies, P.N.M. .... 31 Dec
S Martin, T.F.W. .... 31 Dec

1999

X Knowles, J.M. .... 30 Jun
S Rayner, B.N. .... 30 Jun
E Jaynes, P.R.W. .... 30 Jun
E Hyldon, C.J. .... 30 Jun
X Croke, A. .... 30 Jun
E Hockley, C.J. .... 30 Jun
E Rees, J.B.M. .... 31 Dec
E Jarvis, D.J. .... 31 Dec
X Mervik, C.F. .... 31 Dec
E Hart, J. .... 31 Dec
X Sloan, M.U. .... 31 Dec
X Mathias, P.B. .... 31 Dec
X Gower, J.H.J. .... 31 Dec
X Winstanley, K. .... 31 Dec

2000

X Scorer, S.J. .... 30 Jun
E Williams, N.L. .... 30 Jun
S Quinn, P.A. .... 30 Jun
E Leeming, R.J. .... 30 Jun
X Mansergh, R.J. .... 30 Jun
E Wilkinson, R.M. .... 30 Jun
S MacDonald, G.E. .... 30 Jun
X Cleary, S.P. .... 30 Jun
E Lloyd, S.J. .... 30 Jun
E Peach, G.L. .... 30 Jun
X Lambert, N.R. .... 30 Jun
X Halliday, D.A. .... 30 Jun
X Potts, D.L. .... 30 Jun
X Palmer, C.L. .... 31 Dec
E Watts, R.F. .... 31 Dec
S Crabtree, P.D. .... 31 Dec
X Mansergh, M.P. .... 31 Dec
X Karsten, T.M. .... 31 Dec
E Jess, I.M. .... 31 Dec
S Steel, D.G. .... 31 Dec
E Penny, A.D. .... 31 Dec
E Johns, T. .... 31 Dec
X Windsor, M. .... 31 Dec
X Fraser, T.P. .... 31 Dec

2001

X Dedman, N.J.K. .... 30 Jun
X Steel, P.S.T.C. .... 30 Jun
X Swain, D.M. .... 30 Jun
X Hawkins, R.C. .... 30 Jun
E Mason, R.W. .... 30 Jun
E Langbridge, D.C. .... 30 Jun
X Williams, B.N.B. .... 30 Jun
E Christie, C.S. .... 30 Jun
E Neave, C.B. .... 30 Jun
X Stanford, J.H. .... 30 Jun

CAPTAINS

X Best, R.R. 30 Jun
E Brunton, S.B. 30 Jun
X Chick, S.J. 30 Jun

2002

X Sim, D.L.W. 30 Jun
X Morris, D.S. 30 Jun
S Ross, A.A. 30 Jun
X Turner, I. 30 Jun
E Tate, A.J. 30 Jun
X Dickens, D.J.R. 30 Jun
X Collins, P.N. 30 Jun
E Hughes, R.I. 30 Jun
E Stratton, J.D. 30 Jun
X Tarr, M.D. 30 Jun
S Albon, R. 30 Jun
E Sealey, N.P. 30 Jun
E Gosden, S.R. 30 Jun
X Brown, R.A.M. 30 Jun
X Fraser, E. 30 Jun
X Westwood, M.W. 30 Jun
X Thomas, G.C. 30 Jun
E Burrell, P.M. 30 Jun
X Stanley, N.P. 30 Jun
X Westbrook, J.S. 30 Jun
E Holloway, J.T. 30 Jun
X Wolfe, D.E. 30 Jun
X Cochrane, M.C.N. 30 Jun
E Dearden, S.R. 30 Jun
X Parr, M.J. 30 Jun
X Bell, A.S. 30 Jun
E Parker, H.H. 30 Jun

2003

X Wilson, S.G. 30 Jun
X Bramley, S. 30 Jun
X Durston, D.H. 30 Jun
X Welborn, C.G. 30 Jun
X Upright, S.W. 30 Jun
E Bishop, P.R. 30 Jun
X Hennessey, T.P.D. 30 Jun
E Dannatt, T.M. 30 Jun
X Bevan, S. 30 Jun
X Edgell, J.N. 30 Jun
S Marsh, D.J. 30 Jun
E Costello, G.T. 30 Jun
S Chelton, S.R.L. 30 Jun
X Finney, M.E. 30 Jun
E McElwaine, R.I. 30 Jun
X Wellesley, R.C.R. 30 Jun
E Evans, D.J. 30 Jun
E Rusbridger, R.C. 30 Jun
X Wallace, M.R.B. 30 Jun
E Thompson, R.J. 30 Jun
E Burton, D.S. 30 Jun
X Harding, R.G. 30 Jun
X Lowe, T.M. 30 Jun
E Van Beek, D. 30 Jun
E Beverstock, M.A. 30 Jun
E King, E.M. 30 Jun
X Moores, J.K. 30 Jun
X Morse, J.A. 30 Jun
X Williams, S.P. 30 Jun
S Atherton, M.J. 30 Jun
X Johnstone, C.C.C. 30 Jun
X Ancona, S.J. 30 Jun

2004

S Davis, B.J. 01 Apr
X Chambers, N.M.C. 30 Jun
E King, A.M. 30 Jun
S Hosker, T.J. 30 Jun
E Steel, C.M.H. 30 Jun
E Allwood, C. 30 Jun
X Humphrys, J.A. 30 Jun
E Usborne, C.M. 30 Jun
X Wallace, G.W.A. 30 Jun
E Molyneaux, D.G. 30 Jun
E Rowell, G.E. 30 Jun
X Archibald, B.R. 30 Jun
X James, D.R. 30 Jun
S Whalley, S.D. 30 Jun
X Davies, A.R. 30 Jun
X Evans, M.C. 30 Jun
E Holberry, A.P. 30 Jun
X Richards, C.M. 30 Jun
X Beaumont, I.H. 30 Jun
X Harrap, N.R.E. 30 Jun
X Davis-Marks, M.L. 30 Jun
X Murphie, J.D.D. 30 Jun
E Fulford, J.P.H. 30 Jun
S King, C.E.W. 30 Jun
X Hamp, C.J. 30 Jun
X Thicknesse, P.J. 30 Jun
X Stewart, R.G. 30 Jun
E Holdsworth, H.W. 30 Jun
X Tarrant, R.K. 30 Jun
E Slawson, J.M. 30 Jun
E Beckett, K.A. 30 Jun
X Bennett, P.M. 30 Jun
X Darlington, M.R. 30 Jun
MS Holyer, R.J. 06 Jul
MS Jackson, S.K. 31 Aug

2005

X Lombard, D. 30 Jun
X Greenlees, I.W. 30 Jun
E Coulthard, J.K. 30 Jun
S Nelson, D.T. 30 Jun
X Fletcher, N.E. 30 Jun
E Kenward, P.D. 30 Jun
E Jagger, P.R.A. 30 Jun
E Forsey, C.R. 30 Jun
X Pegg, R.M. 30 Jun
X Keble, K.W.L. 30 Jun
S Bullock, M.P. 30 Jun
E Watts, G.M. 30 Jun
S Smith, M. 30 Jun
X Warren, B.H. 30 Jun
E Taylor, J.J. 30 Jun
X Blunden, J.J.F. 30 Jun
E Lofthouse, I. 30 Jun
X Handley, J.M. 30 Jun
E Wilson, K.P. 30 Jun
E Thistlethwaite, M.H. 30 Jun
X Buckley, P.J.A. 30 Jun
E Farrage, M.E. 30 Jun
E Hay, J.D. 30 Jun
E Newell, J.M. 30 Jun
S Cunningham, P. 30 Jun
X Garrett, S.W. 30 Jun
X Hawthorne, M.J. 30 Jun
X Lemkes, P.D. 30 Jun
X Kenny, S.J. 30 Jun
X Kings, S.J.N. 30 Jun
X Sutton, G.B. 30 Jun
E Toy, M.J. 30 Jun
X Sanguinetti, H.R. 30 Jun
X Clink, J.R.H. 30 Jun
X Kingwell, J.M.L. 30 Jun
E Woodcock, S.J. 30 Jun

COMMANDERS

1985

X Harris, P.N. .... 31 Dec

1987

S Farquhar, J.W. .... 30 Jun
E Binns, J.B. .... 30 Jun
X Robinson, C.P. .... 31 Dec

1988

E Kennaugh, A.J. .... 31 Dec

1989

X Smith, N.P. .... 31 Dec
X Scoles, J.C. .... 31 Dec
X Williams, T.N.E. .... 31 Dec
E Harrison, R.A. .... 31 Dec

1990

E Rogers, M.S. .... 30 Jun
X Turner, S.M. .... 30 Jun
E Issitt, D.J. .... 30 Jun
S Backhouse, A.W. .... 31 Dec
E Milton, G.J.G. .... 31 Dec
X Hibbert, P.N. .... 31 Dec
X Bearne, J.P. .... 31 Dec
S Leatherby, J.H. .... 31 Dec
X Simmonds, R.M. .... 31 Dec
X Crabtree, I.M. .... 31 Dec
E Firth, S.K. .... 31 Dec
X Vaughan, D.M. .... 31 Dec

1991

X Foster, G.R.N. .... 30 Jun
X Boxall-Hunt, B.P. .... 30 Jun
X Ferguson, J.N. .... 30 Jun
X MacDonald, D.H.L. .... 30 Jun
E Hume, C.B. .... 31 Dec
X Williams, N.D.B. .... 31 Dec
E Pancott, B.M. .... 31 Dec
X De Sa, P.J. .... 31 Dec
X Stoneman, T.J. .... 31 Dec
X Fortescue, P.W. .... 31 Dec
X Johnson, G.P. .... 31 Dec
E Gibb, R.W. .... 31 Dec

1992

X Govan, R.T. .... 30 Jun
X Ingham, P.C. .... 30 Jun
E Ratcliffe, J.P. .... 30 Jun
E Stanley, P. .... 30 Jun
X Gregan, D.C. .... 30 Jun
E Adams, R.A.S. .... 30 Jun
E Lankester, T.J. .... 30 Jun
X Lankester, P. .... 30 Jun
E Smith, C.S. .... 30 Jun
X Herman, T.R. .... 30 Jun
X Thoburn, R. .... 30 Jun
X Pepper, M.R. .... 31 Dec
E Usborne, A.C. .... 31 Dec
E Ayers, R.P.B. .... 31 Dec
X Marshall, R.A. .... 31 Dec
S Peilow, B.F. .... 31 Dec
W Robbins, M.J. .... 31 Dec
X Spalton, G.M.S. .... 31 Dec
E Arnold, B.W.H. .... 31 Dec
X Brocklebank, G.P. .... 31 Dec
X Bartholomew, I.M. .... 31 Dec
X Gibson, I.A. .... 31 Dec
E Wormald, R.E. .... 31 Dec
X Powis, J. .... 31 Dec

1993

S Williams, R.E. .... 30 Jun
X Andrew, W.G. .... 30 Jun
X Grant, A.K. .... 30 Jun
E Guy, T.J. .... 30 Jun
X Bell-Davies, R.W. .... 30 Jun
X Chambers, W.J. .... 30 Jun
X Snow, M.C.P. .... 30 Jun
X Holihead, P.W. .... 30 Jun
E Wright, G.N. .... 30 Jun
S Cowdrey, M.C. .... 30 Jun
X Harvey, K. .... 30 Jun
E Cox, P.W.S. .... 30 Jun
X Bateman, S.J.F. .... 30 Jun
E Gubbins, V.R. .... 31 Dec
X Turner, S.E. .... 31 Dec
X Goodwin, D.R. .... 31 Dec
X Thomas, S.A. .... 31 Dec
X Pothecary, R.E. .... 31 Dec
E Stenhouse, N.J. .... 31 Dec
E Lunn, J.F.C. .... 31 Dec
X Curd, T.A. .... 31 Dec
X Trevithick, A.R. .... 31 Dec
X Bosshardt, R.G. .... 31 Dec
X Churchill, T.C. .... 31 Dec
E Parker, I.R. .... 31 Dec
E Hore, R.C. .... 31 Dec
X Riley, M.J. .... 31 Dec

1994

X Hatchard, P.J. .... 30 Jun
E Fisher, M.A.L. .... 30 Jun
X Stanley, C.E. .... 30 Jun
E Fox, K.A. .... 30 Jun
E Brockwell, P.E.N. .... 30 Jun
S Forsyth, A.R. .... 30 Jun
E Whitehorn, I.J. .... 30 Jun
X Cutt, J.J.D. .... 30 Jun
X Reid, M. .... 30 Jun
X Humphreys, J.I. .... 30 Jun
X Arthur, I.D. .... 30 Jun
X Brown, M.K. .... 20 Sep
X Ward, N.J. .... 01 Oct
E Wakeling, J.L. .... 31 Dec
X Hosking, D.B. .... 31 Dec
E Parry, N.T. .... 31 Dec
X Murgatroyd, A.C. .... 31 Dec
E Faulconbridge, D. .... 31 Dec
X Horne, T.K. .... 31 Dec
X Stallion, I.M. .... 31 Dec
X Clark, K.I.M. .... 31 Dec
E Brough, G.A. .... 31 Dec
E White, A.R. .... 31 Dec
S Airey, S.E. .... 31 Dec
X Gillanders, F.G.R. .... 31 Dec

1995

X Carter, K. .... 30 Jun
E Podger, K.G.R. .... 30 Jun
X Phillips, D.G. .... 30 Jun
X McNair, E.A. .... 30 Jun
X Wilson, C.D. .... 30 Jun
X Shrives, M.P. .... 30 Jun
X Thomas, R.P. .... 30 Jun
X Gasson, N.S.C. .... 30 Jun
E Pendle, M.E.J. .... 30 Jun
E Price, F.E.F. .... 30 Jun
E Young, S.S. .... 30 Jun
X Lander, M.C. .... 30 Jun
X Clarke, C.M.L. .... 30 Jun
X Bull, A.J. .... 01 Oct
X Holmes, R. .... 31 Dec
E Cummin, M.A. .... 31 Dec
E Smith, M.A. .... 31 Dec
E Spicer, C.G. .... 31 Dec
S Ireland, R.C. .... 31 Dec
E Sewry, M.R. .... 31 Dec
X Stonor, P.F.A. .... 31 Dec
X Seatherton, E.F.K. .... 31 Dec
S Storrs-Fox, R.N. .... 31 Dec
E Powell, D.C. .... 31 Dec
S Keefe, P.C. .... 31 Dec
E Anderson, R.G. .... 31 Dec
X O'Reilly, S.A. .... 31 Dec
E Wyatt, S.P. .... 31 Dec

COMMANDERS

1996

X	Nicholson, S.C.L.	30 Jun
E	Nixon, P.W.	30 Jun
E	Farrington, S.P.	30 Jun
X	Betteridge, J.T.	30 Jun
X	Langhorn, N.	30 Jun
X	Ayres, C.P.	30 Jun
E	Lovett, M.J.	30 Jun
X	Funnell, N.C.	30 Jun
E	Price, J.P.	30 Jun
E	Bridger, D.W.	30 Jun
X	Sibbit, N.T.	30 Jun
E	Drake, E.D.	30 Jun
X	Furness, S.B.	30 Jun
E	Haley, T.J.	30 Jun
X	Rycroft, A.E.	30 Jun
E	Gourlay, J.S.	30 Jun
X	Perkins, M.J.	30 Jun
X	Corrigan, N.R.	30 Jun
E	Da Gama, J.A.J.	30 Jun
S	Finlayson, A.G.	30 Jun
X	Farrington, R.	30 Jun
E	Erskine, P.A.	30 Jun
E	Yuill, I.A.	01 Oct
X	Lee, D.J.	31 Dec
E	Palmer, J.E.	31 Dec
E	Grafton, M.N.	31 Dec
X	Sullivan, C.	31 Dec
E	Terry, J.M.	31 Dec
S	Nairn, R.	31 Dec
X	Lambert, B.	31 Dec
X	Lambourn, P.N.	31 Dec
S	Church, A.D.	31 Dec
X	Edney, A.R.	31 Dec
X	Pearey, M.S.	31 Dec
X	Hughes, N.J.	31 Dec
S	Tinsley, G.N.	31 Dec
X	Richmond, I.J.M.	31 Dec
X	Lilley, D.J.	31 Dec
X	Hugo, I.D.	31 Dec
E	Jenkin, A.M.H.	31 Dec
X	Abraham, P.	31 Dec
E	Wise, S.D.	31 Dec

1997

X	Horne, T.G.	30 Jun
X	Robinson, A.	30 Jun
X	Balston, D.C.W.	30 Jun
E	Spalding, R.E.H.	30 Jun
E	Whitaker, M.J.	30 Jun
E	Derrick, G.G.J.	30 Jun
E	Foster, M.A.	30 Jun
E	Graham, G.R.	30 Jun
E	Page, D.M.	30 Jun
X	Morgan, P.T.	30 Jun
X	Spence, N.A.	30 Jun
E	Starks, M.R.	30 Jun
X	Scarth, W.	30 Jun
X	Baum, S.R.	30 Jun
X	Pickles, I.S.	30 Jun
S	Richardson, M.P.	30 Jun
X	Barker, R.D.J.	30 Jun
X	Brand, S.M.	30 Jun
S	Crook, A.S.	30 Jun
E	O'Neill, P.J.	30 Jun
E	Braham, S.W.	30 Jun
X	Garratt, M.D.	30 Jun
E	Smithson, P.E.	30 Jun
E	Waterman, J.H.	31 Dec
X	Nail, V.A.	31 Dec
S	Charlton, C.R.A.M.	31 Dec
E	Greenwood, S.	31 Dec
E	Wrightson, H.M.	31 Dec
E	Straughan, H.	31 Dec
E	Peck, I.J.	31 Dec
X	Brooksbank, R.J.	31 Dec
X	Taylor, K.A.	31 Dec
X	MacKay, G.A.	31 Dec
S	White, S.N.	31 Dec
E	Sunderland, J.D.	31 Dec
X	McBarnet, T.F.	31 Dec
E	Pickthall, D.N.	31 Dec
X	Lloyd, P.R.	31 Dec
X	Ameye, C.R.	31 Dec
X	Pettitt, G.W.	31 Dec

1998

X	Pope, C.M.	24 Jun
X	Snook, R.E.	30 Jun
E	Enticknap, K.	30 Jun
E	Clark, D.K.	30 Jun
X	Jardine, G.A.	30 Jun
X	Lade, C.J.	30 Jun
E	McLennan, R.G.	30 Jun
X	Steeds, S.M.	30 Jun
X	Jackman, A.W.	30 Jun
X	Gaunt, N.R.	30 Jun
E	Russell, S.J.	30 Jun
E	Main, E.S.	30 Jun
X	Ewence, M.W.	30 Jun
E	MacDonald, A.I.	30 Jun
E	Taylor, S.A.	30 Jun
X	Cassar, A.P.F.	30 Jun
S	Pattinson, I.H.	30 Jun
E	Quaye, D.T.G.	30 Jun
X	Robertson, K.F.	30 Jun
X	McDonnell, P.W.	30 Jun
E	Wiles, S.J.	30 Jun
X	Reynolds, T.E.	30 Jun
E	Shipperley, I.	30 Jun
X	Ingram, R.G.	30 Jun
X	Cree, M.C.	30 Jun
X	Alcock, C.	30 Jun
E	Elford, D.G.	30 Jun
S	Litchfield, J.F.	30 Jun
E	Gulley, T.J.	30 Jun
E	Danbury, I.G.	30 Jun
E	Sexton, M.J.	30 Jun
E	Hobbs, R.	01 Oct
X	Trundle, N.R.E.	31 Dec
E	Davies, T.G.	31 Dec
S	Spiller, M.F.	31 Dec
X	Newton, D.J.	31 Dec
X	White, M.W.	31 Dec
X	Percharde, M.R.	31 Dec
E	Mason, N.H.	31 Dec
E	Curnow, M.D.	31 Dec
E	Gray, A.J.	31 Dec
X	Woods, R.P.	31 Dec
X	Clark, A.W.C.	31 Dec
E	Stanley-Whyte, B.J.	31 Dec
S	Beard, G.T.C.	31 Dec
E	Fry, J.M.S.	31 Dec
X	Williams, M.H.	31 Dec
S	Redstone, C.	31 Dec
X	Hatch, G.W.H.	31 Dec
X	Evans, K.N.M.	31 Dec
E	Green, A.R.	31 Dec
X	McKendrick, A.M.	31 Dec
E	Chidley, T.J.	31 Dec
X	Muir, K.	31 Dec
E	Green, S.N.	31 Dec
X	McCartain, M.B.W.	31 Dec
X	Shield, S.J.	31 Dec
X	Cook, P.R.	31 Dec
S	Skidmore, C.M.	31 Dec
E	Stokes, R.	31 Dec
X	Adams, A.J.	31 Dec
X	Green, T.J.	31 Dec
E	O'Reilly, T.M.	31 Dec
X	McAlpine, P.A.	31 Dec
X	McQuaker, S.R.	31 Dec
E	Morritt, D.C.	31 Dec
S	Jameson, A.C.	31 Dec
E	Hayes, J.V.B.	31 Dec

COMMANDERS

S Brown, N.L. .... 31 Dec

1999

E Merriman, P.O. .... 30 Jun
E Hadfield, D. .... 30 Jun
X Drewett, R.E. .... 30 Jun
X Haley, C.W. .... 30 Jun
E Ellis, R.W. .... 30 Jun
E Fear, R.K. .... 30 Jun
X Alexander, R.S. .... 30 Jun
E Ranson, C.D. .... 30 Jun
E Darwent, A. .... 30 Jun
E Pett, J.G. .... 30 Jun
X Clarke, N.J. .... 30 Jun
E Haworth, J. .... 30 Jun
E Bisson, I.J.P. .... 30 Jun
E Vandome, A.M. .... 30 Jun
X Spencer, E.A. .... 30 Jun
X Knibbs, M. .... 30 Jun
X Jervis, N.D. .... 30 Jun
S Thomas, F.S. .... 30 Jun
X Carden, P.D. .... 30 Jun
X Northwood, G.R. .... 30 Jun
E Ramshaw, G.W.L. .... 30 Jun
E Simmons, N.D. .... 30 Jun
X Ireland, A.R. .... 30 Jun
X Horn, P.B. .... 30 Jun
S Morton, N.P.B. .... 30 Jun
X Robinson, C.E.T. .... 30 Jun
X Moore, C.I. .... 30 Jun
E Lewis, J.K. .... 30 Jun
E Barton, P.G. .... 30 Jun
X Titterton, P.J. .... 30 Jun
E Daws, R.P.A. .... 30 Jun
X Allen, R.M. .... 30 Jun
X Pollock, D.J. .... 30 Jun
X Weale, J.S. .... 30 Jun
E Roberts, N.S. .... 30 Jun
S Lavery, J.P. .... 30 Jun
X Millward, J.P. .... 31 Dec
E Tindall-Jones, L.D. .... 31 Dec
X Buckland, R.J.F. .... 31 Dec
X Ovens, J.J. .... 31 Dec
E Treanor, M.A. .... 31 Dec
E Maltby, M.R.J. .... 31 Dec
S Isaac, P. .... 31 Dec
E Crossley, C.C. .... 31 Dec
S Tulley, J.R. .... 31 Dec
E Greene, M.J. .... 31 Dec
X Chalmers, D.P. .... 31 Dec
E Mason, A.H. .... 31 Dec
X Tuppen, R.M. .... 31 Dec
X Johnson, A.S. .... 31 Dec
E Plant, J.N.M. .... 31 Dec
X Doyle, G.L. .... 31 Dec
E Thompson, S.J. .... 31 Dec
X Harris, A.I. .... 31 Dec
S Gray, R.S. .... 31 Dec
X Reid, C.I. .... 31 Dec
S Murdoch, S.J. .... 31 Dec
X Race, N.J. .... 31 Dec
E Hodgson, T.C. .... 31 Dec
X Brown, H.S. .... 31 Dec
X Hopper, S.O. .... 31 Dec
E Morris, A.J. .... 31 Dec
X McMichael-Phillips, S.J. .. 31 Dec
E Stubbings, P.R. .... 31 Dec
S Gardner, C.R.S. .... 31 Dec
E Harrison, M.S. .... 31 Dec
E Johnson, J.C. .... 31 Dec
X Sullivan, A.G. .... 31 Dec
E French, S.A. .... 31 Dec
E Wareham, M.P. .... 31 Dec
E Hammond, P.A. .... 31 Dec
X Porter, S.P. .... 31 Dec
X Healy, A.J. .... 31 Dec
X Walliker, M.J.D. .... 31 Dec
S Rance, M.G.W. .... 31 Dec
X Bone, D.N. .... 31 Dec
E Tate, S.J. .... 31 Dec
X Key, B.J. .... 31 Dec
X McGhie, I.A. .... 31 Dec

2000

X Daniels, S.A. .... 30 Jun
E Blake, G.E. .... 30 Jun
E McKenzie, D. .... 30 Jun
E Moreland, M.J. .... 30 Jun
X Snowball, S.J. .... 30 Jun
X Stewart, A.C. .... 30 Jun
X Tilley, D.S.J. .... 30 Jun
X Newton, G.A. .... 30 Jun
X Sephton, J.R. .... 30 Jun
X Cunningham, R.A. .... 30 Jun
E Basson, A.P. .... 30 Jun
X Broadley, K.J. .... 30 Jun
E Atkinson, S.R. .... 30 Jun
E Argent-Hall, D. .... 30 Jun
E Short, G.C. .... 30 Jun
S Tothill, N.M. .... 30 Jun
S Fergusson, H.J. .... 30 Jun
E Harvey, C.A. .... 30 Jun
X Hayes, S.J. .... 30 Jun
E Vanderpump, D.J. .... 30 Jun
S Wunderle, C.A. .... 30 Jun
X Entwistle, S.C. .... 30 Jun
S Spence, A.B. .... 30 Jun
X Carter, I.P. .... 30 Jun
X Stockings, T.M. .... 30 Jun
X Chivers, P.A. .... 30 Jun
E Walker, N.J. .... 30 Jun
E Walker, M. .... 30 Jun
X Heley, D.N. .... 30 Jun
X Pearson, S.J. .... 30 Jun
X Allibon, M.C. .... 30 Jun
S Bath, M.A.W. .... 30 Jun
E Williams, M.J. .... 30 Jun
E Little, G.T. .... 30 Jun
X Talbot, R.P. .... 30 Jun
E Dyer, M.D.J. .... 30 Jun
X Hine, N.W. .... 30 Jun
S Rees, J.H. .... 01 Jul
X McKie, A. .... 31 Dec
E Kerchey, S.J.V. .... 31 Dec
E Welburn, R.S. .... 31 Dec
X Malcolm, S.R. .... 31 Dec
E Stidston, I.J. .... 31 Dec
X Connolly, C.J. .... 31 Dec
E Parsons, C.G. .... 31 Dec
E Deaney, M.N. .... 31 Dec
S Hughes, G.L. .... 31 Dec
E Marmont, K.L. .... 31 Dec
E Abbey, M.K. .... 31 Dec
X Thomas, W.G. .... 31 Dec
X Blowers, M.D. .... 31 Dec
E Risley, J. .... 31 Dec
X Powell, R.L. .... 31 Dec
E Cargen, M.R. .... 31 Dec
E Parsons, B.R. .... 31 Dec
S Bond, N.D. .... 31 Dec
X Durkin, M.T.G. .... 31 Dec
E Martyn, A.W. .... 31 Dec
X Davies, J.H. .... 31 Dec
S Walker, C.L. .... 31 Dec
X Williams, A.P. .... 31 Dec
E Glennie, A.M.G. .... 31 Dec
S Buchan-Steele, M.A. ...... 31 Dec
S Merchant, I.C. .... 31 Dec
S Rigby, J.C. .... 31 Dec
E Corry, S.M. .... 31 Dec
E Jones, H.A. .... 31 Dec
X Reed, A.W. .... 31 Dec
X Williamson, T.J.L. .... 31 Dec
X Denham, N.J. .... 31 Dec
E Heley, J.M. .... 31 Dec

COMMANDERS

X Ashcroft, A.C. 31 Dec
X Milburn, P.K. 31 Dec
X Fulton, C.R. 31 Dec
E Jessop, P.E. 31 Dec
E Moore, M.N. 31 Dec
E Frankham, P.J. 31 Dec
X Cooper, M.A. 31 Dec
E Clough, C.R. 31 Dec
X Fancy, R. 31 Dec
X Blount, K.E. 31 Dec
X Dutton, D. 31 Dec

2001

X Taylor, J.W. 30 Jun
E Parker, M.N. 30 Jun
X Faulkner, J.J. 30 Jun
X Corbett, W.R. 30 Jun
E Gordon, D. 30 Jun
X Knight, D.A. 30 Jun
E Martin, M.T. 30 Jun
X Sheehan, M.A. 30 Jun
E Grieve, S.H. 30 Jun
S O'Grady, M.J. 30 Jun
E Raybould, A.G. 30 Jun
X Payne, R.C. 30 Jun
X Greenwood, P. 30 Jun
E Grantham, S.M. 30 Jun
X Jones, M.C. 30 Jun
E Martin, M.P. 30 Jun
X Mitchell, H.G.M. 30 Jun
E Charlesworth, G.K. 30 Jun
X Doolan, M. 30 Jun
E Wood, J.L. 30 Jun
S Crozier, S.R.M. 30 Jun
E Borland, S.A. 30 Jun
E Podmore, A. 30 Jun
E Haines, P.R. 30 Jun
X Pritchard, G.S. 30 Jun
S Shaw, S.M. 30 Jun
X Foreman, J.L.R. 30 Jun
X Burton, A.J. 30 Jun
X Nolan, A.L. 30 Jun
E St Aubyn, J.D.E. 30 Jun
X Wallace, A. 30 Jun
E Casson, P.R. 30 Jun
X Barker, D.C.K. 30 Jun
E Phenna, A. 30 Jun
X Warwick, P.D. 30 Jun
MS Coulton, I.C. 30 Jun
X Hardern, S.P. 30 Jun
E Prescott, S. 30 Jun
E Kershaw, S. 30 Jun
S Noyes, D.J. 30 Jun
E Corderoy, J.R. 30 Jun

2002

X Schwarz, P.M.G. 30 Jun
E Dawson, S.L. 30 Jun
S Faulks, D.J. 30 Jun
E MacKay, C.R. 30 Jun
E Dumbell, P. 30 Jun
E Birchall, S.J. 30 Jun
X Layland, S. 30 Jun
E Cheesman, C.J. 30 Jun
X Petheram, M.J. 30 Jun
E Tarr, B.S. 30 Jun
E Naden, A.C.K. 30 Jun
E Warden, J.M. 30 Jun
X King, R.W. 30 Jun
X O'Sullivan, A.M. 30 Jun
E Sykes, M. 30 Jun
X Hardy, L.C. 30 Jun
X Hodgkins, J.M. 30 Jun
X Roberts, I.T. 30 Jun
S Laws, P.E.A. 30 Jun
E Jones, R.W. 30 Jun
E Ryan, D.G. 30 Jun
X Mair, B. 30 Jun
E Crago, P.T. 30 Jun
X Fitter, I.S.T. 30 Jun
X Lacey, S.P. 30 Jun
E Gray, A.J. 30 Jun
X Davies, C.J. 30 Jun
X Kelbie, E. 30 Jun
E Moffatt, N.R. 30 Jun
X Turnbull, S.J.L. 30 Jun
S Watts, A.D. 30 Jun
X Hare, N.J. 30 Jun
S Randall, D.F. 30 Jun
X Barrand, S.M. 30 Jun
X Cluett-Green, S.M. 30 Jun
X Gordon, S.R. 30 Jun
E Shaw, K.N.G. 30 Jun
X Gething, J.B. 30 Jun
E Archer, G.W. 30 Jun
X Falk, B.H.G. 30 Jun
X Turnbull, G.D. 30 Jun
X Skeer, M.R. 30 Jun
E Float, R.A. 30 Jun
E Waddington, J. 30 Jun
E Dabell, G.L. 30 Jun
E Grindel, D.J.S. 30 Jun
X Thompson, B.D. 30 Jun
E Haywood, S.A. 30 Jun
X Evans, W.Q.F. 30 Jun
E Magan, M.J.C. 30 Jun
X Turner, D.B. 30 Jun
E French, J.T. 30 Jun
E Streeten, C.M. 30 Jun
E Rhodes, A.G. 30 Jun
E Thompson, A. 30 Jun
S Renwick, J. 30 Jun
E Clifford, T.J. 30 Jun
X Haywood, G. 30 Jun
E Dorricott, A.J. 30 Jun
S Garland, N. 30 Jun
S Lines, J.M. 30 Jun
X Entwisle, W.N. 30 Jun
X Tindal, N.H.C. 30 Jun
X Burke, P.D. 30 Jun
E Scott, N.L.J. 30 Jun
E Wise, G.J. 30 Jun
X Wallis, A.J. 30 Jun
E Jarvis, L.R. 30 Jun
E Childs, D.G. 30 Jun
S Hall, E.C. 30 Jun
X Thomas, R.K. 30 Jun
X Reindorp, D.P. 30 Jun
E Adams, A.M. 30 Jun
X Swannick, D.J. 30 Jun
MS Murphy, A. 30 Jun
X Hodkinson, C.B. 30 Jun
E Robinson, M.P. 30 Jun
X Radakin, A.D. 30 Jun
E Thompson, R.C. 30 Jun
E Course, A.J. 30 Jun
E Annett, I.G. 30 Jun
X Robinson, G.A. 30 Jun
X Wainhouse, M.J. 30 Jun
X Bewick, D.J. 30 Jun
S Lustman, A.M. 30 Jun
X Blackmore, M.S. 30 Jun
X Gilmour, C.J.M. 30 Jun
S Anderson, H.A. 30 Jun
X Thomas, R.A.A. 30 Jun
S Aplin, A.T. 30 Jun

2003

X Murray, S.J. 30 Jun
X Lightfoot, C.D. 30 Jun
E Wyatt, J.M. 30 Jun
X Corner, G.C. 30 Jun
E Cochrane, M.D. 30 Jun
X Leaning, M.V. 30 Jun
X Stanton, D.V. 30 Jun
X Shawcross, P.K. 30 Jun

COMMANDERS

X Powell, S. 30 Jun
E Peacock, S. 30 Jun
E Randall, R.D. 30 Jun
X Suddes, L.A. 30 Jun
E Upton, I.D. 30 Jun
E Claxton, M.G. 30 Jun
E Dustan, A.J. 30 Jun
X Hall, R.L. 30 Jun
X Aiken, S.R. 30 Jun
E Knight, P.R. 30 Jun
X Smith, M.R.K. 30 Jun
E Stewart, J.N. 30 Jun
X Hinch, N.E. 30 Jun
S Flynn, M.T. 30 Jun
X Cunningham, J.G. 30 Jun
E Adams, P. 30 Jun
E Blackman, N.T. 30 Jun
X Brown, W.C. 30 Jun
E Salter, J.A. 30 Jun
E Kirkup, J.P. 30 Jun
X Robertson, M.G. 30 Jun
X Fields, D.G. 30 Jun
E Cropley, A. 30 Jun
E Sumner, M.D. 30 Jun
S David, S.E.J. 30 Jun
E Clark, I.D. 30 Jun
E Saxby, C.J. 30 Jun
X Hutchison, G.B. 30 Jun
X Stangroom, A. 30 Jun
E Smith, K.A. 30 Jun
X Amphlett, N.G. 30 Jun
E Harding, D.M. 30 Jun
X Hawkins, M.A.J. 30 Jun
X Webb, A.J. 30 Jun
E Green, D.P.S. 30 Jun
X Gurmin, S.J.A. 30 Jun
X Johnston, T.A. 30 Jun
X Nisbet, J.H.T. 30 Jun
E Roberts, T.J. 30 Jun
E Kennedy, I.J.A. 30 Jun
X Beardall, M.J.D. 30 Jun
E Jenkins, G.W. 30 Jun
E Burlingham, B.L. 30 Jun
X Aspden, A.M. 30 Jun
X Waddington, A.K. 30 Jun
X Pentreath, J.P. 30 Jun
X Sherriff, D.A. 30 Jun
E Munns, A.R. 30 Jun
X Dyke, C.L. 30 Jun
E Metcalfe, P.G. 30 Jun
X Salisbury, D.P. 30 Jun
E Fieldsend, M.A. 30 Jun
E Gilbert, P.D. 30 Jun
S Straw, A.N. 30 Jun
X Chrishop, T.I. 30 Jun
X Mahony, D.G. 30 Jun
S Taylor, S.J. 30 Jun
X Corbett, A.S. 30 Jun
S Jewitt, C.J.B. 30 Jun
X Coles, A.L. 30 Jun
X Meakin, B.R. 30 Jun
MS Lloyd, C.J. 30 Jun
X Newland, M.I. 30 Jun
S Aitken, K.M. 30 Jun
X Briers, M.P. 30 Jun
E Cran, B.C. 30 Jun
S Hollins, R.P. 30 Jun
S Kyte, A.J. 30 Jun
S Wintle, G.L. 30 Jun
S Hill, R.K.J. 30 Jun
X Harvey, R.M.M.J. 30 Jun
E Dailey, P.G.J. 30 Jun
X Holt, S. 30 Jun
E Kissane, R.E.T. 30 Jun
X Scott, J.A. 30 Jun
E Knight, P.J. 30 Jun
E Rowse, M.L. 30 Jun
E Graham, D.W.S. 30 Jun
X White, J.A.P. 30 Jun
S Burningham, M.R. 30 Jun
S Hood, K.C. 30 Jun
S Trump, N.W. 30 Jun
E Petitt, S.R. 30 Jun
X Titcomb, M.R. 30 Jun
E Roberts, S.D. 30 Jun
X Axon, D.B. 30 Jun
E Pomeroy, M.A. 30 Jun
X Betton, A. 30 Jun

2004

X Rich, J.G. 30 Jun
X Dawson, P.J. 30 Jun
X Riches, I.C. 30 Jun
E Gibson, A. 30 Jun
E Ball, M.P. 30 Jun
X Moss, P. 30 Jun
E Townshend, J.J. 30 Jun
X Bridger, R.J. 30 Jun
X Jones, P. 30 Jun
S Giles, A.R. 30 Jun
S Mellor, B.J. 30 Jun
E Giles, D.W. 30 Jun
E Tarr, R.N.V. 30 Jun
E Shirley, W.P. 30 Jun
X Howell, S.B. 30 Jun
E Denovan, P.A. 30 Jun
X Hunter, N.M. 30 Jun
X Poole, J.L. 30 Jun
E Saunders, T.M. 30 Jun
X Davison, A.P. 30 Jun
X Swarbrick, R.J. 30 Jun
X Hart, M.A. 30 Jun
X Sutcliffe, J. 30 Jun
S Shaw, P.J. 30 Jun
X Lochrane, A.E.R. 30 Jun
S Willis, A.J. 30 Jun
S Carter, S.N. 30 Jun
E Mace, S.B. 30 Jun
S Notley, L.P. 30 Jun
E Toft, M.D. 30 Jun
X Kilby, S.E. 30 Jun
E Hill, P.J. 30 Jun
X Bellfield, R.J.A. 30 Jun
E Stace, I.S. 30 Jun
X Abernethy, J.R.G. 30 Jun
E Harrison, P.G. 30 Jun
E O'Brien, P.M.C. 30 Jun
X Salmon, M.A. 30 Jun
E Lovegrove, R.A. 30 Jun
E Rodgers, S. 30 Jun
X Thorburn, A. 30 Jun
S Philpott, N.E. 30 Jun
E Higgins, G.N. 30 Jun
X Dible, J.H. 30 Jun
X Lister, M. 30 Jun
E Bartlett, D.S.G. 30 Jun
X Ireland, P.C. 30 Jun
S Murrison, R.A. 30 Jun
E Bull, C.M.S. 30 Jun
S Edge, J.H. 30 Jun
E Titcomb, A.C. 30 Jun
X Breckenridge, I.G. 30 Jun
X Woods, J.B. 30 Jun
E MacDonald, J.R. 30 Jun
E Mather, G.P. 30 Jun
X Kyd, J.P. 30 Jun
E Reynolds, A.G. 30 Jun
X Vitali, R.C. 30 Jun
X Bourne, C.M. 30 Jun
E Cree, A.M. 30 Jun
MS Kenney, R.P. 30 Jun
X Hibberd, N.J. 30 Jun
X Rolph, A.P.M. 30 Jun
X Allen, S.M. 30 Jun

COMMANDERS

X Halton, P.V. 30 Jun
E Coulson, P. 30 Jun
X Young, G.L. 30 Jun
E Hill, G.F. 30 Jun
X Dunn, R.P. 30 Jun
X Hatcher, R.S. 30 Jun
S Wood, R. 30 Jun
X Dainton, S. 30 Jun
E Biggs, W.P.L. 30 Jun
E Ferris, D.P.S. 30 Jun
X Burns, D.I. 30 Jun
X Merewether, H.A.H. 30 Jun
X Long, A.D. 30 Jun
X Graham, I.E. 30 Jun
E Band, J.W. 30 Jun
X Stone, P.C.J. 30 Jun
X Haslam, P.J. 30 Jun
E Tritschler, E.L. 30 Jun
MS McAuslin, T.M. 30 Jun
X Thomas, J.E. 30 Jun
S Fisher, C.R.A. 30 Jun
E Marriott, M.N. 30 Jun
X Groves, C.K. 30 Jun
E Lison, A.C. 30 Jun
X Sparkes, P.J. 30 Jun
X Morley, J.D. 30 Jun
MS Durning, W.M. 30 Jun
E Methven, P. 30 Jun
X Warrender, W.J. 30 Jun
E Halliwell, D.C. 30 Jun
E Macleod, J.N. 30 Jun

2005

X Chatwin, N.J. 30 Jun
X Finnemore, R.A. 30 Jun
X Price, T.W. 30 Jun
X Smith, S.L. 30 Jun
X Fox, R.G. 30 Jun
X Langley, E.S. 30 Jun
E McTear, K. 30 Jun
E Murdoch, A.W. 30 Jun
E Smith, G.K. 30 Jun
E Janaway, P. 30 Jun
X Deller, M.G. 30 Jun
E Duncan, I.S. 30 Jun
X Haycock, T.P. 30 Jun
X Abernethy, L.J.F. 30 Jun
E Dowell, P.H.N. 30 Jun
X Swift, R.D. 30 Jun
X Dane, R.M.H. 30 Jun
X George, A.P. 30 Jun
E Boyd, N. 30 Jun
X Thomson, D. 30 Jun
E Grenfell-Shaw, M.C. 30 Jun
E McInnes, J.G.K. 30 Jun
X Pollock, M.P. 30 Jun
X Jones, G.R. 30 Jun
X Williams, D.S. 30 Jun
X Lawler, J.A. 30 Jun
E Rippingale, S.N. 30 Jun
X Cunningham, D.A. 30 Jun
S Walmsley, E.A. 30 Jun
X Furlong, K. 30 Jun
S Hayle, J.K. 30 Jun
E Winkle, S.J. 30 Jun
E Harrop, I. 30 Jun
E Merritt, J.J. 30 Jun
X Maher, M.P. 30 Jun
E Short, J.J. 30 Jun
E Prior, G.M. 30 Jun
E Buckle, I.L. 30 Jun
X Green, P.J. 30 Jun
E Geary, T.W. 30 Jun
E Foster, G.J. 30 Jun
E Cooper, K.P. 30 Jun
X Bowen, N.T. 30 Jun
E Stirzaker, M. 30 Jun
E Jackson, A.S. 30 Jun
X Honnoraty, M.R. 30 Jun
S Chapell, A. 30 Jun
E Mallinson, R. 30 Jun
X Swain, A.V. 30 Jun
X Barker, P.T. 30 Jun
X Bowbrick, R.C. 30 Jun
X Bower, N.S. 30 Jun
E Martin, B.A. 30 Jun
S Mearns, C.M. 30 Jun
X Robertson, D.C. 30 Jun
S Wright, S.H. 30 Jun
X Spiller, V.J. 30 Jun
E McHale, K. 30 Jun
E White, R.F. 30 Jun
E Matthews, D.W. 30 Jun
S Parry, A.K.I. 30 Jun
E Russell, P.R. 30 Jun
E Helliwell, M.A. 30 Jun
X Anstey, R.J. 30 Jun
E Shutts, D. 30 Jun
S Walsh, M.A. 30 Jun
X Hurrell, P.R. 30 Jun
X Cryar, T.M.C. 30 Jun
X Cartwright, D. 30 Jun
E Manson, T.E. 30 Jun
E Forer, D.A. 30 Jun
S Oliphant, W. 30 Jun
X Ward, S.I. 30 Jun
X Price, D.W. 30 Jun
X Huntington, S.P. 30 Jun
S Clark, M.T. 30 Jun
X Olive, P.N. 30 Jun
E Davey, G.S. 30 Jun
S Clark, S.M. 30 Jun
X Orchard, A.P. 30 Jun
E Osmond, J.B. 30 Jun
X Harris, K.J. 30 Jun
X Duffy, H. 30 Jun
S Goldthorpe, M. 30 Jun
X Verney, P.S. 30 Jun
X Beard, H.D. 30 Jun
X Millen, I.S. 30 Jun
X Watt, A.J.L. 30 Jun
S Cole, A.C. 30 Jun
E Cameron, M.J. 30 Jun
X Burns, A.P. 30 Jun
X Guy, T.J. 30 Jun
X Perks, J.L.E.S. 30 Jun
X Henry, T.M. 30 Jun
X Jordan, A.A. 30 Jun
X Paterson, M.P. 30 Jun

LIEUTENANT COMMANDERS

1982

E Murray, R.H. 01 Jan
E Helby, P.F.H. 16 Jul
E Shand, C.M. 01 Nov

1983

X Wilson, R. 01 Jul

1984

X Sinclair, A.B. 01 Feb
E Robinson, D.I. 01 Feb
X Thornton, M.C. 08 Feb
E Smith, A.C. 16 Mar
E Will, A.W. 01 Jun
X Fraser, D.K. 01 Jul
E Lemon, R.G.A. 01 Sep
X King, N.A. 01 Dec

1985

X Archdale, P.M. 16 Mar
X Munday, I.V. 01 Apr
X Stone, C.R.M. 01 May
E Pilsworth, D.S. 01 Jun
S Edwards, C.C. 01 Jul
X Wilson, C.G.T. 01 Aug
S Craven, J.A.G. 01 Sep
E Franks, J.P. 01 Dec
E Coulson, J.R. 08 Dec

1986

X Robertson, F.W. 01 Mar
X Evans, J.W. 06 May
X Mannion, T.S. 01 Sep
X Osman, M.R. 01 Sep
X Field, S.N.C. 01 Sep

1987

X Chandler, S.A. 01 Jan
X Lewis, S.B. 01 Jan
E Fiander, P.J. 01 Feb
X Taylor, N.F. 16 Feb
X Gibson, T.A. 16 Mar
X Creates, K.I. 01 Apr
X Jenks, A.W.J. 16 Apr
X Field, J.D. 16 Apr
X MacNaughton, F.G. 01 May
X Martin, N.D. 01 Jun
E Kirk, T.L. 01 Jun
E Hunter, K.P. 01 Aug
X Peters, A.J.U. 01 Aug
E Lord, A.S. 01 Sep
X Crudgington, P. 01 Sep
X Brown, C.D. 01 Sep
E Newton, M.R. 22 Sep
X Goddard, D.J.S. 01 Oct
X Gaskin, S.E. 01 Nov
X Holmes, G. 01 Dec
E Trotter, S. 01 Dec

1988

S Billington, N.S. 01 Feb
E Edwards, A.D.P. 01 Feb
X Sharpe, G.J. 01 Feb
X Pamphilon, M.J. 01 Mar
E Honey, J.P. 01 Mar
X Nelson, D.E. 01 Apr
X Malin, M.J. 01 Apr
E O'Brien, P.C. 23 Apr
X MacKett, D.G. 01 May
X Johnson, B. 01 May
X Speller, N.S.F. 01 May
E Nurse, M.T. 01 Jun
X Woznicki, S.J. 16 Jun
X Davis, M.P. 01 Jul
X Abbey, M.P. 01 Oct
E Dinham, A.C. 01 Oct
X Chambers, T.G. 01 Oct
X Wrigley, P.J. 16 Oct
S Seddon, J.S.M. 16 Oct
X Smith, K.M. 16 Nov
E Quine, N.J. 01 Dec

1989

E Tweed, C.J. 01 Feb
X Gibbs, P.N.C. 01 Feb
E Denison, A.R.V.T. 01 Feb
X O'Riordan, M.P. 01 Apr
X Pollitt, D.N.A. 01 Apr
X Baudains, T.J. 01 Apr
S Ramsey, J.S. 16 Apr
E Cooper, P.F. 21 Apr
X Newman, P.H. 01 May
E Carver, A.G. 01 May
X Joyner, A. 01 May
X Kent, M.D. 01 May
E Davey, P.J. 01 Jun
X Yates, N.P. 01 Jun
S Almond, D.E.M. 01 Jul
E Jackson, S.H. 01 Jul
X Palmer, P.A. 01 Jul
E Faulkner, R.I. 01 Aug
X Watson, R.J. 01 Aug
S Lewis, G.D. 01 Sep
E Eastaugh, A.C. 01 Oct
X Hipsey, S.J. 01 Oct
X Booker, G.R. 01 Oct
X Carr, D.L. 01 Oct
E Williams, R.C. 01 Oct
E Mant, J.N. 01 Oct
X Grimley, D.M.J. 01 Nov
X Baileff, R.I. 01 Dec

1990

X Wade, N.C. 01 Jan
X Knight, A.W. 01 Feb
X Little, C.S.A. 01 Feb
X Beats, K.A. 16 Feb
X Leaney, M.J. 01 Mar
X Kerr, W.M.M. 09 Mar
X Currie, D.W. 01 Apr
X Britton, N.J. 01 Apr
E Fowler, P.J.S. 01 Apr
X Griffiths, D.T. 01 Apr
E Boraston, P.J. 01 Apr
X Chapple, C.P. 01 May
X Barker, N.J. 01 May
X Chapman, N.J. 01 May
S Cropper, M.A.K. 16 May
X Howarth, D.W. 01 Jun
X Clegg, M.L. 01 Jun
E Howard, K.A. 01 Jul
E Plant, I.R. 01 Jul
X Pringle, A. 01 Jul
X Wass, M.J. 01 Aug
X Davies, C.S. 01 Sep
X Mathias-Jones, P.D. 01 Sep
X Murphy, N. 01 Sep
X Hall, D.W. 01 Oct
X Burgess, S. 01 Oct
X Saunders, J.N. 01 Oct
X Slade, C. 01 Oct
E Squire, P.A. 01 Oct
X Bell, R.P.W. 01 Oct
X Chichester, M.A.R. 01 Oct
E Perry, R. 01 Nov
X Roper, M. 01 Nov
X Straughan, C.J. 01 Dec
X Evans, G.R. 01 Dec
E Maw, M.J. 01 Dec
E Walton, J.C. 01 Dec
X Ferguson, R.G. 12 Dec

1991

S Kingsbury, J.A.T. 01 Feb
S Pike, M.S. 01 Mar
X Eedle, R.J. 01 Mar
X Crowther, K.W. 29 Mar

LIEUTENANT COMMANDERS

E	Martin, E.J.	01 Apr
X	Henderson, T.M.P.	01 Apr
X	Dobson, R.A.	01 Apr
X	Dunlop, P.F.	01 Apr
X	Roberts, D.H.W.	01 Apr
X	Kelly, R.	03 Apr
S	Barnwell, K.L.	23 Apr
X	Naismith, D.H.	01 May
E	Trewhella, G.G.	01 May
X	MacDonald, G.D.	01 May
E	Quick, N.H.	01 May
E	Stott, J.A.	26 May
E	Gibson, D.T.	01 Jun
X	Gomm, K.	01 Jun
E	James, C.	01 Jun
E	Plant, M.G.	13 Jun
E	Lacey, I.N.	16 Jun
E	Stewart, R.W.	01 Jul
X	Smith, N.P.	01 Jul
X	Greenwood, M.J.	01 Sep
E	Canty, N.R.	01 Sep
X	Lawson, S.J.	01 Sep
S	Lloyd, D.P.J.	01 Sep
X	Donaldson, S.B.	01 Sep
E	Clark, A.N.	01 Sep
E	Shaw, I.B.	15 Sep
X	Owen, P.C.	01 Oct
X	Harvey, P.A.	01 Oct
X	Hawkins, R.H.	01 Oct
X	Carrington-Wood, C.G.	01 Oct
X	Graham, D.E.	01 Oct
X	Burden, J.C.	01 Nov
X	Bernau, J.C.	01 Nov
X	Metcalfe, A.P.W.	01 Dec
X	McHale, G.J.	01 Dec

1992

E	Masters, R.H.	01 Jan
X	Morse, A.C.	01 Jan
X	Drylie, A.J.	01 Feb
X	Potts, K.M.	01 Feb
X	Trathen, N.C.	01 Feb
E	White, P.A.	16 Feb
X	Blakey, A.L.	01 Mar
E	Mundin, A.J.	01 Apr
X	Jenkin, J.R.S.L.	01 May
X	Deighton, D.S.	01 May
E	Kennedy, N.H.	01 May
X	Roberts, D.A.	01 May
X	Giles, K.D.L.	01 May
E	Bone, C.J.	01 May
X	Bromige, T.R.J.	19 May
X	Williams, D.I.	29 May
X	Abbott, S.S.C.	01 Jun
E	Burdett, R.W.	01 Jun
X	Emmerson, G.J.	01 Jun
S	Murphy, J.	01 Jun
E	Morris, P.J.	10 Jun
X	Barnes-Yallowley, J.J.H.	16 Jul
E	Sennitt, J.W.	01 Aug
X	West, M.W.	05 Aug
E	John, G.D.	01 Sep
E	King, P.C.	01 Sep
X	Mardon, K.F.	02 Sep
X	Thomas, K.I.	01 Oct
X	Shepherd, P.R.	01 Oct
X	Austin, J.D.	01 Oct
W	Price, T.L.	01 Oct
X	Nelson, D.L.	01 Oct
X	Dunn, N.G.	01 Oct
E	Toon, J.R.	01 Oct
X	Maude, C.P.	01 Oct
S	Chapman, N.P.	01 Oct
E	Shepherd, A.	01 Oct
E	Dalton, D.J.	01 Oct
X	Howorth, K.	01 Dec

1993

X	Bilson, J.M.F.	01 Jan
X	Woolley, M.J.	01 Jan
S	Teasdale, R.M.	16 Jan
X	Walker, N.L.	01 Feb
X	Chesterman, G.J.	01 Feb
X	Fortescue, R.C.	01 Mar
S	Chilman, P.W.H.	01 Mar
X	Hall, A.P.	01 Mar
E	Loring, A.	01 Mar
X	Hobbs, A.R.	01 Apr
S	Lister, S.R.	01 Apr
X	Price, D.J.	01 Apr
E	Tulloch, F.M.	01 Apr
E	Fogg, D.S.	01 Apr
X	Dodds, R.S.	01 May
X	Smith, R.W.R.	01 May
E	Sutton, G.D.	01 Jun
X	Collier, A.S.	01 Jun
X	Witton, J.W.	01 Jun
E	Sneyd, E.P.B.	20 Jun
E	Mullin, P.N.	01 Jul
X	Bennett, G.L.N.	01 Jul
E	McNaughton, J.A.	01 Jul
X	Russell, T.	01 Jul
X	French, K.L.	09 Jul
S	Tyler, P.L.	10 Jul
E	Burnip, J.M.	01 Aug
S	Wiltcher, R.A.	01 Aug
X	Green, D.P.	13 Aug
X	Godfrey, K.R.	01 Sep
X	Landrock, G.J.	01 Sep
E	Udensi, E.A.A.A.	01 Sep
X	Anderson, F.B.	01 Oct
X	Chartres, D.I.	01 Oct
X	Thornton, P.J.	01 Oct
X	Doherty, K.	01 Oct
E	Mills, T.C.	01 Oct
X	Lawrence, S.P.	01 Oct
X	Bradburn, S.J.	01 Oct
E	Franks, P.D.	01 Oct
X	Stacey, H.A.	01 Oct
E	Hamilton, R.A.	01 Oct
X	Robertson, D.M.	01 Oct
X	Bowker, G.N.	01 Oct
E	Pitcher, J.	01 Oct
X	Bird, D.E.	01 Oct
X	Clark, P.M.C.	01 Oct
W	Silver, C.K.	01 Oct
S	McKnight, N.W.	01 Oct
X	Watts, A.P.	01 Oct
X	Acland, D.D.	01 Oct
S	Burt, P.R.	01 Oct
X	Nowosielski, F.	01 Oct
X	James, C.W.	27 Oct
X	Conway, J.J.	01 Nov
S	Taylor, S.M.	01 Nov
X	Wyatt, D.J.	01 Nov
X	Elvin, A.J.	06 Nov
X	Gladwell, T.J.	01 Dec

1994

X	McGrenary, A.	01 Jan
E	Brads, W.	14 Jan
X	Neve, P.C.	11 Feb
X	Saxby, K.A.	24 Feb
X	Newall, J.A.	01 Mar
X	Moorey, C.G.	01 Mar
E	Cattroll, I.M.	01 Mar
X	Meredith, N.	01 Apr
E	Blount, D.R.	01 Apr
X	Crispin, T.A.B.	01 Apr
X	Hailstone, J.H.S.	16 May
X	Eaton, P.G.	01 Jun
E	Bolam, A.G.	01 Jun
X	Andrews, P.N.	01 Jun
X	Lunn, A.C.	01 Jun
X	Hardacre, P.V.	01 Jun
X	Towler, P.J.B.	01 Jun

LIEUTENANT COMMANDERS

X Horsley, A.M.R. 01 Jul
X Houghton, P.J. 01 Jul
S Smerdon, C.D.E. 01 Jul
X Stuttard, M.C. 01 Jul
E Westwood, M.R.T. 01 Jul
E Griffiths, A.J. 26 Jul
X Horner, P.A. 01 Aug
X Denholm, I.G. 13 Aug
X Glass, J.E. 01 Sep
X Robin, C.C.E. 01 Sep
X Fleming, S.A. 30 Sep
X Hands, A.P. 01 Oct
E Alison, L.A. 01 Oct
X Monger, P.D. 01 Oct
X Scott-Dickins, C.A. 01 Oct
X Taylor, L. 01 Oct
X Sewed, M.A. 01 Oct
X Walker, M.C. 01 Oct
X Dowdell, R.E.J. 01 Oct
E Franks, D.I. 01 Oct
E Naden, J.R. 01 Oct
X Burrows, M.J. 01 Oct
X Thompson, N.J. 01 Oct
E Sugden, M.R. 01 Oct
X Savage, S. 01 Oct
X Lee, J.C. 01 Oct
X Elliman, S.M. 01 Oct
E Snow, P.F. 01 Oct
S De La Mare, R.M. 01 Oct
X Hamilton, G.R. 01 Oct
X Disney, P.W. 01 Oct
E De Jonghe, P.T. 01 Oct
X Francis, J. 01 Oct
E Howard, N. 31 Oct
X Gunn, W.J.S. 01 Nov
E Clark, K.C. 01 Nov
X Hurry, A.P. 01 Nov
E Bull, G.C. 01 Nov
E Harding, G.A. 01 Dec
X Hills, A.A. 01 Dec

1995

E Campbell, R.D.H. 01 Feb
X Ovenden, N.S.P. 01 Feb
X Hunt, J.S.P. 05 Feb
X Lewis, T.J. 05 Feb
X Baldwin, C.M. 01 Mar
E Dathan, T.J. 01 Mar
X Pillar, C.D. 01 Mar
X Firth, N.R. 01 Mar
X Jones, M. 01 Mar
E Gillham, P.R. 02 Mar
X Law, J. 27 Mar
E Gray, D.K. 01 Apr
E Munro, K. 01 Apr
X Egeland-Jensen, F.A. 01 Apr
E Gill, M.R. 01 Apr
E Gillan, G.M. 01 Apr
E Holmes, R.W. 01 Apr
X Reed, J.H. 01 Apr
X Greenland, M.R. 16 Apr
X Smith, C.P. 26 Apr
E Reynolds, T.P. 30 Apr
X Birley, J.H. 01 May
E Mills, A. 01 May
X Marshall, R.G.C. 01 May
X Goldsmith, S.V.W. 01 May
X Schnadhorst, J.C. 01 May
S Willis, M.S. 02 May
E Hewitt, A. 01 Jun
E Brown, P.S.J. 01 Jun
X Mannion, R.V. 01 Jun
X Woodward, D.J. 01 Jul
X Cornish, M.C. 01 Jul
X Foster, D.G.S. 01 Jul
E Gibbs, N.D. 01 Jul
E Smith, M.R. 14 Jul
E Rawlings, D.P. 01 Aug
X Greenaway, N.M. 01 Aug
E Juckes, M.A. 16 Aug
E Collins, P.R. 01 Sep
X Burke, M.C. 01 Sep
X Hill, R.A. 01 Sep
X Fitzsimmons, M.B. 01 Sep
X Martin, R.G. 01 Sep
E Murphy, P.W. 01 Sep
X Evans, M.J. 01 Sep
X Evans, A.W. 01 Oct
X Moffatt, R. 01 Oct
X Dean, W.M.H. 01 Oct
X Daniels, I.J.R. 01 Oct
E Nunn, G.E. 01 Oct
E Goble, I.J. 01 Oct
X Carter, R.I. 01 Oct
X Smith, K.J. 01 Oct
X Callister, D.R. 01 Oct
E Hassall, H. 01 Oct
X Pipkin, S.C. 01 Oct
X Mathieson, K.R. 01 Oct
X Brundle, P.R. 01 Oct
X Carretta, M.V. 01 Oct
X Collins, D.A. 01 Oct
E Nelson, A. 01 Oct
X Daniell, C.J. 01 Oct
X Fincher, K.J. 01 Oct
X Bate, D.I.G. 01 Oct
E Andrews, I. 01 Oct
E Roberts, E.W. 01 Oct
S Dobson, B.J. 01 Oct
X Welch, A. 13 Oct
E Lipscomb, P. 01 Nov
X Vickery, T.K. 01 Nov
S Porrett, J.A. 14 Nov
E Stephenson, D. 22 Nov
X Boddington, J.D.L. 16 Dec
X Meeds, K. 16 Dec
X Bath, E.G. 27 Dec

1996

X Atkinson, M. 01 Feb
X Bankier, S. 19 Feb
X Draper, S.P. 26 Feb
S Smith, C.J. 16 Mar
X Harry, A.D. 01 Apr
E Jackson, I.A. 01 Apr
X Lindsay, I.G. 01 Apr
E Withers, J.W. 01 Apr
E Kingsbury, S.H. 01 Apr
X Collins, G.J.S. 07 Apr
S Waters, N.R. 16 Apr
S Marston, P.A. 16 Apr
S McConochie, A.D. 16 Apr
E Walker, P.R. 01 May
E Worthington, J.M.F. 01 May
X Masters, J.C. 01 May
E Scott, J.B. 01 May
E Shepherd, R.G. 01 May
E Carter, J.M. 01 Jun
X Moore, P.H.G. 01 Jun
X Gazzard, J.H. 01 Jun
X Freeman, D.R. 01 Jun
X Hayward, C.E.W. 01 Jun
X Hill, M.R. 22 Jun
E Kempsell, I.D. 26 Jun
X Taylor, B.D. 01 Jul
X McDonough, A.G. 01 Jul
X Simpson, M.J. 01 Jul
X Tetlow, H.S.G. 01 Jul
X McCall, I.R. 01 Jul
E Pooley, S.W. 01 Jul
E Rimmer, H.E. 22 Jul
E Hope, K. 01 Sep
X Benton, A.M. 01 Sep
E Young, M.S. 01 Sep
E Geddis, R.D. 01 Sep

LIEUTENANT COMMANDERS

X Brady, S.E. 01 Sep
X Bark, J.S. 01 Sep
E Woodford, G.I. 01 Sep
E Coles, C.J. 01 Sep
E Goodings, G.J. 01 Oct
X Corbett, G.J. 01 Oct
X Hibbert, M.C. 01 Oct
X Creech, R.D. 01 Oct
X Jefferson, P.M. 01 Oct
E Johns, S.A.B. 01 Oct
X Sykes, R.A. 01 Oct
X Dickson, J.P.E. 01 Oct
X Munro-Lott, P.R.J. 01 Oct
X Hoper, P.R. 01 Oct
X Biggs, D.M. 01 Oct
X Webb, C.M. 01 Oct
X Wilkinson, P.M. 01 Oct
E Ashton Jones, G. 01 Oct
X Armstrong, N.P.B. 01 Oct
W Whetton, J.B.D. 01 Oct
E Clarke, R. 01 Oct
X Slocombe, C.A. 01 Oct
E Lias, C.D. 01 Oct
E Ashton, R.D. 01 Oct
E Bracher, H. 01 Oct
E Rook, D.J. 01 Oct
X Hudson, P.T. 01 Oct
S Olliver, A.J. 01 Oct
X Seymour, K.W. 01 Oct
X Leitch, I.R. 01 Oct
E Dobbin, V.W. 01 Oct
X Saynor, R.M. 01 Oct
E Wood, I.D. 01 Oct
E Galvin, D. 01 Oct
X Van-Den-Bergh, W.L. 01 Oct
E Mockford, J.A. 01 Oct
E Fraser, W.C. 01 Oct
S McGarel, D.F. 01 Oct
E Marson, G.M. 14 Oct
E Watson, P.G.C. 25 Oct
E Burwin, H.L. 01 Nov
S Toomey, N.J. 01 Nov
X Gale, S.P. 01 Nov
E Wilson, C.J. 01 Dec
S Blackwell, R.E. 01 Dec
X Barnbrook, J.C. 16 Dec

1997

X Shepherd, C.S. 01 Jan
X Adam, I.K. 01 Jan
X Carson, N.D.E. 01 Jan
E Harrison, D. 05 Jan
E Irwin, M.A. 09 Jan
X Noyce, N.R. 15 Jan
X Davies, M.B. 24 Jan
X Drysdale, S.R. 01 Feb
E Parvin, P.S. 01 Feb
S Stanton, P.C.M. 16 Feb
X Hulme, T.M. 01 Mar
X Bell, R.D. 01 Mar
X Chandler, N.J. 01 Mar
X Cummings, A.T. 01 Mar
X Hogg, C.W. 01 Mar
S Williams, M.S. 29 Mar
X Cowley, R.M. 01 Apr
E New, C.M. 01 Apr
X Morris, R.J. 01 Apr
E Patterson-Hollis, C. 01 Apr
X Toothill, J.S. 01 Apr
X Lowson, R.M. 01 Apr
X Ryan, R.M. 01 Apr
X Wilson-Chalon, L.M. 01 Apr
X Davison, J.E. 06 Apr
E Harris, A.G. 12 Apr
E Finch, R.L. 01 May
E Feeney, M.L. 01 May
E Clark, S.R. 01 May
X Pethybridge, R.A. 01 May
E Carrick, R.J. 01 May
E King, N.W. 01 May
X Rich, D.C. 20 May
E Thomson, I.R. 22 May
X Woollcombe-Gosson, D.J. 01 Jun
X South, D.J. 15 Jun
X Irons, P.A. 01 Jul
E Peace, R.W. 02 Jul
X Ellis, N.M. 18 Jul
X Forester-Bennett, R.M.W. 24 Jul
X Wells, J.M.C. 01 Aug
E Pearson, N. 01 Aug
X Woollven, A.H. 01 Aug
X Stannard, M.P. 01 Aug
S Horswill, M.N. 01 Aug
S Evans, E.M. 16 Aug
X Webber, C.J. 26 Aug
X Hare, J.H. 01 Sep
E Richardson, M.A. 01 Sep
X Wynn, S.R. 01 Sep
X Petheram, A.J. 01 Sep
X Tebbet, P.N. 01 Sep
X Hutchinson, O.J.P. 01 Sep
X Llewelyn, K. 01 Oct
E Mann, G.D. 01 Oct
X Stringer, R.A. 01 Oct
X Daw, S.J. 01 Oct
W Cobb, J.E. 01 Oct
X Mickleburgh, A. 01 Oct
X Lambourne, D.J. 01 Oct
X Clucas, M.R. 01 Oct
E Morris, S.T. 01 Oct
X James, A.J. 01 Oct
E Morgan, S.A. 01 Oct
X Moys, A.J. 01 Oct
X Fleming, K.P. 01 Oct
X Cook, D.J. 01 Oct
E Price, T.P. 01 Oct
X Cornick, R.M. 01 Oct
X Harmer, J.N.J. 01 Oct
X Hargreaves, N. 01 Oct
E Leonard, M. 01 Oct
E Rowe, P.E. 01 Oct
E Davies, T.M. 01 Oct
E Cole, S.P. 01 Oct
E Downie, A.J. 01 Oct
X Harper, J.A. 01 Oct
X Yarker, D.L. 01 Oct
X Stuttard, S.E. 01 Oct
S Bennett, A.J. 01 Oct
S Finch, T.S.A. 01 Oct
X Morris, P.J. 01 Oct
E Moss, T.E. 01 Oct
E Hellyn, D.R. 01 Oct
X Ward, D.S. 01 Oct
E Morrison, R.W. 01 Oct
X Griffiths, A. 01 Oct
S Knill, R.L. 01 Oct
E O'Flaherty, J.S. 03 Oct
X Wheatley, W.J. 04 Oct
X Surgey, I.C. 26 Oct
X Tabeart, G.W. 01 Nov
X Jones, A.D. 01 Nov
E Morgan, F.S. 01 Nov
X Houlberg, K.M.T. 01 Nov
S Gibson, A.D. 16 Nov
S Asbridge, J.I. 16 Nov
S Hewitt, L.R. 16 Nov
E Faulkner, D.W. 29 Nov
X Dale-Smith, G. 01 Dec
X Ince, D.P. 01 Dec
X Montgomery, M.H. 01 Dec
X Venables, A.N. 01 Dec
S Towler, A. 14 Dec
X Prentice, D.C. 22 Dec

LIEUTENANT COMMANDERS

1998

X Carroll, P.J. 01 Jan
X Peacock, T.J. 01 Jan
E Bartlett, I.D. 01 Jan
E Kitchen, S.A. 01 Jan
X Lea, J. 01 Jan
X Romney, P.D. 01 Jan
X Smith, G.C.S. 01 Jan
E Ward, S.D. 01 Jan
E Hemsworth, K.J. 01 Jan
X Haseldine, S.G. 01 Feb
X Allen, A.D. 01 Feb
X Beadsmoore, J.E. 01 Feb
X Bence, D.E. 01 Feb
X Carroll, B.J. 01 Feb
E Hughesdon, M.D. 01 Feb
X Mugridge, D.R. 01 Feb
E Rogers, A.G. 01 Feb
E Thomas, J.H. 01 Feb
E Wellington, S. 01 Feb
E Franks, C.S. 01 Feb
E Blackburn, S.A. 01 Mar
X Goodman, A.T. 01 Mar
X Mules, A.J. 01 Mar
X Spring, A.R.J. 01 Mar
X Scott, R.J. 02 Mar
X McKenzie, M. 03 Mar
X Stowell, P.I.M. 01 Apr
E Lynn, S.R. 01 Apr
X MacDonald-Robinson, N.U.S. 01 Apr
X Petherick, J.S. 01 Apr
E Rook, G.I. 01 Apr
X Smith, A.P. 01 Apr
X Chapman, S.J. 01 Apr
E Hood, K.M. 01 Apr
E MacGillivray, I. 01 Apr
E Bone, R.C. 01 May
E Green, A.J. 01 May
E Fawcett, F.P. 01 May
E Hepworth, A.W.D. 01 May
X Goodacre, I.R. 01 May
E Hutchison, P.G. 01 May
E Winter, T.M. 01 May
E Dunn, G.R. 01 May
X Royston, S.J. 01 May
E Morshead, C.H. 14 May
E Millar, G.C. 15 May
S Evans, M.D. 16 May
E Philo, J.Q. 01 Jun
E Murray, G.M. 01 Jun
E Baker, M.J. 01 Jun
E Bosustow, A.M. 01 Jun
E Evans, G. 01 Jun
X Green, J. 01 Jun
X Payne, J.D. 01 Jun
X Deacon, S. 01 Jun
E Hanson, N.A. 01 Jun
X Kimberley, R. 01 Jul
X Lowther, J.M. 01 Jul
X Powell, S.R. 01 Jul
X Beech, C.M. 01 Jul
X Price, T.A. 01 Jul
X Bird, R.A.J. 01 Jul
E O'Shea, E.P. 01 Jul
X Badrock, B. 05 Jul
E Hall, A.J. 01 Aug
X Ford, M.J. 05 Aug
X Albon, M. 12 Aug
X Hawkins, J.S. 16 Aug
X McGuire, M.J. 31 Aug
E Stewart, K.C. 01 Sep
X Toor, J.J.S. 01 Sep
X Murphy, S.R.A. 01 Sep
X Savage, M.R. 01 Sep
X May, N.P. 01 Sep
E Humphrey, I.J. 17 Sep
E Wallace, D.J. 01 Oct
E Hart, P.A. 01 Oct
W Hayle, E.A. 01 Oct
X Manson, C.R. 01 Oct
X Reed, M. 01 Oct
E Wilson, D.T. 01 Oct
X Haynes, J.W. 01 Oct
E Davies, L.J. 01 Oct
E Krosnar-Clarke, S.M. 01 Oct
X Tyack, T.J. 01 Oct
E Darling, J.I. 01 Oct
E Mills, G.W. 01 Oct
MS Steel, D.G. 01 Oct
W Whittingham, D.J. 01 Oct
X Neave, A.M. 01 Oct
X Thompson, R.A. 01 Oct
E Bourne, D.S. 01 Oct
X Wilkinson, R.N. 01 Oct
X Shallcroft, J.E. 01 Oct
X Spayne, N.J. 01 Oct
E Dawson, S.N. 01 Oct
S Cunane, J.R. 01 Oct
X Chapman, D.A. 01 Oct
X Franklin, B.J. 01 Oct
X Wheaton, B.J.S. 01 Oct
E Hill, G.A. 01 Oct
E Lord, M. 01 Oct
X Lewis, D.J. 01 Oct
X Barrick, P.V. 01 Oct
S MacDougall, G.R. 01 Oct
X Strathern, R.J. 01 Oct
E McCue, D. 01 Oct
E Simmonds, G.F. 01 Oct
MS Derby, P.J. 01 Oct
E Clarke, J. 01 Oct
E Grace, T.P. 01 Oct
E Jordan, N.S. 01 Oct
E Birbeck, K. 01 Oct
E Rimmer, R. 01 Oct
E Stokes, A.W. 01 Oct
E Arnell, S.J. 01 Oct
E Ferguson, G.H. 01 Oct
S Case, P. 01 Oct
S Pye, P.M. 01 Oct
X Hughes, G.G.H. 01 Oct
X Dawson, W. 01 Nov
S McNally, N.J. 01 Nov
X Reidy, P.A. 01 Nov
E Hall, B.J. 01 Nov
E Smith, M.M. 01 Nov
X Taylor, A.R. 01 Nov
E Vickers, J. 01 Nov
E Corps, S.D. 11 Nov
E Guy, M.A. 13 Nov
E Boulton, N.A. 20 Nov
E Donnelly, J.S. 22 Nov
X Redman, C.J.R. 23 Nov
S Stoffell, D.P. 27 Nov
E Windsar, P.A. 27 Nov
X Davies, I.E. 01 Dec
E MacKay, P. 01 Dec
X Rogers, T.H.G. 04 Dec
E Foster, B.M.T. 07 Dec
X Warn, C.J. 09 Dec
X Powell, W.G. 16 Dec

1999

X Millard, A.R. 01 Jan
E Twine, J.H. 01 Jan
X Hancock, A.P. 01 Jan
X Manfield, M.D. 01 Jan
E Greatwood, I.M. 01 Jan
E Warrington, P.T. 01 Jan
X Ponsford, P.K. 01 Jan
E Roberts, K.E. 01 Jan
X Lees, E.C. 01 Feb
X Osborn, R.M. 01 Feb
X Staley, S.P.L. 01 Feb

LIEUTENANT COMMANDERS

	Name	Seniority
E	Copeland, S.N.	01 Feb
X	Godwin, C.A.	01 Feb
X	Goodsell, C.D.	01 Feb
E	Hancox, M.J.	01 Feb
E	Jackson, P.N.	01 Feb
X	Jones, N.P.	01 Feb
X	Kerslake, R.W.	01 Feb
S	Nairn, A.B.	01 Feb
E	Smith, A.G.	01 Feb
X	Taylor, M.A.	01 Feb
X	Welford, R.C.	01 Feb
E	Wright, N.S.	01 Feb
E	Fergusson, N.A.	01 Feb
E	Crofts, D.J.	01 Feb
X	Holmes, J.D.	04 Feb
X	Pitt, J.M.	17 Feb
W	Kent, I.M.	20 Feb
E	Southern, P.J.	27 Feb
X	Lee, N.F.	01 Mar
E	Lauste, W.E.	01 Mar
E	Casson, N.P.	01 Mar
X	Hussain, S.	01 Mar
X	Burns, R.D.J.	01 Mar
X	McDonnell, D.S.	01 Mar
X	Bingham, D.S.	01 Mar
E	Hill, D.	01 Mar
X	Waller, S.A.	01 Mar
E	Currass, T.D.	01 Mar
E	Douglass, M.C.M.	01 Mar
E	Gray, R.	01 Mar
E	Groom, I.S.	01 Mar
E	Henderson, S.P.	01 Mar
E	Mackie, D.F.S.	01 Mar
E	Rawlinson, S.J.	01 Mar
X	Moss, R.A.	01 Mar
X	O'Flaherty, C.P.J.	01 Mar
E	Bywater, R.L.	01 Mar
X	Hogben, A.L.	01 Mar
E	Briggs-Mould, T.P.	16 Mar
S	Turner, J.S.H.	01 Apr
X	Brooks, G.L.	01 Apr
X	Beck, S.K.	01 Apr
X	Collighan, G.T.	01 Apr
X	Dodd, K.M.	01 Apr
E	Goldman, P.H.L.	01 Apr
S	Mardlin, S.A.	01 Apr
X	Mimpriss, G.D.	01 Apr
E	Roscoe, R.D.	01 Apr
S	Dodd, N.C.	01 Apr
E	Foster, S.J.H.	01 Apr
X	Wood, U.G.S.	01 Apr
E	Waring, J.R.	01 Apr
X	Mahony, C.D.C.	03 Apr
S	Athayde Banazol, C.V.N.	04 Apr
E	Roberts, D.	04 Apr
X	Foster, D.H.	01 May
E	Bowhay, S.	01 May
X	Burstow, R.S.	01 May
E	Scott, M.	01 May
X	Bravery, M.A.E.	01 May
X	Garratt, J.K.	01 May
E	Sansford, A.J.	27 May
X	Golden, D.S.C.	01 Jun
X	Bush, A.J.T.	01 Jun
X	Allen, P.L.	01 Jun
S	Ferns, T.D.	01 Jun
X	Mackey, M.C.	01 Jun
X	Whitley, I.D.B.	01 Jun
E	Wright, B.L.	01 Jun
X	Young, A.	01 Jun
E	West, G.G.	06 Jun
E	Proud, A.D.	11 Jun
S	Rees, J.P.	29 Jun
X	Hewitt, D.L.	01 Jul
E	Jones, D.B.	01 Jul
E	Parkin, M.I.	01 Jul
S	Percival, M.C.	01 Jul
X	Bushell, G.R.	09 Jul
S	Perry, A.J.	16 Jul
X	Allen, R.	20 Jul
X	Southorn, M.D.	21 Jul
E	Richardson, P.S.M.	01 Aug
E	Lee, P.A.	01 Aug
X	Churcher, J.E.	01 Aug
E	Collis, M.J.	01 Aug
E	Currie, S.M.	01 Aug
X	Dreelan, M.J.	01 Aug
E	Owens, D.T.	01 Aug
E	Quekett, I.P.S.	01 Aug
X	Brown, P.A.E.	01 Aug
E	Lowe, J.C.	01 Aug
X	Barnes, J.R.	01 Aug
E	Dyer, J.D.T.	01 Sep
E	Grears, J.	01 Sep
E	McLarnon, C.P.C.	01 Sep
E	Tatham, S.A.	01 Sep
E	Bolton, J.P.	01 Sep
X	Goode, A.N.	01 Sep
E	Greener, C.	01 Sep
E	Taylor, R.	01 Sep
E	Punton, I.M.	01 Sep
X	Whitworth, R.M.	01 Oct
X	Luscombe, M.D.	01 Oct
X	Johns, M.G.	01 Oct
X	Marsh, B.H.	01 Oct
X	Hartley, J.L.	01 Oct
X	Callaghan, P.F.	01 Oct
X	Hayde, P.J.	01 Oct
E	Morris, P.	01 Oct
X	Howard, D.G.	01 Oct
E	Sergeant, N.R.	01 Oct
E	Barrett, S.J.	01 Oct
X	Rae, A.J.W.	01 Oct
X	Goldsmith, D.	01 Oct
X	Anderson, S.C.	01 Oct
X	Cooke, G.J.	01 Oct
E	Preston, M.R.	01 Oct
X	Holden, R.J.	01 Oct
E	Weir, S.D.	01 Oct
X	Yardley, A.P.	01 Oct
X	Barker, J.W.	01 Oct
E	Mason, M.	01 Oct
X	Pegrum, T.A.	01 Oct
X	Cowie, K.M.	01 Oct
E	Linderman, I.R.	01 Oct
E	Matthews, P.B.	01 Oct
X	Avison, M.J.	01 Oct
E	Roberts, S.C.	01 Oct
X	Murray, A.S.	01 Oct
X	Miller, C.R.	01 Oct
E	Gunther, P.T.	01 Oct
E	Nicholls, G.A.	01 Oct
X	Ash, T.C.V.	01 Oct
E	Milsom, J.	01 Oct
E	Appelquist, P.	01 Oct
X	Blythe, P.C.	01 Oct
E	Bougourd, M.A.	01 Oct
X	Lower, I.S.	01 Oct
E	McDermott, O.D.	01 Oct
E	Gazard, P.N.	01 Oct
X	Talbot, C.M.	01 Oct
E	Payne, D.	01 Oct
E	Dutton, P.J.	01 Oct
E	Glennie, B.W.	01 Oct
S	Freegard, I.P.	01 Oct
S	Williams, D.	01 Oct
E	Maude, D.H.	01 Oct
X	Edwards, R.	01 Oct
S	Twist, D.C.	01 Oct
X	Woodruff, A.D.	01 Oct
E	Bassett, N.E.	01 Oct
X	Thomas, L.	01 Oct
E	Jones, D.A.	01 Oct

LIEUTENANT COMMANDERS

X	Stephens, R.P.	01 Oct
X	Horne, A.	01 Oct
E	Norman, P.D.	01 Oct
E	Sugden, S.R.	01 Oct
E	Taylor, K.J.	01 Oct
S	Harris, M.T.	01 Oct
S	Holland, N.R.	01 Oct
W	Graham, P.J.	22 Oct
X	Jones, C.A.	01 Nov
X	Necker, C.D.	01 Nov
X	Baker, A.P.	01 Nov
X	Joyce, T.J.	01 Nov
E	Edmonds, R.M.	01 Nov
S	Ackland, H.K.	01 Nov
X	White, I.F.	18 Nov
E	Chapman, C.L.	29 Nov
X	Smith, B.J.	01 Dec
E	Easterbrook, K.I.E.	01 Dec
E	McRae, P.C.	01 Dec
X	Tennuci, R.G.	01 Dec
E	Woodruff, D.A.	01 Dec
X	Boynton, S.J.	01 Dec
X	Hunkin, D.J.	01 Dec
E	Gayfer, M.E.	01 Dec
S	Talbott, A.H.	01 Dec
X	Moore, C.R.	05 Dec
E	Rose, M.F.	28 Dec

2000

E	Campbell, M.A.	01 Jan
X	Harcourt, R.J.	01 Jan
E	Stamper, J.C.H.	01 Jan
E	Nickolls, K.P.	01 Jan
E	Baxter, I.M.	01 Jan
X	Bryan, R.J.L.	01 Jan
X	Parsons, A.D.	01 Jan
E	Rowland, P.N.	01 Jan
X	Walker, N.M.	01 Jan
X	Washer, N.B.J.	01 Jan
X	Connell, M.J.	01 Jan
E	Higham, J.G.	01 Jan
S	Dunthorne, J.A.	04 Jan
X	Griffiths, M.O.J.	16 Jan
X	Aylott, P.R.F.D.	29 Jan
X	Crosbie, D.E.F.	01 Feb
X	Pierce, A.K.M.	01 Feb
E	Burgess, G.T.M.	01 Feb
E	Gale, M.A.	01 Feb
E	Greenway, S.A.	01 Feb
E	Kelly, J.A.	01 Feb
E	Martin, S.J.	01 Feb
E	O'Brien, K.J.	01 Feb
S	Rae, S.G.	01 Feb
S	Pomeroy, P.M.	01 Feb
E	Lewis, G.D.	03 Feb
E	Bolton, M.T.W.	06 Feb
E	Shaw, M.L.	11 Feb
S	Brenchley, N.G.	17 Feb
S	Ashman, R.G.	28 Feb
S	Sparke, P.R.W.	01 Mar
E	Cotterill, B.M.	01 Mar
E	Balhetchet, A.S.	01 Mar
X	Dominy, D.J.D.	01 Mar
S	Murphy, P.A.	01 Mar
E	Reece, N.D.	01 Mar
E	Teideman, I.C.	01 Mar
E	Whitehead, S.J.	01 Mar
E	Jackson, D.J.	01 Mar
X	Johnson, L.S.	01 Mar
E	Whitfield, K.D.	01 Mar
E	Hartley, A.P.	02 Mar
E	Pugh, J.	08 Mar
E	Bedding, S.W.E.	01 Apr
E	Bignell, S.	01 Apr
X	Bruford, R.M.C.	01 Apr
X	Buck, J.E.	01 Apr
E	Curlewis, A.J.	01 Apr
E	Long, A.M.	01 Apr
X	Firth, R.J.G.	08 Apr
X	Lindsey, R.J.	30 Apr
X	Gurr, A.W.G.	01 May
X	Parry, J.D.F.	01 May
E	Russell, B.	01 May
E	Strutt, J.F.	01 May
X	Wilson, D.R.	01 May
E	Bye, M.D.	01 May
E	Chambers, I.R.	01 May
E	Reah, S.	02 May
E	Prinsep, T.J.	01 Jun
X	Gray, J.A.	01 Jun
E	Bradley, P.M.	01 Jun
E	Howard, N.H.	01 Jun
E	Rogers, C.M.	01 Jun
E	Fleisher, S.M.	01 Jun
X	Moore, M.	01 Jun
E	Mulvaney, P.A.	01 Jun
E	Nicklas, C.J.	01 Jun
X	Wilkinson, D.H.	01 Jun
X	Williams, J.P.	01 Jun
E	Gregory, A.S.	01 Jun
X	Campbell, L.M.	01 Jul
X	Gardner, J.E.	01 Jul
E	Barton, M.A.	01 Jul
E	Crundell, R.J.	01 Jul
E	Lunn, M.H.B.	01 Jul
E	Moody, D.C.	01 Jul
E	Panther, A.M.	01 Jul
E	Atkins, I.	01 Jul
E	Ewen, A.P.	01 Jul
E	Etchells, S.B.	03 Jul
E	Philpot, D.J.	18 Jul
E	Lauchlan, R.A.	01 Aug
X	Dando, J.N.	01 Aug
X	Ley, J.A.	01 Aug
E	Ross, I.	01 Aug
E	Miles, G.J.	07 Aug
E	Thrippleton, M.G.	15 Aug
S	Tothill, R.C.	17 Aug
X	Hutchinson, C.J.	01 Sep
E	Richter, A.S.B.	01 Sep
X	Duff, A.P.	01 Sep
X	Oulds, K.A.	01 Sep
E	Walton, C.P.	01 Sep
E	Wheal, A.J.	01 Sep
X	Wyper, J.R.	01 Sep
X	Wilson, R.	01 Sep
E	Marshall, P.	01 Sep
E	Taylor, A.	01 Oct
X	Watkins, T.C.	01 Oct
X	Cook, G.E.	01 Oct
X	Clarke, A.P.	01 Oct
X	Williams, M.A.	01 Oct
E	Picksley, M.R.	01 Oct
E	Sutcliffe, R.W.	01 Oct
X	Ford, J.A.	01 Oct
X	Higgs, R.J.	01 Oct
S	Walker, N.A.	01 Oct
X	Oddy, D.M.	01 Oct
X	Gardiner, P.F.D.	01 Oct
X	Robertson, P.N.	01 Oct
X	O'Sullivan, B.O.	01 Oct
E	Pears, I.J.	01 Oct
X	Grindon, M.G.	01 Oct
X	Phillips, J.P.	01 Oct
X	Smith, R.C.V.	01 Oct
E	Cook, C.B.	01 Oct
E	Orton, D.M.	01 Oct
E	Lacey, C.M.	01 Oct
E	Moss, P.J.	01 Oct
X	Hinch, D.G.W.	01 Oct
X	Hart, T.G.DE.B.	01 Oct
X	Bennett, W.D.	01 Oct
X	Lynch, S.	01 Oct
X	Howell, H.R.G.	01 Oct

LIEUTENANT COMMANDERS

E	Bissett, I.M.	01 Oct
E	Bissett, P.K.	01 Oct
S	Plaice, G.C.	01 Oct
MS	Trasler, M.F.	01 Oct
X	Finn, G.J.	01 Oct
S	Bell, M.	01 Oct
E	Dyke, K.A.	01 Oct
S	Axon, G.M.	01 Oct
E	Hutchings, J.S.	01 Oct
X	Curtis, R.J.	01 Oct
E	Joyce, D.A.	01 Oct
S	Turner, R.F.	01 Oct
E	Burge, R.G.	01 Oct
E	Hatcher, T.R.	01 Oct
E	Rundle, A.L.	01 Oct
S	Waterhouse, P.	01 Oct
X	Barron, P.J.	01 Oct
X	Billington, T.J.	01 Oct
S	Hall, D.A.	01 Oct
X	Utley, M.K.	01 Oct
E	Aniyi, C.B.J.	01 Oct
E	Love, T.S.N.	01 Oct
X	Lett, J.D.	01 Oct
E	Prince, M.E.	01 Oct
E	Pearson, C.P.B.	01 Oct
S	Pheasant, J.C.S.	01 Oct
E	Phesse, J.P.L.	01 Oct
S	Stillwell-Cox, A.D.R.	01 Oct
X	Walker, E.G.	01 Oct
E	Game, P.G.	01 Oct
E	Hobson, I.S.	01 Oct
E	Finn, I.R.	01 Oct
MS	Gerrell, F.J.	01 Oct
S	Grocott, P.C.	01 Oct
E	Cowper, I.R.	01 Oct
X	Taylor, M.R.	01 Oct
X	Dufosee, S.W.	01 Oct
X	Ahlgren, E.G.	01 Oct
X	Beaumont, S.J.	01 Oct
X	Whitlam, J.	01 Oct
S	Young, S.W.	01 Oct
S	Bunt, K.J.	01 Oct
E	Berry, P.	01 Oct
X	Elsom, G.K.	01 Oct
S	Pocock, D.	16 Oct
E	Norris, J.G.	01 Nov
X	Ramsey, R.T.	01 Nov
X	O'Byrne, P.B.M.	01 Nov
E	Wylie, I.C.H.	01 Nov
S	Hally, P.J.	01 Nov
X	Stockton, K.G.	19 Nov

E	Ballard, M.L.	01 Dec
E	Lowe, S.M.	01 Dec
E	Rayner, A.	01 Dec
X	Broadhurst, M.R.	01 Dec
X	Douglas, P.J.	01 Dec
X	Knight, D.W.	01 Dec
X	Douglas, P.G.	03 Dec
S	Beresford-Green, P.M.	16 Dec
S	Gale, C.V.	24 Dec
E	Rutherford, T.J.	30 Dec

2001

E	McMullan, N.L.	01 Jan
E	Kerr, A.N.	01 Jan
E	Malley, M.P.	01 Jan
X	Smith, G.D.J.	01 Jan
E	Thomas, S.M.	01 Jan
S	Donovan, R.J.	01 Jan
X	MacKinnon, D.J.	01 Jan
X	Varley, I.G.	01 Jan
X	Wills, P.J.	01 Jan
S	Lawrence, S.P.	14 Jan
X	Brown, S.H.	15 Jan
E	Sellers, G.D.	01 Feb
X	Stanton-Brown, P.J.	01 Feb
X	Hopper, S.M.	01 Feb
X	Knott, M.B.	01 Feb
X	Miller, P.D.	01 Feb
X	Thomson, C.D.	01 Feb
X	Tredray, T.P.	01 Feb
E	Woods, T.C.	01 Feb
E	Bowker, I.C.	13 Feb
S	Dudley, S.M.T.	20 Feb
X	Chaston, S.P.	01 Mar
X	Cox, R.J.	01 Mar
S	Hallett, S.J.	01 Mar
E	Head, S.A.	01 Mar
X	Nelson, C.S.	01 Mar
X	Pearson, M.F.	01 Mar
X	Bristowe, P.A.	01 Mar
X	Giles, R.K.	01 Mar
X	George, D.M.	13 Mar
S	Williams, S.W.L.	01 Apr
X	Holden, N.	01 Apr
E	Whyte, I.P.	01 Apr
E	Adams, G.H.	01 Apr
X	Parnell, A.D.	01 Apr
X	Ryan, S.J.	01 Apr
E	Drywood, T.	01 Apr
E	Reid, J.C.J.	01 Apr
S	Whalley, R.J.	01 Apr
E	Holland, S.M.W.	01 May
E	Rand, M.J.	01 May
X	Russell, P.	01 May
X	Bessell, D.A.	01 Jun
X	Williams, C.N.O.	01 Jun
E	Bonnar, J.A.	01 Jun
E	Hutchins, R.F.	01 Jun
E	Keen, N.	01 Jun
X	Newell, P.R.	01 Jun
E	Cropper, F.B.N.	24 Jun
X	Norgan, D.J.	01 Jul
X	Watts, R.	01 Jul
X	Dunn, P.E.	01 Jul
S	Richardson, G.N.	01 Jul
E	Green, A.M.	01 Jul
E	Napier, G.A.	01 Jul
E	Sullivan, M.	01 Jul
E	Towell, P.J.	01 Jul
E	Shirley, A.J.	01 Aug
X	Bower, A.J.	01 Aug
S	Finch, B.A.	01 Aug
X	O'Sullivan, M.L.J.	01 Aug
X	Coyle, G.J.	01 Aug
E	Graham, A.N.S.	01 Aug
S	Preece, D.G.	01 Aug
E	Winter, R.J.	01 Aug
X	Wood, C.	01 Aug
X	Markey, A.P.	01 Aug
E	Campbell, J.C.	01 Sep
E	Lewis, D.J.	01 Sep
E	Laing, I.	01 Sep
X	Dowsett, P.G.	01 Sep
E	Chapman, P.	01 Sep
X	Downes, C.H.	01 Sep
S	Goldsworthy, P.J.	01 Sep
X	Yelland, C.B.	01 Oct
X	Eatwell, R.A.	01 Oct
W	Simpson, E.J.	01 Oct
X	Nicholas, B.J.	01 Oct
S	Ryan, J.B.	01 Oct
X	Turner, K.A.	01 Oct
X	Deverson, R.T.M.	01 Oct
X	Graham, M.A.	01 Oct
X	Knight, A.R.	01 Oct
E	Taylor, S.J.	01 Oct
S	Cottis, M.C.	01 Oct
X	Hannigan, P.F.	01 Oct
X	Scivier, J.S.	01 Oct
X	Bowers, J.P.	01 Oct
X	Duncan, J.	01 Oct
X	Forster, R.A.	01 Oct
E	Horwell, B.B.	01 Oct

LIEUTENANT COMMANDERS

X Tattersall, R.B. 01 Oct
X Westley, D.R. 01 Oct
X Noblett, P.G.A. 01 Oct
X Dunn, P.E. 01 Oct
E Baines, D.M.L. 01 Oct
E Morgan-Hosey, J.N. 01 Oct
X Rowlands, K. 01 Oct
X Richardson, G.A. 01 Oct
X Gough, S.R. 01 Oct
X Rogers, A. 01 Oct
X Brunsden-Brown, S.E. 01 Oct
E Davies, S.P. 01 Oct
E Mountjoy, B.J. 01 Oct
E Wray, A.D. 01 Oct
X Sneddon, R.N. 01 Oct
E Mills, I. 01 Oct
E Procter, J.E. 01 Oct
E Wharrie, E.K.B. 01 Oct
S Wooller, M.A.H. 01 Oct
E Stobie, P.L. 01 Oct
S West, A.W. 01 Oct
E Bannister, A.N. 01 Oct
E Johnson, M.J. 01 Oct
X Griffin, N.R. 01 Oct
E Langrill, M.P. 01 Oct
X Beattie, P.S. 01 Oct
X Dennis, M.J. 01 Oct
S Knock, G.P. 01 Oct
X Houston, D.J.M. 01 Oct
S Joll, S.M. 01 Oct
X Cooke, G.S. 01 Oct
E Barrett, D.L. 01 Oct
E Leaning, D.J. 01 Oct
E Rowan, N.A. 01 Oct
X Kerr, J. 01 Oct
E Hancock, R.T.A. 01 Oct
E Baggaley, J.A.L. 01 Oct
E Farrington, J.L. 01 Oct
S Wilman, D.M. 01 Oct
X Weightman, N.E. 01 Oct
E Dewsnap, M.D. 01 Oct
E Hooper, G.P. 01 Oct
E Cunnane, K.J. 01 Oct
X Green, T.C. 01 Oct
S Melville-Brown, M.G. 01 Oct
X Howe, J.P. 01 Oct
S Walker, D.W.A. 01 Oct
E Cox, D.J. 01 Oct
E Metcalf, R. 01 Oct
X Clink, A.D. 01 Oct
MS Phillips, I.M. 01 Oct

X West, A.B. 01 Oct
X Lintern, R.D. 01 Oct
E Walton, S.P. 01 Oct
X Jaggers, G.G. 01 Oct
S Taylor, I.K. 01 Oct
E Evans, S. 01 Oct
X Kerr, A.T.F. 01 Oct
MS Stead, R.A. 01 Oct
E Dunsby, N.B. 01 Oct
E Mitchell, S.D. 01 Oct
X Clarke, I.B. 01 Oct
X McKernan, J. 01 Oct
X Wilson, G.J. 01 Oct
E Phillips, A.R. 01 Oct
E Walsh, D.G. 01 Oct
X Roberts, P.S. 01 Oct
S Fearnley, A.T. 01 Oct
S Jackson, P.A. 01 Oct
X Smith, N.J. 01 Oct
E Stanham, C.M. 01 Oct
X Smallwood, R.I. 12 Oct
E Wroblewski, J.A. 31 Oct
X Moore, S.K. 01 Nov
X Noyce, V.R.A. 01 Nov
E Palmer, M.E. 01 Nov
X Curry, R.E. 01 Nov
E Chamberlain, N.R.L. 01 Nov
X Castle, A.S. 01 Dec
X Buckingham, G. 01 Dec
E Ford, J.D. 01 Dec
X Edey, M.J. 01 Dec
X Currie, D.G. 16 Dec
X Gritt, L.A. 17 Dec

2002

E Browning, R.S. 01 Jan
E Davies, L. 01 Jan
E Onyike, C.E. 01 Jan
X Pink, S.E. 01 Jan
E Goldsmith, D.T. 01 Jan
E Hutton, K.D. 21 Jan
E Lang, A.J.N. 01 Feb
E Barnett, A.C. 01 Feb
X Fryer, A.C. 01 Feb
S Higgs, T.A. 01 Feb
E Macleod, M.S. 01 Feb
X Hesling, G. 28 Feb
X Wuidart-Gray, S.R. 01 Mar
E Carroll, P.C. 01 Mar
E Clarke, R.W. 01 Mar
E Jose, S. 01 Mar
E Meek, C.S. 01 Mar

E Proctor, W.J.G. 01 Mar
X Stephen, B.M. 01 Mar
X Wallace, S.J. 01 Mar
S Brock, R.F. 01 Mar
E Bugg, K.J. 01 Mar
E Broadbent, P.S. 01 Mar
S Burns, A.C. 04 Mar
X Walker, S.P. 09 Mar
X Ritchie, J.N. 01 Apr
E Derby, B.D. 01 Apr
X Kohler, A.P. 01 Apr
E Cubbage, J. 01 Apr
S Goudge, S.D.P. 01 Apr
E Johnson, C.C.B. 01 Apr
E Kelly, H.C. 01 Apr
X Offord, M.R. 01 Apr
X Childs, J.R. 01 Apr
X Dineen, J.M.G. 01 Apr
S Moore, S.B. 01 Apr
X Hopper, I.M. 09 Apr
X Lynch, R.D.F. 16 Apr
X Brotherton, J.D. 16 Apr
E Flint, H.A. 01 May
E Mandley, P.J. 01 May
X Cull, I. 01 May
X Blackburn, S.J. 01 May
X Hygate, A.M. 01 May
X Maxwell, R. 01 May
X Bradley, M.T. 01 May
X Craig, J.A. 01 May
E Noakes, K.M. 01 May
S Porter, T.B. 01 May
X West, R.J. 01 Jun
X Osborn, C.G. 01 Jun
X Hempsell, A.M. 01 Jun
X Hurley, C. 01 Jun
X McGlory, S.J. 01 Jun
S Moorhouse, S.M. 01 Jun
X Stacey, A.M. 01 Jun
X Waterfield, S.J. 01 Jun
E Prendergast, S.A. 25 Jun
E Cook, M.C. 01 Jul
E Fraser, I.D. 01 Jul
X Russell, T.J. 01 Jul
E Doran, S.E. 01 Jul
X O'Nyons, Y.I. 01 Jul
X Raeburn, M. 01 Jul
X Jacques, M.J. 01 Jul
X Block, A.W.G. 01 Jul
X Gill, M.H. 01 Jul
E Mincher, D.J.F. 01 Jul

LIEUTENANT COMMANDERS

X Payne, P.J. 01 Jul
X Doyle, N.P. 01 Aug
X Goldstone, R.S. 01 Aug
S Nicholson, K.J. 01 Aug
S Dickson, J.I. 01 Aug
S Taylor, C.R. 01 Aug
X Carter, K.S. 27 Aug
E Rose, C.M. 30 Aug
E Marratt, R.J. 01 Sep
X Stephens, R.J. 01 Sep
E Choules, B. 01 Sep
X Aitken, A.J. 01 Sep
E MacDonald, A.J. 01 Sep
E Voyce, J.E. 01 Sep
X Reese, D.M. 01 Sep
X Roberts, M. 01 Oct
E Mason, L.C. 01 Oct
X Suckling, R.L. 01 Oct
X D'Arcy, P.A. 01 Oct
E Gutteridge, J.D.J. 01 Oct
E Thomas, A.L. 01 Oct
E Walker, M.J. 01 Oct
X Crimmen, D.J. 01 Oct
X Davison, G.J. 01 Oct
E Taylor, N.R. 01 Oct
X Gray, P.R. 01 Oct
X Richardson, G.L. 01 Oct
E Moores, C.P. 01 Oct
X Windebank, S.J. 01 Oct
X Slocombe, N.R. 01 Oct
X Richardson, P. 01 Oct
E Ball, S.J. 01 Oct
X Canning, C.P. 01 Oct
X Sparkes, S.N. 01 Oct
X Birse, G.J. 01 Oct
E Solly, M.M. 01 Oct
E Craib, A.G. 01 Oct
E Radbourne, N.I. 01 Oct
W Mayell, J.A. 01 Oct
X Wallis, J.S. 01 Oct
X Brian, N. 01 Oct
X Langrish, G.J. 01 Oct
X Gibbons, N.P. 01 Oct
E Cooke, M.J. 01 Oct
X McTear, N.J. 01 Oct
E Daly, J.M. 01 Oct
E Warr, R.F. 01 Oct
X Soar, G. 01 Oct
X Mould, P. 01 Oct
X Jacques, N.A. 01 Oct
X Sutton, R.M.J. 01 Oct
E McLachlan, M.P. 01 Oct
MS Dell, I.M. 01 Oct
X Harper, I.L. 01 Oct
E Lees, S.N. 01 Oct
E Ireland, J.M. 01 Oct
E Price, T.E. 01 Oct
S Arnold, A.S. 01 Oct
X Miller, G. 01 Oct
E Cheshire, T.E. 01 Oct
E Bradshaw, K.T. 01 Oct
E Wells, B.C. 01 Oct
E Wrenn, M.R.W. 01 Oct
E Wyld, A.W. 01 Oct
S Hart, N.L.W. 01 Oct
E Stephenson, K.J.M. 01 Oct
E Dunningham, S. 01 Oct
X Drodge, A.P.F. 01 Oct
E Snelling, P.D. 01 Oct
E Boyle, J.B. 01 Oct
S Bryant, D.J.G. 01 Oct
X Morgan, D.H. 01 Oct
X Sharpe, T.G. 01 Oct
X Barry, J.P. 01 Oct
X Pitcher, P.P. 01 Oct
E Doull, D.J.M. 01 Oct
X Lamb, A.G. 01 Oct
E Patterson, D. 01 Oct
X Pledger, D. 01 Oct
E McCarthy, S.J. 01 Oct
E Benn, S.W. 01 Oct
E Harwood, C.G. 01 Oct
E Jones, D.L. 01 Oct
X Seward, S.A. 01 Oct
MS Wagstaff, N. 01 Oct
S Ablett, E.L. 01 Oct
E Malkin, S.L. 01 Oct
E Shaughnessy, S.L. 01 Oct
E Keeley, S.P. 01 Oct
X Nash, P.D. 01 Oct
E Holden, P.A. 01 Oct
E Reed, J.C. 01 Oct
X Horne, J.R. 01 Oct
S Dean, J.R. 01 Oct
X Bassett, D.A. 01 Oct
X Rackham, A.D.H. 01 Oct
X Byrne, T.M. 01 Oct
X Marsh, M.P.A. 01 Oct
X Morrison, P. 01 Oct
E Bailey, J.J. 01 Oct
X Smith, M.D. 01 Oct
S Hanson, M.N. 01 Oct
X Capes, S.G. 01 Oct
MS Bradford, T.H.C. 01 Oct
X Easton, D.W. 01 Oct
MS Walton, A.P. 01 Oct
X Smith, A.B.D. 01 Oct
S Scandling, R.J. 01 Oct
S Harris, R.P. 01 Oct
S Barratt, S.M. 01 Oct
S Darlow, P.R. 01 Oct
X Dunne, M.G. 01 Oct
E Weaver, N. 01 Oct
S Bower, J.W. 01 Oct
X Jones, A.E. 01 Nov
X Brown, S.D. 01 Nov
E Cummings, D.J. 01 Nov
E Bird, M.G.J. 01 Nov
X Ripley, B.E. 01 Nov
S White, J.E. 01 Nov
X Kirkwood, T.A.H. 01 Nov
S Murdoch, A.P. 01 Nov
X Sillers, B. 01 Dec
X Brodie, R.W.J. 01 Dec
E Scopes, D. 01 Dec
S Titmuss, J.F. 01 Dec
E Trott, E.A. 01 Dec

2003

E Frost, M.A. 01 Jan
X Braithwaite, J.S. 01 Jan
X Lunn, T.R. 01 Jan
X Allfree, J. 01 Jan
X Jones, M.D. 01 Jan
E Nelson, L.M. 01 Jan
X Laverty, R.E. 01 Feb
X Gray, Y.M. 01 Feb
X Bowden, M.T.E. 01 Feb
E Boyes, M.R. 01 Feb
S Dutton, A.C. 01 Feb
E Gair, S.D.H. 01 Feb
X Maynard, C.I. 01 Feb
X Wiseman, I.C. 01 Feb
X Borbone, N. 01 Feb
X Cooke, J.E. 01 Feb
X Rogers, J.C.E. 01 Mar
E Adams, R.J. 01 Mar
X Foulis, N.D.A. 01 Mar
S Gennard, A. 01 Mar
X Tanner, R.C. 01 Mar
E Burvill, J.P. 01 Mar
E Coope, P.J. 01 Mar
X Goulding, J.P. 01 Mar
E Jennings, W. 01 Mar

LIEUTENANT COMMANDERS

E	Large, S.A.	01 Mar
E	Phillips, J.N.	01 Mar
E	Stagg, A.R.	01 Mar
X	Thompson, M.G.	01 Mar
S	Wales, B.D.	01 Mar
X	Watson, I.	01 Mar
X	Skelley, A.N.M.	01 Mar
X	Herriman, J.A.	01 Apr
E	Rawson, S.M.	01 Apr
X	Foster, T.G.	01 Apr
X	Lovatt, G.J.	01 Apr
X	Stride, J.C.	01 Apr
E	Bowman, R.J.	01 Apr
X	Oliver, G.	01 May
E	Taylor, A.L.	01 May
E	Hardiman, N.A.	01 May
X	Whitfield, R.M.P.	01 May
X	Byron, J.D.	01 May
E	Coulthard, A.J.	11 May
E	Durham, P.C.L.	18 May
X	Peppe, A.G.	01 Jun
X	Asquith, S.P.	01 Jun
X	Euden, C.P.	01 Jun
E	Sharkey, E.R.	01 Jun
X	Ward, A.J.	01 Jun
X	Lee, N.D.	16 Jun
X	Lynn, I.H.	30 Jun
X	Leaver, C.E.L.	01 Jul
X	McKnight, D.J.S.	01 Jul
E	May, S.C.	01 Jul
X	Beacham, P.R.	01 Jul
E	Edward, G.J.	01 Jul
E	Lincoln, K.J.	01 Jul
X	Ruddock, G.W.D.	01 Jul
E	Ryan, N.	01 Jul
X	Smith, R.D.	01 Jul
E	Paulson, R.B.	01 Aug
E	Sandle, N.D.	01 Aug
X	Syrett, M.E.	01 Aug
X	Cahill, K.A.	01 Aug
E	Hickson, M.S.H.	01 Aug
E	Letts, A.J.	01 Aug
S	Russell, G.S.	01 Aug
E	Storey, C.L.	01 Aug
E	Sweeney, K.P.M.	01 Aug
E	Veal, A.E.	01 Aug
X	Tregunna, G.A.	08 Aug
E	Jones, G.D.	01 Sep
E	Edwards, A.G.	01 Sep
X	McWilliams, J.E.	01 Sep
E	Stowell, R.B.M.	01 Sep
E	Collins, S.J.	01 Oct
X	Cobbett, J.F.	01 Oct
X	Bhattacharya, D.	01 Oct
X	Crockatt, S.R.J.	01 Oct
E	Vincent, A.	01 Oct
X	Harrison, P.D.	01 Oct
E	Williams, P.M.	01 Oct
X	Davidson, N.R.	01 Oct
X	Whitfield, J.A.	01 Oct
X	Tetley, M.	01 Oct
X	Hayward, G.	01 Oct
X	Ellwood, P.G.	01 Oct
X	Lindsay, D.J.	01 Oct
X	Logan, J.M.	01 Oct
E	Roberts, I.G.	01 Oct
E	Donovan, P.	01 Oct
X	Neal, S.M.	01 Oct
X	Shrimpton, M.W.	01 Oct
E	Plackett, A.J.	01 Oct
X	Bird, J.M.	01 Oct
E	Wilkins, R.R.	01 Oct
E	Hunt, P.E.R.D.	01 Oct
X	Lambert, A.	01 Oct
E	Cheseldine, D.	01 Oct
S	Fogell, A.D.	01 Oct
X	Woodard, J.R.A.	01 Oct
X	Haigh, A.J.	01 Oct
W	Green, J.L.	01 Oct
E	Higson, B.L.	01 Oct
X	Mercer, D.C.	01 Oct
E	Bedelle, S.J.	01 Oct
E	MacDougall, S.J.	01 Oct
E	Seaman, P.J.	01 Oct
MS	Chilcott, P.L.H.	01 Oct
X	Clements, S.J.	01 Oct
X	Payne, M.J.	01 Oct
E	Byrne, A.C.	01 Oct
E	McQueen, J.B.	01 Oct
X	Crascall, S.J.	01 Oct
E	Butler, L.P.	01 Oct
S	Johnson, M.D.	01 Oct
E	Kies, L.N.	01 Oct
X	Haywood, P.J.	01 Oct
X	Allen, D.J.K.	01 Oct
X	Clarke, D.	01 Oct
X	Mailes, I.R.A.	01 Oct
X	Stembridge, D.P.T.	01 Oct
E	Wicking, G.S.	01 Oct
S	Park, B.C.	01 Oct
X	Hunt, S.C.	01 Oct
E	Hamilton, S.M.	01 Oct
X	Hopkins, S.D.	01 Oct
MS	Howells, M.J.	01 Oct
E	Dawson, N.J.F.	01 Oct
E	Beautyman, A.J.	01 Oct
X	Vartan, M.R.	01 Oct
X	Woolhead, A.L.	01 Oct
E	Bryce, N.A.	01 Oct
E	Midmore, M.J.	01 Oct
E	Craggs, S.	01 Oct
X	Elston, A.J.	01 Oct
E	Deakin, J.	01 Oct
E	Kellett, A.	01 Oct
E	Dawson, A.J.	01 Oct
E	Eddie, A.G.W.	01 Oct
E	Henderson, P.P.	01 Oct
E	Knight, K.J.	01 Oct
X	Gold, J.W.	01 Oct
E	Barrows, D.M.	01 Oct
E	Knight, R.H.	01 Oct
E	Dalton, F.J.	01 Oct
X	Cunningham, N.J.W.	01 Oct
E	Palmer, J.	01 Oct
E	Harrington, J.B.H.	01 Oct
E	O'Neill, P.J.	01 Oct
X	Bosley, B.D.	01 Oct
X	Irons, R.C.S.	01 Oct
S	Matthews, P.K.	01 Oct
X	Wheeler, N.J.	01 Oct
X	Jardine, D.S.	01 Oct
X	Neild, T.	01 Oct
E	Mallen, D.J.	01 Oct
X	Lawson, G.J.	01 Oct
X	Woodrow, K.J.	01 Oct
S	Bollen, J.M.	01 Oct
E	Thompson, M.J.	01 Oct
X	Rimington, A.K.	01 Oct
X	Stride, J.A.	01 Oct
E	Stubbs, M.A.	01 Oct
X	Hunt, F.B.G.	01 Oct
X	Clay, J.C.	01 Oct
S	Nelson, V.	01 Oct
X	Backus, R.I.K.	01 Oct
E	Barrows, S.M.	01 Oct
X	Walker, M.J.	01 Oct
E	Fraser, P.	01 Oct
X	Riggall, A.D.	01 Oct
S	Evans, C.A.	01 Oct
E	Grant, D.J.	01 Oct
E	King, G.C.	01 Oct
X	Hourigan, M.P.	01 Oct
E	Leach, S.J.	01 Oct

LIEUTENANT COMMANDERS

MS Miller, D.E. ....01 Oct
X Richards, F.C. ....01 Oct
S Percival, F. ....01 Oct
E Day, S.N. ....01 Oct
S Gullett, H.R. ....01 Oct
E Fulford, R.N. ....01 Oct
X Clark, A.S. ....01 Oct
MS Finn, D.W. ....01 Oct
X Lewis, K.A. ....01 Oct
X McGrane, R.J. ....01 Oct
S Moores, J. ....01 Oct
E Murchie, A.D. ....01 Oct
X Ellison, T.G. ....01 Oct
E Turle, P.J. ....01 Oct
X Collins, M.C. ....01 Oct
X McEvoy, L.P. ....01 Oct
S Morris, K.I. ....01 Oct
S Strudwick, R. ....01 Oct
X Taylor, J.P. ....01 Oct
X Wilson, A.J. ....01 Oct
E Fitzgerald, C. ....01 Oct
X Holloway, S.A. ....01 Oct
S Noon, D. ....01 Oct
S Stephenson, P.G. ....01 Oct
X Lea, S.A.P. ....01 Nov
X Ley, A.B. ....01 Nov
X Burstow, N.S. ....01 Nov
X Ingram, G.J. ....01 Dec
X Rees, R.T. ....01 Dec
X Foreman, S.L. ....24 Dec

2004

E Beadnell, R.M. ....01 Jan
E Rostron, D.W. ....01 Jan
E Pakes, D.T. ....01 Jan
E Hendrickx, C.J. ....01 Jan
E Field, C.R.H. ....01 Jan
E Perkins, R.J. ....01 Jan
X Brown, A.P. ....01 Feb
X Atkinson, G.C. ....01 Feb
X Dale, A. ....01 Feb
E Powles, D.A. ....01 Feb
S MacKay, A.C. ....01 Feb
X Moorhouse, S.M.R. ....01 Feb
X Peters, W.R. ....01 Mar
X Clark, M.H. ....01 Mar
E Ling, C. ....01 Mar
X Rae, D.G. ....01 Mar
E Screaton, R.M. ....01 Mar
E Stiven, T.D. ....01 Mar
E Lewis, A.J. ....01 Mar
X Lockett, D.J. ....01 Apr
X Readwin, R.R. ....01 Apr
X Shepherd, M.P. ....01 Apr
X Battrick, R.R. ....01 Apr
X Hains, J. ....01 Apr
X Laughton, P. ....01 Apr
E Robertshaw, I.W. ....01 Apr
E Spooner, R.S. ....01 Apr
X Hammond, P.J. ....01 May
E Bell, J.M. ....01 May
E Blair, G.J.L. ....01 May
E Parry, M.R.R. ....01 May
E Smith, M.J. ....01 May
E York, G.R.J. ....01 May
E Flynn, A. ....01 May
X Mowatt, P. ....01 May
X Steadman, R.P. ....01 May
X Griffiths, R.H. ....01 Jun
E Ubhi, W.G. ....01 Jun
E Hedgecox, D.C. ....01 Jun
E Lyons, M.J. ....01 Jun
E Rowlands, A.R. ....01 Jun
X Sturdy, C.C.M. ....01 Jun
E Young, C.J. ....18 Jun
X May, C. ....01 Jul
X Atkinson, R.J. ....01 Jul
E Fraser, H.L. ....01 Jul
E Hope, M.R. ....01 Jul
E Jones, D.M. ....01 Jul
X Parrott, J.P. ....01 Jul
E Thorp, B.T. ....01 Jul
X Tyler, J.C. ....01 Jul
X Dennis, P.E. ....01 Jul
E Woodbridge, R.G. ....01 Aug
E McNamara, I.M. ....01 Aug
X Stroude, P.A. ....01 Aug
E Murphy, S.M. ....01 Aug
X Patterson, J.D. ....01 Aug
X Moules, M.A.J. ....01 Aug
X McGuire, J. ....24 Aug
E Harding, C.S. ....01 Sep
E McCombe, J. ....01 Sep
E Wright, D.I. ....01 Sep
E Puxley, M.E. ....01 Sep
X Read, A.J. ....01 Oct
X Bance, N.D. ....01 Oct
E Forward, D.J. ....01 Oct
X Imrie, P.B. ....01 Oct
E Diver, P.H. ....01 Oct
X Allen, P.M. ....01 Oct
X McIntyre, A.W. ....01 Oct
X Morrell, A.J. ....01 Oct
X Hilson, S.M. ....01 Oct
X Hutton, G. ....01 Oct
X Tidball, I.C. ....01 Oct
X Quinn, S.A. ....01 Oct
E Dyer, G.R. ....01 Oct
E Mitchell, P. ....01 Oct
X King, S.J. ....01 Oct
X Rasor, A.M. ....01 Oct
X Allen, L.B. ....01 Oct
E Dickens, D.S. ....01 Oct
S Cogan, R.E.C. ....01 Oct
X Julian, T.M. ....01 Oct
E Sargent, P.M. ....01 Oct
X Mitchell, M. ....01 Oct
E Rowe, A.J. ....01 Oct
X MacNeil, S.W. ....01 Oct
X Simpson, C.C. ....01 Oct
X Milton, G.P. ....01 Oct
X Stock, C.M. ....01 Oct
X Massey, P. ....01 Oct
E Ellis, J.P. ....01 Oct
X Bolton, S.J. ....01 Oct
X Scott, M.R. ....01 Oct
X Tite, A.D. ....01 Oct
X Chadfield, L.J. ....01 Oct
S Lewins, G. ....01 Oct
X Hoare, P.J.E. ....01 Oct
S Sellars, S.J. ....01 Oct
E Skelton, J.S. ....01 Oct
X Kirkham, S.P. ....01 Oct
E Hodge, C.M. ....01 Oct
E Ajala, A.R.A. ....01 Oct
X Mullen, J.J. ....01 Oct
E Ford, G.R. ....01 Oct
E White, R.L. ....01 Oct
X Russell, N.A.D. ....01 Oct
X Soul, N.J. ....01 Oct
E Carpenter, B.H. ....01 Oct
E Lovering, T.T.A. ....01 Oct
E Cragg, R.D. ....01 Oct
E Abbott, D.A. ....01 Oct
X Atkinson, C.P. ....01 Oct
E Youp, A.T. ....01 Oct
X Noyce, R.G. ....01 Oct
X Doran, I.A.G. ....01 Oct
MS Follington, D.C. ....01 Oct
S Goldsworthy, E.T. ....01 Oct
X Lucocq, N.J. ....01 Oct
X Armstrong, S.T. ....01 Oct
E Le Gassick, P.J. ....01 Oct
E Vincent, D. ....01 Oct

LIEUTENANT COMMANDERS

X Rhodes, M.J. .... 01 Oct
X Harrison, R.S. .... 01 Oct
X Newton, J.L. .... 01 Oct
X Jones, P.D. .... 01 Oct
X Knight, J.D. .... 01 Oct
E Pinder, C.D. .... 01 Oct
E Watson, C.R. .... 01 Oct
X Smith, D.L. .... 01 Oct
S Woodard, N.A. .... 01 Oct
X Crabb, A.J. .... 01 Oct
MS Blocke, A.D. .... 01 Oct
S Carter, S.P. .... 01 Oct
E Potts, G. .... 01 Oct
E McCloskey, I.M. .... 01 Oct
X Monk, S.R. .... 01 Oct
E Sanderson, L.D. .... 01 Oct
E Haworth, J.H.T. .... 01 Oct
X Stuart, E.E.A. .... 01 Oct
X Dickins, B.R. .... 01 Oct
X Essenhigh, A.N.P. .... 01 Oct
E Ashworth, H.J. .... 01 Oct
X Grieve, L.H. .... 01 Oct
E Smith, C.J.H. .... 01 Oct
S Dow, C.S. .... 01 Oct
X Harper, P.R. .... 01 Oct
E Jefferson, T.S. .... 01 Oct
E Miller, M.C. .... 01 Oct
E Cain, C.W. .... 01 Oct
E Ridge, M.H. .... 01 Oct
E Wildin, A. .... 01 Oct
E Mealing, D.W. .... 01 Oct
X Conway, M.J. .... 01 Oct
MS McGunigall, R.J. .... 01 Oct
S Exworthy, D.A.G. .... 01 Oct
S Vogel, L.D. .... 01 Oct
E Cattroll, D. .... 01 Oct
E Shuttleworth, S. .... 01 Oct
E Sargent, L.M. .... 01 Oct
S Welch, K.A. .... 01 Oct
E Richards, J.I.H. .... 01 Oct
S Cox, M.B. .... 01 Oct
X Barraclough, C.D. .... 01 Oct
X Corkett, K.S. .... 01 Oct
E Butler, I.A. .... 01 Oct
S Hendy, R. .... 01 Oct
X Pedre, R.G. .... 01 Oct
S Bull, C.V.R. .... 01 Oct
S Carrigan, J.A. .... 01 Oct
E Benstead, N.W.J. .... 01 Oct
X Higham, S.W.J.A. .... 01 Oct
S Watson, S.B.C .... 01 Oct
E Curtis, D. .... 01 Oct
E Henderson, R.J. .... 01 Oct
S Vollentine, L. .... 01 Oct
S Thomas, D.J. .... 01 Oct
S Prest, N.A. .... 01 Oct
MS Manwaring, R.G. .... 01 Oct
S Reed, N. .... 01 Oct
MS Smith, M.P. .... 01 Oct
E Brunell, P.J. .... 01 Oct
E Sibley, A.K. .... 01 Oct
E Slimmon, K.W. .... 01 Oct
X Trubshaw, C. .... 01 Oct
E Purvis, D.M. .... 16 Oct
E Gordon, N.L. .... 01 Nov
X Balletta, R.J. .... 01 Nov
X McBratney, J.A.G. .... 01 Nov
X Walsh, K.M. .... 01 Nov
W Elborn, T.K. .... 01 Dec
W McBain, M.S. .... 01 Dec
E Mullins, A.D. .... 01 Dec
X Wood, M.L. .... 01 Dec
X Mitchell, C.D. .... 01 Dec
E Ankah, G.K.E. .... 01 Dec
E Brown, A.M. .... 01 Dec
S Reed, D.K. .... 01 Dec
E Whitehouse, N.R. .... 01 Dec

2005

E Boston, J. .... 01 Jan
E Lewis, S.J. .... 01 Jan
X Miles, R.L. .... 01 Jan
X Ottewell, P.S. .... 01 Jan
X Wood, C.R. .... 01 Jan
E Cleminson, M.D. .... 01 Feb
E Kendrick, A.M. .... 01 Feb
X Robertson Gopffarth, A.A.J. .. 01 Feb
E Haddow, T.R. .... 01 Mar
X Butterworth, P.G. .... 01 Mar
E McHugh, R.H. .... 01 Mar
E Thorne, D.J. .... 01 Mar
X Tilden, P.J.E. .... 01 Mar
S Wells, M.P. .... 01 Mar
X Rackham, K.L.M. .... 01 Mar
X Small, R.J. .... 01 Mar
X Arden, V.G. .... 15 Mar
E Rae, A.L. .... 01 Apr
E Foreman, S.M. .... 01 Apr
E Boxall, P. .... 01 Apr
X Brooks, G.C.G. .... 01 Apr
X Hounsom, T.R. .... 01 Apr
X Lumsden, P.I. .... 01 Apr
E Nicoll, A.J. .... 01 Apr
X Jacques, K.M. .... 01 May
X Oakley, S.E. .... 01 May
E Kirk, A.C. .... 01 May

LIEUTENANTS

1982

E Moore, M.R. .... 29 Oct

1984

E Maskell-Bott, J.M. .... 16 Feb

1985

E Halls, B.C. .... 18 Oct
E Schillemore, P.C. .... 18 Oct

1986

E Miller, J.C. .... 17 Oct

1987

X Carne, R.J.P. .... 16 May
E Foubister, R. .... 18 Jun
X Tribe, J.D. .... 16 Oct

1988

E Fisher, R. .... 10 Jun
E White, S.P. .... 10 Jun

1989

E Thomas, M.G. .... 17 Feb
X Boyes, R.A. .... 01 Mar
E Griffiths, A.R. .... 09 Jun
X Swann, J.I. .... 28 Jul
E Lusted, R.P. .... 13 Oct

1990

E Smart, S.J. .... 23 Feb
E Young, K.H. .... 23 Feb
E Allen, D.P. .... 15 Jun
E Davies, G.P. .... 15 Jun
X Davies, A.J.A. .... 01 Aug

LIEUTENANTS

1991

X Eldridge, T.J. ....01 Apr
X Clucas, P.R. ....04 Apr
X May-Clingo, M.S.............04 Apr
E Gilliland, S.S. .... 13 Jun
X Smith, D.T...................... 16 Jun
X Gladston, S.A. .... 01 Jul
X Christmas, S.P. ....16 Aug
X Carnell, G.J.....................01 Sep
X Haworth, C.L.N..............01 Sep
X Milne, P.B........................16 Sep
E Bissett, R.W. ....17 Oct
S Gill, S.C. .... 12 Dec

1992

E Ritsperis, A. .... 01 Jan
X Moulton, S.J. .... 01 Jan
X Poole, T.J. .... 16 Jan
X Thompson, A.R..............01 Feb
X Hatchard, J.P. ....04 Mar
X Murphy, D.A...................01 Apr
X Milligan, R.J.C................16 Apr
X Lawrance, G.M. ....16 May
X Radford, A.J....................01 Jun
E Ellis, D.F. .... 15 Jul
X Jameson, R.M. .... 16 Jul
X Jaques, D.A. ....16 Aug
E Parry, R.J.........................16 Oct
S MacAskill, C.H. .... 11 Dec
X Steele, T.G. .... 11 Dec

1993

E Tomkins, A.B...................19 Feb
E Wooding, G.A. ....19 Feb
E McCaughey, V.J. ....01 Mar
X Darwent, S.A. ....01 Mar
X Gates, N.S. .... 16 Mar
X Bramwell, J.G. ....01 Apr
X Millen, S.C.W..................01 Apr
X Moreby, M.F...................02 Apr
X Harlow, S.R....................01 May
X Gamble, P. ....15 May
X Loane, M.M................... 01 Jun
X White, S.H.W................. 16 Jun
X Morris, A.M. .... 01 Jul
X Mudge, A.M. .... 01 Jul
X Rodgers, D....................... 01 Jul
X Brosnan, M.A. .... 16 Jul
X Norris, G.P....................... 16 Jul
X Hawkes, J.D.................... 23 Jul
E Evison, T. .... 27 Jul
X Cox, S.A.J. ....16 Aug
X Choat, J.H. ....16 Aug
X Willing, N.P. ....16 Aug
X Duncan, C.J. ....01 Sep
X Elwell-Deighton, D.C. .....16 Sep
X Rutherford, K.J. ....01 Oct
E Bowness, P. .... 15 Oct
E Burrows, J.C. .... 15 Oct
X May, P.J..........................29 Oct
X Perry, R.J. .... 01 Nov
X Gamble, N. .... 01 Nov
E Stevenson, J.P. .... 01 Nov
X MacFarlane, I.S.D. .... 01 Nov
X Polding, M. .... 01 Nov
X Simpson, D.K. .... 16 Nov
X Marquis, A.C. .... 01 Dec
X Bing, N.A. .... 16 Dec
X Spence, R.G. .... 16 Dec
X Coyne, J.D. .... 17 Dec
X Wardle, M. .... 17 Dec
S Wyatt, C. .... 17 Dec

1994

X Campbell, P.R. .... 01 Jan
X Hitchings, D.L. .... 01 Jan
X Gotke, C.T. .... 16 Jan
X Buckley, D.D.G...............01 Feb
X Phipps, T.A......................01 Feb
X Bunney, G.J.....................01 Feb
X Taylor, R.J. ....16 Feb
E Brothers, A.H.G. ....18 Feb
E Buckeridge, V.W.............18 Feb
X Bryson, S.A. ....01 Mar
X Hinchcliffe, A. ....01 Mar
X Knight, A.C.F. ....01 Mar
X Corbett, T.J. ....01 Apr
X Barnes, P.A.L. ....01 Apr
E Nicholas, S.P...................01 Apr
S Austen, R.M. ....08 Apr
X Lister, S. ....08 Apr
X Evans, G.B. ....01 May
X Townsend, G.P. ....01 May
X Kennington, L.A. ....01 May
X Matthews, J. ....16 May
X Hedworth, A.J. ....01 Jun
E Page, T.A. .... 10 Jun
X Naylor, A.J. .... 16 Jun
X Oakes, I.J. .... 16 Jun
X Sheils, D.E.T. .... 16 Jul
X Oatley, T.P. .... 16 Jul
X Lee, P.M. .... 16 Jul
X Wingfield, M.J. .... 16 Jul
X Laycock, A. .... 16 Jul
X Wright, D.A. .... 29 Jul
X Garner, S.M. ....01 Aug
E Scott, R.A. ....01 Aug
E Saunders, J.M. ....01 Sep
X Cottee, B.R.J...................01 Sep
X McDonald, N. ....01 Sep
X Mutch, J.R. ....01 Sep
E Balcombe, J.S. ....01 Sep
X Webber, J.P. ....01 Sep
X Downing, I.M. ....16 Sep
X Ling, J.W.L. ....16 Sep
X Penprase, J.M. ....01 Oct
X Lord, R.J. ....01 Oct
X Lamont, N.J. ....06 Oct
X Brayson, M. ....16 Oct
X Ellerton, P........................16 Oct
X Roberts, M.A. .... 01 Nov
X Webster, A.P. .... 01 Nov
X Peachey, R.M. .... 01 Nov
X Allison, G....................... 16 Nov
X Roster, S.P. .... 16 Nov
X Bratby, S.P. .... 16 Nov
X Young, R. .... 01 Dec
X Hardy, L.B. .... 16 Dec

1995

E Jordan, C. .... 01 Jan
E Rogers, P.S. .... 01 Jan
X Mills, S.D.G.................... 01 Jan
X Jones, M.D. .... 16 Jan
X Satterthwaite, B.J............01 Feb
E Langrill, T.J. ....01 Feb
X McCutcheon, G. ....01 Feb
X Barber, C.J.H...................01 Feb
X Johnson, A.R. ....16 Feb
E Fallowfield, J.P................24 Feb
E O'Brien, I.P. ....24 Feb
X Bainbridge, S.D. ....01 Mar
X Gray, J.N.S. ....01 Apr
X Marten, A.D. ....01 Apr
X Humphries, J.E. ....01 Apr
X Stratford, P.J. ....01 Apr
X Reid, M.R........................01 Apr
X McLennan, A. ....01 Apr
E Panic, A. ....15 Apr
X Kelynack, M.T. ....16 Apr
X Cooke-Priest, N.C.R. ......01 May
X Inge, D.J. ....01 May
X Stubbs, I. ....16 May
X Woolsey, K.E.K...............16 May
X Turner, D.N. .... 01 Jun
X Watson, A.H. ....01 Jun

LIEUTENANTS

E	Wilson, J.A.	15 Jun
X	Day, M.K.	15 Jun
X	McCowan, D.J.	16 Jun
X	May, J.W.	01 Jul
X	Parrock, N.G.	01 Jul
X	Deavin, M.J.	01 Jul
X	Bishop, G.C.	27 Jul
X	Higgins, A.J.	01 Aug
X	Yule, M.J.C.	01 Aug
X	Phillips, M.B.	16 Aug
E	Blow, P.T.	01 Sep
E	Mehta, K.L.	01 Sep
E	Proffitt Burnham, J.M.	01 Sep
E	Hambly, B.J.	01 Sep
E	Cullen, N.L.	01 Sep
X	Lanni, M.N.	01 Sep
X	Hayton, S.R.C.	05 Sep
E	Brown, P.A.	07 Sep
X	Baxter, J.C.	27 Sep
E	Welsh, J.	15 Oct
E	Sitton, J.B.	01 Nov
E	Parker, T.S.	01 Nov
X	Chick, N.S.	16 Nov
E	Lee, S.Y.L.	01 Dec
X	Marriott, N.K.	01 Dec
X	Tacey, R.H.	01 Dec
X	West, D.C.	01 Dec
X	Evans, D.A.	20 Dec

1996

E	Collins, T.L.	01 Jan
E	Harrison, T.I.	01 Jan
E	Heighway, M.R.	01 Jan
E	Young, N.A.	01 Jan
X	Okukenu, D.	01 Jan
W	Swan, W.	19 Jan
S	Trinder, S.J.	30 Jan
X	Officer, R.L.	01 Feb
X	Wookey, M.	01 Feb
X	Wilkinson, M.F.	01 Feb
X	Watts, J.N.	01 Feb
X	Segebarth, R.A.	16 Feb
X	Thomas, S.M.	16 Feb
E	Edson, M.A.	22 Feb
E	Hyland, R.A.	22 Feb
X	Packham, C.N.R.	01 Mar
E	Townsend, D.J.	01 Mar
MS	Taylor, N.A.	06 Mar
X	Simms, D.M.	16 Mar
X	Flintham, J.E.	16 Mar
X	Long, M.S.	01 Apr
X	Brailey, I.S.F.	04 Apr
X	Ford, A.J.	04 Apr
X	Campbell, I.A.	16 Apr
X	Fraser, I.E.	16 Apr
E	Evans, P.C.	01 May
X	MacColl, A.A.J.	01 May
E	Marjoram, G.K.	01 May
E	Taylor, I.J.	05 May
X	Robley, W.F.	01 Jun
E	Nimmons, P.	01 Jun
X	Strathie, G.S.	01 Jun
X	Criddle, G.D.J.	01 Jun
X	Fisher, R.J.	01 Jun
X	Gilmore, M.P.	01 Jun
E	Hutchinson, P.	14 Jun
E	Rendell, D.J.	14 Jun
E	Riley, G.A.	14 Jun
X	Vorley, S.W.	15 Jun
X	Wiseman, N.C.	16 Jun
X	Hutchins, T.S.	16 Jun
X	Platt, J.H.	16 Jun
X	Pullan, K.J.	29 Jun
E	Deeks, P.J.	01 Jul
X	Fox, T.M.	01 Jul
X	Spillane, P.W.	01 Jul
X	Wyness, R.S.	01 Jul
X	Pickering, I.J.	01 Jul
X	Davies, H.G.A.	01 Jul
X	Church, S.C.	16 Jul
X	Forbes, P.T.	16 Jul
X	Brember, P.B.	25 Jul
X	Dale, N.R.	25 Jul
X	Smith, S.R.F.	28 Jul
E	Clare, K.	29 Jul
X	Abel, N.P.	16 Aug
X	Clarke, R.J.	16 Aug
X	Hall, D.	16 Aug
X	Whitlum, A.C.	16 Aug
X	Everitt, T.W.	19 Aug
E	Edwards, J.	01 Sep
E	Kelly, G.J.	01 Sep
W	Dobie, F.E.	01 Sep
X	Terry, N.P.	01 Sep
X	Enever, S.A.	01 Sep
X	Williams, R.J.S.	01 Sep
X	Campbell, M.A.M.	01 Sep
X	Hindmarch, S.A.	01 Sep
X	Raeburn, C.	01 Sep
E	Bottomley, S.	06 Sep
E	Donnelly, S.	17 Sep
X	Parr, M.J.E.	01 Oct
X	Donegan, C.L.	01 Oct
X	Hill, A.J.	01 Oct
X	Bonnar, S.M.	01 Nov
E	Davis, S.R.	01 Nov
E	Gothard, A.M.	01 Nov
X	Webber, K.J.	01 Nov
X	Bradley, R.L.	01 Nov
X	Whitlum, S.	01 Nov
X	Ollerton, J.C.	16 Nov
E	Drummond, H.	24 Nov
X	Donworth, D.M.J.	01 Dec
X	Hayden, T.W.	01 Dec

1997

E	Collins, D.R.	01 Jan
E	Dennis, M.J.	01 Jan
E	Dick, C.M.	01 Jan
E	Nelson, P.M.	01 Jan
E	Taylor, C.S.	01 Jan
X	Santrian, K.	01 Jan
E	Hunwicks, S.E.	01 Jan
X	Clague, J.J.	15 Jan
X	Johnson, S.R.D.	16 Jan
E	Smith, K.D.	01 Feb
X	Codd, J.S.	01 Feb
X	Foster, N.P.	01 Feb
E	Kingdom, M.A.	01 Feb
S	Nathanson, H.	01 Feb
X	Thomsen-Rayner, L.L.	01 Feb
E	Collins, S.A.	07 Feb
E	McTaggart, D.A.	07 Feb
E	Sheldon, M.L.	07 Feb
X	Owen, G.	16 Feb
E	Thomson, P.D.	24 Feb
X	Barlow, M.J.	01 Mar
E	Read, P.S.	01 Mar
S	Hefford, C.J.	01 Mar
X	Jackson, I.	01 Mar
X	Mason, D.J.	01 Mar
X	Philip, A.D.	01 Mar
S	Quantrill, S.W.	01 Mar
S	Stockbridge, A.J.	01 Mar
X	Compain, C.H.	21 Mar
E	Cumming, R.A.	01 Apr
X	Bernard, R.A.	01 Apr
X	Green, I.A.	01 Apr
X	Alcindor, D.J.	01 Apr
X	Bennetts, N.	03 Apr
X	Guiver, P.	03 Apr
X	Norford, M.A.	03 Apr
X	Stretton, D.G.	03 Apr
X	Tomlinson, D.C.	03 Apr
E	Brooks, K.M.L.	06 Apr

LIEUTENANTS

X Heaney, M.J. ....16 Apr
E Bennett, D.P. ....01 May
E McGinley, C.T. ....01 May
X Adams, P.N.E. ....01 May
E Adams, G. ....01 May
E Straughan, S.R. ....01 May
E Tracey, A.D. ....01 May
X Jordan, E.L. ....01 May
X Frean, J.P. ....16 May
X Lewis, B.C. ....16 May
E Briggs, M.D. ....01 Jun
S Dobbins, S.J. ....01 Jun
E Lee, W. ....01 Jun
E McCallum, N.R. ....01 Jun
E Sayer, J.M. ....01 Jun
E Burley, M.R. ....01 Jun
E Edwards, J.E. ....01 Jun
X Gamble, S.B. ....01 Jun
E Harvey, B. ....01 Jun
X Leighton, M.R. ....01 Jun
E O'Shaughnessy, D.J. ....01 Jun
S Porter, D.L. ....01 Jun
X Saunders, C.E.M. ....01 Jun
E Finnie, H.M. ....13 Jun
E Jones, M.A. ....13 Jun
E Boyes, G.A. ....01 Jul
E White, K.F. ....01 Jul
X Fitzpatrick, J.A.J. ....01 Jul
X Baines, A.R. ....01 Jul
X McKee, H.M. ....01 Jul
E Patterson, S.D. ....01 Jul
X Pedler, M.D. ....01 Jul
E Saward, J.R.E. ....01 Jul
E Selway, M.A. ....01 Jul
X Wilson, J. ....01 Jul
E Wood, A.G. ....01 Jul
X Boughton, T.F. ....01 Jul
X Birrell, G.C. ....01 Jul
X Canale, A.J. ....01 Jul
X Hughes, S.M. ....16 Jul
E Driscoll, R. ....22 Jul
X McDermott, P.A. ....24 Jul
X Potter, D.J. ....24 Jul
X Rowan, M.E. ....24 Jul
X Southwell, N.P. ....24 Jul
X Vowles, M.J. ....24 Jul
X Whild, D.J. ....24 Jul
X Young, J.N. ....24 Jul
E Mallabone, J.J.K. ....01 Aug
X Chawira, D.N. ....01 Aug
E Evans, M.E. ....01 Aug
X Spinks, D.W. ....01 Aug
X Mennecke-Jappy, G.W.G. 01 Aug
X Northover, A.F. ....01 Aug
E Spiller, S.N. ....01 Aug
E Brutton, J.H. ....01 Aug
X Holder, J.M. ....01 Aug
S Robb, M.E. ....01 Aug
S Pring, S.J. ....14 Aug
X Fuller, C.E. ....16 Aug
X Scott, M. ....16 Aug
E Clark, S.R. ....01 Sep
E Pettigrew, T.R. ....01 Sep
E Ashby, K.J. ....01 Sep
E Strange, S.P. ....01 Sep
E Elsey, D.J. ....01 Sep
X Ward, S. ....01 Sep
S Hayes, C.L. ....01 Sep
X Palethorpe, N. ....01 Sep
X Prole, N.M. ....16 Sep
E Jenner, A.C. ....16 Sep
E Haggerty, S.M. ....01 Oct
X Stevens, A.M.R. ....01 Oct
X Daveney, D.A. ....01 Oct
E O'Toole, M.C. ....01 Oct
E Quade, N.A.C. ....01 Oct
X Livesey, J.E. ....01 Oct
X Shaughnessy, T.E. ....01 Oct
X Walton, S.P. ....01 Oct
S Jenking-Rees, D. ....01 Oct
X Mansfield, J.A. ....01 Oct
X Davey, T.J. ....01 Oct
X Hudson, M. ....10 Oct
E Skittrall, S.D. ....15 Oct
X Alexander, O.D.D. ....01 Nov
X Hancock, Z.M.A. ....01 Nov
X Goulder, J.D. ....01 Nov
X Howe, T. ....01 Nov
X Leadbetter, A.J. ....01 Nov
E McLellan, J.D. ....01 Nov
E Morley, J.I. ....01 Nov
S Sheikh, N. ....01 Nov
E Harrison, M.A. ....01 Nov
S Rickard, J. ....12 Nov
X Richman, P.G. ....16 Nov
E Hawkins, S.R. ....01 Dec
E Hassall, I. ....01 Dec
E Sullivan, M.N. ....01 Dec
E Banham, A.W.D.B. ....01 Dec
X Davies, G.W.T. ....01 Dec
X Witte, R.H. ....01 Dec
S Allsford, K.M. ....01 Dec
E Collen, S.J. ....01 Dec
X Wallace, S.A. ....01 Dec
X Allan, C.R. ....01 Dec
X Anderson, M.E.J. ....01 Dec
E Bamforth, C.J.M. ....01 Dec
X Doig, B.J. ....01 Dec
X Hutchings, R.P.H. ....01 Dec
X Palin, G.R. ....01 Dec
S Webster, R.J. ....01 Dec
E Chambers, P.D. ....01 Dec
E Mealing, S.P. ....01 Dec
E Stevens, A.J. ....04 Dec
X Davies, J.J. ....12 Dec
X Rose, A.D. ....16 Dec

1998

E Auld, D.M. ....01 Jan
E Watkins, K.J. ....01 Jan
X Pickering-Wheeler, C.W. . 01 Jan
X Stilwell, J.M. ....01 Jan
E Ablett, S.D. ....01 Jan
E Chestnutt, J.M. ....01 Jan
X McMichael, J.S. ....01 Jan
X Spoors, B.M. ....01 Jan
X Steen, K.M. ....01 Jan
X Willis, A.S. ....01 Jan
E Goodship, M.T. ....01 Jan
X Blackmore, J. ....16 Jan
X Maley, C.E. ....16 Jan
S Haigh, J.J. ....01 Feb
S Butterworth, C.L. ....01 Feb
X Curry, J.H. ....01 Feb
E D'Silva, D.M. ....01 Feb
X Gibbs, D.J.E. ....01 Feb
E Jacobs, M.P. ....01 Feb
E Millard, J.R. ....01 Feb
S Wood, G.R. ....01 Feb
X Dempsey, S.P. ....01 Feb
X Roberts, N.D. ....10 Feb
X Ward, K.N. ....13 Feb
X Eastwood, R.N. ....15 Feb
X Priest, J.E. ....15 Feb
X Holroyd, J.E.J. ....16 Feb
E McCleary, S.P. ....01 Mar
E Lyons, A.G. ....01 Mar
X Guy, C.R. ....01 Mar
S Haggard, A. ....01 Mar
E Hay, M. ....01 Mar
X Johns, A.W. ....01 Mar
X Richardson, P.C. ....01 Mar
E Thorp, D.B. ....01 Mar
X White, D.J. ....01 Mar

LIEUTENANTS

X	Gray, J.A.	01 Mar
E	Harrington, L.B.	01 Mar
X	Calhaem, R.T.	15 Mar
X	McCormick, P.E.	15 Mar
X	Beech, D.J.	16 Mar
X	Samuels, N.J.	01 Apr
X	Lippitt, S.T.	01 Apr
X	Birchall, J.C.	01 Apr
X	Brotton, P.J.	01 Apr
E	Mountford, P.C.	01 Apr
S	Wright, G.F.	01 Apr
S	Wright, T.M.	01 Apr
X	Hayes, B.J.	03 Apr
X	Peak, M.	03 Apr
S	Platt, N.	03 Apr
X	Wood, J.A.	03 Apr
X	Bates, A.J.	16 Apr
X	Haggo, J.R.	16 Apr
X	Tremelling, P.N.	16 Apr
E	Cameron, F.	24 Apr
E	Buck, S.R.	01 May
E	Dick, F.E.	01 May
E	Goward, R.J.	01 May
E	Hartley, J.H.D.	01 May
X	Rushworth, B.J.	01 May
X	McWilliams, A.R.	01 May
E	Clarke, M.D.	01 May
X	Clay, T.C.D.C	01 May
X	Williams, L.J.	01 May
E	Bartlett, M.J.	01 May
E	Beaver, R.M.S.	01 May
E	Grennan, E.F.	01 May
X	Marshall, M.	01 May
X	Vallance, M.S.	01 May
E	Goodall, M.A.	01 May
S	Sutcliffe, E.D.	01 May
X	Yates, S.E.	01 May
E	Sargent, N.M.	01 May
X	Kurth, R.P.E.	18 May
X	Full, R.J.	01 Jun
E	Humphery, D.	01 Jun
X	Denham, D.J.	01 Jun
S	Gilbert, R.G.	01 Jun
X	Hicks, N.J.I.	01 Jun
X	Coulton, J.R.S.	16 Jun
X	Jenkins, A.R.	16 Jun
E	Jones, R.K.	19 Jun
E	Norgate, P.R.E.	19 Jun
E	Paton, A.J.M.	19 Jun
E	Rankine, I.M.	19 Jun
E	Stone, R.J.	19 Jun
X	Bainbridge, J.R.	30 Jun
E	Simm, C.W.	01 Jul
E	Cross, A.L.	01 Jul
X	Johnson, M.R.E.	01 Jul
X	Howe, C.M.	01 Jul
X	Mason, A.C.	01 Jul
X	Pressdee, S.J.	01 Jul
E	Chilton, J.	01 Jul
X	Rogers, S.J.P.	01 Jul
X	Beale, M.D.	23 Jul
X	Deam, P.A.V.	23 Jul
X	Johns, L.E.	23 Jul
X	Louden, C.A.	23 Jul
X	Parkinson, A.P.	23 Jul
X	Kewley, I.D.	01 Aug
E	Love, R.J.	01 Aug
E	Taylor, K.M.	01 Aug
E	Burns, E.P.	01 Aug
E	Cartwright, J.A.	01 Aug
X	Mansergh, F.A.	01 Aug
S	Cooper, A.	01 Aug
X	Craven, M.W.	01 Aug
X	Heirs, G.G.	01 Aug
X	MacLaughlin, R.A.	01 Aug
X	Muirhead, B.G.	01 Aug
S	Miles, P.J.	01 Aug
S	Park, I.D.	01 Aug
X	Pollard, A.E.	01 Aug
X	Brook, R.L.	11 Aug
X	Hammock, S.G.	16 Aug
X	McTeer, I.J.	16 Aug
E	Bird, T.S.V.	01 Sep
E	Bristow, P.C.	01 Sep
E	Coles, S.P.	01 Sep
E	Jameson, A.J.	01 Sep
E	MacCorquodale, M.A.	01 Sep
E	Rees, A.M.	01 Sep
E	Salim, M.	01 Sep
S	Hardwick, M.J.	01 Sep
X	Bagshaw, J.R.W.	01 Sep
X	Davies, N.M.S.	01 Sep
X	Berry, T.J.	01 Sep
X	Griffiths, N.	01 Sep
X	Howard, N.A.	01 Sep
X	Hutchins, I.D.M.	01 Sep
E	McDonald, D.J.	01 Sep
X	Thomas, M.	01 Sep
X	Williams, A.S.	01 Sep
X	Arkle, N.J.	01 Sep
X	Burbidge, K.	01 Sep
X	Ingham, A.R.	01 Sep
X	Parkin, J.M.B.	01 Sep
E	Brodier, M.I.	04 Sep
E	Metcalfe, R.J.	04 Sep
E	Raynor, S.D.	04 Sep
X	Raynes, C.	16 Sep
X	Ashlin, J.M.	16 Sep
X	Walton, S.D.	01 Oct
X	Osbaldestin, R.A.	01 Oct
X	Anderson, G.S.	01 Oct
X	Crane, O.R.	01 Oct
X	Fletcher, I.J.	01 Oct
X	Gould, J.D.	01 Oct
X	Thomas, D.W.	01 Oct
X	Varty, J.A.	01 Oct
X	Benzie, N.J.E.	01 Oct
X	Densham, M.P.J.	01 Oct
X	Drodge, K.N.	01 Oct
X	Wyness, C.J.	01 Oct
X	Wappner, G.D.	10 Oct
X	Gaskell, H.D.	16 Oct
X	Tazewell, M.R.	16 Oct
X	Doubleday, S.	16 Oct
S	Atwill, J.W.O.	22 Oct
X	Gillett, D.A.	01 Nov
X	Instone, M.J.	01 Nov
X	Chacksfield, E.N.	01 Nov
X	Cowin, T.J.	01 Nov
S	Curwood, J.E.	01 Nov
E	Greig, J.A.	01 Nov
X	McCall, G.	01 Nov
E	McCoy, M.	01 Nov
X	Norgate, A.T.	01 Nov
X	Stein, G.K.	01 Nov
S	Ward, D.J.	01 Nov
X	Iliffe, D.I.	16 Nov
X	Nelson, M.R.	16 Nov
E	McLaughlin, S.	01 Dec
X	Whitehead, P.J.	01 Dec
E	Sangha, R.S.	01 Dec
E	Walsh, A.H.	01 Dec
X	Hartley, B.P.I.	01 Dec
X	Johnston, G.S.	01 Dec
X	Alsop, S.H.	01 Dec
X	Astle, D.S.	01 Dec
E	Blackburn, A.R.J.	01 Dec
X	Crabbe, R.J.	01 Dec
X	Lilly, D.M.	01 Dec
E	McCann, T.	01 Dec
X	Meyer, A.J.	01 Dec
S	Terry, J.H.	01 Dec
X	Webster, R.J.	01 Dec

LIEUTENANTS

X Wright, D.J. .... 01 Dec
E Pine, P.M. .... 06 Dec
X Beard, R.G. .... 10 Dec
X Egerton, S.B. .... 10 Dec
X Martin, A.J. .... 10 Dec
X Routledge, W.D. .... 10 Dec
X Singleton, M.D. .... 10 Dec
X Smith, R.E. .... 10 Dec

1999

E Gibson, S.J. .... 01 Jan
X Ball, A.D. .... 01 Jan
E Carroll, S.L. .... 01 Jan
X Clarke, D. .... 01 Jan
X Conlin, J.A. .... 01 Jan
X Wood, I.L. .... 01 Jan
X Brazier, L.F. .... 01 Jan
X Monachello, P.G. .... 01 Jan
E Newman, D.J. .... 01 Jan
E Ruston, M.R. .... 01 Jan
X Ansell, C.N. .... 01 Jan
S Arend, F.M. .... 01 Jan
X Carrington, V.L. .... 01 Jan
X Croft, D.F. .... 01 Jan
E Hunt, P.S. .... 01 Jan
X Johnson, A.D. .... 01 Jan
E McClement, D.L. .... 01 Jan
X Munro, N.F.H. .... 01 Jan
E O'Shaughnessy, P.C. .... 01 Jan
E Ruddock, J. .... 01 Jan
X Thomson, J.C. .... 01 Jan
X Watts, Z.A. .... 01 Jan
E Smith, A. .... 09 Jan
E Dry, I. .... 31 Jan
E Burns, J.E. .... 01 Feb
X Greenwood, A.W. .... 01 Feb
S Haines, R.J. .... 01 Feb
E Turner, P.L. .... 01 Feb
X Wade, J.M.R. .... 01 Feb
X Bell, C.M. .... 01 Feb
X Denney, J.R. .... 01 Feb
X Hirons, F.D. .... 01 Feb
E Johnson, P.R. .... 01 Feb
E Kilmartin, A. .... 01 Feb
X Mullowney, P. .... 01 Feb
E Moody, A.C. .... 01 Feb
X Wall, S.N. .... 01 Feb
X Morgan, E.J.A. .... 12 Feb
E Jones, L.H. .... 14 Feb
X Sweeney, C. .... 16 Feb
E Todd, D.B. .... 01 Mar
E Northcott, M.K. .... 01 Mar
S Collacott, J.S. .... 01 Mar
X Gibbs, A.M. .... 01 Mar
X Boswell, D.J. .... 01 Mar
X Brewin, D.J. .... 01 Mar
S Conway, S.H. .... 01 Mar
X Fisher, S.J. .... 01 Mar
X Hume, K.J. .... 01 Mar
S Middleton, D.M. .... 01 Mar
X Richards, A.V. .... 01 Mar
S Robertson, S.T. .... 01 Mar
E Wadsworth, R.Y. .... 01 Mar
S Weeks, D.C. .... 01 Mar
E Barton, K.J.A. .... 01 Mar
X Mains, G. .... 18 Mar
X Tighe, S. .... 30 Mar
X Dodds, M.L. .... 01 Apr
X Rawles, J.R. .... 01 Apr
X Twigg, K.L. .... 01 Apr
X Ward, M.T. .... 01 Apr
X Smith, A.J.E. .... 01 Apr
X Stait, B.G. .... 01 Apr
E Thomson, M.L. .... 01 Apr
X Beavis, J.A. .... 01 Apr
X Hilton, S.T. .... 01 Apr
X James, A.W. .... 01 Apr
S Stait, E.J. .... 01 Apr
X Hutchings, J.R. .... 01 Apr
X Percy, N.A. .... 01 Apr
E Grey, E.J.W. .... 03 Apr
X Sparrow, M.J. .... 16 Apr
X Thompson, D.A. .... 16 Apr
X Blacklock, J.F. .... 26 Apr
S Case, A. .... 26 Apr
X Dunkley, S.C. .... 26 Apr
X Harriman, P. .... 26 Apr
X Lovett, S.A. .... 26 Apr
X Pearch, S.M. .... 26 Apr
X Toon, P.G. .... 26 Apr
E Johnston, K.I. .... 01 May
X Ellis, A.C. .... 01 May
X Baldie, S.A.H. .... 01 May
X Breen, D.A. .... 01 May
S Clements, E.J. .... 01 May
S Titcombe, A.J. .... 01 May
X Daly, P. .... 01 May
X Dransfield, J.A.J. .... 01 May
E Stratton, M.P. .... 01 May
X Flatman, T.D. .... 16 May
X Mann, D.M. .... 01 Jun
X Pittard, D.C. .... 01 Jun
E Deal, C. .... 01 Jun
X Hughes, C.B. .... 01 Jun
X Moran, R.J. .... 01 Jun
X Redmayne, M.E. .... 01 Jun
E Stead, A.M. .... 01 Jul
X Kennedy, R.J. .... 01 Jul
S MacKenzie, J.E. .... 01 Jul
E Blackburn, E.C. .... 01 Jul
S Christian, J. .... 01 Jul
X Fennell, C.B. .... 01 Jul
X Gillard, V.A. .... 01 Jul
E Goodship, J.S. .... 01 Jul
S Murphy, V.J. .... 01 Jul
S Relf, K.M. .... 01 Jul
X Saltonstall, P.J.R. .... 01 Jul
X Thomas, D.H. .... 01 Jul
S Caple, J.N. .... 01 Jul
X Kelly, S.P. .... 01 Jul
X Whitwell, N.S. .... 01 Jul
X Swindells, M. .... 16 Jul
E Epps, M.P. .... 17 Jul
E Bailey, S. .... 01 Aug
X Bewley, N.J. .... 01 Aug
X Hughes, J.J. .... 01 Aug
X Neofytou, A.G.K. .... 01 Aug
X Sambrooks, R.J. .... 01 Aug
X Clark, R.A. .... 01 Aug
X Crowe, D.M. .... 01 Aug
X Hannam, D.B. .... 01 Aug
E Holmwood, M.A.G. .... 01 Aug
E Martin, S.W. .... 01 Aug
X Rogers, J.A. .... 01 Aug
X Weston, K.N.N. .... 01 Aug
X Woollven, C.D. .... 01 Aug
X Frazer, H.F. .... 01 Aug
E Molyneux, I.T. .... 01 Aug
X Currie, M.J. .... 16 Aug
E Scotter, C.M. .... 01 Sep
X Bussey, E.L. .... 01 Sep
E Hoather, M.S. .... 01 Sep
X Jordan, A.F. .... 01 Sep
E Alexander, A.L. .... 01 Sep
X Barr, S.P. .... 01 Sep
X Birleson, P.D. .... 01 Sep
X Carnie, M.J. .... 01 Sep
X Cobban, M.J. .... 01 Sep
X Livsey, A.E.J. .... 01 Sep
E Kitt, R.G. .... 01 Sep
X Murphy, R.J. .... 01 Sep
X Buchan, J.A. .... 01 Sep
X Green, J.H. .... 01 Sep
E Healey, M.J. .... 01 Sep

LIEUTENANTS

E Hepplewhite, M.B. ....01 Sep
X Johnson, S. ....01 Sep
E Leivers, A.J. ....01 Sep
S Matthew, M.J. ....01 Sep
S Weare, J.B. ....01 Sep
S Curtis, S.E.H. ....01 Sep
X Knight, D.S. ....01 Sep
S Shepherd, F.R. ....01 Sep
E Booth, W.N. ....02 Sep
E Brennan, P.A. ....02 Sep
E Flatt, L.D. ....02 Sep
E Forshaw, D.R. ....02 Sep
E Leaver, A.M. ....02 Sep
E MacLean, M.T. ....02 Sep
E Millar, K.I. ....02 Sep
E Nicholson, J.C. ....02 Sep
E Nursey, A.P. ....02 Sep
E Penketh, M.G. ....02 Sep
E Quirk, A.T. ....02 Sep
E Rom, S.P. ....02 Sep
E Saywell-Hall, S.E. ....02 Sep
E Scholes, N.A. ....02 Sep
E Spencer, J.C. ....02 Sep
E Stead, J.A. ....02 Sep
E Torney, C.J. ....02 Sep
E Vickers, C.G. ....02 Sep
E Vickery, R.J. ....02 Sep
E Walker, G. ....02 Sep
E Ward, N.A. ....02 Sep
E Watson, A.P. ....02 Sep
X Bull, M.A.J. ....11 Sep
X Netherwood, L.D. ....15 Sep
X Lawrence, L.J. ....16 Sep
X Adams, E.S. ....16 Sep
MS Goodrum, S.E. ....19 Sep
S Baker, N.J. ....20 Sep
X Llewellyn, J.G. ....20 Sep
X Spurdle, A.P. ....20 Sep
MS Welch, A. ....20 Sep
X Martin, N. ....20 Sep
E Osborne, J.M. ....01 Oct
X Cutler, A.R. ....01 Oct
S Black, S.B. ....01 Oct
X Bowen, C.N. ....01 Oct
E Buckenham, P.J. ....01 Oct
X Cornford, M. ....01 Oct
S Cutler, T.P. ....01 Oct
X Hammon, M.A. ....01 Oct
S Rees, K.M.M. ....01 Oct
X Rex, C.A. ....01 Oct
X Sanderson, C.P. ....01 Oct
X Weaver, S. ....01 Oct
X Duncan, K.C.L. ....01 Oct
X Hardman, M.J. ....01 Oct
S Knox, G.P. ....01 Oct
X Thomas, O.H. ....16 Oct
X Greenwood, P.A. ....16 Oct
X Barker, T.J. ....16 Oct
E Clear, N.J. .... 01 Nov
X Finch, I.R. .... 01 Nov
E Andrew, P. .... 01 Nov
X Hayashi, L.R. .... 01 Nov
E Hubschmid, S.R. .... 01 Nov
E Orr, K.J. .... 01 Nov
X Aldous, B.W. .... 01 Nov
S Clarke, A.G. .... 01 Nov
E Jones, I.M. .... 01 Nov
E Lee, S.E. .... 01 Nov
X Rowson, M.J. .... 16 Nov
X O'Neill, J. .... 22 Nov
X Alderwick, J.R.C. .... 01 Dec
E Cessford, R.I. .... 01 Dec
E Derrick, M.J.G. .... 01 Dec
X Marshall, A.J. .... 01 Dec
X Chambers, C.P. .... 01 Dec
X Gray, N.J. .... 01 Dec
E Jenkins, R.C. .... 01 Dec
S Oliver, G.J. .... 01 Dec
X Sloan, I.A. .... 01 Dec
E Ball, M.P. .... 01 Dec
S Carcone, P.N. .... 01 Dec
X Griffiths, C.S.H. .... 01 Dec
X Holden, J.L. .... 01 Dec
X Morse, J. .... 01 Dec
E Pollard, J.R. .... 01 Dec
E Hamilton, M.I. .... 01 Dec
X Taylor, A.I. .... 01 Dec
X Bevan, J.R. .... 16 Dec

2000

E Blethyn, H.P. .... 01 Jan
E Gill, P.S. .... 01 Jan
E Hemingway, D.G. .... 01 Jan
E Muyambo, N.N. .... 01 Jan
E Perryman, I.T.C. .... 01 Jan
E Priestley, C. .... 01 Jan
E White, S.P. .... 01 Jan
E Wood, C.T. .... 01 Jan
E Corderoy, R.I. .... 01 Jan
X Kitteridge, D.J. .... 01 Jan
X Mason, M.J. .... 01 Jan
X Brewer, C.E. .... 01 Jan
X Crew, J.M. .... 01 Jan
E Jackson, S.N. .... 01 Jan
S Lanning, K.A. .... 01 Jan
X Williams, D.L. .... 01 Jan
E Mortlock, P.A. .... 01 Jan
X Rant, O.J. .... 01 Jan
E Russell, C.M.L. .... 01 Jan
X Slattery, D.J. .... 01 Jan
E Bennett, W.E. .... 01 Jan
X Gill, C.D. .... 01 Jan
E Law, R. .... 01 Jan
X McIntyre, L. .... 01 Jan
E Miller, I. .... 01 Jan
E Nicklin, G.J.E. .... 01 Jan
X Phillips, R.M. .... 01 Jan
E Robinson, P. .... 01 Jan
X Boeckx, T.J.F. .... 01 Jan
E Green, R.R. .... 08 Jan
X Francis, D.E. .... 10 Jan
X Irving, D.M. .... 10 Jan
X Lester, R.L. .... 10 Jan
X Moran, C.A. .... 10 Jan
E Stafford, B.R. ....01 Feb
S Brimacombe, L.M. ....01 Feb
S Wall, I.J. ....01 Feb
X Considine, K.J. ....01 Feb
X Harford-Cross, P.J. ....01 Feb
X Jackson, P. ....01 Feb
E Martin, R.J. ....01 Feb
E Risley, J.G. ....01 Feb
X Thatcher, L.F.V. ....01 Feb
X Thompson, W.A. ....01 Feb
E Timbrell, I.P.J. ....01 Feb
X Whitehall, S. ....01 Feb
E Quinn, M.E. ....01 Mar
X Coverdale, P. ....01 Mar
X Hodgson, R.S. ....01 Mar
X Winsor, J. ....01 Mar
X Bennett, C.D. ....01 Mar
E Ellis, C.R. ....01 Mar
X Lanning, R.M. ....01 Mar
E Mathieson, N.B. ....01 Mar
E McDonald, A.W. ....01 Mar
E Milne, W.J.C. ....01 Mar
X Richardson, I.H. ....01 Mar
X Madigan, L. ....01 Mar
X Brown, A.R.A. ....01 Mar
X Holmes, A.M. ....15 Mar
X McGannity, C.S. ....16 Mar
X Barritt, O.D. ....01 Apr
E Pipkin, P.J. ....01 Apr
E Winbolt, N.I. ....01 Apr

LIEUTENANTS

X Lloyd, B.J. ....01 Apr
X MacLean, J.A. ....01 Apr
X Moore, N.J. ....01 Apr
X Murgatroyd, K.J. ....01 Apr
E Barker, P.D. ....01 Apr
X Bates, N.S. ....01 Apr
X Chambers, R. ....01 Apr
X Feeney, M.B. ....01 Apr
E Gilmore, S.J. ....01 Apr
X Hammond, M.M.V. ....01 Apr
X Liddle, R.D. ....01 Apr
X Whitehouse, D.S. ....01 Apr
X Bodman, S.A. ....01 Apr
E England, P.M. ....01 Apr
X Griffen, D.J. ....01 Apr
X Headley, M.J. ....01 Apr
S McLocklan, L.M. ....01 Apr
X Shearn, M.A. ....01 Apr
S Turner, D.J. ....01 Apr
S West, N.K. ....01 Apr
E Bartholomew, D.J. ....01 May
E Free, A.S. ....01 May
E Goodall, J.C. ....01 May
E Hollyfield, P.R. ....01 May
E Holt, J.D. ....01 May
E Padget, J.L. ....01 May
E Ussher, J.H.D. ....01 May
S Halsey, K.E. ....01 May
E Andrews, C. ....01 May
E Baillie, R.W. ....01 May
X Cannell, G.M. ....01 May
X Firth, J.S. ....01 May
S Forge, S.M. ....01 May
X Gardner, M.P. ....01 May
E Newth, C.S. ....01 May
X Page, M.R. ....01 May
X Tok, C.F.L. ....01 May
E Austin, S.T. ....01 May
E Coles, C.P. ....01 May
X Keith, B.C. ....01 May
S Lane, N. ....01 May
X Wood, S.A.H. ....01 May
X Woolhead, C.M. ....01 May
X Stratton, N.C. ....01 May
X Brearley, R.L. ....01 May
X Brown, J.A. ....01 May
X Cromie, J.M. ....01 May
X Hember, M.J.C. ....01 May
X Reid, J.L. ....01 May
X Winand, F.M.J. ....01 May
S Ashley, P.D. ....01 May

E Trueman, B.D. ....01 May
S Benfell, N.A. ....02 May
E Bowser, N.J. ....02 May
E Burton, P.R. ....02 May
E Collins, D.A. ....02 May
E Edwins, M.R. ....02 May
E Hodgson, J.R. ....02 May
E Liddell, M.L. ....02 May
E Lowe, C. ....02 May
E McNair, J. ....02 May
E Moy, D.K. ....02 May
X Paget, S.J. ....02 May
E Ryan, J.P. ....02 May
E Smart, M.J. ....02 May
E Young, P. ....02 May
S Pickering, C.A. ....04 May
X Ballantyne, C. ....07 May
E Pearmain, S.R. ....14 May
E Whetter, R.S. ....14 May
X O'Kane, R.J. ....16 May
E Mantri, A.H. ....22 May
E George, S.D. ....01 Jun
X Beanland, P.L. ....01 Jun
X Bedding, D. ....01 Jun
X Campbell, T.R. ....01 Jun
E Grant, W.G. ....01 Jun
X Higginson, N.J. ....01 Jun
X Ives, D.J. ....01 Jun
X Money, C.J. ....01 Jun
X Mount, J.B. ....01 Jun
X Randles, S. ....01 Jun
X Urwin, S.J. ....01 Jun
X Varley, P.G.S. ....01 Jun
X Irwin, S.G. ....01 Jun
E Lovett, A.R. ....01 Jun
E Jones, M.R. ....01 Jun
E Prest, S.F. ....01 Jun
X Williams, D.E. ....08 Jun
X Sims, A.R. ....15 Jun
X Milles, O.K. ....16 Jun
E Quinn, A.D. ....01 Jul
E Wallace, I.S. ....01 Jul
X Lewis, K.E. ....01 Jul
E Dickinson, P.H. ....01 Jul
X Gare, C.J. ....01 Jul
X Humphries, M. ....01 Jul
S Hynde, C.L. ....01 Jul
E Kitchen, B. ....01 Jul
X Retter, R.L. ....01 Jul
X Bane, N.S.J. ....01 Jul
X Bull, L.P. ....01 Jul

X Jacob, A.W. ....01 Jul
S Stone, N.J.J. ....01 Jul
E Elliott, J.A. ....01 Jul
X Kohn, P.A. ....01 Jul
X Rea, S.D. ....01 Jul
S Roberts, N.S.J. ....01 Jul
E Casson, R.F. ....01 Jul
E Foote, A.S. ....01 Jul
X Harcombe, A. ....16 Jul
E Treharne, M.A. ....01 Aug
X Hewitson, J.G.A. ....01 Aug
S Potts, R.E. ....01 Aug
X Scott, S.L. ....01 Aug
X Sturman, R.W. ....01 Aug
X Ainsley, A.M.J. ....01 Aug
X Anderson, S.R. ....01 Aug
S Clark, C.L. ....01 Aug
S Middleton, W.T. ....01 Aug
X Mc Currach, R.H. ....01 Aug
E Reeves, P.K. ....01 Aug
X Brown, S.G. ....04 Aug
E Collins, L.J. ....01 Sep
E Holmes, R.M. ....01 Sep
X Armstrong, S.M. ....01 Sep
E Blackburn, L.R. ....01 Sep
E Dawson, G.A.E. ....01 Sep
E Dixon, A.K. ....01 Sep
E Dominy, V.L. ....01 Sep
S Lear, S.F. ....01 Sep
X Bailes, K.P. ....01 Sep
X Bullock, R.A. ....01 Sep
X Hearn, S.P. ....01 Sep
X Lynas, J.F.A. ....01 Sep
X Parker, S.A.M. ....01 Sep
X Armstrong, C.D. ....01 Sep
S Johnson, A.C. ....01 Sep
S Peyman, T.A. ....01 Sep
X Ransom, B.R.J. ....01 Sep
E Rooney, M. ....01 Sep
X Wick, H.M.S. ....01 Sep
E Pickard, S.R. ....01 Sep
X Finn, S.A. ....01 Sep
S Flegg, K.G. ....01 Sep
X Stanway, C.A. ....01 Sep
E Geneux, N.S. ....01 Sep
X Hale, A.D. ....01 Sep
X Boon, G.J. ....19 Sep
X Castle, C.D. ....19 Sep
X Cowan, A.R. ....19 Sep
X Griffin, P.J. ....19 Sep
X Howells, S.M. ....19 Sep

LIEUTENANTS

S	Longstaff, T.W.	19 Sep
S	Love, J.D.	19 Sep
X	Lynn, H.W.	19 Sep
X	Mills, G.A.	19 Sep
X	Parton, A.	19 Sep
X	Pirrie, J.A.	19 Sep
X	Stringer, G.E.	19 Sep
X	Walker, R.S.	19 Sep
X	Wilson, G.J.	19 Sep
E	Gould, A.A.	01 Oct
X	Hancock, J.H.	01 Oct
S	Henderson, S.C.	01 Oct
X	Fyfe, K.S.	01 Oct
X	Hadland, G.V.	01 Oct
X	Hampshire, T.	01 Oct
S	Richards, A.J.	01 Oct
X	Robey, J.C.	01 Oct
X	Taylor, T.P.	01 Oct
X	Winn, J.P.	01 Oct
X	Dodd, S.E.	01 Oct
X	Gallimore, R.M.	01 Oct
X	Kroon, Z.	01 Oct
X	Filtness, D.M.	01 Oct
X	King, W.R.C.	01 Oct
E	Grantham, G.J.	01 Nov
X	Hayes, S.	01 Nov
X	Parsons, R.J.	01 Nov
X	Bartram, R.J.	01 Nov
X	Bouyac, D.R.L.	01 Nov
X	Collins, A.C.	01 Nov
X	Crompton, P.J.	01 Nov
X	Owen, S.T.L.	01 Nov
S	Rollason, C.A.	01 Nov
X	Burton, A.	01 Nov
X	Doran, K.E.	01 Nov
X	Horton, J.R.	01 Nov
S	MacDonald, S.B.	01 Nov
E	Seagrave, S.J.	01 Nov
X	Spears, A.G.	01 Nov
X	Simmonite, G.I.	16 Nov
X	Hall, C.J.	01 Dec
X	Partridge, S.C.	01 Dec
E	Wharrie, C.G.	01 Dec
X	Dermody, R.T.	01 Dec
X	Pearson, J.C.	01 Dec
X	Summers, A.J.	01 Dec
X	Fillmore, R.J.	01 Dec
X	Northcote, M.R.	01 Dec
X	Milne, A.P.	16 Dec
	2001	
E	Blackler, S.	01 Jan
E	Oakley, A.J.	01 Jan
E	Sweeney, R.J.	01 Jan
E	Kierstan, S.J.J.	01 Jan
X	Aitken, S.R.	01 Jan
E	Alexander, P.M.D.	01 Jan
X	Butler, P.M.	01 Jan
X	Finn, J.S.	01 Jan
X	Gladwin, M.D.	01 Jan
E	Morphet, K.	01 Jan
X	Turner, J.S.	01 Jan
X	Dingley, P.A.	01 Jan
X	Dixon, R.A.	01 Jan
X	Howie, E.J.	01 Jan
S	Ledward, K.L.	01 Jan
X	Pickles, D.R.	01 Jan
X	Wragg, G.T.	01 Jan
E	Richardson, A.P.	01 Jan
X	Punch, J.M.	01 Jan
E	Robinson, S.L.	01 Jan
E	Satterly, R.J.	01 Jan
X	Davis, G.R.	01 Jan
X	Nicholson, D.A.G.	01 Jan
E	Thomson, J.M.	01 Jan
X	Way, R.A.	01 Jan
S	Grigg, S.K.	08 Jan
S	Harvey, P.J.	08 Jan
X	Lewis, P.L.	08 Jan
S	McGrath, W.J.	08 Jan
E	Austin, P.N.	09 Jan
E	Collins, D.	09 Jan
E	Collins, M.A.	09 Jan
E	Conneely, S.A.	09 Jan
E	Donaldson, A.M.	09 Jan
E	Emms, S.M.	09 Jan
X	Flynn, S.J.	09 Jan
X	Gray, M.J.H.	09 Jan
S	Johnson, K.	09 Jan
E	Jones, P.A.	09 Jan
E	Murphy, A.	09 Jan
E	Stafford, W.	09 Jan
X	White, S.J.	09 Jan
X	Collins, S.J.P.	16 Jan
X	Laurence, S.T.	16 Jan
E	Topham, N.E.	01 Feb
S	New, R.A.	01 Feb
X	Paulet, M.R.	01 Feb
X	Simpson, S.F.	01 Feb
E	Welsh, R.M.K.	01 Feb
X	White, J.P.	01 Feb
X	Hurst, C.N.S.	01 Feb
E	Eaglestone, S.	01 Feb
E	Melville, A.C.	01 Feb
S	Walsh, D.	01 Feb
X	Whitson-Fay, C.D.	15 Feb
X	Lightfoot, R.A.	16 Feb
S	Broadbent, S.E.	01 Mar
E	Billington, S.	01 Mar
X	Dowling, A.J.	01 Mar
X	Knowles, C.J.	01 Mar
E	Wallace, R.P.	01 Mar
X	Price, J.C.	05 Mar
X	Twigg, N.R.	16 Mar
E	Alberts, P.W.	01 Apr
E	Barron-Robinson, D.P.	01 Apr
E	Baxter, F.J.	01 Apr
S	Bell, S.W.	01 Apr
E	Blois, S.D.	01 Apr
S	Brady, T.W.	01 Apr
E	Carter, P.	01 Apr
S	Chilton, D.J.	01 Apr
X	Clarke, M.	01 Apr
S	Cotton, E.L.	01 Apr
E	Crawley, D.A.	01 Apr
X	Daniels, S.P.	01 Apr
E	Dawson, P.	01 Apr
E	Dumbleton, D.W.	01 Apr
X	Dunn, A.	01 Apr
X	Edmondson, J.A.	01 Apr
X	Farr, I.R.	01 Apr
E	Freeman, M.J.	01 Apr
X	Gallimore, J.M.	01 Apr
E	Gibson, M.J.S.	01 Apr
S	Gosling, D.J.	01 Apr
MS	Haughey, J.P.	01 Apr
E	Havron, P.R.	01 Apr
E	Hocking, M.J.E.	01 Apr
E	Holvey, P.J.	01 Apr
E	James, M.	01 Apr
X	Jayes, N.J.	01 Apr
X	Jones, S.S.	01 Apr
MS	Jones, T.M.	01 Apr
X	Jones-Thompson, M.J.	01 Apr
X	Kay, P.S.	01 Apr
E	Matthews, P.R.	01 Apr
X	Meikle, R.B.	01 Apr
E	Meikle, S.A.	01 Apr
E	Metcalf, S.W.	01 Apr
MS	Milburn, V.	01 Apr
X	Molnar, R.M.	01 Apr
X	Moore, M.J.	01 Apr

LIEUTENANTS

S Northeast, P. ....01 Apr
E Nottley, S.M. ....01 Apr
E Parmenter, A.J. ....01 Apr
E Pollard, A.J. ....01 Apr
E Prior, I.A. ....01 Apr
E Prowse, D.G. ....01 Apr
E Rawlings, G.A. ....01 Apr
E Rhodes, A.W. ....01 Apr
MS Robinson, A. ....01 Apr
X Robinson, R.J. ....01 Apr
X Santry, P.M. ....01 Apr
E Shaw, N.A. ....01 Apr
X Smith, P.A. ....01 Apr
S Somerville, S.J. ....01 Apr
E Temple, D.C. ....01 Apr
E Thomson, D.F. ....01 Apr
E Thomson, I.W. ....01 Apr
E Toone, S.A. ....01 Apr
X Tutchings, A. ....01 Apr
E Whitehouse, S.R. ....01 Apr
X Wood, N.R. ....01 Apr
E Cheyne, R.D. ....01 Apr
E Clapham, G.T. ....01 Apr
E Dodd, L. ....01 Apr
E Flegg, M.J. ....01 Apr
E Heal, T.S. ....01 Apr
X Godfrey, S.D.W. ....01 Apr
E Bleasdale, D.R. ....01 Apr
X Cooksley, R.E.C. ....08 Apr
X Gibbs, A.E. ....08 Apr
E Anderson, C.J. ....13 Apr
S Brint, I. ....29 Apr
X Carter, N.R. ....29 Apr
S Christie, A.B. ....29 Apr
E Cooke, R.N. ....29 Apr
X Dainty, R.C. ....29 Apr
E Finch, S. ....29 Apr
E Griffiths, C.J.J. ....29 Apr
X Gwatkin, N.J. ....29 Apr
E Hamilton, G.D. ....29 Apr
E Hardy, R.J. ....29 Apr
E Harrison, A.D. ....29 Apr
X Hattle, P.M. ....29 Apr
E Hewitt, M.J. ....29 Apr
E Loughrey, N.C. ....29 Apr
E Newell, G.D. ....29 Apr
E Nicholson, B.H. ....29 Apr
E Richards, P. ....29 Apr
E Robert, I.A. ....29 Apr
MS Sullivan, T.E. ....29 Apr
S Viney, P.M. ....29 Apr
E Wrennall, E.P. ....29 Apr
E Drew, C. ....01 May
E Farr-Voller, E.M. ....01 May
E Fortt, P.D.J. ....01 May
E Tilsley, D.J. ....01 May
X Leason, N.C. ....01 May
X Reynolds, M.J. ....01 May
X Wilkins, D.P. ....01 May
E Barron, J.M. ....01 May
X Binns, J.F. ....01 May
E Buchanan, R.M. ....01 May
S Carthew, R.J. ....01 May
X Crouch, M. ....01 May
X Duce, M. ....01 May
X Evans, L.S. ....01 May
X Fabik, A.N. ....01 May
X Garreta, C.E. ....01 May
X Gordon, D.I. ....01 May
X Hall, K.J.D. ....01 May
E Holford, S.J. ....01 May
X Hopkins, C. ....01 May
X Humphries, G.D. ....01 May
X Jackson, H.C. ....01 May
X Jones, R.J. ....01 May
E Jordan, M.D. ....01 May
E Kent, M.J. ....01 May
X Klidjian, M.J. ....01 May
E Layton, C. ....01 May
X Little, M.I.G. ....01 May
S Lucocq, C.M. ....01 May
X Martyn, D. ....01 May
S McCowen, P.A.C. ....01 May
E Miller, K.R. ....01 May
E Moon, I.L. ....01 May
X Noonan, C.D. ....01 May
X Nunnen, C.R. ....01 May
X Oakley, C.M. ....01 May
S Ollis, V. ....01 May
S Pearson, S.L. ....01 May
X Pickles, M.R. ....01 May
X Quick, S.J. ....01 May
X Sherwood, G.A.F. ....01 May
X Spencer, A.C. ....01 May
X Spinks, R.J. ....01 May
E Stratton, S.J. ....01 May
X Vickery, B.R. ....01 May
X Waite, T.G. ....01 May
X Watson, B.L. ....01 May
X Wickham, R.J. ....01 May
X Wielopolski, M.L.C.C. .....01 May
X Williams, P.G. ....01 May
X Winterbon, A.R. ....01 May
X Youldon, L.J. ....01 May
E Bland, C.D. ....01 May
E Woods, M.J.P. ....01 May
E Hayden, J.M.L. ....01 May
E Wadge, G.D.E. ....08 May
X Goodman, D.F. ....09 May
S Guilfoyle, V.M. ....15 May
E Crossey, M.D. ....01 Jun
E Cantellow, S.J. ....01 Jun
E Perkins, B. ....01 Jul
E Webb, D. ....01 Jul
X Henaghen, S.J. ....13 Jul
X Malone, J.M. ....29 Jul
X Wightwick, K.H.T. ....01 Aug
X Prosser, M.J. ....01 Aug
X Burghall, R.C. ....01 Aug
X Huxford, S. ....01 Aug
E Barnard, T.J. ....01 Aug
X Perryment, C.P. ....01 Aug
X Robey, S.J. ....01 Aug
S Underwood, R.A.H. ....01 Aug
X Antrobus, S.R. ....05 Aug
E Simpson, M.G. ....05 Aug
E Bennett, B.C.H. ....01 Sep
E Booth, D.P.P. ....01 Sep
E Maxwell, M.S. ....01 Sep
E Miah, J.H. ....01 Sep
X Gadsden, A.C. ....01 Sep
X Menzies, B. ....01 Sep
X Sienkiewicz, M.K. ....01 Sep
X Andrews, I.S. ....01 Sep
E Bass, E.M. ....01 Sep
E Beadling, D.J. ....01 Sep
X Boullin, J.P. ....01 Sep
E Breen, J.E. ....01 Sep
E Brooks, N.R. ....01 Sep
X Brown, A.S. ....01 Sep
E Bulter, D.B. ....01 Sep
E Buxton, D.A. ....01 Sep
S Chapman, M.S. ....01 Sep
S Cole, B.B. ....01 Sep
MS Davies, J.L. ....01 Sep
S De La Rue, A.N. ....01 Sep
X Fraser, M.J.S. ....01 Sep
S Gray, E.J. ....01 Sep
X Hirstwood, J.L. ....01 Sep
X Hulston, L.M. ....01 Sep
X Jackson-Smith, S.P. ....01 Sep
X Jenkins, D.G. ....01 Sep
E King, W.T.P. ....01 Sep

LIEUTENANTS

S Manning, G.P. 01 Sep
X Martin, D.C.S. 01 Sep
X McGowan, A.B. 01 Sep
X Mitchell, J.D. 01 Sep
X Monnox, J. 01 Sep
X Morris, P.J. 01 Sep
MS Murray, A. 01 Sep
E Palmer, C.R. 01 Sep
X Rankin, G.J. 01 Sep
E Ritchie, D.B. 01 Sep
X Scott, N. 01 Sep
E Slowther, S.J. 01 Sep
X Smith, R.A. 01 Sep
X Sterry, J.E.B. 01 Sep
X Stewart, C.H. 01 Sep
MS Wade, A. 01 Sep
X Webb, M.R. 01 Sep
X Wells, J.D. 01 Sep
MS Witt, A.K. 01 Sep
X Colley, R. 01 Sep
X Love, L.E. 01 Sep
S Mawdsley, G.R. 01 Sep
X Stack, E.F. 01 Sep
E Cunningham, D.B. 01 Sep
X Griffin, S. 01 Sep
E Grinnell, J. 01 Oct
S Whale, V.A. 01 Oct
X Renaud, G.A.R. 16 Oct
E Grierson, A.D. 01 Nov
X Hesketh, J.J. 01 Nov
X James, R.M. 01 Nov
X Woad, J.P.R. 01 Nov
X Goddard, I.A. 16 Nov
E Lewis, D. 01 Dec
X Montague, R.J. 01 Dec
X Blythe, J. 01 Dec
X Humphrey, I.R. 01 Dec
X Briggs, C.E. 01 Dec
S Harman, S.J. 01 Dec
E Laidler, P.J. 01 Dec
X Higgins, P.M. 16 Dec
S Jackson, A. 21 Dec

2002

E Atwal, K.S. 01 Jan
E Butler, R.A. 01 Jan
E Moss, R.M. 01 Jan
E Priddle, A.C. 01 Jan
E Ralston, W.A. 01 Jan
E Ross, P.W. 01 Jan
E Saleh, J. 01 Jan
E Stevens, D.G. 01 Jan
S Truelove, S. 01 Jan
E Walker, M.J.E. 01 Jan
E Whitehead, R.J. 01 Jan
X Barrow, C.M. 01 Jan
X Beegan, C.F. 01 Jan
E Berry, S.M. 01 Jan
E Binns, J.R. 01 Jan
X Black, E.J. 01 Jan
S Blick, S.L. 01 Jan
S Boardman, S.J. 01 Jan
X Boulind, M.A. 01 Jan
X Brock, M.J. 01 Jan
E Brodie, D.J. 01 Jan
E Bukhory, H. 01 Jan
E Carbery, S.J. 01 Jan
S Chadwick, K. 01 Jan
X Chandler, P.J. 01 Jan
X Chapman, J.L.J. 01 Jan
X Clarke, M. 01 Jan
X Cooke, S.N. 01 Jan
E Cowie, A.D. 01 Jan
E Creek, S.B. 01 Jan
X Dawson, P.M.D. 01 Jan
X Eaton, D.C. 01 Jan
MS Edwards, D. 01 Jan
X Filshie, S.J. 01 Jan
E Fitzgerald, G.S. 01 Jan
X French, J.H. 01 Jan
E Fry, T.G. 01 Jan
E Gibson, T.A. 01 Jan
E Godley, D.J. 01 Jan
X Grey, C.S. 01 Jan
E Hawkins, S. 01 Jan
X Henry, G.P. 01 Jan
X Holliehead, C.L. 01 Jan
S Holmes, H.J. 01 Jan
S Horwood, N.A. 01 Jan
E Hughes, G.D. 01 Jan
X Hutchinson, N.J. 01 Jan
X Inglis, D.J. 01 Jan
X Issitt, B.D. 01 Jan
E Jarman, P.R. 01 Jan
E Jones, C.D. 01 Jan
S Kingdon, S.C. 01 Jan
X Ladislaus, C.J. 01 Jan
X Latus, S.H. 01 Jan
X Leeper, J.S. 01 Jan
E Louw, L. 01 Jan
E MacIntyre, I.D. 01 Jan
E Mann, A.W. 01 Jan
S Marland, E.E. 01 Jan
E Marshall, G.P. 01 Jan
X Mc Allister, S.E. 01 Jan
E McCamphill, P.J. 01 Jan
X McKay, T.W. 01 Jan
X Moran, B.M. 01 Jan
X Morgan, B.P. 01 Jan
E Morris, D.W. 01 Jan
X Nash, R.D.C. 01 Jan
X Nash, R.P. 01 Jan
X O'Neill, T.J. 01 Jan
X Parsons, R.M.J. 01 Jan
X Pearce, R.J. 01 Jan
MS Pinhey, A.D. 01 Jan
X Quinn, M.G. 01 Jan
E Rand, M.A. 01 Jan
E Richards, S.C.A. 01 Jan
X Rider, J.C.R. 01 Jan
X Rimmer, O.F. 01 Jan
X Rowberry, A.G. 01 Jan
X Russell, M.S. 01 Jan
S Sargent, D.R. 01 Jan
E Sawford, G.N. 01 Jan
E Simpson, W.J.S. 01 Jan
S Smith, L. 01 Jan
E Smye, M.A. 01 Jan
E Snell, D.M. 01 Jan
X Stevenson, S.R. 01 Jan
X Suter, F.T. 01 Jan
E Tait, S.J. 01 Jan
X Tappin, S.J. 01 Jan
X Taylor, G.D. 01 Jan
X Thom, M.F. 01 Jan
X Van Duin, M.I.A. 01 Jan
X Wallace, A.R. 01 Jan
S Wild, R.J. 01 Jan
E Williams, P.A. 01 Jan
X Wood, J.T. 01 Jan
S Cleary, C.M. 01 Jan
X Ludlow, J.A. 01 Jan
E Rooke, Z.S. 01 Jan
E Canty, T.A. 01 Feb
E Marden, T. 01 Feb
S Huynh, C.C. 01 Mar
X Fuller, J.E. 01 Mar
E McClurg, R.J. 01 Mar
E Reynolds, H.F. 01 Mar
E Wickett, R.J. 01 Mar
S Parry, S.D. 05 Mar
E Peasley, H.S. 01 Apr
E Redman, R.J. 01 Apr
E Barr, D.D. 01 Apr

LIEUTENANTS

E	Smith, O.J.	01 Apr
X	Crawford, V.E.	01 Apr
X	Day, B.T.	01 Apr
E	Gaytano, R.T.M.	01 Apr
X	Hopkins, A.E.T.	01 Apr
X	Mountney, G.A.	01 Apr
X	Rawlins, S.T.	01 Apr
E	Abbotts, M.C.	01 Apr
E	Gibbs, M.P.	01 Apr
X	Steadman, R.A.J.	01 Apr
E	Trewinnard, R.M.	01 Apr
E	Walker, S.J.	01 Apr
E	Williams, C.L.	01 Apr
E	Cheal, A.J.	01 Apr
E	Edwards, R.P.	01 Apr
S	Kirwan, J.A.	07 Apr
X	Pearce, E.A.	09 Apr
X	Campbell, A.L.	12 Apr
E	Sharp, C.	12 Apr
E	Sennett, M.C.	01 May
X	Adams, W.J.	01 May
X	Adamson, S.E.	01 May
E	Ainscow, A.J.	01 May
E	Anderson-Cooke, D.C.J.	01 May
E	Andrews, J.P.	01 May
X	Atkinson, L.V.	01 May
E	Bartram, G.J.	01 May
E	Bastiaens, P.A.	01 May
E	Baxter, A.C.	01 May
X	Biggs, P.	01 May
E	Boakes, P.J.	01 May
X	Bond, J.E.	01 May
E	Bowie, R.	01 May
E	Bradley, T.A.	01 May
E	Brooking, R.R.	01 May
X	Buggins, B.	01 May
E	Burdett, V.C.	01 May
E	Carey, T.J.	01 May
E	Collins, D.A.	01 May
S	Cook, N.J.H.	01 May
E	Coyle, R.D.	01 May
S	Elkins, S.S.	01 May
X	Ellis-Morgan, R.T.	01 May
X	Fergusson, I.B.	01 May
X	Flaherty, C.L.	01 May
E	Fuller, S.P.	01 May
E	Fulton, D.M.	01 May
E	Goddard, P.	01 May
X	Hall, S.L.	01 May
X	Hamiduddin, I.	01 May
X	Harrison, J.A.G.	01 May
X	Heaton, H.G.	01 May
S	Holland, C.C.	01 May
X	Holmes, P.J.M.	01 May
X	Hughes, G.E.	01 May
S	Johnston, D.R.	01 May
E	Kestle, M.E.	01 May
X	Kiernan, C.G.	01 May
X	Leeder, T.R.	01 May
E	Leese, J.F.	01 May
X	Lindeyer, M.J.	01 May
E	Livingston, M.P.J.	01 May
X	Lock, W.J.	01 May
E	Lucas, D.P.	01 May
X	Luxford, C.A.	01 May
E	MacCormick, J.	01 May
E	MacQuarrie, G.A.	01 May
X	Marsh, S.D.	01 May
X	Masson, N.G.	01 May
X	Minall, M.L.	01 May
X	Morgan, C.W.	01 May
X	Morgan, D.	01 May
MS	Mundy, A.R.	01 May
X	Newman, C.R.S.	01 May
X	O'Callaghan, P.F.	01 May
S	O'Rourke, R.M.	01 May
X	Oakes, M.C.	01 May
X	Olivey, T.D.	01 May
X	Orme, W.B.	01 May
X	Owen, V.F.	01 May
X	Paston, W.A.	01 May
MS	Patton, R.R.	01 May
S	Peattie, I.W.	01 May
E	Porritt, C.J.	01 May
E	Powne, S.P.W.	01 May
E	Roberts, A.P.	01 May
X	Round, M.J.	01 May
X	Rowe, P.J.	01 May
X	Russell, K.E.F.	01 May
X	Saltonstall, H.F.R.	01 May
X	Seaborn, A.	01 May
E	Sharp, A.P.	01 May
MS	Smyth, C.R.	01 May
E	Snell, A.J.	01 May
X	Spike, A.J.	01 May
E	Standen, G.D.	01 May
X	Steele, M.S.	01 May
X	Stone, J.W.G.	01 May
X	Storey, A.E.	01 May
S	Sturgeon, D.M.	01 May
X	Talbot, R.J.	01 May
E	Tate, N.M.	01 May
X	Taylor, R.P.	01 May
X	Veal, D.J.	01 May
X	Voke, H.L.	01 May
S	Wagstaff, A.	01 May
X	Ware, A.T.	01 May
X	Welsh, G.L.	01 May
E	Woolfe, K.D.	01 May
X	Wynn Jones, I.	01 May
E	Gubby, A.W.	01 May
S	Kennan, N.P.	01 Jun
X	Bradford, G.J.	01 Jun
E	Cooch, T.J.	01 Jul
E	Cross, N.	01 Jul
E	Ramsay, A.J.D.	01 Jul
E	Edge, H.R.	01 Jul
E	Gwilliam, E.K.	01 Jul
S	Bell, L.J.	01 Aug
X	Donovan, S.J.	01 Aug
X	Ritchie, I.D.	01 Aug
X	Smith, E.G.G.	01 Aug
X	Unwin, N.R.F.	01 Aug
X	Voke, C.A.	01 Aug
X	Bullock, J.R.	01 Aug
E	Chang, H.W.	01 Aug
X	Hart, S.D.	01 Aug
E	Holgate, J.A.	01 Aug
X	Leeson, A.R.	01 Aug
X	Walker, N.M.C.	01 Aug
E	French, P.	02 Aug
X	Lippe, P.W.	02 Aug
E	Marrison, G.R.	02 Aug
E	Patch, S.J.	02 Aug
X	Wylie, D.	02 Aug
E	Tait, M.D.	27 Aug
E	Munro, H.L.	01 Sep
S	Chesters, D.M.B.	01 Sep
X	Morey, K.N.	01 Sep
X	Parkinson, J.H.G.	01 Sep
E	Ashton, J.	01 Sep
E	Best, R.M.	01 Sep
X	Botting, N.A.	01 Sep
E	Brierley, S.P.J.	01 Sep
E	Bromwell, M.S.	01 Sep
X	Burrell, D.J.	01 Sep
E	Callis, G.J.	01 Sep
E	Carvosso-White, A.L.	01 Sep
X	Causton, J.F.	01 Sep
E	Chatterjee, S.	01 Sep
E	Cripps, M.J.	01 Sep
X	Crompton, A.P.J.	01 Sep
X	Eling, R.J.	01 Sep

LIEUTENANTS

X	Elliot-Smith, T.J.	01 Sep
E	Ellis, D.R.	01 Sep
X	Feasey, I.D.	01 Sep
X	Fullman, G.	01 Sep
X	Garner, M.E.	01 Sep
E	Gooch, M.D.	01 Sep
E	Goodenough, R.H.	01 Sep
X	Gorman, D.A.	01 Sep
X	Green, L.J.	01 Sep
X	Gulliver, J.W.	01 Sep
E	Hall, C.L.	01 Sep
E	Handoll, G.N.G.	01 Sep
E	Harding, D.V.	01 Sep
E	Heath, S.P.R.	01 Sep
E	Horsted, J.A.	01 Sep
S	Hunt, R.J.C.	01 Sep
E	Hyde, J.W.	01 Sep
E	James, A.G.	01 Sep
X	Johnson, M.W.	01 Sep
E	Keenan, B.F.	01 Sep
X	King, I.A.	01 Sep
X	Kingston, E.A.	01 Sep
E	Lewis, M.D.	01 Sep
S	Lloyd, M.R.	01 Sep
X	Malcolm, P.S.	01 Sep
X	Marriott, M.J.	01 Sep
X	Masterman, A.P.	01 Sep
E	McCarthy, D.J.	01 Sep
E	McEwan, R.D.	01 Sep
X	Molloy, L.	01 Sep
S	Morris, H.S.	01 Sep
X	Moseley, S.H.	01 Sep
X	Murray, G.M.	01 Sep
E	Newall, P.J.	01 Sep
E	Nguyo, D.N.	01 Sep
E	Northcott, P.J.	01 Sep
E	Norton, A.L.E.	01 Sep
X	Owen, D.P.C.	01 Sep
E	Peck, S.R.	01 Sep
E	Reynolds, A.C.J.	01 Sep
X	Riddett, A.O.	01 Sep
E	Rose, A.	01 Sep
X	Ryan, P.D.B.	01 Sep
X	Ryan, P.J.	01 Sep
E	Sturgeon, M.	01 Sep
X	Taylor, J.E.H.	01 Sep
X	Wallace, R.S.	01 Sep
S	Ward, A.J.	01 Sep
S	Webb, E.L.	01 Sep
X	Westwood, A.J.	01 Sep
E	Woodley, S.L.	01 Sep
X	Zipfell, A.J.	01 Sep
X	Abel, L.	01 Sep
X	Baker, J.E.G.	01 Sep
S	Mettam, S.R.	01 Sep
X	Southworth, M.	01 Sep
X	Sykes, M.J.	01 Sep
X	Hudson, A.I.	01 Oct
X	Clee, J.S.	01 Oct
E	Mann, C.A.	01 Oct
X	Baverstock, A.P.	01 Oct
E	Burt, D.J.	01 Oct
E	Ford, B.E.	01 Oct
MS	Green, P.G.	01 Oct
X	Harrison, I.	01 Oct
X	Little, C.M.	01 Oct
X	May, D.M.	01 Oct
X	Monk, K.N.	01 Oct
S	Robinson, D.	01 Oct
E	Stanley, A.B.	01 Oct
X	Vout, D.K.	01 Oct
X	Watson, R.D.	01 Oct
X	Webb, J.P.	01 Oct
X	Morris, D.R.	01 Oct
X	Williamson, P.J.	01 Oct
X	Carpenter, G.E.	01 Oct
X	Doe, J.R.	01 Oct
X	Lupini, J.M.	01 Oct
E	Hallett, D.J.	01 Nov
MS	Sykes, K.D.	01 Nov
X	Skipper, J.A.	01 Nov
S	Harding, E.L.	12 Nov
X	Green, J.	16 Nov
S	Anderson, L.A.	01 Dec
X	Ayrton, R.E.	01 Dec
X	Rees, D.S.J.	01 Dec
X	Shepherd, A.C.	01 Dec
MS	Vines, N.O.	01 Dec
S	Lanigan, B.R.	01 Dec

2003

X	Bergman, B.F.	01 Jan
X	Powell, R.J.	01 Jan
E	Alderton, P.A.	01 Jan
X	Armstrong, R.J.	01 Jan
E	Bailey, T.D.	01 Jan
E	Bass, P.W.	01 Jan
S	Beales, N.S.	01 Jan
X	Bickley, G.N.	01 Jan
X	Birch, P.L.	01 Jan
E	Brindley, M.W.	01 Jan
E	Brooks, P.N.	01 Jan
E	Brown, J.A.	01 Jan
S	Bulmer, W.E.	01 Jan
X	Burns, A.J.	01 Jan
X	Cantellow, R.B.	01 Jan
E	Clarkson, A.M.	01 Jan
S	Conran, N.W.D.	01 Jan
S	Coppin, N.J.	01 Jan
E	Craven, D.	01 Jan
S	Cunnell, R.L.	01 Jan
X	Day, A.	01 Jan
S	Di Maio, M.D.	01 Jan
X	Gascoigne, J.	01 Jan
X	Gater, J.C.	01 Jan
E	Goodsell, D.L.	01 Jan
E	Griffiths, N.C.	01 Jan
X	Hall, G.W.R.	01 Jan
E	Harvey, G.A.	01 Jan
X	Hayes, M.A.	01 Jan
S	Hughes, B.F.M.	01 Jan
E	Hughes, F.C.	01 Jan
X	Hunt, R.E.	01 Jan
E	Inness, M.J.	01 Jan
X	Johnston, J.J.	01 Jan
X	Jones, E.N.L.	01 Jan
X	Kelly, S.	01 Jan
E	Kiff, I.W.	01 Jan
X	L'Amie, C.A.	01 Jan
X	Lancaster, J.H.D.	01 Jan
S	Lawson, A.F.	01 Jan
X	Ligale, E.	01 Jan
X	Lovell, J.E.C.	01 Jan
X	MacPherson, C.A.C.	01 Jan
X	Malone, R.W.	01 Jan
X	McGreal, B.	01 Jan
X	McMaster, G.T.	01 Jan
E	McQuire, D.E.A.	01 Jan
S	Mowat, A.D.J.	01 Jan
X	Notley, E.J.	01 Jan
E	O'Connor, D.P.	01 Jan
X	O'Neill, H.L.	01 Jan
S	Pallett, A.J.	01 Jan
X	Palmer, M.D.	01 Jan
S	Pitman, L.J.	01 Jan
X	Pitt, W.T.	01 Jan
E	Prodger, A.P.	01 Jan
X	Quaite, D.G.	01 Jan
S	Reaves, C.E.	01 Jan
X	Redmayne, M.J.	01 Jan
X	Reynolds, J.	01 Jan
E	Rostron, J.H.	01 Jan
S	Roue, J.L.	01 Jan
E	Savage, D.L.	01 Jan

LIEUTENANTS

X	Semple, B.	01 Jan
X	Shanks, D.Z.	01 Jan
E	Sidebotham, S.C.	01 Jan
E	Trotman, S.P.	01 Jan
E	Walker, I.M.	01 Jan
E	Walker, J.	01 Jan
X	Weaver, T.H.	01 Jan
X	Weston, R.	01 Jan
X	Wheatley, N.S.	01 Jan
X	Wilson, G.P.	01 Jan
E	Wilson, M.G.	01 Jan
X	Worley, T.F.	01 Jan
E	Griffiths, G.	01 Jan
E	Coates, A.J.	01 Jan
E	Maddison, H.R.	01 Jan
X	Reeves, A.P.	01 Jan
E	Holdsworth, R.A.	01 Jan
E	Beverley, A.P.	01 Feb
E	Eldridge, S.J.	01 Feb
E	Ffoulkes, W.M.	01 Feb
E	Moore, S.	01 Feb
E	Stubbs, I.	01 Feb
E	Dyter, R.C.	01 Feb
X	Bannister, J.	01 Feb
X	Benarr, C.M.	01 Feb
E	Boughton, J.A.L.	01 Feb
S	Farrant, J.D.	01 Feb
X	Lynn, S.L.	01 Feb
E	Tomlin, I.S.	01 Feb
E	Cooper, A.	01 Mar
E	Maude, C.D.	01 Mar
E	Peskett, D.M.	01 Mar
E	Thomas, A.J.	01 Mar
S	Roberts, S.	23 Mar
X	Hackland, A.S.	01 Apr
X	Stephenson, C.J.	01 Apr
X	Duffy, M.L.	01 Apr
X	Kilbane, D.K.J.	01 Apr
X	Dobson, A.C.	01 Apr
X	Harrison, L.E.	01 Apr
X	Meacher, P.G.	01 Apr
X	Norman, T.B.	01 Apr
E	Dillon, B.	01 Apr
E	Parker, J.D.	01 Apr
E	Hearty, S.P.	11 Apr
E	Morey, R.G.	11 Apr
X	Anderson, A.E.	01 May
E	Andrews, D.M.	01 May
E	Atkins, P.R.	01 May
E	Ball, W.J.E.	01 May
S	Barnes, N.J.	01 May
X	Becker, R.K.	01 May
MS	Bennett, G.C.	01 May
E	Bingham, A.A.J.	01 May
X	Botterill, H.W.S.	01 May
X	Bowker, J.M.	01 May
E	Briscoe, J.W.A.	01 May
E	Buchanan, D.C.	01 May
MS	Burnett, P.H.	01 May
X	Campbell-Baldwin, J.W.	01 May
S	Chang, C.J.	01 May
X	Chudley, I.V.	01 May
E	Courtney, T.P.	01 May
X	Craig, M.J.	01 May
X	Dray, J.M.	01 May
X	Edwards, T.H.H.	01 May
E	Emery, C.S.	01 May
X	Evans, C.A.	01 May
X	Fairclough-Kay, M.	01 May
E	Fanshawe, E.L.	01 May
X	Ferran, S.H.M.	01 May
X	Fitzpatrick, N.J.	01 May
E	Foster, A.J.	01 May
X	Glendinning, C.J.A.	01 May
X	Gordon, J.	01 May
S	Gott, S.B.	01 May
E	Gould, I.	01 May
E	Green, L.D.	01 May
X	Hall, J.E.	01 May
S	Hannam, S.J.	01 May
X	Hill, T.E.	01 May
X	Hogg, A.J.	01 May
E	Holland, C.J.R.	01 May
S	Irving, T.C.	01 May
S	James, G.C.M.	01 May
S	Jemmeson, S.H.	01 May
S	Jones, D.K.	01 May
E	Jones, S.	01 May
E	Keane, B.M.	01 May
X	Kerley, B.J.	01 May
E	Law, J.S.	01 May
X	Leslie, B.D.	01 May
E	Love, J.J.	01 May
MS	MacPhail, N.M.	01 May
S	Mallinson, L.J.	01 May
S	Malone, M.T.	01 May
E	Markwick, K.W.	01 May
X	McCallum, M.D.	01 May
X	Miall, M.C.	01 May
X	Mitchell, P.J.	01 May
X	Mittins, S.	01 May
E	Nicholls, L.R.	01 May
X	Ottaway, T.A.	01 May
X	Payne, W.D.	01 May
E	Pond, R.J.	01 May
S	Proctor, N.S.	01 May
X	Riches, A.I.	01 May
X	Ronald, E.T.	01 May
S	Rose, S.	01 May
X	Ross, G.D.A.	01 May
E	Royle, N.A.	01 May
E	Russell, M.J.	01 May
MS	Scarborough, D.C.	01 May
X	Scott, N.	01 May
X	Seyd, M.	01 May
X	Shanahan, L.A.	01 May
X	Simmonds, D.D.H.	01 May
X	Skinsley, T.J.	01 May
X	Smith, C.J.	01 May
X	Smith, D.J.	01 May
E	Southwood, S.C.	01 May
X	Spark, S.M.	01 May
X	Stewart, B.C.	01 May
X	Thompson, S.L.	01 May
X	Thornley, J.G.C.	01 May
MS	Todd, G.A.	01 May
E	Tonge, M.S.	01 May
E	Turner, N.B.	01 May
E	Twiselton, M.J.	01 May
X	Walton, G.J.	01 May
X	West, G.A.	01 May
X	White, P.D.	01 May
X	White, S.	01 May
E	Wilkins, R.L.	01 May
E	Wilshaw, G.I.	01 May
X	Wilson, N.A.	01 May
E	Wright, D.W.	01 May
E	Wills, R.H.	01 May
X	Black, J.M.	15 May
E	Anderson, K.B.	01 Jun
E	Atkinson, A.	01 Jun
E	Hignett, G.	01 Jun
E	Sampson, J.P.	01 Jun
S	Wragg, H.C.	01 Jun
E	O'Sullivan, P.B.	01 Jun
E	Vaughan, J.R.	01 Jun
X	Grange, A.B.	27 Jun
E	Smart, C.R.	01 Jul
E	Chappell, M.W.	01 Jul
S	Lai-Hung, J.J.P.	01 Jul
X	Fraser, J.M.	01 Jul
X	Samways, M.J.	01 Jul
X	McKenna, D.R.	01 Jul

LIEUTENANTS

X	Sharp, J.V.	01 Jul
X	Forbes, R.G.	01 Jul
S	Fuller, R.	01 Jul
S	Brown, S.	01 Jul
X	Wrigglesworth, S.M.	01 Jul
S	Boot, S.	01 Jul
E	Bullock, J.B.	01 Jul
X	Nolan, R.J.	01 Jul
E	Bowers, M.R.	01 Aug
E	Burlingham, A.C.R.	01 Aug
X	Holmes, M.D.	01 Aug
E	Robertson, I.W.	01 Aug
S	Rogers, S.M.	01 Sep
X	Shropshall, I.J.	01 Sep
X	Abbot, R.L.	01 Sep
E	Anderson, L.C.	01 Sep
E	Bailey, I.J.	01 Sep
X	Baird, G.M.	01 Sep
X	Barber, M.	01 Sep
X	Barfoot, P.M.	01 Sep
X	Berry, J.T.	01 Sep
S	Boon, S.E.	01 Sep
E	Butler, J.E.	01 Sep
S	Byron, D.C.	01 Sep
E	Caddick, A.	01 Sep
X	Carnew, S.F.	01 Sep
X	Cassidy, S.M.	01 Sep
X	Cloney, J.W.J.	01 Sep
X	Coughlan, S.	01 Sep
E	Cowell, R.J.	01 Sep
X	Cumming, F.S.	01 Sep
E	Dymond, J.R.M.	01 Sep
E	Earle-Payne, G.E.	01 Sep
E	Faulkner, S.G.	01 Sep
E	Fearon, D.J.	01 Sep
E	Fiddock, M.L.	01 Sep
X	Gaskin, D.E.	01 Sep
X	Gilmore, J.E.	01 Sep
E	Gray, J.M.	01 Sep
X	Gray, R.L.	01 Sep
E	Grice, M.G.	01 Sep
E	Hale, B.W.	01 Sep
X	Hodder, P.J.	01 Sep
S	Hughes, G.A.	01 Sep
X	Hulse, R.M.	01 Sep
X	Hunt, B.P.	01 Sep
S	Imrie, S.J.	01 Sep
E	Jerrold, W.H.	01 Sep
X	Jones, G.J.L.	01 Sep
E	Kadinopoulos, B.A.	01 Sep
X	Kirkby, S.J.	01 Sep

S	Law, S.J.	01 Sep
X	Lewis, W.D.	01 Sep
X	MacDonald, K.L.	01 Sep
X	MacLean, G.F.	01 Sep
X	Marjoribanks, C.	01 Sep
X	McCallum, G.P.	01 Sep
E	McCormack, G.	01 Sep
E	Mole, A.J.	01 Sep
X	Nixon, S.E.K.	01 Sep
X	Petch, A.N.	01 Sep
E	Peterson, K.A.	01 Sep
X	Phillips, R.E.	01 Sep
X	Plenty, A.J.	01 Sep
E	Reynolds, M.E.	01 Sep
S	Richardson, S.C.	01 Sep
S	Roberts, B.	01 Sep
X	Royston, J.L.	01 Sep
E	Sharkey, P.J.	01 Sep
X	Sharrott, C.	01 Sep
X	Shears, G.R.	01 Sep
E	Sobers, S.	01 Sep
E	Stevens, J.I.	01 Sep
X	Stubbs, B.D.	01 Sep
E	Tantam, R.J.G.	01 Sep
E	Tough, I.S.	01 Sep
X	Trent, T.	01 Sep
X	Warren, R.A.	01 Sep
X	Weston, H.L.	01 Sep
E	Williams, B.	01 Sep
S	Woosey, D.A.	01 Sep
X	Workman, R.J.	01 Sep
S	Yates, L.O.	01 Sep
E	Woodman, D.P.	01 Sep
X	Pugh, G.N.J.	01 Oct
X	Parry, G.R.	01 Oct
E	Baddeley, R.	01 Nov
E	Selden, J.D.A.	01 Nov
E	Steiger, R.C.	01 Nov
MS	Storey, A-L.	01 Nov
X	George, C.A.	01 Nov
X	McLeod, K.Y.L.	01 Dec
X	Reynolds, Z.A.	01 Dec
X	Voigt, M.A.	01 Dec
X	Bettles, J.	01 Dec
E	Hetherington, T.A.	01 Dec

2004

E	Anderson, K.P.	01 Jan
E	Cripps, N.J.	01 Jan
E	Curtiss, C.J.	01 Jan
E	Devlin, C.J.	01 Jan
E	Webster, A.J.	01 Jan

X	Vincent, P.H.	01 Jan
X	Armstrong, D.M.	01 Jan
X	Banks, M.J.	01 Jan
X	Barrett, S.	01 Jan
X	Barron, P.R.	01 Jan
X	Beard, S.A.	01 Jan
E	Bennett, M.A.	01 Jan
MS	Birkin, K.	01 Jan
E	Boud, C.S.	01 Jan
X	Brace, A.F.	01 Jan
X	Brazenall, B.C.	01 Jan
E	Ciaravella, T.J.	01 Jan
E	Clark, P.A.	01 Jan
S	Clark, S.M.	01 Jan
E	Crosland, S.A.	01 Jan
E	Daly, M.P.	01 Jan
X	Daniel, B.J.E.	01 Jan
X	Davey, C.S.	01 Jan
X	Dewar, M.J.	01 Jan
E	Dixon, M.E.	01 Jan
X	Dodd, P.M.	01 Jan
E	Dooley, M.E.	01 Jan
E	Elliott, S.P.	01 Jan
X	Evans, B.G.	01 Jan
E	Evans, R.P.	01 Jan
X	Fisher, R.V.	01 Jan
S	Flannagan, D.L.	01 Jan
X	Fox, D.J.	01 Jan
S	Gershater, S.C.	01 Jan
E	Gibson, A.	01 Jan
X	Gillett, N.D.	01 Jan
S	Goscomb, P.A.	01 Jan
X	Griffiths, N.M.	01 Jan
E	Harvey, P.G.	01 Jan
MS	Hazard, L.	01 Jan
X	Heward, M.G.	01 Jan
X	Hewitt, R.P.	01 Jan
E	Hogben, M.J.	01 Jan
E	Hopper, G.	01 Jan
X	Hounsome, J.R.	01 Jan
E	Hughes, T.W.	01 Jan
X	Ingamells, S.D.	01 Jan
E	Lee, R.A.	01 Jan
E	Lettington, P.D.W.	01 Jan
S	Marsh, D.R.	01 Jan
S	Marsh, S.W.	01 Jan
X	Marshall, J.M.	01 Jan
X	McMahon, D.S.	01 Jan
E	Mortimer, P.R.	01 Jan
E	Munday, S.W.	01 Jan
E	Nash, R.F.R.	01 Jan

LIEUTENANTS

X	Nekrews, A.N.L.M.	01 Jan
X	Norwood, J.K.	01 Jan
E	O'Brien, T.P.	01 Jan
X	Parker, M.J.	01 Jan
X	Pate, C.M.	01 Jan
E	Pearce, J.	01 Jan
X	Penalver, W.C.	01 Jan
E	Pike, R.T.	01 Jan
S	Richards, G.B.	01 Jan
S	Riggs, M.G.W.	01 Jan
X	Riley, R.A.	01 Jan
X	Roy, C.A.	01 Jan
E	Rucinski, P.G.	01 Jan
E	Say, R.G.	01 Jan
E	Scarlett, C.J.	01 Jan
X	Sedgwick, H.G.	01 Jan
X	Seton, J.	01 Jan
E	Sheehan, T.J.	01 Jan
S	Shortland, K.	01 Jan
E	Shrestha, S.	01 Jan
X	Simpson, C.J.	01 Jan
X	Stead, A.	01 Jan
X	Syson, C.F.	01 Jan
E	Thomas, M.A.	01 Jan
X	Thompson, A.J.	01 Jan
X	Thorley, G.	01 Jan
S	Tibballs, L.R.	01 Jan
E	Torbet, L.	01 Jan
X	Tretton, J.E.	01 Jan
E	Tumilty, K.	01 Jan
S	Turberville, C.T.L.	01 Jan
E	Turner, M.	01 Jan
E	Vardy, K.J.	01 Jan
X	Visram, A.H.	01 Jan
X	Walker, D.H.	01 Jan
S	Walker, M.D.J.	01 Jan
X	Waugh, R.P.	01 Jan
X	Westwood, T.P.	01 Jan
X	Wheen, C.J.D.	01 Jan
E	White, D.	01 Jan
X	White, K.J.	01 Jan
X	Wilkinson, J.R.	01 Jan
X	Wilson, S.A.	01 Jan
X	Yarham, N.P.	01 Jan
S	Jennings, C.R.	01 Jan
X	Gorman, G.K.	15 Jan
E	McLachlan, A.C.	19 Jan
E	Youngman, P.G.	01 Feb
X	Richards, S.T.	16 Feb
X	Thompson, D.J.	20 Feb
E	Braithwaite, G.C.	01 Apr
X	Claxton, A.G.D.	01 Apr
X	Sarkar, T.	01 Apr
X	Culshaw, J.	01 Apr
X	Hill, C.J.	01 Apr
X	Leightley, S.M.	01 Apr
X	Scanlon, M.P.	01 Apr
X	Tregale, J.	01 Apr
MS	Wernham, W.F.	01 Apr
E	Anderson, N.	09 Apr
X	Hart, S.J.	01 May
E	Alder, M.C.	01 May
E	Alderwick, M.E.J.	01 May
S	Baker, H.M.H.	01 May
S	Barclay, M.T.	01 May
X	Bell, D.J.	01 May
X	Bell, N.A.G.	01 May
X	Benbow, J.A.K.	01 May
X	Bladen, C.S.	01 May
X	Blair, L.D.	01 May
X	Bligh, S.L.	01 May
X	Brann, R.W.	01 May
E	Bush, D.J.	01 May
X	Byne, N.	01 May
X	Campbell, A.	01 May
X	Coleman, T.J.A.	01 May
X	Coles, A.J.	01 May
X	Colvin, M.A.T.	01 May
X	Cooper, E.S.	01 May
S	Cooper, L.J.	01 May
X	Cory, N.J.	01 May
X	Cox, M.S.	01 May
E	Crockett, S.K.	01 May
X	Crosby, D.W.M.	01 May
X	Cuthbert, G.	01 May
E	Cutler, D.T.	01 May
X	Dalgleish, G.A.	01 May
X	Dixon, S.P.	01 May
X	Frisby, P.	01 May
X	Gardner, L.P.	01 May
X	Gillard, K.E.	01 May
S	Goddard, D.S.	01 May
X	Goosen, R.D.	01 May
E	Gordon, D.E.	01 May
X	Greenhill, M.C.	01 May
S	Hackman, J.D.	01 May
X	Hanson, S.J.	01 May
S	Harriott, C.L.	01 May
E	Heap, G.G.	01 May
E	Howell, P.C.H.	01 May
X	Hudson, R.E.	01 May
X	Hunnibell, J.R.	01 May
X	Hunt, A.J.	01 May
X	Inglis, G.D.	01 May
X	Isaacs, N.J.	01 May
X	Isherwood, C.R.	01 May
X	Jardine, I.	01 May
X	Jewson, B.D.	01 May
E	Johansen, S.P.	01 May
X	Johnston, A.I.	01 May
X	Koheeallee, M.C.R.C.	01 May
X	Leaker, D.T.	01 May
X	Lindley, J.	01 May
X	Lowe, G.J.	01 May
X	Lucas, N.H.	01 May
X	Martin, R.L.	01 May
E	Maskell, B.M.	01 May
X	Mason, R.J.	01 May
E	Maunder, J.G.	01 May
X	McKee, R.W.	01 May
X	McPhail, T.C.	01 May
S	McPherson, A.	01 May
X	Morris, P.W.	01 May
S	Morrison, J.	01 May
E	Mountjoy-Row, R.E.	01 May
X	Murray, W.J.	01 May
S	O'Reilly, C.A.	01 May
X	Oliver, C.J.	01 May
E	Paton, M.S.	01 May
E	Phillippo, D.G.	01 May
MS	Pickering, D.A.	01 May
X	Robinson, M.S.	01 May
X	Scott, A.J.	01 May
X	Shaw, M.A.	01 May
X	Smith, K.M.	01 May
X	Smith, S.C.	01 May
E	Stanistreet, G.C.	01 May
X	Stewart, N.J.	01 May
S	Street, S.C.	01 May
X	Thomas, J.M.	01 May
X	Thompson, J.	01 May
S	Tomlinson, A.R.	01 May
X	Warren, M.J.	01 May
X	White, A.J.M.	01 May
X	White, R.E.	01 May
S	Williams, G.	01 May
X	Winterton, P.	01 May
X	Wood, M.W.	01 May
E	Wooding, S.J.	01 May
E	Harrison, S.	10 May
X	Williams, T.G.E.	01 Jun
E	Reilly, P.	08 Jun
X	McKeever, S.A.	01 Jul

LIEUTENANTS

E Ainsworth, A.J. 01 Jul
X Bailey, M. 01 Jul
X Balfour, R.D. 01 Jul
E Cheema, S.S. 01 Jul
E Collier, M.J. 01 Jul
S Collins, D.I. 01 Jul
E Collins, G.V. 01 Jul
X Cowlishaw, N.D. 01 Jul
X Edmondson, M. 01 Jul
E Evans, P.J. 01 Jul
E Fidler, M.M.G. 01 Jul
MS Flynn, M.C. 01 Jul
E Frost, L.J. 01 Jul
E Grant, R. 01 Jul
S Grayson, S. 01 Jul
X Grove, J.J. 01 Jul
X Hawkins, S. 01 Jul
S Hine, M.J. 01 Jul
X James, R. 01 Jul
E Jones, M.R. 01 Jul
E King, J.M. 01 Jul
E Lockhart, J.B. 01 Jul
MS Macey, K. 01 Jul
E MacMillan, S.J. 01 Jul
E McDougall, W. 01 Jul
E Munro, M. 01 Jul
X Pirie, I.T. 01 Jul
X Reid, D.R. 01 Jul
E Robinson, L.D. 01 Jul
S Searle, C.R. 01 Jul
E Sneesby, N.J. 01 Jul
E Tall, I.T.G. 01 Jul
E Thwaites, L.W. 01 Jul
E Utting, R.C. 01 Jul
S Vivian, P. 01 Jul
E Williams, L.J. 01 Jul
X Ennis, J.L. 01 Jul
S Evans, A. 01 Jul
X Ivill, S. 01 Jul
MS Parker, D.S. 01 Jul
MS Redding, A.M. 01 Jul
X Walker, J.J. 01 Jul
X Wall, K. 01 Jul
X Wotton, A.C. 01 Jul
MS Abey, J.A. 01 Jul
X Allen, R.W. 01 Jul
X Packer, R.G. 01 Jul
MS Peake, S.P. 01 Jul
S Ward, J.M. 01 Jul
S Wright, J.R. 01 Jul
X Bayliss, R.E. 01 Jul
S Brown, S.M.J. 01 Jul
X Gunter, J.J. 01 Jul
X Hind, K.N. 01 Jul
X Scott, J.V. 01 Jul
S Whittles, G.W. 01 Jul
X Wren, S.J. 01 Jul
E Belcher, D. 01 Jul
E Broster, L.J. 01 Jul
E Caddick, S.A. 01 Jul
E Davidson, J.D. 01 Jul
E Evans, C.C. 01 Jul
E Flitcroft, M. 01 Jul
E Green, W.J. 01 Jul
E Hardy-Hodgson, D.N. 01 Jul
E Heap, S.A. 01 Jul
E Henson, A.J. 01 Jul
E Leaver, A.D. 01 Jul
E Maddison, P. 01 Jul
E Martin, G. 01 Jul
E McNally, N.A. 01 Jul
E Morrison, S. 01 Jul
E Norton, I.A. 01 Jul
E Prideaux, R.J. 01 Jul
E Ripley, S.L. 01 Jul
E Roe, R.J. 01 Jul
E Screen, J.W. 01 Jul
E Stancliffe, A.E. 01 Jul
E Street, P.M. 01 Jul
X Walker, R.P. 01 Jul
E Whittington, R. 01 Jul
E Whyte, G. 01 Jul
E Young, D.A. 01 Jul
MS Klar, P.A. 01 Jul
MS Thornhill, S.M. 01 Jul
X Williams, A.C. 01 Jul
X Ryder, T. 13 Jul
S Deacon, P.R. 22 Jul
X Barrett, B.T. 01 Aug
X Cochrane, D.S. 01 Aug
X Gray, S.D. 01 Aug
X McMahon, D.P. 01 Aug
X Morton, B.A. 01 Aug
X Ray, L.B. 01 Aug
X Rees, R.M. 01 Aug
X Thomson, S.M. 01 Aug
X Westoby, G.T.R. 01 Aug
X Dicker, N.M. 01 Aug
X Greaves, M.R. 01 Aug
X Whitehead, T. 01 Aug
E Gosden, D.R. 01 Aug
X Richardson, M.F. 13 Aug
S Wright, H.J. 13 Aug
MS Burcham, V.L. 13 Aug
MS Fowler, J.E. 13 Aug
X Haley, C.J. 13 Aug
E Keam, I. 13 Aug
E Wright, N.D. 13 Aug
E Parkinson, H.M.L. 01 Sep
X Walker, J.J. 01 Sep
E Weedon, G.A. 01 Sep
E Almond, N.A.B. 01 Sep
X Attwood, K.A. 01 Sep
X Ballard, A.P.V. 01 Sep
X Banfield, S.D. 01 Sep
E Barrie, S. 01 Sep
X Bird, A.W. 01 Sep
X Blackburn, C.J. 01 Sep
E Blake, S. 01 Sep
X Bond, R.D.A. 01 Sep
E Bowers, K.J. 01 Sep
S Bradford, M.J. 01 Sep
X Brannighan, I.D. 01 Sep
X Browett, J.J. 01 Sep
E Brown, A.D. 01 Sep
E Burgess, P.G. 01 Sep
E Colley, I.P. 01 Sep
X Coughlin, P.J.L. 01 Sep
X Dacombe, C.A. 01 Sep
X Dale, N.A. 01 Sep
E Dalglish, K.M. 01 Sep
X Darlington, A. 01 Sep
X Dart, D.J. 01 Sep
X Davies, S.J. 01 Sep
X Davis, P.H. 01 Sep
E Dennard, K.J. 01 Sep
E Downie, D.R.M. 01 Sep
X Duke, A.J. 01 Sep
X Easterbrook, C. 01 Sep
X Elliott, T.D. 01 Sep
E Fickling, J.W.A. 01 Sep
E Fisher, N.D. 01 Sep
X Fleming, D.P. 01 Sep
E Foers, P.S. 01 Sep
X Fooks-Bale, M.E. 01 Sep
E Gahan, R.J. 01 Sep
X Gaunt, A.V. 01 Sep
E Groves, R. 01 Sep
E Harris, R.A. 01 Sep
E Hatton-Brown, O.R. 01 Sep
E Hobbs, T.P. 01 Sep
X Hodgkinson, S.P. 01 Sep
X Holmes, S.M. 01 Sep

LIEUTENANTS

X Ingham, N.H. 01 Sep
E Joyce, D.J. 01 Sep
X Keillor, S.J. 01 Sep
X Kemp, R.L. 01 Sep
X King, D.A. 01 Sep
X Knowles, D. 01 Sep
X Lipson, C.N. 01 Sep
E Lock, A.M. 01 Sep
E Locke, N.M. 01 Sep
E Longman, M.S. 01 Sep
S MacKenow, H.R. 01 Sep
X MacLean, S.M. 01 Sep
X Mallinson, I.P. 01 Sep
X Martin, R.J.W. 01 Sep
E Mawer, K.J. 01 Sep
X Mayberry, P.J. 01 Sep
X McGivern, R.P. 01 Sep
E McLaughlin, V. 01 Sep
X McMillan, N. 01 Sep
X McQueen, P.G. 01 Sep
X Meigh, P.D. 01 Sep
X Morgan, G.L. 01 Sep
E Mullins, N.E. 01 Sep
E Murphy, C.J. 01 Sep
X Neyland, D.A. 01 Sep
E Pearson, I.T. 01 Sep
X Phillips, L.C. 01 Sep
S Phillips, M.R. 01 Sep
E Piaggesi, G.F. 01 Sep
X Pimm, A.R. 01 Sep
X Preece, S.E. 01 Sep
E Pryce, H.C 01 Sep
E Purdy, R.J. 01 Sep
E Ralls, D.W. 01 Sep
X Richardson, J.F. 01 Sep
S Roberts, M.J. 01 Sep
E Roffey, K.D. 01 Sep
X Rugg, C.P. 01 Sep
E Samwell, M.G. 01 Sep
X Seal, M.O. 01 Sep
E Searle, A.J.A. 01 Sep
E Shakespeare, C.A. 01 Sep
S Smith, M.D. 01 Sep
X Stamper, V.L. 01 Sep
X Stevenson, A.P. 01 Sep
E Stevenson, P.M. 01 Sep
X Strawbridge, C.M. 01 Sep
X Stuart, S.A. 01 Sep
S Swift, R.D. 01 Sep
S Tarmey, S.L. 01 Sep
X Taylor, J.E. 01 Sep
X Taylor, J.T. 01 Sep
E Trosh, N. 01 Sep
X Tucker, P.J. 01 Sep
X Vaughan, E.A. 01 Sep
E Wain, A.W. 01 Sep
E Warrick, M. 01 Sep
X Williams, A.M. 01 Sep
E Wood, J.R. 01 Sep
X Wood, R.R.T. 01 Sep
S Wright, J.S. 01 Sep
X Mason-Matthews, A. 01 Sep
X Schofield, J.C. 01 Sep
X Aldous, R.J. 01 Oct
X Bailey, S.G. 01 Oct
X Orton, T. 01 Oct
X Anderson-Hanney, P. 01 Oct
X Crichton, G.S. 29 Oct
X Eacock, J.P. 29 Oct
S Brown, L.E.M. 29 Oct
S Parker, A.R. 29 Oct
X Elesmore, J.D. 29 Oct
X Evans, K. 29 Oct
X Thurston, M.S. 29 Oct
S Jones, A.L. 01 Nov
S Frost, U.E. 01 Nov
E Montgomery, H.E. 01 Nov
X Louis, D.R.A. 01 Dec
X Birkby, C. 01 Dec
X Briant-Evans, T.A.H. 01 Dec
X Carman, F.S.D. 01 Dec
X Duffy, J.C. 01 Dec
X Dunne, J. 01 Dec
X Ealey, N.J. 01 Dec
X Furmston, G.H. 01 Dec
X Green, A.J. 01 Dec
X Hastings, S.B. 01 Dec
X Horobin, P.J. 01 Dec
X Toland, M.J. 01 Dec
X Wilton, M. 01 Dec
X Marshall, C.G. 01 Dec
X Hopwood, A.P. 17 Dec
X Sandy, D.J. 17 Dec
X Snee, P. 17 Dec
S Byrd, L.B. 17 Dec
S Moore, N.G.A. 17 Dec

2005

X Wells, M.N. 01 Jan
X Aitken, L. 01 Jan
E Allan, O.J. 01 Jan
X Armand-Smith, P.H. 01 Jan
X Attwater, R.P. 01 Jan
X Barber, A.S.L. 01 Jan
X Bessant, M. 01 Jan
X Boulton, G.R. 01 Jan
S Brown, E.L. 01 Jan
X Bryson, V.L. 01 Jan
X Bulgin, M.R. 01 Jan
X Capps, J.A. 01 Jan
E Coffey, R.B.D. 01 Jan
X Collier, A.P. 01 Jan
X Corbally, M.L. 01 Jan
X Cunningham, S.I. 01 Jan
X Curd, M.C. 01 Jan
S Davies, D.J. 01 Jan
X Davies, D.T. 01 Jan
X Dixon, S.J. 01 Jan
X Emerson, M.J. 01 Jan
X Franklin, R.W. 01 Jan
X Garey, E.J. 01 Jan
X Hampson, A.G. 01 Jan
X Haskins, B.S. 01 Jan
S Hooper, T. 01 Jan
X Hopkins, N.S. 01 Jan
X Houlston, I.J.E. 01 Jan
E Husband, J. 01 Jan
X Hutchinson, M.R. 01 Jan
X Laidlaw, J.M. 01 Jan
X Lang, A.J.M. 01 Jan
X Mattock, N.J. 01 Jan
X McDermott-Evans, R. 01 Jan
X McDonald, M.J. 01 Jan
X Mifflin, M.J. 01 Jan
X Minnikin, S.B. 01 Jan
S Mitchell, S.E. 01 Jan
X Newby, C. 01 Jan
X Nightingale, S.D. 01 Jan
X Norriss, M.W. 01 Jan
X Owens, J.W. 01 Jan
X Pittock, S.J. 01 Jan
X Pledger, P.M. 01 Jan
X Pope, K.D. 01 Jan
S Savage, A.F. 01 Jan
S Searle, E.L. 01 Jan
X Shakespeare, B. 01 Jan
X Sherry, J.M. 01 Jan
X Sherwin, A.J. 01 Jan
X Smith, L.A. 01 Jan
X Sutcliffe, P.M. 01 Jan
X Tawse, L.O.J. 01 Jan
E Thompson, E.E. 01 Jan
X Tuffin, M.G. 01 Jan
X Ware, P.J. 01 Jan

LIEUTENANTS

X Warr, C.H. .... 01 Jan
X Waters, M.R. .... 01 Jan
X Wheeldon, M.A.J. .... 01 Jan
X Williams, L.A.J. .... 01 Jan
E Wykes, T.E.V. .... 01 Jan
E Ziolo, J.M.C. .... 01 Jan
X Sheals, E.J. .... 18 Jan
X Carter, C.A. .... 18 Feb
X Richardson, G. .... 18 Feb
X Scales, D.R. .... 18 Feb
X Taylor, A. .... 18 Feb
E Mulroy, P.J. .... 18 Feb
X Lewis, J.M. .... 25 Feb
X Perry, C.S.L. .... 01 Mar
E Wood, M.D.J. .... 01 Mar
X Cursiter, J.D. .... 12 Mar
E Floyd, R.E. .... 14 Mar
X Betchley, J.W. .... 01 May
E Winborn, D.J. .... 01 May
X Brettell, J.D. .... 01 May
X Buckley, B. .... 01 May
X Cooke, D.P. .... 01 May
X Cox, A.D. .... 01 May
X Cox, S.J. .... 01 May
X Dunford, L.J. .... 01 May
X Harris, H.J.L. .... 01 May
X Hazlehurst, J.A. .... 01 May
E Leckey, E.H. .... 01 May
X Macaulay, S.C. .... 01 May
X Malster, D.A. .... 01 May
X McCallum, N. .... 01 May
E McCrea, M.J. .... 01 May
X Relf, E.M. .... 01 May
X Scorer, A.J. .... 01 May
X Tasker, A.M. .... 01 May
X Vierow, M.K. .... 01 May

SUB LIEUTENANTS

2001

E Amorosi, R.G.F.L. .... 01 Sep
E Bell, F.J. .... 01 Sep
E Bowen, R.J. .... 01 Sep
E Golden, C.A. .... 01 Sep
E Gordon, A.J. .... 01 Sep
E Huggett, C.L. .... 01 Sep
X O'Neill, C.M. .... 01 Sep
E Tatton-Brown, H.T. .... 01 Sep
E Weil, D.G. .... 01 Sep

2002

X Pearson, A.J. .... 01 Jan
X Wood, C. .... 01 Jan
S Austen, T.V. .... 01 Apr
X Dawe, C.J. .... 01 Apr
X Blake, M.G. .... 01 May
S Boyd, E.M. .... 01 May
S Brooksbank, R. .... 01 May
X Burnet, E. .... 01 May
S Coles-Hendry, F.A. .... 01 May
X Frost, T.S. .... 01 May
X Greenwood, S.J. .... 01 May
S Hanks, O.T. .... 01 May
X Hillier, C.A. .... 01 May
S Hulse, R.J. .... 01 May
S Leech, S.L. .... 01 May
X McLone, S.P. .... 01 May
X McSavage, R.I. .... 01 May
X Milner, L.D. .... 01 May
X Mustafa, H. .... 01 May
X Neil, D.A. .... 01 May
S Parker, D.J. .... 01 May
E Peters, M.K. .... 01 May
X Purvis, S.G. .... 01 May
X Reid, J.A.W. .... 01 May
X Shortall, J.J. .... 01 May
S Smedley, R.L. .... 01 May
X Smith, B. .... 01 May
X Talbot, S.E. .... 01 May
X Talbot, S.J. .... 01 May
X Thomas, D.J. .... 01 May
X Bowman, S.K.J. .... 01 Jun
X Batho, W.G.P. .... 01 Jul
X Borrett, J.E. .... 01 Jul
X Cantrell, S.R.D. .... 01 Jul
X Carr, D.J. .... 01 Jul
X Chisholm, P.J.H. .... 01 Jul
X Driscoll, M.S. .... 01 Jul
X Hairsine, W. .... 01 Jul
X Hall, S.J. .... 01 Jul
X Hay, R.H.I. .... 01 Jul
X Higgins, D.J. .... 01 Jul
X Hopton, M.J. .... 01 Jul
X Jane, S.C. .... 01 Jul
X Johnson, A.M. .... 01 Jul
X Johnson, T.P. .... 01 Jul
E Lawrenson, T.A.H. .... 01 Jul
X Mahoney, A.J. .... 01 Jul
X McKeen, S.A. .... 01 Jul
X Montague, A.D. .... 01 Jul
X Morgan, F.C.F. .... 01 Jul
X Peschardt, C.W.H. .... 01 Jul
X Shaw, S.A. .... 01 Jul
X Smith, M.R.T. .... 01 Jul
X Stacey, E. .... 01 Jul
X Stephens, P.G. .... 01 Jul
X Westlake, K. .... 01 Jul
X Wilcocks, D.N. .... 01 Jul
X Willsmore, S.A. .... 01 Jul
X Wordsworth, J.D. .... 01 Jul
X Herridge, D.J. .... 01 Aug
X Hucker, O.C. .... 01 Aug
X Shropshall, K.A. .... 01 Aug
X Barr, D.J. .... 01 Sep
X Brown, A.P. .... 01 Sep
X Brown, M.A. .... 01 Sep
E Carpenter, G.J. .... 01 Sep
X Chapman, J.R. .... 01 Sep
X Clark, P.J. .... 01 Sep
E Cochrane, C.D. .... 01 Sep
E Cole, S.P. .... 01 Sep
X Cornelio, S.M. .... 01 Sep
S Costain, K.A. .... 01 Sep
X Coxon, H.E.M. .... 01 Sep
X Craven, O.E. .... 01 Sep
X Crombie, S. .... 01 Sep
E Dallas, L.I. .... 01 Sep
X Davidson, S.R. .... 01 Sep
E Dickson, K.G. .... 01 Sep
X Dixon, R.J. .... 01 Sep
E Gearing, R.M. .... 01 Sep
E Goodenough, R.E. .... 01 Sep
X Hagger, M.J. .... 01 Sep
E Hammock, E.R.F. .... 01 Sep
X Hough, P.J. .... 01 Sep
X Hougham, T.N. .... 01 Sep
X Hurman, R.N. .... 01 Sep
X Insley, A.D. .... 01 Sep
X Irving, P.J. .... 01 Sep
X Jenkins, T.R. .... 01 Sep
X Keegan, A.C. .... 01 Sep
E King, I.J. .... 01 Sep
E McBeth, G. .... 01 Sep
X McCavour, B.D. .... 01 Sep
E Mellor, D.P. .... 01 Sep
E Minty, D. .... 01 Sep
X Neale, D.F. .... 01 Sep
E Nicol, A.M. .... 01 Sep

SUB LIEUTENANTS

E Oldfield, C.A.W. 01 Sep
X Ormshaw, M.A. 01 Sep
S Page, C.A. 01 Sep
X Pearce, S.L. 01 Sep
S Poole, D.C. 01 Sep
E Ridgwell, D.R. 01 Sep
E Robertson, A.J. 01 Sep
S Robinson, P.J. 01 Sep
E Rudkin, A.L. 01 Sep
E Rushworth, A.W.E. 01 Sep
S Shaw, S.J. 01 Sep
E Shepherd, C.E. 01 Sep
X Shrubsole, G.M. 01 Sep
X Slight, O.W.L. 01 Sep
X Southall, T.E. 01 Sep
X Taborda, M.A. 01 Sep
E Thomson, P.A. 01 Sep
E Tuhey, J.J.G. 01 Sep
X Warren, A.J.L. 01 Sep
E Watson, J.R. 01 Sep
E Watson, S.C. 01 Sep
S West, T.L. 01 Sep
E Whitaker, R.E. 01 Sep
X Whitehouse, A.P. 01 Sep
E Abel, J.A. 01 Nov
X Coleman, J.M.P. 01 Nov
X Elliott, O.L. 01 Nov
E Farrant, S. 01 Nov
E Hankin, R.S. 01 Nov
X Haywood, A.J. 01 Nov
E Hewlett, P.J.E. 01 Nov
E Ivory, T.J. 01 Nov
E Kay, V.J. 01 Nov
E Lipczynski, B.J. 01 Nov
X Low, S.A.S. 01 Nov
X Perks, A.B. 01 Nov
X Pollock, B.J. 01 Nov
X Sauer, A.C. 01 Nov
X Sharples, J.H. 01 Nov
X Stant, M.S. 01 Nov
E Sutcliff, J.D. 01 Nov
E Sweetman, D.J. 01 Nov
X Taylor, N.S.C. 01 Nov
E Teasdale, J.P. 01 Nov
X Telfer, D.D. 01 Nov
E Tetchner, D.J. 01 Nov
X Whitehouse, M.L. 01 Nov
E Wright, G.J.T. 01 Nov
X Rees, S.G. 01 Dec

2003

X Akers, S.J. 01 Jan
X Alexander, W.A.D. 01 Jan
X Beedle, J.D.S. 01 Jan
X Bird, M.P. 01 Jan
X Burton, J.H. 01 Jan
X Ellison, P.J.P. 01 Jan
X Gill, A.B. 01 Jan
X Harris, R. 01 Jan
X Haynes, J.G. 01 Jan
X Hooper, W.R. 01 Jan
X Jamieson, P.A. 01 Jan
X Knight, J.M. 01 Jan
S Knight, S. 01 Jan
X Lamb, R.J.F. 01 Jan
X Martin, J.N. 01 Jan
X McAteer, D.J. 01 Jan
X Parrott, S.S. 01 Jan
X Parry, S.J. 01 Jan
X Paterson, J.M.A. 01 Jan
X Patrick, J.A. 01 Jan
E Philips, T.J. 01 Jan
X Rogers, M.S. 01 Jan
X Rolls, E.C. 01 Jan
E Shaw, C.R. 01 Jan
X Shields, K.N. 01 Jan
X Snel, K.E. 01 Jan
X Southworth, C. 01 Jan
X Stephens, S.J.R. 01 Jan
X Story, R.S. 01 Jan
X Vereker, R.J.P. 01 Jan
X Vessey, L.M. 01 Jan
X Arbuthnott, E.A.H. 01 Feb
E Baugh, A.J.E. 01 Feb
X Bell, L.G. 01 Feb
E Bent, P.M. 01 Feb
X Brady, M.V. 01 Feb
S Croxton, D.P. 01 Feb
X Dean, J.P. 01 Feb
X Freeman, E.M.R. 01 Feb
X Frith, A.M. 01 Feb
X Hamblin, P.A. 01 Feb
X Harris, A.M. 01 Feb
X Langford, T.D. 01 Feb
E Muir, A. 01 Feb
X Roberts, S.M. 01 Feb
X Royce, R.H. 01 Feb
E Ryder, M.R. 01 Feb
X Sheehan, N.M. 01 Feb
X Sidoli, L.T.A. 01 Feb
X Skinner, J.J. 01 Feb
E Smith, C.A. 01 Feb
X Starkey, D.S. 01 Feb
X Veti, M.A. 01 Feb
X Walker, M.J. 01 Feb
X Yemm, M.A. 01 Feb
X Swann, A.P.D. 01 Mar
X Bond, R.J. 01 Apr
S Grimley, T.P. 01 Apr
X Seal, M.R. 01 Apr
X Seddon, J.D. 01 Apr
X Sheppard, H.C. 01 Apr
X Baker, J.K. 01 May
X Bentley, G.S. 01 May
X Burgoyne, W.L. 01 May
X Cackett, T.E.R. 01 May
E Carlton, P.D. 01 May
S Carver, C.A. 01 May
E Chisholm, D.T. 01 May
X Collie, J.A. 01 May
X Corcoran, R.M. 01 May
X Dobson, S.C.S. 01 May
X Ellicott, M.J. 01 May
X Evered, J.F. 01 May
X Harper, K.J. 01 May
X Keane, J.P. 01 May
X Langmead, B. 01 May
X Marshall, A. 01 May
S Miller, A.D. 01 May
X Noble, R.V. 01 May
E Offord, S.J.J. 01 May
X Pariser, A.M. 01 May
X Parkin, M.J. 01 May
X Peacock, L.G.J. 01 May
X Piper, B.J. 01 May
X Pollitt, A.W. 01 May
X Proudman, M.P. 01 May
X Rawlinson, K.E. 01 May
S Rogerson, A.E. 01 May
X Sharples, M.J. 01 May
X Stephenson, J.M. 01 May
X Thomas, M.P. 01 May
X Tickle, M.J. 01 May
X Tyacke, R.S. 01 May
S Wright, J.N. 01 May
X Ashcroft, K.T. 01 Jun
X Askham, M.T. 01 Jun
X Bate, R.C. 01 Jun
X Batley, J.T. 01 Jun
S Bird, T.M. 01 Jun
S Buchan, L.H. 01 Jun
S Carr, J. 01 Jun
S Charnock, S.J. 01 Jun
X Crowe, P.D. 01 Jun

SUB LIEUTENANTS

X	Drewett, B.J.H.	01 Jun
X	Duncan, J.E.	01 Jun
X	Leaphard, D.P.	01 Jun
X	Lorenz, R.	01 Jun
X	May, O.B.	01 Jun
S	McIntyre, C.	01 Jun
X	Moore, J.P.	01 Jun
X	Paul, G.M.	01 Jun
X	Quick, B.P.	01 Jun
X	Taylor, S.A.	01 Jun
X	Bretten, N.J.	01 Jul
X	Camplisson, O.G.	01 Jul
X	Storton, G.H.	01 Jul
X	Leigh, C.J.	01 Aug
X	Allan, V.E.	01 Sep
X	Allinson, M.D.	01 Sep
X	Barham, E.J.	01 Sep
E	Betts, P.R.	01 Sep
E	Binns, J.B.	01 Sep
E	Blackmore, A.M.	01 Sep
X	Booth, T.O.	01 Sep
X	Cave, J.	01 Sep
E	Church, S.J.	01 Sep
E	Cox, M.J.	01 Sep
X	Cumberland, N.S.	01 Sep
E	Cutlan, S.L.	01 Sep
X	Dale, J.R.	01 Sep
E	Davies, J.S.A.	01 Sep
S	Davison, L.M.	01 Sep
E	Dix, C.P.	01 Sep
X	Dyer, S.D.	01 Sep
X	Ebbern, G.J.	01 Sep
S	Evans, T.W.	01 Sep
X	Farrow, R.D.	01 Sep
X	Ferguson, I.	01 Sep
E	Flannigan, A.	01 Sep
X	Flatt, L.B.	01 Sep
E	Forward, K.L.	01 Sep
E	Fowler, R.	01 Sep
X	Fredrickson, C.A.	01 Sep
X	Gilbertson, C.J.	01 Sep
X	Greaves, T.M.	01 Sep
E	Guild, I.W.	01 Sep
X	Hancox, J.	01 Sep
E	Heywood, R.H.	01 Sep
E	Hitchings, M.J.	01 Sep
X	Holburt, R.M.	01 Sep
E	Howe, J.K.A.	01 Sep
X	Innes, R.	01 Sep
E	Jones, D.P.	01 Sep
X	Lee, D.A.	01 Sep
E	Lister, M.J.L.	01 Sep
E	London, N.J.	01 Sep
E	Marlor, A.	01 Sep
X	Martin, D.L.	01 Sep
X	Maskew, T.A.	01 Sep
X	Matthews, P.J.	01 Sep
X	McEwen, C.J.	01 Sep
E	Moran, J.	01 Sep
S	Morton-Haworth, C.E.J.	01 Sep
X	Moss-Ward, E.G.	01 Sep
X	Nokes, O.	01 Sep
E	North, A.C.	01 Sep
E	Patten, M.L.	01 Sep
E	Payne, J.O.	01 Sep
E	Philipson, M.J.	01 Sep
X	Plunkett, G.N.	01 Sep
X	Power, B.	01 Sep
E	Rooke, A.E.	01 Sep
E	Rooke, K.E.	01 Sep
E	Rose, M.E.	01 Sep
E	Ryan, S.J.	01 Sep
S	Slayman, E.	01 Sep
E	Spacey, C.D.	01 Sep
E	Taberham, H.	01 Sep
E	Taylor, S.R.	01 Sep
X	Thompson, G.C.	01 Sep
E	Westbrook, K.	01 Sep
X	Weston, G.K.	01 Sep
X	Whittle, D.J.	01 Sep
X	Wilcox, C.R.	01 Sep
X	Williams, J.R.	01 Sep
S	Wilson, C.K.	01 Sep
X	Adam, M.W.	01 Nov
X	Ayers, O.R.B.	01 Nov
X	Collins, B.L.	01 Nov
X	Collins, C.A.	01 Nov
X	Cullum, W.E.	01 Nov
X	Edwards, M.I.	01 Nov
X	Flegg, W.J.	01 Nov
X	Fletcher, J.H.G.	01 Nov
X	Mason, D.	01 Nov
X	Muir, K.M.	01 Nov
X	Roberts, D.S.	01 Nov
S	Stephenson, R.J.E.	01 Nov
E	Wilshire, N.L.	01 Nov

2004

E	Adamson, H.J.	01 Jan
E	Allen, A.P.	01 Jan
X	Angliss, R.J.	01 Jan
X	Bakewell, R.A.	01 Jan
S	Barker, P.R.	01 Jan
E	Barter, E.C.	01 Jan
X	Black, K.J.	01 Jan
E	Blatchford, T.P.	01 Jan
X	Bradley, M.J.	01 Jan
S	Brokenshire, S.I.	01 Jan
S	Chatterley, D.A.	01 Jan
X	Cheshire, T.S.	01 Jan
E	Cloherty, A.	01 Jan
X	Cocks, A.E.J.	01 Jan
E	Curnock, T.C.R.	01 Jan
X	Davies, N.S.	01 Jan
E	Deakin, S.M.	01 Jan
E	Duthie, A.G.	01 Jan
MS	Eden, J.R.H.	01 Jan
E	Evans, R.G.	01 Jan
X	Fellows, C.R.	01 Jan
X	Fitzgibbon, J.	01 Jan
S	Forbes, M.P.	01 Jan
X	Gillingham, G.	01 Jan
X	Gooding, D.C.	01 Jan
X	Guy, F.L.	01 Jan
E	Hadley, C.M.	01 Jan
S	Hammond, C.R.	01 Jan
E	Heath, E.J.	01 Jan
X	Henderson, A.G.	01 Jan
E	Herzberg, M.J.	01 Jan
E	Hewitt, N.W.	01 Jan
E	Holland, S.W.	01 Jan
MS	Horlock, A.	01 Jan
X	Inglis, W.S.	01 Jan
E	Jones, H.	01 Jan
S	Jones, M.R.	01 Jan
X	Kelley, A.L.	01 Jan
X	Lake, A.	01 Jan
X	Latchem, A.J.	01 Jan
X	MacRae, K.	01 Jan
E	Maden, S.G.	01 Jan
X	Marlborough, M.J.	01 Jan
E	Martin, C.G.	01 Jan
X	Mason, A.E.	01 Jan
X	McCormack, S.	01 Jan
X	Mehlsen, N.M.N.	01 Jan
X	Montagu, T.B.E.P.	01 Jan
X	Morrow, O.J.	01 Jan
E	Mullis, G.	01 Jan
E	Parkin, B.A.	01 Jan
E	Parnell, D.C.	01 Jan
X	Patterson, P.X.	01 Jan
X	Pearson, R.J.	01 Jan
E	Percival, V.H.	01 Jan
X	Pinnington, A.J.	01 Jan

SUB LIEUTENANTS

E Porteous, R.A. 01 Jan
X Powell, G.M.J. 01 Jan
X Preston, J.N. 01 Jan
E Ray, B.T. 01 Jan
E Reynolds, D.P. 01 Jan
E Rooney, T.M. 01 Jan
E Rose, S.P. 01 Jan
X Smith, J.C. 01 Jan
E Smith, P.M. 01 Jan
X Stackhouse, M.C. 01 Jan
E Stephens, C.P. 01 Jan
X Sykes, H.E. 01 Jan
E Trigwell, S.P. 01 Jan
E Varaitch, S. 01 Jan
E Walter, S.R. 01 Jan
X Waskett, D. 01 Jan
X Whitaker, M.J. 01 Jan
E Wilkinson, S.L. 01 Jan
E Wyper, J. 01 Jan
S Bainbridge, P.A. 01 Feb
X Billings, A.J. 01 Feb
X Broadwith, J.L. 01 Feb
S Crawford, R.I. 01 Feb
X Crocker, D.T.A. 01 Feb
X Elliott, M.E. 01 Feb
S Flinton, A.R. 01 Feb
X Gardner, E.S.E. 01 Feb
X Giles, P.A.I. 01 Feb
X Hardy, J. 01 Feb
X Harrison, A.K. 01 Feb
X Higson, G.R. 01 Feb
X Horn, N.R. 01 Feb
X Jones, T. 01 Feb
X Jones, W.C. 01 Feb
X Knott, T.M. 01 Feb
X McArdle, M.J. 01 Feb
X McIntosh, J.R. 01 Feb
S McKenzie, H.K. 01 Feb
X Mileusnic, C.J. 01 Feb
S Padbury, S. 01 Feb
X Phillips, E.H.L. 01 Feb
X Pilkington, B.M. 01 Feb
X Pyette, M.D.V.C. 01 Feb
X Rowley, T.P. 01 Feb
X Scott, P.D. 01 Feb
X Skinner, A.L. 01 Feb
E Smith, N.D. 01 Feb
X Strickland, T.J. 01 Feb
X Taylor, N.R. 01 Feb
X Tiebosch, N.K. 01 Feb
X Trevethan, C.J. 01 Feb
X Vincent, C. 01 Feb
X Welsh, M.P. 01 Feb
X Williams, J.L. 01 Feb
E Winstone, N.P. 01 Feb
X Webster, M. 01 Apr
S Holloway, B.S.V. 01 May
X Leaman, T.P. 01 May
X Morson, M.G. 01 May
X Murray, J.C. 01 May
X Sinha, R. 01 Jun
X Coleman, A.P.G. 01 Jul
X Hall, R.S. 01 Jul
X Leonard, T.A. 01 Jul
X Magill, A.F. 01 Jul
S Bray, A.J. 01 Sep
X Bryden, D.G. 01 Sep
X Critchley, I.J. 01 Sep
X Gilbert, M.A. 01 Sep
S McLean, D.J. 01 Sep
X Neave, J.R. 01 Sep
X Nugent, H.A. 01 Sep
S Targett, H.A. 01 Sep
X Williams, N.M. 01 Sep
X Reid, J.R. 01 Nov

2005

X Casey, A.M. 01 Jan
X Crofts, A.F. 01 Jan
E Lees, A.C.S. 01 Jan
X Luke, C.J. 01 Jan
X Symcox, C.M. 01 Jan
X Topping, J.A. 01 Jan
X Wotton, R.J. 01 Jan
E Wright, M.G. 01 Jan
X Blunt, C.L. 01 Feb
X Newton, O.R.A. 01 Feb
X Oxley, J.D. 01 Feb
X Walford, L.S. 01 Feb
X West, D.M. 01 Feb

SUB LIEUTENANTS (UCE)

2001

E Reed, P.K. 01 Sep

2002

E Chaudhary, R. 01 Jan
E Simpson, E.L. 01 Jan
E Byers, H.R. 01 Sep
E Cheater, C.J. 01 Sep
X Coatalen-Hodgson, R. 01 Sep
E Errington, R.J.B. 01 Sep
X Fletcher, A.S. 01 Sep
E King, M.A. 01 Sep
E Magzoub, M.M.M. 01 Sep
E Thomas, A.G. 01 Sep
E Turner, V.M. 01 Sep
X Verrecchia, J.R. 01 Sep
E Vowles, I.R. 01 Sep

2003

E Turner, D.L. 01 Jan
E Willmore, S. 01 Jan
X Austin, S.A. 01 Sep
E Betts, A.T.J. 01 Sep
X Blackett, W.P.H. 01 Sep
E Griffiths, F.M. 01 Sep
E Kendall-Torry, G.C. 01 Sep
X Munns, E.N. 01 Sep
E Riordan, S.P. 01 Sep
E Roberts, D.L. 01 Sep
E Westley, A.J.R. 01 Sep
X Williams, O.C.L. 01 Sep

2004

E Blatcher, D.J. 01 Sep
X Holmes, J.J. 01 Sep
E Main, M.G. 01 Sep
E Myatt, M. 01 Sep
X Webb, A.F. 01 Sep
X Wright, J.S. 01 Sep
X Yates, S.P. 01 Sep

MIDSHIPMEN

2003

X Ferris, N. ....01 May
X Kopsahilis, A. ....01 May
X Atyeo, K.E. ....01 Jun
S Hastings, C.S. ....01 Jun
S Whatley, M. ....01 Jul
X Lane, E.H. ....01 Aug
X Amos, J.L. ....01 Sep
X Brown, R.J. ....01 Sep
X Brown, S.S. ....01 Sep
X Burrows, T.G. ....01 Sep
X Butcher, M.W. ....01 Sep
X Edwards, L. ....01 Sep
X Gibson, M.J. ....01 Sep
E Johnson, T. ....01 Sep
E Middleditch, T.C. ....01 Sep
X Peacock, J.D. ....01 Sep
X Revell, A.D. ....01 Sep
X Smith, A.M. ....01 Sep
X Stone, N.S. ....01 Sep
S Thomas, R.D. ....01 Sep
X Tong, S.R. ....01 Sep
X Tottenham, G.J. ....01 Sep
X Witton, O.E.N.J.C. ....01 Sep
X Banning, G.D. ....01 Nov
X Bratt, J.R. ....01 Nov
X Collins, S.J. ....01 Nov
X Knight, A.J. ....01 Nov
X Polhill, J.V. ....01 Nov
X Whittington, C.C. ....01 Nov

2004

X Duff, A.J. ....01 Jan
X Evans, M.R. ....01 Jan
X Kirman, C.R. ....01 Jan
X Howard, J.W. ....01 Feb
X Martindale, H. ....01 Feb
X Ridley, G.E. ....01 Feb
X Hutchinson, A.P. ....01 May
X Bone, M.P.G. ....01 Sep
X Dando, B.J. ....01 Sep
X Edwards, J.D. ....01 Sep
X Garner, R.J. ....01 Sep
X Kendall, P.C. ....01 Sep
X Richardson, D.M. ....01 Sep
X Shepherd, O.J. ....01 Sep
X Smith, L.M. ....01 Sep
X Stevens, C.K. ....01 Sep
X Wallington-Smith, J. ....01 Sep
X Gilbert, J.S.D. ....01 Nov
X Jeffs, S.G. ....01 Nov
X Kenchington, R.A.W. .....01 Nov
X Lane, M.J. ....01 Nov
X McGlone, F.R. ....01 Nov
X Winskell, T.R. ....01 Nov

2005

X Flynn, C. ....01 Jan
X Maumy, J.M. ....01 Jan
X Sloan, P.A. ....01 Feb

MEDICAL OFFICERS

SURGEON VICE ADMIRAL

Jenkins, Ian Lawrence, CVO, MB, BCH, FRCS .... 21 Oct 02
(SURGEON GENERAL (SL 01) OCT 02)

SURGEON REAR ADMIRALS

Farquharson-Roberts, Michael Atholl, CBE, QHS, MB, BS, MA(Lond), LRCP, FRCS, rcds .... 9 Dec 03
(MEDICAL DIRECTOR GENERAL(NAVAL) DEC 03)

Raffaelli, Philip Iain, MSc, MB, BCH, MRCGP, FFOM, rcds, jsdc .... 4 May 04
(CHIEF EXECUTIVE MAY 04)

SURGEON CAPTAINS

1992

- Baldock, N.E. .... 31 Dec

1994

- Howard, O.M. .... 31 Dec

1995

- Tolley, P.F.R. .... 31 Dec

1996

- Douglas-Riley, T.R. .... 31 Dec

1998

- Mugridge, A.R. .... 30 Jun
- Sykes, J.J.W. .... 31 Dec

1999

- Bevan, N.S. .... 31 Dec
- Jarvis, L.J. .... 31 Dec

2000

- Morgan, N.V. .... 30 Jun
- Gabb, J.H. .... 31 Dec
- Johnston, C.G. .... 31 Dec

2001

- Barker, C.P.G. .... 30 Jun

2002

- Brown, D.C. .... 30 Jun
- Campbell, J.K. .... 30 Jun
- McArthur, C.J.G. .... 30 Jun

2003

- Kershaw, C.R. .... 1 Apr
- Runchman, P.C. .... 1 Apr
- Ashton, R.E. .... 1 Apr
- Butterfield, N.P. .... 30 Jun
- Dean, M.R. .... 30 Jun
- Allison, A.S.C. .... 30 Jun

2004

- Walker, A.J. .... 30 Jun
- Pipkin, C. .... 30 Jun
- Hughes, A.S. .... 30 Jun

SURGEON COMMANDERS

1990

- Waugh, P.J. .... 30 Jun

1991

- Lunn, D.V. .... 30 Jun

1993

- Benton, P.J. .... 31 Dec
- Hett, D.A. .... 31 Dec

1994

- Nicol, P.J.S. .... 30 Jun
- Baker, A.B. .... 30 Jun

1995

- Buxton, P.J. .... 31 Dec

1996

- Aitchison, K.J. .... 04 Feb
- Burgess, A.J. .... 30 Jun
- McNeill Love, R.M.C. .... 30 Jun
- Perry, J.N. .... 31 Dec

1997

- Norwood, J.M. .... 01 Mar
- Johnston, R.P. .... 30 Jun
- Edwards, C.J.A. .... 31 Dec

1998

- Hughes, P.A. .... 30 Jun
- Midwinter, M.J. .... 31 Dec
- Risdall, J.E. .... 31 Dec

1999

- Lambert, A.W. .... 30 Jun
- Howell, M.A. .... 30 Jun
- Ross, R.A. .... 31 Dec

2000

- Groom, M.R. .... 30 Jun
- Bree, S.E.P. .... 30 Jun
- Burkett, J.A. .... 01 Jul
- Hill, G.A. .... 31 Dec
- Nicholson, G. .... 31 Dec
- Foster, C.R.M. .... 31 Dec

2001

- Townsend, J.S. .... 31 Jan
- Nichols, E.A. .... 31 Mar
- Turnbull, P.S. .... 30 Jun
- Stewart, M.D. .... 30 Jun
- Birt, D.J. .... 30 Jun

2002

- Pearson, C.R. .... 30 Jun
- Campbell, D.J. .... 30 Jun
- Clarke, J.M. .... 30 Jun
- Stapley, S.A. .... 30 Jun
- Evershed, M.C. .... 30 Jun
- Sharpley, J.G. .... 30 Jun

SURGEON COMMANDERS

- Millar, S.W.S. .... 30 Jun

2003

- Haddon, R.W.J. .... 01 Apr
- Wylie, R.D.S. .... 01 Apr
- Whitehouse, D.P. .... 01 Apr
- Terry, M.C.G. .... 30 Jun
- Hand, C.J. .... 30 Jun
- Smith, S.R.C. .... 30 Jun
- Miles, R. .... 30 Jun
- Tanser, S.J. .... 30 Jun
- Mellor, A.J. .... 30 Jun
- Blair, D.G.S. .... 30 Jun
- Fisher, N.G. .... 30 Jun
- Thomson, R.G. .... 05 Nov

2004

- Wood, G. .... 30 Jun
- Leigh-Smith, S.J. .... 30 Jun
- Cannon, L.B. .... 30 Jun
- Connor, D.J. .... 30 Jun
- Pimpalnerkar, A.L. .... 30 Jun
- Craner, M.J. .... 30 Jun
- Matthews, G.A. .... 30 Jun
- Thomas, L.M. .... 30 Jun
- Rickard, R.F. .... 30 Jun
- Rawal, K.M. .... 30 Jun
- Whittaker, M.A. .... 30 Jun
- Taylor, P.J. .... 30 Jun
- Bowie, A.N. .... 30 Jun

SURGEON LIEUTENANT COMMANDERS

1995

- Randle, M.P. .... 01 Sep
- Batham, D.R. .... 01 Sep
- Evans, G.W.L. .... 17 Oct

1996

- Ramaswami, R.A. .... 27 Jul
- Fowler, P.J. .... 03 Aug
- Neary, J.M. .... 01 Oct

1997

- Palmer, A.C. .... 01 Mar
- Yarnall, N.J. .... 01 Aug

1998

- Masilamani, N.S. .... 14 Jan
- Shrimpton, H.D. .... 04 Feb
- Streets, C.G. .... 01 Aug
- Smith, J.E. .... 01 Aug
- Freshwater, D.A. .... 09 Aug
- Daramola, O. .... 01 Dec

1999

- Baden, J.M. .... 17 Mar
- Duby, A. .... 23 Apr
- Dekker, B.J. .... 01 Aug
- Heames, R.M. .... 01 Aug
- Counter, P.R. .... 01 Aug
- Snowden, M.B.S. .... 01 Aug
- Brinsden, M.D. .... 01 Aug
- Tamayo, B.C.C. .... 01 Aug
- Houlberg, K.A.N. .... 01 Aug
- Gibson, A.R. .... 01 Aug
- Hughes, D.J. .... 01 Aug
- Parry, C.A. .... 12 Aug
- Greenberg, N. .... 01 Sep
- Walker, L.L. .... 04 Sep

2000

- Coltman, T.P. .... 01 Aug
- McCabe, S.E.T. .... 01 Aug
- Siggers, B.R.C. .... 02 Aug
- Bateman, R.M. .... 02 Aug
- Sowden, L.M. .... 02 Aug
- Dickson, S.J. .... 02 Aug
- Mercer, S.J. .... 03 Aug
- Ayers, D.E.B. .... 03 Aug
- McLachlan, J.K. .... 17 Aug
- Lew-Gor, S.T.W. .... 05 Sep
- Tennant, M.I. .... 14 Sep
- Kehoe, A.D. .... 01 Dec

2001

- Shah, R.R. .... 12 Jan
- Crowson, E. .... 06 May
- Webber, R.J. .... 01 Feb
- Matthews, J.J. .... 01 Aug
- Porter, S. .... 01 Aug
- Mantle, M. .... 07 Aug
- Marshall, F.T. .... 07 Aug
- McLean, C.R. .... 07 Aug
- Denholm, J.L. .... 07 Aug
- Smith, J.J. .... 07 Aug
- Reston, S.C. .... 07 Aug
- Bland, S.A. .... 07 Aug
- Milner, R.A. .... 07 Aug
- Schofield, S.R. .... 08 Aug
- Mackie, S.J. .... 12 Aug
- Imm, N.D.H. .... 23 Nov

2002

- Armstrong, E.M. .... 05 Feb
- Pickard, R.J. .... 23 Apr
- Dewar, J.C. .... 30 Apr
- Norris, W.D. .... 20 May
- Prior, K.R.E.J. .... 06 Aug
- Hutchings, S.D. .... 06 Aug
- Beadsmoore, E.J. .... 06 Aug
- Henry, M.F. .... 06 Aug
- Dow, W.A.M. .... 06 Aug
- Rees, P.S.C. .... 06 Aug
- McIntosh, J.D. .... 26 Aug
- Phillips, S.M. .... 03 Sep
- Whybourn, L.A. .... 28 Nov

2003

- Turner, M.J. .... 01 Aug
- Martin, N. .... 04 Aug
- Brodribb, T.J. .... 04 Aug
- Brown, A. .... 05 Aug
- Gay, D.A.T. .... 05 Aug
- Welch, J.F. .... 05 Aug
- Brims, F.J.H. .... 05 Aug
- Allsop, A.R.L. .... 05 Aug
- Evans, G.C. .... 05 Aug
- Cormack, A.J.R. .... 05 Aug
- Collett, S.M. .... 05 Aug
- Doran, C.M.C. .... 07 Aug
- Martin, N.P. .... 26 Aug

2004

- Nelstrop, A.M. .... 10 Feb
- Price, V.J. .... 04 Aug
- Franklyn-Miller, A.D. ...... 04 Aug
- Barton, S.J. .... 04 Aug
- Scott, T.E. .... 04 Aug
- Grainge, C.L. .... 04 Aug
- Keogh, J.M.E. .... 04 Aug
- Read, J.A.J.M. .... 04 Aug
- Coates, P.J.B. .... 04 Aug

SURGEON LIEUTENANTS

2000

- MacKay-Brown, A.L. ......01 Aug
- Cooke, J.M. ....02 Aug
- Gardner, C.B. ....02 Aug
- Hayton, J.C. ....02 Aug
- Harrison, J.C. ....02 Aug
- Stannard, A. ....02 Aug
- Dew, A.M. ....02 Aug
- Lamont, S.N.J. ....02 Aug
- Mercer, S.J. ....02 Aug
- Robin, J.I. ....02 Aug
- Guyver, P.M. ....04 Aug
- Pardoe, E.R. ....06 Aug

2001

- Patel, D.R. ....01 Aug
- Yates, E.H. ....01 Aug
- Bray, K.E. ....01 Aug
- Ruthven, S.C. ....01 Aug
- Beard, D.J. ....01 Aug
- Bains, B.S. ....01 Aug
- Arthur, C.H.C. ....01 Aug
- Bennett, S.A.F.J. ....01 Aug
- Wild, G. ....01 Aug
- Proctor, A.R. ....01 Aug
- Khan, M.A. ....01 Aug
- Wilmott, S.C. ....01 Aug
- Mercer, A.J. ....01 Aug
- Maples, A.T. ....01 Aug
- Bonner, T.J. ....09 Aug

2002

- Pointon B.M. ....04 May
- Cordner, M.A. ....01 Aug
- Phillips, J.C. ....01 Aug
- Wood, A.M. ....01 Aug
- Taylor, R.S. ....07 Aug
- Kershaw, R.J. ....07 Aug
- Barker, V.S. ....07 Aug
- Picken, C.R. ....07 Aug
- Ambrose, R.E.F. ....07 Aug
- Allcock, E.C. ....07 Aug
- Evans, T.E. ....07 Aug
- Edward, A.M. ....07 Aug
- Hemingway, R. ....07 Aug
- Vale, A.J. ....07 Aug
- Hunter, C.R. ....07 Aug
- Westerman, R.W. ....13 Aug
- Gregory, A.E. ....01 Sep

2003

- Calvin, A.J. ....04 Feb
- Leather, N.W.F. ....07 Apr
- Bradley, H.E. ....01 Aug
- Pengelly, S.P. ....06 Aug
- Gardiner, D.R.C. ....06 Aug
- Sargent, D.S. ....06 Aug
- Isbister, E.J. ....06 Aug
- McMenamin, D.M. ....06 Aug
- Gilmartin, K.P. ....06 Aug
- Newton, N.J.P. ....06 Aug
- Lindsay, M.H. ....06 Aug
- Shearman, A.J. ....06 Aug
- Boddy, K.L. ....06 Aug
- Morris, L.E. ....06 Aug
- Jaques, S.C.D. ....06 Aug
- Strachan, R.P. ....06 Aug
- Jones, A.L. ....06 Aug
- Dewynter, A.M. ....06 Aug
- Gordon, D.A. ....06 Aug
- Middleton, S.W.F. ....11 Sep
- Henning, D.C.W. ....19 Sep
- Penn-Barwell, J.G. ....07 Oct
- MacFarlane, G.T. ....08 Oct

2004

- Scutt, M.J. ....04 Feb
- Cockram, A.L. ....04 Feb
- Tayal, M. ....01 Aug
- Morris, A.J. ....03 Aug
- Wrigley, A.J. ....03 Aug
- Hillman, C.M. ....03 Aug
- Roue, K.S. ....03 Aug
- Gokhale, S.G. ....04 Aug
- Potter, D.L. ....04 Aug
- Roscoe, D. ....04 Aug
- Longmore, D. ....04 Aug
- Barnard, E.B.G. ....04 Aug
- O'Shea, M.K. ....06 Sep
- Mellor, R.G. .... 01 Dec

2005

- Philpott, M.C. .... 04 Jan
- McKinlay, J.A.C. ....01 Feb
- Fries, C.A. ....02 Feb

ACTING SURGEON LIEUTENANTS

2003

- Kingsbury-Smith, R.E. ...... 15 Jul

2004

- Herbert, L.J. .... 23 Jun
- Droog, S.J. .... 01 Jul
- Miles, S. .... 02 Jul
- Rainey, O.H. .... 06 Jul
- Halpin, A.C. .... 12 Jul
- Harding, E.J. .... 13 Jul
- Durkin, J.L. .... 15 Jul
- Martin, L.C. .... 16 Jul
- Minshall, D.M. .... 16 Jul
- Robinson, T.G. .... 20 Jul
- Barker, R.J. .... 22 Jul
- Davey, K.L. .... 22 Jul
- Gibbens, C.J. .... 24 Jul
- Hughes, C.L. .... 24 Jul
- Evans, H.J. .... 31 Jul

MEDICAL CADETS SURGEON SUB LIEUTENANTS RN

2002

- Bell, C.S. 01 Jul
- Booth, R.M. 01 Jul
- Brogden, T.G. 01 Jul
- Dowlen, H.T.B. 01 Jul
- Hornby, S.A. 01 Jul
- Warren, J.M. 01 Jul
- Williams, R.J. 01 Jul
- Wood, I.M. 01 Jul
- Howes, R.J. 27 Aug

2003

- Andersson, J.L. 08 Apr
- Wells, L.C. 08 Apr
- Weale, J.H. 29 May
- Bourn, S.J.N. 01 Jul
- Evans, C.V. 01 Jul
- Evans, J.T. 01 Jul
- Hardy, G.D. 01 Jul
- Hughes, R.W. 01 Jul
- Jeffery, S.M.T. 01 Jul
- Oxlade, A.T. 01 Jul
- Rennie, R.A. 01 Jul
- Scorer, T.G. 01 Jul
- Skyrme, L.L. 01 Jul
- Smith, A.H. 01 Jul
- Steer, R.R. 01 Jul
- Bleakley, C.I. 02 Jul
- Tomkins, B.M. 11 Sep
- Holland, T.J. 23 Sep
- Ritson, J.E. 19 Oct

2004

- Smith, F.E. 11 Mar
- Watchorn, J.C. 15 May
- Leong, M.J.L.J. 23 Jun
- Edgar, I.A.M.M. 31 Aug
- Shaw, A.F.H. 06 Sep
- Jamieson, S. 13 Sep
- Towner, S.D.P. 13 Sep
- Lee, R.K. 15 Sep
- Robinson, M.W. 16 Sep
- Fry, R.L. 20 Sep
- Henderson, A.H. 20 Sep
- Kemp, P.G. 20 Sep
- Pillai, S.N. 20 Sep
- Reilly, J.J. 20 Sep
- Denby, W.J. 25 Sep
- Angus, D.J.C. 28 Sep
- Jowett, A.G. 05 Nov
- Hale, A.L. 20 Nov
- Castledine, B.C. 28 Dec

2005

- Wake, C.E.V. 19 Jan
- Ahuja, V.Y. 22 Jan
- Horsburgh, B.A. 07 Feb

DENTAL OFFICERS

SURGEON CAPTAINS(D)

1996
- Morrison, G.L. .... 31 Dec

2000
- Sanderson, R.C. .... 30 Jun

2002
- Weston, M.W. .... 30 Jun

2003
- Thomas, D.L. .... 01 Apr

2004
- Norris, R.E. .... 26 Oct

2005
- Sidoli, G.E. .... 1 Jan

SURGEON COMMANDERS(D)

1990
- Stevenson, R.M. .... 31 Dec

1995
- Gall, M.R.C. .... 30 Jun

1996
- Culwick, P.F. .... 31 Dec

1997
- Aston, M.W. .... 30 Jun

1998
- Howe, S.E. .... 31 Dec
- Jordan, A.M. .... 31 Dec

1999
- Hall, D.J. .... 31 Dec

2000
- McJarrow, D.J. .... 30 Jun
- Redman, C.D.J. .... 31 Dec

2001
- Smith, B.S. .... 30 Jun

2002
- Elmer, T.B. .... 30 Jun

2003
- Turnbull, N.R. .... 30 Jun

2005
- Fenwick, J.C. .... 30 Jun
- James, I. .... 30 Jun

SURGEON LIEUTENANT COMMANDERS(D)

1995
- McMeekin, N.S. .... 15 Jul

1996
- Minall, P.A. .... 24 Jul

1997
- Davenport, N.J. .... 16 Jan
- Everitt, C.J. .... 11 Mar

1998
- Moore, P.G. .... 31 Dec

1999
- Leyshon, R.J. .... 09 Jan
- Stevenson, G.S. .... 14 Jan
- Winch, E.J. .... 24 Jan

2001
- Wingfield, M.H. .... 01 Jul
- Madgwick, E.C.C. .... 23 Jul

2002
- Doherty, M. .... 05 Jan
- Scott, W.A. .... 13 Jan
- Jessiman, S.I. .... 20 Jun
- Hands, A.J. .... 26 Jun
- Verney, K.H. .... 09 Jul
- Chittick, W.B.O. .... 10 Jul
- Dean, T.C. .... 22 Jul

2003
- McDicken, I.N. .... 25 Jun
- Drummond, K.B. .... 13 Jul
- Holmes, P.S. .... 20 Jul
- Murdoch, G.A. .... 20 Jul

2004
- Foulger, T.E. .... 11 Jun
- Burton, T.J. .... 04 Jul

SURGEON LIEUTENANTS(D)

2000
- Williams, B.R. .... 27 Jun
- Wade, C.V. .... 29 Jun
- Bryce, G.E. .... 29 Jun
- Southall, E.L. .... 24 Sep
- Turner, J.C.B. .... 24 Sep

2001
- Hamilton, M.S. .... 26 Jun
- Kershaw, S.H.C. .... 18 Jul

2002
- McNab, G.J. .... 19 Jun
- Short, K.J. .... 04 Jul
- Wells, J.P. .... 04 Jul
- Lovell, A.D. .... 25 Jun
- Williams, D.S. .... 25 Jun
- Stevenson, L.J. .... 27 Jun
- Park, L.K. .... 27 Jun

ACTING SURGEON LIEUTENANTS(D)

2004

- Chan, A. .... 25 Jun
- Hesketh, M.J. .... 25 Jun

ACTING SURGEON SUB LIEUTENANTS(D)

2003

- Hickey, R.M. .... 01 Apr
- Macleod, A.M. .... 01 Apr

CHAPLAINS

DIRECTOR GENERAL NAVAL CHAPLAINCY SERVICE AND THE CHAPLAIN OF THE FLEET

Hammett, Barry Keith, QHC, MA .... 11 Jul 77
(DIRECTOR GENERAL NAVAL CHAPLAINCY SERVICE. FEB 05)

PRINCIPAL ANGLICAN CHAPLAIN

Hammett, Barry Keith, QHC, MA .... 11 Jul 77
(DIRECTOR GENERAL NAVAL CHAPLAINCY SERVICE. FEB 05)

CHAPLAINS

1978

CE Barlow, D. .... 04 Apr

1979

CE Harman, M.J. .... 20 Sep

1980

CE Hilliard, R.G. .... 01 Aug

1981

CE Clarke, B.R. .... 30 Jun

1982

CE Howard, C.W.W. .... 28 Sep

1983

CE Jackson, M.H. .... 19 Apr

1984

CE Brotherton, M. .... 04 Sep

1986

CE Elmore, G.M. .... 30 Sep

1987

CE Luckraft, C.J. .... 05 Aug

1988

CE Thomas, D.W.W. .... 18 Oct

1990

CE Pyne, R.L. .... 23 Jan
CE Callon, A.M. .... 05 Jun
CE Poll, M.G. .... 14 Jun

1991

CE Green, J. .... 04 Jun
CE Scott, J.D.S. .... 03 Sep
CE Springett, S.P. .... 10 Sep

1992

CE Kelly, N.J. .... 26 May
CE Bromage, K.C. .... 02 Aug
CE Morris, J.O. .... 06 Oct

1993

CE Beveridge, S.A.R. .... 28 Apr

1994

CE Hill, J. .... 17 Jan

1997

CE Wheatley, I.J. .... 08 Apr

1998

CE Hills, M.J. .... 21 Apr
CE Evans, M.L. .... 01 Sep
CE Gough, M.J. .... 01 Sep
CE Wylie, D.V. .... 01 Dec

2000

CE Phillips, A.G. .... 14 Feb
CE Heycocks, C.J. .... 24 Sep

2002

CE Hallam, S.P. .... 05 May

2003

CE Hitchins, E.G.D. .... 06 Jan
CE Lamb, S.I. .... 06 Jan

2004

CE Stewart, M.P.M. .... 29 Mar
CE Petzer, G.S. .... 01 Aug
CE Corness, A.S. .... 06 Sep
CE Duff, A.J. .... 04 Oct

2005

CE Simpson, D.J. .... 07 Mar

PRINCIPAL CHURCH OF SCOTLAND AND FREE CHURCHES CHAPLAIN

Maze, Andrew Terence, QHC, BSc .... 11 Sep 79
(PR CHAPLAIN MAY 05)

CHAPLAINS

1981

SF Rae, S.M. .... 02 Feb

1990

SF Eglin, C.A. .... 10 Sep

1992

SF Britchfield, A.E.P. .... 01 Oct

1993

SF Brown, S.J. .... 20 Apr
SF Shackleton, S.J.S. .... 20 Apr
SF Wort, R.S. .... 27 Jul

1995

SF Beadle, J.T. .... 30 Mar

1996

SF Martin, R.C.J.R. .... 03 Sep

1997

SF Wilkinson, T.L. .... 04 Mar
SF Meachin, M.C. .... 07 Jul

1999

SF McFadzean, I. .... 01 Jul

2000

SF Ellingham, R.E. .... 17 Apr
SF Grimshaw, E. .... 02 May
SF Kennon, S. .... 24 Sep
SF Rowe, R.D. .... 24 Sep

2002

SF Goodwin, T. .... 05 May
SF Botwood, T.J. .... 09 Sep

2003

SF Devenney, D.J. .... 06 Jan
SF Dalton, M.F. .... 12 Jan

2004

SF McCulloch, A.J.R. .... 12 Jun
SF Thomson, S. .... 13 Sep

PRINCIPAL ROMAN CATHOLIC CHAPLAIN

Madders, Brian Richard, MBE, QHC 09-Sep 85
(DIRECTOR NAVAL CHAPLAINCY SERVICE (FAITH AUG 02)

CHAPLAINS

1985

RC Donovan, P.A. .... 22 Apr

1990

RC Sharkey, M. .... 01 Oct

1992

RC Couch, P.H.R.B. .... 05 May

1996

RC Bradbury, S. .... 18 Sep
RC McLean, D. .... 18 Sep

1998

RC McFadden, A. .... 01 Sep
RC Yates, D.M. .... 01 Sep

2000

RC Cassidy, M.J. .... 24 Sep
RC Conroy, D.A. .... 24 Sep

NAVAL CAREERS SERVICE OFFICERS (RN)

LIEUTENANTS (CS)

1998

- Drewett, C.E. .... 19 Sep

1999

- Jones, C.R. .... 08 Jan
- Concarr, D.T. .... 19 Sep

NAVAL CAREERS SERVICE OFFICERS (RM)

LIEUTENANTS (CS)

1998

- Rennie, J.G. .... 18 Sep

1999

- Wilcockson, R. .... 07 May

FAMILY SERVICE

LIEUTENANTS (FS)

1999

FS Butterworth, L. .... 16 Jan

ROYAL MARINES

CREST.- The Globe surrounded by a Laurel wreath and surmounted by the Crowned Lion and Crown with 'Gibraltar' on a scroll. The Fouled Anchor imposed on the wreath below the Globe. Motto - 'Per Mare Per Terram'.

THE QUEEN'S COLOUR. - The Union. In the centre the Fouled Anchor with the Royal Cypher interlaced ensigned with the St Edward's Crown and 'Gibraltar' above; in base the Globe surrounded by a Laurel wreath. Motto - 'Per Mare Per Terram'. In the case of Royal Marines Commando units the distinguishing colour of the units is interwoven in the gold cords and tassles.

THE REGIMENTAL COLOUR. - Blue. In the centre the Fouled Anchor interlaced with the Royal Cypher 'G.R.IV' ensigned with the St Edward's Crown and 'Gibraltar' above, in base the Globe surrounded by a Laurel wreath. Motto - 'Per Mare Per Terram'. In the dexter canton the Union in the remaining three corners the Royal Cypher. In the case of Royal Marines Commando units the numerical designation of the unit is shown immediately below the insignia. The distinguishing colour of the unit is interwoven in the gold cords and tassles.

ROYAL MARINES SECRETARY. - Whale Island, Portsmouth Hants PO2 8ER.

CORPS JOURNAL.- 'The Globe and Laurel,' Whale Island Portsmouth, Hants PO2 8ER

ROYAL MARINES ASSOCIATION. - General Secretary, Southsea, Hants, PO4 9PX.

ROYAL MARINES MUSEUM. - Southsea, Hants, PO4 9PX.

ROYAL MARINES

CAPTAIN GENERAL

His Royal Highness The Prince Philip Duke of Edinburgh, KG, KT, OM, GBE, AC, QSO

HONORARY COLONEL

His Majesty King Harald V of Norway, KG, GCVO

COLONELS COMMANDANT

Lieutenant General R H G Fulton, BA, rcds, psc(m), hcsc .... 3 Jun 03
(REPRESENTATIVE COLONEL COMMANDANT ROYAL MARINES)

Brigadier S P Hill , OBE .... 14 Sep 02
(COLONEL COMMANDANT ROYAL MARINES)

LIEUTENANT GENERALS

Fulton, Robert Henry Gervase, BA, rcds, psc(m), hcsc .... 3 Jun 03
(DEP CHIEF OF DEFENCE STAFF (EQUIP CAPABILITY) JUN 03)

Fry, Robert Allan, CBE, BSc, MA, psc(m) .... 7 Jul 03
(DEP CHIEF OF DEFENCE STAFF(COMMITMENTS) JUL 03)

MAJOR GENERALS

Lane, Roger Guy Tyson, CBE, FCMI, rcds, jsdc, psc(m), fsc, hcsc .... 6 Nov 03
(DEPUTY COMMANDER HRF(L) NOV 03)

Dutton, James Benjamin, CBE, BSc, rcds, psc(m) .... 4 May 04
(COMAMPHIBFOR/CGRM May 04

BRIGADIERS

2000
- Rose, J.G. .... 30 Jun

2001
- Thomas, J.H. .... 17 Sep

2003
- Spicer, M.N. .... 16 Jun
- Robison, G.S. .... 15 Sep

2004
- Salmon, A. .... 13 Apr
- Shadbolt, S.E. .... 01 Oct
- Capewell, D.A .... 18 Oct

COLONELS

1996

- Heaver, D.G.V. ....30 Jun
- Hopley, D.A. .... 31 Dec

1998

- Hartnell, S.T. ....30 Jun

1999

- Robbins, J.M.F. ....30 Jun
- Heal, J.P.C. .... 31 Dec
- Noble, M.J.D. .... 31 Dec

2000

- Haddow, F. ....30 Jun
- Bibbey, M.W. .... 31 Dec
- Chicken, S.T. .... 31 Dec

2001

- Thomson, A.B. ....30 Jun
- Mason, J.S. ....30 Jun

2002

- Howes, F.H.R. ....30 Jun
- Dunham, M.W. ....30 Jun
- Huntley, I.P. ....30 Jun
- Messenger, G.K. ....30 Jun

2003

- Stearns, R.P. ....30 Jun
- Denning, P.R. ....30 Jun
- Pickup, R.A. ....30 Jun
- Hook, D.A. ....30 Jun

2004

- Taylor, W.J. ....30 Jun
- Davis, E.G.M. ....30 Jun
- Bevis, T.J. ....30 Jun

2005

- Stewart, D.J. ....30 Jun
- Scott, C.R. ....30 Jun
- Watts, R.D. ....30 Jun

LIEUTENANT COLONELS

1988

- Nunn, C.J. ....30 Jun

1990

- Roy, A.C. .... 31 Dec

1991

- Grant, I.W. ....30 Jun

1992

- Parker, J.V.V. ....30 Jun
- Balm, S.V. ....30 Jun
- Parsons, P.H. .... 31 Dec
- McCabe, J. .... 31 Dec
- Armstrong, R.I. .... 31 Dec

1993

- Crosby, J.P. ....30 Jun
- Canning, W.A. ....30 Jun
- Gelder, G.A. .... 31 Dec
- Martin, P.J. .... 31 Dec

1994

- Beadon, C.J.A. ....30 Jun
- Hughes, S.J. ....30 Jun
- Lovelock, R.B. ....30 Jun
- Wilson, S.R. ....30 Jun
- Wotherspoon, S.R. ....30 Jun
- Taylor, M.K. ....30 Jun

1995

- Guyer, S.T.G. ....30 Jun
- Getgood, J.A. ....30 Jun
- Wilson, A.C. .... 31 Dec
- Tasker, G. .... 31 Dec
- Heatly, R.J. .... 31 Dec

1996

- Bruce, S.L. ....30 Jun
- Leigh, J. .... 31 Dec
- Musto, E.C. .... 31 Dec

1997

- Sampson, P.H. ....30 Jun
- Hutton, J.K. ....30 Jun
- Foster, G.R. .... 31 Dec
- Walker, R.E. .... 31 Dec

1998

- Herring, J.J.A. ....30 Jun
- Arding, N.M.B. ....30 Jun
- Brown, N.P. ....30 Jun
- Newing, S.G. ....30 Jun
- Marino, D.J. ....01 Oct
- Ellis, M.P. .... 31 Dec
- Davies, J.R. .... 31 Dec
- Price, M.J. .... 31 Dec

1999

- Cusack, N.J. ....30 Jun
- Mudford, H.C. ....30 Jun
- Page, M.C. ....30 Jun
- Wolsey, M.A.R. ....30 Jun
- Dechow, W.E. ....30 Jun
- Smith, M.L. .... 31 Dec
- Hall, S.J. .... 31 Dec
- Lindley, N.P. .... 31 Dec
- Spencer, R.A.W. .... 31 Dec

2000

- Summerfield, D.E. ....30 Jun
- Webster, T.J.C. ....30 Jun
- Cawthorne, M.W.S. ....30 Jun
- Salzano, G.M. ....30 Jun
- Burnell, J.R.J. .... 31 Dec
- Barnes, R.W. .... 31 Dec
- Bruce-Jones, N.W. .... 31 Dec
- Middleton, T.P.W. .... 31 Dec
- Matthews, G. .... 31 Dec

2001

- Paul, R.W.F. ....30 Jun
- Syvret, M.E.V. ....30 Jun
- Evans, D.M.M. ....30 Jun
- King, D.C.M. ....30 Jun

2002

- McCardle, J.A. ....30 Jun
- Hudson, J.D. ....30 Jun
- Copinger-Symes, R.S. ....30 Jun
- Harradine, P.A. ....30 Jun
- Marok, J. ....30 Jun
- Maddick, M.J. ....30 Jun
- Cameron, P.S. ....30 Jun
- Ross, J.H. ....30 Jun
- Manger, G.S.C. ....30 Jun
- Curry, B.R. ....30 Jun
- Gray, M.N. ....30 Jun
- Maynard, A.T.W. ....30 Jun

BS Davis, C.J. ....30 Jun

2003

- Daniels, T.N. ....30 Jun
- Taylor, P.G.D. ....30 Jun
- Wilson, D.W.H. ....30 Jun
- Francis, S.J. ....30 Jun
- Birrell, S.M. ....30 Jun
- Holmes, M.J. ....30 Jun
- Pulvertaft, R.J. ....30 Jun

- Stephens, R.J. .... 30 Jun
- Magowan, R.A. .... 30 Jun
- O'Donnell, I.M. .... 30 Jun
- Thorpe, C.D.B. .... 30 Jun
- Dewar, D.A. .... 30 Jun

2004

- Phillips, S.J. .... 30 Jun
- Green, M.G.H. .... 30 Jun
- Bennett, N.M. .... 30 Jun
- Cundy, R.G. .... 30 Jun
- Livingstone, A.J. .... 30 Jun
- Kassapian, D.L. .... 30 Jun
- Oliver, K.B. .... 30 Jun
- Joyce, P. .... 30 Jun
- Stickland, C.R. .... 30 Jun
- Porter, M.E. .... 30 Jun
- Everritt, R. .... 30 Jun
- Pierson, M.F. .... 30 Jun

2005

- Forster, R.M. .... 30 Jun
- Ross, A.C.P. .... 30 Jun
- Scott, S.J. .... 30 Jun
- Saddleton, A.D. .... 30 Jun
- Greedus, D.A. .... 30 Jun
- Maybery, J.E. .... 30 Jun
- White, H.J. .... 30 Jun
- Pressly, J.W. .... 30 Jun
- Morris, J.A.J. .... 30 Jun
- Holt, J.S. .... 30 Jun
- Evans, P.J. .... 30 Jun
- May, D.P. .... 30 Jun

MAJORS

1983

- Simmonds, P.B. .... 01 Aug
- Corner, I.L.F. .... 01 Nov

1984

- Rye, J.W. .... 01 Sep

1985

- Clapson, K. .... 01 Jul

1986

- Tyrrell, R.K. .... 01 Sep

1987

- Ebbens, A.J. .... 01 Sep

1988

- Underwood, N.J. .... 01 Sep
- Milne, A.R. .... 01 Sep

1989

- Milner, H.C. .... 01 Sep

1990

- Walker, G.S.L. .... 01 Sep
- Gittoes, M.A.W. .... 01 Sep
- Hall, R.M. .... 01 Sep
- Parks, E.P. .... 01 Sep
- Grixoni, M.R.R. .... 01 Sep
- Sharland, S.P. .... 01 Sep

1992

- Cook, P.W.J. .... 01 May
- Corrin, C.ST.J. .... 01 Sep
- Bentham-Green, N.R.H. .. 01 Sep
- MacDonald, I.R. .... 08 Feb

1993

- Evans, M.A. .... 01 Sep
- Gwillim, V.G. .... 01 Sep

1994

- Pritchard, S.A. .... 18 Apr

1995

- Allison, K.R. .... 24 Jul
- Smallwood, J.P. .... 05 Sep

1996

- Hood, M.J. .... 25 Apr
- Pelly, G.R. .... 25 Apr
- Cullis, C.J. .... 25 Apr
- Freeman, M.E. .... 01 Sep
- Moore, C.B. .... 01 Sep
- Cooper, R.T. .... 01 Oct
- Thomas, P.W. .... 01 Oct

1997

- Gadie, P.A. .... 01 May
- Thurstan, R.W.F. .... 01 May
- Morris, P.E.M. .... 01 May
- Price, A.M. .... 01 May
- Searight, M.F.C. .... 01 May
- Slack, J.M. .... 01 May
- Hughes, J-P.H. .... 01 Sep
- Cook, T.A. .... 01 Sep
- Hembrow, T. .... 01 Oct
- Maese, P.A. .... 01 Oct
- Ritchie, W.J. .... 01 Oct
- Corbidge, S.J. .... 01 Oct

1998

- Kenworthy, R.A. .... 30 Apr
- Mc Laren, J.P. .... 30 Apr
- Holmes, C.J. .... 01 May
- Litster, A. .... 01 Sep
- Kemp, P.J. .... 01 Sep
- Sear, J.J. .... 01 Sep
- Amos, J.H.J. .... 01 Sep
- Gilding, D.R. .... 01 Sep
- Green, G.M. .... 01 Sep
- Chapman, S. .... 01 Sep
- Jones, M.R. .... 01 Sep
- Cunningham, J.S. .... 01 Oct
- Potter, S. .... 01 Oct
- Crouden, S.F. .... 01 Oct

1999

- Case, A.C. .... 24 Apr
- Kettle, R.A. .... 24 Apr
- Fergusson, A.C. .... 01 May
- Cunningham, J.T. .... 01 May
- Hills, R.B. .... 01 May
- Armour, G.A. .... 01 May
- Manson, P.D. .... 01 Sep
- McInerney, A.J. .... 01 Sep
- Baxendale, R.F. .... 01 Sep
- Hussey, S.J. .... 01 Sep
- Skuse, M. .... 01 Sep
- Stovin-Bradford, M. .... 01 Sep
- Green, M.R. .... 01 Oct
- Tupman, K.C. .... 01 Oct
- Richards, S.W. .... 01 Oct
- Beazley, P. .... 01 Oct

2000

- Murray, A.B. .... 26 Apr
- Robertson, N.B. .... 01 May
- Mattin, P.R. .... 01 May
- Bucknall, R.J.W. .... 01 May
- Cooper-Simpson, R.J. ...... 01 May
- Hammond, M.C. .... 01 May
- Walls, K.F. .... 01 May
- Chattin, A.P. .... 01 May
- Congreve, S.C. .... 01 May
- Cook, M.F. .... 01 May
- Murchison, E.A. .... 01 Sep
- Blythe, T.S. .... 01 Sep

MAJORS

- Wraith, N. 01 Sep
- Kern, A.S. 01 Sep
- Bakewell, T.D. 01 Sep
- Jermyn, N.C. 01 Sep
- Davies, H.C.A. 01 Sep
- Bulmer, R.J. 01 Oct
- Perry, R.W. 01 Oct

BS Watson, P.F. 01 Oct

2001

- Reed, J.J. 01 Jan
- Geldard, M.A. 01 May
- Bestwick, M.C. 01 May
- Walker, A.J. 01 May
- Craig, K.M. 01 May
- King, R.J. 01 May
- Spanner, P. 01 May
- Page, D.C.M. 01 Sep
- Daukes, N.M. 01 Sep
- Dowd, J.W. 01 Sep
- Hedges, J.W. 01 Sep
- Liddle, S.J. 01 Sep
- Hermer, J.P. 01 Sep
- Hughes, M.J. 01 Sep
- Jenkins, G. 01 Sep
- Taylor, M.A.B. 01 Sep
- James, P.M. 01 Sep
- Coomber, J.M. 01 Sep
- De Reya, A.L. 01 Sep
- Harris, C.C. 01 Sep
- Roylance, J.F. 01 Sep
- Thomsett, H.F.J. 01 Sep
- Twist, M.T. 01 Sep
- Fuller, S.R. 01 Sep
- Venn, N.S.C. 30 Sep
- Fraser, G.W. 01 Oct
- Green, G.E. 01 Oct
- Hannah, W.F. 01 Oct
- Kelly, A.P. 01 Oct

2002

- Brighouse, N.G. 24 Apr
- Dresner, R.J. 24 Apr
- Moorhouse, E.J. 24 Apr
- Balmer, G.A. 24 Apr
- Sutherland, N. 24 Apr
- Hardy, D.M. 24 Apr
- Kearney, P.L. 27 Apr
- Hale, J.N. 27 Apr
- Plewes, A.B. 27 Apr
- Lee, S.P. 27 Apr
- Roddy, M.P. 27 Apr
- Tanner, M.J. 01 Sep
- Blanchford, D. 01 Sep
- Read, R.J. 01 Sep
- Turner, S.A. 01 Sep
- Bailey, D.S. 01 Sep
- Harris, T. 01 Sep
- Hammond, D.E. 01 Sep
- Jackson, M.J.A. 01 Sep
- Kelly, P.M. 01 Sep
- McGhee, C. 01 Sep
- Paton, C.M. 01 Sep
- Preston, R.W. 01 Sep
- O'Herlihy, S.I. 01 Sep
- Manning, D. 01 Sep
- Goodridge, T.J. 01 Oct
- Smith, S.F. 01 Oct
- Underwood, P.J. 01 Oct
- Bourne, P.J. 01 Oct

2003

- Gray, J.A. 01 May
- Maltby, R.J. 01 May
- Morley, A. 01 May
- Parvin, R.A. 01 May
- Watkins, A.P.L. 01 May
- Brown, L.A. 01 Sep
- O'Hara, G.C. 01 Sep
- Jepson, N.H.M. 01 Sep
- Muddiman, A.R. 01 Sep
- Whitfield, P.M. 01 Sep
- Devereux, M.E. 01 Sep
- Ethell, D.R. 01 Oct
- Rearden, R.J. 01 Oct
- Stafford, D.B. 01 Oct
- Wilson, A.C. 01 Oct
- Todd, M.A. 01 Oct
- Bowra, M.A. 01 Oct
- Scott, S.C. 01 Oct
- Ward, C.D. 01 Oct

BS Weston, P.A. 01 Oct

2004

- Burrell, A.M.G. 01 Apr
- Collin, M. 01 Apr
- Lock, A.G.D. 01 Apr
- Lee, O.A. 01 May
- Crawford, A.T.S. 01 May
- Duncan, G.S. 01 May
- Somerville, N.J.P. 01 May
- Williamson, A.K. 01 May
- Cheesman, D.J.E. 01 Sep
- Wilson, J.G. 01 Sep
- Cantrill, R.J. 01 Sep
- Penkman, W.A.V. 01 Sep
- Stemp, J.E. 01 Sep
- Nicholls, B.A. 01 Oct
- Parry, J.A. 01 Oct
- Pilkington, A.G.H. 01 Oct
- Thompson, G.M. 01 Oct
- Tulloch, S.W. 01 Oct
- Clark, P.A. 01 Oct
- Fenwick, R.J. 01 Oct
- Rochester, R.W. 01 Oct
- Atherton, B.W. 01 Oct
- Brady, S.P. 01 Oct
- Taylor, S.D. 01 Oct
- Lugg, J.C. 01 Oct
- Merchant, J.M. 01 Oct
- Watson, R.I. 01 Oct
- Alderson, R.J. 01 Oct
- Churchward, M.J. 01 Oct
- Davies, C.R. 01 Oct
- Haw, C.E. 01 Oct
- Lynch, P.P. 01 Oct
- Pruden, I. 01 Oct
- Janzen, A.N. 01 Oct
- Houvenaghel, I.M. 01 Oct
- Jess, A.E.K. 01 Oct
- Middleton, C.S. 01 Oct
- Urry, S.R. 01 Oct
- Clare, J.F. 01 Oct
- Smith, D.M. 01 Oct
- Phillips, M.C. 01 Oct

BS Thornhill, A.P. 01 Oct

- Tarnowski, T.A. 12 Nov

CAPTAINS

1993

- Sharpe, G.A. .... 01 Jan

1995

- Ginn, R.N. .... 01 Jan
- Richardson, M.C. .... 01 Jan

1996

- Nicoll, S.K. .... 01 Jan
- Tyce, D.J. .... 01 Jan

1997

- Shergold, P.J. .... 01 Jan
- Sellar, T.J. .... 01 Jan
- Kilmartin, S. .... 04 Apr
- Sutton, S.J. .... 29 Apr
- Lancashire, A.C. .... 01 Sep

1998

- Holloway, N. .... 01 Jan
- Maddison, J.D. .... 01 Jan
- Westlake, S.R. .... 01 Jan
- Murphy, K.S. .... 01 May
- Baker, M.B. .... 01 Sep
- Coats, D.S. .... 01 Sep
- Fisher, A.G. .... 01 Sep

1999

- Lawton, P. .... 01 Jan
- Pickard, D.M. .... 01 Jan
- Ross, G. .... 01 Jan
- Gosney, C.J. .... 01 Jan
- Cowan, K.G. .... 23 Apr
- Moffat, J.W. .... 23 Apr
- Moran, J.T. .... 28 Apr
- Alexander, G.D. .... 01 May
- Bubb, J.D. .... 01 May
- Edmondson, S.P. .... 01 May
- Garnham, S.W. .... 01 May
- Gibson, A.J. .... 01 May
- Hasted, D. .... 01 May
- Hill, J.P. .... 01 May
- Mawson, J.R. .... 01 May
- Nicholson, D.P. .... 01 Sep
- Bird, G.M. .... 01 Sep
- Boschi, P.H. .... 01 Sep
- Dennis, J.A. .... 01 Sep
- Fuller, J.B. .... 01 Sep
- Hart, S.J.E. .... 01 Sep
- Johnson, M. .... 01 Sep
- Cambridge, G.A. .... 01 Sep
- Leyden, T.N. .... 01 Sep
- Ordway, C.N.M.P. .... 01 Sep
- Thompson, D.H. .... 01 Sep
- Howarth, S.J. .... 01 Sep

2000

- Hazelwood, C.D. .... 01 Jan
- Wiseman, G.R. .... 01 Jan
- Garland, A.N. .... 01 Jan
- Howarth, J. .... 01 Jan
- Cooper, N. .... 01 Jan
- Kenneally, S.J. .... 01 Jan
- Cross, A.G. .... 03 Apr
- Read, C.D. .... 01 May
- Atkinson, N.C. .... 01 May
- Edye, R.F. .... 01 May
- Foster, N.P. .... 01 May
- Gray, K.D. .... 01 May
- Howard, R.D. .... 01 May
- Mears, R.J. .... 01 May
- Thompson, J.P.B. .... 01 May
- Todd, J.W. .... 01 May
- Bowyer, R.J. .... 01 May
- Griffiths, N.A. .... 01 May
- Oura, A.N. .... 01 Sep
- Turner, A.R. .... 01 Sep
- Hardie, M.J. .... 01 Sep
- Totten, P.M. .... 01 Sep
- Foster, B. .... 01 Sep
- Brain, W.J.W. .... 01 Sep
- Durup, J.M.S. .... 01 Sep
- Huntingford, D.J. .... 01 Sep
- Kelly, T.J. .... 01 Sep
- Muncer, R.A. .... 01 Sep
- Todd, O.J. .... 01 Sep
- Ward, A.J. .... 01 Sep
- Davies, RT. .... 01 Sep
- Hopkins, R.M.E. .... 01 Sep
- Smith, G.K. .... 01 Oct

2001

- Stonier, P.L. .... 01 Jan
- Baines, G.A. .... 01 Jan
- Adcock, G.E. .... 01 Jan
- Collins, J. .... 01 Jan
- Fitzpatrick, P.S. .... 01 Jan
- Standen, C.A. .... 01 Jan
- Lucas, S.U. .... 01 Jan
- Giles, G.J. .... 01 Jan

BS Grace, N.J. .... 01 Jan
- Price, D.G. .... 01 Jan
- Tapp, S.J. .... 01 Jan
- Frost, M.J. .... 01 Jan
- Hunt, D. .... 01 Jan

BS Kelly, J.A. .... 01 Jan
- Sutton, D. .... 01 Apr
- Hulse, A.W. .... 01 Apr
- Hall, C.M.I. .... 01 Apr
- McCulley, S.C. .... 01 Apr
- Howe, S. .... 01 Apr
- Wallace, R.S. .... 01 Apr
- Wilcox, T.C. .... 01 Apr
- Fomes, C.J.H. .... 01 Apr
- Cavill, N.R.D. .... 01 May
- Hanson, S.C. .... 01 May
- Lindsay, J.M. .... 01 May
- Roskilly, M. .... 01 May
- Samuel, C.D.R. .... 01 May
- Scanlon, M.J. .... 01 May
- Tamlyn, S.J. .... 01 May
- Baker, A.J. .... 01 Jul
- Hoare, P.F. .... 21 Jul
- Rhodes, P.E. .... 21 Jul
- Tinsley, P. .... 21 Jul
- Barnwell, A.F. .... 21 Jul
- Tidman, M.D. .... 21 Jul
- Perrin, M.S. .... 01 Sep
- Bonney, J.E. .... 01 Sep
- Darley, M.E. .... 01 Sep
- Forbes, D.G. .... 01 Sep
- Francis, T.D.H. .... 01 Sep
- Halsted, B.E. .... 01 Sep
- Hester, J.F.W. .... 01 Sep
- Hopkins, R. .... 01 Sep
- Thompson, P.L. .... 01 Sep
- Mansergh, A.C. .... 01 Sep
- Maynard, P.A. .... 01 Sep
- Morgan, H.L. .... 01 Sep
- Pennington, C.E. .... 01 Sep
- Robinson, P.J.O. .... 01 Sep
- Wallace, S.P. .... 01 Sep
- Liva, A.J. .... 01 Sep

2002

- Clarke, P.M. .... 01 Jan
- Cross, E.J. .... 01 Jan
- Robbins, H.V. .... 01 Jan
- Watson, B.R. .... 01 Jan
- Kemp, A.C. .... 01 Apr
- May, D.J. .... 01 Apr
- Nolan, P.E. .... 01 Apr
- MacPherson, W.G.C. .... 01 Apr
- McLelland, P.H. .... 01 Apr
- Mewes, D.B. .... 01 Apr
- Morton, J.C. .... 01 Apr
- Paterson, T.J. .... 01 Apr

CAPTAINS

- \- Price, R.T. 01 Apr
- \- Usher, A.T. 01 Apr
- \- Usher, B. 01 Apr
- \- Weir, J.R. 01 Apr
- \- Orr, S.D. 03 Apr
- \- Fitzpatrick, P.J. 19 Jul
- BS Smallwood, A.J. 19 Jul
- \- West, D.J. 19 Jul
- \- Abbott, G.P. 01 Sep
- \- Alston, R. 01 Sep
- \- Bartley, D.J. 01 Sep
- \- Brocklehurst, K.P. 01 Sep
- \- Butler, S. 01 Sep
- \- Dean, S.I.R. 01 Sep
- \- Delahay, J.E. 01 Sep
- \- Fidler, J.Q. 01 Sep
- \- Gray, S.A.N. 01 Sep
- \- Hecks, I.J. 01 Sep
- \- Menzies, G.M. 01 Sep
- \- Norman, J.M. 01 Sep
- \- Parker, M.C. 01 Sep
- \- Preston, T.E. 01 Sep
- \- Price, J.E.O. 01 Sep
- \- Rochester, A.D. 01 Sep
- \- Rogers, S.M. 01 Sep
- \- Schleyer, J. 01 Sep
- \- Spink, D.A. 01 Sep
- \- Taylor, N.J. 01 Sep
- \- Tucker, S.J.W. 01 Sep
- \- Waite, M.T. 01 Sep
- \- Venables, D.M. 01 Sep

2003

- \- Bryars, P.M. 01 Apr
- \- Butcher, D. 01 Apr
- \- Dawson, A. 01 Apr
- \- Gibb, A.K.B. 01 Apr
- \- Hembury, L. 01 Apr
- \- Nicholas, J.R. 01 Apr
- \- Peters, A.D. 01 Apr
- \- Phillips, D.G. 01 Apr
- \- Sharpe, M.R. 01 Apr
- \- Stanton, K.V. 01 Apr
- \- Flinn, J.A. 01 Apr
- \- Abbott, D. 01 Apr
- \- Burgess, M.J. 01 Apr
- \- Flower, N.P. 01 Apr
- BS Burcham, J.R. 01 Apr
- BS Dowrick, M.P. 01 Apr
- \- Gordon, R.S. 01 Apr
- \- Noble, K.L. 01 Apr
- \- Carr, P. 01 Jul
- \- Gellender, P.S. 24 Jul
- \- Norton, T.C.H. 01 Sep
- \- Jones, R.P.M. 01 Sep
- \- Axcell, M.F. 01 Sep
- \- Pascoe, J.R.M. 01 Sep
- \- Allan, F.S. 01 Sep
- \- Archer, T.W.K. 01 Sep
- \- Bennet, G.C. 01 Sep
- \- Buczkiewicz, M.J. 01 Sep
- \- Caldwell, D.J. 01 Sep
- \- Copsey, N.R.B. 01 Sep
- \- Coryton, O.C.W.S. 01 Sep
- \- Elliott, M.F. 01 Sep
- \- Eve, L. 01 Sep
- \- Ferrey, R.M. 01 Sep
- \- Galbraith, L.A. 01 Sep
- \- Southern, M.J. 01 Sep
- \- Whitmarsh, A.T. 01 Sep
- \- Johnston, K.G. 01 Sep
- \- MacRae, J.R. 01 Sep
- \- McKeating, P.M. 01 Sep
- \- Metcalfe, L.M. 01 Sep
- \- Moffatt, D. 01 Sep
- \- Morris, R.C. 01 Sep
- \- Newton, R.W. 01 Sep
- \- Payne, M.T. 01 Sep
- \- Shaw, A.T. 01 Sep
- \- Simmons, R.L. 01 Sep
- \- Stitson, P. 01 Sep
- \- Thomas, J.G. 01 Sep
- \- Thorpe, R.M. 01 Sep
- \- Tottenham, T.W. 01 Sep
- \- Waldmeyer, E. 01 Sep
- \- Williams, M.C. 01 Sep
- \- Williams, P.M. 01 Sep
- \- Witts, C.I. 01 Sep
- \- Hilton, J.N. 01 Sep

2004

- \- Brading, R.D. 01 Mar
- \- Bourne, S.W. 01 Apr
- \- Breach, C.E.M. 01 Apr
- \- Buston, D.C. 01 Apr
- \- Campbell, K.R. 01 Apr
- \- Chapple, S. 01 Apr
- \- Gibbins, P. 01 Apr
- \- Knowles, G.R. 01 Apr
- \- Latham, M.A. 01 Apr
- BS Long, R.P. 01 Apr
- \- Priddle, S.M.R. 01 Apr
- \- Roberts, P.A. 01 Apr
- \- Rudd, P. 01 Apr
- \- Watkins, D.T. 01 Apr
- \- Worth, M.C. 01 Apr
- \- Melbourne, S. 02 Apr
- \- Barden, P.E. 01 Jul
- \- Collinson, N.P. 01 Jul
- \- Fenton, G.M. 01 Jul
- \- Gray, T. 01 Jul
- \- Mawer, P.R. 01 Jul
- \- Nielsen, E.M. 01 Jul
- \- O'Connor, D.M. 01 Jul
- \- Titerickx, A.T. 01 Jul
- \- Williams, D.A. 01 Jul
- \- Brown, R. 24 Jul
- \- Curry, P.T. 24 Jul
- \- Curtis, P.J. 24 Jul
- \- Gannon, D.R. 24 Jul
- \- Giles, S. 24 Jul
- \- Milne, J.R. 24 Jul
- \- Rand, M.C. 24 Jul
- \- Ridley, J. 24 Jul
- \- Rutherford, A.T. 24 Jul
- \- Ubaka, P.B.N. 24 Jul
- \- Watson, G.B. 24 Jul
- \- O'Sullivan, M.R.J. 01 Sep
- \- Pinckney, M.R.N. 01 Sep
- \- Apps, J.C. 01 Sep
- \- Bradford, M.H. 01 Sep
- \- Carns, A.S. 01 Sep
- \- Catton, I.C. 01 Sep
- \- Finn, T.A. 01 Sep
- \- George, N.D. 01 Sep
- \- Higham, D.J. 01 Sep
- \- Jamison, J.S. 01 Sep
- \- Kenny, L.E. 01 Sep
- \- Lerwill, S.S.G. 01 Sep
- \- Lewis, B.M. 01 Sep
- \- Lewis, J.A.E. 01 Sep
- \- MacDonald, M.J. 01 Sep
- \- McLaren, S.C. 01 Sep
- \- Moore, W.I. 01 Sep
- \- Norcott, W.R. 01 Sep
- \- Pengelley, T.A.H. 01 Sep
- \- Pennefather, D.C.J. 01 Sep
- \- Precious, A.P. 01 Sep
- \- Renshaw, P.A. 01 Sep
- \- Reynolds, B.K.M. 01 Sep
- \- Ryall, T.A.S. 01 Sep
- \- Simpson, T.W. 01 Sep
- \- Sparks, S. 01 Sep
- \- Suchet, R.J. 01 Sep
- \- Thomson, L.G. 01 Sep

CAPTAINS

- Uprichard, A.J. ....01 Sep
- Vickers, C.H. ....01 Sep
- Winch, J.A. ....01 Sep
- Murray, S.D. ....01 Sep
- Pilkington, W.J. ....01 Sep

LIEUTENANTS

2002

- Carty, M.G. ....01 Sep
- Dow, A.J.R. ....01 Sep
- Postgate, M.O. ....01 Sep
- MacLean, R.G. ....01 Sep
- Thornton, D.M. ....01 Sep

2003

- Ginn, R.D. ....01 Sep
- O'Keefe, T.D. ....01 Sep
- Sharman, M.C. ....01 Sep
- Sutherland, I.D. ....01 Sep
- Trafford, M. ....01 Sep
- White, J.W. ....01 Sep

2004

- Fearn, S.R. ....01 Sep

SECOND LIEUTENANTS

1999

- Hamilton, S.J.D. ....01 Sep
- Hogg, G.D. ....01 Sep

2000

- Pritchard, L.B. ....01 Aug
- Anderson, B.W.D. ....01 Sep
- Armstrong, R.F. ....01 Sep
- Crisp, D.J.D. ....01 Sep
- Davies, L.M.A. ....01 Sep
- Drinkwater, R. ....01 Sep
- Duckitt, J.N. ....01 Sep
- Evans-Jones, T.M. ....01 Sep
- Goss, J.R.C. ....01 Sep
- Lee-Gallon, T.J. ....01 Sep
- Hall, E.C.M. ....01 Sep
- Kyle, R. ....01 Sep
- Lewis, M.J. ....01 Sep
- Long, H.A. ....01 Sep
- MacCrimmon, S.S. ....01 Sep
- Gaffney, B. ....01 Sep
- McCarrick, M.J. ....01 Sep
- Morton, J.H. ....01 Sep
- Noble, T.M.D. ....01 Sep
- Reed, E.C.D. ....01 Sep
- Reid, B.W. ....01 Sep
- Simpson, R.F. ....01 Sep
- Speedie, A.C. ....01 Sep
- Pinney, R.F. ....02 Sep

2001

- Air, C.T.L. ....01 Aug
- Anderson, J.H. ....01 Aug
- Armstrong, C.A. ....01 Aug
- Barrow, J.M. ....01 Aug
- Bowes, N.E. ....01 Aug
- Burgess, L.R. ....01 Aug
- Burr, C.J. ....01 Aug
- Clews, A. ....01 Aug
- Clarke, D.W.D. ....01 Aug
- Cottrell, R.F.G. ....01 Aug
- Cox, S.T. ....01 Aug
- Christie, N.E. ....01 Aug
- Denise, A.M. ....01 Aug
- Dingwall, N.T. ....01 Aug
- Dinsmore, S.J. ....01 Aug
- Eden, C.J. ....01 Aug
- Forrest, P.M. ....01 Aug
- Sayer, R.J. ....01 Aug
- Gray, O.W.J. ....01 Aug
- Hands, E.W.H. ....01 Aug
- Kestle, R.J. ....01 Aug
- Little, G.J.R. ....01 Aug
- MacKenzie-Green, W.H.M.G.. 01 Aug
- Marshall, L. ....01 Aug
- Marston, R.M. ....01 Aug
- Okell, P.M.C. ....01 Aug
- Scott, T. ....01 Aug
- Seaman, A.L. ....01 Aug
- Stephen, T.D.S. ....01 Aug
- Sweny, G.L.H. ....01 Aug
- Waller, R.M. ....01 Aug
- White, A.P.D. ....01 Aug
- Glancy, J.A. ....01 Sep

2003

- Kirkman, T.M. .... 05 Jan
- Goodman, W. ....01 Aug
- Nixon, A.J. ....01 Aug
- Thornton, J.D. ....01 Aug
- Rogers, O. ....01 Sep
- Morris, J.E.D. ....02 Sep

2004

- Argles, E.V. ....01 Aug
- Disney, L.I.W.P. ....01 Aug
- Kidd, R.S. ....01 Aug
- Knight, J. ....01 Aug
- Mallows, J.A. ....01 Aug
- Moore, R.G. ....01 Aug
- Richardson, B.F. ....01 Aug
- Denning, O.W. ....31 Aug

QUEEN ALEXANDRA'S ROYAL NAVAL NURSING SERVICE

CAPTAINS

2001

Bowen, M. .... 27 Mar

2003

Gibbon, L. .... 28 Jul

COMMANDERS

2002

Onions, J.M. .... 30 Jun

2003

Allkins, H.L. .... 30 Jun

2004

Duke, R.M. .... 30 Jun
Howes, N.J. .... 30 Jun

2005

Smith, B.C. .... 30 Jun
Williams, C.M.A. .... 30 Jun
Kennedy, I.J. .... 30 Jul

LIEUTENANT COMMANDERS

1999

Thain-Smith. J.C. .... 31 Mar
Stinton, C.A. .... 01 Oct

2000

Robson, C.J. .... 01 Oct
Spencer, S.J. .... 01 Oct

2001

Baird, E.H. .... 11 Mar
Aldwinckle, T.W. .... 01 Oct
Knight, D.J. .... 01 Oct

2002

Ferguson, V.S. .... 01 Oct

2003

Piper, N.D. .... 01 Oct
Rankin, S.J. .... 01 Oct

2004

England, L. .... 01 Oct
Briggs, C.S. .... 01 Oct
Bagnall, S.A.E. .... 01 Oct
Holland, A.L. .... 01 Oct
Hofman, A.J. .... 01 Oct
Chilvers, L.D. .... 01 Oct

LIEUTENANTS

1996

Johnson, V. .... 25 Jan
O'Maoil-Mheana,P.J. .... 30 Mar
Logan, J.G. .... 27 Jul
James, K.J. .... 26 Nov
Dilloway, P.J. .... 07 Dec

1997

Ouvry, J.E.D. .... 25 Mar
Kiernan, M D .... 30 May
Wilkinson, G. .... 06 Oct

1998

Kennedy, C.H. 07 May 98
Thompson, F. .... 24 Sep
Lang, J.S. .... 30 Sep
Gardner, S.L. .... 05 Nov
Carnell, R.P. .... 06 Nov
Blakeley, A.L. .... 17 Nov

1999

McFarland, N. .... 14 Jan
Kenworthy, L.K .... 01 Apr
Hurley, K.A. .... 26 May
Taylor, L.M. .... 05 Jul
Thorpe, E. .... 03 Aug
Newby Stubbs, R.L. .... 15 Aug
France, S.C. .... 25 Aug
Morgan, R.S. .... 06 Sep
Scott, C.R. .... 12 Sep
Stevens, A.J. .... 24 Sep

2000

Charlton, K.W. .... 14 Jan
McConville, C.W. .... 28 Mar
Brown, B.C. .... 11 Jun
Emmerson, D.M. .... 22 Jun
Geraghty, F. .... 01 Sep
Sutherland, G. .... 25 Oct
Simpson, P.E. .... 27 Oct
Glendinning, A.S. .... 12 Jan
Selwood, P.J. .... 26 Feb
Brodie, S.D. .... 08 Mar
Middleton, J.E. .... 26 Apr
Clarkson, A.M. .... 04 May
Bryce-Johnston, F.L.S. .... 16 Jul
Penney, L.M. .... 16 Sep
Cooper, J.L. .... 01 Nov

2002

Kelly, F.A. .... 01 Feb
Kennedy, I.C. .... 26 May
D'Arcy, T. .... 14 Jul
Swire, B.J. .... 26 Jul
Hodds, S.L. .... 01 Nov
Huggins, K.E. .... 01 Nov
Despres, J.P. .... 19 Nov
Fraser-Smith, A. .... 23 Nov
Wright-Jones, .E.M. .... 29 Nov

2003

Wagstaff, S.E. .... 01 Jan
Ademokun, G.O.A. .... 01 Feb
Gray, S.E. .... 20 Feb
Warburton, A.M. .... 26 Feb

LIEUTENANTS

Martyn, J.M. .... 01 Mar
Claridge, A.M. .... 12 Apr
Adams, S.A. .... 01 Jun
Wesson, M.I. .... 01 Jul
Johnson, S.V. .... 01 Sep
Rea, M.E. .... 01 Oct
Thompson, S.K. .... 01 Nov

2004

Ward, C.J. .... 01 May
Jeffries, B.A. .... 01 Sep
McCullough, K.M. .... 01 Nov

2005

Martyn, J.M. .... 22 Feb
Wardley, T.E. .... 01 Mar
Hale, S.D. .... 01 Apr

SUB LIEUTENANTS

2002

Lees, S.E. .... 01 Sep
James, V.H. .... 01 Aug
Clark, G.R. .... 01 Nov

KEY ROYAL NAVAL PERSONNEL, ATTACHES AND ADVISERS

(See Sec. 1 for Admiralty Board Members and Defence Council Members)

MOD/CENTRAL STAFF

1SL/CNS	Admiral Sir Alan West GCB DSC ADC
CE DEA	Vice Admiral P A Dunt CB
DCDS(C)	Lieutenant General Sir Robert Fry KCB, CBE
DCDS(EC)	Lieutenant General Sir Robert Fulton KBE
DCDS(H)	Vice Admiral R A I McLean CB OBE
DG CAP (CS)	Rear Admiral N C F Guild CB
ACNS	Rear Admiral A M Massey CBE
CM (PA)	Rear Admiral T A Soar OBE
ACDS(RP)	Rear Admiral T J H Laurence MVO
Hd BDS(W)	Rear Admiral A K Dymock CB
SNM RCDS	Rear Admiral R A Mark
DG T&E	Rear Admiral S R J Goodall CBE
DS SEC	Rear Admiral P J Wilkinson
DG JDC	Rear Admiral C J Parry CBE
Cmdt CMT	Rear Admiral N D Latham

CINCFLEET

CINCFLEET	Admiral Sir Jonathon Band KCB
DCINC	Vice Admiral T P McClement OBE
COS(W)	Rear Admiral D G Snelson CB
COM(OPS)	Rear Admiral P Lambert
COS(SPT)	Rear Admiral T C Chittenden
CSO(MPS)/FOSNNI	Rear Admiral N H L Harris MBE
COMUKMARFOR	Rear Admiral C R Style CBE
FOST	Rear Admiral R S Ainsley
CGRM/COMUKAMPHIBFOR	Major General J B Dutton CBE
STLB TL	Rear Admiral N J F RabyOBE

SECOND SEA LORD

2SL/CNH	Vice Admiral Sir James Burnell-Nugent KCB CBE ADC
COS/2SL	Rear Admiral M Kimmons
NAVSEC/DGHR(N)	Rear Admiral R J Ibbotson DSC
FOTR/CE NRTA	Rear Admiral K J Borley
DGNCS	The Venerable B K Hammett QHC

DLO

DG Def Logistics Fleet	Rear Admiral R P Boissier
CE DCSA	Rear Admiral R G J Ward CB
DG Nuclear	Rear Admiral A D H Mathews

PROCUREMENT EXECUTIVE

DPA DLM/CofN	Rear Admiral R F Cheadle CB

NATO

DSACT	Admiral Sir Mark Stanhope KCB OBE
COS MARCOMAFSOUTH	Rear Admiral R P Stevens CB
DEP COMSTRIKFORSTH	Rear Admiral D J Cooke MBE
DCOM HRF(I)	Major General R G T Lane CBE

PJHQ

DCJO(OP SPT)	Rear Admiral P L Wilcocks DSC

AFPAA

CE AFPAA	Rear Admiral T A Spires

MEDICAL

Surgeon General	Surgeon Vice Admiral I L Jenkins CVO QHS
MDG(Navy)	Surgeon Rear Admiral M A Farquharson-Roberts
CE DMETA	Surgeon Rear Admiral P I Raffaelli

ATTACHES AND ADVISERS

NAVAL ATTACHES IN FOREIGN COUNTRIES

Service Mail
All official service mail is to be forwarded in accordance with current instructions.

OFFICERS PROVIDING A NAVAL SERVICE IN FOREIGN COUNTRIES

Albania
Defence Attaché
Tirana

Angola
Defence Attaché
Luanda

Argentina
Defence Attaché
Buenos Aires

Austria
Defence Attaché
Vienna

Bahrain
Defence Attaché
Manama

Belgium
Defence Attaché
Brussels

Brazil
Naval Attaché
Brasilia

Bulgaria
Defence Attaché
Sofia

Chile
Defence Attaché
Santiago

China
Naval Attaché
Peking

Colombia
Defence Attaché
Bogota

Congo (Democratic Republic)
Defence Attaché
Kinshasa

Croatia
Defence Attaché
Zagreb

Czech Republic
Defence Attaché
Prague

Denmark
Defence Attaché
Copenhagen

Egypt
Naval & Air Attaché
Cairo

Finland
Defence Attaché
Helsinki

France
Naval Attaché
Paris

Georgia
Defence Attaché
Tbilisi

Germany
Naval Attaché
Bonn

Greece
Defence Attaché
Athens

Guatemala
Defence Attaché
Guatemala City

Hungary
Defence Attaché
Budapest

Indonesia
Defence Attaché
Jakarta

Ireland
Defence Attaché
Dublin

Israel
Naval & Air Attaché
Tel Aviv

Italy
Naval Attaché
Rome

Japan
Defence Attaché
Tokyo

Jordan
Defence Attaché
Amman

Kazakhstan
Defence Attaché
Almaty

Korea
Naval & Air Attaché
Seoul

Kuwait
Defence Attaché
Kuwait City

Latvia
Defence Attaché
Riga

Lebanon
Defence Attaché
Beirut

Lithuania
Defence Attaché
Vilnius

Macedonia
Defence Attaché
Skopje

Morocco
Defence Attaché
Rabat

Nepal
Defence Attaché
Kathmandu

Netherlands
Defence Attaché
The Hague

Norway
Defence Attaché
Oslo

Oman
Naval & Air Attaché
Muscat

Philippines
Defence Attaché
Manila

Poland
Naval & Military Attaché
Warsaw

Portugal
Defence Attaché
Lisbon

Qatar
Defence Attaché
Doha

Romania
Defence Attaché
Bucharest

Russia

Naval Attaché
Assistant Naval Attaché
Moscow

Saudi Arabia
Naval Attaché
Riyadh

Slovakia
Defence Attaché
BratislSlovakia

Slovakia
Defence Attaché
Ljubljana

Spain
Defence Attaché
Madrid

Sweden
Defence Attaché
Stockholm

Switzerland
Defence Attaché
Berne

Syria
Defence Attaché
Damascus

Thailand
Defence Attaché
Bangkok

Turkey
Naval & Air Attaché
Ankara

Ukraine
Defence Attaché
Kiev

United Arab Emirates
Defence Attaché
Abu Dhabi

United States of America
Naval Attaché
Assistant Naval Attaché
Washington DC

Uzbekistan
Defence Attaché
Tashkent

Venezuela
Defence Attaché
Caracas

Yugoslavia (Federal Republic)
Defence Attaché
Belgrade

OFFICERS PROVIDING A NAVAL SERVICE IN COMMONWEALTH COUNTRIES

Australia
Defence & Naval Adviser
Canberra

Barbados
Defence Adviser
Bridgetown

Brunei
Defence Adviser
Bandar Seri Begawan

Canada
Naval & Air Adviser
Ottawa

Cyprus
Defence Adviser
Nicosia

Ghana
Defence Adviser
Accra

India
Naval and Air Adviser
New Delhi

Jamaica
Defence Adviser
Kingston

Kenya
Defence Adviser
Nairobi

Malaysia
Defence Adviser
Kuala Lumpur

New Zealand
Defence Adviser
Wellington

Nigeria
Defence Adviser
Abuja

Pakistan
Naval & Air Adviser
Islamabad

Singapore
Assistant Defence Adviser & Royal Navy Liaison Officer
Singapore

South Africa
Naval & Air Adviser
Pretoria

Sri Lanka
Defence Adviser
Colombo

Uganda
Defence Adviser
Kampala

Zimbabwe
Defence Adviser
Harare

NON-RESIDENTIAL ACCREDITATIONS

Attaches accredited to the following countries are non-residential

Algeria
(Is resident London (DOMA))

Anguilla
(Is resident Barbados)

Antigua & Barbuda
(Is resident Barbados)

Armenia
(Is resident Georgia)

Azerbaijan
(Is resident Georgia)

Bahamas
(Is resident Jamaica)

Bangladesh
(Is resident India)

Belarus
(Is resident Russia)

Belize
(Is resident Jamaica)

Bermuda
(Is resident USA)

Bolivia
(Is resident Chile)

Botswana
(Is resident Zimbabwe)

British Virgin Islands
(Is resident Barbados)

Burundi
(Is resident Uganda)

Cayman Islands
(Is resident Jamaica)

Cuba
(Is resident Venezuela)

Curacao
(Is resident Barbados)

Dominica
(Is resident Barbados)

Ecuador
(Is resident Venezuela)

El Salvador
(Is resident Guatemala)

Eritrea
(Is resident Kenya)

Estonia
(Is resident Finland)

Ethiopia
(Is resident Kenya)

Fiji
(Is resident New Zealand)

Gabon
(Is resident Congo DR)

Granada
(Is resident Barbados)

Guadeloupe
(Is resident Barbados)

Guinea
(Is resident Sierra Leone)

Guyana
(Is resident Barbados)

Honduras
(Is resident Guatemala)

Ivory Coast
(Is resident Ghana)

Kyrgyzstan
(Is resident Russia)

Lesotho
(Is resident South Africa)

Luxembourg
(Is resident Belgium)

Madagascar
(Is resident London (DOMA))

Malawi
(Is resident Zimbabwe)

Maldives
(Is resident Sri Lanka)

Mauritania
(Is resident Morocco)

Mauritius
(Is resident Kenya)

Mexico
(Is resident Guatemala

Moldova
(Is resident Romania)

Mongolia
(Is resident China)

Montserrat
(Is resident Barbados)

Mozambique
(Is resident Zimbabwe)

Namibia
(Is resident South Africa)

Nicaragua
(Is resident Guatemala)

Panama
(Is resident Venezuela)

Papua New Guinea
(Is resident Australia)

Paraguay
(Is resident Argentina)

Peru
(Is resident Colombia)

Rwanda
(Is resident Uganda)

St Kitts & Nevis
(Is resident Barbados)
St Lucia
(Is resident Barbabos)

St Vincent
(Is resident Barbados)

Senegal
(Is resident Morocco)

Seychelles
(Is resident Kenya)

Suriname
(Is resident Barbados)

Swaziland
(Is resident South Africa)

Tajikistan
(Is resident Kazakhstan)

Tanzania
(Is resident Kenya)

The Gambia
(Is resident Morocco)

Togo
(Is resident Ghana)

Tonga
(Is resident New Zealand)

Trinidad & Tobago
(Is resident Barbados)

Tunisia
(Is resident London (DOMA))

Turkmenistan
(Is resident Russia)

Turks & Caicos Islands
(Is resident Jamaica)

Uruguay
(Is resident Argentina)

Vietnam
(Is resident Malaysia)

Yemen
(Is resident Saudi Arabia)

Zambia
(Is resident London (DOMA))

INTERPRETERS

Name	Rank	Date of Qualifying or Re-qualifying
ARABIC		
Rand, M.C.	CAPT RM	Mar 00
CHINESE		
Gopsill, B.R.	LT CDR	Sep 84
Rayner, B.N.	CAPT	Dec 83
White, S.N.	CDR	Sep 90
DANISH		
Watson, P.H.	CAPT	Oct 76
DUTCH		
Cox, P.W.S.	CDR	Dec 04
Davies, A.R.	CAPT	Mar 84
Ewence, M.W., OBE	CDR	Mar 88
Shipperley, I.	CDR	Oct 93
FRENCH		
Adair, A.A.S.	CDRE	Dec 99
Airey, S.E.	A/CAPT	Mar 80
Bernard, R.A.	LT	Jun 97
Braithwaite, G.C.	LT	Jul 00
Bussey, E.L.	LT	Apr 99
Butcher, M.W.	MID	Jul 04
Butler, N.A.M.	CAPT	Mar 04
Cook, T.A.	MAJ	Jun 01
Craven, J.A.G.	LT CDR	Mar 90
Cree, M.C.	CDR	Feb 95
Davies, H.C.A.	MAJ	Jun 04
Dermody, R.T.	LT	Mar 98
Elliman, S.M.	LT CDR	Oct 92
Ewence, M.W., OBE	CDR	Mar 98
Fieldsend, M.A.	CDR	May 95
Gray, E.J.	LT	Sep 02
Gubbins, V.R., MBE	CDR	Jul 96
Harlow, S.R.	LT	Jun 01
Hollins, R.P.	CDR	Apr 99
Irwin, S.G.	LT	Mar 02
Kettle, R.A.	MAJ	Jun 98
Lawrence, L.J.	LT	Mar 04
Lombard, D.	CAPT	Mar 02
Mansergh, M.P.	CAPT	Mar 91
Newell, J.M., MBE	CAPT	Mar 89
Roddy, M.P., MBE	MAJ	Jun 03
Stewart, A.C.	CDR	Mar 04
Stonor, P.F.A.	CDR	Mar 88
Stride, J.A.	LT CDR	Apr 99
Turner, J.S.H.	LT CDR	Mar 94
Underwood, R.A.H.	LT	Mar 04
Wallace, M.R.B.	CAPT	Jun 03
GERMAN		
Airey, S.E.	A/CAPT	Apr 81
Burstow, N.S.	LT CDR	Jul 96
Durston, D.H.	CAPT	Mar 83
Eberle, P.J.F.	CDRE	Mar 77
Finch, B.A.	LT CDR	Mar 96
Gibbs, N.D.	LT CDR	Mar 04
Hill, D.	LT CDR	Mar 98
Hollins, R.P.	CDR	Mar 98
Howard, D.G.	A/CDR	Apr 00
Knight, P.J.	CDR	Apr 97
Massey, A.M., CBE	CDRE	Mar 80
McGuire, M.J.	LT CDR	Sep 02
Mennecke Jappy, G.W.G.	LT	Dec 04
Nurse, M.T.	A/CDR	Mar 86
Pitcher, P.P.	LT CDR	Nov 97
Robertson Gopffarth, A.A.J.	LT CDR	Mar 95
Robin, C.C.E.	LT CDR	Mar 98
Shropshall, I.J.	LT	May 03
Sparke, P.R.W.	LT CDR	Mar 92
Williams, N.L.	CAPT	Mar 85
GREEK		
Ritsperis, A.	LT	Jul 96
ITALIAN		
Amorosi, R.G.F.L.	SLT	Sep 00
JAPANESE		
Chelton, S.R.L.	CAPT	Oct 88
Norgate, A.T.	LT	Oct 03
Taylor, G.D.	LT	Aug 01
NORWEGIAN		
Stallion, I.M.	CDR	Mar 79
Taylor, W.J., OBE	COL	Mar 91
POLISH		
Tarnowski, T.A.	MAJ	Mar 99

Name	Rank	Date of Qualifying or Re-qualifying
PORTUGUESE		
Harrison, R.A.	CDR	Dec 03
McGlory, S.J.	LT CDR	Jul 96
RUSSIAN		
Airey, S.E.	A/CAPT	Mar 94
Connolly, C.J.	CDR	Mar 89
Davies, A.R.	CAPT	Mar 89
Drewett, R.E., MBE	A/CAPT	Mar 91
Fields, D.G.	CDR	Mar 90
Foreman, J.L.R.	CDR	Mar 92
Green, T.J.	CDR	Mar 89
Gwillim, V.G.	MAJ	Mar 94
Hodgson, T.C., MBE	CDR	Mar 94
Lister, S.R., OBE	CDRE	Mar 90
McTear, K.	CDR	Mar 91
Newton, G.A.	CDR	Mar 94
Peters, W.R.	LT CDR	Mar 00
Priddle, A.C.	LT	Jul 04
Simpson, E.J.	LT CDR	Mar 91
Tarnowski, T.A.	MAJ	Mar 00
SPANISH		
Adam, I.K.	LT CDR	Mar 91
Baker, M.J.	LT CDR	Dec 03
Bussey, E.L.	LT	Mar 98
Croke, A.	CAPT	Jul 00
Curry, B.R., MBE	LT COL	Mar 98
Dedman, N.J.K.	CAPT	Dec 02
Eedle, R.J.	LT CDR	Sep 98
Gannon, D.R.	CAPT RM	Jan 00
Graham, J.E.	CDR	Jun 99
Humphrys, J.A.	CAPT	Mar 98
Lawrence, L.J.	LT	Mar 04
Lynch, R.D.F.	LT CDR	Mar 91
Marsh, B.H., MBE	LT CDR	Jun 03
McGlory, S.J.	LT CDR	Mar 94
McLennan, R.G.	CDR	Mar 94
Reed, J.H.	LT CDR	Jun 02
Sanguinetti, H.R.	CAPT	Mar 90
Turner, J.S.H.	LT CDR	Nov 94
Wolfe, D.E.	CAPT	Mar 95
SWEDISH		
Rigby, J.C.	CDR	Mar 86

OFFICERS OF THE LOGISTICS SPECIALISATION PRACTISING AS NAVAL BARRISTERS

COMMODORES

Fraser R.W. MVO (Director Naval Legal Services)

CAPTAINS

Crabtree, P D, OBE
Steel, D G
Davis, B J, OBE

COMMANDERS

Williams, R E, OBE
Jameson, A C
Brown, N L
Gray, R S
Spence, A B
Crozier, S R M
Anderson, H A
Hollins, R P
Wright, S H
Cole, A C
Wood, R
Taylor, S J

LIEUTENANT COMMANDERS

Kingsbury, J A T
Towler, A
Turner, J S H
Murdoch, A P
Dow, C S
Pheasant, J C S
Axon, G M
Wilman, D M
Reed, D K

LIEUTENANTS

Atwill, J W O
Gilbert, R G
Sheikh, N
Butterworth, C L
Park, I D
Knox, G P

HM SHORE ESTABLISHMENTS

AFPAA(CENTURION)
Centurion Building
Grange Road
GOSPORT
Hants
PO13 9XA

DARTMOUTH BRNC
Britannia Royal Naval College
DARTMOUTH
Devon
TQ6 0HJ

DRAKE SFM
(fao SFM)
HM Naval Base
DEVONPORT
Plymouth
Devon
PL2 2BG

JSU NORTHWOOD
Joint Support Unit
Northwood Headquarters
Sandy Lane
Northwood
Middlesex
HA6 3HP

MWS COLLINGWOOD
Maritime Warfare School
HMS COLLINGWOOD
Newgate Lane
FAREHAM
Hants
PO14 1AS

MWS EXCELLENT
HMS EXCELLENT
PORTSMOUTH
Hants
PO2 8ER

MWS SOUTHWICK PK
MWS (Southwick Park)
Southwick
FAREHAM
Hampshire
PO17 6EJ

NELSON
UPO (PA)
HMS NELSON
Portsmouth
Hants
PO1 3HH

NEPTUNE DLO
HMNB Clyde
Faslane
Argyll and Bute
G84 8HL

RALEIGH
HMS RALEIGH
TORPOINT
Cornwall
PL11 2PD

RNAS CULDROSE
RNAS Culdrose
HELSTON
Cornwall
TR12 7RH

RNAS YEOVILTON
RNAS Yeovilton
ILCHESTER
Somerset
BA22 8HT

SULTAN
HMS SULTAN
GOSPORT
Hants
PO12 3BY

SULTAN AIB
Admiralty Interview Board
HMS SULTAN
GOSPORT
Hants
PO12 3BY

TEMERAIRE
HMS TEMERAIRE
Burnaby Road
PORTSMOUTH
Hants
PO1 2HB

VICTORY
HMS VICTORY
HM Naval Base
PORTSMOUTH
Hants
PO1 3PZ

HM SHIPS

ALBION (Fearless)
BFPO 204
CAPT ....X K Winstanley, MBE

ARCHER (Attacker)
BFPO 208
LT ....X S L Scott

ARGYLL (Type 23)
BFPO 210
CDR....................X W J Warrender

ARK ROYAL (Invincible)
BFPO 212
CDR.................... E S J Thompson

ATHERSTONE (Hunt)
BFPO 215
LT CDR................X R A Pethybridge

BANGOR (Sandown)
BFPO 222
LT CDR................X D R Wilson

BITER (Attacker)
BFPO 229
LT ....X F D Hirons

BLAZER (Attacker)
BFPO 231
LT ....X A E Pollard

BLYTH (Sandown)
BFPO 221
LT CDR................X A K M Pierce

BRECON (Hunt)
BFPO 235
LT CDR................X C P Atkinson

BROCKLESBY (Hunt)
BFPO 241
LT CDR................X A H Woollven

BULWARK (Fearless)
BFPO 243
CAPT ....X J H Stanford

CAMPBELTOWN (Type 22)
BFPO 248
CAPT ....X A S Bell

CARDIFF (Type 42)
BFPO 249
CDR....................X M J D Beardall

CATTISTOCK (Hunt)
BFPO 251
LT CDR................X J R Barnes

CHARGER (Attacker)
BFPO 252
LT ....X A W Johns

CHATHAM (Type 22)
BFPO 253
CAPT ....X S J Chick

CHIDDINGFOLD (Hunt)
BFPO 254
LT CDR................X K M T Houlberg

CORNWALL (Type 22)
BFPO 256
LT CDR................X J J Mullen

COTTESMORE (Hunt)
BFPO 257
LT ....X D S Knight

CUMBERLAND (Type 22)
BFPO 261
CAPT ....X R R Best, OBE

DASHER (Attacker)
BFPO 271

DULVERTON (Hunt)
BFPO 273
LT ....X L R Hayashi

DUMBARTON CASTLE (Castle)
BFPO 274
LT CDR................X A M Stacey

ECHO (Misc)
BFPO 275
CDR....................X A K Waddington

EDINBURGH (Type 42)
BFPO 277
CDR....................X P S Verney

ENDURANCE (Ice Patrol)
BFPO 279
CAPT ....X N R Lambert

ENTERPRISE (Misc)
BFPO 276
CDR....................X V A Nail

EXAMPLE (Attacker)
BFPO 281
LT ....X C J Wyness

EXETER (Type 42)
BFPO 278
CDR....................X A W Reed, OBE

EXPLOIT (Attacker)
BFPO 285
LT ....X M R E Johnson

EXPLORER (Attacker)
BFPO 280
LT ....X A C Mason

EXPRESS (Attacker)
BFPO 282
LT ....X A W James

GLEANER (Gleaner)
BFPO 288
LT ....X S Weaver

GLOUCESTER (Type 42)
BFPO 289
CDR....................X R M Tuppen

GRAFTON (Type 23)
BFPO 291
CDR....................X R J A Bellfield

GRIMSBY (Sandown)
BFPO 292
LT CDR................X N P May

HURWORTH (Hunt)
BFPO 300
LT CDR................X J R Horne

ILLUSTRIOUS (Invincible)
BFPO 305
CDRE..................X R G Cooling

INVINCIBLE (Invincible)
BFPO 308
CDRE..................X N Morisetti

IRON DUKE (Type 23)
BFPO 309
CDR....................X A A Jordan

KENT (Type 23)
BFPO 318
CDR....................X J H T Nisbet

LANCASTER (Type 23)
BFPO 323
CDR....................X J D Morley

LEDBURY (Hunt)
BFPO 324
LT CDR................X R Wilson

LEEDS CASTLE (Castle)
BFPO 325
LT CDR................X C D Goodsell

LIVERPOOL (Type 42)
BFPO 327
CDR....................X G R Northwood

MANCHESTER (Type 42)
BFPO 331
CDR....................X W Q F Evans

MARLBOROUGH (Type 23)
BFPO 333
CDR....................X I E Graham

MERSEY (River)
BFPO 334
LT CDR................X I H Lynn

MIDDLETON (Hunt)
BFPO 335
LT CDR................X P L Allen

MONMOUTH (Type 23)
BFPO 338
CDR....................X J P Kyd

MONTROSE (Type 23)
BFPO 339
CDR....................X A J Webb

NORTHUMBERLAND (Type 23)
BFPO 345
CDR....................X T J Guy

NOTTINGHAM (Type 42)
BFPO 346
CDR....................X S Holt

PEMBROKE (Sandown)
BFPO 357
LT CDR................X S J Ryan

PENZANCE (Sandown)
BFPO 358
LT CDR................X D E F Crosbie

PORTLAND (Type 23)
BFPO 361
CDR....................X S M Allen

PUNCHER (Attacker)
BFPO 362
LT ....X T J Berry

PURSUER (Attacker)
BFPO 363

QUORN (Hunt)
BFPO 366
LT CDR................X R Allen

RAIDER (Attacker)
BFPO 377
LT ....X G R Palin

RAMSEY (Sandown)
BFPO 368
LT CDR................X M C Mackey

RANGER (Attacker)
BFPO 369
LT ....X J M B Parkin

RICHMOND (Type 23)
BFPO 375
LT CDR................X P R Harper

ROEBUCK (Bulldog)
BFPO 376
LT CDR................X J E Churcher

SCEPTRE (Swiftsure)
BFPO 380
CDR....................X M R Titcomb

SCOTT (Hecla)
BFPO 381
CDR....................X S R Malcolm

SEVERN (River)
BFPO 382
LT CDR................X R J Cox

SHOREHAM (Sandown)
BFPO 386
LT CDR................X I S Lower

SMITER (Attacker)
BFPO 387
LT ....X Z A Watts

SOMERSET (Type 23)
BFPO 395
CDR....................X D I Burns

SOUTHAMPTON (Type 42)
BFPO 389
CDR....................X R C Vitali

SOVEREIGN (Swiftsure)
BFPO 390
CDR....................X S R Aiken, OBE

SPARTAN (Swiftsure)
BFPO 391
CDR....................X P V Halton

ST ALBANS (Type 23)
BFPO 399
CDR....................X S Dainton

SUPERB (Swiftsure)
BFPO 396
CDR....................X N J Hibberd

SUTHERLAND (Type 23)
BFPO 398
CDR....................X P J Haslam

TALENT (Trafalgar)
BFPO 401
LT CDR................E J L Farrington

TIRELESS (Trafalgar)
BFPO 402
CDR....................X I G Breckenridge

TORBAY (Trafalgar)
BFPO 403
CDR....................X C K Groves

TRACKER (Attacker)
BFPO 409
LT ....X P A Kohn

TRAFALGAR (Trafalgar)
BFPO 404
CDR....................X M H Williams

TRENCHANT (Trafalgar)
BFPO 405
CDR....................X H D Beard

TRUMPETER (Attacker)
BFPO 407
LT ....X A J E Smith

TURBULENT (Trafalgar)
BFPO 408
CDR....................X A L Coles, OBE

TYNE (River)
BFPO 412
LT CDR................X J M Lowther

UPHLDER TRG TEAM (Upholder)
Capt Sea & Shore Submarine Training
NEPTUNE
HELENSBURGH
Argyll and Bute
GH4 8HL

VANGUARD(PORT) (Trident)
BFPO 418
CAPT ....X J K Moores

VENGEANCE(PORT) (Trident)
BFPO 421
CDR....................X A S Corbett

VENGEANCE(STBD) (Trident)
BFPO 421
CDR....................X M Lister

VICTORIOUS(PORT) (Trident)
BFPO 419
LT CDR................E N A Bryce, MBE

VIGILANT(PORT) (Trident)
BFPO 420
CDR....................X R J Anstey

VIGILANT(STBD) (Trident)
BFPO 420
CDR....................X I T Roberts, OBE

WALNEY (Sandown)
BFPO 423
LT CDR................X J E Beadsmoore

WESTMINSTER (Type 23)
BFPO 426
CDR....................X A Betton

YORK (Type 42)
BFPO 430
CDR....................X R M M J Harvey

RN FISHERY PROTECTION & MINE COUNTERMEASURES SQUADRONS

FISHERY PROTECTION SQN

LT ....X G Cuthbert

FIRST MCM SQN

CDR....................X J A Scott

SECOND MCM SQN

CDR....................X A P Williams, DSC

THIRD MCM SQN

CDR....................X A Wallace

ROYAL NAVAL AIR SQUADRONS

CHFHQ
CAPT ....X G W A Wallace, AFC

LYNX OEU (FAA).
LT CDR................X M A Sewed

702 SQN HERON
A/CDR ....X M B Davies

750 SQN SEAHAWK (FAA)
LT CDR................X C J Daniell

771 SQN (FAA)
LT CDR................X J C Barnbrook

801 SQN (Sea Harrier)
A/CDR ....X A J W Rae

824 SQN (Merlin)
CDR....................X R M H Dane, MBE

845 SQN (Sea King Mk4)
A/CDR ....X C A Slocombe

846 SQN
A/CDR ....X M V Carretta

847 SQN (CDO Support)
MAJ.................RM P E M Morris

848 SQN HERON (FAA)
A/CDR ....X M C Walker

849 SQN A FLT (Sea King AEW)
LT CDR................X D J Lambourne

849 SQN B FLT(Sea King AEW)
BFPO 305
LT CDR................X P M Jefferson

849 SQN HQ
CDR....................X M A J Hawkins

899 SQN HERON (FAA)
LT ....S M D J Walker

ROYAL NAVAL RESERVE UNITS

RNR Air Branch
Cormorant House
Royal Naval Air Station
Yeovilton
BA22 8HL

HMS CALLIOPE
South Shore Road
GATESHEAD
NE28 2BE

HMS CAMBRIA
Hayes Point
Sully
PENARTH
CF64 5XU

HMS CAROLINE
BFPO 806

HMS DALRIADA
Navy Buildings
Eldon Street
GREENOCK
PA16 7SL

HMS EAGLET
RNHQ Merseyside
East Brunswick Dock
LIVERPOOL
L3 4DZ

HMS FERRET
Chicksands
SHEFFORD
Bedfordshire
SG17 5PR

HMS FLYING FOX
Winterstoke Road
BRISTOL
BS3 2NS

HMS FORWARD
42 Tilton Road
Birmingham
B9 4PP

HMS KING ALFRED
Fraser Building
Whale Island
PORTSMOUTH
Hants
PO2 8ER

RNR Media Relations
Fleet Corporate Communications
MP2-4
Fleet Headquarters
Leach Building
Whale Island
Portsmouth
PO2 8BY

HMS PRESIDENT
72 St Katharine's Way
LONDON
E1W 1UQ

HMS SCOTIA
Hilton Road
Rosyth
KY11 2XH

HMS SHERWOOD
Chalfont Drive
NOTTINGHAM
NG8 3LT

HMS VIVID
Building SO40A
HM Naval Base
Devonport
PL2 2BG

HMS WILDFIRE
Brackenhill House
Oxhey Drive South
NORTHWOOD
Middlesex
HA6 3EX

ROYAL MARINES ESTABLISHMENTS AND UNITS

ATTURM
Amphibious Trials & Training Unit
Royal Marines
Instow
BIDEFORD
Devon
EX39 4JH

CDO LOG REGT RM
Commando Logistics Regiment
Royal Marines
RMB Chivenor
BARNSTAPLE
Devon
EX31 1AZ

CTCRM
Commando Training Centre
Royal Marines
Lympstone
EXMOUTH
Devon
EX8 5AR

CTCRM (SEA)
Commando Training Centre
Royal Marines
Lympstone
Nr Exmouth
Devon
EX8 5AR

HQ 3 CDO BDE RM
Headquarters 3 Commando Brigade
Royal Marines
RM Barracks
Stonehouse
PLYMOUTH
Devon
PL1 3QS

RM CONDOR
Royal Marines Condor
ARBROATH
Angus
Scotland
DD11 3SJ

RMB STONEHOUSE
Royal Marines Stonehouse
RM Barracks
Stonehouse
PLYMOUTH
Devon
PL1 3QS

UKLFCSG RM
UKLF CSG
RM Barracks
Stonehouse
Plymouth
Devon
PL1 3QS

1 ASSLT GP RM
1 Assault Group Royal Marines
Hamworthy
POOLE
Dorset
BH15 4NQ

148 FOU BTY RA
RM Poole
Hamworthy
Poole
Dorset
BH15 4NQ

29 CDO REGT RA
29 Commando Regiment Royal Artillery
The Royal Citadel
Plymouth
Devon
PL1 2PD

40 CDO RM
40 Commando Royal Marines
Norton Manor Camp
TAUNTON
Somerset
TA2 6PF

42 CDO RM
42 Commando Royal Marines
Bickleigh Barracks
PLYMOUTH
Devon
PL6 7AJ

45 CDO RM
45 Commando Royal Marines
RM CONDOR
ARBROATH
Angus
Scotland
DD11 3SJ

ROYAL MARINES BAND SERVICE
BRNC BAND
Britannia Royal Naval College
DARTMOUTH
Devon
TQ6 0MJ

ROYAL MARINES BAND SERVICE
CTCRM BAND
EXMOUTH
Devon
EX8 5AR

ROYAL MARINES BAND SERVICE
HQ BAND SERVICE
HQ Band Service RM
Eastney Block
Queen Street
HMS Nelson
PORTSMOUTH
Hants
PO1 3HH

ROYAL MARINES BAND SERVICE
Royal Marines School of Music
Gibraltar Block
Queen Street
HMS NELSON
HM Naval Base
PORTSMOUTH
PO1 3HH

ROYAL MARINES BAND SERVICE
RM BAND PLYMOUTH
RM BAND Plymouth
HMS RALEIGH
TORPOINT
Cornwall
PL11 2PD

ROYAL MARINES BAND SERVICE
RM BAND PORTSMOUTH
RM BAND Portsmouth
HMS NELSON
PORTSMOUTH
Hants
PO1 3HH

ROYAL MARINES BAND SERVICE
RM BAND SCOTLAND
RM BAND Scotland
RNSE HMS CALEDONIA
ROSYTH
Fife
Scotland
KY11 2XH

ROYAL MARINES RESERVE UNITS

RMR BRISTOL
Royal Marines Reserve Bristol
Dorset House
Litfield Place
BRISTOL
BS8 3NA

RMR LONDON
Royal Marines Reserve
City of London
2 Old Jamaica Road
Bermondsey
LONDON
SE16 4AN

RMR MERSEYSIDE
Royal Marines Reserve Merseyside
RNHQ Merseyside
East Brunswick Dock
LIVERPOOL
Merseyside
L3 4DZ

RMR SCOTLAND
Royal Marines Reserve Scotland
37-51 Birkmyre Road
Govan
GLASGOW
G51 3JH

RMR TYNE
Royal Marines Reserve Tyne
Anzio House
Quayside
NEWCASTLE-UPON-TYNE
NE6 1BU

ROYAL FLEET AUXILIARY SERVICE

ARGUS, Aviation Training & Primary Casualty Reception Ship

BAYLEAF, Support Tanker, (AO)

BLACK ROVER, Small Fleet Tanker, (AORL)

BRAMBLELEAF, Support Tanker, (AO)

DILIGENCE, Forward Repair Ship, (AR)

FORT AUSTIN, Support Stores Ship (AFS)

FORT VICTORIA, Combined Fleet Support Tanker & Store Ship(AOR)

FORT GEORGE, Combined Fleet Support Tanker & Store Ship,(AOR)

FORT ROSALIE, Support Stores Ship (AFS)

GOLD ROVER, Small Fleet Tanker, (AORL)

GREY ROVER, Small Fleet Tanker, (AORL)

OAKLEAF, Support Tanker, (AO)

ORANGELEAF, Support Tanker, (AO)

SIR BEDIVERE, Landing Ship Logistics, (LSL)

SIR GALAHAD, Landing Ship Logistics, (LSL)

SIR PERCIVALE, Landing Ship Logistics, (LSL)

SIR TRISTRAM, Landing Ship Logistics, (LSL)

WAVE KNIGHT, Support Tanker,(AO)

WAVE RULER, Support Tanker,(AO)

LARGS BAY, Landing Ship Dock, (Auxiliary)

LYME BAY, Landing Ship Dock, (Auxiliary)

CARDIGAN BAY, Landing Ship Dock, (Auxiliary)

MOUNTS BAY, Landing Ship Dock, (Auxiliary)

KEY ADDRESSES

ARMED FORCES PERSONNEL ADMINISTRATION AGENCY HEADQUARTERS (AFPAA HQ)

AFPAA (Central Office)
Building 182
RAF Innsworth
GLOUCESTER
Gloucestershire
GL3 1HW

AFPAA (Centurion)
Centurion Building
Grange Road
GOSPORT
Hants
PO13 9XA

COMBINED CADET FORCE

Director of Naval Reserves
South Terrace
HM Naval Base
PORTSMOUTH
Hants
PO1 3LS

COMMITTEES

UNITED KINGDOM COMMANDERS IN CHIEF COMMITTEE (HOME)(UKCICC)(H)
Erskine Barracks
Wilton
SALISBURY
Wiltshire
SP2 0AG
(01722 433208)

COMMONWEALTH LIAISON OFFICES

AUSTRALIA
Australia House
Strand
London
WC2B 4LA

BANGLADESH
28 Queens Gate
LONDON
SW7 5JA

CANADA
Macdonald House
Grosvenor Square
LONDON
W1K 4AB

GHANA
13 Belgrave Square
LONDON
SW1X 8PN

INDIA
India House
Aldwych
LONDON
WC2B 4NA

MALAYSIA
45 Belgrave Square
LONDON
SW1X 8QT

NEW ZEALAND
New Zealand House
Haymarket
LONDON
SW1Y 4TQ

NIGERIA
Nigeria House
9 Northumberland Avenue
LONDON
WC2N 5BX

EDUCATIONAL ESTABLISHMENTS

THE ROYAL COLLEGE OF DEFENCE STUDIES
Seaford House
37 Belgrave Square
LONDON
SW1 X8NS
(020 7915 4804)

THE JOINT SERVICES COMMAND AND STAFF TRAINING COLLEGE
BRACKNELL
Berkshire
RG12 9DD
(01344 457271)

JSCSC SHRIVENHAM
Faringdon Road
Watchfield
Swindon
Wiltshire
SN6 8LA
(01793 788001)

MEDICAL SERVICES

The Medical Director General (Naval)
Victory Building
HM Naval Base
PORTSMOUTH
PO1 3LS

Ministry of Defence Hospital Unit Portsmouth
Royal Hospital Haslar
Haslar Road
GOSPORT
Hants
PO12 2AA

Ministry of Defence Hospital Unit Derriford
Derriford Hospital
PLYMOUTH
Devon
PL6 8DH

Institute of Naval Medicine
ALVERSTOKE
Hants
PO12 2DL

MINISTRY OF DEFENCE POLICE HEADQUARTERS

Ministry of Defence Police Headquarters
MDP Wethersfield
BRAINTREE
Essex
CM7 4AZ
(01371 854000)

NAVAL BASES AND SUPPLY AGENCY

CDIRECTOR GENERAL LOG. FLEET
Birch
1-N54c
#3131
FOXHILL
Bath
BA1 5AB

NAVAL BASE COMMANDER CLYDE
HM Naval Base
Clyde
Dunbartonshire
G84 8HL
Defence Munitions
BEITH
Ayrshire
KA15 1JT

CAMPBELTOWN (NATO POL Depot)
Glen Ramskill, Campbeltown
PA28 6RD

COULPORT (RN Armament Depot)
PO Box 1
Cove
Helensburgh
Dunbartonshire
G84 0PD

CROMBIE (RN Armament Depot)
Main Depot
Ordnance Road
Crombie
KY12 8LA

FASLANE (RN Store Depot)
HM Naval Base
Faslane
G84 8HL

GLEN DOUGLAS (NATO Ammunition Depot)
PO Box 1
Arrochar
Dunbartonshire
G83 7BA

LOCH EWE (NATO POL Depot)
Aultbea
Achnasheen
Ross Shire
IV22 2HU

LOCH STRIVEN (NATO POL Depot)
Loch Striven
Scotland
PA23 7UL

ROSYTH (RN Store Depot)
Fife
KY11 2XP

NAVAL BASE COMMANDER DEVONPORT
HM Naval Base
DEVONPORT
Plymouth
PL1 4SL

Devonport (RN Store Depot)
HM Naval Base
DEVONPORT
Plymouth
PL1 4SL

Ernesettle (RN Armament Depot)
Ernesettle Lane
PLYMOUTH
PL5 2TX

Exeter (Support Engineering Facility)
Topsham
EXETER
Devon
EX2 7AH

NAVAL BASE COMMANDER PORTSMOUTH
HM Naval Base
PORTSMOUTH
Hants
PO1 3LT

DIRECTOR SUPPLY (SOUTH)
South Office Block
HM Naval Base
PORTSMOUTH
PO1 3LU

Colerne (RN Store Depot)
Doncombe Lane
Colerne
Wiltshire
SN14 8QY

GOSPORT (RN Armament Depot)
Fareham Road
Gosport
Hants
PO13 0AH

PORTSMOUTH(RN Armament Depot)
Hants
PO1 3LU

MARINE SERVICES SUPPORT

Deputy Director Marine Services Support
Room 92A
Block E
ENSLEIGH
Bath
BA1 5AB

General Manager
HM Mooring Depot
Pembroke Dock
Pembrokeshire
SA72 6TB

NAVY, ARMY AND AIR FORCE INSTITUTES

NAAFI HQ
LONDON Road
Amesbury
SALISBURY
Wiltshire
SP4 7EN

NATO HEADQUARTERS-MILITARY COMMITTEE (UKMILREP)

UKMILREP
NATO Headquarters
BFPO 49

ALLIED COMMAND ATLANTIC (ACLANT)

HEADQUARTERS, SUPREME ALLIED COMMANDER ATLANTIC (SACLANT)
Naval Party 1964
(Saclant)
BFPO 493

REGIONAL HEADQUARTERS EAST ATLANTIC (RHQ EASTLANT)
Eastbury Park
Northwood
Middlesex
HA6 3HP

REGIONAL HEADQUARTERS SOUTH ATLANTIC (RHQ SOUTHLANT)
BFPO 6

SUBMARINE FORCES EASTERN ATLANTIC (SUBEASTLANT)
Eastbury Park
NORTHWOOD
Middlesex
HA6 3HP

ANTI-SUBMARINE WARFARE STRIKING FORCE
Office of COMUKMARFOR
Fieldhouse Building
Whale Island
PORTSMOUTH
Hants

SACLANT UNDERSEA RESEARCH CENTRE
Viale San Bartolomeo 400
I-19026 San Bartolomeo
Italy

ALLIED COMMAND EUROPE (ACE)

SUPREME HEADQUARTERS ALLIED POWERS EUROPE (SHAPE)
BFPO 26

NATO SCHOOL (SHAPE)
Oberammergau
Box 2003
BFPO 105

REGIONAL HEADQUARTERS AFSOUTH
BFPO 8

STRIKFORSOUTH RHQ AFSOUTH
BFPO 8

HQ ALLIED NAVAL FORCES SOUTHERN EUROPE (HQ NAVSOUTH)
BFPO 8

JOINT HQ SOUTHEAST
Sirinyer
Izmir
Turkey

FRENCH COMMANDER-IN-CHIEF MEDITERRANEAN
(CECMED)
Prefecture Maritime
83800 Toulon Naval
France

REGIONAL HEADQUARTERS AFNORTH
BPFO 28
JHQ NORTHEAST
BFPO 150

NAVAL PERSONAL AND FAMILY SERVICE (NPFS)

Area Office (NPFS) Eastern
Swiftsure Block
HMS Nelson
Queen Street
PORTSMOUTH
Hants
PO1 3HH
(02392 722712)

Area Office (NPFS) Western
Fenner Block
H M Naval Base Devonport
HMS DRAKE
PLYMOUTH
Devon
PL2 2BG
(01752 555041)

Area Office (NPFS) Northern
Triton House
1-5 Churchill Square
HELENSBURGH
Argyll and Bute
G84 9HL
(01436 672798)

NAVAL REGIONAL OFFICES

SCOTLAND & NORTHERN IRELAND
REGIONS
HMS CALEDONIA
ROSYTH
Fife
KY11 2XH
(01383 425532)

NORTHERN ENGLAND REGION
Royal Naval Headquarters Merseyside
Brunswick Dock
LIVERPOOL
L3 4DZ
(0151 707 3400/3401/3402)

Naval Regional Sub-Office
HMS CALLIOPE
South Shore Road
GATESHEAD
Tyne & Wear
NE8 2BE
(0191 477 2536)

WALES & WESTERN REGIONS
Naval Regional Management Centre
HMS FLYING FOX
Winterstoke Road
BRISTOL
BS3 2NS
(0117 953 0996)

EASTERN ENGLAND REGION
HMS PRESIDENT
72 St Katharine's Way
LONDON
E1W 1UQ
(020 7481 7324)

REGULAR FORCES EMPLOYMENT ASSOCIATION

(NATIONAL ASSOCIATION FOR EMPLOYMENT OF REGULAR SAILORS SOLDIERS AND AIRMEN)
49 Pall Mall
LONDON
SW1Y 5JG
(020 7321 2011)

ABERDEEN
46A Union Street
ABERDEEN
AB10 1BD

BEDFORD
TA Centre
28 Bedford Road
KEMPSTON
Beds
MK42 8AJ

BELFAST
Northern Ireland War Memorial Building
Waring Street
BELFAST
BT1 2EU

BIRMINGHAM
2nd Floor
Cornwall Buildings
45 Newhall Street
BIRMINGHAM
B3 3QR

BRISTOL
Borough Park Business Centre
Borough Park
Romney Avenue
BRISTOL
BS7 9ST

BURY ST. EDMUNDS
Room 4
90 Guildhall Street
BURY ST EDMUNDS
IP33 1PR

CARDIFF
Maindy Barracks
CARDIFF
CF4 3YE

CHELMSFORD
Springfield Tyrells House
250 Springfield Road
CHELMSFORD
Essex
CM2 6BY

CHELTENHAM
Potter House
St Annes Road
CHELTENHAM
Glos
GL52 2SS

DARLINGTON
67 Duke Street
Darlington
Co. Durham
DL3 7SD

DERBY
Room 18
The College Business Centre
Uttoxeter New Road
DERBY
DE22 3WZ

EDINBURGH
New Haig House
Logie Green Road
EDINBURGH
EH7 4HQ

EXETER
Wyvern Barracks
EXETER
Devon
EX2 6AR

GLASGOW
2nd Floor
The Pentagon Centre
36 Washington Street
GLASGOW
G3 8AZ

LEEDS
Carlton Barracks
Carlton Gate
LEEDS
LS7 1HE

LINCOLN
Unit 4, Oak House
Witharn Park
Waterside South
LINCOLN
LN5 7FB

LIVERPOOL
Suite 43 Oriel Chambers
14 Water Street
LIVERPOOL
L2 8TD

LONDON
49 Pall Mall
LONDON
SW1Y 5JG

MAIDSTONE
Royal British Legion Industries
Royal British Legion Village
Aylesford
Nr MAIDSTONE
Kent
ME20 7NL

MANCHESTER
TA Centre
Belle Vue Street
MANCHESTER
M12 5PW

NEWCASTLE-ON-TYNE
c/o The Queen's Own Yeomanry
Fenham Barracks
Barrack Road
NEWCASTLE-UPON-TYNE
NE2 4NP

NORTHAMPTON
TA Centre
28 Bedford Road
KEMPSTON
Beds
MK42 8AJ

NORWICH
TA Centre
Britannia House
325 Aylsham Road
NORWICH
NR3 2AB

PLYMOUTH
Flat 10
MOD Mt Wise Business Park
Devonport
PLYMOUTH
PL1 4JH

PORTSMOUTH
2B Tipner Road
Stamshaw
PORTSMOUTH
PO2 8QP

PRESTON
Fulwood Barracks
Fulwood
PRESTON
Lancs
PR2 8AA

READING
Watlington House
Watlington Street
READING
RG1 4RJ

SALISBURY
27 Castle Street
SALISBURY
Wilts
SP1 1TT

SHEFFIELD
2nd Floor
9 Paradise Square
SHEFFIELD
S1 2DE

SWANSEA
See Cardiff Branch

QINETIQ, FORMERLY DERA (DEFENCE EVALUATION AND RESEARCH AGENCY) MAJOR ESTABLISHMENTS

From 2 Jul 01, on privatisation, DERA separates into Qinetiq, a plc, and DSTL (Defence Science and Technology Laboratory). DSTL is the MOD-retained part of DERA.

HEAD OFFICE
QINETIQ
Cody Technology Park
Ively Road
FARNBOROUGH
Hampshire
GU14 0LX

DSTL Portsdown West
Portsdown Hill Road
FAREHAM
Hampshire
PO17 6AD

QINETIQ
Winfrith Technology Centre
Newburgh
DORCHESTER
Dorset
DT2 8XJ

DSTL Porton Down
SALISBURY
Wiltshire
SP4 0JQ

QINETIQ
Malvern Technology Park
St Andrews Road
MALVERN
Worcs
WR14 3PS

DSTL Fort Halstead
SEVENOAKS
Kent
TN14 7BP

DEFENCE AVIATION REPAIR AGENCY

HEAD OFFICE
DARA St Athan
St Athan
BARRY
Vale of Glamorgan
CF62 4WA

DARA Almondbank
Almondbank
PERTH
PH1 3NQ

DARA Fleetlands
Fareham Road
GOSPORT
Hampshire
PO13 0AA

DARA Sealand
Welsh Road
DEESIDE
Flintshire
CH5 2LS

DIRECTORATE OF NAVAL RECRUITING REGIONAL CAREERS HEADQUARTERS (RCHQS) AND ARMED FORCE CAREERS OFFICES (AFCOs)

RCHQ NORTH
RN Support Establishment
HMS Caledonia
ROSYTH
KY11 2XH
(01383 425516)

AFCOs NORTH REGION
63 Belmont Street
ABERDEEN
AB10 1JS
(01224 639666)

Palace Barracks
Holywood
BELFAST
Co. Down
BT18 9RA
(02890 423840)

94-96 English Street
CARLISLE
CA3 8ND
(01228 523958)

148 Northgate
DARLINGTON
DL1 1QT
(01325 461850)

29/31 Bank Street
DUNDEE
DD1 1RW
(01382 227198)

TA Centre
Elgin Street
DUNFERMLINE
KY12 7SB
01383 625283

67-83 Shandwick Place
EDINBURGH
EH2 4SN
(0131 221 1111)

Charlotte House
78 Queen Street
GLASGOW
G1 3DN
(0141 221 4852

Britannia Suite
Norwich House
Savile Street
KINGSTON-UPON-HULL
HU1 3ES
(01482 325901)

3 Bridge Street
INVERNESS
IV1 1HG
(01463 233668)

10 - 14 Bond Street
Park Row
LEEDS
LS1 2JY
(0113 2458195)

15 James Street
LIVERPOOL
L2 7NX
(0151 236 1566)

Petersfield House
29 Peters Street
MANCHESTER
M2 5QJ
(0161 835 2923)

67 Borough Road
MIDDLESBROUGH
Cleveland
TS1 3AE
(01642 211749)

New England House
20 Ridley Place
NEWCASTLE UPON TYNE
NE1 8JW
(0191 2327048)

63 College Street
St Helens
MERSEYSIDE
WA10 1TN
(01744 753560)

46 Edward VII Quay
Navigation Way
Ashton on Wibble
PR2 2YF
(01772 555675)

Central Buildings
1A Church Street
SHEFFIELD
S1 1FZ
(0114 272 1476)

RCHQ SOUTH
Ladywood House
45/46 Stephenson Street
BIRMINGHAM
B2 4DY
(0121 634 8508)

AFCOs SOUTH REGION
Unit 46
The Pallasades
BIRMINGHAM
B2 4XN
(0121 633 4995)

244 Holdenhurst Road
BOURNEMOUTH
BH8 8AZ
(01202 311224)

120 Queen's Road
BRIGHTON
BN1 3XQ
(01273 325386)

4 Colston Avenue
BRISTOL
BS1 4TY
(0117 9260233)

2 Glisson Road
CAMBRIDGE
CB1 2HD
(01223 315118)

South Gate House
84 Wood Street
CARDIFF
CF10 1GR
(02920 727626)

3 Dock Road
CHATHAM
ME4 4SJ
(01634 826206)

Sir Henry Parks Road
Canley
COVENTRY
CV5 6TA
(02476 226513)

Fountain House
Western Way
EXETER
EX1 2DQ
(01392 274040)

4th Floor
Britannia Warehouse
The Docks
GLOUCESTER
GL1 2EH
(01452 521676)

Stanford House
91 Woodbridge Road
GUILDFORD
GU1 4LN
(01483 302304)

180A Cranbrook Road
ILFORD
Essex
IG1 4LR
(020 851 858855)

37 Silent Street
IPSWICH
IP1 1TF
(01473 254450)

St George's House
6 St George's Way
LEICESTER
LE1 1SH
(01162 543233)

Sibthorpe House
350/352 High Street
LINCOLN
LN5 7BN
(01522 525661)

Ground Floor
Zone D
St Georges Court
2-12 Bloomsbury Way
LONDON
WC1A 2SH
(020 7305 3329)

Dunstable House
Dunstable Road
LUTON
LU1 1EA
(01582 721501)

22 Unthank Road
NORWICH
NR2 2RA
(01603 620033)

70 Milton Road
Victoria Centre
NOTTINGHAM
NG1 3QX
(0115 9419503)

35 St Giles Street
OXFORD
OX1 3LJ
(01865 553431)

21 - 23 Hereward Cross
PETERBOROUGH
PE1 1TB
(01733 568833)

Mount Wise
Devonport
PLYMOUTH
PL1 4JH
(01752 501790)

Cambridge Road
PORTSMOUTH
PO1 2EN
(023 9282 6536)

Oak House
Chapel Street
REDRUTH
TR15 2BY
(01209 314143)

2nd Floor
Princess House
The Square
SHREWSBURY
Shropshire
SY1 1JZ
(01743 232541)

152 High Street
Lower Bar
SOUTHAMPTON
Hants
SO14 2BT
(023 8063 0486)

36 - 38 Old Hall Street
Hanley
STOKE-ON-TRENT
ST1 3AP
(01782 214688)

Llanfair Buildings
17-19 Castle Street
SWANSEA
SA1 1JF
(01792 654208/642516)

35 East Street
TAUNTON
Somerset
TA1 3LS
(01823 354430)

43A Queens Street
WOLVERHAMPTON
WV1 3BL
(01902 715395)

Halkyn House
21 Rhosddu Road
WREXHAM
LL11 1NE
(01978 263334)

OFFICER CAREERS LIAISON CENTRES (OCLCs)

OCLCs NORTH REGION

RN Support Establishment
HMS CALEDONIA
ROSYTH
KY11 2XH
(01383 425515)

Petersfield House
29-31 St Peter's Street
MANCHESTER
M2 5QJ
(0161 8352916

Palace Barracks
Holywood
County Down
BELFAST or BFPO 806
BT18 9RA
(028 9042 3832)

OCLCs SOUTH REGION

Ladywood House
45/46 Stephenson Street
BIRMINGHAM
B2 4DY
(0121 66348508)

JHQ Building
Northwood HQ
Northwood
MIDDLESEX
HA6 3HP
(01923 833140)

HMS FLYING FOX
Winterstoke Road
BRISTOL
BS3 2NS
(0117 9655251)

ROYAL NAVAL FILM CHARITY

Registered Office
HM Naval Base (PP23)
PORTSMOUTH
PO1 3NH
(023 927 23108)

SEA CADET CORPS

HEADQUARTERS
202 Lambeth Road
LONDON
SE1 7JF
(020 7928 8978)

NORTHERN AREA
HMS CALEDONIA
ROSYTH
Fife
KY11 2XH
(01383 416300)

NORTH WEST AREA
Royal Naval Headquarters Merseyside
East Brunswick Dock
LIVERPOOL
L3 4DZ
(0151 707 3440)

SOUTH WEST AREA
HMS FLYING FOX
Winterstoke Road
BRISTOL
Avon
BS3 2NS
(0117 953 1991)

EASTERN AREA
The Drill Hall
Ropery Road
GAINSBOROUGH
Lincolnshire
DN21 2NS
(01427 614441)

LONDON AREA
HMS PRESIDENT
72 St. Katharine's Way
LONDON
E1W 1UQ
(020 7481 7372)

SOUTHERN AREA
HMS NELSON
PORTSMOUTH
Hants
PO1 3HH
(023 927 24263)

SHIPPING POLICY DIVISION

(DEFENCE PLANNING AND EMERGENCIES BRANCH)
Department for Transport, Local Government and the Regions
Zone 4/21
Great Minster House
76 Marsham Street
LONDON
SW1P 4DR
(020 7944 5148)

YACHT CLUBS USING A SPECIAL ENSIGN

Yachts belonging to members of the following Yacht Clubs may, subject to certain conditions, obtain a Warrant to wear a Special Ensign.

Club	*Address*
WHITE ENSIGN	
Royal Yacht Squadron	Royal Yacht Squadron, Castle Cowes PO31 7QT
BLUE ENSIGN	
Royal Albert Yacht Club	17 Pembroke Road, Portsmouth, PO1 2NT
Royal Brighton Yacht Club	253 St Kilda Street,Middle Brighton, 3186, Victoria,Australia
Royal Cinque Ports Yacht Club	4-5 Waterloo Crescent, Dover, CT6 1LA
Royal Cruising Club	Bywaters, Taylors Lane, Bosham, West Susex, PO18 8QQ
Royal Dorset Yacht Club	11 Custom House Quay, Weymouth, Dorset, DT4 8BG
Royal Engineer Yacht Club	86 Training Squadron, Army Apprentice College, Chepstow, Gwent, NP6 7YG
Royal Geelong Yacht Club	PO Box 156, Geelong, 3220 Victoria, Australia
Royal Gourock Yacht Club	Ashton Gourock PA19 1DA
Royal Highland Yacht Club	Westmanse House, Lichrenan Tanyuilt, Argyl, PH35 1HG
Royal Marines Sailing Club	Poole, Dorset, BH15 4NQ
Royal Melbourne Yacht Club	Lower Esplanade, St Kilda, 3182
Royal Motor Yacht Club	Panorama Road, Sandbanks, Poole, Dorset, BH13 7RN
Royal Naval Sailing Association	Royal Naval Club, 10 Haslar Marina, Haslar Road, Gosport, PO12 1NU
Royal Naval Volunteer Reserve Yacht Club	The Naval Club, 38 Hill Street, London, W1X 8DB
Royal New Zealand Yacht Squadron	Squadron Rooms, Westhaven, PO Box 46128 Herne Bay, Auckland, New Zealand
Royal Northern and Clyde Yacht Club	The Club House, Rhu, Dumbartonshire, G84 8NG
Royal Perth Yacht Club of Western Australia	PO Box 5, Nedlands, West Australia 6009
Royal Port Nicholas Yacht Club	Clyde Quay Boat Harbour, PO Box 9674, Wellington,New Zealand
Royal Queensland Yacht Club	PO Box 21, Manly, Queensland 4179, Australia
Royal Scottish Motor Yacht Club	5 St Vincent Place, Glasgow, G1 2DJ

Club	Address
Royal Solent Yacht Club	Yarmouth, Isle of Wight, PO41 0NS
Royal South Australia Yacht Club	North Haven 5018, South Australia
Royal Southern Yacht Club	Hamble, Southampton, SO3 5HB
Sussex Motor Yacht Club	7 Ship Street, Brighton, East Sussex, BN1 1AD
Royal Sydney Yacht Squadron	PO Box 484, Milsons' Point, NSW 2061, Australia
Royal Temple Yacht Club	6 West Cliff Mansions, Ramsgate, Kent, CT11 9WY
Royal Thames Yacht Club	60 Knightsbridge, London, SW1X 7LF
Royal Western Yacht Club of England	West Hoe, Plymouth, PL1 3DG
Royal Western Yacht Club of Scotland	Lochabar, 20 Barclay Drive, Helensburgh, Dunbartonshire, G84 9RB
Royal Yacht Club of Tasmania	Marieville Esplanade, Sandy Bay, Tasmania 7005
Royal Yacht Club of Victoria	120 Nelson Place, Williamstown, 3016, Australia

BLUE ENSIGN DEFACED BY BADGE OF CLUB

Club	Address
Aldburgh Yacht Club	Aldebrugh, Suffolk
Army Sailing Association	c/o MOD (ASCB), M Block, Clayton Barracks, Aldershot, Hants
Bar Yacht Club	1 Mitre Court Buildings, Temple, London, EC4Y 7BS
City Livery Yacht Club	Shortlands, Bromley, Kent BR2 0LG
Cruising Yacht Club of Australia	New Beach Road, Darling Point, New South Wales 2027
Royal Air Force	Yacht Club Riverside House, Hamble, Southampton,SO3 5HD
Royal Akrana Yacht Club	PO Box 42004, Orakei, Auckland 5, New Zealand
Royal Anglesey Yacht Club	3 Cadnant Court, Rating Row, Beaumaris, Anglesey, Gwynnedd, LL58 8AL
Royal Armoured Corps Yacht Club	Bovington Camp, Wareham, Dorset, BH20 6ND
Royal Artillery Yacht Club	Tamberton, Upton Lovell, Warminster, Wilts, BA12 0JP
Royal Australian Navy Sailing Association	New Beach Road, Edgecliffe, New South Wales 2027, Australia
Royal Bermuda Yacht Club	PO Box 894, Hamilton HM DX, Bermuda
Royal Bombay Yacht Club	PO Box 206, Apollo Bunder, Fort Bombay 400039
Royal Burnham Yacht Club	The Quay, Burnham-on-Crouch, Essex, CM0 8AO
Royal Channel Islands Yacht Club	Le Boulevard, Bulwark, St Aubin, Jersey, Channel Islands, JE5 8AD
Conway Club Cruising Association	5 Furlong Lane, Totternhoe, Nr Dunstable, BEds

Club	Address
Royal Corinthian Yacht Club	Burnham-on-Crouch, Essex
Royal Cornwall Yacht Club	Greenbank, Falmouth, Cornwall
Royal Dee Yacht Club	16 Holford Crescent, Knutsford, Cheshire, WA16 8DZ
Royal Forth Yacht Club	Middle Pier, Granton Harbour, Edinburgh
Royal Freshwater Bay Yacht Club of Western Australia	Keane's Point, Peppermint Grove, Western Australia 6011
Royal Gibraltar Yacht Club	Queensway, Gibraltar
Royal Harwich Yacht Club	Woolverstone, Ipswich, IP9 1AT
Royal Hong Kong Yacht Club	Kellet Island, Hong Kong
Household Division Yacht Club	HQ Welsh Guards, Wellington Barracks, Birdcage Walk, London SW1E 6HQ
Royal Irish Yacht Club	Dun Loaghaire, Co Dublin
Royal Jamaica Yacht Club	Kingston, Jamaica
Little Ship Club	Bell Wharfe Lane, Upper Thames Street, London EC4R 3TB
Little Ship Club (Queensland Squadron)	119 Bank Street, Newmarket, Queensland 4051, Australia
Royal London Yacht Club	The Parade, Cowes, Isle of Wight, PO31 7QS
Medway Cruising Club	Boyses Hill Farm, Newington, Sittingbourne, Kent, ME9 7JF
Royal Malta Yacht Club	Couvre Port, Fort Manoel, Manoel Island, Gzira, Malta
Royal Mersey Yacht Club	Bedford Road East, Rockferry, Birkenhead, Merseyside, L42 1LS
Royal Motor Yacht Club of New South Wales	Wunulla Road, Point Piper, New South Wales 2027
Royal Nassau Sailing Club	PO Box SS 6891, Nassau, Bahamas
Royal North of Ireland Yacht Club	Cultra, 7 Seaford Road, Co Down, Ireland
Royal Northumberland Yacht Club	36 Longridge Drive, Whitley Bay, Tyne & Wear
Royal Ocean Racing Club	20 St James's Place SW1A 1NN
Parkstone Yacht Club	Pearce Avenue, Parkstone, Poole, Dorset, BH14 8EN
Royal Plymouth Corinthian Yacht Club	Madeira Road, Plymouth, PL1 2NY
Poole Yacht Club	New Harbour Road West, Hamworthy, Poole, Dorset
Royal Prince Alfred Yacht Club	PO Box 99, Newport Beach, New South Wales 2106, Australia
Royal Prince Edward Yacht Club	160 Wolseley Road, Point Piper, 2027 New South Wales, Australia
Severn Motor Yacht Club	Bath Road, Broomhall, Worcester, WR5 3HR
Royal Southampton Yacht Club	1 Channel Way, Ocean Village, Southampton, SO1 1XE
Sussex Yacht Club	85-89 Brighton Road, Shoreham by Sea, Sussex
Royal Suva Yacht Club	PO Box 335, Suva, Fiji
The Cruising Association	Ivory House, St Katherine's Dock, London

	E1 9AT
The House of Lords Yacht Club	House of Lords, London, SW1A 0PW
The Medway Yacht Club	Upnor, Rochester, Kent
The Poole Harbour Yacht Club	38 Salterns Way, Lilliput, Poole, Dorset, BH14 8JR
Thames Motor Yacht Club	The Green, Hampton Court, East Molesey, Surrey
Royal Torbay Yacht Club	Beacon Hill, Torquay, Devon
Royal Ulster Yacht Club	101 Clifton Road, BANGOR, Co Down
Royal Welsh Yacht Club	Porth yr Aur, Caernarvon, Gwynedd
Royal Yorkshire Yacht Club	1 Windsor Crescent, Bridlington, YO15 3HY
Old Worcesters Yacht Club	Les Heches, St Peter in the Wood, Guernsey, Channel Islands

RED ENSIGN DEFACED BY BADGE OF CLUB

Brixham Yacht Club	Overgang, Brixham, Devon, TQ5 8AR
Royal Dart Yacht Club	Kingswear, South Devon, TQ6 0AB
Royal Fowey Yacht Club	Fowey, Cornwall, PL23 8IH
House of Commons Yacht Club	RYA House, Romsey Road, Eastleigh, Hants, SO5 4YA
Lloyd's Yacht Club	London, SW6 5DP
Royal Hamilton Amateur Dinghy Club	PO Box 298, Paget PG BX, Bermuda
Royal Lymington Yacht Club	Bath Road, Lymington, Hants, S41 9SE
Royal Norfolk and Suffolk Yacht Club	Royal Plain, Lowestoft, Suffolk, NR33 0AQ
Royal St George Yacht Club	Dun Laoghaire, Co Dublin
St Helier Yacht Club	South Pier, St Helier, Jersey
Royal Victoria Yacht Club	Fishbourne, Isle of Wight, PO33 4EU
Royal Windermere Yacht Club	Fallbarrow Road, Bowness in Windermere, Cumbria, LA33 3DJ
Royal Yachting Association	RYA House, Romsey Road, Eastleigh, Hants, SO5 4YA
West Mersea Yacht Club	116 Coast Road, West Mersea, Colchester,Essex

HONORARY OFFICERS OF THE ROYAL NAVAL RESERVE

Honorary Rear Admiral HRH Prince Michael of Kent, GCVO
Honorary Commodore The Right Honourable The Lord Sterling of Plaistow, GCVO CBE
Honorary Commodore Sir Donald Gosling KCVO
Honorary Captain Mrs Mary Fagan JP
Honorary Captain Mr Eric Dancer CBE JP
Honorary Captain The Lord Browne of Madingley
Honorary Captain Robert B Woods CBE
Honorary Captain Lady Carswell OBE
Honorary Captain R Warwick
Honorary Captain (Supernumerary) The Duke of Buccleugh and Queensberry KT VRD JP
Honorary Commander E J Billington
Honorary Commander P R Moore RD*
Honorary Commander Angus Buchanan
Honorary Commander Stephen Howarth
Honorary Lieutenant-Commander Bear Grylls
Honorary Lieutenant-Commander Dame Ellen MacArthur DBE
Honorary Lieutenant- Commander James Stevens BSc FRIN
Honorary Lieutenant-Commander Ian Robinson
Honorary Commander (Supernumerary) Sir Robin Gillett Bt GBE RD
Honorary Commander (Supernumerary) F A Mason MBE
Honorary Chaplain The Right Reverend Bill Ind
Honorary Chaplain The Reverend John Williams MBE
Honorary Chaplain (Supernumerary) The Right Reverend M A P Woods, DSc, MA, (CofE)

HONORARY OFFICERS OF THE ROYAL MARINES RESERVE

Honorary Colonel E P R Cautley .... 1 Jul 99
Honorary Colonel G M Simmers, CBE, CA .... 01 Apr 00
Honorary Colonel J N Tidmarsh, MBE, JP .... 01 Jan 98
Honorary Colonel Sir David Trippier RD JP DL .... 01 Jan 96
Honorary Colonel Sir Neville Trotter, FCA, JP, DL .... 1 Sep 98

OFFICERS OF THE ACTIVE LIST OF THE ROYAL NAVAL RESERVE, ROYAL MARINES RESERVE, THE QUEEN ALEXANDRA'S ROYAL NAVAL NURSING RESERVE, SEA CADET CORPS AND COMBINED CADET FORCE

ROYAL NAVAL RESERVE

Name	Rank	Branch	Unit	Seniority
A				
Adair, Jonathan	HON MID	URNU	U/A	11.10.01
Adair, Richard Charles	ASLT	NE	WILDFIRE	05.05.05
Adams, Kelly,	HONCADET	URNU	U/A	20.10.00
Adeoye, Ibukunolu,	HONCADET	URNU	U/A	12.10.00
Adeyeye, Ayodeji Olabode,	HON MID	URNU	U/A	24.10.00
Ahlgren, Rebecca	SLT	LOGS	VIVID	08.04.02
Ainsworth, Jeffery,	LT CDR	AIR	RNR AIR BR VL	31.03.01
Aitchison, Ian,	LTCDR	MR	RNR MRS	31.03.03
Aitken, Rebecca,	HONCADET	URNU	U/A	08.10.98
Alcock, Charles Edward Hayes,	LT CDR	AW	PRESIDENT	31.03.00
Alcock, David John, RD GSM	LT CDR	MW	KING ALFRED	18.02.87
Alderson, Victoria,	HONCADET	URNU	U/A	06.11.00
Allan, Richard Michael,	LTCDR	HUMINT	FERRET (RNR)	31.03.02
Allan, Sophie,	HONCADET	URNU	U/A	08.10.98
Allaway, Edward,	HON MID	URNU	U/A	21.10.99
Allen, Clare,	HONCADET	URNU	U/A	07.10.01
Allen, Caroline,	HONCADET	URNU	U/A	20.10.99
Allen, Elinor Jane, RD	LT CDR	OP INT	VIVID	30.09.91
Allen, Ian James, RD	LT CDR	MW,	CAROLINE	31.03.97
Allinson, Graeme,	HON MID	URNU	U/A	11.10.01
Almond, Nicholas,	HON MID	URNU	U/A	07.10.99
Altoft, Kerry,	HONCADET	URNU	U/A	21.10.99
Alvis, Jonathon Geoffrey	ASLT	NE	PRESIDENT	15.10.03
Anderson, Adrian,	LT CDR	AIR	RNR AIR BR VL	31.03.00
Anderson, Graeme,	HON MID	URNU	U/A	27.09.01
Anderson, Isobel,	HONCADET	URNU	U/A	12.10.00
Anderson, John Christopher,	LT	MW	KING ALFRED	06.03.99
Anderson, James,	HON MID	URNU	U/A	08.02.01
Anderson, Kerry McGowan, BSC RD	LT CDR	INFO OPS	CAROLINE	31.03.99
Andersson, James,	HON MID	URNU	U/A	14.10.99

Name	Rank	Branch	Unit	Seniority
Andreou, Alexander,	HON MID	URNU	U/A	12.10.00
Andrews, Mark David,	LT	LOGS	FLYING FOX	03.11.00
Arbeid, Mark Leon,	LT	C4ISR	PRESIDENT	17.04.05
Armstrong, Michael,	LT	AIR	RNR AIR BR VL	14.03.96
Arnold, Christopher,	HON MID	URNU	U/A	19.10.00
Ashby, Maxine Kim	LT	MR	RNR MRS	01.12.97
Ashpole, Richard David,	SG CDR	MED	SHERWOOD	30.09.04
Ashton, Jonathan Richard,	SG CDR	MED	CALLIOPE	11.11.00
Ashwood, Lindsay	ASLT	NE	VIVID	23.11.04
Aslam, Zabeada,	HONCADET	URNU	U/A	22.10.98
Aspden, Mark Charles,	LT	AWNIS	WILDFIRE	01.10.95
Aspinell, Charles Jonathon, RD*	CDR,	NCAGS	KING ALFRED	30.09.97
Aspinell, Pamela Ann, RD	LT CDR	QARNNS(R)	KING ALFRED	31.03.96
Aston, Christopher,	HON MID	URNU	U/A	20.10.98
Athol, Stuart Charles,	LT	NCAGS	PRESIDENT	20.11.01
Attwood, Keith,	HON MID	URNU	U/A	14.10.99
Auld, David,	HON MID	URNU	U/A	05.11.01
Atkinson, James Donald	ASLT	NE	SHERWOOD	23.01.03
Austin, Kevin,	LT CDR	AW	SHERWOOD	31.03.98
Avery, Philip,	LT CDR	AIR	RNR AIR BR VL	31.03.97
Avis, Robert Graeme, RD*	CAPT	AW	PRESIDENT	30.09.97
Aygun, Karyn Stuart RD	LTCDR	NCAGS	FLYING FOX	31.03.01
Awenat, William,	LT CDR	AIR	RNR AIR BR VL	31.03.95

B

Name	Rank	Branch	Unit	Seniority
Babu, Suresh Balasubramanian	ASLT	NE	EAGLET	18.09.03
Backhouse, Jonathan,	LT CDR	AIR	RNR AIR BR VL	01.03.91
Bailey, Stuart,	HON MID	URNU	U/A	12.10.99
Baines, Mark,	LT CDR	AIR	RNR AIR BR VL	01.02.93
Baird, Andrew Wilson,	LT	CIS ENG	CAROLINE	07.08.90
Baker, Henrietta,	HONCADET	URNU	U/A	11.10.01
Baker, Peter Alan, RD	CDR	NCAGS	PRESIDENT	30.09.03
Balchin, Trevor,	HON MID	URNU	U/A	17.10.01
Balmain, Stephen Service,	LT	AW	DALRIADA	01.07.94
Bancroft, David Gideon,	LTCDR	AW	CALLIOPE	31.03.05
Banks, Iain,	LT CDR	AIR	RNR AIR BR VL	31.03.01
Bannister, Mark James	ASLT	NE	WILDFIRE	27.01.05
Barclay, Nicholas,	HON MID	URNU	U/A	12.10.00
Barfield, Kevin Lloyd, RD	LT CDR	CIS ENG	FORWARD	31.01.96
Barham, Edward,	HON MID	URNU	U/A	19.10.00
Barker, Amy,	HONCADET	URNU	U/A	26.10.99
Barker, Elizabeth Charlotte,	LT	NCAGS	PRESIDENT	28.04.02
Barker, Peter,	HON MID	URNU	U/A	11.10.01
Barkhuysen, Edward David	ASLT	NE	FLYING FOX	06.09.02
Barlow, Pauline Elizabeth	SLT	AW	VIVID	09.04.01
Barnes, David,	HON MID	URNU	U/A	07.10.99
Barnes, Judith Margaret,	LT	C4ISR	EAGLET	15.03.03
Barnett, Alison Elaine	ASLT	NE	CAROLINE	15.10.03
Barnwell, Andrew,	ACAPT	AIR	RNR AIR BR VL	05.03.02
Barraclough, Ross,	HON MID	URNU	U/A	24.10.01
Barrand, William,	HON MID	URNU	U/A	07.10.98
Barratt, Stephen James	SLT	AW	FORWARD	23.03.00
Barrett, Mark,	LT CDR	AIR	RNR AIR BR VL	31.03.01
Barter, Emma,	HONCADET	URNU	U/A	10.09.01
Bartlett, David Christopher,	ASG LT	MED	VIVID	27.07.01
Bartlett, David,	HON MID	URNU	U/A	10.09.01
Basis, Rawi,	HON MID	URNU	U/A	11.10.01
Bassett, Nigel Peter, RD	CDR	AW	KING ALFRED	30.09.04
Bate, Rohan,	HON MID	URNU	U/A	18.10.00
Bates, Jodie,	HONCADET	URNU	U/A	07.10.99
Bates, Jocelyn,	HONCADET	URNU	U/A	20.10.00
Battle, Richard John	ASLT	NE	EAGLET	27.11.03

Name	Rank	Branch	Unit	Seniority
Baughan, Philip John, RD	LT CDR	OP INT	SHERWOOD	02.07.89
Baxter, Ross John, RD	LT CDR	NCAGS	FORWARD	31.03.05
Baylis, Clive,	LT CDR	AIR	RNR AIR BR VL	01.10.90
Beaton, Iain William,	ALT	CS(O)	DALRIADA	02.11.04
Beattie, Jane Elizabeth, RD	LT CDR	QARNNS(R)	WILDFIRE	31.03.93
Beauchamp, Martyn,	HON MID	URNU	U/A	01.10.98
Beaumont, Andrew John, RD	LT CDR	MW	EAGLET	31.03.04
Beaumont, Richard,	HON MID	URNU	U/A	10.09.01
Bedford, Helena,	HONCADET	URNU	U/A	21.10.00
Bedford, Johnathon,	SG CDR	MED	SCOTIA	30.09.00
Beech, Eric Edward, RD	LT CDR	DI	FERRET (RNR)	31.03.98
Bell, Charlotte,	HONCADET	URNU	U/A	04.10.01
Bell, Charlotte,	HONCADET	URNU	U/A	25.10.01
Bellamy, Simon,	LT	URNU	U/A	01.10.97
Benmayor Dinah Elizabeth	ASLT	HUMINT	FERRET (RNR)	04.03.04
Benn, Peter Quentin,	LT	MR	RNR MRS	28.02.98
Bennet, Niall Malcolm	A/LT	MW	SCOTIA	22.11.04
Bentall, Estelle,	HONCADET	URNU	U/A	07.10.98
Bentley, David Scott Arthur,	ASLT	MW	FLYING FOX	09.07.98
Benton, Simon,	HON MID	URNU	U/A	09.10.00
Bereznyckyj, Susan Dorothy, RD	LT CDR	QARNNS(R)	SHERWOOD	31.03.94
Bernays, Annie,	HONCADET	URNU	U/A	08.10.98
Berry, Dominic,	HON MID	URNU	U/A	17.10.01
Berry, Ian, RD	LT CDR	MW	CALLIOPE	31.03.96
Betts, Peter,	HON MID	URNU	U/A	10.09.01
Best, Angela Dawn	ASLT	NE	EAGLET	19.11.03
Bewley, Geoffrey, RD	LT CDR	MW	KING ALFRED	31.03.99
Bhanumurthy Sanapala	SGLTCDR	MED	CAMBRIA	03.06.03
Bhimjiani, Ronak,	HON MID	URNU	U/A	12.10.00
Bickerton, Lisa,	HONCADET	URNU	U/A	14.10.99
Bicknell, Richard Anthony, RD	LT CDR	MW	KING ALFRED	31.03.01
Biddlecombe, Amy,	HONCADET	URNU	U/A	14.10.99
Biggerstaff, Adam Graham, RD	LT CDR	OP INT	DALRIADA	03.04.85
Biggs, Nigel, RD	LT	MR	RNR MRS	31.07.95
Billson, Rachel,	HONCADET	URNU	U/A	12.10.00
Binns, James,	HON MID	URNU	U/A	10.09.01
Birch, Anthony,	LT CDR	AIR	RNR AIR BR VL	31.03.99
Bird, Amy,	HONCADET	URNU	U/A	07.10.99
Bird, Graham,	HON MID	URNU	U/A	30.09.99
Bird, Michael,	HON MID	URNU	U/A	09.10.00
Birdsey, Nicola,	HONCADET	URNU	U/A	25.10.01
Birse, Bronwen Louise	LT	MR	RNR MRS	09.02.95
Bishop, Jonathan,	LT CDR	AIR	RNR AIR BR VL	31.03.96
Black, Karen,	HONCADET	URNU	U/A	24.10.01
Black, Simon Mitchell, RD	LT CDR	OP INT	SCOTIA	30.06.83
Blackburn, Claire,	HONCADET	URNU	U/A	18.10.01
Blackburn, John Adam Francis,	SLT	CS(O)	KING ALFRED	12.06.00
Bloom, Michael,	SLT	URNU	U/A	25.03.99
Blyth, Anne Scotland,	SG LTCDR	MED	PRESIDENT	14.08.83
Blythe, Wendy Elizabeth,	LT	LOGS	DALRIADA	29.01.96
Boal, Michael,	LT	MW	CAROLINE	23.02.98
Boardman, Andrew,	HON MID	URNU	U/A	10.09.01
Boardman, Sarah,	HONCADET	URNU	U/A	16.10.97
Boath, Gerard,	HON MID	URNU	U/A	21.10.99
Bolton, Adam Robert	ASLT	NE	VIVID	24.11.04
Bomby, David,	LT CDR	AIR	RNR AIR BR VL	26.03.90
Bonham-Smith, Rupert,	HON MID	URNU	U/A	05.11.98
Booth, Rachael,	HONCADET	URNU	U/A	11.10.01
Boothroyd, Susan Elizabeth,	SLT	LOGS	CALLIOPE	02.05.98
Boswell, Emily Charlotte	ASLT	NE	WILDFIRE	03.06.03
Boulton, Jeremy Charles, RD	LT CDR	SM	PRESIDENT	31.03.01
Bowen, Michael Leslie,	SGLTCDR	MED	PRESIDENT	30.09.98
Bowles, William,	LT CDR	AW	SCOTIA	31.03.98

Name	Rank	Branch	Unit	Seniority
Bown, Anthony Mark,	LT CDR	OP INT	CAMBRIA	08.03.91
Bown, Carol Diane, BA, RD	LT CDR	OP INT	CAMBRIA	31.03.03
Boyd, Edward Russell, RD	LT CDR	AWNIS	KING ALFRED	31.03.03
Boyle, Abigail Elder,	SLT	HUMINT	FERRET	12.12.99
Boyle, Kirk,	LT	DI	FERRET	11.05.96
Boyle, Lucy,	HONCADET	URNU	U/A	22.02.01
Brabner, Susan, RD	LT CDR	DI	FERRET	31.03.94
Bracewell, Anna,	HONCADET	URNU	U/A	09.10.00
Bradburn, James,	HON MID	URNU	U/A	24.10.00
Bradbury, Miles,	ASL	URNU	U/A	29.09.98
Bradford, Christine Mary Patricia, RD	LT CDR	NCAGS	EAGLET	31.03.93
Bradford, Michelle,	HONCADET	URNU	U/A	21.10.99
Bradford, Nigel Stuart, RD	LT	SM	EAGLET	18.12.87
Bradley, Bradley,	HON MID	URNU	U/A	11.11.99
Bradshaw, Francis John C, LVO	CDR	NA	EAGLET	01.02.82
Brady, Matthew`,	HON MID	URNU	U/A	14.10.99
Braine, David,	LT CDR	AIR	RNR AIR BR VL	31.03.98
Brampton, Susan,	LT	QARNNS(R)	PRESIDENT	08.01.97
Brannighan, David Matthew Thomas	MID	NE	CALLIOPE	16.02.04
Branyan, Lawrence, RD	LT	CIS ENG	EAGLET	06.09.89
Breyley, Nigel,	LT CDR	AIR	RNR AIR BR VL	31.03.98
Brierley, Rachel,	HONCADET	URNU	U/A	06.11.00
Brigden, Kevin,	LT CDR	AIR	RNR AIR BR VL	16.04.92
Bright, Jack Thomas	ASLT	NE	PRESIDENT	24.04.05
Bright, James,	HON MID	URNU	U/A	18.10.01
Britton, Jonathan,	HON MID	URNU	U/A	19.10.00
Broadwith, Joanna,	HONCADET	URNU	U/A	11.10.01
Brockie, Alan Fleming	LT	QARNNS(R)	SCOTIA	02.03.01
Brockie, Brian,	CDR	MS	SCOTIA	30.09.01
Brodie, Hazel,	HONCADET	URNU	U/A	08.10.98
Brogan, Gary Edward,	LT	NCAGS	EAGLET	12.10.02
Brook, Roger,	LT	AIR	RNR AIR BR VL	22.02.97
Brooking, Stephen,	LT CDR	AIR	RNR AIR BR VL	11.05.87
Brooks, Alexandra, RD	LT	MR	RNR MRS	10.03.03
Brooks, Richard,	ASLT	NE	PRESIDENT	01.04.04
Broom, Karen,	HONCADET	URNU	U/A	20.10.00
Brothwood, Michael,	LT CDR	AIR	RNR AIR BR VL	03.04.99
Brousil, James Joseph	ASLT	NE	SHERWOOD	18.09.03
Browett, Jon,	ASL	URNU	U/A	16.10.01
Brown, Alastair,	HON MID	URNU	U/A	30.09.99
Brown, Andrew,	HON MID	URNU	U/A	08.10.98
Brown, Andrew,	HON MID	URNU	U/A	18.10.00
Brown, Andrew,	LT CDR	AIR	RNR AIR BR VL	01.10.90
Brown , Andrew David	ASGCDR	MED	SCOTIA	01.05.05
Brown, Colin,	LT CDR	AIR	RNR AIR BR VL	30.04.97
Brown, Gillian,	HONCADET	URNU	U/A	02.10.00
Brown, John Erskine, RD	LT CDR	AWNIS	WILDFIRE	31.03.96
Brown, Katharine Jane,	LT CDR	MR	RNR MRS	12.03.86
Brown, Karl,	LT CDR	AIR	RNR AIR BR VL	31.03.98
Brown, Sabrina,	HONCADET	URNU	U/A	15.10.98
Brown, Timothy,	LT CDR	AIR	RNR AIR BR VL	19.03.93
Brown, Wendy,	HONCADET	URNU	U/A	11.10.01
Browne, Alastair Grant	ASLT	NE	SCOTIA	13.02.03
Browne, Kiera,	HONCADET	URNU	U/A	28.09.00
Browne, Thomas,	HON MID	URNU	U/A	14.10.99
Browning, James,	SLT	CS(O)	PRESIDENT	06.08.00
Brownsword, Lee,	HON MID	URNU	U/A	02.10.00
Bryning, Christopher,	LT CDR	AIR	RNR AIR BR VL	01.03.85
Buchanan, Craig,	HON MID	URNU	U/A	06.12.01
Buchanan, Stuart Bruce	SGLT	MED	VIVID	16.07.99
Buckley, Jonathan Mark,	LT	MW	CAMBRIA	08.11.97
Bucknell, David Ian,	LT CDR	INFO OPS	FLYING FOX	01.07.96
Budd, Christopher,	HON MID	URNU	U/A	20.10.00

Name	Rank	Branch	Unit	Seniority
Bugg, Jennifer,	HONCADET	URNU	U/A	17.10.01
Bugler, Martin,	LT CDR	AIR	RNR AIR BR VL	31.03.97
Bull, Elizabeth,	HONCADET	URNU	U/A	18.10.00
Burchett, Rupert,	HON MID	URNU	U/A	30.11.01
Burchinshaw, Philip,	HON MID	URNU	U/A	07.10.99
Burden, Fraser,	LT	AIR	RNR AIR BR VL	01.04.88
Burgess, Philip,	HON MID	URNU	U/A	06.09.99
Burne, Penelope Jane, RD	CDR	HUMINT	FERRET	30.09.01
Burnet, Alexander,	HON MID	URNU	U/A	30.09.99
Burns, Katherine,	HONCADET	URNU	U/A	19.10.00
Burrow, Adele,	HONCADET	URNU	U/A	22.10.01
Butterworth, James,	HON MID	URNU	U/A	08.10.98
Button, Edward,	HON MID	URNU	U/A	21.10.99
Byers, Penelope,	HONCADET	URNU	U/A	18.10.01
Byrte, James,	HON MID	URNU	U/A	17.10.01

C

Name	Rank	Branch	Unit	Seniority
Cadden, Edward,	ALT	URNU	U/A	01.03.00
Caddock, Matthew,	HON MID	URNU	U/A	09.10.97
Cain, Neal,	LT CDR	AIR	RNR AIR BR VL	31.03.01
Cameron, Anne Louise, RD	LT CDR	NCAGS	KING ALFRED	31.03.01
Cameron, Christopher,	ASL	URNU	U/A	08.12.95
Cameron, James	ALT	HUMINT	FERRET	01.12.04
Campbell, Graham John,	LTCDR	INFO OPS	FORWARD	31.03.05
Campbell, Jonathan,	HON MID	URNU	U/A	25.10.01
Campbell, Mairi,	HONCADET	URNU	U/A	08.10.98
Campbell, William,	LT CDR	AIR	RNR AIR BR VL	01.04.92
Camwell, Barry,	HON MID	URNU	U/A	07.10.98
Canham, Wendy Jacqueline, RD	LT CDR	INFO OPS	SHERWOOD	31.03.98
Capper, Huw,	HON MID	URNU	U/A	07.10.01
Carder, Dorian,	HON MID	URNU	U/A	27.09.01
Carey, Andrew William,	SLT	CS(O)	WILDFIRE	13.08.00
Carey-Jones, Kathryn,	HONCADET	URNU	U/A	11.10.01
Carman, Felix,	HON MID	URNU	U/A	08.10.98
Carnegie, Rebecca,	HONCADET	URNU	U/A	12.10.00
Carpenter, David, RD	LT CDR	MR	RNR MRS	05.06.85
Carruthers, Calum,	HON MID	URNU	U/A	02.11.00
Carss, George Alexander,	SG CDR	MED	KING ALFRED	30.09.01
Carter, David,	ALT	AW	EAGLET	13.10.98
Carter, Richard,	LT	AIR	RNR AIR BR VL	06.01.87
Cartwright, James,	HON MID	URNU	U/A	07.10.01
Carty, David,	HON MID	URNU	U/A	17.10.01
Carty, Jonathan,	HON MID	URNU	U/A	04.10.01
Carvalho, Elaine	ASLT	NE	DALRIADA	01.11.02
Carvasso-White, Helen,	HONCADET	URNU	U/A	21.10.99
Carver, Andrew,	LT CDR	AIR	RNR AIR BR VL	31.03.98
Casey, Graham Peter,	LT CDR	DI	FERRET	31.03.00
Casey, Neil,	LT CDR	AIR	RNR AIR BR VL	31.03.00
Caskie, Iain Neil, RD	LT CDR	SM	SCOTIA	16.05.92
Cass,Geoffrey Philip	LT CDR	NA	FORWARD	03.06.95
Cassells, Jason Bern Costello,	LT	MW	CAROLINE	23.07.04
Casson, Hilary Patricia, RD	LT CDR	NCAGS	VIVID	31.03.96
Castrinoyannakis, Timothy,	HON MID	URNU	U/A	15.02.01
Caulfield, Lee,	HONCADET	URNU	U/A	01.10.99
Challis, Harriet,	HONCADET	URNU	U/A	15.11.01
Chalmers, Amalia Lourdes, RD	CDR	HUMINT	FERRET	31.03.95
Chamberlain, Moira,	LT CDR	QARNNS(R)	KING ALFRED	31.03.05
Chambers, Catherine Louise,	SG LT	MED	KING ALFRED	01.05.05
Chapman, Anthony,	LT CDR	MR	RNR MRS	31.03.03
Chapman, John,	HON MID	URNU	U/A	11.10.01
Chapman, Kate,	HONCADET	URNU	U/A	12.10.99
Chapman, David Quentin,	LT CDR	X	RNR AIR BR VL	01.10.90

Name	Rank	Branch	Unit	Seniority
Charlton, Noel	LT	NCAGS	KING ALFRED	14.10.01
Charters, Emma,	HONCADET	URNU	U/A	28.10.00
Chauvelin, David Coulson Wyllie,	LT	MW	SCOTIA	26.11.98
Cheang, Tia,	HONCADET	URNU	U/A	26.10.99
Cheetham, Ian	ASLT	NE	WILDFIRE	10.11.04
Cheyne, Steven,	LT CDR	AIR	RNR AIR BR VL	01.04.93
Chisholm, David,	HON MID	URNU	U/A	11.09.00
Chua, Jimmy,	HON MID	URNU	U/A	26.10.99
Church, Elizabeth Ann, RD	LT	SM	PRESIDENT	16.11.88
Church, Jonathan,	HON MID	URNU	U/A	15.11.01
Churchley, Richard,	LT CDR	AIR	RNR AIR BR VL	26.04.98
Citrine, Harry,	HON MID	URNU	U/A	11.10.01
Clark, Angela Catherine,	LT	LOGS	KING ALFRED	06.10.92
Clark, Philip,	HON MID	URNU	U/A	30.11.00
Clark, Suzanne,	LT CDR	AIR	RNR AIR BR VL	31.03.97
Clarke, Kathryn Jane	ASLT	NE	EAGLET	18.09.03
Clarke, Laurence Timothy James	SLT	CS(O)	FLYING FOX	10.04.02
Clarke, Peter,	LT CDR	AIR	RNR AIR BR VL	01.10.90
Clarke, Philip James Ian	LT	AW	PRESIDENT	31.10.02
Clarke, Roger Derek, RD	LT CDR	NCAGS	VIVID	31.03.96
Clarke, William Stephen, RD	LT CDR	MW	CAROLINE	31.03.00
Cleary, Deidre,	LT CDR	MR	RNR MRS	31.03.99
Cleary, Sonia,	HONCADET	URNU	U/A	12.10.00
Cleeve, Felicity,	SLT	CS(O)	FORWARD	30.07.01
Clews, Harriet Christine	SLT	CS(O)	WILDFIRE	03.10.02
Cliffe, Daniela Maria,	LT	QARNNS(R)	VIVID	18.05.01
Clifford, Martin,	LT CDR	AIR	RNR AIR BR VL	09.05.98
Coady, Catherine,	HONCADET	URNU	U/A	15.02.01
Cobbold, Andrew Reginald, MA	LT CDR	HUMINT	FERRET	31.03.03
Cochrane, Christopher,	HON MID	URNU	U/A	26.10.99
Cochrane, Mark,	HON MID	URNU	U/A	12.10.00
Cockburn, Frank,	LT CDR	MR	RNR MRS	01.10.89
Cockram, Alice,	HONCADET	URNU	U/A	12.10.00
Cody, William Jonathan Kinsborough,	LT CDR	DI	FERRET	01.07.97
Coe, Morgan,	SLT	MW	PRESIDENT	02.10.97
Coffey, Ralph,	HON MID	URNU	U/A	15.10.98
Cohen, James Seymour Lionel, BSC, RD	LT CDR	NCAGS	PRESIDENT	31.03.97
Cohen, Rachel,	HONCADET	URNU	U/A	22.10.97
Colborne, Raymond,	LT CDR	AIR	U/A	01.01.89
Coldham, David,	HON MID	URNU	U/A	21.10.99
Cole, James,	LT CDR	AIR	RNR AIR BR VL	01.09.84
Coles, Victoria,	HONCADET	URNU	U/A	21.10.99
Coley, Jennifer Marian	LT	MR	RNR MRS	30.07.98
Coley, Simon John	LT	MR	RNR MRS	11.12.98
Colley, Derek,	LT CDR	AW	FORWARD	01.04.94
Collie, James,	ASLT	NE	FLYING FOX	22.10.03
Collier, David,	HON MID	URNU	U/A	04.10.01
Collins, Charles,	HON MID	URNU	U/A	14.10.99
Collins, David,	HON MID	URNU	U/A	12.10.99
Collins, Steven Mark,	CDR	AW	FORWARD	30.09.01
Colquhoun, Rodger,	LT CDR	AIR	RNR AIR BR VL	31.03.01
Colton, Ian,	LT CDR	AIR	RNR AIR BR VL	22.11.92
Colyer, Michael Andrew James,	LT CDR	AW	CALLIOPE	31.03.05
Comins, Amy,	HONCADET	URNU	U/A	27.09.01
Condick, Jodie,	HONCADET	URNU	U/A	19.10.00
Condy, Sallie Louise,	LT CDR	DI	FERRET	31.03.02
Conlon, Rebecca,	HONCADET	URNU	U/A	07.10.01
Connell, John,	LT CDR	AIR	RNR AIR BR VL	01.10.91
Connelly, Shirley,	HONCADET	URNU	U/A	15.11.01
Constable, Thomas,	HON MID	URNU	U/A	04.10.01
Constant, David,	LT	AIR	RNR AIR BR VL	27.03.97
Conway, Keith Alexander, RD	LT CDR	MW	SCOTIA	31.03.99
Cook, Helen	ASLT	NE	CALLIOPE	03.09.02

Name	Rank	Branch	Unit	Seniority
Cook, Simon Geoffrey	ASLT	NE	PRESIDENT	13.05.01
Cook, Simon Hugh Home,	LT	MW	PRESIDENT	31.03.98
Cook, William John,	LT CDR	AW	SCOTIA	01.03.85
Coombes, Kirsty,	HONCADET	URNU	U/A	28.06.99
Coombes, Stewart,	LT CDR	AIR	RNR AIR BR VL	31.03.95
Cooper, David John, RD	LT CDR	OP INT	PRESIDENT	31.03.99
Cooper, Susan, BSC RD	LT CDR	OP INT	PRESIDENT	31.03.01
Copeland-Davis, Terence,	LT	AIR	RNR AIR BR VL	01.05.88
Copleston, Charlotte,	HONCADET	URNU	U/A	11.10.01
Corbett, Edward,	HON MID	URNU	U/A	11.10.01
Corbin, Matthew,	HON MID	URNU	U/A	09.10.00
Corcoran, Robert,	HON MID	URNU	U/A	21.10.99
Cornes, John,	LT	URNU	U/A	01.01.92
Corrigan, Nicholas Timothy	ASLT	NE	SHERWOOD	17.01.04
Corrigan, Paul,	HON MID	URNU	U/A	12.10.00
Corson, Robert John,	SG CDR	MED	CALLIOPE	30.09.04
Cottingham, Neil,	LT CDR	AIR	RNR AIR BR VL	01.10.98
Cotton, Michael,	HON MID	URNU	U/A	14.10.99
Council, Robert,	HON MID	URNU	U/A	18.11.99
Courtney, Kurt David,	SLT	HUMINT	FERRET	14.04.99
Cowan, Andrew Stuart, RD	LT CDR	MW	DALRIADA	31.03.97
Cowan Gray, Duncan,	HON MID	URNU	U/A	11.10.01
Cowen, Alexander,	HON MID	URNU	U/A	04.10.00
Cox, Hugh Jeremy,	SG CDR	MED	KING ALFRED	30.05.94
Cox, Rhoderick,	LT CDR	AIR	RNR AIR BR VL	01.12.88
Cox, Timothy Joseph Edward	ASLT	NE	CAROLINE	20.01.05
Coyle, Mark Francis,	LT	MW	CALLIOPE	14.09.01
Coyle, Stephen,	ASLT	NE	SCOTIA	16.10.01
Craig, Caroline Alexandra,	SLT	LOGS	PRESIDENT	08.08.98
Craig, Graeme,	ALT	URNU	U/A	29.04.98
Craik, Lorna,	HONCADET	URNU	U/A	10.10.97
Crawford, Andrew John, RD	CDR	AW	VIVID	30.09.01
Crawford, Judith,	HONCADET	URNU	U/A	01.10.98
Cribley, Michael,	LT CDR	AIR	RNR AIR BR VL	01.10.91
Crockett, Victor Andrew, RD	LT CDR	DI	FERRET	31.03.95
Crombie, Nicholas,	LT	AIR	RNR AIR BR VL	01.02.93
Crombie, Stuart,	HON MID	URNU	U/A	19.10.00
Crone, David James Edward, RD	CDR	MW	CAROLINE	30.09.04
Cross, Elizabeth Jane Caroline	LT	HUMINT	FERRET	17.06.96
Crossley, Samuel Neil Thomas,	SLT	SM	PRESIDENT	07.05.97
Crump, Peter Charles, RD*	CDR	AW	KING ALFRED	30.09.97
Crumpton, Peter,	HON MID	URNU	U/A	19.10.00
Cumming, Alastair,	HON MID	URNU	U/A	28.09.00
Cunnold, Anne-Marie,	HONCADET	URNU	U/A	12.10.00
Curnock, Timothy,	HON MID	URNU	U/A	07.10.01
Curran, Stuart,	HON MID	URNU	U/A	04.10.00
Currie, Katherine,	HONCADET	URNU	U/A	15.10.97
Curry, Victoria Jane,	HONCADET	URNU	U/A	12.10.00
Curtis, Andrew,	HON MID	URNU	U/A	19.10.00
Curtis, Roger Stafford,	LT	NCAGS	SCOTIA	26.01.94

D

Name	Rank	Branch	Unit	Seniority
Dace, Katherine Elizabeth, RD	LT CDR	DI	FERRET (RNR)	31.03.95
Dady, Simon James,	LT	NCAGS	PRESIDENT	24.01.05
Dalby, Russell	SLT	CS(O)	SHERWOOD	06.04.01
Dale, Marcus,	HON MID	URNU	U/A	12.10.99
Dale, Rebecca,	HONCADET	URNU	U/A	13.10.98
Dalgliesh, Chrstopher,	HON MID	URNU	U/A	24.10.01
Dalton, Neil Jarvis,	LT CDR	MR	RNR MRS	31.03.01
Daly, Karen Lesley	ALT CDR	MR	RNR MRS	27.10.03
Daly, Paul,	LT CDR	AIR	RNR AIR BR VL	31.03.95
Dalziel, Simon Anthony Cannon,	LT CDR	MR	RNR MRS	16.02.89

Name	Rank	Branch	Unit	Seniority
Dann, Adrian Stuart	LT CDR	MCD	KING ALFRED	01.10.98
Dark, Helen RD	LT	OP INT	DALRIADA	16.03.89
Daros, Aloysia,	HONCADET	URNU	U/A	12.10.99
Dashfield, Adrian Kenneth	SGCDR	MED	VIVID	30.06.00
Davies, George,	LT	AIR	RNR AIR BR VL	01.07.91
Davies, Jennifer,	HONCADET	URNU	U/A	24.10.01
Davies, James,	HON MID	URNU	U/A	11.09.00
Davies, Kimberley,	HONCADET	URNU	U/A	18.10.00
Davies, Luke,	HON MID	URNU	U/A	12.10.00
Davies, Nicola,	SLT	LOGS	KING ALFRED	07.12.98
Davies, Robert Michael, RD	ACDR	AW	FORWARD	01.10.04
Davies, Richard Myall,	LT	MR	RNR MRS	17.09.03
Davies, Sarah Elizabeth,	LT	AWNIS	PRESIDENT	19.02.99
Davies, Sarah Jane,	ASLT	NE	PRESIDENT	06.01.00
Davies, Simon Lovat	LT	AW	KING ALFRED	15.09.95
Davies, William,	SLT	URNU	U/A	31.07.95
Davis, Bryan Charles	LT CDR	SM	EAGLET	21.01.96
Davis, Peter,	HON MID	URNU	U/A	12.10.99
Davy, Martin,	HON MID	URNU	U/A	06.11.00
Dawe, Nicholas,	HON MID	URNU	U/A	12.10.00
Dawes, Emma,	HONCADET	URNU	U/A	19.10.00
Dawes, Gawaine,	HON MID	URNU	U/A	14.10.99
Dawes, Helyne,	HONCADET	URNU	U/A	19.10.00
Dawson, Alexander,	HON MID	URNU	U/A	12.10.00
Dawson, Melissa Clare	LT	C4ISR	SCOTIA	21.06.05
Day, Andrew,	HON MID	URNU	U/A	17.10.01
Daye, Angela,	HONCADET	URNU	U/A	22.10.98
De Labat, Victoria,	HONCADET	URNU	U/A	11.10.01
De Silva, Oliver,	HON MID	URNU	U/A	11.10.01
Dean, Mark Christopher	SLT	MW	PRESIDENT	01.12.01
Dear, Joanna,	HONCADET	URNU	U/A	07.10.99
Dedman, Kirstin,	HONCADET	URNU	U/A	11.10.01
Deighton, Graeme	ASLT	NE	CALLIOPE	29.09.04
Delf, Jeannie,	HONCADET	URNU	U/A	14.10.99
Delleur, Laura,	HONCADET	URNU	U/A	07.10.01
Denison-Davies, Edward,	HON MID	URNU	U/A	12.10.99
Denman, Rachel,	HONCADET	URNU	U/A	14.10.99
Dennard, Kieron,	HON MID	URNU	U/A	14.10.99
Dennis, James,	HON MID	URNU	U/A	18.10.01
Dent, John George	ASLT	NE	SCOTIA	15.07.03
Derrick, Malcom, RD	LT CDR	AIR	RNR AIR BR VL	10.12.91
Devereaux, James,	LT CDR	AIR	RNR AIR BR VL	31.03.98
Dick, Steven,	HON MID	URNU	U/A	11.10.01
Dickens Charles Timothy	ASLT	NE	FORWARD	02.11.04
Dickin, Arnie,	HON MID	URNU	U/A	11.10.01
Dickinson, Carolyn,	HONCADET	URNU	U/A	25.10.01
Dilks, Paul David Peter, RD	LT CDR	AW	KING ALFRED	05.04.87
Dilmahomed, Soraya,	HONCADET	URNU	U/A	18.10.01
Dingwall, Donald,	HON MID	URNU	U/A	08.10.98
Dinsmore, Simon,	HON MID	URNU	U/A	01.02.01
Dismore, Oliver,	LT CDR	AIR	RNR AIR BR VL	01.01.88
Ditton, Nathan,	SLT	NCAGS	KING ALFRED	29.07.00
Divers Bsrry,	HON MID	URNU	U/A	30.09.99
Dix, Caroline,	HONCADET	URNU	U/A	17.10.01
Dobson, Serena,	HONCADET	URNU	U/A	11.10.01
Dodds, Nicholas,	HON MID	URNU	U/A	26.10.99
Donahue, Paul John	ASLT	NE	KING ALFRED	10.12.03
Donaldson, John Richard,	LT CDR	DI	FERRET	12.08.94
Donkin, Martin,	HON MID	URNU	U/A	18.10.01
Donnelly, Alexander Harold	ASLT	HUMINT	FERRET	24.11.04
Dorman, Nicholas Roger Vause, RD	LT CDR	MW	SCOTIA	31.03.97
Douglas, Fiona,	HONCADET	URNU	U/A	24.10.01
Douglas, Norman, RD	LT	MW	CALLIOPE	19.01.96

Name	Rank	Branch	Unit	Seniority
Douthwaite, Lisa	SLT	QARNNS(R)	KING ALFRED	13.11.97
Downing, Carl,	LT CDR	AIR	RNR AIR BR VL	16.11.92
Downing, Neil Edmond, RD	LT CDR	MW,	CAROLINE	31.03.00
Downing, Rebecca,	HONCADET	URNU	U/A	28.10.00
Doyle, Lucie,	HONCADET	URNU	U/A	14.10.99
Doyle, Rebecca,	HONCADET	URNU	U/A	25.10.01
Drake, Roderick Allan, RD	LT CDR	NCAGS	FLYING FOX	31.03.98
Driscoll, Claire	SLT	C4ISR	CAMBRIA	19.09.01
Driscoll, Mark,	HON MID	URNU	U/A	01.12.99
Drummond, Andrew Duprose,	SG LT	MED	EAGLET	10.01.02
Dudill, Louise,	SLT	NCAGS	SHERWOOD	27.11.98
Duffey-Price, James,	HON MID	URNU	U/A	07.10.01
Duffield, Gary,	LT CDR	AIR	RNR AIR BR VL	01.02.90
Duffy, John Bernard	LT	DI	FERRET	03.02.92
Duggan, Emily,	HONCADET	URNU	U/A	09.10.00
Duggua, Rodney, RD	LT CDR	OP INT	KING ALFRED	31.03.93
Dukes, Nicholas,	LT CDR	AIR	RNR AIR BR VL	01.10.93
Duncan, Barbara Mary,	LT CDR	AWNIS	EAGLET	31.03.05
Duncan, Euan Maver,	SLT	CS(O)	SCOTIA	13.10.01
Duncan, Keith Julian, RD	CDR	AW	EAGLET	30.09.04
Duncan, Kenneth Robert	LT	CIS ENG	KING ALFRED	02.04.91
Dunford, Victoria,	HONCADET	URNU	U/A	14.10.99
Dunn, Jonathan,	HON MID	URNU	U/A	14.10.99
Dunn, Josephine,	SLT	URNU	U/A	11.11.98
Dunne, James,	HON MID	URNU	U/A	07.10.99
Dunne, Lawrence John,	LT CDR	CIS ENG	FORWARD	31.03.04
Duthie, Charles Euan	ASLT	NE	SCOTIA	25.06.03
Duthie, David James Ralph,	SG CDR	MED	SHERWOOD	30.09.00
Duthie, Ruth Mary Mitchell,	LT	AWNIS	KING ALFRED	16.04.94

E

Name	Rank	Branch	Unit	Seniority
Eacott, Jonathan,	HON MID	URNU	U/A	19.10.00
Eagles, Susan Jane, RD	CDR	MR	RNR MRS	30.09.95
Ealey, Nicholas,	HON MID	URNU	U/A	12.10.99
Earl, Nicholas,	LT	AIR	RNR AIR BR VL	01.12.94
Easen, Sam,	HON MID	URNU	U/A	06.11.00
East, John Howard	ASLT	NE	DALRIADA	10.10.02
Easterbrook, Christopher,	HON MID	URNU	U/A	19.10.00
Eastham, Allam, BSC, RD	LT CDR	NCAGS	KING ALFRED	31.03.94
Ebdy, Carina,	HONCADET	URNU	U/A	27.09.01
Edwards, Michael Steven De La Warr,	ASGCDR	MED	SHERWOOD	01.05.05
Edwards, Tracy,	HONCADET	URNU	U/A	11.10.01
Eldridge, James,	HON MID	URNU	U/A	10.09.01
Ellender, Tony,	LT	URNU	U/A	06.02.92
Elliott, James,	HON MID	URNU	U/A	20.10.00
Elliott, Robin,	LT CDR	AIR	RNR AIR BR VL	01.04.97
ElliSBARry,	HON MID	URNU	U/A	02.10.00
Ellis, Richard Alwyn, RD	LT	OP INT	PRESIDENT	18.08.90
Ellis, Simon Christopher,	ASG SLT	MED	SCOTIA	19.03.02
Elmquist, Anne,	HONCADET	URNU	U/A	12.10.00
England, Robert Frederick Charles,	LT	QARNNS(R)	KING ALFRED	30.08.96
Esfahani, Shahrokh,	LT CDR	INFO OPS	WILDFIRE	31.03.02
Etti, Kehinde,	HONCADET	URNU	U/A	11.10.01
Evans, Ann, RD	LT CDR	DI	FERRET	31.03.94
Evans, Alex,	LT CDR	AIR	RNR AIR BR VL	31.03.99
Evans, Carol,	LT	MR	RNR MRS	12.01.92
Evans, Christian,	SLT	C4ISR	VIVID	02.03.04
Evans, Charlotte,	HONCADET	URNU	U/A	18.10.01
Evans, Dominique,	HONCADET	URNU	U/A	11.10.01
Evans, Ewan,	HON MID	URNU	U/A	01.10.98
Evans, Keith,	HON MID	URNU	U/A	11.10.01
Evans, Louisa,	HONCADET	URNU	U/A	09.10.00

Name	Rank	Branch	Unit	Seniority
Evans, Michael,	LT CDR	AIR	RNR AIR BR VL	17.05.88
Evans, Paul,	HON MID	URNU	U/A	18.10.01
Evans, Rebecca,	HONCADET	URNU	U/A	19.10.00
Everest, Jonathan,	HON MID	URNU	U/A	27.09.01
Eyre, Caroline,	HONCADET	URNU	U/A	11.09.00
Eyres, Jonathon Stuart	ASLT	NE	CALLIOPE	14.01.03

F

Name	Rank	Branch	Unit	Seniority
Fairbotham, Deborah Jane	SLT	NCAGS	FLYING FOX	10.06.01
Falconer, Alistair James,	LT	MR	RNR MRS	16.09.95
Farmer, Gary Gordon,	LT	INFO OPS	SCOTIA	28.06.92
Farrant, Sam,	HON MID	URNU	U/A	19.10.00
Farrington, Mark,	HON MID	URNU	U/A	07.10.01
Faulks, Robert,	LT CDR	AIR	RNR AIR BR VL	17.06.84
Fearon, John,	LT	MW	EAGLET	16.05.03
Fellows, Christopher,	HON MID	URNU	U/A	17.10.01
Ferens, Samantha,	HONCADET	URNU	U/A	18.10.00
Ferguson, Alistair,	HON MID	URNU	U/A	19.10.00
Ferguson, Nicholas Alistair Malcolm,	LT CDR	INFO OPS	VIVID	31.03.99
Fickling, James,	HON MID	URNU	U/A	06.09.99
Filtness, Rosemary Jane, RD	LT CDR	DI	FERRET	31.03.93
Findlay, Alan,	LT CDR	AIR	RNR AIR BR VL	31.03.01
Fisher, Nigel,	HON MID	URNU	U/A	18.10.00
Fisher, Simon,	HON MID	URNU	U/A	25.10.01
Fitchsampson, Steven R,	LT	INFO OPS	FLYING FOX	14.11.02
Fittes, Mark,	HON MID	URNU	U/A	10.09.01
Fitzgerald, Elizabeth,	ASLT	NE	WILDFIRE	03.06.03
Fitzgibbon, John,	HON MID	URNU	U/A	07.10.01
Flanagan, Martin,	LT CDR	AIR	RNR AIR BR VL	01.02.92
Flannigan, Aiden,	HON MID	URNU	U/A	24.10.01
Flatt, Liam,	HON MID	URNU	U/A	20.10.00
Fleming, Samuel,	LT CDR	CIS ENG	KING ALFRED	31.03.02
Fletcher Catriona Rose	ASLT	NE	CALLIOPE	29.04.04
Fletcher, Leigh,	HON MID	URNU	U/A	12.10.00
Fletcher, Richard Paul,	LT	LOGS	EAGLET	31.03.04
Flexer, Richard,	HON MID	URNU	U/A	19.10.00
Flint, Grahame,	HON MID	URNU	U/A	18.10.01
Flintoff Susan Ellen Mariner	ALT	NCAGS	DALRIADA	29.01.04
Flower, Clare,	HONCADET	URNU	U/A	12.10.99
Floyd, Robert,	HON MID	URNU	U/A	26.10.99
Flynn, Joanna,	HONCADET	URNU	U/A	12.10.99
Flynn, Nicola Jane,	LT	MR	RNR MRS	06.12.01
Flynn Stephen Andrew	SLT	AW	CALLIOPE	21.05.02
Foote, Clive,	HON MID	URNU	U/A	18.10.01
Ford, Suzanne,	HONCADET	URNU	U/A	10.09.01
Fordham, Christopher,	HON MID	URNU	U/A	11.10.01
Foreman, Timothy,	LT	AIR	RNR AIR BR VL	04.08.94
Forrest, David,	HON MID	URNU	U/A	11.10.01
Fortey, Louise,	HONCADET	URNU	U/A	20.10.98
Fortey, Melissa,	HONCADET	URNU	U/A	02.10.00
Forward, Kirsty,	HONCADET	URNU	U/A	26.10.99
Foster, Stephen, RD	CDR	NCAGS	FORWARD	30.09.00
Fouracre, Andrew Mark George,	LT	C4ISR	CAMBRIA	18.04.04
Fowler, Alan,	LT CDR	AIR	RNR AIR BR VL	01.06.78
Fox, Gemma,	HONCADET	URNU	U/A	04.10.01
Fox-Roberts, Patrick,	HON MID	URNU	U/A	04.10.01
Foxon, James,	HON MID	URNU	U/A	20.10.00
Franks, James,	HON MID	URNU	U/A	22.10.98
Fraser, Emma,	ASLT	NE	SCOTIA	10.01.02
Fraser, Simon,	HON MID	URNU	U/A	12.10.00
Frodin, David Andrew	ASLT	AW	WILDFIRE	18.03.05
Fry, Christopher Wesley,	LT	OP INT	FORWARD	28.07.95

Name	Rank	Branch	Unit	Seniority
Fry, Stephen Michael, RD	LT CDR	NCAGS	CAMBRIA	31.03.05
Fulford, Spike,	HON MID	URNU	U/A	05.10.00
Fuller, Anna,	HONCADET	URNU	U/A	20.10.00

G

Name	Rank	Branch	Unit	Seniority
Gadsby, Helen,	HONCADET	URNU	U/A	19.10.00
Gaffney, Francis Eugene David	ASLT	NE	WILDFIRE	19.04.04
Galloway, Gareth,	HON MID	URNU	U/A	06.11.00
Galloway, Richard,	HON MID	URNU	U/A	03.12.99
Gardiner, George David,	SGCDR	MED	CAROLINE	30.09.04
Garlick, Alexander,	HON MID	URNU	U/A	17.10.01
Garrod, Michael,	HON MID	URNU	U/A	06.09.98
Gaskin, Matthew,	HON MID	URNU	U/A	11.10.01
Gaskin, Sarah,	HONCADET	URNU	U/A	21.10.00
Gatenby, Chrisopher,	LT	AW	EAGLET	01.10.97
Gausden, Christine,	LT CDR	SM	PRESIDENT	31.03.00
Gavey, Stephen John, RD	LT CDR	NCAGS	VIVID	01.08.88
Gearing, Richard,	HON MID	URNU	U/A	19.10.00
Geary, Michael,	LT	AIR	RNR AIR BR VL	01.07.93
Gee, Michael,	SLT	AW	EAGLET	18.07.99
Geeson, Andrea,	HONCADET	URNU	U/A	22.10.01
Georgeson, Ian,	LT CDR	AIR	RNR AIR BR VL	01.06.91
Georghiou, Marie,	HONCADET	URNU	U/A	22.10.01
Ghaibi, Adam,	HON MID	URNU	U/A	14.10.99
Ghost, Richard Lyell	ASLT	NE	EAGLET	23.07.03
Giaro, Annelyn,	HONCADET	URNU	U/A	18.10.01
Gibb, Peter,	LT CDR	AIR	RNR AIR BR VL	24.01.98
Giblin, Matthew,	HON MID	URNU	U/A	12.02.01
Gibson, Stephen,	LT CDR	AIR	RNR AIR BR VL	31.03.94
Gilbert, Anthony Alexander Leslie	ASLT	NE	FLYING FOX	07.10.04
Gilbert, Geoffrey,	HON MID	URNU	U/A	11.10.01
Giles, Simon,	HON MID	URNU	U/A	15.10.00
Gilligan, James,	HON MID	URNU	U/A	01.10.99
Gleave, Anthony,	HON MID	URNU	U/A	07.10.01
Gleave, James, RD	LT CDR	INFO OPS	DALRIADA	31.03.04
Glover, David,	HON MID	URNU	U/A	06.11.97
Glover, Martyn Richard Timothy, RD, MA	LT CDR	NCAGS	PRESIDENT	31.03.01
Gobey, Christopher Graham	LT CDR	SM	SCOTIA	01.10.95
Gobey, Richard John Allen	ASLT	NE	FLYING FOX	03.06.04
Goldenberg, Alick,	HON MID	URNU	U/A	20.10.00
Golding, Michael Brian	ASLT	NE	CALLIOPE	29.07.03
Goldthorpe, Sally Louise,	LT CDR	MR	RNR MRS	31.03.95
Gooch, Christopher,	HON MID	URNU	U/A	18.10.00
Goodes, Simon Newbury, RD	LT CDR	NCAGS	WILDFIRE	31.03.97
Gopaul, Raul,	HON MID	URNU	U/A	07.10.01
Goram, Malcolm,	LT	AIR	RNR AIR BR VL	05.05.87
Gordon, Kirsten,	HONCADET	URNU	U/A	04.04.01
Gorrod, Richard George,	SG LTCDR	MED	PRESIDENT	28.09.00
Gouldson, Elizabeth J,	SLT	LOGS	FLYING FOX	15.07.98
Govan, Leonie Jane	LT	OP INT	SCOTIA	23.05.97
Govier, Hannah,	HONCADET	URNU	U/A	12.10.00
Grace, Jonathan,	LT CDR	AIR	RNR AIR BR VL	31.03.00
Gracey, Peter Pequignot	LT CDR	SM	PRESIDENT	01.07.96
Graham, Adrian William, RD	LT CDR	DI	FERRET	19.02.89
Graham, Finnbarr,	HON MID	URNU	U/A	19.10.00
Grainger, Julia Catherine Ishbel,	SLT	NCAGS	KING ALFRED	05.04.99
Grainger, Serena Jane,	SLT	SM	PRESIDENT	01.09.99
Grant, David,	HON MID	URNU	U/A	05.10.00
Gray, Andrew Crispian,	LT CDR	AW	PRESIDENT	31.03.99
Gray, Susan Kathryn,	LT CDR	MR	RNR MRS	01.10.93
Gray, William,	HON MID	URNU	U/A	04.10.01
Greaves, Christopher,	LT CDR	AIR	RNR AIR BR VL	01.10.95

Name	Rank	Branch	Unit	Seniority
Greaves, Jeremy Justin,	LT CDR	MR	RNR MRS	31.03.03
Greaves, Michael,	LT CDR	AIR	RNR AIR BR VL	01.04.94
Green, Victoria Susan	ASLT	NE	FORWARD	18.02.03
Greenacre, Richard Paul, RD	LT CDR	AWNIS	VIVID	31.03.97
Greene, Alistair Michael Iyan,	SLT	LOGS	PRESIDENT	13.04.03
Greenhough, Helen,	HONCADET	URNU	U/A	18.10.01
Greenwood, Elizabeth Jane,	LT CDR	MR	RNR MRS	31.03.99
Greenwood, Jeanette,	LT	LOGS	EAGLET	30.03.01
Greenwood, Lauren,	HONCADET	URNU	U/A	16.10.01
Greenwood, Stephen,	HON MID	URNU	U/A	14.10.99
Gregory, Anthony Edward,	ASLT	NE	EAGLET	10.05.01
Gregory, Jonathan,	HON MID	URNU	U/A	17.10.01
Gregory, Simon,	LT CDR	AIR	RNR AIR BR VL	31.03.01
Grierson, Andrew,	ASL	URNU	U/A	29.10.99
Griffin, Alexandra,	HONCADET	URNU	U/A	21.10.99
Griffin, Danielle,	ASLT	NE	KING ALFRED	14.01.03
Griffiths, Charlotte Mary,	LT	LOGS	PRESIDENT	29.09.03
Griffiths, Helen,	HONCADET	URNU	U/A	19.10.00
Griffiths, Michael Edward, BSC, RD	LT CDR	SM	CAMBRIA	31.03.02
Griffiths, Sara Louise,	LT CDR	Q	KING ALFRED	31.03.02
Grist, David Francis Neil,	LT	MS	KING ALFRED	05.07.00
Guild, Ian,	HON MID	URNU	U/A	16.01.01
Guild, Malcolm Donald,	SG LTCDR	MED	SCOTIA	12.07.87
Guilfoyle, Daniel,	HON MID	URNU	U/A	25.10.01
Gunn, Debra Ann, RD	LT CDR	AWNIS	SCOTIA	31.03.94
Gurney, Henry,	HON MID	URNU	U/A	18.10.00

H

Name	Rank	Branch	Unit	Seniority
Hadden, James,	HON MID	URNU	U/A	20.10.00
Hadfield, Marc,	HON MID	URNU	U/A	22.10.01
Hadnett, Edmund Robert,	LT CDR	AW	PRESIDENT	29.01.93
Haffenden, Simon, BSC, MIEE, C.ENG	LT	SM	FLYING FOX	26.04.96
Hagger, Michael,	HON MID	URNU	U/A	01.02.01
Haikin, Peter Harry, BSC	LT	DI	FERRET	02.02.96
Halblander, Craig James Michael, RD, BA, LLB, LLM	LT	MW	KING ALFRED	06.05.94
Hall, Gareth,	HON MID	URNU	U/A	19.10.00
Hall, Neil Jeremy	LT CDR	INFO OPS	KING ALFRED	01.03.93
Hall, Stephen Scott,	SLT	HUMINT	FERRET	16.09.00
Halliday, Ian,	LT CDR	AIR	RNR AIR BR VL	01.09.90
Hamilton, Andrew Robert,	SG LTCDR	MED	SCOTIA	01.08.86
Hamilton, Adam,	HON MID	URNU	U/A	28.10.00
Hamilton, Benjamin,	HON MID	URNU	U/A	11.10.01
Hamilton, Neil David	SLT	AW	PRESIDENT	21.01.01
Hamilton, Stuart,	HON MID	URNU	U/A	19.10.00
Hammond, Christopher,	HON MID	URNU	U/A	06.11.00
Hamnett, Richard,	HON MID	URNU	U/A	09.10.00
Hancock, Angela,	LT CDR	MR	RNR MRS	31.03.00
Handley, Dane,	LT CDR	AIR	RNR AIR BR VL	31.03.96
Hands, Carolyn, RD	LT CDR	NCAGS	FLYING FOX	30.09.85
Hankey, Mark Harold,	LT	MR	RNR MRS	31.07.95
Hankin, Robert,	HON MID	URNU	U/A	30.09.99
Harbour, Karen,	HONCADET	URNU	U/A	19.10.00
Harding, David,	HON MID	URNU	U/A	12.10.00
Harding, James Alexander	ASLT	NE	PRESIDENT	16.03.04
Hardinge, Christopher Harry, MBE	LT CDR	SM	KING ALFRED	31.03.98
Hardy, Gareth,	HON MID	URNU	U/A	07.10.01
Hargreaves, Simon,	LT CDR	AIR	RNR AIR BR VL	01.10.89
Harker, Rebecca,	HONCADET	URNU	U/A	19.10.00
Harper, Kate,	HONCADET	URNU	U/A	11.10.01
Harper, Robert Simon, RD	LT	NCAGS	CAROLINE	27.01.95
Harper, Stephen,	HON MID	URNU	U/A	11.10.01
Harris, Adrian James,	LT	SM	WILDFIRE	30.07.95

Name	Rank	Branch	Unit	Seniority
Harris, Hugh,	HON MID	URNU	U/A	18.10.01
Harris, Mark Edward,	LT	MR	FLYING FOX	15.05.95
Harris, Richard,	HON MID	URNU	U/A	06.09.99
Harris, Rafe,	HON MID	URNU	U/A	19.10.00
Harrison, Mark Alastair Timothy,	SLT	EM	WILDFIRE	12.03.99
Harrison, Peter,	LT CDR	INFO OPS	KING ALFRED	30.05.90
Harrison, Richard William,	SG LTCDR	MED	SHERWOOD	30.09.96
Hart, Daniel,	HON MID	URNU	U/A	07.10.99
Hart, Keith, RD	CDR	AWNIS	WILDFIRE	30.09.01
Hartley, Ann Theresa, RD	LT CDR	DI	FERRET	30.09.87
Hartley, Philip Terence,	LT CDR	DI	FERRET	16.12.88
Hartley, Sheila Ann, RD	LT	OP INT	VIVID	20.01.89
Hartley, Sarah Boyt,	LT	NCAGS	PRESIDENT	06.12.96
Harvey, Paul,	HON MID	URNU	U/A	01.10.98
Harwood, Steven,	LT CDR	MR	EAGLET	31.03.96
Haslam, David,	HON MID	URNU	U/A	01.10.98
Hatch, Lucy,	HONCADET	URNU	U/A	22.10.01
Hathway, Steven,	LT CDR	AIR	RNR AIR BR VL	31.03.98
Hawes, Alison Linda,	LT CDR	MR	RNR MRS	31.03.98
Hawkins, Duncan,	SLT	URNU	U/A	01.03.00
Hawkins, James,	HON MID	URNU	U/A	14.10.99
Hawkins John David	LT	AW	KING ALFRED	01.05.01
Hawkins, Laura,	HONCADET	URNU	U/A	07.10.01
Hawkins, Mitchell,	HON MID	URNU	U/A	18.10.00
Hawksley, Alex,	HON MID	URNU	U/A	20.10.00
Hawthorne, Gillian Louise,	LT	QARNNS(R)	CAROLINE	09.08.99
Haydock, Lynsay,	HONCADET	URNU	U/A	28.09.00
Haynes, Zoe,	ASLT	NE	FORWARD	13.05.04
Hayward, James Douglas, MA, B.ENG	LT CDR	LOGS	FORWARD	31.03.00
Haywood, Andrew,	HON MID	URNU	U/A	21.10.00
Haywood, Paul,	LT CDR	AIR	RNR AIR BR VL	28.08.93
Healey, Philip,	HON MID	URNU	U/A	08.01.02
Healy, Pamela Joyce, BSC	CDR	MR	RNR MRS	30.09.04
Heap, Matthew James,	LT	NCAGS	PRESIDENT	07.04.03
Hearn, Victoria,	HONCADET	URNU	U/A	18.10.01
Heathcote, Paul,	LT CDR	AIR	RNR AIR BR VL	31.03.96
Heavyside, Andrew Philip	MID	NE	WILDFIRE	01.10.03
Heffron, Kirsty,	HONCADET	URNU	U/A	14.11.95
Helsby, Edward,	LT CDR	AIR	RNR AIR BR VL	31.03.96
Henderson, Andrew,	HON MID	URNU	U/A	21.10.99
Henderson, Elizabeth,	LT CDR	AIR	RNR AIR BR VL	01.07.00
Henderson, Guy	ALT	AW	DALRIADA	07.10.04
Hermanson, Stephen	ASLT	NE	WILDFIRE	28.10.04
Hetherington, Simon David Francis,	SLT	NCAGS	PRESIDENT	30.03.99
Hewins, Clive William, RD	LT CDR	AW	SHERWOOD	20.05.91
Hewlett, Philip,	HON MID	URNU	U/A	18.10.00
Hick, David,	LT	AIR	RNR AIR BR VL	20.11.91
Hickey, Gurney,	LT CDR	AIR	RNR AIR BR VL	31.03.99
Hickey, Ruth,	HONCADET	URNU	U/A	05.10.00
Hicks, John David, RD	LT CDR	NCAGS	EAGLET	31.03.00
Hickson, Craig,	LT	AIR	RNR AIR BR VL	27.06.89
Higgins, Rebecca,	HONCADET	URNU	U/A	19.10.00
Higgs, Jane Ann,	LT CDR	QARNNS(R)	EAGLET	31.03.05
Highett, David Francis Trevor,	LT CDR	LOGS	KING ALFRED	02.08.83
Higson, Rennie Malcolm,	SLT	NCAGS	SHERWOOD	10.01.02
Hill, Andrew,	HON MID	URNU	U/A	07.10.01
Hill, Christine,	HONCADET	URNU	U/A	18.10.01
Hill, Douglas,	ASLT	NE	PRESIDENT	20.07.03
Hill, Matthew Charles,	LT	SEA	PRESIDENT	25.01.91
Hill, Paul Terence, RD	LT CDR	SM	PRESIDENT	31.03.00
Hill, Sarah Lyness Dane,	ASLT	NE	SHERWOOD	13.04.00
Hiller, Timothy,	HON MID	URNU	U/A	07.10.01
Hilliard, John Stephen,	ASGCDR	MED	CAMBRIA	01.05.05

Name	Rank	Branch	Unit	Seniority
Hills, Emma,	HONCADET	URNU	U/A	15.11.01
Hilton, Caroline,	HONCADET	URNU	U/A	27.01.00
Hindle, Sean,	LT	SM	EAGLET	18.09.91
Hines, Richard,	HON MID	URNU	U/A	22.11.99
Hines, Stephen Frederic, RD	LT CDR	AW	KING ALFRED	01.08.86
Hiscox Lee Steven	ASLT	NE	FLYING FOX	04.03.04
Hitchings, Michael,	HON MID	URNU	U/A	18.10.00
Hodges, Philip,	HON MID	URNU	U/A	10.09.01
Hodkinson, Alice Clare,	SG LT	MED	PRESIDENT	26.09.01
Hodknson, Krista Louise	ASLT	NE	CAMBRIA	17.11.04
Hogan, Ambrose Dominic,	SLT	SM	PRESIDENT	15.09.99
Hogan, Francis John, RD*	LT CDR	MW	EAGLET	31.03.01
Hogg, Michael,	HON MID	URNU	U/A	21.10.99
Holborn, Carl,	LT	AIR	RNR AIR BR VL	16.09.90
Holbrook, Bryony,	SLT	AW	PRESIDENT	27.03.01
Holley, Steven,	ASL	URNU	U/A	15.11.01
Holliday, Pamela,	HONCADET	URNU	U/A	12.10.00
Hollins, Timothy,	HON MID	URNU	U/A	24.10.00
Hollis, Robert Leslie Graham,	LT CDR	AWNIS	EAGLET	31.03.02
Holman, Emma,	HONCADET	URNU	U/A	08.10.01
Holman, Jonathan,	HON MID	URNU	U/A	20.10.00
Holt, Timothy David	ASLT	NE	CAMBRIA	01.01.03
Honey, Victoria,	HONCADET	URNU	U/A	17.10.01
Hook, Samantha Elisabeth,	SGLTCDR	MED	FLYING FOX	01.05.05
Hooton, Karen,	HONCADET	URNU	U/A	12.10.00
Hopper, Timothy,	HON MID	URNU	U/A	11.09.00
Hopps, Francis,	LT CDR	AIR	RNR AIR BR VL	31.03.98
Horne, Martin,	LT	AWNIS	PRESIDENT	23.05.97
Horner, Benjamin Brian Harold,	LT	SM	PRESIDENT	13.05.02
Horner, Ian David,	LT CDR	DI	FERRET	01.11.83
Hough, Peter,	HON MID	URNU	U/A	05.10.00
Hounsell, Andrew,	HON MID	URNU	U/A	25.10.01
Hounsham, Thomas,	HON MID	URNU	U/A	11.10.01
Howard, Alexander, The Hon	LT CDR	AIR	RNR AIR BR VL	31.03.94
Howard, Benjamin Peter	LT	AWNIS	KING ALFRED	01.04.98
Howe, Jonathan,	HON MID	URNU	U/A	09.10.00
Howell, Colin, RD	LT CDR	OP INT	KING ALFRED	31.03.99
Howes, Simon Tee, RD	LT CDR	DI	FERRET	28.03.84
Howorth, Charles,	HON MID	URNU	U/A	18.10.00
Hoyle, Stephen,	LT CDR	SM	EAGLET	31.03.03
Hubbard, Paul,	LT CDR	LOGS	SCOTIA RNR	22.05.98
Hubbert, Sherard,	HON MID	URNU	U/A	30.09.99
Hubble, Robert,	LT CDR	AIR	RNR AIR BR VL	01.10.97
Huddleston, Eleanor,	HONCADET	URNU	U/A	06.11.00
Huey, Joanne,	HONCADET	URNU	U/A	01.12.00
Hughes, Clare Yvonne, RD*	LT CDR	INFO OPS	PRESIDENT	30.09.90
Hughes, John Fraser,	LT CDR	MR	RNR MRS	14.05.92
Hughes, Jill Elizabeth, RD	LT CDR	NCAGS	CAROLINE	31.03.95
Hughes, Josephine,	HONCADET	URNU	U/A	12.10.99
Hughes, Kai,	LT CDR	DI	FERRET	01.05.92
Hughes, Paul James, RD	SG CDR	MED	KING ALFRED	30.09.95
Hulse, Rebecca,	HONCADET	URNU	U/A	21.10.99
Humphreys, John Martyn, PHD	LT CDR	MW	KING ALFRED	31.03.01
Humphreys, Rosemary Frances	LT	QARNNS(R)	CAMBRIA	13.05.00
Hunot, Michael,	HON MID	URNU	U/A	18.10.00
Hunt, Phillippa,	HONCADET	URNU	U/A	26.10.99
Hunt, Stephen Neil,	LT CDR	MR	RNR MRS	31.03.05
Huntly, Victoria,	HONCADET	URNU	U/A	14.10.99
Hutchings, Carol,	HONCADET	URNU	U/A	07.10.99
Hutchings, Stuart,	LT	URNU	U/A	25.05.00
Hutchinson, Janice Elizabeth,	LT CDR	NCAGS	EAGLET	31.03.93
Hutchison, Peter Patrick	ASLT	AW	SCOTIA	23.05.04
Hyre, Stephanie,	HONCADET	URNU	U/A	12.10.99

Name	Rank	Branch	Unit	Seniority
I				
Insley, Andrew,	HON MID	URNU	U/A	20.10.99
Inwood, John Maxwell,	SG CDR	MED	SCOTIA	30.09.98
Irving, Paul,	HON MID	URNU	U/A	11.10.01
Isted, Lee,	HON MID	URNU	U/A	27.09.01
Ivory, Thomas,	HON MID	URNU	U/A	11.09.00
J				
Jachnik, Clive Vincent, RD	LT CDR	HUMINT	FERRET	31.03.99
Jackson, Graham,	LT CDR	AIR	RNR AIR BR VL	01.10.88
Jackson, Trevor,	LT CDR	AIR	RNR AIR BR VL	01.10.94
Jacobs, Sarah,	HONCADET	URNU	U/A	17.10.01
Jacques, Charlotte,	HONCADET	URNU	U/A	04.10.00
Jaffier, Robert Gary,	LT	C4ISR	FORWARD	26.07.02
James, Nichola,	HONCADET	URNU	U/A	25.10.01
James, Roy Arthur, BSC RD	CDR	SM	FORWARD	30.09.00
Jameson, Susan Catherine,	LT CDR	OP INT	FLYING FOX	31.03.00
Jarrett, Catherine,	HONCADET	URNU	U/A	26.01.00
Jaundrill, Simon,	HON MID	URNU	U/A	07.10.01
Jeffcoate, Richard,	HON MID	URNU	U/A	22.10.01
Jeffery, Samuel,	HON MID	URNU	U/A	18.10.01
Jeffries, Felicity,	ASLT	NE	PRESIDENT	12.04.05
Jeffries, Rebecca,	HONCADET	URNU	U/A	11.10.01
Jenkins, Andrew,	HON MID	URNU	U/A	19.10.00
Jenkins, Clare,	HONCADET	URNU	U/A	06.11.00
Jenner, Alexander,	HON MID	URNU	U/A	20.10.98
Jepson, Zara,	HONCADET	URNU	U/A	25.10.01
Jermy, Richard Alexander,	LT CDR	HUMINT	FERRET	31.03.04
Jobling Stephen Geoffrey	LT	DI	FERRET	31.01.99
Johnson, Catherine,	HONCADET	URNU	U/A	14.10.99
Johnson, David Gerrard,	SLT	AW	EAGLET	05.06.99
Johnson, Edward,	HON MID	URNU	U/A	20.10.99
Johnson, Jill Ena, RD	LT CDR	QARNNS(R)	CAMBRIA	31.03.01
Johnson, Symon,	LT	AIR	RNR AIR BR VL	01.07.96
Johnston, Michael,	HON MID	URNU	U/A	14.10.99
Johnstone, Peter Hughes, RD	LT CDR	LOGS	PRESIDENT	31.03.97
Jones, Anna,	HONCADET	URNU	U/A	11.10.01
Jones, Andrew David,	SLT	MW	KING ALFRED	30.04.01
Jones Carolyn Jane	LT	MR	RNR MRS	04.07.95
Jones, Christopher, RD	LT CDR	AW	PRESIDENT	01.05.88
Jones, Charles David, RD	LT CDR,	SM	DALRIADA	31.03.00
Jones, Geoffrey Mark,	LT CDR	AW	EAGLET	31.03.02
Jones, Hayley,	HONCADET	URNU	U/A	10.09.01
Jones, Iain Stewart	ASLT	NE	KING ALFRED	15.01.04
Jones, Kristoffer,	HON MID	URNU	U/A	01.03.01
Jones, Keith Williams,	LT	LOGS	FORWARD	11.06.03
Jones, Leslie,	LT CDR	HUMINT	FERRET	11.09.93
Jones, Nicholas Thomas Edward	ASLT	NE	FORWARD	15.02.02
Jones, Pauline, RD	LT CDR	LOGS	CALLIOPE	31.03.98
Joshi, Tejas,	HON MID	URNU	U/A	26.01.00
Journeaux, Simon Francis,	ASGLTCDR	MED	EAGLET	28.09.99
Joyce, David,	HON MID	URNU	U/A	06.09.99
Juby, Amy,	HONCADET	URNU	U/A	11.10.01
Judd, Simon,	LT CDR	AIR	RNR AIR BR VL	01.10.96
K				
Kadera, Stephen John,	LT CDR	MR	FLYING FOX	31.03.02
Kay, David,	CDR	LOGS	FLYING FOX	30.09.04
Kay, Victoria,	HONCADET	URNU	U/A	14.10.99
Kaye, Sophie,	HONCADET	URNU	U/A	22.10.01
Kearney, Melian Jane, RD	LT CDR	OP INT	VIVID	31.03.97

Name	Rank	Branch	Unit	Seniority
Keating, Fergus Stephen Jonathon,	SG LTCDR	MED	PRESIDENT	10.01.02
Keating, Guy,	HON MID	URNU	U/A	12.10.00
Kedge, Jennifer,	SLT	CS(O)	WILDFIRE	24.08.01
Keevan, Nina,	HONCADET	URNU	U/A	25.10.01
Keith Gary	CHAPLAIN	CHAP	KING ALFRED	25.11.03
Keith, Rory,	HON MID	URNU	U/A	07.10.99
Kelley, Victoria,	HONCADET	URNU	U/A	18.10.01
Kelly, HNanette Imogene Clare	ASLT	NE	SHERWOOD	22.09.04
Kelly, Sarah Louise,	SLT	MW	SCOTIA	01.02.00
Kelly, Timothy,	LT CDR	X	RNR AIR BR VL	04.07.92
Kembery, Simon John,	LT	AW	CAMBRIA	11.06.93
Kemp, Paul,	HON MID	URNU	U/A	30.05.01
Kemp, Richard,	HON MID	URNU	U/A	07.10.99
Kemp, Simon,	LT CDR	DI	FERRET	31.03.99
Kendall, Martyn, M, J	ASL, nE	EAGLET		31.05.01
Kendall-Torry, Kiri,	HONCADET	URNU	U/A	18.10.01
Kendrick, Katherine Sonia	SLT	AW	PRESIDENT	18.04.01
Kenney, Dawn Elizabeth, RD	CDR	QARNNS(R)	VIVID	30.09.99
Kent, Alan,	LT	AIR	RNR AIR BR VL	15.06.94
Kent, Thomas William Henry, RD	CDR	AW	SHERWOOD	30.09.99
Kenyon, Christopher,	LT CDR	NCAGS	PRESIDENT	03.04.82
Kerby, Robert,	HON MID	URNU	U/A	19.10.00
Kesteven, Ralph,	SLT	CS(O)	EAGLET	24.01.01
Keyte, Lauren,	HONCADET	URNU	U/A	27.09.01
Khan Mohammed Azam	ASLT	NE	EAGLET	17.11.04
Khan, Sophia,	HONCADET	URNU	U/A	06.11.00
Kidd, Alex,	HON MID	URNU	U/A	05.10.00
Kidd, Madeleine,	HONCADET	URNU	U/A	18.10.01
Kilbride, Paul,	HON MID	URNU	U/A	27.09.01
Kim, Michael	LT	C4ISR	FORWARD	05.08.97
King, Andrew Stephen, RD	LT CDR	MW	KING ALFRED	31.03.99
King, Charles Guy Hall,	LT CDR	AW	KING ALFRED	31.03.02
King, David,	HON MID	URNU	U/A	14.10.99
King, Hannah,	HONCADET	URNU	U/A	27.11.01
King, Ian,	LT	OP INT	EAGLET	05.12.97
King, Ian,	HON MID	URNU	U/A	11.09.00
King, Lindsay,	ASL	URNU	U/A	15.10.01
Kirk, William Walter,	LT	NCAGS	SHERWOOD	31.03.96
Kirkham, Anna,	HONCADET	URNU	U/A	07.10.99
Kirkpatrick, Robin,	HON MID	URNU	U/A	08.10.98
Kirwin, Ciara,	HONCADET	URNU	U/A	12.10.00
Kistruck, David,	LT CDR	AIR	RNR AIR BR VL	31.03.00
Kitchen, Catherine Anne,	LT	HQ	WILDFIRE	12.12.92
Knight, David,	ACDR	AIR	RNR AIR BR VL	05.03.02
Knight, Stephen,	HON MID	URNU	U/A	11.09.00
Knopp, Jonathon,	HON MID	URNU	U/A	28.10.00
Knott, Clive,	LT CDR	AIR	RNR AIR BR VL	31.03.98
Knott, Robert,	HON MID	URNU	U/A	10.09.01
Knowles, Donna Maureen,	LT CDR	MW,	CAROLINE	31.03.01
Knowles, Thomas,	LT	SM	SCOTIA	28.02.05
Knupffer, Alexander,	HON MID	URNU	U/A	18.10.01
Kordowski, Nicholas,	SLT	CS(O)	PRESIDENT	01.08.99
Krasun, Charles Robert,	SLT	MW	KING ALFRED	30.10.01
Kyme, Michael John,	LT	DI	FERRET	30.11.93
Kyriakidis, Evangelos,	HON MID	URNU	U/A	12.10.00

L

Name	Rank	Branch	Unit	Seniority
Ladislaus Paul James	SLT	CS(O)	CALLIOPE	30.05.00
Lai, Patrick,	HON MID	URNU	U/A	12.10.00
Laird, William,	HON MID	URNU	U/A	26.10.99
Lamont, Claire,	HONCADET	URNU	U/A	11.10.01
Lancaster, Gavin Kent	SLT	C4ISR	FLYING FOX	24.08.02

Name	Rank	Branch	Unit	Seniority
Lanchbery, Alexandra,	HONCADET	URNU	U/A	11.10.01
Lane, Timothy,	HON MID	URNU	U/A	23.11.01
Lang, Tracey,	HONCADET	URNU	U/A	18.10.00
Langdon, Simon,	HON MID	URNU	U/A	12.10.99
Langmead, Clive Francis, RD	LT CDR	AW	FORWARD	01.07.90
Lapage-Norris, Thomas Richard William,	LT	LOGS	FLYING FOX	31.10.97
Larsen, Thomas,	HON MID	URNU	U/A	11.10.01
Last, Nick, AFC	LT CDR	AIR	RNR AIR BR VL	01.10.91
Lathrope, Jennifer,	HONCADET	URNU	U/A	30.09.99
Laundy, Nicholas,	SG LT	MED	EAGLET	23.05.00
Lauretani, Andrew Stephen David,	LT	MR	RNR MRS	05.10.90
Laverick, Helen Tanya,	LT	LOGS	PRESIDENT	14.10.02
Law, Debbie,	HONCADET	URNU	U/A	18.10.01
Lawrence, Ian Martin,	SLT	AW	KING ALFRED	22.03.02
Lawrence, Jenna,	HONCADET	URNU	U/A	30.05.01
Lawson, Rosemary June	SLT	CS(O)	EAGLET	12.09.01
Le Roux, Gordon,	HON MID	URNU	U/A	19.10.00
Leach, Simon,	LT	AIR	RNR AIR BR VL	22.09.93
Leaphard, Daniel Paul	SLT	CS(O)	FORWARD	10.03.02
Leather, Roger James, RD	LT CDR	AW	EAGLET	01.06.87
Ledwidge, Francis Andrew,	LT CDR	HUMINT	FERRET	31.03.02
Lee, David Antony,	CDR	SM	DALRIADA	30.09.04
Lee, Daren,	HON MID	URNU	U/A	07.10.99
Lee, John, RD	CDR	NCAGS	CALLIOPE	30.09.03
Lee, Robert,	LT	AIR	RNR AIR BR VL	01.10.91
Lee, Thomas William Robert,	LT CDR	HUMINT	FERRET	31.03.05
Legge, Fiona,	HONCADET	URNU	U/A	14.10.99
Leigh, Daniel,	HON MID	URNU	U/A	12.10.00
Lemon, John,	ALT	X	U/A	09.02.88
Lentell, Heather,	LT	QARNNS	EAGLET	03.05.01
Leonard, Jeanette Anne	LT	MR	RNR MRS	07.05.99
Leonard, John Francis,	SG CDR	MED	KING ALFRED	30.09.01
Leonard, Maria,	HONCADET	URNU	U/A	20.10.99
Leong, Melvin,	HON MID	URNU	U/A	11.10.01
Leslie, Sarah,	HONCADET	URNU	U/A	30.09.99
Lewis, Elizabeth,	HONCADET	URNU	U/A	19.10.00
Lewis, John Charles, RD	LT CDR	MR	RNR MRS	31.03.02
Lewis, Jennifer,	HONCADET	URNU	U/A	11.10.01
Lewis, Justine,	HONCADET	URNU	U/A	26.10.99
Lewis, Kathryn Elizabeth, RD	LT CDR	MW	PRESIDENT	31.03.05
Lewis, Richard,	LT CDR	AIR	RNR AIR BR VL	31.03.01
Lewis, Richard	ASLT	NE	CAMBRIA	27.11.03
Lewis, Simon, RD	LT CDR	LOGS	KING ALFRED	31.03.04
Lewis-Simpson Shannon Melinda	LT	MW	CALLIOPE	21.08.97
Leyshon, Sally Louise,	LT CDR	AWNIS	FLYING FOX	31.03.93
Lindsley, Michael James,	LT CDR	AW	CALLIOPE	31.03.99
Lindvall, Kate,	HONCADET	URNU	U/A	04.10.01
Lineham, Samuel,	HON MID	URNU	U/A	11.10.01
Lines, Jessica,	HONCADET	URNU	U/A	07.10.99
Linton, Andrew Malcolm	ASLT	NE	EAGLET	08.03.05
Lipczynski, Benjamin,	HON MID	URNU	U/A	11.09.00
Lippell, Sabrina Rose, RD, BSC	LT CDR	MR	MRS	30.09.89
Lister, Andrew,	LT	AIR	RNR AIR BR VL	16.06.93
Lister, Matthew,	HON MID	URNU	U/A	10.09.01
Little, Julia,	HONCADET	URNU	U/A	18.10.00
Lloyd, David Vernon,	LT CDR	AW	KING ALFRED	31.03.99
Lloyd, Douglas,	HON MID	URNU	U/A	21.10.00
Lloyd, Gareth, RD	LT CDR	OP INT	EAGLET	31.03.98
Lloyd, Peter John,	LT CDR	AW	KING ALFRED	31.03.00
Lloyd, Susan,	LT CDR	MR	RNR MRS	31.03.04
Loates, Mark,	SLT	URNU	U/A	22.01.98
Lock, Alan,	HON MID	URNU	U/A	18.10.01
Lockett, Alex,	HON MID	URNU	U/A	17.10.01

Name	Rank	Branch	Unit	Seniority
Lockwood, Neville Antony,	SLT	MW	KING ALFRED	06.08.00
Lokrantz-Bernitz, Gudmund,	HON MID	URNU	U/A	11.10.01
London, Nicholas,	HON MID	URNU	U/A	18.10.00
Longman, Matthew,	HON MID	URNU	U/A	10.09.01
Lord, Richard,	HON MID	URNU	U/A	30.09.99
Lort, Timothy,	LT CDR	AIR	RNR AIR BR VL	01.10.95
Loughran, Cedric Grenville, RD	CDR	AW	EAGLET	30.09.98
Lovegrove, Richard Edward,	SG LT	MED	WILDFIRE	05.06.01
Low, Simeon,	HON MID	URNU	U/A	01.02.01
Lowry, Claire,	HONCADET	URNU	U/A	15.10.98
Luke, Warren Munro, RD	SG CDR	MED	SCOTIA	30.09.99
Lutman, Charles robert	LT	INFO OPS	CALLIOPE	07.08.01
Lyall, Kenneth Alexander, RD	LT CDR	OP INT	SCOTIA	31.03.97
Lydon, Michael,	LT	LOGS	CALLIOPE	30.09.96
Lyman, David,	HON MID	URNU	U/A	18.10.01
Lynch, Suzanne Marie, RD	LT	LOGS	CAMBRIA	28.05.02
Lyne, James,	HON MID	URNU	U/A	28.09.00

M

Name	Rank	Branch	Unit	Seniority
MacBeth, Jonathan,	HON MID	URNU	U/A	11.10.01
MacDonald, Alastair,	HON MID	URNU	U/A	07.10.99
MacDonald, Fiona,	HONCADET	URNU	U/A	14.10.99
MacDonald, Julie Anne	LT	QARNNS	KING ALFRED	18.05.01
MacHell, Louise,	HONCADET	URNU	U/A	09.10.00
Machin, Peter Charles Clive, RD*	CDR	HQ	CAMBRIA	30.09.00
MacKay, Evan George,	PALT	AW	DALRIADA	06.12.96
MacKenzie, Hannah Louise	ASLT	NE	WILDFIRE	17.06.01
MacKenzie-Philps, Linda,	LT CDR	MR	RNR MRS	31.03.99
Mackie, Robert Charles Gordon,	LT	AW	FORWARD	14.06.03
Mackintosh Zemma Gail	ASGLT	MED	EAGLET	25.06.03
MacLean Graeme Paul	SLT	NE	CAROLINE	15.12.02
MacLean, Marjory Anne	CHAPLAIN	CHAP	SCOTIA	25.11.11
MacLean, Nicholas Peter, RD	LT CDR	SM	PRESIDENT	31.03.97
Macleod, Alistair David, RD*	SG LTCDR	MED	SCOTIA	17.10.78
Macleod, Alanna,	HONCADET	URNU	U/A	08.11.01
MacMillan, Alasdair Iain Macaulay,	SGCDR	MED	SCOTIA	01.05.05
MacRae, Kirk,	HON MID	URNU	U/A	14.10.99
MacSephney Tracy Lee Helen	LT	CS(O)	KING Alfred	01.01.03
MacTaggart, Alasdair Donald, RD	CDR	INFO OPS	DALRIADA	30.09.02
Maddison, Simon,	LT	MCDO	FLYING FOX	19.07.96
Magnay, Claire Georgina,	SLT, SM		FLYING FOX	16.07.94
Mainwaring, Luke,	HON MID	URNU	U/A	25.10.01
Malik, Alia,	HONCADET	URNU	U/A	18.10.01
Malik, Ussamah,	HON MID	URNU	U/A	18.10.01
Malkin, Roy Vyvian,	LT	AW	PRESIDENT	03.07.01
Mallinson, Ian,	HON MID	URNU	U/A	21.10.99
Mallinson, Stuart Jeffry, MSC	LT	MW	PRESIDENT	31.03.96
Malloy, Richard,	HON MID	URNU	U/A	14.10.00
Malone, Keith,	SGLTCDR	MED	EAGLET	12.03.02
Malpas, Peter,	LT CDR,	NCAGS	KING ALFRED	31.03.02
Mann, Barbara Louise,	LT CDR	MR	RNR MRS	31.03.01
Manning, Jacqueline Vera, RD	LT CDR	SM	PRESIDENT	31.03.02
Marandola, Stefan,	LT	AIR	RNR AIR BR VL	17.01.96
Markwell, Jonathan,	HON MID	URNU	U/A	22.10.01
Marland, Helen,	HONCADET	URNU	U/A	14.12.99
Marlor, Andrew,	HON MID	URNU	U/A	11.09.00
Marlow, Stephen, QGM	LT CDR	AIR	RNR AIR BR VL	31.03.97
Marple, Natalie,	HONCADET	URNU	U/A	19.10.00
Marr, David,	LT CDR	AIR	RNR AIR BR VL	01.10.94
Marsh, Timothy,	LT	AIR	RNR AIR BR VL	06.07.87
Marshall, Henry,	HON MID	URNU	U/A	19.10.00
Marshall, Stephen Michael,	LT	MCDO	KING ALFRED	17.04.88

Name	Rank	Branch	Unit	Seniority
Martin, Darren Hinna,	LT CDR	AW	PRESIDENT	31.03.01
Martin, Dion,	HON MID	URNU	U/A	18.10.01
Martin, Nicholas John, RD	LT CDR	MW	CALLIOPE	31.03.95
Maryon, Karen Anne, RD	LT	QARNNS(R)	SHERWOOD	24.12.87
Mason, Andrew Robert,	SLT	MW	PRESIDENT	11.04.98
Mason, Andrew,	HON MID	URNU	U/A	12.10.00
Mason, Ann, RD	LT CDR	LOGS	EAGLET	01.04.99
Mason, David,	HON MID	URNU	U/A	12.10.00
Mason, Grace Victoria,	SLT	AW	PRESIDENT	14.10.99
Mason, Thomas,	LT CDR	AIR	RNR AIR BR VL	01.10.88
Massey, Steven,	LT	AIR	RNR AIR BR VL	01.02.91
Mathers, Fiona Catherine	SLT	AW	VIVID	27.11.02
Mattos, Alexander,	HON MID	URNU	U/A	11.09.00
Mawdsley, Katherine,	HONCADET	URNU	U/A	18.10.01
Mawer, Kieren,	HON MID	URNU	U/A	06.09.99
Maxey, Anna,	HONCADET	URNU	U/A	19.10.00
May, Oliver,	HON MID	URNU	U/A	24.10.00
May, Sarah,	HONCADET	URNU	U/A	06.09.99
Mayo, Guy,	HON MID	URNU	U/A	20.10.00
Mc Alear, Stuart Douglas,	LT CDR	MCD	KING ALFRED	25.10.95
McAlpine, Jeffrey	SLT	CS(O)	EAGLET	22.03.02
McArdell, Steven,	LT	AIR	RNR AIR BR VL	01.04.90
McBride, Andrew,	HON MID	URNU	U/A	27.09.01
McCabe, Jeremy Charles,	LT CDR	AW	VIVID	31.03.02
McCabe, Matthew James	ASLT	NE	PRESIDENT	03.10.03
McCartney, William Robert,	LT	LOGS	PRESIDENT	26.03.03
McClelland, Matthew,	HON MID	URNU	U/A	22.02.01
McCormack, Patrick, RD	LT CDR	NCAGS	DALRIADA	15.07.92
McCormick, Alana,	HONCADET	URNU	U/A	12.12.01
McCormick, Damion Kevin,	SLT	CS(O)	SHERWOOD	20.04.99
McCready, Heather Rachel	ASLT	NE	DALRIADA	22.09.04
McCreery, Robert George, RD	LT	MW	CAROLINE	20.06.89
McDermott Evans, Rachel,	HONCADET	URNU	U/A	29.10.98
McDonald, Roger,	LT CDR	AIR	RNR AIR BR VL	01.09.87
McDonald, Stewart Neil	ASLT	NE	DALRIADA	28.01.03
McEwan, Craig,	HON MID	URNU	U/A	24.10.01
McGee, Alexander,	HON MID	URNU	U/A	25.10.01
McGhee, Stephen James,	LT	AW	DALRIADA	18.12.01
McGinley, Mark Patrick	LT	LOGS	KING ALFRED	09.08.95
McGrath, Gerard Francis,	LT	LOGS	PRESIDENT	08.06.01
McGuire, Dee,	HONCADET	URNU	U/A	08.10.01
McGwinn, Daniel Michael	ASLT	NE	CALLIOPE	27.11.03
McHardy-Roberts, Jaqueline Carole,	SLT	CS(O)	EAGLET	10.02.00
McInnes, Vivian,	LT	QARNNS(R)	DALRIADA	14.12.92
McKeating, John Brendan,	SG CDR	MED	SHERWOOD	31.12.99
McKeever, Kevin,	HON MID	URNU	U/A	11.10.01
McKenzie, Alexander,	HON MID	URNU	U/A	14.10.99
McKenzie, Gary John	LT	AW	CAMBRIA	18.02.05
McKenzie-Boyle, Thomas,	HON MID	URNU	U/A	10.09.01
McKetty, Paul,	HON MID	URNU	U/A	30.09.99
McKinley, Mairi Catriona,	ALT	CS(O)	DALRIADA	01.11.04
McKinnon, Laura,	HONCADET	URNU	U/A	08.10.98
McKinty, Gareth James	ASLT	NE	CAROLINE	05.05.05
McKittrick, Lucinda,	HONCADET	URNU	U/A	18.10.01
McKnight, Christopher,	HON MID	URNU	U/A	18.10.01
McLaughlin, Vincent,	HON MID	URNU	U/A	06.09.99
McLaverty, Karen Anne,	LT	NCAGS	CAROLINE	17.03.99
McLeod, Charles,	HON MID	URNU	U/A	06.10.00
McLeod, Thomas,	HON MID	URNU	U/A	05.10.00
McManus, Peter,	LT CDR	AIR	RNR AIR BR VL	01.10.89
McMaster, Isaac,	HON MID	URNU	U/A	07.10.01
McMinn, Sandra,	ASL	URNU	U/A	01.10.98
McMorkine, Sarah,	HONCADET	URNU	U/A	11.10.01

Name	Rank	Branch	Unit	Seniority
McMurran, Robert Campbell,	LT CDR	OP INT	CAROLINE	31.03.97
McNair, Erin,	HONCADET	URNU	U/A	24.10.01
McNaught, Edward William Gordon, RD	LT CDR	MW	CALLIOPE	31.03.97
McPherson, Emma,	LT	QARNNS	CAROLINE	15.06.00
McQueen, Patrick,	HON MID	URNU	U/A	01.10.98
Mdoe, Charlotte,	HONCADET	URNU	U/A	07.10.01
Meadows, Brian	LT CDR	MR	RNR MRS	01.10.98
Meakin, Matthew,	HON MID	URNU	U/A	18.10.00
Medland, Elizabeth Ellen,	ASLT	NE	VIVID	20.02.01
Meharg, Neil, RD	LT	MW	CAROLINE	11.08.96
Meldram, Sheryl Christine Anne,	LT	QARNNS(R)	PRESIDENT	30.10.93
Mellor, Richard,	HON MID	URNU	U/A	11.10.01
Mellor, Daniel,	HON MID	URNU	U/A	11.09.00
Melson, Janet,	LT	LOGS	KING ALFRED	25.02.96
Mercer, Lara,	HONCADET	URNU	U/A	07.10.99
Meropoulos John,	SLT	HUMINT	FERRET	25.03.04
Merrington, Matthew,	HON MID	URNU	U/A	12.10.99
Millar, Caroline,	HONCADET	URNU	U/A	14.11.00
Miller, Benjamin	SLT	C4ISR	SHERWOOD	02.12.00
Miller, Charles,	HON MID	URNU	U/A	22.10.98
Miller, David,	LT CDR	AIR	RNR AIR BR VL	01.04.95
Miller, Gary,	HON MID	URNU	U/A	01.10.98
Milligan, Kevin,	HON MID	URNU	U/A	14.10.99
Millward, Jonathan,	LT CDR	SM	KING ALFRED	01.09.91
Minto, Paul,	HON MID	URNU	U/A	21.10.00
Minty, Darren,	HON MID	URNU	U/A	18.10.00
Mitchell, Natalie,	SLT	CS(O)	WILDFIRE	19.03.00
Mitchell, Robert,	LT CDR	AIR	RNR AIR BR VL	31.03.93
Mitchell, Samantha,	HONCADET	URNU	U/A	09.11.00
Mitchell, Shouna,	HONCADET	URNU	U/A	07.10.99
Mochar, Melanie,	HONCADET	URNU	U/A	30.09.99
Moghraby, Chetal,	HONCADET	URNU	U/A	20.10.98
Mohyud Din, Nayef,	HON MID	URNU	U/A	09.10.00
Molina, Alexandra,	HONCADET	URNU	U/A	11.10.01
Molyneux Giles Basingthwaite	SGSLT	MED	KING ALFRED	24.01.01
Monkhouse, Joanna,	HONCADET	URNU	U/A	20.10.00
Mooney, Ryan,	HON MID	URNU	U/A	18.10.01
Moore, Christopher	SLT	MW	FORWARD	16.11.00
Moore, Ian,	HON MID	URNU	U/A	18.10.01
Moorthy, Roham Michael,	LT	SM	PRESIDENT	02.03.02
Moran, Simon,	LT	AIR	RNR AIR BR VL	18.02.94
Morden, Hayley,	HONCADET	URNU	U/A	30.09.99
Morgan, Eugene Peter,	LT CDR	DI	FERRET	31.03.05
Morgan, Gareth William, RD	LT CDR	LOGS	CAMBRIA	31.03.01
Morgan, Linda Frances,	LT	QARNNS(R)	WILDFIRE	26.09.96
Morgan, Nicola,	HONCADET	URNU	U/A	18.10.00
Morgan, Richard,	HON MID	URNU	U/A	17.10.01
Morgans, Daniel James,	LT	MW	PRESIDENT	09.05.99
Moriarty, Helen Jean,	LT	QARNNS(R)	PRESIDENT	03.07.97
Morison, Julian Ronald,	ASL, nE		KING ALFRED	17.11.99
Morley, Dietmar Allen,	LT,	NCAGS	SHERWOOD	20.10.98
Morris, Alan Philip,	LT CDR	MR	RNR MRS	01.10.95
Morris, David John, RD	CDR	SM	WILDFIRE	30.09.01
Morris, Jessica,	HONCADET	URNU	U/A	14.10.99
Morris, Rachel,	HONCADET	URNU	U/A	11.10.01
Moseley, Allison,	SLT	NCAGS	CALLIOPE	10.08.96
Mostyn, Isabel,	HONCADET	URNU	U/A	07.11.01
Mouatt, David,	HON MID	URNU	U/A	18.10.00
Mowbray, Roger, QCVSA	LT CDR	AIR	RNR AIR BR VL	01.10.88
Moyes, Peter,	ASL	URNU	U/A	24.03.99
Mullins, Natalie,	HONCADET	URNU	U/A	06.09.99
Mundy, Ross,	HON MID	URNU	U/A	22.10.01
Munn, Claudia,	HONCADET	URNU	U/A	25.10.01

Name	Rank	Branch	Unit	Seniority
Munson, Eileen Patricia, RD	LT	QARNNS(R)	CAMBRIA	23.09.95
Munt, Marcus,	HON MID	URNU	U/A	08.10.98
Murphy, Christian,	HON MID	URNU	U/A	09.10.00
Murphy, Samantha,	ASL	URNU	U/A	16.06.99
Murray, Anita May,	LT	LOGS	VIVID	11.05.03
Murray, Abigail,	HONCADET	URNU	U/A	08.10.98
Murray, Christine,	HONCADET	URNU	U/A	15.11.99
Murray, Edward Charles, RD	LT CDR	HUMINT	FERRET	31.03.99
Murrison, Andrew William, MP	SG CDR	MED	KING ALFRED	31.12.97
Murrison,, Mark Peter , RD	LT CDR	AW	PRESIDENT	31.03.99
Myers, Paul,	LT	AIR	RNR AIR BR VL	01.08.84

N

Name	Rank	Branch	Unit	Seniority
Naaz, Amina,	HONCADET	URNU	U/A	07.12.00
Nadin, Robert,	LT CDR	AIR	RNR AIR BR VL	01.09.95
Nasmyth, James,	HON MID	URNU	U/A	11.10.01
Naylor, Raymond Dean	ASLT	NE	EAGLET	31.10.02
Neale, Andrea,	HONCADET	URNU	U/A	28.10.00
Neale, Daniel,	HON MID	URNU	U/A	19.10.00
Neale, Kirsty A,	LT,	NCAGS	EAGLET	30.11.94
Nelson, Victoria,	HONCADET	URNU	U/A	08.10.98
Newby, Christopher,	HON MID	URNU	U/A	11.09.00
Newton, David Jason,	LT	MR	RNR MRS	28.03.96
Newton, Ingrid Catherine,	LT CDR	LOGS	EAGLET	31.03.99
Newton, Mark,	LT CDR	AIR	RNR AIR BR VL	31.03.01
Newton, Russell Scott Henry,	SLT	SM	PRESIDENT	22.02.00
Newton, Rebecca,	HONCADET	URNU	U/A	06.11.00
Nicholson, John Kempe	SLT	HUMINT	FERRET	26.03.03
Nicolson, Vernon,	LT	HUMINT	FERRET	30.08.02
Nightingale, Samuel,	HON MID	URNU	U/A	09.10.00
Nisbet, James,	SLT	CS(O)	PRESIDENT	24.05.00
Noakes, David Anthony,	LT	LOGS	EAGLET	06.10.00
Noble, Alexander Peter,	SLT	MW	KING ALFRED	09.11.00
Noble, Robert Howard, BSC, RD	LT CDR,	NCAGS	FORWARD	31.03.97
Norris, Andrew,	ALT	NCAGS	KING ALFRED	01.10.90
North, Adam,	HON MID	URNU	U/A	11.09.00
Northcott, John,	LT CDR	LOGS	CALLIOPE	31.03.98
Norton, Rachel,	LT CDR	Q	WILDFIRE	31.03.02
Norwood, Jeffrey Michael,	SG CDR	MED	FORWARD	30.09.97
Nudd, Kathryn Louise,	PSG LT	MED	PRESIDENT	04.04.00
Nunn, James,	LT CDR	AIR	RNR AIR BR VL	31.03.99

O

Name	Rank	Branch	Unit	Seniority
O'Brian, Andrew Telfer	LT	AW	DALRIADA	31.10.02
O'Callaghan, Penelope Jane, RD	LT CDR	QARNNS(R)	KING ALFRED	31.03.96
O'Donohue, Ian,	HON MID	URNU	U/A	09.10.00
O'Dooley, Paul Patrick	SLT	C4ISR	SHERWOOD	01.10.01
O'Driscoll, Edward Hugh,	SLT	HUMINT	FERRET	10.03.98
O'Hara, Katherine,	HONCADET	URNU	U/A	11.10.01
O'Neill, Emily,	HONCADET	URNU	U/A	18.10.00
O'Sullivan, Kathryn Winifred, RD	LT	AWNIS	VIVID	26.07.96
Oag, Denis Cairns,	LT CDR	MW	SCOTIA	31.03.00
Oakley, Richard,	LT	AW	PRESIDENT	22.05.02
Oaten, Timothy John, RD	LT	NCAGS	SHERWOOD	03.06.87
Oates, Edward,	LT CDR	AIR	RNR AIR BR VL	16.02.93
Offords, Stephen,	HON MID	URNU	U/A	01.12.00
Ogden, Braddan,	LT	AIR	RNR AIR BR VL	01.04.95
Oldfield, Christian,	HON MID	URNU	U/A	11.09.00
Oldfield Paul Henry	LT CDR	CISENG	WILDFIRE	22.07.04
Olivant, David Francis, RD	LT CDR	OP INT	SHERWOOD	31.03.99
Omope, Sylvester,	HON MID	URNU	U/A	18.10.01

Name	Rank	Branch	Unit	Seniority
Ord, Elizabeth Mary	LT	DI	FERRET	23.05.97
Ormshaw, Andrew,	LT CDR	AIR	RNR AIR BR VL	23.06.87
Otto, Lucy,	HONCADET	URNU	U/A	18.10.01
Overson, Lauien,	HONCADET	URNU	U/A	11.10.01

P

Name	Rank	Branch	Unit	Seniority
Paddock, Lee David,	LT	SM	FORWARD	01.03.94
Padgham, Philip,	ALT	URNU	U/A	30.06.97
Paffey, Darren,	HON MID	URNU	U/A	05.01.01
Paget-Tomlinson, John Edward	SLT	CS(O)	KING ALFRED	28.02.01
Palmer, Alon, RD	LT CDR	AW	SCOTIA	09.05.91
Palmer, Andrew,	HON MID	URNU	U/A	28.09.00
Palmer, Helen,	ASL	URNU	U/A	01.10.90
Palmer, Helen,	SLT	URNU	U/A	18.04.98
Palmer, James,	HON MID	URNU	U/A	14.10.99
Papaioannou, Theodore,	HON MID	URNU	U/A	07.10.99
Pardoe, Christopher Richard,	LT CDR	MR	RNR MRS	13.09.86
Park, Lindsay,	HONCADET	URNU	U/A	08.02.01
Park, Susanne,	HONCADET	URNU	U/A	24.10.01
Parkins, Jennifer,	HONCADET	URNU	U/A	20.10.98
Parkinson, Amy,	HONCADET	URNU	U/A	18.10.01
Parnell, Rebecca Ann	LT	CS(O)	KING ALFRED	01.01.01
Parry, Angela Lynn	SLT	CS(O)	KING ALFRED	11.06.00
Parry, Christopher John,	LT	CS(O)	WILDFIRE	11.06.03
Parsonage, Neil David, RD LLM	LT CDR	NCAGS	EAGLET	31.03.00
Paterson, Charlotte,	HONCADET	URNU	U/A	18.10.01
Paterson, Gordon Laird,	LT CDR	AWNIS	KING ALFRED	02.11.84
Paterson, Jamie,	HON MID	URNU	U/A	28.09.00
Patterson, Mathew Robert	SLT	MW	FORWARD	27.04.01
Paterson, Stuart,	HON MID	URNU	U/A	08.10.01
Patten, Mark Thomas,	ASGCDR	MED	PRESIDENT	01.05.05
Patten, Nicholas William,	LT CDR	NCAGS	FORWARD	31.03.00
Patterson, Jarrod Lee,	LT CDR	MR	RNR MRS	31.03.01
Patterson, Roger	ASLT	NE	CAROLINE	22.10.03
Paxton, Alan,	HON MID	URNU	U/A	14.10.99
Payne, Christopher John	ASLT	NE	WILDFIRE	05.05.05
Payne, Gareth,	HON MID	URNU	U/A	14.10.99
Payne, Joseph,	HON MID	URNU	U/A	11.10.01
Payne, Robert,	HON MID	URNU	U/A	28.10.00
Payton, Philip John,	CDR	MR	RNR MRS	30.09.00
Pearce, Alexandra,	HONCADET	URNU	U/A	12.11.01
Pearce, Desmond,	ALT	URNU	U/A	12.05.80
Pearson, Craig Antony,	SLT	AW	KING ALFRED	25.10.01
Pearson, Ian,	HON MID	URNU	U/A	01.04.99
Pearson, Paul Austin Kevin,	LT CDR	SM	FLYING FOX	31.03.00
Peart, James,	HON MID	URNU	U/A	10.09.01
Peasley, Helen Susan,	ASLT	NE	SHERWOOD	13.11.01
Pedley, Michael,	SLT	NCAGS	FORWARD	16.01.02
Pellatt, Alison,	HONCADET	URNU	U/A	22.10.01
Percival, Victoria,	HONCADET	URNU	U/A	26.10.99
Perkins, Lucy,	HONCADET	URNU	U/A	14.10.99
Perks, Edward,	HON MID	URNU	U/A	14.10.99
Perry, Daniel,	HON MID	URNU	U/A	12.10.00
Peter, Kathleen Elizabeth,	SLT	MW	WILDFIRE	04.02.00
Pethick, Ian,	LT CDR	LOGS	VIVID	31.03.04
Petrie, Melville,	LT CDR	LOGS	FLYING FOX	09.01.87
Phillips, Katie,	HONCADET	URNU	U/A	19.10.00
Phillips, Nicholas James,	SLT	SM	PRESIDENT	23.10.00
Phillips, Matthew,	HON MID	URNU	U/A	14.10.99
Phillips, Sophia,	SLT	CS(O)	PRESIDENT	13.11.01
Pickard, Amanda,	HONCADET	URNU	U/A	06.11.00
Piddington, Charlotte,	HONCADET	URNU	U/A	22.10.01

Name	Rank	Branch	Unit	Seniority
Pike, Christine Margaret,	LT CDR	DI	FERRET (RNR)	31.03.95
Pike, Daniella,	HONCADET	URNU	U/A	20.10.98
Pike, Stuart,	LT	AIR	RNR AIR BR VL	12.02.95
Pimm, Anthony,	HON MID	URNU	U/A	14.10.99
Pimm, Michael,	HON MID	URNU	U/A	18.10.01
Pink, Karen	ASLT	NE	CALLIOPE	02.12.03
Pirie, Katherine,	LT	AIR	RNR AIR BR VL	15.12.89
Pittaway, Ernest,	HON MID	URNU	U/A	21.10.97
Plant, James,	HON MID	URNU	U/A	10.09.01
Platt, Timothy Samuel,	LT CDR	MCDO	PRESIDENT	01.04.00
Plummer, Ian,	HON MID	URNU	U/A	11.09.00
Pocock, James,	HON MID	URNU	U/A	11.10.01
Pogson, Andrew David	ASLT	NE	SHERWOOD	25.05.04
Poole, Daniel,	HON MID	URNU	U/A	12.10.00
Porter, Jonathan Mitchell Alexander,	SLT	MW	FLYING FOX	22.10.99
Posnett, Dickon,	LT	AIR	RNR AIR BR VL	01.08.88
Poulton-Watt, Andrew Ritchie,	LT	INFO OPS	SCOTIA	03.03.00
Powell, James Nicholas	LT	MR	RNR MRS	22.01.97
Powell, Simon Owen Maxwell	LT CDR	HUMINT	FERRET	31.03.98
Powell, Stephen,	LT CDR	AIR	RNR AIR BR VL	01.10.93
Powell, William,	LT CDR	AIR	RNR AIR BR VL	31.03.99
Powis, Megan,	HONCADET	URNU	U/A	11.09.00
Powley, Simon Owen Maxwell, RD	LT CDR	INTR	FERRET (RNR)	31.03.98
Poynton, Claire,	HONCADET	URNU	U/A	06.12.01
Pratt, Ian Heggie	LT CDR	MR	RNR MRS	06.10.98
Preece, Adam,	HON MID	URNU	U/A	01.02.00
Price, Julian,	LT	AIR	RNR AIR BR VL	16.11.94
Price, Naomi,	HONCADET	URNU	U/A	30.09.99
Price, Susan, RD	LT CDR	NCAGS	FLYING FOX	31.03.97
Pryce, Helen,	HONCADET	URNU	U/A	01.12.00
Pryce, Simon,	LT	AIR	RNR AIR BR VL	05.10.88
Pugh, Hywel Jones,	ALT	AW	PRESIDENT	10.06.90
Pugh, Neil,	LT	LOGS	CAMBRIA	15.05.91
Pugsley, Andrew,	HON MID	URNU	U/A	12.10.99
Puplett, Michael,	ASL	URNU	U/A	06.11.00
Purdy, Helen,	HONCADET	URNU	U/A	25.11.99
Pye, Steven,	ALT	URNU	U/A	21.10.97

Q

Name	Rank	Branch	Unit	Seniority
Quelch, Matthew,	HON MID	URNU	U/A	12.02.01
Quinn Anthony David	ASLT	NE	EAGLET	27.03.03
Quinn Martin Edward	LT CDR	MR	RNR MRS	01.09.03

R

Name	Rank	Branch	Unit	Seniority
Radjenovic, Zeljko	ASLT	NE	EAGLET	28.10.04
Ramsay, Brian, MA, ACMA	LT CDR	SM	PRESIDENT	31.03.01
Ramsdale, Timothy,	LT	AIR	RNR AIR BR VL	16.04.89
Ramshaw, Colin,	HON MID	URNU	U/A	02.11.00
Randles, Philip Neil,	LT	NCAGS	CALLIOPE	22.03.04
Ratzer, Edward,	HON MID	URNU	U/A	28.11.00
Rayne, Jeremy,	HON MID	URNU	U/A	02.11.99
Razaq, Sohail,	HON MID	URNU	U/A	07.10.01
Read, David Arthur, BSC RD	LT CDR	OP INT	PRESIDENT	31.03.97
Read, Edward,	HON MID	URNU	U/A	19.10.00
Redmond, Robert,	LT CDR	AW	PRESIDENT	31.03.00
Reen, Stephen,	LT	AIR	RNR AIR BR VL	01.10.92
Reid, Iain,	LT	AIR	RNR AIR BR VL	01.06.88
Reid, Joseph,	HON MID	URNU	U/A	21.10.98
Reilly, Paul,	HON MID	URNU	U/A	22.11.01
Relf, Elizabeth,	HONCADET	URNU	U/A	10.09.01
Rennell, Ian Joseph,	LT	NCAGS	EAGLET	19.11.96

Name	Rank	Branch	Unit	Seniority
Renouf Robert Jeffrey John	SLT	AW	SCOTIA	28.02.02
Rentoul, Donald,	HON MID	URNU	U/A	08.11.00
Reynolds, Edward,	HON MID	URNU	U/A	07.10.01
Reynolds, Louisa,	HONCADET	URNU	U/A	09.10.97
Reynolds, Nelson James Elliott, RD ADC	CAPT	MW	CAROLINE	30.09.99
Reynoldson, Howard, QVRM	LT CDR	AIR	RNR AIR BR VL	02.11.85
Rhodes, Davina,	HONCADET	URNU	U/A	09.10.00
Richard-Dit-Leschery, Stanley Ernest, RD	LT CDR	AW	VIVID	22.11.92
Richardson, Mark,	HON MID	URNU	U/A	07.10.99
Richards, Anna-Rose,	HONCADET	URNU	U/A	07.10.01
Richards, Guy,	LT CDR	MW	CAMBRIA	31.03.02
Richards Helen Samantha	ASLT	NE	CAMBRIA	11.11.03
Richards, Simon,	LT	AIR	RNR AIR BR VL	10.06.96
Richardson, Ian John,	LT CDR	HUMINT	FERRET (RNR)	15.01.91
Richardson, John,	HON MID	URNU	U/A	14.10.99
Richardson, Margaret Lynda Maither, RD	CDR	QARNNS(R)	DALRIADA	30.09.04
Richardson, Nicholas,	LT CDR	AIR	RNR AIR BR VL	01.10.96
Richmond, Alan,	HON MID	URNU	U/A	18.10.01
Rickard, Margaret Mary,	LT	MS	KING ALFRED	15.05.94
Rigden, James Lee	ASLT	NE	FLYING FOX	29.07.04
Riley, Peter John,	LT CDR	AW	CALLIOPE	31.03.98
Rimay-Muranyi, Gary,	LT	HUMINT	FERRET	18.02.00
Ritchie, David,	LT CDR	AIR	RNR AIR BR VL	01.10.00
Roberts, Emma,	HONCADET	URNU	U/A	22.10.01
Roberts, Helena Enid	ASLT	NE	EAGLET	23.01.03
Roberts James Anthony Frederick	ASLT	NE	FERRET	20.05.04
Roberts, Robert Ellis	ASLT	NE	SCOTIA	23.09.03
Roberts, Sophie,	HONCADET	URNU	U/A	18.10.01
Robertson, Jennifer Louise,	SLT	CS(O)	WILDFIRE	10.07.99
Robertson, Lorne, RD	LT CDR	MW	DALRIADA	17.11.97
Robertson-Nicol, Henry,	HON MID	URNU	U/A	11.10.01
Robinson, Anthony Michael, RD	LT CDR	AW	CAMBRIA	16.06.92
Robinson, Andrew Ronald,	SLT	MW	KING ALFRED	29.01.02
Robinson, Ian Michael, RD	CAPT	NCAGS	SHERWOOD	30.09.01
Robinson, James Brian,	LT	DI	FERRET	24.02.90
Robinson, Jonathon Charles King,	LT CDR	AIR	RNR AIR BR VL	01.11.91
Robinson, Nigel,	LT CDR	AIR	RNR AIR BR VL	31.03.94
Robinson, Paul,	HON MID	URNU	U/A	09.10.00
Robinson, William,	HON MID	URNU	U/A	12.10.00
Robson, Nicholas,	HON MID	URNU	U/A	18.10.01
Rodgers, Beth,	ASLT	NE	DALRIADA	24.11.04
Roll, Susan Margaret,	LT CDR	NCAGS	VIVID	31.03.01
Rollings, David Jonathan, RD*	LT CDR	INFO OPS	CAMBRIA	30.10.87
Rollins Anne	LT	DI	FERRET	20.09.99
Romito, Charles,	HON MID	URNU	U/A	01.03.00
Rooke, Adam,	HON MID	URNU	U/A	06.09.99
Rooke, Zoe,	HONCADET	URNU	U/A	14.01.99
Rose, Norman, RD	LT CDR	URNU	U/A	23.02.90
Rose, Simon,	HON MID	URNU	U/A	25.10.01
Rosindale, Philip Michael, RD	LT	AW	VIVID	19.05.97
Ross, Bruce James,	LT CDR	AW	KING ALFRED	05.05.90
Ross, Jonathan Anthony Duncan, RD	LT CDR	MW	DALRIADA	31.03.98
Ross, Nicholas,	HON MID	URNU	U/A	12.10.00
Roth, Charlotte,	HONCADET	URNU	U/A	04.10.01
Roue, Kathryn,	HONCADET	URNU	U/A	19.10.00
Rowell, Nina,	HONCADET	URNU	U/A	20.10.99
Rowles, Joanne,	LT	INFO OPS	CAMBRIA	21.07.96
Rowley, Andrew,	ASL	URNU	U/A	10.08.00
Rowley, Alexandra,	HONCADET	URNU	U/A	11.10.01
Rowntree, Paul,	HON MID	URNU	U/A	18.10.01
Rudkin, Adam,	HON MID	URNU	U/A	26.10.99
Ruglys, Matthew,	LT	AIR	RNR AIR BR VL	16.11.86
Russ, Philip John, RD	LT CDR	MW	EAGLET	31.03.96

Name	Rank	Branch	Unit	Seniority
Ryan, Amy Jemima,	SLT	SM	FLYING FOX	04.12.99
Ryan, Peter,	ALT	AW	PRESIDENT	18.01.01
Ryan, Simon John D Arcy, RD	LT CDR	OP INT	EAGLET	31.03.99
Ryder, Lucy,	HONCADET	URNU	U/A	25.10.01

S

Name	Rank	Branch	Unit	Seniority
Saffell, Thomas,	HON MID	URNU	U/A	15.10.98
Samwell, Michael,	HON MID	URNU	U/A	21.10.99
San, Howald Kin Loong, RD	LT	SM	PRESIDENT	15.12.90
Sandeman, Lillian,	HONCADET	URNU	U/A	30.09.99
Sanders, Ella,	HONCADET	URNU	U/A	08.02.01
Sanders, Kate,	HONCADET	URNU	U/A	11.09.00
Sanderson, Jennifer Patricia, RD	LT	OP INT	KING ALFRED	08.07.96
Satchell, Peter James, RD	LT CDR	MW	PRESIDENT	31.03.00
Saunders, David James, RD	LT CDR	MW	PRESIDENT	31.03.95
Saunders, Duncan,	ASL	URNU	U/A	10.10.96
Scanlon, Michael Stephen,	SLT	INTR	FERRET (RNR)	13.08.98
Scarth, Martin Richard,	LT	SM	PRESIDENT	18.05.01
Schwab, Robert,	LT CDR	AIR	RNR AIR BR VL	01.10.97
Scivier Paul Kevin	LT	MW	KING ALFRED	04.02.03
Scott, Anthony John	ASLT	NE	PRESIDENT	06.10.03
Scott-Foxwell, Julian, RD	LT CDR, nA	U/A		15.03.98
Scribbins, Christopher John, RD	LT CDR	CIS ENG	CALLIOPE	11.10.91
Scrimgeour John Martin	ASLT	NE	SHERWOOD	31.03.04
Seakins, Patrick Edward,	LT CDR	MR	RNR MRS	31.03.00
Sealy, Douglas Edward,	LT CDR	DI	FERRET	01.10.94
Searle, Geoffrey Derek, RD	LT CDR	MW	KING ALFRED	31.03.00
Seaton, Judith Ann,	SG LT	MED	VIVID	15.10.98
Seldon, John,	HON MID	URNU	U/A	22.10.97
Sellar, Susan,	HONCADET	URNU	U/A	14.10.99
Service, Brian,	LT CDR	AIR	RNR AIR BR VL	31.03.99
Shah, Tanvi,	HONCADET	URNU	U/A	18.10.01
Shakespeare, Christopher,	HON MID	URNU	U/A	04.11.99
Shakespeare, Martin, RD	LT CDR	DI	FERRET	31.03.97
Shannon, Tom, RD	LT CDR	URNU	U/A	01.11.95
Sharpe, Christian Gareth	ASLT	NE	VIVID	28.10.04
Sharples, Derek,	ACDR	AIR	RNR AIR BR VL	05.03.02
Shaw, James Elliot, RD*	CDR	AW	PRESIDENT	30.09.97
Shaw, Katherine,	HONCADET	URNU	U/A	04.10.01
Shaw, Stuart,	HON MID	URNU	U/A	06.11.00
Shaw, Simon,	HON MID	URNU	U/A	06.10.00
Shawcross, Jayne,	LT CDR	AIR	RNR AIR BR VL	03.01.95
Shears, Stephen,	LT CDR	AIR	RNR AIR BR VL	31.03.00
Sheffield, Raphael,	HON MID	URNU	U/A	17.03.99
Shelley, James Charles,	SG LT	MED	PRESIDENT	12.06.01
Shepherd, David,	HON MID	URNU	U/A	11.10.01
Shepherd, Stephen Michael	ALT	LOGS	KING ALFRED	22.08.02
Shepherd, William James, RD	LT	DI	FERRET	25.04.95
Sheppard, Adam James,	SLT	CS(O)	CAMBRIA	18.04.04
Sherman, Christopher James,	LT CDR	MCD	KING ALFRED	24.11.91
Sheriff Jacquiline	LT	MR	RNR MRS	01.12.93
Sherwin, Anthony,	HON MID	URNU	U/A	14.10.99
Shilson, Stuart James,	LT	SM	PRESIDENT	20.03.05
Shiner, David,	LT	DI	FERRET	02.11.99
Shinner, Patrick Anthony, RD	LT CDR	SM	PRESIDENT	31.03.99
Shinner, Stephanie Katherine Fleur, RD	LT CDR	NCAGS	WILDFIRE	31.03.00
Shirtcliffe, Kevin,	HON MID	URNU	U/A	04.10.01
Short, Matthew,	HON MID	URNU	U/A	04.10.01
Shouler, Martin Clifford,	ALT	MW	PRESIDENT	15.11.04
Shrives, Jonathan,	HON MID	URNU	U/A	11.10.01
Sibcy, James Robert William,	ASL, nE	PRESIDENT		03.08.01
Siddiqi, Omar,	HON MID	URNU	U/A	07.10.01

Name	Rank	Branch	Unit	Seniority
Sides James William	SLT	MW	EAGLET	17.04.03
Sides, Susan C., RD	LT CDR	OP INT	FORWARD	30.09.91
Sigley, Arthur David Martin,	LT	AW	SCOTIA	05.07.04
Simmonds, Richard Charles Kenneth,	LT CDR	AWNIS	WILDFIRE	31.03.02
Simmonds, Timothy Paul,	LT CDR	MW	PRESIDENT	31.03.05
Simmons, Annelie,	HONCADET	URNU	U/A	11.10.01
Simons, David,	HON MID	URNU	U/A	09.10.00
Simpson, Alex,	ASL	URNU	U/A	10.01.02
Simpson, James,	HON MID	URNU	U/A	28.09.00
Simpson, Neil William John	ASLT	NE	SHERWOOD	31.07.03
Simpson-Hayes, Gizella Clare	ASLT	QARNNS(R)	PRESIDENT	02.10.02
Sinclair, James,	HON MID	URNU	U/A	30.09.99
Sinnott, Luke,	HON MID	URNU	U/A	24.10.00
Sivagnanam, Piriyah,	HONCADET	URNU	U/A	09.10.00
Skeels-Piggins Talan Stephen	ALT	SM	FLYING FOX	26.11.02
Skelley, Roger Francis	ASLT	NE	VIVID	20.02.03
Skelly, Andrew James	SLT	LOGS	CAROLINE	13.07.03
Skelton, Richard,	HON MID	URNU	U/A	11.10.01
Skidmore, Paul,	ALT	URNU	U/A	01.01.98
Skinner, Christopher,	HON MID	URNU	U/A	28.09.00
Skinner, Nigel Guy, BSC, M.ENG	LT	NCAGS	SHERWOOD	15.11.99
Skuriat, Olenka,	HONCADET	URNU	U/A	23.10.97
Slater, Elizabeth,	HONCADET	URNU	U/A	11.10.01
Slavin, David Eric	SGCDR	MED	KING ALFRED	24.01.97
Slonecki, Adam,	ASLT	NE	PRESIDENT	18.01.05
Small, Peter Kenneth,	SG CDR	MED	CALLIOPE	30.09.97
Small, Pauline,	LT CDR	QARNNS	SCOTIA	31.03.05
Smalldridge, Lindsay,	HONCADET	URNU	U/A	18.10.01
Smith, Andrew,	HON MID	URNU	U/A	06.10.00
Smith, Blair Hamilton,	PSG LTCDR	MED	SCOTIA	13.12.00
Smith, Craig,	HON MID	URNU	U/A	05.10.00
Smith, David,	LT CDR	AIR	RNR AIR BR VL	31.03.00
Smith, David,	LT	LOGS	EAGLET	03.07.01
Smith, Dominic,	HON MID	URNU	U/A	14.10.99
Smith, Gordon,	LT CDR	AIR	RNR AIR BR VL	31.03.01
Smith, Hannah,	HONCADET	URNU	U/A	01.10.98
Smith, Jennifer,	HONCADET	URNU	U/A	06.11.00
Smith, Jillian,	HONCADET	URNU	U/A	12.10.99
Smith, Jane Marion,	ASLT	QARNNS	VIVID	16.04.02
Smith, Kenneth,	HON MID	URNU	U/A	28.09.00
Smith, Lesley Gay Isabel, RD*	CDR	LOGS	VIVID	30.09.96
Smith Martin Richard	ALT	AW	VIVID	13.01.02
Smith, Michael,	LT	URNU	U/A	08.02.95
Smith, Paul,	HON MID	URNU	U/A	17.10.01
Smith, Rebecca,	HONCADET	URNU	U/A	18.10.01
Smith, Stephen,	LT	INFO OPS	WILDFIRE	03.05.97
Smith, Wilfred Donald Fitzroy, RD	SG CDR	MED	EAGLET	30.09.99
Smyth, Kiaran,	ASL	URNU	U/A	06.10.98
Smyth, Michael Paul,	LT	MW	PRESIDENT	05.06.89
Snoddon, Robert,	LT CDR	OP INT	CALLIOPE	31.03.01
Snow, Emma,	HONCADET	URNU	U/A	18.10.01
Souter, Michael David, RD	LT CDR	MR	RNR MRS	01.01.84
Southall, Nicholas,	ASLT	NE	FORWARD	01.04.05
Southern John Stephen	ASLT	NE	EAGLET	28.05.02
Spacey, Craig,	HON MID	URNU	U/A	10.09.01
Spaine, Victor,	HON MID	URNU	U/A	14.10.99
Spencer, Gary,	LT CDR	AIR	RNR AIR BR VL	21.10.94
Spencer, Michael David,	LT	C4ISR	PRESIDENT	25.11.03
Spencer, Philip,	HON MID	URNU	U/A	01.12.00
Spray, Alison, RD	LT CDR	NCAGS	VIVID	31.03.93
Sprowles, K J, RD	LT CDR	NCAGS	PRESIDENT	04.11.90
Stacpoole, Sybil,	HONCADET	URNU	U/A	15.10.98
Staniforth, Claire,	HONCADET	URNU	U/A	19.10.00

Name	Rank	Branch	Unit	Seniority
Stanley, Dermot Alan, RD	LT	SM	CALLIOPE	12.01.96
Staples, David Richard,	PSG LT	MED	WILDFIRE	28.11.01
Staples, Karl James,	ASL, nE		PRESIDENT	25.04.01
Steer, Rebecca,	HONCADET	URNU	U/A	09.10.00
Stephen, Cameron,	HON MID	URNU	U/A	11.09.00
Stephen Lesley Ann	LT	LOGS	DALRIADA	15.12.01
Stephenson, Michael Edward,	SLT	MW	CALLIOPE	19.12.97
Stephenson, Richard, RD	LT CDR	AIR	RNR AIR BR VL	01.03.80
Stevenson, Adam,	HON MID	URNU	U/A	20.10.99
Stevenson, Paul,	HON MID	URNU	U/A	08.09.99
Stewart, Allan,	LT CDR	SM	EAGLET	31.03.02
Stewart, Iain, RD	LT CDR	LOGS	SCOTIA	21.03.87
Stickland, Anthony Charles Robert, RD	LT CDR	AW	KING ALFRED	31.03.98
Stidston, David,	LT CDR	AIR	RNR AIR BR VL	01.10.94
Stocker, Jeremy Richard,	LT CDR	INFO OPS	CALLIOPE	01.06.89
Stocker, John,	HON MID	URNU	U/A	11.10.01
Stopford, Jeremy,	HON MID	URNU	U/A	18.10.01
Stopps, Claire,	HONCADET	URNU	U/A	14.10.99
Storey, David,	HON MID	URNU	U/A	25.10.01
Story, Ruth,	HONCADET	URNU	U/A	12.10.00
Strachan, Robin Kinnear,	SG CDR	MED	PRESIDENT	30.09.95
Strain, Justin Damian Russell,	LT	MW	KING ALFRED	01.05.98
Strawbridge, Chantal,	HONCADET	URNU	U/A	07.10.99
Strawbridge, Rona,	HONCADET	URNU	U/A	19.10.00
Streeter, Pamela,	HONCADET	URNU	U/A	04.02.99
Strike, Peter,	LT	URNU	U/A	30.09.92
Styles, Sarah Jane,	LT	SM	PRESIDENT	29.10.04
Sutcliff, Jonathon,	HON MID	URNU	U/A	11.10.01
Sutton, Gareth,	HON MID	URNU	U/A	18.10.01
Swabey, Matthew,	HON MID	URNU	U/A	06.09.98
Swaby, James,	HON MID	URNU	U/A	18.10.00
Swann, Adam,	HON MID	URNU	U/A	21.10.99
Sweenie, John Fraser,	SG LTCDR	MED	DALRIADA	13.02.90
Sweetman, David,	HON MID	URNU	U/A	18.10.00
Sweetnam, Meriel,	HONCADET	URNU	U/A	24.10.01
Sykes, Andrew,	HON MID	URNU	U/A	18.10.00
Syme, Allan, RD*	LT CDR	NCAGS	DALRIADA	11.02.83

T

Name	Rank	Branch	Unit	Seniority
Tabner, Reuben,	HON MID	URNU	U/A	30.09.99
Tall, Louisa,	HONCADET	URNU	U/A	20.10.98
Tall, Richard Edward,	LT	SM	FLYING FOX	14.12.97
Tarmey, Sarah,	HONCADET	URNU	U/A	08.10.98
Taylor, Dale,	HON MID	URNU	U/A	21.10.99
Taylor, Louise Elizabeth,	LT CDR	NCAGS	EAGLET	31.03.00
Taylor, Neville,	LT CDR	INFO OPS	CALLIOPE	01.04.89
Taylor, Nicholas,	HON MID	URNU	U/A	20.10.98
Taylor, Penelope	SLT	QARNNS(R)	PRESIDENT	18.05.04
Taylor, Rupert James, RD	LT CDR	AW	KING ALFRED	31.03.99
Taylor, Stephen,	HON MID	URNU	U/A	25.10.01
Taylor, Thomas,	HON MID	URNU	U/A	04.10.01
Teasdale, David Andrew,	LT CDR	SM	FLYING FOX	31.03.04
Teasdale, James,	HON MID	URNU	U/A	11.09.00
Telfer, Alison, RD	LT CDR	NCAGS	EAGLET	30.09.91
Temple, Miles,	LT	INFO OPS	WILDFIRE	01.11.94
Templeton, Susan, RD	LT CDR	LOGS	FLYING FOX	31.03.96
Tetchner, David,	HON MID	URNU	U/A	30.11.00
Thomas Andrew	SLT	AW	PRESIDENT	15.03.02
Thomas Brian	LT	AW	CAMBRIA	01.04.04
Thomas, David Graham,	LT	C4ISR	KING ALFRED	12.07.02
Thomas, David James,	SLT	C4ISR	CAMBRIA	27.06.01
Thomas, Emma Margaret,	LT CDR	MR	RNR MRS	31.03.01

Name	Rank	Branch	Unit	Seniority
Thomas, Jeffrey,	LT CDR	AIR	RNR AIR BR VL	01.09.92
Thomas, Neil,	HON MID	URNU	U/A	25.11.99
Thomas, Philip,	HON MID	URNU	U/A	17.10.01
Thomas, Stephen,	LT	MW	CAMBRIA	26.01.97
Thomas, Tenny,	HON MID	URNU	U/A	20.10.99
Thomason, Michael,	LT	LOGS	EAGLET	09.11.97
Thompson, Andrew John, RD	CDR	NCAGS	VIVID	30.09.01
Thompson, Elizabeth,	HONCADET	URNU	U/A	06.09.98
Thompson, Glenn,	LT CDR	AIR	RNR AIR BR VL	31.03.99
Thompson, Huw,	HON MID	URNU	U/A	04.10.01
Thomson, Frederick	SLT	C4ISR	DALRIADA	23.01.03
Thomson, Paul,	HON MID	URNU	U/A	07.10.99
Thomson, Sheena Rosemary, BA	LT CDR	MR	RNR MRS	31.03.00
Thomson, Susie Jane,	LT CDR	MR	RNR MRS	31.03.99
Thorne, Brian John, RD*	CAPT	INFO OPS	CAMBRIA	30.09.97
Thorne, Lee James,	LT CDR	MW	KING ALFRED	31.03.02
Thorne, Stephen Paul, RD	CAPT	INFO OPS	KING ALFRED	30.09.03
Thorpe Alexander David	ASLT	NE	SHERWOOD	24.11.04
Tiffen, Jonathan,	HON MID	URNU	U/A	11.10.01
Tighe, Christopher,	HON MID	URNU	U/A	21.10.99
Tighe, Gary,	LT CDR	AIR	RNR AIR BR VL	01.02.91
Till, Alexander,	HON MID	URNU	U/A	01.11.01
Tilney Duncan Edward	LT	MW	WILDFIRE	13.09.98
Tindall-Jones, Julia Mary, BA	CDR	LOGS	VIVID	30.09.01
Titterton, Jody,	HONCADET	URNU	U/A	02.10.00
Todd, Andrew Harry Campbell, RD	LT CDR	NCAGS	SCOTIA	31.03.98
Todd, Susan,	ASL	URNU	U/A	05.03.96
Tonkin, Neil,	LT CDR	AIR	RNR AIR BR VL	01.10.90
Topping, Mark, RD	LT CDR	INFO OPS	CAMBRIA	31.03.97
Tornambe, Richard,	HON MID	URNU	U/A	07.10.99
Trangmar, Paul,	LT	LOGS	WILDFIRE	22.11.93
Trelawny, Christopher Charles, RD	LT	AW	PRESIDENT	14.12.89
Treloar, Philip,	LT CDR	MR	RNR MRS	16.09.88
Tribe, David,	LT CDR	AIR	RNR AIR BR VL	31.03.99
Trimmer, Patrick David Mark,	LT CDR	OP INT	CALLIOPE	31.03.96
Trosh, Nicholas,	HON MID	URNU	U/A	30.09.99
Tubb, Anna,	HONCADET	URNU	U/A	12.10.00
Tu8ckett Caroline Sybil Elizabeth	SLT	LOGS	SCOTIA	21.07.01
Tudor, Simon,	HON MID	URNU	U/A	12.10.00
Tulloch, Alan,	SLT	X	U/A	08.04.87
Tunstall, Sarah,	HONCADET	URNU	U/A	06.03.00
Tuppen, Heather Jill,	LT	MR	RNR MRS	24.10.94
Turner, Christopher,	LT	URNU	U/A	01.11.96
Turner, Jonathan Andrew McMahon, RD	SGCAPT	MED	KING ALFRED	30.09.03
Turner, Ryan,	HON MID	URNU	U/A	25.10.01
Turner, Simon John,	LT CDR	AW	VIVID	31.03.99
Tutton, Amanda,	HONCADET	URNU	U/A	14.10.99
Tweedie Nicola	ASLT	NE	VIVID	01.03.05
Tyrell, Carol Marguerite,	LT CDR	DI	FERRET	11.04.90

U

Name	Rank	Branch	Unit	Seniority
Upton, Vivienne,	HONCADET	URNU	U/A	22.10.01
Ure Fiona	SLT	C4ISR	CAROLINE	01.11.01
Urquhart Nicola	ASLT	NE	DALRIADA	20.01.04
Urquhart Roderick	ASLT	NE	PRESIDENT	27.11.03
Utting, Penelope Anne,	LT CDR	MR	RNR MRS	31.03.01

V

Name	Rank	Branch	Unit	Seniority
Valentine, Robert Innes,	LT CDR	INFO OPS	SCOTIA	31.03.99
Van Asch, Alexandra,	HONCADET	URNU	U/A	12.10.99
Van Den Bergh, Mark RD	LT	LOGS	WILDFIRE	16.12.92

Name	Rank	Branch	Unit	Seniority
Vardy, Emma,	HONCADET	URNU	U/A	12.10.00
Varley, Peter,	ACDR	AIR	RNR AIR BR VL	05.03.02
Veale, Bryony,	HONCADET	URNU	U/A	19.10.00
Vernon, Michael A, RD	LT CDR	INFO OPS	VIVID	27.08.90
Versallion Mark Anthony	ASLT	NE	PRESIDENT	09.12.99
Villa Nina Louise	ASLT	NE	PRESIDENT	20.01.05
Vincent, Claire Elaine,	LT CDR	AWNIS	KING ALFRED	31.03.04
Vitali, Julie Elizabeth,	LT	DI	FERRET	08.06.96
Vora, Nina,	HONCADET	URNU	U/A	18.10.01

W

Name	Rank	Branch	Unit	Seniority
Wain, Alexis,	HON MID	URNU	U/A	05.07.99
Wainwright, Barnaby,	LT CDR	AIR	RNR AIR BR VL	01.09.89
Wake, Thomas Baldwin, RD	LT CDR	INFO OPS	SHERWOOD	31.03.00
Wakefield David Weldon	ASLT	NE	EAGLET	17.11.04
Wakefield, Gary,	LT CDR	AIR	RNR AIR BR VL	01.03.93
Wakeford, Mark Warren,	LT CDR	MR	RNR MRS	31.03.02
Walden, Geoffery Gerald, RD	LT,	SM	SHERWOOD	10.12.90
Wales, Frederick Anthony, RD	LT CDR	AW	KING ALFRED	31.03.98
Walker, David, RD	LT CDR	LOGS	PRESIDENT	31.03.97
Walker, Graeme,	HON MID	URNU	U/A	10.09.01
Walker, Gail,	HONCADET	URNU	U/A	14.10.99
Walker, Paul MacKenzie,	LT	DI	FERRET	14.03.03
Wallace, Stuart Iain,	LT	AW	EAGLET	23.07.99
Wallace, Simon John,	SLT	AW	SHERWOOD	08.06.00
Waller, James,	LT	C4ISR	PRESIDENT	10.10.03
Waller, Vincent Francis, RD	LT CDR	AW	CALLIOPE	01.09.88
Wallom, Anne,	LT	MR	RNR MRS	13.09.92
Walters, Richard John,	LT CDR	MR	RNR MRS	31.03.04
Walthall, Fiona Elizabeth,	LT CDR	NCAGS	SCOTIA	31.03.02
Walworth, William Michael, OBE	CDR	AW	PRESIDENT	30.09.95
Ward, Eleanore Jane	ASLT	NE	KING ALFRED	04.03.03
Ward, Suzanne,	HONCADET	URNU	U/A	30.09.97
Warner, Adrian,	HON MID	URNU	U/A	11.10.01
Warnock, Gavin,	LT CDR	AIR	RNR AIR BR VL	01.10.95
Warren, Julian,	HON MID	URNU	U/A	28.09.00
Warrick, Mark,	HON MID	URNU	U/A	06.09.99
Wartlier, Lee,	HON MID	URNU	U/A	19.10.00
Waterhouse, Guy,	HON MID	URNU	U/A	22.10.01
Waters, Anna,	HONCADET	URNU	U/A	11.10.01
Waters, Christopher Martin,	LT CDR	NCAGS	KING ALFRED	01.05.86
Waters, Michael,	HON MID	URNU	U/A	14.10.99
Waterworth, Stephen Norman,	LT	CIS ENG	FORWARD	01.04.93
Watson, Catherine, RD	LT CDR	OP INT	EAGLET	31.03.98
Watson, David,	HON MID	URNU	U/A	06.11.00
Watson, Lloyd,	LT CDR	AIR	RNR AIR BR VL	01.10.94
Watts, Alexandra,	HONCADET	URNU	U/A	18.10.01
Watts, Nicholas,	HON MID	URNU	U/A	11.10.01
Waugh, Gillian,	HONCADET	URNU	U/A	11.10.01
Way, Katherine,	HONCADET	URNU	U/A	07.10.99
Weaver, Peter,	ALT	SM	VIVID	23.10.01
Webb Christopher	LT CDR	LOGS	KING ALFRED	03.02.05
Webber, Christina,	HONCADET	URNU	U/A	11.10.01
Webber Stephen John	LT CDR	LOGS	FLYING FOX	01.02.94
Webborn, Elizabeth,	HONCADET	URNU	U/A	17.10.01
Webster Elizabeth Lucy	ASLT	NE	CALLIOPE	06.05.04
Wedgewood, Jonathon James,	ASGCDR	MED	SCOTIA	01.05.05
Weedon, Matthew,	HON MID	URNU	U/A	02.10.00
Wells, Christopher Michael,	LT CDR	AW	KING ALFRED	31.03.94
Wells, Jonathan,	LT CDR	AIR	RNR AIR BR VL	01.12.91
Welsh, Audrey,	LT	CIS ENG	WILDFIRE	17.02.97
Welsh, Nicholas Paul,	ASLT	NE	PRESIDENT	17.10.01

Name	Rank	Branch	Unit	Seniority
Wesley, John R, RD	LT CDR	OP INT	PRESIDENT	12.11.89
West, Nicholas,	LT CDR	AIR	RNR AIR BR VL	31.03.99
West, Susan Elizabeth,	SG CDR	MED	PRESIDENT	30.09.01
Westwood, Steve,	LT CDR	AIR	RNR AIR BR VL	01.10.92
Wheeldon, Matthew,	HON MID	URNU	U/A	26.10.99
Wheeler, Joanne Natalie,	LT	MR	RNR MRS	12.05.03
Wheeler, Robert	SLT	SM	PRESIDENT	13.04.01
Wheeler, Sophia Rebecca Frances,	LT	SM	PRESIDENT	07.03.03
Whitby, Philip,	LT CDR	SM	VIVID	26.12.90
Whitby, Stephen,	LT CDR	INFO OPS	SCOTIA	01.01.92
White, Andrew,	HON MID	URNU	U/A	19.10.00
White, Ian Roy,	LT CDR	NCAGS	CALLIOPE	31.03.96
White, Michael Eaton Lane	LT	AWNIS	VIVID	10.07.95
White, Olivia,	HONCADET	URNU	U/A	19.10.00
Whitehead, Andrea,	HONCADET	URNU	U/A	18.10.00
Whitehead, Keith Stuart, BSC, RD	LT CDR	OP INT	KING ALFRED	31.03.00
Whitehead, Lucy,	HONCADET	URNU	U/A	04.10.01
Whitehouse, Andrew,	HON MID	URNU	U/A	25.11.99
Whitehouse, Marie,	HONCADET	URNU	U/A	21.10.99
Whitney, Camilla,	HONCADET	URNU	U/A	07.10.01
Whittaker, Maime,	HON MID	URNU	U/A	17.10.01
Whittall, Andrew,	LT	AIR	RNR AIR BR VL	15.10.90
Wickens, Ian,	LT CDR	AIR	RNR AIR BR VL	31.03.00
Widdick, David,	HON MID	URNU	U/A	07.10.01
Wilcockson, Alastair Quentin,	ASGCDR	MED	KING ALFRED	27.07.03
Wilkie, Suzanne Ellen,	LT CDR	INFO OPS	SCOTIA	26.06.01
Wilkinson, Douglas,	SGLTCDR	MED	PRESIDENT	01.05.05
Wilkinson, Sarah,	HONCADET	URNU	U/A	01.12.00
Willcox, Joanna,	HONCADET	URNU	U/A	18.10.01
Williams, Andrew Bruce	LT CDR	DI	FERRET	01.07.95
Williams, Alex,	HON MID	URNU	U/A	22.10.01
Williams, Gemma,	HONCADET	URNU	U/A	09.10.00
Williams Julia Elisa Maria	ASLT	NE	FORWARD	11.12.03
Williams, Kate,	HONCADET	URNU	U/A	28.09.00
Williams Kevin Matthew	ASLT	NE	FLYING FOX	15.10.03
Williams, Kristian,	HON MID	URNU	U/A	07.10.01
Williams, Mark Jeremy,	LT	NCAGS	EAGLET	27.10.92
Williams, Owain,	HON MID	URNU	U/A	08.10.98
Williams, Rudolph Stephen,	ASL	NE	VIVID	01.05.02
Williams, Scott,	HON MID	URNU	U/A	11.10.01
Williams, Simon Jeremy	ASLT	NE	FLYING FOX	18.10.02
Williams, Thomas,	ASLT	NE	PRESIDENT	02.12.03
Williams, Timothy Paul, RD	LT	MW	WILDFIRE	22.09.95
Williamson, Helen,	HONCADET	URNU	U/A	12.10.00
Wilson, Gary,	LT CDR	URNU	U/A	10.10.95
Wilson, Garth,	HON MID	URNU	U/A	24.10.01
Wilson, Jonathan,	SLT	MW	SCOTIA	30.05.99
Wilson, Jennifer Maureen,	LT CDR	QARNNS	KING ALFRED	31.03.95
Wilson, Karyn, RD	LT, nCAGS		FLYING FOX	19.07.90
Wilson, Paul,	HON MID	URNU	U/A	19.10.00
Wilson, Peter,	LT CDR	AIR	RNR AIR BR VL	07.09.99
Wilson, Scott McDonald,	ASL, nE		SCOTIA	11.04.02
Wilson, Stephen John,	SGCDR	MED	PRESIDENT	30.09.02
Winder, Nicholas,	ASL, nE		U/A	03.05.00
Window Stephen Harvey	LT CDR	MCD	KING ALFRED	01.09.95
Winfield, Adrian,	LT CDR	AIR	RNR AIR BR VL	31.03.99
Winn, Alexander,	HON MID	URNU	U/A	12.10.00
Winser, Charlotte,	HONCADET	URNU	U/A	11.10.01
Winstanley, Nichola Ann, VRSM	LT CDR	MR	RNR MRS	31.03.95
Winterton, James,	HON MID	URNU	U/A	04.10.01
Wiseman, Anee-Marie,	HONCADET	URNU	U/A	04.10.01
Wiseman, Jane,	LT CDR	AIR	RNR AIR BR VL	31.03.01
Wolstenholme, Clare,	HONCADET	URNU	U/A	25.10.01

Name	Rank	Branch	Unit	Seniority
Wolstenholme, David,	LT CDR	AIR	RNR AIR BR VL	01.10.93
Wolstenholme, Fiona,	HONCADET	URNU	U/A	18.10.01
Wood, Clare,	HONCADET	URNU	U/A	27.11.01
Wood, Graham,	HON MID	URNU	U/A	19.10.00
Wood, John,	LT CDR	CIS ENG	CALLIOPE	31.03.01
Wood, Justin,	LT CDR	AIR	RNR AIR BR VL	01.03.90
Wood, Matthew,	HON MID	URNU	U/A	18.10.01
Wood, Richard,	HON MID	URNU	U/A	20.10.99
Wood, Suzanne,	LT	OP INT	PRESIDENT	05.04.93
Woodham, Jeremy,	LT CDR	AIR	RNR AIR BR VL	02.07.92
Woodman Clare Francesca Jane	LT	MR	RNR MRS	01.09.88
Woodman, Clive Andrew,	LT CDR	MR	RNR MRS	01.09.87
Woods, Fergus,	LT CDR	AIR	RNR AIR BR VL	01.10.88
Wordie, Andrew George Lyon, RD	LT CDR	INFO OPS	SHERWOOD	31.03.95
Wordsworth Helen MArgaret	ASGLT	MED	EAGLET	24.07.01
Worral, Andrew,	HON MID	URNU	U/A	09.10.00
Worsley, Alistair Louis, RD	CDR	MR	RNR MRS	30.09.04
Wray, Ronald Maurice,	LT CDR	NCAGS	KING ALFRED	31.03.99
Wreford, Katrine Patricia,	LT CDR	MR	RNR MRS	31.03.93
Wrigglesworth, Peter John,	SG LTCDR	MED	SHERWOOD	02.08.88
Wright, Alan Howard, RD	LT CDR	AW	EAGLET	01.11.91
Wright, Antony,	LT CDR	AIR	RNR AIR BR VL	01.10.97
Wright, Douglas John,	LT CDR	DI	FERRET	31.03.05
Wright, Gordon, RD	LT CDR	AIR	RNR AIR BR VL	17.04.86
Wright, Gabriel,	HON MID	URNU	U/A	11.10.01
Wright, Iain Alistair MacKay,	LT CDR	DI	FERRET	18.08.97
Wright, Stephen,	LT CDR	INFO OPS	KING ALFRED	31.03.00
Wright, Stephen, GM	LT CDR	AIR	RNR AIR BR VL	31.03.01
Wrightson, Ian,	LT	AIR	RNR AIR BR VL	01.04.93
Wring, Matthew Anthony,	LT CDR	MW	FLYING FOX	31.03.03
Wyatt, Mark Edward, RD	CDR	MW	KING ALFRED	30.09.99
Wyglendacz, Jan Andrew, RD	ACDR	LOGS	CAMBRIA	23.03.03
Wyness, Sharon,	LT	AIR	RNR AIR BR VL	01.09.96

X

Name	Rank	Branch	Unit	Seniority
Xu, Hui,	HONCADET	URNU	U/A	24.10.01

Y

Name	Rank	Branch	Unit	Seniority
Yates, Steven,	LT CDR	MW	FLYING FOX	31.03.00
Yeo, Sophie,	HONCADET	URNU	U/A	18.10.01
Yibowei, Christophe Amaebi,	SLT	LOGS	PRESIDENT	06.02.00
Yong, Andrew,	ASLT	NE	PRESIDENT	01.12.04
Young, Carl,	LT CDR	AIR	RNR AIR BR VL	31.03.98
Young, Duncan, RD	LT CDR	MW	CALLIOPE	31.03.98
Young, Gregory Christian,	LT	MW	PRESIDENT	30.11.02
Young, William David,	LT CDR	LOGS	KING ALFRED	31.03.05
Yule Vt, Victoria,	ASL	URNU	U/A	21.03.96

ROYAL NAVAL RESERVE INTERPRETERS

Name	Rank	Date of Qualifying or Re-qualifying
FRENCH		
Nicholson, P.A.	LT CDR	1980
Pressagh, J.P.	LT CDR	1994
GERMAN		
Cobbold, A.R.	LT	2001
Pressagh, J.P.	LT CDR	1983
ITALIAN		
Pressagh, J.P.	LT CDR	1999
Alcock, M.L.	LT	2001
JAPANESE		
Nicholson, P.A.	LT CDR	1995
PERSIAN		
Cobbold, A.R.	LT	1982
POLISH		
Pressagh, J.P.	LT CDR	1989
RUSSIAN		
Cobbold, A.R.	LT	1989
Pressagh, J.P.	LT CDR	1995
Seakins, P.E.	LT	1995
Jones, L.	LT CDR	1989
SPANISH		
Alcock, M.L.	LT	1995
Nicholson, P.A.	LT CDR	1997
Pressagh, J.P.	LT CDR	1993

ROYAL MARINES RESERVE

Name	Rank	Branch	Unit	Seniority
B				
Baker, AMair,	Lt	M1	LONDON	08.03.00
Barnwell, Barry, RD	Lt Col	M1	SCOTLAND	01.12.90
Billington, Ed,	Capt	M1	MERSEYSIDE	07.06.92
Brooker-Gillespie, Robin,	Loc Maj	M1	LONDON	04.01.95
Brown, Roger,	Capt	M1	MERSEYSIDE	15.07.90
Bruce, Rory,	Lt Col	M1	BRISTOL	30.06.98
Brunskill, Michael,	Lt	M1	MERSEYSIDE	21.05.00
C				
Campbell, Mike,	Act Maj	M1	TYNE	01.04.95
Chamberlain, Henry,	Capt	M1	BRISTOL	28.04.94
Churchill, Colin,	2lt	M2	SCOTLAND	19.04.99
Coard, Thomas, RD	Maj	M1	SCOTLAND	30.06.98
Crichton, Dayle,	2lt	M1	SCOTLAND	11.01.02
D				
Day, Jason,	Lt	M1	LONDON	25.06.99
Doubleday, Iain,	Capt	M1	LONDON	01.04.97
F				
Fielder, David,	Maj	M1	BRISTOL	01.04.99
Figgins, Phil,	Maj	M2	LONDON	01.04.91
Finn, Tristan,	2lt	M1	BRISTOL	11.01.02
Fothergill, Nicholas,	Capt	M1	LONDON	02.11.00
G				
Gardiner, Andrew,	Capt	M1	BRISTOL	03.08.96
Gardner, Andrew,	Lt	M1	MERSEYSIDE	04.04.00
Gibson, Mark,	Capt	M1	MERSEYSIDE	01.02.95
Ginnever, Mark,	Capt	M1	BRISTOL	01.09.01
Guest, Simon,	Capt	M1	LONDON	29.04.93
H				
Halls, Monty,	Capt	M2	BRISTOL	09.11.99
Harker, Andrew,	Capt	M1	TYNE	11.11.01
Hayes, G.M.,	2lt	M1	MERSEYSIDE	09.08.98
Hebron, Bryan,	Capt	M1	TYNE	22.05.90
Hillman, David,	Capt	M1	SCOTLAND	07.01.00
Holt, Andy,	Lt Col	M1	MERSEYSIDE	31.12.93
Hough, Brian, RD	Col	M1	MERSEYSIDE	01.06.97
Hunter, Ben,	Capt	M2	LONDON	15.01.98
Hutchinson, Philip,	Capt	M1	RNR AIR BR VL	
I				
Ilng, John,	Maj	M1	LONDON	01.09.94
J				
Jackson, Fraser,	Capt	M1	SCOTLAND	01.10.92
Jobbins, Paul, GM, OBE, RD* ADC	Col	M2	BRISTOL	28.01.94
K				
Kinninmonth, Craig,	Lt	M1	SCOTLAND	14.09.99
Knox, David,	Maj	M2	TYNE	01.07.99

Name	Rank	Branch	Unit	Seniority
L				
Lacy, Robert,	Act Maj	M1	MERSEYSIDE	01.04.91
Lang, Tom,	Brig	M1	BRISTOL	28.02.95
Langford, Haj,	2lt	M1	LONDON	25.01.00
Lewis, James,	2lt	M1	BRISTOL	07.01.02
Lewis, Robbie,	Capt	M1	BRISTOL	01.07.98
Lindfield, Barry, RD	Maj	M1	MERSEYSIDE	25.10.91
Love, Gavin,	2lt	M1	SCOTLAND	01.07.99
Loynes, Phillip,	Lt Col	M1	MERSEYSIDE	31.12.94
M				
Mannion, Steve,	Maj	M2	LONDON	26.03.96
Martin, Simon,	Capt	M1	LONDON	01.09.01
Mason, Andrew,	Capt	M1	BRISTOL	16.12.96
Mawhood, Christopher,	Maj	M1	MERSEYSIDE	01.09.87
May, Philip,	Act Maj	M1	MERSEYSIDE	02.10.01
McGovern, James,	Lt	M1	SCOTLAND	14.05.01
McLaughlin, Stephen,	Capt	M1	SCOTLAND	18.09.91
Mirtle, Frank, RD	Lt Col	M1	LONDON	01.06.99
Moulton, Frederick,	Maj	M1	BRISTOL	27.04.99
P				
Paul, Thomas, RD	Maj	M1	SCOTLAND	01.06.91
Phillips, Andy,	Capt	M1	BRISTOL	01.09.95
Pike, Andrew,	Lt	M1	TYNE	30.07.95
Pollock, Andrew,	Capt	M1	LONDON	27.03.00
R				
Radford, Barry, MBE	Col	M1	BRISTOL	30.06.94
Reed, Jerry,	Maj	M1	TYNE	01.07.01
Reynolds, Stephen,	Maj		RNR AIR BR VL	01.05.98
Richards, Gavin, RD	Maj	M1	LONDON	16.09.93
Richards, Stephen,	Maj		RNR AIR BR VL	28.04.94
Roberts, John,	Capt	M1	SCOTLAND	22.08.92
Robinson, David, BEM	Maj	M1	TYNE	14.11.95
Rochester, Richard,	Capt	M1	BRISTOL	01.07.95
Rowland, Johnny,	Maj	M1	BRISTOL	25.06.96
Rowlstone, David,	Maj	M1	MERSEYSIDE	01.04.97
S				
Scott, John,	Maj	M1	BRISTOL	01.03.96
Sharp, Gordon,	Maj	M1	LONDON	30.06.98
Smith, Anthony, RD*	Col	M2	BRISTOL	18.07.96
Smith, Fraser,	Act Maj	M1	LONDON	03.08.96
Storrie, Richard,	Capt	M1	BRISTOL	24.04.91
T				
Tayler, Harry,	Act Maj	M1	LONDON	01.07.94
Terry, Stuart,	Maj	M1	BRISTOL	01.02.93
Thompson, Joseph,	Capt	M1	TYNE	07.12.98
Tomkins, Richard,	Maj	M2	BRISTOL	30.06.98
Tonner, Raymond,	Maj	M1	BRISTOL	03.05.95
Travis, Adrian, RD	Maj	M1	LONDON	01.05.96
W				
Waddell, Ian, RD	Capt	M1	SCOTLAND	01.08.91
Watkinson, Neil,	Maj	M1	LONDON	02.09.99
Watt, David,	Maj	M1	BRISTOL	01.08.00
Whitehead, Andrew,	2lt	M1	MERSEYSIDE	01.08.99

Name	Rank	Branch	Unit	Seniority
X				
Xiberras, Maurice,	2lt	M1	MERSEYSIDE	24.05.00

SEA CADET CORPS

Name	Rank	Seniority
A		
Adams, Michael	Lt	05.02.83
Adams, Thomas	Lt	07.09.83
Adey, Kay	3/O W	28.03.04
Agnew, Anthony	Capt RMR	01.11.01
Allam, John	Lt	31.08.87
Allam, Vicki	Lt	18.09.02
Allen, Karen	2/O W	08.10.88
Allen, Leslie	Alt Cdr	01.01.99
Andersen, Kim	Capt RMR	01.11.01
Anderson, Alex	Lt	20.03.00
Anderson, Alison	3/O W	05.07.00
Anderson, Robert	Lt	01.04.99
Annett, Jennifer	2/O W	16.05.96
Appleby, Keith	Lt	21.02.98
Archbold, Dennis	Alt Cdr	11.08.99
Archbold, Theresa	2/O W	20.11.97
Archer, Barry	Lt	08.03.94
Archer, Lynn	2/O W	14.11.96
Argo, James	Lt	30.11.02
Atkins, Doreen	2/O W	08.04.92
Attwood, Anthony	Lt	22.02.87
Avill, Susan	2/O W	01.11.89
Ayers, William	Lt	04.01.02
B		
Bagulay, Alison	3/O W	19.10.02
Bailey, John	Lt	08.04.74
Bailey, Robert	Lt	12.03.91
Bainbridge, Patricia	2/O W	03.11.98
Baker, Michael	Lt RMR	24.05.95
Banks, Paul	Lt	06.06.96
Barber, Anthony	Lt	12.03.91
Barker, David	Lt	21.06.99
Barker, Sandra	2/O W	07.10.98
Barnard, John	Lt	11.04.92
Barnes, Sara-Jane	3/O W	23.11.03
Barr, William	Lt	15.02.00
Barras, Hugh	Lt Cdr	01.08.04
Barron, Edward	Capt RMR	15.10.91
Barrow, Joan	2/O W	05.11.97
Barry, Darren	Mid	31.08.04
Bartlett, Jonathan	Lt Cdr	01.10.04
Bartlweman, Alexander	Lt	25.11.72
Bassett, Gary	Lt	28.10.96
Bayley, George	Lt	24.03.99
Bayliss, John	Lt Cdr	18.02.87
Bayton, Trevor	Lt	25.02.00
Beach, Andrew	Lt	18.07.84
Beal, Peter	Lt	26.03.85
Beddow, Jay	Slt	19.10.02
Bedford, Michael	Lt	01.04.86
Bell, Brian	Lt	25.02.00
Bell, Joseph	Lt	13.09.01
Bell, Veronica	2/O W	29.01.98
Bennett, Angela	2/O W	08.11.00
Bennett, Stephen	Slt	01.12.00
Bentley, Chris	Slt	22.02.04
Benton, Anthony	Capt RMR	01.08.99
Benton, Ruth	1/O W	01.07.04
Beresford-Hartwell, Chritopher	Slt	09.02.04
Bereznyckyj, Nicholas	Maj RMR	01.12.04
Bickle, Margaret	3/O W	05.05.96
Billinghay, Sandra	2/O W	01.07.85
Bilverstone, Brian	Alt Cdr	01.01.01
Bingham, Keith	Alt Cdr	01.01.01
Bingham, Maurice	Lt	01.01.88
Bird, Sarah	3/O W	23.09.01
Birkwood, Geoffrey	Capt RMR	15.10.87
Bishop, Peter	Lt	01.11.95
Blackburn, Alan	Lt	15.06.04
Blackwood, Alan	Lt	09.01.92
Blaker, Carol	1/O W	01.10.81

Name	Rank	Seniority
Blaker, Malcolm	Lt Cdr	03.01.80
Board, Brian	Lt	15.11.91
Boardman, Richard	Lt Cdr	27.04.86
Bolton, David	Slt	05.02.99
Bond, Paul	Lt Cdr	01.01.02
Bonfield, Christopher	Lt	06.11.96
Bonjour, Andre	Lt	27.05.92
Boorman, Nicholas	Lt	12.11.86
Booth, Christina	2/O W	03.12.91
Booth, Dawn	3/O W	13.10.02
Booth, Kenneth	Lt Cdr	02.04.03
Bourne, Jack	Slt	19.01.03
Bowen, Terrence	Lt Cdr	01.01.05
Bowman, Thomas	Alt Cdr	21.11.98
Bowskill, Michael	Lt Cdr	01.07.02
Boyes, Stephen	Lt	25.02.99
Boyne, John	Slt	16.03.94
Bradbury, David	Lt	01.01.88
Bradbury, Jason	Lt	05.05.98
Bradbury, Michelle	3/O W	05.05.02
Bradbury, Scott	Lt Cdr	09.08.04
Bradford, David	Alt Cdr	01.11.00
Bradley, John	Lt	10.09.91
Bramley, Derek	Lt	03.12.88
Bray, John	Lt	07.12.99
Brayford, John	Lt Cdr	02.02.83
Brazier, Colin	1/O W	01.02.03
Brennan-Wright, Alison	3/O W	25.01.04
Bridle, Stephen	Lt	12.11.94
Briggs, Donald	Lt Cdr	01.09.77
Briscoe, Robert	Lt	14.11.96
Britto, Elizabeth	3/O W	31.10.00
Broadbent, Graham	Lt Cdr	01.01.88
Brockwell, Graham	Lt	21.09.90
Brooks, Henry	Lt Cdr	02.05.87
Brotherton, Stephen	Lt	03.07.97
Brown, Alexander	Lt	22.09.86
Brown, Damien	Lt	26.03.02
Brown, David	Lt Cdr	30.03.80
Brown, David	Lt Cdr	02.06.86
Brown, John	Lt Cdr	04.07.78
Brown, Keith	Lt Cdr	01.01.03
Brown, Norman	Lt	01.06.91
Brown, Sylvia	2/O W	01.09.88
Browning, Martin	Lt	02.08.02
Browning, Sharon	2/O W	02.08.02
Browning, Tony	Lt	19.12.93
Broxham, Roy	Lt	21.09.90
Bryant, Charles	Lt	19.02.87
Budden, Paul	Slt	25.01.04
Bullock, Lynn	2/O W	01.12.84
Burbridge, Lee	Lt	08.11.00
Burden, John	Lt Cdr	19.04.78
Burdeyron-Dyster, Ian	Lt Cdr	01.01.88
Burns, Clifford	Lt	01.11.93
Burns, Desmond	Lt	18.02.78
Burns, Philip	Lt Cdr	14.02.03
Burrage, Richard	Lt	25.06.90
Burt, Christopher	Lt	20.08.99
Burton, Andrew	Slt	01.06.04
Burton, Craig	Lt Cdr	01.06.02
Burton, Colin	Lt	07.03.88
Busby, Roger	Lt	19.02.99
Butcher, Colin	Lt	26.11.02
Butler, John	Lt	20.11.97
Butterworth, John	Lt	23.03.87

C

Name	Rank	Seniority
Cadman, John	Lt Cdr	29.04.70
Cadman, Leslie	Lt Cdr	30.06.99
Calvert, Martin	Lt	18.08.92
Campbell, William	Lt	01.01.88
Carney, Robert	Lt	08.08.97
Carr, Barry	Slt	01.12.00
Carr, Leonard	Lt Cdr	19.02.76
Carroll, Paul	Maj RMR	01.05.02
Carter, David	Lt	04.03.92
Cashmore, Matthew	Slt	09.05.04
Caslaw, Paul	Lt	01.08.94
Catterall, Susan	2/O W	20.01.87
Caulfield, Nicola	3/O W	26.05.04
Cea, Franklin	Lt Cdr	01.01.02
Challacombe, Jonathan	Lt Cdr	27.06.90
Challis, Stewart	Slt	09.05.04
Chamberlain, Joanne	2/O W	02.04.99
Chambers, John	Lt Cdr	01.01.88
Chantler, Michael	Lt	01.01.02
Charlton, Adrian	Lt	08.09.86
Chesworth, Howard	Lt	03.12.91
Childs, Paul	Lt	01.06.02
Chinn, John	Lt Cdr	01.01.83
Chittock, Michael	Lt	25.03.94
Chritchlow, Julian	Lt	08.09.95
Cioma, Antoni	Lt Cdr	01.07.90
Clark, Anne	Lt Cdr	01.08.02
Clark, David	Slt	11.05.03
Clark, Ian	Lt Cdr	01.03.92
Clarke, Adam	Lt	17.12.02
Clarke, Leonard	Slt	09.06.94
Clarke, Mark	Lt	03.11.98
Clay, Paul	Slt	05.05.02
Cleworth, Dean	Lt	26.03.02
Clifford, Ian	Lt	11.02.99
Clissold, Mark	Lt	01.04.93
Clyburn, Stephen	Lt RMR	30.12.04
Coast, Philip	Lt Cdr	09.07.90
Coates, Margaret	3/O W	21.01.01
Cockell, Richard	Lt Cdr	04.12.96
Cole, Ain	Slt	08.06.95
Coleman, Keith	Lt	26.11.98
Coles, Thomas	Lt Cdr	19.12.87
Collier, David	Alt	01.09.88
Collins, Ann	2/O W	25.01.91
Collins, David, CENG, MRINA	Lt Cdr	01.01.88
Collins, Raymond	Slt	31.08.94
Collins, Timothy	Slt	27.01.02
Constable, David	Lt	01.03.81
Coombes, Paul	Lt	25.01.94
Cope, Derek	Lt Cdr	16.02.82
Cope, Yvonne	3/O W	01.06.84
Copeland, Phillip	Lt	05.10.97
Copelin, Maureen	1/O W	01.02.05
Corbett, Sandra	2/O W	23.04.99
Cormack, Raymond	Lt	20.11.97
Costerd, David	Lt	08.08.94

Name	Rank	Seniority
Cowell, Christopher	Lt	06.05.87
Cowell, John	Lt	01.04.91
Coxon, John	Lt	14.11.00
Craig, Neil	Lt	01.04.86
Crawley, Stephen	Capt RMR	04.06.95
Creighton, Edward	Lt	26.11.92
Crick, Kenneth	Lt	20.10.92
Critchlow, Jonathan	Lt	05.02.87
Crome, Graeme	Slt	24.03.02
Cross, Stuart	Lt	05.12.97
Crossley, Vincent	Lt Cdr	04.04.77
Crowe, Keith	Slt	25.01.04
Cruse, Gillian	2/O W	16.10.98
Cruse, Malcolm	Lt Cdr	17.10.89
Cummins, Sheila	2/O W	01.11.86
Cumper, Alan	Lt	01.12.98
Curran, Paul	Lt	01.02.88

D

Name	Rank	Seniority
Dale, Philip	Slt	01.03.99
Daly, Martin	Lt	19.11.91
Daly, Shane	Mid	21.11.04
Daniels, Roger	Lt Cdr	14.01.91
Dann, John	Lt	09.07.95
Davies, Bruno	Lt Cdr	15.04.86
Davies, Colin	Lt	18.09.97
Davies, Peter	Lt	19.11.87
Davies, William	Lt Cdr	01.07.04
Davison, Henry	Lt	30.01.00
Daw, Clifford	Lt Cdr	01.01.88
Delderfield, Robin	Lt	01.12.02
Demellweek, Gilbert	Lt	01.01.92
Derbyshire, David	Lt	03.06.92
Devenish, Ian	Capt RMR	12.02.02
Devereux, Edwin	Lt Cdr	31.07.72
Dibben, Michael	Lt	03.11.86
Dibnah, Robert	Lt	05.03.00
Dickinson, Keith	Lt	10.11.85
Dickinson, Simon	Slt	26.09.04
Dixie, Colin	Lt	15.10.00
Dixon, Michael	Slt	19.01.03
Docking, Keith	Lt	07.11.79
Doggart, James	Lt	09.03.01
Doggart, Norman	Lt	01.07.88
Donovan, Terence	Lt	06.11.96
Dorricott, Peter	Lt Cdr	01.10.02
Dowdeswell, Robin	Lt	12.07.86
Dowding, John	Alt Cdr	23.01.73
Dowsett, Mark	Lt	07.06.90
Doyle, Ellen	1/O W	31.03.80
Draper, Philip	Lt	20.12.99
Dryden, Graeme	Lt	26.03.02
Dryden, Stephen	Lt	19.01.81
Dunkeld, Brian	Lt	04.06.97
Dunnings, Mark	Slt	01.09.04
Dyer, Geoffrey	Act Maj RMR	01.05.99
Dyer, Roger	Lt	07.06.97

E

Name	Rank	Seniority
Eaton, Trevor	Lt	01.09.96
Edmondson, Denis	Lt	28.03.01
Edwards, Stuart	Slt	04.06.95
Egan, Terence	Lt	01.01.86
Ellison, Michael	Lt Cdr	01.01.88
English, Michael	Lt Cdr	01.04.88
Erskine, Richard	Lt	20.06.97
Evans, Ivor	Slt	17.07.97
Evans, Janet	1/O W	01.07.94
Evans, John	Lt	28.09.00
Evans, Richard	Lt Cdr	16.09.96
Everard, Gordon	Lt	11.08.89
Every, Paul	Lt	17.04.92
Evison, Christina	3/O W	26.09.04

F

Name	Rank	Seniority
Fairbairn, Rachel	3/O W	22.11.00
Farrell, Michael	Slt	05.05.02
Faulkner, Shelley	3/O W	26.09.04
Fazey, Kate	3/O W	06.05.01
Fenn, Paul	Slt	29.11.99
Fesey, Nicholas	Slt	26.09.04
Fifield, Mark	Lt	14.06.97
Finister, Anthony	Capt RMR	15.08.95
Finlay, David	Lt	21.02.98
Finley, Martin	Capt RMR	27.04.96
Fisher, Barry	Lt Cdr	02.04.03
Fisher, Hazel	Lt Cdr	01.06.02
Fitch, Michael	Lt	28.02.03
Fitzgerald, Terence	Lt RMR	19.08.98
Flaherty, Jeremy	Lt RMR	22.06.03
Fleet, Gordon	Maj RMR	24.06.03
Fleming, Alan	Lt	10.07.93
Fleming, Andrea	2/O W	22.11.02
Fletcher, Carol	1/O W	01.04.80
Fletcher, Jeanette	3/O W	05.02.02
Fletcher, John	Lt Cdr	01.08.87
Fletcher, Malcolm	Lt	20.02.84
Flett, William	Capt RMR	17.11.96
Flynn, John, MBE	Lt Cdr	09.11.75
Ford, Stuart	Lt	02.09.96
Foreman, Waleria	2/O W	20.10.95
Forrest, Norman	Slt	01.10.03
Forrester, Michael	Lt	01.02.79
Forster, Thomas	Lt	19.06.80
Fortune, Colin	Lt	01.10.99
Foster, Andrew	Lt	19.11.91
Foster, Alexandra	2/O W	04.10.96
Foster, Ian	Lt	05.08.85
Foster, James	Lt RMR	09.05.04
Fowler, Alison	2/O W	16.01.97
Fox, Jane	3/O W	27.03.92
Francis, Rebecca	3/O W	01.07.02
Franklin, Patrick	Lt	07.12.02
Freeman, Brian	Lt	16.06.95
Freestone, Andrew	Lt	07.11.95
Fry, Brian	Lt	25.09.78
Fulcher, Diane	2/O W	06.09.94
Fulcher, Graham	Slt	24.04.94
Fuller, Andrew	Lt RMR	20.06.00
Fuller, Keith	Lt Cdr	01.10.01
Fulton, Karen	Lt	20.03.02

Name	Rank	Seniority

G

Name	Rank	Seniority
Gale, Ronnie	Lt	01.11.90
Gallagher, Eamon	Lt	23.06.92
Gambell, Mark	Lt	14.12.96
Gardinerr, John	Lt	04.08.97
Garner, James	Lt Cdr	01.07.01
Garrett, John	Lt Cdr	01.01.02
Garrett, Robert	Slt	06.11.94
Gathergood, John	Lt	17.04.98
Gearing, Robert	Lt Cdr	01.09.77
George, Brian	Lt	01.09.85
Gerald, Anthony	Lt	01.09.98
Gerrard, David	Lt Cdr	01.12.88
Gerrard, Mary	1/O W	01.09.98
Gibson, James	Lt Cdr	25.10.91
Gilbert, John	Lt Cdr	31.12.75
Gilbert, Robin	Maj RMR	01.06.99
Gilbert-Jones, Hilary	3/O W	23.11.03
Gill, Jacqueline	2/O W	28.02.95
Gillard, Terence	Lt Cdr	01.01.95
Gillert, Valerie	2/O W	19.10.91
Gilliam, Kevin	Lt	01.07.93
Gillott, Peter	Slt	23.05.99
Gittens, Susan	Lt	07.12.02
Glanfield, Mark	Lt	06.02.82
Glanville, Barry	Alt Cdr	14.07.00
Glanville, Debra	Lt	23.05.01
Glendinning, Michael	Lt	07.07.99
Goode, Eric	Lt	13.12.97
Goode, Victoria	2/O W	18.11.00
Gooding, Peter	Lt Cdr	01.01.81
Goodleff, Deborah	3/O W	09.05.04
Goodwin, Michael	Lt	08.12.01
Gordon, Andrew	Lt	19.02.89
Gould, Rachael	3/O W	04.12.03
Govier, Adrian	Alt Cdr	27.09.99
Grace, Roger	Lt Cdr	13.07.76
Grainge, Andrew	Lt	09.09.00
Grant, Malcolm	Lt	28.02.95
Gray, Brian	Lt	24.12.87
Green, Cecilia	3/O W	02.12.87
Green, Malcom	Lt	16.08.97
Green, Paul	Lt	01.09.86
Greenaway, Lorna	3/O W	09.05.04
Greenfield, Stephen	Lt	23.05.01
Greenhalgh, Peter, ENGTECH, MINSKSCE, A	Lt	30.04.86
Greer, John	Lt Cdr	01.01.88
Gresty, Stephen	Lt	07.10.98
Grice, Robert	Lt Cdr	05.07.73
Griffin, Paul	Lt	24.10.86
Griffiths, Meirion	Lt Cdr	04.11.88
Griffiths, Nichola	3/O W	05.05.02
Grocott, Alan	Lt	22.05.97
Grogan, Kenneth	Lt	16.09.78
Groves, Richard	Lt Cdr	29.08.86
Guiver, Carl	Maj RMR	01.01.96
Guppy, Graham	Maj RMR	20.06.84

H

Name	Rank	Seniority
Hackett, Clive	Lt Cdr	12.10.90
Hadfield, Philip	Capt RMR	09.04.91
Hagan, George	Slt	29.11.92
Hailwood, Paul	Lt Cdr	01.12.92
Haines, Linda	2/O W	01.11.89
Hale, Ronald	Lt Cdr	23.02.77
Hall, Derek	Lt Cdr	19.01.98
Halliday, Angela	2/O W	20.03.95
Hamilton, Kerry	2/O W	01.05.92
Hanky, Carolyne	2/O W	29.09.99
Hanley, David	Lt	18.11.93
Hanson, David	Lt Cdr	26.07.88
Hanson, Neil	Slt	11.11.01
Hardick, Roger	Lt RMR	05.09.95
Hare, Terence	Lt	17.07.80
Harman, Robert	Lt	04.08.90
Harmer, Robert	Lt	28.10.99
Harris, Brian	Lt Cdr	01.01.02
Harris, Trevor	Lt	05.12.01
Hartwell, Neil	Lt	26.03.02
Harvey, Brian	Slt	01.11.94
Harvey, Lawrence	Lt	27.08.87
Hatchett, Robin	Lt	27.09.86
Hatrick, James	Lt	29.07.93
Hawes, Sandra	2/O W	06.11.95
Hawkins, Leslie	Slt	08.11.99
Hayton, Alan	Lt	20.07.89
Hazeldon, Donald	Slt	28.04.93
Hazzard, Keith	Lt	02.06.98
Headen, Geoffrey	Lt	28.09.00
Healen, Stephen	Lt	05.05.82
Hearl, James	Lt Cdr	01.12.04
Hebbes, Peter	Slt	01.09.91
Helkin, Margaret	Alt Cdr	01.01.01
Hender, Robert	Slt	10.12.86
Henwood, Martin	Lt Cdr	21.10.80
Herbert, Michael	Alt Cdr	01.01.00
Hercock, Norman	Lt	03.11.93
Hewitt, Graham	Lt Cdr	07.04.92
Hide, Brenda	2/O W	17.05.84
Hill, Anthony	Slt	26.06.85
Hill, Ian	Alt	15.03.89
Hill, John	Lt	01.08.75
Hill, Monica	2/O W	18.11.93
Hill, Reginald	Lt Cdr	01.03.88
Hillier, Barbara	Lt	04.09.03
Hinchcliffe, Alan	Slt	28.09.03
Hinds, Michael	Lt	07.04.96
Hithersay, John	Lt	28.10.78
Hoey, David	Lt	10.11.94
Holland, Donald	Lt	15.09.84
Holliday, Anthony	Alt Cdr	01.01.01
Hollywell, Gary	Alt Cdr	01.05.99
Holt, Martin	Alt Cdr	01.01.01
Holt, Wendy	2/O W	29.11.97
Horne, Allan	Lt	16.09.89
Horner, John	Lt Cdr	16.09.92
Horner, Lynda	3/O W	07.08.88
Houlden, Wendy	2/O W	30.09.01
Howie, Thomas	Lt Cdr	01.11.88
Hoyle, Keith	Slt	01.10.86
Hudson, Christopher	Slt	29.11.95
Hughes, Thomas	Lt Cdr	14.09.83
Hulonce, Michael	Lt Cdr	12.03.82

Name	Rank	Seniority
Hunter, Lesley	2/O W	05.05.98
Hunter, Phillip	Lt	01.12.02
Hurst, Paul	Lt	06.06.03
Hurst, Thomas	Lt Cdr	12.07.85
Hutchings, Andrew	Lt	25.11.00
Huyton, Gillian	2/O W	07.10.98

I

Name	Rank	Seniority
Iggo, David	Lt	26.01.96
Ingahm, Mark	Slt	22.11.00
Ingham, Anthony	Slt	24.02.99
Ingham, David	Lt Cdr	28.04.98
Ingram, Thomas	Lt	27.01.03
Izzard, Michael	Lt	25.06.98

J

Name	Rank	Seniority
Jackson, Graeme	Lt	18.09.94
Jaconelli, Nicholas	Lt	12.09.00
James, George	Lt	22.08.78
James, Robert	Lt Cdr	01.01.95
Janner-Burgess, Mark	Slt	21.01.01
Jardine, Roderick	Lt	05.10.95
Jeffery, Stephen	Lt	14.06.92
Jeffrey, Andrew	Slt	30.08.94
Jehan, Paula	3/O W	19.05.91
Jenkins, Ian	Capt RMR	01.09.91
Jenkins, Terence	Slt	06.11.88
Jennings, William	Lt	19.10.84
Johns, Nicholas	Lt	08.04.92
Johnson, Laurence	Lt Cdr	02.08.87
Johnson-Paul, David	Lt	18.04.92
Johnston, Peter	Lt	02.11.84
Johnstone, James	Lt Cdr	01.01.97
Jones, Christopher	Alt Cdr	11.08.99
Jones, Dorothy	2/O W	22.10.94
Jones, Kelvin	Lt	06.05.92
Jones, Lily	2/O W	09.04.91
Jones, Margaret	1/O W	01.07.04
Jones, Mark	Lt	06.11.96
Jones, Nicholas	Mid	26.09.04
Jones, Neil	Lt	03.01.96
Jones, Neil	Lt	24.03.94
Jones, Philip	Slt	23.09.01
Jones, Peter	Lt Cdr	01.02.05
Jones, Trevor	Lt	10.03.00
Jordan, Roger	Lt	22.06.87
Jordan, Sheila	2/O W	26.07.90
Jubb, Elizabeth	3/O W	03.11.02
Juniper, James	Lt RMR	25.01.04
Juniper, Stephanie	3/O W	11.11.01
Jupe, Paul	Slt	02.03.86
Justice, David	Lt	07.02.84

K

Name	Rank	Seniority
Kay, Anne	3/O W	29.05.01
Kaye, Malcolm	Lt	01.11.89
Kearsey, Peter	Slt	01.12.04
Keenan, Robert	Alt Cdr	01.04.91
Keery, Neil	Lt	18.05.01
Keery, William	Lt Cdr	01.01.83
Kemmis Betty, Mark	Lt Cdr	05.05.87
Kemp, David	Lt	23.09.94
Kennedy, Ivan	Lt	16.05.87
Kenrick, Peter	Lt	23.11.94
Kerwin, James	Lt	09.05.97
Kilbey, Susan	3/O W	16.03.03
Killick, Peter	Lt	09.10.85
King, Leslie	Lt Cdr	15.03.98
Kinghorn, Jason	Lt	14.04.98
Knight, Robert	Lt	15.02.00
Kristansen, Karen	2/O W	14.02.98
Kyle, Raymond	Slt	01.11.90

L

Name	Rank	Seniority
Lamkin, John	Lt	15.02.96
Lampert, Brian	Lt Cdr	11.01.85
Lampert, Mark	Slt	25.01.04
Lampert, Susan	2/O W	01.11.89
Lane, John	Lt	31.05.91
Larsen, Colin	Lt	09.05.97
Lawes, Sonia	2/O W	08.03.94
Lawrence, Barrie	Lt	04.10.92
Lawrence, Kevin	Lt	01.05.01
Lea, Garry	Slt	05.05.99
Leatherbarrow, Ronald	Lt	29.03.95
Lee, David	Lt Cdr	31.03.79
Lees, Martin	Slt	19.09.92
Legget, Colin	Slt	19.08.04
Lentell, Heather	2/O W	31.07.01
Lentle, Robert	Lt	01.11.90
Leslie, Harry	Slt	03.03.91
Lewis, Clifford	Lt	04.11.92
Lewis, Christopher	Lt Cdr	01.06.78
Lewis, David	Lt	14.04.98
Lewis, Eleanor	2/O W	23.11.94
Lewis, John	Capt RMR	17.11.98
Lewis, Peter	Lt Cdr	01.01.04
Lewis, Walter	Lt	06.05.79
Light, Michael	Slt	28.02.02
Lincoln, David	Lt	01.01.96
Lincoln, John	Lt Cdr	02.05.02
Lister, Richard	Slt	27.01.02
Lloyd, Terence	Lt	01.01.04
Lock, Keith	Slt	01.12.92
Locke, David	Lt Cdr	01.01.05
Login, Brenda	Lt Cdr	01.10.02
Login, Derek	Lt Cdr	12.12.88
Long, Adam	Lt	01.04.97
Lonsdale, Bryan	Lt Cdr	01.09.90
Lorimer, Deirdre	2/O W	24.06.98
Louch, Stephen	Slt	21.11.04
Louden, Elizabeth	3/O W	01.07.90
Loveridge, Anthony	Lt Cdr	01.12.89
Low, William	Slt	05.04.94
Lowe, David	Lt	23.07.77
Lowe, Stuart	Maj RMR	21.04.02
Lucas, Peter	Lt	24.03.99
Luckman, Bruce	Lt	01.10.92
Lumley, Margaret	2/O W	14.06.97
Luxton, Phillip	Lt	05.11.00
Luxton, Peter	Lt Cdr	20.05.69
Lyster, Cody	Slt	22.06.03

Name	Rank	Seniority

M

Name	Rank	Seniority
MacAusland, Iain	Alt Cdr	01.09.98
MacCallum, James	Lt	18.01.98
MacDonald, Peter	Lt	07.11.91
Macey, Mark	Lt Cdr	01.09.03
Machin, Ian	Act Maj RMR	01.08.96
MacIver, Lynn	2/O W	19.04.96
MacKay, Charles	Slt	01.12.97
MacKay, David	Lt	01.07.84
MacKinlay, Colin	Lt	08.04.92
MacLean, Donald	Lt	28.03.90
MacLennan, Robert	Slt	21.11.04
Madden, Brian	Lt Cdr	01.11.88
Magnall, Edward	Lt Cdr	27.01.81
Mahoney-Brown, Jane	1/O W	01.01.01
Maiden, Philip	Slt	27.01.02
Main, Paul	Lt	12.03.91
Mair, Brian	Lt Cdr	01.01.02
Makepeace, Toby	Slt	11.05.03
Mannough, John	Lt	14.05.90
Mapstone, Arthur	Slt	25.02.02
Marson, Victoria	1/O W	01.02.05
Martin, John	Lt Cdr	01.01.87
Martin, Kevin	Lt	14.03.94
Mason, Edward	Lt Cdr	18.11.69
Mathers, David	Lt	15.02.96
Matson, Christopher	Lt	16.11.97
Mattey, Barry	Lt Cdr	04.02.91
Matthews, Christopher	Lt Cdr	01.10.03
Matthews, John	Lt	19.06.95
Matthews, Philip	Lt Cdr	01.02.89
Matthews, Ronald	Lt	14.01.97
Maynard, Lisa	2/O W	20.03.96
Maynard, Robert	Lt Cdr	21.03.76
McAvady, Andrew	Lt	12.06.98
McAvennie, John	Lt	03.02.90
McAvoy, William	Lt	17.12.79
McBride, Alexander	Lt RMR	03.09.02
McClements, George	Capt RMR	01.01.86
McCune, Barry	Lt	04.06.88
McDonald, Alexander	Slt	01.09.87
McDonald, Peter	Lt	29.06.92
McIntyre, Rosamund	1/O W	11.01.80
McKaig, Alexander	Lt	08.01.87
McKee, David	Lt Cdr	01.04.88
McKenna, Paul	Lt	14.03.96
McKeown, Glenda	2/O W	24.04.96
McLaren, George	Slt	02.12.95
McMaster, George	Lt	06.10.88
McVinnie, Elizabeth	2/O W	06.11.00
Meadows, Paul	Lt	02.02.02
Meek, Caroline	3/O W	06.05.01
Meikle, John	Lt RMR	06.05.01
Meldon, Michael	Lt Cdr	01.03.92
Menhams, Angela	2/O W	02.12.90
Milby, Stuart	Lt Cdr	27.07.93
Milligan, Kevin	Lt	10.06.00
Milligan, Victoria	2/O W	01.05.98
Mills, William	Lt	23.06.93
Minett, Clive	Maj RMR	23.01.05
Mison, Michael	Lt Cdr	25.12.77
Mitchell, Barry	Slt	19.01.03
Mitchell, David	Lt	15.05.98
Mitchell, Jane	2/O W	01.06.00
Mitchell, Ray	Lt Cdr	01.01.04
Mohammed, Barbara	2/O W	07.12.83
Mohammed, John	Lt Cdr	09.09.87
Moir, Brian	Lt	18.09.95
Money, Alan	Lt	25.03.94
Monkcom, Susan	2/O W	01.01.98
Mons-White, Margaret	2/O W	01.09.92
Moody, Roger	Lt Cdr	01.04.74
Moore, Brian	Slt	23.11.03
Moore, Robert	Alt Cdr	01.01.01
Morgan, John	Lt	10.02.90
Morgan, Norman	Lt Cdr	23.07.04
Morgan, Stephen	Lt	13.04.96
Morley, Andrew	Lt	07.10.98
Morley, Carol	2/O W	16.11.01
Morley, Michael	Lt	16.03.88
Morrin, Kevin	Lt	05.04.97
Morris, Angela	3/O W	01.07.02
Morton, Rita	2/O W	13.05.98
Mould, Peter	Lt Cdr	01.08.78
Moulton, Nicholas	Alt Cdr	21.11.98
Mountier, Peter	Lt	19.11.90
Muggeridge, Edwin	Lt	06.05.84
Mugridge, Toni	Lt	15.02.02
Mullin, Anna	3/O W	23.11.03
Mullin, William	Lt	15.11.86
Munro, Gordon	Slt	20.03.91
Murdock, Gordon	Lt Cdr	11.02.76
Murphy, William	Slt	24.05.99
Murray, Donald	Lt	01.05.93
Musselwhite, Ruth	Lt	19.12.02

N

Name	Rank	Seniority
N/a, John	Lt	15.10.71
Newman, Raymond	Lt	24.10.82
Newton, Percy	Slt	28.09.03
Nice, David	Lt	01.01.88
Nicholls, David	Lt	11.09.98
Nichols, David	Slt	15.07.99
Nixon, Joseph	Lt	30.06.84
Nixon, James	Slt	01.01.04
Norman, David	Lt	01.04.86
Norman, John	Lt Cdr	01.08.87
Norris, Anthony	Lt Cdr	20.12.92
Norris, Norman	Lt	01.04.92

O

Name	Rank	Seniority
O' Donnell, Wendy	3/O W	01.02.05
O'Brien, Gary	Lt	30.01.96
O'Connor, Brian	Lt	30.07.85
O'Donnell, Adrian	Lt	06.11.90
O'Donnell, Dominic	Lt	01.12.83
O'Donoghue, Amanda	3/O W	23.11.03
O'Hagan, William	Lt	19.05.86
O'Keefe, Richard	Lt Cdr	29.05.02
O'Neill, Dawn	2/O W	02.12.94
O'Shaughnessy, Helen	3/O W	22.05.95
Oglesby, Simon	Slt	08.12.00
Oldcorn, Geoffrey	Lt	03.11.93

Name	Rank	Seniority
Orfila, Andrew	Lt	11.10.02
Orr, Robert	Lt	26.03.02
Orton, Adrian	Capt RMR	01.07.99
Osborne, Brian	Lt	26.10.83
Osborne, Dawn	2/O W	20.04.83
Osborne, James	Lt Cdr	01.10.74
Owen, William	Lt	05.06.96
Owens, Christopher	Lt	30.05.97

P

Name	Rank	Seniority
Packwood, Shelagh	1/O W	01.12.86
Page, Helen	2/O W	01.10.90
Painter, Lorretta	2/O W	28.01.93
Painting, Peter	Lt	05.10.71
Paling, John	Alt Cdr	01.10.96
Palmer, Alan	Capt RMR	20.11.01
Palmer, Robert	Lt	18.11.93
Palmer, Richard	Lt	23.09.97
Parker, Derek	Alt Cdr	01.06.90
Parker, Simon	Lt Cdr	01.10.02
Parks, Edwin	Lt Cdr	01.01.04
Parks, Martyn	Lt	01.05.99
Parr, Faye	3/O W	27.01.04
Parr, Geoffrey	Lt	28.11.92
Parris, Stephen	Capt RMR	30.01.99
Parry, Michael	Lt	01.06.84
Pascoe, William	Lt	26.07.84
Paterson, Gordon	Alt Cdr	01.12.99
Patterson, Phillip	Lt Cdr	01.12.02
Patterson, Paul	Lt	01.07.00
Paul, Patrick	Slt	12.08.99
Payne, David	Lt	26.11.98
Payne, Derek	Alt Cdr	01.01.01
Payne, David	Lt	18.03.00
Pearce, Peter	Lt	01.06.98
Pearson, James	Lt	09.03.93
Penny, Carl	Lt RMR	04.05.00
Perkins, Jonathon	Lt	09.03.03
Perkins, Kevin	Lt	05.11.97
Perry, Kelly	3/O W	26.09.04
Perry, Paul	Lt Cdr	04.02.94
Perryman, Bowen	Mid	01.09.04
Peters, Kenneth	Lt	15.06.00
Pether, Phillip	Lt	07.07.65
Pettifer, Frank	Lt Cdr	01.01.64
Pettit, Nicholas	Lt	09.03.99
Pettman, Lee	Mid	01.09.04
Phillips, John	Lt	17.03.82
Phillips, Paul	Lt	06.08.98
Philpot, David	Lt RMR	09.02.04
Pickering, Jean	2/O W	03.07.90
Picton, Janet	1/O W	18.09.87
Piercy, Peter	Lt Cdr	25.10.86
Pike, John	Lt	31.05.96
Plummer, Thomas	Lt	25.04.91
Pocock, Stewart	Lt Cdr	01.07.88
Pogson, Godfrey	Lt Cdr	21.05.87
Poke, Claire	2/O W	14.06.97
Poke, David	Maj RMR	01.06.02
Pope, Darren	Lt	22.04.93
Porter, John	Lt Cdr	01.01.02
Postill, John	Lt RMR	19.01.99
Poth, Anthony	Lt Cdr	17.03.86
Pow, David	Lt	06.10.92
Powell, Robert	Capt RMR	24.09.01
Power, Fiona	2/O W	05.03.99
Pownall, Edwin	Slt	25.10.03
Precious, Jason	Slt	17.05.02
Preston, Frank	Slt	01.06.94
Priest, Derek	Slt	21.11.04
Priestley, Gary	Lt	30.11.02
Prince, Ramon	Slt	13.04.97
Pritchard, Carol	2/O W	06.09.94
Pritchard, David	Alt Cdr	01.01.95
Pugh, Heather	1/O W	28.04.98
Puxty, Peter	Lt Cdr	01.01.88

R

Name	Rank	Seniority
Radcliffe, Brian	Lt Cdr	15.01.89
Ramsay, Thomas	Lt Cdr	01.02.89
Rawcliffe, Michael	Lt	17.04.98
Rawlinson, Martin	Lt	01.03.98
Rayson, Trevor	Alt Cdr	01.01.01
Read, Christopher	Slt	21.01.01
Read, Clare	3/O W	13.10.02
Read, Jodie	3/O W	28.06.03
Redhead, Gavin	Lt	28.09.00
Redhead, Julie	Lt	13.06.02
Rees, Andrew	Lt	01.07.87
Reeve, John	Lt	19.11.91
Reeves, Angela	Alt Cdr	01.01.01
Reeves, Mark	Lt	11.05.01
Regan, Paul	Maj RMR	01.10.96
Regler, Stanley	Lt	07.12.82
Reid, Jeffery	Lt	04.11.03
Reid, Morag	Lt	01.09.03
Rhind, Robert	Lt	22.03.90
Richards, Philip	Lt	12.04.01
Richings, David	Lt	15.04.99
Ridgway, Paul	Alt Cdr	21.02.00
Rimmer, Kevin	Lt	30.03.94
Roaf, Alistair	Slt	07.06.96
Robbins, Allan	Lt Cdr	01.10.01
Roberts, Evphemia	Lt Cdr	27.11.03
Roberts, Ronald	Lt Cdr	06.01.86
Robinson, Eric	Lt	18.03.99
Robinson, Paul	Lt	20.07.99
Rock, William	Lt	12.11.00
Rockey, David	Slt	11.03.98
Rodgers, Brian	Slt	28.09.03
Rodgers, Kevin	Slt	11.05.03
Rogan, Christopher	Slt	23.03.00
Rogers, Carol	3/O W	21.11.04
Rogers, Neil	Lt	30.09.00
Rogers, Sallyanne	2/O W	22.11.97
Rollins, Linda	2/O W	03.11.98
Rooney, Frederick	Slt	14.11.96
Roots, Joseph	Lt	21.09.01
Ross, David	Lt	13.10.90
Ross, Malcoln	Lt	09.05.95
Rowe, Raymond	Lt	02.04.99
Rowles, David	Lt Cdr	01.01.88
Rummins, Ann	2/O W	01.01.88
Rundle, Trevor	Lt	26.12.87

Name	Rank	Seniority
Rushton, Steven	Lt	15.03.95
Russell, Audrey	2/O W	01.03.99
Russell, John	Lt	01.11.89
Rutter, Thomas	Lt	30.10.87
Rycroft, Paul	Lt Cdr	08.09.89
Ryder, Jeffrey	Slt	13.10.02
Ryder, Ruth	2/O W	03.11.93

S

Name	Rank	Seniority
Salisbury, Linda	2/O W	02.04.99
Salveson, Anthony	Lt Cdr	01.03.79
Sanders, Christopher	Slt	13.10.02
Saunders, Donald	Lt	28.08.94
Saupe, Peter	Lt	01.01.88
Scanlan, John	Lt	31.03.89
Scarratt, Leslie	Lt RMR	02.09.98
Schofield, George	Slt	01.04.88
Scholes, David	Capt RMR	13.03.91
Scholes, Stephen	Capt RMR	01.07.01
Scott, Francis	Lt Cdr	01.04.92
Scott, Gordon	Lt Cdr	01.12.98
Scourfield, Royston	Lt	01.06.91
Scrivens, Stuart	Lt	03.12.91
Seabury, Paul	Lt	16.08.97
Searles, Andrew	Lt	09.11.96
Sedgwick, Mark	Lt	03.06.00
Seggie, Andrew	Slt	26.06.04
Servis, Thomas	Lt	20.08.85
Shakespeare, William	Lt Cdr	01.04.99
Sharp, Terence	Lt Cdr	08.09.80
Shaw, David	Lt	01.03.88
Shaw, Gail	2/O W	26.10.83
Shaw, Geoff	Lt Cdr	02.12.03
Shaw, James	Lt	14.12.95
Shelton, Clive	Lt Cdr	24.04.98
Shelton, Julie	2/O W	07.10.89
Shepherd, Carl	Lt RMR	05.05.02
Sherwin, Peter	Lt Cdr	01.10.77
Shiel, Garry	Lt	18.03.90
Shiels, Robert	Lt Cdr	08.09.76
Shone, Michael	Lt	15.06.00
Short, Keith	Lt Cdr	06.04.76
Shuttleworth, Tye	Slt	19.10.01
Sickelmore, Barry	Alt Cdr	05.04.99
Sidney, Gerald	Maj RMR	01.01.96
Sigley, Dermid	Lt	01.05.89
Sigley, June	3/O W	21.06.96
Silver, Barry-John	Slt	13.10.02
Silverthorne, Robert	Lt	31.10.91
Simister, Alan	Lt	23.12.98
Simmons, Melvyn	Lt	10.04.93
Simpson, Alfred	Lt Cdr	01.02.74
Simpson, Leonard	Slt	01.05.93
Simpson, Timothy	Lt	01.02.95
Sinden, Daniel	Lt	26.03.02
Skingle, Stephen	Lt	05.05.03
Sloan, Michael	Slt	19.11.02
Smales, Geoffrey	Lt Cdr	01.01.97
Smart, Claude	Lt Cdr	26.04.79
Smedley, Monty	Slt	21.08.04
Smith, Adrian	Lt	21.08.92
Smith, Alan	Capt RMR	02.03.02
Smith, Alan	Slt	01.01.88
Smith, Anthony	Lt	14.09.04
Smith, Graham	Lt	05.04.97
Smith, John	Slt	12.11.98
Smith, James	Lt	09.05.94
Smith, Victoria	1/O W	01.04.80
Soilleux, Peter	Lt	01.09.02
Spear, Keith	Slt	01.04.02
Speariett, Gail	1/O W	16.11.91
Spencer, Allan	Lt	15.10.93
Spencer, Edward	Lt	09.09.76
Spicer, David	Lt	23.02.87
Spicer, Janice	2/O W	10.11.72
Spink, James	Lt	01.09.83
Spong, Victor	Lt Cdr	04.02.02
Sprogis, Alfred	Lt	22.04.94
Squires, John	Lt	06.12.86
Squirrell, Daren	Slt	21.01.01
Standen, Roy	Lt Cdr	31.12.67
Stanier, Tina	Lt RMR	23.09.01
Stanley, Trevor	Lt	21.04.03
Steele, Tommy	Lt	23.11.98
Steggall, Mark	Lt	19.11.91
Steggall, Stephen	Lt	19.05.87
Stevens, Alan	Lt Cdr	04.11.02
Stevenson, Ian	Lt	31.03.87
Stewart, James	Lt	22.05.79
Stewart, Patrick	Lt Cdr	27.07.83
Stewart, Rosaleen	3/O W	01.10.90
Stirrup, William	Lt	18.06.62
Stone, Kathleen	3/O W	21.11.04
Stone, Terrence	Lt	26.02.91
Storey, Hugh	Lt RMR	27.10.01
Stott, Barry	Lt	19.01.96
Straderick, Barbara	2/O W	10.11.95
Street, Brenda	2/O W	14.04.77
Street, Steven	Lt	14.04.99
Strutt, Dupre	Lt Cdr	28.01.98
Stubbs, Edward	Lt	18.11.93
Styles, Marc	Slt	21.11.04
Summers, Andrew	Lt	22.05.87
Sumner, Robert	Lt	06.12.99
Sutherland, Shane	Lt	01.07.94
Sutton, Philippa	2/O W	23.01.04
Svendsen, Peter	Lt Cdr	01.05.02
Swan, Gordon	Lt Cdr	24.01.02
Swarbrick, David	Lt	16.06.83
Sydes, Daniel	Capt RMR	21.09.01

T

Name	Rank	Seniority
Tait, Graham	Lt	12.05.97
Tait, Kevin	Lt	21.03.02
Tanner, Roland	Lt Cdr	21.07.87
Tannock, Andrew	Maj RMR	01.12.04
Tansley, Loreley	3/O W	01.03.04
Tapp, Maria	2/O W	23.10.95
Taylor, Brian	Capt RMR	01.07.91
Taylor, Christopher	Lt	09.02.79
Taylor, Duncan	Lt	22.11.97
Taylor, Fay	3/O W	21.01.01
Teare, Glenys	2/O W	26.08.88
Tebby, Alan	Slt	23.05.99

Name	Rank	Seniority
Tebby, Christine	2/O W	05.09.89
Temple, Edward, MBE	Lt Cdr	01.01.88
Thackery, Richard	Lt	02.03.96
Theobald, Robert	Lt	10.11.87
Theobald, Wendy	A1/O W	01.01.96
Thickett, David	Slt	11.05.03
Thomas, Alan	Lt	14.04.98
Thomas, Derek	Lt	10.10.94
Thomas, Jacqueline	2/O W	31.05.93
Thomas, Michael	Lt	19.07.80
Thomas, Roderick	Lt	26.11.92
Thomas, Valerie	2/O W	22.11.97
Thomas, William	Lt	01.01.82
Thompson, Andrew	Lt	02.08.02
Thompson, John	2/O W	01.03.80
Thompson, Philip	Lt	24.02.00
Thomson, Andrew	Lt	07.04.95
Thomson, Robert	Lt	17.03.71
Thorne, Christopher	Lt	13.07.90
Thornton, Peter	Lt	24.11.79
Timothy, Emile	Maj RMR	20.04.92
Titley, John	Lt	04.07.93
Tomlinson, Alan	Lt	27.10.00
Totty, Paul	Maj RMR	22.03.96
Touhey, Martin	Lt	15.07.87
Townsend, Graham	Lt	01.05.98
Townsend, Steven	Slt	30.03.03
Trahair, Estelle	2/O W	24.04.96
Tranter, Gary	Lt Cdr	01.03.87
Trojan, Margaret	Alt	30.11.99
Trott, Peter	Lt Cdr	02.06.83
Truelove, Gary	Lt Cdr	01.07.04
Truscott, Gary	Lt Cdr	01.01.96
Tubman, Vernon	Slt	18.10.91
Tucker, Neil	Lt	03.11.95
Turner, Ian	Lt	04.11.97
Tuson, Barry	Slt	24.03.97
Tuson, Denise	2/O W	30.03.94
Tweed, Alan	Lt	06.01.93
Tyrrell, Richard	Lt Cdr	19.06.91
Tyson, Michael	Lt	22.03.83

U

Name	Rank	Seniority
Ulrich, Geoffrey	Lt Cdr	27.11.82
Ulrich, Jacquelyn	2/O W	12.03.91
Unsworth, John	Slt	11.05.03
Unwin, Mark	Lt	24.02.01
Urquhart, John	Lt	05.05.97
Utting, Joseph	Lt	21.09.01

V

Name	Rank	Seniority
Vanns, Jonathan	Lt	04.05.92
Vaughan, Jeffery	Lt	10.11.95
Vila, Nina	Lt	08.11.01
Vokes, Simon	Slt	27.01.02

W

Name	Rank	Seniority
Waddleton, Michaél	Lt	09.04.79
Walker, Keith	Lt	05.02.88
Walsh, Brian	Lt RMR	11.05.03
Walsh, Edward	Lt Cdr	01.06.82
Walsh, Maxwell	Lt Cdr	01.03.91
Ward, Eleanore	3/O W	01.06.03
Ward, John	Lt Cdr	01.10.03
Ward, Lesley	2/O W	12.05.95
Ward, Simon	Lt RMR	22.11.00
Waring, Peter	Lt	14.11.96
Warters, David	Slt	10.07.01
Warwick, Lynne	3/O W	23.11.03
Warwick, Stephen	Lt	12.03.98
Waters, Alan	Lt Cdr	01.01.81
Waters, Scott	Lt	21.04.94
Watkins, Colin	Lt Cdr	17.11.03
Watson, Adrian	Slt	06.05.01
Watson, Sheila	2/O W	04.02.00
Watterson, Jeanette	2/O W	26.04.82
Watts, Keith	Slt	26.08.02
Watts, Reginald	Lt Cdr	27.10.91
Waugh, John	Lt	06.09.78
Waylett, Graham	Alt Cdr	01.04.01
Waylett, Matthew	Slt	28.06.03
Webb, Colin	Lt	17.11.95
Webb, John	Lt Cdr	09.11.85
Webster, John	Lt Cdr	14.12.90
Weightman, Eric	Alt Cdr	01.07.00
Welsh, John	Lt	07.11.93
Welsh, Michelle	2/O W	07.11.95
Weobley, Malcolm	Maj RMR	28.08.86
Weston, Mark	Lt	07.11.95
Westover, Robert	Lt	01.04.74
Wheatley, Noel	Lt Cdr	01.01.95
Wheeler, Michael	Lt	22.03.75
White, David	Lt	29.11.02
White, Robert	Lt	29.10.99
White, William	Slt	08.12.00
Whitehead, William	Maj RMR	10.12.02
Whitehouse, Alan	Lt	16.02.90
Whiteman, Mark	Lt	01.01.88
Whitley, Glenda	2/O W	08.05.85
Whitley, Roger	Lt	14.04.99
Whorwood, Julia	2/O W	07.05.97
Wilde, James	Slt	01.03.93
Wilkinson, Christopher	Lt Cdr	01.06.02
Wilkinson Truswell, Jacqueline	3/O W	03.11.02
Wilks, Stephen	Lt	27.07.01
Willett, Marion	2/O W	21.12.86
Williams, Alan	Lt Cdr	01.05.84
Williams, Derek	Lt	13.12.88
Williams, David	Lt	15.03.00
Williams, Deborah	2/O W	04.11.92
Williams, David	Slt	26.03.00
Williams, Susan	Lt	26.03.02
Williams, Suzanne	2/O W	01.03.80
Williamson, William	Lt Cdr	21.04.72
Wilson, David	Lt Cdr	01.09.03
Wilson, Edward	Slt	08.05.89
Wilson, Ethel	2/O W	01.11.98
Wilson, George	Lt	05.06.96
Wilson, George	Lt	01.11.95
Wilson, Ian	Lt Cdr	01.08.02
Wilson, William	Lt	04.11.85
Winn, Julie	3/O W	28.09.98
Wood, Norman	Lt Cdr	01.03.90

Name	Rank	Seniority
Woodage, Alan	Lt	21.10.89
Woodcock, Anthony	Lt Cdr	28.06.84
Woods, Edward	Lt Cdr	01.11.02
Woodward, Stewart	Lt Cdr	14.11.84
Wooldridge, Donald	Lt	03.02.94
Woolgar, Victor	Lt Cdr	01.01.88
Worrall, Ian	Capt RMR	01.07.99
Wylie, William	Lt Cdr	05.12.83
Wynne, David	Lt	21.04.93

Y

Name	Rank	Seniority
Yates, Daniel	Slt	11.05.03
Yorke, Barrie	Lt	01.07.87

Z

Name	Rank	Seniority
Zaccarini, Jason	Lt	26.03.02

COMBINED CADET FORCE

Name	Rank	Date of Appointment	School/College
A			
Adams, Mark	Lt	08/04/99	Churchers
Adams, Steven	A/SLt	01/09/04	Christs College
Adamson, Siobhan	A/SLt	12/12/04	Dollar
Aldridge, Mark	Lt	01/09/92	Trinity
Allan, Richard	A/SLt	17/03/02	St Johns
Allcock, Simon	SLt	15/03/04	Charterhouse
Allen, Brian	SLt	28/02/84	Elizabeth College
Allen, Patrick	A/SLt	08/11/04	Scarborough
Anderson, Laurence	A/SLt	01/04/05	Reigate
Anderson, Robyn	A/SLt	17/09/03	RGS Lancaster
Andrews, Jacqueline	Lt	24/08/93	Re-Call
Armitage, David	SLt	01/10/98	City Of London
Armstrong, Ivan	Lt Cdr	01/09/90	Bangor
Ashfield, David	SLt	10/09/03	King Edward
Ashfield, Noel	SLt	28/11/99	Campbell
Ashton, Stephanie	SLt	13/06/01	Re-Call
Ayers, William	Lt Cdr	06/07/00	HQCCF Re-Call
B			
Baggaley, James	Lt	24/03/03	Ruthin
Bailey, Nicholas	Lt	05/09/00	HQCCF Re-Call
Baker, Piers	Lt	01/01/86	Re-Call
Barker, Janet	Lt	05/05/87	Re-Call
Barlow, Katrina	Lt	10/11/00	Re-Call
Barrett, Rachel	SLt	19/07/02	Re-Call
Barton, Joanne	SLt	01/09/02	Trinity
Bassett, Paul	Lt	12/07/02	Re-Call
Batchelder , Mark	Lt	04/03/99	Berkhamstead
Bate, Christopher	Lt Cdr	08/11/04	Reading Blue Coat
Bateson, Victoria	A/SLt	01/08/04	Oundle
Battison, Clare	SLt	17/09/03	Leys
Beavon, Julie	SLt	01/11/02	Re-Call
Belfield, Peter	2nd Lt RM	01/10/04	Kings Taunton
Bell, Mark	SLt	01/10/03	RGS Newcastle
Benson, Leisle	SLt	01/01/01	Re-Call
Benson, Roger	Lt	07/11/85	Glenalmond
Birch, James	A/SLt	15/08/04	Uppingham
Bird, Jason	Lt	31/07/99	Trinity
Bland, Martin	A/SLt	14/12/04	Ruthin
Bolam, Laura	A/SLt	25/03/01	Langley
Bone, Robert	SLt	27/02/00	Mill Hill
Borking, Graham	Lt	09/01/90	Queen Victoria
Botterill, Marc	Lt	01/04/00	HQCCF Re-Call
Boughton, Charles	SLt	12/09/94	Royal Hospital
Bowen-Walker, Peter	Lt	18/11/01	Perse
Bowles, Michael	Lt	29/10/82	King William
Bownes, Thomas	Lt	19/09/01	Re-Call
Brazier, Colin	Lt Cdr	16/06/97	HQCCF Re-Call
Brazier, Lynda	SLt	01/06/03	Re-Call
Brett, Alison	A/SLt	15/08/04	Kings Wimbledon
Bridgeman, Keith	Cdr	19/06/84	MTS Northwood
Brierley, Louise	Lt	12/09/90	Prior Park
Brittain, Norman	Lt	30/11/72	Oundle
Brooke, Frank	Lt	15/08/04	Ellesmere
Brooks, John	Lt Cdr	01/09/90	St Peters
Brown, Anthony	Cdr	28/09/83	Re-Call
Brown, Thomas	SLt	02/04/01	Arnold
Browne, Niall	SLt	12/10/98	Uppingham
Bryant, Charles	SLt	01/04/03	St Lawrence
Bryant, Marion	Lt	01/04/00	Bournemouth
Burden, Richard	Lt RM	23/11/91	Harrow
Burkert, Andrew	SLt	17/05/02	Seaford
Burns, Derek	Lt Cdr	22/10/70	Re-Call
Burrowes, Christopher	Lt	09/06/90	Winchester
Butt, Robert	SLt	08/02/00	Downside
Butt, Katherine	A/SLt	14/03/05	Downside
Butterworth, Tiffany	SLt	01/02/05	Re-Call
Buttriss, Dave	Lt	12/01/03	Re-Call
Byrom, Matthew	A/SLt	01/10/04	Newcastle
C			
Caldecott, Arabella	A/SLt	10/10/04	Haileybury

Name	Rank	Date of Appointment	School/College
Callow, Martin	Capt RM	29/07/87	Royal Hospital
Campbell, Alexandra	SLt	04/08/01	Re-Call
Cardwell, Alexander	Lt Cdr	30/10/94	Bangor
Carpenter, Richard	Lt	01/11/97	Nottingham
Carr, Deborah	SLt	01/01/03	Edinburgh
Carter, Michael	Lt Cdr	01/09/69	Kelly
Carter, Nicholas	Cdr	01/10/82	Newcastle
Carter, Steven	Lt Cdr	01/04/81	Re-Call
Carter, Sallyanne	A/SLt	15/11/04	Berkhamstead
Cartmell, Keith	Lt Cdr	23/10/96	Arnold
Caves, Richard	Lt	07/12/98	Re-Call
Chandler, Lisa	A/SLt	27/09/04	Dean Close
Chapman, Kenneth	SLt	19/06/84	Stamford
Chapman, Russell	SLt	01/03/04	Plymouth
Chetwood, Jim	Lt	17/06/94	Portsmouth
Clark, Daniel	Alt RM	01/09/01	Bradfield
Clarke, Rueben	Lt	12/03/81	Re-Call
Clifford, Karen	SLt	15/01/01	Pangbourne
Clifford, Neil	A/SLt	01/09/04	Monkton Combe
Clough, Howard	Lt	01/09/97	Re-Call
Coles, John	SLt	11/03/03	Haileybury
Collier, Anthony	SLt	01/01/93	Re-Call
Collins, Micheal	SLt	28/02/83	Magdalen
Collins, Wendy	Lt	26/02/82	Alleyns
Copleston, Michael	Lt	28/03/99	Taunton
Coppleston, Neil	Lt Cdr	01/09/96	Brentwood
Corbould, Leigh	Lt	01/04/95	Stowe
Cornes, Mary	A/SLt	01/08/04	St Edwards
Cox, Damian	SLt	25/03/01	Prior Park
Cox, Jim	Lt Cdr	17/09/97	Birkenhead
Coyle, David	SLt	04/08/01	Framlingham
Coyne, Lucie	Lt Cdr	01/09/96	Brentwood
Crabtree, John	Lt Cdr	11/01/72	Kings Taunton
Crabtree, Ruth	SLt	15/04/02	Re-Call
Craig, Alex	Alt RM	07/04/02	Shrewsbury
Creasey , Peter	Lt	16/06/91	Royal Hospital
Crees, David	Cdr	01/11/72	HQCCF TDO
Crisp, Victoria	A/SLt	15/11/04	Duke Of York
Crocker, Allan	SLt	11/03/01	Clifton
Crook, Patricia	Lt	28/03/99	Haileybury
Crook, Stephen	Lt	11/02/99	City Of London
Curtis, Berwick	Lt	01/01/75	Epsom

D

Name	Rank	Date of Appointment	School/College
Daniels, Paul	Capt RM	01/04/05	Bradfield
De Celis Lucas, Elena	2nd Lt RM	01/09/04	Strathallan
Delpech, Daniel	Lt	01/09/77	Haberdashers
Dickson, Nathalie	A/SLt	23/02/05	RGS High Wycombe
Donaldson, Rhona	A/SLt	27/09/04	Dean Close
Doody, Edwin	SLt	05/02/01	HQCCF Re-Call
Dubbins, Keith	Lt Cdr	19/09/89	Ryde
Dunn, Alex	Cdr	16/03/95	HQCCF Re-Call
Durrans, Howard	Lt	22/05/97	Bridlingto
Durrant, Robert	Cdr	01/03/72	Milton Abbey
Dyer, Paul	SLt	12/03/01	Duke Of York

E

Name	Rank	Date of Appointment	School/College
Eager, Christopher	SLt	05/09/03	Woodbridge
Eames, Andrew	Lt Col	01/11/95	Hereford
Eaton, Diana	A/SLt	01/10/03	St Dunstan
Eaton, Trevor	Lt	01/09/01	St Dunstan
Edwards, Georgina	SLt	01/09/02	Brentwood
Elkington, David	Cdr	12/01/67	Re-Call
Elliott, Lynnette	Lt	01/03/00	Clifton
Emms, Peter	Lt	01/10/96	Magdalen
Erskine, Randal	SLt	21/02/05	Re-Call
Evans, Richard	Lt Cdr	16/09/96	Raleigh
Excell, Steven	SLt	01/09/03	Canford
Eyles, Mark	SLt	18/10/99	Colstons
Eyles, Ruth	SLt	01/09/94	Re-Call

F

Name	Rank	Date of Appointment	School/College
Fabian, Geoffrey	Cdr	15/12/04	Plymouth
Finn, Mark	Lt Cdr	09/11/93	HQCCF(ATO)
Ford, Peter	Lt Cdr	01/07/01	HQCCF Re-Call
Forey, Sarah	SLt	28/06/01	St Peters
Foster, Stella	Lt	07/03/05	Re-Call
Foulger, Tim	Lt	15/12/89	Re-Call
Fountain, Evan	SLt	01/09/00	Whitgift
Fowler, Edith	A/SLt	14/03/05	Alleyns
Francis-Jones, Anthony	Lt	01/04/92	Kings Taun
Fraser, Charles	Lt Cdr	01/06/03	Leys
Freedman, Stephen	Lt Cdr	20/02/91	MTS Crosby
Friend, David	Lt	05/10/90	Kings Bruton
Frost, Rex	Cdr	12/11/79	Exeter
Fullarton, Ian	Lt	07/03/99	RGS High Wycombe
Fuller, David	Lt	26/09/99	Re-Call
Furse, Michael	Lt	17/01/05	HQCCF(ASO)
Fyleman, Keith	Lt	01/11/99	Cheltenham

G

Name	Rank	Date of Appointment	School/College
Geddes, George	Cdr	01/08/03	Kelvinside
Georgiakakis, Nikos	Lt	23/11/89	Charterhouse
Gibson, Claire	A/SLt	15/01/05	St Lawrence
Gilchrist , Simon	Alt RM	01/11/02	Shrewsbury
Gillespie-Payne, Jonathan	Capt RM	06/05/04	Charterhouse
Glasbey, Martyn	Lt	05/09/90	Ryde
Glasspoole, Paul	Lt Cdr	12/06/80	Heles
Goakes, Benjamin	A/SLt	08/11/04	Kimbolton
Gordon, Robin	Lt	07/04/02	Campbell
Gray, John	SLt	18/05/01	Wellingborough
Greatwood, Lisa	SLt	01/02/00	Stowe
Green, George	Cdr	01/01/74	Brighton
Greenhough, Clive	Lt	16/10/97	Re-Call
Grice, Kathryn	SLt	01/04/02	Worksop
Griffiths, Jill	SLt	01/02/04	Pangbourne
Griffiths, Steven	Alt RM	01/06/02	Harrow

H

Name	Rank	Date of Appointment	School/College
Hall, Austin	`Lt	25/06/81	Re-Call
Hall, Kevin	SLt	25/03/01	Re-Call
Hall, Stephen	Lt	01/08/03	Oundle
Halsall, Christopher	A/SLt	10/07/04	Kings Rochester
Hamon, Christopher	Lt Cdr	20/05/94	Sherborne
Hannaford, Rowena	A/SLt	14/07/02	Heles
Hanslip, Michael	Lt Cdr	21/03/03	Re-Call
Harding, Claire	Lt Cdr	07/07/95	Kelly
Hardman, Tom	Lt Cdr	24/02/93	Haberdashers
Harnish, Robert	Lt	17/09/03	Elizabeth
Harris, David	Maj RMR	01/01/01	Kimbolton
Harris, Steven	Lt Cdr	01/08/92	Exeter
Harrison, Anthony	Lt	01/11/88	Re-Call

Name	Rank	Date of Appointment	School/College
Hartley, George	Lt	01/01/91	Ruthin
Hartley, Robin	SLt	01/03/04	Sedbergh
Harvey, Stephen	Capt RM	17/08/97	Bedford Modern
Harvey, Peter	Lt Cdr	21/05/93	HQCCF Re-Call
Hatch, Alistair	Capt RM	01/11/01	Sherborne
Hellier, Jeremy	Cdr	01/08/99	Wellington
Henderson, Joan	Lt Cdr	24/06/93	RGS High Wycombe
Henry, Tom	Lt Cdr	14/09/84	Re-Call
Hewitt, Richard	Lt	25/06/81	Durham
Hill, Hugh	Lt	15/04/97	Winchester
Hill, Peter	Lt	12/03/98	Sevenoaks
Hocking, Barry	SLt	20/03/99	Royal Hospital
Holland, Clare	Lt	12/10/98	Calday Grange
Holland, Julian	A/SLt	01/03/03	Framlingham
Holmes, Matthew	Lt Cdr	17/11/97	Langley
Hooper, Robin	Lt	01/07/02	Re-Call
Horley, Philip	SLt	28/06/99	Sutton Valence
Houghton, Robert	A/SLt	08/11/04	Scarborough
Howard, Ben	Lt	16/04/05	Hqccf
Howard, Susan	A/SLt	22/03/03	Arnold
Hudson, John	Lt Cdr	17/03/94	Re-Call
Hunt, John	SLt	01/09/02	Loughborough
Hutchings, Alan	Lt RMr	01/09/03	Rugby
Hutchinson, Jeremy	Cdr	23/01/77	Re-Call
Huxtable, Nigel	Lt Cdr	31/07/00	Re-Call

I

Name	Rank	Date of Appointment	School/College
Ibbetson-Price, William	Lt Cdr	17/10/89	Re-Call
Ing, John	Maj RMR	01/09/89	Harrow
Iredale, Judy	Lt	28/06/83	Taunton

J

Name	Rank	Date of Appointment	School/College
Jacklin, John	Lt Cdr	08/10/99	NCFBO
Jackson, Howard	Lt	19/04/83	Worksop
Jackson, David	Lt	17/04/96	Bedford
Jago, Peter	Lt	01/09/94	RGS Lancas
Jeans-Jakobsson, Micheal	Lt	23/06/83	Re-Call
Jenkins, David	Lt Cdr	01/01/80	Re-Call
Jethwa, Ashok	SLt	26/01/98	Re-Call
Jones, Chris	Lt	07/04/03	Well Sch
Jones, Lily	SLt	24/07/03	Re-Call

K

Name	Rank	Date of Appointment	School/College
Kay, Anne	SLt	20/03/96	Hqccf
Kearsey, Joanne	SLt	18/12/03	Christs Hospital
Kearsey, Peter	Lt Cdr	15/09/99	Christs Hospital
Kennedy, Caroline	SLt	01/09/02	Whitgift
Kermode, Erica	Lt	26/08/93	Re-Call
Killgren, Carl	Lt Cdr	11/10/85	Stamford
Killgren, Susan	SLt	01/09/00	Stamford
King, Stuart	SLt	02/04/04	Bearwood
Kirby, Michael	A/SLt	03/06/04	Portsmouth
Kirton, Stephanie	Lt	03/07/98	Berkhamstead
Knight, David	Cdr	24/06/04	Re-Call

L

Name	Rank	Date of Appointment	School/College
Lauder, David	SLt	01/01/02	St Edwards
Lawrence, Sarah	Lt RMr	01/06/03	Malvern
Lawson, Derick	Lt	01/12/03	RGS Newcastle
Lawson, Edward	Lt Cdr	28/01/97	Arnold
Lawson, Grant	Lt	06/09/97	Shiplake
Lawson, Matthew	Lt Cdr	01/09/98	St Johns
Leaver, Rebecca	Lt	17/11/01	King Edward
Lee, John	Lt	01/09/88	Hereford
Leyshon, Lara	Lt	04/10/00	Haberdashers
Lilford, Jane	SLt	12/03/01	Bridlington
Lingard, David	Cdr	02/03/99	HQCCF Divi
Little, John	Lt Cdr	11/09/86	Re-Call
Little, Peter	SLt	17/03/02	Re-Call
Lovell, Keith	Lt	07/08/84	Bearwood
Lovell, Stephen	Lt	08/01/92	Royal Hospital
Lowles, Ian	Lt	09/09/02	Exeter
Lowndes, Charles	A/SLt	14/12/04	Shiplake
Lucas, Ian	Cdr	17/11/81	Tonbridge
Lucas, Stuart	SLt	27/02/00	Loretto
Lynch, Jonathan	A/SLt	23/05/05	Harrow

M

Name	Rank	Date of Appointment	School/College
Macbain, Fiona	A/SLt	01/09/04	Strathallan
Maccarthy, Thomas	SLt	05/11/00	Re-Call
Macdonald, Fraser	Lt	29/09/67	Trinity
Macgregor, Karen	Lt	10/10/94	Re-Call
Macintosh, Richard	A/SLt	15/12/04	Ellesmere
Mackie, Alan	Cdr	20/10/81	Bangor
Mackrell, Robin	A/SLt	01/09/03	City Of London
Macleod, Monica	SLt	06/09/01	Re-Call
Maddocks, Jane	SLt	14/02/02	Re-Call
Maiden, Philip	Lt	01/05/02	Christs Hospital
Marsh, Lesley	Lt Cdr	01/01/87	Re-Call
Martin, Brian	Lt	15/07/02	Liverpool
Martindale, Leslie	Lt Cdr	06/08/00	Re-Call
Mason, Julie	SLt	07/04/03	Wellingborough
Matthews, Andrew	SLt	11/10/02	St Margarets
Matthews, Victoria	Lt	02/09/02	Kings Wimbledon
Maxwell, Peter	A/SLt	16/02/03	Kings Rochester
May, Edward	Lt Cdr	05/06/98	HQCCF Re-Call
McCann, John	SLt	17/10/00	Strathallan
McConnell, Sue	Lt	05/12/90	Re-Call
McCFonnell, William	Lt	18/07/88	Re-Call
McDonald, Gary	Lt	03/07/00	Eastbourne
McDonald, Richard	Lt	24/06/99	Re-Call
McGregor, Michael	A/SLt	08/11/04	Oratory
McGuff, Neil	Lt	04/09/91	Wellington
McGuirk, Richard	Lt RMr	01/05/03	Wellingborough
McNeile, Rory	Cdr	01/05/05	Re-Call
Mead, Elizabeth	Lt	30/06/01	Re-Call
Melville, Graham	Lt	21/01/92	Birkenhead
Mercer, Jane	Lt	18/07/99	Rossall
Middleton, Philip	A/SLt	15/08/04	Loretto
Miles, David	Alt RM	01/01/02	Royal Hospital
Millard, Michelle	Lt	15/02/94	Re-Call
Mills, Anita	Lt Cdr	01/02/92	Monkton Combe
Milne, Stuart	SLt	25/06/97	HQCCF Re-Call
Milton, Pippa	Lt	25/06/01	Bedford
Minto, Neil	Lt	08/01/90	Re-Call
Mitchell, Ian	Lt	09/09/93	Wellcol
Mitchell, Robert	Cdr	14/11/83	Kings Wimbledon
Montgomery, Paul	Lt Cdr	25/09/92	Dean Close
Moody, Sue	Lt Cdr	20/09/91	Re-Call
Moore, Adrian	Lt	04/10/01	Re-Call
Moore, David	Lt	27/05/80	Re-Call
Moore, Terry	SLt	11/07/83	Re-Call

Name	Rank	Date of Appointment	School/College
Morgan, Anthony	A/SLt	09/09/04	St Johns
Morgan, Bryn	Lt	01/05/88	Re-Call
Morgan, Giles	Lt Cdr	20/08/01	Re-Call
Morris, Alwyn	A/SLt	14/03/05	Loughborough
Morton, Hilary	Lt	21/01/00	King William
Moss-Gibbons, David	Cdr	01/08/71	Bradfield
Mundill, Robin	Lt	02/01/04	Glenalmond
Murray, Richard	Alt RM	01/10/02	Harrow

N

Name	Rank	Date of Appointment	School/College
Nash, Phillipa	Lt	01/09/02	Kimbolton
Nevin, Paul	A/SLt	17/09/03	Bournemouth
Newton, Ian	Lt Cdr	13/12/95	Re-Call
Nicholson, Robin	Cdr	01/03/75	Milton Abbey
Nicoll, Andrew	SLt	05/07/03	Re-Call
Nurser, Graham	SLt	28/11/99	Wellington

O

Name	Rank	Date of Appointment	School/College
Oatway, Paul	Lt	25/03/04	Aato
Ogilvie, Fergus	Capt RM	03/11/95	Giggleswick
Oldbury, David	Cdr	01/06/73	Re-Call
Olive, Einar	A/SLt	14/12/04	St Edwards
Osmond, Stephen	Cdr	11/01/78	RGS Worcester
Othick, Anthony	SLt	25/05/99	Scarborough
Owen, Elizabeth	SLt	19/01/98	HQCCF Re-Call
Owen, John	Lt Cdr	01/01/98	HQCCF Re-Call

P

Name	Rank	Date of Appointment	School/College
Packer, Thomas	Lt Cdr	17/05/82	Re-Call
Parkinson, Christopher	Lt	06/11/00	Sutton Valence
Parkinson, Michael	SLt	01/06/98	Kings Rochester
Parkinson, Ken	Lt Cdr	26/01/89	HQCCF Re-Call
Paterson, Sheelagh	SLt	01/09/02	Kelvinside
Paton, Gordon	Lt Cdr	21/09/72	Re-Call
Payne, Anthony	Lt	01/12/68	Loughborough
Peak, Edward	A/SLt	22/03/03	Calday Grange
Pearsall, Robert	A/SLt	15/11/04	Heles
Pearson-Miles, Edward	Lt RMr	01/09/03	Wellington
Pegg, Joanne	SLt	01/01/99	Exeter
Peto-Clark, Tim	Lt	16/05/96	Re-Call
Pidoux, John	SLt	21/09/95	Maidstone
Pike, John	Lt	31/01/00	Sandbach
Pitts, Rebecca	A/SLt	01/09/02	Kelly
Pont, Diana	A/SLt	05/07/03	Churchers
Porter, Fiona	Lt	18/05/98	Sutton Valence
Pouder, George	2nd Lt RM	01/12/04	Rugby
Poulet, Gerard	Lt	01/05/01	St Margarets
Poulet-Bowden, Geradine	Lt Cdr	18/07/99	St Margarets
Powell, Andrew	Lt Cdr	16/02/90	Reigate
Price, Thelma	Lt	28/06/98	Dulwich
Prior, Anthony	Lt	01/12/77	Milton Abbey
Prosser, Nicholas	Lt Cdr	24/09/65	Re-Call

R

Name	Rank	Date of Appointment	School/College
Ray, James	A/SLt	01/06/03	Leys
Rennie, Sophie	SLt	27/01/03	Re-Call
Rennison, Clive	Capt RM	01/10/94	Royal Hosp
Rhode, Terry	Lt	01/09/94	Re-Call
Richard, Peter	Lt	01/09/82	Re-Call
Richards, Philip	Lt	16/02/94	Fettes
Ridley-Thomas, Micheal	Lt	06/11/90	Re-Call
Ripley, Myles	Lt	22/02/82	Sedbergh
Robarts, Paul John	SLt	26/06/00	MTS Northwood
Roberts, Derek	Lt	01/11/86	Brighton
Roberts, Martin	Lt Cdr	01/03/67	Re-Call
Robinson, Nigel	SLt	17/09/03	Bedford Modern
Roby, Ron	Cdr	01/02/64	Re-Call
Rooms, Lindsay	Cdr	01/12/77	Re-Call
Rose, Helen	SLt	22/09/00	Bedmod
Rothwell, George	Lt Cdr	07/11/94	HQCCF Re-Call
Russell, James	A/Maj RM	16/06/93	Malvern

S

Name	Rank	Date of Appointment	School/College
Salmon, Tony	SLt	01/04/05	Re-Call
Salt, Graeme	SLt	10/05/02	Kings Wimbledon
Sammons, Keith	A/SLt	15/12/04	Tonbridge
Sanders, Bryant	Cdr	15/11/66	Bournemouth
Sanders, Robert	Lt	19/05/95	Re-Call
Savage, Anthony	Cdr	01/01/97	Portsmouth
Savage, Kirsty	SLt	01/09/02	Re-Call
Schofield, Michelle	Lt	23/11/00	Kings Rochester
Scoins, David	SLt	01/07/02	Re-Call
Scorgie, Stuart	Lt Cdr	01/11/89	Clifton
Sell, Roger	Lt	01/07/98	Re-Call
Shannon, Tom	Lt Cdr	02/09/86	Queen Victoria
Sharpe, Andrew	SLt	01/09/03	Gordons
Shiels, Mary	SLt	01/06/02	Re-Call
Shone, Michael	Lt	01/03/99	HQCCF Re-Call
Shorrocks, Jonathan	Lt Cdr	09/07/81	RGS Worcester
Shortland, Ghislaine	Lt	14/07/02	Gordons
Sibley, Peter Charles	Lt Cdr	15/02/64	Re-Call
Simister, Alan	Lt	01/05/01	Eastbourne
Simms, Julie	A/SLt	01/10/04	Newcastle
Simpson, Philip	Lt	12/07/94	Re-Call
Simpson-Hayes, Gizella	SLt	01/10/01	Re-Call
Sissons, Stewart	Lt	07/07/95	HQCCF Re-Call
Smith, Nicholas	SLt	01/09/04	Woodbridge
Smith, Alison	Lt	01/04/97	Dollar
Smith, John	Lt	01/01/01	HQCCF Re-Call
Smith, Ron	Lt Cdr	30/04/90	Re-Call
Snelgrove, Sarah	A/SLt	14/03/05	Guildford
Spall, Christopher	Lt	07/04/02	Loretto
Spence, Donna	SLt	01/06/95	Bangor
Spence, Richard	Lt	06/09/93	Bangor
Spike, Nigel	Lt	05/10/87	Re-Call
Stanley, John	SLt	08/01/02	Sandbach
Stansbury, William	SLt	01/09/95	MTS Northwood
Stanyer, Richard	A/SLt	15/11/04	Kelly
Stares, Steve	SLt	01/03/03	Re-Call
Stevens, Laurence	Lt	05/07/79	St Bartholomews
Stilwell, Valerie	SLt	24/11/93	Re-Call
Stocker, Paul	Lt	10/09/90	Re-Call
Stratton-Brown, Colin	Lt Cdr	01/09/96	Maidstone
Streatfeild-James, Adam	Capt RM	05/09/00	Strathallan
Stringer, Christopher	Capt RM	16/09/86	Malvern
Sugden, Kara	Lt	08/01/02	Canford
Summers, Peter	SLt	01/09/02	Cheltenham
Sutherland, Peter	Lt	28/06/99	Whitgift
Sweetland, Ashley	A/SLt	14/12/04	Bournemouth

Name	Rank	Date of Appointment	School/College

T

Name	Rank	Date of Appointment	School/College
Taylor, Liam	A/Maj RM	03/03/92	Winchester
Taylor, Martyn	SLt	07/03/02	Victoria
Tear, Richard	Lt	03/04/98	Wellingborough
Temple, Robert	Lt Cdr	08/03/01	HQCCF Re-Call
Tennant, David	Lt Cdr	13/09/85	Tonbridge
Thorn, Simon	SLt	17/10/97	Radley
Tinker, Chris	Cdr	02/06/76	Re-Call
Tiplady, Rod	SLt	01/09/96	Edinburgh
Toase, Stephanie	SLt	01/11/03	Wellington
Toon, Howard	Lt Cdr	21/07/01	Re-Call
Toy, Jolyon	A/SLt	01/01/03	Eastbourne
Trebble, Dennis	SLt	01/01/04	MTS Northwood
Treharne, Andrew	Lt	01/04/03	Re-Call
Triggs, Duncan	Lt	12/07/98	Ruthin
Tucker, Vivien	SLt	12/10/98	Hereford
Turner, Clive	Lt	30/08/99	Re-Call
Turner, Charlotte	SLt	01/07/04	Re-Call
Tweedle, Gordon	A/SLt	05/07/03	Adams Grammmar

U

Name	Rank	Date of Appointment	School/College
Ulrich, Jacquelyn	SLt	01/07/04	Re-Call

V

Name	Rank	Date of Appointment	School/College
Van Der Werff, Tanya	Lt	01/09/91	Reading Blue Coat
Van Zwanenberg, Louise	Lt	15/04/97	Woodbridge
Vanston, Matthew	A/SLt	14/04/05	Langley
Vaughan, Piers	Lt Cdr	05/01/98	Sevenoaks
Vickers, Michael	Lt	02/04/01	Christs College
Vickery, David	Cdr	28/02/84	Re-Call
Vigers, Rose	Lt	15/01/93	Kings Bruton
Vine, Roger	Lt Cdr	01/01/92	Re-Call

W

Name	Rank	Date of Appointment	School/College
Walker, Colin	Cdr	16/06/88	Strathallan
Walker, David	SLt	15/10/01	Woodbridge
Walmsley, Richard	Lt RM	10/01/01	Strathallan
Walsh, George	Lt Cdr	30/09/99	Re-Call
Ward, Sarah	SLt	12/12/00	Mill Hill
Warren, Clive	Lt	18/05/98	Colstons
Waugh, Patrick	Lt	24/04/94	Wellingbor
Webb, Victoria	SLt	01/09/99	Maidstone
Whale, Andrew	Lt	20/12/85	D Of York
Wharton, Neil	2nd Lt RM	01/12/04	Giggleswick
Wilding, Karl	A/SLt	19/09/01	Harrow
Wilkes, Justin	Lt Cdr	29/06/98	Dollar
Wilkinson, Laura	A/SLt	08/11/04	RGS Newcas
Wilkinson, Daren	SLt	08/01/02	Bridlingto
Willetts, Jimnah	A/SLt	31/05/05	Adams Grammar
Williams, Martin	SLt	17/06/01	Clifton
Williams, Robert	Lt Cdr	30/09/82	Glasgow Academy
Wilson, Andrew	SLt	18/09/02	Oratory
Wood, Louise	SLt	11/01/02	Haberdashers
Wright, Duncan	2nd Lt RM	01/01/05	Canford
Wright, Matthew	A/SLt	07/04/03	Mts Crosby
Wylie, John	Lt Cdr	31/07/93	Radley

Y

Name	Rank	Date of Appointment	School/College
Yates, Christopher	Capt RM	01/08/97	Winchester
Yetman, Stephen	A/SLt	01/09/04	Guildford

ADMIRALTY TRIALS MASTERS

Vice Admiral Sir Fabian MALBON, KBE (Rtd) .... 6 Jun 99
Captain E HACKETT (Rtd) .... 30 Jun 85

Qualified in accordance with the International Maritime Organisation (IMO) Convention Regulations in Standards of Training, Certification and Watchkeeping (STCW) 1995, the role of the ATM, is to take command of new-build warships on trials. With their wide experience in working with MoD ship builders and DPA Projects, and because of their individual seamanship skills, ATM are uniquely placed to mediate between all parties during sea trials and to promote the highest standards of safety.

ROYAL NAVAL RESERVE AND OTHER VESSELS AUTHORISED TO FLY THE BLUE ENSIGN IN MERCHANT VESSELS (FOREIGN OR HOME TRADE ARTICLES) AND FISHING VESSELS.

1. A list of Royal Naval Reserve and other vessels authorised to fly the Blue Ensign will no longer be published in the Navy List.

2. Its inclusion was intended for the information of Captains of Her Majesty's Ships with reference to the provisions of Article 9153 of the Queen's Regulations for the Royal Navy under which they are authorised to ascertain whether British Merchant Ships (including Fishing Vessels) flying the Blue Ensign of Her Majesty's Fleet are legally entitled to do so.

3. However, the usefulness of this list serves only a limited purpose as the list of vessels that could fly the Blue Ensign can change frequently. British merchant ships and fishing vessels are allowed to wear the plain Blue Ensign under the authority of a special Warrant, subject to certain conditions being fulfilled, and which are outlined below.

4. Vessels registered on the British Registry of Shipping may wear a plain Blue Ensign providing the master or skipper is in possession of a warrant issued by the Director of Naval Reserves under the authority of the Secretary of State for Defence, and the additional conditions outlined below are fulfilled. The Blue Ensign is to be struck if the officer to whom the warrant was issued relinquishes command, or if the ship or vessel passes into foreign ownership and ceases to be a British ship as defined by MSA 95.

   a. Vessels on Parts I, II, and IV of the Register. The master must be an officer of the rank of lieutenant RN/RMR or Captain RM/RMR or above in the Royal Fleet Reserve or the maritime forces of a United Kingdom Overseas Territory or Commonwealth country of which Her Majesty is Head of State, or an officer on the Active or Retired Lists of any branch of the maritime reserve forces of these countries or territories.

   b. Vessels on Part II of the Register. This part of the Register is reserved for fishing vessels. The skipper must comply with the same criteria as for sub-Clause 4.a. above, however the crew must contain at least four members, each of whom fulfils at least one of the following criteria:

      Royal Naval or Royal Marines reservists or pensioners
      Reservists or pensioners from a Commonwealth monarchy or United Kingdom Overseas Territory
      Ex-ratings or Royal Marines who have completed twenty years service in the Reserves
      Members of the Royal Fleet Reserve

5. Action on sighting a merchant ship wearing a Blue Ensign. The Commanding Officer of one of HM ships on meeting a vessel wearing the Blue Ensign may send on board a commissioned officer to confirm that the criteria outlined above are being met in full. If it is found that the ship is wearing a Blue Ensign, without authority of a proper warrant, the ensign is to be seized, taken away and forfeited to The Sovereign and the circumstances reported to the Director Naval Reserves, acting on behalf of the Commander in Chief Naval Home Command, who maintains the list of persons authorised to hold such warrants.

   However, if it is found that, despite the warrant being sighted, the ship is failing to comply with the criteria in some other particular, the ensign is not to be seized but the circumstances are to be reported to the Director Naval Reserves.

OBITUARY

ROYAL NAVAL SERVICE

Commander

Maughan LVO, OBE, J M C 09.04.02

Lieutenant Commander

Woolliams, M F 28.06.01
Stewart, A M 11.05.01
Hawley, S C 19.05.02

Surgeon Lieutenant

Kershaw, D J E 15.05.01

Lieutenant

Skidmore, R P 12.06.02
Suggett, P R 19.06.01
Lewis, J L M 12.06.02
Paton, D W 25.07.01
Christie, D W 14.03.02

ROYAL MARINES

Brigadier

Bowkett, R M 16.07.02

Captain

Rule, S J 05.04.01

ROYAL NAVAL RESERVE

Lieutenant Commander

Houghton, N G 27.03.01

ABBREVIATIONS OF RANKS AND LISTS

A .... Acting
A/ .... Acting
ACT .... Acting
ADM .... Admiral
ADM OF FLEET .... Admiral of the Fleet
ASL .... Acting Sub-Lieutenant
AT .... Acting Temporary
BRIG .... Brigadier
CAND .... Candidate
CAPT .... Captain
CDT .... Cadet
CHAPLAIN-FLT .... Chaplain of the Fleet
CDR .... Commander
CDRE .... Commodore
CNO .... Chief Nursing Officer
COL .... Colonel
COMDT .... Commandant
(CS) .... Careers Service
(D) .... Dental
E .... Engineering
(FS) .... Family Service
GEN .... General
(GRAD) .... Graduate
HON .... Honorary
I .... Instructor
LOC .... Local
LT .... Lieutenant
LCDR .... Lieutenant-Commander
LT CDR .... Lieutenant-Commander
LT COL .... Lieutenant-Colonel
LT GEN .... Lieutenant-General
MAJ .... Major
MAJ GEN .... Major-General
MID .... Midshipman
(NE) .... New Entry
NO .... Nursing Officer
OFF .... Officer
OFFR .... Officer
P/ .... Probationary
PNO .... Principal Nursing Officer
PR .... Principal
RADM .... Rear-Admiral
REV .... Reverend
RM .... Royal Marines
S .... Supply & Secretariat
(SD) .... Special Duties List

(SDT)........ Special Duties List Temporary
SG........ Surgeon
SURG........ Surgeon
(SL)........ Supplementary List
SLT........ Sub-Lieutenant
SNO........ Senior Nursing Officer
SUPT NO........ Superintendent Nursing Officer
T........ Temporary
T/........ Temporary
TLT........ Temporary Lieutenant
TSLT........ Temporary Sub-Lieutenant
(UCE)........ University Cadet Entrant
VADM........ Vice-Admiral
X........ Seaman
2LT........ Second Lieutenant, Royal Marines

ABBREVIATIONS OF SPECIALISATIONS AND QUALIFICATIONS

(Eur Ing)........ European Engineer
A/TK........ Heavy Weapons Anti-Tank
AAWO........ Anti Air Warfare Officer
ACC/EM........ Accident and Emergency
ACertCM........ Archbishops Certificate Church Music
ACGI........ Associate, City and Guilds London Institute
ACIS........ Associate of The Institute of Chartered Secretaries and Administrators
ACMA........ Associate, Institute of Cost & Management Accountants
ACMI........ Associate of The Chartered Management Institute
(AD)........ Medical and Dental Administration
ADipC........ Advanced Post Graduate Diploma in Management Consultancy
ADIPM........ Associate, Institute of Data Processing Management
adp........ Passed Advanced Adp Course Dadptc
AE........ Air Engineering
AE U/T........ Air Engineering Under Training
AE(L)........ Air Engineering (Electrical)
AE(M)........ Air Engineering (Mechanical)
(AE)........ Assault Engineer
AFIMA........ Associate Fellow, Institute Mathematics & Its Applications
AFOM........ Associate, Faculty of Occupational Medicine
AFRIN........ Associate Fellow Royal Institute of Navigation
AGSM........ Associate of The Guildhall School of Music and Drama
AIEMA........ Associate Member Institute of Environmental Management & Assessment
AIL........ Associate, Institute of Linguists
AIM........ Associate, Institute of Metallurgists
AIMgt........ Associate of The Institute of Management
AInstP........ Associate, Institute of Physics
AKC........ Associate, King's College London
ALCD........ Associate, London College of Divinity

AMASEE .... Associate Member, Association of Electrical Engineers
AMBCS .... Associate Member, British Computing Society
AMBIM .... Associate Member, British Institute of Management
AMHCIMA .... Associate Member, Hotel Catering & Institutional Management Association
AMIAM .... Associate Member, Institute of Administrative Management
AMICE .... Associate Member, Institute of Civil Engineers
AMIEE .... Associate Member, Institute of Electrical Engineers
AMIERE .... Associate Member, Institution of Electronic and Radio Engineers
AMIIE .... Associate Member, Institution of Incorporated Engineers
AMIMarE .... Associate Member, Institute of Marine Engineers
AMIMarEST .... Associate Member Institute Marine Engineers Science & Technology
AMIMechE .... Associate Member, Institute of Mechanical Engineers
AMIMechIE .... Associate Member of Institute of Mechanical Incorporated Engineers
AMInstP .... Associate Member, Institute of Physics
AMINucE .... Associate Member, Institution of Nuclear Engineers
AMIPlE .... Associate Member, Institution of Plant Engineers
AMNI .... Associate Member, Nautical Institute
AMRAeS .... Associate Member, Royal Aeronautical Society
AMRINA .... Associate Member. Royal Institution of Naval Architects
ARAM .... Associate, Royal Academy of Music
ARCM .... Associate, Royal College of Music
ARCS .... Associate, Royal College of Science
ARCST .... Associate, Royal College of Science and Technology (Glasgow)
ARIC .... Associate, Royal Institute of Chemistry
ARICS .... Professional Asssociate, Royal Institution of Chartered Surveyors
ATC .... Air Traffic Control Officer
ATCU/T .... Air Traffic Control Officer Under Training
AV .... Aviation
AWO(A) .... Advanced Warfare Officer(Above Water)
AWO(C) .... Advanced Warfare Officer(Communications)
AWO(U) .... Advanced Warfare Officer(Underwater)
aws .... Qualified Air Warfare College
BA .... Bachelor of Arts
BA(OU) .... Bachelor of Arts, Open University
BAO .... Bachelor of Art of Obstetrics
BAR .... Barrister
BCH .... Bachelor of Surgery (Bch)
BCh .... Bachelor of Surgery
BChD .... Bachelor of Dentistry
BChir .... Bachelor of Surgery
BComm .... Bachelor of Commerce
BD .... Bachelor of Divinity
BDS .... Bachelor of Dental Surgery
BEd .... Bachelor of Education
BEng .... Bachelor of Engineering
BM .... Bachelor of Medicine
BMedSc .... Bachelor of Medical Science

BMS....Bachelor of Medical Science
BMus....Bachelor of Music
BPh....Bachelor of Philosophy
BPharm....Bachelor of Pharmacy
BS....Bachelor of Surgery
BSc....Bachelor of Science
BSC(EH)....Bsc Environmental Health
BSc(Eng)....Bachelor of Science (Engineering)
BTech....Bachelor of Technology
C....Communications
C PHYS....Chartered Physicist
C/T....Clinical Teacher
CA....Caterer
(CA)....Anaesthetics - Consultant
(CA/E)....Accident/Emergency - Consultant
CC....Coronary Care
(CC)....Paediatrics - Consultant
CDipAF....The Certified Diploma in Accounting and Finance
(CDO)....Commando Trained
(CE)....Otorhinolaryngology - Consultant
CEng....Chartered Engineer
Cert Ed....Certificate of Education
CertTh....Certificate in Theology
CGIA....Insignia Award of The City & Guilds of London Insitute
(CGS)....General Surgery - Consultant
CHB....Bachelor of Surgery (Chb)
ChB....Bachelor of Surgery
ChM....Chartered Mathematician
CITP....Chartered It Professional
(CK)....Dermatology - Consultant
(CL)....Pathology - Consultant
(CM)....General Medicine - Consultant
CMA....Management Accountant
CMarSci....Chartered Marine Scientist
CMath....Chartered Mathematician
(CN/P)....Neuro-Psychiatry - Consultant
(CO/M)....Occupational Medicine - Consultant
(CO/S)....Orthopaedic Surgery - Consultant
(COSM)....Oral Surgery/Medicine - Consultant
CPDATE....This Is A 'pay' Only Sq. It Will Not Be Awarded To Personnel.
CPN....Community Psychiatric Nurse
CQSW....Certificate of Qualification in Social Work
(CU)....Urology - Consultant
(CX)....Radiology - Consultant
DA....Diploma in Anaesthesia
DAppDy....Diploma in Applied Dynamics
DCH....Diploma in Child Health

DCHS........Diploma in Community Health Studies
DCL........Doctor of Civil Law
DCP........Diploma in Clinical Pathology
DD........Doctor of Divinity
DDPH........Diploma in Public Dental Health
DEH........Diploma in Environmental Health
df........Qualified Defence Fellowship
DGDP RCS(UK)........Diploma in General Dental Practice Rcs (Uk)
DGDP(UK)........Diploma in General Dental Practice (Uk)
DGDPRCS(Eng)........Diploma General Dental Practice Rcs(Eng)
DHC(PO)........Diploma in Remote Health Care - Polar Option
DHMSA........Diploma in The History of Medicine (Society of Apothecaries)
DIC........Diploma of The Imperial College
DIH........Diploma in Industrial Health
Dip FFP........Diploma of The Facalty of Family Planning
Dip ICN........Diploma in Infection Control Nursing
Dip OHN........Diploma in Occupational Health Nursing
Dip OM........Diploma in Occupational Medicine
Dip SM........Diploma in Sports Medicine
DipA&PPS........Diploma in Academic & Practical Physiotherapy in Sport
DipAvMed........Diploma in Aviation Medicine
DIPCM........Diploma in Clinical Microbiology
DIPCR........Teaching Diploma in Clinical Radiology
DipEcon........Diploma in Economics (Open)
DipEd........Diploma in Education
DipEM........Diploma in Environmental Management
DipEP........Rs Health Diploma in Environmental Protection
DipFD........Diploma in Funeral Directing
DipFM........Diploma in Financial Management
DIPH&S........Diploma in Health and Safety
DipHE(Paeds)........Diploma (He)(Paediatrics)
DipIMC RCSED....Diploma in Immmediate Medical Care of Royal College Surgeons (Edinburgh)
DIPRP........Post Graduate Diploma in Radiation Protection
DipSM........British Safety Council Diploma in Safety Management
DipTh........Diploma in Theology
DLitt........Doctor of Letters
DLO........Diploma in Laryngology and Otology
DM........Doctor of Medicine
DMCMP........Diploma in Medical Centre Practice Management
DMNS........Diploma in Military Nursing Studies
DMRD........Diploma in Medical Radiological Diagnosis
DNE........Diploma in Nursing Education
DNM........Diploma in Nuclear Medicine
DO........Diploma in Ophthalmology
DObstRCOG........Diploma Royal College of Obstetricians and Gynaecologists
DOrth........Diploma in Orthodontics
DP........Diploma in Philosophy

DPH .... Diploma in Public Health
DPHC .... Dental Public Health - Consultant
DPhil .... Doctor of Philosophy
DPhysMed .... Diploma in Physical Medicine
DPM .... Diploma in Psychological Medicine
DRCOG .... Diploma Royal College Obstetricians & Gynaecologists
DRD .... Diploma in Restorative Dentistry
DRRT .... Diploma in Remedial & Recreational Therapy
DSc .... Doctor of Science
DTM&H .... Diploma in Tropical Medicine and Hygiene
ESLog .... European Senior Logistician
Eur Ing .... European Engineer
EW .... Electronic Warfare
FA .... Fleet Analyst
FBCS .... Fellow, British Computer Society
FBIM .... Fellow, British Institute of Management
FC .... Fighter Controller
FCILT .... Fellow of The Chartered Institute of Logistics and Transport
FCIPD .... Fellow of The Chartered Institute of Personnel and Development
FCIS .... Fellow, Institute Chartered Secretaries & Administrators
FCMA .... Fellow, Chartered Institute of Management Accountants
FCMI .... Fellow of The Chartered Management Institute
FDS .... Fellow in Dental Surgery
FDS RCPSGlas .... Fellow in Dental Surgery Royal College of Physicians & Surgeons (Glasgow)
FDS RCS(Eng) .... Fellow in Dental Surgery, Royal College of Surgeons of England
FDS RCS(Irl) .... Fellow in Dental Surgery Royal College of Surgeons in Ireland
FDS RCSEdin .... Fellow in Dental Surgery Royal College of Surgeons of Edinburgh
FDS(RCS) .... Fellow in Dental Surgery, Royal College of Surgeons of England
FFA .... Fellow, Institute of Financial Accountants
FFAEM .... Fellow of The Faculty of Accident and Emergency Medicine
FFARCS .... Fellow, Faculty of Anaesthetists, Royal College of Surgeons of England
FFARCSI .... Fellow, Faculty of Anaesthetists, Royal College of Surgeons in Ireland
FFGDP(UK) .... Fellow of The Faculty of General Dental Practitioners (Uk)
FFOM .... Fellow, Faculty of Occupational Medicine
FHCIMA .... Fellow of The Hotel and Catering Management Association
FIAA .... Fellow, Institute of Actuaries of Australia
FICS .... Fellow of The International College of Surgeons
FIEE .... Fellow, Institute of Electrical Engineers
FIEEIE .... Fellow of The Institute of Electrical and Electronic Incorparated Engineer
FIEIE .... Fellow, Institute of Electrical and Electronic Incorporated Engineers
FIERE .... Fellow, Institution of Electronic and Radio Engineers
FIIE .... Fellow of The Institution of Incorporated Engineers
FIL .... Fellow, Institute of Linguists
FIM .... Fellow of The Institute of Metals
FIMA .... Fellow, Institute of Mathematics and Its Applications
FIMarE .... Fellow, Institute of Marine Engineers
FIMarEST .... Fellow Institute Marine Engineers Science & Technology

FIMechE .... Fellow, Institution of Mechanical Engineers
FIMgt .... Fellow of The Institute of Management
FIMS .... Fellow, Institute of Management Specialists Or Mathematical Statistics
FInstAM .... Fellow Institute of Administrative Management
FInstLM .... Fellow of The Institute of Leadership and Management
FINucE .... Fellow, Institute of Nuclear Engineers
FIOSH .... Fellow of The Institute Occupational Safety & Health
FIPM .... Fellow of The Institute of Personnel Management
FISM .... Fellow of The Institute of Supervision and Management
FITE .... Fellow, Institution Electrical & Electronics Technician Engineers
FNI .... Fellow, Nautical Institute
FRAeS .... Fellow, Royal Aeronautical Society
FRAM .... Fellow, Royal Academy of Music
FRC.Psych .... Fellow of The Royal College of Psychiatrists
FRCA .... Fellow of The Royal College of Anaesthetists
FRCGP .... Fellow Royal College General Practioners
FRCOG .... Fellow, Royal College of Obstetricians and Gynaecologists
FRCP .... Fellow, Royal College of Physicians, London
FRCPath .... Fellow, Royal College of Pathologists
FRCPEd .... Fellow, Royal College of Physicians, Edinburgh
FRCPGlas .... Fellow, Royal College of Physicians and Surgeons of Glasgow
FRCR .... Fellow, Royal College of Radioligists
FRCS .... Fellow, Royal College of Surgeons of England
FRCS(ED)A&E .... Fellow of The Royal College of Surgeons (Edinburgh) Accident & Emergency
FRCS(ORL) .... Fellow Royal College of Surgeons - Otorhinology
FRCS(ORTH) .... Fellow Royal College Surgeons (Orthopaedics)
FRCS(Urol) .... Fellow Royal College of Surgeons (Urology)
FRCSEd .... Fellow, Royal College of Surgeons of Edinburgh
FRCSGlas .... Fellow, Royal College of Physicians and Surgeons of Glasgow
FRCSTr&Orth .... Fellowship of The Royal College of Surgeons (Trauma & Orthopaedics)
FRGS .... Fellow, Royal Geographical Society
FRHistS .... Fellow Royal Historical Society
FRICS .... Fellow Royal Institute Chartered Surveyors
FRIN .... Fellow of The Royal Institute of Navigation
FRINA .... Fellow, Royal Institute of Naval Architects
FRMS .... Fellow, Royal Meteorological Society
FRSA .... Fellow, Royal Society of Arts
fsc .... Qualified Foreign Staff College
GB .... The Gilbert Blane Medal
GCIPD .... Graduate Chartered Institute Personnel & Development
GCIS .... Graduate of The Institute of Chartered Secretaries and Administrators
gdas .... General Duties Areo Systems
GDP .... General Dental Practitioner
GDP UT .... General Dental Practitioner - Specialist U/T
GISVA .... Graduate Institute of Surveyors, Valuers and Auctioneers
GMCIPD .... Graduate Member Chartered Institute Personnel & Development
GMPP .... General Medical Practitioner

GradIMA.............................. Graduate Member, Institute of Mathematics and Its Applications
GradIMS ....Graduate Institute of Management Specialists
GradInstPS .... Graduate Institute of Purchasing and Supply
(GS) .... General Surgery - Senior House Officer
GSX...General Service Executive
gw.. Guided Weapons Systems Course Rmcs Shrivenham
H CH .... Hydrographer (Charge)
hcsc.. Higher Command & Staff College
HDCR ....Higher Diploma of College of Radiographers
HDIPCR.. Higher Diploma in Clinical Radiology
Hf ....Hudson Fellowship
HM...Hydrographer Metoc
HM(AS)...Hydrog/Metoc Advanced Surveyor
HM1 ....Hydrographer/Metoc (First Class)
HM2...Hydrographer/Metoc (Second Class)
HNC ....Higher National Certificate
HND ....Higher National Diploma
HULL.. Hull Engineering
H1 .... Hydrographer (First Class)
H2 .... Hydrographer (Second Class)
I(1)Ab .... Interpreter 1st Class Arabic
I(1)Ch ....Interpreter 1st Class Chinese
I(1)Da..Interpreter 1st Class Danish
I(1)Du ....Interpreter 1st Class Dutch
I(1)Fi .... Interpreter 1st Class Finnish
I(1)Fr..Interpreter 1st Class French
I(1)Ge ....Interpreter 1st Class German
I(1)Id... Interpreter 1st Class Indonesian
I(1)It...Interpreter 1st Class Italian
I(1)Ja.. Interpreter 1st Class Japanese
I(1)Ma.. Interpreter 1st Class Malayan
I(1)No .... Interpreter 1st Class Norwegian
I(1)Pl .... Interpreter 1st Class Polish
I(1)Po...Interpreter 1st Class Portugese
I(1)Ru..Interpreter 1st Class Russian
I(1)Sh .... Interpreter 1st Class Swahili
I(1)Sp .... Interpreter 1st Class Spanish
I(1)Sw .... Interpreter 1st Class Swedish
I(1)Tu .... Interpreter 1st Class Turkish
I(1)Ur .... Interpreter 1st Class Urdu
I(2)Ab ....Interpreter 2nd Class Arabic
I(2)Ch .... Interpreter 2nd Class Chinese
I(2)Da... Interpreter 2nd Class Danish
I(2)Du .... Interpreter 2nd Class Dutch
I(2)Fi .... Interpreter 2nd Class Finnish
I(2)Fr.. Interpreter 2nd Class French
I(2)Ge .... Interpreter 2nd Class German

I(2)Id .... Interpreter 2nd Class Indonesian
I(2)It........ Interpreter 2nd Class Italian
I(2)Ja........ Interpreter 2nd Class Japanese
I(2)Ma........ Interpreter 2nd Class Malayan
I(2)No .... Interpreter 2nd Class Norwegian
I(2)Pl .... Interpreter 2nd Class Polish
I(2)Po .... Interpreter 2nd Class Portugese
I(2)Ru........ Interpreter 2nd Class Russian
I(2)Sh .... Interpreter 2nd Class Swahili
I(2)Sp .... Interpreter 2nd Class Spanish
I(2)Sw .... Interpreter 2nd Class Swedish
I(2)Tu .... Interpreter 2nd Class Turkish
I(2)Ur .... Interpreter 2nd Class Urdu
IC .... Intensive Care
IC/CC........ Intensive Care and Coronary Care
idc .... Qualified Imperial Defence College
IEng .... Incorporated Engineer
ifp........ Qualified, International Fellows Programme
IS .... Information Systems
IS U/T........ Information Systems Under Training
isc........ Initial Staff Course
JCPTGP........ Certificate of Prescribed Experience in General Practice
jsdc........ Joint Service Defence College
jssc .... Joint Services Staff College
LC........ Landing Craft
LCIPD........ Licentiate of The Chartered Institute of Personnel and Development
LDS........ Licentiate in Dental Surgery
LDS RCPSGlas ... Licenciate in Dental Surgery Royal College of Physicians & Surgeons (Glasgow)
LDS RCS(Eng)........ Licentiate in Dental Surgery, Royal College of Surgeons of England
LDS RCS(Irl)........ Licenciate in Dental Surgery Royal College of Surgeons in Ireland
LDS RCSEdin .... Licenciate in Dental Surgery Royal College of Surgeons of Edinburgh
LGSM .... Licentiate, Guildhall School of Music and Drama
LHCIMA........ Licentiate Hotel, Catering and Institutional Management Assn
LICG .... Licentiate of City and Guilds Institute
LIEE........ Licentiate, Institute Electrical Engineers
LIMA........ Licentiate Institute Mathematics & Its Applications
LLB .... Bachelor of Law
LLD........ Doctor of Laws
LLM .... Master of Law
LMCC .... Licentiate, Medical Council of Canada
LMHCIMA........ Licentiate Member of Hotel,Catering and Institutional Management Assn
LMIPD .... Licentiate Member To The Institute of Personnel and Development
LMSSA........ Licentiate in Medicine & Surgery, Society of Apothecaries
LRAM .... Licentiate, Royal Academy of Music
LRCP........ Licentiate, Royal College of Physicians, London
LRCPSGlas .... Licentiate, Royal College of Physicians and Surgeons of Glasgow
LRCS........ Licentiate, Royal College of Surgeons of England

LRPS .... Licentiate, Royal Photographic Society
(LT) .... Laboratory Technician
LTh .... Licentiate in Theology
M ED .... Masters in Education
M.Univ........ Master of The University (Ou)
MA .... Master of Arts
MA(CANTAB)........ Master of Arts Cambridge
MA(Ed) .... Master of Arts in Education
MA(OXON) .... Master of Arts Oxon
MAPM .... Member of The Association of Project Managers
MB .... Bachelor of Medicine
MBA........ Master of Business Administration
MBCS .... Member, British Computer Society
MBIM .... Member, British Institute of Management
MCD........ Mine Warfare Clearance Diver
MCD/MW .... Mine Clearance Diving & Mine Warfare
MCFA .... Member of The Catering and Food Association
MCGI........ Member of City and Guilds Institiute
MCh .... Master in Surgery
MChOrth .... Master of Orthopaedic Surgery
MCIEH .... Member Chartered Institute in Environmental Health
MCIPD .... Chartered Member of The Institute of Personnel and Development
MCIT .... Member, Institute of Training Officers
MCMI........ Member of The Chartered Management Institute
MD .... Doctor of Medicine
MDA........ Master of Defence Administration
MDSc........ Master of Dental Science
mdtc........ Maritime Defence Technology Course
ME........ Marine Engineering
ME U/T .... Marine Engineering Under Training
ME(L)........ Marine Engineering (Electrical)
MEng........ Master of Engineering
MESM........ Marine Engineering (Submarine)
MESMUT .... Marine Engineering (Submarine) Under Training
METOC........ Meteorology & Oceanography
MFCM .... Member, Faculty of Community Medicine
MFDS,RCS ....Membership of The Faculty of Dental Surgery Royal College of Surgeons England
MFGDP(UK) .... Membership in Gen Dent Practice, Facultyof General Dental Practitioners (Uk)
MFOM........ Member, Faculty of Occupational Medicine
MFPM........ Member of Faculty of Pharmaceutical Medicine
MGDS RCS .... Member in General Dental Surgery, Royal College of Surgeons of England
MGDS RCSEd....... Member in General Dental Surgery, Royal College of Surgeons of Edinburgh
MHCIMA .... Member, Hotel Catering & Institutional Management Association
MHSM........ Member of The Institute of Health Services Mamagement
MICE .... Member, Institution Civil Engineers
MIDPM .... Member Institute of Data Processing Management
MIEE........ Member, Insitution of Electrical Engineers

MIEEE ..... Member of The Institution of Electrical and Electronic Engineers
MIEEIE ..... Member of The Institute of Electrical and Electronic Incorporated Engineers
MIERE ..... Member, Institution of Electrical & Radio Engineers
MIExpE ..... Member, Institute of Explosives Engineers
MIIE ..... Member of Institution of Incorporated Engineers
MIIRSM ..... Member of The International Institute of Risk & Safety Management
MIIT ..... Member of The Institute of Information Technology Training
MIL ..... Member, Institute of Linguists
MILDM ..... Member of The Institute of Logistics and Distribution Management
MILog ..... Member of The Institue of Logistics
MILT ..... Member of The Institute of Logistics and Transport
MIM ..... Member, Institute of Metals
MIMA ..... Member of The Institute of Mathematics and Applications
MIMarA ..... Member, Institute of Marine Architects
MIMarE ..... Member, Institute of Marine Engineers
MIMarEST ..... Member Institute Marine Engineers Science & Technology
MIMechE ..... Member, Institution of Mechanical Engineers
MIMechIE ..... Member of The Institute of Mechanical Incorporayed Engineers
MIMgt ..... Member of The Institute of Management
MIMS ..... Member, Institute of Management Specialists
MInsD ..... Member of The Institute of Directors
MinstAM ..... Member, Institute of Administrative Management
MInstFM ..... Member, Institute of Facilities/Resources Management
MINSTP ..... Member, Institute of Physics
MInstPS ..... Member, Institute of Purchasing and Supply
MINucE ..... Member, Institute of Nuclear Engineers
MIOA ..... Member of The Institute of Acoustics
MIOSH ..... Member, Institute of Occupational Safety and Health
MIPD ..... Member of The Institute of Personnel and Development
MIPlantE ..... Member, Plant Engineers
MIPM ..... Member, Institute of Personnel Management
MIProdE ..... Member, Institute of Production Engineers
MISecM ..... Member of The Institute of Security Management
MISM ..... Member of The Institute of Supervisory Management
MITD ..... Member Institute of Training and Development
MITE ..... Member, Institute of Technical Engineers
MLDR ..... Mountain Leader
MLITT ..... Master of Letters
ML2@ ..... Mountain Leader 2 (Rm)
MMedSci ..... Master of Medical Science
MMus ..... Master of Music
MNI ..... Member, Nautical Institute
MNZIS ..... Member of The New Zealand Institute of Surveyors
MOR ..... Heavy Weapons Mortar Course
MOrth ..... Master of Orthodontics
MOrth,RCS ..... Membership in Othodontics Royal College of Surgeons England
MPH ..... Master of Public Health

MPhil .... Master of Philosophy
MPS .... Member, Pharmaceutical Society
MRAeS .... Member, Royal Aeronautical Society
MRCGP .... Member, Royal College of General Practitioners
MRCOG .... Member, Royal College Obstetricians & Gynaecologists
MRCP .... Member, Royal College of Physicians, London
MRCP(UK) .... Member, Royal College of Physicians
MRCPath .... Member, Royal College of Pathologists
MRCPE .... Member, Royal College of Physicians, Edinburgh
MRCPGlas .... Member, Royal College of Physicians and Surgeons of Glasgow
MRCPI .... Member, Royal College of Physicians of Ireland
MRCPsych .... Member, Royal College of Phsyciatrists
MRCS .... Member, Royal College of Surgeons of England
MRCVS .... Member of The Royal College of Veterinary Surgeons
MRIC .... Member, Royal Institute of Chemistry
MRIN .... Member, Royal Institute of Navigation
MRINA .... Member, Royal Institute of Naval Architects
MS .... Master of Surgery
MSc .... Master of Science
MSc gw .... Master of Science Guided Weapons
MSc(Econ) .... Master of Economic and Social Studies
MScD .... Master of Dental Science
MSE .... Member, Society of Engineers
MSRP .... Member of The Society For Radiological Protection
MTh .... Master of Theology
MTO .... Motor Transport Officer
MW .... Mine Warfare
n .... Frigate Navigating Officer's Course
nadc .... Nato Defence College Course
NCAGSA .... Naval Cooperation & Guidance For Shipping(A)
NCAGSB .... Naval Cooperation & Guidance For Shipping (B)
NCAGSC .... Naval Cooperation & Guidance For Shipping (C)
ndc .... National Defence College
NDipM .... National Diploma in Management
NInstC .... Nuclear Instrument Calibration Course
nrf .... Qualified, Nato Research Fellowship
O .... Observer
O LYNX .... Observer (Lynx)
O MER .... Observer (Merlin)
O SKW .... Observer (Seaking Aew)
O SK6 .... Observer (Seaking 6)
O U/T .... Observer Under Training
ocds(Can) .... Qualified Canadian National Defence College
ocds(Ind) .... Qualified Indian National Defence College
OCDS(JAP) .... Overseas National Defence College Japanese
ocds(No) .... Qualified, Norwegian Defence College
ocds(Pak) .... Qualified Pakistan National Defence College

ocds(US) .... Qualified The United States National War College
ocds(USN) .... Qualified, United States Naval War College
odc(Aus) .... Qualified Australia Joint Services Staff College
odc(Fr) .... Qualified French Cours Superieur Interarmees
ODC(SWISS) .... International Training in Security and Arms Control
odc(US) .... Qualified United States Armed Forces Staff College
ONC .... Orthopaedic Nursing
ORTHC .... Orthodontics - Consultant
osc .... Qualified Overseas Staff College
osc(Nig) .... Qualified Nigerian Command & Staff College
osc(us) .... Qualified, Usmc Command & Staff College
OStJ .... Order of St. John
OTSPEC .... Operating Theatre Specialist
P .... Pilot
P GAZ .... Pilot (Gazelle)
P GR7 .... Harrier Gr7 Pilot
P LYNX .... Pilot (Lynx)
P LYN7 .... Pilot (Lynx 7)
P MER .... Pilot (Merlin)
P SHAR .... Sea Harrier Pilot
P SKW .... Pilot (Seaking Aew)
P SK4 .... Pilot (Seaking 4)
P SK6 .... Pilot (Seaking 6)
P U/T .... Pilot Under Training
(P) .... Physiotherapist
pce .... Passed Command Examinations
pce(sm) .... Passed Command Examinations (Sm)
pcea .... Passed Command Examinations (Air)
(PD) .... Pharmacy Dispenser
pdm .... Principal Director of Music
PFOM .... President Faculty of Occupational Medicine
PGCE .... Post Graduate Certificate of Education
PGDip .... Post Graduate
PGDIP .... Post Graduate Diploma
PGDIPAN .... Post Graduate Diploma in Applied Navigation
PGDipL .... Post Graduate Diploma in Law
PGDRP .... Post Graduate Diploma in Radiation Protection
PH .... Helicopter Pilot
PhD .... Doctor of Philosophy
PI .... Photographic Interpreter
PR .... Plotting & Radar
psc .... Passed Staff Course
psc(a) .... Passed Staff Course (Raf)
psc(j) .... Passed Staff Course (Joint)
psc(j)(o) .... Overseas Staff Colleges Except Ndc Rome
psc(j)o .... Overseas Staff Colleges Except Ndc Rome
psc(m) .... Passed Staff Course (Army)

PSC(ONDC) ... Staff Course (Overseas National Defence College)
psc(or) ... Passed Staff Course Overseas Reserves
PT ... Physical Training
ptsc ... Completed Technical Staff Course at The Rmsc Shrivenham
PWO ... Principal Warfare Officer
PWO(A) ... Principal Warfare Officer Above Water
PWO(C) ... Principal Warfare Officer Communications
PWO(N) ... Principal Warfare Officer Navigation
PWO(U) ... Principal Warfare Officer Underwater
rcds ... Royal College of Defence Studies
rcds(fm) ... Royal College of Defence Studies (Foundation Module)
RCPS(Glas) ... Royal College of Phsicians and Surgeons of Glasgow
RCS ... Royal College of Surgeons of England
RCSEd ... Royal College of Surgeons of Edinburgh
REG ... Regulating
REGM ... Registered Midwife
(RGN) ... Registered General Nurse
RMLE/P ... Senior Corps Commission Pilots Only
RMN ... Registered Mental Nurse
RMP1 ... Pilot 1
RMP2 ... Pilot 2
RNT ... Registered Nurse Tutor
S ... S
(S) ... Stores
(SA) ... Anaesthetics - Specialist Registrar
SBS ... Special Boat Squadron
SCM ... State Certified Midwife
SEC ... Secretarial
(SGS) ... General Surgery - Specialist Registrar
SM ... Submariner
SM ... Sm Qualified
SM U/T ... Submarine Unqualified Under Training
SM(n) ... Submarine Navigating Officer
SM(N) ... Submarine (Navigation)
(SM) ... General Medicine - Specialist Registrar
SO(LE) ... Staff Officer Personnel and Logistics
(SO/M) ... Occupational Medicine - Specialist Registrar
SOLE/P ... Senior Corps Commission Pilots/General Duties
sondc ... Senior Overseas National Defence College
sowc ... Senior Officer's War Course
sq ... Rm Major Staff Qualified After Holding Two Specified Staff Appointments
tacsc ... Territorial Army Command and Staff Course
TAS ... Torpedo Anti-Submarine
TDCR ... Teachers Diploma College of Radiographers
TEng ... Certificate of Technical Engineering
TM ... Training Management
TM U/T ... Training Management Under Training

TMSM........ Training Management (Sm)
tp........ Qualified Test Pilots Course
(W)........ Writer
WE........ Weapons Engineering
WE U/T........ Weapons Engineering Under Training
WESM........ Weapon Engineering (Submarine)
WESMUT........ Weapons Engineering (Submarine) Under Training
WTO........ Weapon Training Officer
X........ X

ABBREVIATIONS OF PLACE WHERE OFFICER IS SERVING WHEN NOT SERVING AT SEA

AACC MID WALLOP........ HQ School of Army Aviation Middle Wallop
ACDS(POL) USA........ Assistant Chief of Defence Staff (Policy and Nuclear) USA
AD AIM........ ASSISTANT DIRECTOR AIR INTEGRITY MONITORING
ADAS BRISTOL........ ASSISTANT DIRECTOR ACQUISITION SUPPORT BRISTOL
AFCC........ Armed Forces Chaplaincy Centre
AFPAA HQ........ Armed Forces Personnel Administration Agency Headquarters
AFPAA JPA........ AFPAA (Joint Personnel Administration)
AFPAA WTHY DOWN........ AFPAA (Worthy Down)
AFPAA(CENTURION)........ Directorate of AFPAA (Centurion)
AGRIPPA JFC HQ........ HMS Agrippa JFC HQ (Allied Forces S. Europe (Italy))
AGRIPPA MAR CC........ HMS Agrippa Mar CC (Allied Naval Forces S. Europe (Italy))
AH IPT........ Attack Helicopter Integrated Project Team
AMC........ Aquisition Management Cell
ASM IPT........ Attack Submarine Integrated Project Group
AST(N)........ Area Security Team (North)
ATTURM........ Amphibious Training & Trials Unit Royal Marines
BDLS AUSTRALIA........ British Defence Liaison Staff Australia
BDLS CANADA........ British Defence Liaison Staff Canada
BDLS INDIA........ British Defence Liaison Staff India
BDMT........ Arms CIS Group/Bowman Military Team
BDS WASHINGTON........ British Defence Staff Washington
BF BIOT........ British Forces, British Indian Ocean Territory
BFPO AGENCY DLO........ BFPO Defence Agency Defence Logistics Organisation
BOWMAN IPT........ BOWMAN Integrated Project Team
BRNC BAND........ Band of HM Royal Marines Britannia Royal Naval College
CALEDONIA DLO........ HMS Caledonia
CALLIOPE........ Royal Naval Reserve Tyne (RN Staff)
CAMBRIA........ Royal Naval Reserve South Wales (RN Staff)
CAPT MCTA........ Captain Maritime Commissioning Trials & Assessment
CDO LOG REGT RM........ Commando Logistics Regiment Royal Marines
CENTCOM USA........ Naval Party 1068
CFPS SHORE........ Commander Fishery Protection Squadron (Shore)
CHFHQ(SHORE)........ CDO Helo Force Headquarters (Shore)
CINCFLEET FIMU........ Fleet Information Management Unit
CINCFLEET FTSU........ Commander-in-Chief (Fleet Technical Support Unit)

CLYDE MIXMAN1 .... Her Majesty's Ship NEPTUNE Mixed Manning
CMSG IPT .... CMSG Integrated Project Team
CMT SHRIVENHAM .... College of Management and Technology (inc Defence Leadership Ce
CNNRP BRISTOL .... Chairman Naval Nuclear Regulatory Panel
COM MCC NWD .... Commander MCC Northwood
COS 2SL/CNH .... Chief of Staff to Second Sea Lord/Commander in Chief Naval Home Co
CSIS IPT .... CSIS Integrated Project Team
CSSE USA .... Chief Strategic Systems Executive (USA)
CTCRM .... Commando Training Centre Royal Marines
CTCRM (SEA) .... Commando Training Centre Royal Marines (Sea)
CTCRM BAND .... Band of HM Royal Marines Commando Training Centre Royal Marines
CTS .... Corporate Technical Services
CV(F) IPT .... CVF Integrated Project Team
DA ALGIERS .... Defence Attache Algiers
DA BRIDGETOWN .... Defence Advisor Bridgetown
DA BRUNEI .... Defence Attache Brunei
DA KIEV .... Defence Attache Kiev
DA MANAMA .... Defence Attache Manama
DA SOFIA .... Defence Attache Sofia
DA TBILISI .... Defence Attache Tbilisi
DALRIADA .... Her Majesty's Ship DALRIADA
DARTMOUTH BRNC .... Britannia Royal Naval College Dartmouth
DASC .... Defence Aviation Safety Cell
DCAE COSFORD .... Defence College Aeronautical Engineering (Cosford)
DCCIS BLANDFORD .... Defence College Communications and Information Systems (Blandf
DCCIS FAREHAM .... Defence College of Communication and Information Systems (Fareha
DCDS(C) .... Deputy Chief of Defence Staff (Commitments)
DCL DEEPCUT .... Defence College Logistics (Deepcut)
DCPPA HALTON .... Defence College of Police and Personnel Administration (Halton)
DCSA DHFCS FMR .... DCSA Defence High Frequency Communications Services Forest Moor
DCSA GIBRALTAR .... Defence Communications Services Agency Gibraltar
DCSA NWD REGION .... DCSA Northwood Regional Office
DCTS HALTON .... Defence Centre of Training Support (Halton)
DCTS PORTS .... Defence Centre of Training Support (Portsmouth)
DDA HALTON .... Defence Dental Agency Halton
DDA PLYMOUTH .... Defence Dental Agency Plymouth
DDA PORTSMOUTH .... Defence Dental Agency Portsmouth
DEF EXP ORD SCHL .... Defence Ordnance Disposal School
DEF NBC CENTRE .... Defence Nuclear Biological Chemical Centre
DEF SCH OF LANG .... Defence School of Languages
DFTE PORTSMOUTH .... Director Fleet Time Engineering Portsmouth
DGES LAND .... Director General Equipment Support Land
DGHRN GOSPORT .... Director General Human Resources Navy (Gosport)
DGIA .... Defence Geographic and Imagery Intelligence Agency
DHFS .... Defence Helicopter Flying School
DISC .... Defence Intelligence & Security Centre
DL IPT .... Data Links Integrated Project Group

DLO BRISTOL .... Defence Logistics Organisation Bristol
DLO DEF MUN GP........ DLO Defence Munitions Group
DLO WYTON........ Defence Logistics Organisation Wyton
DLO YEO ....Defence Logistics Organisation Yeovilton
DLO/DG DEF SC .... DLO/Director General Defence Supply Chain
DMSTC........Defence Medical Services Training Centre
DNR DISP TEAM........Director of Naval Recruiting Display Team
DNR EC 2........ Directorate of Naval Recruiting East Central 2
DNR N IRELAND........ Directorate of Naval Recruiting Northern Ireland
DNR NEE 1........ Directorate of Naval Recruiting North East England 1
DNR NWE 2........Directorate of Naval Recruiting North West England 2
DNR PRES TEAMS .... Director of Naval Recruiting Presentation Teams
DNR RCHQ NORTH ....Director of Naval Recruiting Regional Careers Headquarters (Nor
DNR RCHQ SOUTH .... Director of Naval Recruiting Regional Careers Headquarters (Sou
DNR SEE 1 ....Directorate of Naval Recruiting South East England 1
DNR SWE 2........Directorate of Naval Recruiting South West England 2
DNR W CENTRAL........Directorate of Naval Recruiting West Central
DNR WROUGHTON........Director of Naval Recruiting, Wroughton
DOSG BRISTOL........ Defence Ordnance Safety Group Bristol
DPA BRISTOL........Defence Procurement Agency Bristol
DPMD........ Defence Postgraduate Medical Deanery
DRAKE CBS........ Her Majesty's Ship DRAKE - Captain Base Safety
DRAKE COB........Her Majesty's Ship DRAKE - Captain of the Base
DRAKE DIS........Her Majesty's Ship DRAKE - Directorate Infrastructure and Services
DRAKE DPL........ Her Majesty's Ship DRAKE - Area Manpower Management Organisation (AM
DRAKE NBC/DBUS ....Her Majesty's Ship DRAKE - Naval Base Commander/Directorate Bus
DRAKE SFM .... Her Majesty's Ship DRAKE - Superintendent Fleet Maintenance
DSDA........Defence Storage & Distribution Agency
DSFM PORTSMOUTH ....Deputy Superintendent Fleet Maintenance
EAGLET........Royal Naval Reserve Mersey (RN Staff)
EUMS .... European Union Military Staff
EXCH ARMY SC(G) ....Exchange Service British Army On the Rhine
EXCHANGE ARMY UK ....Exchange Service UK Army Units
EXCHANGE AUSTLIA ....Exchange Service Australian Navy
EXCHANGE BRAZIL........ Exchange Service Brazilian Navy
EXCHANGE CANADA ....Exchange Service Canadian Armed Forces
EXCHANGE DENMARK .... Exchange Service Denmark
EXCHANGE FRANCE........ Exchange Service France
EXCHANGE GERMANY ....Exchange Service German Navy
EXCHANGE ITALY .... Exchange Italian Navy
EXCHANGE N ZLAND........ Exchange Service New Zealand Navy
EXCHANGE NLANDS........ Exchange Service Netherlands Forces
EXCHANGE NORWAY ....Exchange Service Norway
EXCHANGE RAF UK........Exchange Service with the Royal Air Force
EXCHANGE SPAIN........Exchange Service Spain
EXCHANGE USA........Exchange Service United States
FDG........Fleet Diving Group

FDU1 .... Fleet Diving Unit 1
FDU2 .... Fleet Diving Unit 2
FDU3 .... Fleet Diving Unit 3
FLEET AV CRANWEL........ Fleet Aviation Cranwell
FLEET AV CU ....Fleet Aviation (HMS Seahawk)
FLEET AV HENLOW ....Fleet Aviation Medical Training Wing Henlow
FLEET AV SULTAN........ Fleet Aviation (SULTAN)
FLEET AV VALLEY .... Fleet Aviation (RAF Valley)
FLEET AV VL........Fleet Aviation Yeovilton
FLEET CIS PORTS .... Fleet Communication & Information Systems (Portsmouth)
FLEET HQ NWD........ Fleet Headquarters Northwood
FLEET HQ PORTS ....Fleet Headquarters Portsmouth
FLEET HQ PORTS 2 ....Fleet Headquarters Portsmouth No. 2
FLEET MINING TM........ Fleet Minewarfare & Patrol Vessels, Diving & Fishery Protectio
FLEET PHOT PORTS ....Fleet Photographic Unit Portsmouth
FLEET ROSYTH .... Fleet (Rosyth)
FLYING FOX .... HMS FLYING FOX
FORT BLOCKHOUSE........The Officer in Charge
FORWARD ....RNR Communications Training Centre (Birmingham) (RN Staff)
FOSNNI........ FOSNNI/Commander Clyde Operations Department
FOST DPORT SHORE........ Flag Officer Sea Training (Devonport)
FOST DSTF ....Flag Officer Sea Training DSTF
FOST FAS SHORE........Flag Officer Sea Training Faslane Shore
FOST NWD (JMOTS)........Joint Maritime Operational Training Staff (Northwood)
FS MASU .... Forward Support Mobile Aircraft Support Unit
FSAST IPT........ Flt Sim & Synth Trnrs/UK Mil Flying Trg Sys Integrated Project Team
FWO DEVONPORT ....Fleet Waterfront Organisation (Devonport)
FWO FASLANE ....Fleet Waterfront Organisation Faslane
FWO PORTSMOUTH........ Fleet Waterfront Organisation Portsmouth
GANNET SAR FLT ....Gannet SAR Flight
HANDLING SQN........ Handling Squadron
HQ ARRC........ HQ Ace Rapid Reaction Corps
HQ BAND SERVICE ....Headquarters Band Service
HQ DCSA........ HQ Defence Communication Services Agency
HQ DMETA ....HQ Defence Medical Education & Training Agency
HQ RHINE/EURO SG........ Headquarters Rhine and European Support Group
HQ SACT ....Headquarters Supreme Allied Comander Transformation
HQ STC........Headquarters Strike Command Ops Support (ATC)
HQ 3 CDO BDE RM........ 3 Commando Brigade Royal Marines
HQBF CYPRUS .... Headquarters British Forces Cyprus
HQ1GP HQSTC .... Headquarters 1 Group
HUMS IPT .... Health & Usage Monitoring Systems Integrated Project Team
IA BRISTOL........ Integration Authority Bristol
IMS BRUSSELS........International Military Staff, Brussels
INM ALVERSTOKE ....Institute of Naval Medicine
JACIG ....Joint Arms Control Implementation Group
JARIC........ Joint Air Reconnaissance and Intelligence Centre

JATEBRIZENORTON .... Joint Air Transport Establishment - Brize Norton
JCA IPT UK.. Joint Combat Aircraft Integrated Project Team
JCA IPT USA.. Future Carrier Borne Aircraft Integrated Project Team USA
JCTS IPT .... Joint Casualty Treatment Ship Integrated Project Team
JDCC .... Joint Doctrine and Concepts Centre
JES IPT .... Joint Electronic Surveillance Integrated Project Team
JF HARROLE OFF .... Joint Force Harrier Role Office
JFCHQ BRUNSSUM .... Joint Force Combined Headquarters Brunssum
JHCHQ.. Joint Helicopter Command Headquarters
JHCNI .... Joint Helicopter Command (Northern Ireland)
JHQ/CIS LISBON .... Joint Headquarters/Communication Information Systems Lisbon
JHQSW MADRID .... JHQ Southwest Madrid
JPS UK .... Joint Planning Staff UK
JSCSC .... Joint Services Command and Staff College
JSSU CHELTENHAM .... Joint Service Signal Unit - Cheltenham
JSSU CYPRUS.. Joint Service Signal Unit CYPRUS
JSU NORTHWOOD .... Joint Support Unit Northwood
JWC/CIS STAVANGR.. Joint Warfare Centre/Communications Information Systems Stava
JWW.. Jungle Warfare Wing
KING ALFRED.. Her Majesty's Ship KING ALFRED
LAIPT .... Logistic Applications Integrated Project Team
LANG TRNG(UK) .... Language Training (UK)
LN BMATT (CEE).. Loan BMATT (CEE) (Vyskov)
LN BPST SAFRICA.. Loan British Peace Support Team (South Africa)
LN SIERRA LEONE.. Loan Sierra Leone
LOAN ABU DHABI.. Loan Service in Abu Dhabi
LOAN BMATT GHANA .... British Military Advisory and Training Team (West Africa)
LOAN BMATT(EC) .... British Military Advisory and Training Team (Eastern Caribbean)
LOAN BRUNEI .... Loan Service in Brunei
LOAN DARA .... Loan DARA
LOAN DESO.. Loan Malaysia
LOAN DSTL.. Loan Defence Science & Tech Labs
LOAN HYDROG .... Loan Hydrographer
LOAN JSOC SLOV .... Joint Services Operations Centre Slovakia
LOAN JTEG BSC DN .... Loan Joint Test Evaluation Group Boscombe Down
LOAN KUWAIT.. Loan Service Kuwait
LOAN NEW ZEALAND .... Loan Service New Zealand
LOAN OMAN .... Loan Service Oman
LOAN OTHER SVCE.. Loan Other Service
LOAN SAUDI ARAB .... Loan Service Saudi Arabia
MARS IPT.. Military Afloat Reach & Sustainability Integrated Project Team
MAS BRUSSELS.. Military Agency For Standardisation (Brussels)
MCME IPT.. MCM Equipment Integrated Project Team
MCTC.. Military Corrective Training Centre
MDC GIBRALTAR .... Maritime Data Centre Gibraltar
MDHU DERRIFORD.. Ministry of Defence Hospital Unit (Derriford)
MDHU FRIMLEY .... Ministry of Defence Hospital Unit (Frimley Park)

MDHU NORTH .... MDHU North Allerton
MDHU PETERBRGH .... Ministry of Defence Hospital Unit (Peterborough)
MERLIN IPT .... Merlin Integrated Project Team
MHRF(F) .... Maritime Higher Readiness Force (France)
MSA .... Medical Supply Agency
MTS IPT .... Maritime Trainers and Simulators Integrated Project Team
MWC PORTSDOWN .... Maritime Warfare Centre (Portsdown)
MWC SOUTHWICK .... Maritime Warfare Centre Southwick
MWS COLLINGWOOD .... Her Majesty's Ship COLLINGWOOD Maritime Warfare School
MWS DEF DIV SCHL .... Maritime Warfare School Defence Diving School
MWS EXC BRISTOL .... Her Majesty's Ship BRISTOL
MWS EXCELLENT .... Her Majesty's Ship EXCELLENT Maritime Warfare School
MWS HM TG (D) .... MWS Hydrographic & Meterological Training Group
MWS RM SCH MUSIC .... Maritime Warfare School Royal Marines School of Music
MWS SOUTHWICK PK .... Maritime Warfare School (Southwick Park)
NAIC NORTHOLT .... Naval Aeronautical Information Cell
NATO DEF COL .... Nato Defence College
NATO MEWSG VL .... NATO Multi-Service Electronic Warfare Support Group Yeovilton
NAVSEC .... Naval Secretary
NBC PORTSMOUTH .... Naval Base Commander (Portsmouth)
NCSA SECTOR NWD .... NCSA Sector Northwood
NC3 AGENCY .... NATO C3 Agency
NELSON .... Her Majesty's Ship NELSON
NELSON WF .... Her Majesty's Ship Nelson-Waterfront
NEPTUNE BNSL .... NEPTUNE - BABCOCK NAVAL SERVICES LTD
NEPTUNE DDA .... Defence Dental Agency Scotland
NEPTUNE DLO .... Captain Base Port (Personnel & Support), HMS NEPTUNE
NEPTUNE DSA .... HMS Neptune - Director of Safety Assurance
NEPTUNE FD .... Facilities Department
NEPTUNE 2SL/CNH .... HMS Neptune (NSC)
NEW IPT .... Naval EW Integrated Project Team
NORTH DIVING GRP .... Northern Diving Group
NP AFGHANISTAN .... Naval Party Afghanistan
NP BOSNIA .... Naval Party BOSNIA Royal Naval Liaison Officer - Banja Luka
NP BRISTOL .... Nuclear Propulsion Bristol
NP DNREAY .... Nuclear Propulsion Dounreay
NS OBERAMMERGAU .... NATO School (SHAPE) Oberammergau
NSRS IPT .... Nato Submarine Rescue System Integrated Project Team
NTE(TTD) .... Naval Training & Education (Training Technology Division)
NW IPT .... Nuclear Weapons Integrated Project Team
NWR .... Nuclear Weapon Regulator
OCLC BIRM .... Officer Careers Liaison Centre, Birmingham
OCLC BRISTOL .... Officer Careers Liaison Centre,Bristol
OCLC MANCH .... Officer Careers Liaison Centre, Manchester
OCLC ROSYTH .... Officer Careers Liaison Centre, Rosyth
OPTAG .... Operational Training and Advisory Group (Warminster)
PAAMS PARIS .... Principal Anti Air Missile System Paris

PJHQ........Permanent Joint Headquarters (Northwood)
PJHQ AUGMENTEES........Permanent Joint Headquarters (Northwood)
PRESIDENT........Royal Naval Reserve London (RN Staff)
PSYOPS TEAM........Psychological Operations Team
QHM CLYDE........Queens Harbourmaster (Clyde)
RAF AWC........Air Warfare Centre RAFC Cranwell
RAF COTTESMORE........Royal Air Force Cottesmore
RAF CRANWELL EFS........Royal Air Force Cranwell (Defence Elementary Flying Training
RAF LINTN/OUSE........Royal Air Force (Linton On Ouse)
RAF SHAWBURY........Royal Air Force Shawbury
RAF WEST DRAYTON........Royal Air Force West Drayton
RAF WITTERING........Royal Air Force Wittering
RALEIGH........Her Majesty's Ship RALEIGH
RCDM........Royal Centre for Defence Medicine
RCDS........Royal College of Defence Studies
RH HASLAR........The Royal Hospital Haslar
RM BAND PLYMOUTH........Band of HM Royal Marines Plymouth
RM BAND PTSMTH........Band of HM Royal Marines Portsmouth
RM BAND SCOTLAND........Band of HM Royal Marines Scotland
RM BICKLEIGH........Royal Marines BICKLEIGH
RM CHIVENOR........Royal Marines CHIVENOR
RM CONDOR........Royal Marines CONDOR
RM NORTON MANOR........Royal Marines NORTON MANOR
RM WARMINSTER........Royal Marines WARMINSTER
RMB STONEHOUSE........Royal Marine Barracks Stonehouse
RMC OF SCIENCE........Royal Military College of Science Shrivenham
RMDIV LECONFIELD........Royal Marines Division Army School of Mechanical Transport
RMR BRISTOL........Royal Marines Reserve Bristol
RMR LONDON........Royal Marines Reserve London
RMR MERSEYSIDE........Royal Marines Reserve Merseyside
RMR SCOTLAND........Royal Marines Reserve Scotland
RMR TYNE........Royal Marines Reserve Tyne
RN GIBRALTAR........Royal Navy Gibraltar
RN SINGAPORE........Royal Navy Singapore
RNAS CULDROSE........Royal Naval Air Station Culdrose
RNAS YEOVILTON........Royal Naval Air Station Yeovilton
RNEAWC........Royal Naval Element Air Warfare Centre
RNLO GULF........Royal Naval Liaison Officer (Gulf)
RNLO JTF4........Royal Naval Liaison Officer for Commander Joint Task Force 4,USN
RNP TEAM........Royal Naval Presentation Team
RNSR BOVINGTON........Royal Naval School of Recruiting, Bovington
RNU RAF DIGBY........Royal Naval Unit RAF DIGBY
RNU ST MAWGAN........Royal Naval Unit St Mawgan
SA ANKARA........Service Attache Ankara
SA ATHENS........Service Attache Athens
SA BERLIN........Service Attache Berlin
SA BRAZIL........Service Attache Brazil

SA BUENOS AIRES........ Service Attache Buenos Aires
SA CAIRO........ Service Attache Cairo
SA COPENHAGEN........ Service Attache Copenhagen
SA ISLAMABAD........ Service Attache Islamabad
SA LISBON........ Service Attache Lisbon
SA MADRID........ Service Attache Madrid
SA MALAYSIA........ Service Advisor Malaysia
SA MOSCOW........ Service Attache Moscow
SA MUSCAT........ Service Attache Muscat
SA OSLO........ Service Attache Oslo
SA PARIS........ Service Attache Paris
SA PRETORIA........ Service Advisor Pretoria
SA ROME........ Service Attache Rome
SA SEOUL........ Service Attache Seoul
SA THE HAGUE........ Service Attache the Hague
SA TOKYO........ Service Attache Tokyo
SABR IPT........ SABR Integrated Project Team
SACLANT ITALY........ Supreme Allied Commander Atlantic, Italy
SACT BELGIUM........ Supreme Allied Commander Transformation, Belgium
SANS IPT........ Sensors, Avionics and Navigation Systems Integrated Project Team
SAT IPT........ Satellite Communications Integrated Project Team
SAUDI AFPS SAUDI........ Saudi Armed Forces Project Sales Saudi
SBS BASE........ Headquarters Squadron Royal Marines Base
SCOTIA........ Her Majesty's Ship SCOTIA
SCU SHORE........ Special Communications Unit (Shore)
SDG PORTSMOUTH........ Southern Diving Unit 2 (Portsmouth)
SETT GOSPORT........ Submarine Escape Training Tank Gosport
SHAPE BELGIUM........ Supreme Headquarters Allied Powers In Europe (Belgium)
SHERWOOD........ RNR Communications Training Centre (Nottingham) (RN Staff)
SONAR 2087 IPT........ Defence Procurement Agency Peer Group G
STG BRISTOL........ Sea Technology Group Bristol
STRIKFORNATO........ Strike Force NATO
STRS IPT........ STRS Integrated Project Team
SULTAN........ Her Majesty's Ship SULTAN
SULTAN AIB........ Admiralty Interview Board
SUPT OF DIVING........ Superintendent of Diving
TCM IPT........ Torpedo Counter Measures Integrated Project Team
TEMERAIRE........ Her Majesty's Ship TEMERAIRE
TORPEDO IPT........ Torpedo Integrated Project Team
T45 IPT........ Type 45 Destroyer Integrated Project Team
UKCEC IPT........ UK Cooperative Engagement Capability
UKLFCSG RM........ United Kingdom Landing Force Command Support Group Royal Marines
UKMCC BAHRAIN........ UK Maritime Battle Staff Bahrain
UKMFTS IPT........ UK MILITARY FLYING TRAINING SYSTEM
UKMILREP BRUSS........ United Kingdom Military Representative Brussels
UKNMR SHAPE........ United Kingdom Military Representative SHAPE
UKSU AFSOUTH........ United Kingdom National Support Unit Allied Forces Southern Europ

UKSU JHQ LISBON .... United Kingdom Support Unit Joint Headquarters Lisbon
UKSU JHQ NORTH .... United Kingdom National Support Element Allied Forces Northern
UKSU SHAPE.............. United Kingdom Support Unit Supreme Headquarters Allied Powers in E
UN AFRICA ....Naval Party Sierra Leone
UNOMIG...UN Monitoring in Georgia
VICTORY..Her Majesty's Ship VICTORY
VIVID ....Her Majesty's Ship VIVID
WILDFIRE ....Her Majesty's Ship WILDFIRE
1 ASSLT GP RM...1 Assault Group Royal Marines
2SL/CNH.................................. Second Sea Lord/Commander-in-Chief Naval Home Command
2SL/CNH FOTR.. Flag Officer Training and Recruiting Headquarters
2SL/CNH RNCMC.. 2SL/CNH Royal Navy Crisis Management Centre
20(R) SQN (RN) .... 20(R) Squadron (RN)
29 CDO REGT RA..29 Commando Regiment Royal Artillery
40 CDO RM...40 Commando Royal Marines
42 CDO RM...42 Commando Royal Marines
45 CDO RM...45 Commando Royal Marines
702 SQN HERON.. 702 Naval Air Squadron Her Majesty's Ship HERON
727 NAS .... 727 Naval Air Squadron
750 SQN HERON...Heron Flight
750 SQN SEAHAWK .... 750 Squadron Seahawk
771 SQN...771 Squadron
815 SQN HQ....................... 815 Headquarters Naval Air Squadron, Her Majesty's Ship HERON
824 SQN...824 Squadron
829 SQN HQ.. 829 Naval Air Squadron Headquarters
848 SQN HERON.. 848 Naval Air Squadron
849 SQN HQ.. 849 Naval Air Squadron Headquarters
899 SQN HERON.. 899 Naval Air Squadron Her Majesty's Ship HERON

Prizes, Testimonials, Etc.

Until further notice silver-gilt medals will be substituted for gold medals)

**Subject to revision consequent upon change in training pattern for Junior Officers.*

THE GEDGE MEDAL, THE CHARLES DARGAVILLE BALLARD PRIZE, THE PAYMASTER-IN-CHIEF EDWARD ROBINSON MEMORIAL PRIZE

These prize funds have had their incomes combined, under a scheme approved by the Charity Commissioners, so that the Managing Trustees may award a medal and a suitable prize annually to the outstanding officer undergoing training on the Junior Officers' Course.

The Gedge Medal was instituted when the members of the Royal Naval Accountant Officers' Dining Club subscribed the sum of £260 to institute a prize for Junior Supply Officers. The Gedge Medal is named in commemoration of Staff Paymaster Joseph T. Gedge, RN, who was killed of the 6th August 1914 when HMS Amphion was sunk by a mine and who was the first British Officer of all the fighting service to be killed during the 1914-18 war.

The Charles Dargaville Ballard Prize was founded in 1954 under the will of the late Captain G. N. Ballard, RN, in memory of his son, Acting Paymaster Sub-Lieutenant Charles Dargaville Ballard, RN, who was killed in action when HMS Manchester was torpedoed by aircraft on 23rd July 1941, while escorting a Malta convoy south of Sardinia.

The Paymaster-in-Chief Edward Robinson Memorial Prize was founded, also in 1954, under the terms of the will of the late Commander A.A.E. Robinson, OBE, RN, in memory of his father, Paymaster-in-Chief Edward Robinson, RN.

The Managing Trustee of these combined prize funds is the Commander, Royal Naval Supply School, HMS Raleigh.

The name of the recipient will be published annually in a DCI.

*THE HUGH CHEETHAM-HILL MEMORIAL TRUST FUND

This fund was established in 1958 by Dr. and Mrs. H.C. Hill, in memory of their son, Lieutenant Commander Hugh Cheetham-Hill, RN, an officer of the Navigation and Direction Branch of the Royal Navy, who died on the 5th October, 1957.

The annual income derived from the Fund's holding in the United Service Trustee Combined Charitable Fund is used to provide a prize to be known as the "Hugh Cheetham-Hill Prize" awarded annually on the recommendation of the Commodore, School of Maritime Operations, to the Officer of the Royal Navy who achieves the best results of the year on the 'n'/SM(n) Course.

The prize will consist of a cheque for the purchase of books or instruments relating to the Science of Navigation, subject to the discretion of the Commodore, School of Maritime Operations.

When two officers are judged to be of equal merit the prize money is shared.

THE ADMIRAL SIR RICHARD CLAYTON MEMORIAL SWORD

The annual award of a presentation sword to the Senior Upper Yardman Warfare Branch Officer who achieves the highest overall marks in the year through initial training at BRNC Dartmouth and the Junior Warfare Officers' Course. The sword is donated by BAE Systems. The Commodore SMOPS approves the award.

The prize winner's name will be published annually in a DCI.

THE CARL ZEISS PRIZE

The annual award of a pair of binoculars, donated by Carl Zeiss, to the Warfare Branch Officer (Naval College Entry or Direct Graduate Entry) who obtains the highest overall marks on the Junior Warfare Officers' Course. Commodore SMOPS approves the award.

The prize winner's name is published annually in a DCI.

THE MARTIN BONIWELL MEMORIAL CUP

This trophy was instituted in 1994 in memory of Lt. Cdr. Martin Boniwell, RN, who died on 20th January 1994 whilst serving in HMS Dryad. The cup is awarded to the top student of each PWO course. Commodore SMOPS approves the award.

THE CUNNINGHAM INITIATIVE AWARDS FUND

In response to an appeal in 1965, a memorial was erected in Trafalgar Square and a plaque in St. Paul's Cathedral to commemorate the life and work of Admiral of the Fleet Viscount Cunningham of Hyndhope. After defraying the costs, there remained a sum of approximately £2,803, and in accordance with the wishes of the donors, the Cunningham Memorial committee set up the Cunningham Initiative Awards Fund.

The object of this Fund is to assist young Royal Naval Officers and Ratings, young Women Naval Service Officers and Ratings, young Royal Marines Officers and other ranks, and QARNNS Officers and Ratings, in defraying the cost of schemes of an adventurous or unconventional nature planned on their own initiative and which will result in the recipients of the awards being more useful members of their Service.

Applications should be forwarded to the Ministry of Defence in accordance with instructions contained in current Defence Council Instructions (Royal Navy).

DARTMOUTH PRIZE (1) FOR OFFICERS ON THEIR INITIAL COMMISSION

This prize is awarded termly to the Officer serving on his Initial Commission in either the Warfare or Supply Specialisations, who obtains the highest marks in the Naval Studies Course examinations in his final term at the Britannia Royal College, Dartmouth.

The prize uses income derived from holdings in the United Service Trustee Combined Charitable Fund attributed to:

a) The Geoffrey Gore-Brown, Midshipman RN, Memorial Scholarship which was founded under the terms of the will of the late Mrs. D.A. Gore-Brown in memory of her son Geoffrey.

b) The Robert Roxburgh Memorial Prize which was founded in 1917, by Mrs. J.B. Roxburgh in memory of her son, Midshipman Robert Roxburgh RN, of HMS Indefatigable, who was killed in action in the Battle of Jutland on the 31st May 1916.

c) The Ryder Memorial Fund was founded in memory of Admiral of the Fleet Sir Alfred Phillips Ryder, KCB, who died on the 30th April 1888.

d) The Wemyss prize which was founded in 1946 by the Hon. Alice Wemyss in memory of her father, Admiral of the Fleet Lord Wester Wemyss, who had been the first Captain of the Royal Naval College at Osborne

DARTMOUTH PRIZE (2) FOR AIRCREW OFFICERS

This prize is awarded termly to the officer of the Aircrew Specialisation who obtains the highest marks in the Naval Studies Course examinations in his final term at the Britannia Royal Naval College, Dartmouth.

The prize uses the income derived from holdings in the United Service Trustee Combined charitable Fund attributed to:

a) The Hickes Memorial Prize, which was founded in 1906 by Miss E.K.T. Hickes in memory of her brother, Cadet Charles Meyrick Hickes, who died in 1862 while under training in HMS Britannia at Portland.

b) The Harold Tennyson Memorial Prize, which was founded in 1917 by Lord Tennyson in memory of his son, Acting Sub-Lieutenant The Hon. Harold Courtenay Tennyson, RN, of HMS Viking, who was killed in action on the 29th January 1916.

THE HEWLETT-PACKARD SWORD

The Hewlett-Packard Company instituted in 1939 the award of a sword to the student who is adjudged to have achieved the best results during the Junior Supply officers course during that year.

The name of the recipient will be published annually in a DCI.

THE WORSHIPFUL COMPANY OF CHARTERED SECRETARIES AND ADMINISTRATORS MEDAL (OFFICER)

This prize is awarded to the Officer on the Junior Supply Officers' Course with the highest examination results in the Secretarial and Law examinations, combined with performance in the Secretarial simulator.

The medal is awarded on the recommendation of the Commander Royal Naval Supply School.

The Officer's name will be published annually in a DCI.

THE COMMANDER EGERTON PRIZE

This Prize was founded in 1901 in memory of Commander Frederick Grenville Egerton, Royal Navy, who was mortally wounded on the 2nd November 1899, in the defence of Ladysmith, whilst acting in the execution of his duty.

The dividends arising from a sum of £500 given by the relatives and invested in Government securities will be employed in providing the prize, to be called "The Commander Egerton Prize", which will be awarded annually at the discretion of the Admiralty Board to the Seaman Officer who achieves the best results of the year in the Above Water Warfare stream of the Principal Warfare Officer Course. Should there be no Officer of sufficient merit, the prize may be withheld at the discretion of the Commodore, School of Maritime Operations.

COMMANDER F.G. EMLEY MEMORIAL FUND

This prize was founded in 1972 in memory of Commander Frank Gordon Emley, RN, who died on the 17th November, 1971.

The annual income derived from the Fund's holding in the United Services Trustee Combined Charitable Fund is employed to provide a prize known as the Commander Emley Prize, in the form of an inscribed silver "Armada" Dish, to be awarded annually to the Naval Officer who gains the highest marks out of the three Nuclear General Courses held each year.

CAPTAIN FARMER MEMORIAL PRIZES

The Captain Farmer Memorial Prizes were founded by the will of Captain Donald William Farmer, RN, who died on the 4th January 1982. The annual income derived from the Charity's holding in the United Services Trustee Combined Charities Fund will be employed to provide five cash prizes annually to Royal Navy Officers as follows:

Officers Under Training	Per cent of annual income
a) The RN Officer in his Initial Commission who gains the highest mark in examinations in professional subjects at Britannia Royal Naval College Dartmouth.	17.5
b) The RN Officer in his Initial Commission who gains the highest aggregate marks at the Fleet Board Examinations	17.5
c) The RN Officer in his Initial Commission of RN or Commonwealth Navies who gains the highest marks on the Principal Warfare Officers Course.	15
Navigation Specialists	
a) The Officer who gains the highest marks on Specialist Navigation Officers Course	25
b) The RN Submarine Service officer who gains the highest marks on Specialist Navigating Officers Course	25

THE GOODENOUGH MEDAL AND FUND

This Prize was founded in memory of Captain James G. Goodenough, CB, CMG, who died on 20th August 1875, while serving as Commodore on the Australian Station, from wounds inflicted with poisoned arrows in an unprovoked attack by natives of Santa Cruz.

The annual income from the fund was formerly used to purchase a gold medal. Now its provides a cash prize awarded annually to the Warfare Branch Officer (Naval College Entry or Direct Graduate Entry) who, having achieved a first class pass at Fleetboard, attains the highest mark in the Warfare Module of the Junior Warfare Officers Course.

Commodore SMOPS approves the award and the prize winner's name is published annually in a DCI.

THE GRAHAM NAVAL HISTORY PRIZE

This Prize was founded in 1909 by Lady Graham in memory of her husband, Admiral Sir William Graham, GCB, formerly Captain HMS Britannia Training Ship.

The annual income, comprising dividends from the Fund's holding in the United Services Trustee Combined Charitable Fund, is employed in providing prizes to be awarded at the Britannia Royal Naval College, Dartmouth, to the Officers of the Seaman or Supply Specialisations for work undertaken in connection with the subject of defence.

Officers of Foreign and Commonwealth navies are eligible to receive this prize.

THE ADMIRAL SIR MAX HORTON PRIZE

The late Admiral Sir Max Horton, GCB, DSO, who served with great distinction in command of submarines during World War 1, and as Flag Officer Submarines from January 1940 to November 1942, left to the Admiralty in his Will, the sum of £500, to be applied for the benefit of Officers of the submarine service of the Royal Navy.

This sum has been invested and the interest is used, in accordance with the Admiral's wishes, to provide a prize annually to the officer of the seaman specialisation of the Royal Navy who achieves the best overall standard on his training course for submarine officer, taking into consideration the results of the examination at the ends of Parts I and II training in the Submarine School and Part III Sea Continuation Training as well as the Commanding Officers' reports from Sea.

The prize will be awarded by the Admiralty Board each year, on the recommendation of the Flag Officer Submarines.

The prize will consist of a tankard bearing a set of dolphins and inscribed with the name of the recipient and the date and nature of the award.

JACKSON-EVERETT PRIZE

In 1927, Signal Officers, past and present, on the Active List, subscribed a sum of approximately £280 to institute a prize for officers qualifying as Signal Specialists, to be known as the "Jackson-Everett Prize".

The Prize is awarded annually to the Warfare Officer who achieves the best results of the year in the Communications and Electronic Warfare Stream of the PWO Course. The prize may not be awarded in any year in which the standard of results obtained by the Officer passing the best examinations is not considered to be of sufficient merit to warrant the award at the discretion of the Commodore SMOPS.

The Prize consists of a sum of money (the income available) for the purchase of books and/or instruments.

The Officer's name will be published annually in a DCI.

THE INSTITUTE OF ADMINISTRATIVE MANAGEMENT (IAM) PRIZE

The IAM Prize was first awarded in 1999. It takes the form of a piece of engraved crystal and a cash award of £100 to the officer achieving the highest overall average examination results on the Junior Supply Officers' Course (JSOC).

THE QUEEN'S GOLD MEDAL

Awarded to the sponsored officer (Naval College Entry, University Cadet Entry or Engineering Sponsorship Scheme) of the Engineering Specialisation achieving the best academic results on degree course. Subject in the case of ESS Officers to subsequent entry to BRNC.

Officers who graduate at Cambridge University are eligible for the award.

THE QUEEN'S SWORD

A sword is awarded each year by Her Majesty the Queen, to the Initial Commission Officer Under Training of either the Warfare or Supply Branch, who achieves the highest overall performance in Naval General Training (and Naval Studies when appropriate) at the Britannia Royal Naval College, Dartmouth, in the preceding year.

A sword is also awarded each year, by Her Majesty the Queen, to the Full Career Commission Officer of the Engineering Specialisation who, on completion of the three/four year degree course and the HMS Collingwood/HMS Sultan phase of SEMC, is adjudged to have achieved the best overall results.

THE QUEEN'S BINOCULARS

Six pairs of binoculars are awarded each year at the Britannia Royal Naval College, Dartmouth, by Her Majesty the Queen, to the Officers Under Training who, on passing out, have obtained the highest score in Naval General Training in the preceding calendar year.

ADMIRALTY PRIZE

A pair of binoculars to be awarded to the best young officer on the Royal Navy Young Officers' Course in the preceding calendar year.

KING GEORGE V PRIZE SCHOLARSHIPS

In accordance with the wishes of His Majesty King George V, that the greater part of the Fund, subscribed for the purpose of commemorating His Majesty's Coronation by subjects of His Majesty bearing the Christian name 'George' in all parts of the Empire, should be utilised for the benefit of junior Officers of the Royal Marines who may find difficulty in meeting the cost of the final stage of their military training, the sum available was invested and the arising income was devoted to the institution of Scholarships termed the 'King George V Prize Scholarships'. Scholarships are awarded each year to the Officers in the Royal Marines who, after passing the Annual Competitive examination, are selected by the Commandant General to attend a British or Commonwealth Staff College.

The annual net income from the Fund will be divided equally between all those awarded a Scholarship in that year.

The first Scholarship was awarded in 1914.

THE MANTLE TROPHY

The Mantle Trophy was presented in 1984 by the Directors of the British Manufacture and Research Company Limited for competition by the Royal Navy in close range gunnery.

The trophy, in the form of a sterling silver cup and cover, is dedicated to the memory of Acting Leading Seaman Jack Mantle who won the Victoria Cross on 4 July 1940, while serving in HMS Foylebank at Portland.

The trophy is awarded every six months to the warship or Royal Fleet Auxiliary which has demonstrated the highest standard or greatest improvement in close range weapon effectiveness. The winners are nominated by the Flag Officer Sea Training.

RONALD MEGAW MEMORIAL PRIZE

This Prize, founded in 1906, is in memory of Midshipman Ronald Megaw, who was killed accidentally while at General Quarters on board HMS Montagu.

The annual income from the memorial fund provides a cash prize awarded annually to the Warfare Branch Officer (Naval College Entry) who obtains the highest aggregate of examination marks in the year. The aggregate total is a summation of the BRNC Professional, BRNC Academic, Fleetboard and Junior Warfare Officers Course marks. Commodore SMOPS approves the award and the prize winner's name is published annually in a DCI

HARWOOD PRIZE

This Prize was founded in 1946 by Sir Eugene Millington-Drake for the purpose of promoting knowledge of Hispanic culture. The annual income derived from the Fund's holding in the United Services Trustee Combined Charitable Fund is used in the provision of prizes to be awarded to the RN General List Officers from the Britannia Royal Naval College, Dartmouth, who demonstrate the highest level of excellence on the Naval Studies Course.

THE HAROLD HUDSON PLATE

The Harold Hudson Plate was donated by Mr. Hudson, a former Deputy Director of MW projects at AUWE Portland, on 15 November 1983. It is a silver plate suitably inscribed which is lodged with the Mine Warfare and Clearance Diving School.

The plate will be awarded to the Royal Naval Officer who gains the highest marks in passing the Mine Warfare Career Training Course, at present the Minewarfare module of the Long MCDO Course.

THE OGILVY MEDAL

This Medal was instituted in 1912 in memory of Captain Frederick Charles Ashley Ogilvy, RN, who died on the 18th December 1909, from typhoid fever, while in command of HMS Natal.

The dividends, arising from a sum of about £240 given by Officers of the Royal Navy and by certain friends and relatives, are employed in providing a medal to be called "The Ogilvy Medal", which is awarded annually, at the discretion of the Admiralty Board, to the Officer who achieves the best results of the year in the Underwater Warfare stream of the Principal Warfare Officer course. Should there be no Officer of sufficient merit the prize may be withheld at the discretion of the Commodore SMOPS.

THE PRENDERGAST PRIZE

It was the wish of Admiral Sir Robert Prendergast, KCB, Commander of HMS Excellent from December, 1901, to December, 1903, to arrange something to further the interest of HMS Excellent but due to ill-health and conditions he was unable to do so during his lifetime.

While it is not possible to achieve Admiral Prendergast's wishes by linking prizes with HMS Excellent, two annual prizes have been instituted as a memorial to him. Both prizes are of equal value and the money available for each will not exceed £100. The two annual prizes are awarded to:

a) The Royal Navy Officer of the WE specialisation who obtained the highest marks in the Weapon Engineering Qualification Oral Board of all the Weapons Engineering Career Courses held at HMS Collingwood in that year.

b) The rating who obtains the highest assessment of the Charge Chief, Weapon Engineering Artificer Qualifying Courses at HMS Collingwood in that year.

SHADWELL TESTIMONIAL PRIZE

The Shadwell Testimonial Prize, founded in 1888 in memory of Admiral Sir Charles F. A. Shadwell KCB, who died 1 March 1886, takes the form of a sum of money (about £100) and a certificate. The first award was made on the plans received during 1899.

The award will be made to Officers who have submitted to the Hydrographer of the Navy through their Commanding Officer or Master the most credible plans of anchorage, harbours, small boat landings or seabed features. Submissions may also include reports and/or data associated with other marine soundings such as passage soundings, amendments to sailing directions or other hydrographic officer publications, or any other form of work in support of the broad aims of improving navigational safety.

It may be awarded to the following:

1) Officers and Warrant Officers of the Royal Navy, Royal Marines or a Commonwealth Navy, of a rank not higher than Lieutenant Commander Royal Navy, Captain Royal Marines, or equivalent,

2) Officers and Warrant Officers of the Royal Naval Reserve (any list) and Royal Fleet Auxiliary, of a rank not higher than Lieutenant Commander or First Officer, serving in one of Her Majesty's Ships or Establishments, Royal Fleet Auxiliaries, or a British-registered ship or vessel,

3) Officers of the Mercantile Marine serving in a British registered ship or vessel, who are not qualified or appointed as Hydrographic Surveyors.

The award will be made on the plans and data received at the Hydrographic Office, Taunton (UKHO), during each calendar year, by a committee consisting of the Hydrographer of the Navy, the Director of Defence Requirements and the Director of Nautical Chartering. No prize will be awarded in any year in which no work of sufficient merit is brought to the notice of the Award Committee.

In the case of cooperation in the production of a plan, a junior officer who has assisted materially in its construction may participate in the award, should the funds be sufficient.

For further information readers are advised to consult DCI RN 198/99.

THE BOYLE SOMERVILLE MEMORIAL PRIZE

A fund has been established in memory of Rear-Admiral Boyle Somerville, for the purpose of awarding a prize which will be known as the 'Boyle Somerville Memorial Prize', and has as its object the encouragement of research or development work in connection with the sciences of meteorology and oceanography.

The prize may be awarded annually to any Officer in the Royal Navy, or one of the Commonwealth navies, whose work during the period under review is adjudged to be of particular merit in connection with the development of meteorology or oceanography and their application to naval operations. Special consideration will be given to any original papers indicating a voluntary effort additional to the author's normal duties.

No prize will be awarded in any year in which no work of sufficient merit is brought to the notice of the Admiralty Board.

The amount of prize is expected to be not less than £100 in any one year and shall be expended in the purchase of books and/or instruments and/or other articles as approved by the Ministry of Defence.

The prize shall not be awarded more than once to the same Officer.

The award will be made on the material received at the Ministry in each calendar year at the sole discretion of the Director of Naval Surveying, Oceanography and Meteorology.

In case of cooperation, an Officer who has assisted in the production of material may participate in the award, should the fund be sufficient.

THE GILBERT BLANE MEDAL

In 1830, Sir Gilbert Blane, Baronet, formerly a member of the Board for Sick and Wounded Seamen, established, with the sanction of the Board of Admiralty, a fund for the encouragement of Naval Medical Science, which is vested in the Corporation of the Royal College of Surgeons of London, in trust.

This fund is employed for the purpose of conferring a Gold Medal annually on the Medical Officer of the Royal Navy who, to a degree which is considered worthy of recognition, has brought about an advance in any branch of Medical Science in its application to Naval Service, or has contributed to an improvement on any matter affecting the health or living conditions of Naval personnel.

Consideration is given to achievements on research, in original articles and reports, criticisms of a constructive character of existing conditions; and information which is brought to notice of meritorious work performed, or suggestions made, by Medical Officers within the scope of the Regulations governing the award of the Medal as stated above.

Special consideration will be given to a specific original work, which should be suitably bound, which has not previously been acknowledged by an award or academic distinction.

The Medal is awarded annually unless no Officer is considered to have qualified, in which event the Medal is held over until the following year or any subsequent year, when, if considered justifiable to do so, it is given as an additional award.

Medical Officers of all ranks are eligible for the award, and an Officer is not restricted to receiving the Medal on one occasion only during his career.

If the un-awarded Medals exceed four, their value is given to the Naval Medical Compassionate Fund.

Nominations for award should be forwarded to the Medical Director General (Navy).

CHADWICK NAVAL PRIZE

Sir Edwin Chadwick KGB, who died in 1890 aged 90, and who devoted his life to Sanitary Science, created in his Will a trust to continue his life's work. Chadwick's wishes, as expressed in the Trust scheme, embrace the promotion of sanitary science, the promotion of health, the prevention of disease and the physical training of the population. The Chadwick Trust supports research and teaching in Public Health Engineering at University College, London. It awards certificates and prizes to students at UCL and the School of Hygiene and Tropical Medicine who have shown merit in subjects within the Trust Scheme. Once in five years, the Trust may make an award to an officer of the Navy, Army or Air Force Medical Services, who has specially assisted in the promotion of the health of the Armed Forces. Nominations for awards are initiated by the Trust in conjunction with the individual Medical Directors-General.

ERROLL-ELDRIDGE FUND

This Fund was formed in June 1910 by a Trust Deed under bequest from Anne Louisa Russel Waldo-

Sibthorp (in memory of her husband Commander George Harry Richard Erroll, RN, who lost his life serving his country), and William Yates Eldridge, whereby the income from, or if required, the capital of £1,500, was to be applied in carrying on at the Royal Naval Hospital at Haslar, original medical research into matters affecting the health of the Navy, especially tuberculosis, and providing and maintaining plant and other requisites for that purpose.

Owing to changed circumstances, the Fund was reconstructed in 1989 as the Erroll-Eldridge Fund to form a prize, the income being devoted to annual "Erroll Prizes" to be awarded to personnel of the Royal Naval Medical Service who have made notable contribution to, or who have carried out useful research on the improvement of the health of Royal Naval personnel.

If, in any year, nobody is nominated whose work is considered to be of specific merit, the income may be applied for any educational charitable purpose for Royal Naval Medical personnel, or it may be re-invested thereby enhancing the value of the prize(s) subsequently awarded.

Medical personnel of all ranks are eligible for the prize; an Officer is not restricted to receiving the prize on one occasion only during his career, nor precluded from receiving the prize in addition to the Gilbert Blane Medal.

THE HARVEY-FLETCHER PRIZE FOR DENTAL OFFICERS

In 1973, a Trust Fund was founded by subscription amongst serving and retired officers of the Naval Dental Services and well-wishers, to provide a prize for award to a Dental Officer of the Active List who is adjudged to have brought about an advance in dental science or the associated sciences in their application to the Naval Service which is worthy of recognition. Under the Trust Deed, any contribution to the greater efficiency of the Naval Dental Service and improvement of the health of the Fleet may be considered. The title of the Prize, which may be awarded not more than once in three years, commemorates both a medical and a dental officer. Fleet Surgeon Christopher Harvey between 1880 and 1890 made the first recorded survey of Naval dental health and urged the need for qualified dentists in Naval Hospitals; Surgeon Rear Admiral (D) E. E. Fletcher, CBE, was the head of the Naval Dental Services from their formation in 1920 until his retirement in 1946.

THE HERBERT LOTT NAVAL TRUST FUND

Mr. Herbert Lott was a member of the London Stock Exchange and was extremely interested in the Royal Navy and the part it played in the defence of the Commonwealth. In 1928 he opened negotiations with the Admiralty for the creation of a Trust Fund and made an initial donation of £20,000, which he increased shortly after by another £5,000. The Herbert Lott Naval Trust Fund was instituted in 1930 to make awards to "those who shall show marked efficiency or shall contribute in signal degree to the improvement of the appliances of the Naval and Marine Forces". When Mr. Lott died in 1948 he left the whole of the residue of his estate (over £100,000) to the Trust Fund that bears his name.

Today, the Herbert Lott Fund is run as six separate Funds, each with its own trustee. Five of these funds make awards on a Command basis to personnel for marked efficiency in their duties or to students of courses and examinations.

The sixth fund makes awards for suggestions or inventions which improve the efficiency of the Naval Service

NORTH PERSIAN FORCES PRIZE

The North Persian Forces Memorial Prize, consisting of a silver medal and a purse, will be awarded for the best paper, published in any journal during the year on tropical medicine or tropical hygiene. Tropical hygiene will be interpreted in its widest sense to include any activity logically classifiable under the heading of tropical, preventative medicine.

Medical Officers of under 12 years' service of the Royal Navy, Royal Army Medical Corps, Royal Air Force and Ministry of Overseas Development are eligible to compete. If no suitable paper is published during the year by an officer of under 12 years service, papers by officers of over 12 years service may be considered. The Award is made by the RAMC Prize Committee.

PARKE'S MEMORIAL PRIZE

The Parke's Memorial Prize, consisting of approximately £50, a silver gilt medal and a purse, may be awarded annually to the Officer who has done most by professional work of outstanding merit, to promote the study of Naval Hygiene or Army Health. This includes any activity logically classifiable under the heading of preventive medicine. First consideration is given to original articles or reports on investigations published in a medical journal.

All regular officers of the Royal Navy or Army, except those on the Staffs of the Institute of Naval Medicine and the Royal Army Medical College, are eligible for this Prize, the award of which is made by the RAMC Prize Committee.

THE SUPERINTENDENT OF DIVING'S TROPHY

This trophy was presented in 1959 by Commander J. R. Carr, OBE, RN, for use as an award for MCD Officers.

The trophy consists of a silver cup, nine inches high, mounted on a plinth, which shows the names of the winners. It will be lodged with the Mine Warfare and Clearance Diving School.

The trophy will be awarded to the Officer gaining the highest marks in the Diving Phase of the Long MCDO Course. The Commodore SMOPS approves the award.

Officers of the Commonwealth navies will be eligible to receive this trophy.

A small sum of money has been invested in trustee stock for the maintenance of the trophy.

THE BEAUFORT-WHARTON TESTIMONIAL

This prize is an amalgamation of two testimonials set up to commemorate Rear Admirals Beaufort and Wharton, both former Hydrographers of the Navy.

The annual income from the memorial fund provides a cash prize awarded annually to the Warfare Branch Officer (Naval College Entry or Direct Graduate Entry) who obtains the highest aggregate marks in the year for Navigation. The aggregate total is a summation of BRNC, Fleetboard and Junior Warfare Officers Course Navigation marks.

Commodore SMOPS approves the award and the prize winner's name will be published annually in a DCI.

THE WILKINSON SWORD OF HONOUR AWARD

An annual award, instituted in 1986 by Wilkinson Sword Limited, to be presented to the Principal Warfare Officer who achieved the best overall results in the year on course. The Commodore SMOPS approves the award. Officers of the Commonwealth are eligible to receive this prize.

The prize winner's name will be published annually in a DCI.

THE WILKINSON SWORD OF PEACE AWARD

The Wilkinson Sword of Peace Award was instituted in 1966 to be presented annually by Wilkinson Sword Limited to the RN or RM unit, establishment or ship, which is judged to have made the most valuable contribution towards establishing good and friendly relations with the inhabitants of any territory within or without the United Kingdom.

Any ship, establishment or unit (including RM Commandos serving under the operational command of the Army) is eligible for this sword.

Nominations for the award are invited annually by DCI.

SIR JAMES MARTIN AWARD

The Sir James Martin Award is presented annually by the Guild of Air Pilots and Air Navigators, to a person who has made an outstanding and practical contribution leading to the safer operation of aircraft or space vehicles, or the enhanced survival of aircrews or passengers. It may also be awarded to a person who has performed an outstanding act in the air or on the ground connected with the survival of aerospace crews, passengers or aircraft, and which can be supported by some positive follow up action leading to the safer operation of aircraft or space vehicles, or the enhanced survival of aircrews or passengers.

Nominations for the award are invited annually by DCI.

DEFENCE SURVEYORS' ASSOCIATION ANNUAL PRIZE

A prize of £150 and a certificate may be awarded to the person who, in the opinion of the Council, has made a significant contribution to the advancement of the technology associated with mapping, data acquisition and management of spatial data. Consideration will also be given to those who have made a contribution to raising the profile of the Defence Geographic Community in general.

Nominations, with supporting written recommendations by Commanding Officers, are to sent to the Captain Hydrographic Surveying Squadron. The Captain will then make his proposal to the Board for the most deserving candidate. This is then considered by the Defence Surveyors' Association at their AGM, which is usually held in June.

ROYAL INSTITUTION OF CHARTERED SURVEYORS HYDROGRAPHIC SURVEY PRIZE

The Land and Hydrographic Survey Division of the RICS will award a prize of a £40 book token to the Officer gaining the highest marks on the Long Hydrographic Course held at the Royal Naval Hydrographic School, HMS Drake each year. The Commander RNHS will forward a nomination to the RICS in October.

ROYAL MARINES SWORD OF HONOUR

The Royal Marines' Sword of Honour is awarded to the Young Officer who is placed first overall in the order of merit on completion of basic training. The Sword is suitably engraved to commemorate the occasion. There is also a Sword of Honour awarded to the Officer placed first in the Special Duties Course order of merit.

ANNUAL COMPETITION FOR NAVAL HISTORY PRIZES

The aim of this competition is to encourage naval personnel to take an greater interest in naval history.

The competition is open to all officers and ratings serving in the RN, RM or QARNNS, officers and ratings of Commonwealth navies who are serving on exchange or loan service in the RN, RM or QARNNS, and officers and ratings of Commonwealth or foreign navies undergoing training with the RN, RM or QARNNS.

Prizes will be awarded in two sections as follows:

Officers First Prize	£500
Second Prize	£250
Third Prize	£150
Ratings First Prize	£500
Second Prize	£250
Third Prize	£150

All competitors submitting essays of sufficient merit will be awarded certificates. The Directorate of Naval Service Conditions, sponsors of this competition, reserves the right to increase the value and number of the prizes, to withhold the award of some or all of the prizes if essays of insufficient merit are submitted, and to combine prizes and divide them equally where prizewinning essays are of equal merit.

Essays are to be on one of the stipulated subjects and are to be in English, typed and of not more than 12,000 words.

Authorship of essays must be strictly anonymous. Each competitor is to use a 'nom de plume' which is to appear on the title page of the essay. The author's name must not appear on the essay.

Each essay is to be accompanied by a sealed envelope with the author's 'nom de plume' typed on the outside. The envelope is to contain a declaration signed by the author, that the essay is his/her unassisted work: this is to be countersigned by the author's Commanding Officer. The envelope should also contain a sheet of paper on which the competitor's 'nom de plume', name, rank/rate, official number and address have been typed.

Essays are to be sent to: Naval History Prize, Defence Studies Department, Joint Services Command and Staff College, Bracknell, Berks RG12 9DD, to arrive by 31st December of the year of the competition.

The subject for the essay for each year and the titles of the book recommended for study will be published in Defence Council Instructions (RN).

Competitors are advised to consult the note 'Naval History Prize - Advice for Competitors' which may be obtained from the Defence Studies Department, Joint Services Command and Staff College, Bracknell, Berks RG12 9DD.

Provision of Books. Authority cannot be given for the provision at official expense of books recommended for study in prize competitions. Full use should be made of the facilities afforded by the public library system, Admiralty Library, 3-5, Great Scotland Yard, London SW1A 2HW (which lends books of reference on a limited scale), and the Central Library, Drake Circus, Plymouth PL4 8AL (which lends Naval History Prize essays from previous competitions)

THE HOWARD-JOHNSTON SWORD

A Fund was established in 1985 by Rear Admiral C. D. Howard-Johnston, CB, DSC in memory of his son, Sub Lieutenant Richard Howard-Johnston who was lost at sea in HMS Affray in 1952.

The purpose of the fund is to present a sword annually to the best overall student on the Submarine Advance Warfare Course held at the Royal Naval Submarine School. The Managing Trustees have the discretion to award the prize in cash if there is insufficient income to purchase a sword.

The prize may not be awarded in any year in which the standard of results obtained by the best overall student is not considered to be of sufficient merit to warrant the award. The prize is awarded on the recommendation of the Commander, Royal Naval Submarine School, HMS Raleigh.

THE LORD FIELDHOUSE MEMORIAL PRIZE

Established by term mates of the Admiral of the Fleet the late Lord Fieldhouse, GCB, GBE, the prize will be awarded annually to the top student on the Submarine Intermediate Warfare Course on the recommendation of the Commander, Royal Naval Submarine School,. The prize takes the form of books to the value of £50.00.

SUBMARINE OFFICERS LIFE MEMBERS COMMITTEE FIELDHOUSE PRIZE

Established by the Submarine Officers Life Members Committee to commemorate Admiral of the Fleet the late Lord Fieldhouse, GCB, GBE, two prizes are awarded annually on the recommendation of the Commander, Royal Naval Submarine School, to the top student of the following courses:

a. Deputy Weapons Engineering Officer (SM) Course

b. Weapon Engineering Rating (SM) Courses for OM(WSM), OM(SSM), OM(TSM)

The prize takes the form of books to the value of £100 for officers and £50 for ratings.

THE COMMODORE'S WARFARE PRIZE

An annual award, instituted in 1984 by Ferranti Computer Systems Limited, to the Principal Warfare Officer who demonstrated outstanding achievement on course. Commodore SMOPS approves the award. Officers of the Commonwealth are eligible to receive this prize.

The prize winner's name will be published annually in a DCI

THE MARY TALBOT PRIZE

A book prize is awarded termly to the officer who demonstrates the best overall performance in leadership exercises during Terms 1 and 2 at the Royal Naval College, Dartmouth.

THE DORIS GRAHAM PRIZE

A book prize is awarded termly to the officer who achieves the highest aggregate score in the Assessed Command Exercise during Term 1 Leadership training at the Royal Naval College, Dartmouth.

ROYAL INSTITUTE OF NAVIGATION PRIZE

The Royal Institute of Navigation Prize is a silver salver which is presented annually by a representative of the Royal Institute of Navigation to the best Student on each SPEC(N) Course.

The following prizes are administered by the Officers' Training Centre at HMS SULTAN:

INSTITUTE OF MARINE ENGINEERING SILVER JUBILEE MEDAL

The Institute of Marine Engineering Silver Jubilee Medal is awarded annually to the graduate Marine Engineer Officer, of either the surface or sub-surface specialisation, who achieves the best overall results from initial and professional training.

BAE SYSTEMS SWORD

The BAE Systems Sword is awarded annually to the Senior Upper Yardman of the Engineering Specialisation who, on completion of the Britannia Royal Naval College and specialist school phases of post promotion courses, is judged to have achieved the best overall academic and professional results.

WESTLAND HELICOPTERS SWORD

The Westland Helicopters Sword was founded in 1994. The prize is awarded annually to a graduate Air Engineer Officer who, on completion of the Britannia Royal Naval College and professional courses, is judged to have achieved the best overall academic and professional results.

A W FORMAN BOOK PRIZE

The A W Forman Book Prize was founded by the Institution of Mechanical Engineers in 1982. The prize is awarded annually to the group of graduate Marine Engineer Officers, of either the surface or sub-surface specialisation, who achieves the best overall results for their Design, Make and Evaluate project during the Systems Engineering and Management Course.

ROYAL NAVAL ENGINEERS' BENEVOLENT SOCIETY CHATHAM MEMORIAL PRIZE FUND

The Chatham Memorial Fund was founded soon after World War II from the voluntary subscriptions of the Chatham Branch members of the Royal Naval Engineers' Benevolent Society. The annual income derived from the Fund's holdings is employed to provide a cash prize to the group of Senior Upper Yardman Marine Engineer Officers who achieve the best overall results for their Design and Evaluate project during the Systems Engineering and Management Course.

THE YARD PRIZE

The YARD Prize Fund was founded in 1987 by Yarrow Admiralty Research Development Limited with the object of promoting excellence in project work. The annual income derived from the Fund's holdings is employed in providing a cash prize to a graduate Marine Engineer Officer who, on completion of the Masters of Science program at University College London, is judged to have achieved the best post-graduate project.

Commonwealth are eligible to receive this prize.

FLEET AIR ARM PRIZES AND AWARDS

Note:

1. *Nominations for prizes will be based on courses qualifying in a calendar year.*
2. *Should nominees not achieve a sufficiently high standard the respective trophy will not be awarded.*
3. *Details of Trophies and Awards are contained in Naval Air Command General Orders - Chapter 13.*
4. *Administration of a particular award is indicated by brackets after the award title.*

THE ARMSTRONG-WHITWORTH TROPHY (RNAS Culdrose)

Originally presented by Armstrong Whitworth in 1956. It is awarded to the student obtaining best air mark on the Basic Observer Course.

THE AUSTRALIA SHIELD (COMNA)

The Australia Shield was bought from trust monies originally donated by the people of Australia and is awarded annually by the FOMA to the Front Line Squadron achieving the highest degree of operational capability over the year 1st December to 30th November.

The Silver Challenge Shield is retained in the ship or establishment having the winners on its strength. The Commanding Officer of the winning squadron has authority to spend a cash prize of £500 on amenities for the benefit of the squadron as a whole.

THE BAMBARA FLIGHT SAFETY TROPHY (COMNA)

The Bambara Flight Safety trophy, a silver cup, was allocated to the Naval Air Command in 1959 from funds made available from the paying off of HMS BAMBARA in Sri Lanka.

The trophy, and a shield for the runner-up, is awarded annually by FOMA to the unit with the best flight safety record.

THE BOYD TROPHY (COMNA)

The Boyd trophy, a silver model of a Swordfish, was presented to the Naval Air Command in 1946 by the Fairey Aviation Company Limited in commemoration of Vice Admiral Sir Dennis Boyd, KCB, CBE, DSC.

It is awarded annually to the Naval pilot(s) or aircrew(s) who, in the opinion of FOMA, has achieved the finest feat of aviation during the previous year. It is retained by the unit in which the winner was serving at the time the winning feat was achieved.

THE HENRY LEIGH CARSLAKE PRIZE (COMNA)

This is awarded annually for the best article on the subject of the work and development of the FAA. It is open to RN and RNR personnel of any specialisation who have completed their training and are currently serving in the Naval Air Command.

DAEDALUS TROPHY (RNAS Culdrose)

Originally presented by HMS Daedalus in 1956, it is awarded to the student gaining the best overall mark on each Basic Observer Course.

THE FAIRCHILD HILLER TROPHY (COMNA)

A silver "Comyns Cup" inscribed "Helicopter Ground School Trophy" presented in 1967 to the RNHGS by the Fairchild Hiller Corporation to mark the long association between the School and the Corporation.

The trophy is awarded annually to the student pilot who gains the highest marks in ground subjects on the previous years Basic Flying Training Course at DHFS.

THE FULMAR TROPHY (RNAS Culdrose)

The trophy consists of a silver, two-handled cup approximately 11 inches high on a plinth. It is awarded to the best observer completing AEW OFT.

THE PHILIP HALLAM TROPHY ((RNAS Yeovilton)

The Hallam Trophy, consisting of a silver model of a Hunter aircraft, was presented to the Fleet Air Arm in 1964 by Mr. V. Hallam in memory of his son Lieutenant P. C. G. Hallam who was killed in a flying accident at Lossiemouth in 1960. It is awarded annually to the best pilot completing Harrier OFT.

THE HARGREAVES TROPHY (RAF Cranwell)

This is a silver cup presented by Commander C. F. Hargreaves in 1968. It is awarded at the end of each course to the student pilot who obtains the best results in flying at the RNEFTS.

THE KELLY MEMORIAL PRIZE (COMNA)

The prize was founded in 1958 from the residue of donations given to erect a memorial plaque in the Chapel at BRNC Dartmouth to the late Lieutenant Commander (P) D. P. W. Kelly, Royal Navy.

The Prize consists of a silver model of a Sea Hawk mounted on a plinth carrying plaques to be inscribed with the winners' names, and is awarded annually to the best Aviator qualifying for the award of "wings".

THE KELMSLEY TROPHY (RNAS Culdrose)

This trophy was presented by the FAA Officers' Association. It is to be held at RNAS Culdrose and awarded to the best pilot completing ASW AFT.

THE MIDSHIPMAN M SIMON TROPHY (RAF Cranwell)

This trophy was presented to the RNEFTS in 1979 by Mr. and Mrs. Simon in memory of their son, Midshipman M. Simon, RN, who was killed in a flying accident at RAF Leeming in 1978. It is awarded at the end of each course to the student pilot who obtains the best results in ground school.

THE 141 NAVIGATION TROPHY (RAF Cranwell)

A wooden shield, approximately 12 inches high with a silver scroll and silver nameplates surrounding it. It was presented by the RAF Officers of 141 HSP Course in November 1968, and is awarded to the student who achieves the best overall marks in Navigation including the Final Navigation Test at the end of each course at RNEFTS.

THE LOUIS NEWMARK FLYING TROPHY (COMNA)

A silver salver presented to the Royal Naval Helicopter School in 1967 by Louis Newmark Limited in recognition of the close ties over several years between RN Helicopter Squadrons and the Company. It is awarded annually to the student pilot who achieves the highest mark in flying on the previous years' Basic Flying Training Course at DFHS.

THE ADMIRAL SIR DUDLEY POUND PRIZE FUND (COMNA)

This prize fund was established in 1955 out of monies from the Admiral Pound Memorial Fund.

Seven prizes annually are awarded to the four pilots and three observers who achieve the greatest success at an Operational Flying School in each of the following groupings:

1) SK6/Merlin (O)
2) SK6/Merlin (P)
3) AEW (O)
4) Lynx (O)
5) Lynx (P)
6) SK 4 (P)
7) FA 2 (P)

The selection of Officers is made at the end of each calendar year, and award is restricted to ab-initio students.

The prize money, currently £75, is made available for the purchase of books or instruments (including such things as watches), the choice being subject to Ministry of Defence approval.

THE ROBERT SANDISON TROPHY (COMNA)

The trophy, a silver model of a Wyvern aircraft, was presented to the Fleet Air Arm by Mr. P. Sandison in memory of his son, Lieutenant R. E. Sandison, RN, who was killed in a flying accident in September 1956. It is awarded by FOMA to the aircrew making the most valuable contribution to the development of weapons, weapon tactics or methods of delivery.

THE WALLROCK TROPHY (BRNC Dartmouth)

This trophy was presented in 1949 by Mr. Samuel Wallrock on the institution of the Short Service Commission (Aircrew) entry. The trophy consists of a bronze plaque on an oak background and is awarded to the Supplementary List midshipman obtaining the highest marks in passing out examination for each course of general naval and air training at BRNC Dartmouth. The recipient also receives a WALLROCK tankard by British Aerospace.

THE SOPWITH PUP TROPHY (COMNA)

The Sopwith Pup trophy is a silver model of a Sopwith Pup Aircraft, which was presented to the Flag Officer Carriers and Amphibious Ships by Hawker Siddley Aviation (now British Aerospace) to mark the firm's long association with the Fleet Air Arm.

The trophy is awarded annually by COMNA to the ship whose flight achieves and maintains the highest degree of Operational Capability over the year from 1st December to 30th November. The trophy is normally to be retained in the ship, but may be transferred to the flight's parent air station at the discretion of the Commanding Officer.

THE WESTLAND PRIZE (RNAS Culdrose/RNAS Yeovilton)

The trophies are a Silver Cup, which was first awarded in 1965 by the then Westland Aircraft Company, and a Silver Salver, which was presented in 1997 by GKN Westland Helicopters Limited. Both trophies mark the company's long and close association with the rotary wing aviation in the Fleet Air Arm. They are awarded annually at RNAS Culdrose and RNAS Yeovilton, to the aircrew officer or rating who has achieved the best all-round results in Operational Flying Training on Helicopters. A prize tankard is presented to the individuals to mark the award.

THE FERRANTI BLUE FOX RADAR TROPHY (RNAS Yeovilton)

This trophy, a table model of the Blue Fox radar approximately 8.5 inches high, was presented to the Fleet Air Arm in 1982 by Ferranti Limited (Radar Systems Department) The trophy is awarded annually to the officer or rating judged to have made the most valuable engineering contribution to the Sea Harrier Weapon System.

Recipients also receive a cash award of £25.

THE ROBIN BOSTOCK TROPHY RNAS Culdrose)

A silver salver presented in 1987 by Mrs. F. J. H. Rathbone in memory of her brother-in-law who was killed in action while attacking German warships at Trondheim in 1940. It is awarded to the observer who achieves the best overall flying marks on each OFT course.

THE ROLLS ROYCE ENGINEERING EFFICIENCY TROPHY (COMNA)

The directors of Rolls Royce presented a silver trophy to be awarded annually by FOMA to the Squadron or Ship's Flight judged to have achieved the best overall standards of engineering efficiency and effectiveness. The award takes into account all aspects of engineering activities and covers the period 1 Dec to 30 Nov.

THE RACAL ORANGE CROP TROPHY (COMNA)

The Racal Orange Crop Trophy, a silver model of the Orange Crop control indicator, was presented to the Royal Navy by Racal Defence Electronics (Radar). It is awarded annually by COMNA to the front line helicopter crew who have contributed most to the Orange Crop database or tactical progression, in the year from 1 Feb to 31 Jan. The trophy is normally to be retained in the parent ship or squadron of the current holder.

THE THORN EMI TROPHY (RNAS Culdrose)

Awarded annually to the individual within 849 Naval Air Squadron contributing most to the development of the AEW Sea King or its tactical employment during the previous year.

THE REAL TIME TROPHY (RNAS Yeovilton)

A meridian clock mounted upon a mahogany base plate and covered by a glass dome. The Real Time Trophy was presented by Singer Link-Miles and is to be awarded to the Officer or Rating who has made the most outstanding contribution to the development, improvement or use of the Sea Harrier Simulator.

THE RACAL CTS TROPHY (RNAS Yeovilton)

The Trophy, a silver salver, was presented by Racal Avionics in 1990 on the commissioning of 700L Squadron. It is awarded annually to the aircrew(s) or maintainer(s) who have contributed most to the development or tactical exploitation of the Lynx Central Tactical System Software improvements.

TRENCHARD MEMORIAL TROPHY (COMNA)

The trophy is a silver model of three pilots, on a suitable base, with an inscribed plaque. The trophy was entrusted to the Central Flying School in memory of Lord Trenchard in 1959. It lay dormant until 1978 when it was first awarded on a three-yearly basis (last awarded 1993) for "outstanding written contributions to the art of flying instruction". The criteria are deliberately very broad to cast the net as wide as possible. Previous entries have included entries on "Helicopter Flight Simulation in the RN", "Economy in Flying Training", and "Teaching the Art of VSTOL Flying".

THE LEWIS TROPHY (RNAS Culdrose)

The trophy, an 18-inch silver salver, was presented to the Fleet Air Arm in November 1980 by Mr & Mrs H A Lewis in memory of their son, Lieutenant Greg Lewis who was killed in a Wessex HAS Mk3 flying accident in June 1980. It is to be retained by 810 Squadron and awarded at the end of AFT to the student Maritime Helicopter Observer who achieves the best flying pass in the Advanced Flying Training Course.

THE DOLPHIN TROPHY (RNAS Culdrose)

Sponsored by Ferranti-Thompson, the trophy is a piece of engraved glass depicting a dolphin. It is awarded, at Wings Parade, to the student showing most improvement during ASW Operational Flying Training.

THE GEOFFREY TURNER TROPHY (RNAS Culdrose)

The prize commemorates a pilot lost with his Gannet aircraft on a night sortie over the sea in 1957 and is awarded, at Wings Parade, to the best pilot completing ASW OFT.

THE PILKINGTON DAW TROPHY (RNAS Culdrose)

Presented in memory of Lt James Daw and Sub Lt David Pilkington who were killed in a car accident in 1992. The Pilkington Daw Trophy is awarded, at Wings Parade, to the student achieving best marks for character and leadership during ASW AFT/OFT.

THE ROUE TROPHY (RNAS Culdrose)

The Roue Trophy, a Caithness Glass bowl, was presented by Mrs Gill Roue in memory of her husband, Lieutenant Commander D Roue, who was killed in a flying accident in 1981. It is awarded annually to the best observer completing AEW OFT.

THE ROB MORRIS TROPHY (RNAS Culdrose)

The Rob Morris Trophy was presented to commemorate Lt Rob Morris (pilot) who died in a canoeing accident in Jan 92 whilst serving in 814 Squadron. It is awarded to the aircrew member of 814 Squadron achieving the highest mark at their Certificate of Competence Board.

THE FERGUSON SHIELD (RNAS Yeovilton)

The Ferguson Shield is a wood/silver shield and was originally presented in 1958 by the widow of Lt Cdr W A M Ferguson RN. It is presented annually to the best qualifying AWI of the year.

THE BRITISH AEROSPACE SEA SKUA TROPHY (RNAS Yeovilton)

This trophy was presented by British Aerospace Air Weapons Division in 1986. It is a silver model of a Skua and is presented annually to the best qualifying HWI of the year.

THE ADAM CAWTHORNE TROPHY (RNAS Yeovilton)

The trophy was presented by the parents of Sub Lt Adam Cawthorne (Observer) who was killed in a Lynx accident in 1985. It is awarded annually to the best ab-initio Observer gaining wings.

THE RICHARD HARPER MEMORIAL TROPHY (RNAS Yeovilton)

Awarded (on a course basis) to the 702 Squadron student who in the opinion of the staff is considered to have "worked the hardest" to pass the course.

BRITISH AEROSPACE TROPHY

Presented in 1986 by Lieutenant Commander Dave Eagles, then Chief Test Pilot with BAe Warton. Awarded to the best overall student groundschool and flying.

THE KELVIN HUGHES VECTAC TROPHY (COMNA)

The "Little Admiral" trophy, awarded annually to the ship, squadron or ship's flight which has been the most efficient in the conduct and assessment of VECTACs.

THE RENWICK SWORD (FOMA)

Presented by Mrs Renwick to FONAC in 1983. The sword, belonging to the late Captain Renwick, is awarded to the most promising Sea Harrier pilot passing through flying training. It is retained by the winner until he leaves the Service at which time it is returned to FOMA for subsequent presentation to another Sea Harrier pilot.

Societies, Institutions and Charities

THE ROYAL NAVAL ASSOCIATION

Headquarters: 82 Chelsea Manor Street, LONDON SW3 5QJ
(Tel: 020 7352 6764. Fax: 020 7352 7385)
e-mail: rna@netcomuk.co.uk
Patron: Her Majesty the Queen

The Royal Naval Association was formed in 1950 from the Royal Naval Old Comrades Association and other naval organisations, to be the principal recognised Association of serving, and ex-serving officers, ratings and other ranks of the RN, RM, WRNS, QARNNS and all Reservists who have served for six months. A Royal Charter was granted in 1954. In 1974 the Association became a Registered Charity.

The aims of the Association are to further the efficiency of the Service in which members of the Association have served or are still serving; to perpetuate comradeship by bringing together the greatest possible number of Naval people, in Branches at home and Overseas; and to relieve members of the Association who are in conditions of need, hardship or distress.

There are currently over 38,000 members in over 490 Branches, providing focal points for the preservation of the traditions of the Service, and to perpetuate the memory of members of Her Majesty's Naval Forces who have died in the service of our Country. Many Branches run Clubs: money is raised for service charities, and members and their families in need of help receive not only financial support but continuing practical friendship. For those unable to join a Branch but who wish to demonstrate their support, a Headquarters Roll is available. Associate Membership may also be available to those who do not qualify for Full Membership but are in sympathy with the aims of the Association.

Application for Membership should be made initially to the General Secretary at the above address. The basic subscription is £6.00 per annum, but money should not accompany the initial application.

KING GEORGE'S FUND FOR SAILORS (KGFS)

8 Hatherley Street, LONDON, SW1P 2YY
(Tel: 020 7932 0000 Fax: 0120 7932 0095)

KGFS - the seafarers' charity - was founded by King George V in 1917. KGFS is the only central fund making grants to nautical charities which look after the welfare needs of seafarers and their dependants in the Royal Navy, Merchant Navy and the Fishing Fleets. Help ranges from care of elderly seafarers to financial help for those still serving who hit problems brought on by ill-health, disability, homelessness, unemployment, broken homes or bereavement. Seafarers' children also benefit with help in education.

Applications for grants are received each year from the nautical charities. Grants now being made total almost £3 million annually and are made to over 80 charities.

KGFS receives income from three sources:-

1. Voluntary contributions to fund-raising events, flagdays, donations and annual appeals.
2. Legacies.
3. Interest on Investments.

Help is always needed to raise voluntary contributions in order to meet the ever increasing amounts required to take care of the elderly seafaring veterans and those who serve today and who require help with the complex problems that beset our society. If you can help please telephone on 020 7932 0000. The Fund does not make grants to individuals but if help is needed the Fund can direct an individual to the appropriate charity through its Nautical Welfare Guide.

ROYAL NAVAL BENEVOLENT SOCIETY FOR OFFICERS

1, Fleet Street, London, EC4Y 1BD
(Tel: 020 7427 7471)

Object: To afford financial assistance to officers of the Royal Navy, Royal Marines, QARNNS and their respective reserves and their dependants when they are in need. The Executive Committee of the Society meets quarterly and can normally make grants, at the moment, of up to £1,950 for members and £650 for non-members, many of which are repeated at six-monthly intervals. Additional grants may be made for each dependent member of the family. RNBSO is now formally associated with the ARNO.

Membership and Subscription: All commissioned officers on the active list of the Royal Navy, Royal Marines and QARNNS and all officers on the retired list, who held such rank whilst still serving on the active list, are eligible for membership, which is available on payment of a single life subscription of £50. For those who might find it hard to pay £50 the subscription may be paid in two instalments of £25.

Further information can be obtained from the Secretary at the above address.

NAVY SPECIAL FUND

Room 49, Old Naval Academy, HM Naval Base, Portsmouth, Hampshire, PO1 3LS

The Navy Special Fund is a small charitable fund, which was formed and maintained by gifts from various non-public sources, including a grant from the Naval Prize Fund. Its primary object is the temporary relief of need, hardship or distress arising amongst persons who are serving or who have served in the Royal Navy, the Royal Marines, the Women's Royal Naval Service or Queen Alexandra's Royal Naval Nursing Service, and their dependants. Assistance takes the form of single grants or, exceptionally, loans; the latter to serving personnel only.

The fund does not conflict with the functions of the Royal Naval Benevolent Trust and applications for ratings should be made to the Trust in the first place. The Navy Special Fund may be able to supplement any assistance given by the Trust or may be able to assist when the Trust has been precluded by its rules from doing so.

Applications for assistance, giving full particulars supported by any available evidence and stating, in the case of ratings, whether application has been made to the Royal Naval Benevolent Trust, should be forwarded by Commanding Officers or the Naval Personal Family Service to The Secretary.

WRNS BENEVOLENT TRUST

311 Twyford Avenue, Portsmouth PO2 8PE
(Tel: 023 9265 5301)

The object of the trust is to provide financial relief in cases of necessity or distress amongst ex-serving or serving female officers and ratings who joined the WRNS or Royal Navy between 1 September 1939 and 1 November 1993.

The Trust is managed by the Central Committee whose members are elected at each Annual General Meeting. With the exception of Honorary legal and financial advisors, all members are either serving or ex female members of the service. The Trust is reliant on grants and donations for its existence.

Applications for assistance should be forwarded in writing to the General Secretary.

QUEEN ALEXANDRA'S ROYAL NAVAL NURSING SERVICE - TRUST FUND

c/o DNS Room 133, Victory Building, HM Naval Base, Portsmouth PO1 3LS.

Object: To promote efficiency and relieve hardship amongst serving or former members of QARNNS or their dependants.

Membership: Serving or former members of QARNNS or those who have been recalled for service in war or emergency.

Management: Two Managing Trustees, namely Matron in Chief QARNNS and the Medical Director General (Naval), and the Hon. Secretary.

Custodian of the Fund: The United Services Trustee.

Assistance: The Managing Trustees will approve grants at their discretion to eligible applicants.

Further information can be obtained from the Hon. Secretary, at the above address.

NAVAL MEDICAL COMPASSIONATE FUND

c/o Sec MDG(N), Room 114, Victory Building, HM Naval Base, Portsmouth PO1 3LS

The Naval Medical Compassionate Fund was founded by Order in Council in 1915 to help the widows and orphans of Medical Officers of the Royal Navy, active or retired, who were subscribers to the Fund at the time of their death, or were not more than nine months in arrears with the subscriptions.

In addition to a grant payable on the death of the subscriber, the Directors have powers to grant relief to widows and orphans of dependants who find themselves in necessitous circumstances.

Medical Officers on the Active List of the Royal Navy, including those holding Short Service Commissions, who have not yet subscribed, are invited to do so.

All correspondence regarding the NMCF should be addressed to the Assistant Secretary NMCF at the above address.

ROYAL MARINES CHARITIES

CORPS SECRETARY HEADQUARTERS ROYAL MARINES
HMS EXCELLENT WHALE ISLAND PORTSMOUTH PO2 8ER
(Tel: 023 9254 7214. Fax: 023 9254 7207)
E-mail: royalmarines.charities@charity.vfree.com

The Royal Marines Corps Secretariat centrally administers Royal Marines Charities and prize funds, the main charities are listed below. Full details of all funds are listed in Royal Marines Instructions (BR 1283).

The Royal Marines Benevolent Fund. The principal purpose of the Fund is to benefit persons who are serving or who have served in the Royal Marines, or their dependants, to relieve need, hardship or distress. The Fund was formed in 1997 and subsumed the following funds and their purposes:

The Upton Kelly Memorial Fund. The aim of this fund is to relieve distress or necessity amongst retired officers and officers' widows and their dependants.

Royal Marines Tercentenary Relief Fund. The purpose of this fund is to provide widows, or next of kin, with a sum of money on death. This is applicable to serving Royal Marines or reservists on duty.

Royal Marines Welfare Fund. The income to this fund may be used to relieve distress among serving and retired Warrant Officers, non-commissioned officers and men of the Royal Marines, their widows and dependants.

Royal Marines Band Benevolent Fund. The fund is used to relieve need or distress for serving and retired RM Band Service ranks or their dependants by making grants.
Contact: Officers - The Corps Secretary, Tel: 023 9254 7214
SNCOs, Cpls and Marines - HQRM Welfare SNCO, Tel 023 9254 7544

1939 War Fund. The deed of trust allows this fund to be used for maintaining and increasing the efficiency and esprit de corps of the Royal Marines. It may also assist in the relief of distress for past and present members of the Corps and their relatives and dependants and for making grants to other charities which may directly or indirectly assist members of the Corps.

Royal Marines Reserve 50th Anniversary Relief Fund. This Fund was formed in 1998 with an initial grant from the Royal Marines Benevolent Fund. Its object is to relieve the need, distress or hardship of serving or retired members of the RMR, or their widows, dependants or immediate close family, as a result of death, disability or other tragic circumstances; these circumstances will normally be in part or wholly attributable to Crown Service.
Contact: HQRM SO2 Reserves, Tel 023 9254 7655

Royal Marines' Association. The object of the RMA is to maintain and promote fellowship and esprit de corps among Royal Marines, serving and retired. The Association keeps members in touch with each other through world wide branches and assists in the investigation of cases of hardship and distress. Further information on membership and subscriptions can be obtained from The General Secretary, RMA Central Office, Eastney Esplanade, Southsea, Hants, PO4 9PX - Tel: 023 9273 1978, Fax: 023 9229 6945.

THE OFFICERS' ASSOCIATION

PATRON: HER MAJESTY THE QUEEN

48 Pall Mall, London, SW1Y 5JY (Tel 020 7389 5204)

The Officers' Association provides services which are available to ex-officers of the Royal Navy (including Royal Marines), the Army and the Royal Air Force, and their widows and dependants including those who held commissions in the Women's Services.

Services include:
Employment - an efficient Employment Department to assist ex-officers of all ages and ranks to find suitable employment, both those just leaving the Services and those who are changing their civilian jobs. Many hundreds of ex-officers are found jobs every year over a wide salary range.

Benevolence - financial assistance is given in a number of ways such as cash grants and allowances for the elderly in Residential or Nursing Home Care and towards shortfalls in Home fees.

Homes advice - advice and information on independent sector Homes and Homes run by service charities and other voluntary organisations; sheltered accommodation for the elderly; convalescence homes; advice on financial assistance toward Home fees.

A Country Home - running "Huntly", a delightful country home at Bishopsteignton, South Devon, which affords comfort and security for ex-officers at or over the age of 65, both male and female, who do not need special nursing care. Selection is made with due regard to need.

Bungalows - running a 12-bungalow estate at Leavesden, Herts, for disabled ex-officers and their families.

The Association has offices in London and Dublin; the Officers' Association (Scotland) has offices in Glasgow and Edinburgh.

All enquiries should be made to: The General Secretary at the above address

SSAFA FORCES HELP (THE SOLDIERS, SAILORS, AIRMEN AND FAMILIES ASSOCIATION - FORCES HELP)

19 Queen Elizabeth Street, LONDON, SE1 2LP
(Tel: 020 7403 8783 Fax: 020 7403 8815)
E-mail: public-awareness@ssafa-forces-help.org.uk
Website: www.ssafa-forces-help.org.uk
Registered Charity Number 210760. Est 1885

Object: The national charity helping serving and ex-Service men, women and their families, in need. SSAFA Forces Help is not primarily a grant making organisation but all Branches have funds always available for emergency issue. Where there is a financial need, SSAFA Forces Help first ensures that a family is getting all they are entitled to from statutory sources and then puts up the case to the appropriate Service or Regimental benevolent funds. The Royal Navy Benevolent Trust and other Service charities use SSAFA Forces Help's nation-wide network of voluntary workers to visit their family cases and carry their generosity over the doorstep.

To carry out this work SSAFA Forces Help has a network of volunteers at home and abroad. SSAFA Forces Help provides both professional and voluntary support to Service personnel and their families in the UK and overseas. In the UK, SSAFA Forces Help supplies a social work advisory service to the Army and Royal Air Force. All enquiries and applications to the Welfare Department at the above address.

THE ROYAL HOMES FOR OFFICERS' WIDOWS AND DAUGHTERS

Queen Alexandra's Court, St. Mary's Road, Wimbledon
LONDON, SW19 7DE
(Tel 020 8946 5182)

Queen Alexandra's Court is managed by a Committee responsible to SSAFA Forces Help Council.

The accommodation comprises unfurnished self-contained flats for widows, divorcees or unmarried daughters of deceased officers or warrant officers, or women who are retired officers or warrant officers, of all three Services.

For full particulars application should be made to the Manager at the above address.

CHARITY OF WILLIAM KINLOCH

(The Kinloch Bequest)
(Tel: 020 7240 3718)

The Charity is administered by the Royal Scottish Corporation.

Candidates for the benefits of the Charity must be Scotsmen or women who have served in the Royal Navy, Army or Air Force who have become disabled through no fault of their own, who are in need and deserving. Preference will be given to those who have been maimed or wounded in the service of their country.

Application for the benefits must be made in the first place in writing to the Secretary, Royal Scottish Corporation, 37 King Street, Covent Garden, London WC2E 8JS. Every applicant must state his name, address, age and occupation, and the date of his entry into the Navy, Army or Air Force and the date and cause of his discharge therefrom, and must produce evidence of his qualification for the appointment.

QUEEN ADELAIDE NAVAL FUND

Guildford Cathedral Office, GUILDFORD GU2 5UP

The objects of the Fund are the provision of help by financial grants to needy serving or retired Officers of the Royal Navy, Royal Marines, Women's Royal Naval Service and Queen Alexandra Royal Naval Nursing Service and of the Reserves of those forces and their spouses, former spouses, families and dependants.

Applications for help, preferably by letter, should be made to the Secretary at the above address.

THE MARINE SOCIETY

202 Lambeth Road, LONDON SE1 7JW
Tel: 020 7261 9535 Fax: 020 7401 2537
e-mail: enq@marine-society.org

THE MARINE SOCIETY was founded in 1756 to encourage poor men and boys to join the Royal Navy at the start of the Seven Years War. Today it is the oldest public maritime charity in the world. It is dedicated to the education, training, and well-being of professional British seafarers from all the sea services. It operates a 154 grt power-driven training ship ts Earl of Romney (formerly HMS Echo); provides tuition to Royal Navy personnel through the Forces Distance Learning Scheme; operates a free and impartial educational advice service; provides books and videos on loan or for sale at discount prices; offers financial assistance for vocational development and scholarships for academic studies in pursuit of professional goals.

For further information contact the Director or visit its website at www.marine-society.org

ARGYLL NAVAL FUND

Royal Highland and Agricultural Society of Scotland, Ingliston
NEWBRIDGE, Midlothian, EH28 8NF

Financial grants may be made at the discretion of the Directors of the Royal Highland and Agricultural Society of Scotland, as Trustees of the above fund, to the parents or guardians of young men and women from the Highlands of Scotland or with Highland connections, who are successful in applying for a place at BRNC Dartmouth.

Application for a grant may be made to the Treasurer, after applying for a place at BRNC Dartmouth. A grant will be conditional upon award of a place at BRNC Dartmouth and will be entirely at the discretion of the Trustees.

KING WILLIAM IV NAVAL FOUNDATION.

Royal Naval Cottages, SOUTHWICK, Hants, PO17 6HE

Situated on the approach road to HMS DRYAD, the foundation comprises twelve cottages, for widows and orphan daughters, over the age of 40, of officers of the Royal Navy, Royal Marines and their Reserves. Lady residents are elected by the Governors as vacancies occur. Applicants, who must be in good health and capable of looking after themselves, should apply to the Resident Secretary at the above address.

THE ROYAL STAR AND GARTER HOME FOR DISABLED SAILORS, SOLDIERS AND AIRMEN

RICHMOND, Surrey, TW10 6RR
(Tel: 020 8940-3314)
REGISTERED CHARITY NO: 210119

The Royal Star and Garter Home was founded in 1916 as an independent charity to care for servicemen disabled in the Great War. Today the Home cares for up to 200 disabled ex-service men and women of all ranks and from all parts of the country, whose disability may be the result of active service, chronic illness or serious accident, providing the very best in medical and nursing care as well as being a true home in every sense of the word.

The Home also offers short term respite care or a period in the excellent rehabilitation unit which includes physiotherapy, hydrotherapy, speech and occupational therapy.

The Home urgently needs funds to maintain the high standards of care and facilities and to replace and update equipment. Please help us to continue this good work either by donation, or a covenant, or by a bequest in your will. All donations will be gratefully received by the Director of Fundraising, Patsy Willis, The Royal Star & Garter Home, Richmond, Surrey, TW10 6RR.

ERSKINE HOSPITAL

BISHOPTON, Renfrewshire PA7 5PU
(Tel: 0141 812 1100, Fax: 0141 812 3733
Web: www.erskine.org

For eight decades, through two World wars and the conflicts of the twentieth century, Erskine Hospital, a registered charity, has cared for more than 60,000 sailors, soldiers and airmen.

The Hospital is situated on the south bank of the River Clyde, near Bishopton in Renfrewshire and some 12 miles west of Glasgow.

As the foremost ex-Service care facility in the United Kingdom, it provides unique medical, nursing and residential and respite care for more than 500 men and women each year. Ex-Service personnel, who are war pensioners, and their families also enjoy independent living in 56 cottages within the Hospital grounds and the Erskine Workshops provide rewarding employment for those able to work. In addition there are two fully equipped holiday flats for couples (one to be ex-Service) available throughout the year for short holiday lets at modest cost.

Dignity, Privacy and respect are of paramount importance in delivering Eskine Care for both young and old ex-service personnel. As a registered charity (SC006609) outwith the NHS, Eskine needs more than £2 million in donations each year to continue its work.

In recent years, a strategic review determined that the old buildings no longer met modern care regulations and that there was no alternative but to rebuild. A £16 million 180-bed centre of nursing care excellence opening in July 2000 will replace the outdated original buildings in the estate close to the current location with a 30-bed unit a few miles away in the Erskine New Town. In addition, Erskine care will be taken to other areas of Scotland to enable ex-Service personnel to be cared for in a facility closer to their own community, family and friends. The first of these is scheduled to open in Edinburgh at the end of the year 2000.

Applications for admission and enquiries about all facilities should be addressed to the Admissions Coordinator and donations to the Director of Finance both at the above address.

THE SIR OSWALD STOLL FOUNDATION

446 Fulham Road, LONDON, SW6 1DT
(Tel. 020 7385 2110)

The Foundation consists of 138 flats, some designed for wheelchairs, with supporting services for disabled ex-servicemen and women.

For full particulars apply to the Housing Manager.

WILLIAM SIMPSON'S HOME

Main Street, Old Plean, STIRLING FK7 8BQ
(Tel: 01786 812421; Fax: 01786 815970

This Residential Home caters for the Social needs of men, irrespective of colour, creed, religion or age. It is situated in pleasant country surroundings between Stirling and Falkirk. The Home is registered with Central Regional Social Work Dept., and is subject to the Quality Assurance Inspection and Guidelines. Clients unable to meet the charges from their own resources will be able to apply for DSS and Social Work funding.

Applications for admission or for further particulars should be made to Miss J P A Lyon BA., Chief Executive, at above address.

LADY GROVER'S HOSPITAL FUND FOR OFFICERS' FAMILIES

48 Pall Mall, LONDON, SW1Y 5JY
(Tel. 020 7925 0539)

The object of the Fund is to help Officers defray expenses incurred by the illness of their dependants. Officer subscribers are NOT THEMSELVES eligible for benefit.

Membership is open to: Any Officer, male or female, of the three Services, who holds or has held a regular commission for a minimum of five years.

Membership is also open to: Widows or widowers of Officers, divorced wives or husbands of Officers, for their own benefit or that of their own children, and for descendant carers of Officers (all within certain criteria).

Annual Subscription: £30.00 per annum.

Grants: The amount of each grant is assessed on the basis of the actual expenses incurred with maximum rates as follows:-

Temporary Hospital or Nursing Home accommodation - up to £1,050.00 per week.

Temporary employment at home of a qualified nurse - up to £280.00 per week.

Convalescence away from home - up to £280.00 per week.

Temporary employment of a Home Help - up to £140.00 per week.

Ex gratia grants at the discretion of the Committee. The maximum period for which benefit is payable in a period of twelve months is eight weeks, except in the case of Home Help, when the maximum period is twelve weeks.

Applications for membership should be made to the Secretary at the above address.

THE ROYAL NAVAL AND ROYAL MARINES CHILDREN'S FUND

RN & RM Children's Fund, Swiftsure Block, HMS NELSON,
Portsmouth, PO1 3HH.
(Tel and Fax: 023 9281 7435)

This Fund was formed on 1st April 1999 from the former charities known as The RN & RM Children's Trust and The RN & RM Children's Home.

The object of the charity is the relief of Beneficiaries who are in need, hardship or distress. The Trustees may relieve Beneficiaries by:

a. Making grants of money to them.

b. Providing or paying for goods, services or facilities for them.

c. Making grants of money to other persons or bodies who provide goods, services or facilities to those in need.

Beneficiaries must be sons or daughters under the age of 25 of serving or former serving members of the Royal Navy, Royal Marines, Queen Alexandra's Royal Navy Nursing Service, the former Women's Royal Naval Service and the Reserves of those forces.

The majority of children are maintained at boarding schools, but some attend local schools. Subject to the financial circumstances of the family, fees and uniform expenses are met by the Trust.

Subscriptions, donations and applications should be addressed to The Administrator at the above address.

SAILORS' FAMILIES' SOCIETY

NEWLAND, Hull, HU6 7RJ
(Tel: 01482-342331)
Patron: Her Majesty Queen Elizabeth The Queen Mother

The Society's work for seafarers' children throughout the British Isles extends to those who remain in the care of a widowed parent or other relations. Apart from financial assistance, the Seafarers' Families Support Scheme assists with gifts of clothing and the provision of holidays at seaside resorts.

As well as its work for children, the Society provides homes for elderly seafarers or their widows in Hull.

Enquiries and applications for help should be addressed to the Chief Executive, Graham J Powell.

ALEXANDRA HOUSE

(Royal United Services Short Stay Residence for Service Children)
6-8 Berthon Road, Bull Point, St. Budeaux, PLYMOUTH PL5 1EX
(Tel: 01752 365203)
Patron: H.R.H. Princess Alexandra, The Hon. Lady Ogilvy GCVO
President: Naval Base Commander, HM Naval Base Devonport

The Foundation (formerly at Newquay) has since 1839 looked after children of men and women in the Armed Services. Its short stay home is now established in a modern house to meet the immediate temporary need that arises when a family crisis occurs, such as injury to the father serving abroad, sudden departure of the mother to join him, and lack of relatives or friends to care for the children. The problem is met AT ONCE, at any hour of day or night, and the children are cared for, placed in schools and, by arrangement, given whatever special instruction, treatment or maintenance they need for up to three months, while family affairs are settled.

The House is run as a family home, not as an Institution, and the Housemother-in-Charge has long experience in schools, nursing and catering in UK. It is supported by voluntary contributions and by a modest scale of payments by the parents. Financial help can sometimes be given or lent by the Foundation.

Urgent and emergency inquiries should be made by telephone as above. Routine correspondence should be addressed to the Comptroller, Alexandra House.

Grants, covenants, donations and legacies are especially valuable to the Foundation as a Charity under current law, and an outline of the tax advantages to the donor or his estate may be obtained from the Comptroller.

It is hoped to occupy new and better premises in Autumn 2000. The telephone number will remain unchanged.

ROYAL CALEDONIAN SCHOOLS TRUST

Unit 75 Wenta Business Park
Colne Way
Watford
WD24 7ND
Telephone: 01923 215350
Email: RCST@nildram.co.uk

The Royal Caledonian Schools Trust is able to consider applications from the children of Scottish Service men and women and from children of needy Scots currently resident in London. Grants have to be for educational purposes and range from school fees to book allowances. Enquiries should be made to the Chief Executive at the above address.

QUEEN VICTORIA SCHOOL

DUNBLANE, Perthshire FK15 OJY
Telephone: 01786 822288 (Exchange)
0131-310-2901 (Direct Line to Headmaster's Secretary)
Fax No: 0131-310-2926
Email address: enquiries@qvs.pkc.sch.uk
Web Address: www.qvs.pkc.sch.uk
Patron: HRH The Duke of Edinburgh KG, KT, OM, GBE

The School, which is set in 45 acres of beautiful Perthshire countryside, provides boarding school education for the children of Scottish servicemen and women and those who have served in Scotland. It is easily accessible by road, rail or air.

Quality education is provided at a low cost of £167 per term.

Pupils may be registered for entry from the age of seven and normally admitted to Primary 7 (i.e. age 10.5/11 years). Applications must reach the School by 31 December so that they may be considered for the Admissions Board which convenes in February. However, consideration will also be given, in particular circumstances, to applications made after these dates.

The School offers a wide curriculum following the Scottish educational system and includes courses at Standard and Higher grade as well as Certificate of Sixth Year Studies and SCOTVEC modules. Increasingly pupils move on to Higher and Further Education but career links with the Services remain strong. Pastoral care is afforded a very high priority along with careers guidance and personal and social education. In addition, there is a very full programme of sporting, cultural and spiritual development.

Queen Victoria School is a unique boarding school which seeks to achieve the best that is possible academically for all its pupils. The School prides itself also on developing the pupil in the widest possible sense and aims to achieve success academically, in sport, music, drama and many other extra-curricular areas. A very special and unique dimension of Queen Victoria School is the ceremonial side which preserves the very best of the School's traditions.

For futher information write to theHeadmaster at the above address.

GREENWICH HOSPITAL

40, Queen Anne's Gate, London, SW1H 9AP
(Tel: 020 7396 0140/0150; Fax 020 7396 0149)Patron:
HRH The Duke of York

Greenwich Hospital is a Crown Charity founded in 1694 for the benefit of seafarers and their dependants. It is managed by the Admiralty Board, on behalf of the Secretary of State for Defence, who is the sole trustee. The following is a summary of the main benefits provided by Greenwich Hospital. Further information about the benefits and Greenwich Hospital's other activities may be obtained from the Director of Greenwich Hospital.

a) The Royal Hospital School, Holbrook, Suffolk (Headmaster H Blackett)

RHS is a thriving, independent HMC co-educational boarding school maintained by Greenwich Hospital primarily for the benefit of children or grandchildren of seafarers. The School is proud of its Royal connections and celebrates its naval heritage. Today there are some 700 pupils aged from 11 to 18 and entry is normally dependent on success in the school's entrance examination. Fees for serving members of the Royal Navy and Royal Marines match the level of parental contribution for those qualifying for the Services Boarding School Allowance. Fees for the children and grandchildren of ex-seafarers are assessed on the parents' ability to pay. This can allow for a continuity of education when parents leave the Services which might not otherwise be possible.

The School offers a wide curriculum to A level and has excellent modern teaching, boarding and recreational facilities on a 200-acre site overlooking the River Stour.

b) **Education grants.** Grants are available towards the maintenance and education of the children of deceased or distressed officers and ratings of the Royal Navy and Royal Marines and of members of their Reserve Forces who died in service.

c) **Officers' pensions.** These are means-tested pensions which may be awarded to retired permanent officers of the Royal Navy and Royal Marines in cases of need.

d) **Special pensions.** These are means-tested pensions for certain seamen and marines who are in poor health or otherwise unable to support themselves.

e) **Widows' pensions.** These are means-tested pensions for the widows of seamen and marines, and are normally restricted to widows over 65 years of men who gave long service, or who died in service or who were invalided.

f) **Jellicoe Annuities.** These annuities, funded by Greenwich Hospital, are paid by the Royal Naval Benevolent Trust to ratings and ratings' widows who are ineligible for the pensions outlined above. Further details may be obtained from; the Secretary of RNBT, 311 Twyford Avenue, Portsmouth, Hampshire PO2 8PE (Tel 023 9269 0112)

THE ROYAL NAVAL AND ROYAL MARINES DEPENDANTS' FUND

RNDF, Centurion Building, Grange Road, GOSPORT
Hants, PO13 9XA
(Tel. 023 9270 2101)

Objects: To make an immediate and substantial grant to the widow, widower or dependant of RN, RM and QARNNS personnel, who die while serving, on the active list/on regular engagements. Subscriptions: £1.80 per year payable in advance on 1st August. Subscriptions are deducted from service pay.

Further information may be obtained from BR 8588, UPOs or from the Secretary at the above address.

THE ASSOCIATION OF ROYAL NAVY OFFICERS

70 Portchester Terrace, Bayswater,
LONDON, W2 3TP

Aims: To provide all possible and speedy help to members, their wives and dependants who may be in financial or other distress. ARNO is now formally associated with the RNBSO.

To give financial assistance in the form of grants where there is essential expenditure beyond the member's means, and bursaries to enable children to continue their planned education where there has been a change in circumstances. To offer financial assistance to members themselves towards further education and re-training after they have left the Service.

To assist members, their wives and dependants by arranging medical, legal and financial consultations.

To keep members in touch with one another socially, and to keep the Secretary informed in cases where fellow members, their widows and dependants are in distress of any kind.

Membership: Open to serving and retired Commissioned Officers of the RN, RM, QARNNS, WRNS and their respective Reserves. Widows and Widowers of members become Honorary Members without the need to subscribe.

Subscription: £10 per annum. Life Membership £150.

Full information can be obtained from the Secretary. Tel: 020 7402 5231, Fax: 020 7402 5533.

ASSOCIATION OF WRENS

8 Hatherley Street, LONDON, SW1P 2YY
(Tel: 020 7932 0111)
Patron: HRH The Princess Royal

The Association, founded in 1920 (celebrating its 80th Anniversary in 2000), is open to all ex-members of the WRNS, WRNR, WRNVR, QARNNS, former Naval VADs, Commonwealth and South African Women's Naval Services and serving female members of the Royal Navy. The aim of the Association is to perpetuate comradeship by bringing together the greatest possible number of Wrens and Ex-Wrens at home and overseas and to help former members of the said services by bringing to the notice of Service charities persons who are in conditions of need, hardship or distress.

Applications for membership should be made to the Secretary at the above address.

ROYAL UNITED SERVICES INSTITUTE FOR DEFENCE STUDIES

Whitehall, LONDON SW1A 2ET
(Tel: 020 7930 5854 Fax: 020 7321 0943)
e-mail: defence@rusids.demon.co.uk.
Web site: www.rusi.org

An independent centre free of political ties, the RUSI is the professional association of the armed forces. It is dedicated to the study, and debate of issues affecting defence, technology, the military sciences and regional and international security. The RUSI arranges lectures, conferences, public and private seminars and has a wide range of publications. When in London members may have access to the reading room and library and are able to attend the Institute's programme of events.

Subscriptions Rates: Basic Membership £48.00. (Receipt of Journal, use of library and attendance at lectures). Members may choose from a wide range of publications and membership options to suit their needs.

For further information please contact the Membership Secretary.

ROYAL NAVAL LAY READERS' SOCIETY

Royal Naval Lay Readers' Society, Room 203, Victory Building,
HM Naval Base, Portsmouth, Hants PO1 3LS.
(Tel: 023 9272 7902. Fax Number: 023 9272 7112)

Licensed Readers assist in the work of the Anglican Church amongst men and women of the Royal Navy and their families. In ships at sea and in naval establishments ashore, they work alongside Naval Chaplains in the furtherance of the Christian Faith and the welfare of the Navy's people.

The Society is dependent financially on voluntary contributions for the maintenance of its work.

Subscriptions and donations may be sent to the Treasurer at the above address

THE WHITE ENSIGN ASSOCIATION LIMITED

(President Cmmodore Sir Donald Gosling, RNR)
(Chairman Admiral Sir Jock Slater, GCB, LVO, DL)
HMS BELFAST, Tooley Street, London SE1 2JH.
(Tel: 020 7407 8658, MOD Main Building 81945, FAX: 020 7357 6298)

The White Ensign Association formed in 1958 with Admiralty Board endorsement is a registered charity. The activities of the Association are supervised by a Council of Management, representing a distinguished body drawn from the City of London, Commerce, Industry and the Royal Navy.

Its functions are to provide independent and unbiased help on all matters of personal finance including investment and financial planning for resettlement. Also to give assistance on all matters of civilian employment including job search.

This is available to all serving and retired officers, men and women of the Royal Navy, Royal Marines, QARNNS or any of the Naval Services and their respective Reserves. It is also available to dependants of natural beneficiaries.

The White Ensign Association maintains links with the City of London, Industry and Commerce through its White Ensign Association Membership Scheme.

Enquiries to: Captain J O Roberts Royal Navy, Chief Executive, The White Ensign Association Ltd., HMS BELFAST, Tooley Street, London SE1 2JH. Tel: 020 7407 8658, MOD Main Building 81945, FAX: 020 7357 6298

THE QARNNS ASSOCIATION

2 Longwater Drive, Alverstoke, GOSPORT, Hants PO12 2UP.

Objects: The objects of the Association shall be to further the efficiency of the Queen Alexandra's Royal Naval Nursing Service for the public benefit by fostering esprit de corps amongst its members and by providing relief for past and present members and their dependants who are in conditions of need, hardship and distress.

Administration: President: A senior retired Matron-in-Chief QARNNS is invited to assume the office of President and she is given Honorary Life Membership of the Association: The Committee of the Association consists of eight Association members, the Matron-in-Chief, QARNNS, four members elected by members of the Association, and ex-officio officers appointed by the Committee to act as Chairman, Secretary and Treasurer. The organisation of subsidiary Branches will follow the same general pattern as that of the Main Association.

Membership: Open to all serving and former Nursing Officers, QARNNS and QARNNS(R)

Subscriptions: £5.00 Payable annually on 1st January.

Further information can be obtained from the Secretary, Lieutenant Commander S. Clements ARRC, at the above address.

FLEET AIR ARM OFFICERS' ASSOCIATION

FAAOA, 4 St. James' Square, LONDON SW1Y 4JU.

Full Membership is open to all Officers (Male and Female) of all Specialisations who are serving, or have served, in the Fleet Air Arm or the Royal Naval Air Service. Officers of all other UK armed services who have had, or still have, connections with the Fleet Air Arm are also eligible to join. Associate Membership is available to such persons, including Officers of foreign armed services, who are, or were, attached to, or had a close connection with, the Fleet Air Arm.

The Association originally came into being in 1957 and is a means of keeping in touch, not only for all former Naval aviators but also for serving officers. The name of the Association was given official Admiralty approval and there are now almost 3,000 members representing the entire spectrum of naval aviation from the early days of the RNAS to the present day.

The Fleet Air Arm Officers' Association exists as a focal point for all who are professionally and socially bound together by their common interest and vocation in Naval Aviation. It provides a link of friendship between the serving and the retired, the young and the old, not provided in any other form.

We keep a keen interest in Naval Air Power and can advise at high level if their is any sign of degradation or denigration to our national defence interests.

Considerable sums have been regularly donated to both Service and Maritime Charities, including the FAA Benevolent Trust, the FAA Museum, St. Bartholomew's Church, Yeovilton, the RNLI and other smaller Charities. The Association also has a substantial involvement with youth training and development such as the Sail Training Association and the Ocean Youth Club. The FAAOA Aviation Scholarship Trust, Registered Charity No. 298817, was established in 1986 to fund the Association Gliding Scholarship Scheme, which provides gliding courses for young people between 16 and 20 years of age who have a wish to join the RN as a career.

The annual subscription entitles members to receive a "FLY NAVY" Journal issued annually, News Sheets twice yearly and a Membership Book every three years. Local First of the Month Meetings are held and Association representatives can be found all over the world.

For Further information apply to the Admin Director.

THE MISSIONS TO SEAMEN

ST. Michael Paternoster Royal, College Hill, LONDON EC4R 2RL
(Tel: 020 7248 5202 ; Fax: 020 7248 4761)
Welfare officer: Canon Ken Peters

The Missions to Seamen is a voluntary society of the Anglican Church which cares for the welfare of navy and merchant navy seafarers of all races and creeds in over 300 ports worldwide.

Working through an international network of chaplains and staff, it makes some 90,000 ship visits a year to offer friendship, practical and spiritual support, and help in emergencies.

BRITISH LIMBLESS EX-SERVICE MEN'S ASSOCIATION (BLESMA)

Frankland Moore House, 185-187 High Road, Chadwell Heath, Romford, Essex RM6 6NA
Telephone: 020 8590 1124 Fax: 020 8599 2932
e-mail: blemsa@btconnect.com
Patron: HRH PRINCES ALICE, Duchess of Gloucester
General Secretary R R Holland MBE, BEM, MBIM

BLESMA is a national charity catering specifically for Serving and Ex-Service limbless men and women. The Association also accepts responsibility for the dependants of its Membership and in particular their widows.

The objects of the Association are to promote the welfare of all those of either sex who have lost a limb or limbs or one or both eyes as a result of Service in any branch of Her Majesty's Forces or Auxiliary Forces and to assist their dependants.

The Association:

a) Through its Branches spread over the country, operates a Welfare Visiting Service to its Members and Widows.

b) Provides permanent residential and convalescent holiday accommodation through its two Nursing and Residential care homes at Blackpool and Crieff in Perthshire.

c) Provides a counselling service to individuals pre and post amputation.

d) Furnishes advice on pensions, allowances and, where necessary, represents Members and their dependants at Pension Appeal Tribunals.

e) Provides financial assistance to Members and Widows in the form of grants.

f) Plans and organises rehabilitation programmes for amputees.

g) Assists in finding suitable employment for amputees.

h) Provides limited funding for research and development into artificial limbs and in the training of Prosthetists and Orthotists.

i) Acts as Consumer Watchdog in respect of the provision of artificial limbs, wheelchairs and appliances.

NAUTICAL INSTITUTE

202 Lambeth Road, LONDON SE1 7LQ or phone 020 7928-1351.

The Nautical Institute is an independent professional body for qualified mariners which is directed by a Council of whom the majority must be actively employed at sea. The Institute is recognised as an authoritative body for consultation on matters concerning the Nautical Profession; its aims are to encourage high standards of competence and knowledge and facilitate the exchange and publication of information. The Institute publishes a monthly journal.

Further details may be obtained from The Secretary, The Nautical Institute at the above address.

NAVY RECORDS SOCIETY

Department of War Studies, Kings College, LONDON WC2R 2LS.

This Society was founded to combine the practical interests of the service with the academic rigour of historians in a mutually beneficial synthesis. Since then it has published over one hundred and forty volumes dealing with all aspects of naval service over the last five hundred years. Recent volumes have covered the careers of Admirals Beatty, Cunningham and Somerville, together with the Battle of the Atlantic, Signals Intelligence and the development of shipboard organisation. Forthcoming volumes address the development of the submarine service, Henry VIII's Navy and a variety of 20th century subjects.

The Annual Subscription is £30.00, which entitles members to receive copies of all volumes published in that year, on average one or two appear each year, and to purchase copies of volumes already in print at special rates.

Those interested are invited to apply to the Hon. Secretary, Professor A. D. Lambert at the above address.

V

Y

Amendments to Navy List Entry

Editor of the Navy List
DNCM
Room 208
Jago Road
HMNB Portsmouth
PO1 3LU

Please ensure that you state your Service Number and use the spaces provided next to each incorrect field to insert what you believe to be the correct entry. All potential inaccuracies will be investigated.

The information contained in Sections 2 and 3 of this edition was extracted from the Naval Manpower Management Information System and is corrected to include those promotions, appointments etc. promulgated on or before 9 April 2005 which will be effective on or before 30 June 2005.

Service Number (mandatory) ....

Surname ....

Forenames ....

Titular Address ....

Post-Nominals* ....

Rank ....

Commission ....

Branch ....

Spec ....

Seniority ....

* Please note that documentary evidence (for example, a supporting certificate) will be required if any amendments to your post-nominal details are to be made.

Signed .... Date ....

Once completed, please return this form to the above address, marked for the attention of your Career Manager.

Every effort will be made to correct errors and omissions notified to the Editor but regrettably receipt of this form cannot be acknowledged.